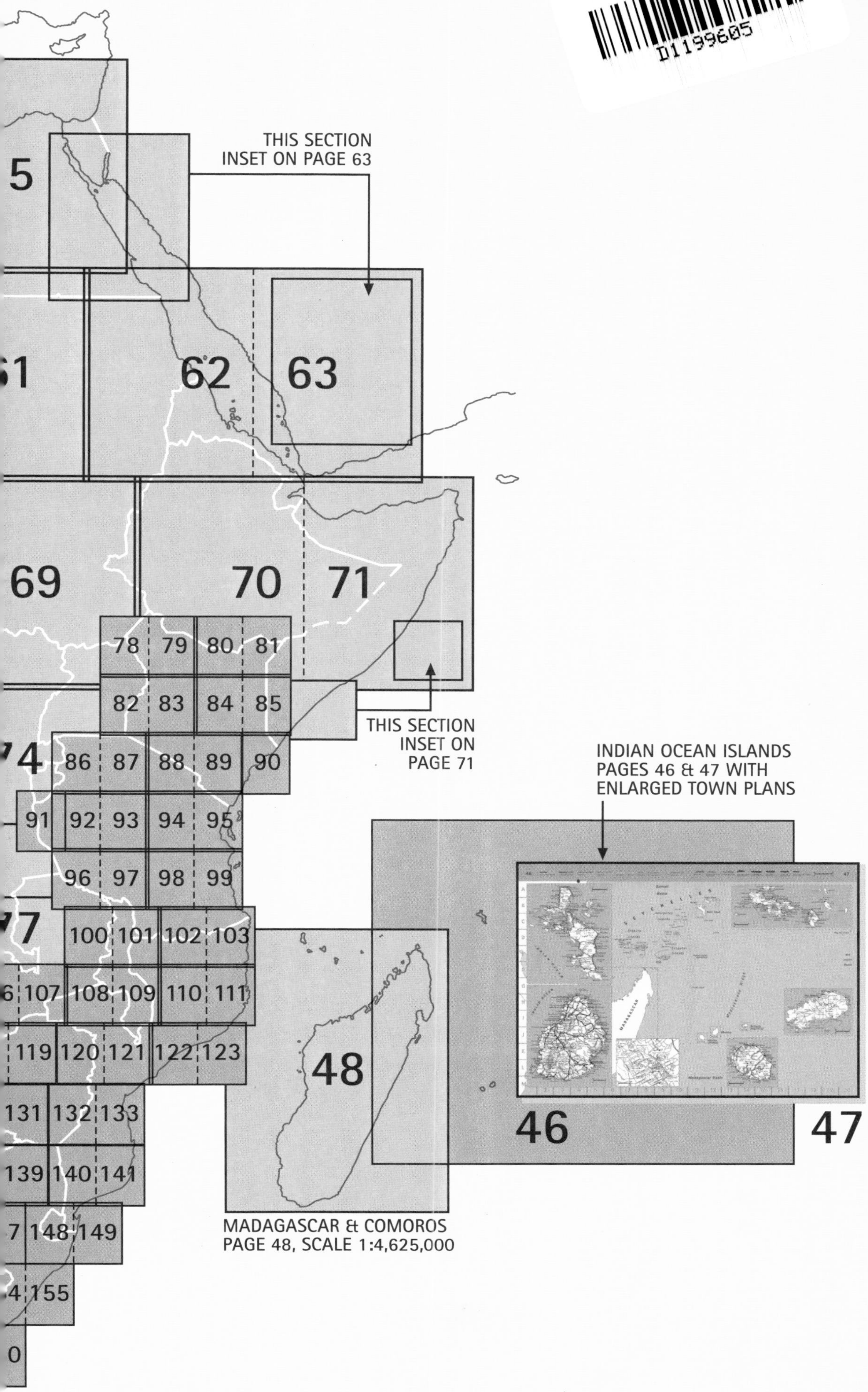
THIS SECTION INSET ON PAGE 63
5
61
62
63
69
70
71
78 79 80 81
82 83 84 85
THIS SECTION INSET ON PAGE 71
74 86 87 88 89 90
91 92 93 94 95
96 97 98 99
77 100 101 102 103
6 107 108 109 110 111
119 120 121 122 123
131 132 133
139 140 141
7 148 149
4 155
0
48
MADAGASCAR & COMOROS PAGE 48, SCALE 1:4,625,000
INDIAN OCEAN ISLANDS PAGES 46 & 47 WITH ENLARGED TOWN PLANS
46
47

REGIONS IN THIS ATLAS

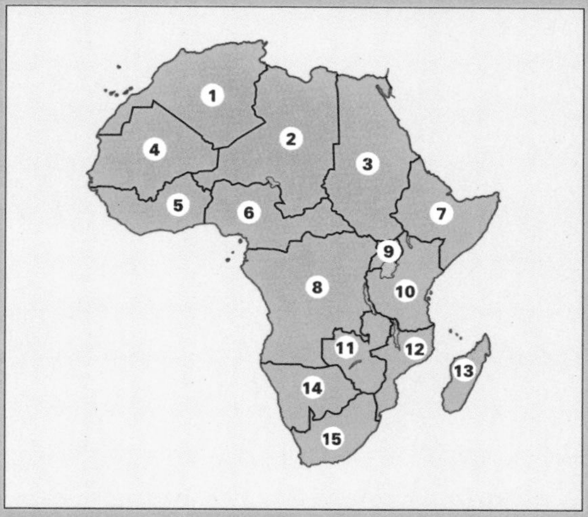
1
2
3
4
5
6
7
8
9
10
11
12
13
14
15

CONTENTS

NATIONAL GEOGRAPHIC

African Adventure Atlas

Africa

The Indian Ocean Islands
The Atlantic Ocean Islands

Contents

A weary 4x4 enthusiast trudges upstream through a lonely forest river in the Democratic Republic of the Congo in search of clean water for his vehicle's radiator can.

Exploring Africa

The vastness of the African landscape, the diversity of its cultures and the irrepressible spirit of adventure that pervades the great continent make it an adventurer's paradise. Exploring the desert dunes, thickly wooded forests and dry, dusty plains of Africa is unparalleled in its rewards: an endless sea of 'undiscovered' tribal lands, horizonless savanna dotted with rural villages and towering skylines of bustling modern cities that marry the thrill of the unknown with the pioneering spirit of the traveller. Everything in Africa is bigger and better: the glowing sunsets, the pristine beaches and the indomitable fire of its people. Mighty rivers wind their way across rugged mountainscapes and through lush or stony valleys en route to the ocean, while long, apparently abandoned roads stretch as far as the eye can see, branching off beyond hills and desert plains. It is a land of spectacular beauty and unpredictable passion, where – for the most part – its people live much as they have for centuries, if not millennia.

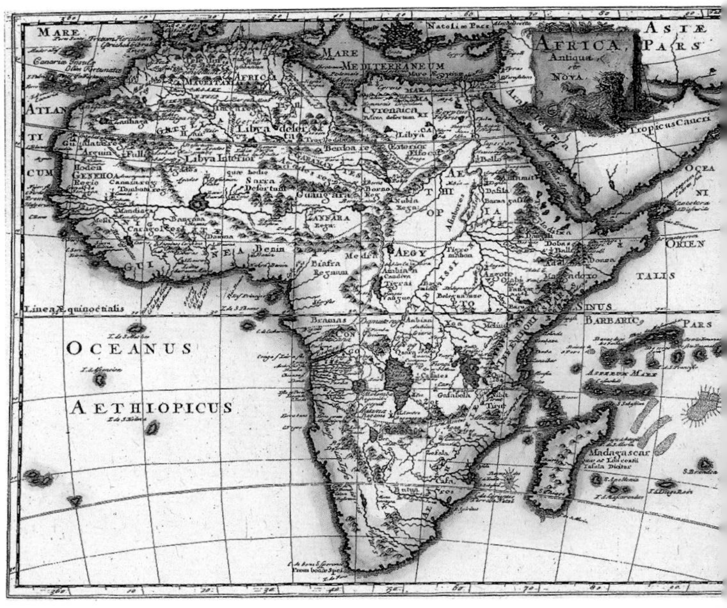

A hand-coloured reproduction of Africa Antiqua et Nova, *published in 1711, by the esteemed German geographer Philipp Cluver (1580–1622).*

WHILE THE CONTINENT CERTAINLY HAS ITS FAIR SHARE of troubles, (and travel here has indeed its downfalls), Africa remains in the realms of the magical. Despite the precarious nature of the economy, the fragility of government and the all-too-common threat of war and unrest in many parts of the continent, the nations of Africa are united in more than simple gloom and pessimism. Given a shared history of foreign oppression and cultural looting from so much of the Western world, there is a passion and a commitment here that seems to overshadow even the most ominous predictions of its future.

From the baking sands of the Sahara to the emptiness of the Kalahari, the marshlands of the Nile Delta to the wetlands of St Lucia, Africa is the quintessential playground for intrepid adventurers. Much remains unexplored and free of the commercialism that pervades the Developed World, yet the deep-rooted hospitality and welcome offered by its citizens are hard to match in even the most sophisticated holiday destinations in Europe, Asia and even the Americas. Despite often pitiful home conditions and an all-pervading poverty, the rural – and, to some degree, urban – people of Africa have retained an almost noble outlook on life. Although there is no denying that corruption is indeed rife, bureaucratic red-tape can be more than simply irritating, and certain parts of the continent do in fact pose health and safety risks for the Western traveller, that indefinable sense of 'untramelled terrain' – discovering a new world – is what entices adventurers of every persuasion to what was once known as The Dark Continent. Today, with a little determination and dollars in the pocket, it is not difficult to conquer the challenges of Africa: wade through its wetlands, raft its white waters, climb its towering peaks, leap off its precipices, and hike through the dense undergrowth of its rainforests.

While the romantic, pastoralist notion of 'unspolit' Africa is all but gone – more than half the population of about 340 million Africans survive on less than US$1 a day, and by the end of the last century, the world's most indebted countries owed no less than US$200 billion – what remains is an unshakable intrigue in what the continent still hides and nurtures, way beyond the all-seeing eye of the camera, the international film crews and wildlife documentors. This ill-defined quality has ensured that the intrepid adventures of colonial explorers, such as David Livingstone and others of his ilk, continue to enthrall and captivate their latter-day counterparts: environmentalists and social commentators such as David Attenborough, and modern adventurers such as Jim Rogers, Michael Palin and Fiona Walker. Because Africa still grapples with encroaching desert sands, deforestation, poaching and the decimation of wildlife herds, and so many of its people still face famine, drought and oppression, it may thus be the adventure – both literal and figurative – offered by its rivers and forests, deserts and grasslands that will prove to be the continent's saving grace, the light at the end of a long tunnel that has seen untold destruction in the pre- and post-colonial era of both Africa's lands and the civilisations that have arisen here. The success of Africa's tentative steps toward embracing foreign travel, of course, depends largely on those foreign travellers, and their sense of responsibility and morality.

On a continent where so many people subsist on little more than a handful of grain, it is relatively easy for the unscrupulous traveller to take advantage of the desperation and, for the price of a T-shirt or a ballpoint pen, take home a handsome trophy, be it a lion pelt, zebra hide, tortoise shell or hand-carved sculpture and other ancestral treasures that fetch inestimable prices on the

ABOVE *Egypt's grand Sphinx at El Giza has endured the test of time and witnessed countless travellers pose with her for photographs.*
RIGHT *Darkest Africa retains a degree of the tribal tradition of previous decades (as seen in this village scene from the former Belgian Congo, now the DRC), albeit usually with a touch more commercialism.*

Travellers enjoying the colonial benefits of a relaxed mule ride on a palm-tree lined road on the way to Saqqara in Egypt, near the pyramids.

Dr. David Livingstone (missionary, doctor, explorer, scientist and anti-slavery activist) was the first white man to lay eyes on Victoria Falls (one of the great wonders of the world) in the course of charting most of Africa in the late-1800s. Millions have since gazed upon the Falls, including The Prince of Wales in 1925.

Western market. Such has been the plight of Africa for centuries - and most conspicuously over the last few decades - and it has brought untold misfortune to the continent. And yet, in return for such great reward, travellers today may reap enormous benefit from the experience alone, leaving nothing but footprints in the sand and taking nothing but photographs.

"Travellers today may reap enormous benefit from the experience alone, leaving nothing but footprints in the sand and taking nothing but photographs."

Africa boasts a complexity of geology, climate, culture and biodiversity shared by no other continent, and the remarkable portfolio of adventures it offers reflects the many extraordinary faces of the land and its peoples.

The vastness of the landmass, covering more than 30 million square kilometres (some 12 million square miles), and the rich and complicated heritage of its indigenous people - over 1400 languages are spoken in Africa - are undoubtedly its most treasured assets. Across the entire length and breadth of this remarkable continent, from mountain to sea, desert to savanna, are endless vistas of breathtaking landscapes peopled by an enormous cultural diversity. From remote, virtually isolated spots deep in the hills are age-old customs that defy Western interpretation, while the blinking lights on busy streets of its great cities reflect a contemporary urban culture unmatched anywhere else in the world. And yet, despite all the variations in colour, shape, texture and temperament in an ever-changing social and geographical landscape, there is an extraordinary affinity with the spirit of the land, a long-cherished legacy of diversity that, ironically, embraces the unity of it all. This is the face of the Real Africa.

SEAN FRASER, author

Hollywood has always been enthralled by Africa's jungles and deserts. This scene from the 1926 classic Beau Geste shows three French Foreign Legionnaires battling the desert winds to set up their overnight camp.

How To Navigate Through This Atlas

SEE LEGEND ON FLAP

This Atlas has been designed to guide you easily to your chosen destination, adventure or area of interest. An easy-to-use contents page appears at the start of each section to help you find well-known places of interest (see page 3). The atlas is split into five colour-coded sections (shown on this page). The best starting point is the regional (blue) spreads: coloured index tabs direct you to relevant town plans, parks and adventure activities for each region (as shown on this page).

The regional spreads include map reference page numbers for the touring section (main mapping). The legend appears on the flap to allow the reader to access this information while referring to any page.

Go Directly to Regional Sections Page 8

Locator

Colour coded chapters

Picture Captions
Captions for all pictures on the regional pages appear under the heading Picture Captions. These bullets provide a cross-reference to the text (where relevant) as well as on the map.

Country Information
Vital statistics for each country within the Region

Map References
Each Top Attraction has a page number below it which directs you to the relevant page of the Main Map Touring Section.

Go Directly to Town Plans Page 162

Town Plan Maps
Detailed street plans of major African cities and towns, featuring a map of the city surrounds where relevant. PAGES 166–207

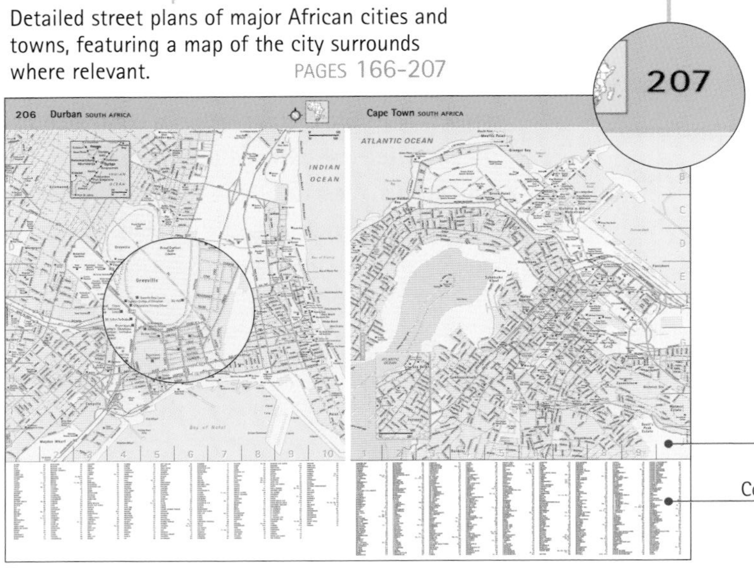

- Places of interest
- City surrounds map
- Historical and cultural areas
- Accommodation options

Index grid

Concise street index

Go Directly to Touring Section Page 40

Main Map Touring Section
Detailed, contiguous topographic maps of the entire African continent (1:1,000,000 and 1:3,500,000), featuring finely crafted relief terrain and all major and minor routes and their distances. PAGES 44–160

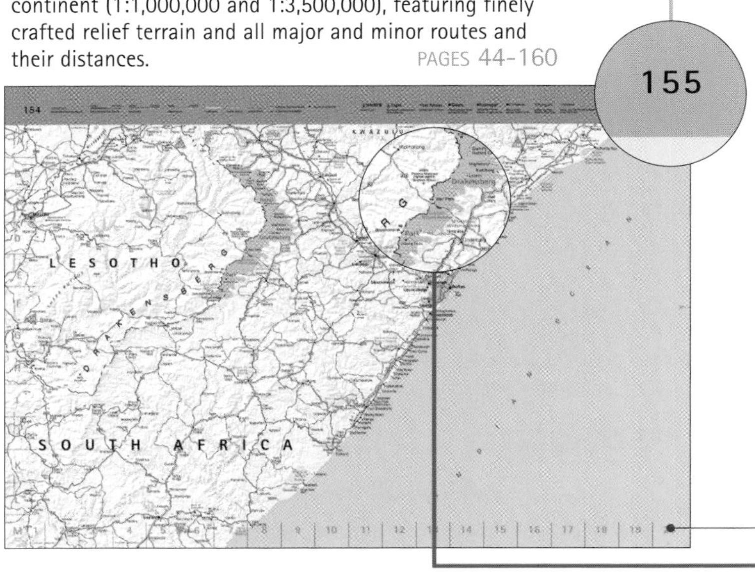

- Places of interest
- Border posts
- Airports and airfields
- Distance pins
- Scenic and adventure routes
- Trails
- National parks and reserves
- Cross-references for all parks and adventures found elsewhere in this atlas

Index grid

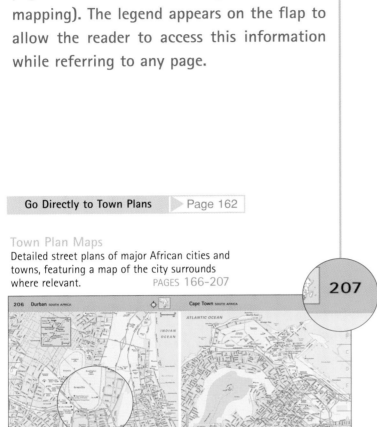

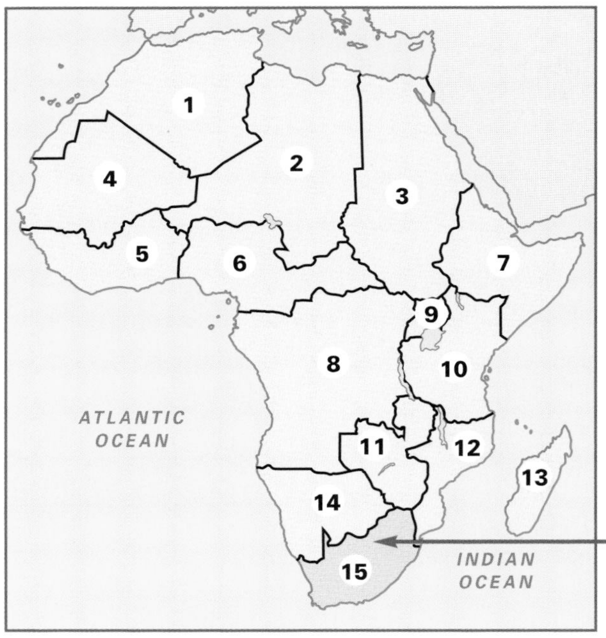

Go Directly to National Park Introductions ▶ Page 208

National Parks

The national parks and reserves of each region (as well as individual flora and fauna) are introduced in this section. All parks and reserves in the region are listed with a cross-reference to the bulleted map. PAGES 212–241

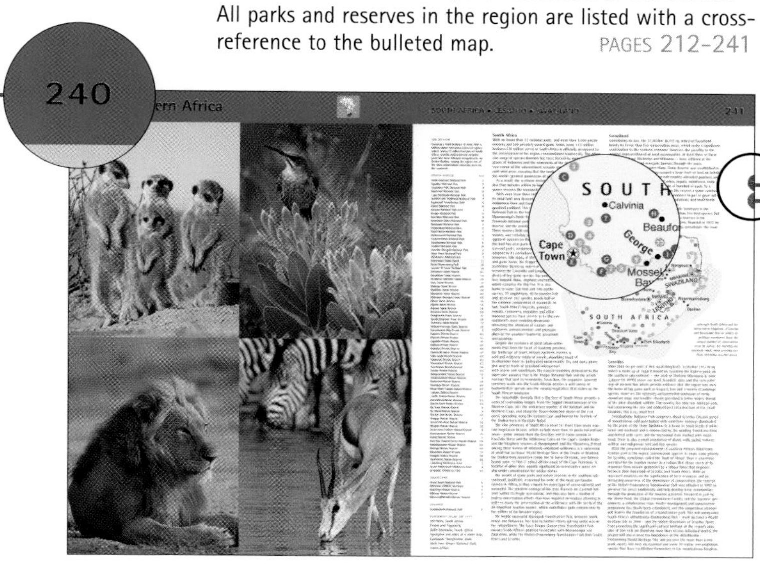

Index Tabs
Coloured tabs guide the reader to the National Parks and Adventures covered in each Region.

- Full colour photographs
- Map indicating park and reserve location
- List of all parks in the region

Regional Section

This atlas introduces the African continent in a selection of 15 geographical regions which are introduced over 30 pages. The Regional Section focuses on people and places (past and present), providing a basic feel for the countries within each region. PAGES 10–39

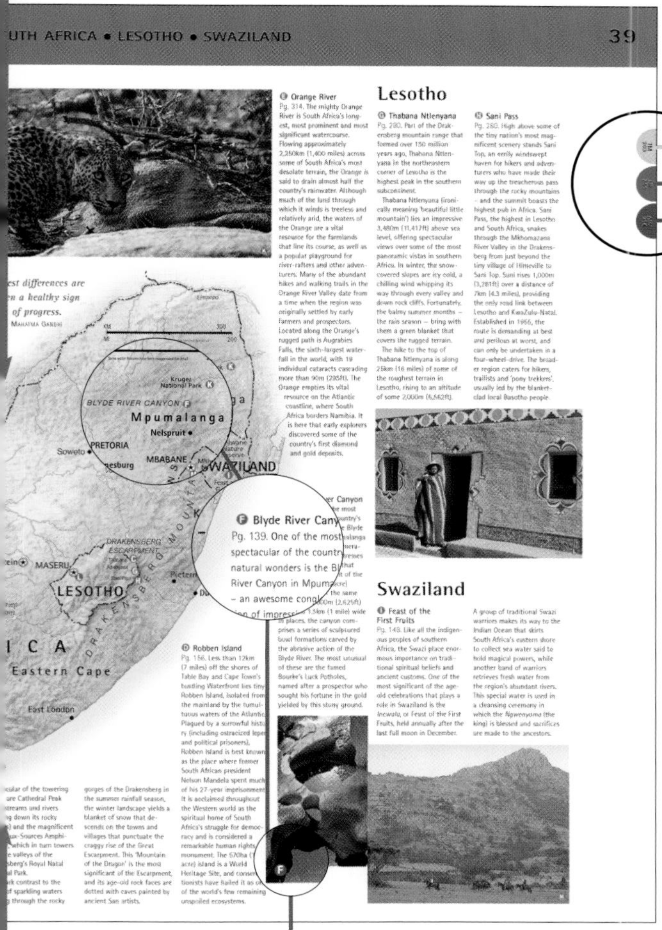

Go Directly to National Parks ▶ Page 242

Index Tabs
Coloured tabs provide an easy guide to the start of the relevant Town Maps, National Parks and Adventure for each Region.

National Park and Key Tourist Maps

Detailed, large-scale maps covering selected national parks and conservation areas spread throughout Africa, including enlarged insets of areas of particular interest and cross-references to adventure activities. PAGES 244–281

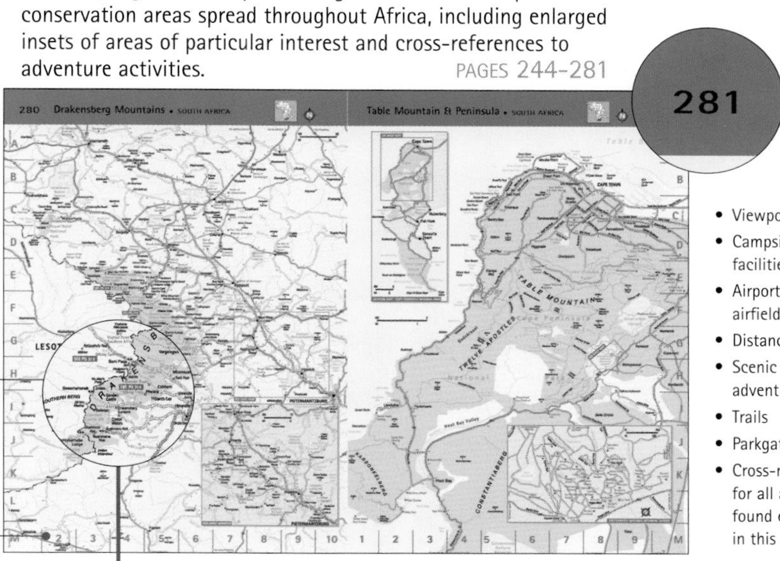

Detailed park map

Index grid

- Viewpoints
- Campsites and facilities
- Airports and airfields
- Distance pins
- Scenic and adventure routes
- Trails
- Parkgate
- Cross-references for all adventures found elsewhere in this Atlas

Top Attractions

The main centres and places of interest are described on the regional pages. A bullet ties in with the relevant picture and its location on the map.

Go Directly to Adventure Activities ▶ Page 282

Adventure Activities

Six adventure activities are explored for each region, covering a wide variety of relevant adventure possibilities. PAGES 286–315

THE REGIONS OF AFRICA AS USED IN THIS ATLAS

1. The Maghreb
2. The Sahara
3. The Nile Valley
4. The Taoudenni Basin
5. The Ivory Coast
6. The Equatorial Interior
7. The Horn of Africa
8. The Congo Basin
9. The Great Lakes
10. The Great Rift Valley
11. The Great Zambezi
12. The Mozambique Coast
13. The Indian Ocean Islands
14. The Skeleton Coast
15. Southern Africa

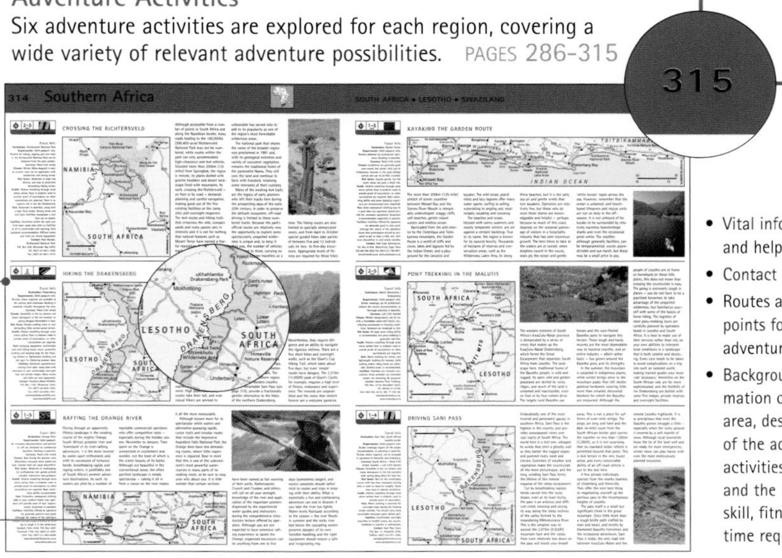

Map indicating route

- Vital information and helpful hints
- Contact details
- Routes and access points for all adventures
- Background information on the area, description of the adventure activities available and the level of skill, fitness or time required

Countries of Africa by Region

A lone pirogue navigates through the gentle, reeded waters of the Okavango Delta, Botswana.

The Maghreb

MOROCCO

(including Western Sahara)
Capital: Rabat
Area: 712,550 km^2/ 275,112mi^2
Population: 30 million
Main ethnic groups
- Arab and Berber (99%)
- European (1%)

Main languages:
- Arabic
- Berber
- French

Main religion:
- Muslim (99%)

Currency: Moroccan dirham (100 centimes)

CANARY ISLANDS (Spain)

Capital:
- Santa Cruz de Tenerife (Western Islands)
- Las Palmas – Gran Canaria (Eastern Islands)

Area: 7 major and 6 minor islands, cover 7,050km^2/2,720mi^2 of the Atlantic Ocean
Population: 1.83 million
Main ethnic groups:
- Canarios (96%)

Main language:
- Castilian Spanish

Main religion:
- Roman Catholic (96%)

Currency: Euro (100 cents)

ALGERIA

Capital: Algiers
Area: 2,381,740 km^2/ 919,590mi^2
Population: 31.4 million
Main ethnic groups:
- Arab and Berber (99%)
- European (1%)

Main languages:
- Arabic
- Berber
- French

Main religions:
- Muslim (99%)
- Christian and Jewish (combined, 1%)

Currency: Algerian dinar, DZD (100 centimes)

TUNISIA

Capital: Tunis
Area: 163,610 km^2/ 63,170mi^2
Population: 9.8 million
Main ethnic groups:
- Arab and Berber (98%)
- European (1%)

Main languages:
- Arabic
- French

Main religions:
- Muslim (98%)
- Christian (1%)

Currency: Tunisian dinar, TND (1,000 millimes)

The Maghreb is an area of fertile coastal plains, olive groves, towering mountain ranges and baking desert sands, and the latter-day politics of the region remains as varied as its landscape. Morocco, which includes the Western Sahara (its occupied territory since 1975), is a constitutional monarchy, while Tunisia is a multiparty republic and Algeria is governed by a military regime. The people of the region are predominantly of Arabic and Berber descent, with a scattering of Europeans, largely because of the area's proximity to Europe and colonial ties with France. These ties were only fairly recently severed, with Morocco gaining independence in 1956 and Algeria in 1962. Off the coast of Western Sahara lie the Canary Islands, a self-governing protectorate of Spain. Despite these close associations with the West, the Maghreb remains distinctly African, bustling with markets and punctuated with palm-fringed oases linked by nomadic desert caravans.

The Maghreb has been embroiled in conflict between the various powers seeking control of the region during its long and often turbulent history, yet the territory is one of the most stable on the continent. Tunisia, Morocco and the Canary Islands are relatively prosperous and cater well for tourist travel, while Algeria is a notable exception.

D

B

'He who does not travel does not know the value of men.'

MOORISH PROVERB

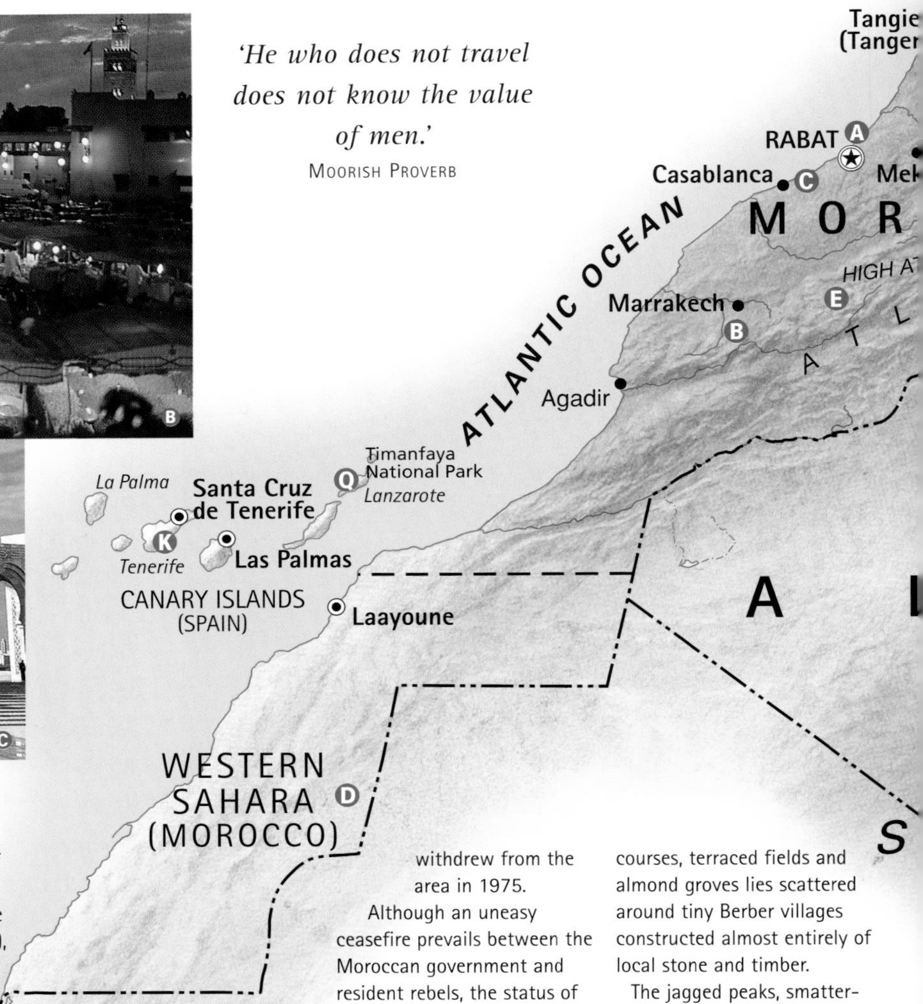

Morocco

C

Ⓐ Rabat

Pg. 168. Steeped in a long and colourful history, the modern city of Rabat is every inch the nation's capital. Unmistakably influenced by the distinct flavours of Phoenicia and Carthage, the cosmopolitan centre is the country's administrative hub and, as such, lacks the same exotic appeal as enticing Marrakech and Casablanca. The contrasting faces of the old and the new in Rabat, however, remain a fascinating tribute to the history of the nation, and it continues to play a significant role in latter-day Morocco.

Ⓑ Marrakech

Pg. 168. Framed by the snow-covered peaks of the High Atlas Mountains, ancient Marrakech is virtually surrounded by some 13,000 hectares (32,000 acres) of palm and olive groves. In the heart of the city is the market square of Djemaa el Fna, a heady mix of bustling stalls selling everything from dates and oranges to carpets and traditional aphrodisiacs. A parade of snake charmers and belly dancers, monkey trainers and henna artists weaves through the haphazard tent-like booths. Winding alleys lead off the market into a maze of cubicles and shop-fronts, while above looms the towering 70-metre (230-foot) minaret of Koutoubia, its magnificent proportions and elaborate design a breathtaking monument to Islam that has influenced many of Morocco's architectural masterpieces.

Ⓒ Casablanca

Pg. 168. Considered to be the nation's unofficial capital, Casablanca is a thriving modern city far removed from the exotic literature emanating from the West. Scattered along its panoramic shore are beach clubs and nightclubs, fashionable cafés and exclusive boutiques. Many public buildings were built in authentic Art Deco style, and there are a number of monuments and mosques (principal among them the ornate Mosquée Hassan II), cathedrals and theatres. Casablanca is permeated throughout with the rich and distinct flavour of its colourful past, but nowhere is this more evident than in the Old Medina. This provides a fascinating insight into the history of the old city with its eclectic mix of opulent and dilapidated markets and malls.

Ⓓ Western Sahara

Pg. 287. The expansive stretch that is the Western Sahara is officially considered by Morocco as its 'Saharan provinces', but the sparsely populated region has been disputed territory since Spain withdrew from the area in 1975.

Although an uneasy ceasefire prevails between the Moroccan government and resident rebels, the status of the Western Sahara remains undecided. Morocco retains a firm hold over the extensive lands, having erected a 1,600-kilometre (1,000-mile) sand wall to curb militant activity. The Moroccans have also injected considerable capital into the development projects that will help uplift both the desert infrastructure and the city of Laayoune. There are roadblocks and police cordons, yet traffic between the Western Sahara and Morocco remains relatively unimpeded, and local and tourist travel are encouraged.

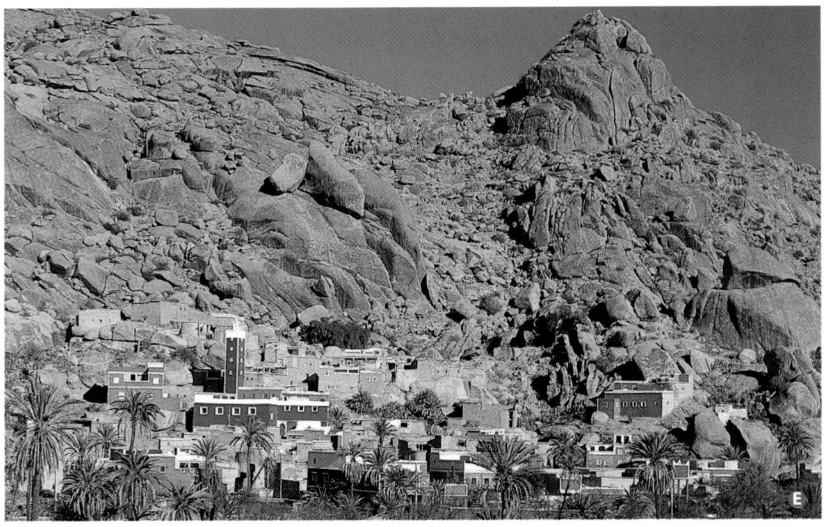

E

Ⓔ High Atlas

Pg. 245. The Atlas is the highest mountain range in North Africa, its forests, crests, peaks and valleys a climber's dream and an adventure paradise. Long, winding rivers carve their way through deep granite gorges, while a series of watercourses, terraced fields and almond groves lies scattered around tiny Berber villages constructed almost entirely of local stone and timber.

The jagged peaks, smattering of sacred shrines and derelict palaces lure adventurers and sightseers to the zigzagging tracks and trails towered over by the impressive Jebel Toubkal. At a height of 4,167 metres (13,670 feet), the looming massif is the highest in the Atlas range and provides some of the world's greatest treks. Both challenging and inspiring, the steep valleys and sheer rock faces attract ardent climbers, while a number of lesser walks and hikes cater for the casual hiker.

Interspersed along this web-like network of mule trails are numerous Berber settlements, isolated pockets of an age-old culture that has seen little change over the centuries. The emphasis here is on the warmth and hospitality for which the deeply spiritual Berbers are renowned. Visitors should adhere to the rather strict local code of conduct.

Tunisia

Ⓕ Monastir
Pg. 49. Tracing its history to Punic and Roman times, Monastir is a popular resort destination and vital centre of tertiary education. It boasts all the amenities of prominent tourist stopovers, including an airport, a variety of watersports and night-time entertainment for the throngs of holiday-makers.

Ⓖ Tunis
Pg. 170. Once little more than a small fishing village, Tunisia's capital is the most cosmopolitan of all North African cities. Within its ancient walls are the souks and minarets of old, but the expanding city includes a sophisticated network of wide boulevards, busy streets, chic pavement cafés and lush parks well accustomed to the tourist traffic.

Ⓗ Chott el Jerid
Pg. 246. As flat as glass, the crystalline Chott el Jerid is the most expansive of the salt lakes characteristic of central Tunisia and spans some 250 kilometres (150 miles) by 20 kilometres (13 miles). These pans form soggy marshes in winter, attracting an array of water birds to the wetlands. In summer, the salt crystallizes to form a gleaming crust.

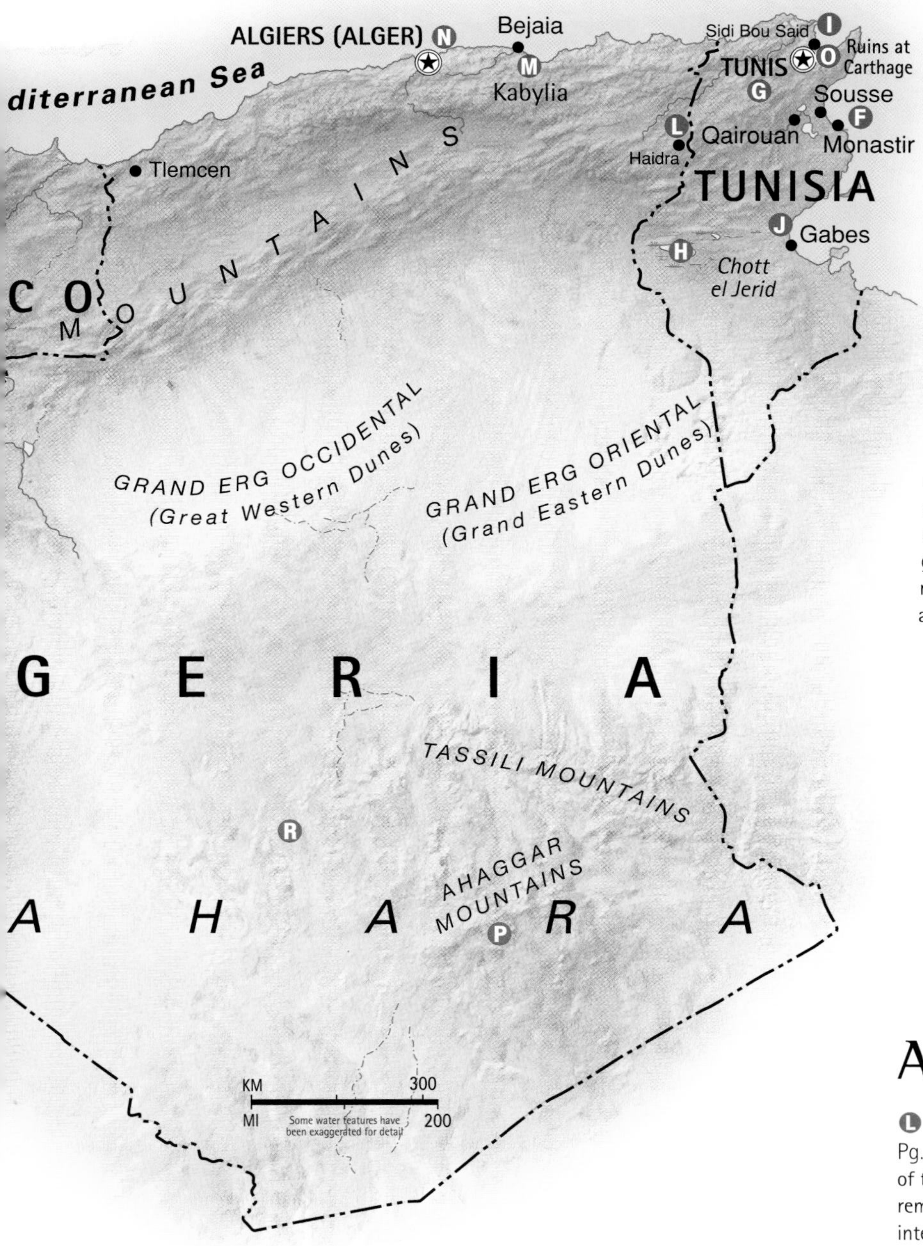

Ⓘ Sidi Bou Said
Pg. 49. Picturesque Sidi Bou Said is blessed with uninterrupted views dotted with whitewashed cottages cascading with pink bougainvillea, and the landscape is straight from a picture postcard. High up on the hill overlooking the quaint little village stands the old Arab fort around which the settlement developed in the 13th century. Famed as a popular modern-day retreat for acclaimed artists rather than for its unique beauty, the art galleries of Sidi Bou Said remain the village's top attractions.

Ⓙ Gabes
Pg. 246. The Gulf of Gabes sweeps down from Sfax to the isle of Jerba in a deep crescent and offers a welcome respite from the more frenetic tourist spots. The settlement here comprises a thriving little town that reached its peak in the Middle Ages, but today its principal functions include heavy industry and commerce rather than the tourism market. Gabes has nevertheless retained much of its old-world charm and remains unspoilt, long sandy beaches baking under the North African sun.

PICTURE CAPTIONS
Ⓑ Marrakech market, Morocco
Ⓒ Casablanca, Morocco
Ⓓ Dunes, Western Sahara, Morocco
Ⓔ High Atlas mountains, Morocco
Ⓗ Dry salt waves, Chott el Jerid, Tunisia
Ⓘ Sidi Bou Said, Tunisia
Ⓞ Ruins at Carthage, Tunisia
Ⓟ Ahaggar Mountains, Algeria
Ⓠ Timanfaya National Park, Canary Islands
Ⓡ Camels, Sahara desert, Algeria

Algeria

Ⓛ Haidra
Pg. 49. Although very little of the original Roman town remains, a number of small interesting sites hint at Haidra's affiliation with the old Empire: an ancient forum, citadel, Roman baths and fluted columns, and an enormous Byzantine fort.

Ⓜ Kabylia
Pg. 49. Like much of the country, Algeria's Kabylia region has been ravaged by the continuing civil war. It is perhaps best renowned for its traditional Berber communities and for the extraordinary riding skills of the Berber horsemen. By far the majority of Algeria's population is of Arab-Berber origin, and the locals still speak an area-specific dialect, with only a smattering of French. Custom plays a fundamental role in the daily lives of these people, who are relatively isolated from 'civilization'. They place much importance on their means of transport – camels and horses – and have developed remarkable skills as riders.

Ⓝ Algiers
Pg. 169. Algiers is the capital of war-torn Algeria, Africa's second-largest country, where Islamic fundamentalists are intent on bringing the national economy and the government to its knees in their quest for an Islamic state. Travel in and around the capital remains perilous and is ill-advised, in particular for casual sightseers and tourists with little or no comprehension of the political complexities that continue to ravage Algeria.

Canary Islands (Spain)

Ⓚ Tenerife
Pg. 44. As the largest island in the Canary archipelago, Tenerife is also the capital of the Western Islands, a striking conglomeration of 13 islands set in the sparkling waters of the Atlantic. The rocky ridge that forms Tenerife's spine is covered in the most part with lush banana plantations, orchards and fields of green, and culminates in the 3,718-metre (12,198-foot) Mount Teide – still heralded (ironically) as the highest point 'in Spain'. The islands are administered as part of Spain, yet lie just 96 kilometres (60 miles) off the African coast and some 1,120 kilometres (696 miles) from the European mainland.

The island of Tenerife, with its own capital at Santa Cruz de Tenerife on the northeast coast, is quite spectacular, lined with popular holiday resorts, pristine beaches and leafy old villages. Each of the hamlets has its own town square that hints at its connection to colonial Spain, and sprinkled across the island are historic sites and places of interest for holiday-makers.

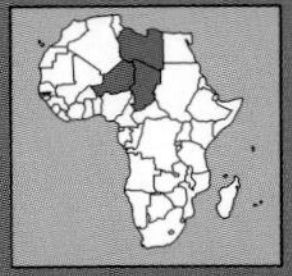

The Sahara

The central corridor extending from the Mediterranean south to the heart of Africa offers some of Africa's finest desert panoramas, covering as it does so much of the great Sahara, which reaches across North Africa to create the world's most extensive desert. The proximity to Europe and the cultural diversity of nations that occupy this stark but beautiful space have meant that the sands of Libya, Chad and Niger have seen an endless stream of hard-fought battles and fruitless wars, the remnants of which still plague parts of the region today. The long-standing disputes that have arisen as a result of Chad's long civil war, Libya's dubious foreign policy and Niger's Tuareg uprising have meant that security is at times precarious, causing concern for the safety of Western travellers. Because of the volatility of the political situation, Libya is, perhaps not altogether fairly, considered a rather risky travel destination.

The desert landscape, harsh climate and troubled histories of Libya, Niger and Chad have prevented them from becoming booming tourist destinations, but although there are indeed very real dangers, in many cases these may not be life-threatening, especially as each nation emerges to take advantage of the potential offered by a growing tourism industry.

NIGER

Capital: Niamey
Area: 1,267,000km²/ 489,190mi²
Population: 11.6 million
Main ethnic groups:
- Hausa (56%)
- Djerma (22%)
- Fulani (9%)

Main languages:
- French
- Hausa
- Djerma
- Fulani
- Tuareg
- Teda

Main religions:
- Muslim (85%)
- Traditional beliefs (14%)
- Christian (1%)

Currency: Franc CFA (100 centimes)

LIBYA

Capital: Tripoli
Area: 1,759,540km²/ 679,360mi²
Population: 5.4 million
Main ethnic groups:
- Arab and Berber (97%)

Main languages:
- Arabic
- Tuareg

Main religion:
- Muslim (97%)

Currency: Libyan dinar (1,000 dirhams)

CHAD

Capital: N'Djamena
Area: 1,284,000km²/ 495,755mi²
Population: 9.0 million
Main ethnic groups:
- Bagirmi/Kreish/Sara (32%)
- Sudanic Arab (25%)
- Teda (7%)

Main languages:
- French
- Sara
- Maba

Main religions:
- Muslim (44%)
- Christian (33%)
- Traditional beliefs (23%)

Currency: Franc CFA (100 centimes)

Niger

Ⓐ Niamey

Pg. 171. Nestled on the edge of the Sahara and enclosed by the stark beauty of the desert, Niamey is a delightful blend of the old and new. With a population of over half a million (mostly Hausa), the city was declared the nation's capital in the 1920s and boasts adequate visitor's facilities, while retaining much of its desert character and African charm.

The second-largest country in West Africa, and Africa's main producer of uranium, Niger plays an important role in the regional economy. It is a pretty enough place with great markets, such as the Grand and Petit Marchés, and a few surprising highlights, most notably the National Museum complex.

Ⓑ Ténéré Desert

Pg. 249. The rolling dunes of this remote region – dotted with little else than small herds of gazelle, occasional oases and small fields of vegetables and wheat – hide centuries-old tracks of camel caravans. The panorama of massive dunes is ever changing, and all life is susceptible to the whims of a sandstorm and the rare downpour of seasonal rains. The winds that whip across the vast emptiness produce a strange hum or whistle, almost unnoticed by the groups of nomadic Tuareg (a proud race of the Sahara's Berber people). Dressed in flowing robes like Lawrence of Arabia, Berbers live a Spartan life, constantly on the move across the searing sands. Great stretches are rarely broken by a single bush, shrub or tree, and pivotal to existence here is the hardy camel, bought, sold and milked at every oasis or village. Vast tracts of sand alternate with rock-strewn piste, many decorated with rock paintings (some 10,000 years old) illustrating cattle, giraffe, and even ostrich.

B

E

D

PICTURE CAPTIONS
Ⓑ Ténéré Desert, Niger
Ⓓ Mosque, Agadez, Niger
Ⓔ Niger River, Niger
Ⓖ Leptis Magna, Libya
Ⓗ Acacus Mountains, Libya
Ⓚ Lake Chad, Chad
Ⓛ Coastline near Bardia, east of Tobruk, Libya
Ⓜ Desert town, Libya
Ⓝ Scimitar-horned oryx, Zakouma National Park, Chad

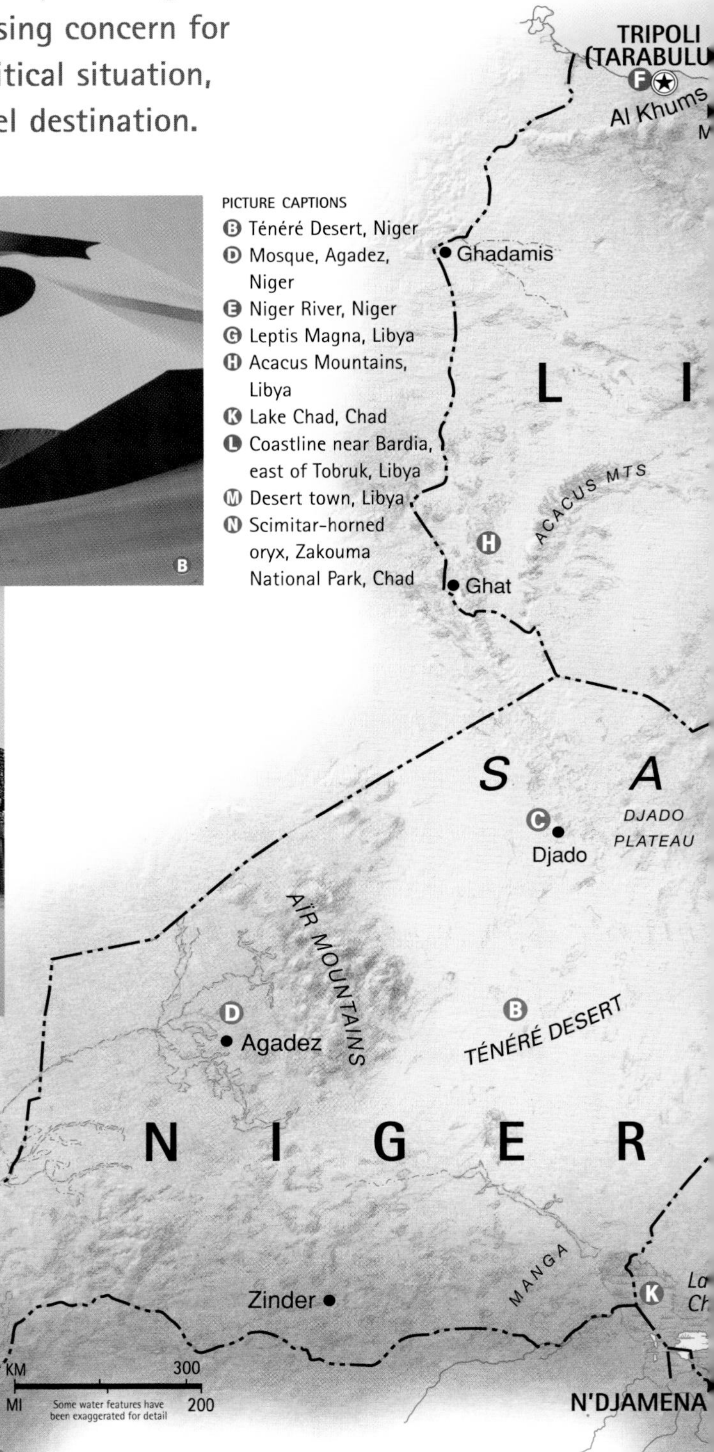

Ⓒ Djado

Pg. 249. Well off the beaten tourist track is one of the country's most intriguing, yet least visited, cultural attractions. This is the village of mud huts erected some 700 years ago by the Toubou people. Set against a breathtaking backdrop of rugged mountainscape and barricaded from civilization by a measureless expanse of wild and windy wasteland, dry and virtually featureless, the sense of isolation here is bewildering, the long-abandoned homes of crumbling mud and primitive bricks haunted by an eerie silence. Virtually unchanged since the convoluted labyrinth of cave-like dwellings were deserted by their occupants more than two centuries ago, the wind and elements have taken their toll on the walls and foundations of the huts that still stand atop the hill. The mystical aura that pervades the mud homes of Djado is one that can only be found on the desert dunes of Africa at its emptiest.

Ⓓ Agadez

Pg. 249. In a region of desolate plains circled by imposing volcanic peaks, framed by the distant massif of the Aïr mountains, ancient Agadez was one of the most vibrant centres in the southern desert. For centuries, the booming town was the congregation point for travellers and Tuareg and Hausa traders, and an important centre for desert wanderers and merchants. The bustling town is as picturesque as any cinematographer would have us believe, while centuries of trade and travel have created a latter-day population that is a mix of people and languages. The desert architecture is typical of the Sahel, and the 500-year-old minarets of the Grand Mosque were revered as one of the finest Muslim places of worship on the continent.

Ⓔ Niger River

Pg. 288. One of Niger's few reliable water sources, the Niger River is the lifeblood of a nation plagued by drought and uncertain rainfall. It passes through Mali into the southwest corner of Niger and on to Nigeria, its waters integral to the survival of fishing villages, farming communities and settlements on its banks. The river's course remains one of the least explored in modern history, despite the many camel caravans, intrepid explorers and modern-day adventurers that ply its waters.

The river's waters – only navigable in small areas – irrigate the lands alongside, helping to balance the erratic rains, leaving the rice paddies lush and verdant. The health of the river is preserved largely by the bourgou grass that covers sections of its flood plains, providing the staple fish diet of locals, fodder for cattle and a breeding ground for aquatic life.

TM 171
NP 214
ADV 288

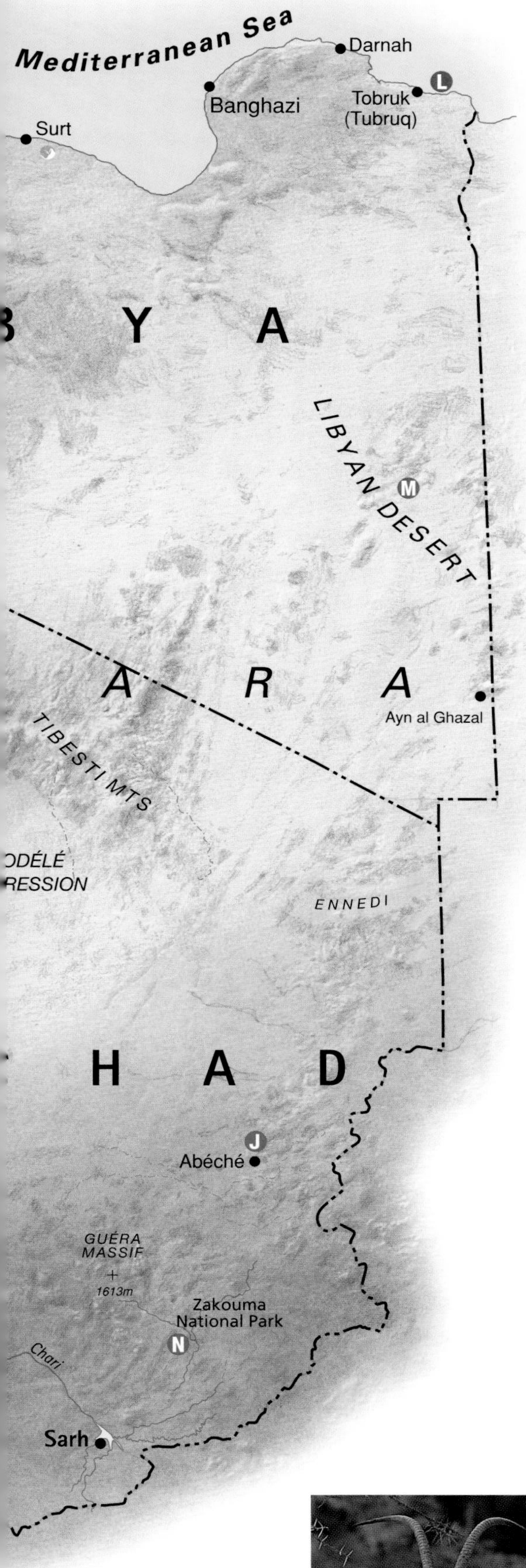

Libya

Ⓕ Tripoli

Pg. 172. With a population of just over 1.5 million, Tripoli – with Banghazi, the joint capital of Libya – is one of the most alluring and atmospheric of Africa's great capitals. A thoroughly modern city, with tall contemporary structures, a well-planned infrastructure and latter-day tourist traps, the old section was built on the original site of ancient Oea. The grand old medina is a maze of side streets, darkened doorways and haphazard souks. With a staunchly Muslim community, alcohol is hard to come by, a strict dress code is rigidly adhered to and the rowdy thoroughfares are dotted with a series of charming old minaret-adorned mosques that date from the heyday of the Ottomans. The most impressive is the stately Karamanli Mosque off Green Square which, in turn, is guarded over by the most recognized landmark in Tripoli: the Old Castle – known locally as Assai al Hamra – overlooking both the harbour front and the ancient medina. The city itself is perhaps the region's safest stopover, with a friendly and generally hospitable community who welcome visitors to their almost forgotten home ground. The city and the country can be frustrating to navigate, especially if you are unfamiliar with the language, culture and geography, but as long as you observe the traditions and customs of the locals and reserve judgment on the political situation, it may prove to be one of the safest and most enjoyable destinations in North Africa.

Ⓖ Leptis Magna

Pg. 288. Widely acknowledged as one of the very best surviving Roman ruins in the region – if not the world – and, along with the ancient Greek metropolis of Cyrene, offering some of the finest historical experiences in Africa, the crumbling city of Leptis Magna is undoubtedly one of the highlights on the country's tour route. Situated not far from the town of Al Khums and no more than 120km (75 miles) to the east of the capital, it is a masterpiece of ancient architecture that covers a relatively large stretch of the Libyan interior.

Originally erected by the Carthaginian invaders, the Roman town at the mouth of the Wadi Lebda – conveniently positioned on the bustling trade route – quickly mushroomed into a burgeoning merchant town, dealing in olive oil and grain supplies. Circled by a forest of stately pine trees and stands of olive trees – and within easy access to some of Libya's finest beaches – the ancient archaeological site was well preserved by the encroaching sands and was only discovered in the 20th century.

Ⓗ Acacus Mountains

Pg. 289. Although the political instability of the broader region hinders access to the Acacus Mountains, the hilly landscape in the far south remains one of Libya's most enduring natural heritage sites, boasting a remarkable array of outstanding prehistoric rock art. The principal human settlement in this desolate wilderness is the small, historic town of Ghat, a dull place aside from the extraordinary desert architecture and some of the Sahara's most spectacularly scenic vistas. The town and the surrounding hillsides are populated by the nomadic Tuareg, many of whom now act as travel guides.

Chad

Ⓘ N'Djamena

Pg. 171. The principal city of one of the most impoverished nations in Africa, N'Djamena has few natural resources, endures a punishing climate and has suffered enormously through a 25-year civil war – yet it is one of the most gratifying destinations on the outskirts of the Sahara. Its buildings are scarred by bullets and shrapnel, and many are dilapidated and run down. The central urban district still struggles with substandard accommodation, petty crime, prostitution, and soldiers who will not hesitate to draw their weapons for the slightest transgression. Nonetheless, a renewed life pervades the city streets, and the severely pillaged National Museum is taking on a more alluring look, boasting some fine exhibits and displays.

Ⓙ Abéché

Pg. 248. Surrounded by the desert sands of Libya and some 800km (497 miles) east of N'Djamena, Abéché's stone inlaid walkways and shaded alleys are a long way from its bustling days as a devoutly Muslim settlement (capital of the Ouadaï sultanate and its vital slave trade, and a critical stop on the merchant route that crossed the country en route to the shipping ports along the Indian Ocean). An important Islamic centre, Abéché offers a fascinating insight into the history of both the immediate precinct and the broader region, but is not particularly accommodating to visitors.

Ⓚ Lake Chad

Pg. 289. Although scenically splendid and uniquely picturesque, in stark contrast to the natural splendour of the magnificent Tibesti mountain range in the country's northern reaches, Lake Chad is a popular getaway for locals in southern Libya. For foreigners, getting to and from the lake is an arduous task, caught up in red tape and bureaucratic authorities' suspicions of even the most innocuous traveller. The lake shore is a truly beautiful stretch of African landscape, and travel here is considerably safer than in the northern regions. Fed predominantly by the waters of the Chari River, Lake Chad has no clear outlet and, depending on the seasonal rains, covers between 10,000 and 26,000km^2 (4,000 to 10,000 sq. miles), considerably less than it once did. During the frequent and extended droughts the lake tends to sink and has been known to disappear almost entirely.

EGYPT
Capital: Cairo
Area: 1,001,450km²/ 386,660mi²
Population: 71.2 million
Main ethnic groups:
- Eastern Hamitic (90%)
- Other (10%)

Main languages:
- Arabic
- French
- English
- Berber
- Greek
- Armenian

Main religions:
- Muslim (95%)
- Other (5%)

Currency: Egyptian pound (100 piastres)

SUDAN
Capital: Khartoum
Area: 2,495,712km²/ 963,600mi²
Population: 32.6 million
Main ethnic groups:
- Arab (51%)
- Dinka (13%)
- Nuba (9%)
- Beja (7%)
- Other (20%)

Main language:
- Arabic

Main religions:
- Muslim (70%)
- Christian (5%)
- Other (including traditional spiritual beliefs) (25%)

Currency: Sudanese pound (100 piastres)

Nestled in the bowl of the great Nile Basin, Egypt and Sudan are both hot and, at times, stifling. Both nations have as many differences as similarities and, although they may be neighbours, the topography of the land and the political landscape are quite disparate. Although rain is scarce throughout much of Egypt and northern Sudan, the southern reaches of Sudan – covered by grassland, savanna, forest and marsh – may experience rainfall for as much as eight months of the year. Their governments are equally diverse – Egypt is a relatively stable republic, largely pro-West and with a history of ethnic tolerance, while military Islamic fundamentalists have governed Sudan since 1989. Sudan has also been plagued by civil unrest between Arab Muslims in the north and African Christians in the south since 1983. Although travel to Egypt remains an important earner of foreign income, security fears have had some effect in recent years, and travel in Sudan may still be risky.

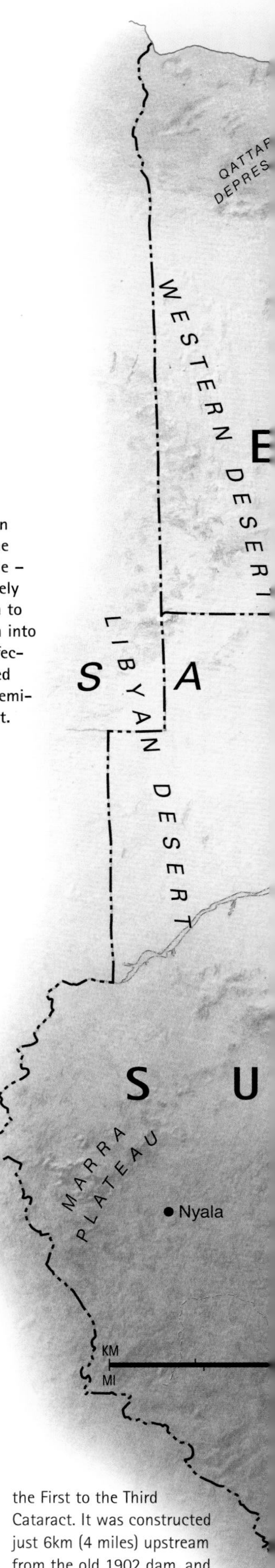

Although rain remains an often painfully scarce commodity, the fertile valley of the mighty Nile – flowing north from the relatively green lands of southern Sudan to the delta that forms its mouth into the Mediterranean – is the effective divide between the parched desertscape of Libya and the semi-arid lands of the eastern desert.

A

B

F

Egypt

Ⓐ Cairo

Pg. 173. The largest city in Africa as well as the Middle East, Cairo is a delightful clamour of taxis and traffic, sights, sounds and smells, and is home to 16 million Egyptians. Its shimmering skyline is a rich amalgamation of modern highrises and rickety flat-topped dwellings, many of which trace their origins back centuries and even tens of centuries.

Cairo is a traveller's delight, providing a fascinating look into the age-old empire of the pharaohs, with markets, museums and music conjuring up the spirits of the ancients. Among Cairo's great treasures is the mosque of El Azhar, founded more than 1,000 years ago and still the religious centre of Islamic Cairo. Another is the bustling Khan el Khalili bazaar, the commercial heart of the city.

Ⓑ Pyramids at Giza

Pg. 251. Approximately 17km (10.5 miles) to the west of Cairo's famed university, and accessible from the capital by either bus or taxi, stand the Great Pyramids at Giza, acclaimed by the ancients as one of the Seven Wonders of the World. The entire conurbation of antediluvian tombs, seemingly swathed in mystery, is spellbinding in its stature. The monumental Sphinx (with the head of a woman atop a lion's body), along with the conical mausoleums of Cheops and Chephren that pierce the desert sky, form El Giza's imposing centre.

So ancient are these magnificent structures that, though they were built adjacent to the Nile, over the centuries the river has meandered over 5km (3 miles) away.

Greek myth has it that the Sphinx (meaning 'to hold fast') guarded ancient Thebes, killing any traveller unable to answer her puzzling riddle – until the mythological Oedipus correctly answered the riddle. The Sphinx then killed herself.

Ⓒ Valley of the Kings

Pg. 250. Although the valley on the west bank of Luxor is barren and apparently lifeless, it is home to one of the most unashamed treasures of the ancient world: a series of long-forgotten crypts crowned by the breathtaking tomb of Tutankhamun, the boy-god-king who died at the tender age of 19. This most spectacular of all the ancient tombs – unseen and unopened for 3,200 years – was first discovered and opened in 1922 by Howard Carter. The four diminutive rooms within the tomb revealed an unparalleled hoard of astounding artefacts and magnificent jewels that had been buried with the young pharaoh who lived during one of the most splendid periods of ancient Egypt.

Ⓓ Sinai

Pg. 290. The rocky, undulating landscape of this mountainous peninsula in northeastern Egypt is situated at the northern end of the Red Sea, neatly flanked by the gulfs of Suez and Aqaba.

The imposing edifice of Jebel Musa stands 2,285m (7,497ft) high, making it one of Egypt's highest mountains and the spiritual heart of the rugged peninsula. It was immortalized in scripture as Mount Sinai, where God gave the Judaic leader Moses the stone tablets that bore the Ten Commandments.

Ⓔ Red Sea

Pg. 290. The blue water of the Red Sea – a long, narrow stretch of water separating Arabia from northeast Africa – is an underwater wonderland of marine gardens, mesmerizing schools of fish, spectacular dive sites and some of the finest coral reefs in the world. Fringing the bewitching desert and the jagged horizon of the highlands, the 438,000km² (169,000 sq. miles) of the Red Sea is said to be anything from 20 to 40 million years old. It links with the Mediterranean in the north via the Suez Canal and spills out into the Indian Ocean in the south. It takes its name from its occasional red appearance as algae congregate in surface waters. The reefs here are festooned with magnificent corals and bursts of colour that originate from the amazing aquatic life. The sandy depths of the great sea are hunted by lionfish and spotted stingray, and the region is so abundant in wildlife that some of the most respected marine scientists of modern time have spent lifetimes studying the enormous biodiversity of this bowl of water.

Ⓕ Aswan

Pg. 250. Situated just below the Nile's First Cataract, Aswan remains a relatively small town, with a population of about 200,000, yet it plays a vital role in the lives of millions of Egyptians, most of whom draw their power from the Aswan High Dam. Officially opened in 1971, the huge dam forms a reservoir on Lake Nasser and stretches some 480km (300 miles) from the First to the Third Cataract. It was constructed just 6km (4 miles) upstream from the old 1902 dam, and the water remains the centre of life here, with domestic cattle and water buffalo gently grazing on its endless banks. Mystery writer Dame Agatha Christie penned a portion of *Murder on the Nile* from her suite in the still-gracious Cataract Hotel overlooking the First Cataract.

E

Ⓖ Nile River

Pg. 250. In the west lies the great Qattara Depression, a remarkable 133m (436ft) below sea level, and to the east stretches the Red Sea. While the upper reaches of the river are often very

TM 173
NP 216
ADV 290

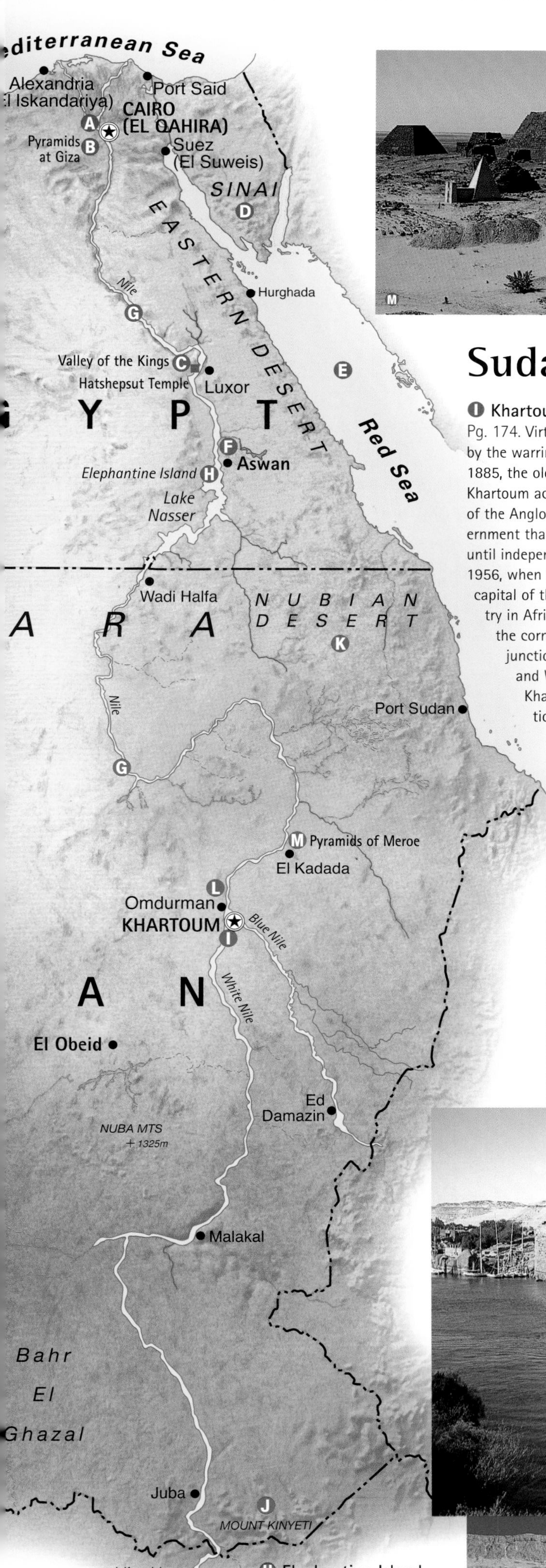

narrow and lined by precipices, the lower valley emerges into the expansive and heavily populated Nile Delta. In contrast to the dry and dusty sands beyond the relatively lush course of the river, no less than 95 per cent of Egypt's population have made their home in the Nile Valley from what comprises only three per cent of the country's landmass.

H Elephantine Island
Pg. 250. In the middle of the mighty Nile, opposite the Aswan High Dam – the latter-day successor to the original dam built in 1902, and twice raised during the course of the 20th century – is the ancient settlement of Elephantine Island, whose island fortress of Yebu acted as the border post between Egypt and Nubia.

Sudan

I Khartoum
Pg. 174. Virtually decimated by the warring Mahdists in 1885, the old city of Khartoum acted as the seat of the Anglo-Egyptian government that ruled Sudan until independence in January 1956, when it became the capital of the largest country in Africa. Nestled into the corner formed by the junction of the Blue and White Nile, Khartoum's population is less than one million, yet it remains the economic hub of the Sudan. Battered by dust storms and suffering precariously low water supplies, the city is picturesque in its own distinct way and surprisingly cosmopolitan. Some 80 per cent of the workforce is occupied in farming on just five per cent of the land, growing cotton, peanuts, gum arabic, sugar and the like. Weak global agricultural prices, a limited infrastructure and ruthless climatic conditions have taken their toll on the once-mighty capital, but an increase in oil production (its first surpluses came in 1999), regular rainfall and foreign investment in local irrigation projects have brought some respite.

J Mount Kinyeti
Pg. 78. Standing proudly on Sudan's border with Uganda, Mount Kinyeti is perhaps Sudan's most significant natural landmark, and the 3,187m (10,456ft) peak of the great mountain is the nation's tallest. It covers much of the flat countryside to the south of the rather featureless plain, and is bound in the east and west by separate mountain ranges. Surrounded by the tropical landscape of the southern reaches, its relatively lush slopes are sheltered from the harshness that pervades the aridity of the northern plains and stand in stark contrast to the inhospitable terrain that stretches north. Mount Kinyeti is a remarkable island of unspoiled wilderness but is virtually inaccessible to all but the bravest and most determined traveller.

K Nubian Desert
Pg. 62. Commonly considered a desert, the Nubian is little more than a vast, virtually horizonless sandstone plateau that stretches across northeastern Africa from the cliffs of the Nile Valley to the shores of the Red Sea. The people here have always been an amalgamation of nomadic groups and subsistence farmers. In recent times the lives of many Nubians were adversely affected by the construction of the reservoir projects at Aswan, when the waters were dammed and thus flooded their traditional farmlands. Fortunately, commerce and the tourist trade now provide the bulk of employment.

L Omdurman
Pg. 62. Situated on the banks of the Nile just north of the capital in central Sudan, this centre of industry and finance is the largest town in the country and, along with Khartoum, forms the nation's greatest urban conurbation. Omdurman was the setting for the great Battle of Omdurman in 1898, in which the Mahdi was expelled by the armed forces of British field marshall Lord Horatio Herbert Kitchener (the 1st Earl of Khartoum and, at that time, the head of the Egyptian army). Enjoying a stark yet surprisingly beautiful setting, Omdurman is a significant contributor to the national economy – largely thanks to its proximity to Khartoum and its location on the course of the Nile.

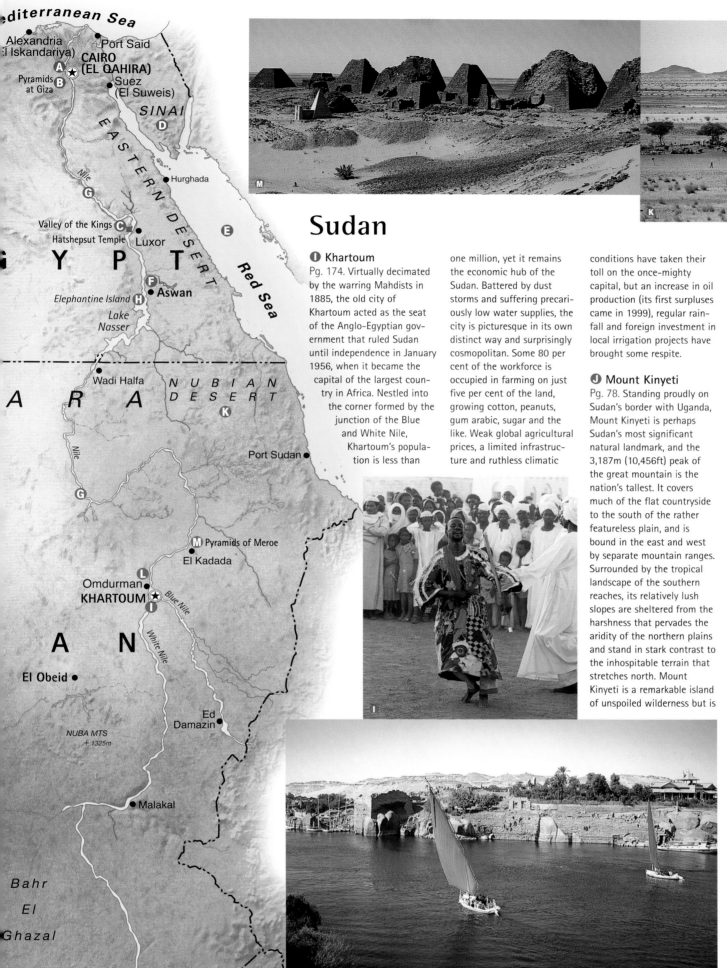

PICTURE CAPTIONS
A Tutankhamun's death mask, Egyptian Museum
B Pyramids at Giza, Egypt
C Hatshepsut Temple, Thebes, Egypt
E Hurghada, Red Sea, Egypt
F Abu Simbel, Egypt
G Feluccas, Nile River, Egypt
I Religious Ceremony, Khartoum, Sudan
K Nubian Desert, Sudan
M Pyramids of Meroe, Sudan

'There was no answer, save the incessant angry murmer of the Nile as it raced around a basalt-walled bend and foamed across a rock ridge half a mile upstream. It was as though the brown weight of the river would drive the white men back to their own country.'
SIR RUDYARD KIPLING, 1890

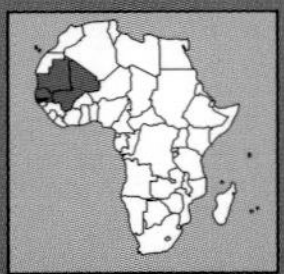

The Taoudenni Basin

SENEGAL

Capital: Dakar
Area: 196,720km²/ 75,950mi²
Population: 9.9 million
Main ethnic groups:
- Wolof (46%)
- Fulani (25%)
- Serer (16%)

Main languages:
- French
- Wolof
- Fulani

Main religions:
- Muslim (92%)
- Traditional beliefs (6%)
- Christian (2%)

Currency: CFA franc (100 centimes)

GAMBIA

Capital: Banjul
Area: 11,300km²/ 4,363mi²
Population: 1.5 million
Main ethnic groups:
- Mandinka (41%)
- Fulani (14%)
- Wolof (13%)

Main language:
- English

Main religions:
- Muslim (85%)
- Christian (9%)
- Traditional beliefs (6%)

Currency: Dalasi (100 butut)

MAURITANIA

Capital: Nouakchott
Area: 1,030,700km²/ 397,955mi²
Population: 2.6 million
Main ethnic groups:
- Maure (80%)
- Wolof (7%)

Main languages:
- French
- Hassaniyah Arabic
- Wolof

Main religion:
- Muslim (100%)

Currency: Ouguiya (5 khoums)

MALI

Capital: Bamako
Area: 1,240,190km²/ 478,840mi²
Population: 11.3 million
Main ethnic groups:
- Bambara (31%)
- Fulani (13%)

Main languages:
- French
- Bambara
- Fulani

Main religions:
- Muslim (80%)
- Traditional beliefs (18%)
- Christian (2%)

Currency: CFA franc (100 centimes)

CAPE VERDE

Capital: Praia
Area: 4,030km²/ 1,556mi²
Population: 500,000
Main ethnic group:
- Mestico (Creole) (71%)

Main language:
- Portuguese

Main religion:
- Roman Catholic (98%)

Currency: Cape Verdean escudo (100 centavos)

From the Fulani to the Wolof people, the sands of the Sahara to the Caribbean-like beaches of the Cape Verde Islands, the ancient mosques to the towering office blocks, the vast lands covered by the western Sahara are as diverse as anywhere on the continent. It is a lively mix of vibrant markets, skyscraper-like minarets and charming little museums all clustered together in surprisingly modern cities, which otherwise have little appeal to the holiday-maker, yet it has an inexplicable attraction to those bent on experiencing a very real Africa that contrasts enormously with the desert dunes further north, the tropical forests of the central interior and the savanna plains of the south. Although plagued with political instability in parts, and ravaged by drought and poverty in others, the western Sahara is, in its own way, gentle and unassuming, its rugged landscape crisscrossed by age-old caravan routes and modern highways characteristically lined with stands of palm trees and dusty little villages.

Although the region covered by the western sands of the great Sahara is a wide-open expanse of desert landscape – fringed in parts by rocky outcrops and isolated stands of scrappy vegetation – it remains one of the most culturally diverse areas on the continent.

A

B

The truth is like gold: keep it locked up and you will find it exactly as you first put it away.
SENEGALESE PROVERB

Senegal

Ⓐ Dakar

Pg. 175. In parts colonial and in others distinctly African in mood and temperament, Dakar is possibly the finest capital in West Africa. Still suffering the effects of a deeply troubled history of slavery and human misery, the functional city is a frenzy of energetic crowds and lively banter. High-rise buildings stand proudly alongside charming little homes circled by ramshackle vehicles weaving in and out of a body of traffic that shows no signs of order or control. As the world slave capital, ancient Dakar – with its otherworldly landscape and unprepossessing salt pan that is Lac Rose – is at once very French and very Muslim, with the distinctive influences of both cultures emerging in the architecture and the cultural heritage of the million-plus population (the majority are made up of the tall and dignified Senegalese). There is a series of small but picturesque beaches and a number of pretty little parks, along with museums and places of worship – most notably the Grand Mosque in the old city, or medina. Many of the typical tourist sites are the most impressive in all of West Africa, but it is the life of the city and the ambience lent to it by its people that remain the main attraction. Busy markets, such as at Kermel and Sandaga, remain the lifeblood of the capital.

Ⓑ Île de Gorée

Pg. 56. The tiny stretch of volcanic rock – no more than 800m (2,625ft) long and 300m (984ft) wide – that emerges from the ocean a few kilometres offshore from Dakar Peninsula is the World Heritage Site known as the Island of Tears, Île de Gorée. As the centre of the mammoth and highly lucrative slave trade that once ravaged much of Africa, the island remains soaked in the tears of human pain and suffering, and the House of Slaves forms the focal point of this living museum. There are no vehicles on the island, which is punctuated with slave museums, the impressive architecture of the colonial occupants and the much publicized Guns of Navarone. Despite this tormented heritage, there is a passion among the people seldom seen anywhere else in Africa.

Gambia

Ⓒ Banjul

Pg. 175. Dry, dusty and far from beautiful in the conventional sense, the Gambian capital can hardly be considered the tourist hot spot it purports to be, yet it offers a refreshingly relaxing holiday and UK tourists inject vital foreign currency into Gambia annually. The flooding of the river means that Banjul's urban centre is small and compact, with a distinctly colonial feel, despite the change in street names that now claim to be more representative of the heritage of Gambia's indigenous people. The buildings may be dilapidated and the rains may bring mud along with an uncomfortable humidity, but there are interesting excursions into the interior. Banjul is often overlooked by the more worldly traveller, despite its attractive beaches lined with fields of peanut plantations.

Ⓓ Gambia River

Pg. 292. In an otherwise empty countryside, the Gambia River is undoubtedly the most prominent feature of the endless landscape and is virtually the only worthwhile attraction. Its fairly modest origins are to be found in the Fouta Djallon highlands of Guinea, more than 500km (310 miles) from its exit into the Atlantic Ocean. The life of virtually every Gambian revolves around the movements of the river, from its tides to its floods. The vast majority of the nation's people eke out their meagre living in attractive but placid little villages, characteristically rural in nature, on the banks of the river. The shanty towns, rice paddies, water pumps and occasional colonial ruins give some indication of the pivotal role played by the river in the day-to-day lives of Gambians. Mangrove swamps are alive with mud-skippers and crabs, and the towering tree-tops are inhabited by troops of small primates, best seen further inland on the Kombo Peninsula in the Abuko Nature Reserve. The surrounding wildlife sanctuaries comprise either mud flats or dusty savanna, but prove to be gems of indigenous fauna.

D

J

TM 175
NP 218
ADV 292

Mauritania

Ⓔ Nouakchott
Pg. 176. The capital city of Nouakchott ('place of the wind') is truly unremarkable and is laid-back in every sense, although it is perhaps one of the richest cultural centres in West Africa. Occupied largely by nomadic Moors who still harbour rigidly defined class structures, the itinerant lifestyle of the nation's people means that there are few tangible examples of artistic expression. It is the day-to-day customs and traditions of the locals that make it such a fascinating stopover, particularly for those who are still amazed by the intricacies of African culture and the latter-day adaptions that have ensured the survival of near-forgotten civilizations. Nouakchott today is home to some 30 per cent of the country's population, and the urban development forms the eye of the dust storm and endless sands that surround the biggest city in the Sahara. Slums and plain, rather unremarkable buildings are counteracted by well-to-do commercial and suburban districts that are home to dignitaries and government officials. There is none of the frenetic activity of other capitals, and the wide, windswept streets offer very little interesting activity for tourists or locals. Quiet and even lonely, the only real life focuses on the busy markets that remind you that you are indeed in the heart of Africa. The favourite drawcard is the expansive beach, enclosed by a wall of dunes separating the city from the cold waters of the ocean.

Ⓕ Adrar Plateau
Pg. 293. Although never extending higher than 1,000m (3,300ft), the Adrar Plateau must be Mauritania's most promising wilderness attraction. Blessed with exceptional vistas and never-ending panoramas of sweeping dunes and rough-hewn escarpments, the vast flatlands are wild and isolated, dotted with welcoming oases and groves of date palms that inevitably indicate the existence of some sort of urban settlement. Some of the lonely little towns are rather dour and uninviting, many no more than ghost towns. The surrounding landscape, punctuated on occasion with the odd attraction – such as the ancient Berber ruins at Azougui – is best traversed by 4x4 vehicle, donkey or the ever-present camel, and features some fine examples of indigenous rock art.

Atar provides a pleasant diversion, covering a wide-open space and acting as the centre of life in the country's northern reaches. The prominent tourist stop is the town of Chinguetti, graced with an extraordinary backdrop and once considered one of Islam's most venerated cities, preceded only by Jerusalem, Mecca and Medina.

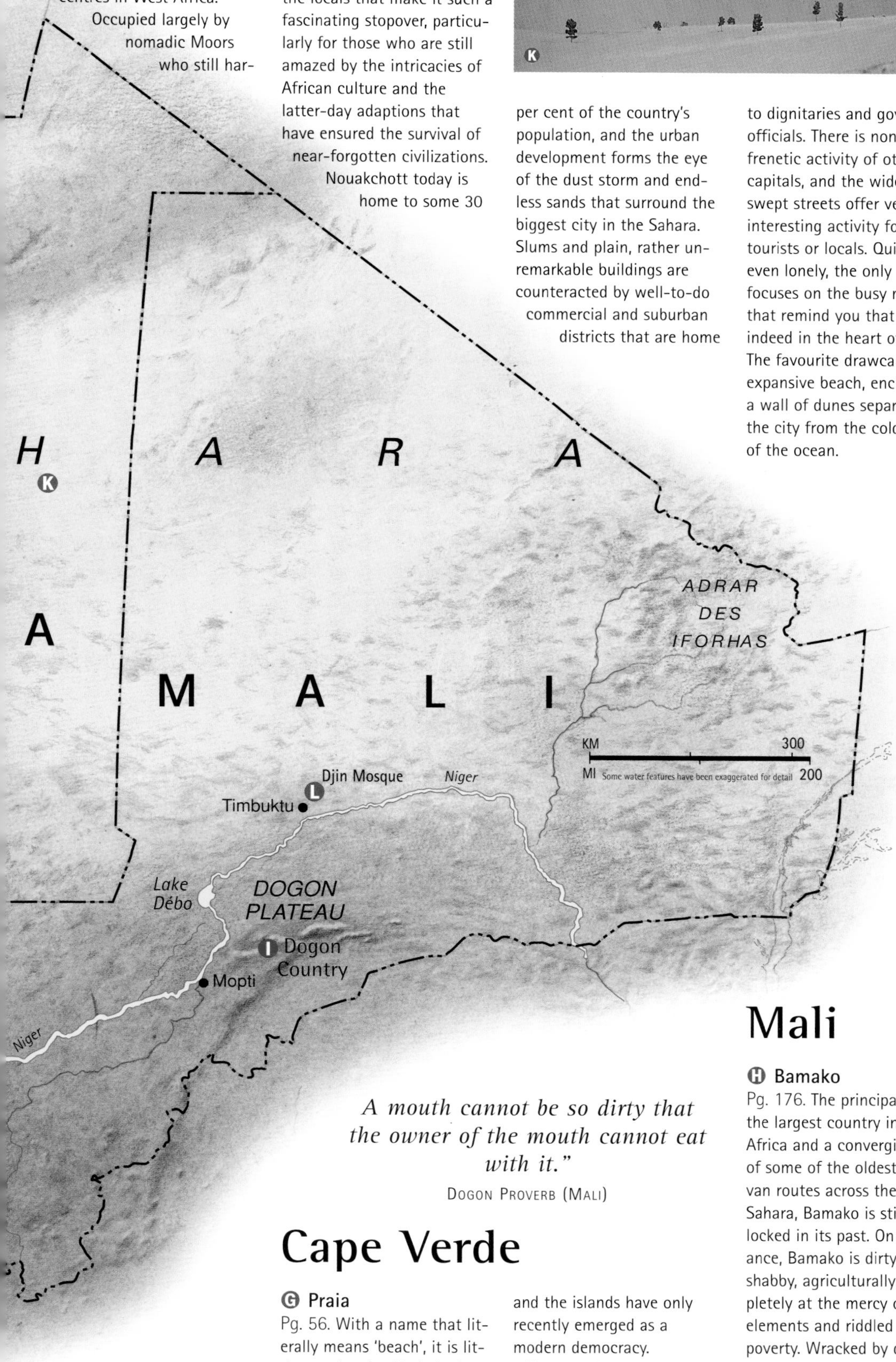

A mouth cannot be so dirty that the owner of the mouth cannot eat with it."
DOGON PROVERB (MALI)

Cape Verde

Ⓖ Praia
Pg. 56. With a name that literally means 'beach', it is little wonder that Praia is the pride of Cape Verde, a small conglomeration of nine main islands, separated into the Barlaventos (Windwards) and Sotaventos (Leewards). São Tiago is the largest of the islands and, like the others in the group, has only been occupied for the last 500 years. The approximately 4,000km² (1,550 sq. miles) of land covered by the islands is populated largely by the descendants of emancipated slaves who settled during the reign of Portuguese explorers, and the islands have only recently emerged as a modern democracy.

The coastline of São Tiago, on which Praia is situated, is remarkably untainted by modern development and offers a number of pleasant swimming beaches, with some of the most picturesque coastal landscape of Africa's offshore islands. Boa Vista's beaches are spectacular, and the main attractions are the island's rugged east coast and mountainous interior, an adventure-lover's delight. Hopping from island to island is also a relatively hassle-free process.

Mali

Ⓗ Bamako
Pg. 176. The principal city of the largest country in West Africa and a converging point of some of the oldest caravan routes across the great Sahara, Bamako is still very locked in its past. On appearance, Bamako is dirty and shabby, agriculturally completely at the mercy of the elements and riddled with poverty. Wracked by drought and other natural plagues, it is both hot and oppressive, crowded and uninviting, with its modernisation process lamentably slow. In the same breath, Bamako is slowly emerging from the dust and sand to take its rightful place as a promising indication of what can transpire in even the most desolate of African destinations.

The oases of the desert fringes occur naturally where underground watercourses break through the ground surface, and it is here that tall palm trees flourish, providing the all-important shade and shelter for orchards and vegetable patches that help sustain the local people. Large areas are given over to the commercial cultivation of date palms, which plays a pivotal role in the latter-day economy.

Ⓘ Dogon Country
Pg. 247. The open landscape of Mali's southern reaches is a vast, empty country most noted for the unusual mud configurations that are the dwellings of the Dogon people, elaborately constructed along the forms of a female body and steeped in centuries of mystery and wonder. This is Dogon Country, or Pays Dogon, where every Dogon family fashions their collection of mud huts and animal pens according to the structure and scheme of the village. These fascinating remnants of an ancient culture, with their numerous granaries and outbuildings, bear testimony to a rich cultural heritage that remains relatively intact. High above the endless Seno Plain is a series of cave homes meticulously carved into the towering rock face of the escarpment.

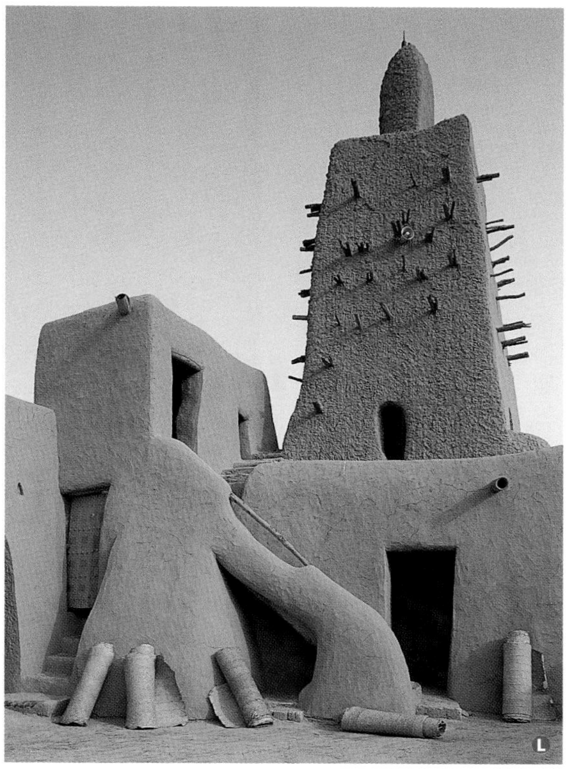

PICTURE CAPTIONS
Ⓐ Wood carving, Dakar, Senegal
Ⓑ Slave House, Île de Gorée, Senegal
Ⓓ Stilt Lodge, Gambia River, Gambia
Ⓘ Cliff houses, Dogon Country, Mali
Ⓙ Wassu Stone Circles, Wassu, Gambia
Ⓚ Sahara Desert, Mauritania
Ⓛ Djin Mosque, Timbuktu, Mali

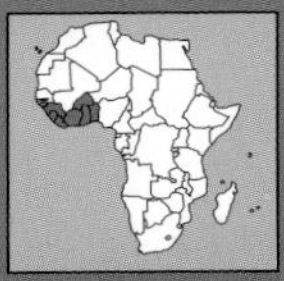

The Gulf of Guinea was the centre of the world's most notorious slave trade for centuries, during which the vast majority of its population lived in terror. The modern countries that exist here have survived years of repressive colonialism, and – despite the considerable political turmoil and extreme poverty that continue to pervade many of these nations – are slowly re-establishing their own identities and emerging as popular, if not entirely sophisticated, travel destinations. The cities may be small, the architecture unremarkable, the industries economically vulnerable and the societies still struggling to throw off the shackles of their past, but even the capitals are rich in a cultural diversity found in few other places in Africa. Traditional beliefs have survived centuries of colonialism along with the imposed structures of Christianity and Islam, and indigenous cultures and customs remain the dominant feature on the social landscape of the far western reaches of West Africa.

With few natural resources and economies that are struggling to shed the bleak image that blanketed West Africa over the last 100 years of revolutions and civil wars, the development of the hospitality industry may provide a valuable source of foreign income for the impoverished countries of the Ivory Coast.

'It was like walking into a steam laundry. Moisture hung in the atmosphere so heavily that my skin and shirt were soaked within minutes.'

DAVID ATTENBOROUGH, 1980

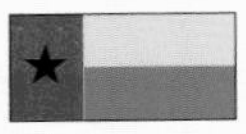

GUINEA-BISSAU

Capital: Bissau
Area: 36,120km²/ 13,940mi²
Population: 1.3 million
Main ethnic groups:
- Balante (27%)
- Fulani (22%)
- Malinke (12%)

Main language:
- Portuguese

Main religions:
- Traditional beliefs (54%)
- Muslim (38%)
- Christian (8%)

Currency: CFA franc (100 centimes)

GUINEA

Capital: Conakry
Area: 245,860km²/ 94,927mi²
Population: 8.4 million
Main ethnic groups:
- Fulani (40%)
- Malinke (25%)

Main languages:
- French • Fulani

Main religions:
- Muslim (85%)
- Christian (8%)

Currency: Guinean franc (100 centimes)

SIERRA LEONE

Capital: Freetown
Area: 71,740km²/ 27,699mi²
Population: 5.6 million
Main ethnic groups:
- Mende (34%)
- Temne (31%)
- Limba (9%)

Main languages:
- English
- Krio (Creole)

Main religions:
- Traditional beliefs (52%)
- Muslim (40%)
- Christian (8%)

Currency: Leone (100 cents)

LIBERIA

Capital: Monrovia
Area: 111,370km²/ 43,000mi²
Population: 3.3 million
Main ethnic groups:
- Kpelle (20%)
- Bassa (14%)
- Americo-Liberians (5%)

Main languages:
- English
- Kpelle • Bassa

Main religions:
- Traditional beliefs (70%)
- Muslim (20%)

Currency: Liberian dollar (100 cents)

CÔTE D'IVOIRE

Capital: Yamoussoukro (designated), Abidjan (seat of government)
Area: 322,463km²/ 124,504mi²
Population: 16.8 million
Main ethnic groups:
- Baoule (23%)
- Bété (18%)

Main languages:
- French • Akran

Main religions:
- Traditional beliefs (63%)
- Muslim (25%)

Currency: CFA franc (100 centimes)

BURKINA FASO

Capital: Ouagadougou
Area: 274,200km²/ 105,870mi²
Population: 12.6 million
Main ethnic group:
- Mossi (45%)

Main languages:
- French
- Mossi

Main religions:
- Traditional beliefs (65%)
- Muslim (25%)

Currency: CFA franc (100 centimes)

GHANA

Capital: Accra
Area: 238,540km²/ 92,100mi²
Population: 20.2 million
Main ethnic groups:
- Akan (52%)
- Mossi (15%)

Main languages:
- English
- Akan
- Mossi

Main religions:
- Traditional beliefs (38%)
- Muslim (30%)
- Christian (24%)

Currency: Cedi (100 pesewas)

TOGO

Capital: Lomé
Area: 56,790km²/ 21,927mi²
Population: 5.3 million
Main ethnic groups:
- Ewe (43%)
- Kabye (26%)

Main languages:
- French
- Ewe

Main religions:
- Traditional beliefs (70%)
- Christian (20%)

Currency: CFA franc (100 centimes)

BENIN

Capital: Porto-Novo
Area: 112,620km²/ 43,480mi²
Population: 6.6 million
Main ethnic group:
- Fon (39%)

Main languages:
- French
- Fon

Main religion:
- Traditional beliefs (70%)

Currency: CFA franc (100 centimes)

Guinea-Bissau

Ⓐ Bissau

Pg. 177. One of the smallest countries in Africa, Guinea-Bissau has emerged as a nation that continues to balance the atrocities of a colonial past with the latter-day uncertainties that plague so much of undeveloped Africa. Home to a relatively small population, the port city is still under strict military control. The waterfront boasts some architectural gems, yet cosmopolitan Bissau is not a pretty city. One of the last of the West African states to achieve independence from Portugal, it is run-down and lacks the glamour of other great capitals, and is a dangerous place to visit. On the outskirts of the city are some picturesque beaches and impressive scenery, but the inner city has a distinct lack of cultural attractions. Bissau's annual carnival in February sees the city spring to life as citizens parade their floats and lavish costumes down the city streets.

Guinea

Ⓑ Conakry

Pg. 177. Despite a rich history, the capital offers only an inkling of what lies beyond the urban settlement. The first of France's colonies in Africa to become independent, Guinea was closed to foreign travel for many years. Situated on a promontory 20km (12 miles) offshore and with a population of about one million – no less than 10 per cent of the country's total – the capital's cultural diversity is vast, with many of its people well versed in the politics of the day. A good base from which to explore the surrounding hills and countryside, the city is not pleasant, a dirty and muggy settlement riddled with corruption and violence. Conakry is far more inviting now than a few decades ago, and attractions such as the Grand Mosque offer respite from the littered streets. The offshore islands of Îles de Los, Île de Kassa, Île Tamara and, most notably, Île Roume offer a great diversion from one of the least exciting of Africa's capital cities.

Sierra Leone

Ⓒ Freetown

Pg. 177. Freetown's very name is symbolic of its history, its present and, quite possibly, its future. Established in the 18th century, the capital of Sierra Leone is peopled largely by the half a million citizens descended from the emancipated slaves returning from the USA and Britain, who founded the settlement. Sierra Leone remains unsafe for travellers in the aftermath of the civil war of the 1990s and it is one of the poorest nations in the world, yet the cosmopolitan make-up of Freetown is a refreshing change. The dominant Creole culture is influenced by its Anglo-American heritage, yet modern-day Sierra Leone remains rich in tradition and staunch in its authenticity. It has always been at the centre of a majestic countryside with an abundance of wildlife and within easy access of some outstanding beaches, most notably Lumley. Freetown is surprisingly clean and efficient, with plenty of restaurants and fast-food outlets in addition to nightclubs of every description.

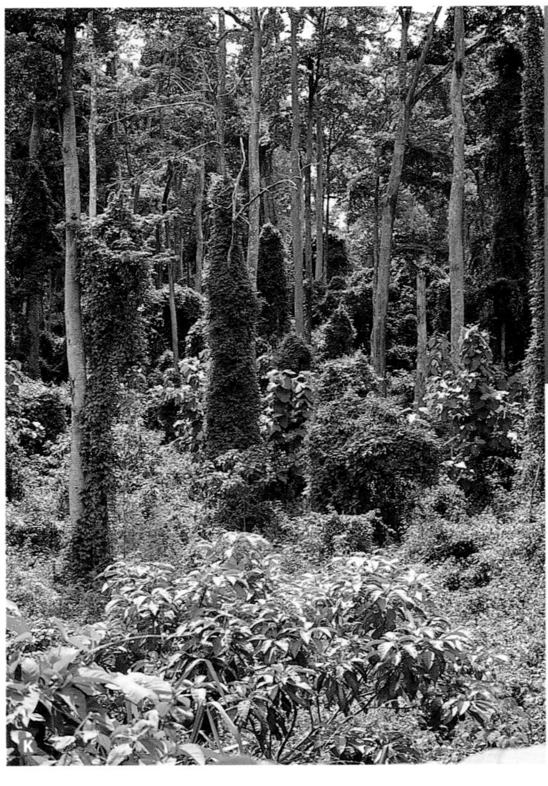

Côte d'Ivoire

Ⓓ Yamoussoukro

Pg. 65. Hailed as one of the largest of the continent's western countries, with a relatively stable economy and a good reputation as one of Africa's most hospitable, Côte d'Ivoire (formerly known as the Ivory Coast) has essentially two separate – and very different – capitals. Although Abidjan is the biggest city, the most glamorous and more inviting, Yamoussoukro is today the official principal city, having usurped Abidjan as the capital in 1983. Yamoussoukro is, for the most part, a conglomeration of uninspiring government buildings with aspirations of grandeur and, although it is dotted with some grand hotels, accommodation standards vary from poor to fair, with only a handful of the luxury variety. Perhaps the only really successful attempt at splendid architecture during its years of transformation is the massive Basilique de Notre Dame de la Paix (the highlight of a

TM 177
NP 220
ADV 294

Liberia

F Monrovia
Pg. 64. Founded in 1847, Monrovia is the capital of the oldest republic in Africa and promises to become one of the continent's most desirable destinations. Having survived the misery imposed by the slave trade, the half a million Americo-Liberian citizens continue to struggle with sociopolitical issues. As the country's principal port and the seat of the 150-year-old University of Liberia, Monrovia should be a lively centre, with an abundance of offerings for tourists.

Unfortunately, little of the old city remains intact and the infrastructure is a shadow of its former self. Blessed with extraordinary scenery and surrounded by some of the continent's last remaining rainforests, Monrovia is still not safe, and independent travel is riddled with dangers and uncertainties.

Burkina Faso

G Ouagadougou
Pg. 179. Previously known as the Upper Volta (up until 1984), Burkina Faso epitomizes the very worst of Africa's most destitute.

The capital at Ouagadougou may be hot and dirty, poor and ramshackle, dusty and crowded, yet its half a million citizens have made it surprisingly inviting and welcoming to the visitor. Living up to the virtues extolled by the very name of the country – honour, dignity, nobility and integrity – the people of Ouagadougou, amidst all that squalor, have energetically set about transforming their city. As the traditional seat of the nation's Mossi emperors, Ouagadougou is today a rich tapestry of cultures and customs, reflecting most of the country's population groups, while welcoming newcomers and sightseers to a growing collection of hotels, museums and restaurants, with clubs and bars catering for the intrepid traveller.

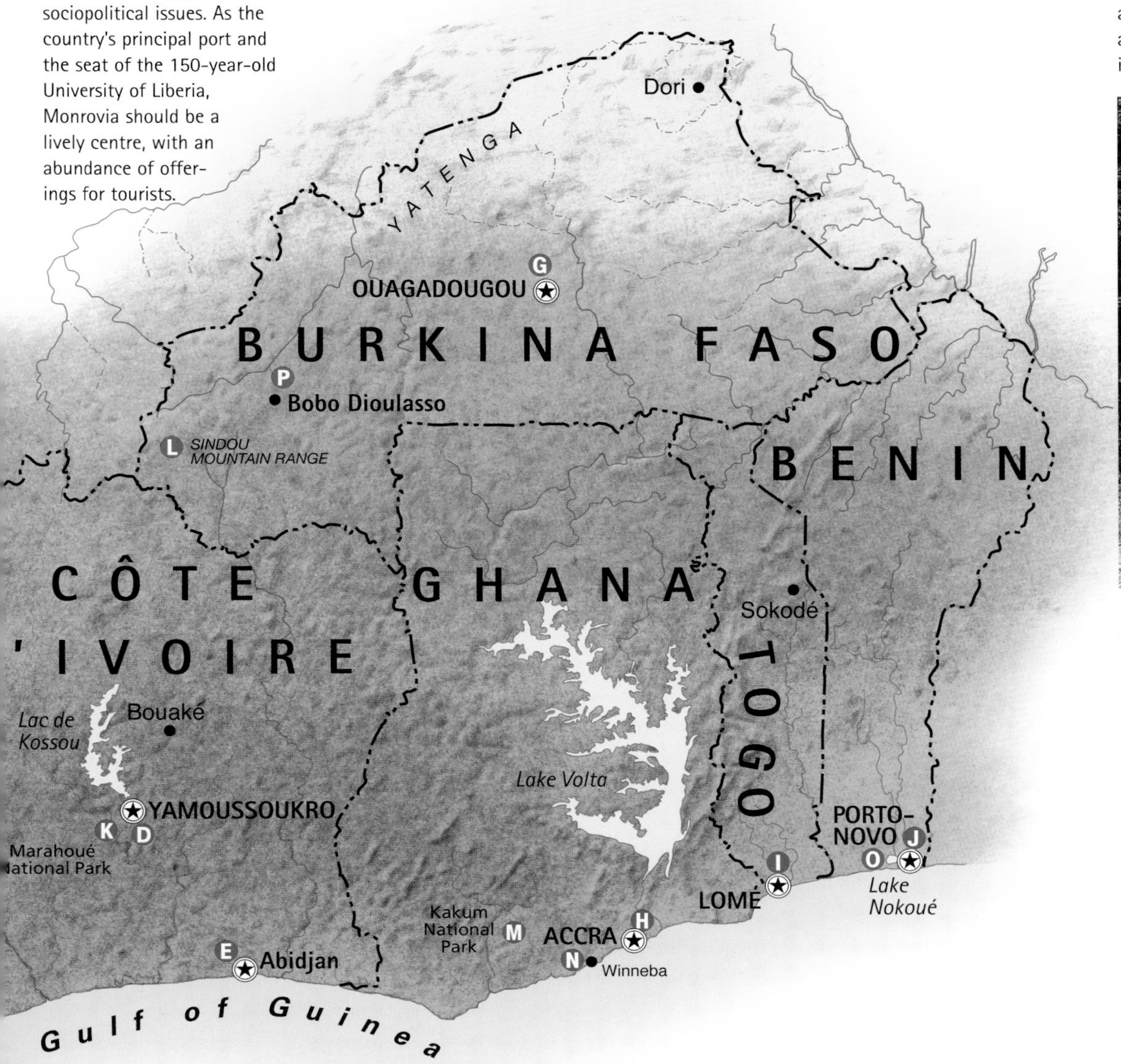

visit to the capital), paid for by the late President – Félix Houphouët-Boigny – and consecrated, albeit somewhat reluctantly, by the Pope.

E Abidjan
Pg. 178. No longer the capital city of Côte d'Ivoire, Abidjan is a lively, inviting and relatively prosperous city, and the second-largest in West Africa. The ancient city has retained some of the colonial charm evident in its architecture, but it has also developed a glamorous and rather cosmopolitan feel, which – together with an overriding sense of the exotic and mysterious that is part of traditional culture – has meant that its tourism infrastructure is one of the most sophisticated in Africa. Located on Ebrié lagoon, the modern and industrialized city forms the focus of the local tourism industry, and its contemporary skyline sets it far apart from the country's true capital at Yamoussoukro.

Ghana

H Accra
Pg. 180. The diamond on the Gold Coast is historic Accra, capital of one of Africa's most prosperous nations in former times. It was founded on a site on the Gulf of Guinea that was the original location of three fortresses erected by English, Dutch and Danish colonists in the 1600s. Accra's population, numbering about one million, originated from no fewer than 74 ethnic groups, resulting in a varied cultural mix. The buildings are rather dull, but a committed attempt at rehabilitation has seen a number of development programmes that have reintroduced some of its glamour. Alive with energy, the city is remarkably green and has few of the big-city problems of other capitals.

Togo

I Lomé
Pg. 181. Once considered the financial powerhouse of the western region, the port of Togo is the capital of what was one of Africa's most politically constant countries. Togo is a tiny nation and, although always relatively stable, it saw its fair share of suffering towards the end of the 20th century. Despite a moderate climate and pretty beaches along its 56km (35-mile) coast – the beach at Lomé still has the air of a sleepy seaside town – the settlement that once served as a crossroads for travellers began to crumble after conflict set in. Slowly rebuilding, there is still a long way to go to restore its reputation as a travellers' haven. The old French quarter remains the heart of Lomé and, apart from a handful of bars, clubs and discos, there is little to lure visitors beyond the bustling marketplaces that sell anything from fresh produce and handicrafts to traditional medicines and handmade clothing. Despite a certain charm, Lomé – as with most politically volatile cities – is increasingly dangerous for the naïve.

PICTURE CAPTIONS
- E Abidjan, Côte d'Ivoire
- K Marahoué National Park, Côte d'Ivoire
- L Sindou mountain range, Burkina Faso
- M Kakum National Park, Ghana
- N Local fishermen, Winneba, Ghana
- O Stilt village, Ganvie, Lake Nokoué, Benin
- P Grand Mosque, Bobo Dioulasso, Burkina Faso

Benin

J Porto-Novo
Pg. 181. Benin can be justifiably proud that, after a long and bitter struggle against oppression by Portuguese colonists, it was one of the first of the West African countries to embrace democracy. As a port city situated on a coastal lagoon, Porto-Novo also served as an important centre of West Africa's slave trade. Porto-Novo has a post office and hospital and provides a refreshing change from life in most big cities as it is delightfully unaffected by bustling tourist traffic. Spread out along the banks of a lagoon and the surrounding foothills, Porto-Novo was the ancestral seat of the Gun kingdom and boasts an extraordinarily rich cultural legacy, most clearly discerned in traditional craft work such as wood carvings, musical instruments, traditional weapons and even the architecture of its simple homes and luxurious palaces.

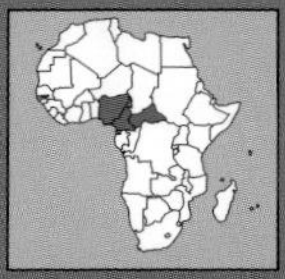

NIGERIA

Capital: Abuja
Area: 923,770km²/ 356,669mi²
Population: 129.9 million
Main ethnic groups:
- Hausa (21%)
- Yoruba (20%)
- Ibo (17%)

Main languages:
- English • Hausa
- Yoruba

Main religions:
- Muslim (50%)
- Christian (40%)

Currency: Naira (100 kobo)

SAO TOME & PRINCIPE

Capital: São Tomé
Area: 964km² / 372mi²
Population: 170,372
Main ethnic groups:
- Mestico • Angolares
- Forros • Servicais
- Tongas • Europeans (primarily Portuguese)

Main language:
- Portuguese

Main religion:
- Christian (largely Catholic) (80%)

Currency: Dobra (STD)

CAMEROON

Capital: Yaoundé
Area: 475,440km²/ 183,568mi²
Population: 16.2 million
Main ethnic groups:
- Bamileke/Manum (20%)
- Fang (19%)

Main languages:
- English • French • Fang

Main religions:
- Traditional beliefs (51%)
- Christian (33%)
- Muslim (16%)

Currency: CFA franc (100 centimes)

EQUATORIAL GUINEA

Capital: Malabo
Area: 28,050km²/ 10,830mi²
Population: 500,000
Main ethnic groups:
- Fang (72%)
- Bubi (14%)
- Duala (3%)

Main languages:
- Spanish • Fang

Main religion:
- Christian (largely Catholic) (89%)

Currency: CFA franc (100 centimes)

CENTRAL AFRICAN REPUBLIC

Capital: Bangui
Area: 622,980km²/ 240,530mi²
Population: 3.6 million
Main ethnic groups:
- Baya (34%) • Banda (27%) • Mandija (21%)

Main languages:
- French • Sangho

Main religions:
- Christian (50%)
- Traditional beliefs (27%)
- Muslim (15%)

Currency: CFA franc (100 centimes)

The central region of West Africa is a land of extremes: prosperity versus dire poverty, harmony and reconciliation versus anarchy and disorder, peace and stability versus corruption and outright civil warfare. Whereas some of the towns and even the capital cities are lively places, with a warm, generous and welcoming reception for visitors, others are alarmingly hostile and dangerous to the uninitiated, where even the marketplaces – usually Africa's great melting pots of indigenous culture – have been taken over by gangs of thugs and thieves. In some instances, such as the Central African Republic (CAR), policies adopted by government have simply exacerbated these problems, with corruption and crime rife in CAR, posing a very real threat to the traveller – and the future of the nation's tourism industry. That said, cities such as Yaoundé in Cameroon and even Malabo in Equatorial Guinea are a delight, epitomizing the very best of what Africa has to offer the adventurer.

The western and central regions, although in large parts riddled with instability and corruption, are some of the most scenically spectacular in Africa, awash with vast stretches of lush rainforests, gently undulating hills, and endless sandy coastlines blessed with balmy beaches and lively and colourful locals.

'The edge of a colossal jungle, so dark green as to be almost black ... The sun was fierce, the land seemed to glisten and drip with steam.'
JOSEPH CONRAD, *HEART OF DARKNESS*, 1902

B

C

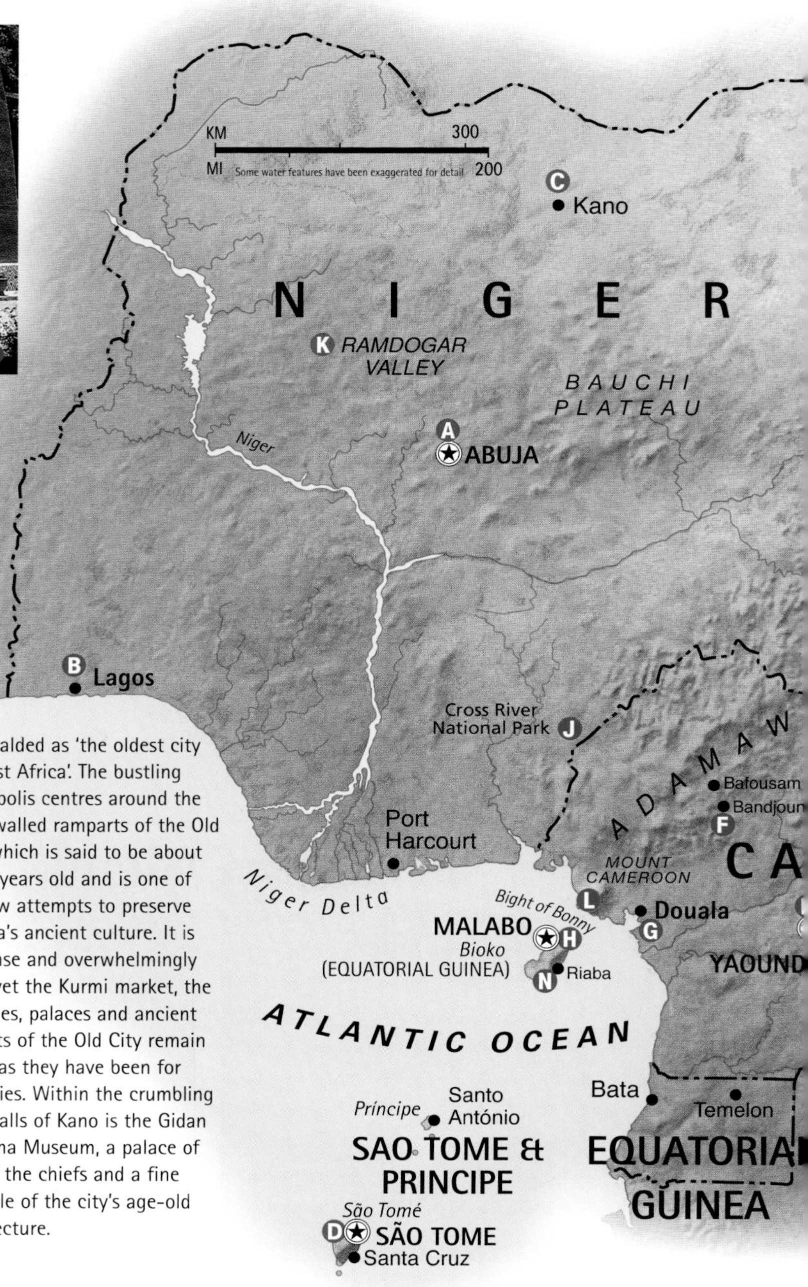

Nigeria

Ⓐ Abuja

Pg. 183. Given its size and population – a phenomenal 130 million spread out over nearly a million square kilometres (390,000 square miles) – Nigeria understandably exerts enormous clout over the entire region, affecting the broader economy and, to some degree, even the politics. Abuja acts as an influential powerhouse and is the economic heart of West Africa, as well as boasting the greatest number of museums in the world. Nigerians are, on average, the most highly educated people in Africa, yet the nation is still suffering the effects of a severe depression, a corrupt and inefficient government system, and a serious lack of basic commodities. Despite all it has to offer – a fertile cultivated landscape with magnificent views set against a lush mountain and savanna backdrop – Abuja is not a spot for extensive sightseeing. Its streets are tree lined and dotted with towering office blocks and some prestigious hotels, but inexpensive accommodation is hard to come by and the transport infrastructure is chaotic. As a multicultural centre, Abuja is so varied in flavour that it seems to lack the charm of other similar cities. One of the few reminders of its mystical past is provided by the distinctive profile of the landmark Central Mosque.

Ⓑ Lagos

Pg. 182. As the previous capital of Nigeria, Lagos's congested streets, crowded pavements and high levels of crime have made it Africa's most notorious city, a scattered settlement that includes a portion of the mainland and the islands of Lagos, Ikoyi and Victoria, originally separated by wetlands now filled in to form one seething mass of humanity. Lagos is a sad reflection of the continent and, although considered a vital cultural and economic centre, its more than eight million citizens – living within some 200km² (80 sq. miles) – live lives of despair, threatened daily by armed thugs, and the global underworld of drugs has Lagos as the base of its distribution network. In the city's defence, there are a few highlights: a proliferation of markets, most notably the Jankara market; beautiful beaches; an intriguing Brazilian Quarter; and a fine selection of theatres and museums, including the Onikan National Museum. It is, however, the contagious rhythms and unique styles of Nigeria's music that remains Lagos's great asset, a vibrant music tradition that has evolved into one of the country's most significant cultural treasures.

Ⓒ Kano

Pg. 66. On a continent where everything is ancient, it is no small feat for Kano (Nigeria's second-largest settlement) to be heralded as 'the oldest city in West Africa'. The bustling metropolis centres around the mud-walled ramparts of the Old City, which is said to be about 1,000 years old and is one of the few attempts to preserve Nigeria's ancient culture. It is immense and overwhelmingly busy, yet the Kurmi market, the mosques, palaces and ancient dye pits of the Old City remain much as they have been for centuries. Within the crumbling clay walls of Kano is the Gidan Makama Museum, a palace of one of the chiefs and a fine example of the city's age-old architecture.

J

K

Sao Tome & Principe

Ⓓ São Tomé

Pg. 72. The capital city is a dreamy destination: laid back and with a tiny population, lack of development has lent it an old-world charm, yet it is extremely pretty and clean. The largely unknown islands of Sao Tome and Principe offer an equatorial paradise, with lush jungles, pristine waters, volcanoes and abundant bird species.

PICTURE CAPTIONS
- Ⓑ Rush hour market, Lagos, Nigeria
- Ⓒ Adobe house, Kano, Nigeria
- Ⓙ Cross River National Park, Nigeria
- Ⓚ Rocky mountain outcrop, near Ramdogar Valley, Nigeria
- Ⓛ Mount Cameroon, Cameroon
- Ⓜ Footbridge north of Lomié, Cameroon
- Ⓝ Woodtrading schooners, Riaba, Bioko, Equatorial Guinea
- Ⓞ Forest pool, CAR
- Ⓟ Goliath bullfrog, CAR

TM 182
NP 222
ADV 296

Cameroon

E Yaoundé
Pg. 183. Cameroon's capital, Yaoundé, is the great gem in the crown of Africa. Blessed with breathtaking beauty, Yaoundé is the lifeline of one of the continent's most prosperous nations. No fewer than 130 different ethnic groups have made their home here, to create Africa's richest cultural mix.

Cameroon's capital – with its moderate clime and hospitable people – remains one of the most vital cities. Located on a dramatic plateau, Yaoundé was custom built as a national showcase and is easy to navigate. There is an exciting calendar of festivals, some fine local architecture, glorious beaches and impressive museums. The Musée d'Art Camerounais, on the city's outskirts, displays the world's best West African art.

F Bandjoun
Pg. 67. Just a little way from the provincial capital at Bafousam stands Bandjoun, one of the greatest centres of authentic Cameroonian culture – a boisterous and spirited nucleus of commercial activity. The ancient Bamileke settlement, some 3km (2 miles) beyond the limits of the town's boundaries, is the area's principal attraction, an impressive tribute to the history and people of the region. The imposing chief's compound – known as the *chefferie* – at Bandjoun is the best preserved of the age-old settlements that were home to the chiefs of the Bamileke, famed across the globe as one of the great trading nations of their time. The chief's compound at Bandjoun, the biggest of the remaining historical sites in Cameroon, comprises a fascinating series of ancient Bamileke homes – separated by squares and marketplaces – dotted around the picturesque countryside and fenced in by a bamboo enclosure for protection.

G Douala
Pg. 67. Douala (Cameroon's principal city) is not a favourite destination of travellers, but it remains an important hub for cross-country travelling in Cameroon. The nation's most prosperous urban centre, Douala is the epitome of a big African city: a magnificent location surrounded by a chain of starkly beautiful black-sand beaches counterbalanced by a steadily growing urban population, and all the crowds and crime. Hot and humid, with annual precipitation levels exceeding 4,000mm (158in), the jostling city is a churning, blistering metropolitan centre that is one of the most significant in the entire region. Despite being spread across a wide, open landscape that is scenically enchanting, the business districts of the huge inner city are generally the home territory of gangs of petty thieves and thugs. Visitors should not be discouraged and should make some effort to see the museums and markets of contemporary Akwa, a thriving modern centre structured around the Boulevard de la Liberté, with its landmark Catholic cathedral.

L

M

N

Hold a true friend with both your hands.
NIGERIAN PROVERB

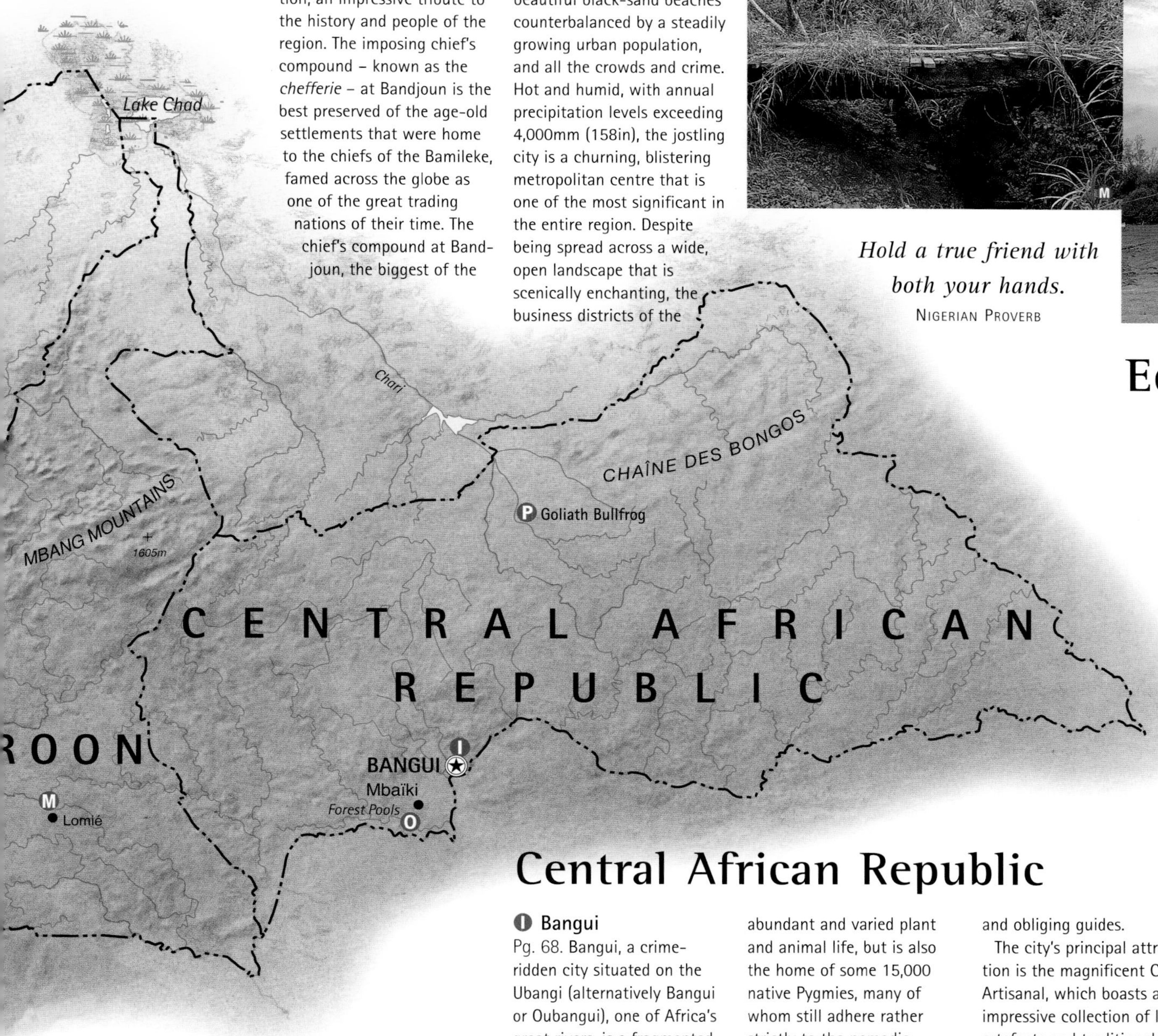

Equatorial Guinea

H Malabo
Pg. 297. The capital of beautiful but impoverished Equatorial Guinea, Malabo is situated on the attractive island of Bioko and is gentle but rustic, laid-back yet lively, nestling in an awe-inspiring landscape ringed by a selection of pretty beaches and charming little fishing hamlets. Exploring the formerly dilapidated little town is a richly rewarding adventure, and one that can be achieved in comfort. Malabo is upmarket and vibrant – a refreshing change in the heart of Africa – and local festivals are celebrated with verve, a spirited mix of traditional music and dance highlighted by *Balélé* performances. Beyond the city limits, the rich, dark soils and verdant vegetation are typical of a volcanic landscape. The mountainside is laced with walking paths and hiking trails, although making the 3,106m (10,200ft) ascent to the summit of Pico Malabo (a military zone, so a permit is necessary) remains one of the most popular of the local adventures.

Central African Republic

I Bangui
Pg. 68. Bangui, a crime-ridden city situated on the Ubangi (alternatively Bangui or Oubangui), one of Africa's great rivers, is a fragmented quagmire of political tensions, lawlessness and destitution. It offers a vast and unfathomable contrast to the remarkable beauty of the country and the wealth of mineral deposits that lies beneath its soils, largely unexploited and virtually forgotten.

The CAR is a truly beautiful country, its rugged splendour unexplored by masses of tourists, and vast stretches of its landscape remain as they have been for hundreds, if not thousands, of years. The ecological grandeur of its lush rainforest environment is not only a natural haven for an abundant and varied plant and animal life, but is also the home of some 15,000 native Pygmies, many of whom still adhere rather strictly to the nomadic lifestyle pursued by their hunter-gatherer forefathers.

Bangui is one of the most crime-infested capitals in Central Africa. There are indeed highlights, many of which remain unexplored and unexploited. Plenty of venues in the west of Bangui are devoted entirely to the promotion of innovative indigenous music, and there are a number of enticing theatres, galleries and museums, the most significant of which must be the Musée de Boganda. Here the story of Pygmy culture is carefully explained by knowledgeable and obliging guides.

The city's principal attraction is the magnificent Centre Artisanal, which boasts an impressive collection of local artefacts and traditional items that is representative of most of the countries in Central Africa and the Congo Basin. There is also a truly remarkable assembly of local art in the unique collection of unusual art created using the wings of butterflies.

O

P

The Horn of Africa

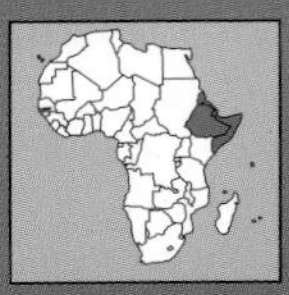

ERITREA

Capital: Asmara
Area: 121,320km²/ 46,842mi²
Population: 4.5 million
Main ethnic groups:
- Nine main population groups

Main languages:
- Tigrinya
- Arabic
- Tigre
- Bilen
- Kunama

Main religions:
- Coptic Christian (45%)
- Muslim (45%)

Currency: Eritrean nakfa (100 cents)

ETHIOPIA

Capital: Addis Ababa
Area: 1,100,574km²/ 424,934mi²
Population: 67.7 million
Main ethnic groups:
- Oromo (40%)
- Amhara/Tigrean (32%)

Main languages:
- Amharic
- English
- Arabic

Main religions:
- Muslim (43%)
- Christian (37%)
- Traditional beliefs (16%)

Currency: Ethiopian birr (100 cents)

SOMALIA

Capital: Mogadishu
Area: 637,660km²/ 246,200mi²
Population: 7.8 million
Main ethnic groups:
- Somali (98%)
- Bantu (0.75%)
- Arab (0.75%)

Main languages:
- Somali
- Arabic

Main religion:
- Sunni Muslim (99%)

Currency: Somali shilling (100 cents)

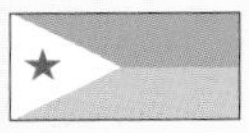

DJIBOUTI

Capital: Djibouti
Area: 23,200km²/ 8,958mi²
Population: 700,000
Main ethnic groups:
- Issa (35%)
- Afar (20%)
- Gadabourists/Isaaks (28%)

Main languages:
- Arabic
- French
- Somali
- Afar

Main religion:
- Christian (87%)

Currency: Djiboutian franc (100 centimes)

The Horn of Africa has, in recent years, seen untold misery, ranging from drought and famine to civil war and border disputes that resulted in a huge displacement of the population and a serious problem with refugees intent on escaping the turmoil of their home territories, and with Ethiopia surviving as the only African country never to be colonized. With the possible exclusion of Somalia – which remains a difficult, treacherous and unpredictable place for foreign visitors – it is a region that is slowly rejuvenating itself, rebuilding its infrastructure not only for its long-suffering citizens but also for the steady trickle of tourists slowly making their way back to an area that harbours considerable potential for peace and prosperity.

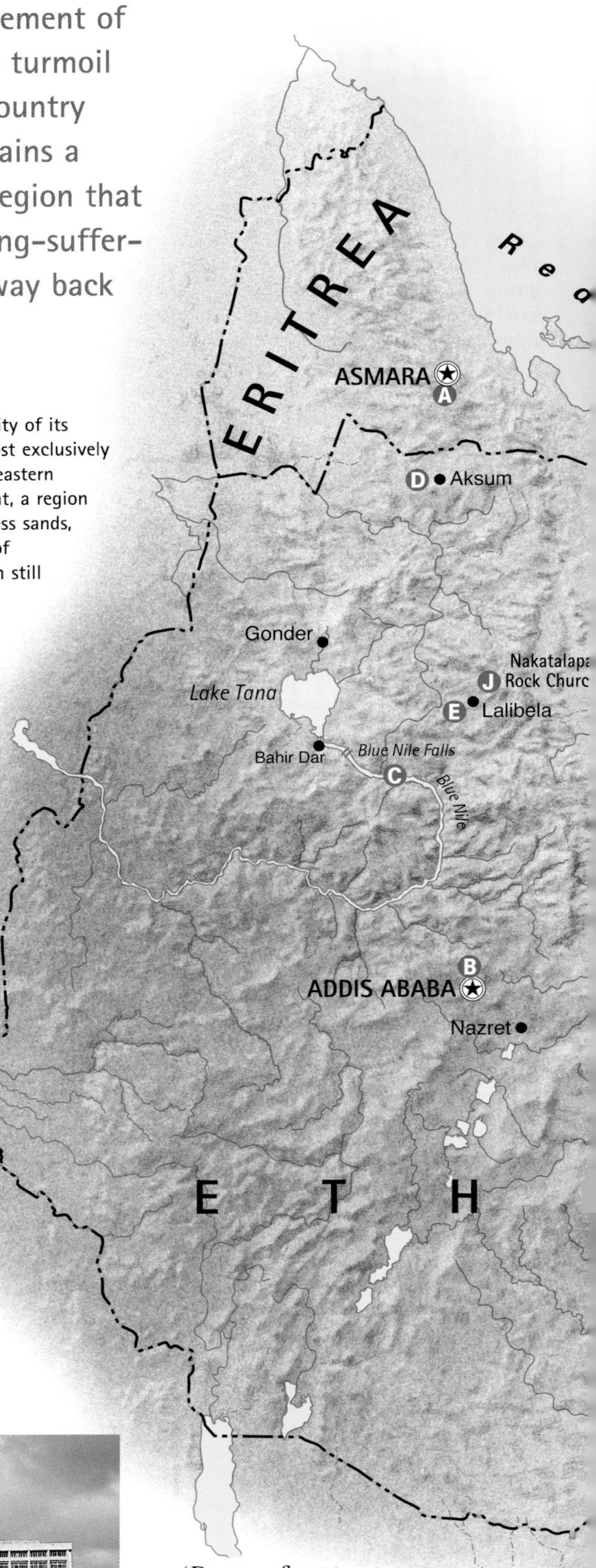

Eritrea

Ⓐ Asmara

Pg. 185. Established in 1993, Eritrea is the youngest nation on the continent, emerging from extended civil strife and a long-standing border dispute with Ethiopia. One of the shining lights in Africa, it has survived a tormented past to step boldly into a promising future. Its capital at Asmara is relaxed, friendly and peaceful, and the suburban thoroughfares of the old quarter are lined with gracious old buildings and flowering trees of every hue. The most valiant attempt at civil engineering is the great Massawa-Asmara highway: its extensive length (with 65 bridges and 30 tunnels) was all but destroyed during the war, but is being restored entirely by the Eritreans without Western assistance. The city is pleasantly uncrowded, remarkably uncluttered, clean, efficient and very safe by African standards.

A

Although the vast majority of its people are engaged almost exclusively in agriculture, the northeastern stretches of the continent, a region of desert dune and endless sands, has a surprising wealth of resources, much of which still needs to be harnessed.

C

Ethiopia

B

Ⓑ Addis Ababa

Pg. 184. Widely recognized as one of Africa's greatest capitals, Addis Ababa – isolated by grassland, mountains and desert – originated in pre-Christian times and was formally established just over 100 years ago. The city is the spiritual centre of the Land of Cush. Despite the pressures on its natural resources, Addis Ababa has a relatively stable economy based on agriculture that supports a population of about three million.

Given its historical significance, the outskirts are scattered with archaeological sites, while the city confines have a collection of temples and churches decorated with medieval paintings, murals and mosaics, all of which make this the starting point for historical routes that wind across the country. Its international status is signified by the acclaimed Addis Ababa University and the headquarters of the Organisation of African Unity and United Nations Economic Commission for Africa. The hospitality industry is Ethiopia's second-largest income earner. Streets are dangerous at night, and markets popular among thieves and pickpockets, yet the capital can be a delight. Addis Ababa boasts a number of significant museums, notably the university's Ethnological Museum.

Ⓒ Blue Nile

Pg. 258. Virtually synonymous with Africa, the Nile is Africa's greatest asset and the Blue Nile Ethiopia's most significant watercourse. The mighty Blue Nile Falls is one of the continent's great waterfalls. Some 400m (1,312ft) in width and plummeting an impressive 45–50m (148–164ft), the falls are known by the locals as Tis Isat, which translates as 'Smoke of the Nile' – an apt description of the spray that emanates from the gushing chasm. Although indeed an awesome spectacle year-round, the falls reach their full potential following the often torrential rain in November and December. The natural splendour of the Blue Nile Falls is, therefore, one of Ethiopia's premier drawcards, and the tourism infrastructure that has developed around the falls is one of the country's most advanced. Still in use is the bridge erected by the Portuguese nearly 400 years ago, and the surrounds are intertwined with a network of paths and trails, a popular walking route. Voyages are offered on the river in a vessel made almost entirely from papyrus.

Further along the course of the Blue Nile, some 30km (19 miles) from the falls, is the lively port town of Bahir Dar on the southern banks of 3,600km² (1,390 sq. miles) Lake Tana, both of which offer an equally rewarding experience.

Ⓓ Aksum

Pg. 62. The holy city of Aksum is acclaimed far and wide as the nation's most significant religious centre. Founded some 1,000 years ago by Menelik, apparently the bastard son of the legendary Queen of Sheba and wise King Solomon, Aksum has a vital Christian heritage that is very orthodox in nature. Ethiopians are devout believers and claim that the Arc of the Covenant remains hidden at Aksum.

The history of the city is largely unexplored and many archaeological sites have yet to be excavated, but there is

'Dregs of water ... were measured out among us, in Danakil, as though they had been the contents of the last bottle of some priceless vintage wine.'

LM Nesbitt, *Desert and Forest*

TM 184
NP 224
ADV 298

Djibouti

Ⓕ Djibouti
Pg. 185. The Monaco of Africa, Djibouti is a lively and bustling city-state barely 100 years old and peopled by an eclectic mix of cultures. Until 1977 the commercial port was a French colony and, despite being home to nearly 70 per cent of the nation's population, it retains some of its colonial flavour.

Once little more than extensive pastures for itinerant herders that roamed the hinterland, the tranquil streets are lined with fine mansions and its harbour-cum-marina is dotted with traditional fishing boats, dhows and modern sailing vessels. Le Marché Centra, the city's principal market district, is its most enduring attraction, while an interesting drawcard is the African Quarter which, although seedy, is inexpensive and offers fascinating insight into the lives of the trading locals. Lack of luxuries aside, the tiny city-state is an undiscovered treasure of mainland Africa.

H

Somalia

Ⓖ Mogadishu
Pg. 185. As Hammawein, old Mogadishu was a sprawling spectacle of grand cathedrals and architectural masterpieces set amid a splendid African landscape of sweeping sands and pristine, cove-dotted beaches that should have made it a highlight of the continent. Founded by the Arabs approximately 1,000 years ago, Mogadishu reached its greatest potential in the 1200s, when much of the city's early wealth originated as a result of a flourishing trade with China, Persia and India. Today, Somalia is one of the least developed nations in the world, and the capital continues to suffer as a result of political, geographic and social problems. The once impressive architecture of an old African capital is now riddled with bullets and is steadily decaying, and tourist travel is extremely limited. This nation of traders and farmers is, however, slowly creeping towards some semblance of peace. Situated on the longest shoreline of any African country, Mogadishu's fishing industry remains vital to the local economy, and the city also has a relatively small but thriving industry in frankincense, myrrh, henna and a local perfume base known as *unce*, all of which may be found at Mogadishu's street markets, ablaze with brightly painted signboards.

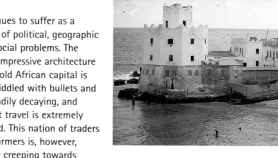

As a consequence of floods, famine, drought and political unrest, the southern reaches of the country remain far less accessible and rewarding than the northern stretch, which itself remains painfully susceptible to the turbulence permeating the rest of the country.

I

G

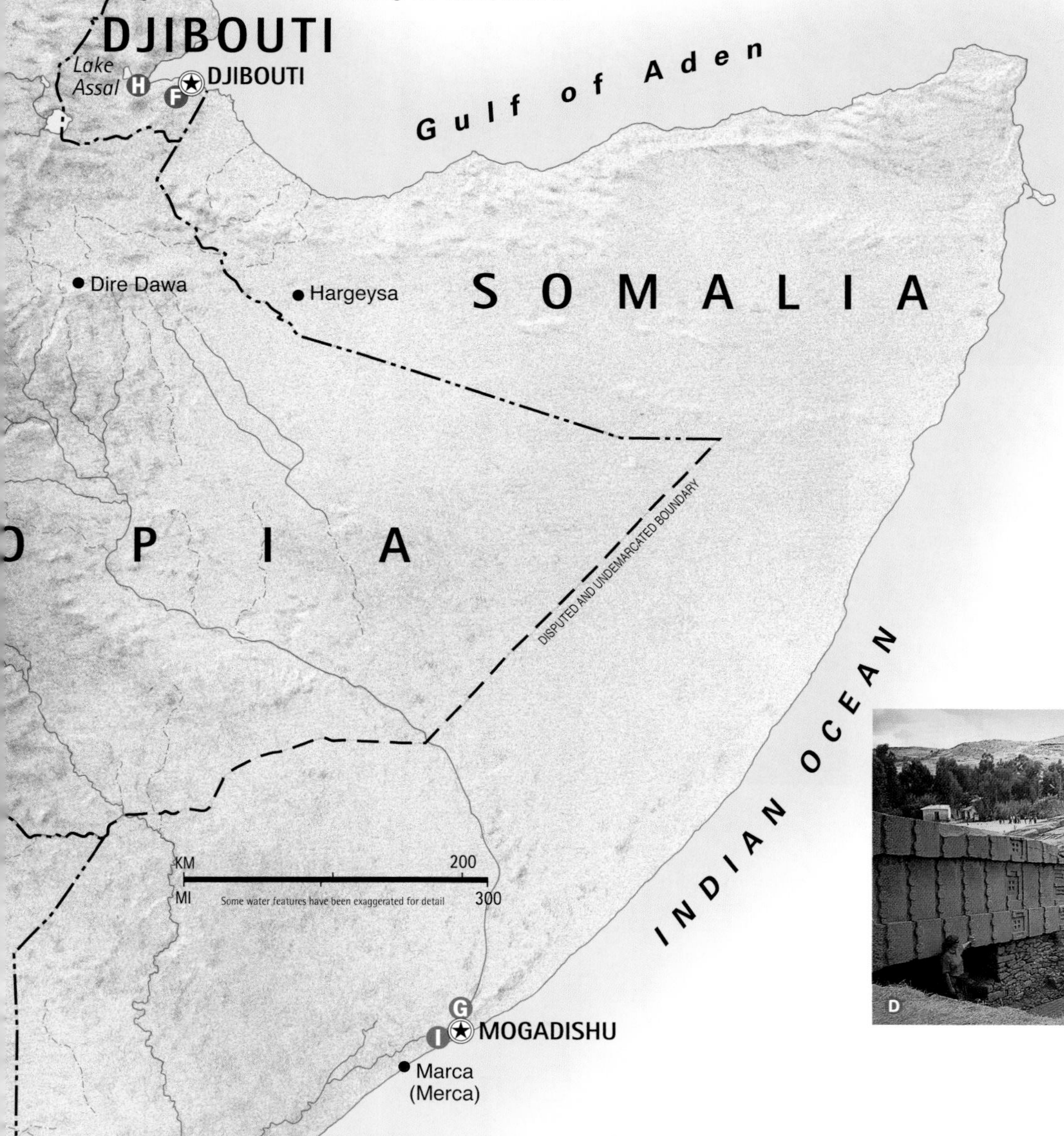

little doubt that Aksum is at least 500 years old, the collection of granite monoliths in the stele field on the outskirts of the town dating back some 2,000 years. The site is an impressive tribute to the history of the region, the adjacent museum providing a fascinating look at finds excavated from local sites.

The 7th-century church of St Mary of Zion, the country's most sacred site, is said to house the elusive Arc of the Covenant. The landscape is further dotted with ancient monasteries, churches, palaces and a complex of meticulously crafted catacombs.

Ⓔ Lalibela
Pg. 258. Scattered across Ethiopia is a series of rugged cave-like churches painstakingly carved from the rock face by human hands. The most celebrated of these is the series of 11 churches dotted around ancient Lalibela. There are similar conglomerations of rock-hewn churches around Ethiopia – notably at Tigray – but those at Lalibela have been most widely acclaimed as great architectural gems. The chapel-like subterranean caverns house treasures of historical and religious significance. The labyrinth of stone, which took nearly 50,000 worshippers a decade to complete, still hums with the haunting chants of monks and other orthodox Ethiopians celebrating mass, while priests carefully guard the relics from desecration and theft. The largest of the churches, Bet Medhane Alem, looms 11.5m (38ft) and covers an area of 800m² (8,611 sq. ft). Other sites include the Bet Abba Libanos and Bet Giorgis, in the shape of a 15m (50ft) cross.

PICTURE CAPTIONS
Ⓐ Asmara, Eritrea
Ⓑ Addis Ababa, Ethiopia
Ⓒ Blue Nile Falls, Ethiopia
Ⓓ Fallen stele, Aksum, Ethiopia
Ⓔ St George Cross, Lalibela, Ethiopia
Ⓖ Mogadishu, Somalia
Ⓗ Lake Assal Falls, Djibouti
Ⓘ Bread queue, Somalia
Ⓙ Nakatalapa rock church, Ethiopia

D

J

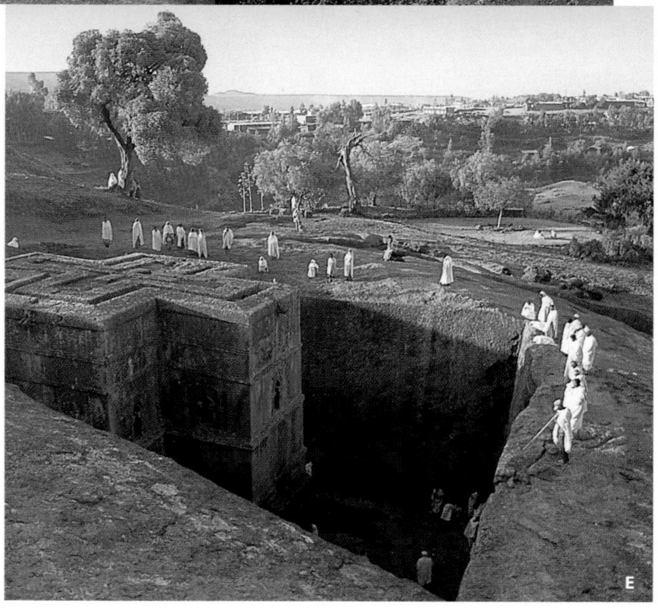
E

The Congo Basin

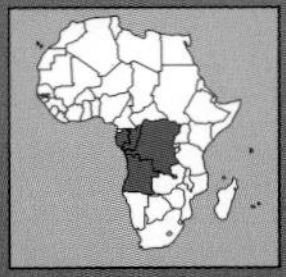

With the exception of oil-rich Gabon, a prosperous and relatively stable nation, the south-central region of the continent – with its profusion of rainforest and swamps, perhaps the epitome of the romantic notions of the African jungle – is one that has seen great suffering among its people, due almost entirely to the series of civil wars, revolution and instability that have come to symbolize the temperament of the region. Even by African standards, Congo, the Democratic Republic of the Congo (DRC) and Angola – but, again, with the exception of Gabon – are vast countries, with a total population of some 70 million people. This results in much strain on existing natural resources and leads to extreme poverty, especially among rural peoples who rely almost entirely on what the earth yields. The high cost of travel and the issue of personal safety remain areas of concern for international visitors, but the rewards are no less gratifying.

While Gabon has made best use of its mineral resources to build up considerable wealth from its oil fields, the vast oil reserves and diamond deposits to be found in Congo, Angola and the DRC (some 85 per cent of its foreign income) have remained largely unexploited while these countries have battled civil war and economic collapse.

GABON

Capital: Libreville
Area: 267,670km²/ 103,347mi²
Population: 1.2 million
Main ethnic groups:
- Fang (36%)
- Mpongwe (15%)
- Mbete (14%)

Main languages:
- French
- Fang

Main religions:
- Christian (96%)
- Muslim (2%)

Currency: CFA franc (100 centimes)

CONGO

Capital: Brazzaville
Area: 342,000km²/ 132,047mi²
Population: 3.2 million
Main ethnic groups:
- Bakongo (48%)
- Teke (17%)
- Mboshi (17%)
- Sangha (5%)

Main languages:
- French
- Kongo

Main religions:
- Catholic (50%)
- Traditional beliefs (48%)

Currency: CFA franc (100 centimes)

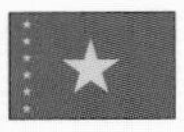

DEMOCRATIC REPUBLIC OF THE CONGO

Capital: Kinshasa
Area: 2,345,410km²/ 905,567mi²
Population: 55.2 million
Main ethnic groups:
- Baya (34%)
- Banda (27%)

Main languages:
- French
- Sangho

Main religions:
- Christian (50%)
- Traditional beliefs (27%)
- Muslim (15%)

Currency: Congolese franc (100 centimes)

ANGOLA

Capital: Luanda
Area: 1,246,700km²/ 481,354mi²
Population: 12.7 million
Main ethnic groups:
- Ovimbundu (37%)
- Kimbundu (25%)
- Bakongo (13%)

Main language:
- Portuguese

Main religions:
- Christian (64%)
- Traditional beliefs (34%)

Currency: Kwanza (100 lwei)

I

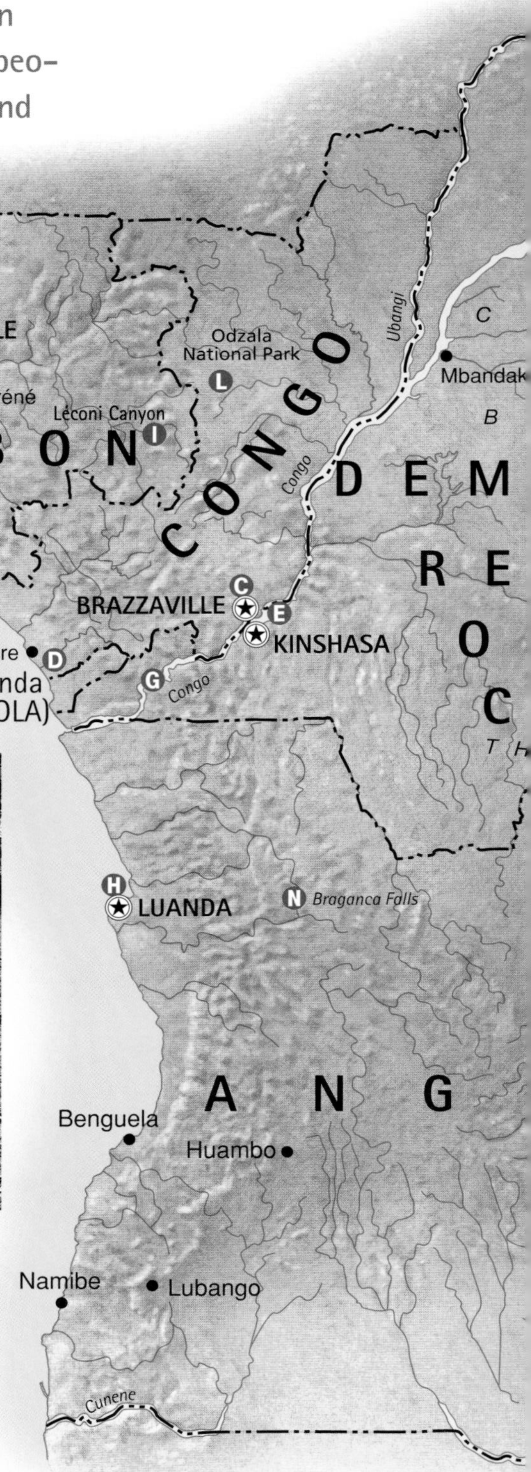

Gabon

Ⓐ Libreville

Pg. 186. Established as a French trading colony in the mid-1800s, Libreville saw considerable development following its lucrative slave trade to Brazil and other South American nations towards the end of the 19th century. Situated on an estuary of the Gabon River, it is one of the most modern capitals on the continent, and the principal city of one of the richest countries in Africa south of the Sahara – its more than one million people enjoy the fruits of Gabon's extensive oil reserves. The wide thoroughfares and leafy boulevards stand in stark contrast to the rustic little villages scattered on the outskirts. Although the charm of the rural settlements seems to have eluded Libreville's commercial districts, its African quarters are alive with a buzz more typical of the continent. Highlights are the impressive St-Michel's Church, with its mosaic and wood-carved façade, the traditional utensils and handiwork for sale at Le Village des Artisans, and the indigenous art on display at the Musée des Arts et Traditions. Along the northern coastal stretch is a series of truly beautiful beaches and resort towns, such as the famed Cap Estérias and Pointe-Dénis.

Ⓑ Lambaréné

Pg. 259. Steeped in a popular history that has become the focal point of the entire area, the town of Lambaréné – situated on the banks of an island in the Ogooué River – is gentle and laid-back, despite the fact that it is the third-largest settlement in Gabon. No more than a tiny rural community half buried in the lush rainforest that surrounds it, Lambaréné was put on the map by its most famous citizen, the doctor and philanthropist Albert Schweitzer, whose remains were laid to rest here in 1965. When he arrived in 1913, he set about establishing one of Gabon's finest medical facilities. The famed doctor's home, his original office, laboratory and treatment centre, some 8km (5 miles) outside of the town, are now a little dilapidated but the Schweitzer Hospital, its annex and the adjacent museum, with its guided tours, are still popular among visitors. Additional excursions in the immediate vicinity include a pirogue trip to see the wildlife in the famed lake region. Hippos – along with other animals and birds – are prolific here during the dry season, when they tend to congregate at the all-important water sources.

B

'Better to keep peace than to make peace'
ALBERT SCHWEITZER

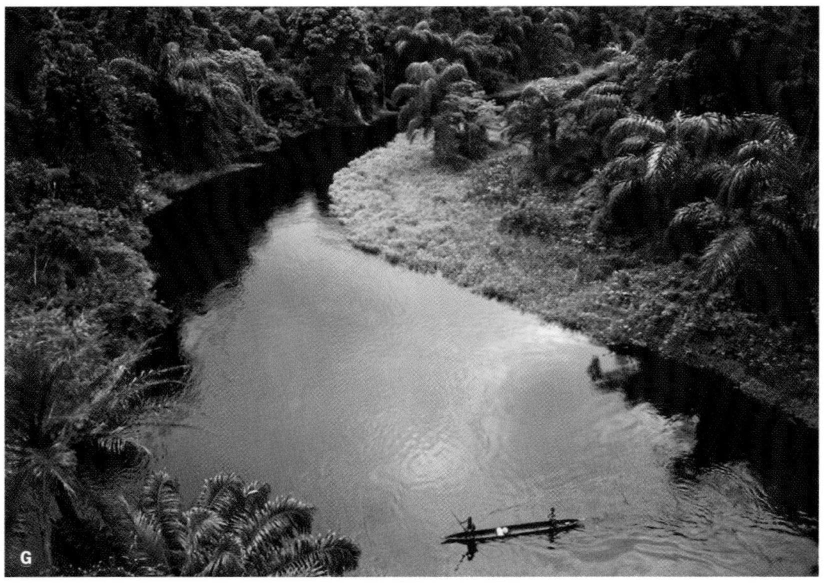
G

Congo

Ⓒ Brazzaville

Pg. 186. Following at least a decade of political turbulence and sustained bloodshed at the hands of revolutionaries, Brazzaville (located on the Congo River) has both its advantages and disadvantages for any tourist brave enough to venture into the very heart of Africa. Congo is famed for its short stretch of pristine coastline and its vibrant and innovative local music industry, yet the overriding feeling is one of despair. The capital of Congo is a spread-out mass of urban decay, where big city meets tiny village. Well greened, there are small pockets of tranquil solitude unblemished by the scars of war that ravaged the people and their environment, especially the Congo River. Just 10km (6 miles) from the city centre are the celebrated rapids on the Congo river.

Ⓓ Pointe-Noire

Pg. 72. In a country best known for its tropical forest and hot and humid interior, it is a refreshing change to discover that large parts of its

TM 186
NP 226
ADV 300

Democratic Republic of the Congo

Ⓔ Kinshasa

Pg. 188. Known by its colonists as Léopoldville, what is today Kinshasa became the capital of the Belgian Congo in 1929 and is now one of the most dynamic of Africa's modern cities. Set amid rainforests and volcanic mountains and peopled by over five million (mostly Kongo), the city vacillates between a thriving metropolis and a dusty little backwater, incorporating the good and the bad of virtually every contemporary urban settlement. It has a very reputable university, a number of impressive museums – most significantly the Museé de Kinshasa – and a proud heritage of fine art, the finest examples of which may be seen at the Académie des Beaux-Arts. The local music scene is Kinshasa's most enduring highlight. Musicians continue to perform at popular nightspots in the Cité area and the thumping music and laughter emanating from the *ngandas* (open-air dance venues) continue to draw crowds of revellers.

Kinshasa's detractions include being hot, humid and chaotic with a horribly inept public transport system, an extremely intimidating (and often corrupt) military and police presence, and vast numbers of visitors reporting incidents of harassment.

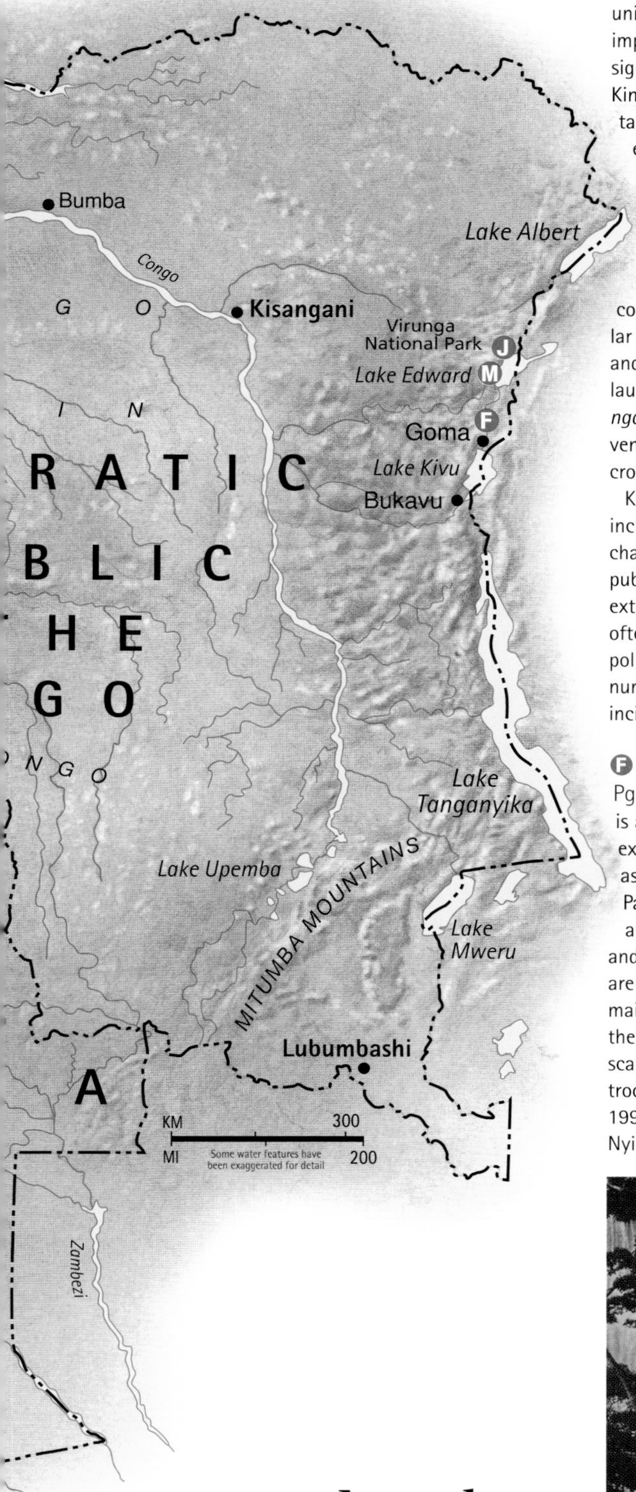

Ⓕ Goma

Pg. 260. The town of Goma is a good base from which to explore national parks such as Kahuzi-Biega National Park. Although the outskirts are undeniably attractive and the shores of Lake Kivu are lined with grand, well-maintained private homes, the inner Cité still bears the scars left by marauding troops in the mid- to late 1990s. More recently, Nyiragongo Volcano, which forms the majestic backdrop of the town, erupted in early 2002 and resulted in one of the country's most horrific tragedies. Goma is still struggling to overcome the massive geological as well as political and social devastation. It can, nevertheless, be a charming little stopover.

Ⓖ Congo River

Pg. 301. The length of the Congo River's winding, 4,800km (3,000-mile) course delineates the political boundary between Congo and the DRC and lies in a basin of some 3,000,000km² (1,160,000 sq. miles) lined with lush equatorial forest and punctuated intermittently with swamp and savanna plain. The great river, hailed as the second-longest in Africa, rises on the Katanga Plateau, where it is known locally as the Lualaba and, together with the Ubangi River, channels most of the DRC's run-off to the sea. One of the greatest benefactors of the waters of the Congo River is Kisangani, the all-important urban settlement nestling on the water's edge and an important crossroads for cross-country travellers. A large proportion of local travel centres on the much vaunted Stanley Falls (Boyoma Falls), one of the area's most significant tourism drawcards.

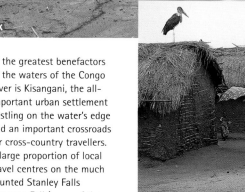

PICTURE CAPTIONS
- Ⓑ Albert Schweitzer's gravestone, Lambaréné, Gabon
- Ⓖ Congo River, Democratic Republic of the Congo
- Ⓗ Old Christian Church, Luanda, Angola
- Ⓘ Léconi Canyon, Gabon
- Ⓙ Virunga National Park, Democratic Republic of the Congo
- Ⓚ Army ants, Democratic Republic of the Congo
- Ⓛ Mountain gorillas, Odzala National Park, Congo
- Ⓜ Marabou storks, Lake Edward, Democratic Republic of the Congo
- Ⓝ Braganca Falls, Angola

shoreline are little short of idyllic, such as Pointe-Noire. One of Congo's many popular beach towns, the laid-back milieu and breathtaking setting of turquoise waters and deserted beaches are incomparable. Pointe-Noire is relaxed and friendly, with a succession of beach clubs and pubs. The days are balmy, but the gentle sea breeze is refreshing. With the blue sea and pristine beaches dotted with thatched umbrellas just a few kilometres beyond the urban limits, it is little wonder that the resort town is enjoying increasing attention.

Angola

Ⓗ Luanda

Pg. 187. Still bearing the evidence of its Portuguese colonial heritage and fighting a continuing battle against crime and civil unrest, Luanda – officially known as São Paulo de Loanda – was founded in 1576 and, in less than 100 years, had become the nucleus of the thriving slave trade to the plantations of Brazil. Originally established to accommodate no more than 30,000 settlers, what is now the capital of Angola is wholly unable to meet the needs of its 2.8 million citizens, many of whom made their way here from farmland during the civil war towards the end of the 20th century. The overcrowded city streets spill over into a series of dirty and dusty shanty towns on its outskirts. Luanda has managed to retain at least some of its centuries-old charm. The old Portuguese Quarter, known as Cidade Alta, is undoubtedly the most picturesque, a series of Victorian- and Edwardian-style buildings housing museums and galleries, restaurants and even government offices. Sadly, this is virtually the only evidence of a profusion of indigenous cultures in the city, where most of the citizens have adopted Western lifestyles.

The Great Lakes

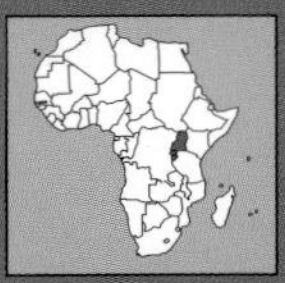

R

RWANDA

Capital: Kigali
Area: 26,340km²/ 10,170mi²
Population: 7.4 million
Main ethnic groups:
- Hutu (90%)
- Tutsi (9%)
- Twa pygmy (1%)

Main languages:
- Kinyarwnada
- French
- Kiswahili

Main religions:
- Catholic (65%)
- Traditional beliefs (25%)
- Protestant (7%)

Currency: Rwandan franc (100 centimes)

BURUNDI

Capital: Bujumbura
Area: 27,830km²/ 10,745mi²
Population: 6.7 million
Main ethnic groups:
- Hutu (85%)
- Tutsi (13%)
- Twa pygmy (1%)

Main languages:
- Kirundi
- French
- Swahili

Main religions:
- Catholic (62%)
- Traditional beliefs (32%)
- Protestant (6%)

Currency: Burundi franc (100 centimes)

UGANDA

Capital: Kampala
Area: 236,036km²/ 91,134mi²
Population: 24.7 million
Main ethnic groups:
- Buganda (18%)
- Banyoro (14%)
- Teso (9%)

Main languages:
- English
- Luganda
- Nkole
- Chiga
- Lango
- Acholi
- Teso

Main religions:
- Roman Catholic / Protestant (66%)
- Traditional beliefs (18%)
- Muslim (16%)

Currency: Ugandan shilling (100 cents)

The warm, tropical climate and mostly fertile lands of Rwanda, Burundi and Uganda provide an ideal habitat for the gorillas and chimpanzees for which the region is justifiably famed, but it is also blessed with an abundance of other wild animals so characteristic of equatorial Africa and more than its fair share of avifauna. The rainforests of the west and savanna plains of the east create a surprising contrast in landscape and mood, but despite the flaming sunsets sinking over an unblemished wilderness, the recent history of its human inhabitants is unfortunately less inspiring. Although showing remarkable recovery, all three nations have been ravaged by war and drought and, as a result, famine and poverty. Today, Rwanda, Burundi and Uganda suffer the worst of the worldwide AIDS epidemic, and huge numbers of locals live with HIV/AIDS. As a result, population estimates are dramatically affected by low life expectancy, high infant mortality, and low population growth.

The landmass covered by Uganda, Burundi and Rwanda is some of the most densely populated in the world and, although there are small pockets of valuable parks and reserves, much of it is given over to cultivation in order to feed the region's 37-odd million people.

Rwanda

Ⓐ Kigali

Pg. 189. Despite the horrors of the genocide that took place in Rwanda, Kigali has emerged as a promising focal point of the country's rehabilitation process. Standing high on a ridge, Kigali lies in the centre of a country that is surrounded by other nations that have seen equally devastating conflict in recent times. With a relatively small citizenship of about a quarter million, the capital remains the nation's most important cultural, economic and academic centre. Although many of the buildings in the urban hub still bear the scars of the war, there has been a very real attempt to resurrect the beauty of the old city, and a number of small but pretty parks have been established to help enhance the face of Kigali. Although post-war Kigali boasts a mobile cellular service that connects the national capital with the capitals of the prefectures, the infrastructure is basic, and there are no more than 1,000 television sets in the city.

Ⓑ Lake Kivu

Pg. 302. Lake Kivu lies at 1,460m (4,790ft), covering an impressive 2,698km² (1,042 sq. miles) and plunging to depths of 475m (1,558ft). The grand body of water is navigated by small vessels and shallow barges, many of which play no small role in the tea and cotton processing industries around Kamembe. The lake shore is equally spectacular. To the south lies the Nyungwe Forest. The surrounds are quite beautiful, dotted intermittently with the gems of Rwanda's natural attractions, including the 100m (330ft) falls of Les Chutes de Ndaba, the waterfalls on the Rusizi River, Nyakabuye's hot springs, and the wildlife of Rugege Forest, including chimpanzees, leopard and even elephant.

The shores are studded with pretty towns, from Cyangugu on Kivu's southernmost shore to Gisenyi in the north, noted for the 3,407m (11,180ft) peaks of Nyiragongo.

H

'A magnificent sight, that ages, added to the greatest length of human life, would not erase or eradicate from my memory.'
James Bruce, Scots Traveller, 1700s

Burundi

Ⓒ Bujumbura

Pg. 189. Situated on hill slopes stretching up from the northern shore of Lake Tanganyika and blessed with a balmy climate, Bujumbura is a treasure house of cultural gems. Comparatively small, but beautiful, it has a rich history moulded by the developments of the entire country. Although it boasts magnificent views across Lake Tanganyika's northern reaches, the former colonial town remains unmistakably the capital of one of the world's most populated nations.

Attractive and even beautiful in parts, albeit simple, its most intriguing tourist magnet is the Musée Vivant, a reconstruction of a model Burundian village with a reptile park and market.

Ⓓ Gitega

Pg. 74. One of the few centres that continue to attract Burundi's share of travellers is Gitega, Burundi's second-largest settlement.

A certain charm infiltrates the multi-sensory streets. There is a small but interesting National Museum. The surrounds are rugged but picturesque, and dotted on the outskirts of town are a selection of diversions and day trips that offer a very pleasant glimpse of unspoilt Burundi. Among the natural splendours are the magnificent falls of Kagera Falls, little more than a relaxed day trip from the town and its most popular drawcard. The falls are at their most striking during the rainy season from about October to January.

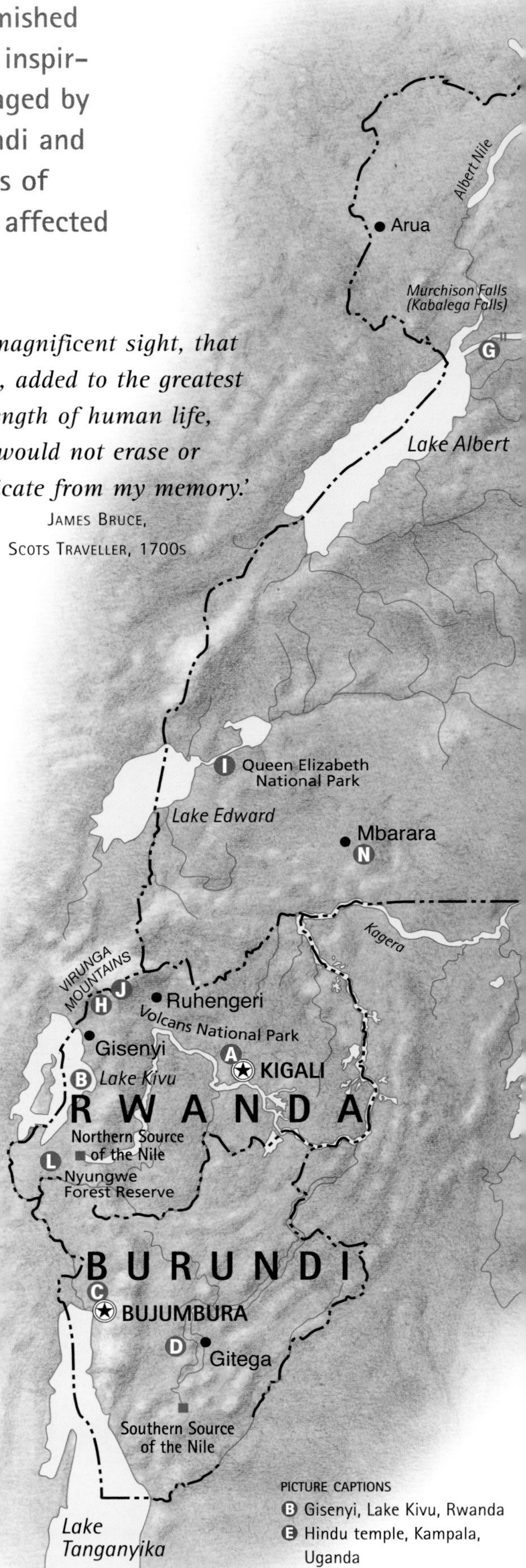

B

I

J

PICTURE CAPTIONS
- Ⓑ Gisenyi, Lake Kivu, Rwanda
- Ⓔ Hindu temple, Kampala, Uganda
- Ⓖ Murchison Falls, Uganda
- Ⓗ Virunga Mountains, Rwanda
- Ⓘ Papyrus, Chamura River, Queen Elizabeth NP, Uganda
- Ⓙ Gorilla, Volcans National Park, Rwanda
- Ⓚ Jinja, source of the Victoria Nile, Uganda
- Ⓛ Colobus monkey, Nyungwe Forest Reserve, Rwanda
- Ⓜ Shoebill stork, Uganda
- Ⓝ Ankole cattle, Mbarara

TM 189
NP 228
ADV 302

'Uganda is truly the pearl of Africa'.
WINSTON CHURCHILL,
MY AFRICAN JOURNEY, 1908

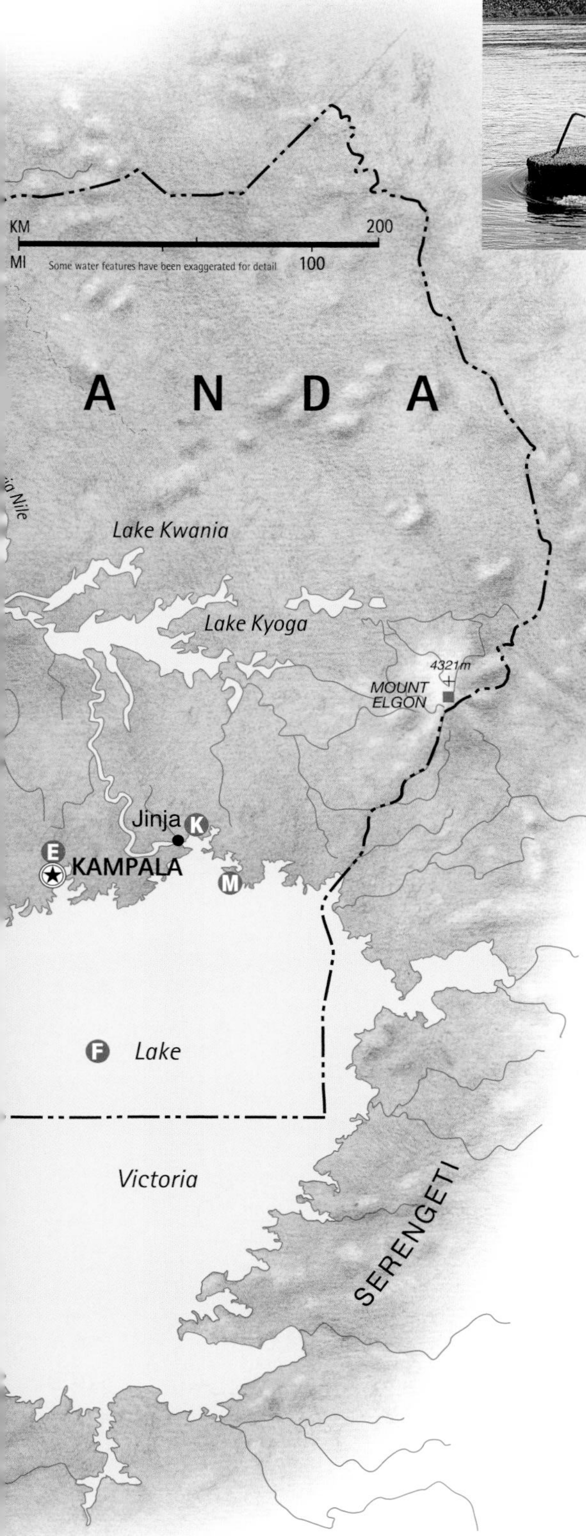

Uganda

E Kampala

Pg. 189. Despite the crumbling walls of the ghetto areas, bullet-riddled and shrapnel-scarred, what was once considered the Pearl of Africa is re-emerging as one of the gems in Africa's crown. Located on the undulating landscape so typical of Central Africa, the seven hills on which Kampala stands are lush and fertile, and the city itself is fast becoming a burgeoning modern centre, along with the impressive National Museum and enthralling Kasubi Tombs. Grand places of worship for all the prominent faiths include the Kibuli Mosque, Rubaga Catholic Cathedral, Namirembe Anglican Cathedral and a typically ornate Hindu Temple.

The city is peopled with an eclectic mix of colourful characters, a human parade of lively vendors and an avian population of marabou storks who alight on every conceivable vantage point. Kampala experienced pitiful degradation during the bloody reign of dictator Idi Amin, but its people have returned to the city, and brought with them a stability and even 'prosperity'. The streets are still filled with the widows, orphans and refugees that are Amin's legacy, but the broken windows are slowly being replaced, the buildings patched up and reinforced, and the inner city of Kampala is no longer a place to be avoided for fear of your life. In fact, it is lush, pretty, friendly and safe – something not many African capitals can claim.

F Lake Victoria

Pg. 74. The papyrus-fringed shores and intermittent swamps along Lake Victoria have contributed considerably to its image as one of the most striking in all of Africa. As the largest of the continent's great lakes, Lake Victoria is delightfully free of fishing, sailing and water-sport enthusiasts. A vast, gentle and tranquil body of water that borders Kenya, Tanzania and Uganda, Lake Victoria lies a relatively short distance from both Rwanda and Burundi. It is into this great lake that the beginning of the mighty Nile empties, and then leaves again at Jinja as the Victoria Nile. The great river moves on to feed the swamplands of Lake Kyoga in the centre of the country and spills into Lake Albert in the northwest of Uganda en route to the north of Africa. Together with the Victoria Nile, Lake Victoria is at the heart of some of the best-watered lands on the African continent and is the home territory of an endless variety of wildlife, notably the black-and-white pied kingfishers at home in the bird sanctuaries dotting the shore, and the common Nile perch, which was introduced into Lake Victoria. Locals harvest the waters by casting fishing nets from small handcrafted rowboats to eke out their meagre living. Lake Victoria remains very much a place for the people of Uganda, offering little evidence of the tourist market.

G Murchison Falls

Pg. 262. Unmistakable as one of Uganda's most recognizable faces, the Murchison Falls (or Kabalega Falls) on the Victoria Nile River lie at the heart of 3,900km^2 (1,500 sq. miles) of natural splendour, neatly divided by the waters of the Victoria Nile as it snakes its way from Lake Kyoga to Lake Albert. The outlying countryside comprises mostly savanna and grassland, but along the banks of the river are stands of densely packed forest, including mahogany, with acacia trees and papyrus reeds filling in the gaps. The terrain is stalked by predators such as lion and leopard, trod by those great African giants, the elephant and the giraffe, and grazed by bushbuck and waterbuck, while crocodiles and hippos wallow in the river waters. Waders and other waterfowl are common and it is not unusual to spot shoebills, African skimmers, red-throated bee-eaters, herons and kingfishers among the more than 380 bird species to be found in the national park. However, the most enduring asset of the park is the spectacular falls, which tumble about 43m (140ft). Even more remarkable is the enormous force of the water of the usually 50m-wide (165ft) Nile as it is thrust through a mere 7m (23ft) gap between the rocks that form the Rift Valley escarpment. A three-hour boat trip from Paraa (leaving twice a day) takes enthralled visitors right up to the foot of the falls, while an intriguing diversion may be to hunt for the latter-day survivor of the timeless *African Queen*, the humble vessel that carried Katherine Hepburn and Humphrey Bogart to the heights of stardom. The original vessel was unearthed from the banks of the Victoria Nile during the reclamation of the park and continues to ply the waters of the river.

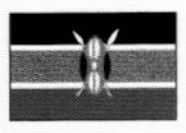

KENYA

Capital: Nairobi
Area: 592,747km²/ 228,861mi²
Population: 31.1 million
Main ethnic groups:
- Kikuyu (21%)
- Luhya (14%)
- Kamba (11%)

Main languages:
- Swahili
- English
- Kikuyu
- Luo
- Kamba

Main religions:
- Catholic (34%)
- Protestant (32%)
- Traditional beliefs (26%)
- Muslim (6%)

Currency: Kenyan shilling (100 cents)

TANZANIA

Capitals: Dar es Salaam (administrative), Dodoma (legislative)
Area: 945,087km²/ 364,900mi²
Population: 37.2 million
Main ethnic groups:
- ± 120 Bantu groups (99%)

Main languages:
- Swahili
- English

Main religions:
- Traditional beliefs (42%)
- Muslim (31%)
- Christian (27%)

Currency: Tanzanian shilling (100 cents)

The Great Rift Valley

At its most dramatic in East Africa, the Great Rift Valley was formed some 20 million years ago when violent subterranean shifts resulted in the collapse of mammoth tracks of land situated along parallel fault lines, causing volcanic eruptions of molten rock. Today, this massive fissure in the earth's crust stretches 9,500km (6,000 miles) from Lebanon to Mozambique, and no less than 800km (500 miles) between Lake Manyara and the Red Sea. The dramatic inclines of its valley walls slice between 50km (30 miles) and 500km (300 miles) through the width of the African landscape. Apart from Ethiopia on the Horn of Africa, the two countries that are home to the most theatrical inclines of the great valley are Kenya and Tanzania, both of which are characterized by high-lying inland plateaux and fertile coastal belts dotted with tropical islands.

Cutting through the heart of both Kenya and Tanzania is the colossal trench of the Rift Valley, its extraordinarily vertical walls looming up from the wide golden plain below and the cliff-like ramparts broken by cross fractures. The length of the great scar that has been forged down one-sixth of the earth's circumference is characterized by a succession of great lakes.

'I felt as if we had stumbled on a race that had survived simply because Time had forgotten to finish them off.'

John Hillaby, *Journey to the Jade Sea*, 1964

Kenya

A Nairobi
Pg. 190. One of the most cosmopolitan and certainly one of the youngest of all of Africa's capitals, Nairobi is a metropolis of museums and malls interspersed with market stalls, galleries and game reserves, boutiques and bars, curios and criminals. The city's two million inhabitants come from a variety of tribal cultures, and the noise, colour and squalor of the older portions contrast greatly with modern structures such as the Kenyatta Conference Centre. Nairobi National Park lies on the city perimeter, with the Aberdare National Park nearby and river rafting on the Athi River.

B Mount Kenya
Pg. 83. Sacred Kirinyaga (Mount Kenya) on the central Highlands is a playground for hikers, mountaineers and climbers. The snowcapped summit of its three-million-year-old bulk stands at 5,199m (17,058ft), already eroded by 2,000m (6,500ft) through glaciation. Topped by three main peaks – Batian, Nelion and Lenana – the slopes of this extinct volcano are covered in snow and ice, with 600km² (230 sq. miles) of protected land above the 3,200m (10,500ft) forest line.

The region is the traditional home to the Kikuyu people, and the park is home to birds, elephant, buffalo, lion, black rhino and bushbuck.

C Lake Turkana
Pg. 79. Kenya's long, narrow lake covers 7,104km² (2,743 sq. miles). Known by many locals as Basso Narok (Black Lake), in Kenya's colonial heyday it was known as Lake Rudolf, a ribbon of water 250km (155 miles) long and 56km (35 miles) wide, enclosed by the cliffs of the Rift Valley, cutting through the parched northern reaches of endless horizons and volcanic outcrops. Fed by Ethiopia's Omo River and, to some degree, by the Turkwel, Lake Turkana is the world's largest desert lake, and one of the largest alkaline lakes. Volcanic islands in the middle of the lake are the territory of hippos and some 22,000 crocodiles, while the waters shelter huge Nile perch. Migrant birds visit in such great numbers that their breeding sites on South and Central Island have been declared national parks.

D Lake Victoria
Pg. 82. Also known as Victoria Nyanza, Lake Victoria falls within the boundaries of Kenya, Tanzania and Uganda. Covering 69,485km² (26,828 sq. miles), Victoria is Africa's largest lake and the world's second largest. Lying at an altitude of 1,134m (3,720ft) in the populated highlands of Kenya, it averages a depth of only 78m (255ft), and its waters are drained by the Victoria Nile. The lake is dotted with little islands such as Ndere (a national park in the middle of the lake) and Saa Nane (a reserve harbouring island wildlife like rock agamas and hyraxes), while the 240km² (93-sq.-mile) Rubondo Island reserve boasts sitatunga, elephant, bushbuck and chimps. The lake shore is lined with reeds, papyrus and flamingoes, while its banks are settled mostly by the Luo, farmers and fishermen who ply the lake for Nile perch.

E Mombasa
Pg. 89. A romantic port on a coral island, Mombasa has retained much of its 12-centuries-old charm. Like Zanzibar, it has remained virtually unchanged for about 100 years, with its floating market skirting the shores of Mombasa Island. With a population of half a million, old Mombasa has a long history of conquerors and colonists. Guarding the Old Harbour is historic Fort Jesus, and beyond lie spectacular reefs only 640m (2,000ft) offshore. These reefs are lined with white, pebble-free beaches such as Tiwi and Diani, circled by dhows and schools of tropical fish. This makes for excellent snorkelling and scuba diving.

F Lamu Archipelago
Pg. 90. The islands of Lamu, Manda and Apte form the Lamu Archipelago, site of some of the best diving off East Africa. The lesser-known isles include Manda – best known for its Takwa Ruins covering 5ha (12 acres) – and Pate Island, home to the mystical 8ha (20 acres) Swahili state of Shanga. Most prominent of the trio is Lamu Island, a 9th-century settlement of cobbled streets and flagstoned courtyards. The island, 19km (12 miles) long, is a mix of traditional Islam and Swahili and offers a fascinating glimpse into old Africa. The lively harbour front is also the hunting ground of the island's many feral cats.

TM 190
NP 230
ADV 304

Tanzania

G Dar es Salaam
Pg. 191. Established in 1870 by Sultan Majid of Zanzibar as his 'Haven of Peace', the spiritual heart of Tanzania is magical Dar es Salaam, the nation's most important harbour city and its largest urban settlement. More acclaimed for its splendid beaches such as at Oyster Bay and Kunduchi, dynamic Dar remains every inch the contemporary city. It has a wonderful mix of people and cultures (the legacy of German and English colonists), as well as noisy but mesmerizing markets and unparalleled, upmarket tourist facilities. It also boasts impressive historic sites that are, in the most part, only a few decades old.

H Mount Kilimanjaro
Pg. 265. Mighty Kilimanjaro, with an altitude of 5,895m (19,340ft), emerged 750,000 years ago as a result of volcanic activity to create the world's highest freestanding mountain. The precise origin of Kili's name remains lost in time – the local word *kilima* (from which the name apparently stems) means 'hill' rather than 'mountain'.

Rising from the plains of the Masai, the mountain peak – a dormant volcano – is snowcapped (although just 3° south of the equator) and the make-up of the slopes varies enormously. From the foot to about 1,800m (5,900ft), the inclines comprise volcanic soils, while the vegetation up to 2,800m (9,200ft) is rainforest, which receives over 2,000mm (79in) of rain, followed — to an altitude of 4,000m (13,100ft) — by a moorland of heather and giant lobelias.

I Zanzibar
Pg. 191. Zanzibar is a separate Swahili city-state within Tanzania and consists of two islands which lie about 40km (25 miles) off the coast – Unguja (or Zanzibar) is the more famous, but there is also Pemba. Both share a sad history of trade in ivory and slaves. Known as the Spice Island, Zanzibar is a beach idyll, at the centre of which stands Stone Town, the old quarter of Zanzibar Town, the island's largest settlement. The maze of narrow streets, paths and alleys is littered with the history of its Swahili, Arabic, Asian and European residents.

Stone Town boasts a romantic skyline of towering minarets, an Arab fort, lavish 19th-century palaces, and Portuguese churches, the most prominent landmarks being St Joseph's Cathedral and the Victorian clock tower of the House of Wonders. The outskirts are ringed with clove plantations, and the harbour is dotted with Swahili fishing dhows that flit across the offshore reefs.

J Ngorongoro Crater
Pg. 264. The Ngorongoro Crater, the largest intact volcanic caldera in the world, forms the heart of the Ngorongoro Conservation Area, the expansive tableland that covers the 265km² (102 sq. miles) of the crater floor. Hedged in by 600m (2,000ft) walls that tower high above the open savanna, this is a sweep of untamed wilderness across which herds numbering hundreds of zebra and wildebeest charge, and huge flocks of pink flamingoes wade the seasonal waters. The plains and montane forest are home to a breathtaking array of Africa's most recognized wildlife, with no fewer than a quarter million large mammals scattered across the emptiness. The abundance of antelope species means that this is also prime big cat country, with cheetah, leopard and the world's densest population of over 100 lions. The rest of the Big Five have also settled here: elephant bulls, 3,000 head of buffalo, and roughly 20 black rhinos.

K Serengeti
Pg. 264. The dramatic natural arena in which Africa's greatest display plays itself out, the horizonless plains of the Serengeti are a spectacular wildlife sanctuary without parallel. Known by the local Masai as 'The Great Open Place', the plateau of the 15,000km² (5,800 sq. mile) grassland is covered by the short grasses of the Serengeti National Park, acclaimed as the finest game reserve in Africa. This extraordinary ecosystem – adjoined by the Masai Mara Reserve, Maswa Game Reserve, Ngorongoro and Loliondo Controlled Area – is home to enormous populations of mammals.

The Serengeti's annual wildebeest migration begins on the southern plateau during the summer rains (December to May) when herds of 100,000 animals – reaching 40km (25 miles) – begin their 800km (500-mile) trek to the western territories, only to make the gruelling return trip to the southern plains between October and November.

'As wide as all the world, great, high and unbelievably white in the sun...'
ERNEST HEMINGWAY ON TANZANIA'S MOUNT KILIMANJARO

PICTURE CAPTIONS
A Nairobi, Kenya
B Mount Kenya, Kenya
C Lake Turkana, Kenya
E Fort Jesus, Mombasa, Kenya
F Mosque, Lamu, Kenya
G Dar es Salaam, Tanzania
H Mount Kilimanjaro, Tanzania
I Stone Town, Zanzibar, Tanzania
J Lion pride, Ngorongoro Crater, Tanzania
K Gong Rock, Serengeti, Tanzania

'Treat the earth well. It was not given to you by your parents, it was loaned to you by your children.'
KENYAN PROVERB

The Great Zambezi

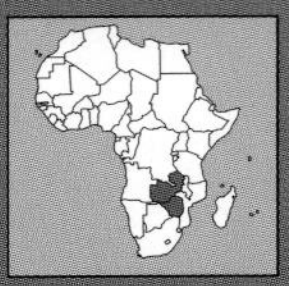

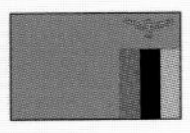

ZAMBIA

Capital: Lusaka
Area: 752,610km²/ 290,584mi²
Population: 10 million
Main ethnic groups:
- Bemba (36%)
- Maravi (18%)
- Tonga (15%)

Main languages:
- Bemba
- Tonga
- Nyanja
- Lozi
- Lunda
- English

Main religions:
- Christian (63%)
- Traditional beliefs (37%)

Currency: Zambian kwacha (100 ngwee)

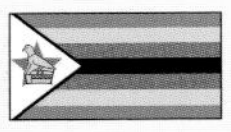

ZIMBABWE

Capital: Harare
Area: 390,580km²/ 150,800mi²
Population: 12.3 million
Main ethnic groups:
- Shona (71%)
- Ndebele (16%)
- White (1.5%)
- Asian (0.5%)

Main languages:
- English
- Shona
- Ndebele

Main religions:
- Syncretic (combination Christian/traditional beliefs) (50%)
- Christian (26%)
- Traditional beliefs (24%)

Currency: Zimbabwean dollar (100 cents)

Steeped in a long and erratic history of colonial occupation, Zambia and Zimbabwe were once known as Northern and Southern Rhodesia respectively, settler outposts that continue in many ways to struggle against the legacy left behind by empirical Britain after independence. Ethnically diverse and culturally extremely rich, both Zambia and Zimbabwe rely to a large degree on the land that has since been reclaimed from colonial powers. Zambia's greatest asset is its copper reserves and, although these are gradually declining, copper exports still account for some 80 per cent of the nation's foreign income. Zimbabwe, on the other hand, has historically relied almost entirely on the harvest of its cash crops, most notably tobacco, which have created one of the most broadly based economies of the region.

Both Zambia and Zimbabwe are spectacular in their natural beauty and, despite the political turmoil in which they have been — and, in the case of Zimbabwe, still are — embroiled, the potential of the tourism industry remains virtually the only shining light on what may otherwise be rather bleak futures.

'The loveliest thing in all Africa; my own personal paradise.'
STUART GORE-BROWN

J

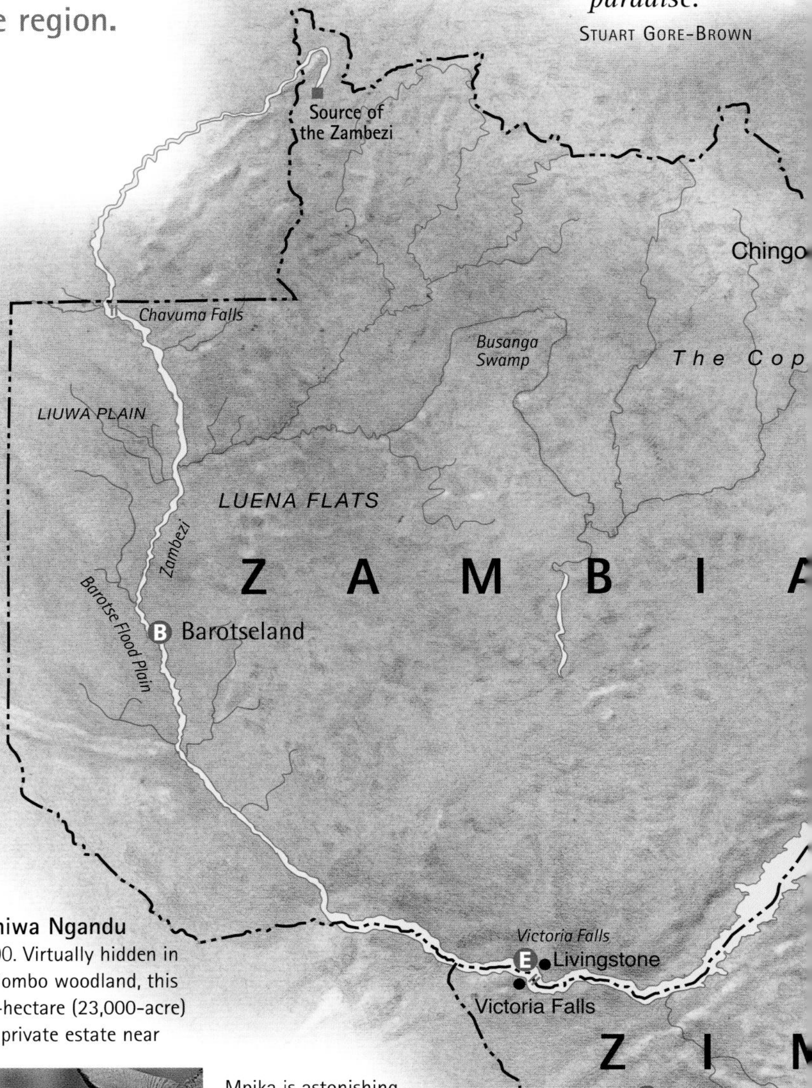

Zambia

Ⓐ Lusaka

Pg. 192. Having originated as little more than a single general store serving workers building a railway siding in the early 1900s, the modern city – succeeding Livingstone as the nation's capital in 1930 – has mushroomed into a hub of activity conveniently situated at one of the most important crossroads in southern Africa. Lusaka is every inch a modern urban settlement with all the charm and scourges that entails: open-air markets, tree-lined boulevards and dusty side streets lurking with muggers and less innocuous criminals. In reality, apart from a network of travel-orientated facilities such as the airport, bus terminals and tourist offices, there is little to attract the casual sightseer. Lusaka's citizens are nevertheless widely acknowledged as the friendliest and most hospitable on the continent.

Ⓑ Barotseland

Pg. 104. Fiercely independent and devout followers of tradition, the people of Barotseland remain one of the most authentic indigenous groups in Zambia. Barotseland once extended far and wide, but now centres around the Zambezi's flood plains. The most engrossing feature of the region is the rituals of its people, epitomized in the Kuomboka, a lavish parade that sees the Lozi king take to the waters in an ornate barge in his ceremonial evacuation of the flood plain in favour of higher ground. The ritual is repeated every year as a highlight of the ceremonial calendar.

Ⓒ Luangwa Valley

Pg. 267. The Luangwa Valley follows the course of the Luangwa River: one side is wild, unpredictable and remote, the other an expanse of picturesque nature reserve abounding with wild animals.

The northern reaches of the valley, occupied mostly by the Bemba people, is dominated by the untamed wilderness of North Luangwa National Park: difficult to access, nature reigns supreme in the Park. Predators and scavengers lurk in murky waters and scour the plains. It is from the fauna-rich miombo woodlands of the Zambian plateau that the escarpment dips 1,000m (330ft) to the floor of the Luangwa Valley.

Hippo and crocodile still inhabit the Luangwa River, but along the 200km (124 miles) that separate North Luangwa from its southern counterpart there is a noticeable change. South Luangwa National Park is one of Africa's best reserves and is far more developed than the north. Although no 'walk in the park', it is much more accessible, dry river beds and hard-baked soils opening into woodland and grassy plains populated with lion, leopard, elephant, buffalo, zebra and Thornicroft's giraffe. The Save the Rhino Trust continues to combat the poaching of elephant and rhino in the area.

Ⓓ Shiwa Ngandu

Pg. 100. Virtually hidden in the miombo woodland, this 9,350-hectare (23,000-acre) grand private estate near Mpika is astonishing. In 1914 Stuart Gore-Brown, ex-soldier, mentor and explorer, laid claim to 4,900ha (12,000 acres), later adding 4,450ha (11,000 acres) to the property. He went on to play a pivotal role in the story of Zambia and remains the only European settler to have been honoured with a state funeral and to be buried according to the ritual reserved for a tribal chief.

The grand old Shiwa House is in a sad state of disrepair, but the surrounding wilderness is quite breathtaking.

C

A

B

Ⓔ Victoria Falls

Pg. 307. Located on the majestic Zambezi River (within the boundaries of Zambia and Zimbabwe), the dramatic Victoria Falls has been hailed as the greatest spectacle on earth. Situated amid a small rainforest, which forms part of the surrounding national park, Victoria Falls has become one of the continent's most enduring legacies and is today big business. Thousands of visitors flock here annually to look out over the spectacular 2km (1-mile) wide falls and down into the Zambezi Gorge: for the privilege they suffer the spray of water as it tumbles 100m (330ft). The rainforest that skirts the edge

TM 192
NP 232
ADV 306

of Victoria Falls is washed in parts by 500m (1,640ft) of spray and is laced with a convoluted network of walks and trails, at times stepping out onto the lip of the great basin and at others receding into the woods, or winding down the tracks to the gorge below. Zambia's vantage points offer a much closer look at the 545 million litres (144 million gallons) that gush down the rock face every minute during heavy rains. A rainbow hangs semi-permanently above the falls between April and June, enhancing the breathtaking view over the hinterland.

PICTURE CAPTIONS
- Ⓐ Lusaka, Zambia
- Ⓑ Festival, Barotseland, Zambia
- Ⓒ White rhino, Luangwa Valley, Zambia
- Ⓔ Victoria Falls, Zambia
- Ⓕ Cave paintings, Crocodile Rock, Harare, Zimbabwe
- Ⓖ Lake Kariba, Zimbabwe
- Ⓗ Great Zimbabwe, Zimbabwe
- Ⓘ Matobo Hills, Zimbabwe
- Ⓙ Sandbank, Zambezi River, Zambia
- Ⓚ Kudu, Hwange National Park, Zimbabwe

H

I

Zimbabwe

Ⓕ Harare

Pg. 193. Founded just over 100 years ago, Zimbabwe's capital was once hailed as the most African of the continent's principal cities. Harare – known as Salisbury until independence in 1980 – was pronounced the official capital of Southern Rhodesia in 1923 and was declared a city in 1935. It has seen better days and is plagued intermittently with fuel shortages and near empty supermarket shelves. Despite the latter-day problems (including a growing urban crime rate), the capital remains a beautiful city that has retained at least some of its charm. Harare is an important centre of the country's arts and crafts industry, most notably the soapstone sculptures synonymous with Zimbabwe, the best of which may be found about 8km (5 miles) from town at Chapungu Kraal, a model Shona village that offers a glimpse of tribal life.

Harare is set against an inspiring backdrop of bushveld savanna punctuated with a series of rock formations – the most famous of which are the Epworth Balancing Rocks – and an impressive number of rock-art sites.

F

Ⓖ Lake Kariba

Pg. 306. Constructed between 1955 and 1958, and opened by Queen Elizabeth II in 1960, Lake Kariba remains one of the continent's most ambitious water projects, and is the third-largest artificial body of water in Africa. The massive walls span a perimeter of 579m (1,900ft) and stretch 282km (175 miles) across the landscape to cover a total of 5,000km² (1,930 sq. miles). The walls are 24m (79ft) thick at the base and 128m (420ft) high. A fascinating diversion is to take a walk along the top of the dam wall to feel the pounding of the massive turbines.

The shores of the great lake are a wildlife haven and are surrounded by some of Zimbabwe's finest parks, reserves and wilderness areas, all of which are rich in game and popular drawcards.

Ⓗ Great Zimbabwe

Pg. 269. Perhaps the country's most significant legacy, the majestic stone-walled ruins of Great Zimbabwe comprise the most impressive medieval site in Africa south of the Sahara. This architectural and archaeological gem, about 30km (19 miles) from Masvingo, was established more than 1,000 years ago by the Karonga, ancestors of the local Shona, and comprises a fascinating series of stone walls. The walled city harboured no fewer than 10,000 citizens – a fatal mistake that led to overpopulation and the abandonment of the citadel in the 1450s. Excavation of the site has provided evidence that medieval Africa was indeed highly sophisticated. Guided tours take visitors through the Hill Complex – once known as the Acropolis – thought to have been the monarch's residence. The walls of the Great Enclosure are 5m (16ft) thick and 11m (36ft) high and were built with nearly a million stone 'bricks' over 100 years in the 14th and 15th centuries.

G

K

E

Ⓘ Matobo Hills

Pg. 131. Despite the stark beauty of their horizonless vistas, the granite hills of Matobo are best known in the Western world as the final resting place of Cecil John Rhodes, the mining pioneer and statesman who played a significant role in the troubled history of southern Africa. His grave tablet stands in the middle of a wide circle created from the boulders that lie strewn across the hillsides. The spot at Malindidzimu is known as the View of the World and provides one of the most impressive panoramas in southwestern Zimbabwe.

Backed by austere, cold-faced mountains weathered by rain and wind and sand, the Matobo National Park – 50km (31 miles) south of Bulawayo – is a breathtaking wilderness, home to a relatively small assortment of wild and rare animals.

The giant granite outcrops and precariously balanced rock formations characterize the landscape, and boast arguably the world's most astounding collection of indigenous rock art.

The Mozambique Coast

MOZAMBIQUE

Capital: Maputo
Area: 799,380km²/ 308,642mi²
Population: 19.6 million
Main ethnic groups:
- Makua-Lomwe (47%)
- Tsonga (23%)
- Malawi (12%)

Main language:
- Portuguese

Main religions:
- Traditional beliefs (60%)
- Christian (30%)
- Muslim (10%)

Currency: Metical (100 centavos)

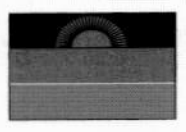

MALAWI

Capital: Lilongwe
Area: 118,480km²/ 45,745mi²
Population: 10.9 million
Main ethnic groups:
- Maravi (55%)
- Lomwe (17%)
- Yao (13%)
- Ngoni (7%)

Main languages:
- English
- Chewa

Main religions:
- Protestant (34%)
- Catholic (32%)
- Traditional beliefs (18%)

Currency: Malawian kwacha (100 tambala)

Mozambique and Malawi are desperately poor nations, with up to 80 per cent of their rural people engaged in farming, and the majority of citizens living on the shores of Lake Malawi depending on its waters for subsistence and livelihood. This vital body of water is called Lago Niassa in Mozambique and Lake Nyasa in Tanzania. Mozambique and Malawi are both covered by large stretches of endless savanna and have proven remarkable in their resilience. Malawi, the landlocked 'Warm Heart of Africa', and Mozambique — some of the continent's finest coastline makes it one of Africa's premier beach destinations — are a traveller's dream: wild animals crossing an unspoiled wilderness easily accessible to the visitor, and all very, very cheap. The diverse cultural heritage of both countries is an eclectic mix of fascinating customs and traditions still practised with enthusiasm by the vast majority of the population, making for a memorable exploration of the eastern reaches of southern Africa.

B

D

E

Mozambique

Ⓐ Maputo

Pg. 196. No more than a small, haphazard collection of temporary shelters in the 16th century, Maputo (known in fairly recent times as Lourenço Marques) is a lively port city criss-crossed with palm-fringed avenues lined with jacaranda and flame trees. Following a period of civil strife and political uncertainty that ended only in 1992, many of Maputo's grand palaces and synagogues, markets and museums, and even humble Creole-style homes – particularly in the larger urban centres — bear the physical scars of civil war to this day. However, Maputo is emerging from the ashes to slowly regain some of the glory of its heyday. Home to a thriving population of bohemian artists and a steady trickle of travellers, Maputo's vigorous nightlife centres around the late-night bars of Rua do Bagamoio, the revelry spilling over into the evening markets and brightly lit seafront. The city – rather dilapidated in parts – is dotted with historic Portuguese forts and highlighted by its must-see Museum of the Revolution.

Ⓑ Inhaca Island

Pg. 308. The idyll that is Inhaca is a series of beautiful beaches lined with brightly coloured offshore reefs and shores dotted with stands of mango trees. About 24km (15 miles) from the mainland and easily accessible via the ferries departing from the capital, Inhaca Island is the largest in the Gulf of Maputo and its pretty village presents a fascinating look at island life. Dominated by the upgraded Inhaca Hotel, the narrow streets have a good selection of restaurants and cafés interspersed with the odd — laid-back — attraction. Situated in extraordinarily rich waters, the island's coastal attractions have proven its most popular drawcards. Apart from the marine research centre, which offers a different perspective to the conventional island idyll, Inhaca's shores are peppered with striking beaches and a fascinating reef life that offers some of the finest diving, snorkelling and underwater explorations on Africa's east coast.

Ⓒ Zambezi Delta

Pg. 122. The 3,000km (1,860-mile) Zambezi River winds for 820km (510 miles) of its route across Mozambique before reaching the ocean. Its broad valley slices the country in two, beginning at Feira and ending, after having accumulated run-off waters from five other countries, in the wetlands of the delta. By the time the waters reach Mozambique they have been tamed by Zimbabwe's Lake Kariba and are again dammed by the 160m (525ft) walls of the 270km-long (168-mile) Cahora Bassa, Mozambique's most ambitious dam. Having coursed through the hinterland, waters guarded by crocodiles and hippos, the Zambezi begins to disperse about 600km (373 miles) downstream on the buffalo plains of Marromeu, where it spreads into a network of streams, channels and tributaries covering 4,000km² (1,544 sq. miles). Today, the delta spans only 100km (62 miles), but is nevertheless breathtaking – especially from the air – and is home to big game such as elephant, buffalo, rhino and roan antelope.

Ⓓ Ibo

Pg. 103. Heavily fortified during its Portuguese occupation, Ibo has a history as the region's most important supplier of slaves to the sugar plantations of Île de France and, along with Ilha de Mozambique, was hailed as the colonists' most vital trading grounds off the African coast. Although the island has seen better days,

A

PICTURE CAPTIONS
- Ⓐ Eiffel House, Maputo, Mozambique
- Ⓑ Pomene Beach, Inhaca Island, Mozambique
- Ⓓ Fort, Ibo, Mozambique
- Ⓔ Lighthouse, Barra Peninsula, Mozambique
- Ⓕ Elephants, Lilongwe, Malawi
- Ⓖ Local paddling a mokoro (dugout boat), Lake Malawi, Malawi
- Ⓗ Shire River, Malawi
- Ⓙ São Sebastião, Ilha de Mozambique, Mozambique
- Ⓚ Cahora Bassa dam, Mozambique
- Ⓛ Church, Blantyre, Malawi

TM 195
NP 234
ADV 308

Although both Malawi and Mozambique are covered largely by extensive savanna plains, these are fringed by forested highlands and, in the case of Mozambique, a lush coast of lagoons and coral reefs that continue to attract travellers and adventurers to some of southern Africa's wildest and most undeveloped landscape.

Malawi

F Lilongwe

Pg. 271. Although it is Malawi's vast natural heritage that is its enduring drawcard, the appeal of its large centres – in particular its capital at Lilongwe – should not be underestimated. Blantyre stretches for about 20km (12 miles) into Limbe, and is the social and commercial heart of Malawi. Lilongwe, on the other hand, is gentle, laid-back and utterly predictable in character. Although only of limited interest to the casual visitor, the sprawling city — home to about a half million Malawians — is a refreshing mix of old and new, with little clutter, noise and commotion. The older sectors of Lilongwe have retained much of their original charm, while the modern parts are a surprisingly sedate collection of malls, tourist traps and official buildings merging well with the islands of green that form the residential districts. A notable example is Capital City, initiated by President Banda with the financial assistance of the South African government during the height of the latter's apartheid regime. Not only is the climate of the city moderately warm, but Lilongwe is very accessible, very cheap and, in the heart of southern Africa, a convenient base from which to explore the subcontinent.

G Lake Malawi

Pg. 271. Known as Lake Nyasa or Lago Niassa, depending on which bank you are standing, the 23,000km² (8,900 sq. mile) Lake Malawi is the third-largest inland body of water on the continent and covers nearly half the country's territory. The 585km (364 miles) of its length along the southern Rift Valley comprises a diversity of habitats for an array of wildlife. As a result, the waters of the lake — encircled by mountain slopes — have formed the mainstay of the nation's economy and the nucleus of Malawi's tourism industry. Blessed with tranquil beaches, the most important human settlement along the shore is the fishing community at Chember, who depend on Lake Malawi for their livelihood. Numerous dugout vessels ply the lake surface, netting fish that form the staple diet of Malawi. The lake has one of the world's richest populations of freshwater fish and many of the species found here are endemic. Casual angling is forbidden in areas, including Cape Maclear National Park and the surrounding islands, although water-based leisure activities are encouraged.

H Shire River

Pg. 271. The 596km (370-mile) Shire, flowing from Lake Malawi through Malawi and Mozambique to the Zambezi, is the country's longest river. It winds through Malawi's Liwonde National Park, crossing some of the country's most abundant wildlife territories, and through wild open spaces. The river is the hunting and grazing waters of crocodile and hippo, while the surrounding wilderness has a small but healthy population of elephant and even two black rhinos, introduced into the area in recent years. The shallows, wooded shores and expansive sky are home to waders, waterfowl and migrant birds during the summer months. Although much of the Shire offers boat rides for visitors, the southern valley remains largely undiscovered, top attractions being the wild expanses of Majete Wildlife Reserve and Lengwe National Park.

I Likoma Island

Pg. 271. Although Likoma lies just off Mozambique, the island remains the property of Malawi, its coastline — dotted with lone baobabs alongside crystal waters — taking on the flavour of the motherland. The sandy 17km² (6.5 sq. mile) island, with its mango trees and rugged mountain peaks, is flat and unprepossessing, but its languid beaches are lapped by clear waters. Lying in splendid isolation off the mountain-backed beach of Mozambique's mainland, Likoma can be difficult to reach and the only proper — albeit rather unreliable — way to reach the island is via the MV *Ilala II*, the dilapidated but enchanting old lake steamer that once a week ferries passengers between Likoma and Mozambique. The island itself is tranquil and laid back and, apart from the weekly performance of the *malipenga* dancers pandering almost exclusively to a tourist audience, there are few notable landmarks. The most significant is the cavernous St Peter's Cathedral, built along the lines of Winchester Cathedral by Anglican missionaries in the early 1900s. St Peter's remains the focal point of the island today, with many of the locals working virtually all year every year on maintaining the colossal remnant of Likoma's colonial past.

F

L

H

J

its wide streets are lined with quaint Mediterranean-style buildings. Many of these stately structures were erected in the 1800s and, although the whitewashed walls of the once grand but long abandoned Portuguese villas and palaces are fading, it is the very isolation that is the island's charm. The centuries-old churches and ancient bulwarks that fringe the streets and line the waterfront are but half the attraction — the other is the surrounding ocean, alive with turtles and dolphins that can easily be spotted from the dhows that ferry visitors around Ibo's romantic coastline.

E Barra Peninsula

Pg. 141. Barra is the site of Inhambane (the capital of the province) and is one of Mozambique's most popular holiday meccas — the azure waters, coves, bays and sands provide a spectacular backdrop to the beach life. The landscape of Barra and the adjoining Cape Inhambane is dotted with coconut plantations and mangrove swamps, and the wave-washed shores are a vivid invitation to the marine wonderland. The waters are warm but unpredictable, and powerful rip currents and volatile waves make it an exhilarating but precarious water-sport base.

K

G

The Indian Ocean Islands

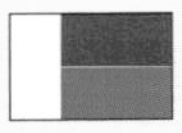

MADAGASCAR

Capital: Antananarivo
Area: 587,041km²/ 226,658mi²
Population: 16.9 million
Main ethnic groups:
- Merina (26%)
- Betsimisaraka (15%)

Main languages:
- Malagasy
- French

Main religions:
- Catholic (21%)
- Protestant (20%)

Currency: Malagasy franc (0.2 ariary)

COMOROS

Capital: Moroni
Area: 1,862km²/ 719mi²
Population: 600,000
Main ethnic groups:
- Comorian (96%)
- Makua (2%)

Main languages:
- Arabic
- French

Main religions:
- Muslim (86%)
- Catholic (14%)

Currency: Comoran franc (100 centimes)

MAURITIUS

Capital: Port Louis
Area: 2,040 km²/ 788mi²
Population: 1.2 million
Main ethnic groups:
- Creole (55%)
- South Asian (40%)

Main languages:
- English
- French Creole
- Hindi

Main religions:
- Hindu (52%)
- Catholic (26%)
- Muslim (17%)

Currency: Mauritian rupee (100 cents)

RÉUNION (France)

Capital: St-Denis
Area: 2,510km²/ 970mi²
Population: 700,000
Main ethnic groups:
- Creole (90%)
- Indo-Chinese (7%)

Main languages:
- French Creole (92%)
- French (7%)

Main religions:
- Catholic (90%)
- Hindu (6%)

Currency: French franc (100 centimes); Euro

SEYCHELLES

Capital: Victoria
Area: 453km²/ 175mi²
Population: 100,000
Main ethnic groups:
- Seychellois (95%)
- South Asian (3%)

Main languages:
- Creole
- French
- English

Main religion:
- Catholic (90%)

Currency: Seychelles rupee (100 cents)

Virtually all the tropical islands that dot the Indian Ocean off the east coast of the continent have a long history of colonization that has had a deep and lasting influence on their local communities. These comprise a vast mix of people descended from African, Arab, European and Asian settlers who have made their home here over the centuries. The larger nations like Madagascar, Mauritius and Seychelles are multiparty republics, while Réunion remains a French Overseas Department, and their cultural legacies are extremely varied and contribute enormously to the social fabric of the island populations. The islands of the Seychelles (colonized first by the French and then the British) make up a relatively wealthy nation where poverty is rare and the standard of living one of the highest in the Third World. Nonetheless, some 80 per cent of the people of politically volatile Comoros depend exclusively on subsistence farming, making it one of Africa's poorest countries.

The hot and humid conditions and varying topography of the Mascarenes (Mauritius, Rodrigues and Réunion) range from mountainous highlands to low-lying coral atolls. The other small islands of the Indian Ocean are ideally suited to the production of exotic crops such as vanilla, coffee, sugar and spices, the export of which forms the basis of local economies and the centre of the largely farming communities.

'You gather the idea that Mauritius was made first and then heaven, and that heaven was copied after Mauritius.'
MARK TWAIN

A

B

Madagascar

Ⓐ Antananarivo
Pg. 198. 'Tana' is charmingly dishevelled in appearance, its cobbled thoroughfares traversed by rickety carts – still drawn by oxen – and jam-packed with French colonial-style buildings housing anything from souvenir shops to family-owned produce stores. Quaint and laid-back, Tana is the capital of Madagascar and boasts the Ivato international airport, its population of some 2 million citizens relying on income derived from a small but thriving tourism industry. Considering the extraordinary wildlife for which the island is most renowned, many visitors are conservationists and wildlife enthusiasts, and it is the uniqueness of the indigenous flora and fauna that remains the principal attraction. This is despite the bustling urban development and the fact that Tana is relatively cheap as a holiday destination, and its zoological gardens provide fascinating insights into the wildlife. The centre is home to the prolific Madagascar nightjar as well as the scavenging hedgehog tenrec.

Ⓑ Nosy Be Archipelago
Pg. 274. The heart of Madagascar's hospitality industry, the island of Nosy Be is at the centre of the archipelago off the northwest shore that takes its name. Dotted with tourist hotels and amenities, the hilly 280km² (110 sq. mile) island is easily accessible from the capital and, as such, has taken on many of its more popular elements: boat excursions to neighbouring islands, open-air markets and a vibrant nightlife.

For a glimpse of the natural heritage of Madagascar, take a pleasant walk through the luxuriant vegetation that covers much of Nosy Be or visit the fascinating rainforest stand on the Lokobe Peninsula. Lokobe is home to the cryptically shaped and coloured endemic thorn spider and *Isoxya* species, the blue-coloured Parson's chameleon, as well as subspecies of the black lemur.

C

Ⓒ Fort Dauphin
Pg. 48. Relatively isolated by unforgiving terrain and an underdeveloped road network and infrastructure, Tôlañaro (Fort Dauphin) was the landing site of the first European travellers in the 16th century and is the centre of Madagascar's lobster industry. The scrubland and relatively high rainfall predominant in much of the area make it inhospitable to the casual tourist, although the reef-protected beaches allow for a great adventure for naturalists, most notably at Libanona, the rugged slopes of Pic St Louis and the protected splendour of the nearby Berenty reserve. Those on the lookout for nocturnal species such as the greater dwarf lemur will be richly rewarded.

L

Ⓓ Isalo Mountains
Pg. 48. Pinnacle of the impressive national park that takes their name, the sandstone mountains of Isalo offer a different view to the conventional image of lush Madagascar. Small patches of grassland break the rather bleak landscape, and the occasional green belts are interspersed with strange rock configurations. Punctuated with a number of ancient burial sites held sacred by locals, the recently upgraded network of roads affords access to splendid views of the highlying landscape. Visitors' amenities are in a sad state and the region is largely the domain of hikers, campers and wildlife enthusiasts. They are able to take full advantage of the country's top trails and camp sites – petty crime notwithstanding – as well as the wildlife, especially the lemurs and the endemic Benson's rock thrush.

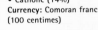

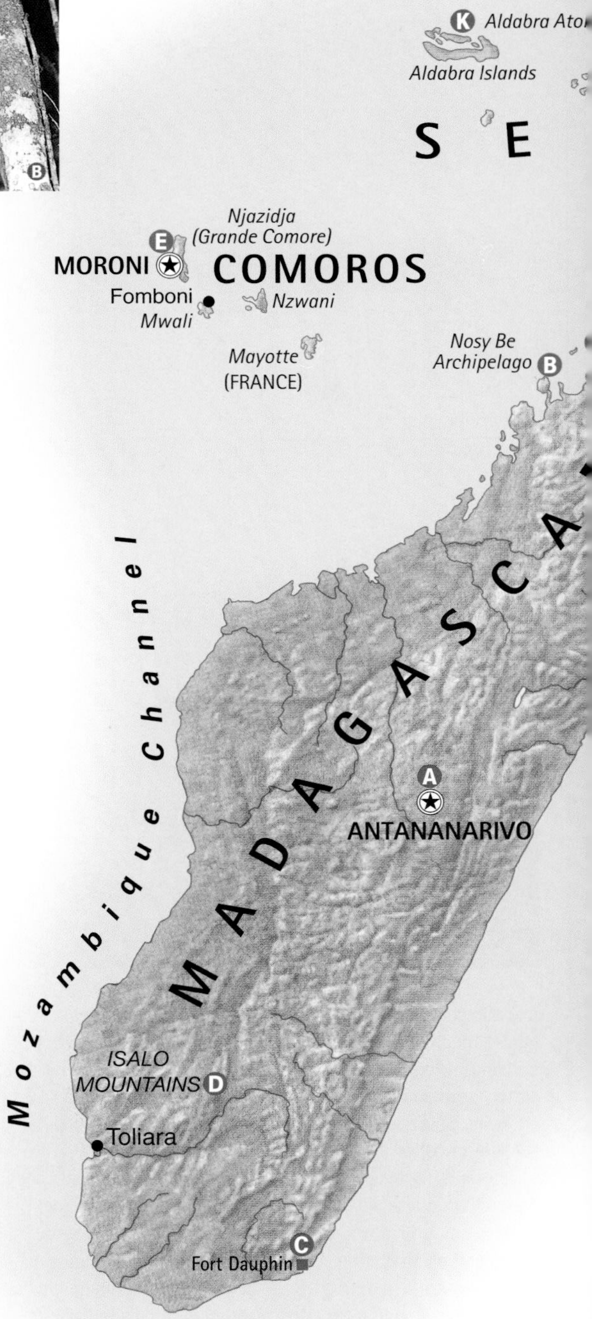

PICTURE CAPTIONS
Ⓐ Antananarivo, Madagascar
Ⓑ Lemur, Nosy Be Archipelago, Madagascar
Ⓒ Shipwreck, Fort Dauphin, Madagascar
Ⓔ Thatch hut, Moroni, Comoros
Ⓕ Port Louis, Mauritius
Ⓗ Le Morne Peninsula, Mauritius
Ⓘ Valley, St-Denis, Réunion
Ⓙ Mahé, Seychelles
Ⓚ Aldabra Atoll, Seychelles
Ⓛ Northwest coastal swamps, Madagascar

TM 198
NP 236
ADV 310

Comoros

E Moroni

Pg. 48. Moroni, the capital of Comoros, is situated on the island of Grande Comore, the most prominent of the three main volcanic islands surrounded by a number of picturesque coral atolls best known for their fine diving opportunities. Moroni and the islands are all scenically beautiful – heavily wooded and cultivated with aromatic crops such as cloves and vanilla that perfume Comoros. Although tourism is a burgeoning industry and a vital earner of foreign exchange, most of the 25,000 impoverished citizens of Moroni are involved in some way with the farming of cash crops. The capital is rustic in appearance and there is little urban lifestyle, yet it is lively and colourful – a true 'island paradise'. The magnificent scenery and the unspoiled island wilderness are Moroni's primary attractions.

E

H

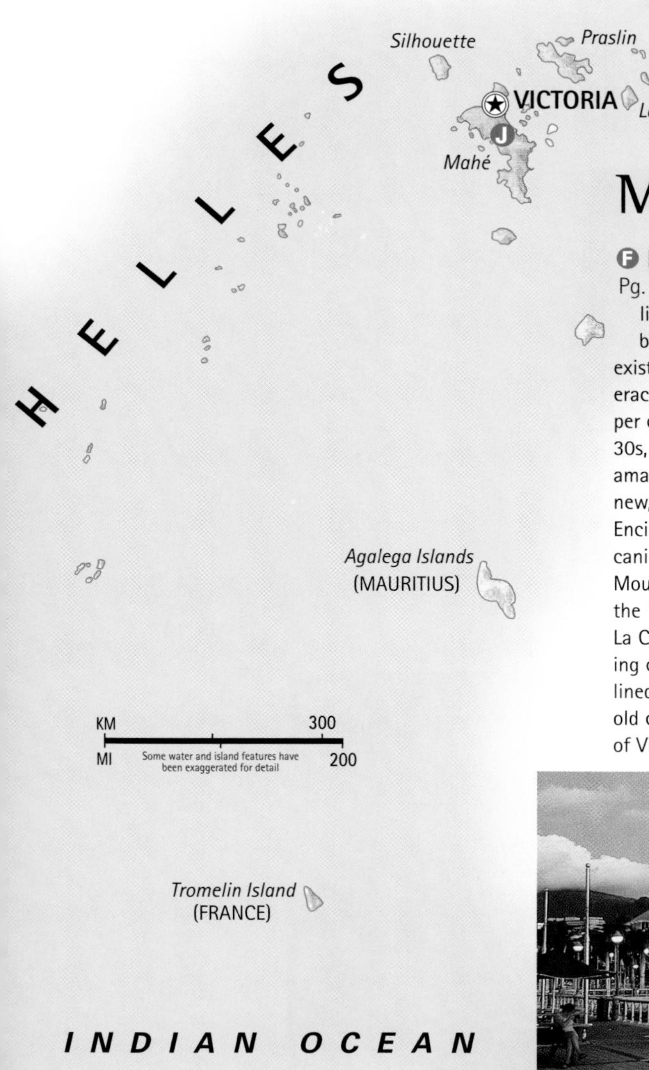

Mauritius

F Port Louis

Pg. 199. As the heart of idyllic Mauritius, a democracy boasting a virtually non-existent crime rate and a literacy rate of more than 90 per cent among the under-30s, Port Louis is a quaint amalgamation of old and new, wild and sedate. Encircled by the craggy volcanic peaks of the Moka Mountains and overlooked by the 19th-century ramparts of La Citadelle, the few remaining clearings and gardens are lined with banyan trees and old colonial buildings, legacy of Victoria's Empire. Port Louis remains every inch the capital, home to 20 per cent of the island's population and bustling with pedestrian traffic. The city has retained a distinct village charm, yet the increasingly modern skyline is dotted with ever popular fast-food and souvenir shops. Its impressive Caudan Waterfront is a thoroughly contemporary tourist development.

G Tamarind Falls

Pg. 46. The hot and dry Sunset Coast is pummelled on occasion by tropical storms and lashed by waves that lure surfers of all abilities. Inland lie the decidedly more tranquil environs of Mare aux Vacoas, a mountain lake encircled by forests of pine and palm, green woods and tea plantations with breathtaking views of the Black River Gorges.

The sometimes demanding forest trails are the domain of deer and monkey, and many visitors hike to the spectacular 295m (968ft) Tamarind Falls, the island's biggest and most impressive waterfall. The area is restricted primarily because of the presence of all-important hydroelectric power stations. Hikers and trailists will need to obtain permission from the Forestry Department or the Electricity Board.

H Le Morne Peninsula

Pg. 46. In the early days of settlement, Le Morne was relatively isolated, inaccessible and unpopulated and a haven for runaway slaves. The scenic peninsula is widely considered the last remaining outpost of African-Creole culture. The rocky landscape, pinpointed by the 556m (1,824ft) Le Morne Brabant, offers spectacular views of the 14km (9-mile) coast and is a popular tourist drawcard. Access to the mountain slopes is restricted and permission must be obtained. Fashionable hotels boast golf courses, horse-riding, big-game fishing, diving, water-sports and evening entertainment.

F

Seychelles

J Mahé

Pg. 46. The largest of the 40 islands and 75 low-lying atolls that make up the Seychelles, Mahé is home to 90 per cent of the population, the seat of the nation's capital, Victoria, and the nucleus of the all-important tourism industry. Visitors are drawn to Mahé by the picturesque environs, most notably exceptional beaches such as Beau Vallon, and the unique plant and animal life, and it is Victoria that acts as a base for most excursions into the island wilderness of sea and sand. Blessed with an old-world charm, the capital has rapidly developed a sound infrastructure geared toward the hospitality industry.

K Aldabra Atoll

Pg. 46. Aldabra is the most removed atoll, situated 1,200km (750 miles) from the frenetic activity of Mahé and the capital. This small collection of 14 islets is best accessed via a three-hour boat trip from the nearest airstrip on Assumption. The large coral lagoon and the immediate environs of mangrove are a sanctuary for flora and fauna, including pemphis scrub and giant land tortoises. The crystal waters and well-preserved corals around the 100km (62-mile) coast of Aldabra's islands are a much admired haven for water adventurers, who consider the atoll to be the most pristine in all Seychelles.

Réunion (France)

I

I St-Denis

Pg. 46. Located on the scenic north coast of the island, Réunion's capital is most admired for its mountain and volatile volcano, yet boasts picturesque beaches and is a lively centre of social activity. The highest mountain in the Indian Ocean is Piton des Neiges – 3,069m (10,068ft) – separating St-Denis from the urban hub of St-Pierre on the southern coast. St-Denis is a trendy resort town bordering foothills of the rugged hinterland and skirted by cultivated lands of grapevines, lentil crops and geraniums. Geranium oil is a vital element of Réunion's economy. The island's varied climate lends itself to an equally diverse landscape, from tropical lushness to more temperate vegetation. Most travellers visit the three cirques, the natural amphitheatres that form the island's heart.

J

K

The Skeleton Coast

NAMIBIA

Capital: Windhoek
Area: 824,290 km²/ 318,260mi²
Population: 1.8 million
Main ethnic groups:
- Ovambo (50%)
- Kavango (9%)
- Herero (7%)
- Damara (7%)
- White (6%)

Main languages:
- English
- Afrikaans
- Ovambo
- Kavango
- German

Main religion:
- Christian and Lutheran (90%)

Currency: Namibian dollar (100 cents)

BOTSWANA

Capital: Gaborone
Area: 600,372 km²/ 231,805mi²
Population: 1.6 million
Main ethnic groups:
- Tswana (75%)
- Shona (12%)
- San (3%)
- White (1%)

Main languages:
- English
- Tswana
- Shona
- San
- Ndebele

Main religions:
- Traditional beliefs (50%)
- Christian (mostly Anglican) (50%)

Currency: Pula (100 thebe)

The multiparty republics of neighbouring Botswana and Namibia cover the arid western and central interior of the southern subcontinent (including the Kalahari) and offer two rather different impressions of Africa. Botswana is entirely landlocked and punctuated with occasional pockets of bushveld, while Namibia is flanked by coastal desert plains. However, there are a number of important similarities that contribute to making this expansive region one of the wealthiest and most spectacular on the continent. Both countries have a long history of European settlement and domination, and the remnants of the colonial era continue to influence their latter-day sociopolitical landscape. The first to gain independence was Botswana, which until 1966 was known as the British protectorate of Bechuanaland. Namibia (formerly South West Africa) remained under the control of neighbouring South Africa until it gained independence in 1990, following protracted guerilla activity.

Although the portion of the southern African subcontinent covered by Namibia and Botswana is generally rather dry (and, in places, inhospitable) terrain, the land is rich in diamonds and other minerals (uranium, copper, nickel and coal). The national economies of both countries rely considerably on these valuable exports.

'Here, in this sacred house of silence, I can lose myself – the sky is as endless as it is containing, and here the water teases land.'
IAN McCALLUM, 1999

Namibia

Ⓐ Namib Desert

Pg. 124. Namibia's most conspicuous drawcard is the Namib, an endless stretch of red sand interrupted with sparse vegetation. The desert comprises the Skeleton Coast and the Namib-Naukluft parks, covering 15 per cent of the country's landmass, including about 6.5 million hectares (16 million acres) of some of the southern hemisphere's driest and most inhospitable terrain. These abandoned stretches of sand and gravel, hemmed in by relentless dune, are home to a range of unique flora and fauna, with nearly 200 vertebrates found nowhere else. Despite its desolation, it is a living desert, inhabited by gemsbok (oryx), bird flocks, succulent plants, insects and over 20 endemic reptiles.

Ⓑ Fish River Canyon

Pg. 312. The Fish River Canyon comprises wind-carved depressions, inclines and rock formations moulded from the inland plateau. The Canyon is dramatic in its simplicity, with valleys and gullies slicing through its geological foundations laid 2,000 million years ago. The Canyon is some 160km (99.7 miles) long and, in parts, nearly 600m (1,968ft) deep, putting it second in size only to the Grand Canyon in North America.

Ⓒ Skeleton Coast

Pg. 312. The most extraordinary of Namibia's many spectacles is the bone-white sands that comprise the great Skeleton Coast, an eerie expanse of beach that extends from the country's northern border to the Namib-Naukluft Park in the south. Hemmed in by the cold Atlantic in the west and the dry interior to the east, the 1.6 million hectares (4 million acres) of the Skeleton Coast Park is an untamed wilderness divided into two main regions. The baking sand of the Namib covers the northern stretch, while the south is made up of dry gravel plains scattered with boulders and laced, in part, with seasonal rivers. Although there are few mammal species, it is renowned for its abundant bird life. The volatility of the elements and the relentless battering of wave and wind lend to this landscape an almost surreal beauty. The coast can be shrouded in mist for days, which helped to earn it the reputation as the world's largest shipping graveyard — over 100 vessels have run aground here.

Ⓓ Walvis Bay

Pg. 201. Positioned between the searing sands of the Namib in the south and the windswept shore of the Skeleton Coast in the north, Walvis Bay is the unofficial capital of Namibia's coastal stretch. Much of the social and economic activity of this thriving little city centres on its all-important natural harbour, the deepest in south-western Africa. For centuries, small indigenous settlements remained undisturbed in this forgotten corner until Dutch, German and British colonial powers stumbled across the treasure that is its natural harbour. The town was only reincorporated into official national boundaries four years after independence, remaining an essential 'outpost' of South Africa until 1994. Walvis Bay acts as a vital instrument in the national economy, servicing the freight and fishing industries, and is an ideal base for adventure activities offered by its immediate environment, including four-wheel-drive and desert exploration, and bird-watching.

Ⓔ Kaokoland

Pg. 312. Kaokoland refers to the vast rocky, mountainous terrain bordered in the north by the Cunene River and by the Hoanib in the south, and immediately inland of the northern Skeleton Coast. It is a wild and unpredictable wilderness populated largely by the Himba and Herero-speaking people, who gave the area its name. Kaokoland's river waters are the home of crocodiles, and small herds of Kaokoland elephant continue to roam this desolate landscape. The region fell victim to devastating drought in the 1970s and much of its wildlife was decimated, but the land is slowly recovering and Kaokoland remains a popular tourist drawcard, especially to view the lumbering great elephants.

TM 200
NP 236
ADV 312

Botswana

Ⓖ Okavango Delta

Pg. 277. The Okavango Delta is the world's largest, spreading over 15,000km² (5,790 sq. miles). This wetland wilderness creates a vast green oasis in the middle of otherwise inhospitable terrain. It is here that the waters of the country's only perennial river, the Okavango, spread across its flood plain, soaking deep into the surrounding lands. The river should fulfil all Botswana's water requirements, but not only is it shared with Namibia, much of the water is lost to evaporation. Drawing on the water supply for irrigation and domestic consumption also encroaches on the river and its delta. Conservationists are fighting to have the delta declared a World Heritage Site to secure its protection.

G

H

Ⓗ Makgadikgadi Pans

Pg. 277. The Makgadikgadi Pans form part of Botswana's 7,000km² (2,700 sq. mile) Makgadikgadi Pans Game Reserve and Nxai Pan National Park, and it is the world's largest natural salt pans, covering 12,000km² (4,633 sq. miles). The pans once formed part of a massive inland lake, but all that exists today on the remaining plains is an endless sea of cracked, empty, salt-encrusted pans, most notable among them the Sowa, Ntwetwe and Nxai pans of Makgadikgadi. Summer rains fill the depressions to create the lifeblood of the wildlife that flocks here during the rainless winter.

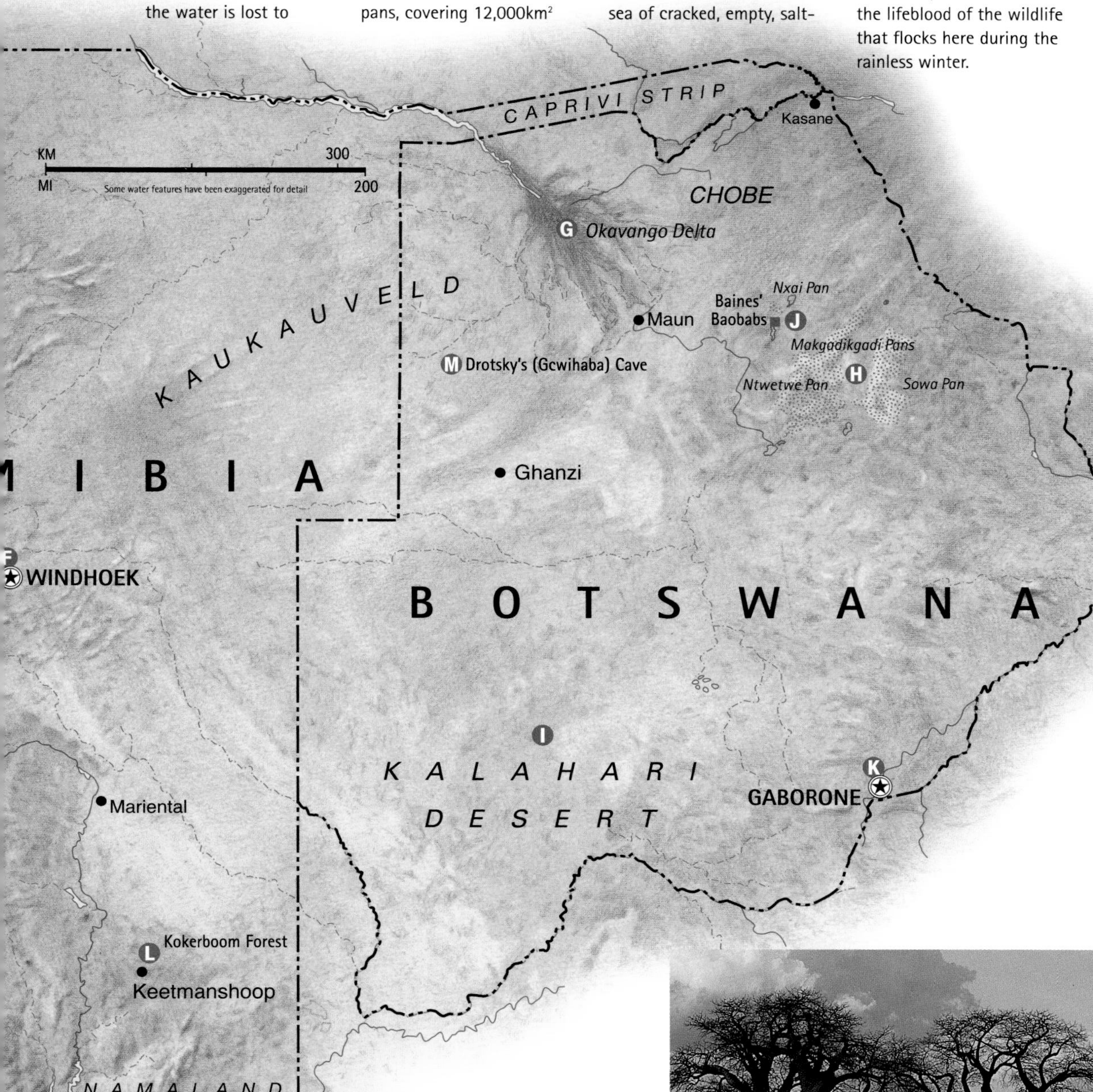

Ⓘ Kalahari Desert

Pg. 136. The Kalahari is the largest continuous stretch of sand in the world. Flat, dry and empty, it covers more than 80 per cent of Botswana, stretching from the Orange River towards the more equatorial regions. This wide-open expanse – whipped by clouds of dust, lashed by the summer rains and baked by the sun – was formed 200 million years ago when the supercontinent Gondwana began to break up to form the landmasses of the southern hemisphere. The foundation of sandstone, shale and coal is 300 million years old, while some rocks date back three billion years.

Ⓙ Baines' Baobabs

Pg. 277. The stands of baobabs that dot pockets of the otherwise empty interior symbolize the grandeur of this sparse country. From the outskirts of settlements to the featureless pans, the horizon is broken by the silhouette of a baobab, indigenous resident for thousands of years. The most prominent of these are the Seven Sisters. Referred to as Baines' Baobabs, this cluster of 'upside down' trees is named in honour of the artist and explorer, Thomas Baines, who captured them on canvas in 1862. Baines' Baobabs stand on the rim of Kudiakam Pan.

Ⓚ Gaborone

Pg. 202. The capital is a relatively small, compact city, and although there may be few conventional tourist sites, Gaborone has enjoyed phenomenal growth since it was appointed the capital of the new nation in the 1960s. Back then, the rather insignificant village had no more than a scattering of homes, but it boasted one important resource – water. As a result, it was declared a city within 20 months of becoming the capital and, largely because of its considerable mineral wealth, is one of the fastest-growing urban settlements on the African continent.

Its road infrastructure lends Gaborone a modern appearance, with impressive restaurants, hotels, casinos and other entertainment centres. The modern city has retained at least some of its distinct African flavour – its side streets are filled with craft markets and vending stalls, and few other urban centres of similar status can boast the same number of small reserves and conservation land on its doorstep.

J

Ⓕ Windhoek

Pg. 200. The Namibian capital – although small and underdeveloped compared to other world capitals – is the great tourist centre and economic hub of the nation, a vibrant, colourful and modern city catering well for the international traveller. The nightlife is lively, the facilities adequate and the infrastructure impressive for such a small nation. The colours, cultures and panoramic vistas are a photographer's dream, and in recent years there has been a healthy resurgence in the tourism market. Windhoek lies at the very heart of this burgeoning industry and has, as a result, become every inch the modern city, with its fair share of attractions and detractions. Nonetheless, the city remains the gateway to the adventures promised by the coast, desert and wild expanse beyond waiting to be explored.

I

M

PICTURE CAPTIONS
- Ⓑ Fish River Canyon, Namibia
- Ⓒ The Skeleton Coast, Namibia
- Ⓓ Greater Flamingoes, Walvis Bay, Namibia
- Ⓔ Epupa Falls, Kaokoland, Namibia
- Ⓖ Okavango Delta, Botswana
- Ⓗ Makgadikgadi Pans, Botswana
- Ⓘ Gemsbok, Kalahari Desert, Botswana
- Ⓙ Baines' Baobabs, Botswana
- Ⓛ Kokerboom Forest, Namibia
- Ⓜ Drotsky's Cave, Botswana

Southern Africa

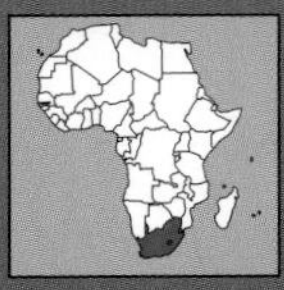

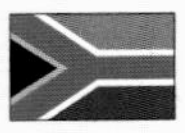

SOUTH AFRICA

Capitals: Pretoria (administrative), Cape Town (legislative) and Bloemfontein (judicial)
Area: 1,221,040 km²/ 471,446mi²
Population: 43.6 million
Main ethnic groups:
- Black (75%)
- White (14%)
- Coloured (mixed race) (9%)
- Asian (2%)

Main languages:
- 11 official languages, including nine indigenous black languages, English and Afrikaans

Main religions:
- Protestant (55%)
- Catholic (9%)
- Hindu (1%)
- Muslim (1%)
- Other (including traditional spiritual beliefs) (34%)

Currency: Rand (100 cents)

LESOTHO

Capital: Maseru
Area: 30,350 km²/ 11,718mi²
Population: 2.2 million
Main ethnic group:
- Basotho (99%)

Main languages:
- Sesotho
- English
- Zulu

Main religions:
- Christian (combined) (80%)
- Indigenous beliefs (20%)

Currency: Loti (100 lisente)

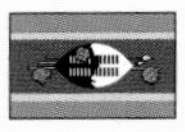

SWAZILAND

Capital: Mbabane
Area: 17,360 km²/ 6,703mi²
Population: 1.1 million
Main ethnic group:
- Swazi (95%)

Main languages:
- Siswati
- English
- Zulu

Main religions:
- Christian (combined) (60%)
- Other (including traditional spiritual beliefs) (40%)

Currency: Lilangeni (100 cents)

The southernmost sweep of the subcontinent comprises South Africa and the independent kingdoms of Lesotho and Swaziland that fall within its boundaries. For the most part this is a wilderness of wide-open spaces stretching from mountain to sea, desert to savanna. The undulating grasslands, wooded valleys, open bushveld and towering cityscapes combine to create a rich tapestry that forms a breathtaking backdrop to the natural wonder of southern Africa and the diverse cultural heritage of its many peoples – from the Zulu to the San – as they embrace full democracy. For intrepid travellers and adventurers, the prime attraction is the region's unrivalled wildlife heritage, at its most impressive in the big-game regions of Mpumalanga, KwaZulu-Natal and the Eastern Cape. The landscape is arid and desolate in parts, while other areas are verdant and bountiful. Such contrasting faces offer a unique look at a region that varies from First World sophistication to pastoralist Africa.

The spectacle of southern Africa's varied wildlife, the diversity of its extraordinary landscape and the rich cultural heritage of its indigenous peoples has ensured that the region has enjoyed an unprecedented resurgence in its tourism and hospitality industries. South Africa in particular has now emerged as one of the leading players in Africa's social, political and economic arena.

PICTURE CAPTIONS
- Ⓐ Kirstenbosch National Botanical Garden, Cape Peninsula National Park, South Africa
- Ⓑ Wilderness, Garden Route, South Africa
- Ⓒ Drakensberg Escarpment, South Africa
- Ⓓ Robben Island, South Africa
- Ⓔ Bourke's Luck Potholes, Blyde River Canyon, South Africa
- Ⓙ Groot Constantia, Cape Town, South Africa
- Ⓚ Leopard, Kruger National Park, South Africa
- Ⓛ Ndebele artwork, Lesotho
- Ⓜ Mlilwane Nature Reserve, Swaziland

J

B

D

'... the most stately thing, and the fairest cape we saw in the whole circumference of the earth.'
SIR FRANCIS DRAKE, 1580

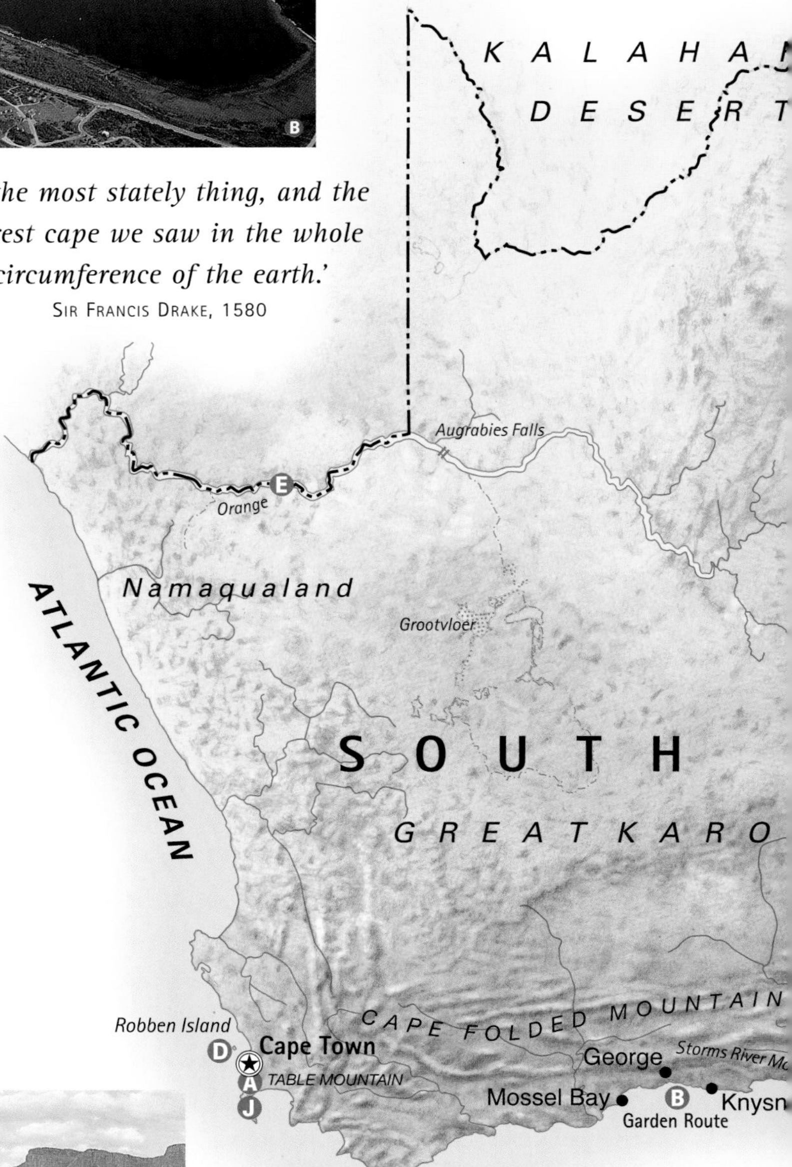

South Africa

Ⓐ Table Mountain
Pg. 281. The distinctive flat-topped summit of Table Mountain is the most recognizable landmark in Cape Town (the Mother City) and lies in the heart of the Cape Floral Kingdom, the smallest but richest of the world's six broad floral regions. Fynbos (hardy, fine-leaved shrubs and plants that have taken root in these nutrient-poor soils) accounts for about 80 per cent of the 8,500-plus plant species on the mountain slopes. The world-famous Kirstenbosch National Botanical Garden lies on the slopes of Table Mountain.

Many wild animals once roamed these rocky slopes, including Africa's great cats and a number of antelope species. It is currently the domain of the dassie, or rock hyrax, easily viewed from the ever popular revolving cable car that carries sightseers up the mountain. The highest point on Table Mountain is MacClear's Beacon, 1,086m (3,564ft) above sea level, and at the foot lies Table Bay.

Ⓑ Garden Route
Pg. 315. The Garden Route is an extraordinarily beautiful stretch of countryside that winds along the southwestern contour of the subcontinent for some 200km (124 miles) between the town of Mossel Bay and the mouth of the Storms River. The route is dotted with charming little towns and villages, including some of the country's most notable holiday resorts, such as Knysna and Plettenberg Bay. The Garden Route boasts an astounding array of indigenous flora and fauna and attracts adventurers and holiday-makers from far afield. Flanked in the east by the warm Indian Ocean and in the west by the sometimes parched hinterland, the tranquil coves and sandy dunes are a traveller's paradise. The coastline is battered in parts by wind and pummelled by the ocean, yet much of it is traversed via well-developed roads, with only an occasional dirt road leading to out-of-the-way beachside havens.

A

C

Ⓒ Drakensberg Escarpment
Pg. 280. The western boundary of KwaZulu-Natal is demarcated by a series of crests that comprise the spectacular Drakensberg range. This in turn forms the Great Escarpment that separates the province from the mountain kingdom of Lesotho beyond. The scenic splendour of these impressive mountain slopes and lush valleys is also the picturesque setting for some of the country's finest national parks and game reserves, which are characterized by towering peaks and rolling hills. Among the most

TM 203
NP 240
ADV 314

Honest differences are often a healthy sign of progress.
MAHATMA GANDHI

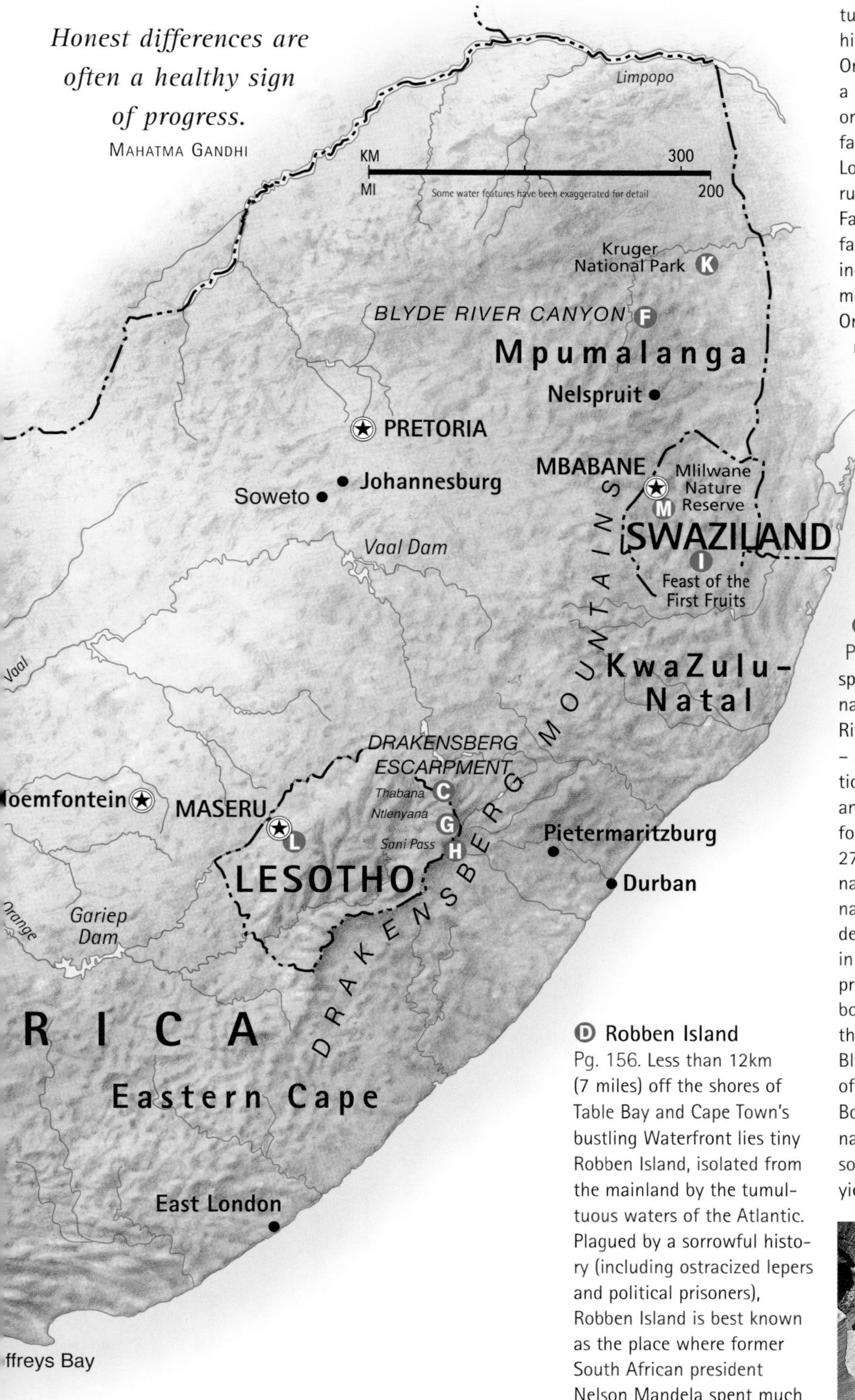

spectacular of the towering ridges are Cathedral Peak (with streams and rivers coursing down its rocky inclines) and the magnificent Mont-Aux-Sources Amphitheatre, which in turn towers over the valleys of the Drakensberg's Royal Natal National Park.

In stark contrast to the vision of sparkling waters gushing through the rocky gorges of the Drakensberg in the summer rainfall season, the winter landscape yields a blanket of snow that descends on the towns and villages that punctuate the craggy rise of the Great Escarpment. This 'Mountain of the Dragon' is the most significant of the Escarpment, and its age-old rock faces are dotted with caves painted by ancient San artists.

Ⓓ Robben Island

Pg. 156. Less than 12km (7 miles) off the shores of Table Bay and Cape Town's bustling Waterfront lies tiny Robben Island, isolated from the mainland by the tumultuous waters of the Atlantic. Plagued by a sorrowful history (including ostracized lepers and political prisoners), Robben Island is best known as the place where former South African president Nelson Mandela spent much of his 27-year imprisonment. It is acclaimed throughout the Western world as the spiritual home of South Africa's struggle for democracy and is considered a remarkable human rights monument. The 570ha (1,409 acre) island is a World Heritage Site, and conservationists have hailed it as one of the world's few remaining unspoiled ecosystems.

Ⓔ Orange River

Pg. 314. The mighty Orange River is South Africa's longest, most prominent and most significant watercourse. Flowing approximately 2,250km (1,400 miles) across some of South Africa's most desolate terrain, the Orange is said to drain almost half the country's rainwater. Although much of the land through which it winds is treeless and relatively arid, the waters of the Orange are a vital resource for the farmlands that line its course, as well as a popular playground for river-rafters and other adventurers. Many of the abundant hikes and walking trails in the Orange River Valley date from a time when the region was originally settled by early farmers and prospectors. Located along the Orange's rugged path is Augrabies Falls, the sixth-largest waterfall in the world, with 19 individual cataracts cascading more than 90m (295ft). The Orange empties its vital resource on the Atlantic coastline, where South Africa borders Namibia. It is here that early explorers discovered some of the country's first diamond and gold deposits.

Ⓕ Blyde River Canyon

Pg. 139. One of the most spectacular of the country's natural wonders is the Blyde River Canyon in Mpumalanga – an awesome conglomeration of impressive buttresses and forested inclines that forms the centrepoint of the 27,000ha (66,718-acre) nature reserve of the same name. Some 800m (2,625ft) deep and 1.5km (1 mile) wide in places, the canyon comprises a series of sculptured bowl formations carved by the abrasive action of the Blyde River. The most unusual of these are the famed Bourke's Luck Potholes, named after a prospector who sought his fortune in the gold yielded by this stony ground.

Lesotho

Ⓖ Thabana Ntlenyana

Pg. 280. Part of the Drakensberg mountain range that formed over 150 million years ago, Thabana Ntlenyana in the northeastern corner of Lesotho is the highest peak in the southern subcontinent.

Thabana Ntlenyana (ironically meaning 'beautiful little mountain') lies an impressive 3,480m (11,417ft) above sea level, offering spectacular views over some of the most panoramic vistas in southern Africa. In winter, the snow-covered slopes are icy cold, a chilling wind whipping its way through every valley and down rock cliffs. Fortunately, the balmy summer months – the rain season – bring with them a green blanket that covers the rugged terrain.

The hike to the top of Thabana Ntlenyana is along 25km (16 miles) of some of the roughest terrain in Lesotho, rising to an altitude of some 2,000m (6,562ft).

Ⓗ Sani Pass

Pg. 280. High above some of the tiny nation's most magnificent scenery stands Sani Top, an eerily windswept haven for hikers and adventurers who have made their way up the treacherous pass through the rocky mountains – and the summit boasts the highest pub in Africa. Sani Pass, the highest in Lesotho and South Africa, snakes through the Mkhomazana River Valley in the Drakensberg from just beyond the tiny village of Himeville to Sani Top. Sani rises 1,000m (3,281ft) over a distance of 7km (4.3 miles), providing the only road link between Lesotho and KwaZulu-Natal. Established in 1955, the route is demanding at best and perilous at worst, and can only be undertaken in a four-wheel-drive. The broader region caters for hikers, trailists and 'pony trekkers', usually led by the blanket-clad local Basotho people.

Swaziland

Ⓘ Feast of the First Fruits

Pg. 148. Like all the indigenous peoples of southern Africa, the Swazi place enormous importance on traditional spiritual beliefs and ancient customs. One of the most significant of the age-old celebrations that plays a role in Swaziland is the *Incwala*, or Feast of the First Fruits, held annually after the last full moon in December.

A group of traditional Swazi warriors makes its way to the Indian Ocean that skirts South Africa's eastern shore to collect sea water said to hold magical powers, while another band of warriors retrieves fresh water from the region's abundant rivers. This special water is used in a cleansing ceremony in which the *Ngwenyama* (the king) is blessed and sacrifices are made to the ancestors.

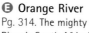

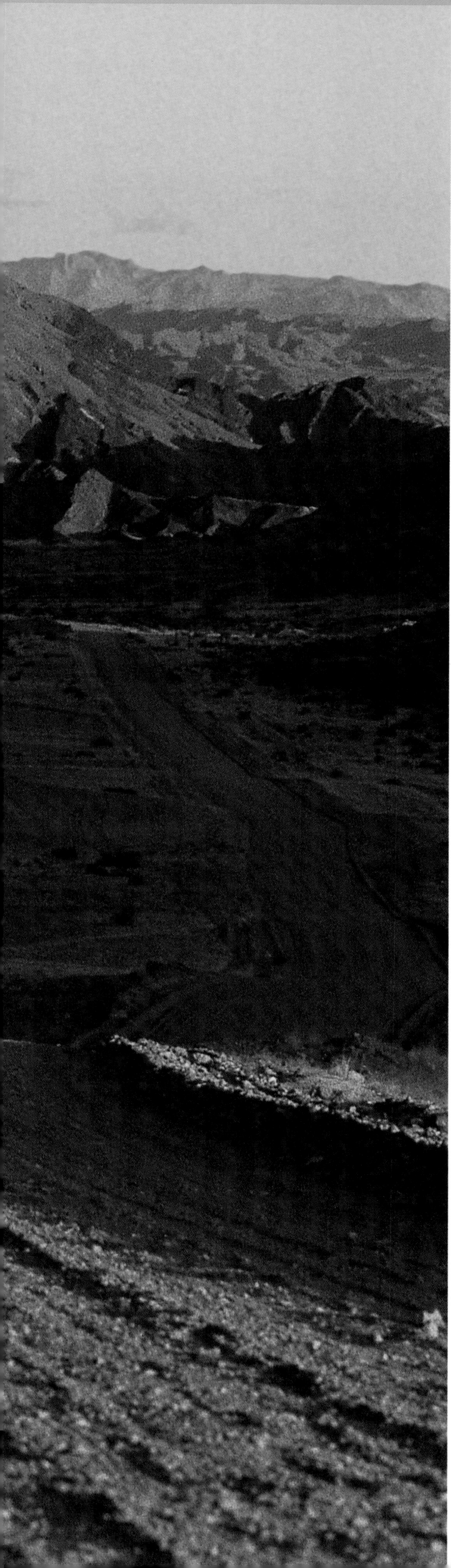

Touring the countries of Africa

COUNTRIES OF AFRICA AND THEIR CAPITALS

Algeria	Algiers	49
Angola	Luanda	75
Benin	Porto-Novo	66
Botswana	Gaborone	138
Burkina Faso	Ouagadougou	58
Burundi	Bujumbura	74
Cameroon	Yaoundé	67
Canary Islands (Spain)	Las Palmas (eastern islands)	
	Santa Cruz de Tenerife (western islands)	50
Cape Verde	Praia	56
Central African Republic	Bangui	68
Chad	N'Djamena	67
Comoros	Moroni	46
Congo	Brazzaville	72
Côte d'Ivoire	Yamoussoukro+/Abidjan++	65
Democratic Republic of the Congo	Kinshasa	72
Djibouti	Djibouti	70
Egypt	Cairo	55
Equatorial Guinea	Malabo	66
Eritrea	Asmara	62
Ethiopia	Addis Ababa	70
Gabon	Libreville	72
Gambia	Banjul	56
Ghana	Accra	65
Guinea	Conakry	64
Guinea-Bissau	Bissau	64
Kenya	Nairobi	88
Lesotho	Maseru	154
Liberia	Monrovia	64
Libya	Tripoli	53
Madagascar	Antananarivo	48
Malawi	Lilongwe	109
Mali	Bamako	57
Mauritania	Nouakchott	56
Mauritius	Port Louis	46
Morocco (incl. Western Sahara)	Rabat	49
Mozambique	Maputo	149
Namibia	Windhoek	134
Niger	Niamey	58
Nigeria	Abuja	66
Réunion (France)	St-Denis	46
Rwanda	Kigali	74
Sao Tome and Principe	São Tomé	66
Senegal	Dakar	56
Seychelles	Victoria	71
Sierra Leone	Freetown	64
Somalia	Mogadishu	71
South Africa	Pretoria+/Cape Town++/Bloemfontein+++	147
Sudan	Khartoum	62
Swaziland	Mbabane	148
Tanzania	Dar es Salaam+/Dodoma++	94
Togo	Lomé	66
Tunisia	Tunis	49
Uganda	Kampala	82
Zambia	Lusaka	106
Zimbabwe	Harare	120

+ Administrative, ++ Legislative, +++ Judicial

The isolation of touring through Namibia's Kaokoland confronts the four-by-four enthusiast with the greatest challenges and most enduring highlights.

PAGE NUMBER REFLECTS THE NUMBER OF THE PAGE WHERE YOU WILL FIND THE CAPITAL OF EACH COUNTRY

PLEASE CONSULT PAGES 42–43 FOR A COMPLETE LAYOUT OF PAGES AND ROUTE PLANNER

Touring Maps Route Planner

The main map data in this Atlas is presented in contiguous format (from page 44 to 160), running from the top left of Africa (starting with the Canary Islands and Indian Ocean islands before moving onto the mainland, starting with Morocco) all the way down to the Eastern Cape and KwaZulu-Natal coastline in South Africa. The boxes over each section of the map of Africa on this page are numbered to indicate the page of this Atlas on which the mapping is presented. Due to the nature of North Africa being sparsely populated or relatively underdeveloped (in terms of urban centres and transport infrastructure) and covered by so much desert, the Northern and Central sections are presented at 1:3,500,000 scale, while the Southern and South-Central countries are covered at 1:1,000,000. The Indian Ocean Islands and the Canary Islands are covered separately at varying scales, while the very top of Africa (upper Morocco, Algeria and Tunisia) as well Egypt's Red Sea coastline and the bottom of Somalia, are all shown as insets. The grids over the map on this page are a simple guide for you to pinpoint the page location of your destination of interest, as well as the page to turn to for extended coverage on either side of each page map. This information appears on the individual pages as well, but is supplied here for faster and clearer reference.

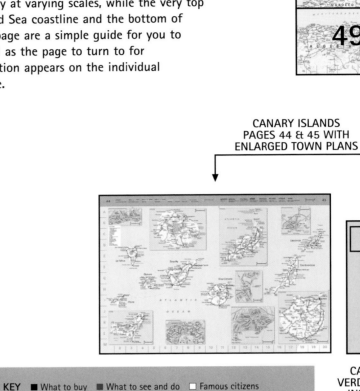

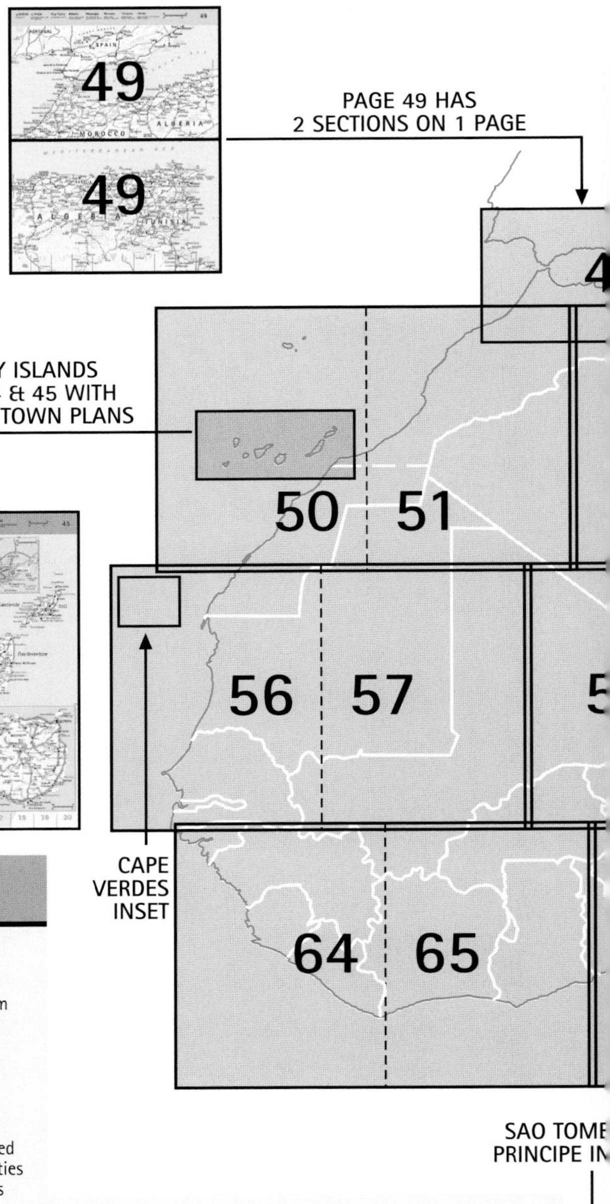

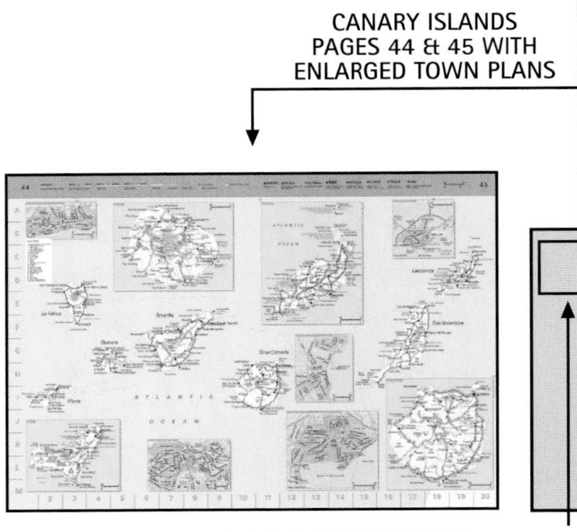

WHAT TO LOOK OUT FOR IN AFRICA

KEY ■ What to buy ■ What to see and do □ Famous citizens

Algeria
■ Carpets in El Oued ("Town of a Thousand Domes")
■ Roman ruins; horse-riding with the Berbers
□ Writer/philosopher Albert Camus

Angola
■ Masks and fabric in Luanda
■ Palm-fringed beaches at Mussulo Island; ride Benguela Railways' No.1 train to Lobito city
□ Angolan rebel leader Jonas Savimbi; journalist Rafael Marques

Benin
■ Sculptures, wall hangings
■ Abomey's Royal Palace; Ouidah's voodoo museums; cycle the countryside
□ Singer Angelique Kidjo

Botswana
■ Traditional Tswana food; home-baked bread (Shakawe)
■ San rock art (Tsodilo Hills), Mokoro and elephant rides
□ Sir Seretse Khama; Mpule Kwelagobe (Miss Universe 1999)

Burkina Faso
■ Beads and carvings at Bobo-Dioulasso's Grand Marché
■ Vistas at Goram-Goram; cultural festivals at Bobo Dioulasso and Ouagadougou
□ Captain Thomas Sankara (the man who named Burkina Faso)

Burundi
■ Basketware, pottery, drums
■ Kagera Falls in winter; Bujumburu's cultural exhibits
□ The Drummers of Burundi (music group)

Cameroon
■ Woodwork, local music CDs
■ Maroua's villages and mountains; attend Yaoundé's open-air mass; Foumban's end-of-Ramadan celebrations
□ Poet/musician/writer Francis Bebey; soccer star Roger Mila

Canary Islands (Spain)
■ Woven baskets
■ Whale-watching, flora-gazing
□ Singer Pedro Guerra

Cape Verde
■ Local books and music CDs
■ Volcanic Mount Fogo; Mindelo's city carnival
□ Author Teixeira de Sousa; singer Cesaria Evoria

Central African Republic
■ Postcards – taking photographs is not always welcomed by officials or locals! Butterfly wing collages are a must
■ Boali Falls (50m high!) in the rainy season; Bouar's megalithic stone monuments
□ Artisan trainer Cyr Perroni

Chad
■ Local stamps which feature celebrities from Elvis to Bill Clinton to Madonna!
■ Sao-Kotoko's museum with ancient artefacts and contemporary fishing, farming and household items; N'Djamena's African quarter nightlife and Grand Marché market
□ François Tombalbaye, Chad's first head of state, who was assassinated in 1975

Comoros
■ Comorian cuisine
■ Empty yet glorious beaches; watch the endangered green turtles laying eggs
□ Ali Soilih, who led a successful coup before being shot dead by Bob Denard's mercenaries

Congo
■ Local music CDs
■ Pointe-Noire's tranquil beaches; Congo river rapids; take time to wander Brazzaville's food and market stalls
□ Soccer star Lomana LuaLua

Cote d'Ivoire
■ Musical instruments, woven clothing at Korhogo
■ Waterfalls and countryside in the Man region; experience the masked-dancing festival
□ Author and social psychologist Albert Taïeb

Democratic Republic of the Congo
■ Local music CDs; local art in Kinshasa
■ Mountain gorillas, volcanoes, the great lakes; see the Congo River on *Le Grand Pousseur* boat
□ Laurent Kabila

Djibouti
■ Qat (if you're over 18), a mild stimulant
■ Lake Abbé's flamingoes and belching steam chimneys; scenic drive from Berbera to Hargeysa
□ Author Abdourahman A Waberi

Egypt
■ Postcards from the Egyptian (Cairo) Museum
■ Giza's pyramids and Sphinx; snorkel in the Sinai
□ Tutankhamun; author Naguib Mahfouz

Equatorial Guinea
■ A photography permit!
■ Malabo's Spanish-colonial architecture; walk Bioko's rainforests, beaches and volcanoes
□ Infamous Olympic swimmer Eric "The Eel" Moussambani

Eritrea
■ Local cuisine
■ Asmara's National Museum; travel the dramatic Massawa-Asmara Railway
□ Local women, one-third of whom were freedom fighters

Ethiopia
■ Gold and silver jewellery at Addis Ababa's Mercato open-air market
■ Addis Ababa from high up on Entoto NP; explore Lalibela's rock churches
□ Olympic gold medallist Haile Gebrselassie

Gabon
■ Wooden masks, statues, bowls, plates and sandstone carvings
■ Gabon's flourishing wildlife; pirogue trip near Lambaréné
□ Doctor and philanthropist, Albert Schweitzer (USA)

Gambia
■ A $1 ticket to the famed no-holds barred boreh wrestling bouts in Serekunda
■ Wassu's Stone Circles; cruise the Gambia River
□ Alex Haley (author of *Roots*)

Ghana
■ Ashanti wood-carved stools, basketware and leather goods, Kente cloth
■ Beaches, forts and fishing villages; walk Accra's vibrant markets and streets
□ Ama Ata Aidoo (writer/feminist/politician) and Kofi Annan (UN Secretary General)

Guinea
■ Delicious poisson and poulet yassa
■ The Fouta Djalon Plateau; watch street music in Conakry
□ Former president Sekou Touré

Guinea-Bissau
■ Arts and crafts
■ Cacheu's ruined fort; visit Bijagós Archipelago by boat
□ Revolutionary hero Amílcar Cabral

Kenya
■ Carved gourds, beads, makonde wood carvings
■ The endangered black rhino in Amboseli NP; explore Lake Turkana
□ Authors Kuki Galman and Ngugi wa Thiong'o; World Cup cricket captain Steve Tikolo; President Daniel Arap Moi

Lesotho
■ Basotho grass hat; carpets and woven jerseys from Teyateyaneng ('the place of quick sands')
■ Thabana Ntlenyana's views; pony trekking
□ Author Thomas Mofolo

Liberia
■ Local replica masks
■ The Firestone rubber plantation, the largest in the world; hike around Mount Nimba
□ Artist Leslie Lumeh; soccer star George Weah

Libya
■ Traditional jewellery
■ The Sahara, cave paintings; explore the many ancient Roman and Greek cities
□ Colonel Muammar Gaddafi

Madagascar
■ Local wine; a ticket to a hira gasy performance
■ Fianarantsoa to Manakara by train; Périnet's endemic wildlife
□ Author Michèle Rakotoson

Malawi
■ Roasted locusts in Lilongwe
■ Liwonde's wildlife & scenery; boat around Lake Malawi
□ Author Paul Tiyambe Zeleza; Hastings Banda

Mali
■ Dogon masks; Fulani wedding blankets
■ Djenné's Grand Mosquée; wander Timbuktu's streets
□ Singer Habib Koite

Mauritania
■ Wooden chests, old arrow heads
■ Birds in Arguin Bank NP; visit the Adrar's oases
□ First president Mokhtar Ould Daddah, overthrown in 1978

Mauritius
■ A T-shirt with a dodo on it
■ Sir Seewoosagur Ramgoolam Botanical Gardens; enjoy the beaches & water activities
□ Author Édouard J Maunick

Morocco
■ Spices, dhurries and rugs
■ Dadés Gorge's ochre-coloured cliffs; wander the medieval cities of Fez, Marrakech and Meknes
□ Author Tahar Ben Jelloun

Mozambique
■ A donation to the landmine clearing fund; leatherwork
■ Mozambique Island's WHS buildings; Maputo nightlife
□ Joaquim Chissano & Samora Michel; author Mia Couto

Namibia
■ Local 'German' beer, woodcarvings and baskets
■ Fish River Canyon, rock paintings, petrified forest; explore Kolmanskop ghost town
□ athlete Frank Fredericks; Miss Universe Michele McLean

Niger
■ Traditional metalwork, woven and leather goods
■ Niamey's Grand Marché; Gerewol ceremony near Agadez
□ Singer/songwriter Ismael Lô, dubbed Senegal's "Bob Dylan"

Nigeria
■ Fabrics; suya (spiced brochettes)
■ Museum at Jos; walk the Sacred Groves at Oshogbo's rainforest
□ Soccer star JJ Okocha; General Sani Abacha; author and activist Ken Saro-Wiwa

Réunion (France)
■ Creole meals
■ Gorgeous tropical scenery; enjoy Cilaos' hot springs
□ Poet and painter Léon Dierx

Rwanda
■ A copy of *Gorillas in the Mist*
■ Gorillas, colobus monkeys; wander Nyungwe Forest
□ Author Dian Fossey (USA); singer Cécile Kaiyrebwa

Sao Tome and Principe
■ Post a letter to anywhere in the world for under a dollar
■ Portuguese colonial buildings; enjoy the beaches & water; walk around Príncipe in a day
□ Pianist José Vianna da Motta

Senegal
■ Local music CDs
■ Local wrestling (les luttes); Île de Gorée's slave gate; enjoy a party in Dakar
□ Soccer star Patrick Vieira

Seychelles
■ A coco de mer nut!
■ Exotic vegetation & wildlife; enjoy the beaches & water
□ Artist Michael Adams; Esmeralda (the island's 150-year-old tortoise)

Sierra Leone
■ Bullet-proof jacket; giant saucepans and monkey skulls at Freetown's Basket Market
■ Flavourful Freetown; hike Mount Bintumani
□ Author Syl Cheney-Coker

Somalia
■ Qat, leather sandals
■ War ravaged towns; sleep in beach huts at Sinsusi Beach
□ Author Nuruddin Farah; model Imam

South Africa
■ Decorated ostrich eggs
■ Table Mountain, the Cango Caves, the Drakensberg, Namaqualand in full bloom
□ Human rights icon and former president Nelson Mandela; author Wilbur Smith; former rugby captain Francois Pienaar

Sudan
■ A camel at the daily camel markets near Omdurman
■ Visit Khartoum's Ethnographic Museum; wander Suakin's "ghost port", explore the Blue Nile
□ Madhist warrior and local hero, Osman Dinga

Swaziland
■ Local craftwork
■ Walking Hlane Royal National Park; white-water rafting
□ King Sobhuza II

Tanzania
■ Makonde (ebony) carvings
■ Olduvai Gorge, site of presumed evolution of early humans
□ The late Freddie Mercury, lead singer of rock group *Queen*

Togo
■ Woodwork
■ Kpalimé for hikes and excursions; explore voodoo sites
□ Singer, actor and storyteller King Mensah

Tunisia
■ Rugs, carpets and leather
■ Exploring the ancient medinas of Chabbi; singer/actress Amina; movie director Ali Laâbidi

□ National poet Abu el Kcem el Chabbi; singer/actress Amina; movie director Ali Laâbidi

Uganda
■ Batiks, wooden spoons, elephant-shaped soapstones
■ Enjoy a close-up view of the Murchison Falls from a hire boat
□ Former dictator Idi Amin; playwright Charles Mulekwa

Zambia
■ Reed and papyrus mats, semi-precious stones, chitenjes cloth, wooden carvings, basketwork
■ Experience the thrill of a game park night drive
□ Cecil John Rhodes; journalist and poet Gideon Nyirendra; singer Samantha Mumba

Zimbabwe
■ Handicrafts, pottery, woven goods, soapstone and wood carvings, African carved faces (wood or stone)
■ Watch someone bungee-jump off the Zambezi Bridge; wander the breathtaking Zimbabwe ruins; photograph the San rock paintings at Matobo Hills
□ Robert Mugabe; cricket stars Henry Olonga and Andy Flower; author/activist/former Zimbabwe Liberation Army member, Freedom Nyamubuya

HITCHHIKING

While hitchhiking may be perilous in any corner of the globe, it has both its advantages and disadvantages in Africa, a continent where most locals must rely on passing trucks and heavy-duty vehicles to move from A to B. Hitchhiking may well provide an unparalleled opportunity to see the wonders of the continent first-hand and to meet its people, yet it would be foolish to chance your luck in regions (particularly in Central and North Africa) known for their corrupt officialdom and where there is a strong military presence or any form of unrest.

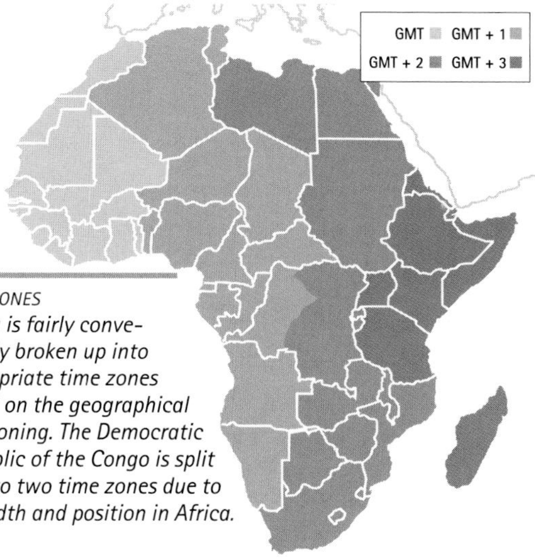

TIME ZONES
Africa is fairly conveniently broken up into appropriate time zones based on the geographical positioning. The Democratic Republic of the Congo is split up into two time zones due to its width and position in Africa.

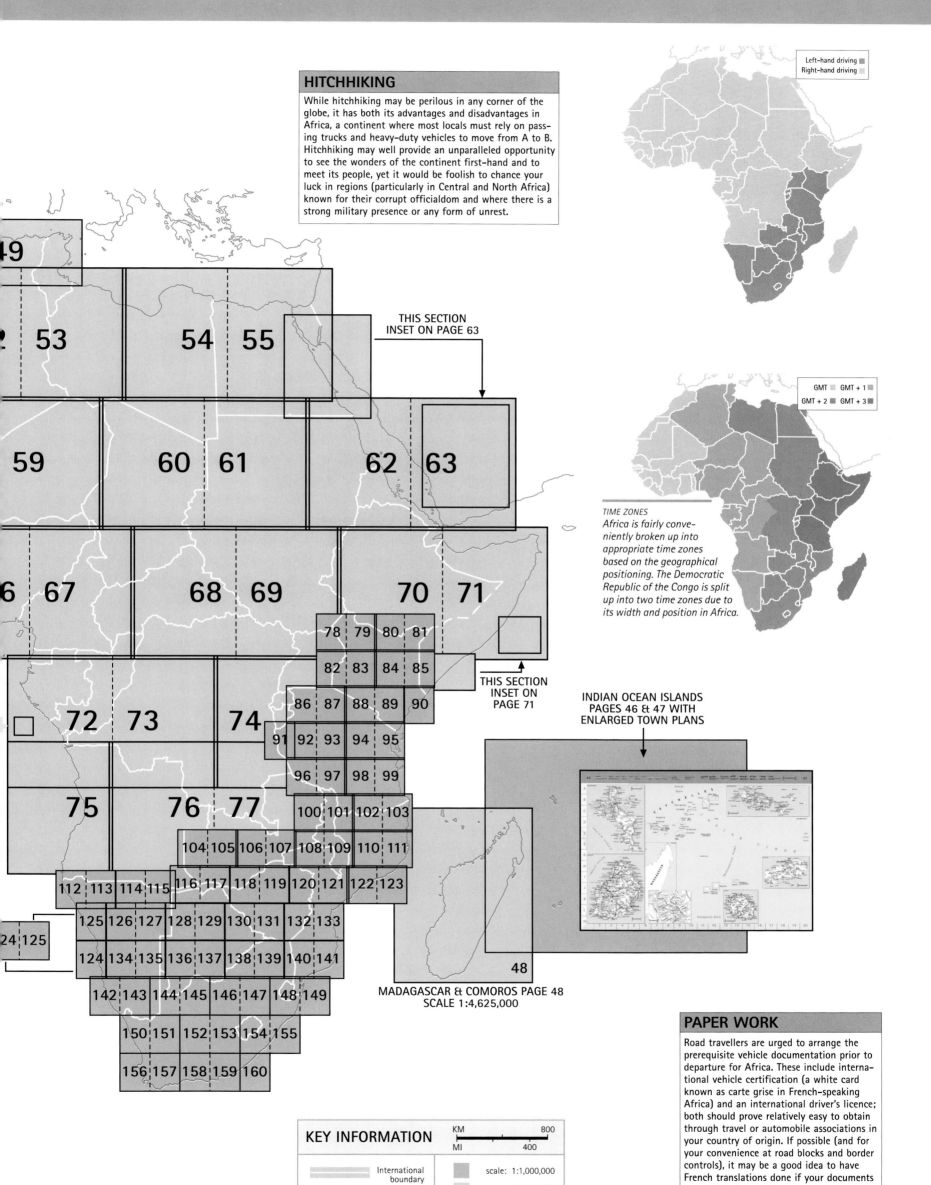

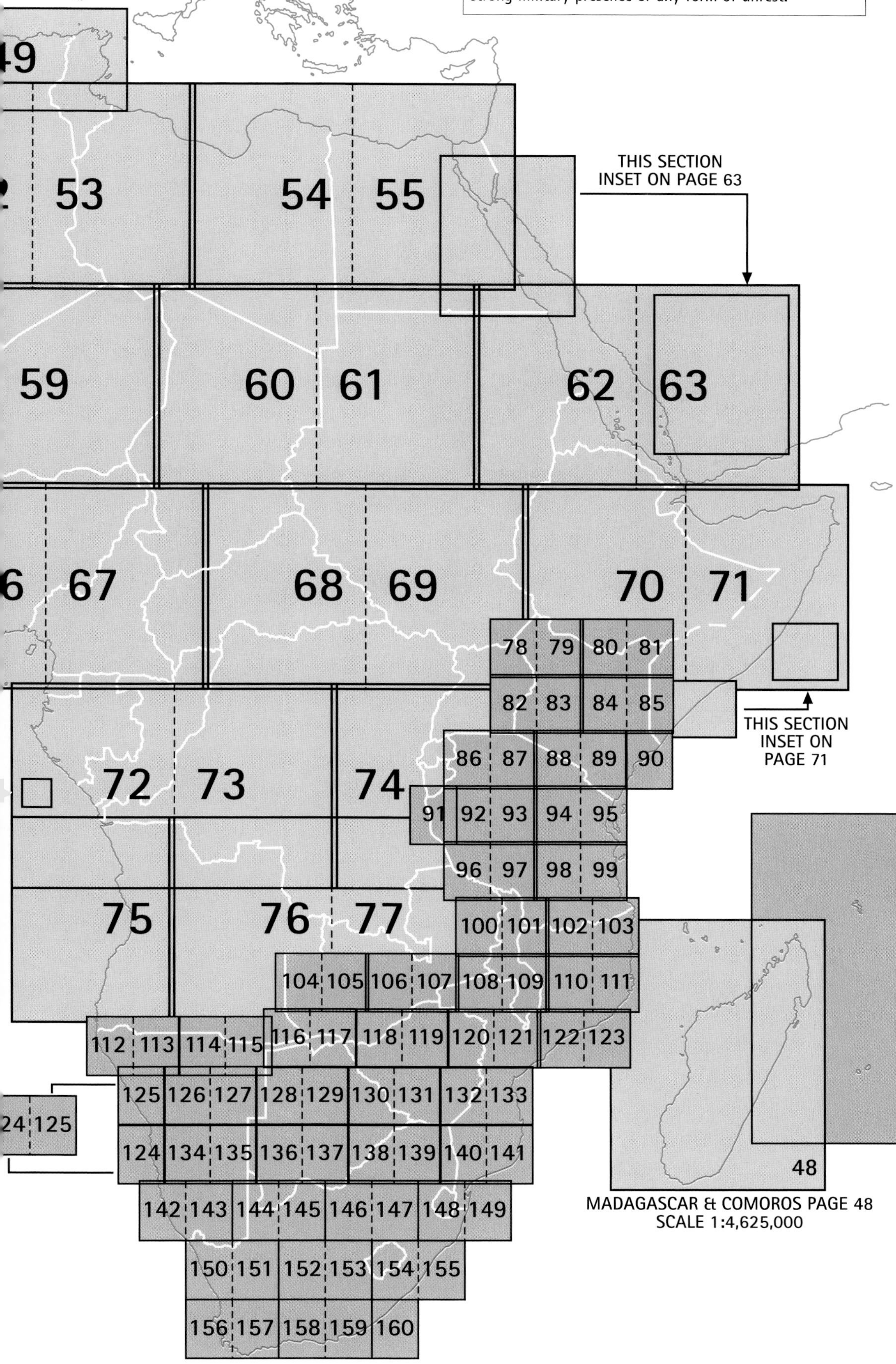

KEY INFORMATION

KM 800
MI 400

International boundary
scale: 1:1,000,000
scale: 1:3,500,000

PAPER WORK

Road travellers are urged to arrange the prerequisite vehicle documentation prior to departure for Africa. These include international vehicle certification (a white card known as carte grise in French-speaking Africa) and an international driver's licence; both should prove relatively easy to obtain through travel or automobile associations in your country of origin. If possible (and for your convenience at road blocks and border controls), it may be a good idea to have French translations done if your documents are entirely in English.

SCENIC ROUTE — MAJOR CONNECTING ROUTE
TARRED / UNTARRED — MAIN CONNECTING ROUTE
TARRED / UNTARRED — MAIN ROAD
TARRED / UNTARRED — MINOR ROAD
4WD ROAD
LOCAL TRACK
HIKING TRAIL
DIVE CENTRE
SCUBA AREA / SITE
SWIMMING BEACH / AR

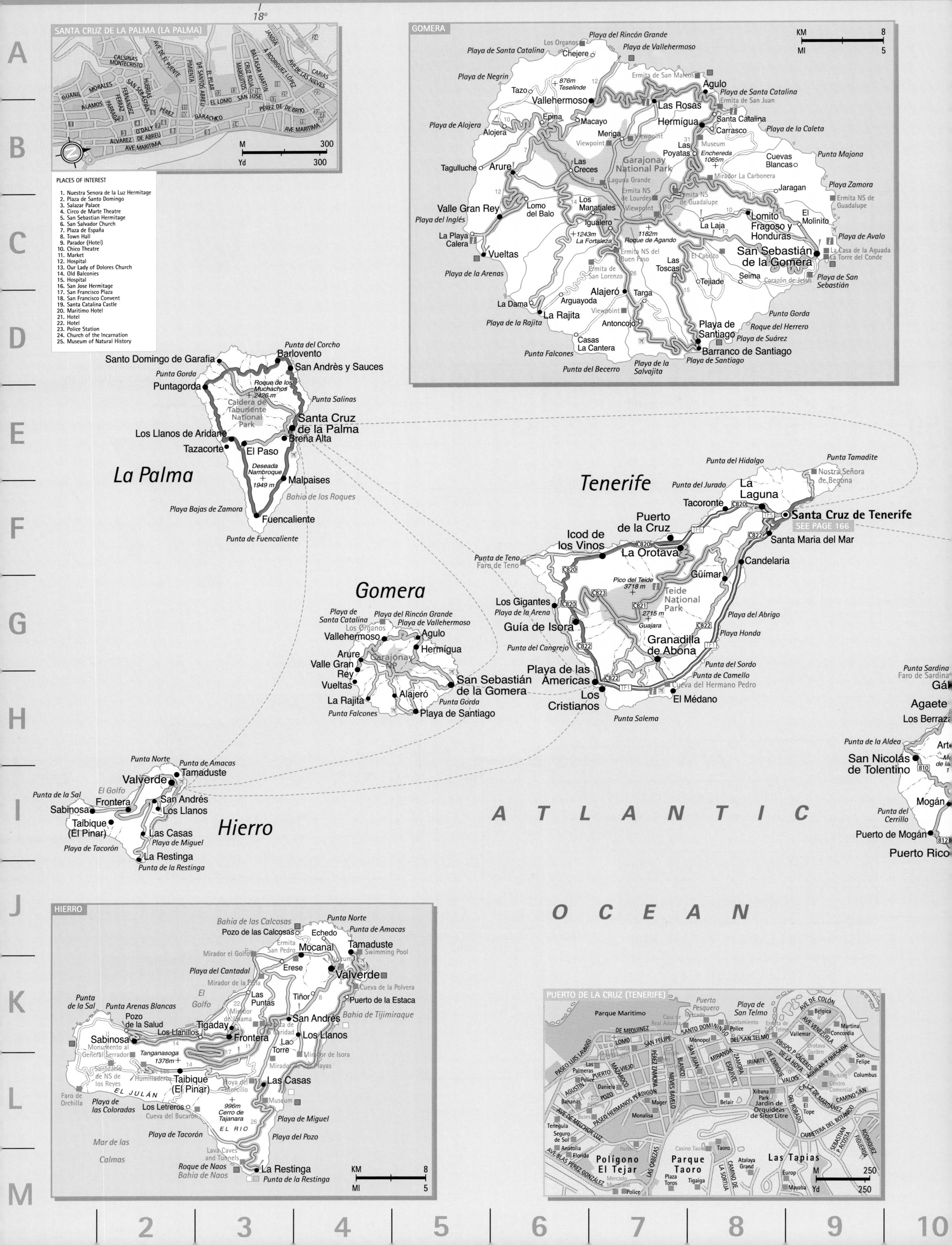

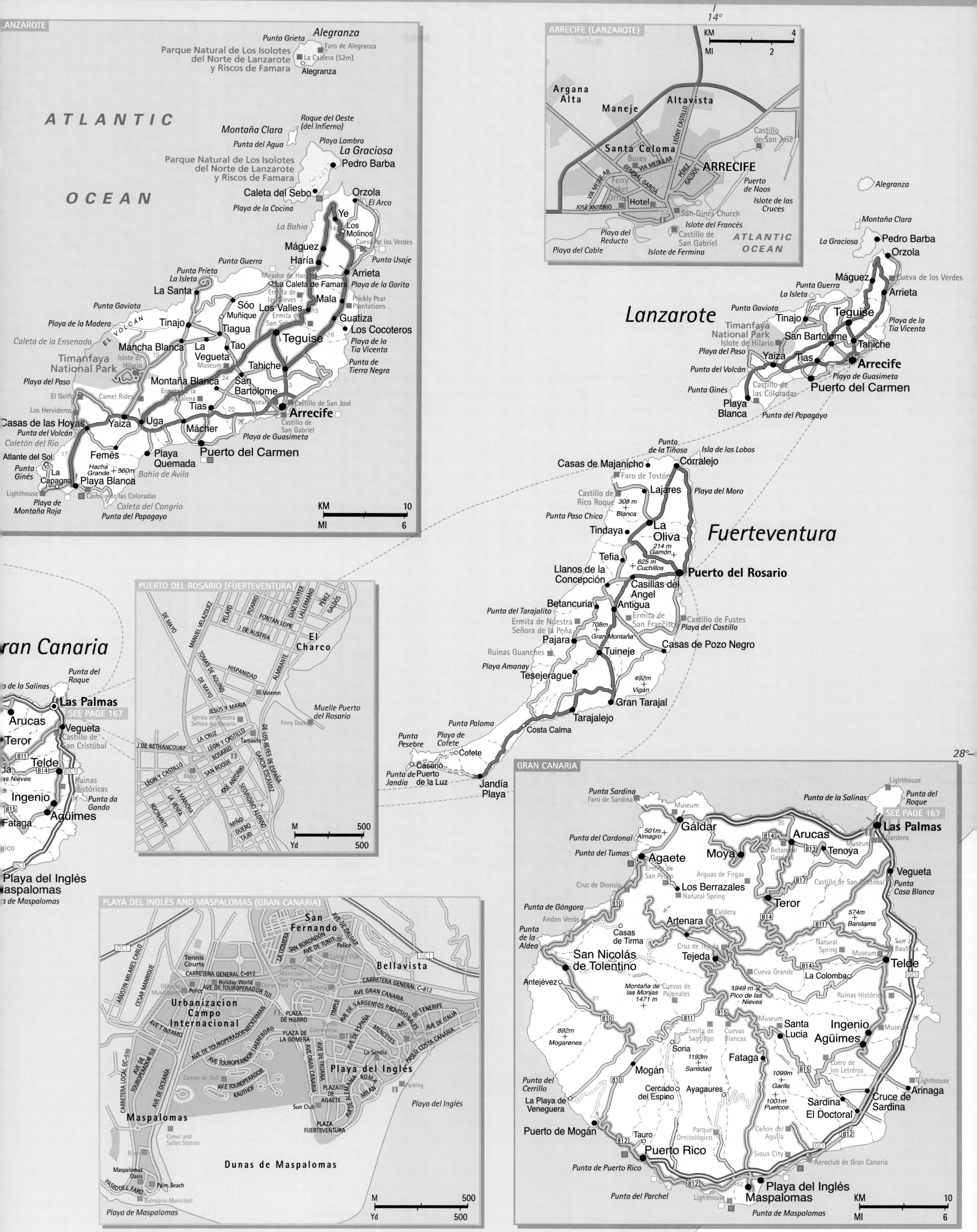

LANZAROTE
Alegranza
Punta Grieta
Faro de Alegranza
La Caldera (52m)
Parque Natural de Los Isolotes del Norte de Lanzarote y Riscos de Famara
ATLANTIC
OCEAN
Roque del Oeste (del Infierno)
Montaña Clara
Punta del Agua
Playa Lambra
La Graciosa
Pedro Barba
Caleta del Sebo
Orzola
El Arco
Playa de la Cocina
La Bahía
Ye
Los Molinos
Cueva de los Verdes
Máguez
Haría
Punta Usaje
Punta Guerra
Punta Prieta
La Isleta
La Santa
Arrieta
La Caleta de Famara
Playa de la Garita
Ermita de las Nieves
Mala
Prickly Pear Plantations
Punta Gaviota
Sóo
Muñique
Los Valles
Ermita de San Sebastián
Guatiza
Los Cocoteros
Playa de la Madera
Tinajo
Tiagua
Teguise
Playa de la Tía Vicenta
Caleta de la Ensenada
El Volcán
Mancha Blanca
La Vegueta
Tao
Timanfaya National Park
Islote de Hilario
Museum
Punta de Tierra Negra
Tahiche
Playa del Paso
Montaña Blanca
Ermita de la Magdalena
San Bartolomé
El Golfo
Camel Rides
Museum
Castillo de San José
Los Hervideros
Tías
Arrecife
Castillo de San Gabriel
Casas de las Hoyas
Yaiza
Uga
Mácher
Punta del Volcán
Playa de Guasimeta
Caletón del Río
Puerto del Carmen
Atlante del Sol
Femés
Playa Quemada
Punta Ginés
La Capagna
Hacha Grande + 560m
Bahía de Ávila
Lighthouse
Playa Blanca
Castillo de las Coloradas
Playa de Montaña Roja
Caleta del Congrio
Punta del Papagayo
KM 10
MI 6
ARRECIFE (LANZAROTE)
14°
KM 4
MI 2
Argana Alta
Maneje
Altavista
Castillo de San José
Santa Coloma
Buses
Vía Medular
León y Castillo
ARRECIFE
Ferry Ticket Office
General García
Pérez Galdós
Puerto de Naos
Islote de las Cruces
José Antonio
Hotel
San Ginés Church
Islote del Francés
Playa del Reducto
Castillo de San Gabriel
ATLANTIC OCEAN
Playa del Cable
Islote de Fermina
Alegranza
Montaña Clara
La Graciosa
Pedro Barba
Orzola
Máguez
Cueva de los Verdes
Punta Guerra
La Isleta
Arrieta
Punta Gaviota
Lanzarote
Tinajo
Teguise
Timanfaya National Park
Islote de Hilario
San Bartolomé
Playa de la Tía Vicenta
Playa del Paso
Yaiza
Tías
Tahiche
Arrecife
Punta del Volcán
Playa de Guasimeta
Punta Ginés
Castillo de las Coloradas
Puerto del Carmen
Playa Blanca
Punta del Papagayo
Punta de la Tiñosa
Isla de los Lobos
Casas de Majanicho
Corralejo
Faro de Tostón
Lajares
Playa del Moro
Castillo de Rico Roque
308 m Blanca
Punta Paso Chico
Tindaya
La Oliva
Fuerteventura
214 m Gamón
Tefía
625 m Cuchillos
Llanos de la Concepción
Puerto del Rosario
Casillas del Angel
Betancuria
Antigua
Punta del Tarajalito
Ermita de Nuestra Señora de la Peña
Ermita de San Francisco
Castillo de Fustes
Playa del Castillo
708m Gran Montaña
Pajara
Casas de Pozo Negro
Ruinas Guanches
Tuineje
Playa Amanay
Tesejerague
492m Vigán
Gran Tarajal
Tarajalejo
Punta Paloma
Costa Calma
Punta Pesebre
Playa de Cofete
Cofete
Caserío
Punta de Jandía
Puerto de la Luz
Jandía Playa
28°
PUERTO DEL ROSARIO (FUERTEVENTURA)
El Charco
Valerón
Muelle Puerto del Rosario
Ferry Dock
M 500
Yd 500
Gran Canaria
Punta del Roque
Punta de la Salinas
Las Palmas
SEE PAGE 167
Arucas
Vegueta
Teror
Castillo de San Cristóbal
Telde
Ruinas Históricas
Punta da Gando
Ingenio
Agüimes
Fataga
Playa del Inglés
Maspalomas
Punta de Maspalomas
PLAYA DEL INGLÉS AND MASPALOMAS (GRAN CANARIA)
San Fernando
Tennis Courts
Bellavista
Urbanizacion Campo Internacional
Playa del Inglés
Campo de Golf
Sun Club
Playa del Inglés
Maspalomas
Camel and Safari Station
Dunas de Maspalomas
Maspalomas Oasis
Palm Beach
Balneario Municipal
Playa de Maspalomas
M 500
Yd 500
GRAN CANARIA
Lighthouse
Punta Sardina
Faro de Sardina
Punta de la Salinas
Punta del Roque
Museum
SEE PAGE 167
Gáldar
501m Almagro
Las Palmas
Punta del Cardonal
Arucas
Gardens
Punta del Tumas
Agaete
Moya
Tenoya
Ermita de San Pedro
Arguas de Firgas
Vegueta
Botanical Garden
Castillo de San Cristóbal
Punta Casa Blanca
Cruz de Dionsio
Los Berrazales
Natural Spring
Punta de Góngora
Teror
Caldera
Anden Verde
574m Bandama
Punta de la Aldea
Casas de Tirma
Artenara
Natural Spring
Cruz de Tejeda
San Juan Bautista
San Nicolás de Tolentino
Tejeda
Museum
Telde
Antejévez
Cueva Grande
La Colombaq
Montaña de las Monjas 1471 m
Cuevas de Pajonales
1949 m Pico de las Nieves
Ruinas Históricas
892m Mogarenes
Museum
Ermita de Santiago
Cuevas Blancas
Santa Lucía
Ingenio
Agüimes
Museum
Soria
1193m Santidad
Fataga
Lomo de los Letreros
Mogán
Punta del Cerrillo
1099m Garita
Lighthouse
Arinaga
Cercado del Espino
Ayagaures
1001m Puercos
La Playa de Veneguera
Sardina El Doctoral
Cruce de Sardina
Puerto de Mogán
Tauro
Parque Ornitológico
Cañon del Águila
Sioux City
Puerto Rico
Aeroclub de Gran Canaria
Punta de Puerto Rico
Playa del Inglés
Punta del Parchel
Lighthouse
Maspalomas
Punta de Maspalomas
KM 10
MI 6

SCENIC ROUTE — MAJOR CONNECTING ROUTE
TARRED / UNTARRED — MAIN CONNECTING ROUTE
TARRED / UNTARRED — MAIN ROAD
TARRED / UNTARRED — MINOR ROAD
4WD ROAD
LOCAL TRACK
HIKING TRAIL
DIVE CENTRE
SCUBA AREA / SITE
SWIMMING BEACH / AF
SNORKEL AREA

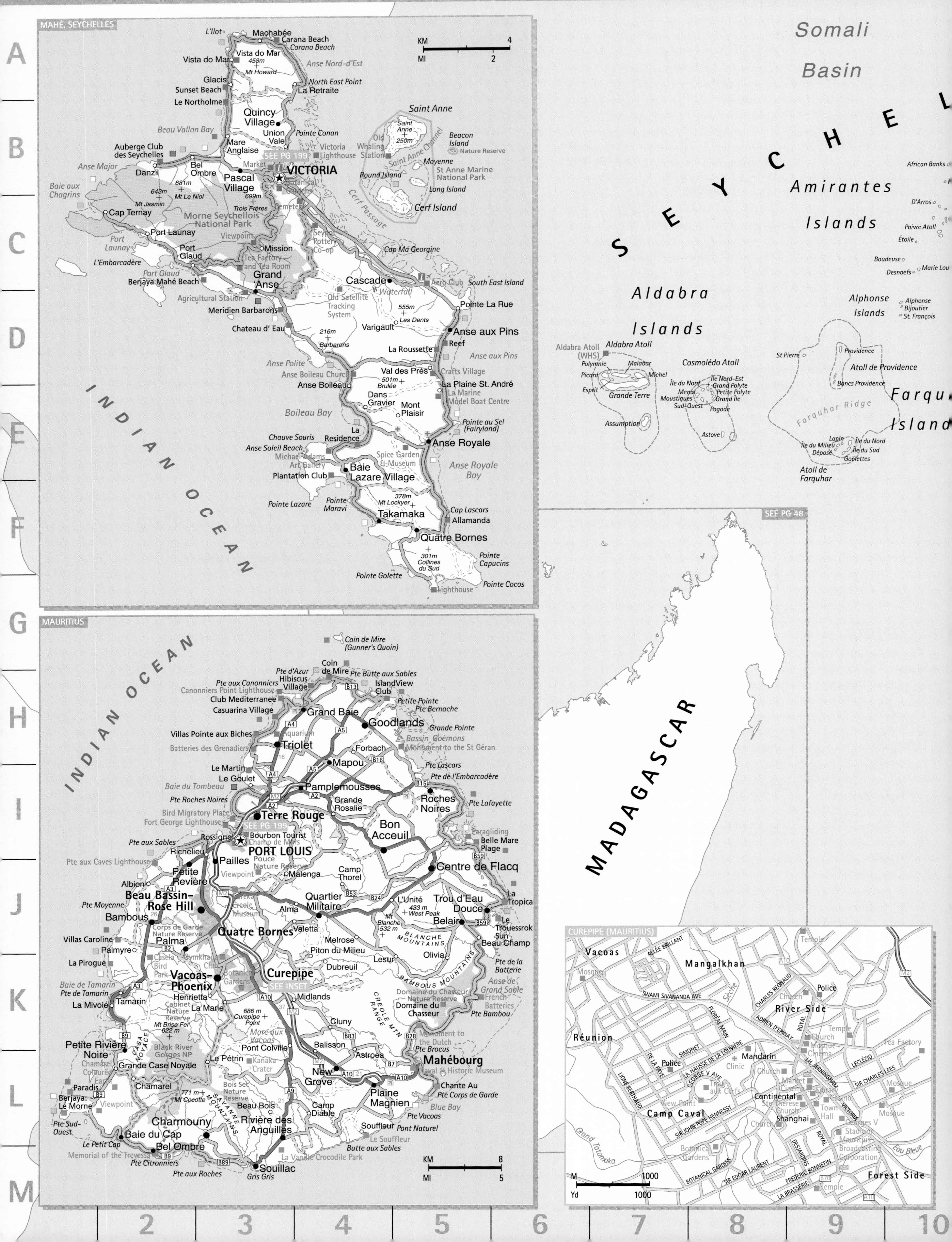

NAIROBI — CAPITAL CITY
Abidjan — SECONDARY CAPITAL CITY When Applicable
Las Palmas — DEPENDANCY CAPITAL
Gweru — LARGE / MAJOR TOWN Over 50,000 people
Ruhengeri — SECONDARY TOWN Between 10,000 & 50,000
El Kadada — SMALL TOWN Between 5,000 &10,000
Chinguetti — LARGE VILLAGE Between 500 & 5,000
Winneba — SMALL VILLAGE OR SETTLEMENT Under 500 people

KM 250
MI 150

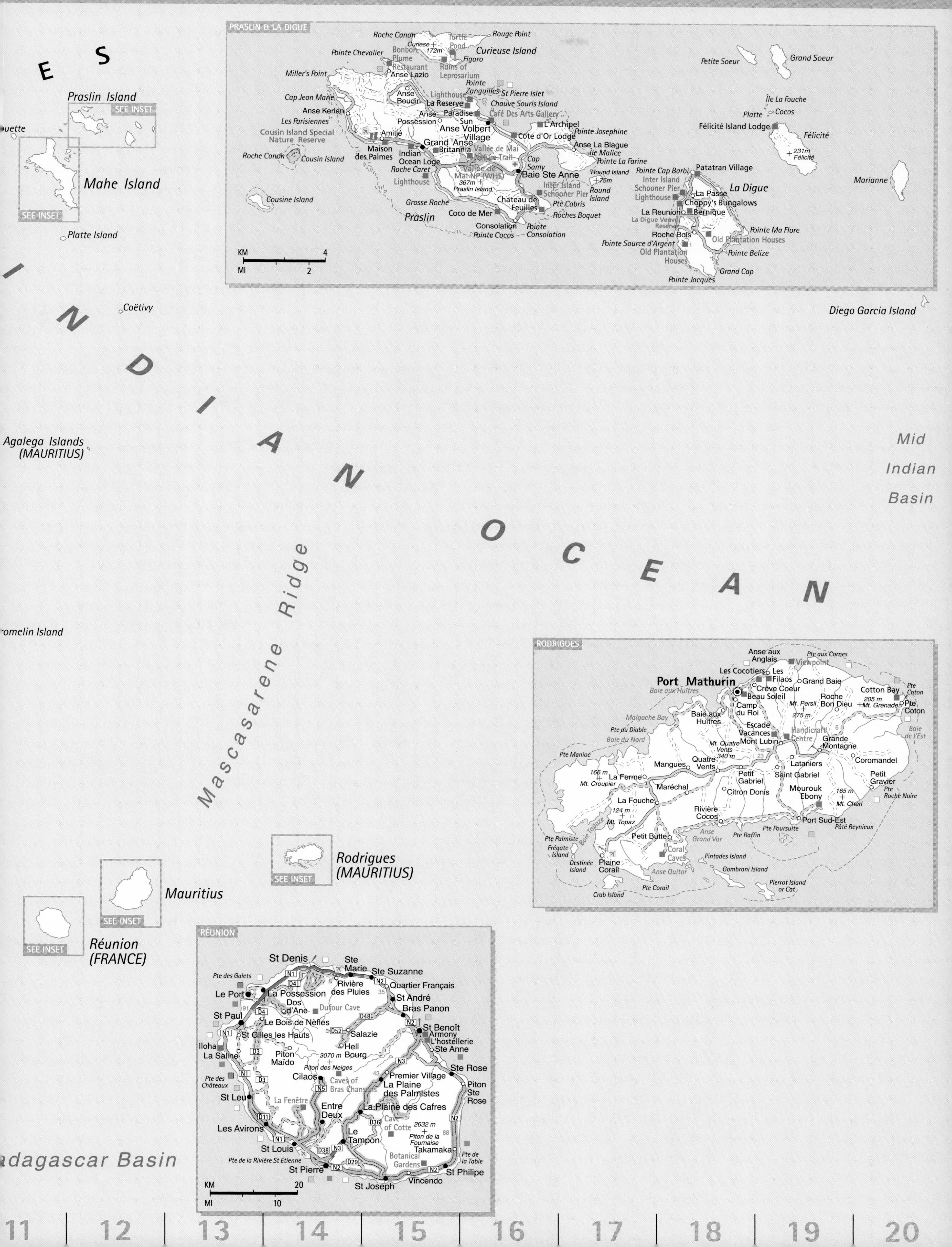

SCENIC ROUTE / MAJOR CONNECTING ROUTE · TARRED / UNTARRED MAIN CONNECTING ROUTE · TARRED / UNTARRED MAIN ROAD · TARRED / UNTARRED MINOR ROAD · 4WD ROAD · LOCAL TRACK · HIKING TRAIL · 234 NATIONAL ROUTE NUMBER · 234 OTHER ROUTE NUMBER · PLACE OF INTEREST

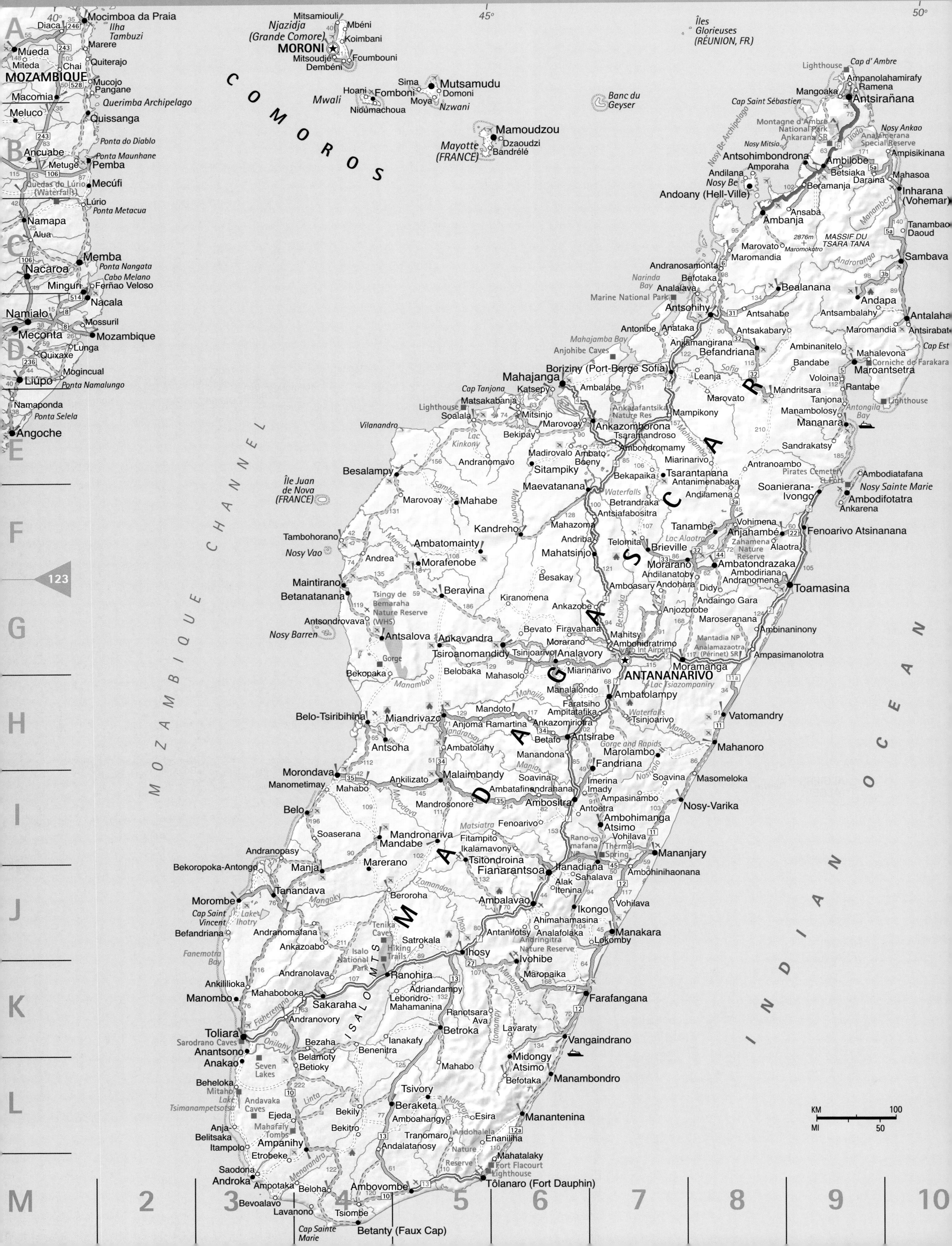

NAIROBI CAPITAL CITY | Abidjan SECONDARY CAPITAL CITY When Applicable | Las Palmas DEPENDANCY CAPITAL | Gweru LARGE / MAJOR TOWN Over 50,000 people | Ruhengeri SECONDARY TOWN Between 10,000 & 50,000 | El Kadada SMALL TOWN Between 5,000 &10,000 | Chinguetti LARGE VILLAGE Between 500 & 5,000 | Winneba SMALL VILLAGE OR SETTLEMENT Under 500 people | KM 100 MI 50

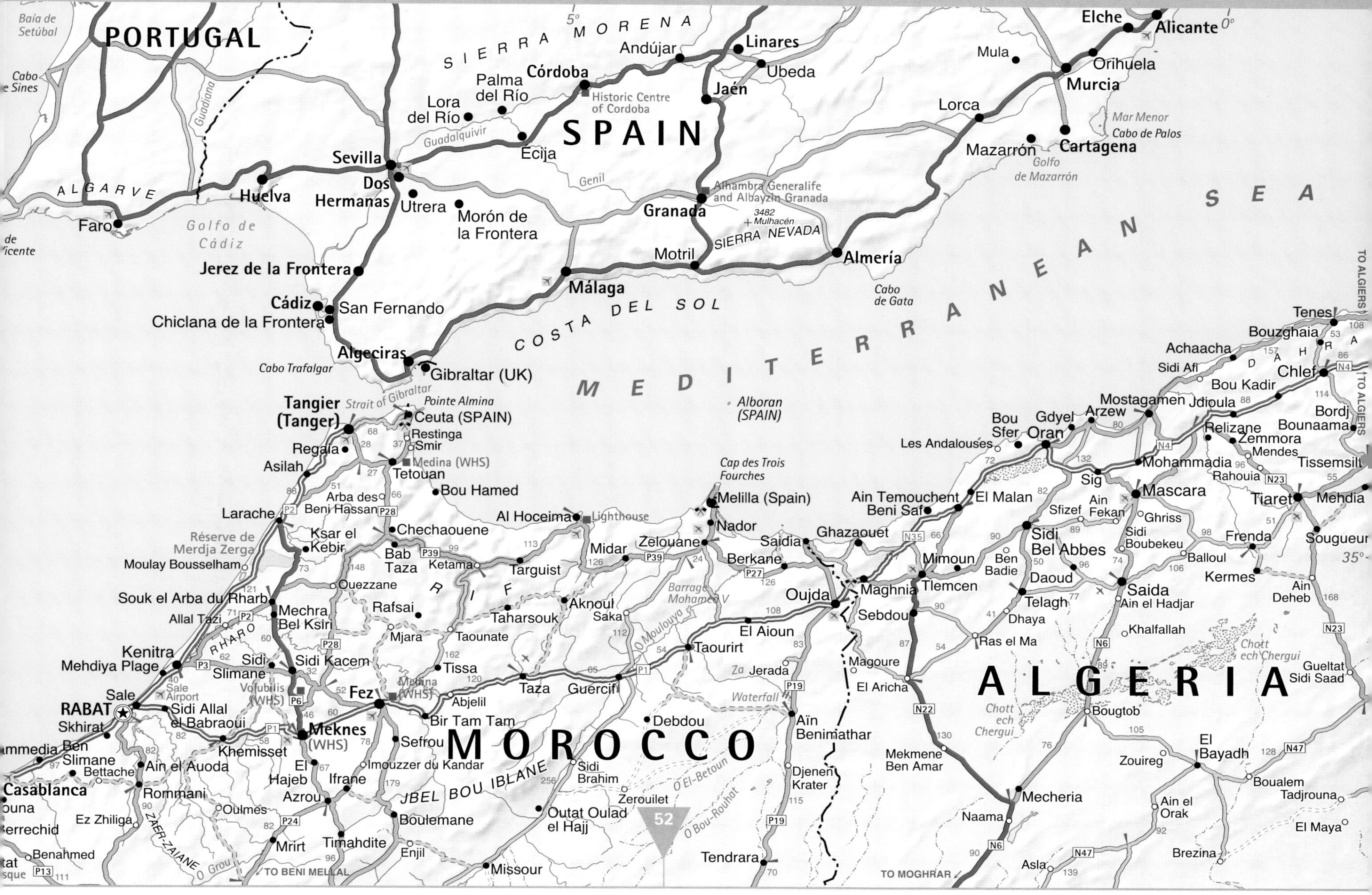

SCENIC ROUTE — MAJOR CONNECTING ROUTE
TARRED / UNTARRED — MAIN CONNECTING ROUTE
TARRED / UNTARRED — MAIN ROAD
TARRED / UNTARRED — MINOR ROAD
4WD ROAD
LOCAL TRACK
HIKING TRAIL
234 NATIONAL ROUTE NUMBER
234 OTHER ROUTE NUMBER
PLACE OF INTEREST

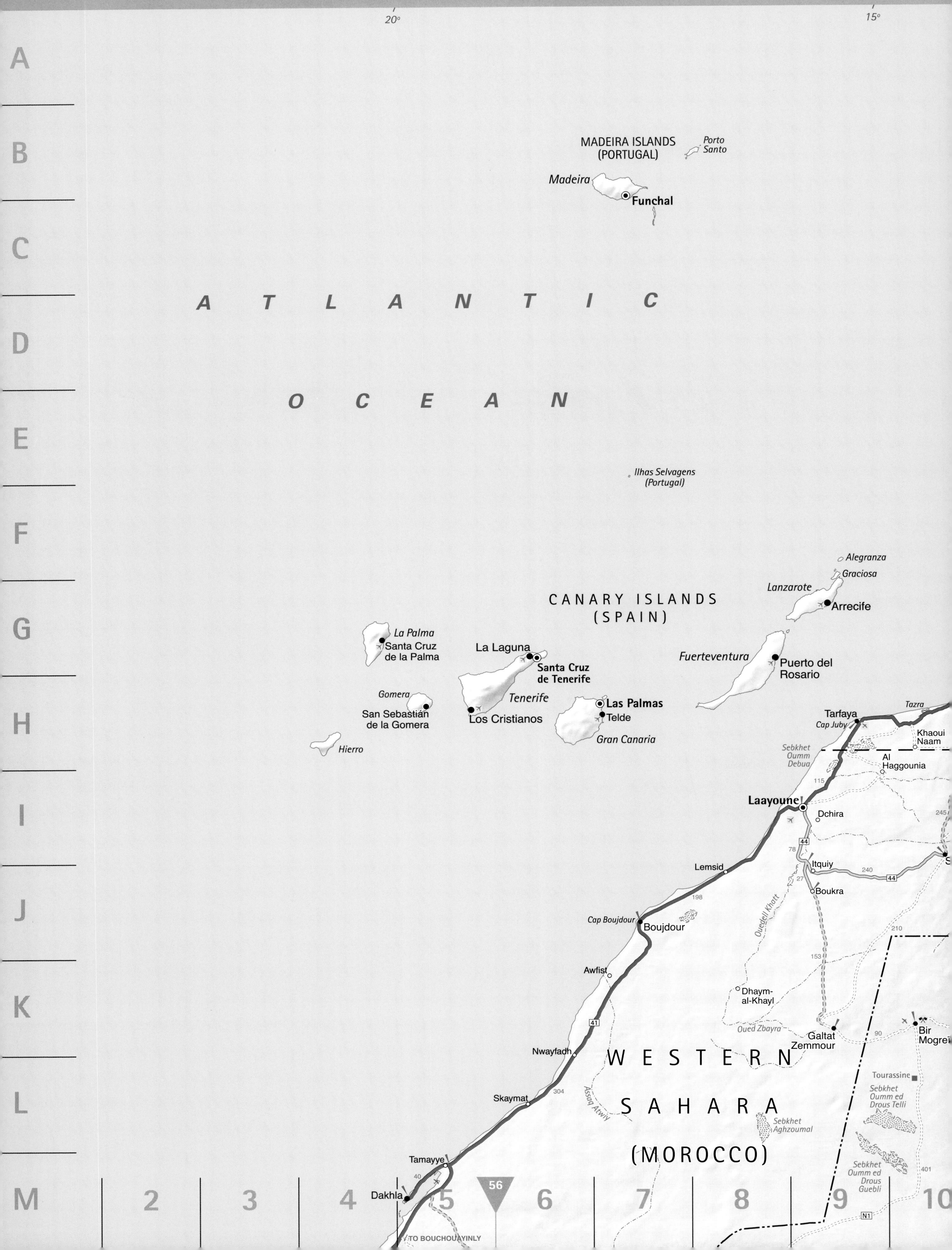

NAIROBI — CAPITAL CITY
Abidjan — SECONDARY CAPITAL CITY When Applicable
Las Palmas — DEPENDANCY CAPITAL
Gweru — LARGE / MAJOR TOWN Over 50,000 people
Ruhengeri — SECONDARY TOWN Between 10,000 & 50,000
El Kadada — SMALL TOWN Between 5,000 &10,000
Chinguetti — LARGE VILLAGE Between 500 & 5,000
Winneba — SMALL VILLAGE OR SETTLEMENT Under 500 people

KM 100
MI 50

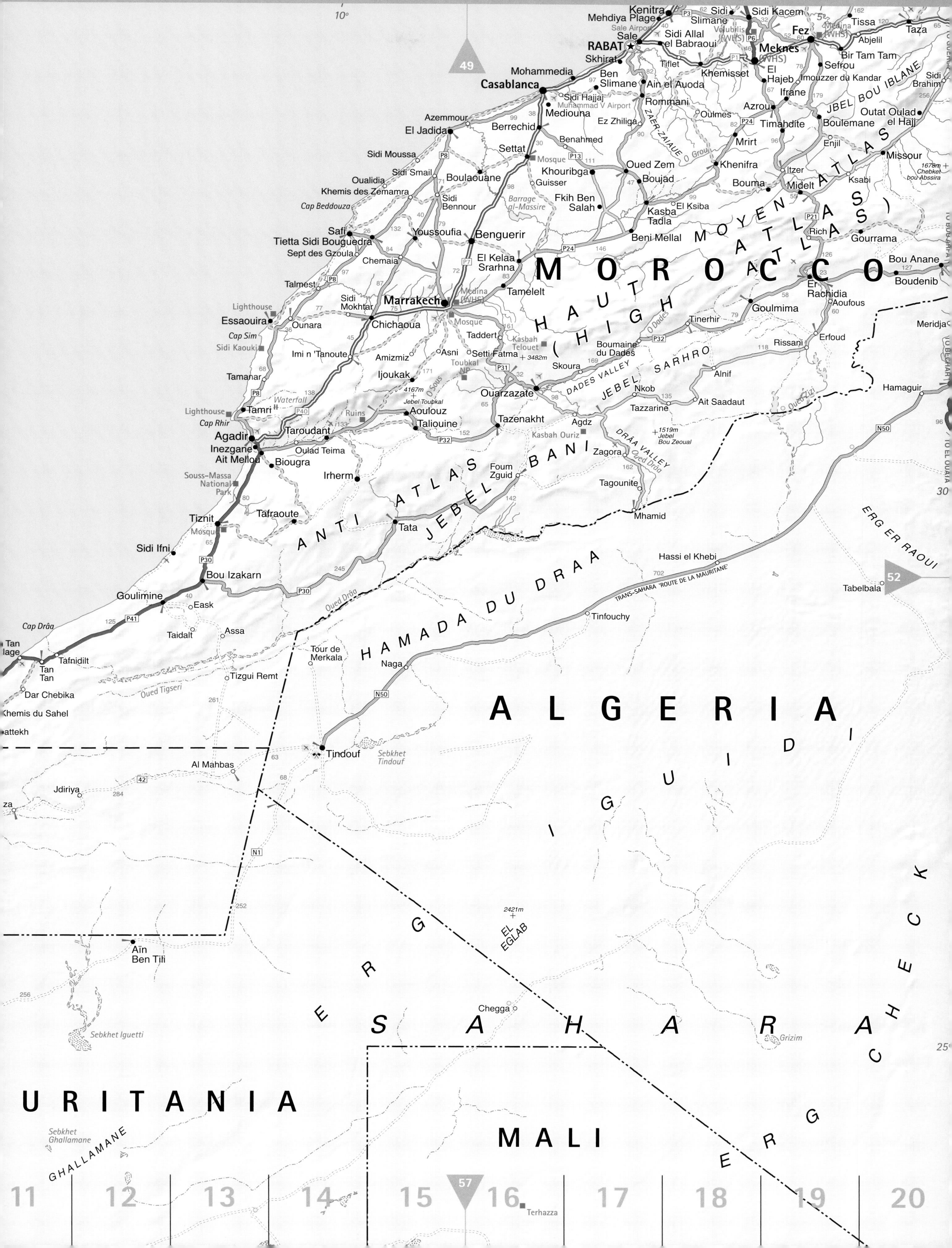

SCENIC ROUTE
MAJOR CONNECTING ROUTE
TARRED UNTARRED
MAIN CONNECTING ROUTE
TARRED UNTARRED
MAIN ROAD
TARRED UNTARRED
MINOR ROAD
4WD ROAD
LOCAL TRACK
HIKING TRAIL
234 NATIONAL ROUTE NUMBER
234 OTHER ROUTE NUMBER
PLACE OF INTEREST

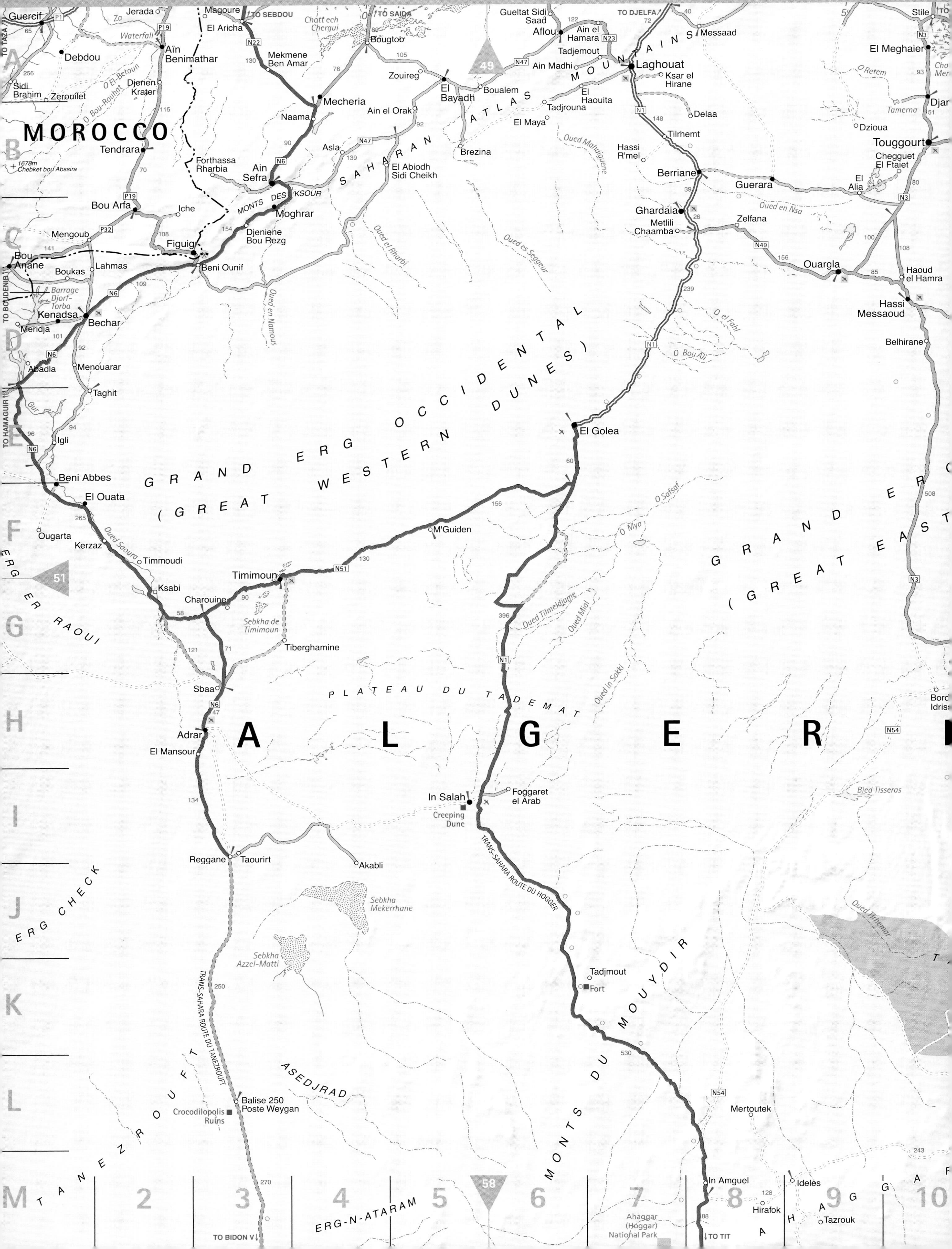

NAIROBI CAPITAL CITY | Abidjan SECONDARY CAPITAL CITY When Applicable | Las Palmas DEPENDANCY CAPITAL | Gweru LARGE / MAJOR TOWN Over 50,000 people | Ruhengeri SECONDARY TOWN Between 10,000 & 50,000 | El Kadada SMALL TOWN Between 5,000 &10,000 | Chinguetti LARGE VILLAGE Between 500 & 5,000 | Winneba SMALL VILLAGE OR SETTLEMENT Under 500 people

KM 100 MI 50

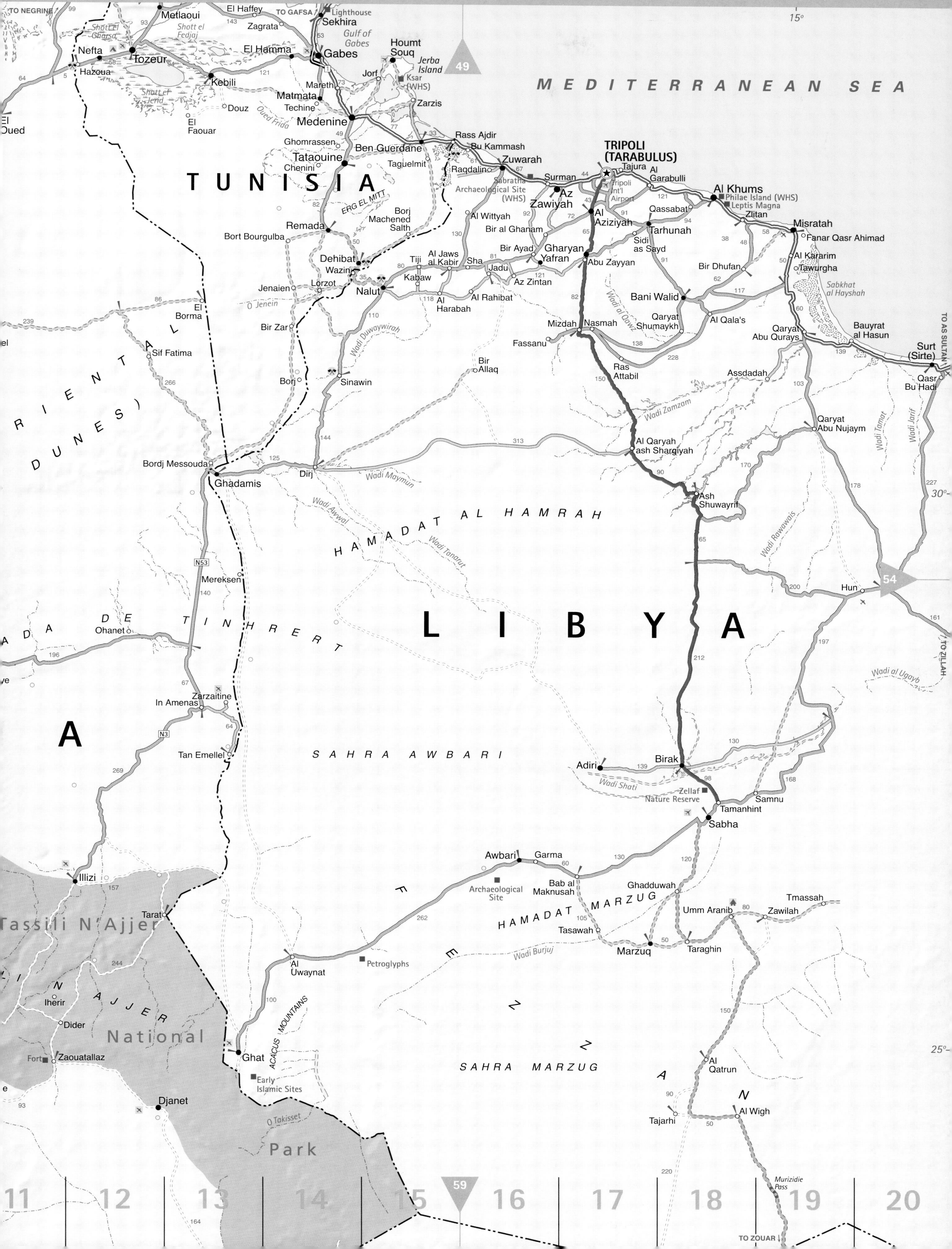

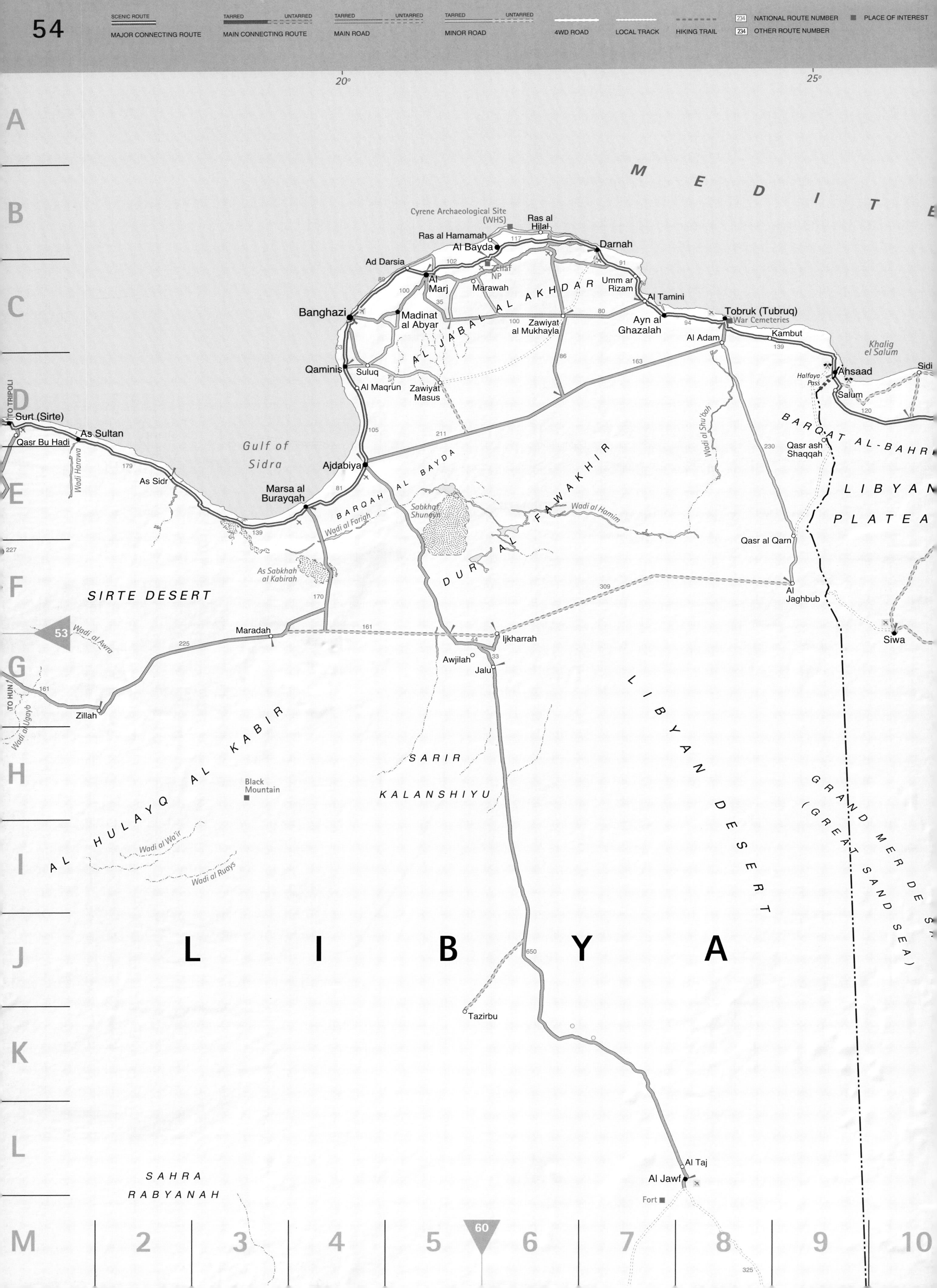
SCENIC ROUTE
MAJOR CONNECTING ROUTE
TARRED UNTARRED
MAIN CONNECTING ROUTE
TARRED UNTARRED
MAIN ROAD
TARRED UNTARRED
MINOR ROAD
4WD ROAD
LOCAL TRACK
HIKING TRAIL
234 NATIONAL ROUTE NUMBER
234 OTHER ROUTE NUMBER
PLACE OF INTEREST
20°
25°
MEDITE
Cyrene Archaeological Site (WHS)
Ras al Hilal
Ras al Hamamah
Al Bayda
Darnah
Ad Darsia
Al Marj
Marawah
Umm ar Rizam
Al Tamini
Banghazi
Madinat al Abyar
AL JABAL AL AKHDAR
Zawiyat al Mukhayla
Ayn al Ghazalah
Tobruk (Tubruq)
War Cemeteries
Al Adam
Kambut
Khalig el Salum
Halfaya Pass
Ahsaad
Salum
Sidi
Qaminis
Suluq
Al Maqrun
Zawiyat Masus
TO TRIPOLI
Surt (Sirte)
As Sultan
Qasr Bu Hadi
Wadi Harawa
Gulf of Sidra
Ajdabiya
As Sidr
Marsa al Burayqah
BARQAH AL BAYDA
Wadi al Farigh
Sabkhat Shunayn
DUR AL FAWAKHIR
Wadi al Hamim
Wadi al Shu'bah
BARQAT AL-BAHR
Qasr ash Shaqqah
LIBYAN PLATEA
Qasr al Qarn
Al Jaghbub
As Sabkhah al Kabirah
SIRTE DESERT
53
Wadi al Awra
Maradah
Ijkharrah
Awjilah
Jalu
Siwa
TO HUN
Wadi al Ugayb
Zillah
LIBYAN DESERT
AL HULAYQ AL KABIR
Black Mountain
SARIR KALANSHIYU
GRAND MER DE S (GREAT SAND SEA)
Wadi al Wa'ir
Wadi al Ruays
LIBYA
Tazirbu
Al Taj
Al Jawf
Fort
SAHRA RABYANAH
60
117 102 91 89 100 35 80 100 94 139 86 163 53 211 105 230 120 81 179 139 227 309 170 161 225 44 33 161 650 325
A B C D E F G H I J K L M
2 3 4 5 6 7 8 9 10

LEBANON
BEIRUT
DAMASCUS
SYRIA
Sea of Galilee
Haifa
Tel Aviv
AMMAN
JERUSALEM
PALESTINIAN AUTHORITY
Dead Sea
Gaza
Beer Sheva
ISRAEL
JORDAN
Pillars of Solomon
Maan
TO TRIPOLI
TO HOMS
TO SAB ABAR
TO QASR AL AZRAQ
TO TABUK
TO JIDDAH
TO BIR SHALATEIN
RANEAN SEA
Matruh
Fuka
El Daba
Sidi Abdarrahman
El Alamein
War Cemetery
Alexandria (El Iskandariya)
Bourg El-Arab
Lake Maryut
Khalig el Arab
El Hammam
Rosetta (Rashid)
Lake Burullus
Lighthouse
Baltim
Lake Idku
Fuwa
Damanhur
Kafr el Sheikh
Shirbin
El Kubra
Dumyat (Damietta)
El Matariya
Port Said
El-Tina Bay
Lake Manzala
SUEZ CANAL
El Mansura
Tanta
Zifta
Abu Kebir
El Salhiya
Zagazig
Ismailia
Romani
El- Arish
Minuf
Benha
Bilbeis
El Khatatba
Wadi Natrun
135m Qarat el Mashruka
163m Mingar el Magabra
185m Gebel Hadid
QATTARA DEPRESSION
Gt. Bitter Lake
Khatmia Pass
Giddi Pass
Mitla Pass
Bir Hasana
Cairo International Airport
El Giza
CAIRO (EL QAHIRA)
Pyramids at Giza Sphinx (WHS)
Helwan
Suez (El Suweis)
Sudr
Nakhl
El Thamad
Elat
Taba
Al Aqabah
Dahshur
Birket Qarun
Sinnuris
Gerza
El Saff
Ain Sukhna
SINAI
Crocodilopolis
El Faiyum
Maimum
Beni Suef
St Anthony's Monastery
Zafarana
Gulf of Suez
Coloured Canyon
Nuweiba
Gulf of Aqaba
Sitra
Biba
El Fashn
St Paul's Monastery
Abu Durba
Gebel Musa 2285m
St Catherine's Monastery
Ras Abu Gallum NP
SAUDI ARABIA
Al Jadidah
Bawiti
Maghagha
Beni Mazar
Samalut
483m Khasm el Raqaba
Ras Gharib
Wadi el Tarfa
EGYPT
El Minya
Beni Hasan (Rock Tombs)
Northern Tombs
Southern Tombs
El Ashmunein
Mallawi
EASTERN
Tiran & Sanafir Islands Protectorate
Sharm el Sheikh
Ras Mohammed National Park
Ras Mohammed
Ras al Ushsh
Gez Shadwan
GHARD ABU MUHARIK
Nile
Abnub
Manfalut
Asyut
Hurghada
RED SEA
Qasr Farafra
WESTERN
Abu Tig
Tahta
El Badari
Antaeopolis
Wadi Qena
DESERT
Bur Safaga
Akhmim
Sohag
El Araba el Madfuna
Temples of Sethos I & Ramses II
Dishna
Temple of Hathor
Qena
Bir Seiyala
Quseir
Qift
Qus
Valley of the Kings & Queens
Necropolis of Thebes (WHS)
Karnak
Luxor
Armant
El Rizeiqat
El Bayadiya
El Idisat
697m Gebel el Shalul
Hibis Archaeological Site
El Qasr
Tombs
Balat
Tunaydah
Mut
El Kharga
Aphroditopolis
El Deir
Isna
El Mahamid
El Basaliya Qibli
El Kanayis
Marsa Alam
Idfu
Temple of Horus
El Kanayis Temple
El Gaga
Baris
Dush
ABU BALLAS
El Nasser
Kom Ombo
1st Cataract
Tombs of the Nobles
Aswan
Elephantine Island
Aswan High Dam
Kalabsha Temple
BAB EL KALABSHA
Lake Nasser
TO ABU SIMBEL
Bir Quleib
30°
35°
25°
63
61
11
12
13
14
15
16
17
18
19
20

SCENIC ROUTE — MAJOR CONNECTING ROUTE
TARRED / UNTARRED — MAIN CONNECTING ROUTE
TARRED / UNTARRED — MAIN ROAD
TARRED / UNTARRED — MINOR ROAD
4WD ROAD
LOCAL TRACK
HIKING TRAIL
234 NATIONAL ROUTE NUMBER
234 OTHER ROUTE NUMBER
■ PLACE OF INTEREST

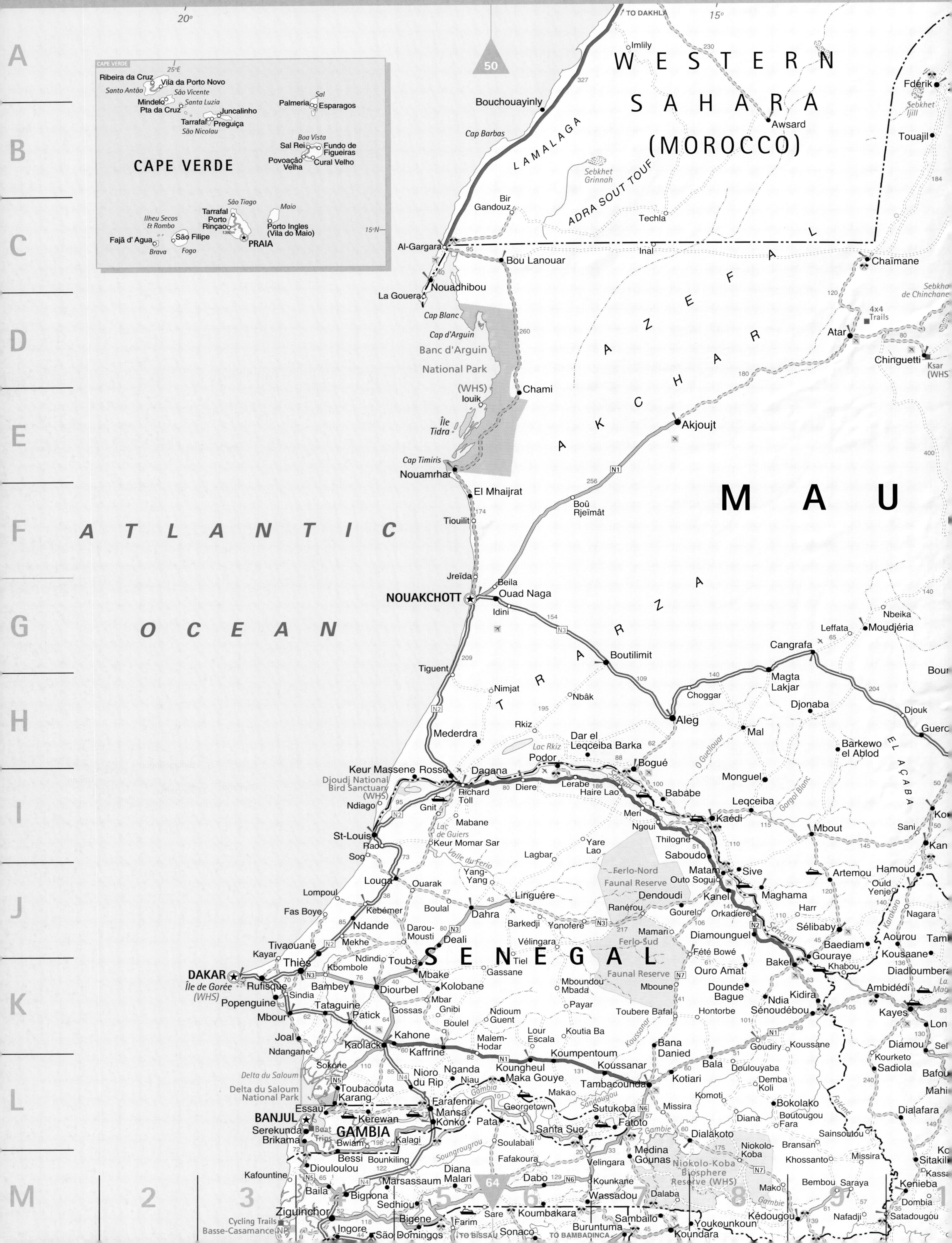

NAIROBI CAPITAL CITY | Abidjan SECONDARY CAPITAL CITY When Applicable | Las Palmas DEPENDANCY CAPITAL | Gweru LARGE / MAJOR TOWN Over 50,000 people | Ruhengeri SECONDARY TOWN Between 10,000 & 50,000 | El Kadada SMALL TOWN Between 5,000 &10,000 | Chinguetti LARGE VILLAGE Between 500 & 5,000 | Winneba SMALL VILLAGE OR SETTLEMENT Under 500 people

KM 100 MI 50

SCENIC ROUTE / MAJOR CONNECTING ROUTE · TARRED / UNTARRED MAIN CONNECTING ROUTE · TARRED / UNTARRED MAIN ROAD · TARRED / UNTARRED MINOR ROAD · 4WD ROAD · LOCAL TRACK · HIKING TRAIL · 234 NATIONAL ROUTE NUMBER · 234 OTHER ROUTE NUMBER · PLACE OF INTEREST

NAIROBI CAPITAL CITY | Abidjan SECONDARY CAPITAL CITY When Applicable | Las Palmas DEPENDANCY CAPITAL | Gweru LARGE / MAJOR TOWN Over 50,000 people | Ruhengeri SECONDARY TOWN Between 10,000 & 50,000 | El Kadada SMALL TOWN Between 5,000 &10,000 | Chinguetti LARGE VILLAGE Between 500 & 5,000 | Winneba SMALL VILLAGE OR SETTLEMENT Under 500 people

KM 100 MI 50

SCENIC ROUTE — MAJOR CONNECTING ROUTE · TARRED / UNTARRED — MAIN CONNECTING ROUTE · TARRED / UNTARRED — MAIN ROAD · TARRED / UNTARRED — MINOR ROAD · 4WD ROAD · LOCAL TRACK · HIKING TRAIL · 234 NATIONAL ROUTE NUMBER · 234 OTHER ROUTE NUMBER · ■ PLACE OF INTEREST

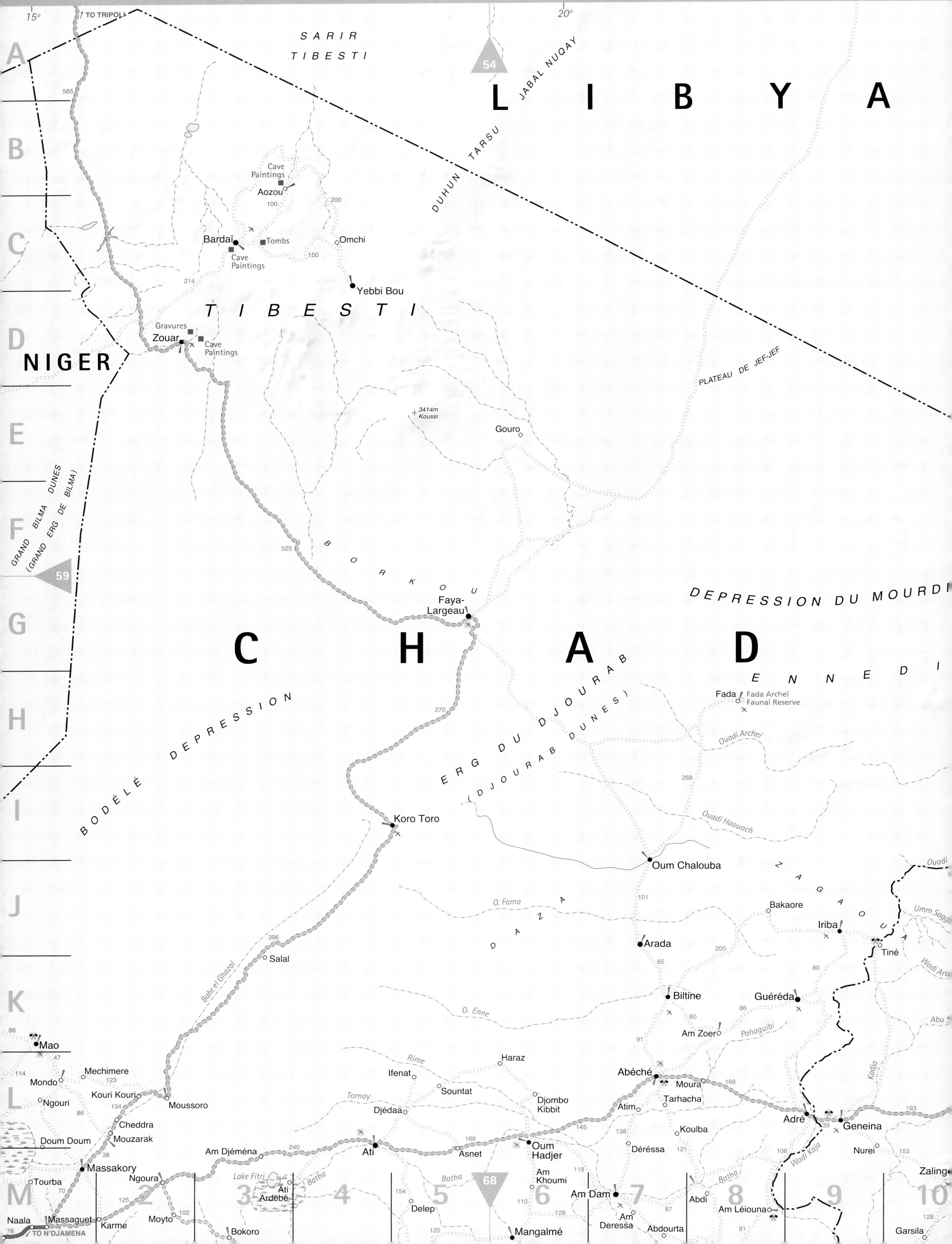

NAIROBI — CAPITAL CITY | Abidjan — SECONDARY CAPITAL CITY When Applicable | Las Palmas — DEPENDANCY CAPITAL | Gweru — LARGE / MAJOR TOWN Over 50,000 people | Ruhengeri — SECONDARY TOWN Between 10,000 & 50,000 | El Kadada — SMALL TOWN Between 5,000 &10,000 | Chinguetti — LARGE VILLAGE Between 500 & 5,000 | Winneba — SMALL VILLAGE OR SETTLEMENT Under 500 people

KM 100 MI 50

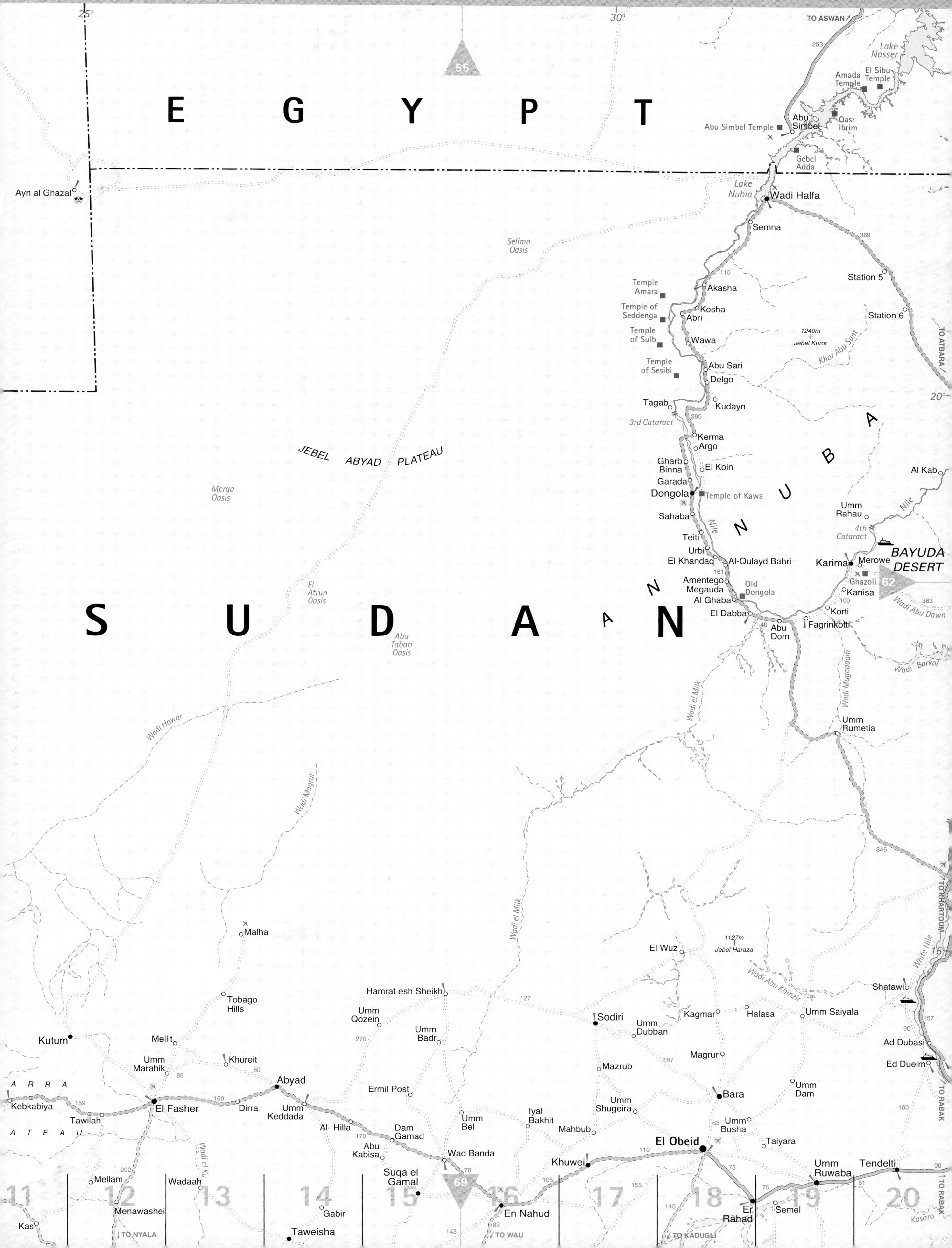

SCENIC ROUTE — MAJOR CONNECTING ROUTE
TARRED / UNTARRED — MAIN CONNECTING ROUTE
TARRED / UNTARRED — MAIN ROAD
TARRED / UNTARRED — MINOR ROAD
4WD ROAD
LOCAL TRACK
HIKING TRAIL
234 NATIONAL ROUTE NUMBER
234 OTHER ROUTE NUMBER
■ PLACE OF INTEREST

NAIROBI CAPITAL CITY | Abidjan SECONDARY CAPITAL CITY When Applicable | Las Palmas DEPENDANCY CAPITAL | Gweru LARGE / MAJOR TOWN Over 50,000 people | Ruhengeri SECONDARY TOWN Between 10,000 & 50,000 | El Kadada SMALL TOWN Between 5,000 &10,000 | Chinguetti LARGE VILLAGE Between 500 & 5,000 | Winneba SMALL VILLAGE OR SETTLEMENT Under 500 people

KM 100 MI 50

SCENIC ROUTE — MAJOR CONNECTING ROUTE
TARRED / UNTARRED — MAIN CONNECTING ROUTE
TARRED / UNTARRED — MAIN ROAD
TARRED / UNTARRED — MINOR ROAD
4WD ROAD
LOCAL TRACK
HIKING TRAIL
234 NATIONAL ROUTE NUMBER
234 OTHER ROUTE NUMBER
PLACE OF INTEREST

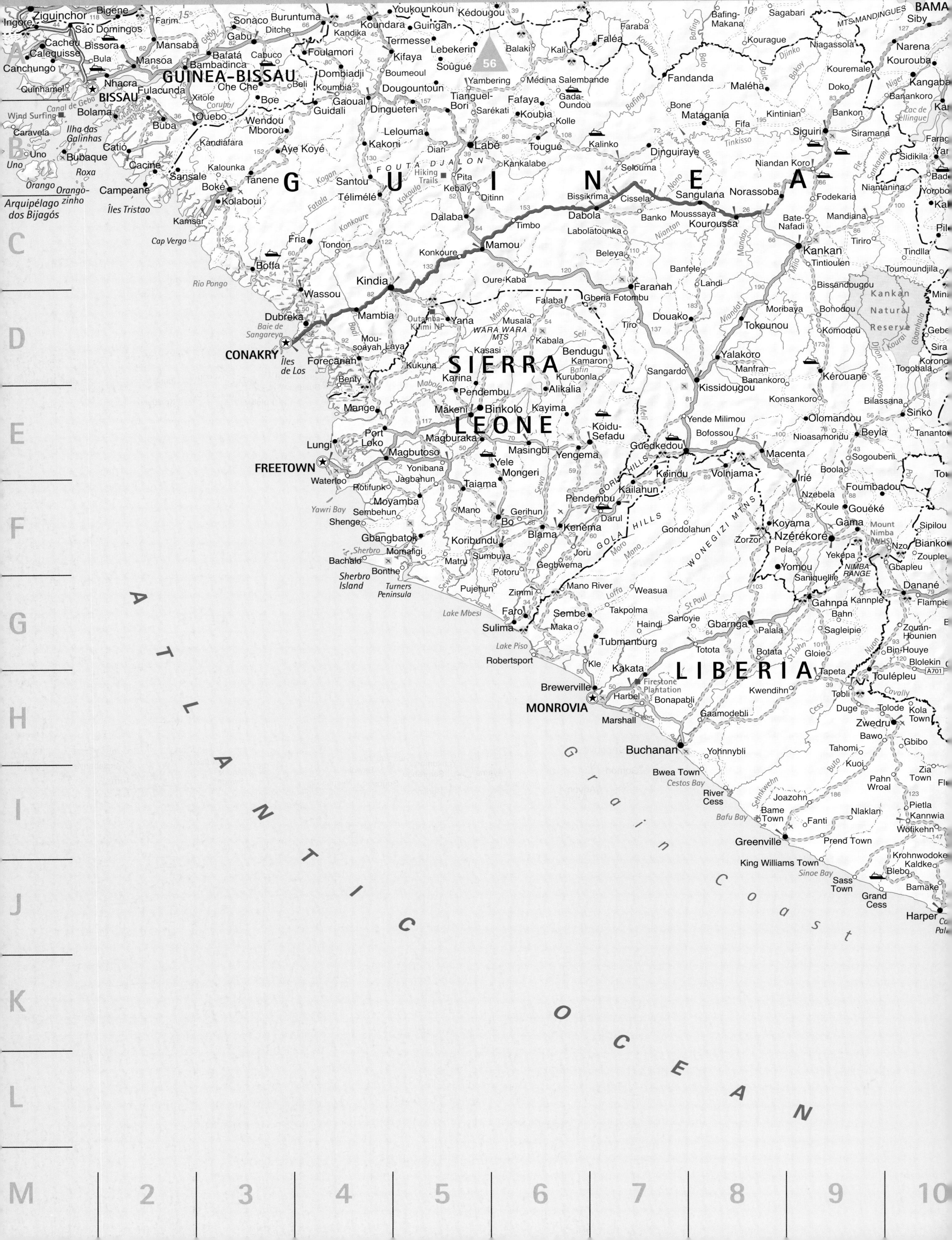

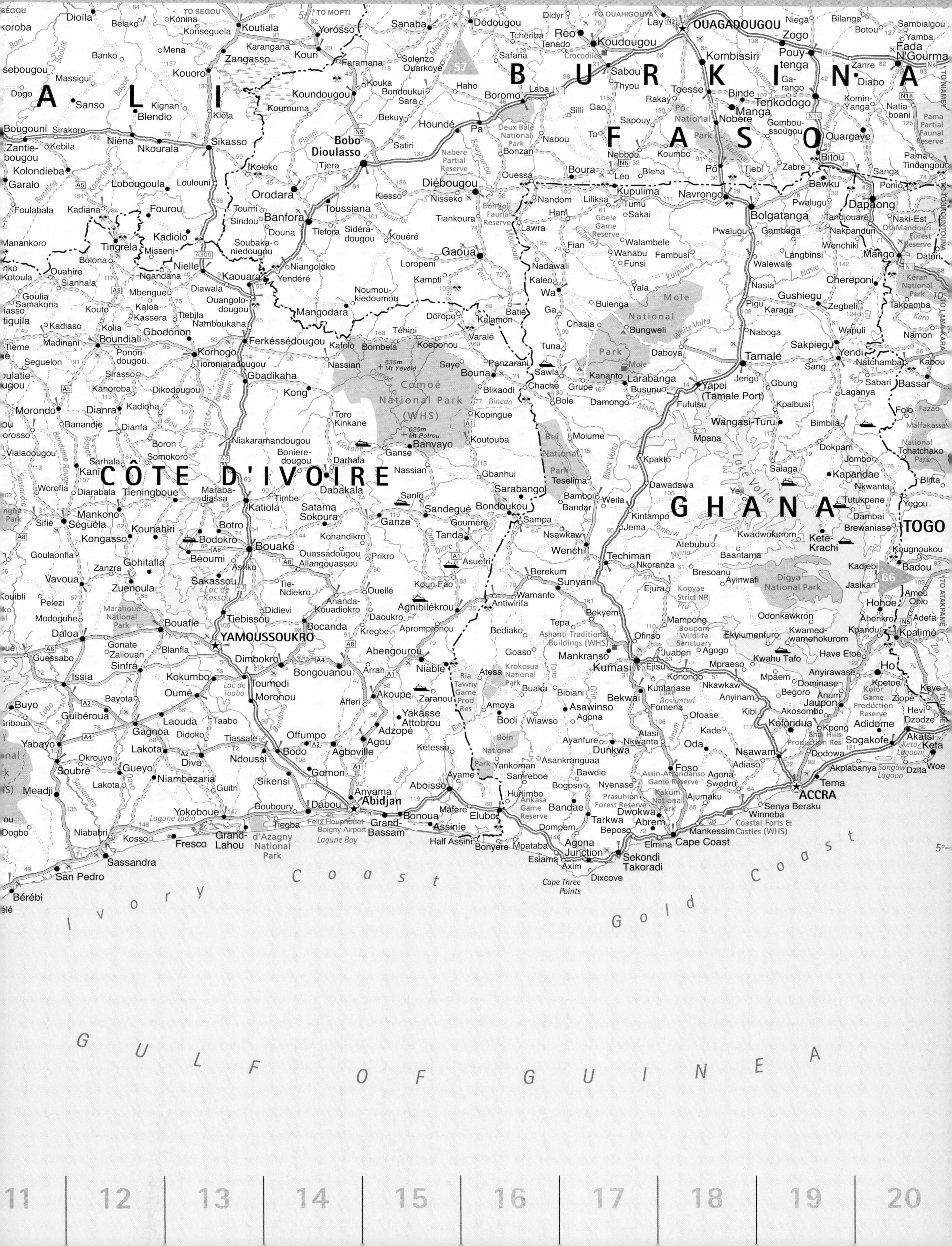

M A L I
B U R K I N A F A S O
CÔTE D'IVOIRE
GHANA
TOGO
G U L F O F G U I N E A
Ivory Coast
Gold Coast
OUAGADOUGOU
Koudougou
Bobo Dioulasso
Banfora
Orodara
Gaoua
Diébougou
Boromo
Houndé
Dédougou
Reo
Kombissiri
Manga
Tenkodogo
Zogo
Pouytenga
Fada N'Gourma
Diabo
Ouargaye
Bitou
Pô
Léo
Sapouy
Dapaong
Mango
Koutiala
Sikasso
Kadiolo
Zangasso
Koundougou
Sanaba
Yorosso
Korhogo
Ferkéssédougou
Katiola
Bouaké
YAMOUSSOUKRO
Abidjan
Grand-Bassam
Dabou
Tiassalé
Agboville
Abengourou
Bondoukou
Bouna
Séguéla
Daloa
Bouaflé
Gagnoa
Divo
Lakota
Soubré
Sassandra
San Pedro
Grand-Lahou
Fresco
Dimbokro
Bongouanou
Tanda
Dabakala
Boundiali
Odienné
Tingréla
Kong
Comoé National Park (WHS)
Bolgatanga
Navrongo
Tamale
Yapei (Tamale Port)
Wa
Bole
Damongo
Larabanga
Mole National Park
Salaga
Yeji
Kintampo
Techiman
Wenchi
Sunyani
Berekum
Kumasi
Ejisu
Mampong
Obuasi
Dunkwa
Konongo
Nkawkaw
Koforidua
ACCRA
Tema
Winneba
Cape Coast
Elmina
Sekondi Takoradi
Axim
Tarkwa
Ho
Kpalimé
Hohoe
Keta
Akatsi
Ada
Kete-Krachi
Kpandu
Yendi
Bimbila
Lake Volta
Digya National Park
Kakum National Park
Bui National Park
Half Assini
Elubo
Aboisso
Bonoua
Assinie
Cape Three Points
Dixcove
Senya Beraku
Nsawam
Akosombo
Sogakofe
Dzodze
Badou
Atakpamé
57
66
11 12 13 14 15 16 17 18 19 20

SCENIC ROUTE — MAJOR CONNECTING ROUTE
TARRED / UNTARRED — MAIN CONNECTING ROUTE
TARRED / UNTARRED — MAIN ROAD
TARRED / UNTARRED — MINOR ROAD
4WD ROAD
LOCAL TRACK
HIKING TRAIL
234 NATIONAL ROUTE NUMBER
234 OTHER ROUTE NUMBER
PLACE OF INTEREST

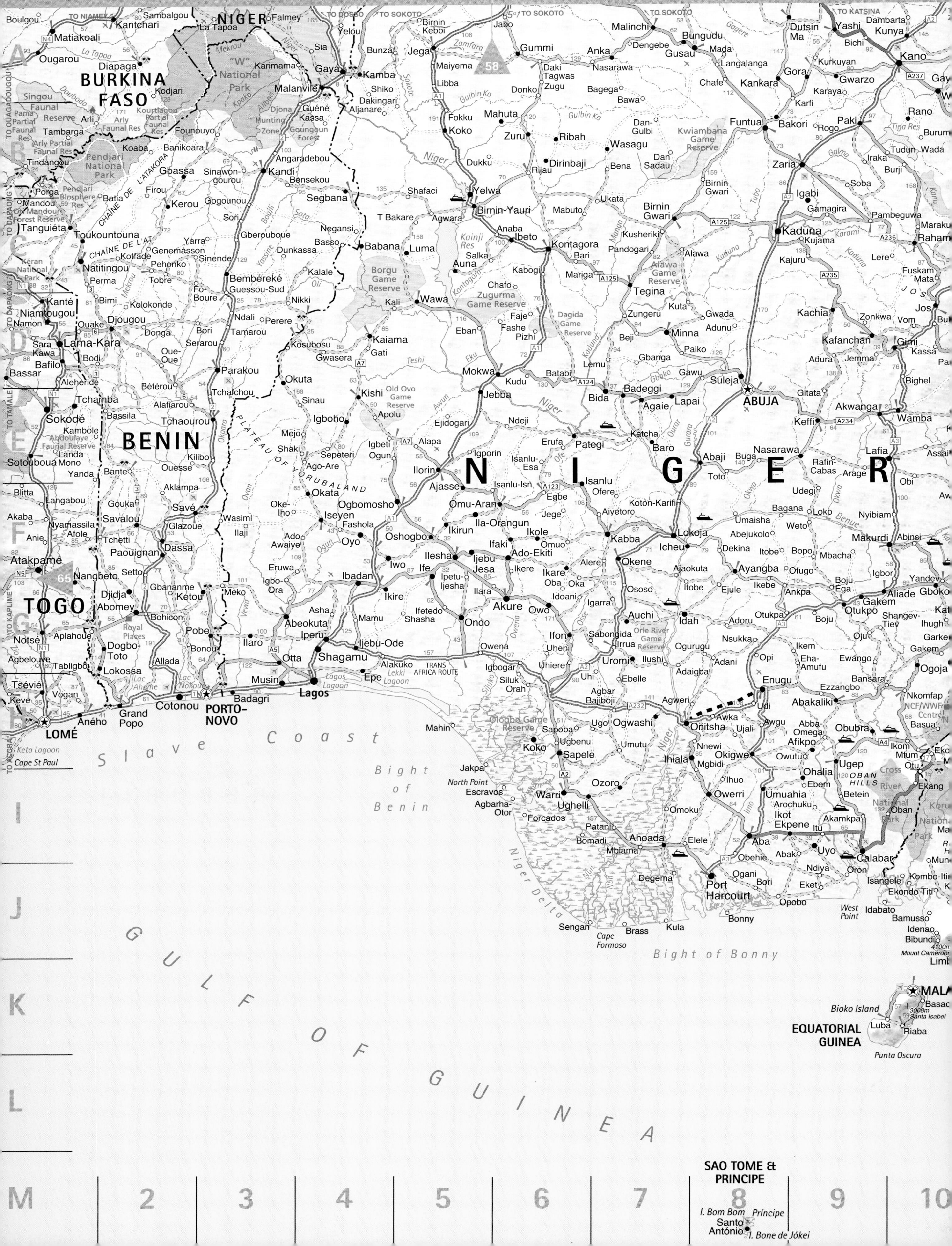

A B C D E F G H I J K L M
2 3 4 5 6 7 8 9 10

NAIROBI CAPITAL CITY | Abidjan SECONDARY CAPITAL CITY When Applicable | Las Palmas DEPENDANCY CAPITAL | Gweru LARGE / MAJOR TOWN Over 50,000 people | Ruhengeri SECONDARY TOWN Between 10,000 & 50,000 | El Kadada SMALL TOWN Between 5,000 &10,000 | Chinguetti LARGE VILLAGE Between 500 & 5,000 | Winneba SMALL VILLAGE OR SETTLEMENT Under 500 people

KM 100
MI 50

SCENIC ROUTE — MAJOR CONNECTING ROUTE
TARRED / UNTARRED — MAIN CONNECTING ROUTE
TARRED / UNTARRED — MAIN ROAD
TARRED / UNTARRED — MINOR ROAD
4WD ROAD
LOCAL TRACK
HIKING TRAIL
234 NATIONAL ROUTE NUMBER
234 OTHER ROUTE NUMBER
PLACE OF INTEREST

KORDOFAN
NUBA MOUNTAINS
U D A N
SUDAN
HR EL GHAZAL
ETHIOPIA
UGANDA
HAUT-ZAÏRE
TO EL OBEID
TO KHARTOUM
TO WAD MEDANI
TO GHIMBI
TO GORE
TO LODWAR
TO BAFWASENDE
TO KISANGANI
TO KASENYE
TO NAKASONGOLA
TO MBALE
El Odaiya
Abu Zabad
Dilling
Kortala
Karling
Rashad
Delami
El Lagowa
Babanusa
Muglad
Kadugli
Talodi
Heiban
Abu Gubeiha
Abu Hashim
Tosi
Qurayd
Renk
Ed Damazin
Al Barun
Kukur
Bobuk
Kambal
Bigori
Agaru
Kayli
Kurmuk
Ulu
Shaykh Gok
Tingya
Paloich
Abaiat
Ban Donige
Kungila
Asosa
Belgo
Fama
Kodok
Aboke
Malakal
Taufikia
Tonga
Wunagak
Kan
Abwong
Ding Ding
Nasir
Jokau
Gambela
Gambella National Park
Abebo
Gog
Akobo
Bambesi
Begi
Daga Post
Gidami
Waat
Ayod
Fathai
Fatitet
Duk Faiwil
Fangak
Bentiu
Puig
Lake No
Rangnom
Umm Sagura
Tungaru
Qurdud
Turda
Gabras
Safaha
As-Sumay
Naam
Abyei
El Melemm
Wer Ping
Mashar
Nyamlell
Madol
Aweil
Gogrial
Aluk
Ghama
Kangi
Kajok
Dugdug
Gadein
Akop
Meshra er Req
Wun Shwai
Adok
Atiedo
Agwok
Madier
Gunna
Bisellia
Wau
Kawajena
Bir Di
Wal Athiang
Tonj
Peili
Gemmeiza
Kashwal
Rumbek
Southern National Park
Akot
Lol
Aluakluak
Yirol
Madbar
Mvolo
Dogoba
Shambe
Alel
Nyiel
Bor
Malek
Minkamman
Tali Post
Gemmeiza
Lamindo
Terakeka
Amadi
Mundri
Rokom
Mongalla
Medi
Juba
Ngangala
Pibor Post
Pochala
Akelo
Lopaye
Lodein
Toworth
Kenamuke Swamp
Kasangor
Nangolet
Kapoeta
Nagpotpot
Loming
Torit
Lobira
Nagichot
Ikoto
Lokichokio
Kidepo Valley National Park
Lopodi
Agoro
Madi Opei
Naam Okora
Apoka
Kaabong
Koputh
Loyoro
Orom
Kotido
Panyangara
Matheniko Game Reserve
Gatanga
Tambura
Obo
Bassigbiri
Bambouti
Selim
Ezo
Bokoko
Ukwatutu
Doruma
Bire Kpatua GR
Nzara
Yambio
Mbarizunga GR
Bakordi
Maridi
Ibba
Garmabe
Mendopolo
Garamba National Park (WHS)
Babia
Berebuda
Mandoro
Duru
Bangadi
Pilipili
Togo
Gangale
Faradje
Aba
Yei
Loga
Lalyo
Gobur
Araka
Sirsiri
Nimule National Park
Nimule
Moyo
Laropi
Morobo
Oraba
Yumbe
Koboko
Arua
Ajai Game Reserve
Rhino Camp
Okollo
Mutir
Pakelle
Atiak
Padibe
Kitgum
Acholibur
Paimol
Pajule
Gulu
Bobi
Patongo
Adilang
Alerek
Wiawer
Niangara
Amadi
Mangada
Makilimbo
Dungu
Denge
Sesenge
Dingba
Tibo
Gabu
Dili
Baranga
Tapili
Ndedu
Nzopi
Makoro
Poko
Rungu
Mawa-Geti
Ngina
Wanga
Watsa
Dubela
Adranga
Maie
Aru
Mava
Egbunda
Isiro
Penge
Gao
Gombari
Arebi
Maituri
Djalasiga
Mambunga
Betongwe
Vube
Andudu
Mungbere
Ngoa
Arumbi
Pawa
Medje
Babonde
Wamba
Matete
Mboro
Bula
Akokora
Mangbiwalu
Goli
Mahagi
Nioka
Mahagi Port
Fataki
Pakwach
Wangkwar Gate
Murchison Falls Nat. Park
Karuma Game Reserve
Bulisa
Wairingo Gate
Rabongo
Kitwanga
Butiaba
Biso
Masindi
Kihande Palace
Nakitoma
Lalem
Anyeke
Ogur
Lira
Atura
Apac
Aduka
Kaberamaido
Ocheró
Soroti
Serere
Kumi
Orumo
Aloi
Omoro
Kuju
Amuria
Dokolo
Wera
Katakwi
Bokora Game Reserve
Iriri
Nabilatuk
Pian Upe Game Reserve
Chepsikunya
Kokeris
Turutoko
Marakesa
Chutes Akambo Falls
Okapi National Park
Bomili
Nizi
Bunia
Blukwa
Kaisu
Lake Albert
White Nile
Blue Nile
Bahr el Arab
Bahr el Jebel (White Nile)
Mountain Nile
Sobat
Pibor
Akobo
Dinder National Park
Roseires Dam
Al Garef
Wad an Nail
J Bozi
J Mazmum
Ar-Ruat
Sharafa
Haskanit
Ghabeish
Wad Hassib
Bukhit
Abu Gabra
Gharig
1325m
1697m Mogila
2795m Lotuke
3187m Mt Kinyeti
1594m Nyeri
1292m Rabongo
11 12 13 14 15 16 17 18 19 20
61
70
74

SCENIC ROUTE · MAJOR CONNECTING ROUTE · TARRED · UNTARRED · MAIN CONNECTING ROUTE · TARRED · UNTARRED · MAIN ROAD · TARRED · UNTARRED · MINOR ROAD · 4WD ROAD · LOCAL TRACK · HIKING TRAIL · 234 NATIONAL ROUTE NUMBER · 234 OTHER ROUTE NUMBER · PLACE OF INTEREST

NAIROBI — CAPITAL CITY
Abidjan — SECONDARY CAPITAL CITY When Applicable
Las Palmas — DEPENDANCY CAPITAL
Gweru — LARGE / MAJOR TOWN Over 50,000 people
Ruhengeri — SECONDARY TOWN Between 10,000 & 50,000
El Kadada — SMALL TOWN Between 5,000 &10,000
Chinguetti — LARGE VILLAGE Between 500 & 5,000
Winneba — SMALL VILLAGE OR SETTLEMENT Under 500 people

KM 100 / MI 50

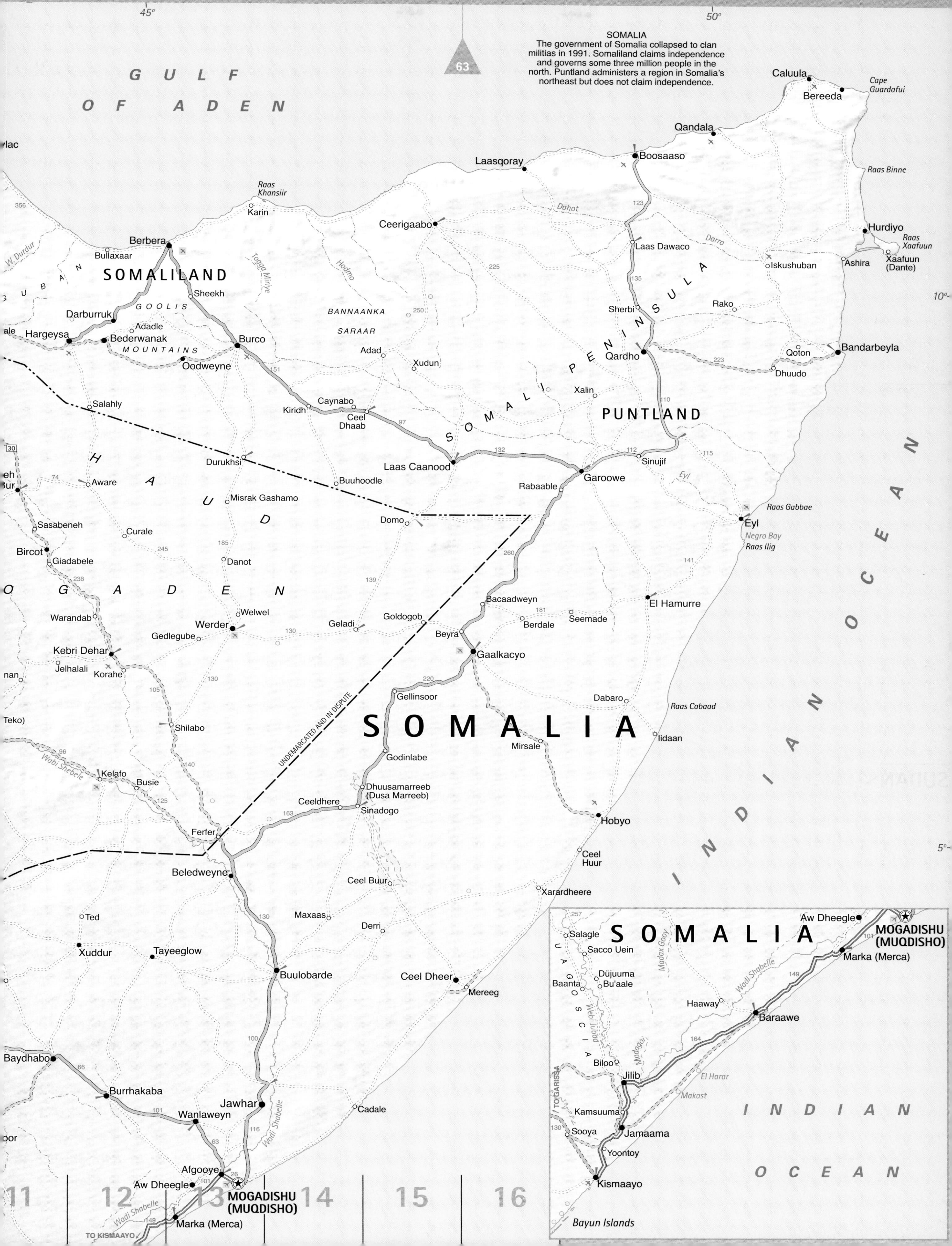

SCENIC ROUTE — MAJOR CONNECTING ROUTE
TARRED / UNTARRED — MAIN CONNECTING ROUTE
TARRED / UNTARRED — MAIN ROAD
TARRED / UNTARRED — MINOR ROAD
4WD ROAD
LOCAL TRACK
HIKING TRAIL
234 NATIONAL ROUTE NUMBER
234 OTHER ROUTE NUMBER
■ PLACE OF INTEREST

NAIROBI CAPITAL CITY · Abidjan SECONDARY CAPITAL CITY When Applicable · Las Palmas DEPENDANCY CAPITAL · Gweru LARGE / MAJOR TOWN Over 50,000 people · Ruhengeri SECONDARY TOWN Between 10,000 & 50,000 · El Kadada SMALL TOWN Between 5,000 &10,000 · Chinguetti LARGE VILLAGE Between 500 & 5,000 · Winneba SMALL VILLAGE OR SETTLEMENT Under 500 people

KM 100 MI 50

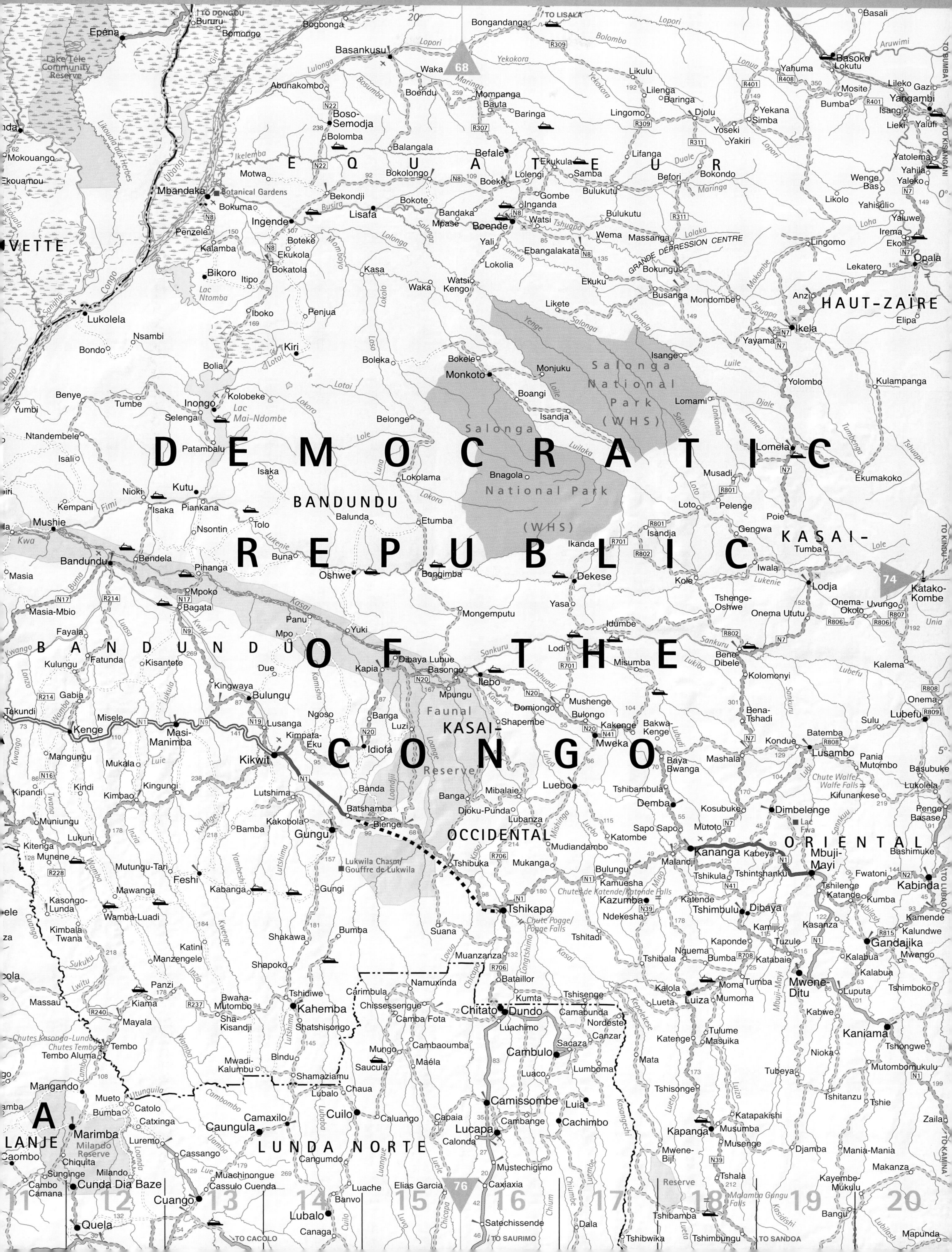

SCENIC ROUTE / MAJOR CONNECTING ROUTE — TARRED / UNTARRED MAIN CONNECTING ROUTE — TARRED / UNTARRED MAIN ROAD — TARRED / UNTARRED MINOR ROAD — 4WD ROAD — LOCAL TRACK — HIKING TRAIL — 234 NATIONAL ROUTE NUMBER — 234 OTHER ROUTE NUMBER — ■ PLACE OF INTEREST

NAIROBI — CAPITAL CITY
Abidjan — SECONDARY CAPITAL CITY When Applicable
Las Palmas — DEPENDANCY CAPITAL
Gweru — LARGE / MAJOR TOWN Over 50,000 people
Ruhengeri — SECONDARY TOWN Between 10,000 & 50,000
El Kadada — SMALL TOWN Between 5,000 &10,000
Chinguetti — LARGE VILLAGE Between 500 & 5,000
Winneba — SMALL VILLAGE OR SETTLEMENT Under 500 people

KM 100
MI 50

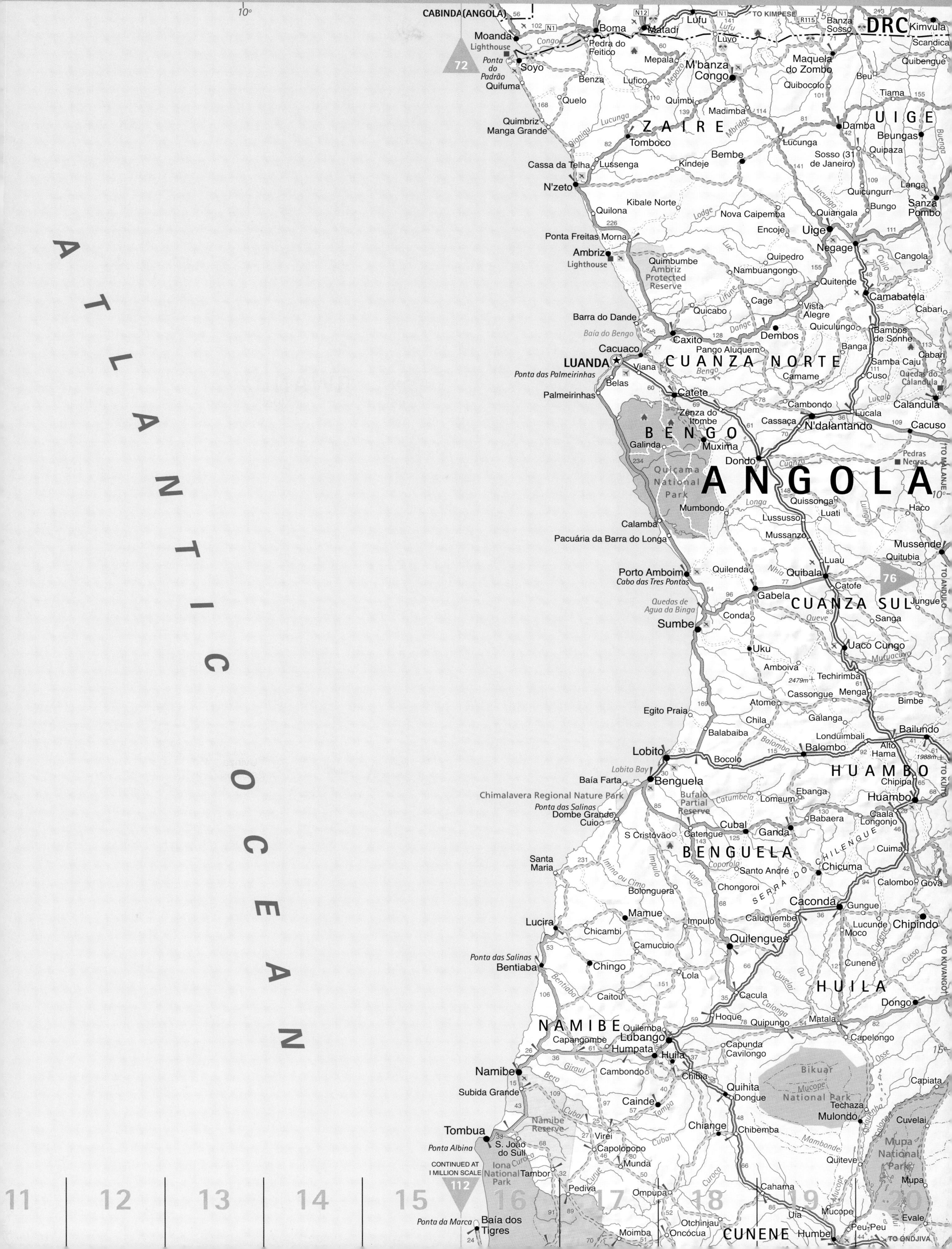

SCENIC ROUTE — MAJOR CONNECTING ROUTE
TARRED / UNTARRED — MAIN CONNECTING ROUTE
TARRED / UNTARRED — MAIN ROAD
TARRED / UNTARRED — MINOR ROAD
4WD ROAD
LOCAL TRACK
HIKING TRAIL
234 NATIONAL ROUTE NUMBER
234 OTHER ROUTE NUMBER
PLACE OF INTEREST

NAIROBI — CAPITAL CITY
Abidjan — SECONDARY CAPITAL CITY When Applicable
Las Palmas — DEPENDANCY CAPITAL
Gweru — LARGE / MAJOR TOWN Over 50,000 people
Ruhengeri — SECONDARY TOWN Between 10,000 & 50,000
El Kadada — SMALL TOWN Between 5,000 &10,000
Chinguetti — LARGE VILLAGE Between 500 & 5,000
Winneba — SMALL VILLAGE OR SETTLEMENT Under 500 people

KM 100
MI 50

SCENIC ROUTE — MAJOR CONNECTING ROUTE | TARRED / UNTARRED — MAIN CONNECTING ROUTE | TARRED / UNTARRED — MAIN ROAD | TARRED / UNTARRED — MINOR ROAD | 4WD ROAD | LOCAL TRACK | HIKING TRAIL | 234 NATIONAL ROUTE NUMBER | 234 OTHER ROUTE NUMBER | ■ PLACE OF INTEREST

NAIROBI CAPITAL CITY | Abidjan SECONDARY CAPITAL CITY When Applicable | Las Palmas DEPENDANCY CAPITAL | Gweru LARGE / MAJOR TOWN Over 50,000 people | Ruhengeri SECONDARY TOWN Between 10,000 & 50,000 | El Kadada SMALL TOWN Between 5,000 &10,000 | Chinguetti LARGE VILLAGE Between 500 & 5,000 | Winneba SMALL VILLAGE OR SETTLEMENT Under 500 people

KM 30 MI 20

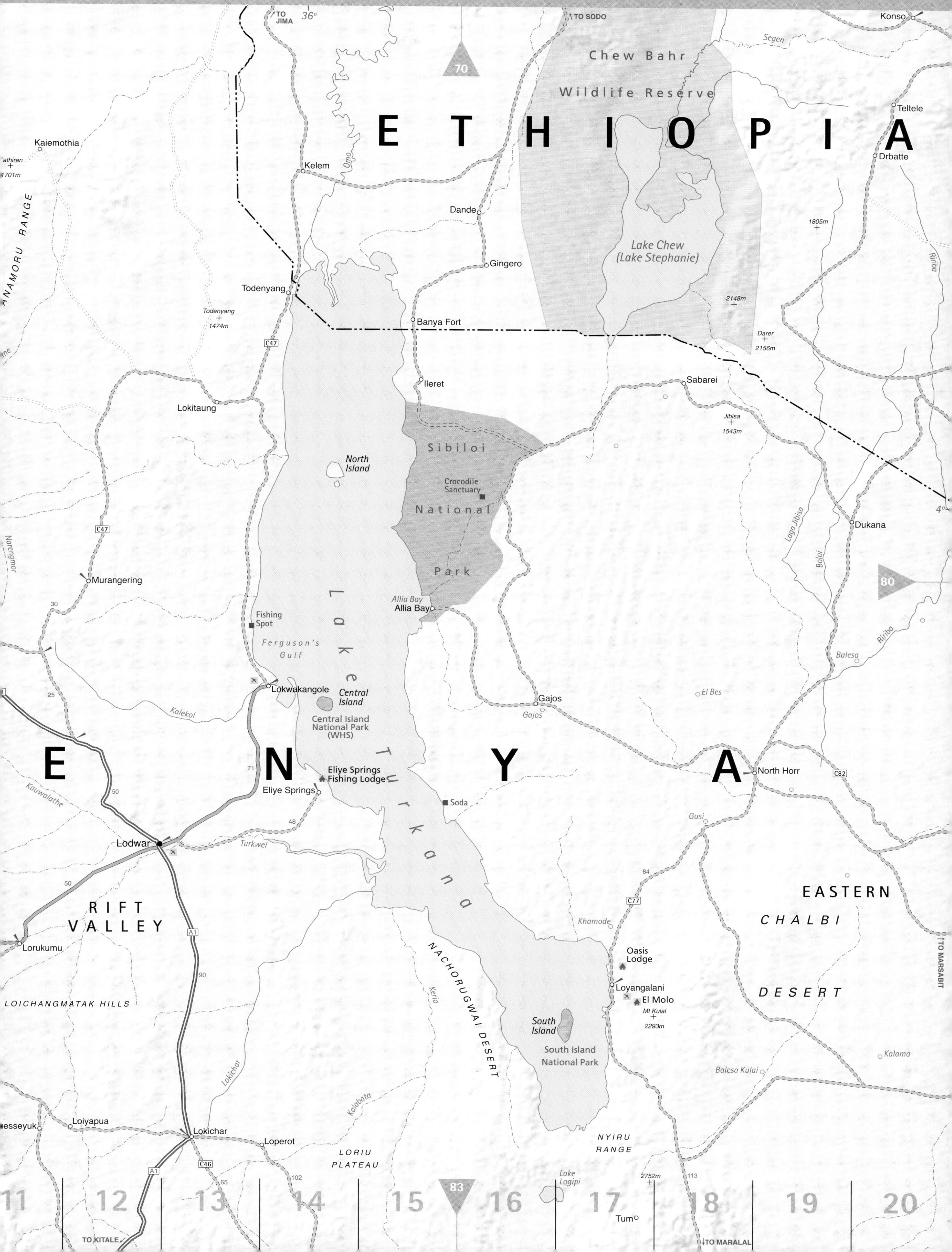

SCENIC ROUTE MAJOR CONNECTING ROUTE
TARRED UNTARRED MAIN CONNECTING ROUTE
TARRED UNTARRED MAIN ROAD
TARRED UNTARRED MINOR ROAD
4WD ROAD
LOCAL TRACK
HIKING TRAIL
234 NATIONAL ROUTE NUMBER
234 OTHER ROUTE NUMBER
PLACE OF INTEREST

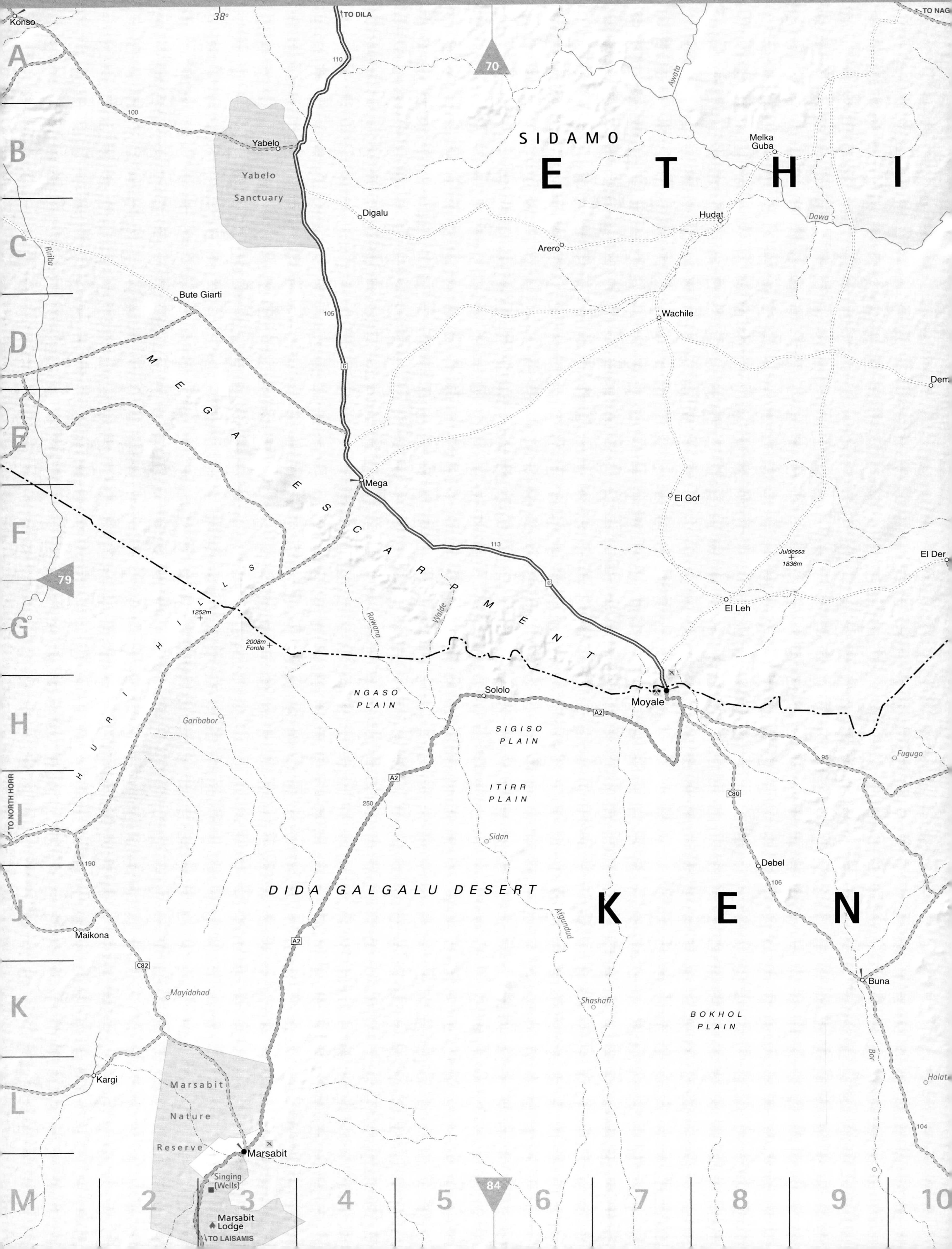

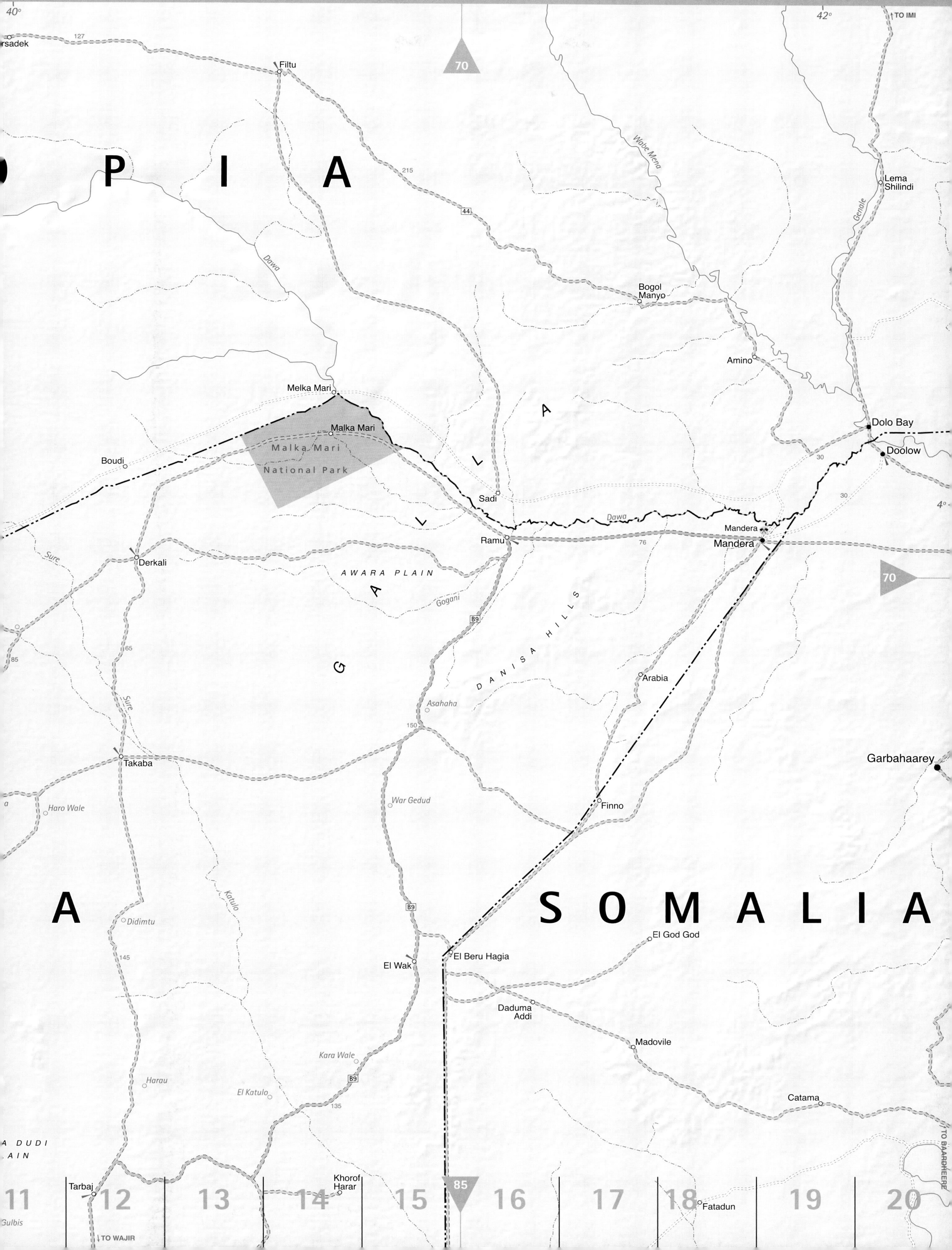
PIA
SOMALIA
A
GALLA
Filtu
Lema Shilindi
Bogol Manyo
Amino
Melka Mari
Malka Mari
Malka Mari National Park
Boudi
Dolo Bay
Doolow
Sadi
Ramu
Mandera
Mandera
Derkali
AWARA PLAIN
DANISA HILLS
Arabia
Asahaha
Takaba
Garbahaarey
Haro Wale
War Gedud
Finno
Didimtu
El God God
El Beru Hagia
El Wak
Daduma Addi
Madovile
Kara Wale
Harau
El Katulo
Catama
Tarbaj
Khorof Harar
Fatadun
Wabe Mena
Genale
Dawa
Sure
Gogani
Katulo
TO IMI
TO WAJIR
TO BAARDHEERE
A DUDI AIN
Gulbis
rsadek
11 12 13 14 15 16 17 18 19 20

SCENIC ROUTE — MAJOR CONNECTING ROUTE
TARRED / UNTARRED — MAIN CONNECTING ROUTE
TARRED / UNTARRED — MAIN ROAD
TARRED / UNTARRED — MINOR ROAD
4WD ROAD
LOCAL TRACK
HIKING TRAIL
234 NATIONAL ROUTE NUMBER
234 OTHER ROUTE NUMBER
■ PLACE OF INTEREST

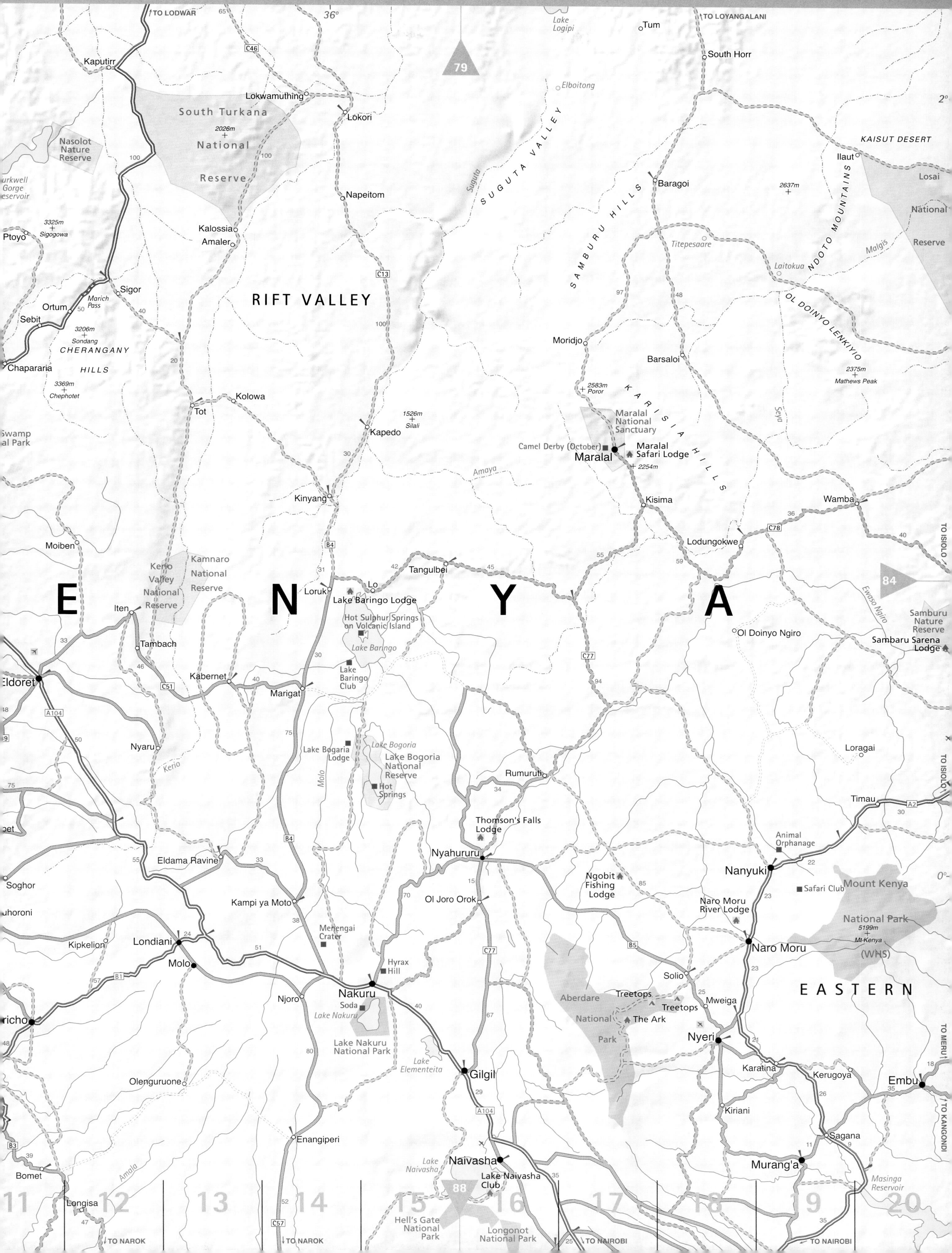
TO LODWAR
TO LOYANGALANI
Lake Logipi
Tum
South Horr
79
Kaputirr
Lokwamuthing
Lokori
Elboitong
South Turkana National Reserve
2026m
Nasolot Nature Reserve
Kerio Valley Gorge Reservoir
SUGUTA VALLEY
Suguta
Baragoi
KAISUT DESERT
Ilaut
Losai National Reserve
NDOTO MOUNTAINS
2637m
Napeitom
SAMBURU HILLS
Titepesaare
Malgis
Laitokua
3325m Sigogowa
Ptoyo
Kalossia
Amaler
Sigor
Marich Pass
Ortum
Sebit
RIFT VALLEY
OL DOINYO LENKIYIO
3206m Sondang
CHERANGANY HILLS
Chapararia
Moridjo
Barsaloi
2375m Mathews Peak
3369m Chephotet
Kolowa
Tot
2583m Poror
KARISIA HILLS
1526m Silali
Kapedo
Seya
Swamp National Park
Maralal National Sanctuary
Camel Derby (October)
Maralal
Maralal Safari Lodge
2254m
Amaya
Kinyang
Kisima
Wamba
Moiben
Lodungokwe
TO ISIOLO
Kamnaro National Reserve
Kerio Valley National Reserve
Tangulbei
84
K E N Y A
Loruk
Lo
Lake Baringo Lodge
Iten
Hot Sulphur Springs on Volcanic Island
Lake Baringo
Ewaso Ngiro
Samburu Nature Reserve
Sambaru Sarena Lodge
Ol Doinyo Ngiro
Tambach
Eldoret
Kabernet
Marigat
Lake Baringo Club
Nyaru
Kerio
Lake Bogaria Lodge
Lake Bogoria
Lake Bogoria National Reserve
Hot Springs
Molo
Loragai
Rumuruti
Timau
Thomson's Falls Lodge
Animal Orphanage
Eldama Ravine
Nyahururu
Soghor
Nanyuki
Safari Club
Mount Kenya National Park
5199m Mt Kenya
(WHS)
Ngobit Fishing Lodge
Kampi ya Moto
Ol Joro Orok
Naro Moru River Lodge
Menengai Crater
Londiani
Kipkelion
Molo
Hyrax Hill
Naro Moru
Solio
EASTERN
Nakuru
Njoro
Soda
Lake Nakuru
Aberdare National Park
Treetops
The Ark
Mweiga
Lake Nakuru National Park
Kericho
Nyeri
Lake Elementeita
Gilgil
Karatina
Kerugoya
Embu
TO MERU
Olenguruone
Kiriani
Enangiperi
Sagana
TO KANGONDI
Bomet
Amala
Lake Naivasha
Naivasha
Lake Naivasha Club
Murang'a
Masinga Reservoir
88
Longisa
Hell's Gate National Park
Longonot National Park
TO NAROK
TO NAROK
TO NAIROBI
TO NAIROBI
11 12 13 14 15 16 17 18 19 20

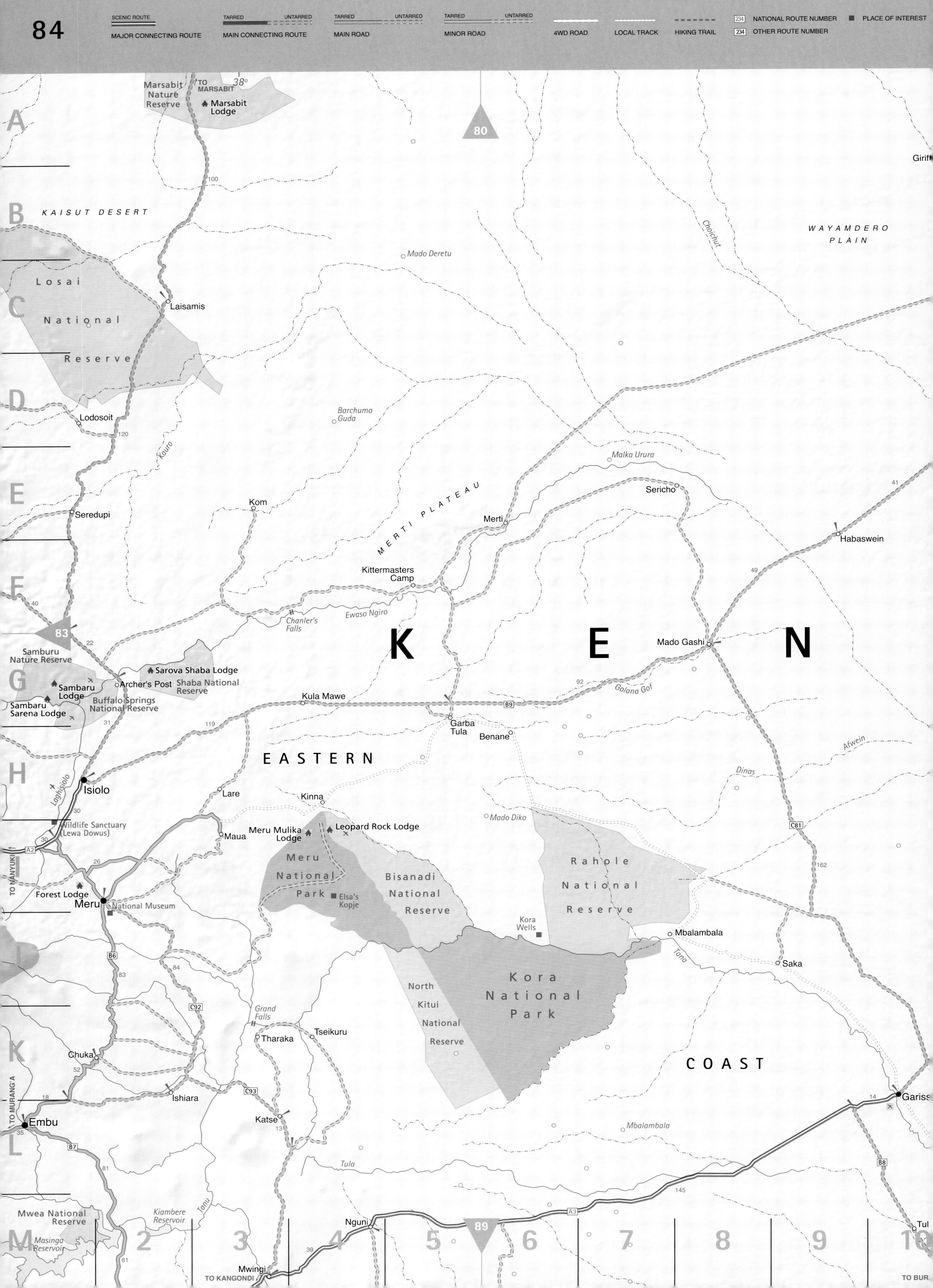
SCENIC ROUTE
MAJOR CONNECTING ROUTE
TARRED UNTARRED
MAIN CONNECTING ROUTE
TARRED UNTARRED
MAIN ROAD
TARRED UNTARRED
MINOR ROAD
4WD ROAD
LOCAL TRACK
HIKING TRAIL
234 NATIONAL ROUTE NUMBER
234 OTHER ROUTE NUMBER
PLACE OF INTEREST
Marsabit Nature Reserve
TO MARSABIT
38°
Marsabit Lodge
80
Girif
KAISUT DESERT
WAYAMDERO PLAIN
Choichut
Mado Deretu
Losai National Reserve
Laisamis
Barchuma Guda
Lodosoit
Kauro
Malka Urura
Sericho
Seredupi
Kom
MERTI PLATEAU
Merti
Habaswein
Kittermasters Camp
Ewaso Ngiro
Chanler's Falls
83
Samburu Nature Reserve
K
E
N
Mado Gashi
Sarova Shaba Lodge
Samburu Lodge
Archer's Post
Shaba National Reserve
Buffalo Springs National Reserve
Sambaru Sarena Lodge
Kula Mawe
B9
Golana Gof
Garba Tula
Benane
EASTERN
Afwein
Dinas
Isiolo
Laghisiolo
Lare
Kinna
Mado Diko
C81
Wildlife Sanctuary (Lewa Dowus)
Maua
Meru Mulika Lodge
Leopard Rock Lodge
A2
TO NANYUKI
Meru National Park
Bisanadi National Reserve
Rahole National Reserve
Elsa's Kopje
Forest Lodge
Meru
National Museum
Kora Wells
Mbalambala
Tana
Saka
B6
C92
Kora National Park
North Kitui National Reserve
Grand Falls
Tharaka
Tseikuru
Chuka
COAST
Ishiara
C93
Garissa
TO MURANG'A
Embu
Katse
Mbalambala
B7
Tula
B8
A3
Mwea National Reserve
Kiambere Reservoir
Tanu
Nguni
89
Tul
Masinga Reservoir
Mwingi
TO KANGONDI
TO BUR
A
B
C
D
E
F
G
H
I
J
K
L
M
2
3
4
5
6
7
8
9
10

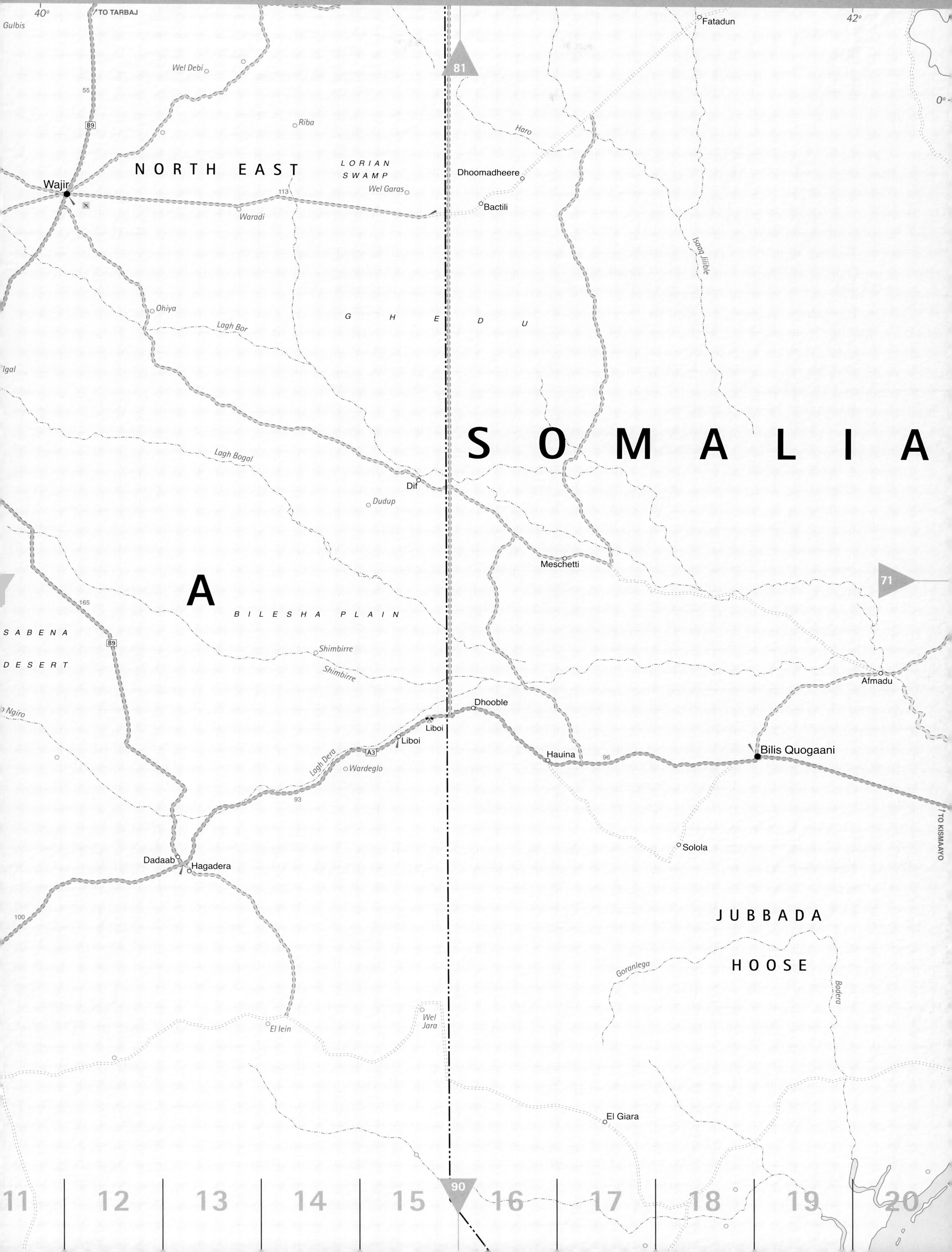
TO TARBAJ
Gulbis
Wel Debi
Riba
NORTH EAST
LORIAN SWAMP
Wel Garas
Wajir
Waradi
Fatadun
Haro
Dhoomadheere
Bactili
Isaaq Jiible
Ohiya
Lagh Bor
G H E D U
Igal
SOMALIA
Lagh Bogal
Dif
Dudup
Meschetti
A
BILESHA PLAIN
SABENA DESERT
Shimbirre
Afmadu
Ngiro
Dhooble
Liboi
Hauina
Bilis Quogaani
Lagh Dera
Wardeglo
TO KISMAAYO
Solola
Dadaab
Hagadera
JUBBADA HOOSE
Goranlega
Badera
El Iein
Wel Jara
El Giara

SCENIC ROUTE — MAJOR CONNECTING ROUTE
TARRED / UNTARRED — MAIN CONNECTING ROUTE
TARRED / UNTARRED — MAIN ROAD
TARRED / UNTARRED — MINOR ROAD
4WD ROAD
LOCAL TRACK
HIKING TRAIL
234 NATIONAL ROUTE NUMBER
234 OTHER ROUTE NUMBER
■ PLACE OF INTEREST

NAIROBI CAPITAL CITY
Abidjan SECONDARY CAPITAL CITY When Applicable
Las Palmas DEPENDANCY CAPITAL
Gweru LARGE / MAJOR TOWN Over 50,000 people
Ruhengeri SECONDARY TOWN Between 10,000 & 50,000
El Kadada SMALL TOWN Between 5,000 &10,000
Chinguetti LARGE VILLAGE Between 500 & 5,000
Winneba SMALL VILLAGE OR SETTLEMENT Under 500 people
KM 30
MI 20

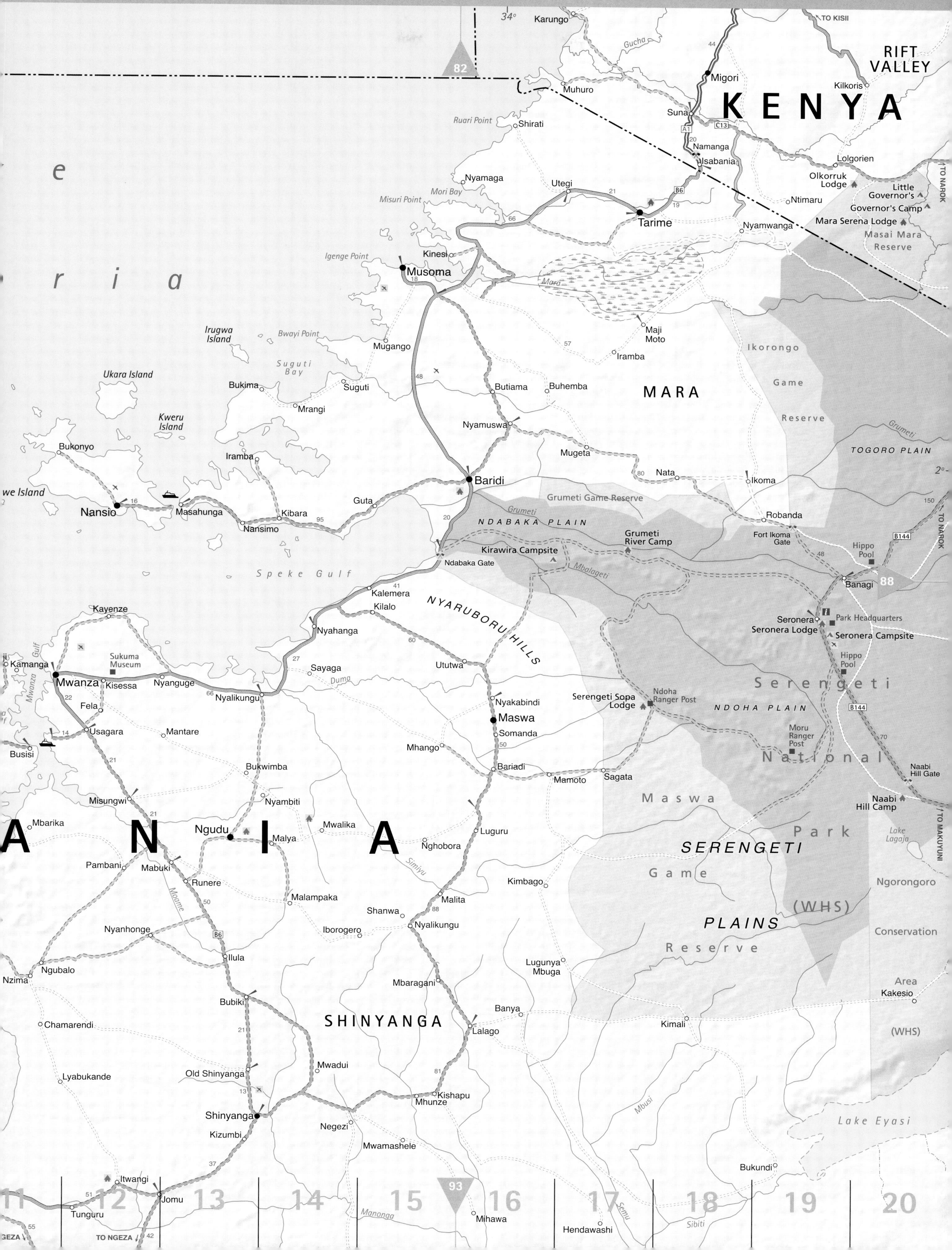

SCENIC ROUTE / MAJOR CONNECTING ROUTE · TARRED / UNTARRED MAIN CONNECTING ROUTE · TARRED / UNTARRED MAIN ROAD · TARRED / UNTARRED MINOR ROAD · 4WD ROAD · LOCAL TRACK · HIKING TRAIL · 234 NATIONAL ROUTE NUMBER · 234 OTHER ROUTE NUMBER · PLACE OF INTEREST

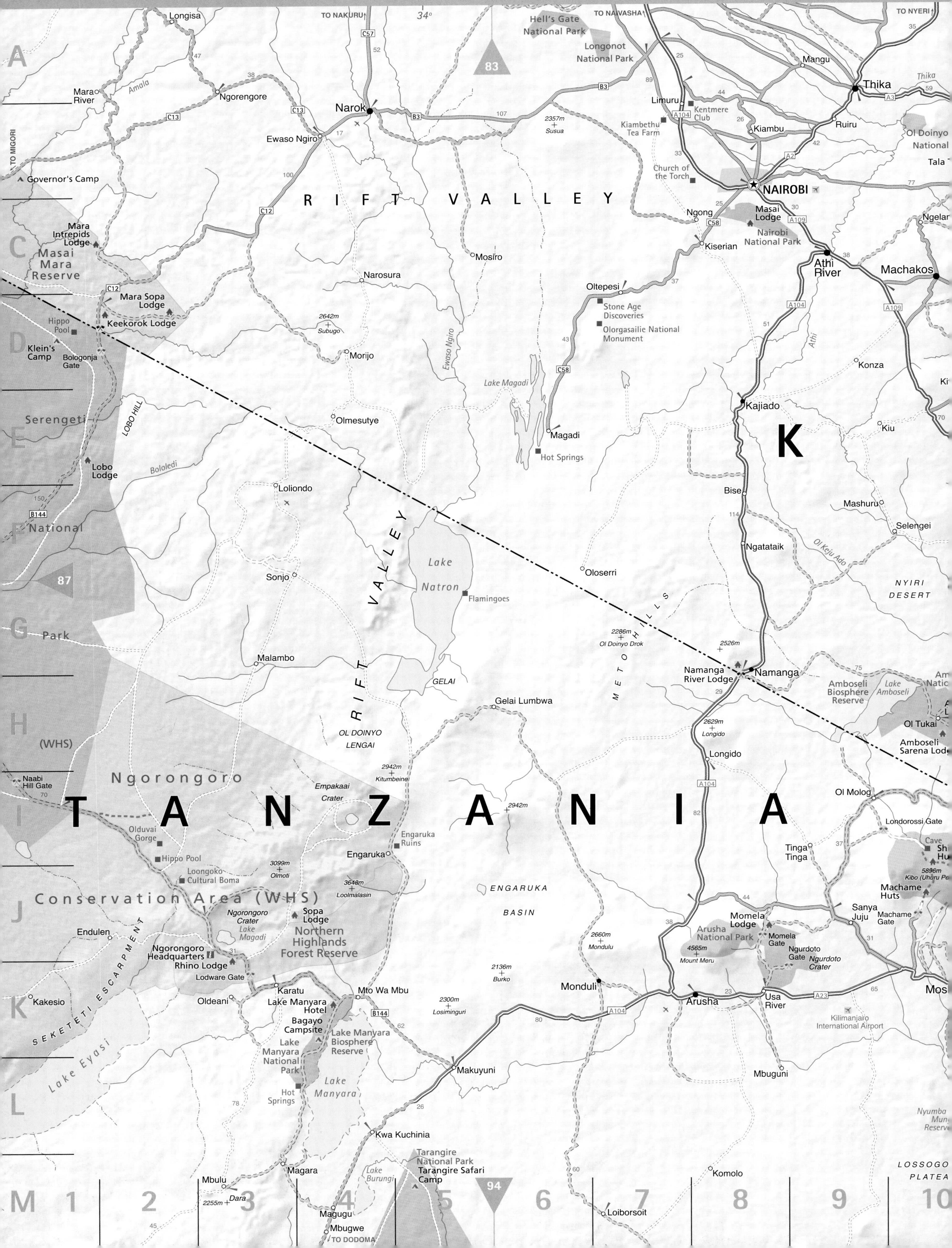

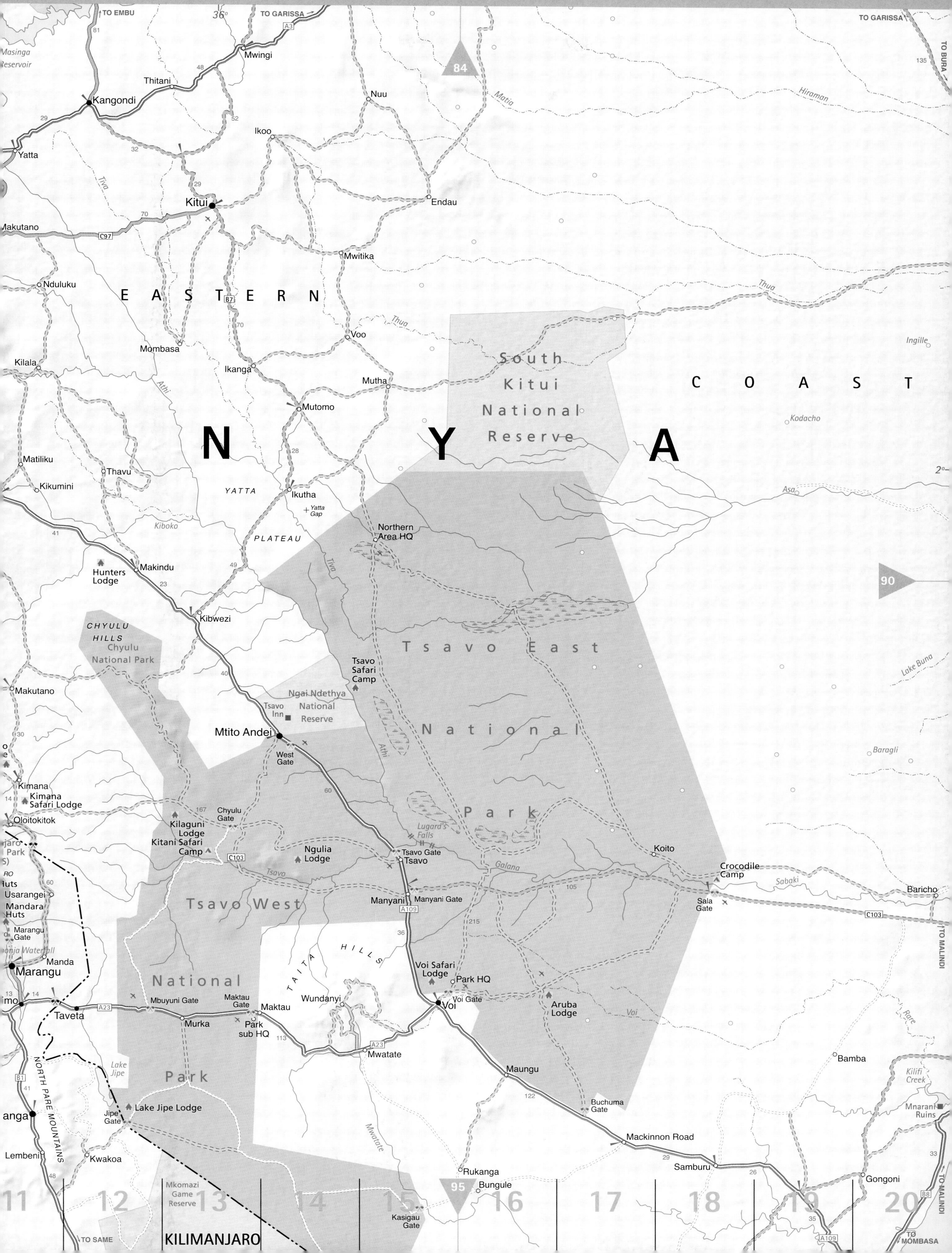

TO EMBU
TO GARISSA
TO GARISSA
TO BURA
Masinga Reservoir
Mwingi
Thitani
Kangondi
Nuu
Ikoo
Yatta
Kitui
Endau
Makutano
Mwitika
Nduluku
EASTERN
Mombasa
Voo
Kilala
Ikanga
Mutha
Mutomo
South Kitui National Reserve
COAST
Kodacho
Ingille
N Y A
Matiliku
Thavu
Kikumini
YATTA
Ikutha
Yatta Gap
PLATEAU
Kiboko
Northern Area HQ
Hunters Lodge
Makindu
Kibwezi
CHYULU HILLS
Chyulu National Park
Tsavo East National Park
Tsavo Safari Camp
Ngai Ndethya National Reserve
Tsavo Inn
Mtito Andei
West Gate
Makutano
Kimana
Kimana Safari Lodge
Oloitokitok
Chyulu Gate
Kilaguni Lodge
Kitani Safari Camp
Ngulia Lodge
Lugard's Falls
Tsavo Gate
Tsavo
Koito
Crocodile Camp
Sala Gate
Baricho
Manyani
Manyani Gate
Tsavo West National Park
TAITA HILLS
Voi Safari Lodge
Park HQ
Voi Gate
Voi
Aruba Lodge
Usarangei
Mandara Huts
Marangu Gate
Manda
Marangu
Mbuyuni Gate
Maktau Gate
Maktau
Wundanyi
Taveta
Murka
Park sub HQ
Mwatate
Maungu
Bamba
Kilifi Creek
Lake Jipe
NORTH PARE MOUNTAINS
Lake Jipe Lodge
Jipe Gate
Buchuma Gate
Mnarani Ruins
Mackinnon Road
Samburu
Gongoni
Lembeni
Kwakoa
Rukanga
Bungule
Mkomazi Game Reserve
Kasigau Gate
TO SAME
KILIMANJARO
TO MALINDI
TO MALINDI
TO MOMBASA
Baragli
Lake Buna
Athi
Tiva
Thua
Galana
Sabaki
Voi
Rare
Mwatate
Matia
Hiraman
Asa
84
90
95
11 12 13 14 15 16 17 18 19 20

SCENIC ROUTE — MAJOR CONNECTING ROUTE | TARRED / UNTARRED — MAIN CONNECTING ROUTE | TARRED / UNTARRED — MAIN ROAD | TARRED / UNTARRED — MINOR ROAD | 4WD ROAD | LOCAL TRACK | HIKING TRAIL | 234 NATIONAL ROUTE NUMBER | 234 OTHER ROUTE NUMBER | ■ PLACE OF INTEREST

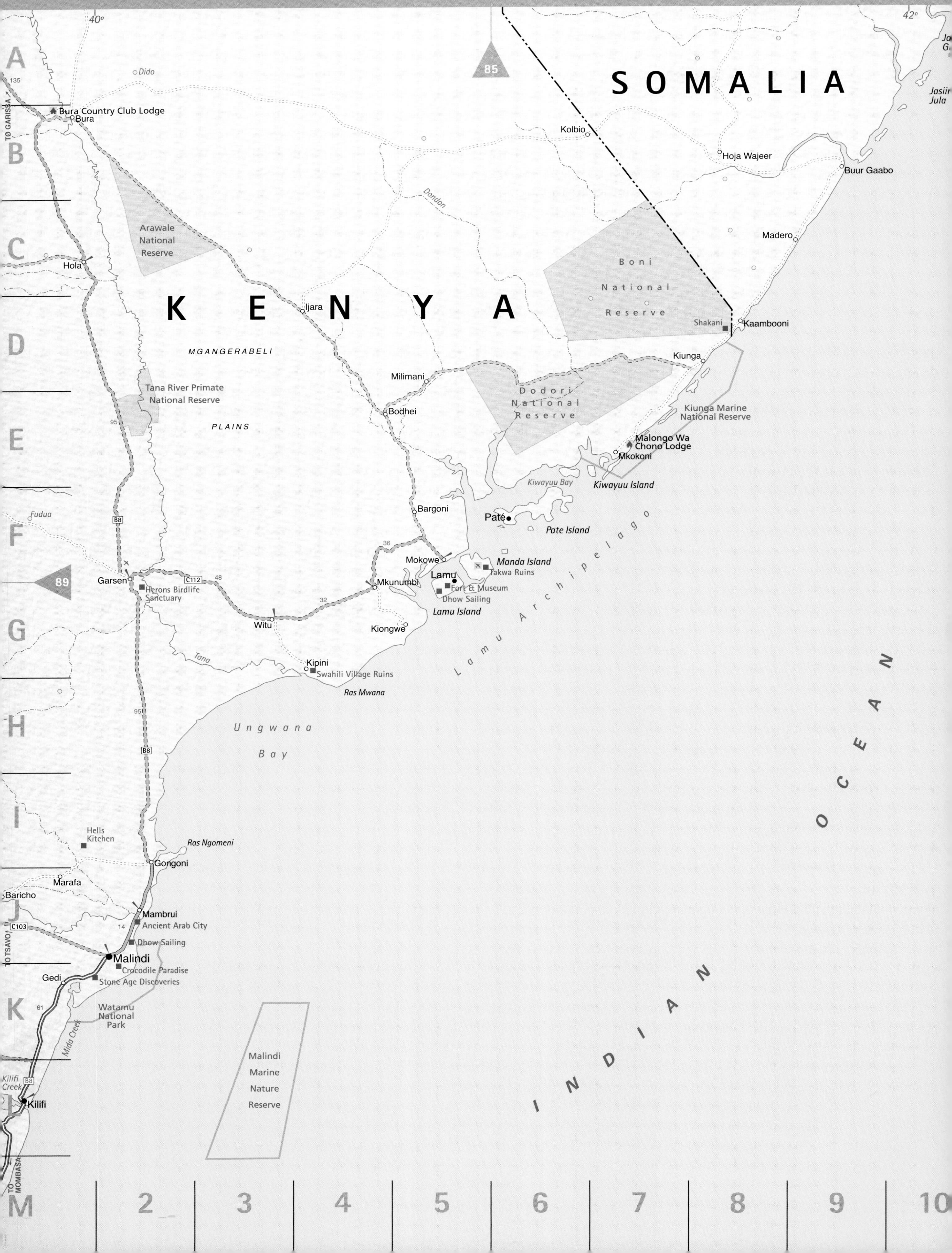

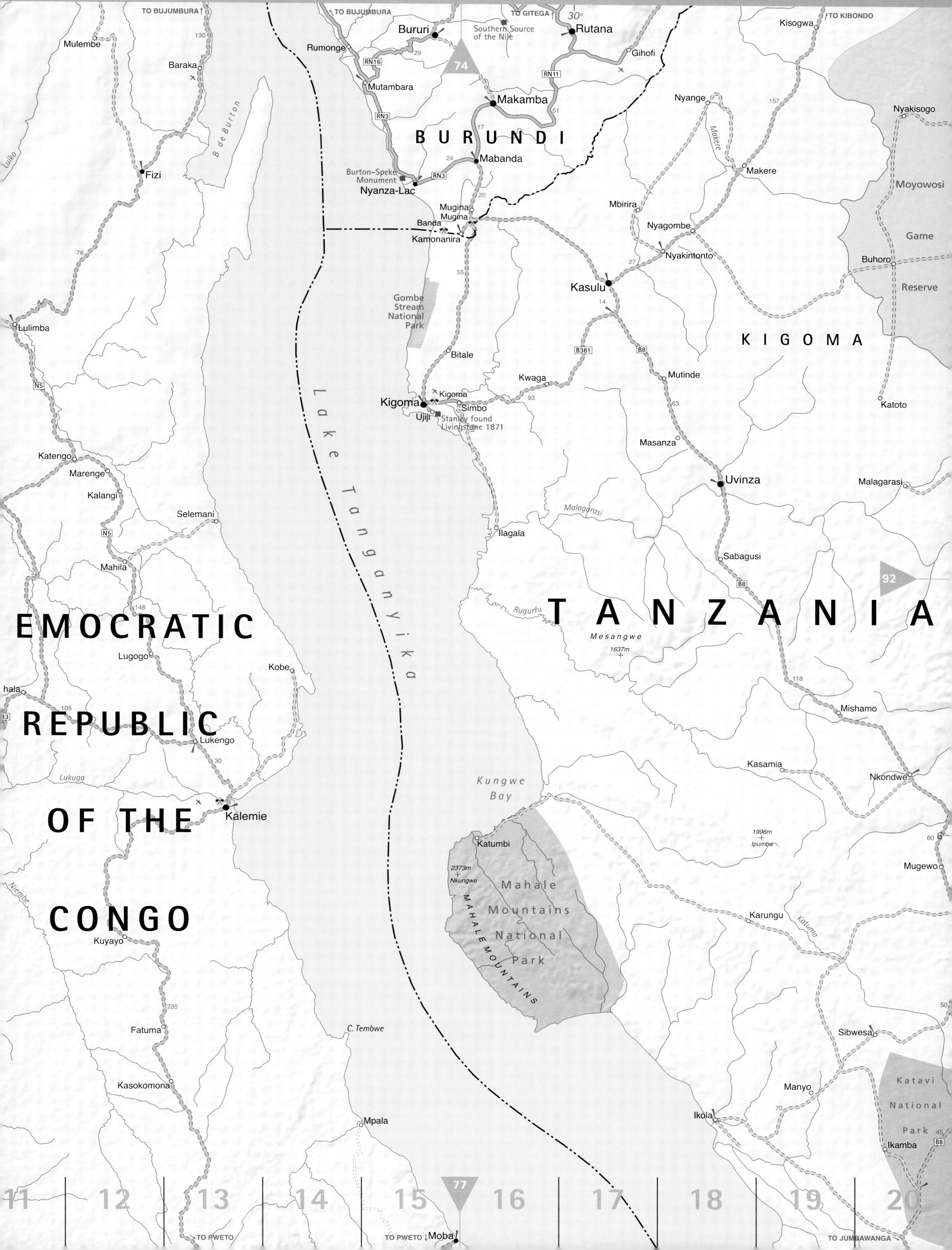
BURUNDI
KIGOMA
TANZANIA
DEMOCRATIC REPUBLIC OF THE CONGO
Lake Tanganyika
Bururi
Rutana
Makamba
Mabanda
Nyanza-Lac
Burton-Speke Monument
Southern Source of the Nile
Rumonge
Mutambara
Gihofi
Kisogwa
TO KIBONDO
TO BUJUMBURA
TO GITEGA
Mulembe
Baraka
Fizi
Lulimba
Katengo
Marenge
Kalangi
Selemani
Mahila
Lugogo
Kobe
Lukengo
Kalemie
Kuyayo
Fatuma
Kasokomona
Mpala
Moba
TO PWETO
Mugina
Banda
Kamonanira
Gombe Stream National Park
Bitale
Kigoma
Ujiji
Simbo
Stanley found Livingstone 1871
Kwaga
Kasulu
Nyakintonto
Nyagombe
Mbirira
Makere
Nyange
Nyakisogo
Moyowosi Game Reserve
Buhoro
Katoto
Mutinde
Masanza
Uvinza
Malagarasi
Ilagala
Sabagusi
Rugufu
Mesangwe
1637m
Mishamo
Kasamia
Nkondwe
Kungwe Bay
Katumbi
2373m Nkungwe
Mahale Mountains National Park
MAHALE MOUNTAINS
1996m Ipumba
Mugewo
Karungu
Katuma
Sibwesa
Manyo
Ikola
Katavi National Park
Ikamba
TO JUMBAWANGA
C. Tembwe
Lukuga
Niembe
B de Burton
74
77
92
RN16
RN3
RN11
B381
B8
N5
11 12 13 14 15 16 17 18 19 20

SCENIC ROUTE — MAJOR CONNECTING ROUTE
TARRED / UNTARRED — MAIN CONNECTING ROUTE
TARRED / UNTARRED — MAIN ROAD
TARRED / UNTARRED — MINOR ROAD
4WD ROAD
LOCAL TRACK
HIKING TRAIL
234 NATIONAL ROUTE NUMBER
234 OTHER ROUTE NUMBER
■ PLACE OF INTEREST

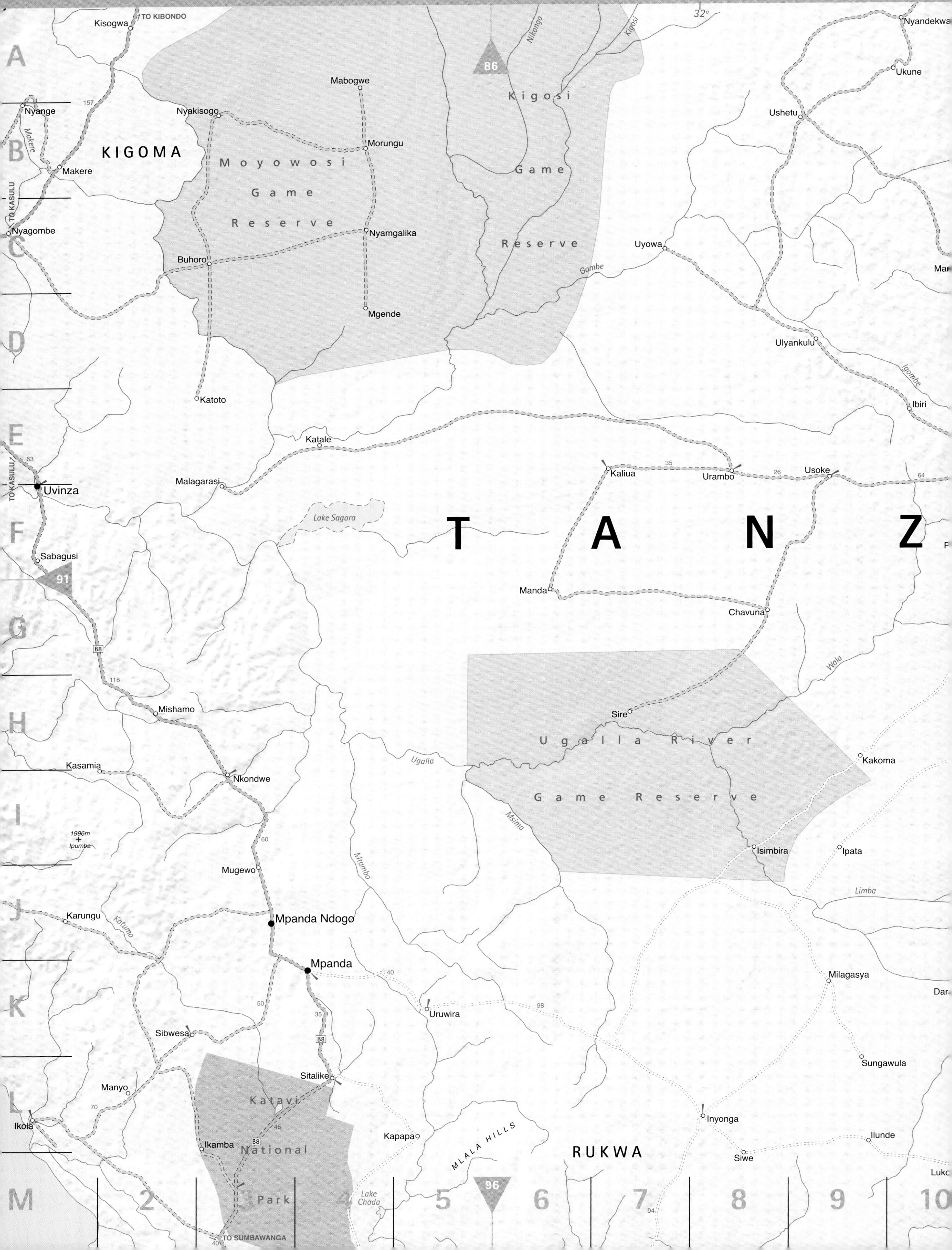

TO KAHAMA
TO SHINYANGA
Tunguru
Manonga
Mihawa
Hendawashi
Semu
Sibiti
Igurubi
87
Chomachankale
Lake Kitangiri
Matongo
Mkalama
Tulia
Haidom
Itobo
Bukene
Nzega
B3
Ziba
Sakamaliwa
Mbutu
Igunga
Sekenke
Nduguti
Kiomboi
Bulunde
Kirondatal
Shelui
Lambi
Basotu
B6
Ngongoro
Wembere
Duruma
Kiniyangiri
Mwisi
Cheli
Mtinko
Iguguno
Endesh
Simba
Susijinda
Usure
Ilongero
Igombe
Sepuka
Malandala
TO BABATI
Ndala
Mpiringa
Mohenge
Singida
Mgori
Salimu
Mwaru
A B O R A
Isiksisia
Mwaru
Loya
Mngaa
Puma
Tabora
Mgongila
Misughaa
Mhowala
Kwasasa
Kigwa
Misaki
Matari
A N I A
S I N G I D A
Taru
B141
Mpondo
Mihama
Mkurusi
94
Mitundu
Kisengi
Issuna
Nyahua
Makuru
Tumbili
Ikunga
Jabolo
Chona
B129
Kitaraka
Kapatu
Itigi
Manyoni
Saranda
Mabondeni
Nwahua
B141
TO DODOMA
Mkinga
Ilunga
Kilimatinde
Ukimbo
Msalalo
Kisigo
Mwanisenga
Makasuko
Jiwe La Singa
Jamkola
Bahi Swamp
Mahaka
Kalangali
Msisi
Magiro
Kipili
Ilewiro
Kilumbi
Nkonko
Muhesi
Usuhilo
Iseke
Miaroye
Itumba
Shame
Madyo
Kisigo
Bagamayo
K i z i g o G a m e
B141
R e s e r v e
aswa
1520m
Rungwa
Game Reserve
1356m Nguru
Itende
Kitunda
Igumira
Ipera
Ilangali
Rungwa
97
Njombe
Ruaha National Park
Mdalula
TO CHUNYA
11 12 13 14 15 16 17 18 19 20

SCENIC ROUTE — MAJOR CONNECTING ROUTE
TARRED / UNTARRED — MAIN CONNECTING ROUTE
TARRED / UNTARRED — MAIN ROAD
TARRED / UNTARRED — MINOR ROAD
4WD ROAD
LOCAL TRACK
HIKING TRAIL
234 NATIONAL ROUTE NUMBER
234 OTHER ROUTE NUMBER
PLACE OF INTEREST

NAIROBI CAPITAL CITY | Abidjan SECONDARY CAPITAL CITY When Applicable | Las Palmas DEPENDANCY CAPITAL | Gweru LARGE / MAJOR TOWN Over 50,000 people | Ruhengeri SECONDARY TOWN Between 10,000 & 50,000 | El Kadada SMALL TOWN Between 5,000 &10,000 | Chinguetti LARGE VILLAGE Between 500 & 5,000 | Winneba SMALL VILLAGE OR SETTLEMENT Under 500 people

KM 30 MI 20

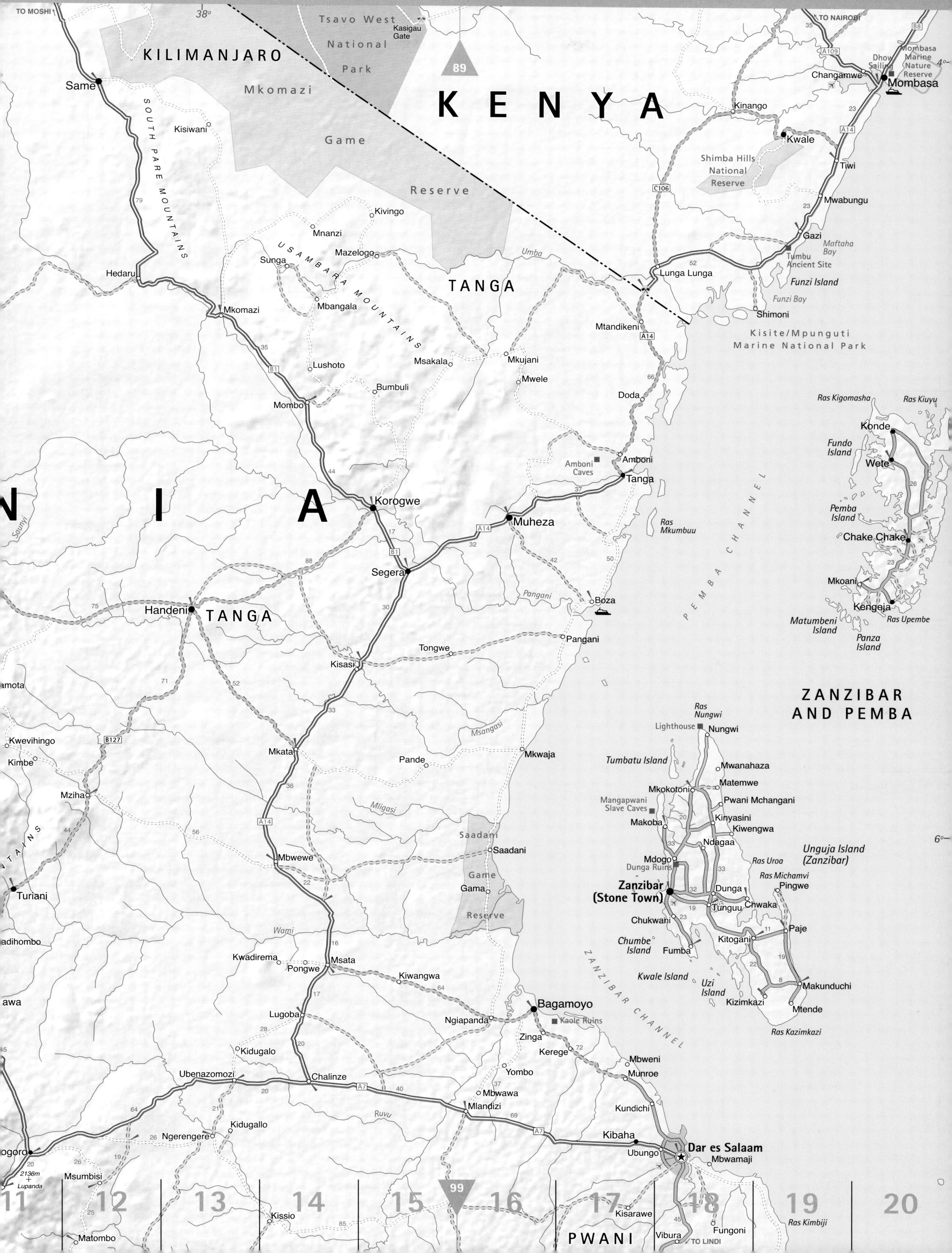

SCENIC ROUTE — MAJOR CONNECTING ROUTE
TARRED / UNTARRED — MAIN CONNECTING ROUTE
TARRED / UNTARRED — MAIN ROAD
TARRED / UNTARRED — MINOR ROAD
4WD ROAD
LOCAL TRACK
HIKING TRAIL
234 NATIONAL ROUTE NUMBER
234 OTHER ROUTE NUMBER
PLACE OF INTEREST

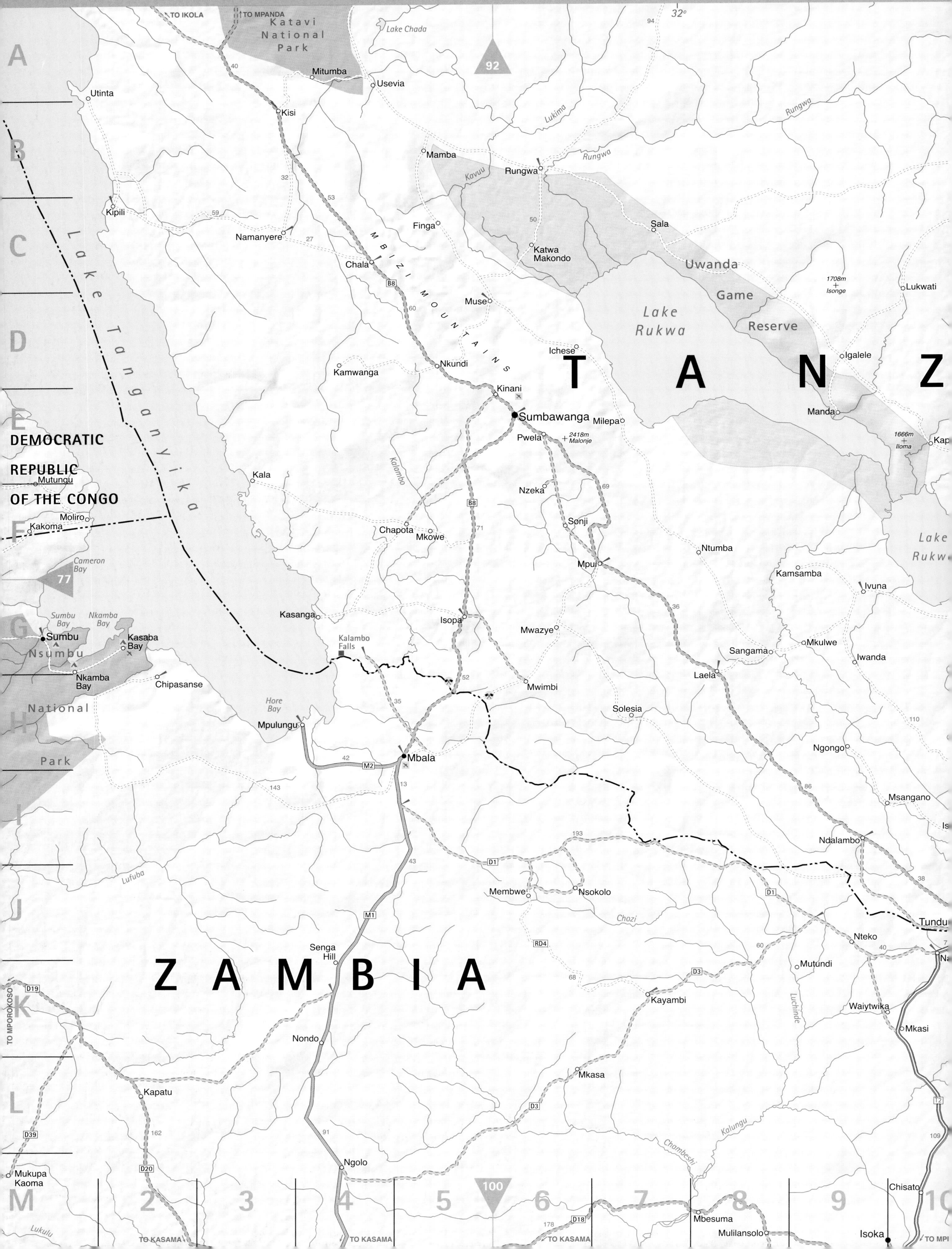

NAIROBI CAPITAL CITY | Abidjan SECONDARY CAPITAL CITY When Applicable | Las Palmas DEPENDANCY CAPITAL | Gweru LARGE / MAJOR TOWN Over 50,000 people | Ruhengeri SECONDARY TOWN Between 10,000 & 50,000 | El Kadada SMALL TOWN Between 5,000 &10,000 | Chinguetti LARGE VILLAGE Between 500 & 5,000 | Winneba SMALL VILLAGE OR SETTLEMENT Under 500 people

KM 30 MI 20

SCENIC ROUTE — MAJOR CONNECTING ROUTE
TARRED / UNTARRED — MAIN CONNECTING ROUTE
TARRED / UNTARRED — MAIN ROAD
TARRED / UNTARRED — MINOR ROAD
4WD ROAD
LOCAL TRACK
HIKING TRAIL
234 NATIONAL ROUTE NUMBER
234 OTHER ROUTE NUMBER
PLACE OF INTEREST

PWANI
LINDI
Selous Reserve
TANZANIA
(WHS)
MOROGORO
TO DAR ES SALAAM
TO NACHINGWEA
TO MTWARA
Kisarawe
Fungoni
Ras Kimbiji
Vibura
Mkuranga
Mbezi
Buyuni
Masaki
Kissio
Matombo
Mkulazi
Mvuha
Magogogoni
Maneromango
Binga
Mazomora
Kisiju
Lukanga
Kilimahera
Nyuruandanga
Bungu
Kisangire
Kisaki
Mgeta
Selous Grave
Mbuyu Rufiji Camp
Mtemere Gate
Impala Safari Camp
Rufiji River Camp
Stiegler's Gorge Safari Camp
Mpanga
Mtanza
Mloka
Logeloge
Kilimani
Kibiti
Mahege
Mchungo
Mchukwi
Kikale
Mbumi
Ikwiriri
Ndundu
Utete
Ferries across Rufiji do not operate between March and July
Lake Utenge
Rufiji
Niangandu
Msomemi
Mbwera
Nyamwage
Mohoro
Nyakitasi
Marendego
Somanga
Mohoro Bay
Nangulangwa
Kipatimu
Songo Songo Island
Bweni
Jimbo
Baleni
Mafia Island
Kilindoni
Ghole
Nwera
Kua Ruins
Juani Island
MAFIA CHANNEL
Kilwa Kivinje
Njinjo
Mitole
Nangurukuru
Mpara
Rugombera
Naiwangaa
Kilwa Masoko
Kilwa Kisiwani
Sangarungu Haven
Songo Mnara Island (WHS)
Ruins
Chema
Miguruwe
Mpatora
Kiwatama
Mtandura
Kiwawa
Miembwe
Matandu
Mihungu
Mirahi
Likawage
Zinga Mulika
Roango
Ras Mombi
Mitumbati
Kimambi
Ruhangino
Lihimalyao
Grant Point
Kihundo
Kiswere
Mtandi
Mavuji
Mitumbati
Kinjacha
Mlowoka
Nambunju
Kitumbini
Mkata
Ndembo
Maboyo
Nanjirinji
Nambiranji
Liwale
Ngangora
Mkunya
Mirui Chini
Mbemkuru
Ruawa
Mchinga
Nangaru
Ras Mbanura
Namichiga
Mandawa
Lindi Bay
Lindi
Mihumo Chini
Milola
Mitengi
Mingoyo
95
103
11 12 13 14 15 16 17 18 19 20

SCENIC ROUTE — MAJOR CONNECTING ROUTE
TARRED / UNTARRED — MAIN CONNECTING ROUTE
TARRED / UNTARRED — MAIN ROAD
TARRED / UNTARRED — MINOR ROAD
4WD ROAD
LOCAL TRACK
HIKING TRAIL
234 NATIONAL ROUTE NUMBER
234 OTHER ROUTE NUMBER
PLACE OF INTEREST

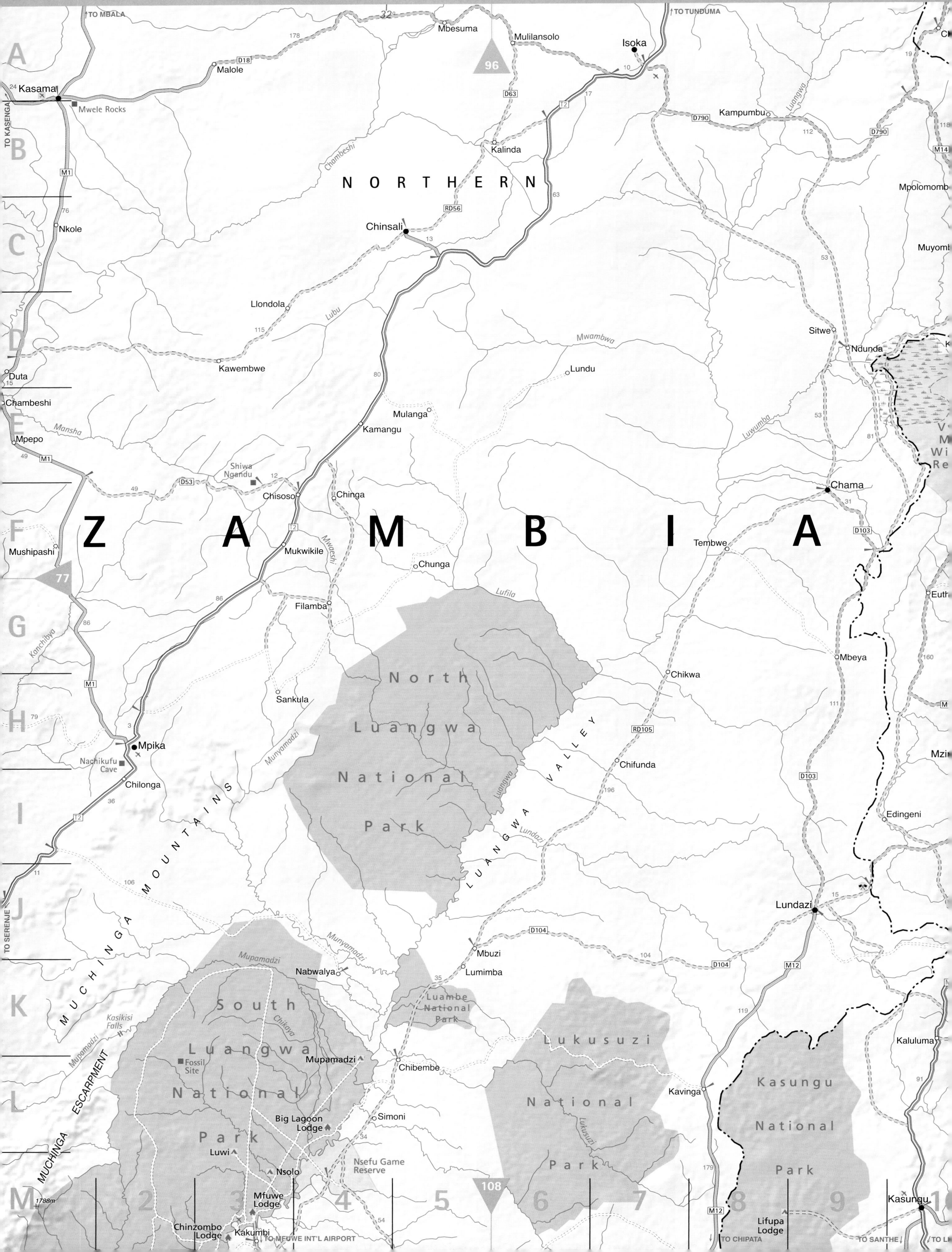

NAIROBI — CAPITAL CITY
Abidjan — SECONDARY CAPITAL CITY When Applicable
Las Palmas — DEPENDANCY CAPITAL
Gweru — LARGE / MAJOR TOWN Over 50,000 people
Ruhengeri — SECONDARY TOWN Between 10,000 & 50,000
El Kadada — SMALL TOWN Between 5,000 &10,000
Chinguetti — LARGE VILLAGE Between 500 & 5,000
Winneba — SMALL VILLAGE OR SETTLEMENT Under 500 people

KM 30
MI 20

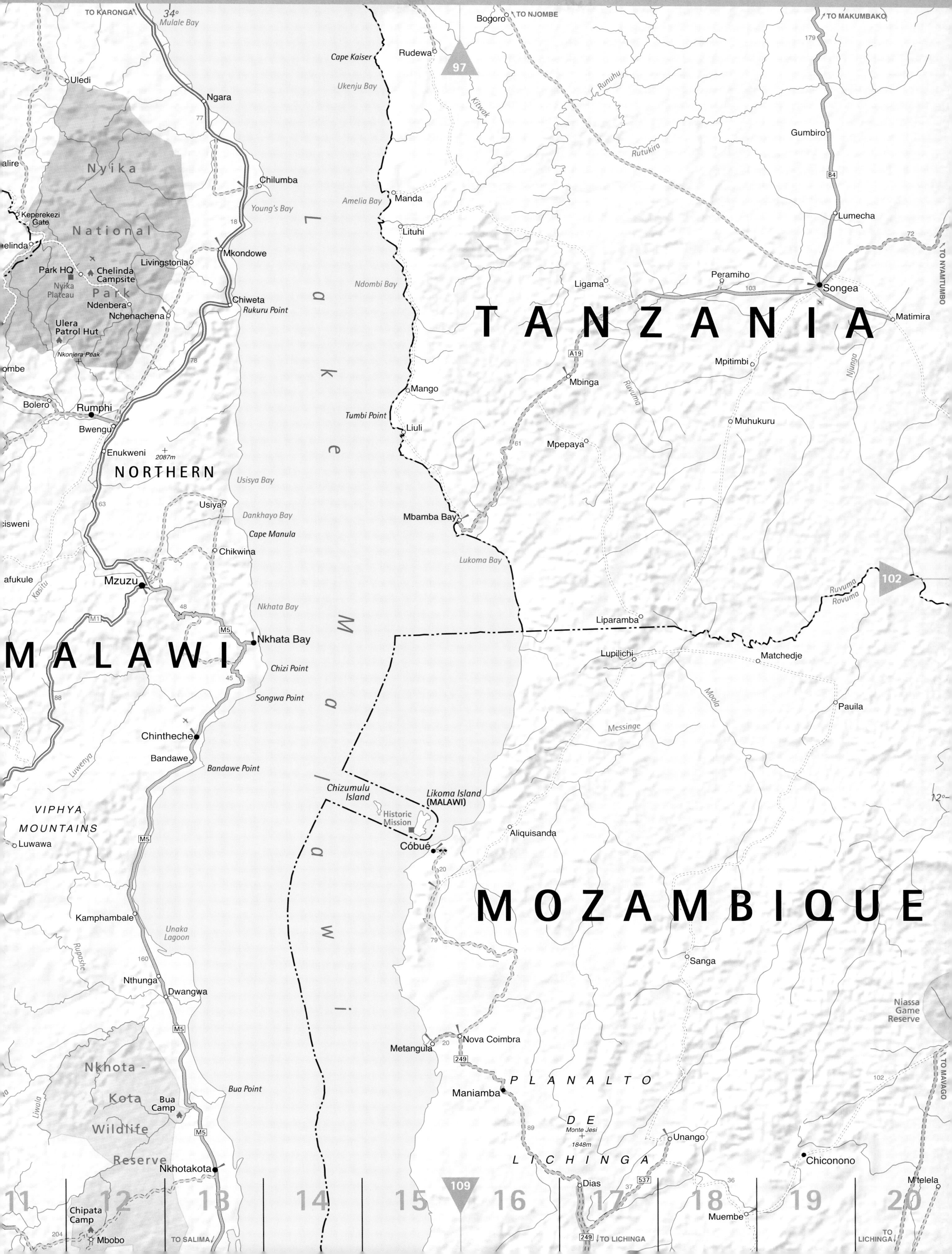

SCENIC ROUTE — MAJOR CONNECTING ROUTE | TARRED / UNTARRED — MAIN CONNECTING ROUTE | TARRED / UNTARRED — MAIN ROAD | TARRED / UNTARRED — MINOR ROAD | 4WD ROAD | LOCAL TRACK | HIKING TRAIL | 234 NATIONAL ROUTE NUMBER | 234 OTHER ROUTE NUMBER | PLACE OF INTEREST

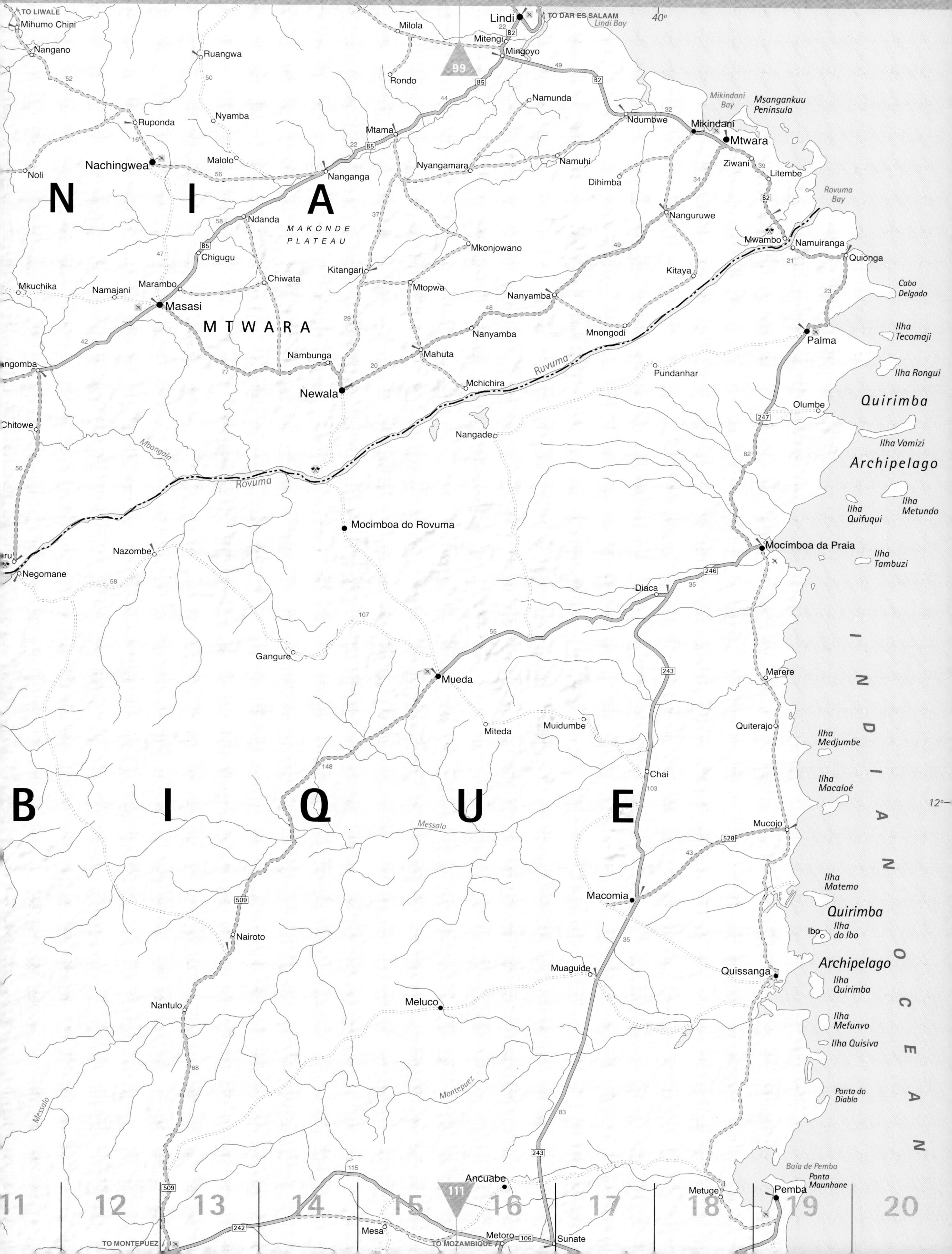
TO LIWALE
Mihumo Chini
Nangano
Ruangwa
Lindi
TO DAR ES SALAAM
Lindi Bay
Milola
Mitengi
Mingoyo
Rondo
Namunda
Mikindani Bay
Msangankuu Peninsula
Ndumbwe
Mikindani
Mtwara
Ruponda
Nyamba
Mtama
Nachingwea
Malolo
Nyangamara
Namuhi
Ziwani
Litembe
Noli
Nanganga
Dihimba
Rovuma Bay
N I A
Ndanda
MAKONDE PLATEAU
Nanguruwe
Mwambo
Namuiranga
Quionga
Chigugu
Mkonjowano
Kitangari
Kitaya
Mkuchika
Chiwata
Cabo Delgado
Namajani
Marambo
Mtopwa
Nanyamba
Masasi
MTWARA
Ilha Tecomaji
Mnongodi
Nanyamba
Palma
Nambunga
Mahuta
Ilha Rongui
ngomba
Pundanhar
Mchichira
Ruvuma
Newala
Olumbe
Quirimba
Chitowe
Nangade
Mbangala
Ilha Vamizi
Archipelago
Rovuma
Ilha Metundo
Ilha Quifuqui
Mocimboa do Rovuma
Mocímboa da Praia
Ilha Tambuzi
Nazombe
ru
Negomane
Diaca
Gangure
Mueda
Marere
Miteda
Muidumbe
Quiterajo
Ilha Medjumbe
Chai
Ilha Macaloé
B I Q U E
Messalo
Mucojo
Ilha Matemo
Macomia
Quirimba
Ibo
Ilha do Ibo
Nairoto
Archipelago
Muaguide
Quissanga
Ilha Quirimba
Nantulo
Meluco
Ilha Mefunvo
Ilha Quisiva
Montepuez
Messalo
Ponta do Diablo
INDIAN OCEAN
Baía de Pemba
Ponta Maunhane
Ancuabe
Metuge
Pemba
Mesa
TO MONTEPUEZ
Metoro
TO MOZAMBIQUE
Sunate
40°
12°
99
111

SCENIC ROUTE — MAJOR CONNECTING ROUTE
TARRED / UNTARRED — MAIN CONNECTING ROUTE
TARRED / UNTARRED — MAIN ROAD
TARRED / UNTARRED — MINOR ROAD
4WD ROAD
LOCAL TRACK
HIKING TRAIL
234 NATIONAL ROUTE NUMBER
234 OTHER ROUTE NUMBER
PLACE OF INTEREST

NAIROBI
CAPITAL CITY

Abidjan
SECONDARY CAPITAL CITY When Applicable

Las Palmas
DEPENDANCY CAPITAL

Gweru
LARGE / MAJOR TOWN Over 50,000 people

Ruhengeri
SECONDARY TOWN Between 10,000 & 50,000

El Kadada
SMALL TOWN Between 5,000 &10,000

Chinguetti
LARGE VILLAGE Between 500 & 5,000

Winneba
SMALL VILLAGE OR SETTLEMENT Under 500 people

KM 30
MI 20

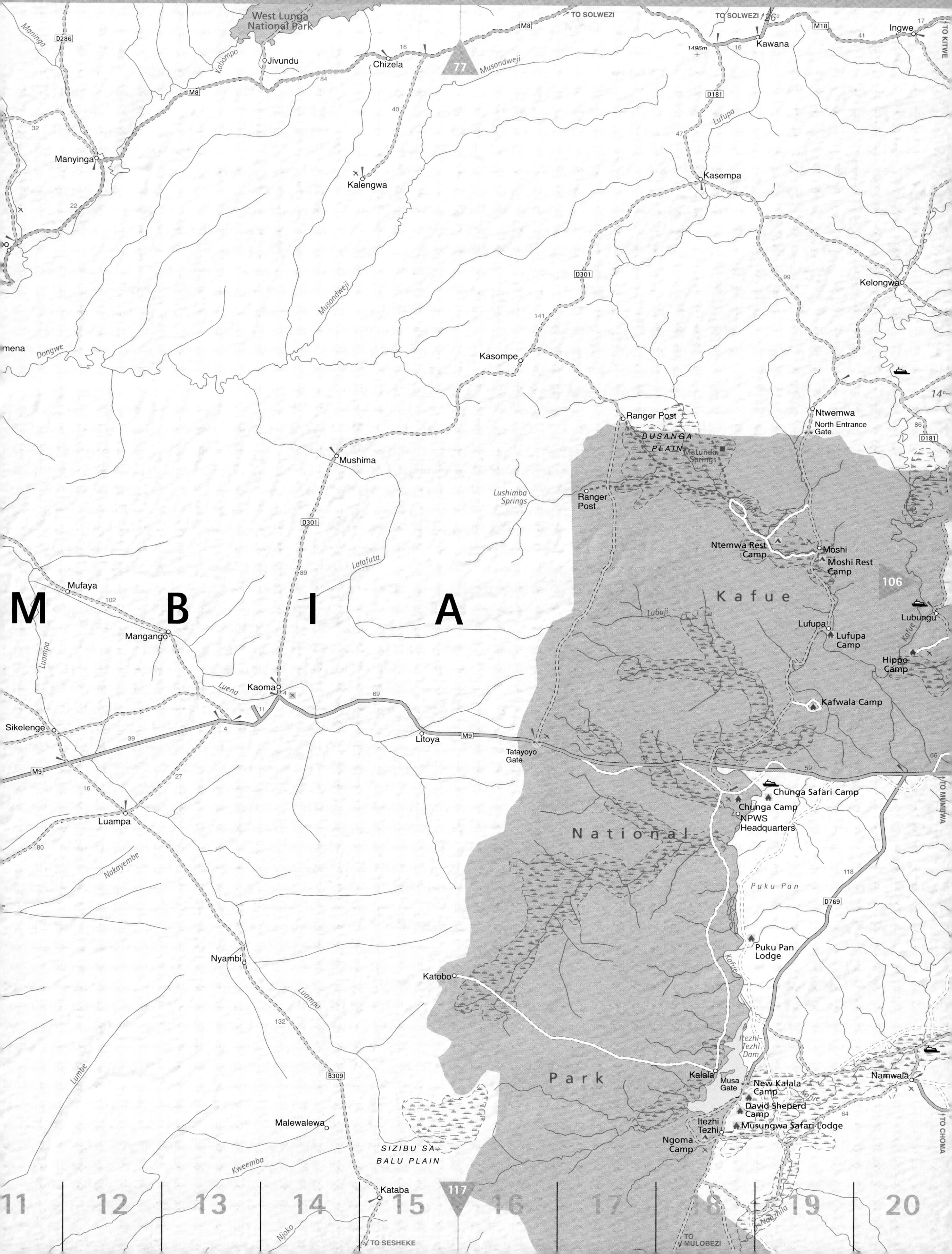

SCENIC ROUTE · MAJOR CONNECTING ROUTE · TARRED UNTARRED MAIN CONNECTING ROUTE · TARRED UNTARRED MAIN ROAD · TARRED UNTARRED MINOR ROAD · 4WD ROAD · LOCAL TRACK · HIKING TRAIL · 234 NATIONAL ROUTE NUMBER · 234 OTHER ROUTE NUMBER · ■ PLACE OF INTEREST

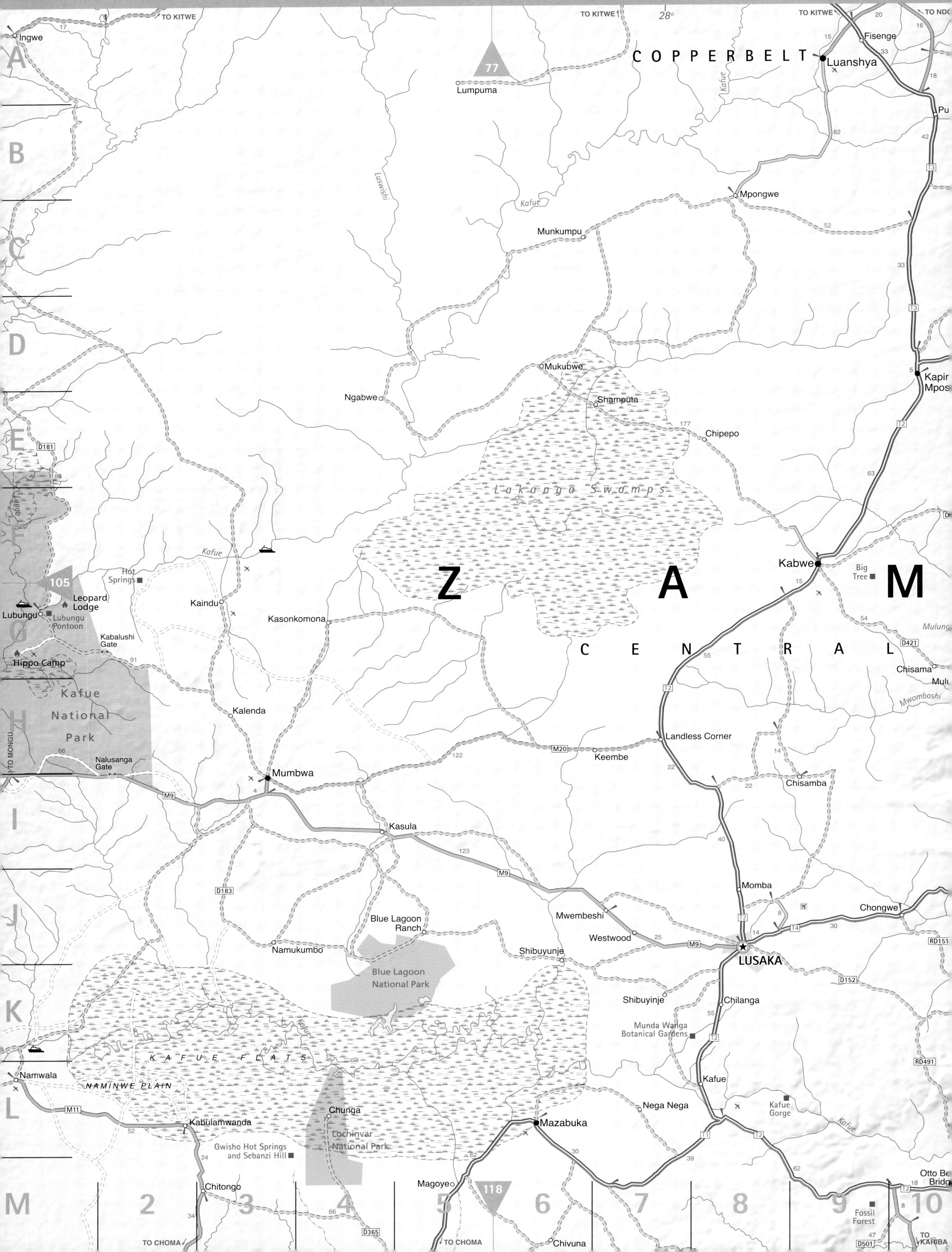

NAIROBI CAPITAL CITY | Abidjan SECONDARY CAPITAL CITY When Applicable | Las Palmas DEPENDANCY CAPITAL | Gweru LARGE / MAJOR TOWN Over 50,000 people | Ruhengeri SECONDARY TOWN Between 10,000 & 50,000 | El Kadada SMALL TOWN Between 5,000 &10,000 | Chinguetti LARGE VILLAGE Between 500 & 5,000 | Winneba SMALL VILLAGE OR SETTLEMENT Under 500 people | KM 30 MI 20

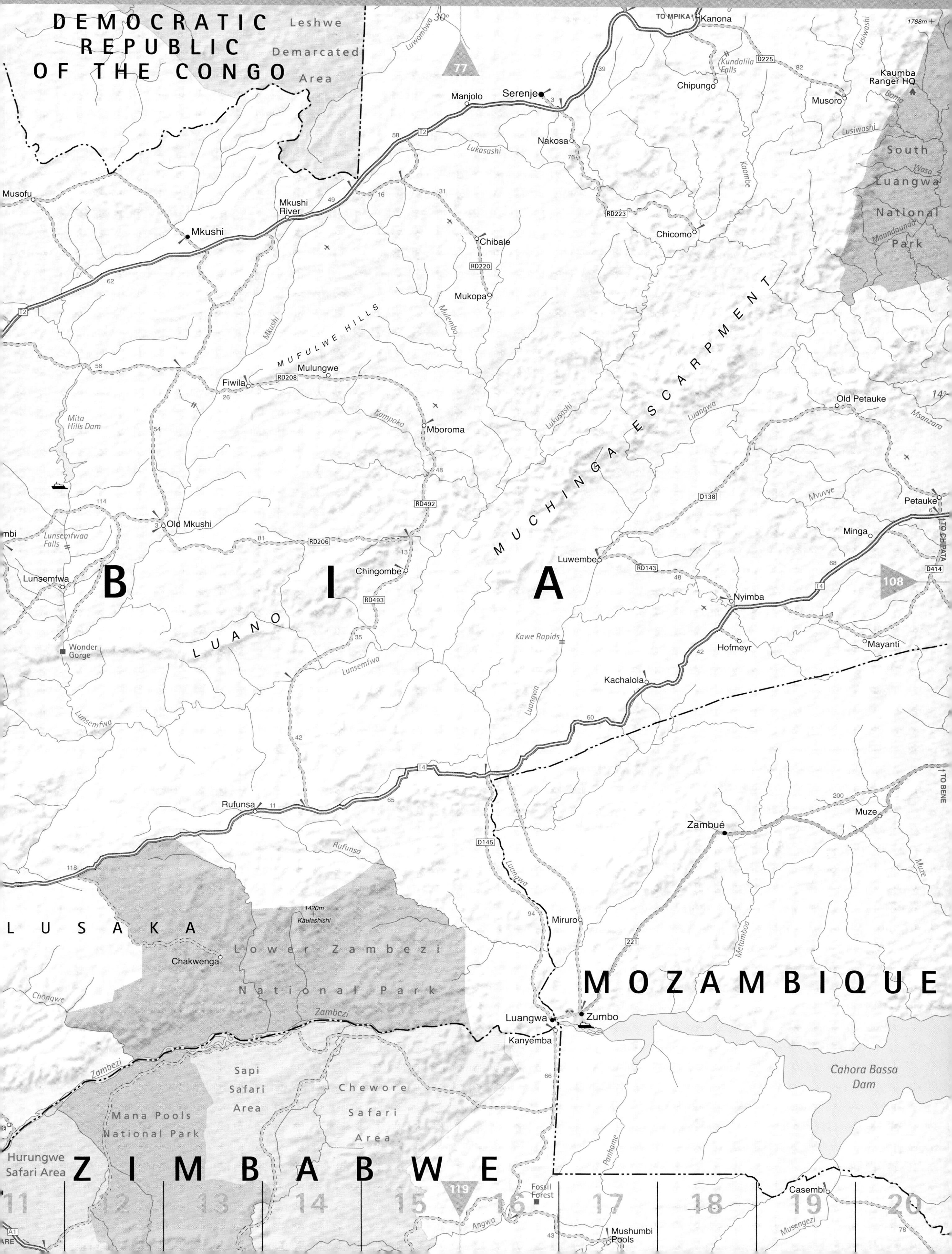

SCENIC ROUTE — MAJOR CONNECTING ROUTE
TARRED / UNTARRED — MAIN CONNECTING ROUTE
TARRED / UNTARRED — MAIN ROAD
TARRED / UNTARRED — MINOR ROAD
4WD ROAD
LOCAL TRACK
HIKING TRAIL
234 NATIONAL ROUTE NUMBER
234 OTHER ROUTE NUMBER
PLACE OF INTEREST

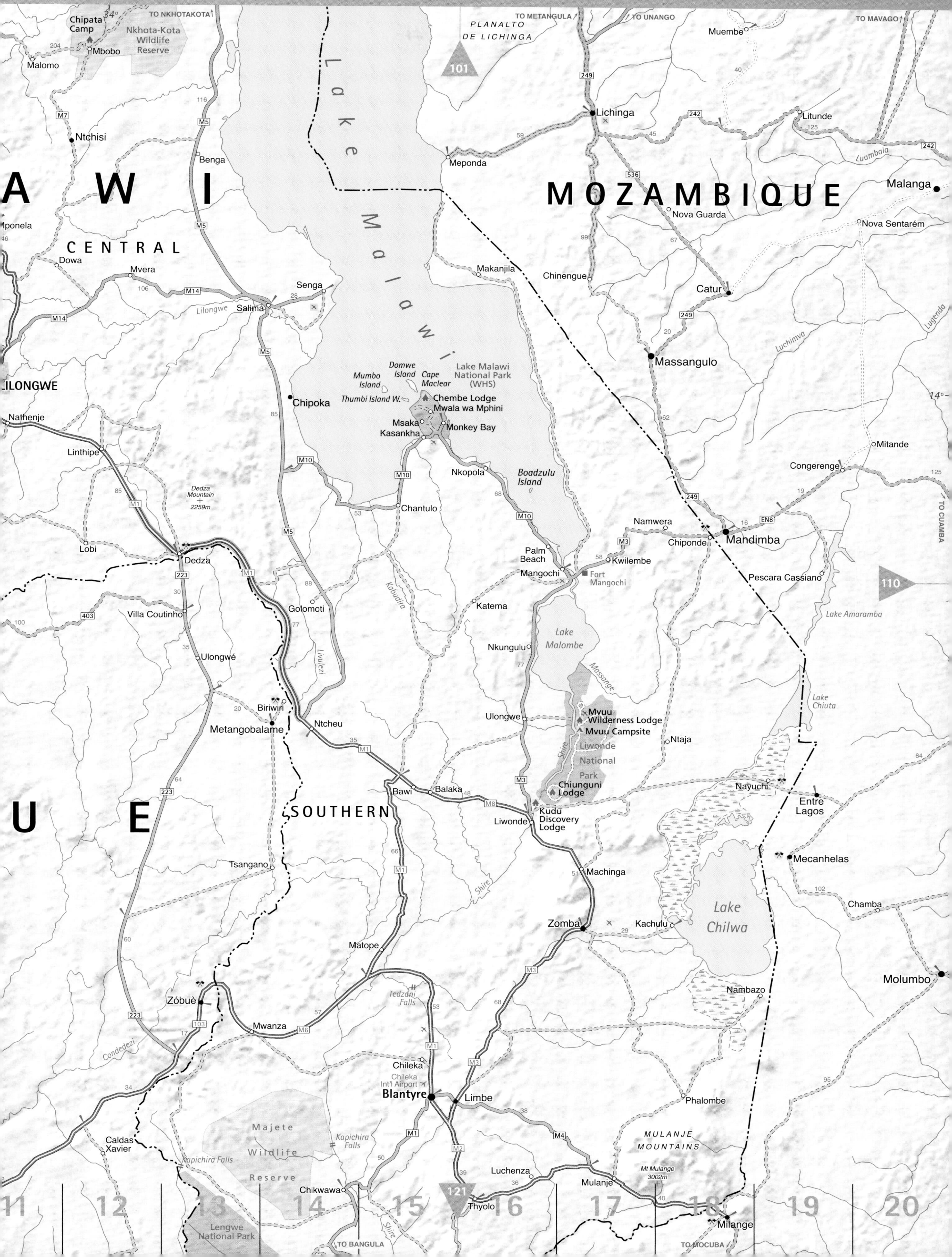

MOZAMBIQUE
CENTRAL
SOUTHERN
Lake Malawi
Lake Malawi National Park (WHS)
Liwonde National Park
Majete Wildlife Reserve
Lengwe National Park
Nkhota-Kota Wildlife Reserve
PLANALTO DE LICHINGA
MULANJE MOUNTAINS
Lake Chilwa
Lake Malombe
Lake Chiuta
Lake Amaramba
Lichinga
Mandimba
Massangulo
Zomba
Blantyre
Limbe
Salima
Dedza
Ntcheu
Mangochi
Liwonde
Machinga
Mulanje
Milange
Molumbo
Mecanhelas
Entre Lagos
Malanga
TO NKHOTAKOTA
TO METANGULA
TO UNANGO
TO MAVAGO
TO CUAMBA
TO BANGULA
TO MOCUBA
101
110
121

SCENIC ROUTE — MAJOR CONNECTING ROUTE
TARRED / UNTARRED — MAIN CONNECTING ROUTE
TARRED / UNTARRED — MAIN ROAD
TARRED / UNTARRED — MINOR ROAD
4WD ROAD
LOCAL TRACK
HIKING TRAIL
234 NATIONAL ROUTE NUMBER
234 OTHER ROUTE NUMBER
■ PLACE OF INTEREST

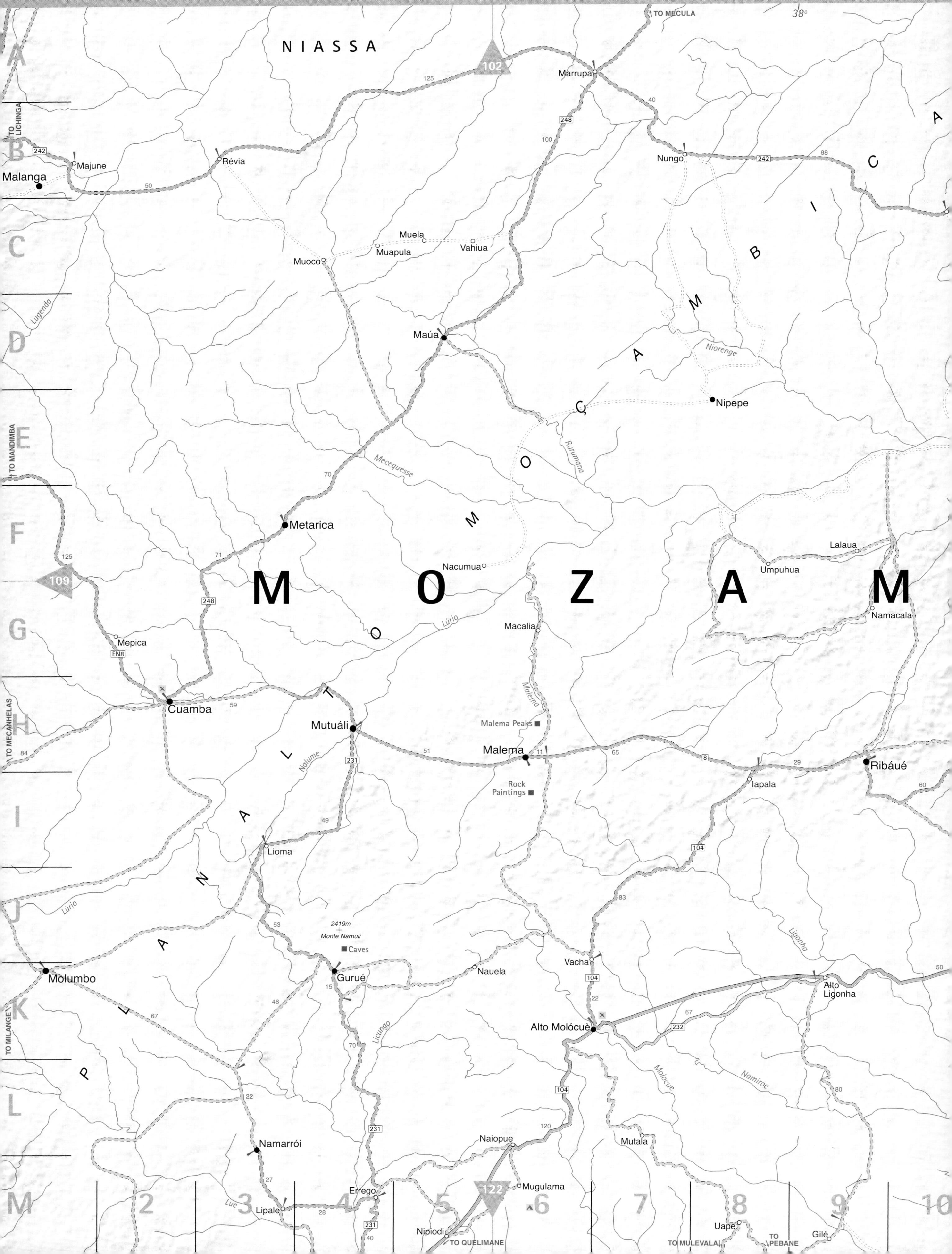

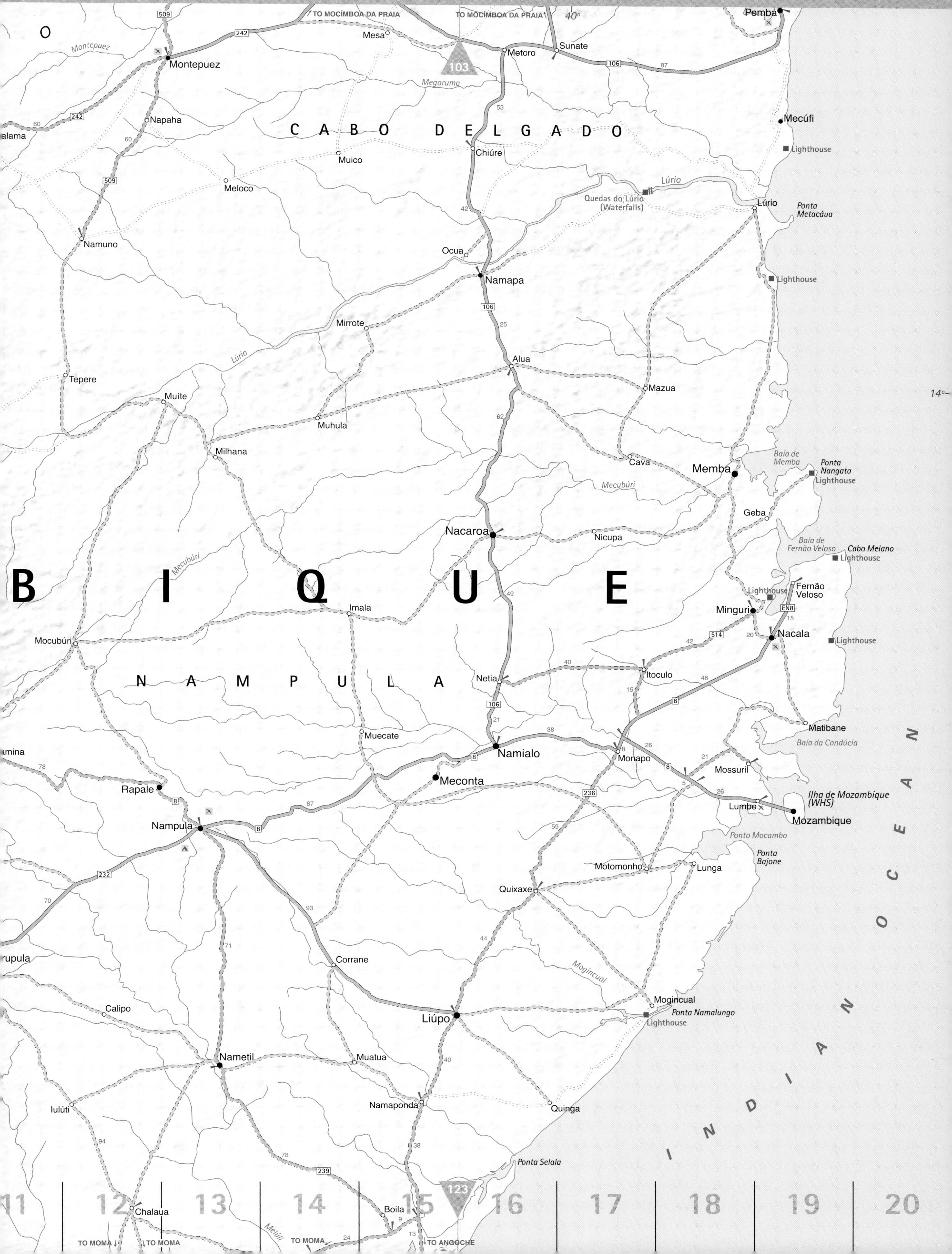

TO MOCÍMBOA DA PRAIA
TO MOCÍMBOA DA PRAIA
40°
Pemba
Mesa
Montepuez
Metoro
Sunate
103
Megaruma
Napaha
CABO DELGADO
Mecúfi
Lighthouse
Muico
Chiúre
Meloco
Lúrio
Quedas do Lúrio (Waterfalls)
Lúrio
Ponta Metacáua
Namuno
Ocua
Namapa
Lighthouse
Mirrote
Alua
Tepere
Mazua
Muíte
14°
Muhula
Milhana
Cava
Baía de Memba
Memba
Ponta Nangata Lighthouse
Mecubúri
Geba
Nacaroa
Nicupa
Baía de Fernão Veloso
Cabo Melano Lighthouse
BIQUE
Fernão Veloso
Imala
Lighthouse
Minguri
Mocubúri
Nacala
Lighthouse
NAMPULA
Netia
Itoculo
Matibane
Baía da Condúcia
Muecate
Namialo
Monapo
Mossuril
Rapale
Meconta
Nampula
Lumbo
Ilha de Mozambique (WHS)
Mozambique
Ponto Mocambo
Ponta Bajone
Motomonho
Lunga
Quixaxe
Corrane
Mogincual
Mogincual
Ponta Namalungo
Lighthouse
Calipo
Liúpo
Nametil
Muatua
Iulúti
Namaponda
Quinga
Ponta Selala
INDIAN OCEAN
123
Chalaua
Boila
Meluli
TO MOMA
TO MOMA
TO MOMA
TO ANGOCHE
11
12
13
14
15
16
17
18
19
20

SCENIC ROUTE — MAJOR CONNECTING ROUTE
TARRED / UNTARRED — MAIN CONNECTING ROUTE
TARRED / UNTARRED — MAIN ROAD
TARRED / UNTARRED — MINOR ROAD
4WD ROAD
LOCAL TRACK
HIKING TRAIL
234 NATIONAL ROUTE NUMBER
234 OTHER ROUTE NUMBER
■ PLACE OF INTEREST

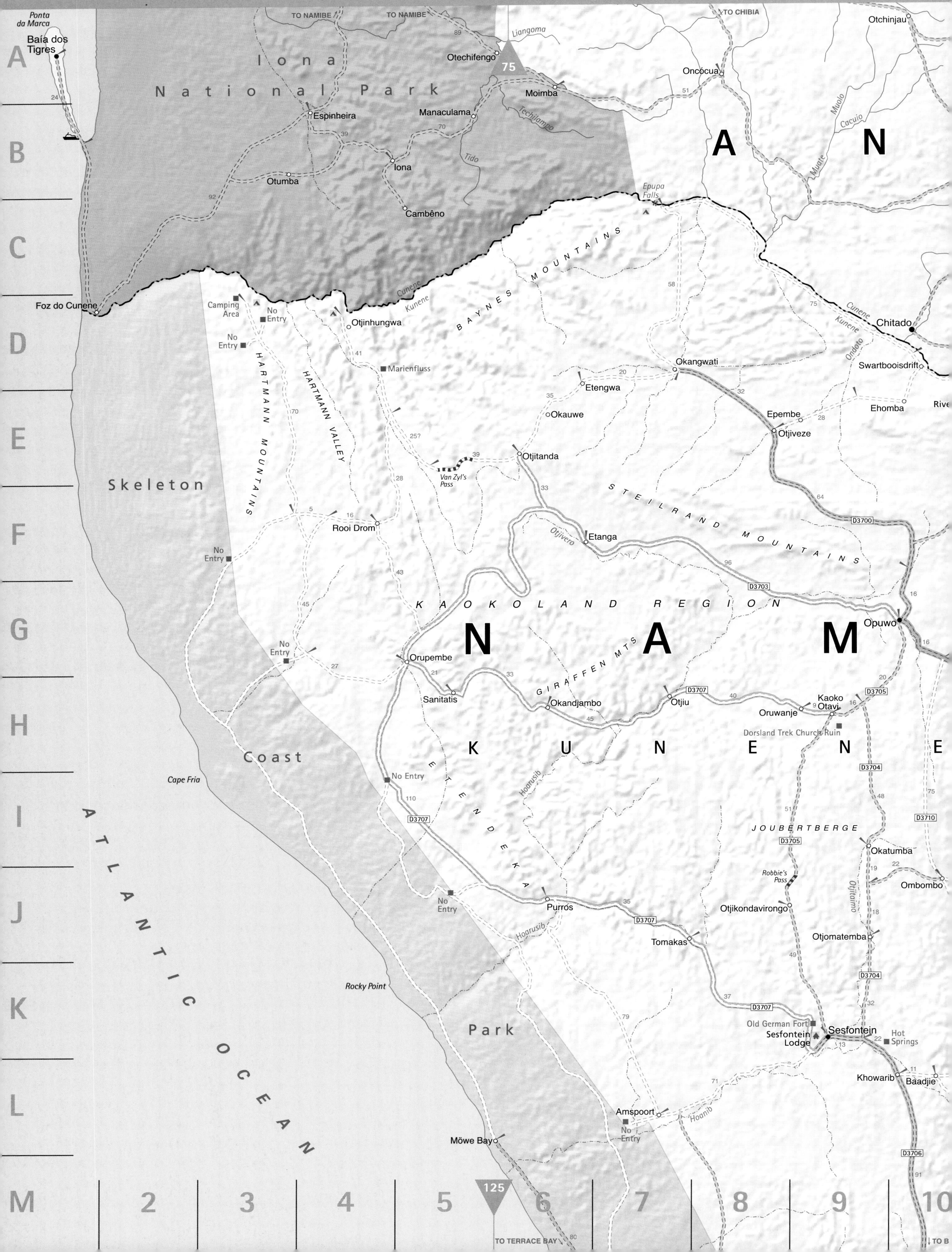

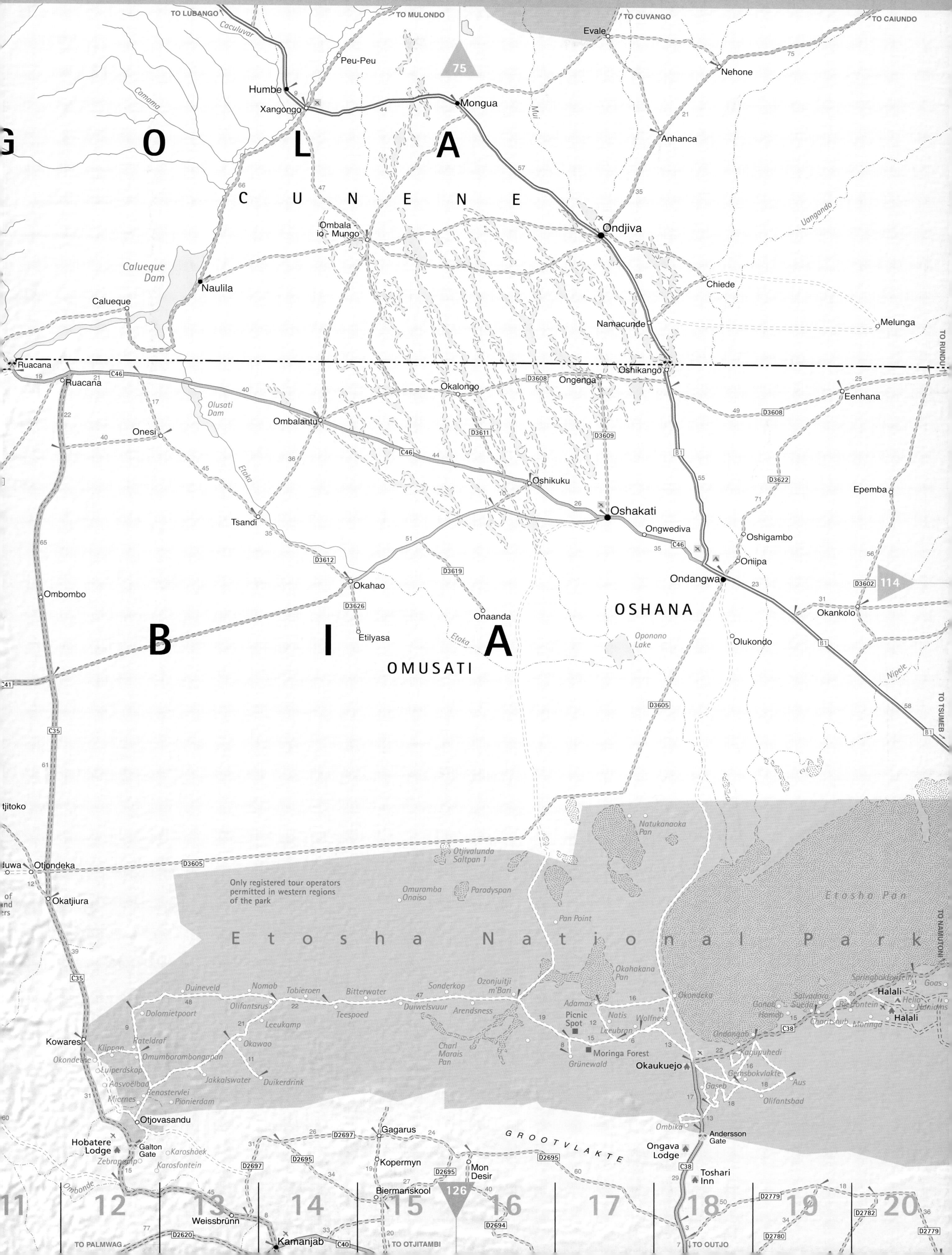
TO LUBANGO
TO MULONDO
TO CUVANGO
TO CAIUNDO
ANGOLA
CUNENE
Humbe
Xangongo
Mongua
Peu-Peu
Evale
Nehone
Anhanca
Ondjiva
Ombala io - Mungo
Calueque Dam
Naulila
Calueque
Chiede
Namacunde
Melunga
Oshikango
Ruacana
Okalongo
Ongenga
Eenhana
Ombalantu
Onesi
Olusati Dam
Oshikuku
Oshakati
Ongwediva
Tsandi
Epemba
Oshigambo
Oniipa
Ondangwa
Okankolo
Okahao
Onaanda
Etilyasa
Ombombo
Olukondo
Oponono Lake
OSHANA
OMUSATI
NAMIBIA
TO RUNDU
TO TSUMEB
Otjondeka
Okatjiura
Natukanaoka Pan
Otjivalunda Saltpan 1
Only registered tour operators permitted in western regions of the park
Omuramba Onaiso
Paradyspan
Etosha Pan
Pan Point
Etosha National Park
TO NAMUTONI
Okahakana Pan
Duineveld
Nomab
Tobieroen
Bitterwater
Sonderkop
Ozonjuitji m'Bari
Dolomietpoort
Olifantsrus
Teespoed
Duiwelsvuur
Arendsness
Adamax
Picnic Spot
Natis
Wolfsnes
Okondeka
Halali
Helio
Goas
Kowares
Leeukamp
Okawao
Rateldraf
Klippan
Okondeka
Omumborombongaan
Luiperdskop
Aasvoëlbad
Jakkalswater
Duikerdrink
Renostervlei
Pionierdam
Miernes
Charl Marais Pan
Leeubron
Moringa Forest
Grünewald
Okaukuejo
Kapupuhedi
Gemsbokvlakte
Aus
Gaseb
Olifantsbad
Ombika
Andersson Gate
Otjovasandu
Hobatere Lodge
Galton Gate
Karoshoek
Karosfontein
Zebrapomp
Ombonde
Gagarus
Kopermyn
Mon Desir
GROOTVLAKTE
Ongava Lodge
Toshari Inn
Biermanskool
Weissbrünn
Kamanjab
TO PALMWAG
TO OTJITAMBI
TO OUTJO
C46
C35
C41
C38
C39
C40
B1
D3608
D3609
D3611
D3612
D3619
D3622
D3626
D3602
D3605
D2697
D2695
D2620
D2694
D2779
D2780
D2782
75
114
126
11 12 13 14 15 16 17 18 19 20

SCENIC ROUTE — MAJOR CONNECTING ROUTE
TARRED / UNTARRED — MAIN CONNECTING ROUTE
TARRED / UNTARRED — MAIN ROAD
TARRED / UNTARRED — MINOR ROAD
4WD ROAD
LOCAL TRACK
HIKING TRAIL
234 NATIONAL ROUTE NUMBER
234 OTHER ROUTE NUMBER
PLACE OF INTEREST

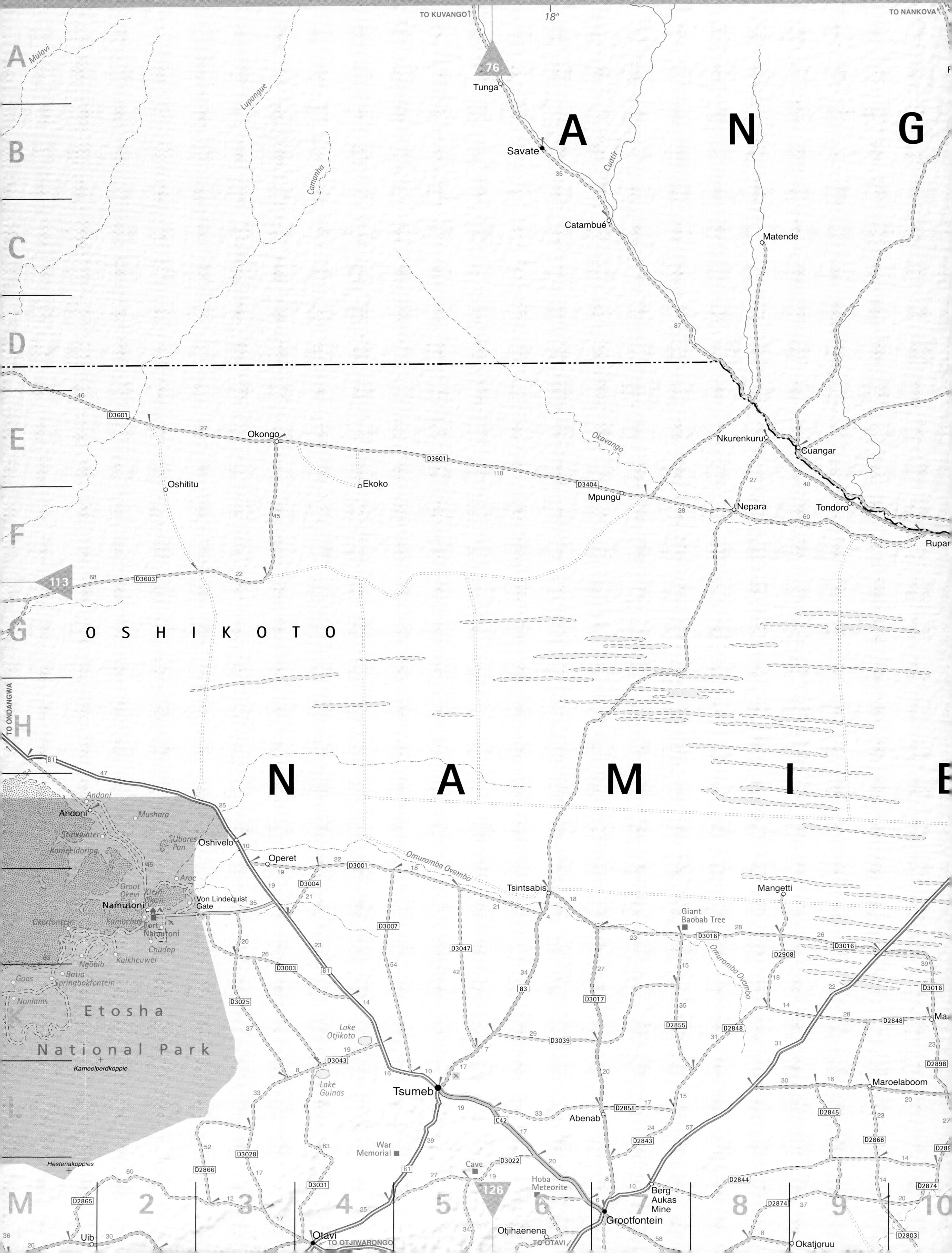

NAIROBI CAPITAL CITY | Abidjan SECONDARY CAPITAL CITY When Applicable | Las Palmas DEPENDANCY CAPITAL | Gweru LARGE / MAJOR TOWN Over 50,000 people | Ruhengeri SECONDARY TOWN Between 10,000 & 50,000 | El Kadada SMALL TOWN Between 5,000 &10,000 | Chinguetti LARGE VILLAGE Between 500 & 5,000 | Winneba SMALL VILLAGE OR SETTLEMENT Under 500 people

KM 30
MI 20

SCENIC ROUTE — MAJOR CONNECTING ROUTE
TARRED / UNTARRED — MAIN CONNECTING ROUTE
TARRED / UNTARRED — MAIN ROAD
TARRED / UNTARRED — MINOR ROAD
4WD ROAD
LOCAL TRACK
HIKING TRAIL
234 NATIONAL ROUTE NUMBER
234 OTHER ROUTE NUMBER
PLACE OF INTEREST

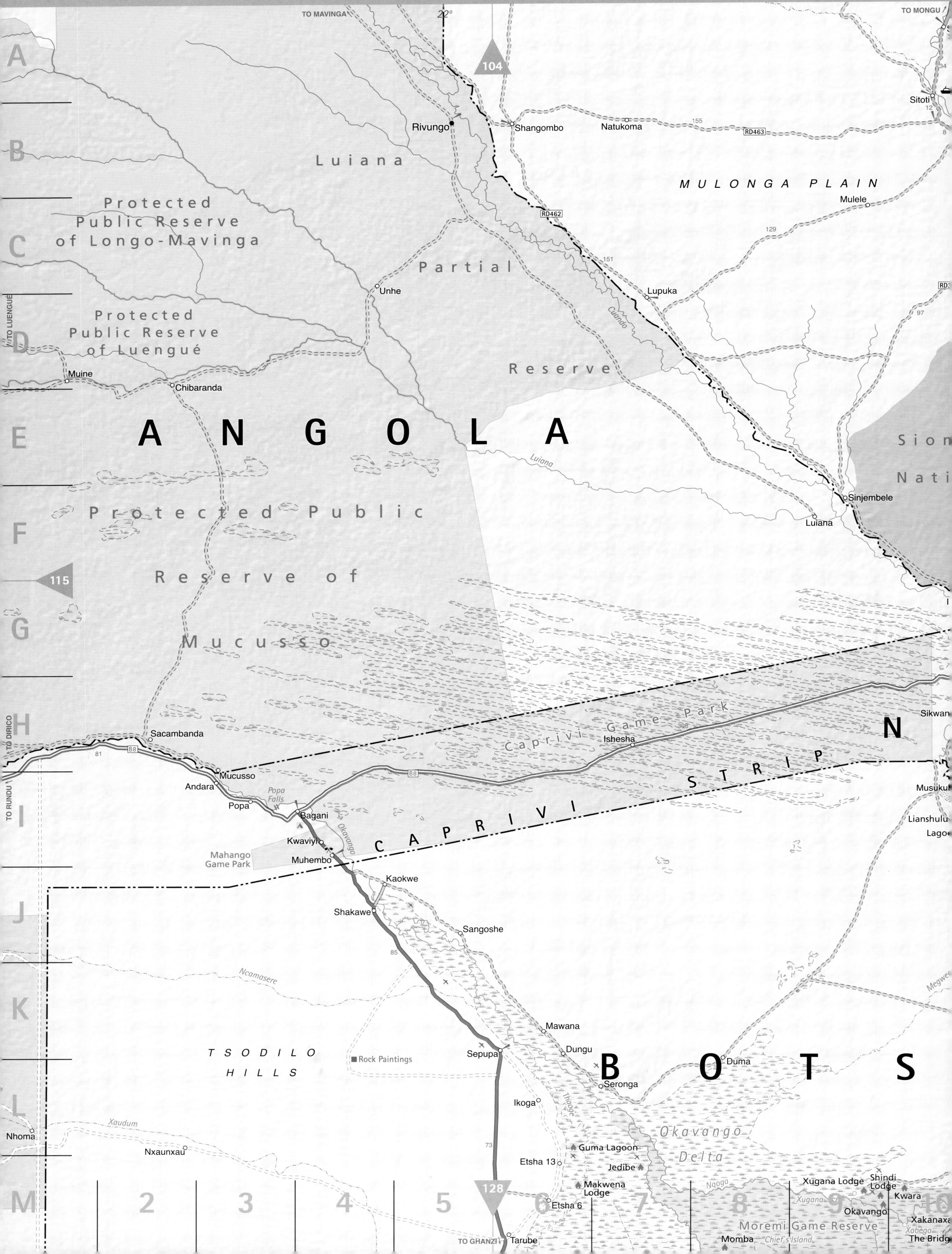

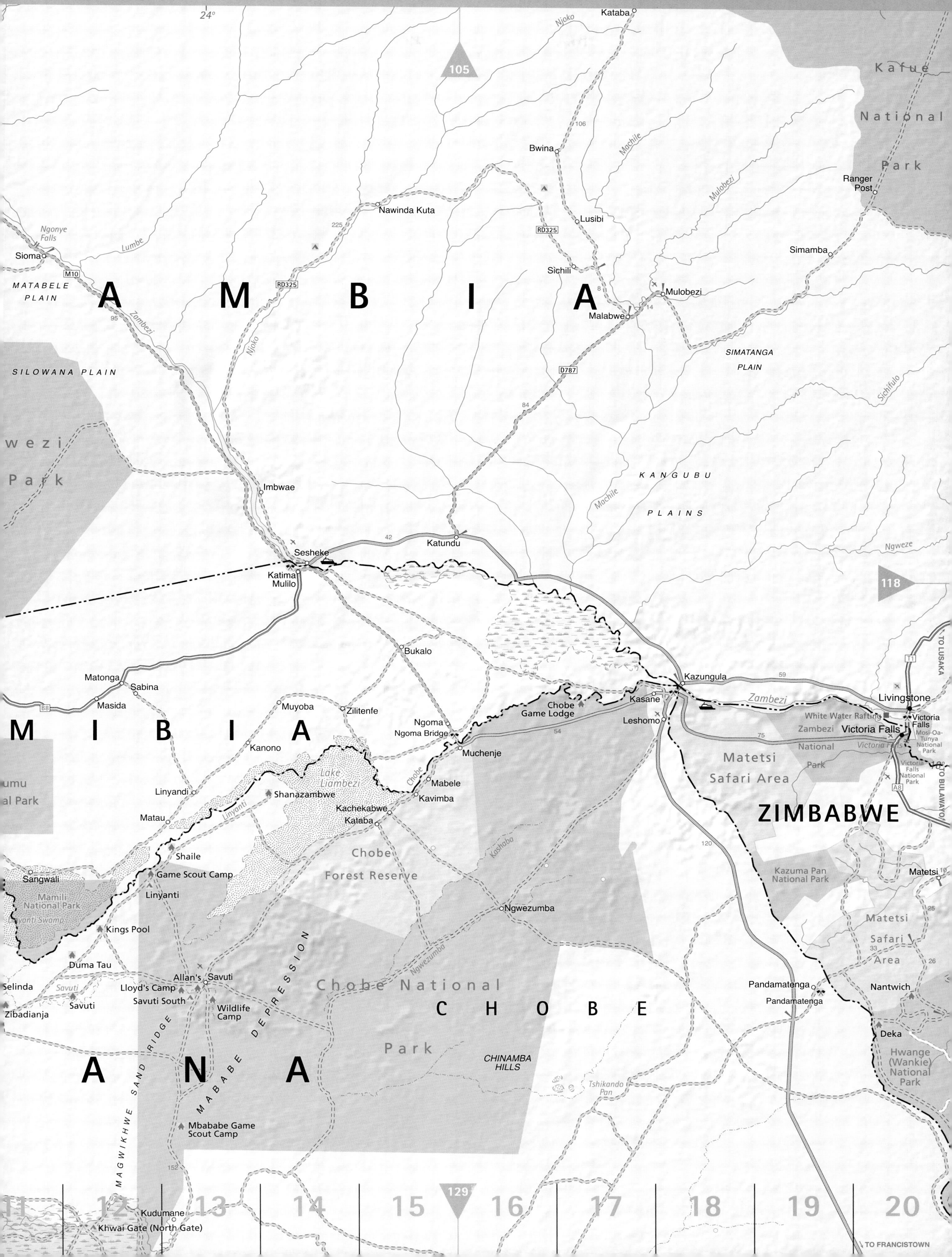

24°
105
Kataba
Njoko
Kafue
National
Park
106
Bwina
Machile
Mulobezi
Ranger Post
Nawinda Kuta
Lusibi
RD325
Ngonye Falls
Lumbe
225
Sioma
Simamba
Sichili
M10
Mulobezi
MATABELE PLAIN
A M B I A
Malabwe
RD325
95
Zambezi
Njoko
SIMATANGA PLAIN
D787
SILOWANA PLAIN
Sichifulo
84
wezi
Park
KANGUBU
Machile
PLAINS
Imbwae
Katundu
42
Ngweze
Sesheke
Katima Mulilo
118
Bukalo
Kazungula
59
T1
TO LUSAKA
Matonga
Sabina
Masida
B8
Muyoba
Zilitenfe
Chobe Game Lodge
Kasane
Zambezi
Livingstone
Leshomo
White Water Rafting
Victoria Falls
Ngoma
Ngoma Bridge
54
Zambezi
Victoria Falls
Mosi-Oa-Tunya National Park
M I B I A
Kanono
Muchenje
National
75
Victoria Falls
Matetsi
Park
Victoria Falls National Park
TO BULAWAYO
Lake Liambezi
Safari Area
umu
al Park
Linyandi
Shanazambwe
Chobe
Mabele
Kavimba
A8
ZIMBABWE
Matau
Linyanti
Kachekabwe
Kataba
Chobe
Shaile
Kashaba
120
Forest Reserve
Sangwali
Game Scout Camp
Kazuma Pan National Park
Matetsi
Mamili National Park
Linyanti
Linyanti Swamp
Ngwezumba
Kings Pool
Matetsi
Safari
Area
Duma Tau
Ngwezumba
Selinda
Savuti
Allan's Savuti
Lloyd's Camp
Savuti South
Wildlife Camp
Chobe National
Pandamatenga
Pandamatenga
Nantwich
Zibadianja
Savuti
C H O B E
Deka
MAGWIKHWE SAND RIDGE
MABABE DEPRESSION
Park
Hwange (Wankie) National Park
A N A
CHINAMBA HILLS
Tshikando Pan
Mbababe Game Scout Camp
152
129
11 12 13 14 15 16 17 18 19 20
Kudumane
Khwai Gate (North Gate)
TO FRANCISTOWN

SCENIC ROUTE · MAJOR CONNECTING ROUTE · TARRED / UNTARRED MAIN CONNECTING ROUTE · TARRED / UNTARRED MAIN ROAD · TARRED / UNTARRED MINOR ROAD · 4WD ROAD · LOCAL TRACK · HIKING TRAIL · 234 NATIONAL ROUTE NUMBER · 234 OTHER ROUTE NUMBER · PLACE OF INTEREST

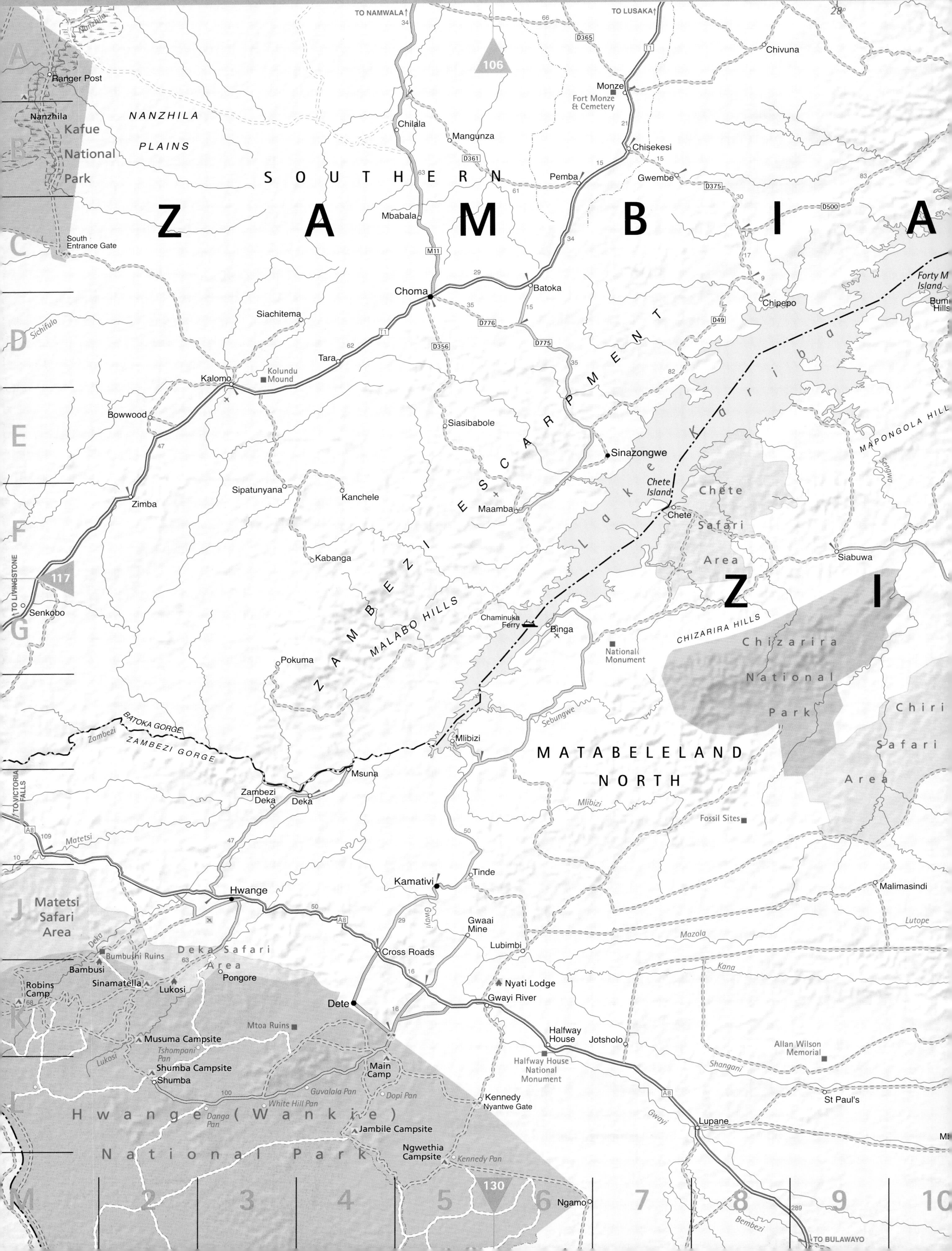

NAIROBI CAPITAL CITY | Abidjan SECONDARY CAPITAL CITY When Applicable | Las Palmas DEPENDANCY CAPITAL | Gweru LARGE / MAJOR TOWN Over 50,000 people | Ruhengeri SECONDARY TOWN Between 10,000 & 50,000 | El Kadada SMALL TOWN Between 5,000 &10,000 | Chinguetti LARGE VILLAGE Between 500 & 5,000 | Winneba SMALL VILLAGE OR SETTLEMENT Under 500 people

KM 30 MI 20

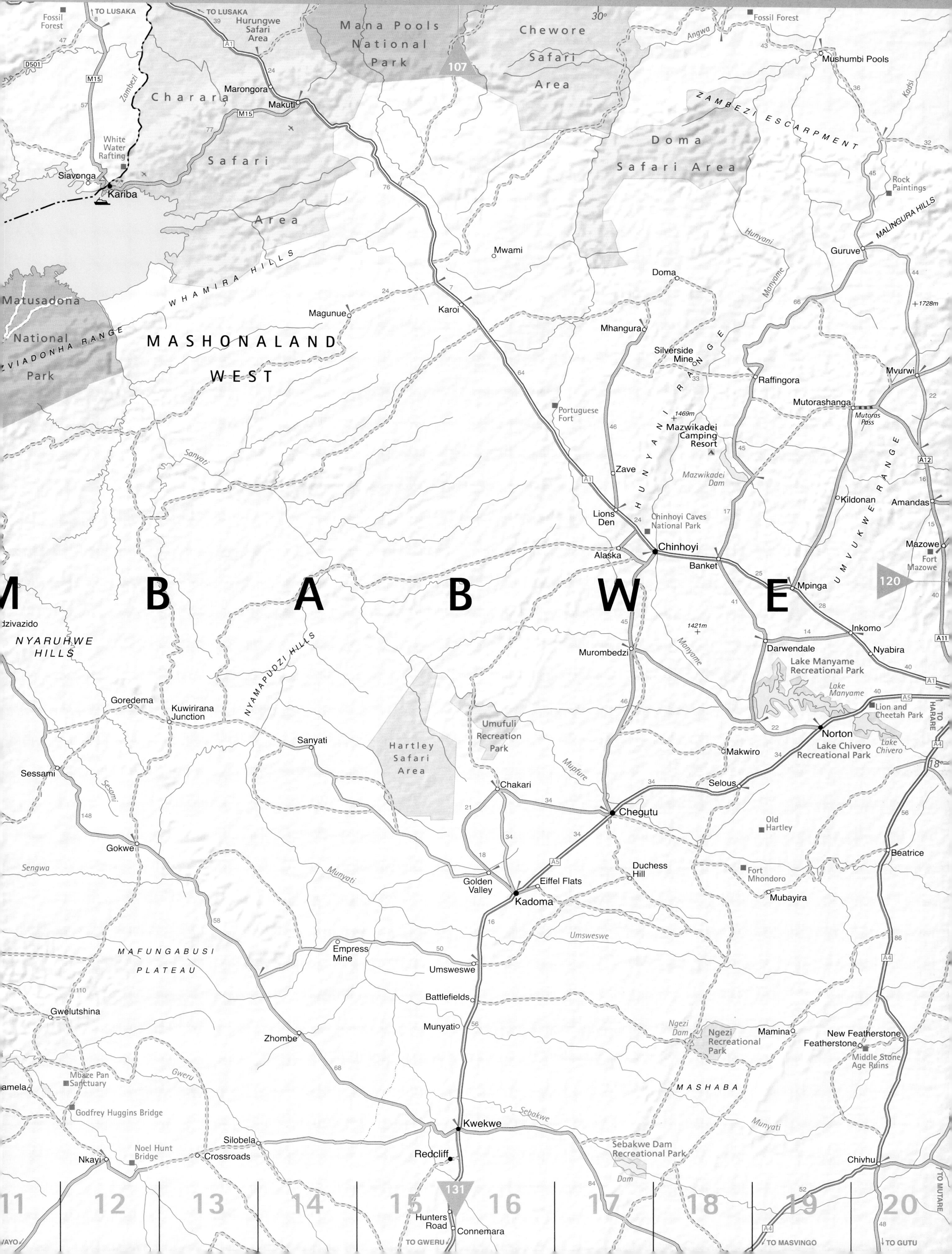

SCENIC ROUTE MAJOR CONNECTING ROUTE | TARRED UNTARRED MAIN CONNECTING ROUTE | TARRED UNTARRED MAIN ROAD | TARRED UNTARRED MINOR ROAD | 4WD ROAD | LOCAL TRACK | HIKING TRAIL | 234 NATIONAL ROUTE NUMBER | 234 OTHER ROUTE NUMBER | PLACE OF INTEREST

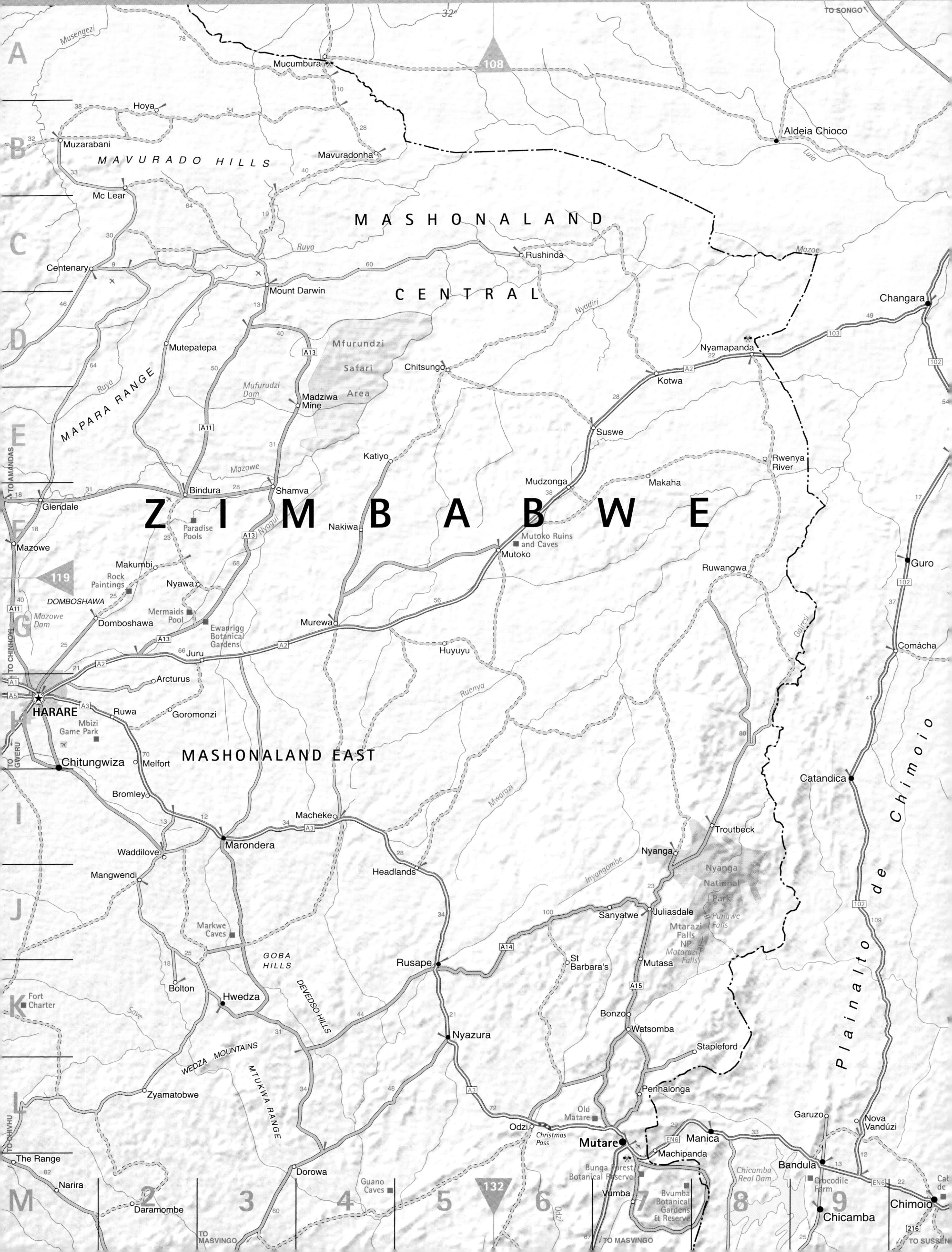

NAIROBI CAPITAL CITY | Abidjan SECONDARY CAPITAL CITY When Applicable | Las Palmas DEPENDANCY CAPITAL | Gweru LARGE / MAJOR TOWN Over 50,000 people | Ruhengeri SECONDARY TOWN Between 10,000 & 50,000 | El Kadada SMALL TOWN Between 5,000 &10,000 | Chinguetti LARGE VILLAGE Between 500 & 5,000 | Winneba SMALL VILLAGE OR SETTLEMENT Under 500 people

KM 30 MI 20

SCENIC ROUTE — MAJOR CONNECTING ROUTE
TARRED / UNTARRED — MAIN CONNECTING ROUTE
TARRED / UNTARRED — MAIN ROAD
TARRED / UNTARRED — MINOR ROAD
4WD ROAD
LOCAL TRACK
HIKING TRAIL
234 NATIONAL ROUTE NUMBER
234 OTHER ROUTE NUMBER
PLACE OF INTEREST

NAIROBI CAPITAL CITY | Abidjan SECONDARY CAPITAL CITY When Applicable | Las Palmas DEPENDANCY CAPITAL | Gweru LARGE / MAJOR TOWN Over 50,000 people | Ruhengeri SECONDARY TOWN Between 10,000 & 50,000 | El Kadada SMALL TOWN Between 5,000 &10,000 | Chinguetti LARGE VILLAGE Between 500 & 5,000 | Winneba SMALL VILLAGE OR SETTLEMENT Under 500 people

KM 30 MI 20

SCENIC ROUTE — MAJOR CONNECTING ROUTE
TARRED / UNTARRED — MAIN CONNECTING ROUTE
TARRED / UNTARRED — MAIN ROAD
TARRED / UNTARRED — MINOR ROAD
4WD ROAD
LOCAL TRACK
HIKING TRAIL
234 NATIONAL ROUTE NUMBER
234 OTHER ROUTE NUMBER
■ PLACE OF INTEREST

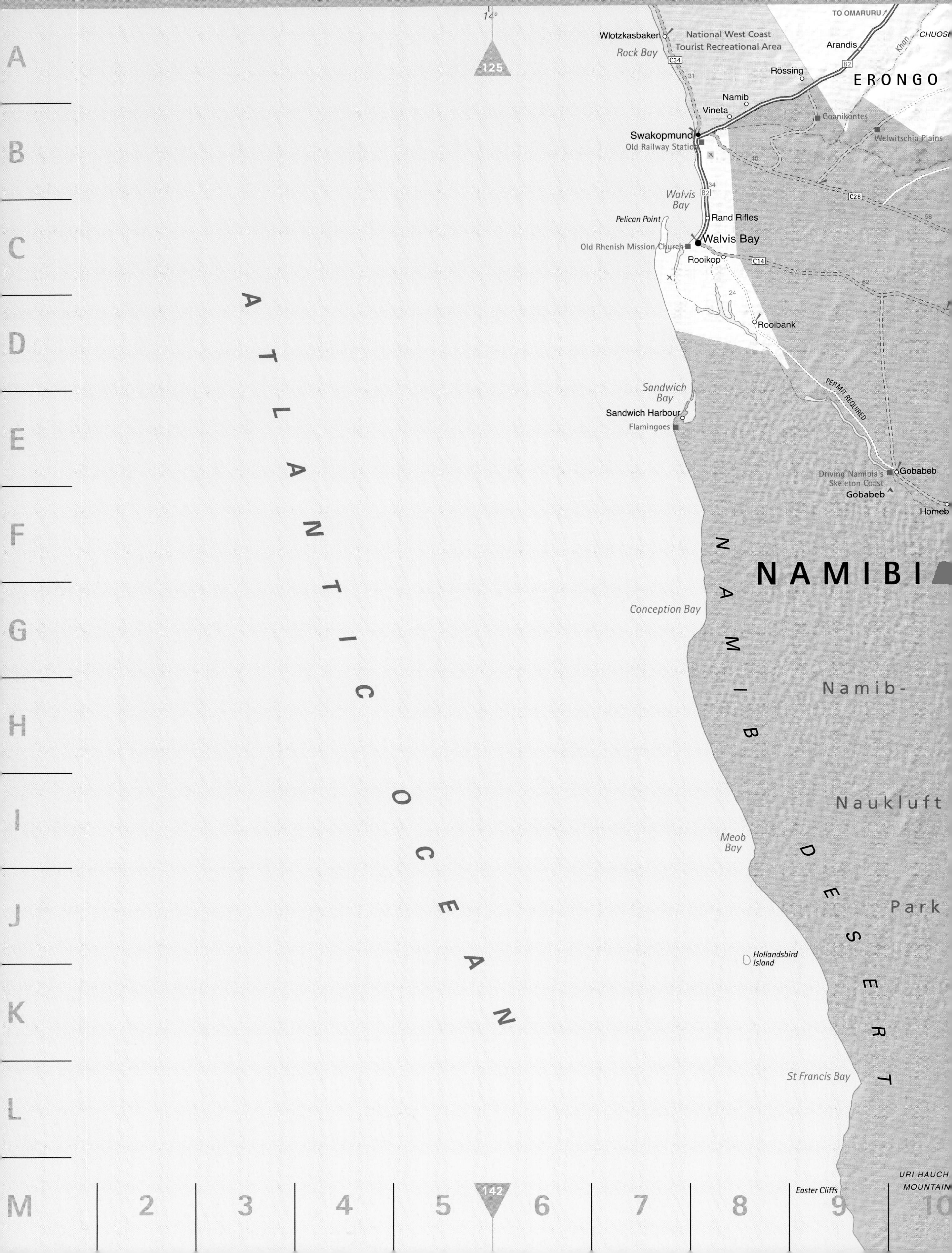

NAIROBI CAPITAL CITY | Abidjan SECONDARY CAPITAL CITY When Applicable | Las Palmas DEPENDANCY CAPITAL | Gweru LARGE / MAJOR TOWN Over 50,000 people | Ruhengeri SECONDARY TOWN Between 10,000 & 50,000 | El Kadada SMALL TOWN Between 5,000 &10,000 | Chinguetti LARGE VILLAGE Between 500 & 5,000 | Winneba SMALL VILLAGE OR SETTLEMENT Under 500 people

KM 30 MI 20

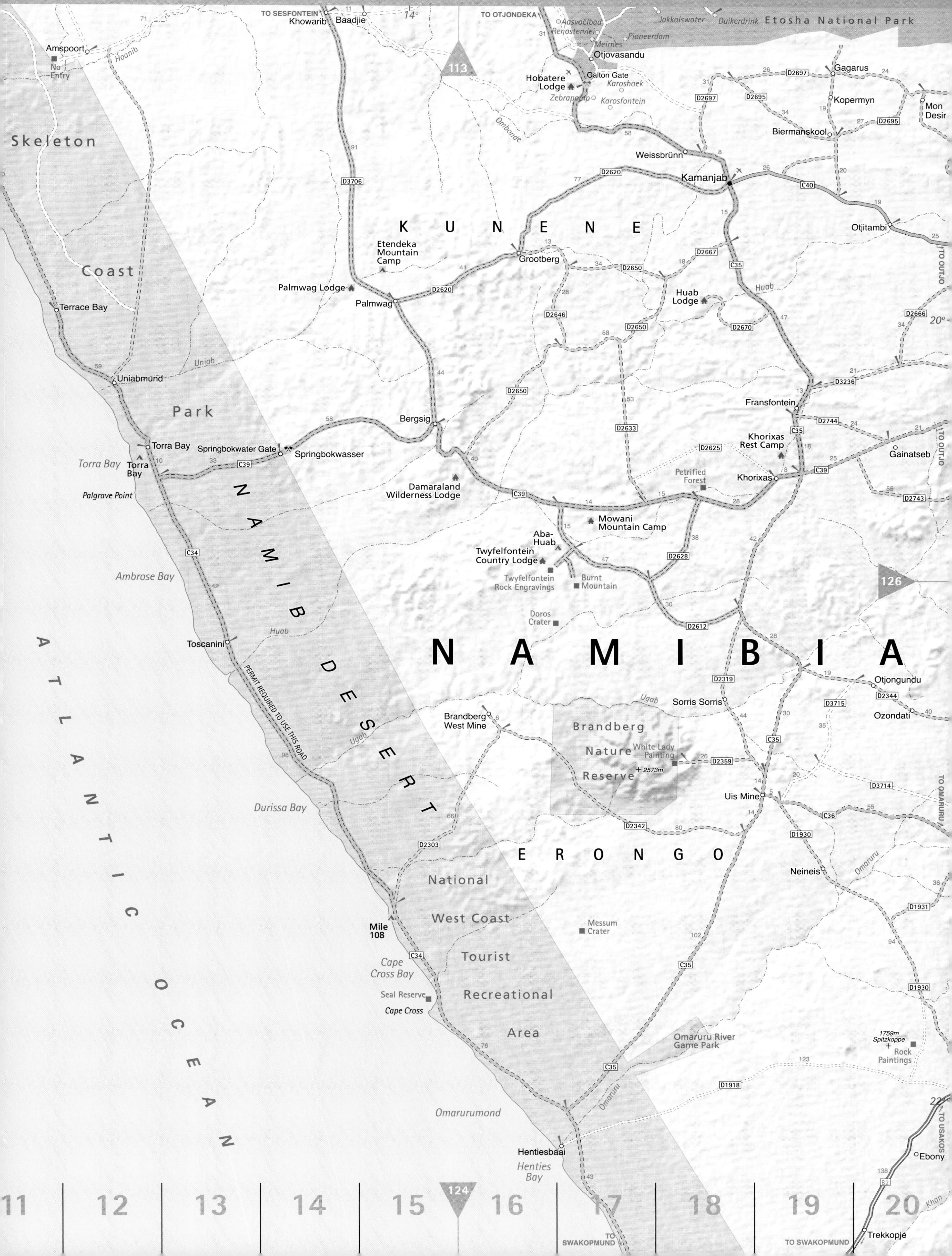

SCENIC ROUTE — MAJOR CONNECTING ROUTE
TARRED / UNTARRED — MAIN CONNECTING ROUTE
TARRED / UNTARRED — MAIN ROAD
TARRED / UNTARRED — MINOR ROAD
4WD ROAD
LOCAL TRACK
HIKING TRAIL
234 NATIONAL ROUTE NUMBER
234 OTHER ROUTE NUMBER
PLACE OF INTEREST

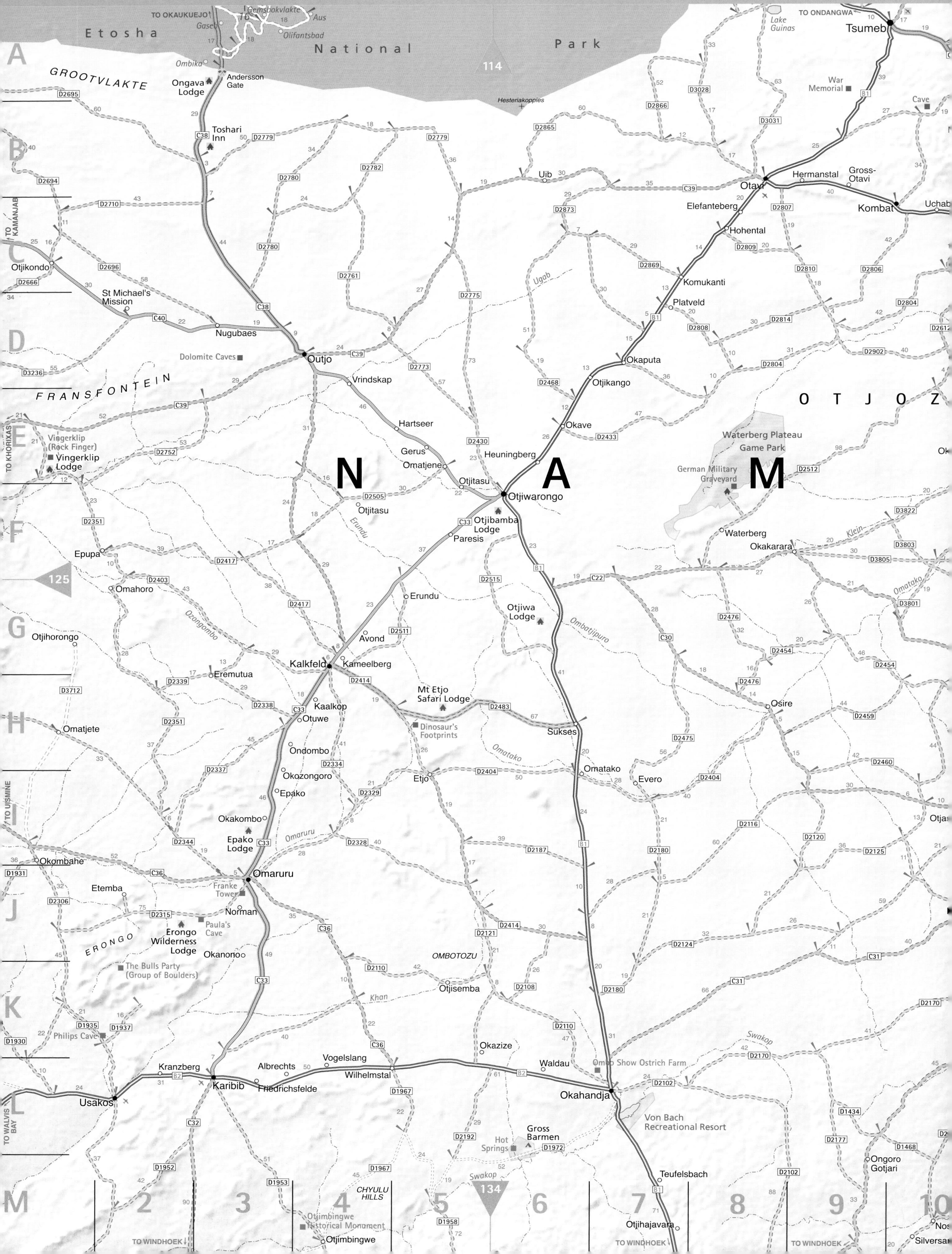

NAIROBI CAPITAL CITY | Abidjan SECONDARY CAPITAL CITY When Applicable | Las Palmas DEPENDANCY CAPITAL | Gweru LARGE / MAJOR TOWN Over 50,000 people | Ruhengeri SECONDARY TOWN Between 10,000 & 50,000 | El Kadada SMALL TOWN Between 5,000 &10,000 | Chinguetti LARGE VILLAGE Between 500 & 5,000 | Winneba SMALL VILLAGE OR SETTLEMENT Under 500 people

KM 30 MI 20

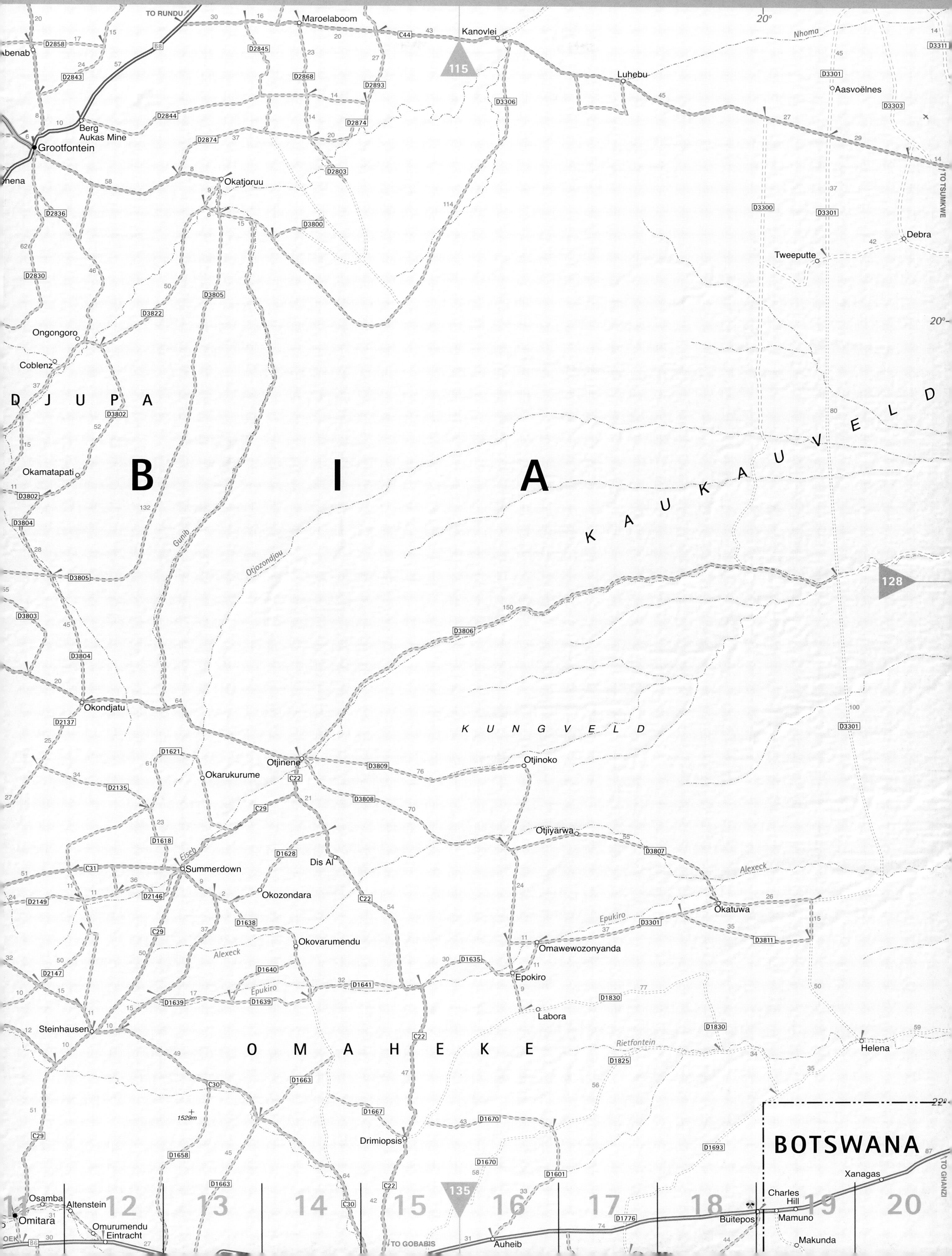

SCENIC ROUTE MAJOR CONNECTING ROUTE | TARRED UNTARRED MAIN CONNECTING ROUTE | TARRED UNTARRED MAIN ROAD | TARRED UNTARRED MINOR ROAD | 4WD ROAD | LOCAL TRACK | HIKING TRAIL | 234 NATIONAL ROUTE NUMBER | 234 OTHER ROUTE NUMBER | PLACE OF INTEREST

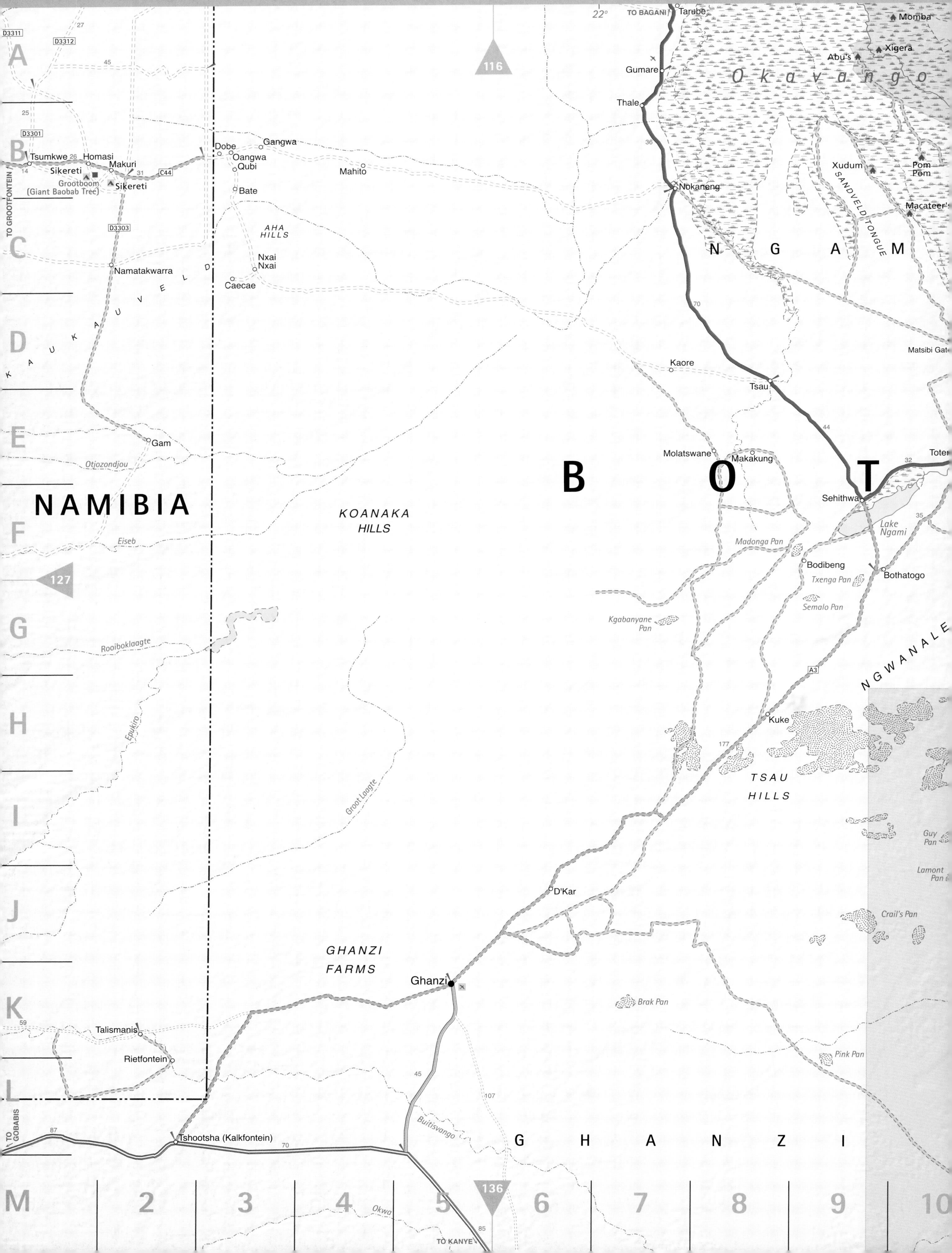

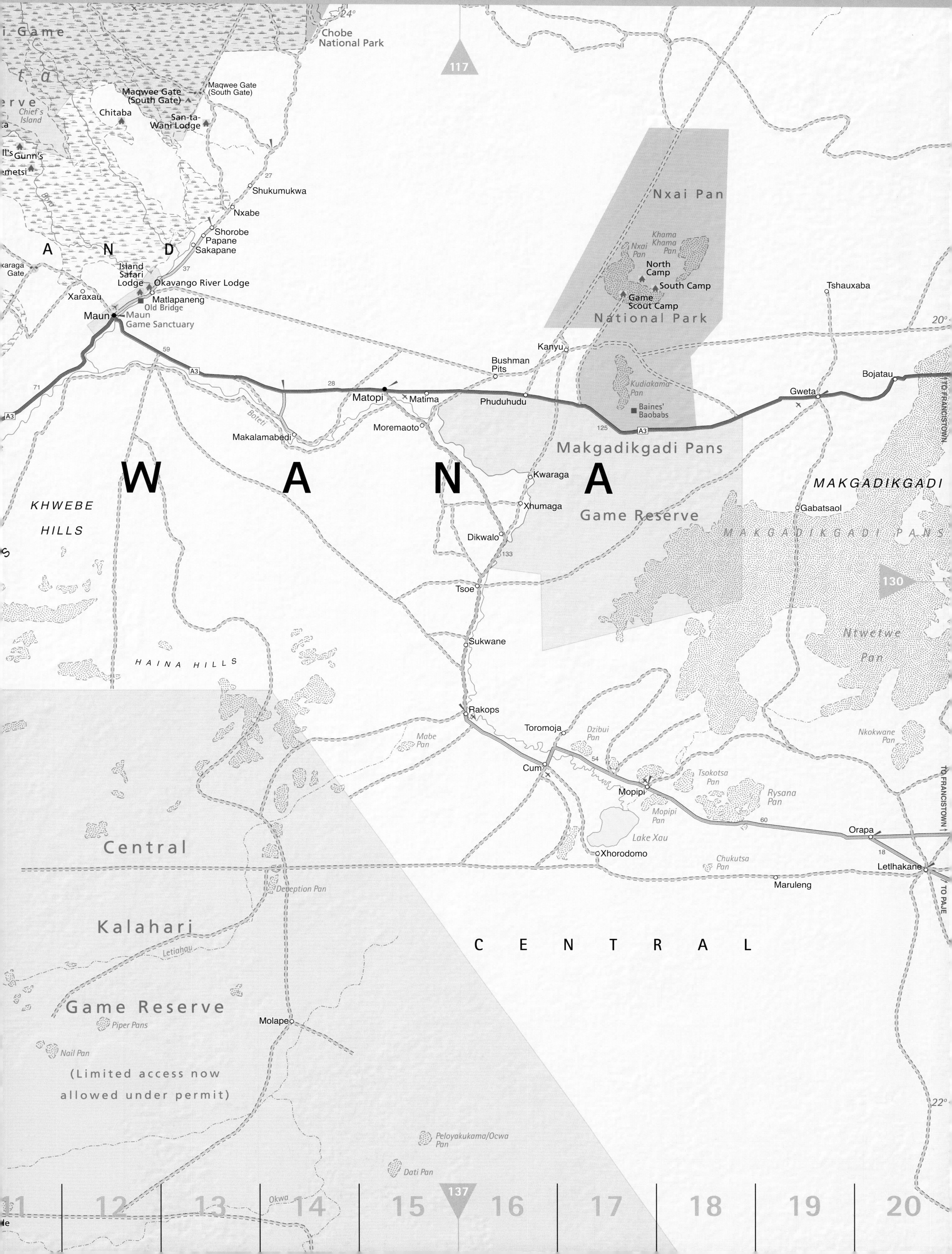
Chobe National Park
117
Maqwee Gate (South Gate)
Chitaba
San-ta-Wani Lodge
Chief's Island
Gunn's
Shukumukwa
Nxabe
Shorobe
Papane
Sakapane
Island Safari Lodge
Okavango River Lodge
Xaraxau
Matlapaneng
Old Bridge
Maun
Maun Game Sanctuary
A3
Nxai Pan
Khama Khama Pan
Nxai Pan
North Camp
South Camp
Game Scout Camp
National Park
Tshauxaba
Kanyu
Bushman Pits
Matopi
Matima
Phuduhudu
Kudiakama Pan
Baines' Baobabs
Makalamabedi
Moremaoto
Boteti
Bojatau
Gweta
TO FRANCISTOWN
Makgadikgadi Pans
Game Reserve
Kwaraga
Xhumaga
Dikwalo
W A N A
KHWEBE HILLS
MAKGADIKGADI
Gabatsaol
MAKGADIKGADI PANS
130
Tsoe
Sukwane
Ntwetwe Pan
HAINA HILLS
Rakops
Toromoja
Dzibui Pan
Mabe Pan
Nkokwane Pan
Cum
Mopipi
Tsokotsa Pan
Rysana Pan
Mopipi Pan
Lake Xau
Orapa
Central
Xhorodomo
Chukutsa Pan
Letlhakane
Maruleng
TO PAJE
Deception Pan
Kalahari
C E N T R A L
Letiahau
Game Reserve
Molape
Piper Pans
Nail Pan
(Limited access now allowed under permit)
Peloyakukama/Ocwa Pan
Dati Pan
137
Okwa
11 12 13 14 15 16 17 18 19 20

SCENIC ROUTE
MAJOR CONNECTING ROUTE
TARRED UNTARRED
MAIN CONNECTING ROUTE
MAIN ROAD
MINOR ROAD
4WD ROAD
LOCAL TRACK
HIKING TRAIL
234 NATIONAL ROUTE NUMBER
234 OTHER ROUTE NUMBER
PLACE OF INTEREST
TO KASANE
Hwange (Wankie) National Park
118
Libuti Camp
Chemuumi
Korondziba
Sihazela
Gwaai
Regina Mundi Mission
Jimila
Dhlamini
MATABELELAND NORTH
Pamula
Tsholotsho
Tamasanka Pan
Nemtungu Pan
Kaukaka
Sepako
Tsuli
Maitengwe
Tegwani
Manzamnyama
Gwayi
Fossil Dinos
Z I
TO MAUN
A3
Zoroga
Nata
Nata Lodge
Sowa Pan Lodge
Maitengwe
Tsigara
MAKGADIKGADI PANS
Tutume
Plumtree
Plumtree
Vakaranga
Sowa
Dukwe
Ramokgwebane
129
Mosetse
Masunga
Tshesebe
Thabatshukudu
Sowa Pan
Tshwagong
Sebina
Fort Empandeni Earthworks
Shashe
NORTH EAST
Ramokgwebane
Ingwese Dam
Ntsokotska Pan
Mmatshumo
Thakadu
Francistown
Dumela
Ngwesi
Mphoengs
TO ORAPA
Tlalamabele
Mokobela Pan
Matsiloje
BOTSWANA
Ditsinane Pan
Shashe
Tonota
Tati
Foley
CENTRAL
Motloutse
Serule
Mmashoro
Selebi Phikwe
Sefophe
Paje
138
Maope
Thataganyana Rock
TO PALAPYE
TO MAHALAPYE
Mogapinyana
Mogapi
TO SHERWOOD

NAIROBI CAPITAL CITY | Abidjan SECONDARY CAPITAL CITY When Applicable | Las Palmas DEPENDANCY CAPITAL | Gweru LARGE / MAJOR TOWN Over 50,000 people | Ruhengeri SECONDARY TOWN Between 10,000 & 50,000 | El Kadada SMALL TOWN Between 5,000 &10,000 | Chinguetti LARGE VILLAGE Between 500 & 5,000 | Winneba SMALL VILLAGE OR SETTLEMENT Under 500 people

KM 30 MI 20

SCENIC ROUTE — MAJOR CONNECTING ROUTE
TARRED / UNTARRED — MAIN CONNECTING ROUTE
TARRED / UNTARRED — MAIN ROAD
TARRED / UNTARRED — MINOR ROAD
4WD ROAD
LOCAL TRACK
HIKING TRAIL
234 NATIONAL ROUTE NUMBER
234 OTHER ROUTE NUMBER
PLACE OF INTEREST

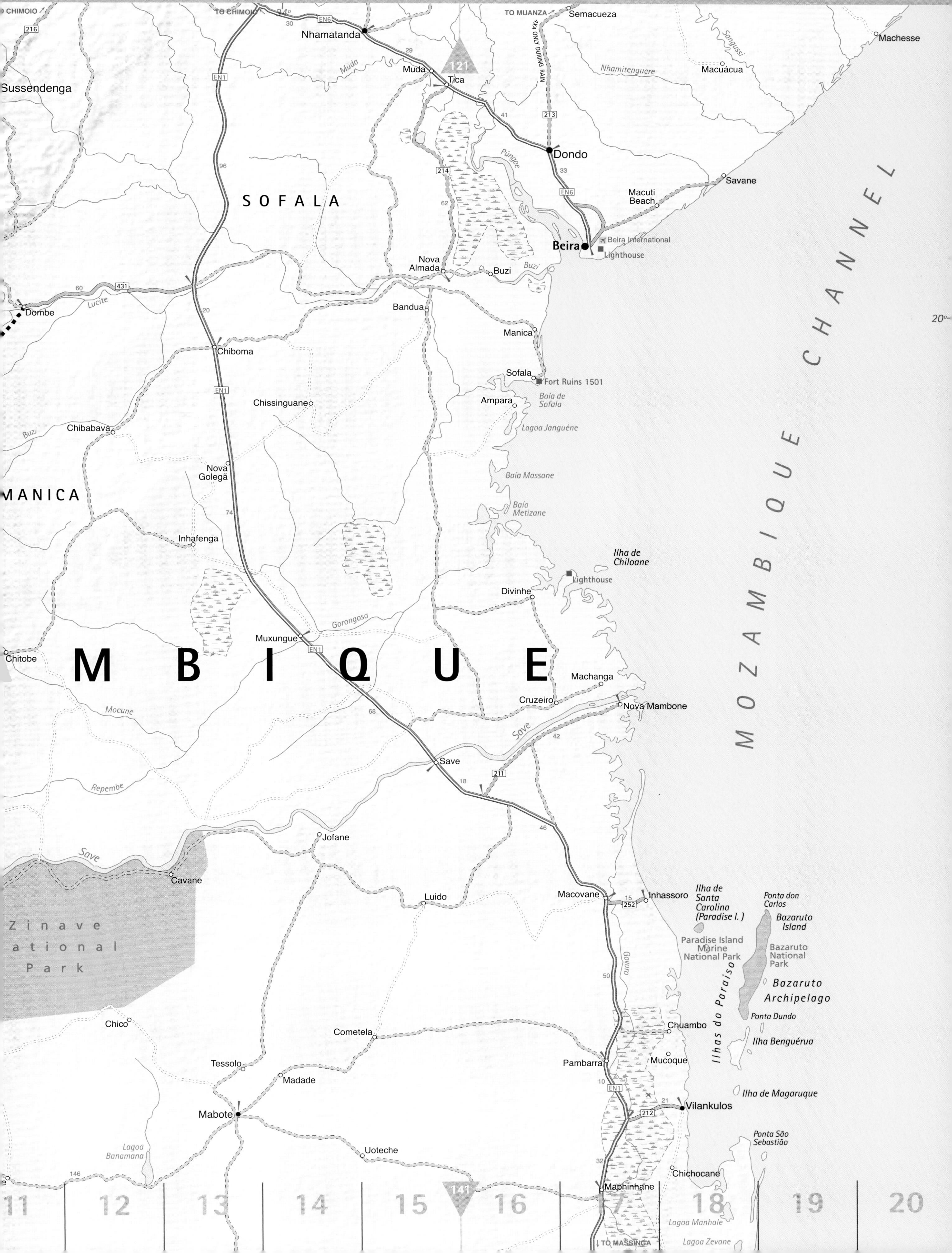

CHIMOIO
TO CHIMOIO
TO MUANZA
Semacueza
4x4 ONLY DURING RAIN
Nhamatanda
Muda
Tica
121
Machesse
Macuácua
Nhamitenguere
Sangussi
Sussendenga
Dondo
Púngoè
SOFALA
Macuti Beach
Savane
Beira
Beira International
Lighthouse
Nova Almada
Buzi
Dombe
Lucite
Bandua
Manica
Chiboma
Sofala
Fort Ruins 1501
Baía de Sofala
Ampara
Chissinguane
Lagoa Janguéne
Chibabava
Nova Golegã
Baía Massane
Baía Metizane
MANICA
Inhafenga
Ilha de Chiloane
Lighthouse
Divinhe
Gorongosa
Muxungue
Chitobe
M B I Q U E
Machanga
Cruzeiro
Nova Mambone
Mocune
Save
Save
Repembe
Jofane
Cavane
MOZAMBIQUE CHANNEL
Zinave National Park
Luido
Macovane
Inhassoro
Ilha de Santa Carolina (Paradise I.)
Ponta don Carlos
Bazaruto Island
Paradise Island Marine National Park
Bazaruto National Park
Bazaruto Archipelago
Govuro
Ilhas do Paraíso
Ponta Dundo
Chico
Cometela
Chuambo
Ilha Benguérua
Tessolo
Pambarra
Mucoque
Madade
Ilha de Magaruque
Mabote
Vilankulos
Ponta São Sebastião
Lagoa Banamana
Uoteche
Chichocane
Maphinhane
141
Lagoa Manhale
Lagoa Zevane
TO MASSINGA
11 12 13 14 15 16 17 18 19 20

SCENIC ROUTE · MAJOR CONNECTING ROUTE
TARRED · UNTARRED · MAIN CONNECTING ROUTE
TARRED · UNTARRED · MAIN ROAD
TARRED · UNTARRED · MINOR ROAD
4WD ROAD
LOCAL TRACK
HIKING TRAIL
234 NATIONAL ROUTE NUMBER
234 OTHER ROUTE NUMBER
PLACE OF INTEREST

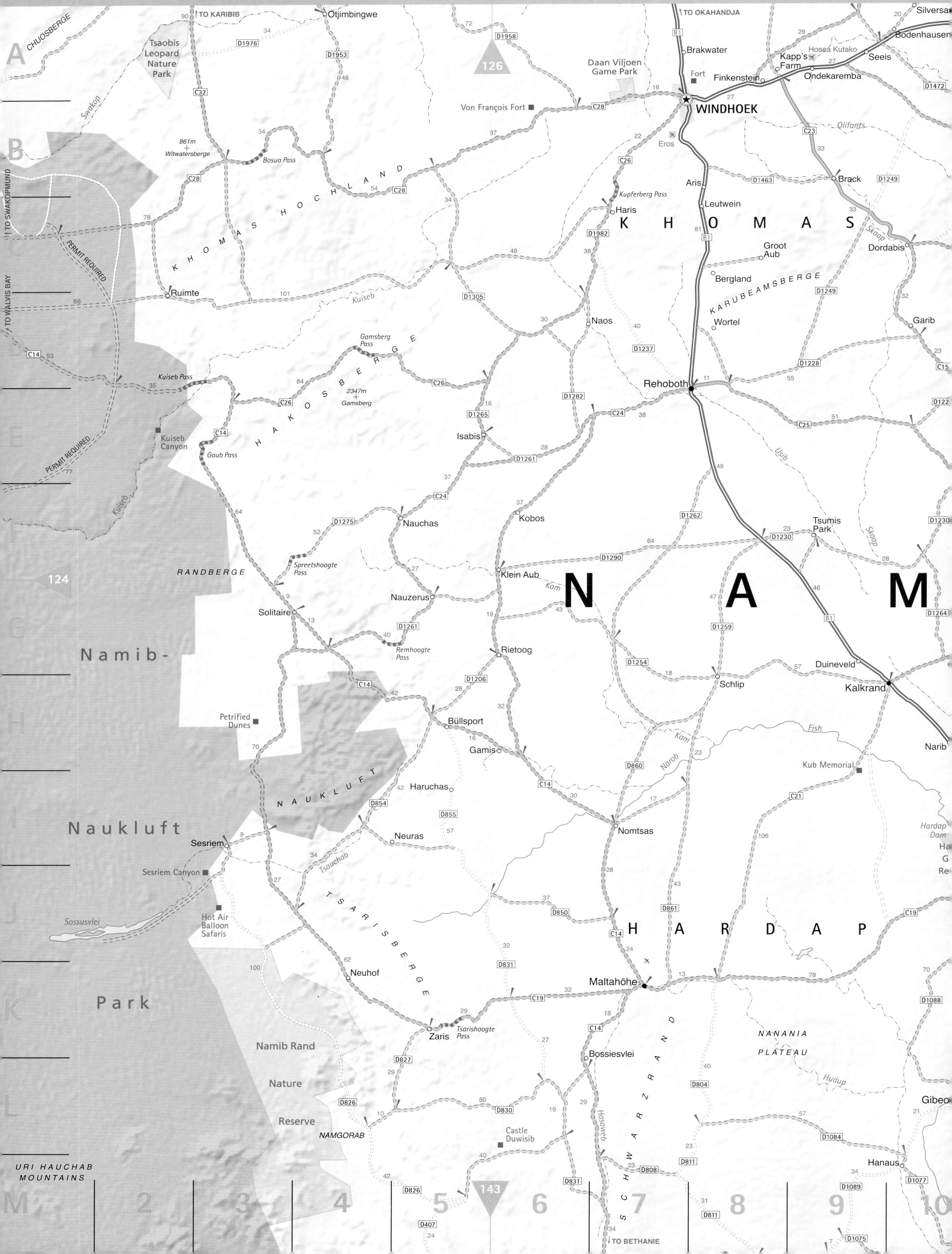

NAIROBI — CAPITAL CITY | Abidjan — SECONDARY CAPITAL CITY When Applicable | Las Palmas — DEPENDANCY CAPITAL | Gweru — LARGE / MAJOR TOWN Over 50,000 people | Ruhengeri — SECONDARY TOWN Between 10,000 & 50,000 | El Kadada — SMALL TOWN Between 5,000 &10,000 | Chinguetti — LARGE VILLAGE Between 500 & 5,000 | Winneba — SMALL VILLAGE OR SETTLEMENT Under 500 people

KM 30 / MI 20

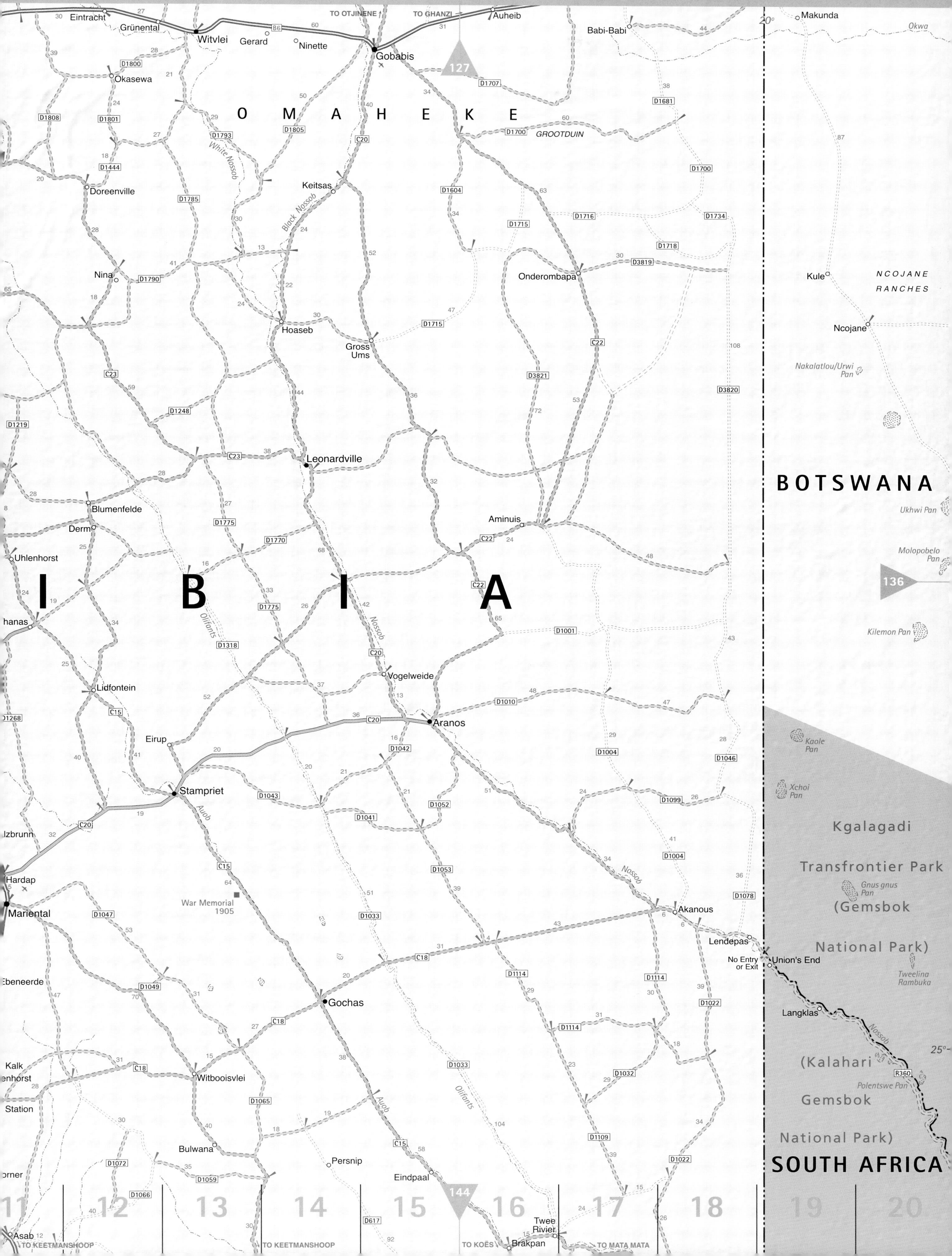

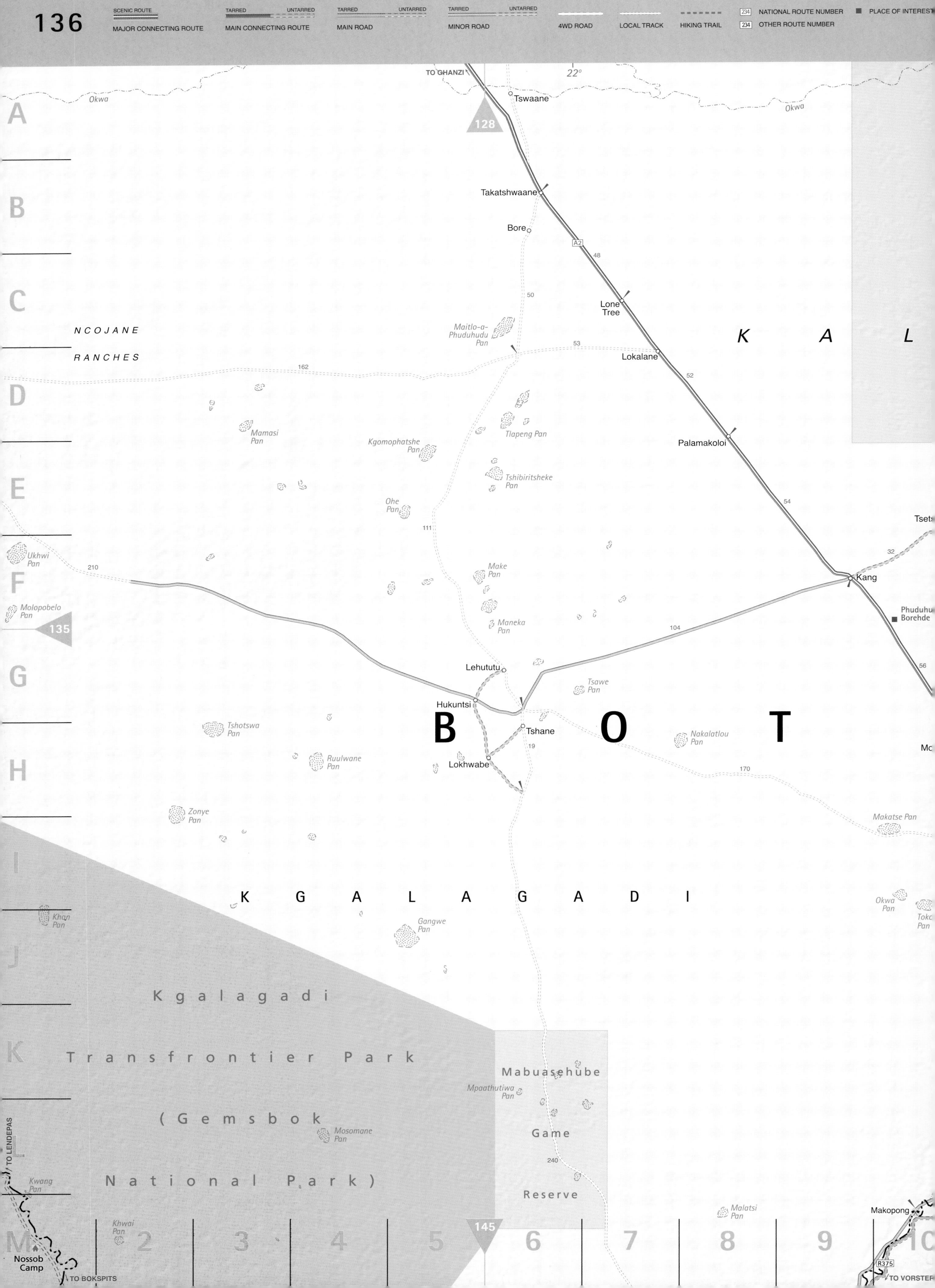
SCENIC ROUTE
MAJOR CONNECTING ROUTE
TARRED UNTARRED
MAIN CONNECTING ROUTE
TARRED UNTARRED
MAIN ROAD
TARRED UNTARRED
MINOR ROAD
4WD ROAD
LOCAL TRACK
HIKING TRAIL
234 NATIONAL ROUTE NUMBER
234 OTHER ROUTE NUMBER
PLACE OF INTEREST
TO GHANZI
22°
Okwa
Tswaane
128
Okwa
A
B
C
D
E
F
G
H
I
J
K
L
M
Takatshwaane
Bore
A2
48
50
Lone Tree
Maitlo-a-Phuduhudu Pan
NCOJANE
RANCHES
K A L
53
Lokalane
162
52
Mamasi Pan
Tlapeng Pan
Kgomophatshe Pan
Palamakoloi
Tshibiritsheke Pan
Ohe Pan
54
111
Tsets
Ukhwi Pan
210
32
Make Pan
Kang
Molopobelo Pan
135
Maneka Pan
104
Phuduhudu Borehde
Lehututu
56
Tsawe Pan
Hukuntsi
Tshane
B O T
Tshotswa Pan
Nakalatlou Pan
19
Ruulwane Pan
Lokhwabe
170
Mc
Zonye Pan
Makatse Pan
K G A L A G A D I
Khan Pan
Okwa Pan
Toko Pan
Gangwe Pan
Kgalagadi
Transfrontier Park
(Gemsbok
National Park)
Mabuasehube
Mpaathutiwa Pan
Game
Reserve
Mosomane Pan
240
TO LENDEPAS
Kwang Pan
Malatsi Pan
Makopong
Khwai Pan
145
2
3
4
5
6
7
8
9
10
Nossob Camp
R375
TO BOKSPITS
TO VORSTER

Central Kalahari Game Reserve
Khutse Game Reserve
KALAHARI DESERT
KWENENG
BOTSWANA
SOUTHERN
SOUTH EAST
SOUTH AFRICA
Gcingha Pan (Mazeamanong)
129
138
146
Bape
Okwa
Meratswe
Khanke Pan
Khwakwa Pan
Sekushuwe Pan
Matallane Pan
Kutse Pan
Mareswe Pan
Mabuakolobe Pan
Tsunuye Pan
Ngohowe Pan
Sehohu Pan
Tsia
Salajwe
Tswaane Pan
Khang Pan
Lokaakwe Pan
Tsesame
Khudumalapye
Motokwe
Dutlwe
Takatokwane
Sekono Pan
Botlhapatlou
Letlhakeng
Naledi
Kgari Pan
Moshaweng
Dikokwana Pan
Petrified Forest
Livingstone's Cave
Rock Engravings
Molepolole
Kamaku Pan
Tshinka Pan
Seletsa Pan
Mabutsane
Sekoma
Sekoma Pan
TRANS-KGALAGADI HIGHWAY
Jwaneng
Thamaga
Livingstone's Mission
Khakhea Pan
Khakhea
Khakhaiwa Pan
Malote Pan
Mosopo
Mathalsa Tree
Rock Paintings
Ranaka
Khwekhwe Pan
Tswaing Pan
Selokolela
Moshaneng
Kanye
Otse
Moselebe
Sita Pan
Lobatse
Werda
Molopo
Selokolela
Tsatsu
Skilpadshek
Mmathethe
Hildavale
Bray
Sekhutlane
Pitsane
Good Hope
TO GABORONE
TO ZEERUST
TO MAFIKENG
TO MMABATHO
24°
A1
A2
N4
R375
R378
11 12 13 14 15 16 17 18 19 20

SCENIC ROUTE — MAJOR CONNECTING ROUTE
TARRED / UNTARRED — MAIN CONNECTING ROUTE
TARRED / UNTARRED — MAIN ROAD
TARRED / UNTARRED — MINOR ROAD
4WD ROAD
LOCAL TRACK
HIKING TRAIL
234 NATIONAL ROUTE NUMBER
234 OTHER ROUTE NUMBER
PLACE OF INTEREST

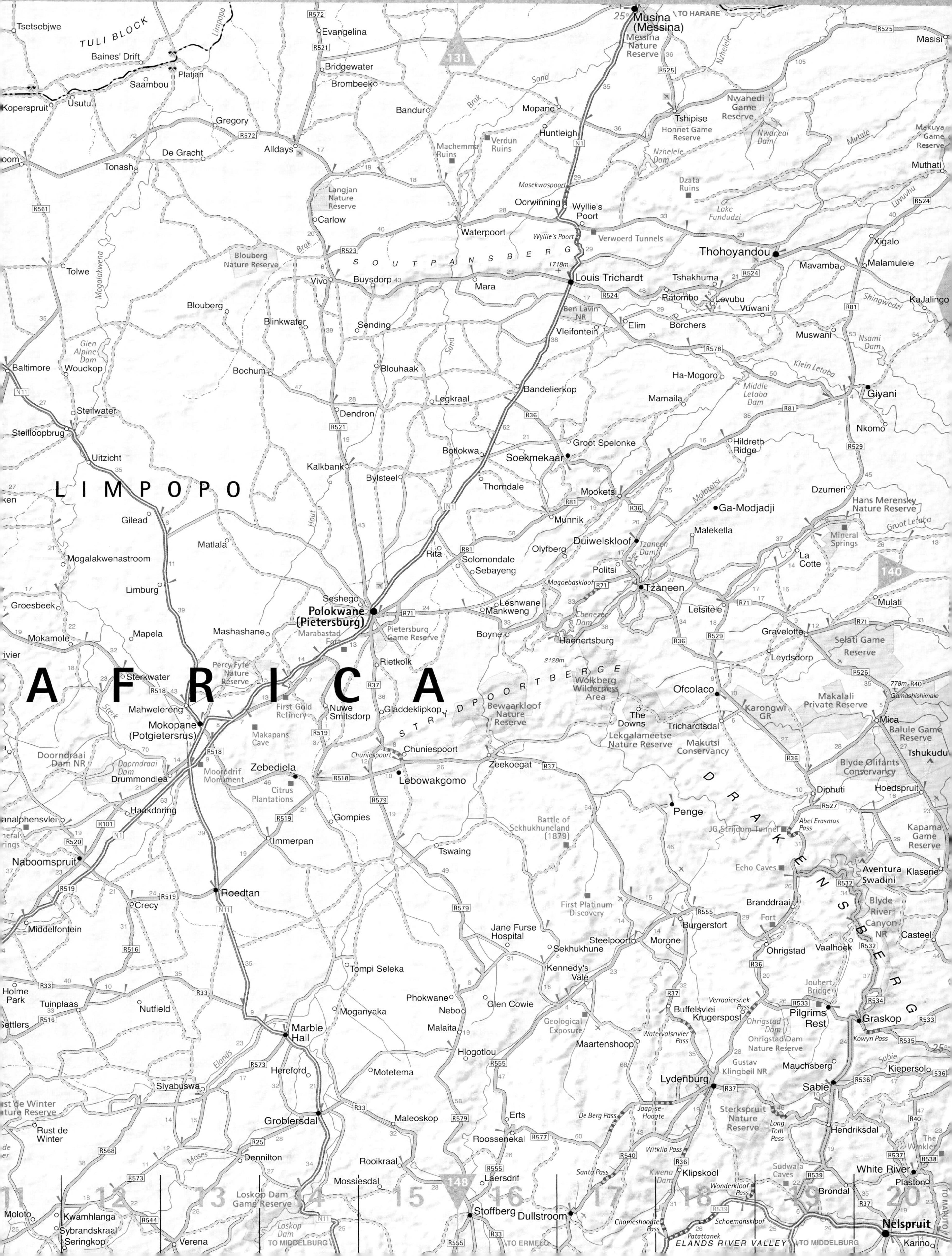

LIMPOPO
AFRICA
TULI BLOCK
SOUTPANSBERG
STRYDPOORTBERGE
DRAKENSBERG
Musina (Messina)
Messina Nature Reserve
TO HARARE
131
140
148
Tsetsebjwe
Baines' Drift
Platjan
Saambou
Kopersspruit
Usutu
Evangelina
Bridgewater
Brombeek
Bandur
Mopane
Huntleigh
Verdun Ruins
Machemma Ruins
Gregory
De Gracht
Alldays
Tonash
Langjan Nature Reserve
Carlow
Tshipise
Honnet Game Reserve
Nwanedi Game Reserve
Nwanedi Dam
Nzhelele Dam
Makuya Game Reserve
Masisi
Muthati
Dzata Ruins
Lake Fundudzi
Masekwaspoort
Oorwinning
Wyllie's Poort
Verwoerd Tunnels
Waterpoort
Thohoyandou
Xigalo
Malamulele
Mavamba
Blouberg Nature Reserve
Tolwe
Vivo
Buysdorp
Mara
Louis Trichardt
Tshakhuma
Ratombo
Levubu
Vuwani
KaJalingo
Blouberg
Blinkwater
Sending
Ben Lavin NR
Elim
Borchers
Vleifontein
Muswani
Nsami Dam
Glen Alpine Dam
Baltimore
Woudkop
Bochum
Blouhaak
Ha-Mogoro
Middle Letaba Dam
Giyani
Bandelierkop
Legkraal
Mamaila
Steilwater
Steilloopbrug
Dendron
Nkomo
Uitzicht
Kalkbank
Botlokwa
Soekmekaar
Groot Spelonke
Hildreth Ridge
Bylsteel
Thorndale
Mooketsi
Dzumeri
Ga-Modjadji
Hans Merensky Nature Reserve
Gilead
Munnik
Maleketla
Mineral Springs
Matlala
Mogalakwenastroom
Duiwelskloof
Olyfberg
Tzaneen Dam
La Cotte
Rita
Solomondale
Sebayeng
Politsi
Limburg
Magoebaskloof
Tzaneen
Mulati
Groesbeek
Seshego
Polokwane (Pietersburg)
Leshwane
Mankweng
Letsitele
Mapela
Mashashane
Marabastad Fort
Pietersburg Game Reserve
Boyne
Ebenezer Dam
Haenertsburg
Gravelotte
Selati Game Reserve
Mokamole
Leydsdorp
Percy Fyfe Nature Reserve
Sterkwater
Rietkolk
2128m
Wolkberg Wilderness Area
Ofcolaco
Makalali Private Reserve
Mahwelereng
First Gold Refinery
Nuwe Smitsdorp
Gladdeklipkop
Bewaarkloof Nature Reserve
Karongwi GR
The Downs
Trichardtsdal
Mica
Balule Game Reserve
Mokopane (Potgietersrus)
Makapans Cave
Lekgalameetse Nature Reserve
Makutsi Conservancy
Tshukudu
Doorndraai Dam NR
Drummondlea
Moorddrif Monument
Zebediela
Chuniespoort
Zeekoegat
Blyde Olifants Conservancy
Citrus Plantations
Lebowakgomo
Diphuti
Hoedspruit
Haakdoring
Gompies
Penge
Abel Erasmus Pass
JG Strijdom Tunnel
Kapama Game Reserve
Naboomspruit
Immerpan
Battle of Sekhukhuneland (1879)
Tswaing
Echo Caves
Aventura Swadini
Klaserie
Roedtan
Crecy
Branddraai
Blyde River Canyon NR
First Platinum Discovery
Fort
Middelfontein
Jane Furse Hospital
Burgersfort
Steelpoort
Morone
Ohrigstad
Vaalhoek
Casteel
Sekhukhune
Tompi Seleka
Kennedy's Vale
Holme Park
Tuinplaas
Nutfield
Phokwane
Nebo
Glen Cowie
Joubert Bridge
Buffelsvlei
Verraaiersnek Pass
Krugerspost
Pilgrims Rest
Graskop
Moganyaka
Malaita
Geological Exposure
Waterval Pass
Ohrigstad Dam
Ohrigstad Dam Nature Reserve
Kowyn Pass
Marble Hall
Maartenshoop
Hlogotlou
Gustav Klingbeil NR
Mauchsberg
Kiepersol
Hereford
Motetema
Lydenburg
Sabie
Siyabuswa
Groblersdal
Maleoskop
Erts
De Berg Pass
Jaap-se-Hoogte
Sterkspruit Nature Reserve
Long Tom Pass
Hendriksdal
Rust de Winter
Roossenekal
Dennilton
Witklip Pass
The Winkler
Rooikraal
Laersdrif
Santa Pass
Kwena Dam
Klipskool
Sudwala Caves
White River
Plaston
Mossiesdal
Loskop Dam Game Reserve
Wonderkloof Pass
Brondal
Moloto
Kwamhlanga
Sybrandskraal
Seringkop
Verena
Loskop Dam
TO MIDDELBURG
Stoffberg
Dullstroom
TO ERMELO
Chameshoogte Pass
Schoemanskloof
Patattanek
ELANDS RIVER VALLEY
TO MIDDELBURG
Nelspruit
Karino
Limpopo
Sand
Brak
Nzhelele
Mutale
Luvuvhu
Shingwedzi
Klein Letaba
Mogalakwena
Hout
Molototsi
Groot Letaba
Steelpoort
Elands
Moses
Sabie
N1
N11
R572
R521
R523
R524
R525
R561
R578
R81
R36
R71
R37
R518
R519
R520
R101
R516
R33
R573
R25
R568
R544
R555
R579
R577
R540
R539
R532
R533
R534
R535
R536
R537
R538
R40
R526
R527
R528
R529
R533
1718m
778m
25°
11 12 13 14 15 16 17 18 19 20

SCENIC ROUTE MAJOR CONNECTING ROUTE · TARRED UNTARRED MAIN CONNECTING ROUTE · TARRED UNTARRED MAIN ROAD · TARRED UNTARRED MINOR ROAD · 4WD ROAD · LOCAL TRACK · HIKING TRAIL · 234 NATIONAL ROUTE NUMBER · 234 OTHER ROUTE NUMBER · ■ PLACE OF INTEREST

NAIROBI CAPITAL CITY | Abidjan SECONDARY CAPITAL CITY When Applicable | Las Palmas DEPENDANCY CAPITAL | Gweru LARGE / MAJOR TOWN Over 50,000 people | Ruhengeri SECONDARY TOWN Between 10,000 & 50,000 | El Kadada SMALL TOWN Between 5,000 &10,000 | Chinguetti LARGE VILLAGE Between 500 & 5,000 | Winneba SMALL VILLAGE OR SETTLEMENT Under 500 people

KM 30 / MI 20

SCENIC ROUTE MAJOR CONNECTING ROUTE
TARRED UNTARRED MAIN CONNECTING ROUTE
TARRED UNTARRED MAIN ROAD
TARRED UNTARRED MINOR ROAD
4WD ROAD
LOCAL TRACK
HIKING TRAIL
234 NATIONAL ROUTE NUMBER
234 OTHER ROUTE NUMBER
PLACE OF INTEREST

NAIROBI CAPITAL CITY
Abidjan SECONDARY CAPITAL CITY When Applicable
Las Palmas DEPENDANCY CAPITAL
Gweru LARGE / MAJOR TOWN Over 50,000 people
Ruhengeri SECONDARY TOWN Between 10,000 & 50,000
El Kadada SMALL TOWN Between 5,000 &10,000
Chinguetti LARGE VILLAGE Between 500 & 5,000
Winneba SMALL VILLAGE OR SETTLEMENT Under 500 people
KM 30 MI 20

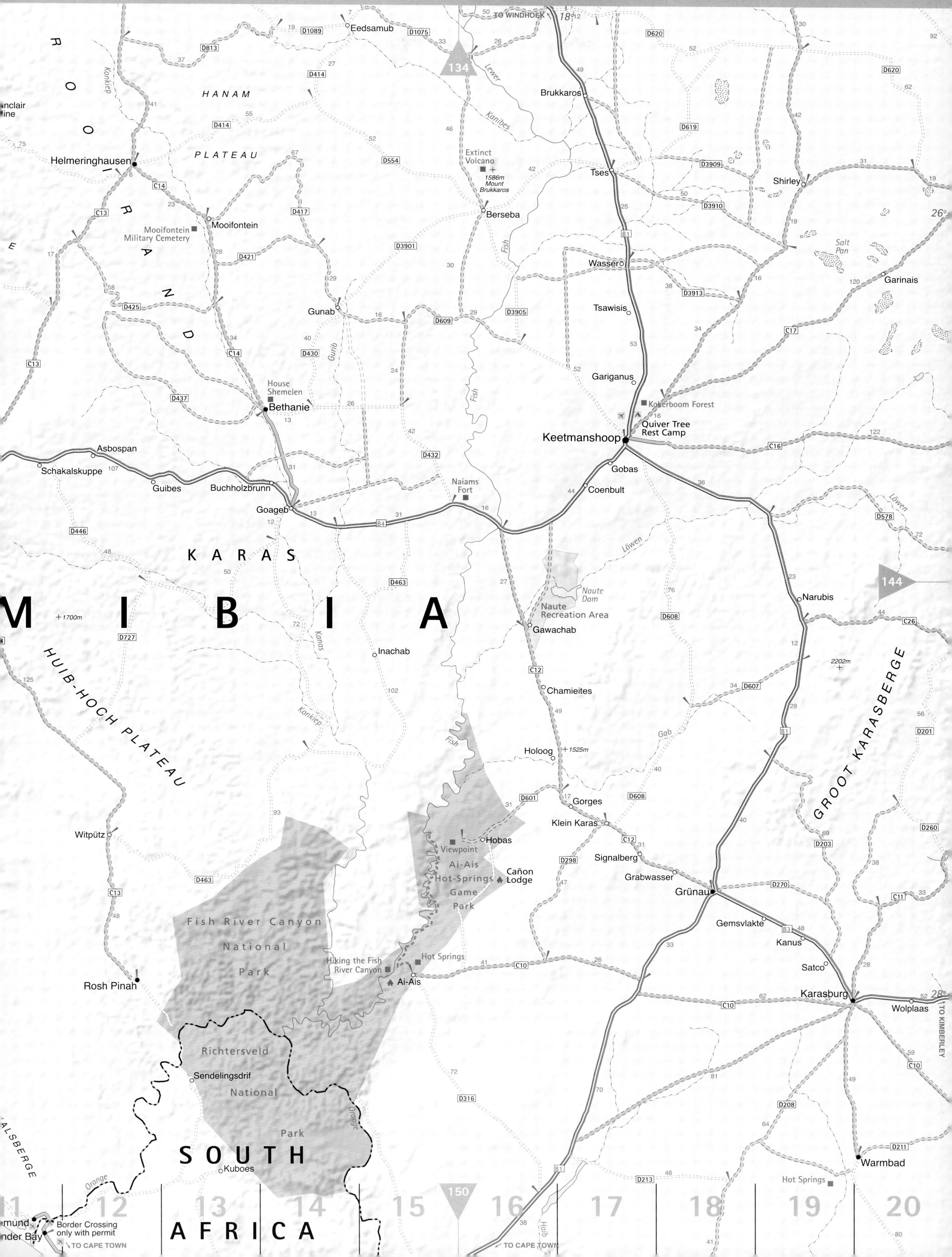

SCENIC ROUTE — MAJOR CONNECTING ROUTE
TARRED / UNTARRED — MAIN CONNECTING ROUTE
TARRED / UNTARRED — MAIN ROAD
TARRED / UNTARRED — MINOR ROAD
4WD ROAD
LOCAL TRACK
HIKING TRAIL
234 NATIONAL ROUTE NUMBER
234 OTHER ROUTE NUMBER
PLACE OF INTEREST

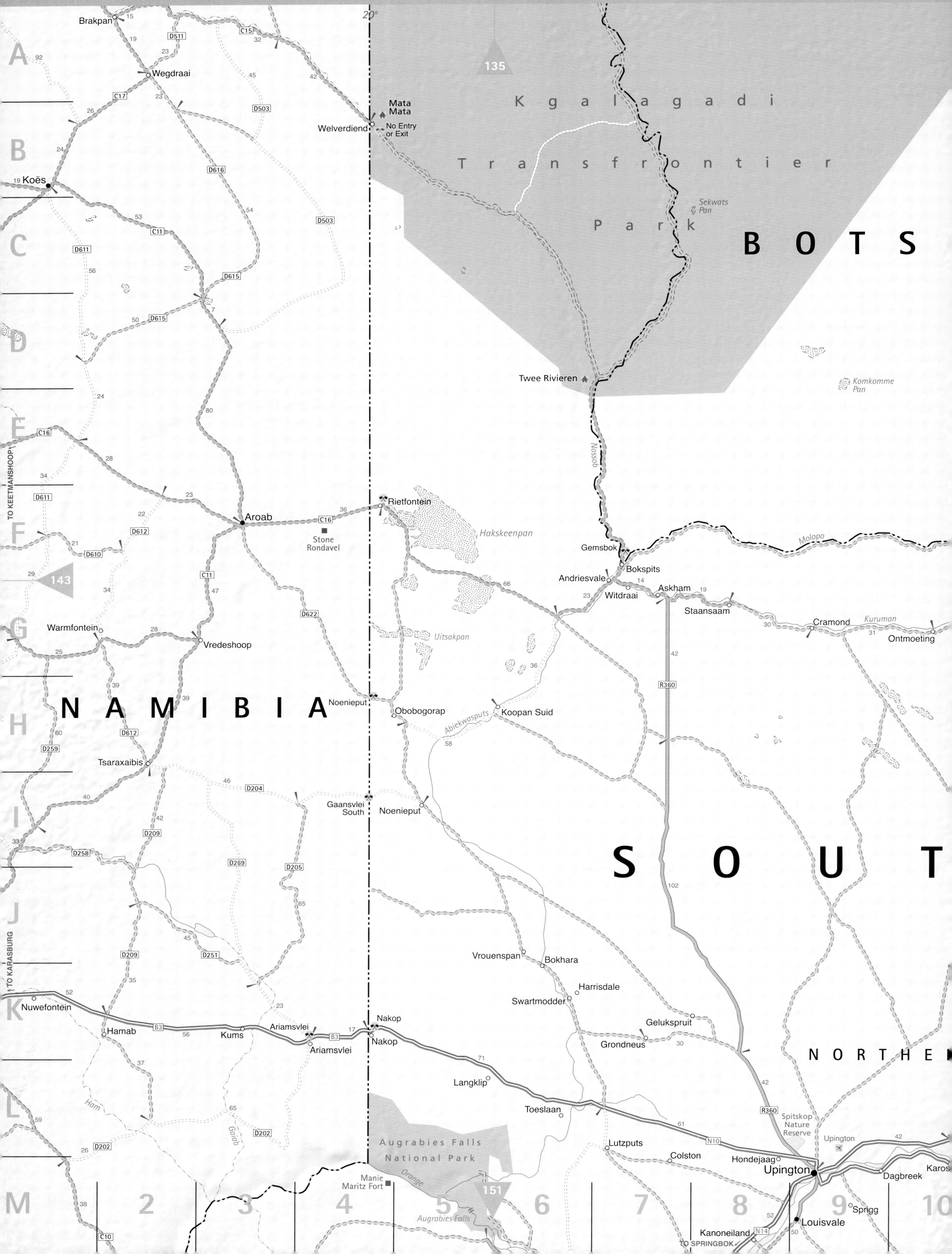

BOTSWANA
KALAHARI DESERT
SOUTH AFRICA
Molopo Nature Reserve
Vorstershoop
Terra Firma
Pomfret
Senlac
Tosca
Moloporivier
Vergeleë
Maleshe
Tshabong
McCarthy's Rest
Morokweng
Voorspoed
Madiakgama
Ewbank
Heuningvlei
Langehorn
Crafthole
Tlhakgameng
Severn
Ganyesa
Aansluit
Kuruman
Avontuur
Coetzersdam
Van Zylsrus
Maswehatshe
Ditshipeng
Louwna
Bothithong
Takoon 1823
Geluk
Black Rock
Tsineng
Sonstraal
Ga-Mopedi
Hotazel
Lykso
Faans Grove
Witloop
Mamathwane
Moffat's Mission Church 1833
Mothibistad
Seoding
Steekdorings
KORANNABERG
Sutton
Kuruman
Markramsdraai
Eye of Kuruman
Dibeng
Wincanton
Kathu
Reivilo
War Graves 1897
Sishen
Bekker
Blesmanspos
Moeswal
Langkloof
War Graves 1877
Droëspruit
Blinkfontein
Wonderwerk Caves
KURUMAN HILLS
Langberg
Madipelesa
Olifantshoek
Lohatlha
Vroeggedeel
Glosam
Palingpan
Swartputs
Daniëlskuil
Koopmansfontein
Beeshoek
Blinkklip
Owendale
Ulco
Postmasburg
Silver Streams
Lime Acres
Delportshoop
Longlands
Papkuil
Bermolli
ASBESBERGE
LANGBERG
Sydney-on-Vaal
Vaalbos National Park
Vaal
TO VRYBURG
TO JOHANNESBURG
TO KIMBERLEY
136
146
152
Sekhutlane
Molopo
1550m
1855m
1682m
1615m
22°
24°
26°
28°
11 12 13 14 15 16 17 18 19 20

SCENIC ROUTE — MAJOR CONNECTING ROUTE
TARRED / UNTARRED — MAIN CONNECTING ROUTE
TARRED / UNTARRED — MAIN ROAD
TARRED / UNTARRED — MINOR ROAD
4WD ROAD
LOCAL TRACK
HIKING TRAIL
234 NATIONAL ROUTE NUMBER
234 OTHER ROUTE NUMBER
PLACE OF INTEREST

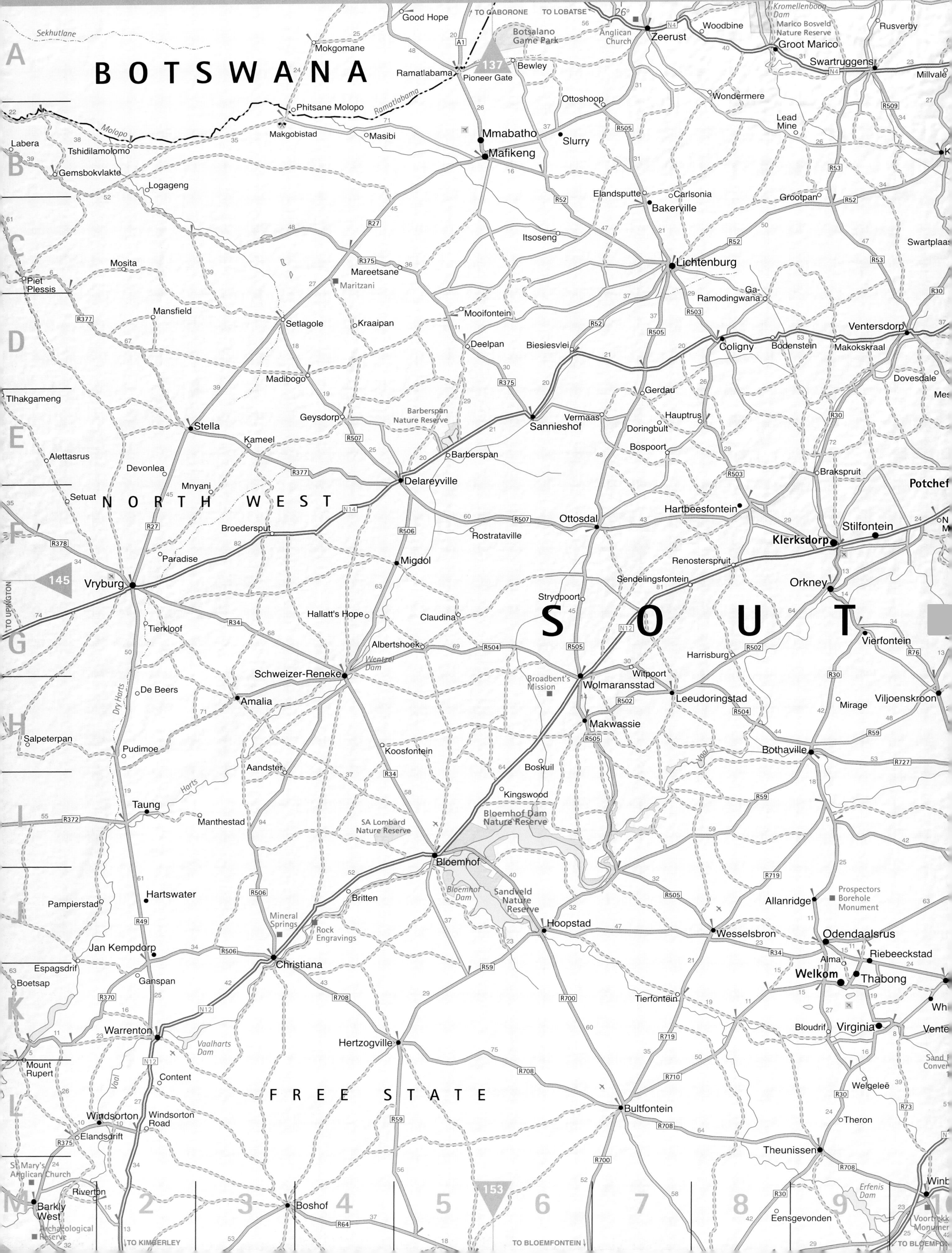

NAIROBI CAPITAL CITY | Abidjan SECONDARY CAPITAL CITY When Applicable | Las Palmas DEPENDANCY CAPITAL | Gweru LARGE / MAJOR TOWN Over 50,000 people | Ruhengeri SECONDARY TOWN Between 10,000 & 50,000 | El Kadada SMALL TOWN Between 5,000 &10,000 | Chinguetti LARGE VILLAGE Between 500 & 5,000 | Winneba SMALL VILLAGE OR SETTLEMENT Under 500 people

KM 30
MI 20

SCENIC ROUTE — MAJOR CONNECTING ROUTE | TARRED / UNTARRED — MAIN CONNECTING ROUTE | TARRED / UNTARRED — MAIN ROAD | TARRED / UNTARRED — MINOR ROAD | 4WD ROAD | LOCAL TRACK | HIKING TRAIL | 234 NATIONAL ROUTE NUMBER | 234 OTHER ROUTE NUMBER | PLACE OF INTEREST

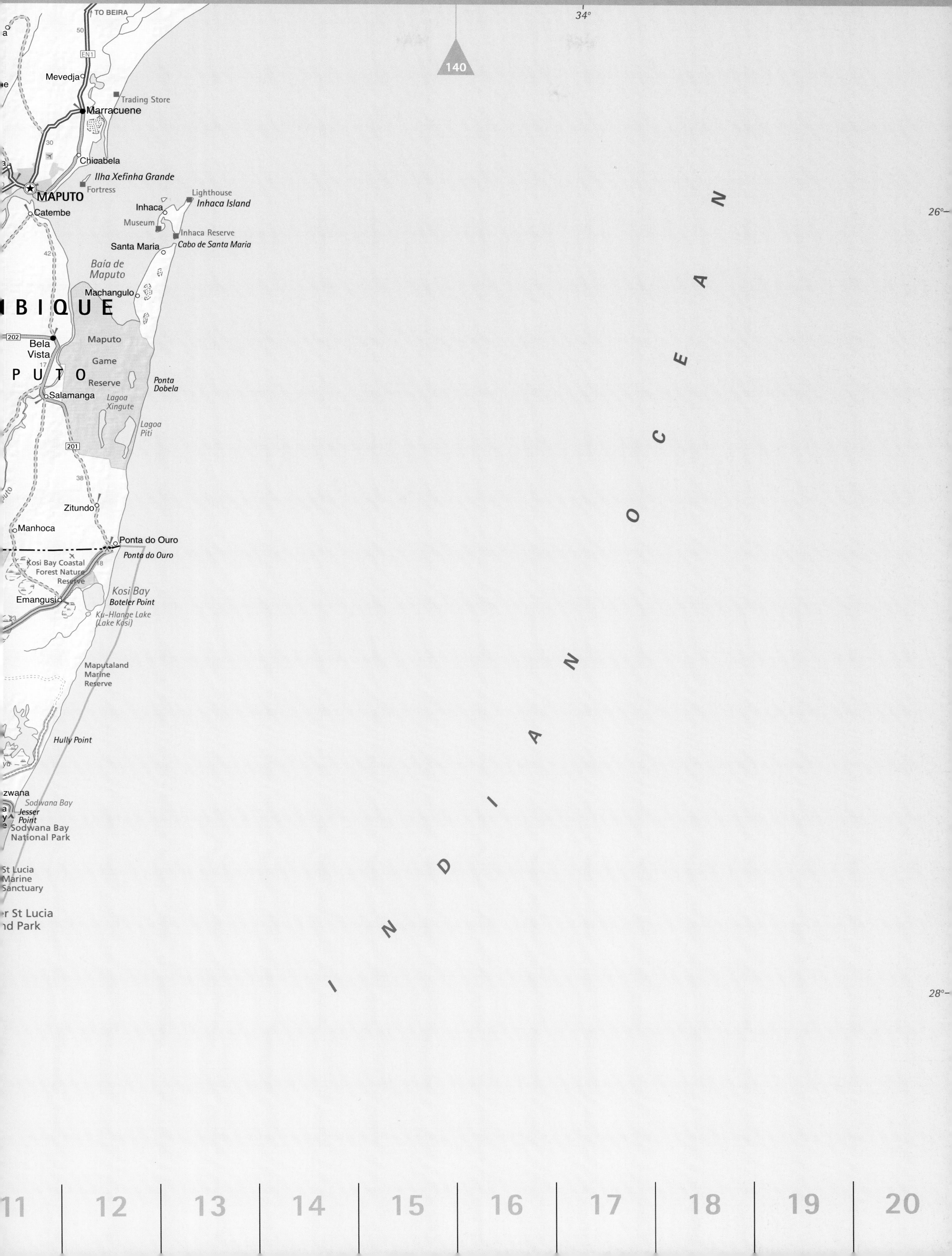
TO BEIRA
EN1
Mevedja
Trading Store
Marracuene
Chicabela
Ilha Xefinha Grande
Fortress
MAPUTO
Lighthouse
Inhaca Island
Inhaca
Museum
Catembe
Inhaca Reserve
Santa Maria
Cabo de Santa Maria
Baía de Maputo
Machangulo
BIQUE
202
Bela Vista
Maputo Game Reserve
P U T O
Ponta Dobela
Salamanga
Lagoa Xingute
Lagoa Piti
201
Zitundo
Manhoca
Ponta do Ouro
Ponta do Ouro
Kosi Bay Coastal Forest Nature Reserve
Kosi Bay
Boteler Point
Emangusi
Ku-Hlange Lake (Lake Kosi)
Maputaland Marine Reserve
Hully Point
zwana
Sodwana Bay
Jesser Point
Sodwana Bay National Park
St Lucia Marine Sanctuary
r St Lucia
nd Park
140
34°
26°
28°
I N D I A N O C E A N
11 12 13 14 15 16 17 18 19 20

SCENIC ROUTE — MAJOR CONNECTING ROUTE | TARRED / UNTARRED — MAIN CONNECTING ROUTE | TARRED / UNTARRED — MAIN ROAD | TARRED / UNTARRED — MINOR ROAD | 4WD ROAD | LOCAL TRACK | HIKING TRAIL | 234 NATIONAL ROUTE NUMBER | 234 OTHER ROUTE NUMBER | PLACE OF INTEREST

AFRICA
NORTHERN CAPE
GREAT KAROO
TO KARASBURG
Onseepkans
River Rafting
Augrabies
144
Kakamas
TO JOHANNESBURG
Kanoneiland
Keimoes
Neilersdrif
Trooilapspan
TO UPINGTON
Kalkwerf
Josling
Wegdraai
Kleinbegin
Oorkruis
Boksputs
Koegrabie
Sonderpan
Putsonderwater
TO PRIESKA
Bladgrond
Pofadder
Hartebeest
Sout
Houmoed
Bossiekom
Tuins
Kenhardt
Rooiberg Dam
Kolke
Jaght Drift
Diemansputs
Verneuk Pan
Granaatboskolk
Halfweg
Grootvloer
152
Zwartkop
Katkop
Onderstedorings
Van Wyksvlei
Brandvlei
Riet se Vloer
Rock Paintings
Krom
Swartkolkvloer
Sakrivier
Tontelbos
Loeriesfontein
Corbelled Houses
Klein Doring
Sak
Sterling
Hantam
1673m
HANTAMSBERG
Calvinia
Oorlogskloof
Williston
Bloukrans Pass
Bloukrans
Fish
157
Quaggasfontein Poort
TO CARNARVON
TO CERES
TO FRASERBURG
Saaifontein
N14
N10
R358
R27
R383
R361
R357
R353
R355
R354
R364
R63
R308
11
12
13
14
15
16
17
18
19
20
20°
30°

SCENIC ROUTE / MAJOR CONNECTING ROUTE
TARRED / UNTARRED MAIN CONNECTING ROUTE
TARRED / UNTARRED MAIN ROAD
TARRED / UNTARRED MINOR ROAD
4WD ROAD
LOCAL TRACK
HIKING TRAIL
234 NATIONAL ROUTE NUMBER
234 OTHER ROUTE NUMBER
PLACE OF INTEREST

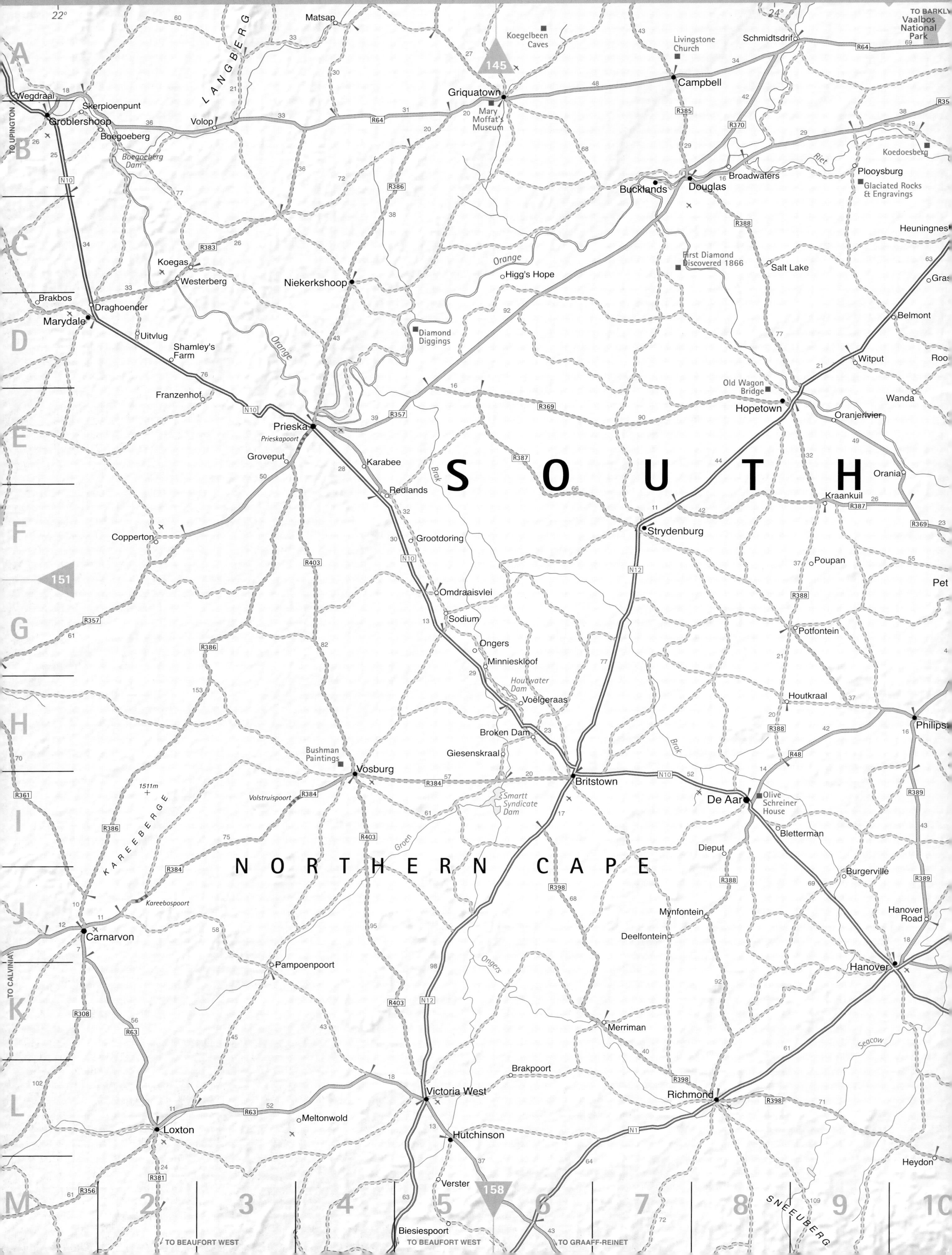

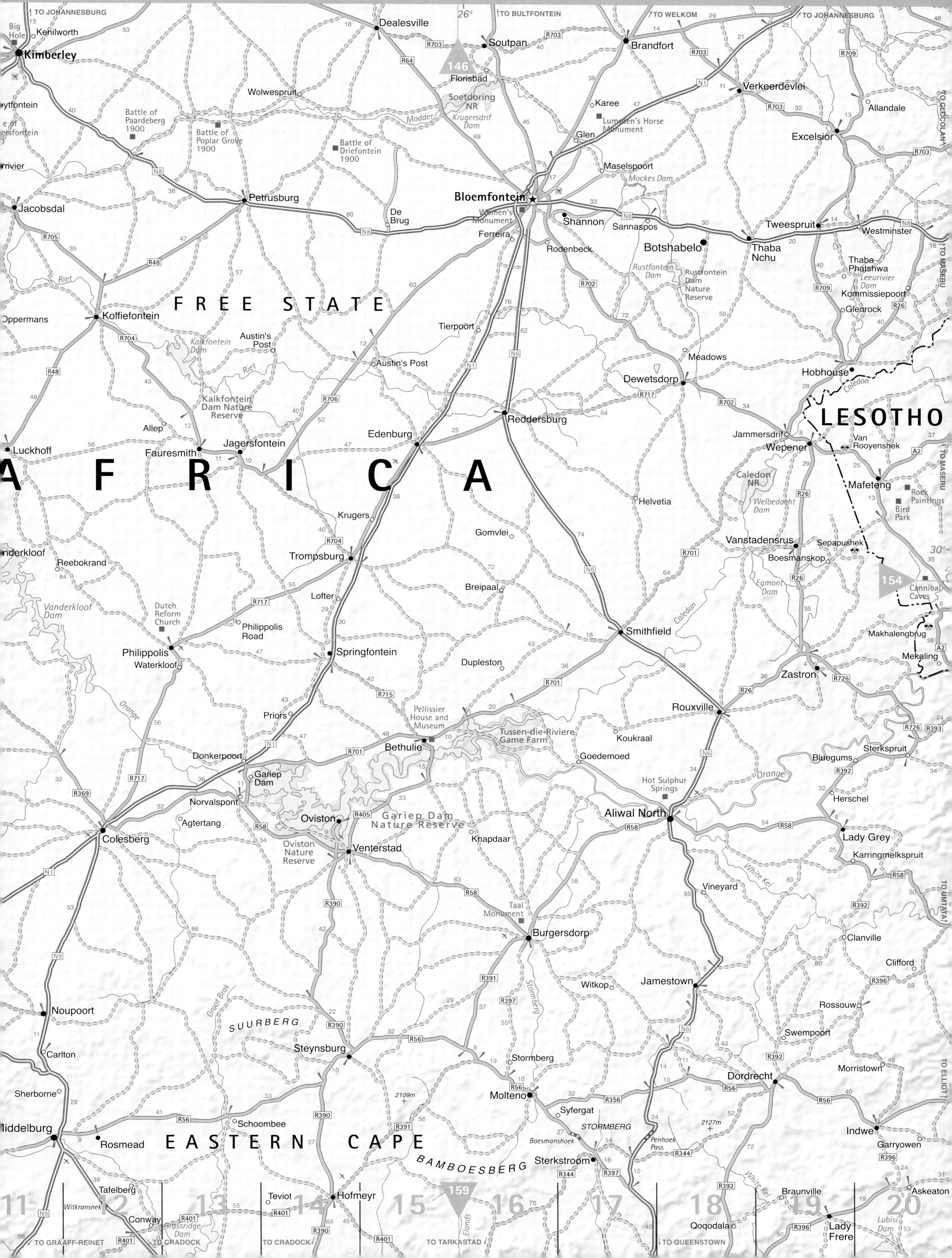
TO JOHANNESBURG
Big Hole
Kenilworth
Kimberley
Dealesville
Soutpan
TO BULTFONTEIN
TO WELKOM
Brandfort
TO JOHANNESBURG
146
Florisbad
Soetdoring NR
Krugersdrif Dam
Modder
Wolwespruit
Battle of Paardeberg 1900
Battle of Poplar Grove 1900
Battle of Driefontein 1900
Karee
Lumsden's Horse Monument
Glen
Verkeerdevlei
Allandale
Excelsior
TO CLOCOLAN
Maselspoort
Mockes Dam
Jacobsdal
Petrusburg
De Brug
Bloemfontein
Women's Monument
Shannon
Sannaspos
Tweespruit
Westminster
Ferreira
Rodenbeck
Botshabelo
Thaba Nchu
Rustfontein Dam
Rustfontein Dam Nature Reserve
Thaba Phatshwa
Leeurivier Dam
Kommissiepoort
Glenrock
TO MASERU
Riet
FREE STATE
Koffiefontein
Oppermans
Kalkfontein Dam
Austin's Post
Tierpoort
Austin's Post
Meadows
Dewetsdorp
Hobhouse
Caledon
LESOTHO
Kalkfontein Dam Nature Reserve
Allep
Edenburg
Reddersburg
Jammersdrif
Wepener
Van Rooyenshek
Luckhoff
Fauresmith
Jagersfontein
AFRICA
Caledon NR
Welbedacht Dam
Mafeteng
Rock Paintings
Bird Park
Helvetia
Krugers
Gomvlei
Vanstadensrus
Sepapushek
Boesmanskop
Vanderkloof
Reebokrand
Trompsburg
Egmont Dam
154
Cannibal Caves
Vanderkloof Dam
Lofter
Breipaal
Dutch Reform Church
Philippolis Road
Smithfield
Makhalengbrug
Philippolis
Waterkloof
Springfontein
Dupleston
Mekaling
Zastron
Orange
Rouxville
Priors
Pellissier House and Museum
Tussen-die-Riviere Game Farm
Koukraal
Sterkspruit
Bethulie
Donkerpoort
Gariep Dam
Goedemoed
Bluegums
Hot Sulphur Springs
Herschel
Norvalspont
Agtertang
Oviston
Gariep Dam Nature Reserve
Aliwal North
Lady Grey
Colesberg
Oviston Nature Reserve
Venterstad
Knapdaar
Karringmelkspruit
White Kei
Vineyard
TO UMTATA
Taal Monument
Burgersdorp
Clanville
Clifford
Groot Brak
Witkop
Jamestown
Stormberg
Rossouw
Noupoort
SUURBERG
Swempoort
Steynsburg
Stormberg
Carlton
Morristown
Dordrecht
TO ELLIOTT
Sherborne
2109m
Molteno
Syfergat
STORMBERG
Middelburg
Schoombee
Rosmead
EASTERN CAPE
Boesmanshoek
2127m
Penhoek Pass
Indwe
Garryowen
BAMBOESBERG
Sterkstroom
Tafelberg
Teviot
Hofmeyr
159
Braunville
Askeaton
Witkransnek
Conway
Grassridge Dam
Elands
Qoqodala
Lady Frere
Lubisi Dam
TO GRAAFF-REINET
TO CRADOCK
TO CRADOCK
TO TARKASTAD
TO QUEENSTOWN
11
12
13
14
15
16
17
18
19
20
26°
30°

SCENIC ROUTE — MAJOR CONNECTING ROUTE
TARRED / UNTARRED — MAIN CONNECTING ROUTE
TARRED / UNTARRED — MAIN ROAD
TARRED / UNTARRED — MINOR ROAD
4WD ROAD
LOCAL TRACK
HIKING TRAIL
234 NATIONAL ROUTE NUMBER
234 OTHER ROUTE NUMBER
PLACE OF INTEREST

WAZULU-NATAL
TO DUNDEE
TO PIET RETIEF
Tugela Gorge
Dlolwana
Ndundulu
Nkwalini
Mposa
Tugela Ferry
Keate's Drift
Cetshwayo's Grave
148
Bulawayo Site of Shaka's Kraal
Empangeni
Enseleni Nature Reserve
Richards Bay
Mhlatuzi Lagoon
Richards Bay Game Reserve
Felixton
Coward's Bush Monument
Toll
The Ranch
Entumeni
Eshowe
Fort Kwa-Mondi
Muden
Kranskop
Ntunjambili
Fort Nongqai
Battle of Gingindlovu
Mtunzini
Greytown
General Louis Botha's Birthplace
Ahrens
KwaSizabantu Mission
Gingindlovu
Amatikulu
Nyoni
Umlazi Nature Reserve
Craigie Burn Dam
Fort Mtombeni
Mapumulo
Otimati
Mandini
Tugela
Battle of Tugela 1838
Tugela Mouth
Rietvlei
Sevenoaks
Mvoti
Fort Pearson
Ultimatum Tree
Darnall
Zinkwazi Beach
Dalton
Fawnleas
York
New Hanover
Mpolweni
Albert Falls Nature Reserve
Albert Falls
Wartburg
Valley of 1000 Hills
Shaka's Memorial
Aldinville
Stanger
Shakaskraal
Umhlali
Sheffield Beach
Salt Rock
Shaka's Rock
Ballito
Queen Elizabeth Park
Colenso Mission Station 1854
Pietermaritzburg
Ndwedwe
Tongaat
Verulam
Inanda
Umdloti
Umhlanga
Phoenix
Ashburton
Camperdown
Kranskloof Nature Reserve
KwaMashu
Clermont
Mpumalanga
Hammarsdale
Pinetown
Nshongweni Dam
Durban
The Bluff
Queensburgh
Umlazi
Isipingo
Umbumbulu
Adams Mission
Umbogintwini
Amanzimtoti
Kingsburgh
Mkomazi
Umgababa
Dududu
Umkomaas
Clansthal
Vernon Crookes Nature Reserve
Umzinto
Braemar
Scottburgh
Park Rynie
Kelso
Pennington
Sezela
Ifafa Beach
Mtwalume
Turton
Hibberdene
Umzumbe
Southport
Sea Park
Umtentweni
Port Shepstone
Shelley Beach
Uvongo
INDIAN OCEAN
30°
11
12
13
14
15
16
17
18
19
20

SCENIC ROUTE | MAJOR CONNECTING ROUTE | TARRED UNTARRED MAIN CONNECTING ROUTE | TARRED UNTARRED MAIN ROAD | TARRED UNTARRED MINOR ROAD | 4WD ROAD | LOCAL TRACK | HIKING TRAIL | 234 NATIONAL ROUTE NUMBER | 234 OTHER ROUTE NUMBER | ■ PLACE OF INTEREST

NAIROBI CAPITAL CITY | Abidjan SECONDARY CAPITAL CITY When Applicable | Las Palmas DEPENDANCY CAPITAL | Gweru LARGE / MAJOR TOWN Over 50,000 people | Ruhengeri SECONDARY TOWN Between 10,000 & 50,000 | El Kadada SMALL TOWN Between 5,000 &10,000 | Chinguetti LARGE VILLAGE Between 500 & 5,000 | Winneba SMALL VILLAGE OR SETTLEMENT Under 500 people

KM 30
MI 20

SCENIC ROUTE — MAJOR CONNECTING ROUTE
TARRED / UNTARRED — MAIN CONNECTING ROUTE
TARRED / UNTARRED — MAIN ROAD
TARRED / UNTARRED — MINOR ROAD
4WD ROAD
LOCAL TRACK
HIKING TRAIL
234 NATIONAL ROUTE NUMBER
234 OTHER ROUTE NUMBER
PLACE OF INTEREST

EASTERN CAPE
AFRICA
OCEAN
TO MIDDELBURG
TO STEYNSBURG
TO ALIWAL NORTH
TO TSOMO
TO KOMGA
TO EAST LONDON
Queenstown
Tarkastad
Cradock
Bedford
Adelaide
Cookhouse
Somerset East
Pearston
Fort Beaufort
Alice
Fort Hare
Seymour
Whittlesea
Sada
Cathcart
Stutterheim
King William's Town
Bisho
Zwelitsha
Breidbach
Berlin
Peddie
Grahamstown
Alicedale
Paterson
Kirkwood
Addo
Uitenhage
Despatch
Port Elizabeth
Summerstrand
Port Alfred
Bathurst
Alexandria
Kenton-on-Sea
Boesmansriviermond
Colchester
Coega
Algoa Bay
Cape Padrone
Cape Recife
St Francis Bay
Great Fish Point
Hamburg
Addo Elephant National Park
Mountain Zebra National Park
Groendal Wilderness Area
Shamwari Game Reserve
Great Fish River Nature Reserve
WINTERBERGE
BANKBERG
Cofimvaba
Bolotwa
Qamata
St Marks
Southeyville
Lubisi Dam
Xonxa Dam
Bailey
Bowker's Park
Sunken Garden
Driver's Drift
Tylden
Waqu
Spitskopvlei
Visrivier
Baroda
Post Chalmers
Agter Sneeuberg
Petersburg
Halesowen
Mortimer
Drennan
Swaershoek
Witmos
Daggaboersnek
Glenrock
Cameron's Glen
Spring Valley
Elandsdrif
Lake Arthur
Kommandodrif Dam
Eastpoort
Golden Valley
Long Hope
Middleton
Sheldon
Carlisle Bridge
Riebeek East
Klipfontein
Ann's Villa
Suurberg
Bellevue
Coerney
Sunland
Bluecliff
Glenconnor
Ncanaha
Salem
Langholm
Southwell
Kasuka Road
Kariega
Boknesstrand (Richmond)
Dias Cross
Bluewater Bay
Swartkops
Bethelsdorp
Thornhill
Witteklip
Sea View
Skoenmakerskop
Van Stadens Wild Flower Reserve
Committees
Breakfast Vlei
Lekfontein
Kwa-Pita
Middledrift
Keiskammahoek
Hogsback
Balfour
Liddleton
Blinkwater
Braunschweig
Kei Road
Amabele
Bethel
Dohne
Mgwali
Sittingbourne
Chalumna
Kidd's Beach
Bell
Wooldridge
Wesley
Fallodon
Settlers Church
Old Provost
Fort Selwyn
Fort Brown
Ecca Pass
Martello Tower
Fort Willshire
Sundial
Nico Malan Pass
Katberg Pass
Devil's Bellows
Waterdown Dam
1820 Settlers Milestone
Gaika's Grave
Rooikrans Dam
Historic Buildings
Bruintjieshoogte
Old Parsonage
Olive Schreiner's Grave
Swaershoek Pass
Lootsberg Pass
Grassridge Dam
Darlington Dam
Olifantskop
2013m
2371m
153
160
11 12 13 14 15 16 17 18 19 20

SCENIC ROUTE — MAJOR CONNECTING ROUTE | TARRED / UNTARRED — MAIN CONNECTING ROUTE | TARRED / UNTARRED — MAIN ROAD | TARRED / UNTARRED — MINOR ROAD | 4WD ROAD | LOCAL TRACK | HIKING TRAIL | 234 NATIONAL ROUTE NUMBER | 234 OTHER ROUTE NUMBER | PLACE OF INTEREST

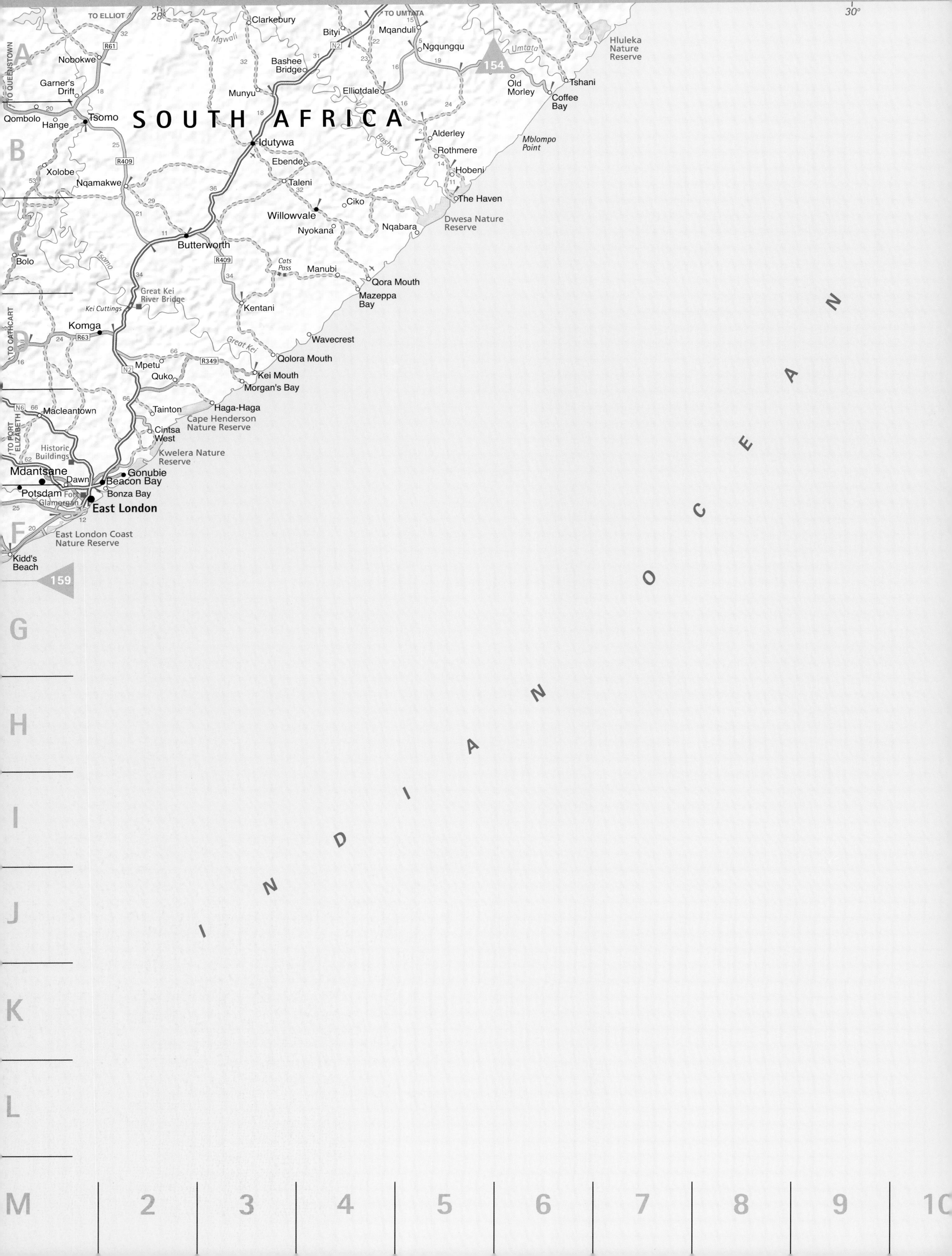

Gear For Africa

The right equipment and comfortable but practical clothing will make travel through Africa much more enjoyable. For the vast majority of their time spent in Africa, travellers will find themselves without the conveniences of familiar territory, such as an unlimited supply of fresh water, a comfortable place to rest, modern toilets (and toiletries) and the luxury of simply calling for any help you might require. Although specialised adventures such as rock climbing, river rafting, diving, snorkelling and forest and river exploration will require additional gear specific to the adventure of your choice, the standard options of bush and desert treks, walking tours or horse-, camel- and elephant-back safaris will require little more than the usual safari get-up. The backpacks and rucksacks of most travellers exploring the rainforests, trekking across the desert, hiking through the bush or touring Africa's landmark cities will be filled with items that need to last for anything from a few days to a few weeks (sometimes even longer), so particular care needs to be taken in the packing process. For guidelines on what to take along on extended trips that will involve out-of-the-ordinary adventures, it would be wise to consult either a reputable travel agent or someone who has travelled to the same places as you intend to explore.

What to Wear

- Backpack / rucksack (with well-padded straps) that is durable, water resistant and as light as possible.
- Boots and / or shoes that strap or tie up around the ankles. Walking strap sandals for hot conditions.
- Long-sleeved, lightweight (cotton is best) shirt that allows air-flow.
- Full-legged trousers that are lightweight and have wide pockets to carry essentials.
- Heavy-duty vest with plenty of pockets to carry essentials and luxuries.
- Headgear (wide-brimmed), sunglasses and sunscreen for protection from the sun.
- Thick socks to cushion your feet on long treks as well as for city-based tours. These will provide additional warmth for those cold African nights.
- Jacket (or coat) that is wind-proof and waterproof to protect against steep drops in temperature.
- Waterproof rain gear.
- A strong belt may also be used to secure baggage, as a lynch of sorts, or serve as a carrying handle for awkward equipment and / or luggage. And you never know what use you might find for such an item in an African emergency!

5 Essentials

- Passport / identity documents
- Water bottle and / or purification tablets
- Compass
- Malaria prophylactics
- Sturdy walking boots

5 Toiletries

- Toothpaste / toothbrush
- Soap / shower gel / shampoo
- Razors / shaving cream
- Lip balm and sunscreen
- Personal medication, protection and tampons

Good Idea!

- A sarong can serve as an extra 'blanket' or pillow, headgear, scarf, towel, skirt... or even as a rope.
- Carry a padlock and chain to secure your belongings where necessary.
- Take extra batteries for cameras, mobile phones and other electronic equipment. Charge them fully if possible before beginning any African adventure.
- Depending on your destination and the nature of the adventure, thermal underwear may be either a luxury or a necessity.
- Where possible, pack individual items in plastic bags - this serves to help protect your belongings while taking up no additional space in your luggage. They will also prove to have an endless number of uses. Naturally, your sense of environmental conscience will remind you not to discard of these items improperly.
- Make photocopies (preferably certified) of ALL your travel documents, and keep these separate from the originals (which you must carry at all times).
- A small mirror can act as a reflector to summon help in case of emergencies.
- Amateur photographers will do well to take compact disposable cameras, which are cheaper and lighter to carry than their more sophisticated counterparts, which are easily damaged and just as easily stolen.

Out of the Ordinary

Certain expeditions will call for specialised equipment and gear. These should be of the best quality you can afford and, where possible, as light and portable as possible. Adventure-specific equipment is, generally, virtually unobtainable in remote parts, and such items are thus susceptible to theft (proving an irresistable magnet for light fingers). The following leisure-sport activities will require specialised equipment (as well as advice on which items to obtain from trained professionals and / or reputable sports dealers) prior to departure:

- Diving
- Snorkelling
- Angling
- Rock climbing
- 4x4 driving
- Windsurfing
- Mountain biking

(See New Holland's range of Adventure titles or National Geographic's books for more comprehensive details)

5 Luxuries

- 2-ply toilet paper
- Deodorant
- Binoculars
- Inflatable pillow
- Washing detergent

5 Conveniences

- Phrase book / travel guide
- Torch / flashlight
- Portable table stove
- Small tent
- Compact foldup chair

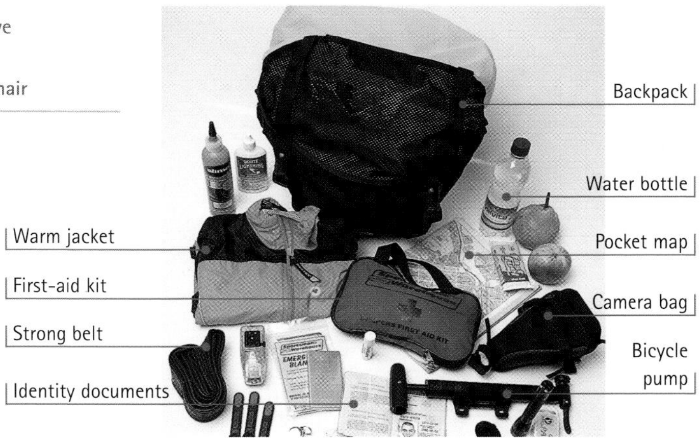

Don't Leave Home Without These

- Multi-purpose pocket tool (Leatherman / Swiss Army knife)
- Eating and drinking utensils (non-breakable)
- First-aid kit
- Compass
- Sunscreen
- Insect repellent
- Protective headgear
- Water canister
- Water purification tablets
- Hip bag / money belt
- Sunglasses
- Length of nylon cord
- Towel and face-cloth

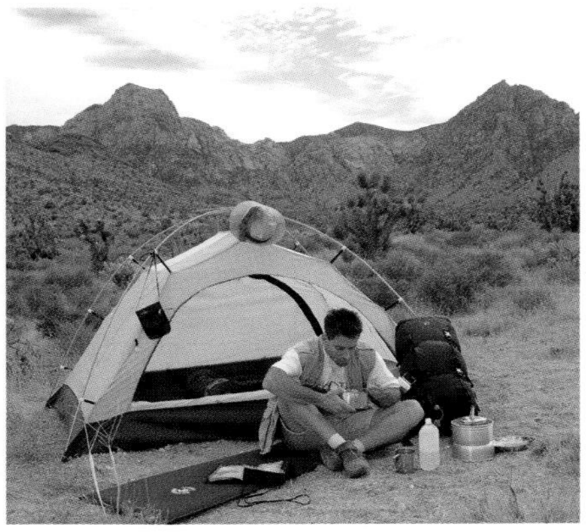

Overnight

- Zip-up sleeping bag
- 'Space blanket' (the foil type - they provide incredible insulation)
- Woollen gloves and headgear (a 'beanie' will serve you well)
- Thick socks
- Mosquito net

Leave at Home

- Jeans and towels are rather heavy and take a long time to dry.
- Jewellery — such as rings, chains, pendants, as well as other valuables — are simply an invitation for theft.
- Pillows are awkward to pack and to carry, and there will always be a substitute (such as a sarong, see **Good Idea!** above).
- Big, heavy (often expensive) travel books? Ideally photo-copy the necessary sections, unless you really intend to cover a large part of the country concerned, or are assured of safe (and, ideally, somewhat luxurious) accommodation and transport.
- Cash! Ideally carry a credit card (and a backup, if possible, stored seperately) as well as traveller's cheques-carry only small amounts of hard cash.

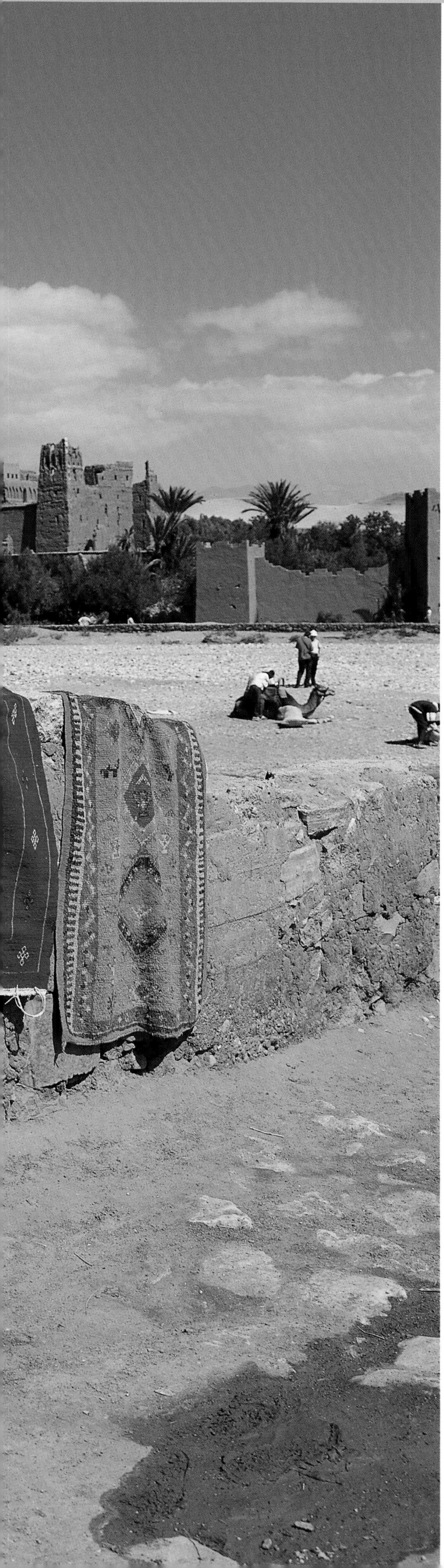

Town Maps

ALPHABETICAL LISTING FOR MAPS OF TOWNS AND CITIES

An assortment of locally-produced rugs and kelims for sale near the Atlas Mountains, Morocco.

Africa's Towns

- Africa's most ethnically diverse country is the Democratic Republic of the Congo, boasting more than 200 ethnic groups.
- Nigeria has the highest population growth rate in Africa, gaining more than 9,000 citizens a day!
- Chad's annual population growth rate is the highest in Africa (3.3%), while South Africa has the lowest figure (0.02%).

Urban Africa is a world of extremes, the capital cities and large centres acting as melting pots of cultural diversity, mixing the ancient and the modern. For many Westerners travelling across the face of Africa, the cities are the only bow to 'civilisation' and serve as vital springboards for adventures beyond the urban limits.

Africa's cities and large towns combine the charm of traditional Africa with the convenience of modern development: crumbling old edifices lie interspersed with high-rise office blocks, lively market squares - spilling over with fresh produce, brightly coloured fabrics, intricately carved curios and live poultry - dotted here and there with telephone booths. Tucked away amid the dusty side streets and cobbled alleys are islands of green, where statues of honoured statesmen stand proudly alongside mosques, shrines and cathedrals. Scattered among museums and galleries showcasing a nations' rich cultural history are contemporary additions to the social life of the local people: vibrant nightclubs, late-night eateries and popular meeting places.

While modern Africa means entertainment and excitement for travellers, for locals it is simply 'home' ... and with it comes the everyday trials and tribulations that face citizens of every big city in the world. Earning a living, feeding a family and making ends meet are also basic needs of every African, and nowhere is this more noticeable than in the urban centres. Despite the fact that most of Africa's big cities - especially the capitals - have seen enormous growth and a burgeoning of free enterprise, poverty is rife in even the most developed cities, bringing with it a pitifully low standard of living. Petty theft and prostitution offer highly favourable returns for many of the most impoverished of Africa's inner-city dwellers. This is the Africa many prospective travellers hear most about, and yet it is an element that few ever encounter. Despite dwindling national economies and a generally impoverished population, most Africans are proud and hospitable people with the habit of welcoming visitors (and their dollars) warmly to their homeland. The majority will happily invite travellers into their homes, escort them around and show them what Africa has to offer. After all, the locals know where to find the finest fabrics, the plumpest fruit, the nearest post office or a safe bed for the night. Don't shy away from making their acquaintance — but try to establish from the authorities or travel agents which areas or sorts of characters or hospitality to avoid. Despite its warmth and charm, elements of Africa can be brutal and unsympathetic.

SAY 'PLEASE'!

While some communities will welcome clicking cameras — often for a small fee — others will refuse to be photographed, either for religious or cultural reasons. It is safest to ask permission from local leaders before hauling out your camera in rural villages and snapping away. This is essential in urban areas, where military installations and government buildings abound (and which are often entirely off-limits to Westerners and locals alike).

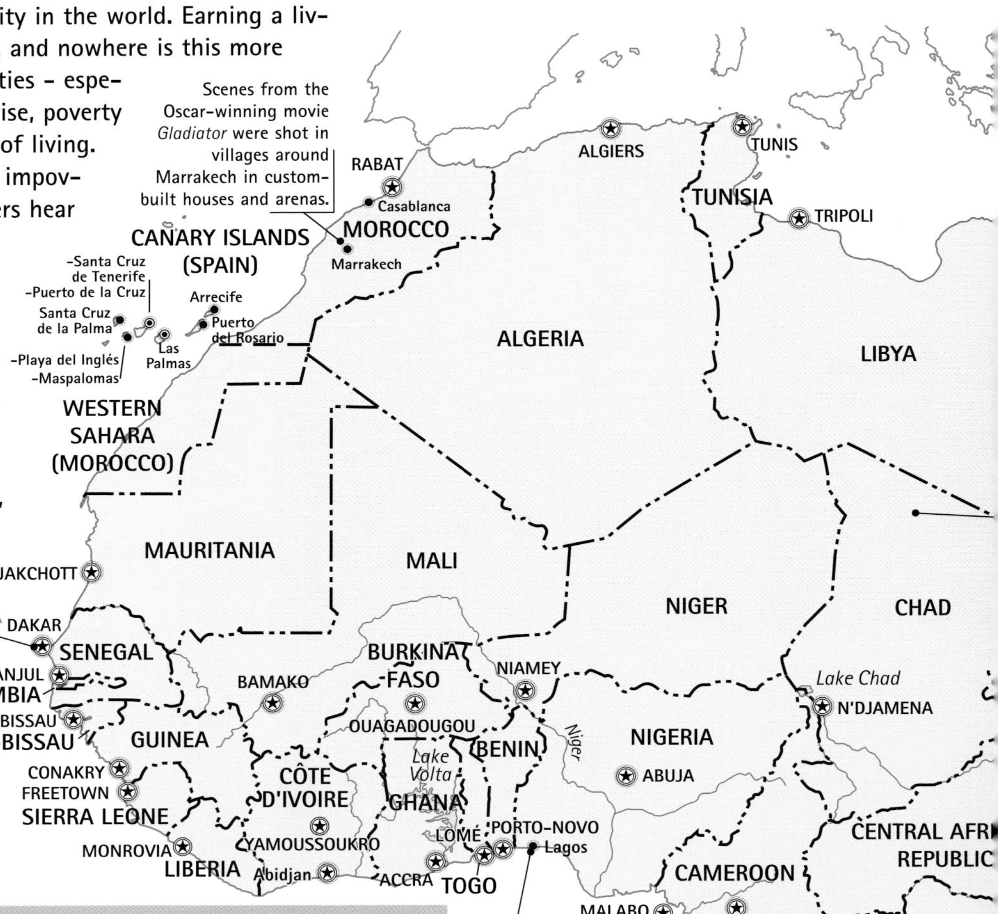

Scenes from the Oscar-winning movie *Gladiator* were shot in villages around Marrakech in custom-built houses and arenas.

The famed Paris to Dakar Rally covers 9,500km and is driven in two separate marathon stages across some of Africa's toughest terrain. Arguably the most arduous motor-vehicle race in the world, competitors number around 450, some 80 per cent of which are amateurs intent on conquering the continent's most demanding off-road race.

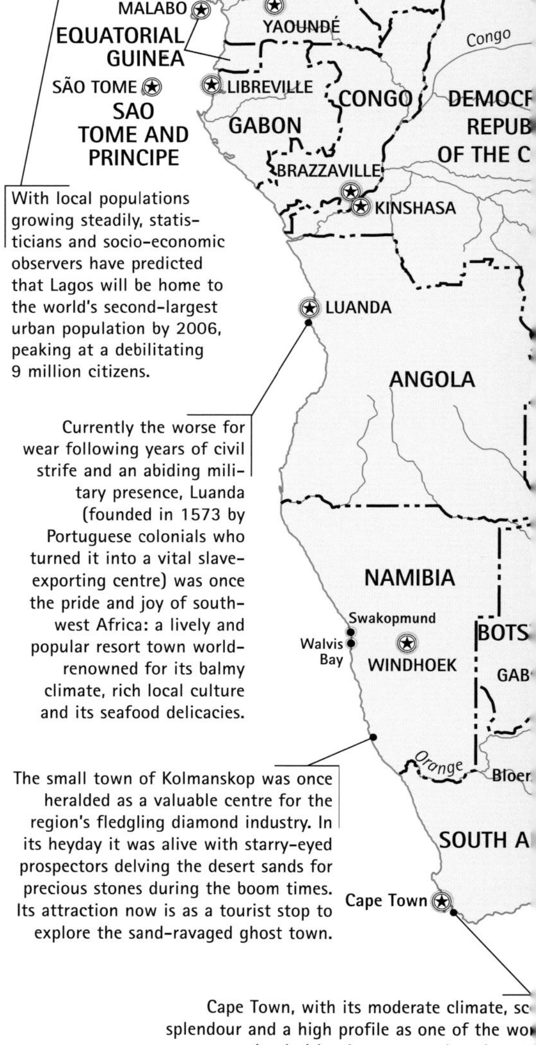

With local populations growing steadily, statisticians and socio-economic observers have predicted that Lagos will be home to the world's second-largest urban population by 2006, peaking at a debilitating 9 million citizens.

Currently the worse for wear following years of civil strife and an abiding military presence, Luanda (founded in 1573 by Portuguese colonials who turned it into a vital slave-exporting centre) was once the pride and joy of south-west Africa: a lively and popular resort town world-renowned for its balmy climate, rich local culture and its seafood delicacies.

The small town of Kolmanskop was once heralded as a valuable centre for the region's fledgling diamond industry. In its heyday it was alive with starry-eyed prospectors delving the desert sands for precious stones during the boom times. Its attraction now is as a tourist stop to explore the sand-ravaged ghost town.

Cape Town, with its moderate climate, sc
splendour and a high profile as one of the wo
top tourist desitinations, currently enjoys e
growing acclaim in the international holiday
hospitality industry and, especially a
September 11, has a new-found status as on
the safest destinations in the world. Accordin
the World Trade Organisation, South Africa
moved up from the 52nd most popular destina
in the early 1990s to 25th in 20

REGION	COUNTRY	CAPITAL	EUROPEAN LANGUAGE	MAJOR RELIGION	CURRENCY	GOVERNMENT
THE MAGHREB	Morocco (incl Western Sahara)	Rabat	French	Muslim	Dirham	Constitutional monarchy
	Canary Islands (Spain)	Las Palmas	Castilian Spanish	Catholic	Euro	Constitutional monarchy (Spain)
	Algeria	Algiers	French	Muslim	Dinar	Military regime
	Tunisia	Tunis	French	Muslim	Dinar	Multiparty republic
THE SAHARA	Niger	Niamey	French	Muslim	CFA franc	Multiparty republic
	Libya	Tripoli	Arabic	Muslim	Dinar	Socialist state
	Chad	N'Djamena	French	Muslim	CFA franc	Transitional government
THE NILE VALLEY	Egypt	Cairo	French/English	Muslim	Egyptian pound	Multiparty republic
	Sudan	Khartoum	Arabic	Muslim	Sudanese pound	Military regime
THE TAOUDENNI BASIN	Senegal	Dakar	French	Muslim	CFA franc	Multiparty republic
	Gambia	Banjul	English	Muslim	Dalasi	Military regime
	Mauritania	Nouakchott	French	Muslim	Ouguiya	Multiparty republic
	Mali	Bamako	French	Muslim	CFA franc	Multiparty republic
	Cape Verde	Praia	Portuguese	Catholic	Escudo	Multiparty republic
THE IVORY COAST	Guinea-Bissau	Bissau	Portuguese	Traditional	CFA franc	Multiparty republic
	Guinea	Conakry	French	Muslim	Guinean franc	Multiparty republic
	Sierra Leone	Freetown	English	Traditional	Leone	Military regime
	Liberia	Monrovia	English	Traditional	Liberian dollar	Transitional
	Côte d'Ivoire	Yamoussoukro	French	Traditional	CFA franc	Multiparty republic
	Burkina Faso	Ouagadougou	French	Traditional	CFA franc	Multiparty republic
	Ghana	Accra	English	Traditional	Cedi	Multiparty republic
	Togo	Lomé	French	Traditional	CFA franc	Multiparty republic
	Benin	Porto-Novo	French	Traditional	CFA franc	Multiparty republic
THE EQUATORIAL INTERIOR	Nigeria	Abuja	English	Muslim	Naira	Military regime
	Sao Tome & Principe	São Tome	Portuguese	Catholic	Dobra	Multiparty republic
	Cameroon	Yaoundé	French/English	Traditional	CFA franc	Multiparty republic
	Equatorial Guinea	Malabo	Spanish	Catholic	CFA franc	Multiparty republic
	Central African Republic	Bangui	French	Christian	CFA franc	Multiparty republic
THE HORN OF AFRICA	Eritrea	Asmara	Arabic	Coptic Christian	Eritrean nakfa	Provisional military government
	Ethiopia	Addis Ababa	English	Muslim	Ethiopian birr	Multiparty republic
	Somalia	Mogadishu	Arabic	Sunni Muslim	Shilling	Transitional
	Djibouti	Djibouti	French	Christian	Djiboutian franc	Single-party republic
THE CONGO BASIN	Gabon	Libreville	French	Catholic	CFA franc	Multiparty republic
	Congo	Brazzaville	French	Catholic	CFA franc	Multiparty republic
	Democratic Republic of the Congo	Kinshasa	French	Christian	Congo franc	Single-party republic
	Angola	Luanda	Portuguese	Christian	Kwanza	Multiparty republic
THE GREAT LAKES	Rwanda	Kigali	French	Catholic	Rwandan franc	Multiparty republic
	Burundi	Bujumbura	French	Catholic	Burundi franc	Multiparty republic
	Uganda	Kampala	English	Catholic	Shilling	Multiparty republic
THE GREAT RIFT VALLEY	Kenya	Nairobi	English	Catholic	Shilling	Multiparty republic
	Tanzania	Dar es Salaam	English	Traditional	Shilling	Single-party republic
THE GREAT ZAMBEZI	Zambia	Lusaka	English	Christian	Kwacha	Multiparty republic
	Zimbabwe	Harare	English	Syncretic	Zimbabwean dollar	Multiparty republic
THE MOZAMBIQUE COAST	Mozambique	Maputo	Portuguese	Traditional	Metical	Multiparty republic
	Malawi	Lilongwe	English	Christian	Kwacha	Multiparty republic
THE INDIAN OCEAN ISLANDS	Madagascar	Antananarivo	French	Christian	Malagasy franc	Multiparty republic
	Comoros	Moroni	French	Muslim	Franc	Islamic republic
	Mauritius	Port Louis	English	Hindu	Rupee	Multiparty republic
	Réunion (France)	St-Denis	French	Catholic	Franc	Multiparty republic
	Seychelles	Victoria	French	Catholic	Rupee	Multiparty republic
THE SKELETON COAST	Namibia	Windhoek	English	Christian	Namibian dollar	Multiparty republic
	Botswana	Gaborone	English	Traditional	Pula	Multiparty republic
SOUTHERN AFRICA	South Africa	Pretoria	English	Christian	Rand	Multiparty republic
	Lesotho	Maseru	English	Christian	Loti	Constitutional monarchy
	Swaziland	Mbabane	English	Christian	Lilangeni	Executive monarchy

A little respect

Despite the enormous diversity of cultures and customs spread across the continent, Africans are generally conservative, adhering to devout religious practices, rather rigid moral values and strict hierarchical social structures. This is particularly true of the largely Muslim populations in North and East Africa, and the followers of ancient traditional belief systems.

For many Africans any unnecessary display of human flesh is offensive (especially by women) – most notably in staunchly Muslim countries – but modern society has encouraged some leniency to the "dress code", although exposed arms and legs are generally frowned upon, unless you are on a beach in a resort area.

Much the same is true of alcohol and drugs, especially in Muslim communities. Both are widely used across the continent, yet small rural communities – despite the proliferation of home brews and the like – may frown upon excessive use, especially when it flies in the face of religious intolerance.

Adultery is widely forbidden while, beyond the city limits, close-knit (and mostly religious) communities condemn promiscuity as the scourge of Africa. HIV/AIDS has reached pandemic proportions in many parts and and prostitution is rife, a sorrowful indictment on the levels of poverty and destitution in Africa.

Political leaders and others often proclaim homosexuality as 'un-African' and entirely absent from traditional culture, yet it is as common here as anywhere in the world. Even heterosexual displays of affection are generally frowned upon, which makes the largely closeted gay community even more cautious.

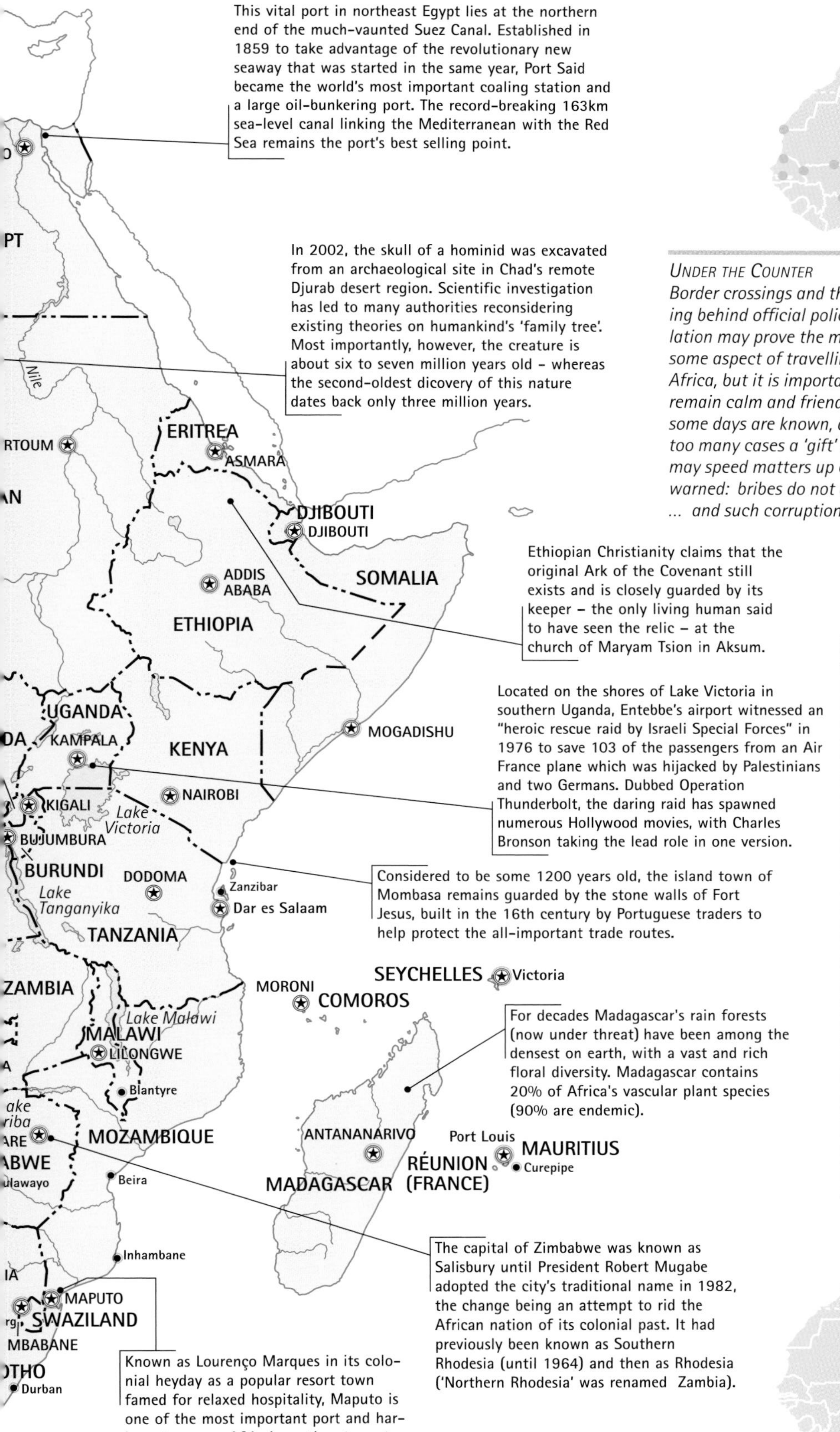

This vital port in northeast Egypt lies at the northern end of the much-vaunted Suez Canal. Established in 1859 to take advantage of the revolutionary new seaway that was started in the same year, Port Said became the world's most important coaling station and a large oil-bunkering port. The record-breaking 163km sea-level canal linking the Mediterranean with the Red Sea remains the port's best selling point.

In 2002, the skull of a hominid was excavated from an archaeological site in Chad's remote Djurab desert region. Scientific investigation has led to many authorities reconsidering existing theories on humankind's 'family tree'. Most importantly, however, the creature is about six to seven million years old – whereas the second-oldest dicovery of this nature dates back only three million years.

Ethiopian Christianity claims that the original Ark of the Covenant still exists and is closely guarded by its keeper – the only living human said to have seen the relic – at the church of Maryam Tsion in Aksum.

Located on the shores of Lake Victoria in southern Uganda, Entebbe's airport witnessed an "heroic rescue raid by Israeli Special Forces" in 1976 to save 103 of the passengers from an Air France plane which was hijacked by Palestinians and two Germans. Dubbed Operation Thunderbolt, the daring raid has spawned numerous Hollywood movies, with Charles Bronson taking the lead role in one version.

Considered to be some 1200 years old, the island town of Mombasa remains guarded by the stone walls of Fort Jesus, built in the 16th century by Portuguese traders to help protect the all-important trade routes.

For decades Madagascar's rain forests (now under threat) have been among the densest on earth, with a vast and rich floral diversity. Madagascar contains 20% of Africa's vascular plant species (90% are endemic).

The capital of Zimbabwe was known as Salisbury until President Robert Mugabe adopted the city's traditional name in 1982, the change being an attempt to rid the African nation of its colonial past. It had previously been known as Southern Rhodesia (until 1964) and then as Rhodesia ('Northern Rhodesia' was renamed Zambia).

Known as Lourenço Marques in its colonial heyday as a popular resort town famed for relaxed hospitality, Maputo is one of the most important port and harbour towns on Africa's southeast coast. Maputo acts as the departure point for much of southern Africa's gold bullion destined for the rest of the world.

KEY INFORMATION

KM 800 / MI 400

TUNIS	Capital city		Inland water
Lagos	Other city		Major river
	International boundary		

City and town plans featured in this book

UNDER THE COUNTER
Border crossings and the reasoning behind official policy and regulation may prove the most bothersome aspect of travelling within Africa, but it is important to remain calm and friendly. Delays of some days are known, although in far too many cases a 'gift' of a few dollars may speed matters up considerably. Be warned: bribes do not always work as intended … and such corruption is punishable by law.

BE SAFE

Most of the capital cities in Africa are generally as safe as anywhere in the world, but nonetheless the issue of personal safety and security remains an area of some concern in many parts of the continent. Generally, throngs of people - both locals and visitors - tend to discourage serious crime, but they may also attract chancers, with pickpockets, muggers and other petty criminals taking advantage of unsuspecting Westerners porting cameras and other sophisticated equipment.

Where such incidents have been reported (as opposed to being brushed off due to the travellers' time constraints or fear of reprisal), these tend to be restricted to more secluded or out-of-the-way places, and in general to the hours after darkness has fallen. This is particularly true of the seedier areas, such as cities' unofficial drug enclaves and red-light districts catering for a sex industry which, more often than not, caters almost exclusively for the tourism market. Be warned.

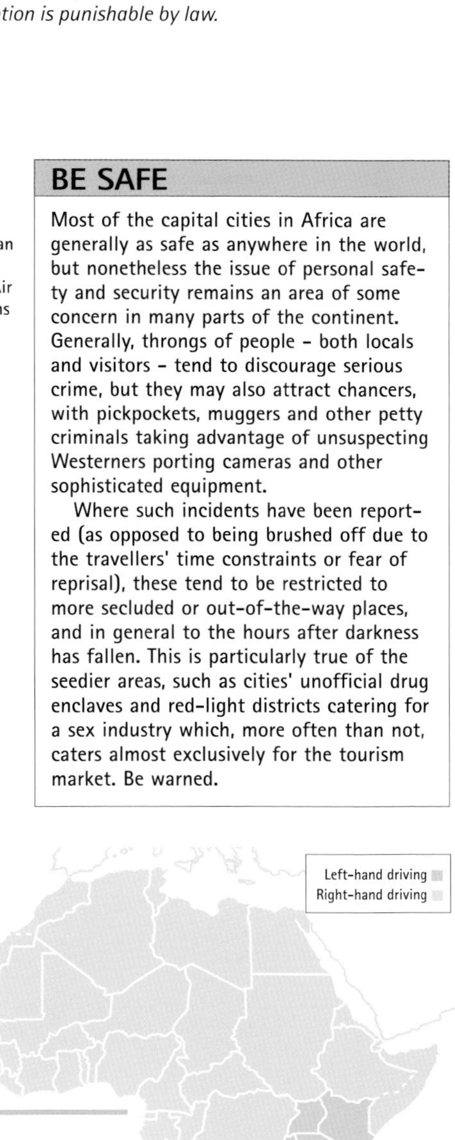

LEFT OR RIGHT?
In many parts of Africa, drivers are required to drive on the left-hand side of the road, which requires an unusual 'acclimatisation' period for many foreign travellers. It is important to ascertain the rules of the road for your destination prior to departure, and to bear in mind that neighbouring countries sometimes have opposing regulations – this can make road travel from one country to the next quite harrowing.

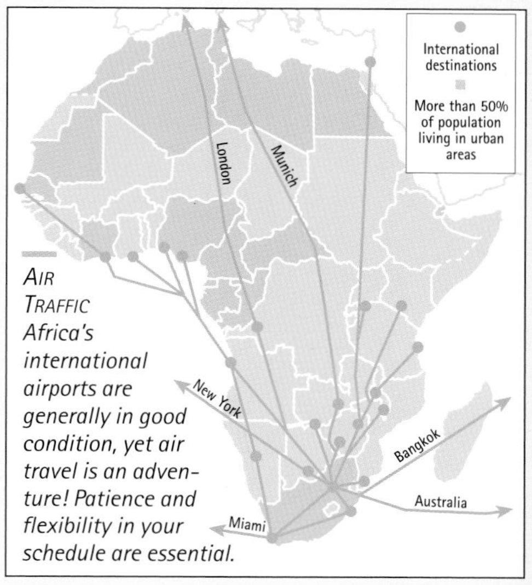

AIR TRAFFIC
Africa's international airports are generally in good condition, yet air travel is an adventure! Patience and flexibility in your schedule are essential.

Meeting traveller's needs

While many of the continent's urban centres remain delightfully undeveloped and unaffected by the growing tourism industry, most will cater well for the needs of travellers. Although some are less efficient than others and tend to operate at their own pace (on the legendary hourglass of 'African time'), all the capital cities and many of the larger towns offer at least some semblance of an infrastructure that is - at worst – adequate.

Although Internet connections and e-mail facilities can hardly match those of more developed countries, a surprising number of African cities have seen considerable technological growth in recent years and virtually all have a generally sound post and telecommunications infrastructure, with telephone and fax facilities. It will be wise to carry an international telephone connection card (ie AT&T) or similar internet connection separate from your wallet in the event of theft or an emergency (and perhaps to combat inflated call charges from shopkeepers or locals, where public facilities are non-existent or highly-inflated).

Depending on the state of the local economy and its development, most African nations should offer a constant and reliable electricity supply to their urban centres, although further afield the supply may be somewhat more erratic. Much the same is true of the commercial and financial sectors, with most cities and towns boasting any number of banks and exchange bureaux – restricted largely to central business districts – which offer a far more reliable and honest service than the ever-growing black market for currency exchange.

The basic urban infrastructure of roads, hospitals and other community services varies enormously, from the sophisticated developments of Nairobi and Johannesburg to the often deplorable state of affairs in Monrovia and Lagos, for example. Although roads and road signs may be a little worse for wear even in the inner cities, public transport systems are generally satisfactory for the basic needs of independent travellers, with fairly regular bus, train and taxi services connecting the most prominent tourist spots and local attractions.

Apart from the handful of countries that have been declared danger zones by Western nations – or which have severed political ties with the West – national embassies, consulates or honorary consulates are represented in most of Africa's capitals, many of which are very well serviced by both international and domestic airports, hotels, restaurants and popular entertainment venues such as cinemas, theatres and nightclubs.

It is important to remember, however, that – apart from those kept almost universally – individual countries may celebrate any number of public holidays specific to the nation, most often in commemoration of their independence, the birthday of a founding father or days – and even extended periods – of religious significance, such as the Muslim fasting at Ramadaan, during which time business hours may vary and trade restricted.

Biblioteca Municipal
PLAZA DEL ARQUITECTO
Mencey
RAMBLA DEL GENERAL FRANCO
Contemporáneo
Taburiente
Parque Municipal García Sanabria
El Toscal
Church
Bar Cristobel
Salamanca
PLAZA DE LA PAZ
PLAZA DE TOROS
Sanidad
PLAZA 25 DE JULIO
Ayuntamiento (Town Hall)
PLAZA DE LA PATOS
Gobierno Militar
Capitanía General
PLAZA DE GENERAL WEYLER
Parque de Artillería
Parking
Cinema
Horizonte
Principe Paz
Parque Municipal de la Granja
PLAZA DE R DOMINICANA
Catedral de la Concepción
PLAZA DE DUGGI
Barranco de los Santos
Hospital Militar
Hospitalito de Niños
Duggi
Parlamento
PLAZA DEL PRINCIPE
PLAZA ALFEREZ PROVISIONAL
Iglesia de San Francisco
Museo Municipal de Bellas Artes
Juzgados
Austriaco
Atlantico
Palacio de Carta
Océano
Casino
PLAZA SANTO DOMINGO
PLAZA DE ESPAÑA
Teatro Guimerá
Monumento de los Caídos
PLAZA DE LA CANDELARIA
PLAZA DE LA MADERA
Anaga
Correos y Telegrafos
Palacio Insular (Cabildo)
Alamada del Duque de Santa Elena
Estación Maritima
Police
ATLANTIC OCEAN
Estadio Heliodoro Rodriguez López
Instituto Nacional de Meteorologia
Tanausu
PLAZA DE LA IGLESIA
Iglesia de Nuestra Señora de la Concepción
Nueva Dársena Sur
PLAZA DEL MERCADO
Mercado de Nuestra Señora de Africa
Museo de la Naturaleza y el Hombre
Parque de Don Quijote
PLAZA GRAVINA
GLORIETA DE PEDRO MENDOZA
Parque de Bomberos
PLAZA DE LA VICTORIA
Bar Mercado
Cuartel de San Carlos
Estación de Guaguas
El Cabo
Zona Industrial
TO LA LAGUNA
TO AIRPORT
TO SANTA MARIA DEL MAR
DIQUE NUEVO
DÁRSENA COMERCIAL
MUELLE
Santa Cruz de Tenerife
Tenerife
Las Palmas
Gran Canaria
Lanzarote
Arrecife
Puerto del Rosario
Fuerteventura
M 300
Yd 300
KM 60
MI 30

CONTINUED ON INSET MAP
CONTINUED ON MAIN MAP
Ciudad Jardín
Altavista
La Rehoya
San Antonio
Barrio De La Paz
Lugo
Arenales
Triana
Ciudad del Mar
San Lázaro
San Bernardo
San Francisco
San Nicolás
Miller Bajo
Guiniguada
San Roque
Vegueta
Puerto
Santa Catalina
Alcaravaneras
Puerto de la Luz
Playa de las Canteras
Playa de Alcaravaneras
Punta Gorda
Punta del Arrecife
La Barra
Naval Base
ATLANTIC OCEAN
HOTEL NAMES
1 Corinto
2 Imperial Playa
3 Nautilus
4 Tenesoya
5 Rocamar
6 Melia
7 Cristina Sol
8 Utiaca
9 Cantur
10 Verol
11 Sol
12 Reina Isabel
13 Los Bardinos
14 Atlanta
15 Concorde
16 Tigaday
17 Fataga
TO TAFIRA
TO AIRPORT
M 600
Yd 600
M 300
Yd 300

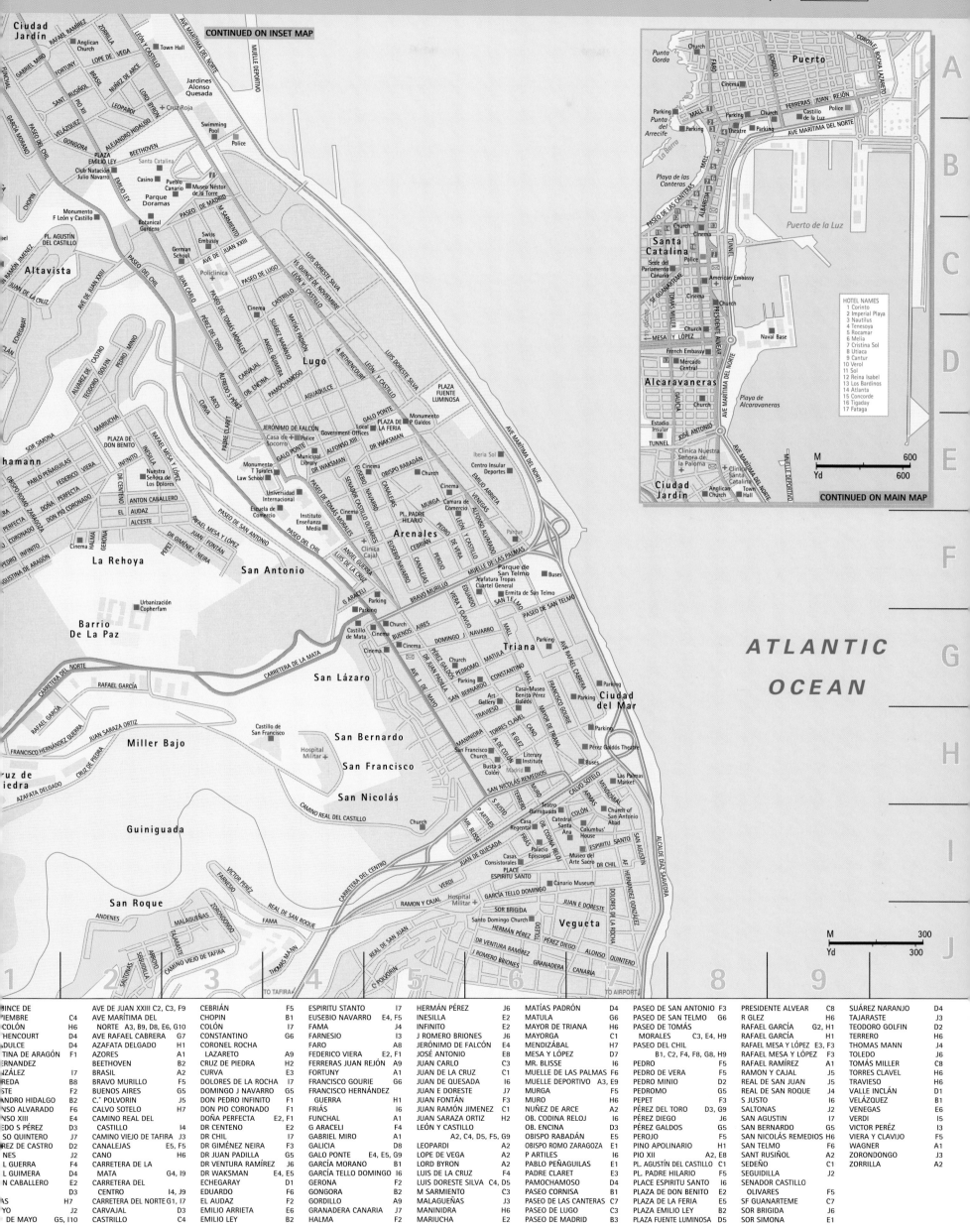

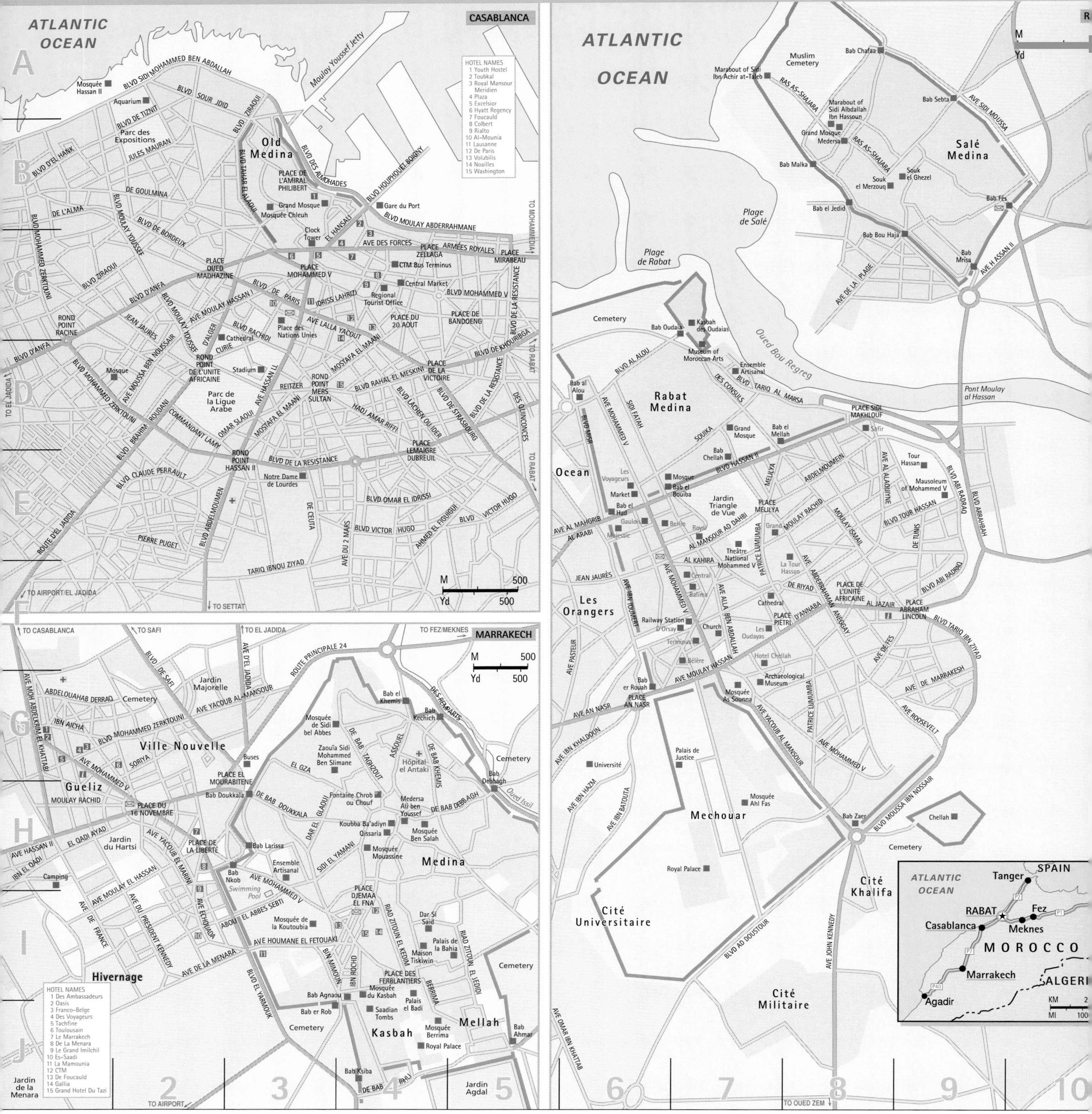

Casablanca

- AHMED EL FIGUIGUI E4
- AVE DES FORCES ARMÉES ROYALES C4
- AVE DU 2 MARS E4, F4
- AVE HASSAN II D3
- AVE LALLA YACOUT C3
- AVE MOULAY HASSAN I C2
- AVE MOUSSA BEN NOUSSAIR D2
- BLVD ABDELMOUMEN E2
- BLVD BRAHIM ROUDANI D2
- BLVD CLAUDE PERRAULT E2
- BLVD D'ANFA D1, C2
- BLVD D'EL HANK B1
- BLVD DE BORDEAUX B2
- BLVD DE KHOURIBGA D5
- BLVD DE LA RESISTANCE C5, D3, D5
- BLVD DE PARIS C3
- BLVD DE STRASBOURG D5
- BLVD DE TIZNIT A2, B2
- BLVD DES ALMOHADES B3
- BLVD HOUPHOUET BOIGNY B4
- BLVD LACHEN OU IDER D4
- BLVD MOHAMMED V C5
- BLVD MOHAMMED ZERKTOUNI B1, D2
- BLVD MOULAY ABDERRAHMANE B4
- BLVD MOULAY YOUSSEF B1, C2
- BLVD OMAR EL IDRISSI E4
- BLVD RACHIDI C3
- BLVD RAHAL EL MESKINI D4
- BLVD SIDI MOHAMMED BEN ABDALLAH A2
- BLVD SOUR JDID A2
- BLVD TAHAR EL ALAOUI B3
- BLVD VICTOR HUGO E4, E5
- BLVD ZIRAOUI A3, C1
- COMMANDANT LAMY D2
- CURIE D3
- D'ALGER C2
- DE CEUTA E3
- DE GOULMINA B2
- DE L'ALMA B1
- EL HANSALI C3
- HADJ AMAR RIFFI D4
- IDRISS LAHRIZI C4
- JEAN JAURÈS C2
- JULES MAURAN B2
- MOSTAFA EL MAANI D3, D4
- OMAR SLAOUI D3
- PIERRE PUGET E2
- PLACE DE BANDOENG C5
- PLACE DE L'AMIRAL PHILIBERT B3
- PLACE DE LA VICTOIRE D4
- PLACE DU 20 AOUT C4
- PLACE LEMAIGRE DUBREUIL D4
- PLACE MIRABEAU C5
- PLACE MOHAMMED V C3
- PLACE OUED MADHAZINE C2
- PLACE ZELLAGA C4
- REITZER D3
- ROND POINT DE L'UNITE AFRICAINE D2
- ROND POINT HASSAN II E3
- ROND POINT MERS SULTAN D3
- ROND POINT RACINE C1
- ROUTE D'EL JADIDA F1
- TARIQ IBNOU ZIYAD F3

Marrakech

- ABDELOUAHAB DERRAQ G1
- ABOU EL ABBES SEBTI I3
- ASSOUEL G4
- AVE D'EL JADIDA F3
- AVE DE FRANCE I1
- AVE DE LA MENARA I2
- AVE DU PRESIDENT KENNEDY I2
- AVE ECHOUADA I2
- AVE HASSAN II H1
- AVE HOUMANE EL FETOUAKI I3
- AVE MOHAMMED ABDELKRIM EL KHATTABI F1, G1
- AVE MOHAMMED V G1, I3
- AVE MOULAY EL HASSAN H2
- AVE YACOUB AL MANSOUR G2, G3
- AVE YACOUB EL MARINI H2
- BERRIMA I4
- BIN MIMOUN I3
- BLVD DE SAFI F2
- BLVD EL YARMOUK I3
- BLVD MOHAMMED ZERKTOUNI G2
- DAR EL GLAOUI H3
- DE BAB DOUKKALA G3
- DE BAB DEBBAGH G5
- DE BAB IRHLI J4
- DE BAB KHEMIS G4
- DE BAB TAGHZOUT G4
- DES REMPARTS G4
- EL GZA G3
- EL QADI AYAD H1
- IBN AICHA G1
- IBN EL QADI H1
- IBN ROCHD I4
- MOULAY RACHID H1
- PLACE DE LA LIBERTÉ H2
- PLACE DES FERBLANTIERS I4
- PLACE DJEMAA EL FNA I4
- PLACE DU 16 NOVEMBRE H2
- PLACE EL MOURABITENE G3
- RIAD ZITOUN EL JEDIDI I5
- RIAD ZITOUN EL KEDIM I4
- ROUTE PRINCIPALE 24 F3
- SIDI EL YAMANI H3
- SORIYA G2

Rabat

- ABDELMOUMEIN E8
- AL JAZAIR F8
- AL KAHIRA F7
- AL MANSOUR AD DAHBI E7
- AVE ABDERRAHMAN ANEGGAY F8
- AVE AL ALAOUIYNE E8
- AVE ALLA BEN ABDALLAH F7
- AVE AL MAHGRIB AL ARABI E6
- AVE AN NASR G6
- AVE DE FES F8
- AVE DE LA PLAGE C8
- AVE DE MARRAKESH G9
- AVE HASSAN II C9
- AVE IBN BATOUTA H6
- AVE IBN HAZM H6
- AVE IBN KHALDOUN G6
- AVE IBN TOUMERT F6
- AVE JOHN KENNEDY I8
- AVE MOHAMMED V D6, F6, G8
- AVE MOULAY HASSAN G7
- AVE OMAR IBN KHATTAB J6
- AVE PASTEUR F6
- AVE ROOSEVELT G9
- AVE SIDI MOUSSA A9
- AVE YACOUB AL MANSOUR G7
- BLVD ABI RADRAQ E9, F9
- BLVD AD DOUSTOUR I7
- BLVD AL ALOU D6
- BLVD ARRAHBAH E9
- BLVD HASSAN II E7
- BLVD MISR D6
- BLVD MOUSSA IBN NOSSAIR H8
- BLVD TARIQ AL MARSA D7
- BLVD TARIQ IBN ZIYAD F9
- BLVD TOUR HASSAN E8
- D'ANNABA F8
- DE RIYAD F8
- DE TUNIS E9
- DES CONSULS D7
- JEAN JAURÈS F6
- MELIYA E7
- MOULAY ISMAIL E8
- MOULAY RACHID E8
- PATRICE LUMUMBA F7, G8
- PLACE ABRAHAM LINCOLN F9
- PLACE AN NASR G6
- PLACE DE L'UNITÉ AFRICAINE F8
- PLACE MELIYA E7
- PLACE PIETRI F7
- PLACE SIDI MAKHLOUF D8
- RAS AS-SHAJARA A8, B8
- SIDI FATAH D6
- SOUIKA D7

MEDITERRANEAN SEA
Pointe el Kettani
Ilot de la Marine
Bab El Oued
Casbah
Oued Koriche
Les Tagarins
Telemly
Deux Entêtés
El Kettar Cemetery
Jardin de Prague
Fort de la Casbah
Palais du Dey
National Library
Dar Hassan Pacha
Ketchaoua Mosque
Grand Mosque
PLACE DES MARTYRS
Chambre de Commerce
Darse de l'Amirauté
Môle de Pêche
Jetée du Nord
Gare Maritime Transatlantique
Môle el Djefna
Algiers Railway Station
Ferry Terminal
Môle de France
Bassin de Vieux Port
Bassin du Radoub
Jetée de l'est
Môle des Combustibles
Môle Amiral Mouchez
PLACE EMIR ABDELKADER
Palais du Gouvernement
Esplanade de l'Afrique
Main Post Office
PLACE GRANDE POSTE
University of Algeria
Institut d' Études Nuclaires
Casino Music Hall
National Algerian Theatre
PLACE MOHAMED TOURI
PLACE PORT SAID
Palais de Justice
Palais de l'Assemblée Nationale
Airport Buses
Casino Municipal
TO CHERCHELL
TO BLIDA
TO HOUARI BOUMEDIENNE AIRPORT
M 300
Yd 300
A B C D E F G H I J
1 2 3 4 5 6 7 8 9
Bologhine Ibnou Ziri
Pointe Pescade
Pointe des Consuls
Les Deux Moulins
SEE STREETPLAN
ALGIERS
KM 4
MI 2

Jardin Zoologique
Cimetiére Sidi Yahia
Stade Taib Ben Ammar
Cimetiere Chrétien
Parc des Sporte
Palais de la Foire
Parc J Kennedy
Lake Tu
Palais des Congrès
Sports Grou
Bab el Khadra
Halfaouine
Bab Souika
Medina
Bab Bhar
Kasbah
Jardin Habib Thameur
Charles Nicolle
Faculté de Medicine
Lycée Technique de Tunis
Palais de Justice
Ancien Cimetière de Sidi Ahmed Sakka
Collège Sadiki
Museum 9 April
Faculté des Lettres
Bab Sidi Kacem
Bab Sidi Abdallah
Bab Sidi Abdessalem
Bab Benat
Nelson Mandela Metro Station
République Metro Station
Tripoli Louage Station
Bab El Khadra Metro Station
Ibn Rachid Metro Station
Habib Thameur Metro Station
Place Barcelone Metro Station
Tunis Railway Station
Town Hall
Cathedral
National Theatre
French Embassy
British Embassy
Bourse de Travail
Buses to Airport, Bardo Museum
Dar Ben Abdallah Museum
Great Mosque (Zitouna)
Dar Lasram
Dar Othman
Dyer's Souks
Second Hand Clothes Souk
Market
Parking
TO ARIANA
TO QAIROUAN
M 50
Yd 500

N'Djamena CHAD • Niamey NIGER

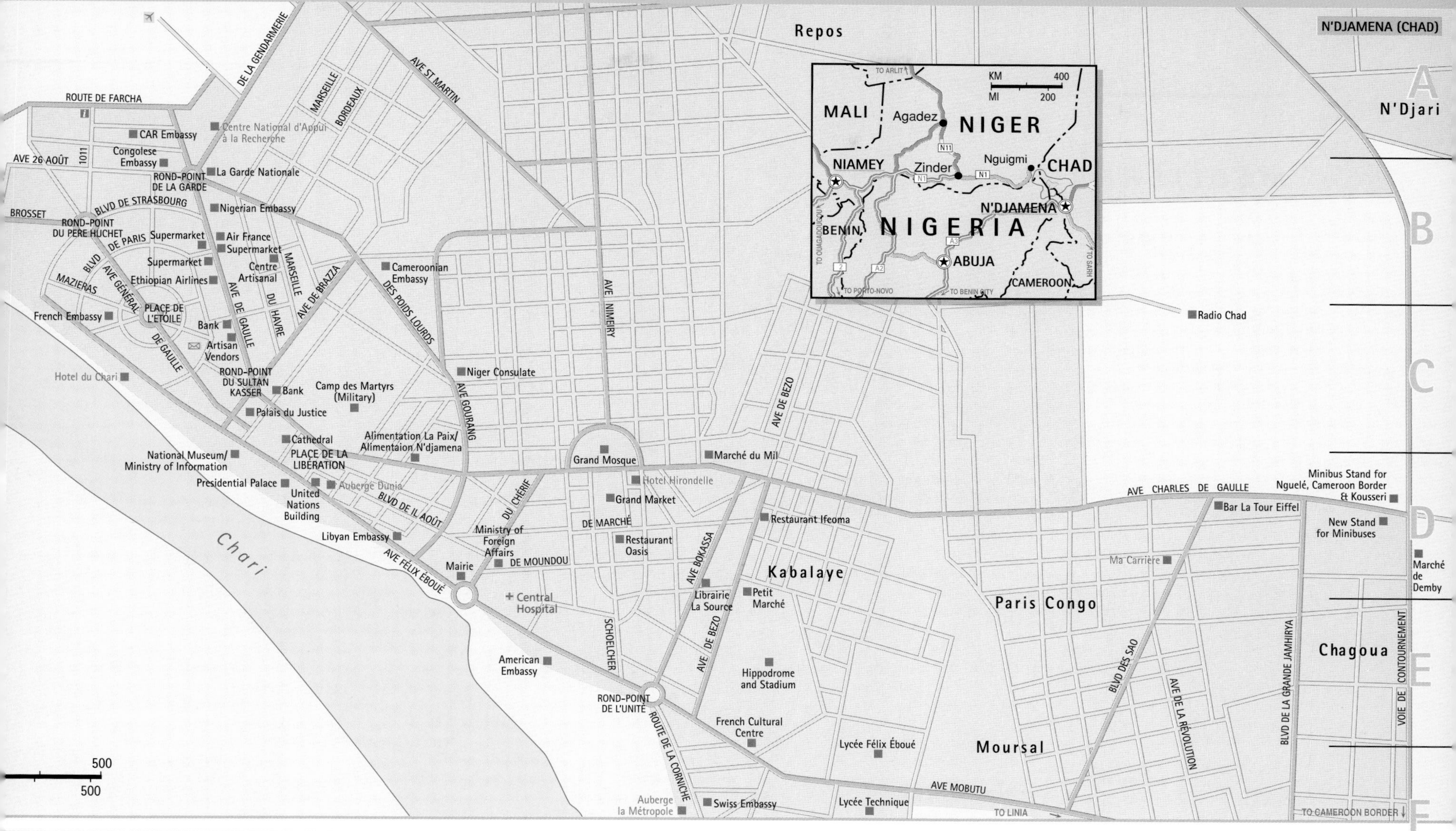

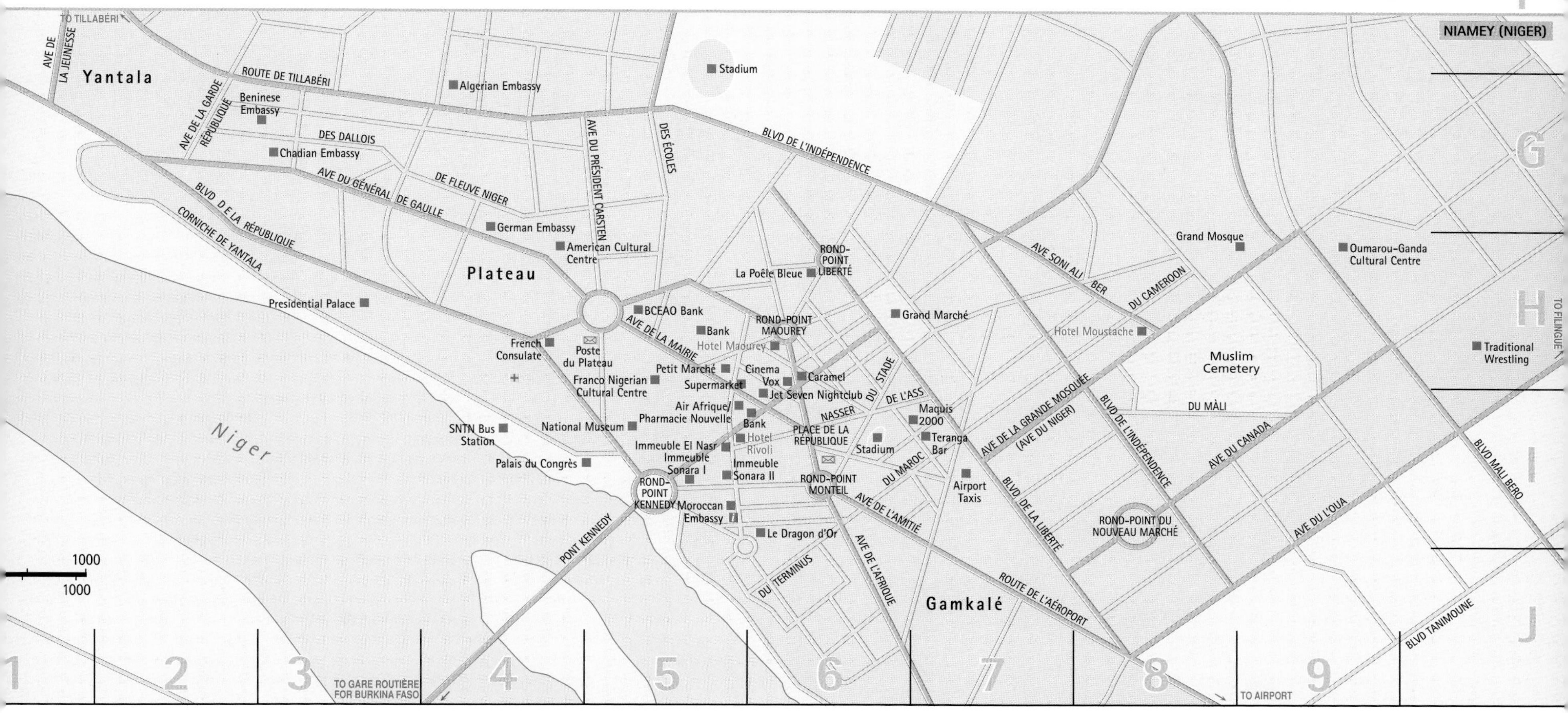

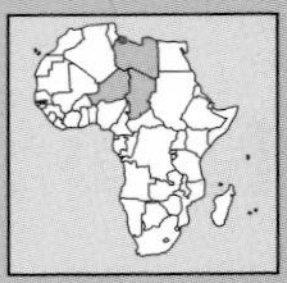

A
B
C
D
E
F
G
H
I
J
2
3
4
5
6
7
8
9
10
M 600
Yd 600
MEDITERRANEAN
SEA
Customs
Fishing Harbour
Harbour
AL KURNISH
Al Kurnish
Arch of Marcus Aurelius
Gurgi Mosque
Clock Tower
Carpenters Market
Central Bank of Lybia
Medina (Old City)
Assai al Hamra (Old Castle)
Jamahiriya Museum
At Turk Market
Al Mushir Market
An Naqa Mosque
Karamanli Mosque
AL FATAH
Islamic Call Society
Bab al Bahr
Bab al Madinah
Central Bus and Taxi Station
AL MA'MUN
AR RASHID
SIDI OMRAN
ASSAHA AL KHADRAH
People's General Committee
AL BALADIYAH
IMHIMMID AL MQARYIF
1ST SEPTEMBER
City Bus Station
OMAR AL MUKHTAR
Cinema
Al Kabir
Gazelle Fountain
Jazzayat Building
Municipality
ALGERIAN SQUARE
Main Post Office
Daru Al Ifta' House
Africa
AHMAD ASH SHARIF
ADH-DHAHRA AL KABIRA
Funduq Ayyusar
Marhaba
Catholic Church
Cleopatra
Palace
San Francisco Church
Italian Embassy
Waddan
British Embassy
ZAWIYAT AL DAHMANI
SIDI ISSA
Turkish Embassy
Al Mahari
IBN 'UQAYL
AN NASR
Football Club
City Bus Station
AL JAMAHURIYAH
Market
Cemetery
FASHLOUM
Garden City
KHALID IBN AL WALID
Tunisian Embassy
People's Palace
Syrian Embassy
Japanese Embassy
Yemen Arab Republic E
Maltese Embassy
Lebanese Embassy
Moroccan Embassy
Bulgarian Embassy
AL QADISIYAH SQUARE
Pakistani Embassy
Finnish Embassy
Jordanian Embas
Kuwaiti Embassy
DRC Embassy
German Embassy
Iranian Embassy
Romanian Embassy
French Embassy
BIN 'A
AL MA'ZI MOSQUE
Chinese Embassy
Tripol International Fair
AL MA'ARRI
TARIQ
AL KURNISH
Public Beach
Continental
SIDI AL BAHLUL
ABDUN NASR
SHAWOY
AL MASIRAH AL KUBRAH
KHALIFA AZZAYDI
Assahary
Libyan Historic Society
AMR BIN AL A'SS
MIZRAN
Bank
Al Wahah
Rex
Mediterranean
Municipal Club
Sports Centre
Government Printing Press
SIDI MUNEDIR
Sidi Munedir Islamic Cemetery
PALESTINE SQUARE
AS SARIM
ABU HRIDAH
AL JAMAHURIYAH
Ibn Annatis Hospital
Shopping Centre
AZ ZAWIYAH
ASSAYIDI
SIDI KHALIFAH
AL JALA'
Bab Akkarah
Head Post Office
Bab Bin Ghashir
SUQ ATH THALAT
Annasr Forest (Zoo & Recreation Area)
AL HADHBAH
KM 2
MI 1
SEE STREETPLAN
Al Annakhil Holiday Resort
AL FATAH HIGHWAY
Fishing Club
Horse Racing
Planetarium
Radio & Television Station
Garden City
TO TUNISIA
TO TAJURA
ARADAH
JAMA'A ASSAQA'A
AWLADA BIN AL HAJ RPAD
11TH JUNE
Sidi Al Marsri
Annasr Forest
SECOND RING
Al Khadra' Hospital
Market
AIRPORT HIGHWAY
TO TRIPOLI INTERNATIONAL AIRPORT
Shopping Centre
University Hospital
AL KHUMS
TO AL FIRNAJ
Police Academy
AL HADHBAH
THIRD RING
TO BIN GHASHIR

CTOBER	B6	BAYN AL-SAYARIG	C8	EL GAMIA	G2	EL FUSTAT	H5, I5	EL MUWASALAH	H8, J9	HAMDI	A8	LUFTI HASSANA	D2	NOQTET EL POLIS	C2	SARWAT	F1
.Y	A2, C5	BEIN EL GHANAYIN	A10	BAYN AL-SAYARIG	C8	EL GAMIL	B8	EL NASIRIYA	F6	HARAT EL BAHNASAWI	I6	MADINAT ABBAS	A5	NUBAR	E5	SAYYALAT EL RODA	H4
L HALIM HUSAIN	C1	BEIRAM EL TONSI	G6	BEIN EL GHANAYIN	A10	EL GEISH	B9, D7	EL NIL	C2, D3, F2, H2	HARUN	F2	MAGLIS EL SHA'AB	E5	NUBAR	E6	SHANAN	A5
L MAGID EL LABBAN	F6	BIRKET EL RATLI	B8	BEIRAM EL TONSI	G6	EL GEZIRA	B3, C4	EL QAL'A	D7, E8, F8	HASSAN ASSIM	A3	MAGRA EL UYUN	H5	NUR EL ZALAM	F7	SHEIKH EL ARUSI	B7
L RAHIM SABRI	D2	BOULOUS HANNA	E2	BIRKET EL RATLI	B8	EL GIZA	F2, H2	EL QARAFAH EL KUBRA	H8	HASSAN EL ANWAR	I4	MANSUR	E5	NUZHA	A10	SHEIKH QAMAR	A9
ADRAN	H3	BULAQ EL GADID	B4	BOULOUS HANNA	E2	EL GUMHURIYA	B6, D6	EL QASR EL AINI	F5, G4	HASSAN SABRI	B3	MASNA EL TARABISH	B10	OM KOL THUM	B2	SHEIKH RIHAN	E5, E7
L MAATI	B2	CHAMPOLLION	C5	BULAQ EL GADID	B4	EL HADAI'Q EL ZUHRIYA	D3	EL QOLALI	A6	HUSEINIYA	B9	MATHAF EL NIL	G4	ORABI	A1, B6	SHUBRA	A6
. MAHASIN EL SADILI	B1	CLOT BEY	B7	CHAMPOLLION	C5	EL HADAIQ	D1	EL QUBEISI	A8	HUSSEIN WASIF	F2	MAWARDI	F5	PORT SAID	A9, C8, F6	SIDI MALIK	I5
A'UD	I4	DARB EL HUSR	G7	CLOT BEY	B7	EL HILMIYAH	F7	EL RODA	I4	IBN EL FARID	I8	MIDAN ABDIN	E6	QASR EL NIL	D6	SIKKET EL HADID	H5
AYFAYN	H4, I4	DARB NASSER	A5	DARB EL HUSR	G7	EL HUSN	H2	EL SABTIYA	A5	IBN KHALDUN	A10	MISR EL QADIMA	J7	RAMSES	A8, B6	SIKKET EL ZAHIR	B8
ALIB	C5	DR MOHAMMED SHAHEEN	C2	DARB NASSER	A5	EL IMAM EL LAYTI	H8	EL SADD EL BARRANI	G5	IBN YAZID	H6	MOHAMMED BEY EL ALFI	C6	RUSHDI	D6	SULEIMAN GOHAR	E2
	C6	EL ABBASIYA	A10	DR MOHAMMED SHAHEEN	C2	EL IMAM EL SHAF'I	I8	EL SAHAFA	B5	IBN ZANKI	B3	MOHAMMED EL DURRI	C2	S ABDEL AZIZ RADWAN	C1	SULEIMAN EL KHADIM	A4
.D ALI SATURI	F1	EL ADAWIYA	B5	EL ABBASIYA	A10	EL IMAM EL SHATBI	B5	EL SALIBAH	F7	IBRAHIM EL GIBALI	J4	MOHAMMED FAIRD	E6	S AMIN BEY AR-RAFI'I	E2	SULTAN AHMAD	E10
.D MAHIR	D8, I1	EL AHRAR	C1	EL ADAWIYA	B5	EL KHADRI	B4	EL SAMMAKIN	B9	IDARAT EL MURUR	C10	MOHAMMED IZZ EL ARAB	F5	S AMIN AR-RAFEL	F2	SUQ EL SILAH	F8
.D OMAR	E7	EL ASHRAF	G7, H7	EL AHRAR	C1	EL KHALIG EL MASRI	F5	EL SARAY	G4	IMAD EL DIN	C6	MOHAMMED MAHMUD	D5	S AS-SAAD AL-ALI	E2	SUWAIQA EL LALA	F6
S-SIRA	H5	EL AZHAR	D8, D10	EL ASHRAF	G7, H7	EL MADRASA EL QAWMIYA	H3	EL SAYYIDA 'AISHA	G8	IRAN	E1	MOHAMMED MAZHAR	A3	S EL AHRAM	I1	TALAAT HARB	C6
. SIRA	I7	EL BAHR EL AZAM	I2	EL AZHAR	D8, D10	EL MAGHAR	F8	EL SAYYIDA NAFISA	H7	ISA MOHAMMED	C1	MOHAMMED RUSHDI	A2	S EL GAMIA	G2	TANTA	B1
USA	H5	EL BAIYUMI	B9	EL BAHR EL AZAM	I2	EL MAHATTA	J1	EL SHARABIYA	A8	ISMAIL ABAZA	E5	MOHAMMED SABRI ABU EL ALAM	D6	S EL MUQATTAM	G10	TARIQ-AN-NASR	E10, I10
RAHIM	G5	EL BAQLI	G8	EL BAIYUMI	B9	EL MAHRUSA	A1	EL SIRGANI	B10	ISMAIL MOHAMMED	A3			S GAMIAT-EL QAHIRA	G1	TULUN	G7
BN EL AS	I5	EL BUSTAN	D5	EL BAQLI	G8	EL MALIK ABD EL AZIZ EL SU'UD	H3, I3	EL TAHAWIYYAH	I8	ISMAIL SIRRI	F5	MOHAMMED SUKRI	C2	S MUSTAFA ABD AR-RAZIQ	E7	UMAR TUSUN	A1
A'QUB	H7	EL CORNICHE EL NIL	A4, C4, E4, H4	EL BUSTAN	D5			EL TAHRIR	D5, E1, E3	KAMIL MUHSIN	I9	MOHAMMED TALAT	C2	SABIL EL KHAZINDAR	A10	USEF SULIMAN	B8
HEIKH ALI YUSAF	F5			EL CORNICHE EL NIL	A4, C4, E4, H4	EL MALIK EL MUZAFFAR	I3	EL TAMBATI	B8	KAMIL SIDQI	B7	MUH. QADRI	F6	SABRI	A8	YUSSUF NAGIB	C7
L BAHR	B7	EL DARB EL AHMAR	E8			EL MALIK EL SALIH	J3	EL TAWASHI	B7	KHAIRAT	F6	MUHAMMED KHALAF	E2	S'AD ZAGHLUL	I2	YUSUF EL DIGAWI	H3
L-WAZIR	F8, F9	EL DIYURA	G5	EL DARB EL AHMAR	E8	EL MANSURI	A5	EL TAWIL	A7	KUBRI 6 OCTOBER	D2	MUMTAZ	G5	SAKAKINI	A9	ZEIN EL ABIDIN	G6
AD-DIN AR-RIFA'I	G7	EL DUQQI	D1,E1	EL DIYURA	G5	EL MANSURIYA	C10	EL ZAHAR	A6	KUBRI 26 JULY	B4	MURAD	H2	SALAH AD-DIN	G8		
ALA	B9	EL FALAKI	F5	EL DUQQI	D1,E1	EL MANYAL	H3, I3	EL ZAHIR	A8, B7	KUBRI EL GAMIA	G3	NADI AS-SAID	D1	SALAH EL DIN	B2		
AD-DIN	D9	EL FALONGA	B1	EL FALAKI	F5	EL MASI	F7	EL ZUHUR	A6	KUBRI EL GIZA	I3	NAGIB RIHANI	C7	SALAH SALIM	D10, F9, I6, J1		
RI EL UYUN	H7	EL FARIQ ABD EL MUN'IM RIYAD	B1	EL FALONGA	B1	EL MIQYAS	I3	GA'FAR	B5	KUBRI EL MANYAL	F4	NAGM AD-DIN	F7	SALAMA	G6		
AT ALI	A2			EL FARIQ ABD EL MUN'IM RIYAD	B1	EL MISAHA	E2	GALAL	C10	KUBRI GHAMRA	A9	NASRA	E6	SAMI EL BARUDI	D7		
WI	E1	EL FATIH	I2			EL MUIZZ	C9, E8	GEZIRET BADRAN	A6	KUBRI QASR EL NIL	D4	NAWAL	D2	SAQQAIYIN	E6		
HILAL	H5	EL FUSTAT	H5, I5	EL FATIH	I2	EL MUSKI	C8	GOHAR EL QA'ID	D8	KUBRI ZAMALEK	A2	NIGM EL DIN	B9	SARIF EL KABIR	D7		

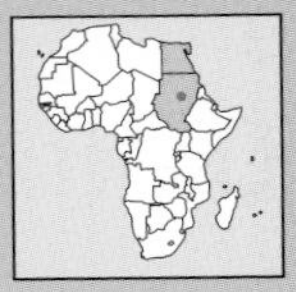

1ST ST	J10
10TH STREET	E8
10TH STREET SOUTH	I5
16TH STREET SOUTH	I4
17TH STREET	E7, F2
18TH STREET	F7
19TH STREET	E7, F2
31ST AVENUE EAST	G8
33RD AVENUE EAST	H8
35TH AVENUE	H7
35TH AVENUE EAST	H8
37TH AVENUE	H7
39TH AVENUE EAST	I5, H7
41ST AVENUE EAST	H7
43RD AVENUE EAST	H7
45TH AVENUE EAST	I7
46TH STREET	E2
47TH AVENUE EAST	I7
48TH STREET	E2
49TH AVENUE EAST	I7
50TH STREET	E1
51ST AVENUE EAST	I7
52ND STREET	E1
53RD AVENUE EAST	I7
54TH STREET	E1
55TH AVENUE EAST	I7
57TH AVENUE EAST	J7
59TH AVENUE EAST	J7
61ST AVE EAST	J7
63RD AVE EAST	J7
65TH AVE EAST	J7
67TH AVE EAST	J7
69TH AVE EAST	J7
ABU SINA	E6
AFRICA	H9
ALI ABDUL LATIF	E2
ALI ABDUL LATIF SOUTH	I3
ALI NAR	D7
ARMY ROAD (RING ROAD)	G2, G6
ATBARA	E6
BABIKER BADRI	E6
BALADIYA	D8, E2, E6
BARLAMAN	D3
BLUE NILE BRIDGE	A10
BURI	C10
BUSTAN	H8
CONTOMICHOLOS	E6
EL GEISH (RING ROAD)	E9
EL HURRIYA	E3
EL HURRIYA SOUTH	I4
EL NUGUMI	D7, E8
EL QASR	D5, F6
EL QASR SOUTH	I6
EL TAIYAR EL GAMEIL	F3
GAMAA	C6, C9, D1
GAMHURIYA	D4, D8
HASIM BEY	F4, I5
HOSPITAL	F6, G3
JAMI	F5
KHALIFA	D5
KULLIYAT AT TIBB	G5
MAHDI	E8
MALIK	F4
MEK NIMIR	D7, E7, H8, I7
MIDDLE	J10
NILE	B8, C3, C6
OTHMAN DIGNA	E9
SALEH PASHA EL MEK	F3
SAYED ABDUL RAHMAN	F3, F6
SINKAT	D3
TAIYAR MORAD	D4
TAIYAR ZULFU	
TAIYAR ZULFU SOUTH	
TAIYER IZZ ED DIN SOUTH	
TAYER IZZ ED DIN	
ZUBEID HAG EL AMIN	
ZUBIER PASHER	D8

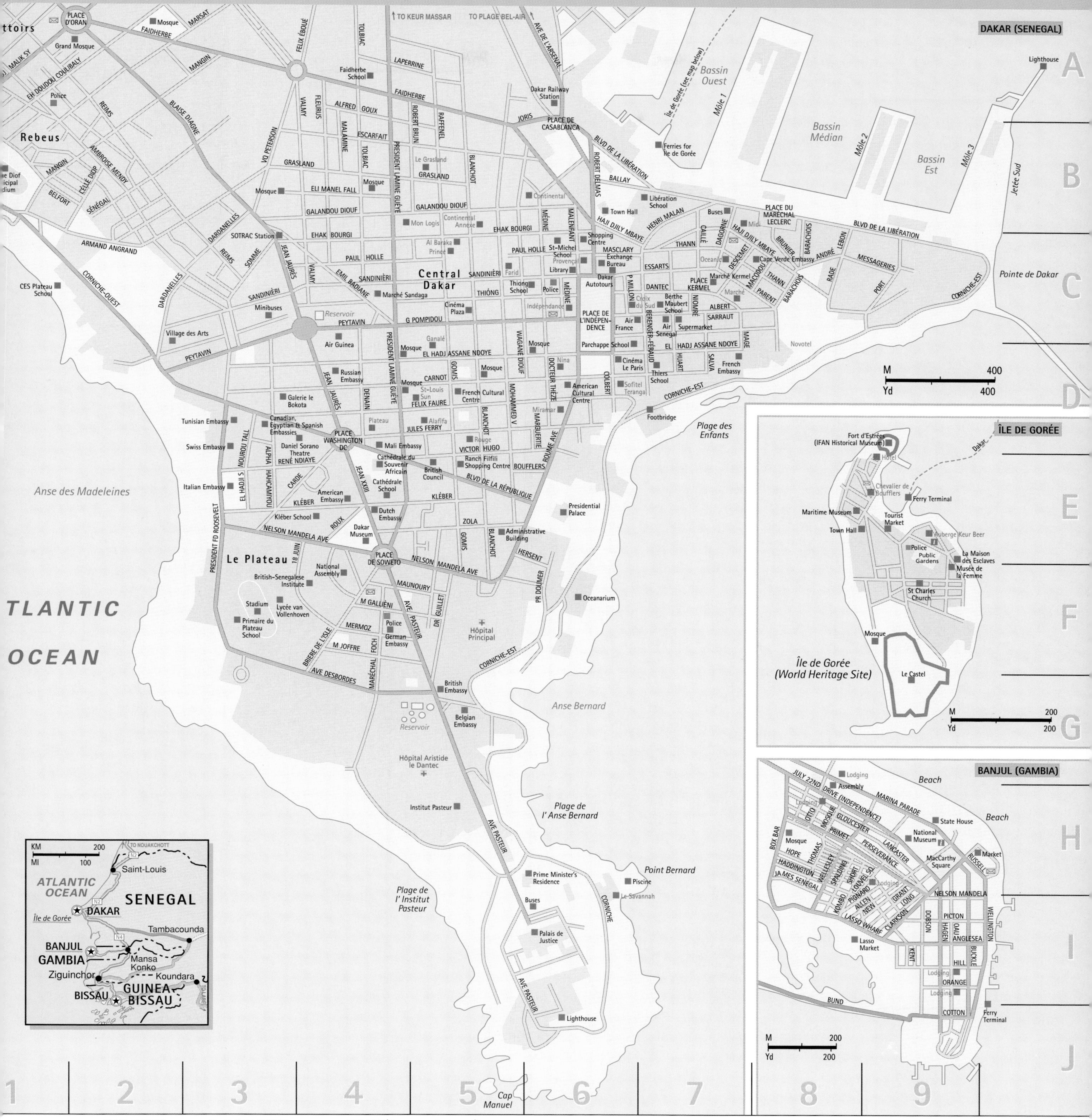
DAKAR (SENEGAL)
ÎLE DE GORÉE
BANJUL (GAMBIA)
Central Dakar
Le Plateau
Rebeus
ATLANTIC OCEAN
Anse des Madeleines
Anse Bernard
Bassin Ouest
Bassin Médian
Bassin Est
Môle 1
Môle 2
Môle 3
Jetée Sud
Lighthouse
Pointe de Dakar
Plage des Enfants
Plage de l' Anse Bernard
Plage de l' Institut Pasteur
Point Bernard
Cap Manuel
TO KEUR MASSAR
TO PLAGE BEL-AIR
Île de Gorée (see map below)
Ferries for Île de Gorée
Dakar Railway Station
PLACE DE CASABLANCA
PLACE D'ORAN
PLACE DE L'INDÉPENDENCE
PLACE WASHINGTON DC
PLACE DE SOWETO
PLACE DU MARÉCHAL LECLERC
PLACE KERMEL
Grand Mosque
Faidherbe School
Town Hall
Libération School
Shopping Centre
Marché Sandaga
Marché Kermel
Cathédrale du Souvenir Africain
Presidential Palace
Oceanarium
Hôpital Principal
Hôpital Aristide le Dantec
Institut Pasteur
Prime Minister's Residence
Palais de Justice
Stadium
Dakar Museum
National Assembly
Mosque
Fort d'Estrées (IFAN Historical Museum)
Chevalier de Boufflers
Ferry Terminal
Maritime Museum
Tourist Market
Town Hall
Auberge Keur Beer
Police
Public Gardens
La Maison des Esclaves
Musée de la Femme
St Charles Church
Le Castel
Île de Gorée (World Heritage Site)
Beach
State House
National Museum
MacCarthy Square
Market
Lasso Market
Ferry Terminal
ATLANTIC OCEAN
SENEGAL
Saint-Louis
DAKAR
Île de Gorée
Tambacounda
BANJUL
GAMBIA
Mansa Konko
Ziguinchor
Koundara
GUINEA-BISSAU
BISSAU
TO NOUAKCHOTT
KM 200
MI 100

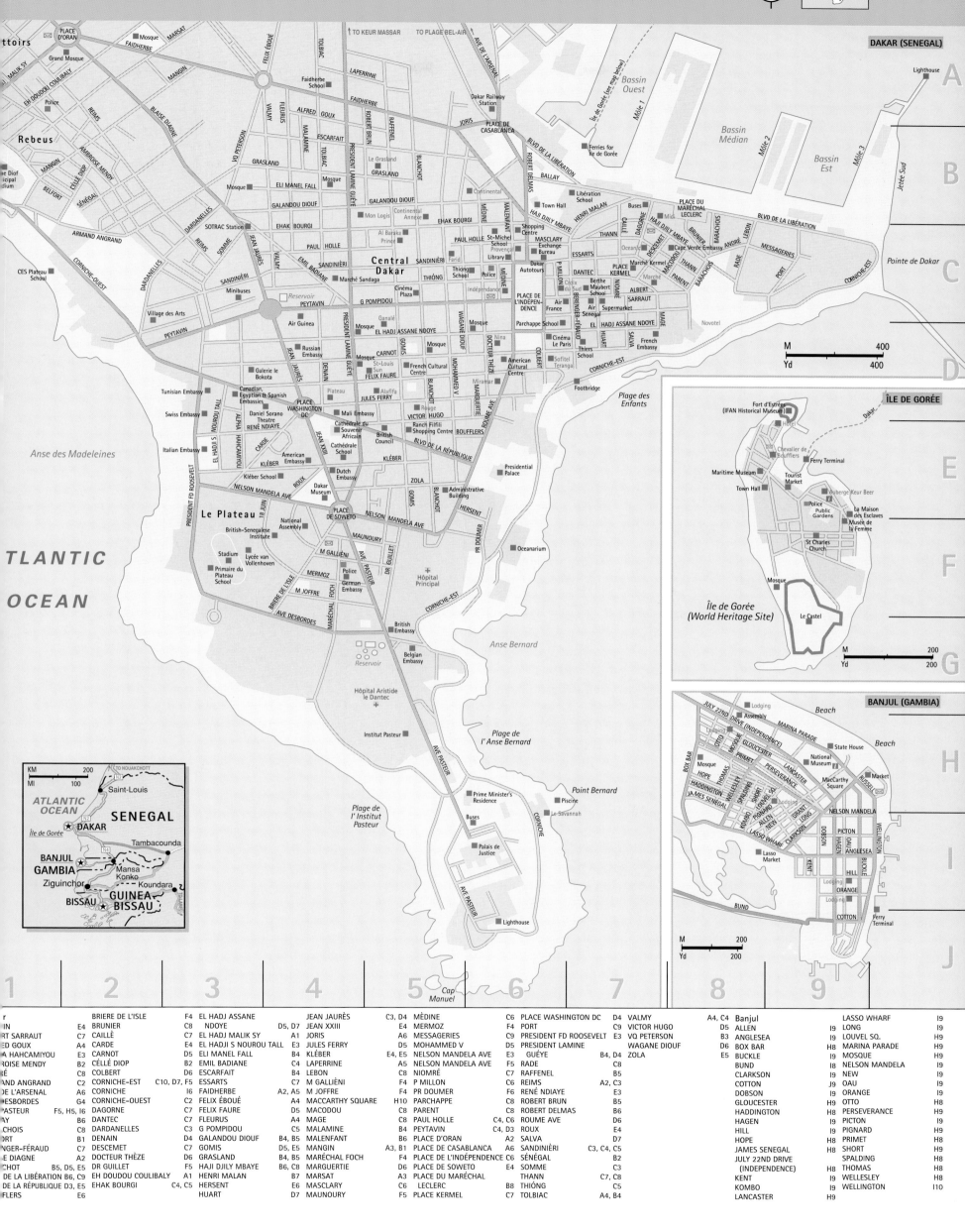

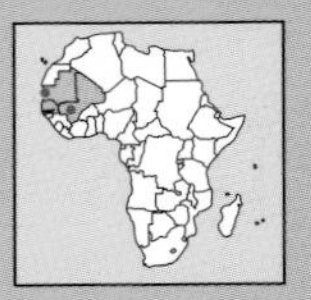

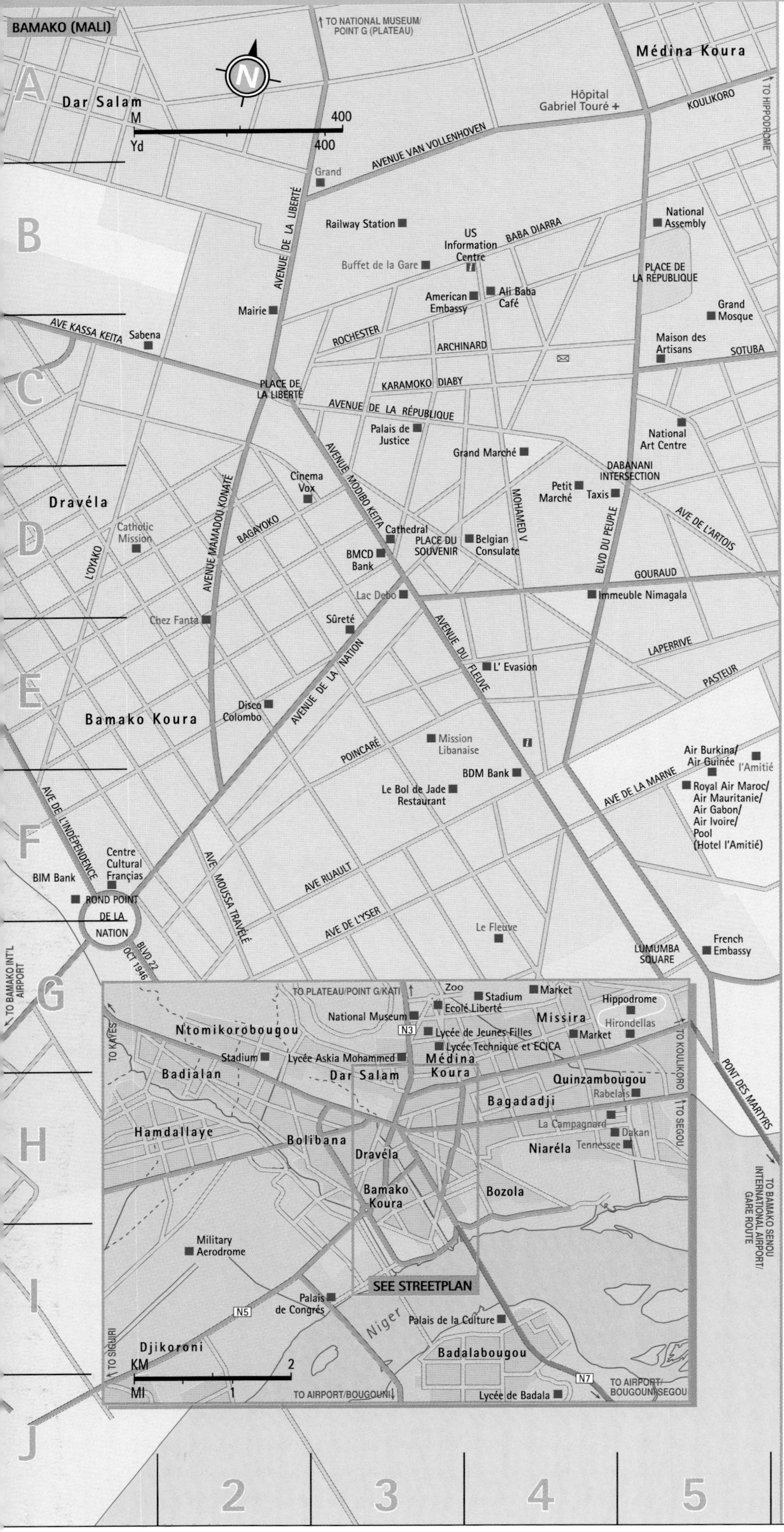

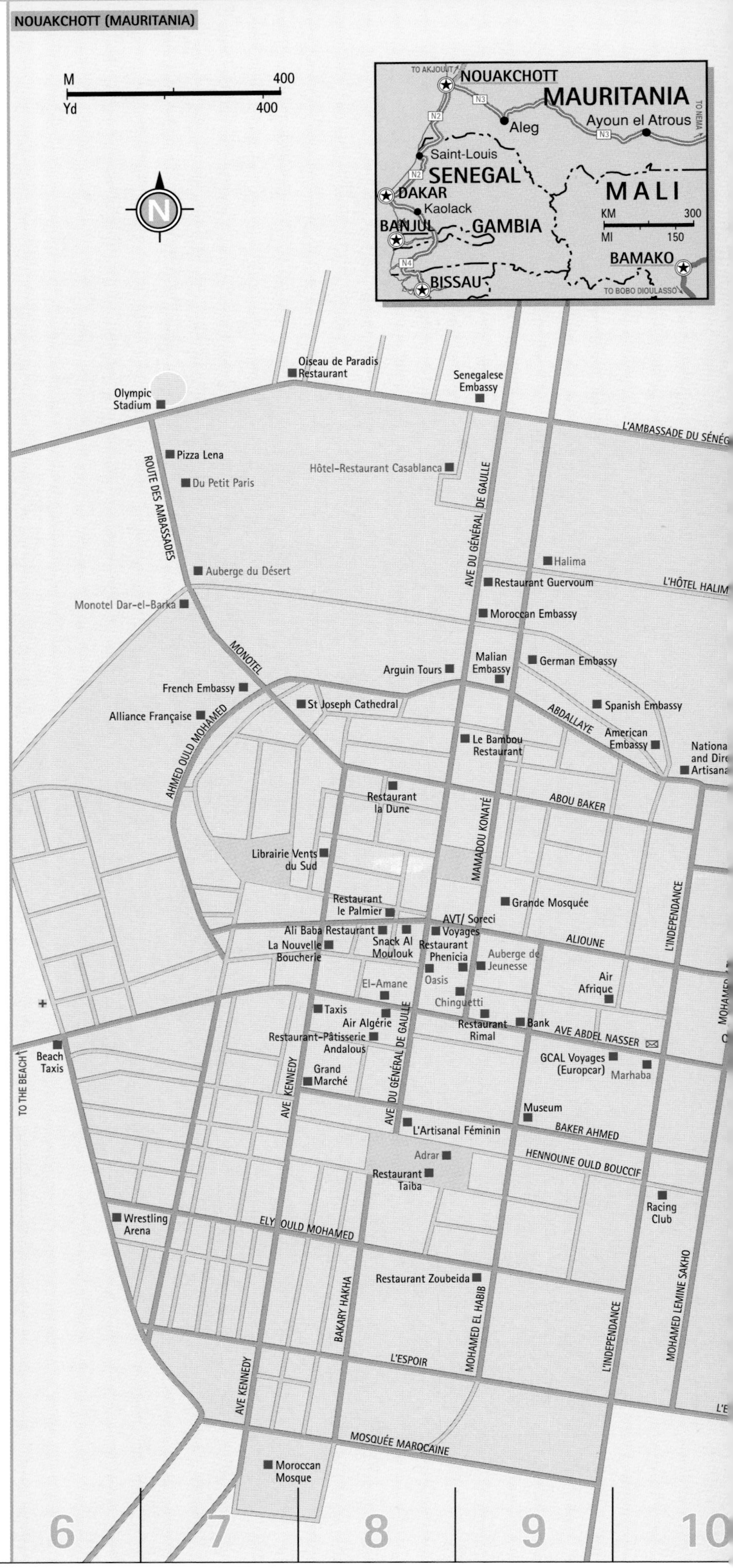

Bamako

ARCHINARD C3
AVE DE L'ARTOIS D5
AVE DE L'INDÉPENDENCE F1
AVE DE L'YSER G3
AVE DE LA LIBERTÉ B2
AVE DE LA MARNE F5
AVE DE LA RÉPUBLIQUE C3
AVE KASSA KEITA C1
AVE MOUSSA TRAVÉLÉ F2
AVE RUAULT F3
AVE VAN VOLLENHOVEN A3
AVENUE DE LA NATION E2
AVENUE DU FLEUVE E4
AVENUE MAMADOU KONATÉ D2
AVENUE MODIBO KEITA C3
BABA DIARRA B4
BAGAYOKO D2
BLVD 22 OCTOBRE 1946 G1
BLVD DU PEUPLE D4
DABANANI INTERSECTION D5
GOURAUD D5
KARAMOKO DIABY C3
KOULIKORO A5
L'OYAKO D1
LAPERRIVE E5
LUMUMBA SQUARE G5
MOHAMED V D4
PASTEUR E5
PLACE DE LA LIBERTÉ C2
PLACE DE LA RÉPUBLIQUE B5
PLACE DU SOUVENIR D3
POINCARÉ E3
PONT DES MARTYRS H5
ROCHESTER C3
ROND POINT DE LA NATION F1
SOTUBA C5

Nouakchott

ABDALLAYE E9
ABOU BAKER F9
AHMED OULD MOHAMED F7
ALIOUNE G9
AVE ABDEL NASSER H9
AVE DU GÉNÉRAL DE GAULLE D9, H8
AVE KENNEDY H7, J7
BAKARY HAKHA I8
BAKER AHMED H9
ELY OULD MOHAMED I7
HENNOUNE OULD BOUCCIF H9
L'AMBASSADE DU SÉNÉGAL D10
L'ESPOIR J8, J10
L'HÔTEL HALIMA E10
L'INDEPENDANCE G10, J9
MAMADOU KONATÉ F9
MOHAMED EL HABIB I9
MOHAMED LEMINE SAKHO G
MONOTEL
MOSQUÉE MAROCAI
ROUTE DES AMBASSA

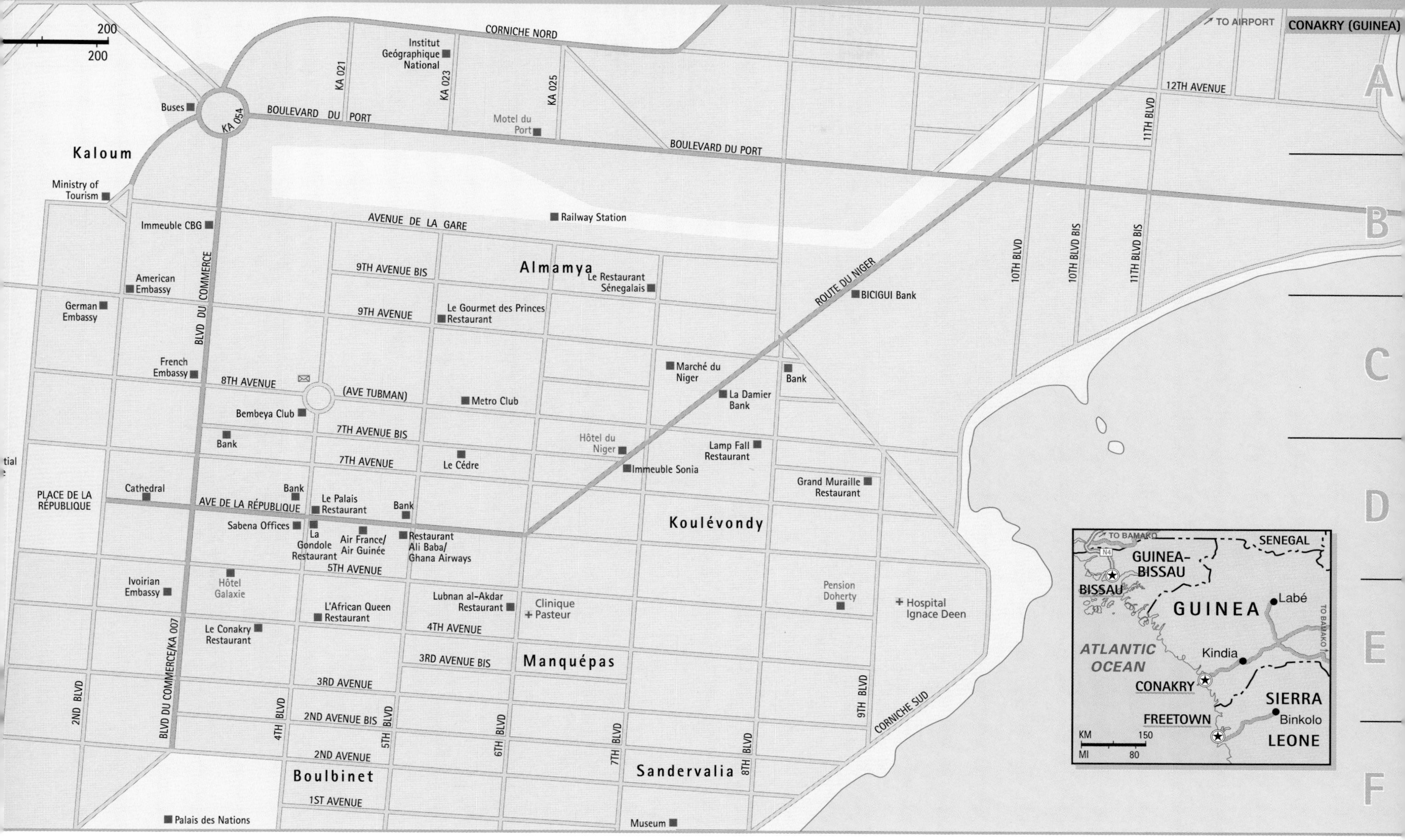

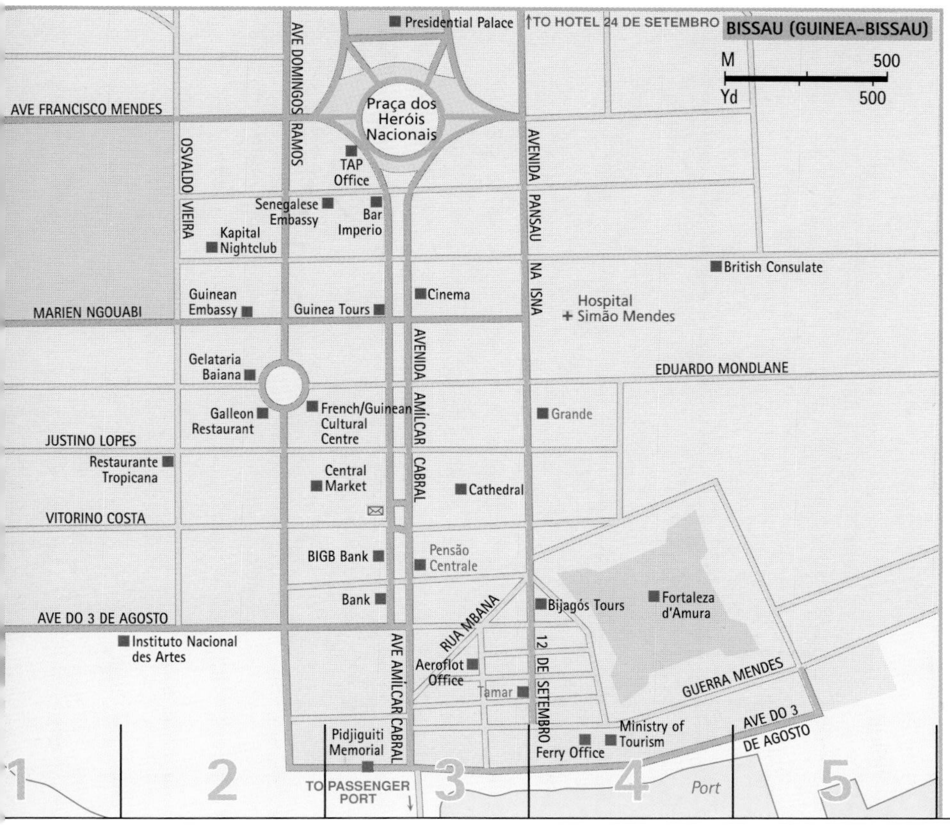

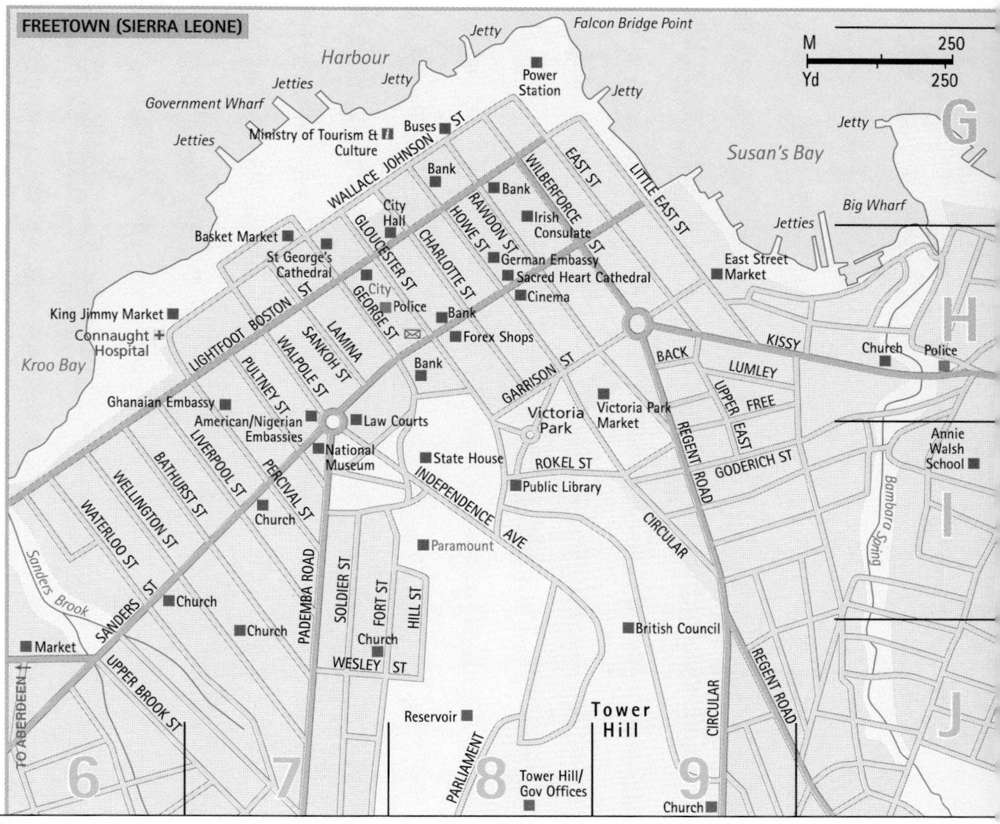

ry
ENUE F3
/D E1
VENUE F3
VENUE BIS F3
VD E1
ENUE E3
ENUE BIS E5
ENUE E4
VD E3
ENUE D3
VD E4
VD F4

7TH AVENUE D3
7TH AVENUE BIS C3
7TH BLVD F5
8TH AVE (AVE TUBMAN) C1
8TH BLVD E6
9TH AVENUE C3
9TH AVENUE BIS B3
9TH BLVD E7
10TH BLVD B8
10TH BLVD BIS B8
11TH BLVD A9
11TH BLVD BIS B9
12TH AVENUE A9

AVE DE LA GARE B3
AVE DE LA RÉPUBLIQUE D2
BLVD DE COMMERCE/ KA007 F2
BLVD DU COMMERCE E6
BOULEVARD DU PORT A3, A5
CORNICHE NORD A4
CORNICHE SUD F6
KA 021 A3
KA 023 A4
KA 025 A5
KA 054 A2

PLACE DE LA RÉPUBLIQUE D1
ROUTE DU NIGER B7

Freetown
BACK H9
BATHURST ST I6
CHARLOTTE ST G8
CIRCULAR I9, J9
EAST ST H9
FORT ST I7
FREE H9
GARRISON ST H8
GEORGE ST H7
GLOUCESTER ST H7
GODERICH ST I9
HILL ST J8
HOWE ST G8
INDEPENDENCE AVE I8
KISSY H9
LAMINA SANKOH ST H7
LIGHTFOOT BOSTON ST H7
LITTLE EAST ST G9
LIVERPOOL ST I7
LUMLEY H9
PADEMBA I7
PARLIAMENT J8
PERCIVAL ST I7
PULTNEY ST H7
RAWDON ST G8
REGENT I9, J9
ROKEL ST I8
SANDERS ST J6
SOLDIER ST I7
UPPER BROOK ST J6
UPPER EAST H9
WALLACE JOHNSON ST H7
WALPOLE ST H7
WATERLOO ST I6
WELLINGTON ST I6
WESLEY ST J7
WILBERFORCE ST H9

Bissau
12 DE SETEMBRO J4
AVE DO 3 DE AGOSTO I1, J4
AVE DOMINGOS RAMOS G2
AVE FRANCISCO MENDES G1
AVENIDA AMÍLCAR CABRAL I3, J3
AVENIDA PANSAU NA ISNA G4
EDUARDO MONDLANE H4
GUERRA MENDES J4
JUSTINO LOPES I1
MARIEN NGOUABI H3
OSVALDO VEIRA G2
RUA MBANA J3
VITORINO COSTA I1

ALLEE DES ANC COMBS C8
AUTOROUTE DE L'AEROPORT I9
AVE 4 G9
AVE 5 G9
AVE 6 G9
AVE 7 G9
AVE 9 G9
AVE 10 G9
AVE 12 H9
AVE 13 H9
AVE 15 H9
AVE 17 H9
AVE 19 H9
AVE CHARDY C8
AVE ANOMA D8
AVE CHRISTIANI / AVE 1 F8
AVE DE LA REINE POKOU H10
AVE DE MARCHORY H10
AVE DELAFOSSE D8
AVE DU DOCTEUR CROZET B8
AVE DU DOCTEUR JAMOT B8
AVE FRANCHET D'ESPEREY C8
AVE GÉNERAL DE GAULLE E8
AVE JEAN PAUL II A8
AVE LAMBLIN D8
AVE LAURENT CLOUZET/ AVE 27 I9
AVE MARCHAND C8
AVE OUEZZIN COULIBALY / AVE 21 H9
AVE TERASSON DE FOUGERES C8
AVE TREICH LA PLENE E8
AVE VICTOR BIAKA/ AVE 2 G8
BLVD ANGOULVANT D7
BLVD BOTREAU ROUSSEL D9
BLVD CARDE B7
BLVD DE LA PAIX – AUTOROUTE DE L'OUEST C6
BLVD DE LA RÉPUBLIQUE B8, D8
BLVD DE MARSEILLE H7
BLVD GBON COULIBALY H9
BLVD GÉNÉRAL DE GAULLE B9, E8
BLVD JEAN DELAFOSSE G8
BLVD LAGUNAIRE A9
BLVD ROUME B8
BLVD VALÉRY GISCARD D'ESTAING G7
JESSE OWENS C8
PLACE DE LA RÉPUBLIQUE E7
PONT GENERAL DE GAULLE E9
PONT HOUPHOÉT-BOIGNY F7
RUE 7 G8
RUE 9
RUE 12
RUE 13
RUE 15
RUE 21
RUE 23
RUE 25
RUE 44

SEE STREETPLAN
Tampoui
Tanghen
Somgandé
Wayalghen
Bois de Boulogne
Dassasgo
Kolgo Naba
Zogona
Oumtenga
Gounghen
Samanden
Pissi
Sissen
Patte d'Oie
BOULEVARD CIRCULAIRE
AVE YATENGA
AVE DE LA LIBERTÉ
AVE DU GÉN. DE GAULLE
AVE KADIOGO
University
Grand Marché
Presidential Palace
St Camille
Palais du Moro Naba
Mosque
International Airport
N3
N4
N5
N6
TO QUAHIGOUYA/KAYA
Barrage 3
Gardens
Canal
Yalgado Hospital
TO FADA N'GOURMA/NIAMEY
Cathédrale de Dapoya
AVE DE LA LIBERTÉ
AVE DIMDOLOBSAM
Paspanga
MON GREMASSOM
ÉCOLES
AVE D'OUBRITENGA
Nigerian Embassy
Ghanaian Embassy
AVENUE HO CHI MINH
BLVD DU FASO
BLVD CHARLES DE GAULLE
STMB Buses
COMMERCE
Moemmin
AVE NIANDÉ OUÉDRAOGO
AVENUE KOUANDA
Railway Station
Bank
Centre Artisanal
Institut Géographique
Presidential Palace
French Embassy
DIONGOLO TRAORÉ
Maison du Peuple
ONATEL
AVE DE L'INDÉPENDENCE
Hôtel de l'Indépendence
Air France
Ran
AVE NELSON MANDELA
PLACE DES NATIONS UNIES
Relax
French Cultural Centre
Camp Militaire
AVENUE YATENGA
AGOSTINO NETO
Supermarket
DU TRAVAIL
BISHOP
AVE RAOUL FOLLEREAU
American Embassy
PLACE DU 2 OCTOBRE
PLACE DU CINÉASTE AFRICAIN
Bank
Air Afrique
Grand Marché
Restaurant La Gourmandise
Restaurant Le Vert Galant
Billiard Club
Restaurant Ciné Burkina
Continental
BICIAB
Sabena
Zangouetin
Delwendé
Grand Mosque
Café de la Paix
Belle Vue
AVE HOUARI BOUMEDIENNE
AVENUE KADIOGO
Air Burkina
AVENUE THÉVENOUD
DE LA CHANCE
AVE HOUARI BOUMEDIENNE
AVE LÉO FROBENIUS
AVE KWAME NKRUMAH
AVE DE LA RÉSISTANCE DU 17 MAI
Kouloubа
JOSEPH BADOUA
Cemetery
Idéal
Café Chez Salif
Fondation Charles Dufour
DE LA MOSQUÉE
AVE YENNENGA
Pension Guigsème
AVE LOUDUN
DU DR GOURMISSON
AVENUE MORO-NABA
AVENUE BASSAWARGA
Cathedral
Municipal Stadium
DU DR GOURMISSON
Hôtel de la Paix
Mosque
Sahel's
Peuloghin
Palais du Moro Naba
St Léon
AVENUE COULIBALY
AVENUE COULIBALY
Buses
AVE DE L'AÉROPORT
M 500
Yd 500
Aeroport International de' Ouagadougou
TO GARE ROUTIÈRE
TO CFA BAR
A B C D E F G H I J
1 2 3 4 5 6 7 8 9

Kokomlemle
Asylum Down
North Ridge
Ringway Estate
Cantonments
West Ridge
East Ridge
Christiansborg
Ussher Town
James Town
Gulf of Guinea
Accra Beach
Korle Lagoon
Klotey Lagoon
TO KUMASI
TO ABURI
TO KOTOKA INTERNATIONAL AIRPORT
KWAME NKRUMAH CIRCLE
SANKARA CIRCLE
DANQUAH CIRCLE
AFRICAN LIBERATION SQUARE
MUSEUM CIRCLE
MAKOLA CIRCLE
LUTTERODT CIRCLE
INDEPENDENCE SQUARE
Independence Arch
Accra Sports Stadium
Osu Cemetery
State House
Kwame Nkrumah Conference Centre
Accra International Conference Centre
Ministry of Interior
National Theatre
Novotel
Accra Polytechnic
Museum of Science
National Museum
National Archives
Cathedral
Ridge Hospital
Swiss Embassy
UK High Commission
German Embassy
Canadian High Commission
Dutch Embassy
French Embassy
American Embassy
Goethe Institute
Police Hospital
Cantonments Hospital
Christiansborg Castle (Osu Castle)
Department of Wildlife
Riviera Beach
Akuma Village
Art Centre (Centre for National Culture)
Kwame Nkrumah Mausoleum
Kwame Nkrumah Memorial Park
Former Parliament House
Makola Market
Tudu Station
Tema Station
Accra Railway Station
Princess Marie-Louise Children's Hospital
Ussher Fort
James Fort
Lighthouse
GNTC Shopping Centre
Kwame Nkrumah Memorial
Mental Hospital
Accra Technical Training Centre
Aquinas Secondary School
Kumordzie Hospital
M
Yd
600

PORTO-NOVO (BENIN)
800
800
Houinmè
Hounsouko
Catholic Mission
Tokpota
Catholic Mission
FounFoun
Kandévié
Djègan-Daho
Hôtel Dona
Château d'Eau
CATCHI
Bank
BOULEVARD EXTÉRIEUR
École Normale Supérieure
D'OUANDO
Protestant College
Dèguè-Gare
ADJARA-DOCADJI
Lycée Toffa1
Lycée Behanzin
Disused Railway Station
Comme Chez Soi
OBALÉDÉ
Stadium
PLACE KOKOYÉ
ROND-POINT ATAKÉ
Police
Ethnographic Museum
Bank
Ouinlinda
Catholic Mission
National Assembly
PLACE JEAN BAYAL
Zèbou
Mosque
Ataké
Casa Danza
AVE VICTOR BALLOT
Grand Market
BOULEVARD LAGUNAIRE
Cathedral
DU PONT
Ilèfié
École Coranique
TOFFA
Hôtel La Détente
Bank
Buvette la Royauté/ Escale du Musée
Gare Routière
Palais Royal du Roi Toffa
Gare Routière
Buvette Escale du Pont
Agbokou
Akron
Lagoon
TO RAMCO SUPERMARKET/ TOKOIN/UNIVERSITY DU BENIN
LOMÉ (TOGO)
TO AIRPORT/ GARE DE KARA/ATAKPAMÉ
Tokoin
Lagoon
Amoutivé
Military Camp
BOULEVARD DU 13 JANVIER
D'ATAKPAMÉ
Restaurant de la Paix
Hôtel du Boulevard
Restaurant Sénégalais
Bank
DE LA MARNE
Le Phoenicien
Nyekonakopé
AVE NICOLAS GRUNITSKY
ROUTE DE KPALIMÉ
Railway Station
AVE DU NOUVEAU MARCHÉ
AVE DE LA LIBÉRATION
Relais de la Poste
Fouta Djalon
Place de l'Indépendence
National Museum/ Palais du Congrès
La Bodega
Bank
Hôtel du 2 Février Sofitel
Place des Martyrs
AVE DU 24 JANVIER
French Cultural Centre
DE BÉ
D'ANÉHO
Bar 50/50
SGGG Supermarket
DU CHEMIN DE FER
AVE MAMAN N'DANIDA
Stadium
Sûreté (Immigration)
ONTAGNE
BOULEVARD DU 13 JANVIER
ALSACE LORRAINE
Lebanese Restaurant
Le Byblos
Bar Panini
BOULEVARD NÔTRE DAME
Quartier Administratif
AVE SARAKAWA
Goethe Institute
AVENUE DUISBERG
AVENUE DE GAULLE
French Consulate
DU GOLFE
AVENUE GEORGES POMPIDOU
DE KOUROMÉ
DE LA GARE
VAUBAN
DE LA PAIX
Le Galion
American Cultural Centre
DE L'OCAM
joviakope
DU GRAND MARCHÉ
Bank
Air Afrique
Grand Market
DU MARÉCHAL FOCH
Nigerian Airways
American Embassy
Dutch Embassy
BOULEVARD CIRCULAIRE
DU LAC TOGO
AVENUE SARRAUT
Goyi Score Supermarket
Du Golfe
Bank
Bank
Librairie Bon Pasteur
Cathedral
Marox Restaurant
Securina
Presidential Palace
Gare de Contonou
DU COMMERCE
LASSEY
Palm Beach
Le Boké Restaurant
BOULEVARD DE LA MARINA
Beach
Hôtel le Bénin
Auberge le Galion
BOULEVARD DE LA MARINA
ROUTE D'AFLOA
Beach
Gulf of Guinea
M 250
Yd 250
A
B
C
D
E
F
G
H
I
J
1 2 3 4 5 6 7 8 9

TO SHAGAMU
Lagos Lagoon
Lagos Island
Ikoyi Island
Victoria Island
Lagos Harbour
Five Cowrie Creek
Kuramo Waters
Iddo Market
Oba's Palace
Central Mosque
St John's Church
Jankara Market
Cemetery
State House
Golf Course
Lagos Polo Club
National Library
City Hall
Supreme Court
Ministry of External Affairs
Ferry Station
Lagos Lawn & Tennis Club
Onikan National Museum
Lagos Yacht Club
Lagos Motor Boat Club
American Embassy
German Embassy
Australian High Commission
Cameroonian Embassy
Beninese & Ivoirian Embassies
Chadian Embassy
Embassy of Niger
Federal Palace
Goethe Institute
1004 Apartments Housing Complex
French Embassy
UK High Commission
Boats for Tarwa Bay & Lighthouse Beach
Murtala Mohammed Int'l Airport
Oshodi
Mende
Mushin
Somolu
Surulere
Yaba
Iganmu
Badia
Apapa
Tin Can Island
University of Lagos
Lagos University Teaching Hospital
National Stadium
National Theatre
SEE STREETPLAN
KM 2
MI 1
M 600
Yd 600

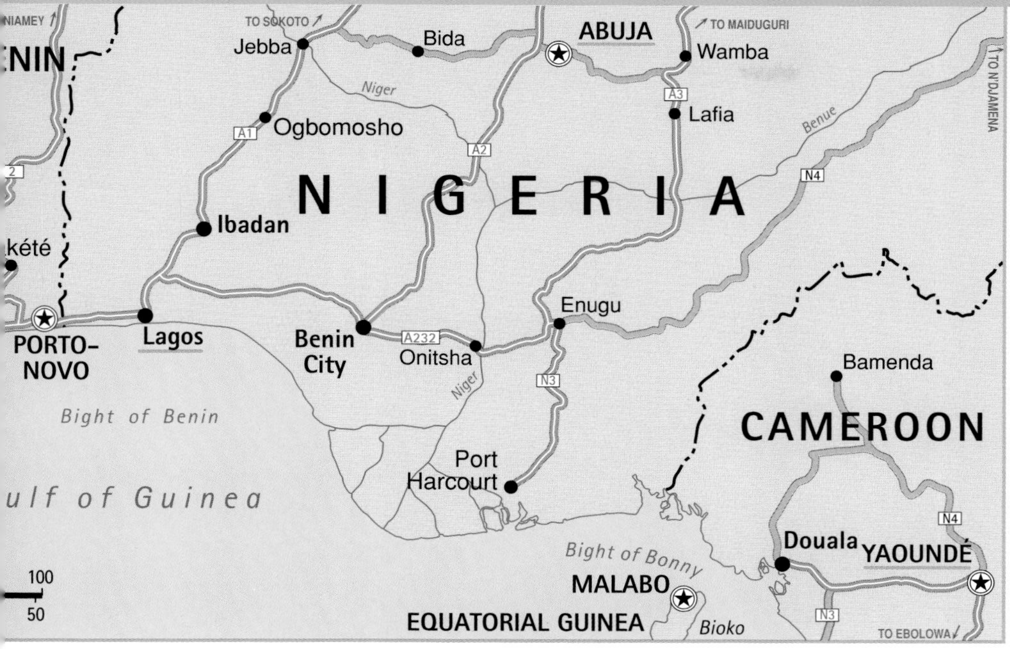

NIGERIA
CAMEROON
ABUJA
Jebba
Bida
Wamba
Lafia
Ogbomosho
Ibadan
Lagos
PORTO-NOVO
Benin City
Onitsha
Enugu
Port Harcourt
Bamenda
Douala
YAOUNDÉ
MALABO
EQUATORIAL GUINEA
Bioko
Bight of Benin
Gulf of Guinea
Bight of Bonny
Niger
Benue
TO SOKOTO
TO MAIDUGURI
TO N'DJAMENA
TO EBOLOWA

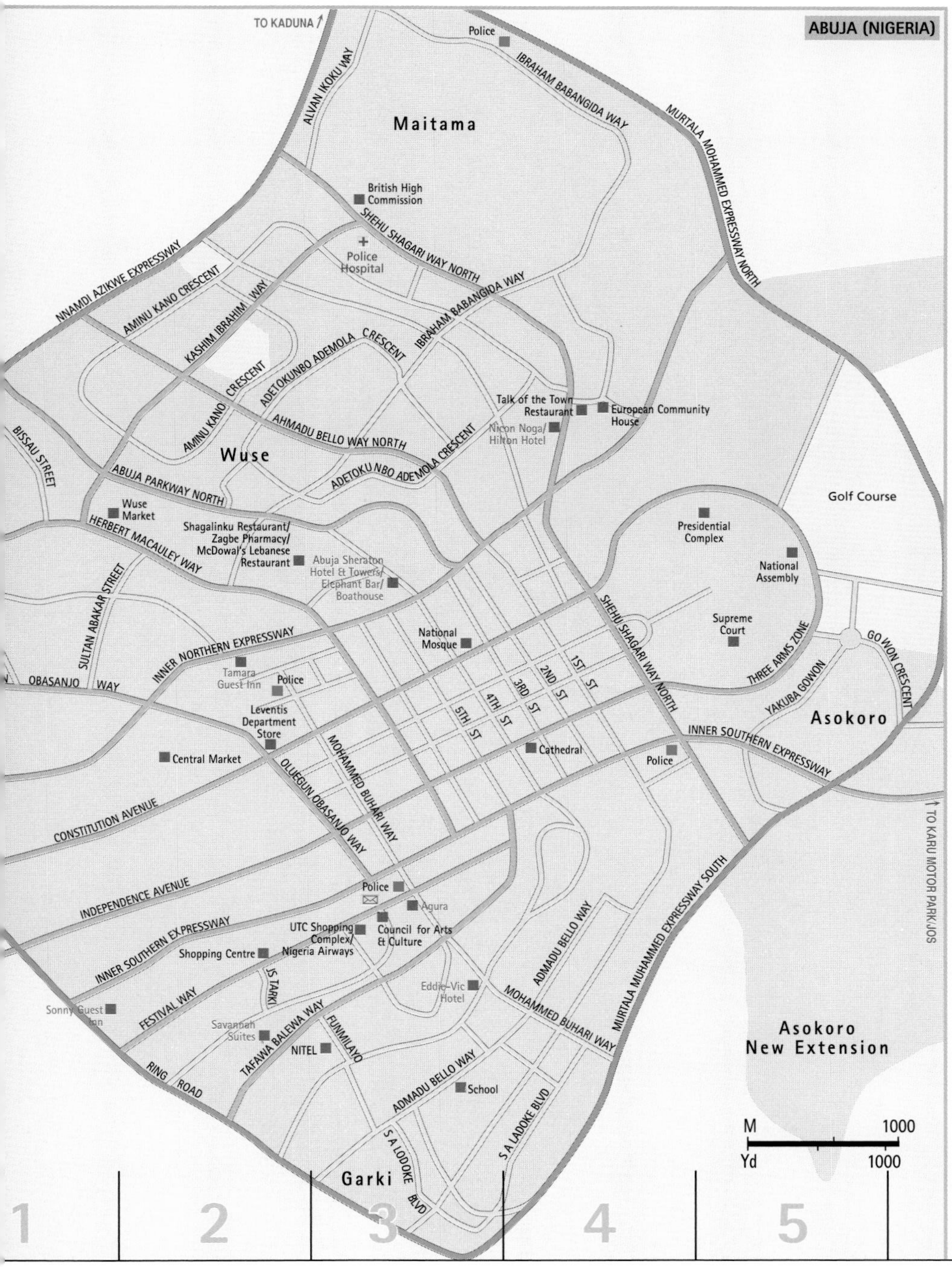

ABUJA (NIGERIA)
TO KADUNA
Maitama
Wuse
Asokoro
Asokoro New Extension
Garki
Golf Course
Presidential Complex
National Assembly
Supreme Court
British High Commission
Police Hospital
Talk of the Town Restaurant
European Community House
Nicon Noga/Hilton Hotel
Wuse Market
Shagalinku Restaurant/Zagbe Pharmacy/McDowal's Lebanese Restaurant
Abuja Sheraton Hotel & Towers/Elephant Bar/Boathouse
National Mosque
Tamara Guest Inn
Police
Leventis Department Store
Central Market
Cathedral
UTC Shopping Complex/Nigeria Airways
Council for Arts & Culture
Shopping Centre
Eddie-Vic Hotel
Savannah Suites
NITEL
School
IBRAHAM BABANGIDA WAY
MURTALA MOHAMMED EXPRESSWAY NORTH
MURTALA MUHAMMED EXPRESSWAY SOUTH
SHEHU SHAGARI WAY NORTH
NNAMDI AZIKWE EXPRESSWAY
INNER NORTHERN EXPRESSWAY
INNER SOUTHERN EXPRESSWAY
CONSTITUTION AVENUE
INDEPENDENCE AVENUE
HERBERT MACAULEY WAY
ABUJA PARKWAY NORTH
AHMADU BELLO WAY NORTH
MOHAMMED BUHARI WAY
OLUEGUN OBASANJO WAY
TO KARU MOTOR PARK/JOS
M 1000
Yd 1000

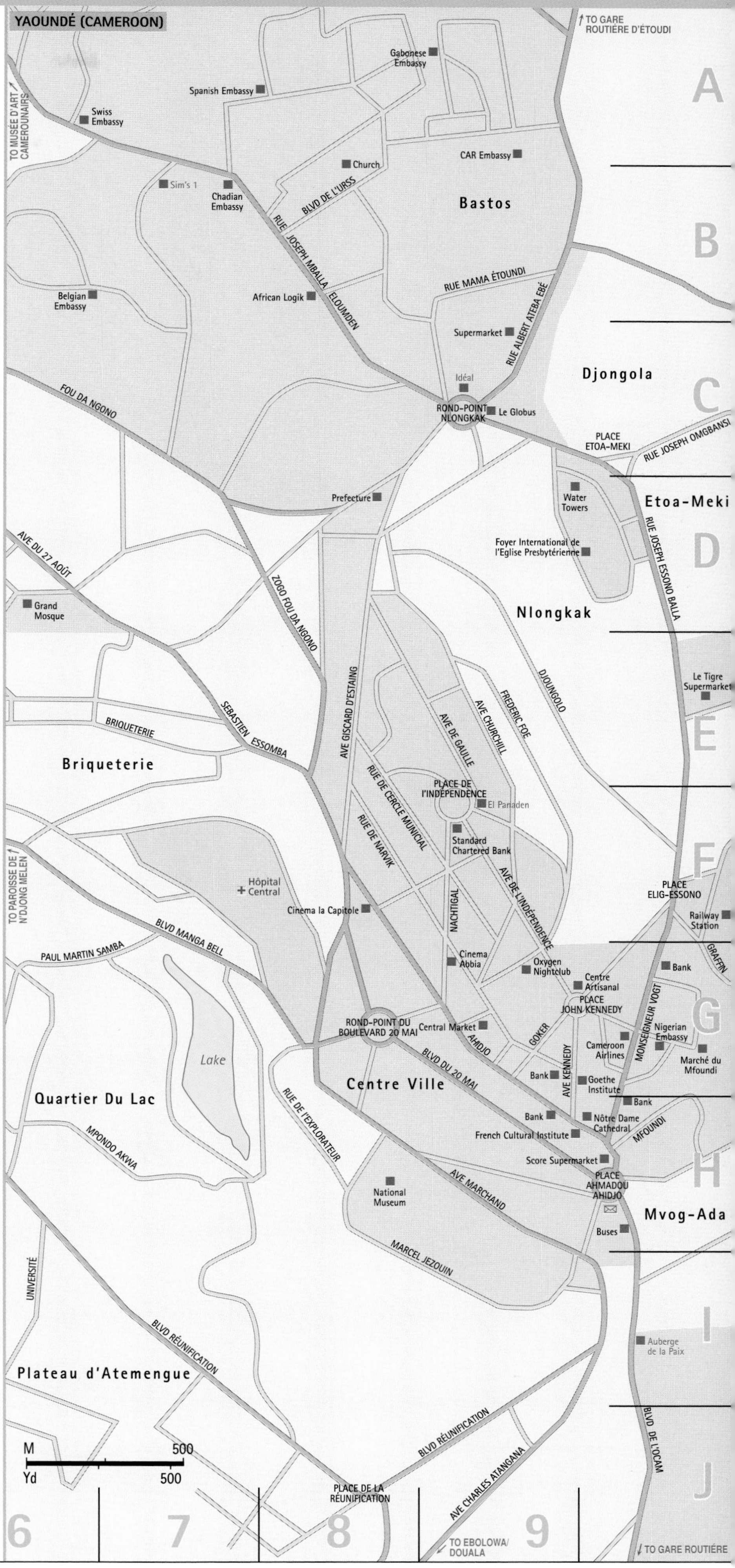

YAOUNDÉ (CAMEROON)
TO GARE ROUTIÈRE D'ETOUDI
Bastos
Djongola
Etoa-Meki
Nlongkak
Briqueterie
Centre Ville
Quartier Du Lac
Plateau d'Atemengue
Mvog-Ada
Gabonese Embassy
Spanish Embassy
Swiss Embassy
Church
CAR Embassy
Chadian Embassy
Sim's 1
Belgian Embassy
African Logik
Supermarket
Idéal
ROND-POINT NLONGKAK
Le Globus
PLACE ETOA-MEKI
Water Towers
Prefecture
Foyer International de l'Eglise Presbytérienne
Grand Mosque
Le Tigre Supermarket
PLACE DE L'INDÉPENDENCE
El Panaden
Standard Chartered Bank
Hôpital Central
Cinema la Capitole
PLACE ELIG-ESSONO
Railway Station
Cinema Abbia
Oxygen Nightclub
Centre Artisanal
PLACE JOHN KENNEDY
Bank
ROND-POINT DU BOULEVARD 20 MAI
Central Market
Cameroon Airlines
Nigerian Embassy
Marché du Mfoundi
Goethe Institute
Notre Dame Cathedral
French Cultural Institute
Score Supermarket
PLACE AHMADOU AHIDJO
Buses
National Museum
Lake
Auberge de la Paix
PLACE DE LA RÉUNIFICATION
TO EBOLOWA/DOUALA
TO GARE ROUTIÉRE
M 500
Yd 500

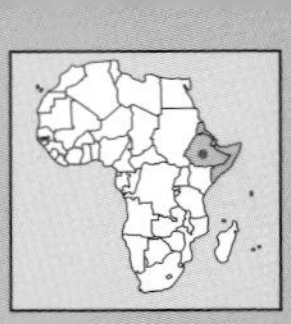

A
B
C
D
E
F
G
H
I
J
2
3
4
5
6
7
8
9
10
ARBEYNOCH
Ras Desta Hospital
DEJAZMACH BELAY ZELEKA
DEJAZMACH HAILE SELASSIE
Kostre
Italian School
Arose
Afincho Ber Bridge
Addis Ababa University
Ethnological Museum
Museum
John F Kennedy Library
St Marks Church
Karl Marx Park
Egyptian Embassy
OMEDLA
GENERAL MULUGETA BULI
TENAGNEWORK
WEATHERAL
Tourist
Yekatit 12 Hospital
YEKATIT 12 SQUARE
Lion House
Yared Music School
Ministry of Finance
RUSSIA
Armenian Church
TEWODROS
St John Church
DEJAZMACH NESIBU
Aba Koran
Ras Mekonen Bridge
Faculty of Technology
Makane Iyesus Church
School of Post Graduate Studies
Fasika
WELETE YOHANIS
National Museum
HAILE MARYAM MAMO
SYLVIA PANKHURST
GAL HAILU KEBEDE
ADWA SQUARE
Cinema
Theatre
American Church
Greek Church
Bakata
Clinic
JOHN MELLY
St George Church
MENELIK II SQUARE
SAHLE SILASIE
St Mary Church
Art School
GEZACHEN HAILE
Idget Mall
KING GEORGE
Balehadin Mosque
Hashim Mosque
Bus Terminal
DEJAZMACH ZEWDU ABE KORAN
ABUNE PETROS SQUARE
Monument
City Hall
Sunshine
DEJAZMACH AFEWERK
ADWA AVENUE
Library
Menelik II Comprehensive Secondary School
QUEEN SHEWAREGED GEDLE
Habte Giyorgis Bridge
Piazza
African Terrere
EDEN
Arada
St George
English Church
FITAWRARI HABTE GIYORGIS
Police
FITAWRARI GEBEYEHU
MEGABIT 28 SQUARE
Faculty of Science
UMMER SEMETER
Adis Ketema Park
Al-Anwar Mosque
St Raguel Church
Shopping Mall & Ethiopian Airlines
CUNNINGHAM
DE GAULLE SQUARE
Ethiopian Airlines
Indian National Community School
Tourist
QUEEN ELISABETH
Adis Ketema
Nur Mosque
BERGOYANE
Yilma
Kechene
GOBENA ABA TIGU
Chelika
Yeka
Continental
Trinity Cathedral
Catholic Cathedral
WAVEL
Bank
MUNIY
Telda
Taitu
Awraris
Baro
DEJAZMACH JOTE
Market
Cinema
Theatre
Mercato
MAHATMA GANDHI
Parliament
GENERAL WINGATE
Bekentu Bridge
Cemetery
Rahma Mosque
Husein Mosque
ARBEYNOCH SQUARE
GASTON GUEZ
Curio Stalls
Congress Hall
DEJAZMACH MEKONIN
Teke Haimanot
Extreme
Indian Community School
TEWODROS SQUARE
COLSON
Gola Sefer
Church
Cemetery
Kurtume
Kere Bridge
DEVELOPMENT THROUGH COOPERATION AVE
Clinic
Awar
St Michael Church
Menelik II Mausoleum
Fitber
TESEMA ABA KEMAW
DEJAZMACH BALCHA ABA NEFSO
Tewodros Shopping Centre
Lycee Franco Ethiopian School
Municipal Technical College
St Gabriel Church
Grand Palace
Wele Mosque
Geja Sefer
DEJAZMACH WOLDE MIKAEL
Tikur Anbesa School
FITAWRARI WENDMENEH
SABA SQUARE
General Post Office
ZEWDITU
Baher Dar
Black Lion Hospital
Libyan Embassy
YARED
National Postal Museum
TAITU
Zewditu Hospital
Sheraton
Hilton International
Archaeological Museum
National Library
Harambee
YOHANIS
Filwoha
Adwa Park
MENELIK II AVENUE
ANDINET SQUARE
SUDAN
Ethiopia
Finfina
National Palace
TITO
Baro Shopping Centre
Ministry of Development
Police
Ministry of Health
Lido
National Theatre
Cinema
Ras
Gandhi Hospital
Malawian Embassy
Clinic
Lideta Mekane Iyesus
Deste
Africa
CHURCHILL AVENUE
GENERAL ABEBE DUMTEW
Red Cross Society Clinic
RAS DESTA DAMTEW
Ghion
LENIN SQUARE
Africa Hall
DEJAZMACH BEKELE WEYA
Library
Canadian Embassy
Commercial College
Wabi Shebele
Holy Saviour Church
Nile
Addis Ababa Stadium
Bantyiketu
National
RAS ABEBE AREGAY
St Stephen Church
Ethiopian Tourist Commission
JOMO KENYATTA AVENUE
Dejaz Balcha Hospital
SMUTS
Technical School
Clinic
ELENI SQUARE
RAS MEKONIN AVENUE
TIKUR ANBESA SQUARE
Yordanis
Tanzanian E
MEXICO SQUARE
Lion of Judah Statue
YILMA DEMISE
ABIOT MESKAL SQUARE
Bantyiketu Bridge
Lideta Church
Police General Headquarters
Addis Ababa Railway Station
RAS BIRU AVE
St Yossef School
Ministry of State Farms
Lideta
Exhibition Halls
Addis Ababa Museum
AFRICA AVENUE
Almaz Pension
ROOSEVELT
RAS LUISEGED
Wanza
Sudanese Embassy
Kirkos
M 500
Yd 500
Buche
St Kirkos Church
Cemetery
Guenet
Shimels Habte Comprehensive Secondary School
Liberian Embassy
TO DEBRE ZEIT
TO AIRPORT

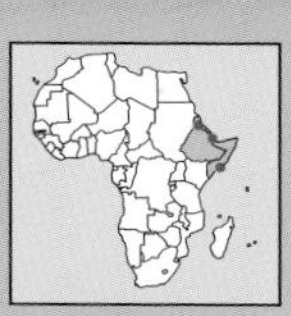

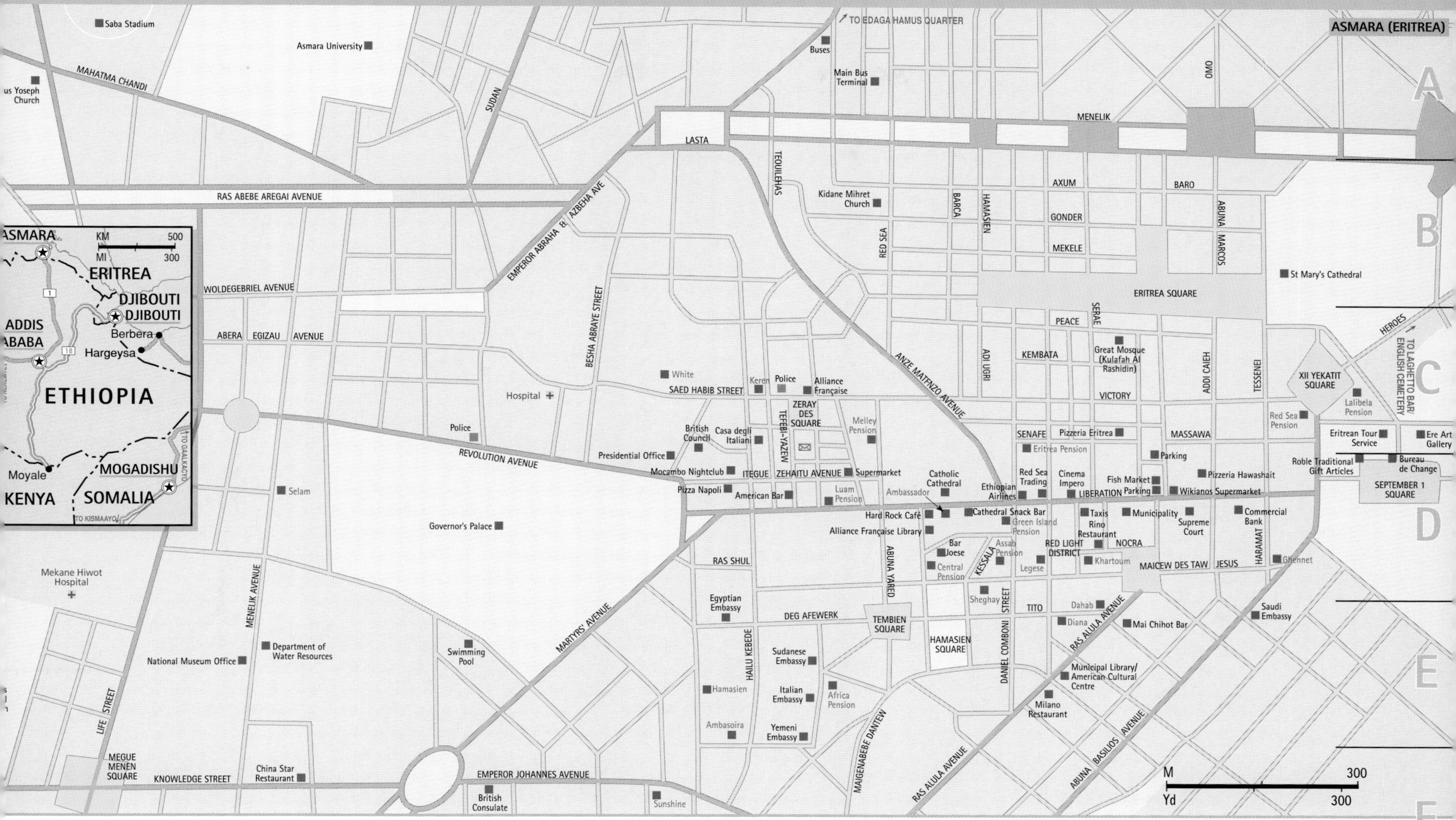

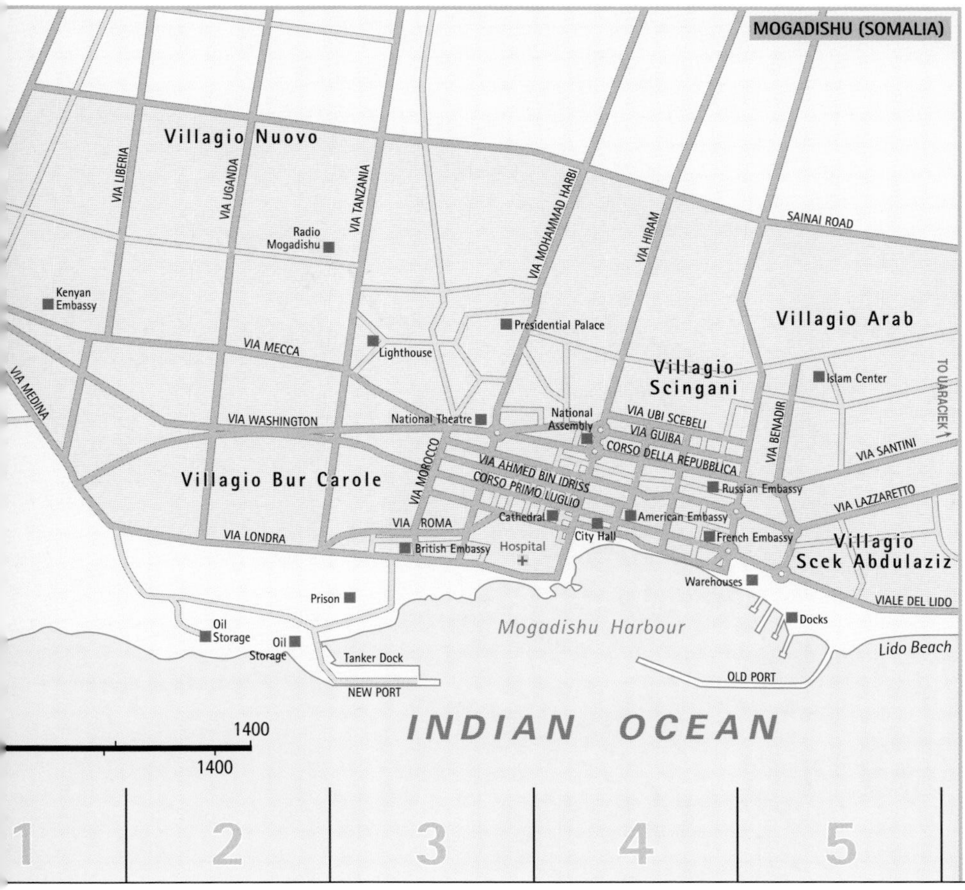

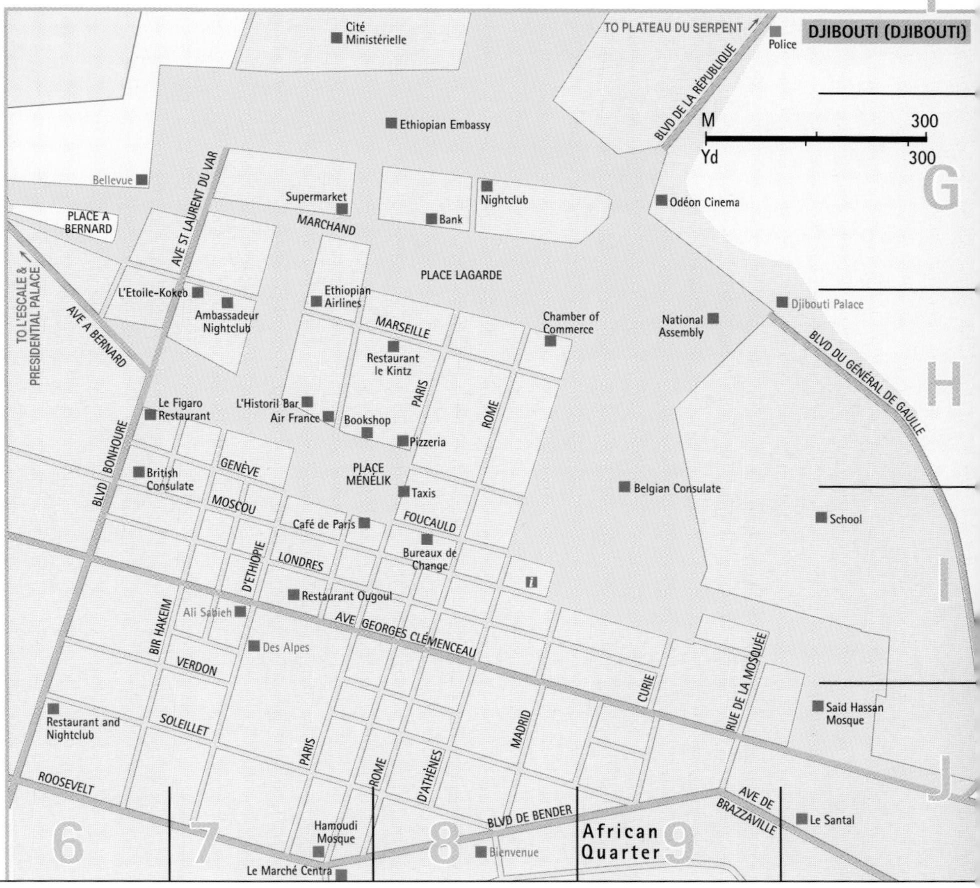

a
EGIZAU AVENUE C3
BASILIOS AVENUE F8
MARCOS B9
YARED D7
AIEH C9
GI C7
ATFNZO AVENUE C7
B8
B7
B9
ABRAYE STREET C5
EWERK E6
OR ABRAHA &
HA AVE B4
OR JOHANNES
AVENUE F4
ERITREA SQUARE B8
GONDER B8
HAILU KEBEDE E6
HAMASIEN B7
HAMASIEN SQUARE E7
HARAMAT D9
HEROES C10
ITEGUE ZEHAITU
AVENUE D6
KEMBATA C8
KESSALA D7
KNOWLEDGE STREET F2
LASTA A5
LIBERATION D8
LIFE STREET F2
MAHATMA CHANDI A1
MAICEW DES TAW
JESUS D8
MARTYRS' AVENUE E5
MASSAWA C9
MEGUE MENEN SQUARE F1
MEKELE B8
MENELIK A8
MIAGENABEBE
DANTEW F6
NOCRA D8
OMO A9
PEACE C8
RAS ABEBE AREGAI AVE B3
RAS ALULA AVENUE E8, F7
RAS SHUL D6
RED LIGHT DISTRICT D8
RED SEA A7
REVOLUTION AVE C4
SAED HABIB STREET C5
SENAFE C8
SEPTEMBER 1 SQUARE D10
SERAE C8
SUDAN A4
TEFEBI-YAZEW C6
TEMBIEN SQUARE E7
TEOUILEHAS A6
TESSENEI C9
TITO E8
VICTORY C8
WOLDEGEBRIEL AVENUE B3
XII YEKATIT SQUARE C10
ZERAY DES SQUARE C6

Djibouti
AVE A BERNARD G6
AVE DE BRAZZAVILLE J9
AVE GEORGES
CLÉMENCEAU I7
AVE ST LAURENT
DU VAR G6
BIR HAKEIM I6
BLVD BONHOURE I6
BLVD DE BENDER J7
BLVD DE GÉNÉRAL DE
GAULLE H10
CURIE J9
D'ATHÈNES J8
D'ETHIOPIE J7
FOUCAULD I8
GENÉVE H7
LONDRES J7
MADRID J8
MARCHAND G7
MARSEILLE H7
MOSCOU I7
PARIS H8, J7
PLACE A BERNARD G6
PLACE LAGARDE G8
PLACE MÉNÉLIK H7
ROME H8, J7
ROOSEVELT J6
RUE DE LA MOSQUÉE J9
SOLEILLET J6
VERDON I6

Mogadishu
CORSO DELLA
REPUBBLICA H4
CORSO PRIMO LUGLIO H3
NEW PORT I3
OLD PORT I4
SAINAI ROAD G5
VIA AHMED BIN IDRISS H3
VIA BENADIR H5
VIA GUIBA H4
VIA HIRAM G4
VIA LAZZARETTO I5
VIA LIBERIA G2
VIA LONDRA I2
VIA MECCA H2
VIA MEDINA H1
VIA MOHAMMED HARBI G4
VIA MOROCCO I3
VIA ROMA I3
VIA SANTINI H5
VIA TANZANIA G3
VIA UBI SCEBELI H4
VIA UGANDA G2
VIA WASHINGTON H2
VIALE DEL LIDO I5

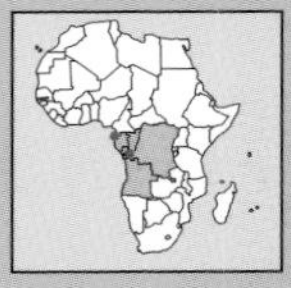

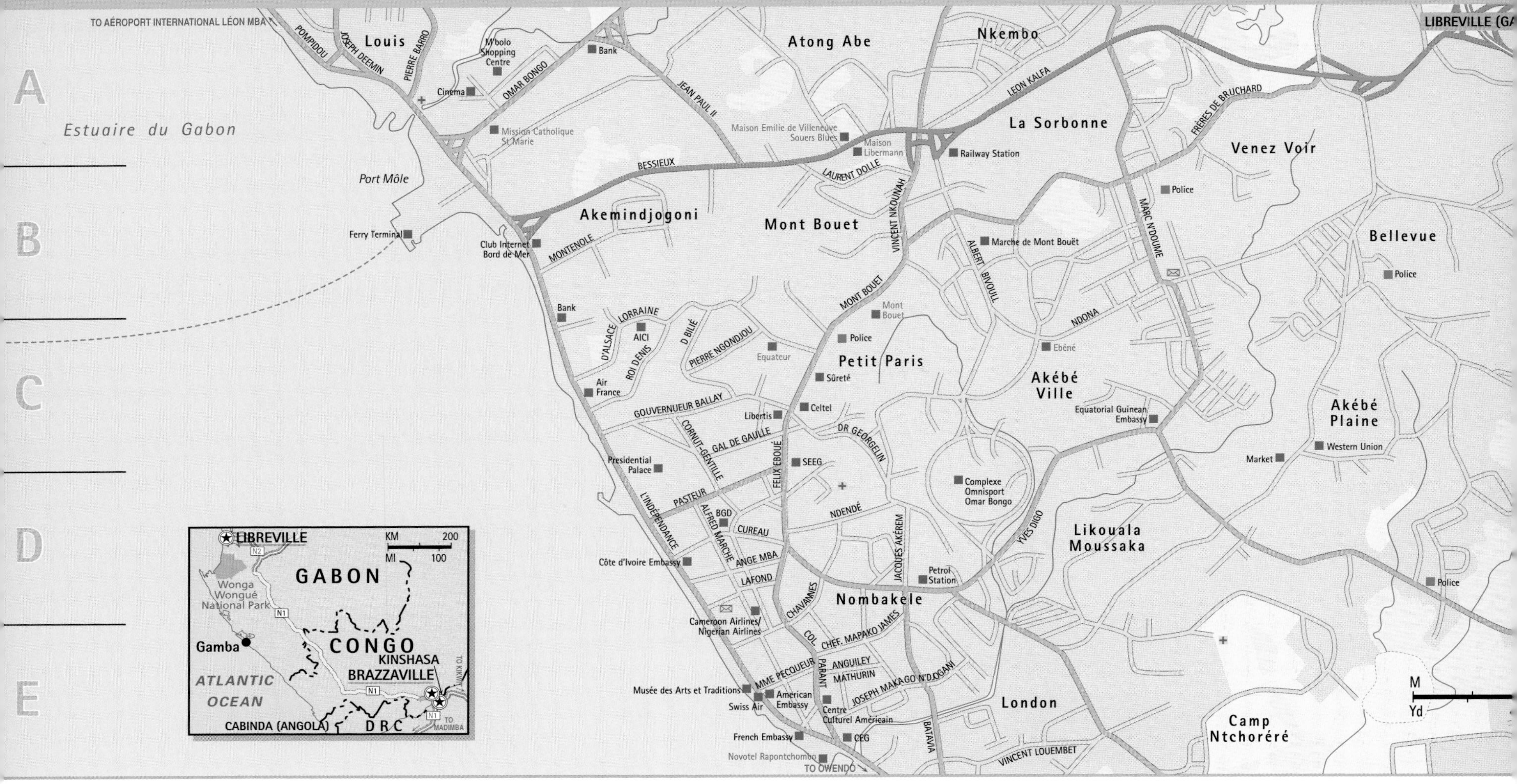
LIBREVILLE (GA
TO AÉROPORT INTERNATIONAL LÉON MBA
Louis
Atong Abe
Nkembo
Estuaire du Gabon
Port Môle
Ferry Terminal
La Sorbonne
Venez Voir
Akemindjogoni
Mont Bouet
Bellevue
Petit Paris
Akébé Ville
Akébé Plaine
Likouala Moussaka
Nombakele
London
Camp Ntchoréré
M'bolo Shopping Centre
Bank
Cinema
Mission Catholique St Marie
Maison Emilie de Villeneuve Souers Blues
Maison Libermann
Railway Station
Police
Club Internet Bord de Mer
Marche de Mont Bouët
Mont Bouet
Ebéné
AICI
Air France
Equateur
Sûreté
Celtel
Libertis
Equatorial Guinean Embassy
Western Union
Market
Presidential Palace
SEEG
Complexe Omnisport Omar Bongo
BGD
Côte d'Ivoire Embassy
Petrol Station
Cameroon Airlines/ Nigerian Airlines
Musée des Arts et Traditions
Swiss Air
American Embassy
Centre Culturel Américain
French Embassy
CEG
Novotel Rapontchombo
TO OWENDO
M
Yd
LIBREVILLE
GABON
Wonga Wongué National Park
Gamba
CONGO
KINSHASA
BRAZZAVILLE
ATLANTIC OCEAN
CABINDA (ANGOLA)
DRC
KM 200
MI 100
A
B
C
D
E

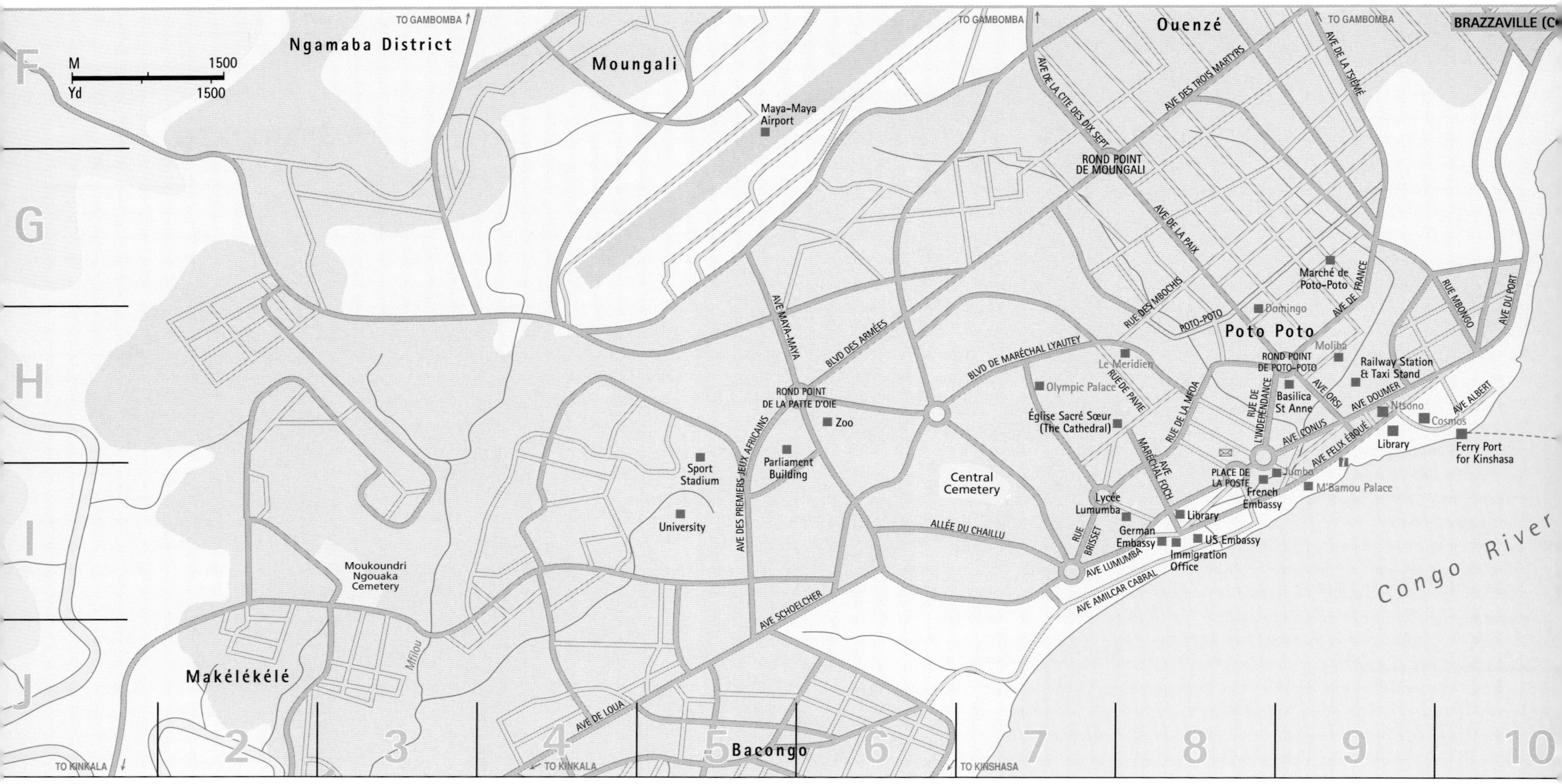
BRAZZAVILLE (C
TO GAMBOMBA
Ngamaba District
Moungali
Ouenzé
M 1500
Yd 1500
Maya-Maya Airport
ROND POINT DE MOUNGALI
Marché de Poto-Poto
Domingo
Poto Poto
Moliba
ROND POINT DE POTO-POTO
Railway Station & Taxi Stand
Le Meridien
Olympic Palace
Église Sacré Sœur (The Cathedral)
Basilica St Anne
Ntsono
Cosmos
Library
Ferry Port for Kinshasa
ROND POINT DE LA PATTE D'OIE
Zoo
Sport Stadium
Parliament Building
Central Cemetery
University
Lycée Lumumba
PLACE DE LA POSTE
Jumbo
French Embassy
M'Bamou Palace
Library
German Embassy
US Embassy
Immigration Office
Congo River
Moukoundri Ngouaka Cemetery
Makélékélé
Bacongo
TO KINKALA
TO KINSHASA
F
G
H
I
J
2
3
4
5
6
7
8
9
10

Luanda ANGOLA

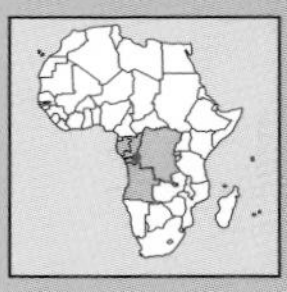

24 NOVEMBRE E5, H6, I6
30 JUIN C10, D6, E3, F1
ACTION D10
AKETI G7
AKULA J10
AMBASSADEURS E1
ASSOLONGO J1
AVE DU FLEUVE CONGO C3
AVIATEURS B9
BAKONGO D10, E10
BANDUNDU B8
BANGALA C10
BARAKA G9
BARON JACQUES C9
BAS-CONGO C9
BATETELA E1
BEAUX ARTS G6
BOENDE G6
BOKASSA D10, F10
BOLOBO H9
BOLONGO H7
BOYATA E6
BUKAMA H7
BUNGU J1
BUTA G7
CAISSE D' EPARGNE C4
CAMP MILITAIRE J4, J5
CATARACTES B9
CERCLE D4, E5
CITOYENNE BONONGE I5
CITRONNIERS E5
CLINIQUES E1
COCOTIERS F4
COLONEL EBEYA C10, D7
COLONEL LUKUSA I4
COLONEL TSHATSHI C3, D1
COLONEL VANGU D4
COMANDANT KABONGO I4
COMANDANT PONGO I4
COMMERCANTS D10
COMMERCE D9
COMMUNE D5
COTEAU F1
CROIX-ROUGE G9
DIBAYA J9
DILOLO H10
DIMA H10
DODOMA F9
DOUANE B8
DRACEANA E4
DUMI B10
ÉCOLE F10, G10
ENSEIGNMENT J8
EQUATEUR B9, C9
ETHIOPIE J10
ETOILE C4
FLAMBOYANTS E4, F4
FLEURS C5
FLEUVE CONGO C2
GAMBELA J9
GECAMINES B8
GOMA C2, D1
GOMBARI J10
GOMBE F1, F3, F4
HAUT-CONGO C10, D9
HEROS NATIONAUX C2
HÔPITAL D8
HOTEL B10
HUILERIERS D7, F8, H8, J8
INZIA J9
IPENGE C9
ISANGI G7
ITAGA E8, E9, F6
ITURI F3
JACARANDAS E5
JUSTICE C5, D3, E2, F1
KABALO G7, G9
KABAMBARE G9, H7
KABINDA G10, H7
KALEMBELEMBE G9, H7
KALEMIE B7, C5, C7
KANDA-KANDA J9
KAPANGA H9
KASAI C10
KASA-VUBU D8, F9, H10
KASONGO LUNDA G6
KATANGA C5, J8
KATO E8, E10, F6
KAUKA F3
KIBATI G9
KIDICHO C3
KIGOMA F9
KIKWIT H7
KILO-MOTO C5
KILOSA F9
KINDU G9
KISANGANI D3
KITEGA G6
KITEGE F9
KITOKO C1
KITONA C8
KOLWEZI C6
KONGOLO G9
KUTU F6, H7
KWANGO F3
KWILU G7
LAC MOERO F6
LEMERA C1, C3, C5
LIBENGE G7
LIKASI E3
LILAS C5
LINGBANGA I3
LODJA J9
LOKOLAMA J9
LOWA D10, E8
LT COLONEL LUKUSA C6, C8
LUALABA E8
LUAPULA G9
LUBEFU F2
LUIZA F6
LUKENIE G8
LUKOLELA H10
LUOZI J10
LUPUNGU B9
LUTUMBA C3
LUVUA E8, E10, F6
LUVUNGI G9
MAHENGE F9
MALEMBANKUNLU G2
MALUKU H9
MANDARINIERS E4
MANGAI J8
MARAIS D9, F10, G10
MARCHÉ C9, D9, F9, G10
MASIMANIMBA J9
MATEBA I10
MAYUMBE G6
MBANZA- NGUNGU H9
MBOMU E10, F5, F8
MBUJI-MAYI C6
MFUMU LUTUNU C7
MILLS E3
MISSION C6
MOERO E8, E9
MONGALA C8
MONT DES ARTS E6
MONTS VIRUNGGA D2
MPOLO C8, I9, J10
MUAI KABARE C3
MUSHIE F6, H7
MUTOMBO KATSHI C9
MWEKA F6
MWENE-DITU F2, H5
NATION B9
NATIONS UNIES C1
NELSON MANDELA E4, G3
NGABU C4, D4
NGABU MICHEL C3
NGELE G6
NGONGO LUTETE C7
NKOKINA B10
NYAMURAGIR C10
NYANGWE H7
NYANZA F9
OFFICE DES ROUTES D2
OKITO C2
OMS D4
ORANGERS E4
OSWE J9
OUGANDA F1
PAIX B9
PALMIER E3
PANIA MUTOMBO F6
PERE BOOKA D3
PETIT PONT F1
PLACE DE L'AFRIQUE CENTRALE C10
PLACE DE L'INDÉPENDENCE E2
PLACE DE LA GARE B10
PLACE DE LA JUSTICE C5, G8
PLACE DE LA RÉPUBLIQUE C2
PLACE DE RÉVOLUTION E9
PLACE DES SAFOUTIERS E4
PLACE DES TRAVAILLEURS B8
PLACE DU MARCHÉ D9
PLACE DU 27 OCTOBRE B9
PLACE DU 4 JANVIER J10
PLACE NELSON MANDELA E4
PLATEAU C9, F10, G10
PONT KASA-VUBU I10
PORT B9, C8
PRESIDENCE H4
PROVINCE D7
PUMBU E2
REGION F8, H8
REPUBLIC CENTRAFRIQUE C10
ROND-POINT DE BATETELA F2
ROND-POINT PETIT PONT G1
RP MOLS E3
RUAKANDINGI D10, E8
SAFOUTIERS E4
SAIO J7
SANKURU F8, G9
SAPUSAPU
SCIENCE
SENDWE
SERGENT EKOMONO
SERGENT MOKE
SERGENT TSHIKALA
SHABA
SONGOLOLO
TCHAD
TITULE
TOKO
TOMBALBAYE C9,
TRAVAILLEURS
TSF
TSHELA
TSHIKAPA
TSHUAPA
UBANGI
USOKE
UVIRA
VICTOIRE
VILLAGE
VISTA
WAGENIA
WANGATA D8,
ZONGO-NTOLO

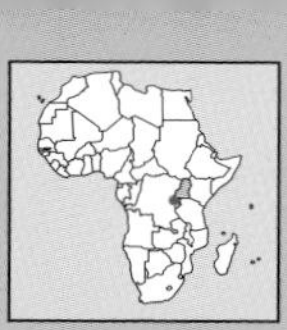

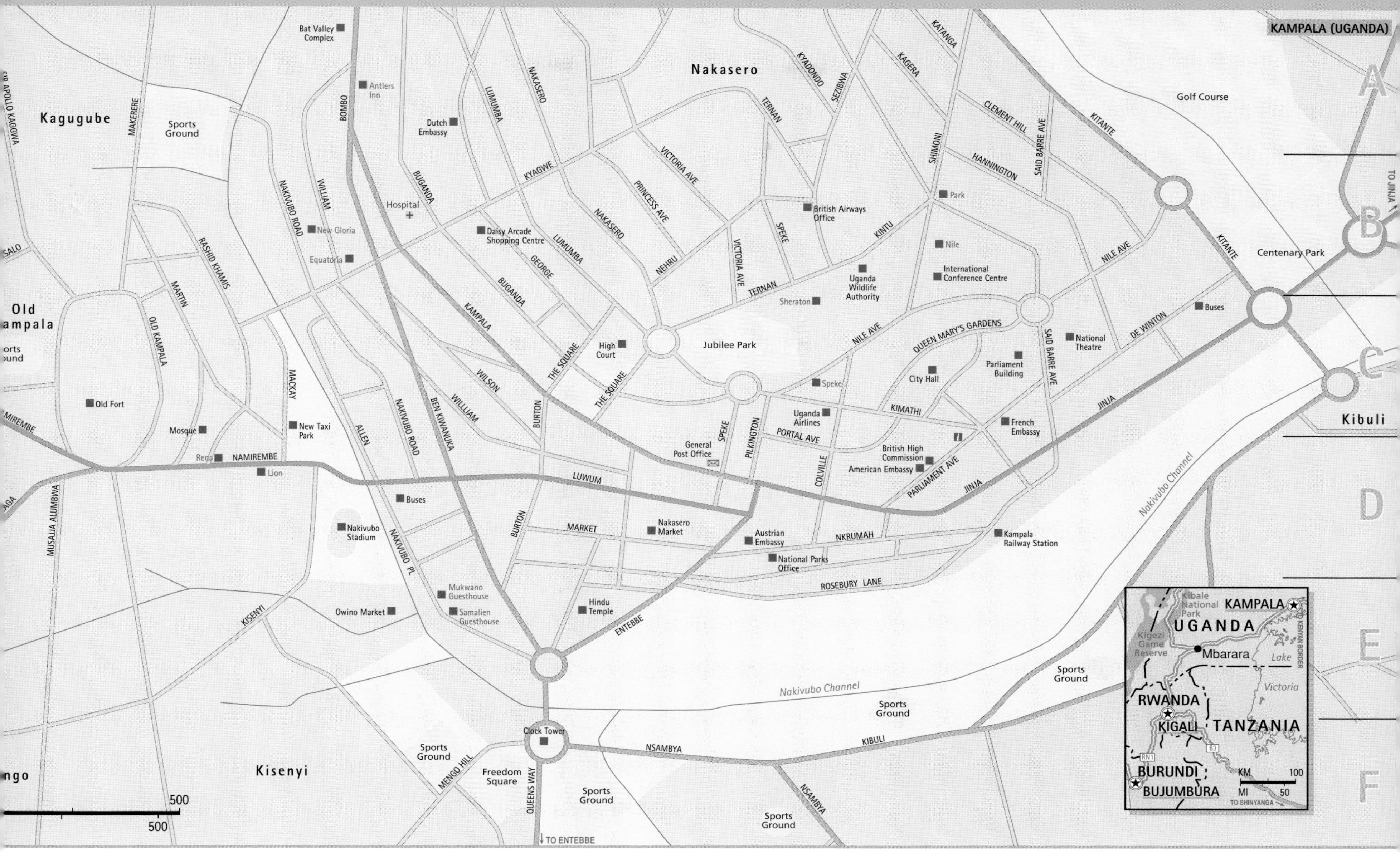
KAMPALA (UGANDA)
Nakasero
Kagugube
Old Kampala
Kisenyi
Kibuli
Golf Course
Centenary Park
Jubilee Park
Sports Ground
Old Fort
Mosque
Bat Valley Complex
Antlers Inn
Dutch Embassy
Hospital
New Gloria
Equatoria
Daisy Arcade Shopping Centre
British Airways Office
Park
Nile
International Conference Centre
Uganda Wildlife Authority
Sheraton
Buses
National Theatre
High Court
Parliament Building
City Hall
Speke
French Embassy
Uganda Airlines
General Post Office
British High Commission
American Embassy
New Taxi Park
Lion
Nakivubo Stadium
Nakasero Market
Austrian Embassy
National Parks Office
Kampala Railway Station
Mukwano Guesthouse
Samalien Guesthouse
Hindu Temple
Owino Market
Clock Tower
Freedom Square
Nakivubo Channel
TO ENTEBBE
TO JINJA
KAMPALA
UGANDA
Mbarara
RWANDA
KIGALI
TANZANIA
BURUNDI
BUJUMBURA
Lake Victoria
TO SHINYANGA
500

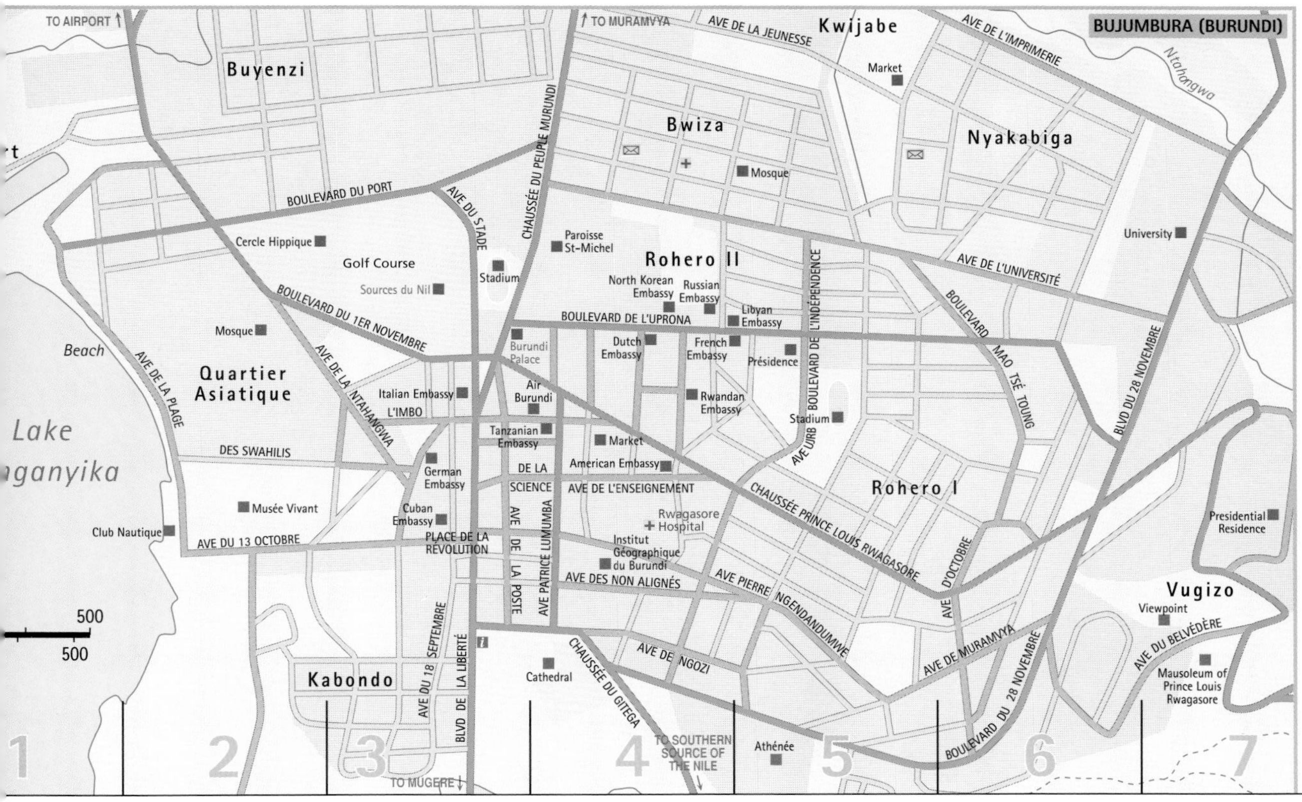
BUJUMBURA (BURUNDI)
Buyenzi
Bwiza
Kwijabe
Nyakabiga
Rohero II
Rohero I
Quartier Asiatique
Kabondo
Vugizo
Lake Tanganyika
TO AIRPORT
TO MURAMVYA
Market
Mosque
Cercle Hippique
Golf Course
Sources du Nil
Stadium
Paroisse St-Michel
North Korean Embassy
Russian Embassy
Libyan Embassy
University
Dutch Embassy
French Embassy
Présidence
Burundi Palace
Italian Embassy
Rwandan Embassy
Tanzanian Embassy
German Embassy
Musée Vivant
Cuban Embassy
Club Nautique
American Embassy
Rwagasore Hospital
Institut Géographique du Burundi
Presidential Residence
Viewpoint
Mausoleum of Prince Louis Rwagasore
Cathedral
Athénée
TO SOUTHERN SOURCE OF THE NILE
TO MUGERE
500

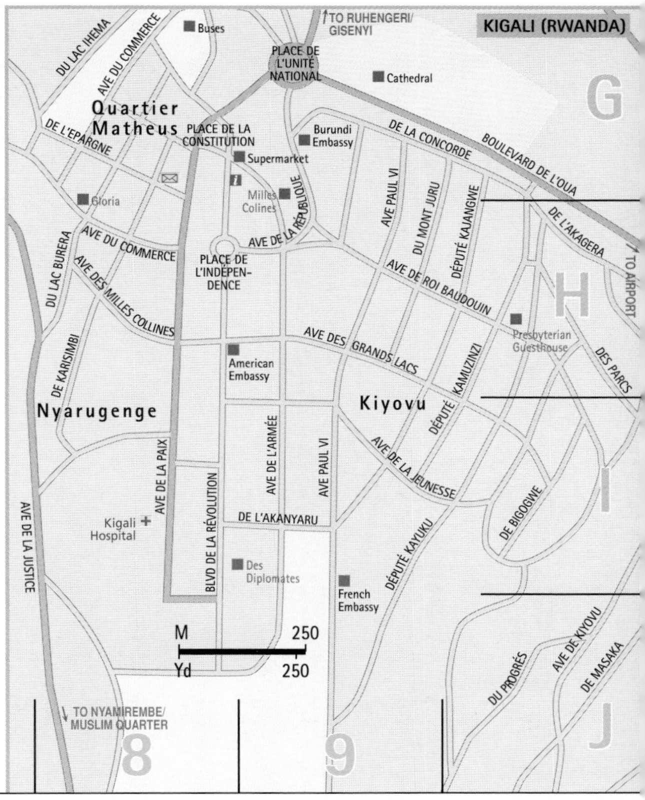
KIGALI (RWANDA)
Quartier Matheus
Nyarugenge
Kiyovu
TO RUHENGERI/ GISENYI
TO AIRPORT
Buses
PLACE DE L'UNITÉ NATIONAL
Cathedral
PLACE DE LA CONSTITUTION
Burundi Embassy
Supermarket
Gloria
Milles Collines
PLACE DE L'INDÉPENDENCE
Presbyterian Guesthouse
American Embassy
Kigali Hospital
Des Diplomates
French Embassy
TO NYAMIREMBE/ MUSLIM QUARTER
M 250
Yd 250

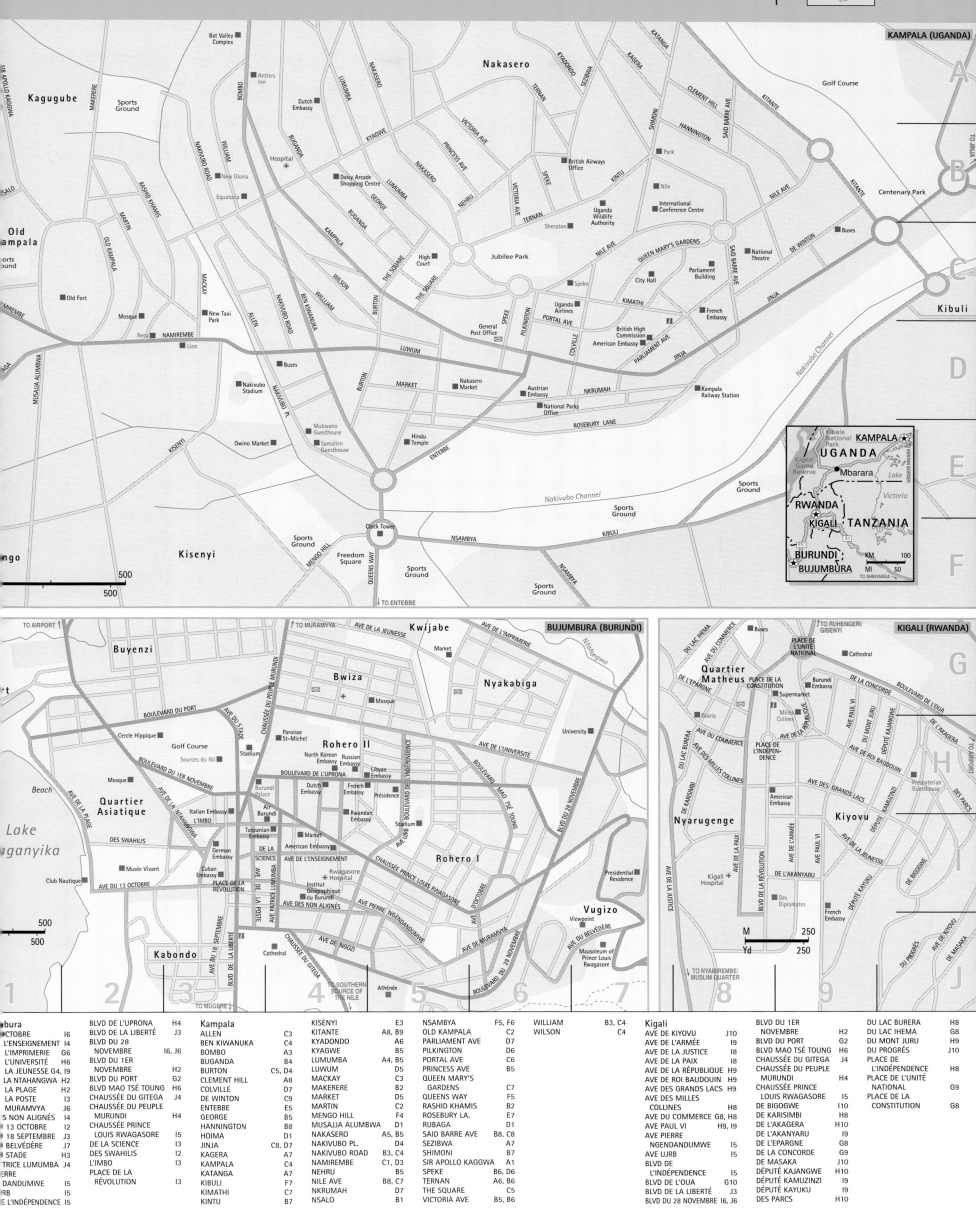

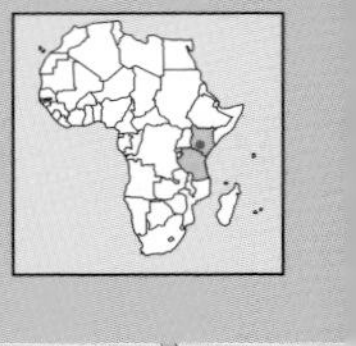

ABIDJAN	C9
ACCRA	F8
AERODROME	J8
AMBALA	F9
ARBORETUM DR	D3
ARBORETUM RD	E3
ARGWINGS KODHEK	I3
ARGWINGS KODHEK GR	I2
ARGWINGS KODHEK CL	I2
ARGWINGS KODHEK RD	H1
ASHOK LA	A6
BAIYA	C10
BANDA	F7
BARICHO	J8
BATU BATU GDNS	B6
BATU BATU RD	B7
BHANDARI	B5
BIASHARA	F7
BISHOPS	H4
BORAN	D8
BROOKSIDE CL	A1
BUJUNI	D8
BULEMIA	A5
BUNYALA	I8, J7
CATHEDRAL	H5
CEDAR	C2
CHAMBERS	D7
CHANAN SINGH	D9
CHEMILIL	D6
CHEPKORIO	J9
CHIROMO LA	C4
CHIROMO ROAD	C4
CHOGORIA	J10
CHYULU	I5
CITY HALL	G7
CITY PARK	B9, B10
COMMERCIAL	I9
CORK	C5
CRESCENT LA	B4
CROSS LA	F9
CROSS RD	F9
CROSSWAY	B3
DAVID OSIELI	B1
DENIS PRITT	G2
DESAI	C8, E9
DOROBO	F4
DUBOIS	F8
DUNGA	J9
DURUMA	F9
EAST CHURCH	B1
ELGON	J6
ENTERPRISE	I10
EXCHANGE	G9
EXPRESS	G9
FACTORY	I9
FAIRVIEW	B10
FIFTH NGONG	I4
FIFTH PARKLANDS	A8
FIRST NGONG	H5
FIRST PARKLANDS	A4, B7
FORCES	A4
FOREST LA	C7
FOREST RD	C9
FOURTH NGONG	H4
FOURTH PARKLANDS	A7
GABORONE	F8
GALBEROBE	C10
GALLA	C6
GARDEN	C2
GEDI	G8
GENL WARUINGI	E10
GEORGE PADMORE	I1
GICHUNG	D1
GITHUNGIRI	E1
GUINEA BISSAU CRES	C10
GWASI	F9
HAILE SELASSIE	G9, H6, H8
HAKATI	G9
HARAMBEE	G7
HARRY THUKU	E6
HILL	I6
HIMALAYA	B4
HOMBE	D10
HOSPITAL	I4, J5
IRUNGU RIIKA LA	E9
IRUNGU RIIKA RD	D9
ISEBANIA	H2
ITA	B7
JABAVU LA	H2
JABAVU RD	H1
JAIRO OWINO	E10
JODONGO LA	E8
JODONGO RD	E8
JUJA	C10
KABETE	A2
KAMBURU	I1
KARANTIN	D10
KARUNA	A1, A2
KASKAZI	B4
KASUKU	H1
KAUNDA	G7
KEEKOROK	E8
KEIYO	C6
KENYA	J6
KENYATTA	F7, G5
KIAMBERE	J7
KIBERA LA	J1
KIBERA RD	J1
KIBO	I5
KIEJEKU	D7
KIJABE	E6
KILIMANJARO	J6
KILOME	E7
KIMATHI	F7
KINDARUMA LA	I2
KINDARUMA RD	I1
KINSHASA	D9, D10
KINYANJUI	E10
KIPANDE	D7
KIPIPRI	C10
KIPKOBUS	D7
KIRICHWA	C1
KIRINYAGA	E7, E9
KIVEMIA	E4
KIVULI	D7
KOINANGE	F6
KOLOBOT	C7, D4
KOMBO MUNYIRI LA	F10
KOMBO MUNYIRI RD	F10
KULALU	D9
KUMASI	F9
KUSI	A6
LAGOS	F8
LAIKIPIA GR	D1
LAIKIPIA LA	D2
LAIKIPIA RD	D2
LANDHIES	G10
LANTANA	B1
LATEMA	F8
LENANA	G1, H2
LIMURU	B8, C7
LOITA	F6
LOLDAIKA	D8
LOME	D9
LONGONOT	J5
LOSAI	C10
LOWER HILL	I7
LUSAKA	J10
LUTHUDI	F9
M DADDAH	F6
MACHAKOS	I10
MADAME CURIE	C6
MADRAS	C9
MAGATHA	A5
MAKUVU	G1
MAMA NGINA	G7
MAMLAKA	E4, F5
MANDERA	D1
MARA	I5, I6
MARATHA	B5
MARKET	F6
MARUNDU	A1
MASABA	J7
MASARI	A6
MATUMBATO RD	J6
MAUA	A3
MBAGATHI WAY	J3
MBAGATHI	J3
MBOGO	D7
MBONO CRES	C10
MBONO RD	C10
MBUYU	D7
MENENGAI	J5
MFANGANO LA	G9
MFANGANO ST	G9
MIGORI	D1
MILIMANI LA	G4
MILIMANI RD	G2, G4
MKUNGU	A3
MOGIRA	D10
MOGOTIO	B4
MOI	F7, H9
MONROVIA	F6
MPAKA	A4, B3
MPESI	B4
MSANAKA	A5
MSAPO CL	B4
MSAPO LA	B4
MSHALE	C9
MTAMA	A7
MTITO ANDEI	H1
MUCAI DR	J2
MUCAI RD	J2
MUGA	E10
MUHUGU LA	C6
MUHUGU RD	C6
MUINDI MBINGU	F7
MUKINDURI	A3, B4
MUKUI	C6
MUNAE	C6
MURANG'A	C9
MURANGA	E7
MURANGA LA	D8
MUSEUM HILL	D5
MUSHEMBI	D7
MUSINDI LA	E9
MUSINDI RD	E9
MUSLIM	D10
MUTATI	A6
MUTHITHI	B4, C5
MVULI	B1
MWIMBI	F9
NAHAR SINGH	D9
NDEGE	C9
NDUMBERI	F8
NGAIRA	H8
NGARA	D6, D8, E9
NGARA LA	D8
NGARIAMA	F8
NGARIAMA LA	E8
NGIRIAM RD	E8
NGONG	H5, I2
NGONG	I2
NJEMA	C9
NJUGU	F7
NKRUMAH AVE	G8
NKRUMAH LA	G8
NOSHABA	C4
NYERERE	F5
OJIJO CL	B5
OJIJO RD	C5
OKOTHAURA	C9
ORCHARD CL	A10
PARK	D9
PARKLANDS	A3, B6
PARLIAMENT	H7
PATE BAY	H8
PEMBE	C9
PLUMS	C5
POKOT	C7
POPO LA	F10
POPO RD	F10
POSTA	G6
PROCESSIONAL	G6
PUMWANI	F10
QUARRY	E10, F10
RACE COURSE	E10
RAGATI	H5, I5
RAILWAY	G9
RALPH BUNCHE	G3, I4
RAMESH GAUTAMA	E7
RHAPTA	B1, B2
RING ROAD KILELESHWA	D1
RING ROAD NGARA	C10, D10
RING ROAD PARKLANDS	A3
RING ROAD PUMWANI	F10
RING ROAD RIVERSIDE	D2
RING ROAD WESTLANDS	B2
RIVER	F8, F9
RIVERSIDE DR	C2, D3
RIVERSIDE LA	C1
RONALD NGALA	F9
ROSE AVE	G1, H1, I1
ROSE CL	G1
SAMBURU	D6
SCHOOL GR	A2
SCHOOL LANE	A1
SECOND NGONG	H5
SECOND PARKLANDS	A5, B7
SERENGETI	A10
SHEIKH KARUME	F8
SHILLINGI	D7
SHIVACHI	A5
SIMBI	D9
SIONA	C9
SOIT OLOLOL	C9
SOLAI	J8
SONGOT LA	D9
SONGOT WALK	D10
SPORTS	B1, B2, C5
STANDARD	F7
STATE HOUSE AVE	G4
STATE HOUSE CRES	G4
STATE HOUSE RD	E4, G2
STATION	H8
TAARIFO	C6
TABERE	E1, F1
TAIFA	G8
TEMPLE LA	
TEMPLE RD	
THE CRESCENT	
THETA	
THINGIRA	
THIRD NGONG	
THIRD PARKLANDS	
TIMBOROA	
TIWI	
TOM MBOYA	
TSAVO	
TUBMAN	
TUMBO	
UHURU	E5
UNIVERSITY	
UPPER HILL	H5
UYOMA	
VALE	
VALLEY	H4
VOI	
WABERA	
WAIYAKI WAY	
WAJIR	
WAKULIMA	
WAMBUGU GDNS	
WAMBUGU GR	
WAMBUGU LA	
WAMBUGU RD	
WATO	
WERUGA	
WESTLANDS	B2
WOODLANDS GR	
WOODLANDS LA	
WOODLANDS RD	G2,
WOODVALE	
WORKSHOP	H8

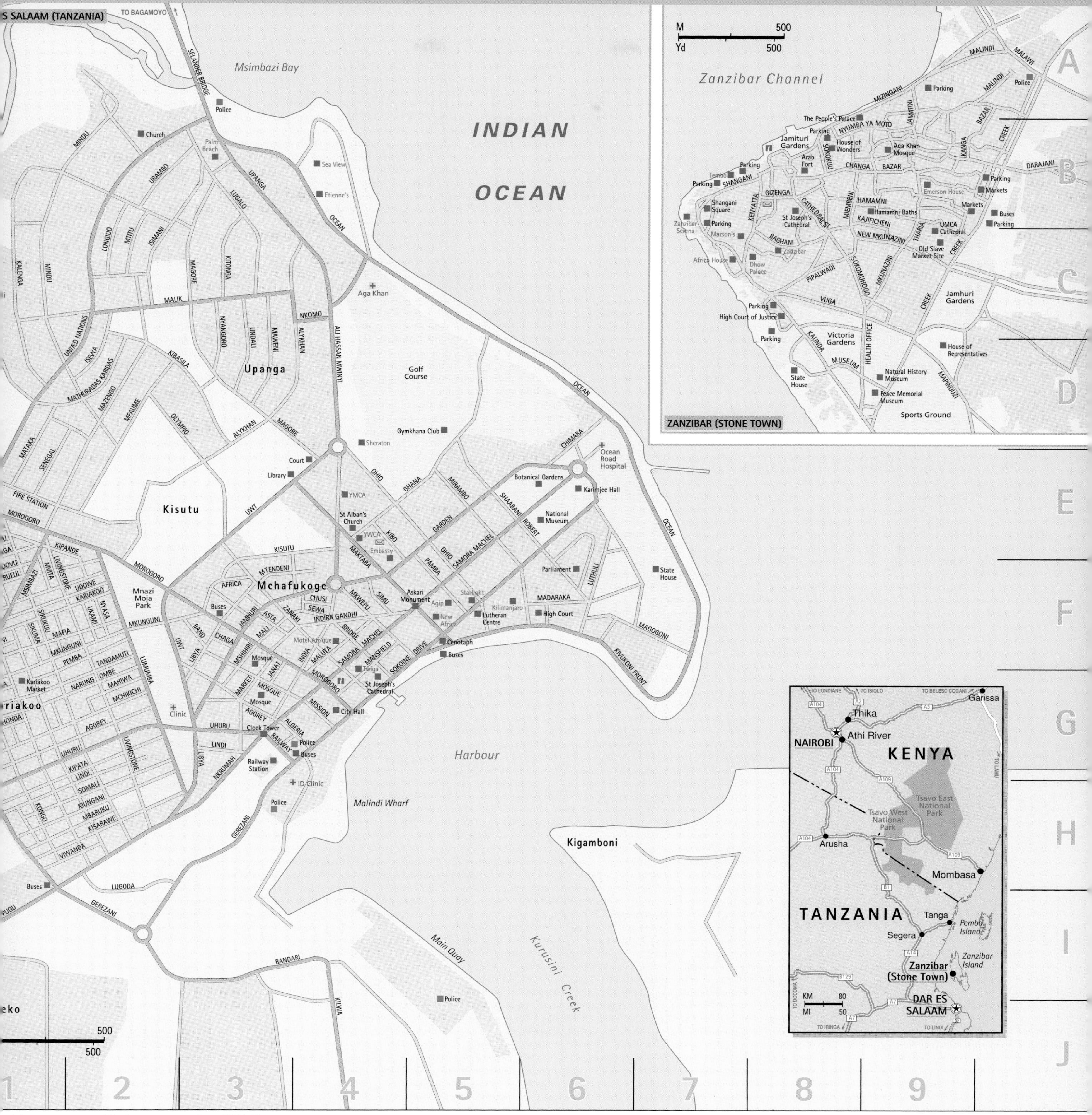
S SALAAM (TANZANIA)
TO BAGAMOYO
Msimbazi Bay
INDIAN
OCEAN
Zanzibar Channel
Upanga
Kisutu
Mchafukoge
Harbour
Malindi Wharf
Kigamboni
Main Quay
Kurusini Creek
Aga Khan
Golf Course
Gymkhana Club
Sheraton
Ocean Road Hospital
Botanical Gardens
Karimjee Hall
National Museum
State House
Parliament
High Court
Askari Monument
Kilimanjaro
Lutheran Centre
Cenotaph
Buses
St Joseph's Cathedral
City Hall
Clock Tower
Railway Station
ID Clinic
Police
Mnazi Moja Park
Kariakoo Market
ZANZIBAR (STONE TOWN)
The People's Palace
Jamituri Gardens
House of Wonders
Aga Khan Mosque
Arab Fort
Emerson House
Markets
Shangani Square
St Joseph's Cathedral
UMCA Cathedral
Old Slave Market Site
Zanzibar Serena
Africa House
Dhow Palace
Jamhuri Gardens
High Court of Justice
Victoria Gardens
House of Representatives
Natural History Museum
Peace Memorial Museum
State House
Sports Ground
KENYA
NAIROBI
Thika
Athi River
Garissa
Tsavo East National Park
Tsavo West National Park
Arusha
Mombasa
TANZANIA
Tanga
Pemba Island
Segera
Zanzibar Island
Zanzibar (Stone Town)
DAR ES SALAAM
TO IRINGA
TO LINDI
TO DODOMA

Lusaka ZAMBIA

Street	Grid
ADDIS ABABA DRIVE	E6
ALEX MASALA	D6
ALICK NKHATA	E9
ANDREW MWENYA	F4
ASH	J10
ATAKATA	A6
AZIKIWI	D4
BAKAVU	D1
BEIT	F5
BEN BELLA	H1
BENAKALE	D4
BIRDCAGE	G6
BOLI	J7
BOMBAY	I2
BRENTWOOD	I10
BROADS	F3
BUCHI	D3
BURMA	I5, J7
BUSANGA	A10
BUSUMA	H10
BUTEKO	G2
BUWA	D2
BWEMBELELO	B1
BWINJIMFUMU	E4
CAIRO	F1
CEDAR	J10
CHACHACHA	H1
CHAHOLI	E5
CHAINAMA	A5
CHAINDA	H2
CHAKELUKA	B5
CHAKUNKULE	I6
CHAKWA	H3
CHALA	D3
CHANDE	D2
CHANGA	H3
CHAPITA	B1
CHIBWA	I5
CHIFINGA	E1
CHIGWILIZANO	D5
CHIKANKATA	A1
CHIKUNI	D3
CHIKUPI	A6
CHIKWA	F5
CHILEBE	E2
CHILEKWE MWAMBA	F6
CHILIMBULU	I4
CHILUBI	G4
CHILUFAYA MULENGA	G6
CHIMANGA	G5
CHIMUKOKO	A1
CHINGALIKA	E4
CHINGOMBE	F4
CHINYUNYU	A1
CHIPANDA	A2
CHIPARAMBA	G1
CHIPEMBELE	J6
CHIPOMA	F5
CHIPOVU	E5
CHIPUSHI	G10
CHISIDZA	H8
CHISOKONE	D5
CHITE	I8, J8
CHITEMENE	D5
CHITUKUKO	J10
CHITULI	D5
CHIWALAMABWE	A6
CHIWAYA	B2
CHIYANGA	E2
CHONGWE	I2
CHOZI	D4
CHURCH	F2, F4
CIP	I2
CONAKRY	B1
CONGO	G10
DAR ES SALAAM	G1
DEDAN KIMATHI	G2
DELHI	H3
DOKO	D2
DONGWE	I2
DR AGGREY	J5
DUSHAMBE	G3
ELM	J10
ENOCK KAVU	E6
EULWE	E5
FAIRLEY	H6
FREEDOM WAY	G1
FREETOWN	E5
GANDHI	H3
GOVERNMENT	H6
GREAT EAST	C6, E4, E9
GREAT NORTH	C1
HAILE SELASSIE AVE	F7
HEROES	G2
HIBISCUS	I6
INDEPENDENCE AVE	G4, I8
INDUS	I4
ISUNGA	H3
ITUNA	G4
JACARANDA	H6
JOHN MBITA	I6
JOSEPH	E4
KABANGA	F6
KABELENGA	E2
KACHA	D4
KAFUE	I1
KAJA	I3
KAKUZI	I3
KALAMBO	E1
KALANGA	A1
KALEMBWE	D5
KALUNDWE	F1
KALUNGWISHI	I2
KAMBA	E2
KANGO	J6
KANSOKOMA	J5
KAPOCHE	A1
KAPUMPE	I8
KARACHI	H2
KARIBA	A8
KASEMPA	G10
KASISI	F7
KASIYA	A10
KATEMO	E4, F5
KATIMA MULILO	A4, A7, B2
KATONDO	G1
KATOPOLA	D6
KATUNJILA	G1
KAUMBWE	A1
KAWIMBWE	B1
KAYOMBO	G3, G4
KIBILE	A6
KWACHA	B6, C6
KWAME NKRUMAH	H3
KWANDO	I3
LAGOS	E4, E5
LANDA	D4
LEWANIKA	I10
LIMBE	D4
LIVINGSTONE	J5
LONGOLONGO	E2
LOS ANGELES BLVD (SADDAM HUSSEIN BLVD)	F6, G8
LOUMOE	D2
LUAMPA	J2
LUANGWA	I3
LUANO	F4
LUANSHYA	E1
LUAPULA	I3
LUBAMBE	D3
LUBANSENSHI	B8
LUBU	E6
LUBUTO	E5
LUBWA	F4
LUCHELE	I4
LUENA	I3
LUFUBU	A9
LUFUPA	A8
LUI	J3
LUKASA	E7
LUKOMA	B1
LUKULU	G10, I3
LUKUSUZI	A8
LUMBE	E3
LUMEZI	I3
LUMUMBA	G1
LUNG	I3
LUNGWEBUNGU	E5
LUNSEMFWA	A9
LUNU	J3
LUNZUA	D6
LUONGO	A9
LUPANDE	A10
LUSITU	J3
LUSIWASI	A8
LUTEMPWE	I2
LUZI	E2
MACH	I3
MACHA	E5
MAGOYE	A8
MAKANTA	F3
MAKISHI	D2, E3
MALAMBO	C1
MALASHA	F1
MALATA	I4
MALILA	D3
MAMBULIMA	E5
MANCHICHI	C5, D3
MANDA HILL	B7, C6
MANENEKELA	I7
MANSANSA	E3
MANSHYA	I3
MAPEPE	A5
MAPOMPO	A5
MARTIN MWAMBA	C7
MASA	J6
MATABA	J6
MATALA	J6
MBERERE	A6
MBIYA	E3
MBOYA	H3, I5
MIBYA	I5
MILIMA	J10
MKUSHI	I4
MOGADISHU	G5
MOPANI	I5
MPANGWE	G7
MPULUNGU	B5, C6
MSANZARA	A8
MTANDANI	E4
MUCHISHA	G4
MUFUNDA	J6
MUKONTEKA	D6
MUKOSA	D2
MUKUPE	H3
MULOBEZI	B6
MULOMBWE	F3
MULULU	B1
MUMANA	A6
MUNGULUBE	D2
MUSANYA	J2
MUSENGELE	G10
MUSHEMI	F6
MUSI	J2
MUSONDE	D1
MVULE	I8
MVUWE	A10
MWAIMWENA	G5
MWALESHI	B5
MWALULE	D2
MWAMBESHI	D3
MWAMBWA	J3
MWANSABOMBWA	A5
MWATIYAMVU	A1
MWILWA	E4
MWINILUNGA	G10
MZEE KENYATTA	H7
NAIROBI	G2
NALUBUTU	E6
NAMAMBOZI	E4
NAMBALA	E3
NANGOMBE	I3
NANGWENYA	D7
NANYAKATOLO	D4
NATIONALIST	I7, J7
NCHENJA	D3
NGIBE	A1
NGOSA	E1
NGULUBE	I8
NGUMBO	H7, H8
NGWEE	G7
NGWEREMA	C6
NINTH	J6
NJOKA	A5
NKAN DABWE	I6
NKANA	J3
NKANCHIBAYA	E5
NKATENGA	J6
NKWAZI	G1
NSATO	C1
NSEMBE	B1
NSUMBU	I8
NSUNZE	H4
NYAKASEYA	G4
NYATI	E6
NYIMBA	G10
OBOTE	H3, I4
OMELO	E4
PANGANINI	E1
PARIRENYETWA	F3
PARLIAMENT	B6
PASELI	D4
PAUL BANDE	I6
PRESIDENTS	H9
PROTEA	F3
PROVIDENT	E3
RAPHAEL KOMBE	H4
SADZU	F2
SAISE	F6
SAPELE	G2
SEKOU TOURE	
SESHEKE	
SEVENTH	J
SHEKI-SHEKI	
SIBWENI	
SIND	
SIXTH	
SPEAKERS	
SUEZ	
TEAK	
TENTH	
TITO	F
TUKULUHO	
TULETEKA	
TWATOTELA	
TWIKATANE	
UFULU	
UNDI	
UNITED NATIONS	
VIMBE	
VUBU	
WAMALUNGA	
WAMULWA	
WUSIKILI	
YOTAM MULEYA	
ZAMBEZI	
ZIMBABWE	
ZIMBA	
ZIN	
ZINNIA	
ZUNGULU	

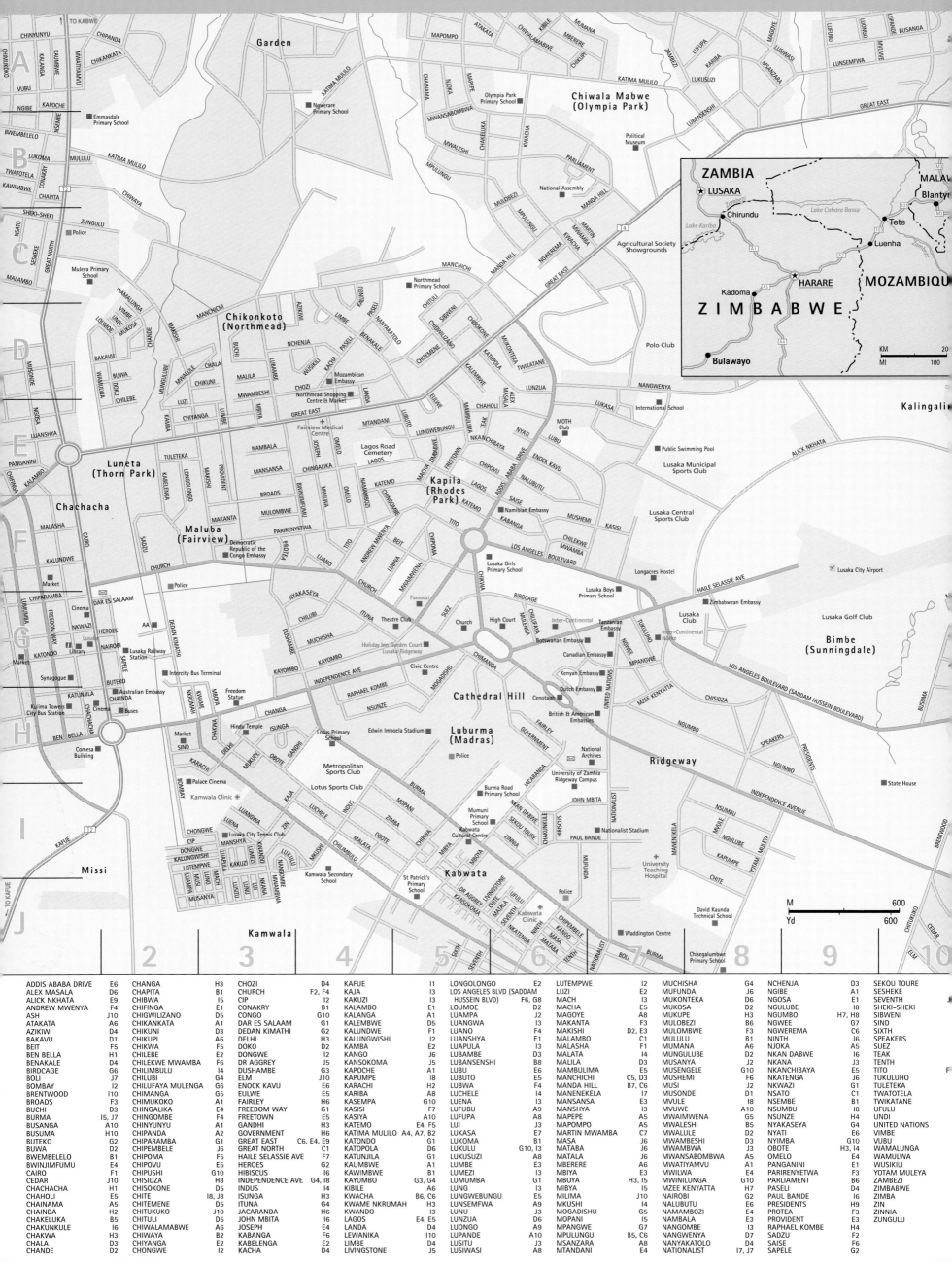

Milton Park
Belvedere North
Avenues
Harare Gardens
Braeside
Arcadia
Mbare
Graniteside
Old Hararians Sports Club
Alexandra Sports Club
Royal Harare Golf Club
Harare SportsClub
Zimbabwe House (President's Residence)
State House
Parirenyatwa Hospital
Sekuru Kaguvi Hospital
Mbuyu Nehanda Hospital
Old Central Hospital
St Giles Primary School
St Giles Hospital
Wilkins Hospital
Prince Edward Secondary School
Allan Wilson Secondary School
Selbourne Rootledge Primary School
St Josephs House
Harare Polytechnic
Girls High Secondary School
Queen Elizabeth Secondary School
City Bowling Club
National Art Gallery
Les Brown Swimming Pool
Greenwood Park
David Livingstone Primary School
Golf Driving Range
Chapman Golf Club
Raylton Sports Club
Zimbabwe Agricultural Showgrounds
Glamis Stadium
National Sports Centre
Conference Centre
Queen Victoria Museum (Zimbabwe Museum of Human Science)
Library
Courtauld Theatre
College of Music
Magistrates' Court
Louis Mountbatten Primary School
Harare Railway Station
Eastgate Mall
Town House
Reservoir
Toposcope
Magaba Shopping Centre
Cemetery
Rufaro Stadium
ZBC Studios
Danny Bismark Stadium
Mukuvisi
TO KARIBA/ZAMBIA
TO EWANRIGG BOTANICAL GARDENS
TO MUTARE
TO BEITBRIDGE/ JOHANNESBURG
TO HARARE INTERNATIONAL AIRPORT
M 500
Yd 500

Bulawayo ZIMBABWE

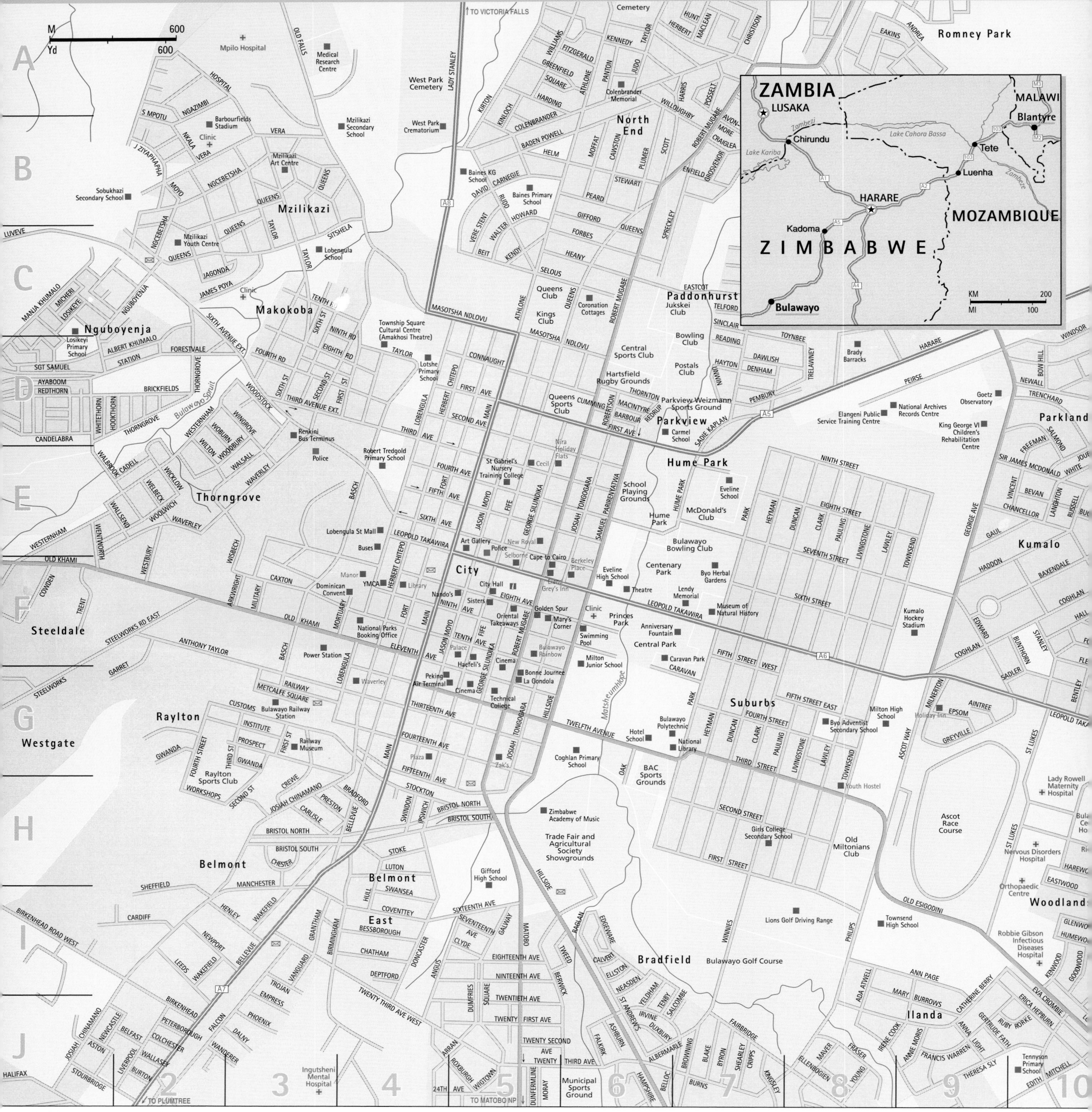

24TH AVE	J5
ADA ATWELL	I8
AINTREE	G9
ALBERMARLE	J6
ALBERT KHUMALO	D2
ANDREA	A9
ANGUS	I4
ANN PAGE	I9
ANNA LIGHT	J9
ANNIE MORIS	J9
ANTHONY TAYLOR	F2
ARKWRIGHT	F3
ARRAN	J5
ASCOT WAY	J9
ASHBURN	J6
ASTON	J1
ATHLONE	A6, C5
AVONMORE	B7
AYABOOM	D1
BADEN POWELL	B5
BARBOUR	D6
BASCH	E4, F3
BAXENDALE	F10
BEIT	C5
BELFAST	J2
BELLEVUE	H4, I3
BELLOC	J6
BENTLEY	G10
BERWICK	I5
BESSBOROUGH	I4
BEVAN	E10
BIRKENHEAD ROAD WEST	I1
BIRKENHEAD	J2
BIRMINGHAM	I3
BLAKE	J7
BOW HILL	
BRADFORD	H4
BRICKFIELDS	D2
BRISTOL NORTH	H3, H5
BRISTOL SOUTH	H3, H5
BROWNING	J7
BUCKNALL	E10
BUNTHORN	F10
BURNHAM	E10
BURNS	J7
BURTON	J2
BYRON	J7
CADELL	E2
CALVERT	I6
CANDELABRA	D1
CARAVAN	G7
CARDIFF	I2
CARLISLE	H3
CATHERINE BERRY	J9
CAWSTON	B6
CAXTON	F3
CHANCELLOR	E10
CHAPLIN	F10
CHATHAM	I4
CHESTER	H3
CHRISTISON	A7
CLARK	E8, G7
CLYDE	I5
COGHLAN	F9, F10
COLCHESTER	J2
COLENBRANDER	B5
CONNAUGHT	D5
COVENTTEY	I4
COWDEN	F1
CRAIGLEA	B7
CREWE	H3
CUMMING	D6
CUSTOMS	G3
DALNY	J3
DAVID CARNEGIE	B5
DAWLISH	D7
DENHAM	D7
DEPTFORD	I4
DUMFRIES SQUARE	J5
DONCASTER	I4
DUNCAN	E8, G7
DUNFERMLINE	J5
DUXBURY	J6
EAKINS	A8
EASTCOT	C7
EASTWOOD	H10
EDGEWARE	I6
EDITH MITCHELL	J10
EDWARD	F9
EIGHTEENTH AVE	I5
EIGHTH AVE	F5
EIGHTH RD	D3
EIGHTH STREET	E8
ELEVENTH AVE	F5
ELLENBOGIEN	J8
ELLSTON	I6
EMPRESS	J3
ENFIELD	B7
EPSOM	G9
ERICA HEPBURN	J10
EVA CROMBIE	J10
FAIRBRIDGE	J7
FALCON	J2
FALKIRK	J6
FIFE	E5, F5
FIFTEENTH AVE	G4
FIFTH AVE	E4
FIFTH STREET EAST	G8
FIFTH STREET WEST	F7
FIRST AVE	D5, D6
FIRST ST	D3, G3, H7
FITZGERALD	A6
FLETCHER	F10
FORBES	C6
FORESTVALE	D2
FORRESTER	F10
FORT	E4, F4
FOURTEENTH AVE	G4
FOURTH AVE	E4
FOURTH RD	D3
FOURTH STREET	G2, G7
FRANCIS WARREN	J9
FRASER	J8
FREEMAN	E10
GALWAY	I5
GARRET	G2
GAUL	E9
GEORGE AVE	E9
GEORGE SILUNDIKA	E5, G5
GERTRUDE FATH	J9
GIFFORD	B6
GLENWOOD	I10
GOODWOOD	I10
GRANTHAM	I3
GREENFIELD SQUARE	A5
GREYVILLE	G9
GROSVENOR	B7
GWANDA	G2, G3
HADDON	F9
HALIFAX	J1
HALL	F10
HAMPSHIRE	J6
HARARE	D9
HARDING	A5
HAREWOOD	H10
HARRIS	A7
HAYTON	D7
HEANY	C6
HELM	B5
HENLEY	I3
HERBERT	A7
HERBERT CHITEPO	D4, F4
HEYMAN	E7, G7
HILLSIDE	G5, H5
HOOKTHORN	D2
HOSPITAL	A2
HUDSON	F10
HULL	I4
HUME PARK	E7
HUMEWOOD	I10
HUNT	A7
INGLEWOOD	I10
INSTITUTE	G3
IPSWICH	H4
IRENE COOK	J8
IRVINE	J6
J ZIYAPHAPHA	B2
JAGONDA	C2
JAMES POYA	C2
JASON MOYO	F4, E5
JOSIAH CHINAMANO	H3, J1
JOSIAH TONGOGARA	E6, G5
JOUBERT	E10
JUDO	A6
KENDY	C5
KENNEDY	A6
KENWOOD	I10
KINGSLEY	J7
KINGSWOOD	I10
KINLOCH	B5
KIRTON	A5
LADY STANLEY	A5
LANGDON	G10
LANGHTON	E10
LAWLEY	E8, G8
LEED	SI2
LEOPOLD TAKAWIRA	E4, F7, G10
LIVERPOOL	J2
LIVINGSTONE	E8, G8
LOBENGULA	D4, F4
LOCKWOOD	J10
LOSIKEYE	C1
LUDLOW HEWITT	E10
LUTON	H4
LUVEVE	C1
LYNNWOOD	I10
MACINTYRE	D6
MACLEAN	A7
MAIN	D5, G4
MANCHESTER	H3
MANJA KHUMALO	C1
MARY BURROWS	J9
MASOTSHA NDLOVU	C4, D6
MATOBO	I5
MAVER	J8
METCALFE SQUARE	G3
MICHERI	C1
MILITARY	F3
MILNERTON	G9
MOFFAT	B6
MORAY	J5
MORTUARY	F3
MOYO	B2
NEASDEN	I6
NEWALL	D10
NEWCASTLE	J1
NEWPORT	I2
NGAZIMBI	A2
NGCEBETSHA	B2, C2
NGUBOYENJA	C2
NINETEENTH AVE	I5
NINTH AVE	F5
NINTH RD	C3
NINTH STREET	E8
NKALA	B2
OAK	G6
OLD ESIGODINI	I9
OLD FALLS	A3
OLD KHAMI	F1, F3
PANTON	A6
PARK	E7, G7
PAULING	E8, G7
PEARD	B6
PEIRSE	D9, D10
PEMBURY	D7
PETERBOROUGH	J2
PHILIPS	I8
PHOENIX	J3
PLUMER	B6
PORTA	D10
POSSELT	A7
PRESTON	H3
PROSPECT	G3
QUEENS	B3, C2, C3, C6
RAGLAN	I6
RAILWAY	G3
READING	D7
REDRUP	D6
REDTHORN	D1
ROBERT MUGABE	B7, C6, F5
ROBERTSON	D6
ROXBURGH	J5
RUBY RORKE	J10
RUDD	B5
RUSSELL	E10
S MPOTU	B2
SADIE KAPLAN	D7
SADLER	G10
SALCOMBE	J6
SALMOND	D10
SAMUEL PARIRENYATWA	E6
SCOTT	B6
SECOND AVE	D5
SECOND ST	D3, H3, H7
SELOUS	C5
SEVENTEENTH AVE	I5
SEVENTH STREET	E8
SGT SAMUEL	D1
SHEARLEY CRIPPS	J7
SHEFFIELD	I2
SHERWOOD	I10
SINCLAIR	C7
SIR JAMES MCDONALD	E10
SITSHELA	C3
SIXTEENTH AVE	I5
SIXTH AVE	E4
SIXTH AVENUE EXT.	C2
SIXTH ST	C3, D3, F8
SPRECKLEY	C6
ST ANDREW'S	J6
ST LUKES	G10, I9
STANLEY	F10
STATION	D2
STEELWORKS RD EAST	F2
STEELWORKS	G1
STEWART	B6
STOCKTON	H4
STOKE	H4
STOURBRDIGE	J1
SWANSEA	I4
SWINDON	H4
TAYLOR	A6, C3, D4
TELFORD	C7
TENBY	J6
TENTH AVE	F5
TENTH RD	C3
THERESA SLY	J9
THIRD AVE	D4
THIRD AVENUE EXT.	D3
THIRD ST	G3, G7
THIRTEENTH AVE	G4
THORNGROVE	D2
THORNTON	D6
TOWNSEND	F9, G8
TOYNBEE	D8
TRELAWNY	D8
TRENCHARD	D10
TRENT	F1
TROJAN	I3
TWEED	I6
TWELFTH AVENUE	G6
TWENTIETH AVE	J5
TWENTY FIRST AVE	J5
TWENTY SECOND AVE	J5
TWENTY THIRD AVE WEST	J4
TWENTY THIRD AVE	J5
UNWIN	D7
VANGUARD	
VERA	
VERE STENT	
VINCENT	
WAKEFIELD	
WALBROOK	
WALLASEY	
WALLSEND	
WALSALL	
WALTER HOWARD	
WANDERER	
WAVERLEY	
WELBECK	
WENTWORTH	
WESTBURY	
WESTERNHAM	
WHITE	
WHITETHORN	
WICKLOW	
WIGTOWN	
WILLIAMS	
WILLOUGHBY	
WILTON	
WINDSOR	
WINGROVE	
WINNIES	
WISBECH	
WOBURN	
WOODBURY	
WOODSTOCK	
WOOLWICH	
WORKSHOPS	
WYCHWOOD	
YELDHAM	
YOUNG	

TO TETE/LILONGWE
TO CHILEKA AIRPORT
TO CHIKWAWA
TO BLANTYRE COLLEGE
TO ZOMBA/THYOLO/MULANJE
Mbayani
Mussa
Nayambadwe
Ndirande
Kabula
Mandala
Blantyre
Sunnyside
Mount Pleasant
Ginnery Corner
Chichiri
Chitawira
Njamba Park
Soche
Central
Manase
Zingwangwa
Nkolokosa
Kamoto
Welemu
Kapeni
Chinyonga
Kampala
Ndirande Forest Reserve
Mudi Dam
Chimwankhunda Dam
Malamulo Blantyre Clinic
Cathedral of St Paul
Hong Kong Restaurant
Le Meridien Mount Soche
Supermarket
Foreign Exchange Bureau
Hindu Temple
Library
Petrol Station
South African Airways
British Airways
Malawi Institute of Tourism
National Bank
British Consulate
District Commissioner's Office
Map Sales Office
Monument
Old Boma
Food Stalls
Municipal Market
Clock Tower
Blantyre Railway Station
Hotel Blantyre
Mwaiwanthu Private Hospital
St Michael's and All Angels Church
Henry Henderson Institute
Kapeni Theological School
Blantyre Girls' Primary School
Grace Bandawe Hostel
Blantyre Secondary School
Nyambadwe Primary School
St Andrew's Secondary School
Makata Primary School
Ndirande Primary School
Namalimwe School
Market
Dharad School
Blantyre Sports Club
Golf Course
Rangely Gardens
Mandala House
St Andrew's Primary School
Greek Club
Museum
Sports Ground
Chichiri Conference Centre
Trade Fair Grounds
Chichiri Showgrounds
Chichiri Stadium
Portuguese Club
Wanderers Club
Chichiri Secondary School
Chichiri Secondary School
Chichiri Cottage
Independence Arch
Red Cross
College of Medicine
Queen Elizabeth Central Hospital
Polytechnic
French Cultural Centre
Multi-Country Post & Telecommunications Training Centre
Jubilee Park
Catholic School
Seventh Day Adventist Primary School
Chitawira Homecraft Centre
Chitawira Primary School
Njamba MCDE School
MOTH Club
Zoo
South End School
St Pius School
Traditional Court
Kwacha International Conference Centre
Soche Technical School
Zingwangwa Primary School
Chimwankhunda School
Cemetery
M1
M2
M 800
Yd 800

TO AIRPORT 6 KM
M
Yd
Mikandjuine
Mafalala
Coop
Sommerchield
Malhangalene
Alto Maé
Central
Polana Cimento
Catembe
Rio Espírito Santo
Baía de Map
(Maputo Ba
PRAÇA 21 DE OUTUBRO
PRAÇA DO OMM
PRAÇA DO MERCADO
PRAÇA DA INDEPENDÊNCIA
PRAÇA DOS TRABALHADORES
PRAÇA 25 DE JUNHO
PRAÇA DA TRAVESSIA DO ZAMBEZE
PRAÇA ROBERT MUGABE
Police
Mercado
Cinema
Cemetery
Cooperativa De Arte Maconde
Mercado Janet
Museu de Revolução (Museum of the Revolution)
Moçambicano
Universo
Residencial Taj Mahal
Casa da Cultura
Louis Tregardt Trek Memorial Garden
Museu de Arte
Bazar do Povo
City Hall/ Civic Centre
Estadio do Ferroviário
Railway Station
Cathedral
Rovuma
Samora Machel Statue
French Cultural Centre
Casa do Ferro (Eiffel's 'House of Steel')
Mercado Central
Jardim Tunduru Botanical Gardens
British High Commission
Supreme Court
Tamariz
Archives
Central
Hotel Carlton
Bank
Turismo
Saturday Craft Market
Museu da Moeda
Buses
Fortaleza da Nossa Senhora da Conceição
Library
Tivoli
ENT
Theatre
Feira Popular
Stadium
Ferry to Catembe and Ponta do Ouro
Sports Ground
Maputo
FACIM Complex
Escola Nautica
Pensão Alegre
Santa Cruz
Andalucia
Girassol
Aviz
Pensão Martins
Intercape Bus Terminus
The Base Backpackers
Club Desportivo de Maxaquene (Swimming Pool)
Instituicão de Siencias
Maputo Central
Fatima's
Extravancia Crafts
Zambian High Commission
German Embassy
American Embassy
Santo Antonio Da Polana Church
Zimbabwean High Commission
President Palace
'Artedif' Crafts
Buses
Car Rental
Parque José Cabral
Instituto Nacional de Meteorologia
Observatorio
Polana
Canadian High Comnission
Dutch Embassy
Tanzanian High Commission
Hoyo-Hoyo
Bureau de Informação Público
Cinema
Terminus
SA Embassy
Museu de Geologia
Avenida
Villa Itália
Clube Naval
Museu de Historia Natural
Núcelo de Arte
Cardoso
Associação Cultural Tchova Xitaduma
AVENIDA DO PRESIDENTE CARMONA
AVENIDA 25 DE SETEMBRO
AVENIDA 10 DE NOVEMBRO
AVENIDA DA MARGINAL
AVENIDA EDUARDO MONDLANE
AVENIDA KENNETH KAUNDA
AVENIDA MARIEN NGOUAMBI
AVENIDA 24 DE JULHO
AVENIDA JULIUS NYERERE
AVENIDA MARTIRES DE INHAMINGA
A
B
C
D
E
F
G
H
I
J
2
3
4
5
6
7
8
9
10

AGOSTI C5
PEIO H5
O DE PAIVA I3
DO LAWLEY F4, F6
DE CORVO H3
RMANDO TIVANE E3, G5
ANIEL NAPATIMA F2
AHORA BASSA H4
ATEUS SANSÃO
HEMBA I3

AVE DE MAIO E3
AVE DE NAMPULA I6
AVE EDUARDO MONDLANE E4, G3
AVE PERO DE NAYA F3
AVE PODER POPULAR F2
AVE 24 DE JULHO D6, G5
AVE BASE N'TCHINGA B5, D3
AVE INDEPENDÊNCIA B9
B DIAS I5
BALTZAR DE ARAGÃO C5, E4

BRITO CAPELO I6
CCCXXXI G5
CHAIMITE C4, D5
COMANDANTE DIOGO DE SA E4
D FRANCISCO GORIAO I4
D FRANCISCO BARRETO G2
D FRANCISCO DE ALMEIDA H3
D JOAO DE CASTRO H4
DA BEIRA F2
DA ESTREMADURA D4

DE LOURENÇO MARQUES E4
DE PA CABRAL G2
DE PORTO AMÉLIA H6
DE S TOMÉ F2
DE SOFALA F4
DE TIMOR C5
DG DE SILVEIRA H3
DO ALENTEJO D4, C5
DO ALGARVE D4
DO COMANDANTE GAIVÃO H3
DO CORREIA F5

DO DOURO E3
DO GENERAL MACHADO H2
DOS AÇORES E2
DOS CAPITÃES DE SOFALA H5
DOS VICE REIS F4
ENG. ARTUR DO CANTO RESENDE F3
ESTEVAO DE ATAIDE H4
ESTRADA ACORDAS DE LUSAKA C5
ESTRADA K GOMES C6

ESTRADA MANGA A7
F DE MAGALHÃES H5
FERNÃO VELOSO F5
FERRAZ H3
FJ DOS SANTOS I4
FM PINTO I4
FREI JOÃO MADEIRA E5
GENERAL TEIXEIRA BOTELHO D4
GENERAL VIERA D4
JOÃO DE RESENDE E2

JOÃO QUIERO I6
L DE ALMEIDA H4
MACHADO I4
MAJOR SERPA PINTO F2
MARTIN AFONSO MELO I6
MÁRTIRES DE MASSANGANO E3
MOUZINHO DE ALBUQUERQUE G3, H4
N COELHO H3
NEVES FERREIRA F4
PEDRO NUNES H3

PRAÇA DA INDIA I5
RENATO BATISTA H3
ROBERTO IVENS H6
RUA I G2
SANCHA DE TOAR H3
SANCHEZ MIRANDA C4
SERPA PINTO I3
VASCO DA GAMA H6
VF DES ROMEN I4

Inhambane
3 DE FEVEREIRO B8
AVE ACORDOS DE LUSAKA C9
AVE DA VIGILANCIA B9
AVE REVOLUCÃO C9
DOS CONTINUADORES B9
MAIN ROAD C8, C9, D9

M 300
Yd 300
TO L'AÉROPORT D' IVATO/AMBOHIDRATRIMO
Antohomadinika
Behoririka
Lac Behoririka
Andravoahangy Ambony
Besarety
Beton
Soarano
Antananarivo Railway Station
Ambondrona
Faravohitra
Ankadivato
Tsaralanana
Isoraka
Ampefiloha
Lac Anosy
Monument aux Morts
Ambohidahy
Amparibe
Antsakaviro
Ambohijatovo
Antsahabe
Ankorahotra
Andohalo
Ankazotokana
Ambanidia
Ankadibevava
Stade Municipal de Mahamasina
Antsahatsiroa
Ambavahadimitafo
Befelatanana
Antsahondra
Canal
TO ARIVONIMAMO
TO AMBATOLAMPY
RN1
RN3
RN4
RN7
KENYA
TANZANIA
MOZAMBIQUE
INDIAN OCEAN
SEYCHELLES
VICTORIA
Praslin Island
Mahé
Zanzibar
Agalega Island (Mauritius)
COMOROS
Tromelin Island (France)
ANTANANARIVO
MADAGASCAR
MAURITIUS
PORT LOUIS
Réunion (Fr.)
KM 600
MI 300

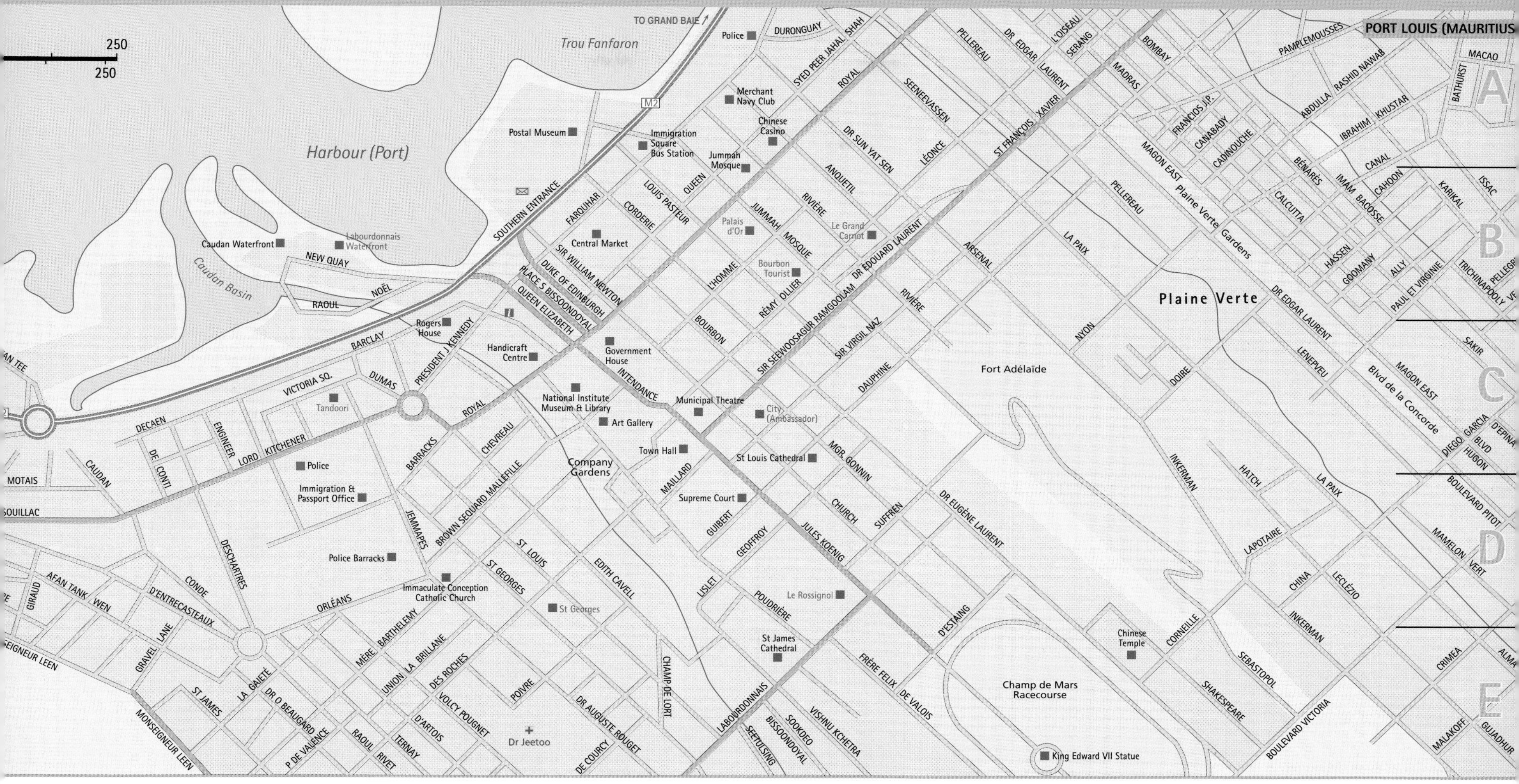

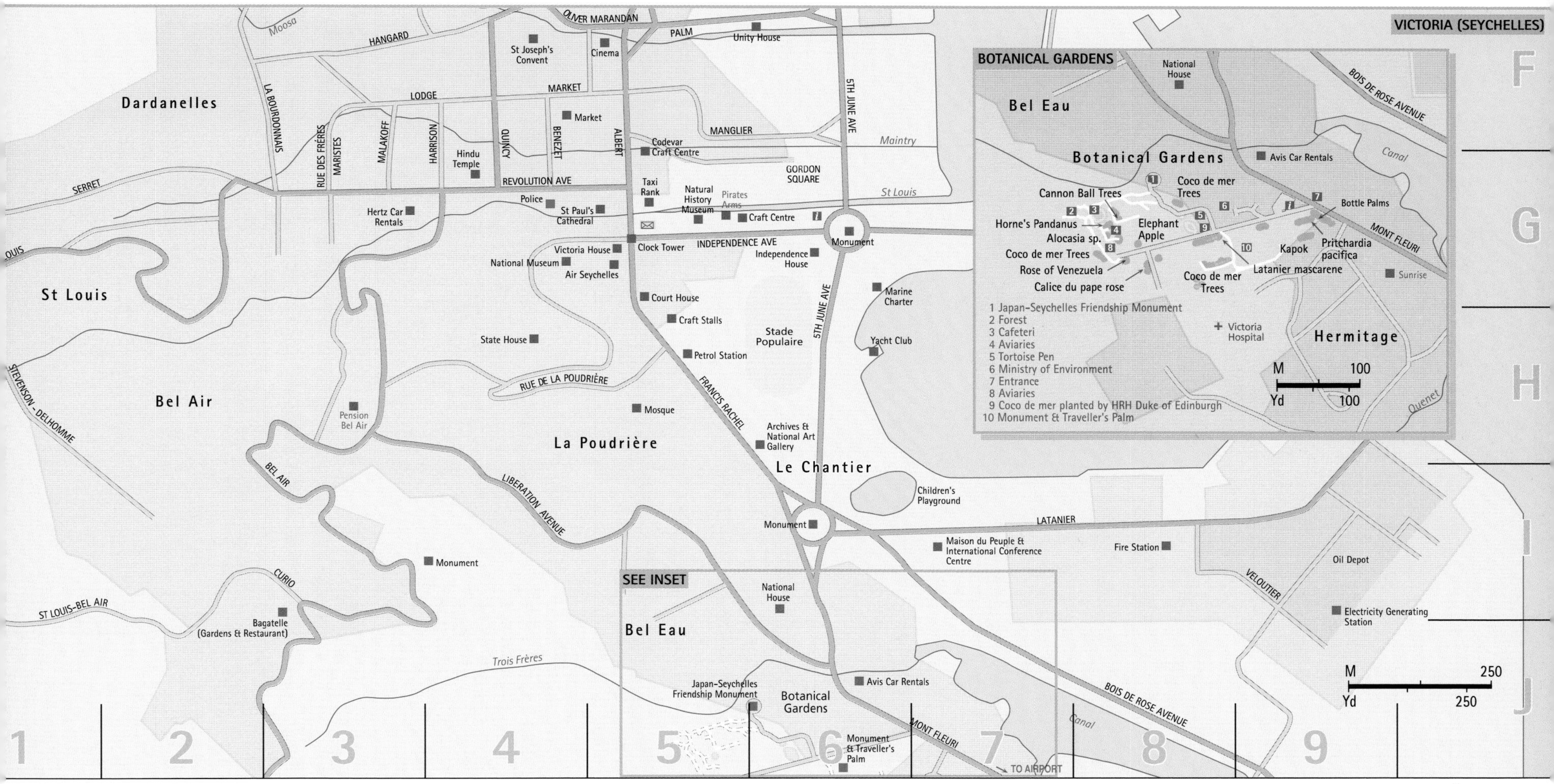

Port Louis

LLA RASHID NAWAB A9
TANK WEN D1
B10
E10
ETIL B6
NAL B7
LAY C3
ACKS C3
URST A10
ÈDÈRE D1
RÈS A9
BAY A8
EVARD HUGON C10
EVARD PITOT D10
EVARD VICTORIA E9
BON B5
WN SEQUARD
LLEFILLE D4
NOUCHE A9
ON B10

CALCUTTA B9
CANABADY A8
CANAL A10
CAUDAN C1
CHAMP DE LORT E5
CHEVREAU D4
CHINA D9
CHURCH D6
CONDE D2
CORDERIE B5
CORNEILLE E8
CRIMEA E10
D'ARTOIS E4
D'ENTRECASTEAUX D2
D'EPINAY C10
D'ESTAING D7
DAUPHINE C6
DE CONTI D2
DE COURCY E5
DECAEN C2
DES ROCHES E4
DESCHARTRES D2

DOIRE C8
DR AUGUSTE ROUGET E5
DR EDGAR LAURENT A7, B9
DR EDOUARDO LAURENT B6
DR EUGÈNE LAURENT D7
DR O BEAUGARD E3
DR SUN YAT SEN A6
DUKE OF EDINBURGH B4
DUMAS C3
DURONGUAY A6
ENGINEER C2
FARQUHAR B5
FRANCIOS J.P. A8
FRÈRE FELIX DE VALOIS E6
GEOFFROY D6
GIRAUD D1
GOOMANY B9
GRAVEL LANE E2
GUIBERT D5
GUJADHUR E10
HASSEN B9

HATCH C9
IBRAHIM KHUSTAR A9
IMAM BACOSSE B9
INKERMAN C8, E9
INTENDANCE C5
ISSAC A10
JEMMAPES D3
JULES KOENIG D6
JUMMAH MOSQUE B6
KARIKAL B10
KWAN TEE C1
L'HOMME B5
LA GAIETÉ E2
LA PAIX B8, D9
LABOURDONNAIS E5
LAPOTAIRE D9
LECLÉZIO D9
LENEPVEU C9
LÉONCE A7
LISLET D5
L'OISEAU A7
LORD KITCHENER C2

LOUIS PASTEUR B5
MACAO A10
MADRAS A8
MAGON EAST A8, C10
MAILLARD D5
MALAKOFF E10, G3
MAMELON VERT D10
MAUPIN D1
MGR. GONNIN C6
MÈRE BARTHELEMY E3
MONSEIGNEUR LEEN E1, E2
MOTAIS D1
NEW QUAY B3
NOËL B3
NYON C8
ORLÉANS D3
P DE VALENCE E3
PAMPLEMOUSSES A9
PAUL ET VIRGINIE B10
PELLEGRIN B10
PELLEREAU A7, B8
PLACE S BISSOONDOYAL B4

POIVRE E4
POUDRIÈRE D6
PRESIDENT J KENNEDY C4
QUEEN ELIZABETH B4
QUEEN B5
RAOUL B3
RAOUL RIVET E3
RÉMY OLLIER B6
RIVIÈRE B6, B7
ROYAL A6, C4
SAKIR C10
SEBASTOPOL E9
SEENEEVASSEN A7
SEETULSING E6
SERANG A8
SHAKESPEARE E8
SIR SEEWOOSAGUR RAMGOOLAM C6
SIR VIRGIL NAZ C6
SIR WILLIAM NEWTON B4
SOOKDEO BISSOONDOYAL E6
SOUILLAC D1

SOUTHERN ENTRANCE B4
ST FRANÇOIS XAVIER A8
ST GEORGES D4
ST JAMES E2
ST LOUIS D4
SUFFREN D6
SYED PEER JAHAL SHAH A6
TERNAY E3
TRICHINAPOOLY B10
UNION LA BRILLANE E3
VELE B10
VICTORIA SQ. C3
VISHNU KCHETRA E6
VOLCY POUGNET E4

Victoria

5TH JUNE AVE F6, H6
ALBERT G5
BEL AIR I3
BENEZET F4
BOIS DE ROSE AVENUE F10, J8
CURIO I3
FRANCIS RACHEL H5
GORDON SQUARE G6
HANGARD F3
HARRISON G4
INDEPENDENCE AVE G5
LA BOURDONNAIS F3
LATANIER I7
LIBERATION AVE I4
LODGE F3
MONT FLEURI G10, J7
OLIVER MARANDAN F4
PALM F5
QUINCY F4
REVOLUTION AVE G4

RUE DE LA POUDRIÈRE H4
RUE DES FRÉRES MARISTES G3
SERRET G1
ST LOUIS G1
ST LOUIS-BEL AIR I1
STEVENSON-DELHOMME H1
VELOUTIER I9

A KLOPPERS	E1
A RUPERT	A5
AANDBLOM	B2
ABT	D5
ADLER	F5
AJ TITUS	D1
AKWAMARYN	B8
ALBATROSS	I2
ALEXANDER	E3
ALIES	D3
AMASONIET	A9
ANDERSON	F8
ANDRADIET	C8
ANDREW KLOPPERS	D2
ANDROMEDA	G2
ANEMONE	D1
ANGELIER	B3
ANTILIA	G2
ANZ	I10
APUS	F2
ARA	E2, E3
ARIANS	H10
ARIES	F3, G2, G3
ARMSTRONG	J6
ASBLOM	B2
ASTER	B2
ATLAS	C8
AUGUST GOTZ	D5
AUOB	C9
AUSSPAN	I7
AUSSPANPLATZ	I7
AUSWÄRTS	D1, F2
B PHILLIPS	E1
BACH	E3, F3, G3, G4, H5
BAHNHOF	F6
BALLOT	J8
BAMBOOPALM	E2
BANTING	F4
BARBET	I4
BARELLA	G9
BASSINGTH-WALGHTE	G10
BEETHOVEN	F4
BEHRING	F4
BELL	J7
BERG	G10
BERKER	G9
BEST	F3
BISMARCK	G6, H6
BLENKINSOP	D5
BOHR	J5
BOK	I6
BORGWARD	B2
BOTTLEPALM	E3
BOWKER	F9, F10
BRAHMS	G5
BRANDBERG	D6
BREITING	H9
BRITS	E8
BROCK	E10
BRUG	A1, A2
BÜLOW	F5, G6
BURG	I8
CAMPBELL	J7
CANDYPALM	E3
CAPRIVI	E9
CENTAURUS	J8
CHAPMAN	G9
CHATEAU	I8
CHOPIN	H5
CHRISTIAN	I9
CHRYSLER	B1, C2
CHURCH	H6
CLEOPATRA	F2
COCOPALM	E2
COETZÉ	J3
COLUMBIA	G1
CONRAD RUST	F10
CORVUS	H2
CRATER	G2
CROHN	F7
CRUX	G3
CURIE	F4
D MUNAMAWA	G7
DALTON	J5
DAVID BEZUIDENHOUT	C1
DE JAGER	D9
DE VILIERS	D5
DE WILT	D5
DELFOS	B4
DELPHINIUS	G2
DIAMANT	C2
DINTER	E9, E10
DODGE	C2
DOLLAR	B2
DR VAN ECK	B4
DR W KÜLZ	I6
DRAKENSBERG	C8, D9
E MENZAH	E2
E OPPENHEIMER	A4
EADIE	I9
EDELVALK	H4
EDISON	J5, J6
EDSEL	B2
EGRET	I4
EINSTEIN	J5
EISEB	D8
ELLIS	E6
ERIKSON	H6
ERNST WEISKE	D4
ERONGO	D7
EROS	C8, D7
ESSEN	B5
ETIENNE ROSSEAU	A4
ETNA	C6
EULEN	H4
EVEREST	C8
F FERRIS	D1
FALKEN	I2
FARADAY	J7
FARGO	B2
FELD	I7, J8
FERRY	J7
FESTE	I9
FLAMINK	H2
FLORENCE NIGHTINGALE	C1,D3
FORBES	C2
FORSYTHE	J3
FORTUNA	E2
FRANC	B3, C3
FREUD	F6
FREYN	E8
FRIEDEN	I9
G DIERGAARD	D2
GALEN	F4
GALILEI	J7
GARNET	F1
GARTEN	H7
GATHEMANN	F9
GAUSNIP	I2
GEMINI	G2
GESELL	E6
GEVERS	G10
GIRAFFE	C5
GLÜCK	G5
GOSHAWK	H4
GREGOROWSKI	C4
GRENDON	J7
GRIEG	G5
GRIMM	E7
GUSINDE	E9
GUTENBERG	I7
GUTSCHE	C9, D9
H VAN ECK	D1
HADDY	H5
HAHNEMANN	E3
HAKOS	C8
HAMERKOP	I3
HAMMAN	F10
HANEKAM	B1
HARVEY	E4, E5
HAYDN	G5
HEINITZBURG	H8
HELIODOOR	C7
HENDRIK WITBOOI DRIVE	G2, I2
HERCULES	F2
HERZINGER	F10
HIPPOKRATES	F3
HOCHLAND	I5, J1
HOCHLAND	J2
HOLDEN	C1
HOOGENHOUT	H6
HOSEA KUTAKO DRIVE	A5, E6, J5
HÜGEL	H8
HUGO HAHN	H10
HUGO	D5
HYDRA	G3
IBIS	I1
INDEPENDENCE AVE	A4, C6, E6
IRLE	I9
ISABELLA	B2
J HAUPT	D2
J JULIUS	D1
J VRIES	D2
JAAP SNYDER	C3
JADE	E1
JAGUAR	B1
JAN JONKER	I7, J9
JAN MARAIS	A4
JASMYN	B2
JENNER	F3, F5
JOHANN ALBRECHT	D5, E5
JOHN MEINERT	F5, F6
JOHN SIMMS	D4
JORDAN	J3
JP ANDRIES	D1
KALIE ROODT	A4
KALK	H7
KASINO	G7
KASTELL	I9
KELKIEWYN	I3
KELLER	E7
KEPLER	I5
KERBY	H6
KESTREL	H3
KEVIN	I5
KILIMANJARO	C7
KINGFISHER	H2
KINOPALM	E3
KOCH	H10
KOESTER	D1
KONING	E9
KORHAAN	I1
KORNALYN	E1, F1
KÖRNER	E7, F7
KORT	I6
KROON	B2
KUISEB	C9, D8
KUNENE	D9
KUPFERBERG	C8
KWÊVOËL	H2
L HENDRICKS	D1
LAZARETT	I7, J6
LE ROUX	H10
LEO	G2
LEWERIK	J2
LEWIS	I6
LIBRA	H2
LILIENCRON	C7, E7
LINDEQUIST	G7
LISTER	E5
LISZT	I6
LORENTZ	E9
LOSSEN	I7
LOTZ	G10
LOUIS BOTHA	G5
LÜDERITZ	F7
LUTHER	E7
MAHEM	I4
MALAGIET	E1
MANDUME NDEMFAYO AVE	J6
MARABOE	J2
MARAIS	E7
MARCH	E5
MARCONI	J5
MARITZ	H10
MAYO	E3
MEASS	C2
MENSA	G2
MERCEDES	B2
MERCURY	G3
MERENSKY	I7
METJE	E9, F9
MIDDLEWICK	D5
MOKKE	G9
MOLTKE	F7
MONT BLANC	D7
MOZART	G5
MU GREEF	C2
NACHTIGAL	I6
NAUKLUFT	C8
NELSON MANDELA AVE	D7, G10
NESER	I8
NEWTON	I8
NGAMI	E8
NOBEL	J6
NOSSOB	C7
OKAVANGO	D9
OMARURU	B7
OMATAKO	D8
ONIKS	F1
OOIEVAAR	D4, D5
ORANGE	D9
ORBAN	H8
ORIOLE	H3
OSLER	E6
OSPREY	I3
OSSMANN	E8
OTTO NITZSCHE	H10
OUTENIQUA	D7
P VAN HARTES	D2, E2
PALOMAR	C8
PAPAGEIEN	I4, I5, H4
PARK	G7
PASTEUR	F3, F5
PATTERSON	J7
PAVLOV	F5
PAVO	G1
PELIKAN	H1
PENGUIN	J2
PÊREL	D9
PERLHUHN	I1
PERSEUS	G2
PETER MÜLLER	G6
PETTENKOFER	E5
PHOENIX	G2
PIENAAR	J3
PIETERSEN	B5, C2, C3
PLAATJIES	C2
PLANCK	J5
POND	B2
POST	G6
PRINCESSPALM	E3
PROMENADEN	D7
PULLMAN	C6
PURCELL	H5
QUAIL	H2
R HERCULES	E1
RABEN	H3, I3
RAND	A2, B3, C3
REHOBOTHER	I7
REIHER	H2
REV. M SCOTT	H7, I7
RHINO	C5
RIETHAAN	H2
ROBERT MUGABE AVE	E7, I8
ROBIN	I1, I2
ROBYN	A9
ROENTGEN	G4
ROLLS ROYCE	B1
ROMBERG	G6
ROSS	E5
ROSSING	C8
ROSSINI	F6
ROWAN	D6
RUDOLPH HERTZOG	I5
RUGGENBACH	D6
RUHR	A6
RUSCH	H9
RYKVOET HOEPFNER	G9
SAFFIER	A9
SAGITIA	G3
SALK	F4
SAM NUJOMA DRIVE	H2, H6, H8
SANDERBURG	I9
SANDPIPER	H4
SARD	E1
SAUERBRUCH	E3
SAUER	C5
SCHANZEN	E7, E8
SCHILLER	E7
SCHMEREMBECK	H5
SCHOEMAN	D5
SCHÖNLEIN	E4
SCHUBERT	G5
SCHWABE	I10
SCHWEITZER	F5
SCHWENRINSBURG	H8
SCORPIA	H3
SCULPTOR	G2
SEITZ	J8
SEKRETAR	J2
SHAKESPEARE	D7
SHANGHAI	A1
SHEFFIELD	B5
SHEPPMANN	J1
SHINZ	I6
SHWABE	I10
SIMPSON	F4
SINCLAIR	F8
SPEGT	H1
SPITSKOP	C8
STARK	E9
STEIN	H10
STEIN	I10
STELZEN	H1
STEPHENSON	C5
STERLING	B2, C2
STOKE	J7
STORCH	G5
STRAUSS	G4
STÜBEL	G6
STURROCK	C4
SUNBIRD	I4
SWARTBERG	C8
T LOUW	A5
TAL	G6
TARPEY	D4
TAUBEN	H1, I2
TAURUS	
THOMPSON	
THORER	
TOMMIE MULLER	
TREVITHICK	
TROTHA	
TROUPAND	
TURKOOIS	
UGAB	
UHLAND	E7,
VAN COLLER	
VAN DER BIJL	
VAN ECKENBRECHER	
VAN RHIJN	
VEDDER	
VELA	
VENNING	
VERBENA	
VERDI	
VESTA	
VILJOEN	
VIRGO	
VOIGTS	
VOLANS	
VON BRAUN	
VON BURGDORFF	
VORAL	
W BOTHA	
W CAMM	
W KAPUENENE	
WAGNER	
WARD	
WATT	
WEBB	
WEBER	
WECKE	
WELLS	
WESTERN BYPASS	
WILLAN	
WILLIAMS	
WINTERBERG	
WOERMANN	
YSKOR	
ZIEGENFUSS	
ZIEGLER	E
ZWARTS	

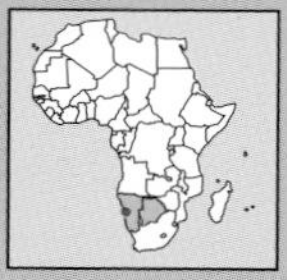

STREETPLANS
Swakopmund
ATLANTIC OCEAN
Namib-
Naukluft
Park
Walvis Bay
Dolphin Beach
Surfer's Paradise
Bird Rock
Lighthouse
Willis Beach
Dune Seven
Bird Paradise
Marine Deposits Fossilized Shells
Walvis Bay Nat Res
Kuiseb River Delta
Rooibank
DUNES
TO WINDHOEK
Welwitschia Plains
Camel Farm
Rossmund Golf Course
Goanikontes
Swakop
Kuiseb
KM 15
MI 8
WALVIS BAY
Kuisebmond
Industrial
ATLANTIC OCEAN
Jetty
Harbour
Walvis Bay Railway Station
Walvis Bay Lagoon
Meersig
Golf Course
Lagoon Lodge
Langholm
Courtyard
The Spawning Ground
Protea Lodge
Atlantic
Cinema
Town Hall
Municipal Offices
Library
Museum
Police
North Hospital
Jan Wilken Stadium
Civic Centre
Magistrates' Court
Church
Casa Mia
Asgard House
Kuisebmond Municipal Offices
South Hospital
TO SWAKOPMUND
1000
SWAKOPMUND
M 500
Yd 500
ATLANTIC OCEAN
Tamariskia
Vineta
Central Sports Field
Industry
Kramersdorf
Cemetery
Mole
Swimming Bath
Strand
Museum
Magistrates' Office
Lighthouse
State House
Kristall Galerie
Police
Swakopmund
Swakopmund Railway Station
Kalabash Sports Bar
Schweizerhaus
Hansa
Atlanta
Air Namibia
Rapmund
Wildlife/Conservation
Woermannhaus
Library
Buses
Jay Jays
Tug Boat Pub
Jetty
Deutches Haus
Omeg
Grüner Kranz
Schütze
D'Avignon
Europa Hof
Prinzessin-Rupprecht-Heim
Youth Hostel
Garni Adler
National Marine Aquarium
Sculletus House
TO HENTIES BAY
TO WINDHOEK
TO DUNES & MUNICIPAL CAMPSITE
Swakop
C34
B2
1 2 3 4 5 6 7 8 9
A B C D E F G H I J

BOTSWANA
Molepolole
Thamaga
GABORONE
Kanye
Lobatse
Mmathethe
SOUTH AFRICA
Groot Marico
Zeerust
Mafikeng
TO MAHALAPYE
TO RUSTENBURG
KM 40
MI 20
TO INTERNATIONAL AIRPORT
TO FRANCISTOWN
TO MOLEPOLOLE
TO THAMAGA
TO LOBATSE
TO TLOK
Broadhurst
Tsholofelo Park
Segoditshane
Madibeng
Phologolo
Badiri
Mmaraka
Dilalelo
Selamela
Boitshoko
Sekgwa
Mophato
Village
Bontleng
Madirelo
Babusi
Old Naledi
Naledi
Ngotwane
Golf Course
National Stadium
Former BDF Airport
University of Botswana
Princess Marina Hospital
Gaborone Sun
National Museum & Art Gallery
The Mall
Government Enclave
National Assembly
Office of the President
Gaborone Railway Station
Showgrounds
Cemetery
Botswana Polytechnic
Botswana Technology Centre
Automotive Training School
Nalendi Secondary School
Bokamoso Community Secondary School
Sports Fields
M 500
Yd 500

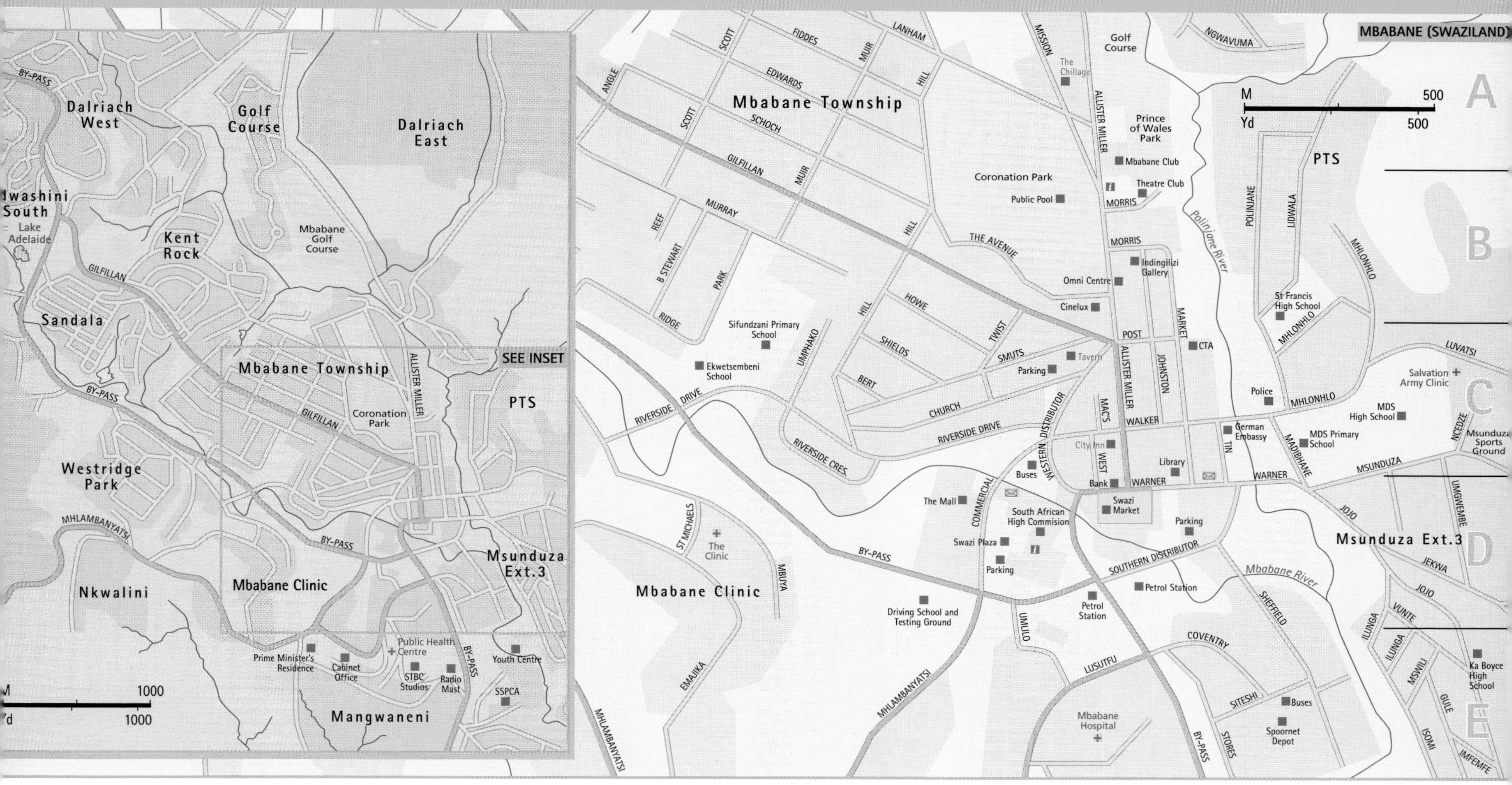

MBABANE (SWAZILAND)
Dalriach West
Golf Course
Dalriach East
Mbabane Golf Course
Kent Rock
Sandala
Westridge Park
Nkwalini
Mbabane Township
Coronation Park
SEE INSET
PTS
Mbabane Clinic
Msunduza Ext.3
Mangwaneni
Prime Minister's Residence
Cabinet Office
Public Health Centre
STBC Studios
Radio Mast
Youth Centre
SSPCA
M 1000
Yd 1000
Mbabane Township
Coronation Park
Public Pool
Golf Course
The Chillage
Prince of Wales Park
Mbabane Club
Theatre Club
Indingilizi Gallery
Omni Centre
Cinelux
Tavern
Parking
CTA
St Francis High School
Salvation Army Clinic
Police
MDS High School
MDS Primary School
German Embassy
Msunduza Sports Ground
Sifundzani Primary School
Ekwetsembeni School
City Inn
Library
Bank
Buses
The Mall
South African High Commission
Swazi Market
Swazi Plaza
Parking
The Clinic
Mbabane Clinic
Msunduza Ext.3
Petrol Station
Driving School and Testing Ground
Mbabane River
Ka Boyce High School
Mbabane Hospital
Buses
Spoonret Depot
M 500
Yd 500

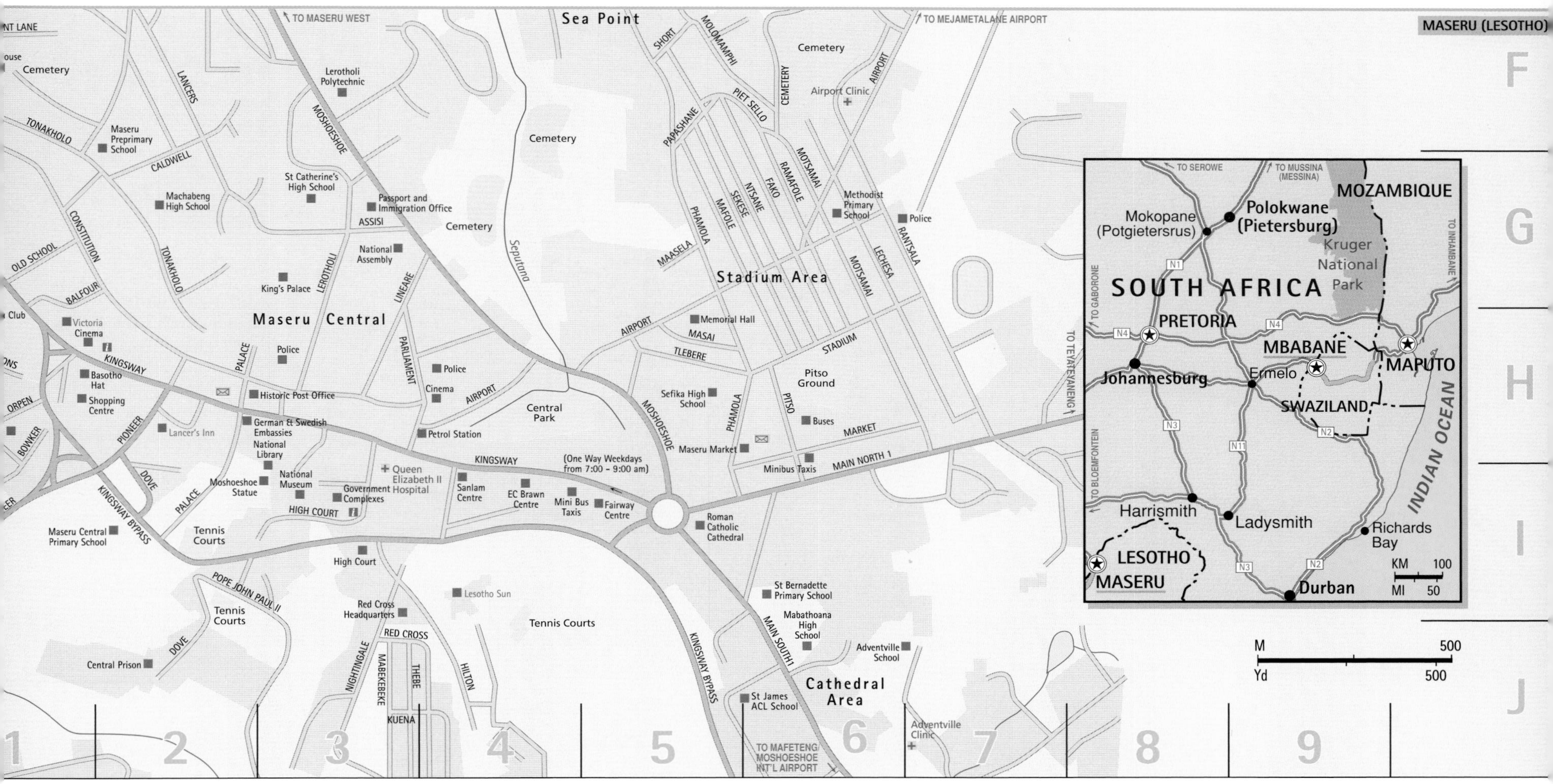

MASERU (LESOTHO)
TO MASERU WEST
Sea Point
TO MEJAMETALANE AIRPORT
Cemetery
Airport Clinic
Lerotholi Polytechnic
Maseru Preprimary School
Machabeng High School
St Catherine's High School
Passport and Immigration Office
National Assembly
King's Palace
Maseru Central
Victoria Cinema
Basotho Hat
Shopping Centre
Police
Historic Post Office
German & Swedish Embassies
National Library
Lancer's Inn
Moshoeshoe Statue
National Museum
Government Complexes
Queen Elizabeth II Hospital
Cinema
Petrol Station
Central Park
Sanlam Centre
EC Brawn Centre
Mini Bus Taxis
Fairway Centre
(One Way Weekdays from 7:00 – 9:00 am)
Methodist Primary School
Police
Stadium Area
Memorial Hall
Sefika High School
Pitso Ground
Buses
Maseru Market
Minibus Taxis
Roman Catholic Cathedral
Maseru Central Primary School
Tennis Courts
High Court
Red Cross Headquarters
Lesotho Sun
Tennis Courts
Central Prison
St Bernadette Primary School
Mabathoana High School
Adventville School
St James ACL School
Cathedral Area
Adventville Clinic
TO MAFETENG/ MOSHOESHOE INT'L AIRPORT
TO TEYATEYANENG
M 500
Yd 500
MOZAMBIQUE
Polokwane (Pietersburg)
Mokopane (Potgietersrus)
Kruger National Park
SOUTH AFRICA
PRETORIA
MBABANE
Ermelo
MAPUTO
Johannesburg
SWAZILAND
INDIAN OCEAN
Harrismith
Ladysmith
Richards Bay
LESOTHO
MASERU
Durban
TO SEROWE
TO MUSSINA (MESSINA)
TO GABORONE
TO BLOEMFONTEIN
TO INHAMBANE
KM 100
MI 50

ALBANY	C4
ALBERT	H6, H8
ALBRECHT	G9
ALEXANDER	H4
ALYTHENZIE	A4
AMESHOFF	D4
ANDERSON	H5, H7
ANDERSON WEST	H4
ANDRIES	F10
ANGLE	F9
ANNET	D1
ASCOT	E10
AURET	G9, H10
AVENUE	G2, G3
AVENUE	G3
BANKET	E7
BARBARA	I7
BARKLY	B2, B3
BARRY HERTZOG	B1
BEACON	F9
BEAUFORT	F10
BEIT	E8
BEIT	E9
BEREA	G9
BERTHA	E4
BERTRAMS	E10
BETTY	G9, H9
BEZUIDENHOUT	F10, G4
BICCARD	D5, F5
BITCON	J6
BLACKWOOD	B5
BOK	E6, E7
BONANZA	I2
BOOYSENS	I5
BREE	F7, G1, G3, G5
BROAD	J5
BUNTING	D1
BURGERSDORP	G2
BUSWAY	I3
BUXTON	E8, F8
CAMPBELL	B2
CARLOW	A1
CARR	F2, F4
CENTRAL	G1, G2, H2
CHARLES	F8
CITY AND SUBURBAN	H9
CLAIM	E7
CLARE	H2
CLARE	H3
CLARENCE	F10
CLUNY	A4
COMMERCIAL	G1
COMMISSIONER	G7, G10
CORNELIUS	H7
COWIE	A4
CROWN	H1
CURREY	F8, F9
DARCY	H5
DARNAWAY	A5
DAVIES	E8, F8
DAWE	F10
DE BEER	E4
DE KORTE	E4, E6
DE LA REY	E1
DE VILLIERS	F6, F7
DE VILLIERS GRAAFF	B5, F3
DELVERS	G7
DENNIS	I7
DERBY	E10
DF MALAN	B6
DIAGONAL	G5
DORA	E9
DOVETON	B2
DUMP	J5
DUNCOMBE	A4
DURBAN	H8, H9
DURRIS	A4
DU TOIT	G1
EARP	J3
EASTERN BYPASS	B9
EDITH CAVELL	E7
EENDRACHT	E3
EIGHTH	E1, F9, H1
ELEVENTH	F1
ELOFF	E6, F6, G6, I6
ELOFF EXT.	J6
EMPIRE	C1, C3, C6
END	E8, F8, G8
END STREET EXT.	H8
ENOCH SONTONGA	E2
EPLER	G3
EPPING	A5
ERIN	E10
ERROR	F9
ESCOMBE	B2
ETON	B4
FALKLANDS	C3
FARADAY	I6, I7
FAWCUS	H9
FENNEL	J7
FERREIRA	H5
FIFTEENTH	F1
FIFTH	E1, F10, G1
FIRST	E1, E10
FOUNTAIN	H2
FOURTEENTH	F1
FOURTH	E1, F10, G1
FOX	G6, G7, G9, G10, H4
FRASER	G5
FREDERICK	H6
FRERE	C3, E10
FROST	D1
FULLER	E10
GALE	C2
GARRETT	B3
GILLIES	G2
GIRTON	C5
GOCH	G3
GODFREY	I5
GOUD	G7, H8
GOUS	F10
GRAF	E3
GRAHAMSTOWN	H7
GUILD	C1
GUS	G10, H10
HADFIELD	E7
HALL	H5
HANAU	H10
HANCOCK	F7
HANOVER	G1, H1
HANS PIROW	J4
HANS	G10, H10
HARDY	H7
HARRIES	H6
HARRIS	H4
HARRISON	F5
HARRISON EXT.	H5
HEIDELBERG	I7
HEIDELBERG	J9
HEIGHT	E8
HEIGHT	F8
HENRI	E4
HERB	F9
HIGH	G2, H2
HILLCREST	A1
HILLSIDE	C5
HOEK	E6
HOOFD	D4, D5
HOOP	J1
HOSPITAL	E6
HUBERT	H4
HULBERT	J7
HULL	E1, F1
IBIS	D1
IGNATIUS	I4
JAN SMUTS	B3, D4
JANIE	G10, H10
JAY	D1
JEPPE	F7, G3, G5
JOHN PAGE	G10
JOHN WEST	J4
JORISSEN	E4
JOUBERT	D5, E6, G6, H6
JUBILEE	B5
JULES	H10
JUTA	E4, E5
KARL	G10, H10
KAY	H5
KERK	G6, G8
KERK ST MALL	G4
KING GEORGE	E6, F6
KLEIN	E6, F7
KOCH	F6, F7
KORT	G5
KRAUSE	F1
KRUGER	G9
KRUIS	F6, G6, H6
LANGERMAN	G1, H1
LARK	D1
LAUB	J7
LAWLEY	A3
LAWRENCE	A1
LEMON	C1
LEWIS	C1
LEYDS	E5, E6, E7
LIDDLE	E10
LILIAN	G2, H2
LIME	C1
LOCH	B2, B3
LONDON	J5
LOVEDAY	D5, E5, F5, H6, I6
LOVEDAY ST SOUTH	J6
LOVERS WALK	H2
LOWER PAGE	G9
LOWER RAILWAY	F9
LOWER ROSS	G9
LUTTIG	G2
MACINTYRE	G10, H10
MADISON	G10, H10
MAIN	G3, G7, G10, H5
MAIN RD EAST	B1
MAIN REEF	H3, I1
MALAN	G2
MALHERBE	G2
MARITZBURG	H9
MARKET	G4, G6, G8, G9, G10
MARSHALL	G10, H4, H7
MARTIN	I4
MAY	H2
MEIKLE	H8
MELLE	D4, E4
MELROSE	H7
MILLBOURNE	E10
MILLER	F10
MINNAAR	G3
MINT	G2, H2
MOOI	G7, H7
MOSELEY	F8
NAPIER	B2
NARMADA	I1
NEW N	H6
NEW S	H6
NEWTON	I7
NIND	E8
NINTH	E1, F9, H1
NOORD	F5, F6, F7
NORTH PARK	F9
NUGGET	E8, G8, H8
NURSERY	H3
ORANGE	C1
OVE	F9
OVERBEEK	F9
OWL	C1
OXFORD	A5, B4, B5
PALALA	A3
PALLINGHURST	A3, B3
PARIS	J5
PARK	F10, G10, H8
PARK DRIVE	H1
PARK LANE	G3
PARK RD	G3
PARKTOWN-WESTCLIFF HERITAGE WALK	B5
PAT MBATHA BUS & TAXIWAY	J3
PEARSE	E8
PHILLIP	H8
PIETERSEN	E7
PIM	F4, G3
PINE	H3
PIONEER	H2
PLEIN	F5, F7
POLLY	G7, H7
PRESIDENT	G4, G7
PRESS	J1, J2
PRINCESS	F10
PRITCHARD	G5, G7
PROP	J5
QUARTZ	E7, F7
QUEEN ELIZABETH	E4
QUEENS	C1, C6
QUINCE	C1
QUINN	F3
RAIKES	E2
RAILWAY	G1
RHODES	C3
RICHARDS	J5
RING	F1, G1
RISSIK	F5, G5, H6
ROCK RIDGE	B4
ROCKEY	F8
ROGERS	J4
ROPER	J7
ROSETTENVILLE	H7, J7
RUARGH	J5
SALISBURY	H6
SANS SOUCI	B1
SARATOGA	E8
SAUER	G5
SAUER EXT.	H5
SCHOOL	H8
SCRAPER	J3
SEYMOUR	C3
SHAFT	H3
SHERBORNE	B4
SHORE	G9
SECOND	E1,F10
SEVENTEENTH ST	F1
SEVENTH	E1, F9, G1
SHERWELL	E8, F8
SHERWOOD	A4
SIEMERT	E8
SIMMONDS	D5, E5, G5, H5
SIMMONDS SOUTHWAY	J5
SIVEWRIGHT	E9
SIXTEENTH	F1
SIXTH	E1, F10, G1
SMAL	F6, H7
SMAL ST MALL	G6
SMIT	E3, E5, E6, E7, F2
SOLOMON	E2
SOMERSET	G1, H1
SOUTH PARK	F9
SOUTHERN BYPASS	D8
SOWETO HIGHWAY	D6
SPRINZ	I7
ST ANDREWS	C4
ST DAVIDS	C4
STAIB	F9
STANLEY WEST	C1
STATION	E4
STEPHENSON	I6, I7
STIEMENS	E4
STOTT	I6
SUBWAY	F1
SUTHERLAND	E6
SYDENHAM	G3
TENTH	E1, H1
TERRACE	H2
THAMES	E10
THE OVAL	C5
THE VALLEY ROAD	A2, A4
THIRD	E1, F10
THIRTEENTH	F1
THORPE	H5
TORRANCE	E2
TORWOOD	A4
TREMATON	B5
TREU	
TROYE	
TRUMP	
TRUMP WEST	
TWELFTH	F
TWIST	
UPPER RAILWAY	
UPPER ROSS	
USSHER	
USUTU	
VAN BEEK	E
VERWEY	
VICTORIA	
VILLAGE	
VLAK	
VON BRANDIS	
VON WIELLIGH	
VOORHOUT	
WABORD	
WALL	
WANDERERS	
WATERFALL	
WAUCHOPE	
WEBBER	I4,
WELLINGTON	
WEMMER JUBILEE	
WEMMER PAN	
WESTCLIFF	
WESTERN	
WESTERN BYPASS	
WESTEX	
WEST	F4, G4, H
WILHELMINA	
WINCHESTER	
WOLHUTER	H4
WOLMARANS	E
WYCHWOOD	
YALE	D
YAMUNA	

ES	D5, F5, H5, I5	BROWN	D5	DU TOIT	C6, F7	HANS PIROW	J8	LOVEDAY	J10	ORCHARD	F10	PROES EAST	D7	SKIETPOORT	I3	VAN DER BYL	F6
BOTHA	A10	BUREAU	E4	DWARS	H9	HOPP	H4	LUDO	I1	PADNOLLER	G7	QUEEN	E5	SKINNER	F2, F6, G1	VAN DER WALT	D5, F5, H6, I6
ERY ROW	H2	CAPE	J2	EDMOND	D8	HOSPITAL	D7	LUKAS	J10	PALACE	E4	READ	H6	SKINNER LANE	G2	VERMEULEN	E1, E3
DEL	J1	CELLIERS	G8, I8	EDWARD	D7, E7	INEZ	G7	MAGASYN	J2	PAPAWER	J2	REITZ	H10	SOETDORING	I2	VERMEULEN EAST	E5
ST	B10	CENTRAL	E5	ELANDSPOORT	J7	JACOB MARE	H4, H5	MALAN	A9	PARK	F10	RELLY	H10	SOUTPANSBERG	B7, B10	VILJOEN	A10, B10
	D8	CHRISTINA	H4	ELEVENTH	C2	JAN SMUTS	J6	MARGARETHA	C5	PARK LANE	G5	RHODES	H6	SPUY	G10	VISAGIE	G3, G5
	E4	CHURCH	E3, E5, E8	ERICA	G7	JEPPE	F8	MEARS	G7	PARLIAMENT	E4	RIDGE	J7, J9	ST PATRICKS	J7	VLOK	G10, I10
R ST EAST	C1	CHURCH SQUARE	E4	ESSELEN	F7, G9	JERUSALEM	C1	MEINTJIES	G7	PAUL KRUGER	A4, D4, F4, H4	RISSIK	H7, H9	STAND	D2	VOLKSTEM	F4
R	C1	COWIE	E1	FAURE	D9	JORISSEN	G8, H10	MENTS	I8	PERKS	A7	RIVERDALE	C5	STRUBEN	D1, D3, D5	VOORHOUT	J1
X	C8	DF MALAN	G1	FIFTH AVE	J3	JOUBERT	G7, H7	MIDDELBERG	J10	PIET UYS	H6	ROSE	A10	TANGO	J1	VOORTREKKERS	A8
DERE	C8	DE KOCK	H10	FIRST	I2	JUBILEE	G8	MINNAAR	G3, G6	PLEIN	G10	SCHEIDING	H5	TENTH	C2	VOS	H10
CHOEMAN	J3	DE RAPPER	G9	FIRST ST	I3	JUBILEE SQUARE	G8	MOGUL	C1	POMONA	J8	SCHOEMAN	F2, F6, F9	THIRD	I1	WALKER	H7, I10
	I7, I8, I10	DE VEER	D7	FOURTH AVE	J3	KERK	E1	MOSCA	B5	POTGIETER	D2, G2	SCHUBART	D3, G3, H3	THIRD AVE	I3	WELLS	B10
	A10	DE VRIES	H9	GEDENK	J2	KLAWER	J1	MUCKLENEUK	J9	PRELLER	J7	SECOND	I1	TORONTO	J1	WESSELS	E10
	D2	DE WAAL	C5	GERHARD MOERDYK	G7	KOCH	J4	MUTUAL	E4	PRETORIUS	E7, E10, F3	SECOND AVE	I3	TREVENNA	F8	WILLEM PUNT	J8
	C1	DEQUAR	H2	GOVERNMENT	D10	KOTZE	G7, G9	NELSON MANDELA	G6, I6	PRINCES PARK	F2	SECOND ST	J3	TROYE	F9, H8, I7, J7	WILLOW	J6
	E3	DORLAS	E7	GREEF	G8	LENNEN	G6	NORMAAL	I6	PRINSHOF	C6	SEVENTH	D1	UMVOTI	J1	WIMBLEDON	I2
AN	D3, G4	DOUGALL	J10	HAMILTON	C8, D8	LEWIS	C5	OCKERSE	D7	PRINSLOO	D6, F6, G6	SHEPHERD	D6	UNION	A9, B9	WYLAND	F9
E	G9, I9	DR SAVAGE	A7, B7, C6	HAMILTON AVE	D9	LEYDS	E9, G9, I8	OASIS	I2	PROES	D3, D5, E1	SILVER	I9	VALLEY	G10	ZEEDERBERG	E9

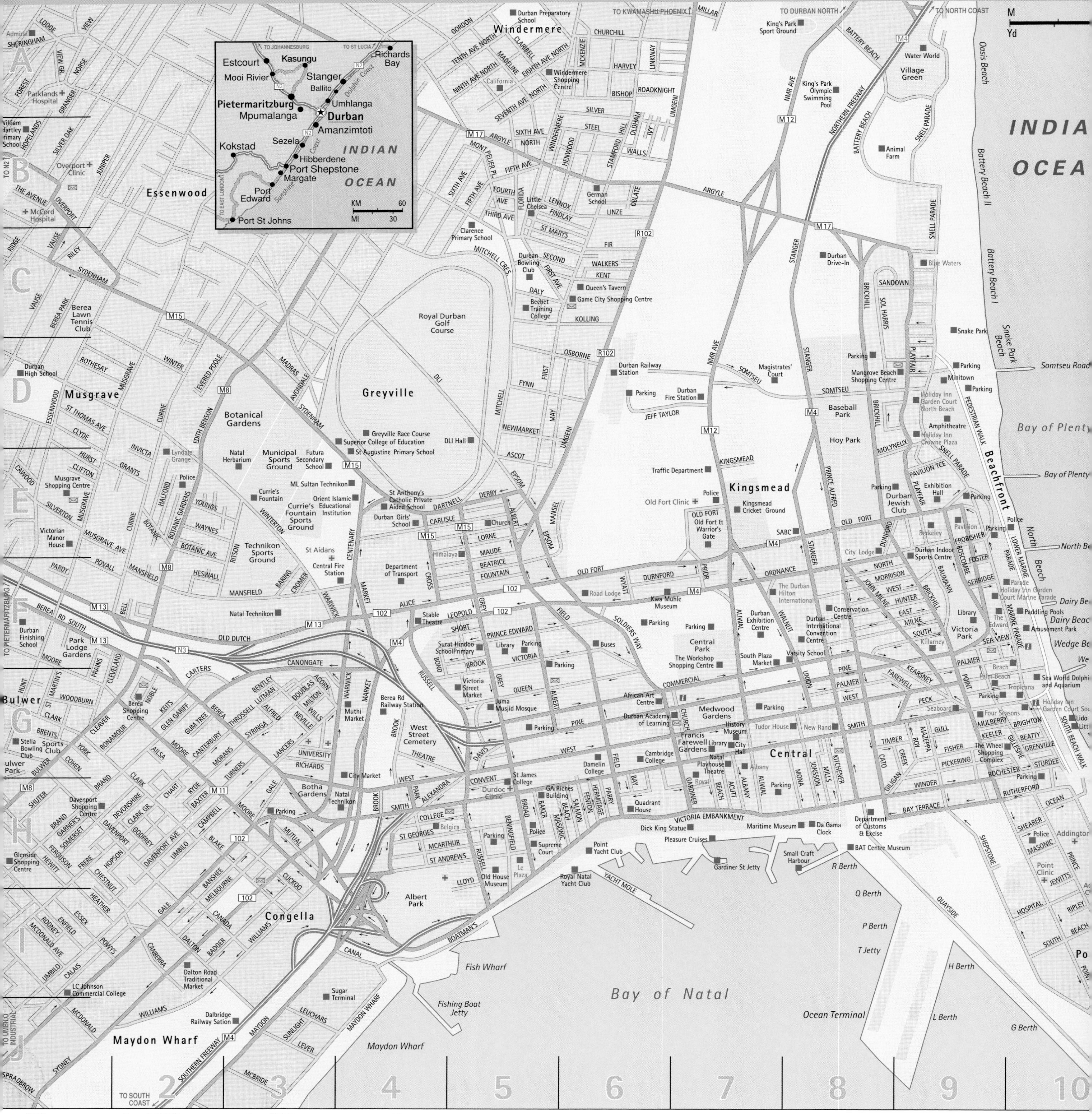

ACORN G3
ACUTT H7
AILSA G2
ALBANY H7
ALBERT E5, G5
ALBERT TCE I10
ALEXANDRA H4
ALFRED G3
ALICE F4
ALIWAL F7, H7
ANSON J10
ARGYLE B5, B7
ASCOT E5
AVONDALE D3
BADGER I2
BAKER H5
BANSHEE H2
BARING F3
BATTERY BEACH A8, B8
BAUMANN F9
BAXTER H2
BAY H6
BAY TCE H9
BEACH H6, H7
BEATRICE F5
BEATTY G10
BELL F2, I10
BENINGFIELD H5
BENTLEY G3
BEREA G2
BEREA PARK C1
BEREA RD SOUTH F1
BISHOP A6
BLAKE H2
BOATMAN'S I4
BONAMOUR G1
BOND F4
BOSCOMBE E9
BOTANIC E2
BOTANIC AVE E2
BOTANIC GARDENS E2
BRAND H1
BRENTS G1
BRICKHILL C8, D8,F9
BRIGHTON G10
BROAD H5
BROOK F5, G4, H4
BULWER G1
CALAIS I1
CAMPBELL H2
CANADA I2
CANAL I4
CANBERRA I2
CANONGATE F3
CANTERBURY G2
CARLISLE E4
CARTERS G2
CATO G8
CAWOOD E1
CENTENARY E4
CHART H2
CHESTNUT H1
CHURCH G7
CHURCHILL A6
CLARIBELL A5
CLARK G1, H2
CLARK GR. H2
CLEAVER G1
CLEVELAND G1
CLIFTON E1
CLYDE D1
COHEN G1
COLLEGE H4
COMMERCIAL G6
CONVENT H5
CREEK G9
CROMER F3
CROSS F4
CUCKOO H3
CURRIE D2, E2
DLI D4
DALTON I2
DALY C5
DARTNELL E4
DAVENPORT H1
DAVENPORT AVE H2
DAVIS G5
DERBY E5
DEVONSHIRE H2
DOUGLAS G3
DUNFORD E8
DURNFORD F6
EAST F9
EDITH BENSON D2
EIGHTH AVE NORTH A5
ENFIELD I1
EPSOM E5
ERSKINE H10
ESSENWOOD D1
ESSEX I1
EVERED POOLE D2
FAREWELL G9
FENTON H6
FERGUSON H1
FIELD F6, G6
FIFTH AVE B5
FINDLAY B5
FIR C6
FIRST D5
FIRST AVE C5
FISHER G9
FLORIDA B5
FOREST A1
FOSTER F9
FOUNTAIN F5
FOURTH AVE B5
FRERE H1
FROBISHER E9
FYNN D5
GALE H3, I2
GARDINER H7
GARNER'S H1
GILIGAN H8
GILLESPIE G10
GLEN GARIFF G2
GODFREY H2
GORDON A5
GRANGER A1
GRANTS E2
GRENVILLE G10
GREY F5, G5
GULL G9
GUM TREE G2
HALFORD E2
HARVEY A6
HEATHER I1
HENWOOD B6
HERMITAGE H6
HESWALL F2
HEWITT H1
HOPELANDS B1
HOPSON H1
HOSPITAL I10
HUNT G1
HUNTER F9
HURST E1
INVICTA E2
IVY B6
JEFF TAYLOR D6
JEWITTS H10
JOHN MILNE F8
JONSSON G8
JUNIPER B1
KEARSNEY G9
KEELER G9
KEITS G2
KENT C6
KINGSMEAD E7
KITCHENER G8
KOLLING C6
LANCERS G3
LENNOX B6
LEOPOLD F5
LEUCHARS J3
LEVER J3
LINKWAY A6
LINZE B6
LLOYD H5
LODGE A1
LORNE E5
LOWER MARINE PARADE E10
LUTMAN G3
MADELINE A5
MADRAS D3
MANSEL E5
MANSFIELD F2, F3
MARINE PARADE F10
MARKET F4, G4
MASONIC H5, H10
MAUDE E5
MAY D5
MAYDON J3
MAYDON WHARF J4
MAZEPPA G9
MCARTHUR H4
MCBRIDE J3
MCDONALD J1
MCDONALD AVE I1
MCKENZIE A6
MELBOURNE I2
MILLAR A7
MILLS G8
MILNE F8
MILTON G3
MITCHELL D5
MITCHELL CRES. C5
MOLYNEUX E8
MONA G8
MONTPELIER PL. B5
MOORE F1, G2, H3
MORANS G2
MORRISON F8
MULBERRY G9
MUSGRAVE D2, E1
MUSGRAVE AVE E1
MUTUAL H3
NEVILLE G3
NEWMARKET D5
NINTH AVE NORTH A5
NMR AVE A8, D7
NOBLE G2
NORSE A1
NORTH F8
NORTHERN FREEWAY B8
OBLATE B6
OCEAN H10
OLD DUTCH F3
OLD FORT E7, E8, F6
OLDHAM B6
ORDNANCE F7
OSBORNE D6
OVERPORT B1
PALMER F9, G8
PARDY F1
PARK H4
PARRY H6
PAVILION TCE E9
PECK G9
PICKERING G9
PINE G6, G8
PLAYFAIR D9, E9
POINT G9, I10
POVALL F1
POWYS I1
PRAINS G1
PRINCE H10
PRINCE ALFRED E8
PRINCE EDWARD F5
PRIOR F7
QUAYSIDE I9
QUEEN G5
RICHARDS G3
RIDGE C1
RILEY C1
RIPLEY I10
RITSON E3
ROADKNIGHT A6
ROCHESTER G9
RODNEY I1
ROTHESAY D1
ROY G9
RUSSELL G4, H5
RUTHERFORD H10
RYDE H2
SALMON H6
SANDOWN C8
SEA VIEW F9
SECOND C5
SERRIDGE F9
SEVENTH AVE NORTH A5
SHEARER H10
SHEPSTONE H9
SHERINGHAM A1
SHORT F5
SHUTER H1
SILVER A6
SILVER OAK B1
SILVERTON E1
SIXTH AVE B5
SIXTH AVE NORTH B5
SMITH G8, H4
SNELL PARADE B9, C9, E9
SOLDIERS WAY F6
SOL HARRIS C8
SOMERSET H1
SOMTSEU D7, D8
SOUTH F8
SOUTH BEACH AVE I10
SOUTH BEACH WALK G10
SOUTHERN FREEWAY J2
SPRADBROW J1
ST ANDREWS H4
ST GEORGES H4
ST MARTIN'S G1
ST MARYS C5
ST THOMAS AVE D1
STAMFORD HILL B6
STANGER C8, D8, F8
STEEL B6
STURDEE G10
SUNLIGHT J3
SYDENHAM C1, D3
SYDNEY J1
SYRINGA G3
TENTH AVE NORTH A5
THE AVENUE B1
THEATRE
THIRD AVE
THROSSELL
TIMBER
TURNERS
UMBILO
UMGENI
UNION
UNIVERSITY
VAUSE
VICTORIA
VICTORIA EMBANKMENT
VIEW
VIEW GR.
WALKERS
WALLS
WALNUT
WARWICK
WAYNES
WEST F9, G6,
WILLIAMS
WILLS
WINDER
WINDERMERE
WINTER
WINTERTON
WOODBURN
WYATT
YACHT MOLE
YORK
YOUNGS

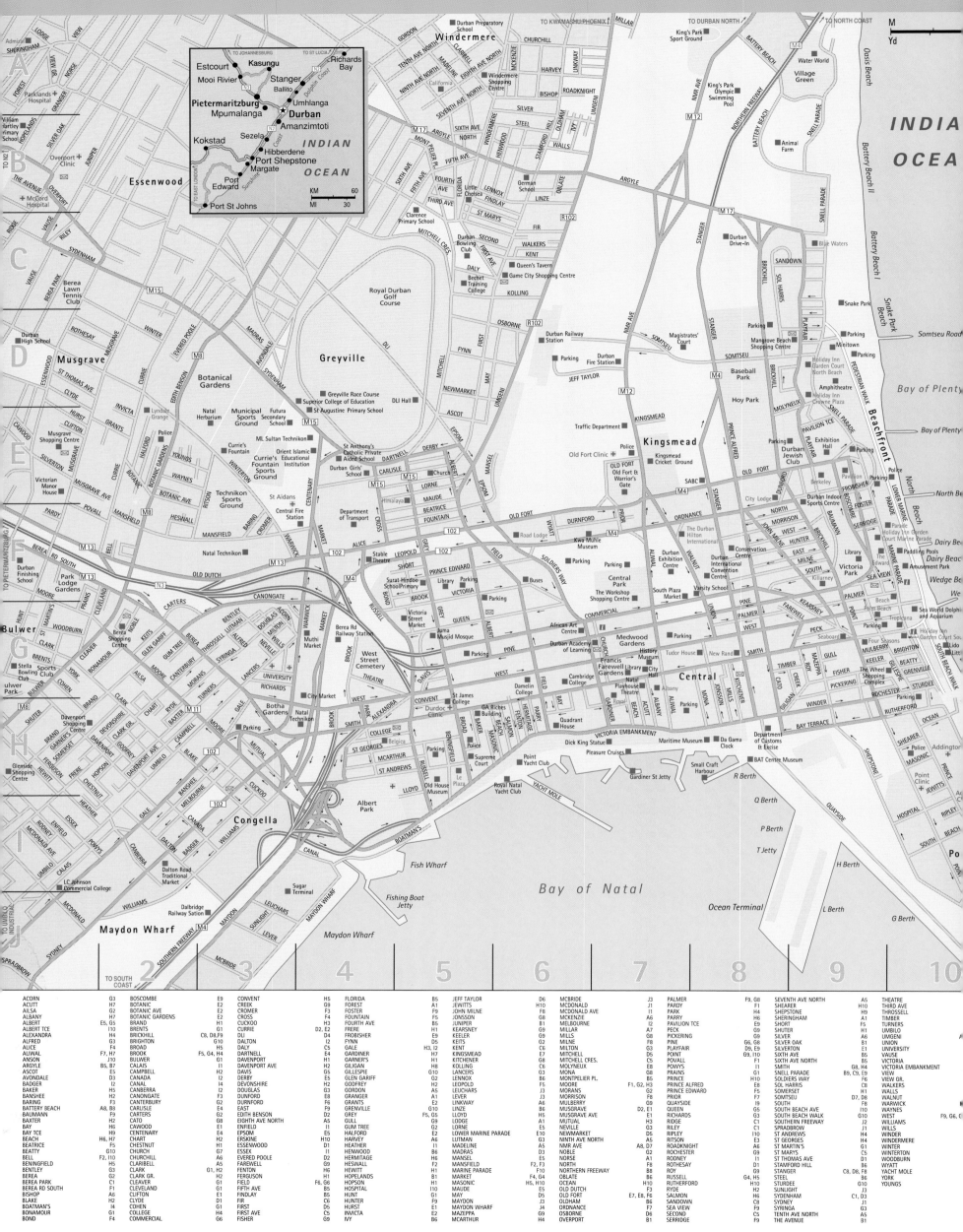

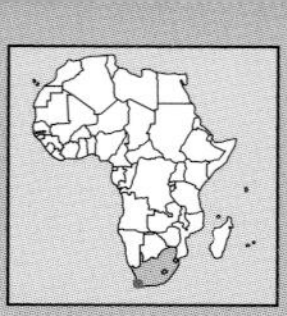

LOM	I8
LEY	F7
NTHUS	J9
E	J7
Y	E1
	H3
US	G7
NDRA	B3, I2, J5
	D7, E6
KIRK	H3
	J8
DALE	H5
M	C3
RP	D2
R'S	E1
	I8
NG CALLANDER	H9
T	E5
A	D1
E	H6
ALE	C3
EY	E1
BAS	I4
T	H6
AM	I9
CK	G7
	G10
	I4
Y	D2, D7
EW	H3
	A4, B3
	A3, B6, C2
AM	H5
ONNA	J9
R	J8
OMBRE	H4
UE	E1, J3
OOD	I2
NT	J5
ERE	J5
EVIS	D4
TT	D6
NGTON	G4
	F6
EY	J6
Y	D1
TERS	B3, B5
HEATH	D2
ROCK	C1
	I10
	G6
HOF	H8
	H3
AUX	F1
BOUNDARY	D5
BOUQUET	G6
BOWLERS	C3
BRADWELL	J7
BRAEMAR	C5
BRAESIDE	C4
BRANDWEER	I7
BREAKWATER BLVD	B6
BREDA	I6, J6
BREE	E7, F6, G5
BRITTANY	J2
BROMPTON	I1
BROWNLOW	G4
BRYANT	F5
BUITEN	G5, G6
BUITENGRACHT	F6
BUITENKANT	H7, I6
BUITENSINGEL	G5
BURG	F7
BURNSIDE	G4
BUXTON	J5
BYRON	H4
CALAIS	D2
CALEDON	G8,H8
CAMBERWELL	C2
CAMDEN	H3
CAMP	H4, I5
CANTERBURY	H8
CARISBROOK	G5
CARL	E5
CARREG	D5
CARSTENS	G4
CASSELL	H2
CASTLE	F8, G8
CAUVIN	I10
CAVALCADE	C5
CHAPEL	H9, H10
CHATEAU	F1
CHELSEA	I7
CHEPSTOW	D5
CHEVIOT	C4
CHIAPPINI	E6, E7
CHRISTIAAN	I10
CHURCH	F6, F7, H3
CIVIC	F9
CLARE	H7
CLARENS	H2
CLIFFORD	E2
CLOVELLY	I8
CLYDEBANK	C4
CLYDE	C4
COBURN	D6
COEN STEYTLER	E8
COMMERCIAL	G7
CONIFER	D1
CONSTANTIA	I3
CONSTITUTION	H9, I10
CORPORATION	G7
COURVILLE	I6
CRASSULA	I8
CROXTETH	C4
CULVER	J6
DF MALAN	E9
DA GAMA	E8
DARLING	G7
DASSEN	E2
DAVENPORT	J7
DAWES	E6
DE BARRANGE	G1
DE HOOP	I3
DE KORTE	H8
DE L'HERMITE	F1
DE LONGUEVILLE	I2
DE LORENTZ	I4
DE SMIT	D6
DE VILLIERS	H8
DE WAAL	I9
DEANE	E2
DEAUVILLE	G1
DELPHINIUM	I8
DENHOLM	J7
DERRY	J8
DERWENT	I4
DES HUGUENOTS	I3
DEVONPORT	G4
DIAS	E8
DISANDT	G1, I3
DIXON	E6
DOCK	C6, D7
DOLLS HOUSE	B3
DORMAN	H5
DORMEHL	G10
DORP	F6
DORSET	G10
DOVER	E2
DRELINGCOURT	G1
DRURY LANE	H8
DUNCAN	D8, E9, F1
DUNKLEY	H6
DYSART	C4
EAST PIER	A8
EASTERN BOULEVARD	H10
EATON	H4
EBENEZER	D6
EDWARD	E1
ELLA	E5
ELLIS	E1
EXNER	J8
FAURE	H5
FAWLEY	I9
FIFTH	D2
FIRDALE	E2
FIRDALE	I4
FIRMOUNT	D2
FISH	F7
FISH MARKET	C7
FLOWER	J6
FONTAINBLEAU	F1
FOREST HILL	J6
FORT	C2
FORT WYNYARD	B6
FRANCAIS	H3
FRANCIS	H10
FREDERICK	E5, G3
FREESIA	J8
FRERE	C2
FRESNAYE	G1, I2, I3
FRIARS	E2
FRITZ SONNENBERG	B5
GARDENIA	I8
GILMOUR HILL	H4
GLADIOLUS	J8
GLADSTONE	J6
GLEN AVE	J3
GLENGARIFF	C2, D3
GLYNN	H7
GLYNVILLE	H6
GORDON	I6
GORE	G9
GORLESTON	F1
GOVERNMENT AVE	H6
GRAHAM	D1
GRAY	H10
GREEN	G6
GREY'S PASS	H6
GRIMSBY	C2
GRISNEZ	J7
GROVE	C4
HALL	D1, H10
HANOVER	H3, H8
HANS STRIJDOM	E7
HARRINGTON	H7
HASTINGS	H4
HATFIELD	C3, H6
HEAD	H1
HEATHFIELD	E1
HEERE	I10
HEERENGRACHT	E8
HERBERT	E1
HERTZOG BLVD	F8
HIDDINGH	I6
HIGGO	J2, J3
HIGGO CRES.	J3
HIGH LEVEL	C3, D2, F1
HIGHFIELD RD	D6
HILL	C3
HILLSIDE	D6, G4
HOF	I5, J4
HOFMEYR	D2, I4, I5
HOLMFIRTH	E1
HOPE	H6
HOPEVILLE	I6
HOSPITAL	D7
HOUT	F6
HUDSON	E6
ILKLEY	D3
IRWINTON	F1
JACK CRAIG	F9
JAGERSFONTEIN AVE	I6
JAMIESON	G5
JAN SMUTS	E9
JARVIS	D6
JASPER	I6
JETTY	E8
JORDAAN	F5
JOUBERT	D3
JUSTISIE	I9
JUTLAND	I7
KEEROM	G6
KEI APPLE	H2
KEIZERSGRACHT	H9
KELVIN	D3, I4
KENMORE	G4
KENSINGTON	J4
KIEWIET	B3
KING	H4
KINGS	I2
KLOOF	H2
KLOOF AVE	I4
KLOOF NEK	H4
KLOOF ST	H5
KOETZE	I4
KOHLING	H5
KORT	D3
KREUPELHOUT	J9
KRYNAUW	I5
KUYPER	I8
LAMBERT	J8
LAW	C3
LE SUEUR	I3
LEEUKLOOF	G3
LEEUKOP	I3
LEEUWEN	F6
LEEUWENDAL	I4
LEEUWENHOF	J3, J4
LEEUWENVOET	G4
LEINSTER	C5
LELIE	E7
LEWIN	G10
LINCOLN	D1
LINGEN	I5
LION	F5
LION'S HEAD WALK	I1
LOADER	D6, E6
LODGE	I6
LONDON	D1
LONG	E7, G6
LONGMARKET	E5, F7
LOOP	F7, G6
LOUIS GRADNER	F9
LOWER PLEIN	G7
LUDLOW	J7
LUTON	I7
LWR PYPIES	I8
LYMINGTON	I9
MAIN	C2, C4, D2, E1
MALAN	I4
MAPLE	I4
MARAIS	D1
MARTIN HAMMERSCHLAG	F9
MAYNARD	I7
MCKENZIE	H7
MECHAU	E6
MELLISH	J7
MERRIMAN	D5
MILITARY	E5, G4
MILL	I7
MILNER	E1, G4
MOLTENO	J5
MONASTERY	F1
MORAY	J6
MORKEL	I5
MOUNT	H8
MT NELSON	D2
MUIR	H9
MUNNIK	H10
MUTLEY	D2
MYRTLE	I6
NAPIER	D7, E6
NELSON	G10, H10
NEW CHURCH	G5, H5
NEW MARKET	G10
NEWPORT	I4
NICOL	H4
NOORDELIK	J8
NORFOLK	D1
NORMANDIE	F1
OCEAN VIEW	D2, D3, D4, D5, F1, G1
OESTER	H8
OLD MARINE	F8
OLDFIELD	D2
ORANGE	H5
ORPHAN	G5
ORPHAN ST	G6
OSWALD PIROW	F9
PADDOCK	H6
PARADE	G7
PARK	B3, H5
PARK HOUSE	H5
PARLIAMENT	G7
PEAK	I9
PENARTH	C2
PENTZ	F5
PEPPER	F6
PERTH	I10
PINE	C4
PINEOAK	J9
PLANTATION	I9
PLEIN	G7
PONTAC	H10
PORT	D7
PORTSWOOD	C6
POYSER	G4
PRESTWICH	D6, E7
PRINCE	J6
QUARRY HILL	I3
QUEEN	H10
QUEENS	G4, I1, I2
QUEEN VICTORIA	G6
QUENDON	I2
RABBI MIRVISH	J7
RAEL	H3
RAVENSCRAIG	C3
RAYDEN	J5
REFORM	H9
REGENT	H2, I3
RHEEDE	H5
RHINE	D2
RICHMOND	C3
RIEBEECK	E7
ROCHESTER	I1
ROCKLANDS	C2
ROELAND	H7
ROGER	H9, H10
ROMNEY	C3
ROODEHEK	H7
ROOS	D4
ROSE	E6
ROSEMOUNT	J6
ROSMEAD	J4
ROTHESAY	A3
RUGLEY	J7
RUSSELL	G10, H10
SADDLE	I9
SALAZAR	E8
SCHOLTZ	C3
SCHOONDER	I6
SCOTT	I6, I7
SELKIRK	G9
SHORTMARKET	F6
SIDNEY	H9
SIGNAL HILL	E3
SIR GEORGE GREY	J6
SIR LOWRY	G9
SMART	G8
SOLAN	H7
SOLOMONS	H1
SOMERSET	D6
SOPHIA	J6
SOUTH ARM	C8
SPARTA	E2
SPRINGBOK	D3
ST BARTHOLOMEW	G1
ST BREDE'S	C3
ST CHARLES	F1
ST DENIS	F1
ST GEORGES	C4
ST GEORGES MALL	F7
ST JAMES	C1, J8
ST JOHNS	F1, H3, H6
ST LOUIS	J3
ST MICHAEL'S	H3
ST PATRICK	I2
STAL	G7
STANLEY	B2, D7
STEPHAN	B4
STERLING	H8
STRAND	F7
STUCKERIS	G9
SUMMERSEAT	J3
SURF	H2
SURREY	A4
SYDNEY	C4
TABLE BAY BOULEVARD	E9
TAMBOERSKLOOF	H4
TANABARU	E5
TENNANT	H8
THE GLEN	E1
THORNHILL	C5
THREE ANCHOR BAY	C2
TRAMWAY	I2
TRENT	I4
TUIN	I4
UNION	I5
UPPER BLOEM	F5
UPPER BUITENGRACHT	H4
UPPER BUITENKANT	J6
UPPER CANTERBURY	H7
UPPER CLARENS	H3
UPPER HILLSIDE	D5
UPPER KLOOF	J4
UPPER LEEUWEN	F5
UPPER MAYNARD	I7
UPPER MILL	I7
UPPER ORANGE	J6
UPPER PEPPER	F5
UPPER PORTSWOOD	C5
UPPER RHINE	D2
UPPER UNION	H4
VAN RYNEVELD	I8
VARNEYS	C4
VARSITY	I3
VERNON KENT	H8
VESPERDENE	C5
VICTORIA	G5
VINE	I5
VIRGINIA	I7
VLEI	B4
VOETBOOG	E5
VOGELGEZANG	H10
VOS	E6
VREDE	H6
VREDEHOEK	J7, J8
VRIENDE	I6
WALE	F5, F6
WANDEL	H6
WARRENVILLE	H7
WARREN	H3
WATERKANT	E6, E7
WATSONIA	I8
WELGEMEEND	I5
WELTEVREDEN	H5
WEMBLEY	I7
WERF	H8
WESLEY	H7
WESSELS	D5
WEST QUAY	C7
WESTERN BOULEVARD	C4, C6
WESTMORE	J3
WEXFORD	J8
WHARF	E8
WHITFORD	G5
WICHT	G8
WIGTOWN	C4
WILKINSON	H5
WISBEACH	D1
WOODSIDE	G3, H4
WYNYARD	J6
YEOVILLE	J7
YORK	C5
YUSUF	E5

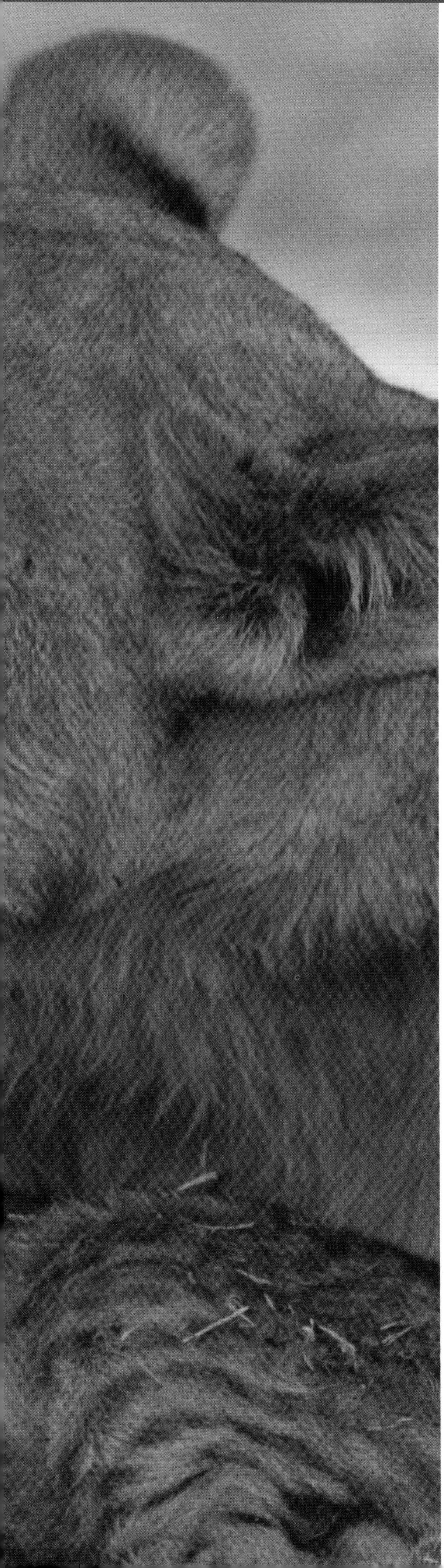

National Parks by Region

COUNTRIES OF AFRICA

A lioness grooms her young cub, Kruger National Park, South Africa. The baby only leaves its mother's care after two years of life and learning.

Africa's National Parks

Covering a total land mass of 30,330,000km^2 (11,700,000 sq miles), the wilderness landscape of Africa undoubtedly comprises some of the most unspoilt and undeveloped on the planet, stretching some 8000km (5000 miles) from north to south and 7500km (4500 miles) east to west. The continent – including the surrounding Indian Ocean Islands – is divided into some 54 political zones, and while about five of these have no protected areas currently recognised by the United Nations (and some smaller nations have perhaps only one or two), no fewer than 818 official conservation areas lay scattered across this vast continent, with additional reserves, parks and other protected areas being gazetted on a regular basis. Africa's conservation land today exceeds 230 million hectares (570 million acres), which also covers a large percentage of its 30,500km (19,000 miles) coastline, and although many of these have indeed been sadly neglected as a result of political skirmishes, the devastation of war, the ever-present scourge of poaching and environmental degradation and the growing demands of the continent's human population of some 800 million. Only 12 per cent of the land is arable, leaving a remarkable proportion untainted by human intervention, allowing for enormous potential in both tourism and ecotourism – and, perhaps more importantly, in conservation.

Africa's existing national parks, game and nature reserves, conservation areas, wetlands and wildlife sanctuaries vary in size and stature, covering, for example, only 5000ha (12,350 acres) on the island of Reunion to 25.43 million hectares (63 million acres) in Tanzania. They thus remain the most sought-after adventure and safari destinations in the world. To cater for the requirements of a growing interest in the continent's wild places, African nations are paying increasing attention to the possibilities offered by their land. These vary from the floral reserves of Indian Ocean Islands to the vastness of the Serengeti plains, with the thousands-strong herds of migrating wildebeest. Game-viewing and bird-watching are unparalleled and, despite even the threats posed by the possibility of malaria infection – the list of adventures and more leisurely pastimes appears seemingly endless. As a result, the infrastructure of these national assets are slowly becoming more and more developed in terms of visitors' facilities and public amenities, with a growing awareness of governments – initially spurred on by the rapid development of the tourism trade to Africa in about the 1970s – of the economic potential of these vast stretches of natural splendour.

In a world beset by conflict and division, peace is one of the cornerstones of the future. Peace parks are building blocks in this process, not only in our region, but potentially in the entire world.

– Nelson Mandela

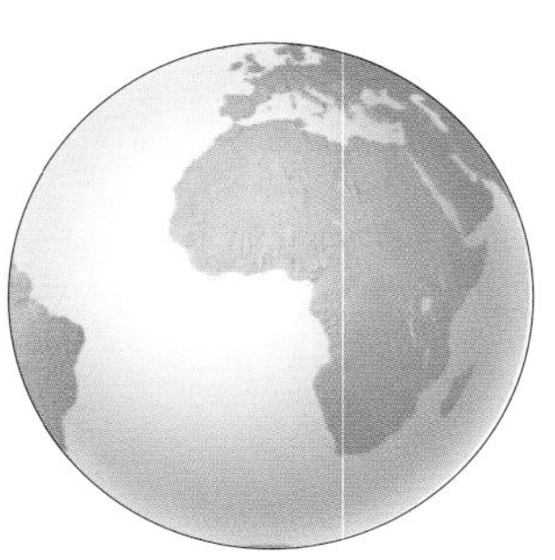

- The African elephant is the world's heaviest terrestial mammal (7,000kg/14,400lb)
- Mauritius has three entries in the list of the world's 10 most rare birds: the Echo Parakeet, the Pink Pigeon and the Mauritius Kestrel
- Somalia boasts the greatest number of camels in the world, 5,800,000 in 2000, almost a third of the world's total camel population.

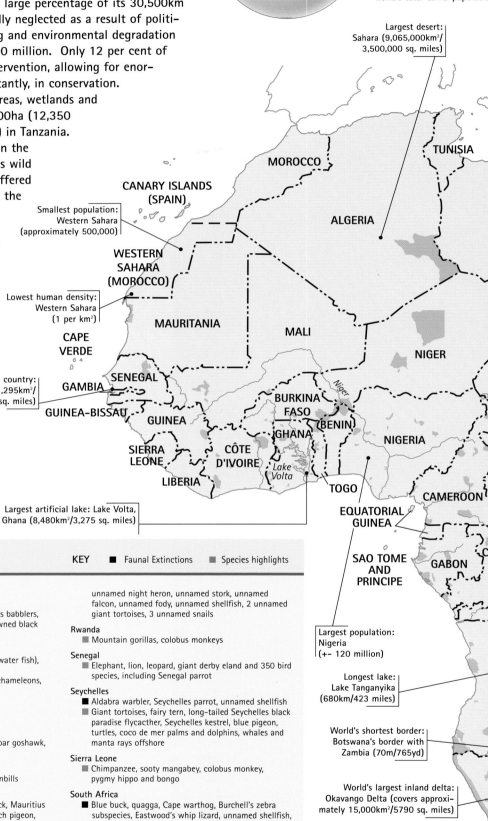

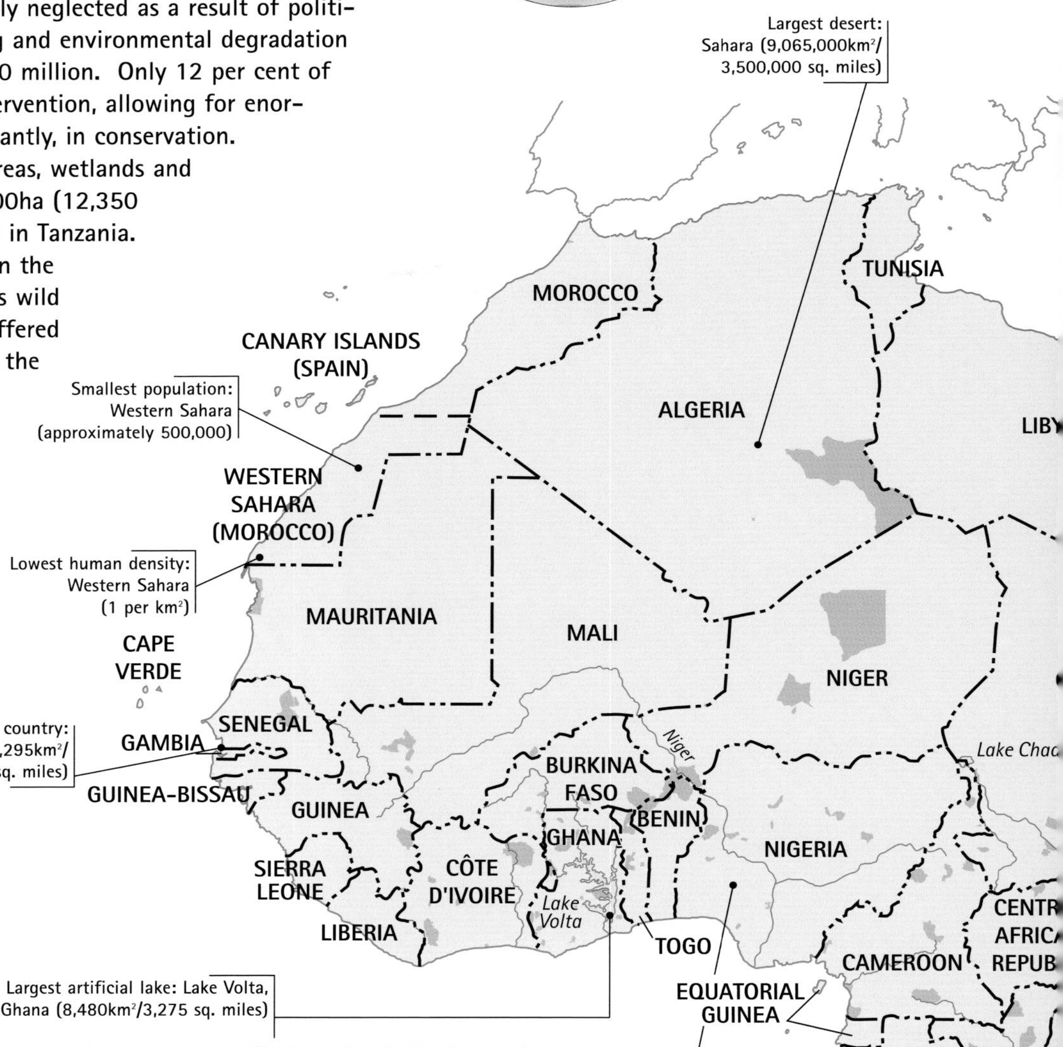

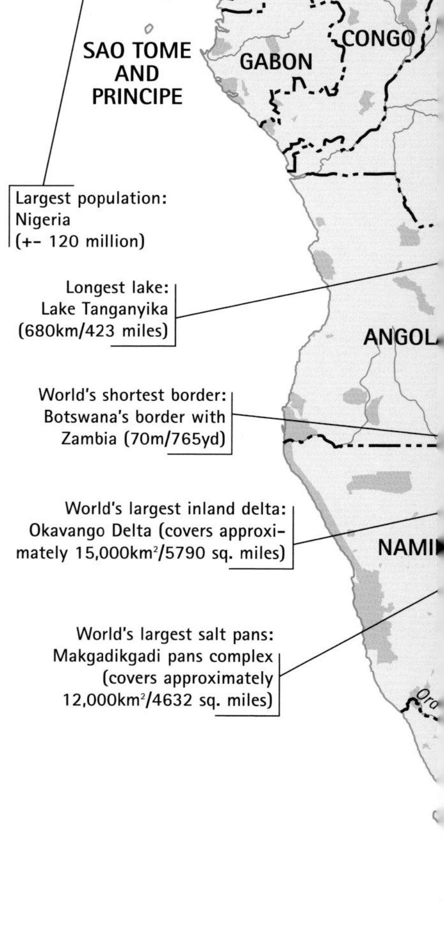

THE OLD AND THE BEAUTIFUL

KEY ■ Faunal Extinctions ■ Species highlights

Algeria
- ■ Bubal hartebeest, red gazelle

Benin
- ■ Baboon, elephant, hippo, warthog

Botswana
- ■ Burchells zebra subspecies
- ■ Elephant, buffalo, wildebeest, giraffe, hippo, kudu, puku

Burkina Faso
- ■ Elephant, hippo and birdlife

Cameroon
- ■ Elephant, giraffe, hippo, lion, ostrich and other birds

Cape Verde
- ■ Cape Verde giant skink

Comoros
- ■ Green turtle

Congo
- ■ Gorillas

Côte d'Ivoire
- ■ Lion, elephant, hippo and savanna bird species

Democratic Republic of the Congo
- ■ Mountain and lowland gorillas, chimpanzees

Djibouti
- ■ Flamingoes and other birdlife of Lac Abbé

Egypt
- ■ Bubal hartebeest, Egyptian barbary sheep
- ■ Marine and coral life in the Red Sea

Ethiopia
- ■ Simien wolf/fox, ibex, baboon, raptors (ie lammergeier)

Gabon
- ■ Primates such as gorillas, chimpanzees, mandrils and monkeys, hippo, elephant crocodile and humpback whales offshore

Gambia
- ■ Sitatunga, duiker, vervet monkeys, red colobus

Ghana
- ■ Elephant, antelope, lion and bird species

Kenya
- ■ Kenyan rocky river frog, Kenya oribi
- ■ Wildebeest, black rhino, reticulated giraffe, beisa oryx, flamingoes

Lesotho
- ■ Rhebok, baboon, bearded vulture

Libya
- ■ Bubal hartebeest
- ■ Fennecs, and desert birds such as fulvous babblers, great and lesser grey shrikes, white-crowned black wheatear and desert larks

Madagascar
- ■ Pygmy hippo, elephant bird, zona (freshwater fish), snail-eating coua, 2 unnamed shellfish
- ■ Lemur (such as indri and sifaka), fossa, chameleons, baobab, traveller's palm

Malawi
- ■ Hippo, crocodile, elephant, kudu

Mali
- ■ Senegal parrot, long-tailed parakeet, gabar goshawk, lappet-faced vulture

Mauritania
- ■ Pelicans, flamingoes, terns, herons, spoonbills

Mauritius
- ■ Dodo, Mauritian shelduck, Mauritian duck, Mauritius night heron, Rodrigues night heron, Dutch pigeon, Rodrigues pigeon, Rodrigues solitaire, Mauritian red rail, Leguat's rail, Mascarene coot, Rodrigues starling, Mauritius grey parrot, Broadbilled parrot, Rodrigues parrot, Rodrigues ring-necked parakeet, Rodrigues little owl, Mauritian barn owl, Commerson's scops owl, dark flying fox, giant day gecko, Round Island burrowing boa, Hoffstetter's worm snake, unnaned butterfly, unnamed bulbul, unnamed petrel, unnamed lizard, 4 unnamed giant tortoises, 13 unnamed snails
- ■ Mauritius fody, Mauritius fruit bat, Mauritius kestrel, pink pigeon, Telfair skink,

Morocco (incl. Western Sahara)
- ■ Bubal hartebeest, barbary lion
- ■ African parrot, Argan trees, leopard and panther colonies

Namibia
- ■ Burchell's zebra subspecies, unnamed shellfish
- ■ Desert rhino, elephant, Damara tern, gemsbok, mountain zebra

Niger
- ■ Some 300 aquatic bird species

Nigeria
- ■ Elephant, hippo, crocodile and even lion

Réunion (France)
- ■ Réunion flightless ibis, Réunion solitaire, Réunion crested starling, Mascarene parrot, dark flying fox, unnamed night heron, unnamed stork, unnamed falcon, unnamed fody, unnamed shellfish, 2 unnamed giant tortoises, 3 unnamed snails

Rwanda
- ■ Mountain gorillas, colobus monkeys

Senegal
- ■ Elephant, lion, leopard, giant derby eland and 350 bird species, including Senegal parrot

Seychelles
- ■ Aldabra warbler, Seychelles parrot, unnamed shellfish
- ■ Giant tortoises, fairy tern, long-tailed Seychelles black paradise flycacther, Seychelles kestrel, blue pigeon, turtles, coco de mer palms and dolphins, whales and manta rays offshore

Sierra Leone
- ■ Chimpanzee, sooty mangabey, colobus monkey, pygmy hippo and bongo

South Africa
- ■ Blue buck, quagga, Cape warthog, Burchell's zebra subspecies, Eastwood's whip lizard, unnamed shellfish, 2 unnamed butterflies, 3 unnamed worms
- ■ Lion, leopard, cheetah, buffalo, elephant, hippo, rhino, giraffe

Spain (Canary Islands)
- ■ Fuertaventuran houbara, Canarian buzzard, blue chaffinch

Swaziland
- ■ Burchell's zebra subspecies
- ■ White rhino, elephant, lion, zebra, crocodile

Tanzania
- ■ Lion, leopard, cheetah, wild dog, rhino, elephant, chimpanzee

Togo
- ■ Butterfly species

Tunisia
- ■ Bubal hartebeest
- ■ Fennec, wild boar, porcupine, fox

Uganda
- ■ Gorillas, chimpanzees, hippo, pelicans

Zambia
- ■ Robert's lechwe
- ■ Thornicroft's giraffe, lion, leopard, elephant, buffalo, zebra, puku, sitatunga

Zimbabwe
- ■ Elephant, giraffe, buffalo, sable, kudu

WAR ZONES
These are the countries in Africa that are in conflict, either ethnic or political. Such conflicts makes travel and especially game viewing particularly difficult and hazardous. Be sure to consult your travel agent.

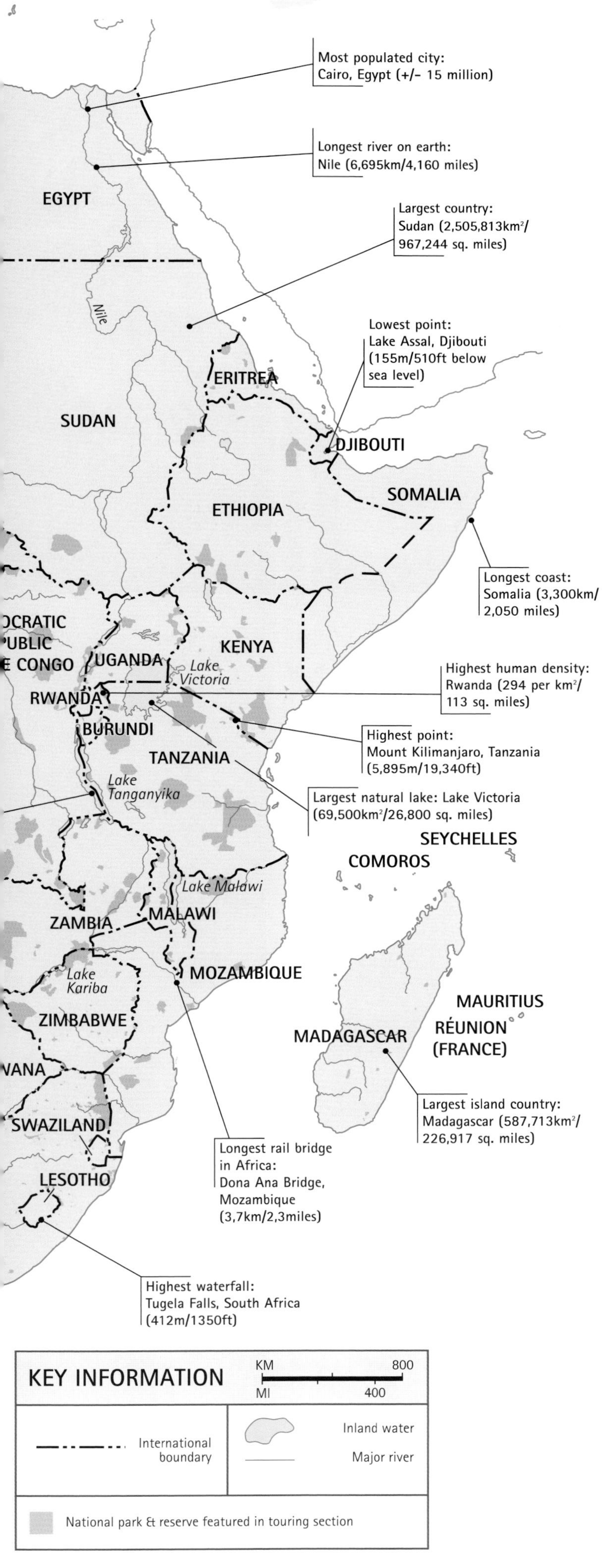

Forest Clumps

While many of the continent's forests remain some of their custodian nations' most prized attractions – and the backdrop of a plethora of adventure activities and recreational excursions – the dangers that threaten their existence cannot be ignored. In 1999, the WWF helped coordinate an agreement (The Yaoundé Forest Summit, held in Cameroon), which brought together Cameroon, Gabon, the Central African Republic, the Democratic Republic of the Congo and Equatorial Guinea. These nations all committed themselves to establishing future transfrontier conservation areas. Their intention is to preserve natural assets and utilise environmental and mineral wealth to the benefit of all Africans.

SAY CHEESE!

The cities, parks and unexplored parts of Africa present countless opportunities to capture photographic evidence of Africa's beauty, charm and power (as well as proof that you've been there, done that). It's always good to seek out your own original images from your travels, but here are some must-take photo opportunities for any traveller to capture.

KEY fauna flora landscapes

COUNTRY	SITE
Algeria	desert dunes of Timimoun
Angola	palm-fringed Ilha do Mussolo
Benin	Pendjari National Park
Botswana	majestic wetlands of the Okavango Delta
Burkina Faso	"W" National Park
Burundi	Kagera Falls
Cameroon	the peaks of Mount Cameroon
Canary Is (Spain)	the snow-capped volcano, Mount Teide
Cape Verde	Fogo's volcanic peak
CAR	famed waterfalls of Boali Falls
Chad	the waters of Lake Chad
Comoros	beaches of Grand Comore
Congo	seascape of Pointe-Noire
Côte d'Ivoire	wilderness of Man
DRC	gorillas and volcanoes of Virunga National Park
Djibouti	birdlife of Lake Abbe
Egypt	coral reefs off the Sinai Peninsula
Equatorial Guinea	Bioko's rainforest wonderland
Eritrea	marine life of the Dahlak Archipelago
Ethiopia	Blue Nile Falls near Bahir Dar
Gabon	wildlife splendour of Lopé Faunal Reserve
Gambia	winding waterway of the Gambia River
Ghana	big game at Mole National Park
Guinea	the plateau of Fouta Djalon
Guinea-Bissau	the archipelago of Bijagós
Kenya	wildebeest migrations of the Masai Mara
Lesotho	stony slopes of Thabana Ntlenyana
Liberia	the hilly country of Mount Nimba
Libya	prehistoric countryside of the Acacus mountains
Madagascar	rainforest inhabitants of Analamazaotra (Périnet) Special Reserve
Malawi	the water world of Lake Malawi
Mali	wasteland wonder of the Falaise de Bandiagara World Heritage Site
Mauritania	avifaunal haven of Banc d'Arguin National Park
Mauritius	rugged terrain of Black River Gorges
Morocco (incl W.Sahara)	remote spectacle of the High Atlas
Mozambique	diving splendour of the Bazaruto Archipelago
Namibia	stark beauty of the Skeleton Coast
Niger	endless sands of the Ténéré
Nigeria	Oshogbo rainforest's Sacred Groves
Réunion (France)	volcanic landscape of the cirques
Rwanda	tropical haven that is Volcans National Park
Sao Tome & Principe	turtles laying eggs at Praja de Micolo
Senegal	fertile river valley of the Casamance
Seychelles	Praslin's Vallée de Mai
Sierra Leone	the wildlife heritage of Tiwai Island
Somalia	Bushbush Game Reserve neighbouring Kenya
South Africa	unparalleled wildlife spectacle of the Kruger National Park
Sudan	uncharted waters of the Blue Nile
Swaziland	gentle grandeur of Mkhaya Nature Reserve
Tanzania	legendary savannas of the Serengeti
Togo	hill country of Kpalimé
Tunisia	stark desert landscape of Douz
Uganda	the spectacle of the Murchison Falls
Zambia	the untamed valley of the mighty Zambezi
Zimbabwe	the giant cascades of world-famous Victoria Falls

Peace Parks

The Peace Parks Foundation is dedicated to creating a vast network of transfrontier conservation areas in southern Africa, promoting regional cooperation, job creation and biodiversity conservation.

The foundation may be contacted at:
PO Box 12743, Die Boord, Stellenbosch 7613, South Africa; tel: (27-21) 887-6188, fax: (27-21) 887-6189, e-mail: parks@ppf.org.za, website: www.peaceparks.org

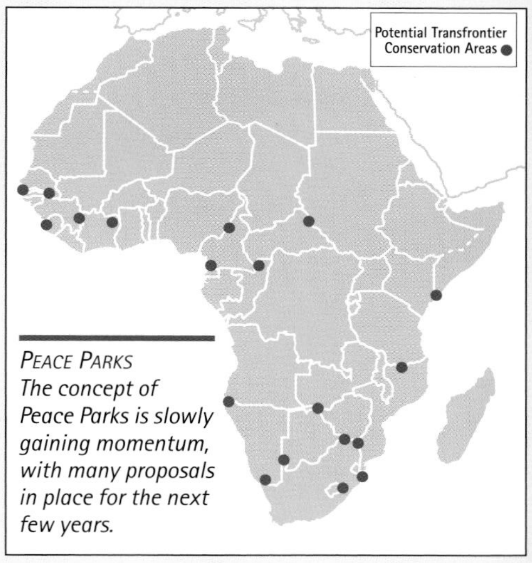

PEACE PARKS
The concept of Peace Parks is slowly gaining momentum, with many proposals in place for the next few years.

The Transfrontier Parks

One of the most inspiring and successful of Africa's conservation initiatives is the establishment of transfrontier parks, international cooperation agreements between neighbouring countries on land that crosses national boundaries. These 'collaborations' rely on mutual cooperation between participating nations, thus encouraging peace and regional development which should see a marked improvement in living standards of the communities directly involved in such ecotourism projects.

While a number of these efforts enjoy the financial and administrative support of global organisations such as the World Bank, the most promising outcome has been the direct involvement of the participating countries' governments. Numerous other initiatives, backed by visionary political leaders, conservation officials and private donors, have followed, which in turn allows a level of stability and growth that encourages further foreign investment and development.

The concept of transfrontier parks that involve a partnership agreement between cooperating nations now offers what is termed a 'global solution' to dwindling herds, encroaching human populations and land degradation with, for example, the relocation of wildlife to areas where they were once common but are now facing extinction. The original intention was to establish no more than six such parks, yet the new millennium saw nearly 20 individual sites being considered as transfrontier conservation areas, thereby carefully marrying the commercial potential of a far broader region with the demands of an economically viable and sustainable environment.

The most notable of the success stories has been the development of southern Africa's transfrontier parks. The Kgalagadi Transfrontier Park between South Africa and Botswana was Africa's first formal transnational reserve, and has been followed with equally successful ventures in the 100,000km² (40,000 sq miles) Great Limpopo Transfrontier Park between South Africa, Mozambique and Zimbabwe, in addition to the Maloti-Drakensberg Transfrontier Park between South Africa and Lesotho.

These extraordinary efforts have aligned allies determined to preserve indigenous habitats and the wildlife and human populations they sustain. With a series of international agreements already ratified and implemented (and a number on the cards), the success rate is a continued source of inspiration for conservation focussed on the future of the continent.

ADV 285
NP 244

THE REGION

Algeria may not be the safest or the most popular tourist destination in the Maghreb, but it boasts the most impressive conservation record of the entire region. Algeria has nearly 13 million hectares (32 million acres) of its 2.3 million square kilometres (900,000 sq. miles) of land protected for conservation purposes. By comparison, Tunisia has 250,000 hectares (600,000 acres) and Morocco 400,000 hectares (990,000 acres) of conservation lands.

TUNISIA	Key
Boukornine National Park	D
Bou-Hedma National Park	F
Chambi National Park	E
El Feidja National Park	A
Ichkeul National Park	B
Zembra and Zembretta National Park	C
Sebkhet Sidi El Hani Wetland	G
Sebkhet Kelbia Natural Reserve	G
Kneiss Islands Nature Reserve	1
Ichkeul Ramsar Wetland	B
Ichkeul Biosphere Reserve	B
Ichkeul World Heritage Site	B

ALGERIA	
Ahaggar (Hoggar) National Park	A
Belezma National Park	G
Chrea National Park	D
Djudjura National Park	E
El Kala National Park	H
Gouraya National Park	F
Tassili N'Ajjer National Park	B
Taza National Park	F
Theniet El Had National Park	C
Macta Ramsar Wetland	1
Mergueb Nature Reserve	2
Tassili N'Ajjer Biosphere Reserve	B
Tassili N'Ajjer World Heritage Site	B

MOROCCO	
Souss-Massa National Park	A
Toubkal National Park	B
Bouarfa Protected Area	5
Bokkoyas Biosphere Reserve	3
d'Afennourir Lake Ramsar Wetland	4
Khnifiss Bay Ramsar Wetland	6
Merja Sidi Boughaba Ramsar Wetland	2
Merja Zerga Ramsar Wetland	1

CANARY ISLANDS (SPAIN)	
Dunes National Park	E
Palmitos National Park	E
Garajonay National Park	C
Caldera de Taburiente National Park	A
Timanfaya National Park	D
Teide National Park	B

CLOCKWISE FROM TOP LEFT
Merzouga dunes, Morocco.
Volubilis Ruins, Morocco.
Ahaggar Mountains, Algeria.
Keel-billed toucan, Gran Canaria.

Tunisia

Balancing the demands of a growing tourism industry with the requirements of a precarious ecology so easily unbalanced by human intervention is a continuing issue for Tunisian wildlife and conservation authorities. With over 60 per cent of the country situated less than 350m (1,150ft) above sea level – and just one per cent above 1,000m (3,300ft) – Tunisia has only one river of any real significance. It also has a wide range of natural habitats, which extend from coastal wetlands and characteristically Mediterranean landscape to mountain and desert sands. These habitats are threatened by the growing problems of desertification, creeping urbanization and industrial pollution. In addition, cultivation for farmland and the accompanying use of insecticides poses further dangers.

These problems are exacerbated by plantations such as pine and the invasive Australian wattle and eucalyptus species, as well as the continuing decline in numbers of wildlife that were once prolific in the region. Wild boar and desert gazelle continue to be hunted, while fennec – one of the area's most distinguishing species – are still trapped illegally. These unsanctioned practices, many of which have continued over the centuries as a legacy of colonization, have resulted in the extinction of the leopard and lion in this region, while the lynx is rare today.

Locals overfish Tunisian waters, and land- and boat-based spearfishing is promoted as a tourist pastime. The national fishing industry is highly regulated and is one of the best managed in the entire Mediterranean region, carefully maintaining the sustainability of its fishing waters.

Considering its vast landmass, Tunisia is surprisingly low on indigenous avian species, and its bird numbers only surge during the annual migration periods, when the birds inevitably become vulnerable to hunting sportsmen.

Conservation needs are enjoying some priority among local authorities and a number of reserves and protected areas have been proclaimed, with a series of environmental education programmes established. One of the most significant is the reintroduction of the larger desert antelopes, such as oryx and addax, at Bou-Hedma National Park, where populations have been drastically reduced as a result of irresponsible hunting practices and other human intervention. The area around Meknassy and the terrain covered today by Bou-Hedma were once well wooded, with plenty of wildlife, and it is said that Hannibal might have sourced his famed elephants from this area. In order to retain some semblance of their former glory, regions such as this will require decisive intervention by conservation authorities. Such success has already been achieved at Ichkeul, a national park, as well as a Ramsar Wetland area and a World Heritage Site.

Algeria

The second-largest country in Africa, Algeria not only has the greatest landmass devoted to environmental protection on the continent, but also boasts one of the biggest national parks in Africa. This is despite its civil conflict and political turbulence. Separated into four broad regions – the Tell Atlas, High Plateau, the mountains of the Sahara Atlas, and the seemingly endless Sahara Desert – Algeria is home to nearly 30 million citizens. The population is plagued by a number of environmental concerns that demand urgent attention, not only to ensure the sustainability of the relatively small proportion of arable land – a mere three per cent (the Sahara covers some 85 per cent of the country) – but also for the benefit of conservation.

Inland waters and the nearly 1,000km (620 miles) of coastline, skirted by the mountains and valleys of the Tell Atlas, face pollution from sewerage, petroleum waste and other industrial effluent. Hydrocarbons account for 30 per cent of the GDP and 90 per cent of the nation's export earnings, and Algeria is one of the world's most important producers of gas and oil. The national coffers take priority over what many Algerian officials may consider peripheral concerns, such as conservation and ecotourism. However, considerable effort is being put into diversifying the local economy by encouraging foreign investment in areas beyond its fossil fuel industries.

More than 10 per cent of the population are occupied in the farming sector, while a further 10 per cent live in the non-arable Sahara, either in oasis settlements or small oil towns, or they are nomads whose lifestyle has been considerably disrupted by the drought-like conditions plaguing the region. Age-old pastures have been lost and the already limited water supplies (especially in urban settlements around which nomadic herders have congregated) have thus dwindled. This has affected both the quality of traditional life and the orchards of date palms (palmeraie) so vital to life in the desert.

It is thus no small feat that the biosphere reserves at Tassili and El Kala, the Ramsar Wetland areas at Lake Oubeïra and Lake Tonga, and the World Heritage Site of Tassili N'Ajjer National Park have been declared protected areas. Tassili N'Ajjer, in southeastern Algeria, lies within the Sahara and extends about 700km (450 miles) northwest to the Amguid, and the massive 80,000km² (31,000-sq.-mile) stretch of plains and valleys is the site of some of the finest rock paintings and engravings to have survived in North Africa. Some of these paintings date from 9000 to 2500 BC. With its unique rock formations carved by the erosive nature of the elements over aeons, the park is majestically beautiful and the gem in Algeria's conservation crown.

Morocco

Morocco boasts an extraordinary biodiversity and is home to a wide range of endemic floral and faunal species. Many of these are specific to the unique environments and ecosystems in which they naturally appear. The country has a fine collection of nearly 40 national parks, protected areas and nature reserves aimed at preserving an area once abounding with an equally impressive array of game and wildlife such as the leopard and Barbary lion. They have now either been all but eradicated from the region or hunted to extinction. Leopard populations in the northwest of the continent have, for example, dwindled dramatically in recent decades following the alarming increase in the trade of bushmeat and animal skins. Morocco and the Western Sahara – along with Egypt – still have limited numbers but, like so many countries on the continent, head counts of existing populations are either nonexistent or unreliable. Natural or man-made phenomena such as desertification have caused more than 20 mammal species to be classified as endangered.

Nonetheless, Morocco boasts a varied wildlife that justifies a sound and comprehensive environmental protection policy. The so-called Barbary ape, otters and wild boar are commonly found in the mountain foothills, while on the edge of the desert are herds of antelope and gazelle, and populations of fennec, jackal and hyena. Birds abound in every form, with approximately 300 resident and migrant species,

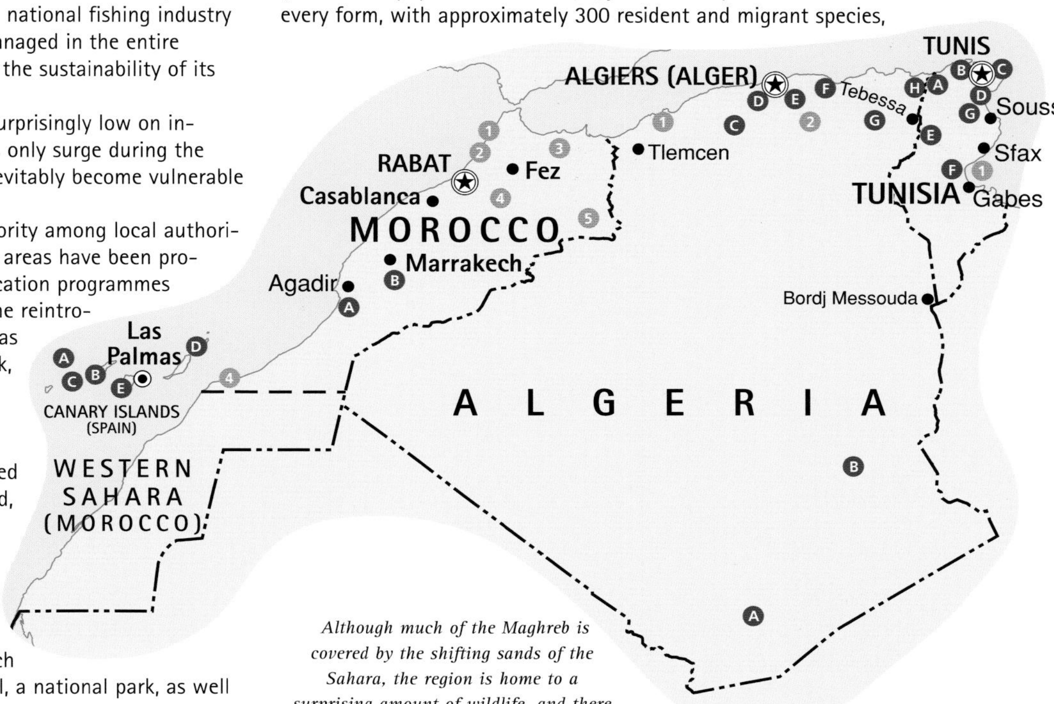

Although much of the Maghreb is covered by the shifting sands of the Sahara, the region is home to a surprising amount of wildlife, and there is a growing awareness among its custodian nations of the universal importance of this often desolate landscape.

ranging from the rare and endangered bald ibis and Eleanora's falcon to woodpeckers, gulls and waterfowl. The country is a vital stopover for migrating flocks of storks and cranes, as well as raptors, which make their home here in the spring and autumn months.

Human influences such as deforestation have resulted in plant life facing the same fate as the wildlife. This is particularly true of the oak, cedar and olive species with which Morocco is most commonly associated, the endemic wild pear (occurring only in the Mamora forest near Meknès and Rabat) and the indigenous forests of argane, now threatened by the advancement of cultivated stands of eucalyptus and pine.

The government has set aside areas that serve as sanctuaries for local plant and animal life found naturally across its varied terrain, from Toubkal to the sea shores of Tamri and the dune sea of the Sahara's Iriqui. Protected areas include biological, botanical, hunting and marine reserves, forest sanctuaries and Ramsar Wetlands such as Merja Zerga, Merja Sidi Boughaba, d'Afennourir Lake and Khnifiss Bay (Puerto Cansado). Prime among these conservation areas are the 36,000ha (90,000 acres) of mountain and forest that make up the great Toubkal National Park, and the impressive Souss-Massa National Park, some 60km (38 miles) south of Agadir. In a united effort with conservation authorities based in Europe, breeding pairs of addax and oryx have been reintroduced at Souss-Massa.

Canary Islands

These islands off the west coast of Morocco, acclaimed for their largely unspoilt natural heritage, have some 300 bird species, about 70 of these resident on the islands, and considerable effort – notably at Dunes National Park – has gone into preserving their bird life: these include rare and endangered species such as the laurel pigeon and Canarian oystercatcher, and even common species, such as the canary. Many of the reserves – such as Timanfaya and Caldera de Taburiente – have established small but successful environmental programmes intended to preserve wildlife species such as the Hierro giant lizard. Intensive efforts have also been established in the untamed forest wilderness – declared a natural heritage site by UNESCO – of the National Park of Garajonay, right in the middle of La Gomera, and Teide National Park. Established on the island of Tenerife in 1954, the bulk of Teide covers the 3,718m (12,198ft) Mount Teide and the Las Cañadas volcanic crater.

THE REGION

All three nations in the northern central regions of Africa (Niger, Libya and Chad) have designated a number of national parks and nature reserves – most notably the faunal and partial faunal reserves – to preserve both the scenic splendour and indigenous wildlife. Animal stocks are today extremely limited, and it is the unspoiled landscapes of these protected areas that remain the main attraction.

NIGER	Key
"W" National Park	A
Addax Sanctuary Strict Nature Reserve	4
Aïr and Ténéré Natural Reserves	3
Gadabéji Total Faunal Reserve	2
Tamou Total Faunal Reserve	1
Dosso Partial Faunal Reserve	1
"W" Ramsar Wetland	A

LIBYA	
Kouf National Park	A
Zellaf Nature Reserve	1
Garabulli Protected Area	3
Nefhusa Protected Area	2

CHAD	
Manda National Park	B
Zakouma National Park	A
Abou Telfane Faunal Reserve	3
Bahr Salamat Faunal Reserve	4
Binder-Léré Faunal Reserve	6
Fada Archeï Faunal Reserve	1
Mandélia Faunal Reserve	7
Ouadi Rimé-Ouadi Achim Faunal Reserve	2
Sinianka-Minia Game Reserve	5
Massaguet Pastoral Reserve	9
Lake Fitri Ramsar Wetland	8

Niger

In a land made up largely of mountain and desert, Niger's natural attractions – from the distant peaks of the Aïr Mountains to the endless sand sea of the Ténéré and the scenic gem that is Niger's "W" National Park, which is both a national park and Ramsar Wetland – comprise one of its greatest assets. With nearly 10 million hectares (3,850,000 sq. miles) of its land set aside for conservation, much of the countryside – empty and barren, but ecologically and geologically unique – remains largely untrammelled. Not only are these areas spectacularly beautiful, but vast stretches remain much as they have been for centuries. It is for this reason that areas such as the rugged Aïr Mountains to the northeast of Agadez and the great Ténéré continue to attract only the most intrepid of adventurers intent on exploring some of Africa's last remaining wilderness areas. Although the Ténéré Desert stretches to within 500km (310 miles) of the town of Agadez, it is an immense wasteland that is, by and large, extremely isolated from any semblance of civilization and thus presents an enormous challenge for even the bravest of travellers. As a result, the wild landscapes of Niger do not see many travellers venturing beyond the standard tourists routes or even into the country's parks and reserves. There is also the very real threat of physical danger, posed not by the wild animals or the harsh and unforgiving environment but by the militant hardliners and bandits that patrol so much of the country's northern and eastern hinterland. Travellers who do venture to isolated areas such as the Aïr Mountains and Ténéré Desert should thus never risk travelling alone – and not without the necessary permission from local authorities. Even despite the fact that so much of its landmass is devoted to the preservation of the landscape and the wildlife it harbours, conservation in Niger is fraught with issues that continue to dog progress. With less than four per cent of Niger's land considered suitable for agriculture, the constant creep of the desert is undoubtedly the nation's greatest dilemma, and this is further exacerbated by the continued denuding of wooded areas for both the production of charcoal for industrial purposes and wood for home fires. Vast stands of already restricted vegetation have thus been lost to deforestation and this, combined with overgrazing (the vast majority of the population is employed in one way or another in the agricultural sector), has demanded at least some attention from state authorities. As a result, small but generally successful efforts at re-greening have been granted official sanction by the government so that areas such as Guesselbodi (not far from Niamey) have seen considerable change for the better. Here, locals have been employed to plant seedling trees and other forms of indigenous vegetation and have built windbreaks to protect these from the wind and desert sands.

By far the most successful of the government's conservation programmes is the "W" National Park (Parc National W du Niger), named after the double U-bend in the Niger River that winds through the northern reaches of the park. "W" National Park – and the adjacent Tamou Reserve – is indeed a wonderland of beauty and is widely acknowledged as the country's finest wildlife reserve and one of the best in all of West Africa. It may lack the vast herds of big game safari-goers can expect to see further south, but the great park provides some good game-viewing and is a birding paradise that boasts no fewer than 300 avi-fauna species, including herons, storks and ibis, which flock to the river between February and May. There are also some remnants of the ubiquitous
Big Five, which are still Africa's greatest attraction. Small herds of buffalo patrol the plains, while elephant have congregated in the Tapoa Valley and solitary leopards and prides of lion have also been recorded in the park.

"W" National Park extends into both Benin and Burkina Faso and, at 2,200km² (850 sq. miles), is Niger's largest park. Situated less than 150km (93 miles) from Niamey, it is the most accessible to visitors and sees the most tourist traffic.

Libya

Surrounded by the water of the Mediterranean and the sands of the Sahara, Libya is the fourth-largest country in Africa, with a long and fascinating history peppered with Roman and Greek occupation that has resulted in a rich cultural legacy.

Although Libya may have been far more fertile in Roman times, it is now a largely barren and uninspiring wilderness that ranges from semidesert to vast rock-strewn plains, imposing mountains to deep Sahara, with just one flowing river – the Wadi Ki'am, which is little more than a 2km (1-mile) stream. What little vegetation there is is limited to palm and olive groves, citrus orchards and stands of tamarisk and wild fig interspersed with thin, straggly grasses. The 170,000ha (420,000 acres) of conservation land is largely the home territory of mammals such as small antelopes and gazelles, with a healthy population of porcupines, reptiles and birds. Birdlife includes warblers, larks, hoopoes, flamingoes, finches, and the white-crowned black wheatear, and birds of prey, including eagles and falcons.

The investment of vast resources is ploughed into farmland rather than national parks and wildlife sanctuaries. Despite brave government-backed attempts at vegetating the encroaching sand dunes and sourcing additional fresh water supplies for domestic, industrial and agricultural consumption – the latter relieved somewhat by the development of the Great Manmade River Project, which poses threats of its own when it comes to the run-off waters of the Sahara – the ecology of the land is the least of Libya's problems and the proposed solutions are slow in producing effective results. Libya's conservation record is rather dismal in relation to those of neighbouring countries. In many ways, the damage has already been done – much of the indigenous wildlife has been hunted to near extinction and the natural habitats ravaged by the grazing patterns of domestic livestock – and reversing the process is almost impossible. By far the most serious concern in Libya is the enormous problem of desecrated cultural sites and public littering, which has not only infiltrated the dune sea but also left its mark on other natural attractions, including the beaches and oases. From the unusual lakes of Awbari Sand Sea to the fascinating rock formations that punctuate the Acacus range in the remote west and the ancient rock art to be found at Wadi Matkhandoush, it is the very isolation of Libya's unspoiled terrain that makes it so attractive to adventure travellers. Parks and reserves such as Kouf, Zellaf, Garabulli and Nefhusa – and the geologically complex plateau that stretches between Al-Khums and Al-Qusbat – are beginning to emerge as promising tourist destinations. Travelling through Libya is not an easy task, especially given the political intrigue and the unpredictability of its socio-economic climate. Not only is spoken English a rarity beyond the major urban settlements, but travellers need special permission to drive both on and off the roads and into the desert. It is also a very expensive destination, with very little in the way of hotels or indeed any other accommodation, and organized tours are the only real way to travel through Libya. This does not make for a very inviting prospect, but once the potential of its protected areas has been realized and acted upon, it will become an extremely rewarding wildlife and travel destination.

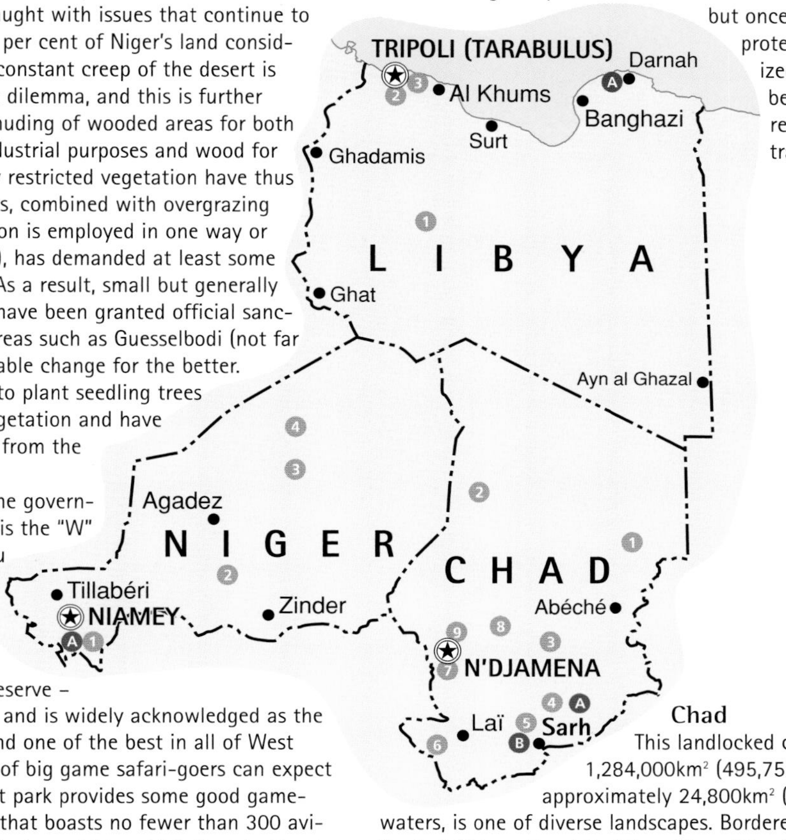

Although scenically beautiful, the desert sands that cover Niger, Libya and Chad once teemed with wild animals that are still to be seen south of the Sahara. Sadly, many have long been locally extinct, and only small pockets of big cat populations, for example, remain in the northern reaches.

Chad

This landlocked country that covers some 1,284,000km² (495,755 sq. miles), excluding approximately 24,800km² (1,575 sq. miles) of inland waters, is one of diverse landscapes. Bordered by Cameroon, the Central African Republic, Libya, Niger, Nigeria and Sudan, the massive lake that shares its name is the Sahel's most vital body of water, but Chad's vistas comprise mostly dry, wide plains encircled by mountain and desert, tapering towards lowland plateaux in the south. As a result, the environmental issues faced by national parks such as Manda and Zakouma and the eight smaller faunal reserves are equally broad, varying from the desertification of the northern reaches to the availability of drinkable water, as well as soil and water pollution and a wholly inadequate system of waste disposal. These concerns are further aggravated by the extreme poverty of the largely farming population and the economic instability posed by the country's geographic isolation, the periodic and debilitating drought, virtually non-existent infrastructure and the political conflict it has seen over the last few decades. The success of conservation efforts concentrated in and around Manda National Park, Zakouma National Park and faunal reserves such as Abou Telfane, Bahr Salamat, Binder-Léré and others of their ilk, and even the Ramsar Wetland at Lake Fitri, is being severely hampered by insufficient funds to carry even the few existing projects to fruition. The local strain of malaria is becoming increasingly resistant to chloroquine. With resources stretched to the limit, poachers continue to hunt and destroy the indigenous wildlife that has remained after nearly 20 years of decimation during the civil war.

The good news is that the wildlife reserves and national parks are steadily – albeit painstakingly slowly – being restocked and monitored with the aim of attracting an upmarket tourism clientele. This is particularly rewarding when one considers that countries such as Chad – as well as Benin and the Democratic Republic of Congo – boast the world's most rapidly growing populations of big cats, the growth rate of which stood at more than three percent for the year 2000. The impressive 3,000km² (1,150-sq.-mile) Zakouma National Park just beyond the southern fringe of the Sahara counts healthy if not thriving populations of Africa's three biggest cats – lion, leopard and cheetah – and a number of smaller feline species, including servals.

CLOCKWISE FROM TOP LEFT
Niger Desert, Niger.
Cheetahs, Chad.
Aïr Mountains, Niger.
Horned adder, Libya.

ADV 288
NP 248

THE REGION

Although it is rated by many to be one of the leading nations on the African continent, Egypt has allocated less than a million hectares of its land to conservation, whereas Sudan, the largest nation in Africa and long considered the pariah, has set aside an impressive – or, at least, potentially impressive – 10.35 million hectares as national park or conservation area.

EGYPT	Key
Ras Abu Gallum National Park	C
Ras Mohammed National Park	A
Nabq National Park	B
Zerenike Protectorate (Lake Bardawil)	3
St Catherine's Protectorate	4
Gebel Elba Protectorate	6
Lake Qarun Protectorate	1
Tiran and Sanafir Islands Protectorate	5
El Omayed Protectorate	2
Lake Bardawil Ramsar Wetland	3
Lake Burullus Ramsar Wetland	2

SUDAN	
Bandingilo National Park	E
Boma National Park	D
Dinder National Park	B
Nimule National Park	F
Radom National Park	H
Sanganeb Atoll Marine National Park	A
Shambe National Park	C
Southern National Park	G
Arkawit Wildlife Sanctuary	2
Arkawit-Sinkat Wildlife Sanctuary	1
Ashana Game Reserve	12
Bengangai Game Reserve	9
Chelkou Game Reserve	11
Fanyikango Island Game Reserve	5
Juba Game Reserve	8
Numatina Game Reserve	10
Rahad Game Reserve	4
Sabaloka Game Reserve	7
Tokar Game Reserve	3
Zeraf Game Reserve	6
Dinder Biosphere Reserve	B
Radom Biosphere Reserve	H

CLOCKWISE FROM TOP LEFT
Clownfish, Red Sea, Egypt.
Pyramid and Sphinx at El Giza, Cairo, Egypt.
Camel, Sudan.
Rock face, Sinai Desert, Egypt.

Egypt

With a climate that is, in the most part, hot and dry, and a rainfall that is quite negligible when it comes to its water requirements, Egypt's main source of revenue is its oil and gas reserves rather than the tourism potential of its parks and conservation areas. Egypt enjoys – to some degree, at least – a high-profile reputation as one of the most popular holiday destinations in Africa and can boast more than 10 individual protected areas designed to help protect the wildlife and natural heritage as well as the priceless antiquities that are the nation's cultural heritage. The country nevertheless has a deplorable conservation record, especially when contrasted with other comparable nations.

To the east of the lush river valley lies the Eastern (Arabian) desert – a rather sterile desert plain skirted in the east by high mountains – while in the west stretches the Western (Libyan) Desert, a wide and largely empty tableland dotted intermittently with the odd oasis of green and a series of strange geological formations. Blessed, too, with engaging coves, white beaches and the crystal waters of the Mediterranean, Egypt's desiccated interior is punctuated with the goatskin tents and humble mud-brick structures that are home to the Bedouins and farmers who continue to uphold the ancient traditions of their forefathers, in so doing making considerable contributions to the local economy. It is this dichotomy of need and function that has ensured that conservation remains low on Egypt's list of priorities.

The precious reefs and offshore islands of the Red Sea were declared national protected areas in 1995, and recreational diving was limited to designated areas only. However, the Red Sea – with its brightly coloured underwater gardens of coral and marine creatures of every imaginable size and shape – remains under serious risk from a largely unregulated tourism industry and development projects intended to supplement the national economy rather than the natural heritage on which it depends. A number of national marine parks have been planned, but there appears to be little attempt to enforce the existing environmental laws, and progress is slow. In the meanwhile, other dive areas – such as Sharm el-Sheikh and Ras Mohammed in the south of the Sinai Peninsula – remain under equal threat, and the country continues to be plagued by environmental issues that could, with some effort, be avoided, eradicated or diminished through a long-term commitment by the national authorities.

Although it is a signatory to a number of international environmental agreements initiated to help stabilize natural habitats and safeguard rare, vulnerable or endangered species, Egypt – sadly – is far removed from a sound environmental programme. Although many Egyptians tend to follow the guidelines presented by the recycling programme promoted in the big cities, Cairo is, quite literally, littered with refuse. This is a sad indictment on the tourist market, but is not helped by ineffective waste removal and a blatant disregard for urban environmental issues. The pollution that fills Cairo's skies has already begun to erode the great monuments and antiquities that make up its ancient skyline, and desertification has effectively pushed the pyramids 5km (3 miles) into the desert. Growing tourist numbers have led to mementoes being chiselled and splintered from the façades of ancient monuments, while visitors have brazenly looted corals and other marine creatures from the surrounding reefs. Illegal animal products such as elephant ivory, long since banished from the marketplaces of many other African countries, are still available on the streets of Egypt's urban centres, and the country's inland water sources such as freshwater lakes – all important in a country that is painfully dry beyond the Nile Valley – are being adversely affected by toxins emitted by agriculture and industry. In addition, far too many birds en route from Europe to the African continent still meet a cruel fate here in Egypt, and the water birds that succeed in settling on protected wetlands in the north of Africa are hunted for the pot as well as, in many cases, purely for recreation.

Fortunately there has been at least some attempt to conserve the country's natural heritage, and the Egyptian government has, in recent years, gazetted additional reserve areas such as the Red Sea's Elba region, the Zerenike area of Lake Bardawil, and the Naqb, Ras Abu Gallum and Dahab regions in Sinai. In fact, the Sinai – a region of stark splendour between the peaks of Mount Sinai and, at 2,642m (8,700ft) Egypt's highest mountain, Mount St Catherine in the south and the coastal plains of the desert to the north – boasts the best conservation record, seen at its finest in the Ras Mohammed National Park where, unlike most other parks, a team of rangers is employed on a full-time basis. In order to protect the fragile ecosystem, off-road driving is strictly forbidden. Another heartening conservation project is the Wind, Sand and Stars Project, which has initiated the renovation of age-old Bedouin gardens, providing drinking water for locals, while foreign visitors are taught about the sustainability of life in the desert. The monumental grandeur of ancient Luxor has also escaped the worst of the ravages, and much of its architectural splendour remains largely untouched. Despite the fact that it is one of the nation's premier tourist destinations, the settlement – erected on and around the 4,000-year-old site of ancient Thebes – is a relatively well-protected conglomeration of historic wilderness and modern commercialism.

Covering perhaps the driest and most parched desert landscape in all of Africa, both Egypt and Sudan face enormous challenges when it comes to the conservation of their wildlife heritage.

Sudan

Consisting mostly of hot, dry plateau dotted intermittently with marshland in the north and highlands skirting the Red Sea, the Sudan stretches from the Nubian Desert through swampland to the southern rainforests. All-important rains fall for only two months of the year in the central regions, and up to eight months in the far south. As a result, much of the country is frequently ravaged by the food shortages brought on by the drought conditions that continue to plague plantations of cotton, gum arabic and sesame seeds that form the mainstay of the national economy. Combined with the effects of a debilitating civil war and the fact that at least two million of its citizens are constantly on the move across nomadic tribal lands, such climatic conditions mean that, like Egypt, the Sudan cannot afford – economically, socially or politically – to give precedence to its natural heritage over its mostly impoverished peoples, no matter how urgent the call for environmental protection of its wildlife and apparently endless landscape. In many regions where vast expanses of dry desert support little life, all effort is generally channelled into the day-to-day requirements of Sudan's population of some 28 million, 75 per cent of whom reside almost entirely in the country's rural areas. In far-flung reaches of the country, where the climate ranges from hot and dry to humid and tropical, water remains the source of all life and priority is given to the harvesting of this natural resource. In the northern deserts, diesel engines pump water from the Nile while, far from the river banks, where rains seldom fall, locals have built small dams for domestic and agricultural use.

In the light of these very real logistical issues, it is little wonder, then, that the national parks and other conservation areas have suffered considerably in favour of more pressing matters. Even the best of the protected lands – covering a variety of contrasting landscapes, from Bandingilo and Shambe national parks, the Arkawit Wildlife Sanctuary and the Chelkou Game Reserve, to the Sanganeb Atoll Marine National Park, the Radom Biosphere Reserve and the national park and biosphere reserve at Dinder – continue to fight an uphill battle to preserve their integrity as wildlife havens. The situation has not been helped by the years of conflict that have discouraged tourist traffic to a multitude of hot spots noted for their uncertain security and thus the personal safety of visitors. The Sudan is, nevertheless, a signatory to a number of international environmental agreements on biodiversity, climate change, desertification, protection of both endangered species and the ozone, as well as the ban on nuclear testing. Although all these agreement have been signed, none of them have been ratified and, consequently, little progress has been made in the area of conservation and development.

Sudan is the largest country in Africa and borders no fewer than nine African countries. However, as forest and woodland covers approximately 20 per cent of the land, less than 6 per cent in total is arable. It is hardly surprising that nature spots aimed at the tourism and lesiure industries come a poor second in the race for land. One spot that has seemed to conquer the adversities is the wilderness of Nyala, for some 400 years the seat of the Fur sultanate and now little more than a far-flung desert settlement. This picturesque satellite is, however, the popular starting point for expeditions up the Sudan's second-highest mountain, the 3,088m (10,150ft) Marra Mountain. Although not easily navigable on foot (less so by vehicle!), the topography – which includes an imposing, extinct volcano – does offer some very good hiking terrain, with spectacular vistas of natural splendour interspersed with cultivated lands that are well watered by the rivers of the immediate region. It is thus the more than 20 protected oases of wilderness (covering more than 10 million hectares), that contribute a little to the varied face of the Sudan and its natural heritage.

ADV 290
NP 250

THE REGION

In what is arguably the most impoverished region of North Africa, the countries that cover the western reaches of the Sahara are nevertheless extremely rich in desert wildlife. Senegal, Mauritania and The Gambia are world renowned for the extraordinary diversity of their bird life, making them popular destinations not only for the mass tourism market, but also the adventurer and naturalist.

SENEGAL	Key
Basse-Casamance National Park	E
Delta du Saloum National Park	D
Djoudj National Park	A
Madeleines Island National Park	C
Langue de Barbarie National Park	B
Niokolo-Koba National Park	F
Ferlo-Nord Faunal Reserve	1
Ferlo-Sud Faunal Reserve	2
Ndiael Faunal Reserve	A
Bandia Game Reserve	4
Maka-Diama Hunting Reserve	3
Niokolo-Koba Biosphere Reserve	F
Delta du Saloum Biosphere Reserve	D
Delta du Saloum Ramsar Wetland	D
Djoudj Ramsar Wetland	A
Gueumbeul Ramsar Wetland	B
Bassin du Ndiael Ramsar Wetland	A
Djoudj National Bird Sanctuary WHS	A
Niokolo-Koba World Heritage Site	F

GAMBIA	
Kiang West National Park	A
Niumi National Park	B
River Gambia National Park	C
Sine Saloum National Park	B
Abuko Nature Reserve	1

MAURITANIA	
Banc d'Arguin National Park	A
Diawling National Park	B
Baie du Lévrier (Cap Blanc) Integral Reserve	1
Banc d'Arguin Ramsar Wetland	A
Banc d'Arguin World Heritage Site	A

MALI	
Boucle du Baoulé National Park	A
Badinko Faunal Reserve	3
Bafing Faunal Reserve	2
Banifing-Baoulé Faunal Reserve	11
Douentza Partial Faunal Reserve	6
Fina Faunal Reserve	4
Kénié-Baoulé Faunal Reserve	1
Kongossambougou Faunal Reserve	5
Soussan Faunal Reserve	11
Talikourou Faunal Reserve	12
Ansongo-Menaka Partial Faunal Reserve	10
Gourma Eléphant Partial Faunal Reserve	8
Falaise de Bandiagara Sanctuary	7
Lake Horo Ramsar Wetland	9
Walado Debo/Lake Debo Ramsar Wetland	9
Falaise de Bandiagara World Heritage Site	7

CAPE VERDE ISLANDS

No UN-recognized protected areas

CLOCKWISE FROM TOP LEFT

Baobab, Palmarin, Senegal.
Pelicans, Bird Island, Langue de Barbarie National Park, Senegal.
Gazelle, Gueumbeul Ramsar Wetland, Senegal.
Rock art, Bandiagra, Mali.

Senegal

Boasting no less than 2.24 million hectares (5.5 million acres) of formally protected land, Senegal's conservation record is varied. Although it is no longer home to the vast numbers of large mammals that once roamed its plains, it is justifiably proud of a number of its parks and reserves, which have made valiant attempts in preserving what remains of its wildlife. Senegal already has two World Heritage Sites: Djoudj National Bird Sanctuary and Niokolo-Koba, the latter also officially designated a national park and biosphere reserve, while parts of Delta du Saloum have been declared a national park, biosphere reserve and Ramsar Wetland. Other gazetted reserves focus either on the wetland deltas on which they are situated or on the extensive bird life of the broader region. One such example is Madeleines Island National Park, the three islets just offshore from Dakar, which serve as a vital breeding site for sea birds such as cormorants.

Senegal's great showpiece is, however, Niokolo-Koba National Park, which – at 950,000ha (2,350,000 acres) – is the largest national park in the region, harbouring a number of species that are either rare or endangered beyond its borders. Top on its list are breeding herds of elephant, buffalo, giant eland, waterbuck and duiker, some 20 packs of wild dog, families of side-striped jackal, lion prides, and troops of primates such as chimpanzees and Temminck's red colobus. Although some of the larger mammals are present only in limited numbers, certain antelope species are found here in their thousands.

Niokolo-Koba National Park is also known for a prolific bird life of about 350 individual species, including black-crowned cranes, Abyssinian ground hornbills, and saddle-billed and woolly-necked storks, but it is Djoudj – a national park, Ramsar Wetland and officially designated bird sanctuary – that is the jewel in Senegal's birding crown. Covering no less than 16,000ha (40,000 acres), the swampy flatlands and delta streams of the Senegal River have created one of Africa's most significant wetlands, especially as it lies directly within the flight path of flocks of migrating birds. Of equally global significance, and just as renowned for its avifauna, is Langue de Barbarie National Park, located at the mouth of the Senegal River in the southernmost reaches of the peninsula that shares its name. It is one of the better protected of Senegal's bird sanctuaries. Although the wetlands are easily accessible via boat, visitors' numbers are restricted and no overnighting is permitted within the boundaries of the national park. This contrasts considerably with the delta of Basse-Casamance National Park, the most fertile of all Senegal's parkland, which no longer sees the same tourist figures since an increasing number of attacks on tourists in recent years. Comprising rather impressive stretches of savanna, tidal wetland, swamp and woodland, the protected area of Basse-Casamance is set somewhat apart from the rest of the country by the waters of the Gambia River, but is nevertheless home to a good number of small rainforest inhabitants such as duiker, colobus monkeys, flying squirrels and pangolins.

Conservation efforts in these parks are undoubtedly noble, if not entirely successful, and there is at least some attempt to control both the wildlife populations and the numbers of visitors who may interact with the localized ecosystem. The Bandia Game Reserve is considerably less rigid. In fact, this 700ha (1,750-acre) private reserve has taken full advantage of tourism potential. Whereas privately owned Bandia has managed to accumulate the resources to maintain its lands, many state-owned reserves simply do not have that capital.

Gambia

Although Gambia cannot claim to have any park or reserve that matches the expanses of East and Central Africa, the 18,000ha (45,000 acres) of its 11,300km² (4,350 sq. miles) that make up its conservation areas are a haven for a huge variety of avifauna, with no less than 400 bird species making their home in and around the capital alone. Although the landscape comprises mostly open plain and occasional salt swamps along the river, the varied climatic conditions allow for a distinct variation in mood and temperament in the country's parks.

While guided walks among the birds and monkeys of Bijilo Forest Park are popular among nature-lovers, it is the marshy banks of the Gambia River that remain the primary destination for birders, who flock here to spot the localized Egyptian plover and observe the nesting sites of the red-throated and northern carmine bee-eaters.

Principal among Gambia's national parks is the bushveld and forest of Kiang West National Park. Large mammals and big game are not prominent features here, although the riverine forest and open bush that line parts of the river course are home to a number of small primate species, antelope and a total of nearly 600 bird species. The Gambian wildlife experience is varied, with some extraordinary highlights and some extreme disappointments. One of the highlights is Abuko Nature Reserve. Not only does its varied landscape boast an impressive array of primate, antelope and bird species – from vervet and colobus monkeys to duiker and sitatunga – but it is well cared for, with a sound record in conservation, much of which focuses on the remarkable bird life. A large proportion of the avifauna comprises migrating species that make their home here at certain times during the year, and visiting species – including flycatchers and kingfishers – are those most at home around the water sources.

Mauritania

Even with a total of nearly two million hectares (five million acres) of its land given over to conservation, Mauritania faces a series of very real threats when it comes to the ecology of the region.

Far off the beaten tourist track, it enjoys very limited patronage from worldwide travellers, and suffers enormously from a very serious lack of resources, both in the immediate sense of conservation and tourism and in the broader economic status of the country as a whole.

It was once the home of great prides of lion, herds of elephant and giraffe, and impressive populations of cheetah, leopard and a variety of prey species, but this is no longer the case. Many animals and plants are locally extinct, endangered or present only in limited numbers, their home territories having shrunk enormously over the last century. The eastern reaches of the desert are, for example, home to the endangered addax, while there are only occasional sightings of elephant or leopard – which once thrived here – in Ayoun el Atrous.

Standing head and shoulders above Mauritania's few conservation areas – two national parks, an integral reserve and Ramsar Wetland – is Banc d'Arguin, a national park and Ramsar Wetland, in addition to its status as a World Heritage Site. Banc d'Arguin National Park is not an easy place to visit. Quite desolate and isolated, it is best known as a birding paradise, studded throughout with the nests of mammoth flocks of birds, most notably aquatic and migratory species such as flamingoes. The park is also the home ground of the Imragen, fishermen who earn their living by plying local waters for fish such as sardines and yellow mullet. The constant activity of foreign fishing trawlers, such as Korean and Japanese vessels, in Mauritanian waters means that marine stocks are waning.

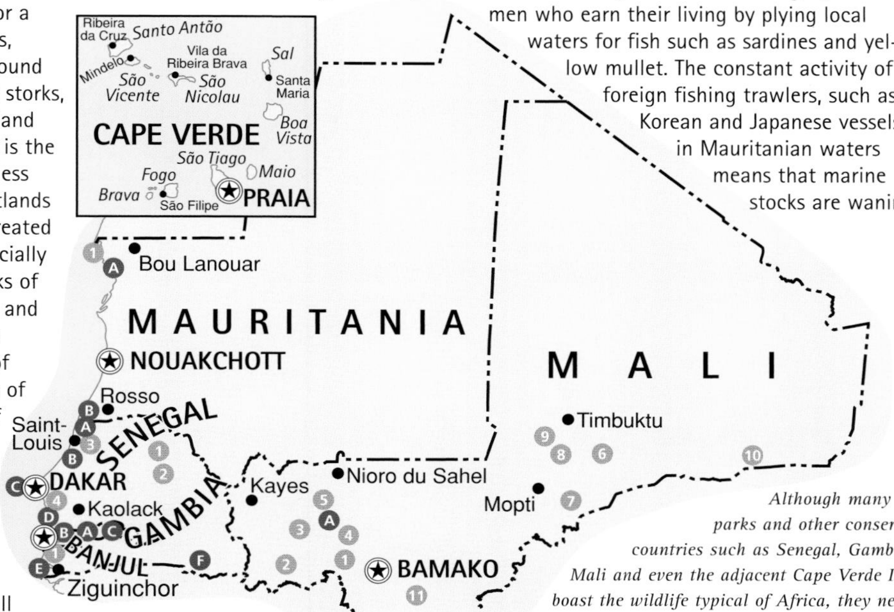

Although many of the national parks and other conservation areas in countries such as Senegal, Gambia, Mauritania, Mali and even the adjacent Cape Verde Islands may not boast the wildlife typical of Africa, they nevertheless have a fine array of bird and mammal species that continue to attract the attention of environmentalists and conservationists.

Mali

Ravaged by extreme poverty and the effects of debilitating drought that, at various times in recent history, has brought the country to its knees, Mali nevertheless has nine faunal reserves, three partial faunal reserves and three classified forests. Along with its famed Boucle du Baoulé National Park and the Falaise de Bandiagara – both a partial faunal reserve and World Heritage Site – these cover a total of 5.75 million hectares. Vast, impoverished Mali is extremely rich in a cultural heritage that forms the very heart of its most widely recognized assets. The Mali landscape is, in parts, both bleak and austere, but there is a prepossessing charm that overrides the emptiness of its desert. Although it is home to a rather different selection of big game and other wildlife species than may typically be seen in the continent's great game reserves, the sweeping dunes and savanna bushveld have, over the centuries, come to harbour an extraordinary diversity of wildlife particular to the gulf of Africa. There are indeed species that remain threatened, rare or endangered, but Mali has one of the most successful conservation records in West Africa. The wild open spaces are an important haven for big game, predators and large groups of other mammal species that appear to be thriving here. There is still an impressive number of hippos at home in the waters of the Niger, and the elephant population even seems to be increasing. The limited number of visitors to the rather isolated countryside of Boucle du Baoulé National Park has undoubtedly helped the conservation and preservation process, allowing for healthy herds of elephants to establish themselves here and a population of some 600 individuals around Gossi. Fortunately for the elephant 'community', the Tuareg people have traditionally concentrated on other big game, instead of hunting these great beasts.

Cape Verde

Cape Verde's 10 islands and eight surrounding islets – covering some 4,035km² (1,560 sq. miles) – have made little effort to preserve what remains of the environment. Indigenous wildlife does not extend much beyond the primate populations of Brava and Santiago – with some interesting bird species and a limited number of reptiles (such as the giant gecko and localized skink) – yet the islands have no UN-recognized protected areas and are something of an ecological wasteland, albeit not entirely as a result of simple neglect by government officials. The very location and geological make-up of the islands mean that they are highly susceptible to all sorts of climatic variations and the forces of nature that sweep across their coastal landscape.

THE REGION

The far western reaches of West Africa are a world of contrast, densely populated stretches of savanna adjoining wild expanses of open African veld, with some fine wildlife reserves juxtaposed against some of the most exploited and depleted natural landscapes in the world.

GUINEA-BISSAU	Key
Lagoa de Cufada Ramsar Wetland	1

GUINEA	
Badiar National Park	A
Haut Niger National Park	B
Massif du Ziama Strict Nature Reserve	1
Mount Nimba Strict Nature Reserve	2
Mount Nimba Biosphere Reserve	2
Massif du Ziama Biosphere Reserve	1
Mount Nimba World Heritage Site	2

SIERRA LEONE	
Outamba-Kilimi National Park (OKNP)	A
Kangari Hills Forest Reserve	2
Loma Mountains Forest Reserve	4
Sankan Biriwa (Tingi Hills) Forest Reserve	3
Western Area Forest Reserve	1

LIBERIA	
Sapo National Park	A

CÔTE D'IVOIRE	
d'Azagny National Park	F
Banco National Park	G
Comoé National Park	E
Îles Ehotile National Park	H
Marahoué National Park	C
Mont Péko National Park	B
Mont Sangbé National Park	D
Taï National Park	A
Haut Bandama Flora and Fauna Reserve	3
N'zo Partial Faunal Reserve	1
Comoé Biosphere Reserve	E
Taï Biosphere Reserve	A
Comoé World Heritage Site	E
Mont Nimba World Heritage Site	2
Taï World Heritage Site	A

BURKINA FASO	
Deux Balé National Park	A
Kabore-Tambi National Park	B
"W" National Park	C
Arly Faunal Reserve	8
Bontioli Faunal Reserve	1
Singou Faunal Reserve	6
Arly Partial Faunal Reserve	7
Kourtiagou Partial Faunal Reserve	8
Pama Partial Faunal Reserve	5
Sahel Partial Faunal Reserve	3
Mare aux Hippopotames Bird Reserve	2
Mare aux Hippopotames Ramsar Wetland	2
Mare d'Oursi Ramsar Wetland	4
"W" National Park Ramsar Wetland	C

GHANA	
Bia National Park	B
Bui National Park	E
Digya National Park	D
Kakum National Park	C
Mole National Park	F
Nini-Suhien National Park	A
Kogyae Strict Nature Reserve	5
Ankasa Game Reserve	1
Assin-Attandanso Game Reserve	3
Bia Game Reserve	B
Gbele Game Reserve	6
Kalakpa Game Reserve	4
Bia Biosphere Reserve	B
Owabi Ramsar Wetland	2

TOGO	
Fazao-Malfakassa National Park	C
Fosse aux Lions National Park	A
Kéran National Park	B
Abdoulaye Faunal Reserve	1
Akaba Forest Reserve	3
Haho-Yoto Forest Reserve	5
Kpessi Forest Reserve	2
Oti Mandouri Forest Reserve	6
Togodo Faunal Reserve	4
Kéran Ramsar Wetland	B
Togodo Ramsar Wetland	4

BENIN	
Pendjari National Park	A
"W" National Park	B
Atakora Hunting Zone	1
Djona Hunting Zone	2
Pendjari Hunting Zone	3
Pendjari Biosphere Reserve	3

CLOCKWISE FROM TOP LEFT
Man River, Sierra Leone.
Elephant, Mole National Park, Ghana.
Rope bridge, Côte d'Ivoire.
Wattled Crane, Comoé National Park, Côte d'Ivoire.

Guinea-Bissau

Few areas of Guinea-Bissau have been set aside for protection, and certainly none recognized by the United Nations. Much of the country comprises flat tableland interspersed with forests and a surprising number of wetlands, varying from swamps to flood plain. The landscape has rather healthy populations of reptiles and antelope, hippo, primates and other small mammal species, but has seen better days. The larger wildlife species are now locally extinct, having succumbed to overpopulation and the widespread decimation of natural resources during the war years, but many of the offshore islands, most notably those of the Bijargos Archipelago, remain remarkably intact and boast a rich diversity of marine-based animals such as turtles and manatees.

Guinea

While Guinea boasts Mount Nimba – World Heritage Site, Biosphere Reserve and Strict Nature Reserve – and a few impressive nature reserves, its two national parks are the most worthy of exploration. Guinea has, however, seen considerable decline in its wildlife populations but most of the larger mammals – elephant, lion, hippo, buffalo and chimpanzees – remain despite any real effort to protect them.

The fairly recently established national parks of Badiar and Haut-Niger do, however, have at least some history of conservation worthy of recognition. Whereas prides of lion were quite common in Haut-Niger National Park during the 1960s and 1970s, their numbers began to dwindle in the decades that followed. Today, however, following a relatively conscientious attempt at rehabilitating their natural habitat, small prides are making their way back to the area, and the Mafou Forest is now the home of a number of resettled prides. Haut-Niger hosts elephant, buffalo, hippo, chimps, waterbuck and other antelope, and its populations are healthy and growing. Both parks offer the opportunity to spot wild animals such as lion and leopard.

Sierra Leone

The most outstanding of Sierra Leone's protected areas is Outamba-Kilimi National Park, an isolated wilderness that owes much of its success to a remote location that limits accessibility. The park is roughly divided into two contrasting sections: one, around Outamba, of wooded hills and grassland laced with rivers; the other, the Kilimi portion, a broad, featureless plain stretching across the west. Both boast species typical of the region, including the pygmy hippo and primates.

Sierra Leone also has four forest reserves in which no hunting is permitted. These are Kangari Hills, Western Area, Sankan Biriwa (also known as Tingi Hills) and Loma Mountains, which is crowned by the 1,945m (6,380ft) peak of Mount Bintumani. The latter reserve was specifically established to help preserve the woodland and its primate species. Not as impressive as the national park at Outamba-Kilimi, it is nevertheless an extraordinarily picturesque area with some success in its conservation effort. The Sierra Leone Conservation Society has taken a proactive stance on the state of the local ecology, anticipating and preventing any further damage to the country's wild habitats.

Liberia

Liberia is covered mostly by forested plains and a series of small but prominent mountain ranges, its rugged shoreline the outlet to a number of rivers and streams that wind their way to the sea across the wide coastal plain and a lush and thickly wooded interior. Although Liberia is widely recognized as a sanctuary of one of the last remaining virgin rainforests in the entire region, conservation here is far from a priority and is restricted to just one protected area. The 0.13-million-hectare Sapo National Park sees very few foreigners exploring its untamed wilderness, and its conservation record is virtually non-existent. The only feature of significance here is the relatively unspoiled forest and the small animals it harbours. Gone are the visitor facilities and infrastructure that once made Sapo a fine African wilderness.

Côte d'Ivoire

Much of Côte d'Ivoire's landscape is utilized as agricultural land, yet there are eight national parks, four official reserve areas and three World Heritage Sites. The main parks have sound populations of elephant, lion, hippo, buffalo and a variety of antelope species. The 3,600km^2 (1,400-sq.-mile) Taï National Park hosts the only remaining virgin rainforest – less than a fifth of the rainforest that existed only decades ago remains, and it is reported that Côte d'Ivoire has sacrificed nearly half its woodland to unregulated logging in fewer than 30 years.

Isolated and inaccessible to the ordinary traveller at the best of times, most of the conservation areas have closed at some time or another, only to reopen with few real improvements to the existing structures. However, there are indeed very real attractions to Côte d'Ivoire's parks. The 11,500km^2 (4,500-sq.-mile) Comoé National Park – also a Biosphere Reserve and World Heritage Site – is the largest and most visited of the parks, a savanna woodland boasting a good population of elephant, lion, hippo and thriving bird populations. Much the same can be said for both Mount Sangbé National Park and the 1,000km^2 (390-sq.-mile) Marahoué National Park which is ideal for walking safaris, although it does not boast the big cats and other big game is not readily spotted among the vegetation.

Burkina Faso

Like Côte d'Ivoire, Burkina Faso is losing its natural forest at a distressing rate. Matters are further exacerbated by the desertification and erosion that has followed the deforestation brought by logging activities, and the antiquated farming still practised by uneducated locals. Having to deal with vital issues such as these has meant that Burkina Faso's numerous national parks, faunal reserves (there are no fewer than eight), and other protected areas, spread across vast tablelands that are difficult to cross and densely populated, have had to take a back seat. The wildlife here is not as abundant as it once was, although elephant are fairly common in readily accessible parks such as Deux Balé National Park, "W" National Park and Arly Faunal Reserve, which has healthy populations of monkey, hippo and even lion.

ADV 294
NP 252

Ghana

If it weren't for the enormous potential of a thriving and successful tourism industry, Ghana may well have gone the way of Burkina Faso and Côte d'Ivoire. Although it does face problems of its own, it remains one of the shining lights of West Africa. One community project that has enjoyed considerable success is the conservation programme put into effect at the Boabeng-Fiema Monkey Sanctuary. Members of the local community traditionally have a high regard for the primates that inhabit groves of forest in the immediate vicinity, and they have thus been entrusted to safeguard these monkey populations and to manage the guesthouse and other tourist facilities in the area.

Although the Bia, Bui and extensive Digya national parks, with their elephant, antelope and hippo, are yet to regain their original glory, parks such as Kakum are showing promising signs of improvement. But it is Mole National Park that is Ghana's top wildlife destination. Established some 30 years ago, the 5,100km^2 (2,000-sq.-mile) national park is not only the nation's oldest and most expansive, but also the best maintained and best stocked, with considerable populations of big game, among them healthy herds of elephant, buffalo and other antelope, plenty of bird species and small mammals such as baboons, warthogs and monkeys.

While some nations in West Africa, such as Burkina Faso, are so riddled with poverty that very little of their natural resources remain untouched by development or the ravages of over-population, others, such as Benin, have developed a fine legacy of conservation.

Togo

Although there are nine conservation areas recognized by the United Nations, the existing parks and reserves are all in shocking condition, with pitifully low populations of indigenous wildlife and severe degradation of the landscape ravaged by poachers, hunters and timber plantations. Even Kéran National Park, once Togo's finest wildlife area, has seen better days, with much of it having been reclaimed as farmland, and the few remaining animals struggling to survive. Although it was once rich in wildlife, today only a handful of antelope and the occasional small mammal such as baboon may be seen here. Even parks such as Fazao-Malfakassa National Park, which has seen considerable rehabilitation of its land and wildlife stocks, have a far way to go and many of the game reserves and national parks are extremely disappointing for the game-viewer.

Benin

Although Benin, with its impressive coastline of over 100km (60 miles), has experienced many of the negative influences of deforestation, desertification, drought and poaching, it has a remarkably sound and steadily improving environmental policy that, it is hoped, will save it from the devastation seen in so many nations on the continent. Only a few insignificant areas of indigenous rainforest survive here, and continued wildlife poaching still threatens existing animal populations. However, it is one of the few African countries that rightfully boasts a rapidly increasing population of big cats, and is home to Pendjari, a biosphere reserve, hunting zone and, as Pendjari National Park, one of the finest wildlife sanctuaries in the entire region. The northern region in which Pendjari is situated is refreshingly untainted by the ravages of human populations, and much of its wildlife remains as it has been for decades, making for some of the best game-viewing in West Africa. Pendjari has a fine array of smaller mammal species such as warthog and baboon, and good herds of elephant, hippo and other big game. Plans are afoot for Pendjari to merge with similar parks in Benin as well as in neighbouring Burkina Faso.

ADV 296
NP 255

THE REGION

Covering a total area of more than 2 million square kilometres (792,000 sq. miles) and harbouring a population of no fewer than 132 million, some 12 million hectares (30 million acres) of the central region of West Africa have been given over to conservation. While this may seem impressive, however, Equatorial Guinea can lay claim to none of it, having no officially recognized protected areas within its borders.

NIGERIA	Key
Chad Basin National Park	F
Cross River National Park	D
Gashaka Gumti National Park	E
Kainji Lake National Park	A
Old Oyo National Park	B
Yankari National Park	C
Baturiya Wetlands Game Reserve	5
Dagida Game Reserve	1
Falgore (Kogin Kano) Game Reserve	3
Gilli-Gilli Game Reserve	9
Kambari Game Reserve	5
Kashimbila Game Reserve	6
Kwiambana Game Reserve	2
Lame-Burra Game Reserve	4
Orle River Game Reserve	10
Pai River Game Reserve	7
Pandam Game Reserve	8
Okumu Nature Sanctuary	12
Omo Biosphere Reserve	11

SAO TOME AND PRINCIPE	
Obo National Park	A

CAMEROON	
Bénoué National Park	E
Bouba Ndjidah National Park	D
Kalamaloué National Park	A
Korup National Park	F
Lobeke National Park	G
Mozogo-Gokoro National Park	B
Waza National Park	C
Campo Faunal Reserve	1
Dja Faunal Reserve	3
Douala-Edéa Faunal Reserve	2
Faro Reserve	4
Lake Lobeke Faunal Reserve	G
Bénoué Biosphere Reserve	E
Dja Biosphere Reserve	3
Waza Biosphere Reserve	C
Dja World Heritage Site	3

EQUATORIAL GUINEA	
No UN-recognized protected area	

CENTRAL AFRICAN REPUBLIC	
André Félix National Park	D
Bamingui-Bangoran National Park	B
Dzanga-Ndoki National Park	A
Manovo-Gounda-Saint Floris National Park	C
Vassako-Bolo Strict Nature Reserve	6
Aouk-Aoukale Faunal Reserve	8
Gribingui-Bamingui Faunal Reserve	4
Koukourou-Bamingui Faunal Reserve	5
Nana-Barya Faunal Reserve	3
Ouandjia-Vakaga Faunal Reserve	9
Yata-Ngaya Faunal Reserve	10
Zemongo Faunal Reserve	11
Dzanga-Sangha Special Reserve	1
Avakaba Presidential Park	7
Bamingui-Bangoran Conservation Area	B
Basse-Lobaye Forest	2
Manovo-Gounda-Saint Floris World Heritage Site	C

CLOCKWISE FROM TOP LEFT
Waza National Park, Cameroon.
Roumsiki Mountains, Cameroon.
Kempe Falls, Central African Republic.
Mandril, Korup National Park, Cameroon.

Nigeria

Despite its status as one of the world's leading oil producers, Nigeria remains extremely impoverished, the vast majority of its 115 million citizens eking a meagre living as subsistence farmers. It does, however, have some of the most beautiful landscapes on the continent. Its equatorial forests are the focus of its six national parks and 12 game reserves, which cover an impressive three million hectares (7½ million acres). One of its finest is the much vaunted Cross River National Park which, although scattered with palm plantations – a mainstay of the economy – is comprised largely of indigenous rainforest. The park lays claim to a diversity of wild animals, but is also the location of some of the most innovative and successful conservation programmes on the continent. One of Cross River's most portentous assets is the dense growth of plant species particular to rainforests, and it is globally recognized as vital in the preservation of floral species considered endangered or threatened in other areas on the continent. It is also an important sanctuary for 1,500 faunal species, such as chimpanzees and antelope, typical of equatorial woodland. While the animal life of its Oban Division – the park is roughly divided into two sections – is fairly standard, its Okwangwo Division plays host to four separate gorilla groups, said to number about 400 individuals, monitored by the WWF.

Kainji Lake National Park also comprises two areas – Borgu and Zugurma – both of which have viable populations of baboon, green monkey, waterbuck, hippo and crocodile, and even lion and leopard. While these are fairly easily spotted in the Zugurma section, they are less prolific in much neglected Borgu, a sparse 4,000km² (1,500 sq. miles) of indigenous vegetation ravaged by poaching and hunting.

Yankari is Nigeria's most rewarding wildlife destination, with the first two months of the year proving best for game viewing – dry conditions force animals to make regular visits to water sources. The animals in this 2,200km² (850-sq.-mile) park are elusive, yet populations appear to be healthy and thriving, a far cry from the near obliteration of indigenous wildlife in Nigeria during its years of guerilla activity. While only small numbers of big cats such as lion and leopard still exist in Yankari, game drives do ensure regular sightings of a variety of antelope and gazelle species, and even elephant, hippo, monkeys and warthog.

Nigeria has vast stretches of land officially designated as protected, but there are also small, unofficial wildlife havens yet to receive official sanction or government funds, but which have played a significant part in preserving threatened habitats. One such project is the Okumu Nature Sanctuary, a tiny refuge for indigenous wildlife, such as the now endangered white-throated monkey. Although it is virtually surrounded by rampant development, Okumu is fiercely hanging on to its indigenous wildlife.

Sao Tome and Principe

The relatively unknown islands offer abundant rainforests, jungles, bamboo and cocoa plantations, volcanoes, glorious tropical beaches and baobab trees in the drier regions. Its amazing array of flora and fauna includes sea turtles, a fabulous array of birdlife and more than 800 plant species (120 endemic) – the Giant Begonia reaches 3 metres (9,8 feet) in height. Obo National Park on São Tome is an unspoilt gem, displaying endemic fauna and flora amidst a wide diversity of landscapes: Pico Cão Grande, roughly five kilometres (3 miles) inland from the splendid coastline, stands 2,024 metres (6,641 feet) above sea level.

Cameroon

Although more than 2 million hectares (5 million acres) of Cameroon are protected, even the best intentions have done little to conserve one of the most sensitive ecosystems in Africa. Although evidence suggests that even government is making some effort to address conservation issues, the state of the country's wildlife has been sorely neglected, and its biodiversity is under very serious threat from indiscriminate land usage and poorly maintained rural projects. According to recent accounts, population numbers of the local subspecies of black rhino – the most endangered – have dropped from more than 600 individuals to no more than 12 in 40 years. Although some contingency plans are in place, the conservation ethic depends on a restricted tourism infrastructure that is insufficiently funded and inadequately staffed. The good news is that small pockets of land remain untouched, thanks to the actions of international conservation groups. In recent years, Cameroon put its signature to the Yaoundé Declaration which, together with the involvement of other West African nations, proclaimed its commitment to an ongoing programme of environmental care in the broader region that will help protect areas of increasingly threatened natural forest, other indigenous vegetation and endemic wildlife. The WWF remains extremely active in the conservation of Cameroon's natural heritage – its local agency is the continent's biggest – and has brought about significant change in the local conservation ethic. The national government and WWF established the 2,000km² (772-sq.-mile) Lobeke National Park in 2001 and declared its support of – if not practical involvement in – the Northern Savanna Project which, underwritten by the WWF and other non-governmental organizations, is set to establish further parkland in the country's northern reaches. This is in stark contrast to the healthy populations of forest elephants, buffalo, duiker, gorillas, chimps and other primates in the southeast.

Situated in the undeveloped north are the comparatively developed national parks of Bénoué and Bouba Ndjidah and the very limited facilities of Faro, for which there are plans to develop a sufficiently user-friendly infrastructure that will help encourage additional tourist traffic to the region. The most promising of Cameroon's national parks remains Waza (in the far north) and Korup (further south). The herds of elephant, antelope, gazelle and giraffe, hippo, lion and prolific bird life of Waza are Cameroon's most widely acclaimed and the park is the country's most visited, but innovative efforts in Korup are ensuring that the park is enjoying increased attention. As a result of community policing, instances of poaching are being reduced, wildlife numbers – especially primates and elephant herds – are steadily increasing, and the trade in bush meat is slowly being addressed. These efforts have been incorporated under the umbrella known as the Korup Project, financed in part by the conservation arm of the EU and, like the rest of the park, is governed largely by the WWF, which also helped fund the establishment of the 3,000km² (1,160-sq.-mile) park in the mid-1980s.

Equatorial Guinea

With no UN-recognized protected areas anywhere across 28,050km² (10,830 sq. miles), little has been done to conserve this tiny nation's natural heritage and, with the exception of a few determined individuals, even the philanthropic agencies and non-governmental organizations so active in neighbouring countries are largely absent from Equatorial Guinea. As a result, the steady degradation of the otherwise picturesque landscape continues unchecked, and the wildlife populations that once roamed freely across its vast wilderness have been reduced to small pockets of insignificant numbers. Equatorial Guinea suffers the same environmental problems – and to about the same degree – as many of the surrounding states, but many of the conservation issues still need to be addressed with the determination hitherto reserved for the economic development of urban settlements. Research programmes focusing on Bioko Island have, for example, recorded an alarming increase in such environmental tragedies as the trade in bush meat, a problem that plagues many undeveloped nations in Africa. Today, informal markets in Malabo appear to be flooded with bush meat, with increasingly more rodents and small mammals on offer, including chimpanzees – this is especially disturbing considering the ecological status of primates in this part of Africa.

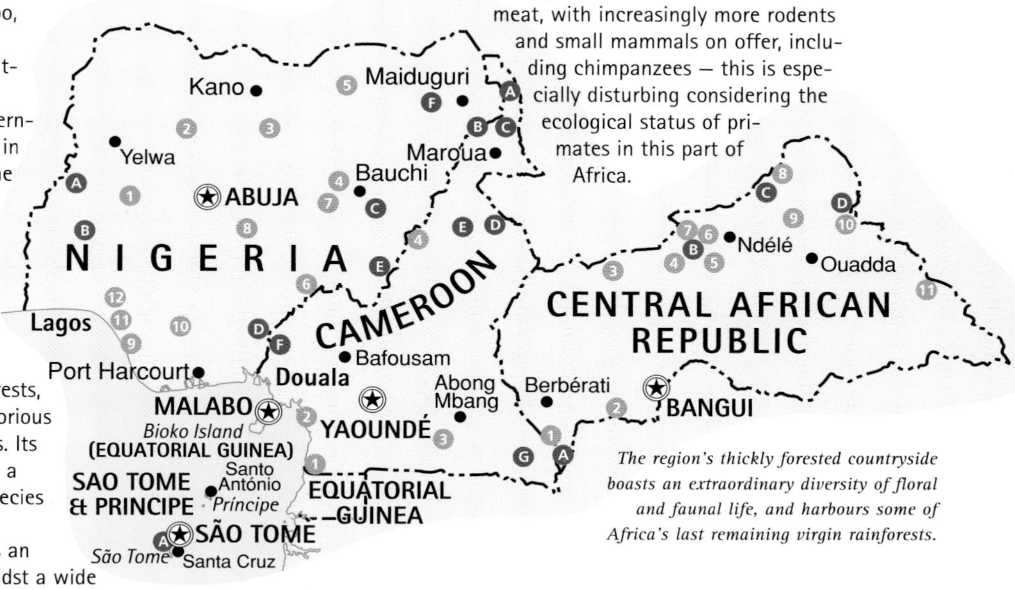

The region's thickly forested countryside boasts an extraordinary diversity of floral and faunal life, and harbours some of Africa's last remaining virgin rainforests.

Central African Republic

In the heart of Africa's forest land, the Central African Republic (CAR) is everything literature and Hollywood movies make of equatorial Africa: densely treed, steamy rainforests buzzing with insects, populated by elephants, lowland gorillas and chimpanzees, and difficult to negotiate. It is the epitome of Africa's jungle, but it is also symbolic of Africa's worst: high population densities of humans who are both poor and desperate, governed by a corrupt and inefficient bureaucracy that, spurred on by a legacy of opportunism, seems to pay scant attention to the demands of its land, its people and its natural heritage.

The CAR is remarkably beautiful, with much of its landscape unexplored and the real wealth of its natural treasures yet to be discovered. Dzanga-Sangha Reserve harbours one the continent's few surviving virgin rainforests, a haven for impressive numbers of the region's threatened and endangered primate species. Recent surveys indicate that the Dzanga section of Dzanga-Ndoki National Park – adjacent to Dzanga-Sangha Special Reserve and southwest of Bangui – is one of the most significant areas for the preservation of Africa's remaining ape populations, including chimpanzees and the region's lowland gorillas. A nest count has revealed fewer than two gorillas per square kilometre (⅓ mile) – Africa's highest population density of Western lowland gorilla – in addition to some 0.16 chimpanzees per square kilometre. Considering the current status of these primates in Africa, the CAR appears to be one of the safest havens for these endangered mammals.

Prime among the country's wildlife sanctuaries – numbering four national parks, nine reserves of various classifications and other conservation areas, including a World Heritage Site – is Dzanga-Ndoki National Park, still home to truly wild populations of rainforest animals. Because of its situation close to the equator, the park is hot, humid, densely wooded and thick with undergrowth, so faunal life such as elephants, gorillas, bongos, buffalo and sitatunga are easily hidden among the vegetation, emerging occasionally into regular clearings among the forest terrain. Both the forest floor and canopy play host to a wide variety of insects, amphibian species and reptiles such as pythons and green mambas.

THE REGION

With the exception of Ethiopia, which has nine national parks, 10 wildlife sanctuaries and no fewer than 13 controlled hunting areas, plus the Simien World Heritage Site – covering a total of nearly 19 million hectares (7 million acres) – the nations that make up the Horn of Africa are largely devoid of national parks. Tracts of conservation land here are few and are restricted to smaller wildlife sanctuaries and reserves.

ERITREA	Key
Gash-Setit Wildlife Reserve	3
Nakfa Wildlife Reserve	2
Yob Wildlife Reserve	1

ETHIOPIA	
Abijatta-Shalla Lakes National Park	F
Awash National Park	G
Bale Mountains National Park	I
Gambella National Park	B
Mago National Park	D
Nechisar National Park	E
Omo National Park	C
Simien Mountains National Park	A
Yangudi Rassa National Park	H
Babile Elephant Sanctuary	15
Yabelo Sanctuary	9
Afdem-Gewane Controlled Hunting Area	17
Akobo Controlled Hunting Area	4
Arsi Controlled Hunting Area	10
Awash West Controlled Hunting Area	G
Bale Controlled Hunting Area	I
Borana Controlled Hunting Area	8
Chercher & Arba Gugu Controlled Hunting Area	16
Dabus Valley Controlled Hunting Area	2
Eastern Hararghe (Harar-Wabi Shebelle) Hunting Controlled Area	18
Erer-Gota Controlled Hunting Area	14
Jikao Controlled Hunting Area	3
Murle Controlled Hunting Area	6
Omo West Controlled Hunting Area	5
Tedo Controlled Hunting Area	4
Alledeghi Wildlife Reserve	11
Bale Wildlife Reserve	I
Chew Bahr Wildlife Reserve	7
Gewane Wildlife Reserve	12
Mille-Sardo Wildlife Reserve	13
Shire Wildlife Reserve	1
Tama Wildlife Reserve	7
Simien Mountains World Heritage Site	A

SOMALIA	
Alifuuto (Arbowerow) Nature Reserve	2
Bushbush Game Reserve	1

DJIBOUTI	
Fôret du Day	1

CLOCKWISE FROM TOP LEFT
Blue Nile Falls, Ethiopia.
Ethiopian wolf, Simien Mountains, Ethiopia.
Simien Mountains, Ethiopia.
Lobelia, Bale Mountains, Ethiopia.

Eritrea

Considering that the State of Eritrea is no more than a decade old and is still struggling to counter years of famine, drought, poverty and political dissension, it is little wonder that this semiarid country has cast no more than a cursory glance at the issues of environmental conservation. Its tourism industry, although growing, remains but a fledgling enterprise that is still to prove its potential for government coffers. The dry landscape has no permanent river systems and no inland water sources of any consequence, so it should come as no surprise that Eritrea has only three wildlife sanctuaries and no national parks. State officials have shown little enthusiasm for the few but generally promising ecological programmes established by non-governmental organizations and international environmental agencies. Priority, it seems, is given to economic development within or around existing urban settlements and, to some degree, to the mostly impoverished rural areas that depend on agriculture. Although these elements of Eritrea's sociopolitical development do indeed demand dedicated attention and resources, it would do the national government well to consider the potential of the nation's unexplored wilderness and the wealth of endemic wildlife it harbours.

Ethiopia

Although Ethiopia must be one of the most ravaged of all African nations, still suffering from drought and famine, poverty and political uncertainty, its conservation efforts – meagre as they are – are the most commendable in the entire region, with the state having set aside more than 18 million hectares (45 million acres) as protected sanctuaries for the nation's flora and fauna. No less than 20,756km² (8,014 sq. miles) of the country has been allocated for national parks and, in addition, Ethiopia has a remarkably rich bird life, yet the country is not particularly well known for the abundance and diversity of its wildlife. The small animal population is primarily restricted to out-of-the-way places further inland.

Much of Ethiopia's faunal resources are today threatened by a series of environmental concerns, ranging from the rapidly growing human population and the steady decline of its existing forests and woodlands to the day-to-day demands of agriculture and a massive foreign debt. This debt burden has driven the nation to grow and export flowers while, tragically, huge numbers of people are starving because not enough food is grown for domestic use. At the same time, thousands and thousands of indigenous trees are being systematically cut down for domestic fuel as well as to accommodate the timber requirements of both the agricultural sector and the construction industry. Statistics show that more than two-thirds of Ethiopia's trees have been felled in less than 30 years.

Government departments and the Ethiopian Wildlife Conservation Organization have at least taken some responsibility for the country's wildlife resources. However, the preservation and maintenance of Ethiopia's natural ecosystems, the conservation of the indigenous vegetation and wild animal species they harbour, and the education of the masses – including farmers, students and other non-governmental organizations – is left largely to specialized organizations such as the Ethiopian Wildlife & Natural History Society. The Society's volunteers continue to green a countryside that is now considerably damaged by alien species such as the Australian eucalyptus. Other wildlife organizations have now also taken up the plight of the Ethiopian wolf, a fox-like mammal previously known as the Simien wolf that, although once fairly common, is now one of the most endangered canine predators in the world. Flag-bearer of this cause is the Ethiopian Wolf Conservation Programme, an offshoot of Oxford University's Wildlife Conservation Research Unit that is funded in part by the UK-based Born Free Foundation. Endemic to the highlands, the Ethiopian species is the only wolf to be found naturally in Africa, and most recent records indicate that there are fewer than 600 individuals left in Ethiopia's wilds.

The area that can lay claim to the greatest number of these canines is the spectacular Simien Mountains National Park which, although it has plenty of gelada baboon, ibex and, most notably, a number of birds of prey, is perhaps best known as a popular hiking destination. Like Simien Mountains, Bale Mountains National Park – also designated a Controlled Hunting Area and Wildlife Reserve – serves as a haven for these and a number of other creatures, but its greatest attraction for visitors is its 2,400km² (925 sq. miles) of scenic splendour, which includes the Sanetti Plateau and the 4,377m (14,360ft) peak of Tullu Demtu. Although Simien and Bale parks both boast some good populations of endemic animals, it is the rugged terrain of the mountain landscape and the series of hiking trails that enjoy more attention than the limited wildlife.

While parks such as the Abijatta-Shalla Lakes National Park have very little to offer the safari-goer, the other three parks in the Rift Valley – Yangudi Rassa, Awash and Nechisar – and even remote areas such as the great Omo Valley and the adjoining Mago National Park, report significant numbers of birds, game such as gazelle and zebra, and even elephants and other large mammals, including predators. Despite its rather parched wilderness and its thinly spread animal life, the 2,162km² (7,100-sq.-mile) Mago also counts waterbuck, gerenuk, black-backed jackal, lesser kudu, and bushbuck among its 100 species, although its once impressive numbers of buffalo herds have now been reduced to little more than 400 head. Mago may well be Ethiopia's single most important national park when it comes to tourism potential, but many of the smaller reserves have highlights of their own that may only be accessible to visitors once facilities across the country's protected areas have been upgraded.

Somalia

Like Eritrea, Somalia has no national parks, and conservation efforts are restricted to the Alifuuto (Arbowerow) Nature Reserve and the Bushbush Game Reserve, both of which are to be found in the southern reaches of the country. Covering the very 'horn' that gives its name to the broader region, this sliver of land – like much of the wider area – once teemed with an extraordinary variety of indigenous animal life. Sadly, forces of nature and the encroachment of human settlement have taken their toll on Somalia and the landscape it covers today. Desertification is as prolific here as it is further inland, and is exacerbated by escalating deforestation. Large tracts of land that were once dotted with acacia species have, for example, been denuded in favour of charcoal production, which has proved to be an important export – albeit unofficially – with vast quantities shipped out to neighbouring countries where wood fuels are equally rare.

Despite the ecological importance of the marine and coastal environment off Somalia's shores, the exploitation of these resources is equally important to the national economy. The waters off the coast are extraordinarily rich and can't yet be seen as threatened by the existing levels of human activity, but they are nevertheless affected – mostly adversely – by the harvesting of marine life that is currently taking place. Diving and fishing for lobster and the hunting of sharks for their fins are widespread in these waters, and the export of these items contributes enormously to the local economy, drawing huge amounts of foreign capital to the country.

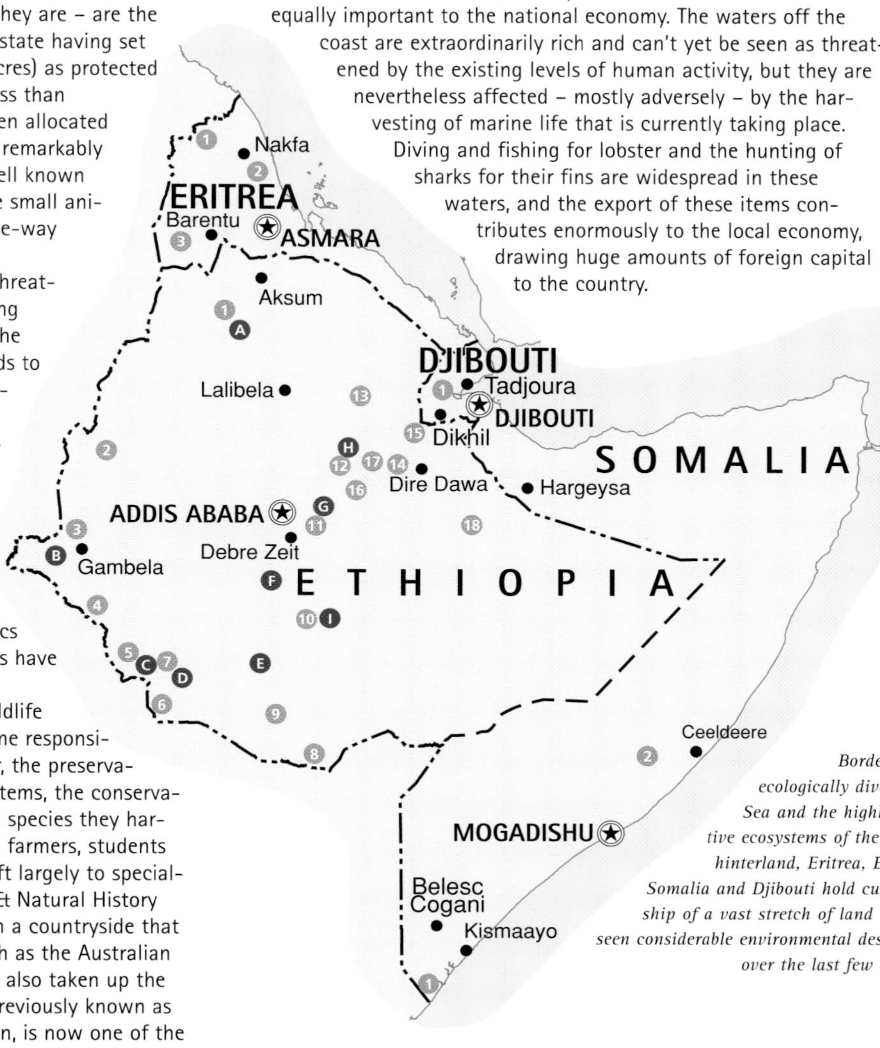

Bordering the ecologically diverse Red Sea and the highly sensitive ecosystems of the African hinterland, Eritrea, Ethiopia, Somalia and Djibouti hold custodianship of a vast stretch of land that has seen considerable environmental destruction over the last few decades.

Wildlife that once found its home on the parched hinterland has now, for all intents and purposes, long disappeared, leaving only selected species to roam the dry and dusty terrain. Of those wild animals that do remain, however, there are still healthy and, in some isolated areas, thriving populations. While jackal, hyena, oryx, dik-dik, warthog, ostrich and other bird life are indeed fairly common, and there are good numbers of elephant, buffalo, antelope and even, to some degree, big cats such as cheetah, Somalia has already lost a number of species – most notably its wild ass, which is today one of the world's most threatened mammals.

Djibouti

The tiny city-state of Djibouti comprises little more than the urban settlement that is its capital, bordering the Gulf of Aden at the southern end of the Red Sea. The dry and wild landscape that makes up the state of Djibouti's 23,200km² (9,000 sq. miles) of coastal plain and mountainous plateau is renowned more for its leisure and adventure activities than for the wildlife that inhabits the interior. Apart from the scenic beauty of the land and the ecological importance of certain areas, such as its lakes – Lake Assal, Lac Goubet and Lac Abbé – there is little to distinguish a terrain that is mostly a simple westerly extension of neighbouring Eritrea, Ethiopia and Somalia. Djibouti has no national parks, no game or nature reserve – either state-owned or private – and no wildlife sanctuaries. It is mostly a wasteland of arid, inhospitable land, and its sole contribution to the protection of the region's ecological status is to be found its only protected area, the unremarkable Fôret du Day, which skirts the bay on which the entire nation is focused.

ADV 298
NA 257

THE REGION

Both in its varied history and in its rather precarious present, Central Africa has been the centre of much turmoil that has seen its people suffer at the hands of civil war along with the rape of large tracts of land considered – by many – to be some of the most remarkable on the continent. While some 8 million hectares of Angola's acacia-dotted plains have now been set aside as protected land, less than 2 million hectares of Congo's equatorial rainforest is under official protection.

GABON	Key
Ipassa-Makokou Strict Nature Reserve	1
Lopé Faunal Reserve	3
Moukalaba-Dougoua Faunal Reserve	5
Ouanga Plain Faunal Reserve	6
Petit Loango Faunal Reserve	5
Iguela Hunting Reserve	4
Moukalaba Hunting Reserve	5
Ngové-Ndogo Hunting Reserve	4
Setté-Cama Hunting Reserve	6
Wonga-Wongué Presidential Reserve	2
Ipassa-Makokou Biosphere Reserve	1
Petit Loango Ramsar Wetland	5
Setté-Cama Ramsar Wetland	6
Wonga-Wongué Ramsar Wetland	2

CONGO	
Nouabalé-Ndoki National Park	A
Odzala National Park	B
Conkouati Faunal Reserve	4
Lefini Faunal Reserve	2
Lekoli-Pandaka Faunal Reserve	B
Mont Fouari Faunal Reserve	5
Tsoulou Faunal Reserve	3
M'boko Hunting Reserve	B
Mont Mavoumbou Hunting Reserve	5
Nyanga Sud Hunting Reserve	5
Dimonika-Mayombe Biosphere Reserve	1
Odzala Biosphere Reserve	B

DEMOCRATIC REPUBLIC OF THE CONGO (DRC)	
Garamba National Park	F
Kahuzi-Biega National Park	C
Kundelungu National Park	A
Maiko National Park	D
Okapi National Park	H
Salonga National Park	G
Upemba National Park	B
Virunga National Park	E
Bili-Uere Hunting Reserve	2
Bombo-Lumene Hunting Reserve	4
Bushimaie Hunting Reserve	5
Luama Hunting Reserve	1
Maika-Penge Hunting Reserve	G
Mangai Hunting Reserve	6
Mondo Missa Hunting Reserve	F
Rutshuru Hunting Reserve	7
Swa-Kibula Hunting Reserve	8
Valle De La Lufira Biosphere Reserve	9
Luki Forest Reserve	10
Yangambi Forest Floral Reserve	11
Garamba World Heritage Site	F
Kahuzi-Biega World Heritage Site	C
Salonga World Heritage Site	3
Virunga World Heritage Site	E

ANGOLA	
Bikuar National Park	C
Cangandala National Park	E
Iona National Park	A
Kameia National Park	F
Quiçama National Park	D
Mupa National Park	B
Luando Integral Nature Reserve	4
Bufalo Partial Reserve	2
Luiana Partial Reserve	6
Mavinga Partial Reserve	5
Mocamedes Partial Reserve	1
Chimalavera Regional Nature Park	3

CLOCKWISE FROM TOP LEFT
Gabon turtle, Gabon.
Nouabalé-Ndoki National Park, Congo.
Okapi, DRC.
Makao Forest, Congo.

Gabon

Of the nations that fall within the equatorial band of Central Africa, Gabon is perhaps the shining light, largely because it is blessed with a growing economy, an abundance of indigenous resources and a relatively sophisticated infrastructure. With the burgeoning economy, however, come the responsibilities of a developing nation and Gabon is still struggling to maintain an adequate balance, the timber industry – and the accompanying logging activities – taking its toll on the fragile ecosystems. The thickly wooded forests see as much as 3,000mm (118in) of rain in a year, giving rise to a diversity of plant and animal life. Because its human population remains relatively low, species such as gorillas, chimps, leopard, mandrills, monkeys, buffalo, antelope and elephant thrive here. Gabon once enjoyed extensive protection from government and non-profit conservation bodies, but the activity on the logging concessions in the interior remains a concern, as does the trade in bush meat. Logging is nevertheless one of the nation's most vital income-producers and its importance has grown with the decline in the oil price. Whereas tree-felling was once limited to land within easy reach of industry, the Trans-Gabon Express has meant that more areas are now accessible, with an increasing number of roads – many exclusively for logging vehicles – crisscrossing areas that were once virtually uninhabited. Timber concessions show signs of making considerable profits in the foreseeable future, and the alarming growth in the industry affects not only Gabon's woodlands, but also animal populations. The expanding road network has, in turn, meant an increase in poaching of hitherto unaffected areas, and nearly 50 per cent of the Lopé Faunal Reserve has fallen victim to the chain saws as a result of its negotiations and land-swap agreements with logging companies. Environmental custodians of the Wildlife Conservation Society arranged in 2000 for a logging operation to work some 650km^2 (250 sq. miles) of Lopé and, in return, about 400km^2 (155 sq. miles) reserved for the timber industry were incorporated into the reserve.

This has meant that some areas remain untouched by bulldozers, and the government has proclaimed certain areas 'inviolate'. The concession areas have, however, not been favourably received by all parties. Some conservationists have expressed concern that the compromise is too lenient, others have rejected it outright, while others have been spurred on to establish formal programmes. One such operation is the ECOFAC (the Programme for Conservation and Rational Utilization of Forest Ecosystems in Central Africa), founded largely as a result of a grant from the European Union in the early 1990s. Operating in at least five other countries in Central Africa, ECOFAC has a research station in Lopé, which not only keeps an eye over the wildlife sanctuary, but also promotes sustainable development.

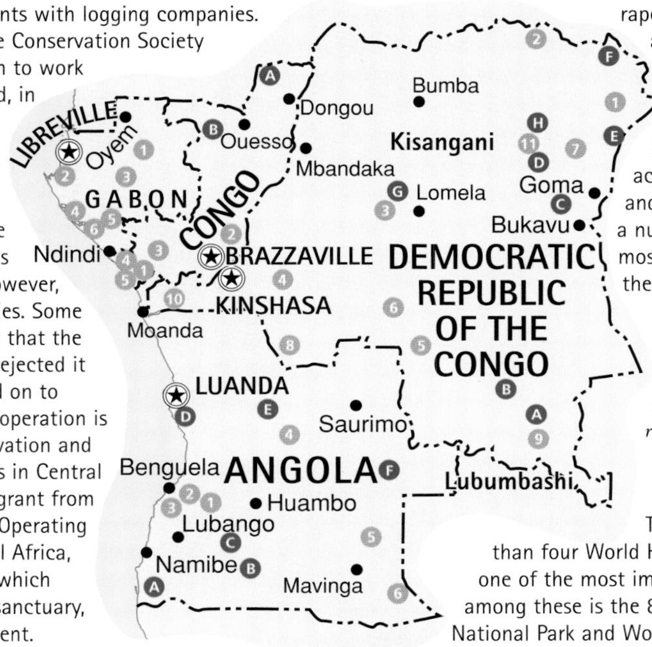

Congo

The Congo River boasts a watershed of more than 4 million square kilometres (15,5 million square miles) and comprises a series of tributaries with no less than 12,500km (7,750 miles) of navigable inland waters. Flanked by forested mountain slopes, the river remains relatively unblemished by the human population on its banks. Although there is evidence of some degradation – sited here is the massive Inga Dam and hydroelectricity scheme, and certain regions do suffer as a result of isolated pollution issues – a more serious problem in Congo is the growing reliance on the trade in bush meat. A distressing number of families, most notably in and around the Nouablé-Ndoki National Park, depend on bush meat for daily sustenance and even income. For many, the trade in primates and other small mammals is the primary source of income, especially considering that vast areas of farming land have been lost and areas that were once inaccessible have now been opened by the development of logging routes. The animals of the forest – itself in danger of being lost to development – are killed, dismembered, smoked and cured, and then sold on local streets to be eaten, their skins sold to traders and body parts used to make traditional medicines and potions. The growing human population and increasing urbanization have also meant that the activity has stretched beyond subsistence hunting, the traps and snares – some horrifically brutal – earning millions of US dollars in local and urban communities.

Although Africa boasts no temperate rainforests, the Congo Basin lays claim to the continent's largest tropical rainforest. Congo, with its high-lying grasslands and forested plateaux, also continues to wrestle with the issue of tree-felling for commercial purposes, and the forest canopy is slowly being whittled away, and with it the natural habitat of the country's primate population. Congo's wooded landscape provides outstanding opportunities for gorilla watching, and Odzala National Park is one of the world's finest parks of its kind, with reports of no fewer than 100 of these beasts spotted during a single visit. The 'gorilla industry' remains one of the nation's few 'lifelines' and is slowly re-establishing itself following the political turbulence of the late 20th century, which saw the decimation of any sort of safe travel within the Congo. For decades, Uganda's Bwindi Impenetrable Forest provided the only viable option to see Africa's wild gorillas, but matters have changed in recent years. Although there is still a long road ahead, the economic potential of ecotourism is slowly being realised and certain areas are being opened to adventure travellers and naturalists.

Democratic Republic of the Congo

Much maligned and one of the most recent victims of the world view that Africa is dark, dangerous and unpredictable in both terrain and temperament, the Democratic Republic of the Congo (DRC) – formerly Zaïre – is nevertheless a magnificent country. It boasts many hidden treasures, not the least of which are the diamonds that form one of the mainstays of the national economy. Like Gabon and Congo, the DRC, which falls largely within the forest-bedecked basin of the river from which it takes its name, is rich in an indigenous wildlife that roams its grass plains and vast mountain slopes. But nature has also taken its toll here and in early 2002, Mount Nyiragongo, which overlooks the town of Goma, erupted, causing not only untold human suffering but also catastrophic environmental devastation. According to the Dian Fossey Gorilla Fund International, the volcanic eruption resulted in a crisis of tremendous proportions and it will take decades for the rehabilitation programmes to restore the landscape here to its former glory. Despite the magnificent natural beauty of the country, it would be foolish to disregard the volatility of the nation's political situation, which has been responsible for so much of the destruction inflicted upon the environment here.

Whereas the stable tourist trade of the mid- to late 20th century ensured that the biodiversity of the local ecosystem remained relatively unscathed by either development or human settlement, the growing tensions and resultant civil unrest that followed in the 1990s and beyond meant that this soon dwindled to virtually nothing, and environmental concerns have little significance in the modern nation. The thickly wooded rainforest was rampantly raped and pillaged by both the militia and unchecked trophy hunters, poachers and subsistence hunters – despite the survival in even latter-day DRC of controlled hunting areas. This, together with activities of the ever-present mining and logging industries, has resulted in a number of plant and animal species, most notably primates, emerging on the endangered list.

While some nations in Africa have made valiant attempts to protect their wildlife heritage, much of Central Africa has a less than impressive conservation record, with vast tracts of land decimated by the legacy of degradation left by military forces in recent years.

There are, nonetheless, no fewer than four World Heritage Sites in the DRC, surely one of the most impressive records in Africa. Principal among these is the 8,000km^2 (3,000-sq.-mile) Virunga National Park and World Heritage Site, the nation's first park established some 80 years ago. Sadly, however, many of the parks, wildlife sanctuaries and conservation areas saw untold destruction during the civil war, and very little remains of the once thriving wildlife populations of lion, elephant, giraffe, hippo, hyena, buffalo and antelope. Although some areas today may well have been re-opened to visitors – such as the breathtaking mountains of the Ruwenzoris – at the time of writing, the military retain a significant presence and matters remain somewhat tenuous, so travellers are advised to make extensive enquiries before venturing in and around the DRC.

Angola

Although some two-thirds of Angola is covered by stark but magnificent plateau, and much of the remaining land consists largely of coastal desert, the extraordinary splendour of the countryside has seen little tourism, embroiled as it has been in years of political insecurity. Sadly, Angola is one of the casualties of instability and uncertainty that continues to bedevil Africa. This is all the more pitiful considering the location and natural beauty of this African republic, which only recently saw the backs of its colonial occupiers. The arid desert sands are golden, sparsely populated and rich in unique fauna and flora, the seas a splendid blue and the offshore islands lined with spectacular beaches dotted with inexpensive hotels and restaurants, desperate to capitalize on the meagre tourist trade. Unfortunately, the wholly inadequate response to the hospitality industry means that even promising holiday destinations are plagued with litter, inefficient bureaucracy, a lack of security and poor service. Only time will tell whether Angola will be able to emerge from the quagmire of ineptitude in which it finds itself in the 21st century, but a small number of conservation bodies and non-profit environmental organizations continue to hold out hope for the future of this country. In an attempt to bring about rehabilitation in Angola, conservationists in 2000 relocated to the Kissama Reserve a number of elephants from Tuli in Botswana, where they had been mistreated. The operation took more than two years to be finalized, and their presence in Angola has been hailed as a symbol of peace, hope and renewal in a country in the throes of civil war. The Kissama Foundation was specifically established to facilitate the relocation of animals to Angola and to rebuild populations decimated during the years of military action and rampant poaching. It has been the driving force behind not only the introduction of the Tuli elephants, but also the reintroduction of other wildlife that was once common in these parts, including ostriches, zebra herds and even camels.

ADV 300
NP 259

THE REGION

Considered by many to be the most volatile region in all of Africa, the central area of the continent that includes Rwanda, Burundi and Uganda is also one of the most picturesque, an extraordinary landscape of lush forest and fertile savanna that is slowly re-emerging as one of Africa's great treasures. Today, the three nations together boast no less than five million hectares of officially protected land, a promising indication for the economic stability of the broader region.

RWANDA	Key
Akagera National Park	B
Volcans National Park	A
Mukura Hunting Reserve	1
Volcans Biosphere Reserve	A
Nyungwe Forest Reserve	2

BURUNDI	
Kibira National Park	A
Rusizi National Park	B
Ruvubu National Park	C
Gisagara Nature Reserve	1
Makamba Nature Reserve	2
Rusizi Ramsar Wetland	B

UGANDA	
Bwindi Impenetrable National Park	H
Gorilla (Mgahinga) National Park	E
Kibale National Park	F
Kidepo Valley National Park	A
Lake Mburo National Park	C
Mgahinga Gorilla National Park	E
Mount Elgon National Park	G
Murchison Falls National Park	B
Queen Elizabeth National Park	D
Ruwenzori Mountains National Park	I
Kasagala Nature Reserve	16
Ajai Game Reserve	14
Bokora Game Reserve	5
Bugungu Game Reserve	17
Karuma Game Reserve	15
Katonga Game Reserve	22
Kigezi Game Reserve	1
Kyambura Game Reserve	22
Matheniko Game Reserve	7
Pian Upe Game Reserve	3
Toro Game Reserve	19
Mount Kei White Rhino Sanctuary	11
Otze Forest White Rhino Sanctuary	10
Zoka Nature Reserve	23
Central Karamoja Controlled Hunting Area	4
East Madi Controlled Hunting Area	13
Kaiso Tonya Controlled Hunting Area	18
Karuma Controlled Hunting Area	15
Katonga Controlled Hunting Area	21
Lipan Controlled Hunting Area	9
North Karamoja Controlled Hunting Area	8
Sebei Controlled Hunting Area	2
Semliki Controlled Hunting Area	20
South Karamoja Controlled Hunting Area	6
North Teso Controlled Hunting Area	24
West Madi Controlled Hunting Area	12
Queen Elizabeth / Ruwenzori Biosphere Reserve	D
Lake George Ramsar Wetland	D

CLOCKWISE FROM TOP LEFT

Murchison Falls, Uganda.
Hippo, Queen Elizabeth National Park, Uganda
Hiker, Nyungwe Forest, Rwanda
Butterflies, Bwindi Impenetrable National Park, Uganda.

Rwanda

For a nation that has only in recent years emerged from one of the most sickening genocides in living history, Rwanda is slowly but most assuredly rebuilding itself and is today as safe as anywhere else in Africa. Following years of carnage, crime levels are gratifyingly low, the sociopolitical situation relatively stable, and the all-important tourism steadily re-establishing itself as a cornerstone of the national economy. In fact, the contribution of the hospitality industry may prove to be the great saviour of a country intent on reconstruction and development as it emerges in the 21st century. In the years that preceded the internal conflict in which more than a million Rwandans lost their lives, Rwanda was hailed as one of the continent's favoured destinations, not the least of which was for the attraction of its mountain gorillas. Today, the forested mountain slopes, which occupy the 26,500km^2 (10,000 sq. miles) of the country, are one of the last remaining sanctuaries of gorillas and, as a result, tourists on a quest to see these primates once formed Rwanda's third-largest source of foreign capital. Today, following the stability that has settled since the mid-1990s, it is not difficult to trek to see at least two of the five significant family groups thriving here. In fact, given the recent history of the place, it is remarkable that it is the breathtaking landscape of forest, mountain, lakes and savanna and an impressive array of wildlife that are now drawing the visitors back — if not in droves then, certainly, in far greater numbers than seen towards the end of the 1900s.

In the new era of economic growth and reconstruction, the importance of the country's parks and reserves is slowly re-establishing its foothold, and parks such as Akagera, Nyungwe and Volcans National Park are enjoying a higher priority than ever before.

As Rwanda's only savanna reserve, gazetted in 1932, Akagera National Park — a wide stretch of savanna punctuated with lakes and swamps — is best known for its mammal and bird life, the latter numbering nearly 700 species, including great flocks of storks and pelicans and other water-based avifauna. Although some 60 per cent of the plains that formed part of the original national park were reclaimed in order to settle refugees returning after the genocide (a trend that put paid to Gishwati Forest Reserve, which was once acclaimed as the second-largest remaining rainforest in Rwanda), the breeding herds of the big game that remained now form the nucleus of the park, and Akagera is the setting for some of the country's best wildlife experiences. Great herds of buffalo, zebra, eland and duiker graze the grasslands, and pods of hippo have re-established themselves in local waters, while sitatunga, giant forest hogs, spotted hyena and side-striped jackal, and even Masai giraffe and leopard, have made their home here.

Equally impressive are the 270-plus bird species and equal number of tree species, a prolific insect life and the apes of Nyungwe Forest, which is said to harbour no fewer than 500, and possibly as many as 1,000, of the of the nearly 200,000 wild primates of Central Africa, and boasts more than a dozen species of monkey, many of which are considered endangered. Consequently, the forest reserve, which at 970km^2 (375 sq. miles) is one of the largest mountain rainforest protectorates on the continent, is Rwanda's top wildlife drawcard. It was, however, also the centre of an important conservation effort, established here in 1988 to help preserve the forest habitat. Known as the Nyungwe Forest Conservation Project and supported financially by the Rwandan government as well as by both the US Peace Corps and the New York Zoological Society, the future of the project is uncertain, but there are still tours to see Nyungwe's colobus monkeys.

Once acknowledged as the best of Rwanda's protected parks and the centre of the 'gorilla-spotting industry', the slopes of Volcans National Park — covered with rainforest — are home to four of the surviving troops of mountain gorilla and the park was re-opened to the public at the turn of the new millennium. Conservationists based here still, however, face an ongoing struggle with hunters and poachers, and constantly have to square up against government bureaucrats. As a result, the number of adventurers allowed to visit the home pockets of the gorillas is limited and visitors need a special permit.

Burundi

All of Burundi suffered greatly during the wars, the national economy and sociopolitical climate plunging into complete disarray. Today, the society — and, indeed, the government — is still trying to pick up the pieces, with only limited success. Although parts of Burundi are indeed safe to visit, notably some urban centres that remain relatively stable, tribal factions mean that the country remains unstable and ecotourism is virtually non-existent. Much of the country's 27,835km^2 (10,750 sq. miles) is covered by mountain, and it boasts a variable climate and a high rainfall. Despite the fact that Burundi covers some magnificent landscape, the risks may be too many for the casual visitor. Although the nation's three national parks — Kibira, Rusizi and Ruvubu — and the Gisagara and Makamba nature reserves cover some 0.14 million hectares, resources are limited and conservation is, in practice, hardly a priority. In the years of political turmoil, even the mountain gorilla suffered enormously, populations severely affected by the movement of troops and the blood that bathed the forests. In fact, even the claim that Source du Nil (The Source of the Nile) near Rutana, which is perhaps the nation's greatest drawcard — albeit little more than a rather disappointing brook — is the southernmost source of the Nile is disputed. Burundi is, thus, one of the unfortunate casualties of war-torn Africa and its woodland and tropical climes remain, for the most part, lost to adventurers.

Uganda

Once hailed as one of the finest wildlife havens in Africa, Uganda reeled under the scourge of dictator Idi Amin, and its much vaunted wildlife experience and conservation record began to falter to such a degree that vast populations of its fauna were decimated, and along with them tracts of indigenous vegetation, from semidesert brush to verdant plains. Fortunately, however, decades later — and despite the fact that some 25 per cent of its 236,580km^2 (91,320 sq. miles) of land cover is considered arable — Uganda is slowly regaining some of its scenic glory and along with it restocking its wildlife heritage. The road may still prove to be long and arduous, but there is evidence (albeit sporadic) that at last something right is being done, and for every annoyance — from the tsetse fly to the destructive water hyacinth choking the life out of Lake Victoria — there is a heart-warming success story, no matter how apparently insignificant it may be.

Today, Uganda boasts no fewer than 35 gazetted conservation areas, from national parks and reserves to game sanctuaries and controlled hunting areas. In fact, despite the protestations of staunch conservationists, there are a number of hunting areas, all of which are — in theory, at least — regulated by government, with limited access to the tourist market. The country seems, however, to have successfully skirted the controversy, and leaned toward the potential of the ecotourist rather than the casual holiday-maker. As a result, the sustainability of the environment and even indigenous culture are not sacrificed for the needs of the tourism industry.

Although some of Uganda's reserves are still susceptible to the legacy of recent years, many have become acclaimed wildlife destinations, most noticeably the majestic Murchison Falls. Desperadoes still work some of the roads that snake through Murchison Falls National Park, yet despite this it remains the showpiece of all of Uganda's parks, its largest (at 3,900km^2/ 1,500 sq. miles) and its most impressive, harbouring a diversity of wildlife from endangered birds to chimpanzees. Whereas the latter half of the 20th century saw untold damage to reserves — thousands of animals met their fate here during these years of mismanagement and political instability — Murchison Falls and other national parks, such as the 34km^2 (13-sq.-mile) Mgahinga and the 2,000km^2 (770-sq.-mile) Queen Elizabeth, are steadily recovering from declining tourist numbers, and some of the upmarket lodges may even be considered too crowded during the peak holiday seasons. Fortunately, wildlife populations are now seeing the fruits of the most recent conservation projects and, whereas poaching once helped the local environment to recover from the natural damage executed by elephants in their foraging, it is now the efforts of conservationists that have helped rebuild faunal populations. The population numbers are still a lot fewer than during the early 1900s, but parks such as Murchison Falls and Queen Elizabeth are now in fairly good ecological shape, which bodes well for the future of ecotourism. Although many of the safari lodges on the outskirts of the reserves were virtually destroyed during the unrest, most have now recovered to become some of Africa's most luxurious.

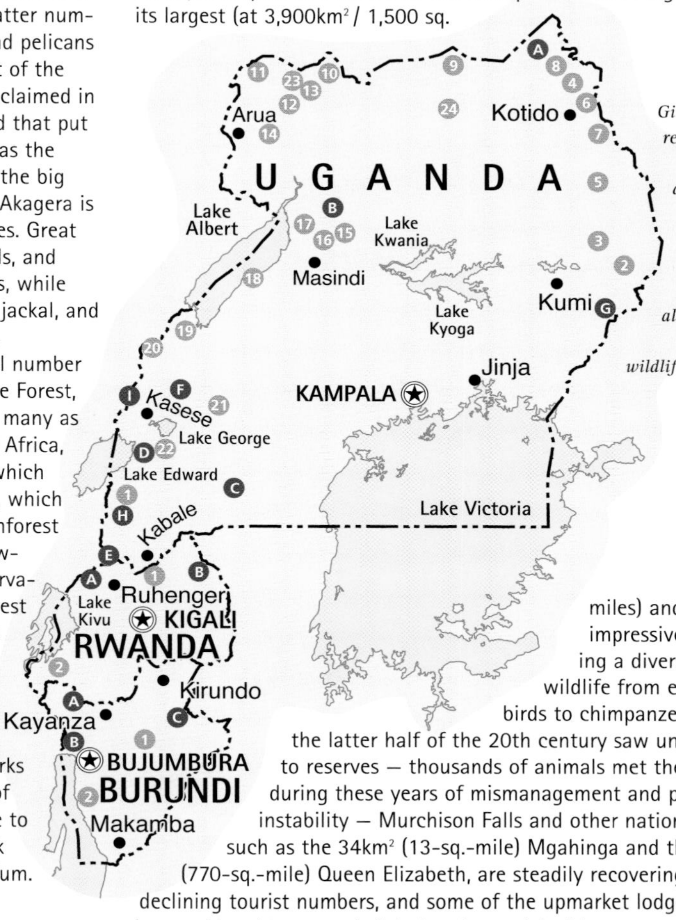

Given the political volatility in recent years of the region that includes Rwanda, Burundi and Uganda, it is the foreign revenue of its national parks, other protected areas and tourist attractions that promises to help alleviate the strife of war-torn communities – and indeed wildlife populations that have also suffered as a result.

A small number of parks and reserves also act as the base for conservation efforts aimed at preserving what remains of the country's natural resources, most notably the region's chimp population. Ngamba Island in Lake Victoria is the home of the chimpanzee orphanage established by the Born Free Foundation as part of the Chimpanzee Sanctuary and Wildlife Conservation Trust, while the rainforests of Gorilla (Mgahinga) National Park that (together with Rwanda's Volcans National Park and Congo's Virunga National Park) form the 420km^2 (162-sq.-mile) Virunga Conservation Area, are home to nearly 650 individuals. In addition, recent plans to focus attention on Uganda's extensive wetlands saw fruit when the National Wetlands Programme (NWP) spearheaded the launch of the Wetlands Sector Strategic Plan with the nation's government. With political backing and through careful management, the environmental programme will help to assure this treasure house – labelled the 'Pearl of Africa' by Sir Winston Churchill – remains one of the continent's most enduring assets.

ADV 302
NP 262

ADV 304
NP 264

THE REGION

In a region perhaps best known for the phenomenon of its wildlife, Kenya and Tanzania have, in the process of capitalizing on their extraordinarily rich natural heritage, both achieved an enviable record of conservation. Kenya has devoted some 4.5 million hectares to protected land, while Tanzania has dedicated a phenomenal 25.5 million hectares — no less than a third of its land area — to the cause.

KENYA	Key
Aberdare National Park	H
Amboseli National Park	E
Hell's Gate National Park	K
Kisite / Mpunguti Marine National Park	A
Kora National Park	S
Lake Nakuru National Park	I
Longonot National Park	J
Malka Mari National Park	P
Meru National Park	R
Mombasa Marine National Park	V
Mount Elgon National Park	M
Mount Kenya National Park	Q
Nairobi National Park	F
Ol Doinyo Sabuk National Park	G
Ras Tenewei Marine National Park	U
Ruma National Park	L
Sibiloi National Park	O
South Island National Park	N
Tsavo East National Park	C
Tsavo West National Park	B
Watamu National Park	T
Chyulu National Park	D
Southwestern Mau Nature Reserve	5
Arawale National Reserve	18
Bisanadi National Reserve	14
Boni National Reserve	23
Buffalo Springs National Reserve	12
Dodori National Reserve	22
Lake Bogoria National Reserve	6
Losai National Reserve	10
Marsabit Nature Reserve	8
Masai Mara Reserve	4
Ngai Ndethya National Reserve	3
North Kitui National Reserve	16
Rahole National Reserve	15
Samburu Nature Reserve	11
Shaba National Reserve	13
Shimba Hills National Reserve	2
South Kitui National Reserve	17
South Turkana National Reserve	7
Tana River Primate National Reserve	19
Kiunga Marine National Reserve	21
Malindi Marine Nature Reserve	20
Mombasa Marine Nature Reserve	1
Amboseli Biosphere Reserve	E
Kiunga Biosphere Reserve	21
Malindi-Watamu Biosphere Reserve	T
Mount Kenya Biosphere Reserve	Q
Mount Kulal Biosphere Reserve	9
Lake Nakuru Ramsar Wetland	I
Lake Naivasha Ramsar Wetland	K
Mount Kenya National Park WHS	Q

TANZANIA	
Arusha National Park	J
Gombe Stream National Park	E
Katavi National Park	C
Kilimanjaro National Park	K
Lake Manyara National Park	H
Mahale Mountains National Park	D
Mikumi National Park	A
Ruaha National Park	B
Rubondo Island National Park	F
Serengeti National Park	G
Tarangire National Park	I
Udzungwa Mountains National Park	L
Biharamulo Game Reserve	11
Burigi Game Reserve	10
Ibanda Game Reserve	8
Kilimanjaro Game Reserve	K
Kizigo Game Reserve	3
Maswa Game Reserve	12
Mkomazi Game Reserve	15
Mount Meru Game Reserve	14
Moyowosi Game Reserve	7
Rumanyika Game Reserve	9
Rungwa Game Reserve	4
Saadani Game Reserve	2
Selous Game Reserve	1
Ugalla River Game Reserve	6
Umba Game Reserve	16
Uwanda Game Reserve	5
Ngorongoro Conservation Area	13
Lake Manyara Biosphere Reserve	H
Serengeti-Ngorongoro Biosphere Reserve	G
Kilimanjaro World Heritage Site	K
Ngorongoro World Heritage Site	13
Selous World Heritage Site	1
Serengeti World Heritage Site	G

CLOCKWISE FROM TOP LEFT

Olduvai Gorge, Serengeti, Tanzania.
Flamingoes, Ngorongoro Crater, Tanzania.
Gerenuk, Meru National Park, Kenya.
Buffalo, Amboseli National Park, Kenya.

Kenya

With nearly 60 separate officially designated conservation areas, including national parks, reserves, marine reserves and wetlands covering some 10 per cent of Kenya's land and waters, Kenya boasts the largest, best stocked and most accessible protected areas in all of Africa. The word 'safari' is taken from the local Swahili language and, appropriately, the safari industry is now one of the nation's most important income producers.

Kenya's central plateau is divided by the Great Rift Valley, and the semidesert stretches south of the equator to the fertile east coast. The varying geology of the region means that the national parks controlled by the Kenya Wildlife Service, the game reserves and private wildlife conservancies cover an extraordinary range of landscapes, from wide-open plains to densely wooded forests and marine environments. Unfortunately, despite the sterling efforts initiated by government authorities, foreign conservation organizations and private benefactors, wildlife areas remain under constant threat as a result of numerous scourges that continue to plague wild Kenya and, indeed, much of Africa. As elsewhere, poaching, an evergrowing population and consequent evergrowing land use mean that there is enormous pressure on the wild spaces as a result of encroachment by human settlement. The Masai Mara's wildebeest population has dropped from about 120,000 to some 22,000 in less than 20 years, their seasonal stomping grounds having given way to farm land and cattle pastures. Situations such as this are further exacerbated by what appears to be irresponsible and narrow-minded decisions made by non-aligned government officials in the face of conservation. Despite enormous opposition from local, international and non-governmental conservation organizations in recent years, the Kenyan government announced that it would excise about 67,000ha (165,500 acres) of the country's unique woodlands, including some 270ha (670 acres) of Nakuru, 1,825ha (4,500 acres) of Mount Kenya, 2,837ha (7,000 acres) of Marmanet and 900ha (2,220 acres) of Molo. Leading environmental groups have lashed out as a result, pointing out that, apart from the irreparable damage to the immediate environment, also affected would be the national economy and the ecology of the broader region. Felling these forests would alter local rainfall, thus affecting the water system and, therefore, agriculture — not to mention the other industries dependent on hydro-electric power. In fact, Kenya's rivers are already suffering from natural deterioration. Originating in the forests of the Eastern Mau Escarpment are the Njoro, Makalia and Enderit rivers, which drain into the great lake that forms the heart of Lake Nakuru National Park and provides sustenance for more than half a million Kenyans. The lake itself, which now flows for only one third of the year, has been reduced to dust no fewer than six times in the last decade. Only dedicated and meticulous management programmes can alleviate such disasters. Fortunately, the overall sentiment is one of concern and, following a steadfast campaign led by fishermen and conservationists, the government's Fisheries Department has taken steps to help preserve the nation's marine life. Not only did it declare a short moratorium on trawling, it also established a task force, including representatives from non-governmental and private research programmes, the Kenyan Wildlife Service, coastal development authorities, fishing associations, conservation groups and fishing communities. This task force was charged with investigating the status of marine resources for future utilization.

At the same time, however, Kenya does have some of the finest national parks and reserves in the world. Parks such as Aberdare, Amboseli, Meru, Tsavo East and West, and Samburu provide, in the most part, outstanding wildlife experiences unparalleled anywhere else on earth. Although the tourist trade does have numerous downfalls — parks such as Amboseli and Masai Mara are crisscrossed with tracks and trails carved by the caravan of tourists — in most cases a percentage of the revenue generated by safari operations and the entrance fees to government parks and reserves is allocated to local inhabitants and the establishment of wildlife research programmes and education centres teaching conservation ethics.

Mount Kenya National Park, for example, is not only one of the country's top safari spots, but also a popular recreation destination much favoured among climbers determined to ascend Africa's second-highest peak. Visitors' facilities here are more than adequate. The four main hiking routes across Mount Kenya — Naro Muru, Sirimon, Timau and Chogoria — all vary in distance and accessibility, demanding various degrees of fitness. Whereas some climbs are not particularly arduous, others demand all the skills and equipment — including ice axes and ropes — utilized by dedicated mountaineers. The trails, camps and huts on the trail circuit are not the mountain's only nod to visitors; it is also serviced b y a number of fine hotels and plush safari lodges, offering excellent game-viewing, including night drives.

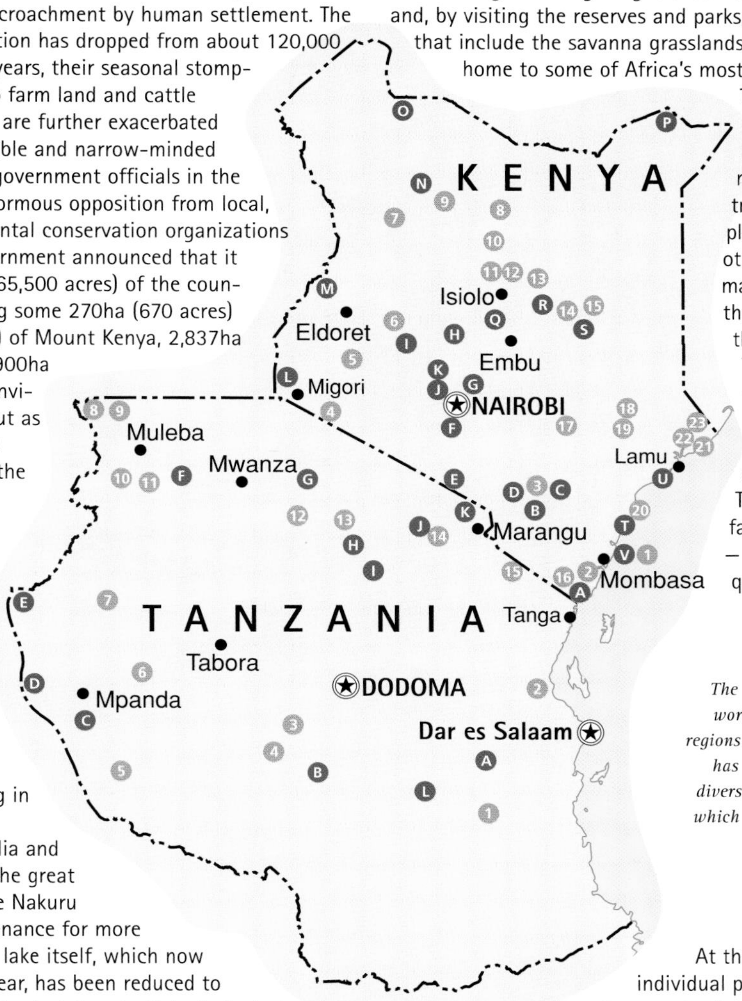

Tanzania

Consisting mostly of wide plains spreading east of the Great Rift Valley, high-lying mountainscapes in the north and south, and a lushly wooded coastal strip, Tanzania can justifiably claim to have one of the most remarkable conservation records in Africa. With approximately 30 per cent of the land dedicated to the conservation efforts concentrated in wildlife sanctuaries, the country does, however, continue to struggle with juggling the requirements of its largely impoverished citizens and the demands of conserving the nation's natural heritage. The more than 35 parks, reserves and conservation areas — from the tropical coast to the semiarid central plateau, the semitemperate highlands to the forested woodlands — constantly have to compete for funds reserved mostly for the all-important agricultural sector, which includes livestock and cash crops such as cotton, coffee, tea, cloves, and the lucrative diamond-mining industry, all of which contribute enormously to the national coffers.

Although government authorities are indeed committed to conservation, in a Third World country such as Tanzania, fulfilling that commitment is easier said than done. Casual visitors, holiday-makers, tourists and safari-goers bring sought-after foreign currency into the country and, by visiting the reserves and parks, help to preserve vital habitats that include the savanna grasslands and endless plains that are home to some of Africa's most recognized wildlife species. Tanzanians, therefore, rely in many ways on the influx of naturalists and ecotourists who make their way to the huge tracts of land that remain unexplored. In comparison to many other African nations, including many that rely on the attraction of their wildlife to foreign visitors, the tourist infrastructure in Tanzania is relatively sophisticated, and travel in and around the game reserves, national parks and World Heritage Sites — such as Arusha, Gombe, Kilimanjaro, Tarangire, Selous and the world-famous Serengeti and Ngorongoro — is generally a pain-free and quite luxurious experience.

The Great Rift Valley is one of the world's most spectacular volcanic regions and the area's latter-day geology has given rise to an extraordinary diversity of landscape and faunal life, which reaches its pinnacle on the wild plains of Kenya.

At the same time, the conservation of individual parks is not enough to ensure the long-term protection of vast ecosystems. Like elsewhere in Africa, the focus needs to shift from particular parks to wider conglomerations of conservation areas, where the preservation of regional biodiversity is closely married with sustainable development that is beneficial to local communities. So far, this has been sadly lacking in much of Africa, and during the 1980s Tanzania was a disaster zone when it came to conservation. As a result, indigenous animals such as Ader's duiker — restricted to the island of Zanzibar and the stands of forests along Kenya's coast — remains threatened by the loss of its habitat as well as its demand as bush meat. The huge prices of horn and ivory in the East have resulted in the vast elephant populations being decimated and endangered rhinos massacred to the point of extinction. The scourge of poaching — occasionally simply to provide daily sustenance for locals — has been exacerbated by the continued lack of resources and funds, ineffective and corrupt management, and the low morale of underpaid wardens, scouts and rangers. Fortunately, with the assistance of wildlife organizations, world conservation bodies and even the Tanzanian Army, as well as pressure of world opinion, officials from the National Parks and Game Department have drastically reduced the incidence of serious poaching. Apart from the constant threat posed by illegal hunting, the expanding boundaries of cultivated lands stretching well into the natural habitats of indigenous fauna, and irresponsible practices such as dynamite fishing, poor irrigation and the like, one factor that continues to plague the protected lands of the country's parks and reserves – and even the wild expanses of unprotected areas – is the deforestation of huge tracts of land for human settlement. This goes hand in hand with the supply of tropical wood to timber dealers prepared to pay for the privilege and to provide invaluable charcoal for domestic consumption, particularly in high-demand areas such as large urban settlements like Dar es Salaam. In a nation whose individual household income is pitifully meagre, coal is the least expensive form of energy available to locals who are unaware that no fewer than 10 tons of timber is required to produce one ton of charcoal. As a result, the forests of Tanzania are dwindling at an alarming rate of 400,000ha (1,500 sq. miles) a year.

THE REGION

In order to preserve its extraordinary natural heritage, Zambia has set aside no less than 22.65 million hectares of land as protected area, while Zimbabwe claims more than 6 million hectares of conservation land, including a number of specially designated safari areas rich in some of the most impressive wildlife populations in Africa.

ZAMBIA	Key
Blue Lagoon National Park	M
Isangano National Park	H
Kafue National Park	L
Kasanka National Park	J
Lavushi Manda National Park	N
Liuwa Plain National Park	P
Lochinvar National Park	K
Lower Zambezi National Park	A
Luambe National Park	C
Lukusuzi National Park	B
Lusenga Plain National Park	G
Mweru-Wantipa National Park	F
North Luangwa National Park	D
Nsumbu National Park	E
Sioma Ngwezi National Park	O
South Luangwa National Park	I
Mosi-Oa-Tunya National Park	Q
West Lunga National Park	R
Bangweulu Game Management Area	14
Bilili Springs Game Management Area	19
Chambeshi Game Management Area	12
Chibwika-Ntambu Game Management Area	29
Chisomo Game Management Area	16
Chizera Game Management Area	31
Kafinda Game Management Area	15
Kafue Flats Game Management Area	23
Kalaso Mukoso Game Management Area	13
Kansonso-Busanga Game Management Area	27
Kaputa Game Management Area	9
Luano Game Management Area	1
Lukwakwa Game Management Area	30
Lumimba Game Management Area	5
Lunga-Luswishi Game Management Area	26
Lupande Game Management Area	4
Luwingu Game Management Area	10
Machiya-Fungulwe Game Management Area	25
Mansa Game Management Area	11
Mazabuka Game Management Area	17
Mulobezi Game Management Area	21
Mumbwa Game Management Area	24
Munyamadzi Game Management Area	6
Musalangu Game Management Area	7
Musele-Matebo Game Management Area	28
Namwala Game Management Area	22
Nkala Game Management Area	18
Sandwe Game Management Area	3
Sichifula Game Management Area	20
Tondwa Game Management Area	8
West Petauke Game Management Area	2
West Zambezi Game Management Area	32
Kafue Flats Ramsar Wetland	23
Bangweulu Swamps Ramsar Wetland	14
Victoria Falls / Mosi-Oa-Tunya WHS	Q

ZIMBABWE	
Chimanimani National Park	B
Chizarira National Park	I
Gonarezhou National Park	C
Hwange (Wankie) National Park	E
Inyanga and Mtarazi Falls National Park	A
Kazuma Pan National Park	F
Mana Pools National Park	K
Matobo (Matopos) National Park	D
Matusadona National Park	J
Nyanga National Park	A
Victoria Falls National Park	H
Zambezi National Park	G
Mushandike Sanctuary	2
Mutirikwi Game Park	16
Charara Safari Area	5
Chegutu Safari Area	10
Chete Safari Area	6
Chewore Safari Area	14
Chipinge Safari Area	7
Chirisa Safari Area	I
Dande Safari Area	15
Deka Safari Area	4
Doma Safari Area	13
Hurungwe Safari Area	9
Malapati Safari Area	1
Matetsi Safari Area	3
Mfurundzi Safari Area	12
Sapi Safari Area	14
Tuli Safari Area	17
Darwendale Recreation Park	11
Lake Kariba Recreation Park	8
Lake Kyle Recreation Park	16
Umufuli Recreation Park	18
Mana Pools / Sapi / Chewore WHS	K
Great Zimbabwe World Heritage Site	16
Victoria Falls / Mosi-Oa-Tunya WHS	G

CLOCKWISE FROM TOP LEFT
Great Zimbabwe Ruins, Zimbabwe.
Elephants at a water hole,
Hwange National Park, Zimbabwe.
Epworth Balancing Rocks, Harare, Zimbabwe.
Zebra, South Luangwa NP, Zambia.

Zambia

With kilometre after endless kilometre of wide-open plain, vast stands of indigenous woodland and lush riverine vegetation – most of which remains mercifully unblemished and packed with enormous herds of game and an abundance of predators – it is no surprise that Zambia enjoys much acclaim as one of Africa's finest wildlife destinations. Despite the difficulties of travel across the rugged countryside, years of inept government, and a poor conservation record during its formative years, it is considered by many today as a fine example of a developing nation that is making at least some effort in preserving its natural heritage. Not only are its national parks and game management areas set in what may well be some of Africa's most authentic wilderness areas, but the backdrop of Zambia's landscape is arguably the most breathtaking in the subcontinent. It boasts at least two of the continent's most celebrated natural phenomena: the magnificent Victoria Falls (known locally — and more appropriately — as Mosi-Oa-Tunya – "the smoke that thunders") and the mighty Zambezi River.

Zambia covers an impressive 750,000km² (290,000 sq. miles) and has about 20 national parks, more than 30 game management areas and countless numbers of small private and state-run reserves. Perhaps because most are separated from each other by vast distances and, in some cases, are virtually inaccessible or difficult to get to, they represent some of southern Africa's most pristine wilderness areas. Sadly, many of these areas suffered enormous devastation during the decades of poaching and some of the parks are still pitifully low on wildlife. Although poaching (especially of the region's elephants) remains an ongoing problem, the last decade or so has seen some impressive attempts to rehabilitate the landscape and bolster the wildlife populations that had been decimated in the preceding years. This has been made possible not only by the practical and, more importantly, financial assistance of private donors, but also thanks to an increasing awareness of the importance of conservation by government officials and others in positions of authority. Wildlife services have recently taken another look at the requirements of the country's environment and have made at least some attempt to balance this with the needs of the locals by establishing community projects that allow the human population to derive some benefit from conservation efforts in the region. Attempts to rehabilitate the depleted land and reintroduce depleted game stocks after many years of neglect and mismanagement are ongoing and, although there may be a long way to go, Zambia's parks are nevertheless a bounty of treasure and the impressive populations of birds and mammals have made it one of the continent's top safari, hiking and wildlife photography destinations.

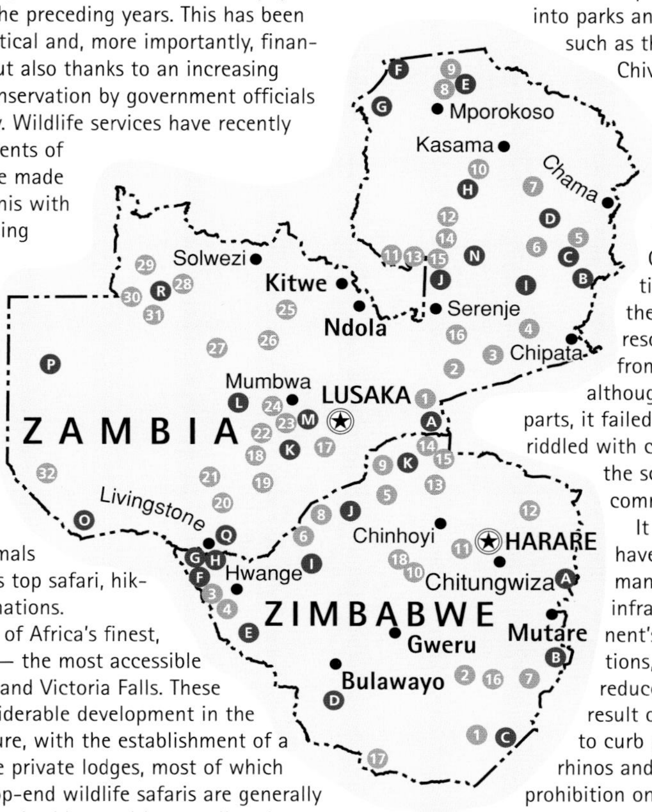

Zambia's top parks include some of Africa's finest, such as South Luangwa and Kafue — the most accessible of the parks — and Lower Zambezi and Victoria Falls. These most popular parks have seen considerable development in the way of roads and other infrastructure, with the establishment of a number of camp sites and exclusive private lodges, most of which are affiliated to safari operators. Top-end wildlife safaris are generally rather expensive and most are patronized by wealthy travellers, but exchange rates are usually very favourable for overseas visitors, and more and more budget travellers are finding their way through Zambia's parks with considerable ease and without too much damage to their pocket.

The superb wilderness areas harbour massive herds of game, including Africa's most recognized wildlife species such as lion, leopard, buffalo and elephant. Throughout the history of Zambia — and, in fact, much of Africa — wildlife resources were traditionally controlled by tribal laws and custom; however, with the settlement of Europeans and the increase in poaching, game reserves were set aside to control hunting, poaching and the growth of population numbers. By the end of the 19th century, elephant and black rhino populations had been virtually decimated by the ivory and horn trades, but hunting safaris slowly began to make way for photographic and walking safaris and, as a result, populations climbed dramatically by the late 20th century. The success was, however, short-lived and many valiant attempts saw little fruit with a sudden resurgence of destructive forces in the late 1900s. Wildlife numbers are once again low and conservation authorities will have to revive their initial attempts in order to save Zambia's wild animals. Fortunately, game numbers are still impressive enough to attract safari-goers and other adventurers to the country's bushveld, and the wild countryside remains virtually intact. As a result, the future of Zambia's wild spaces may well rest in the hands of the visiting public. Nearly a third of the country's land is now protected by law and, although hunting still takes place with government consent, it is more controlled, with the national parks and game management areas much more carefully maintained. The level of amenities in these areas tends to vary considerably, ranging from very basic to super-luxurious, but a number of prominent, well-established safari operators based in and around the parks offer plenty of opportunities for self-drive excursions, with local guides and scouts available on request. Zambia has become an acclaimed ecotourism destination, and the government-run parks are accessible only with the required permit in hand.

Zimbabwe

Despite the rather poor roads and lack of a sophisticated infrastructure, the natural wonders, fascinating diversions and extraordinary diversity of landscapes and wildlife remain Zimbabwe's top attractions. It is a nation blessed with some of sub-Sahara's most impressive conservation areas, and even the political, social and economic turmoil under the government of Robert Mugabe has not detracted from this. Although international travel to and from Zimbabwe has dwindled, virtually all the visitors make their way to reserves, such as Hwange — at 14,620km² (5,625 sq. miles), Zimbabwe's largest — and Gonarezhou, at 5,000km² (1,935 sq. miles), the second largest. More than 30,000 elephant, 15,000 buffalo, 3,000 giraffe and 400 bird species have settled here, and the intrinsic value of the land and its resources is gradually making its importance felt. Fortunately, Zimbabwe's conservation officials and private groups are preserving the habitat not only for its economic value, but also for aesthetic and ecological reasons. Although hunting is still allowed — and, in some areas, encouraged — it is generally limited to the natural growth of wildlife populations. In this way, wild animals are protected not only for conservation purposes, but also for the millions of dollars hunting introduces to the national coffers and, in theory at least, these revenues are channelled back into local communities. In fact, one of the priorities of Zimbabwe's conservation bodies is the utilization of systems introduced to help sustain and educate locals most likely to be affected by fencing operations and wildlife management. Mukuvisi Woodlands, Cecil Kop and Tshabalala, for example, were established as reserves and used as wilderness schools in the cities where urban children can learn about conservation. Another positive step has been the incorporation into parks and reserves of cultural heritage sites, such as the ruins of Great Zimbabwe and Lake Chivero's rock art. The Communal Areas Management Programme for Indigenous Resources (CAMPFIRE) was formed as a result of skirmishes among a community that had been forcibly removed from its land in the 1960s in order to establish the Gonarezhou National Park. Today, it continues to empower rural people so that they are better able to manage natural resources and thus benefit economically from tourism and hunting. However, although the project has been successful in parts, it failed to make the impact predicted in areas riddled with corruption and where the profits from the schemes failed to reach the pockets of community members.

It is, however, the animal populations that have been most affected by irresponsible management and the lack of funds and infrastructure. During the 1980s, the continent's most expansive black rhino populations, which numbered some 3,000, were reduced to no more than 300 individuals as a result of poaching, but there have been efforts to curb poaching activities by dehorning the rhinos and hunting down poachers. Although the prohibition on the trade in rhino horn seems to have met with little success, there has been some attempt — with limited success — to translocate rhino and other species to safer grounds. Efforts are still under way to ban ivory trade entirely.

Considering the vast tracts of untamed wilderness and the breathtaking, scenic beauty of the region, it is little wonder that Zambia and Zimbabwe have rapidly become two of the most acclaimed wildlife and safari destinations on the continent.

It is with relief that many of these efforts have yielded some rewards. For example, the elephant populations in Zimbabwe are now growing, some having been reintroduced with the establishment of the Gaza-Kruger-Gonarezhou Transfrontier Park, the 'Superpark' that spans the boundaries of three countries – South Africa, Zimbabwe and Mozambique. At an impressive 100,000km² (40,000 sq. miles), this is the world's largest conservation area and 'Operation Ark' saw some 1,000 elephants translocated from the Kruger National Park in South Africa to both Mozambique and Zimbabwe.

From the challenging hikes of Chimanimani to the abundance of wildlife at Hwange — baboons, vultures and jackals to crocodiles, lion, buffalo and elephants — there is plenty in Zimbabwe's national parks to attract the visitor. Mana Pools – on the banks of the Zambezi and surrounded by mopane veld – is, for example, not only one of the country's most isolated parks, but has also been declared a World Heritage Site by UNESCO. Matobo National Park, in turn, is hailed as the site of one of the country's most important monuments to the region's early inhabitants, the San, who left as their legacy remarkable art on the rock faces scattered across the 43,000ha (106,000 acres) just outside Bulawayo. As is evidenced by Nyanga, Gonarezhou, Hwange and Chimanimani national parks, much of Zimbabwe is still wild, and yet it has made the necessary concessions in certain of its conservation areas to the mass tourism market. Although both are protected by law, Lake Kariba and Victoria Falls cannot, in all fairness, be considered 'untamed'. Damming operations at Kariba have made it a popular holiday spot, while Victoria Falls is undisputed as one of the continent's key drawcards.

The latter, although beautiful and breathtaking in its magnitude, is a long way from the romantic notion of 'wildest Africa'.

ADV 306
NP 267

ADV 308
NP 271

THE REGION

With more than 8 million hectares of protected wildlife area between them, both Mozambique and Malawi — despite the considerable odds posed by the socio-political history of the region — have a wide range of national parks and game reserves that bode well for the economic future of the two struggling nations.

MOZAMBIQUE	Key
Banhine National Park	B
Bazaruto National Park	D
Gorongosa National Park	E
Limpopo National Park	A
Paradise Island Marine National Park	F
Zinave National Park	C
Gile Game Reserve	4
Maputo Game Reserve	1
Marromeu Game Reserve	3
Niassa Game Reserve	5
Pomene Game Reserve	2

MALAWI	
Kasungu National Park	B
Lake Malawi National Park	C
Lengwe National Park	E
Liwonde National Park	D
Nyika National Park	A
Majete Wildlife Reserve	3
Mwabvi Wildlife Reserve	4
Nkhota-Kota Wildlife Reserve	2
Vwaza Marsh Wildlife Reserve	1
Lake Malawi World Heritage Site	C

CLOCKWISE FROM TOP LEFT

Aloe plant, Nyika National Park, Malawi.

Nosestripe clownfish hiding in an anemone, Bazaruto Archipelago, Mozambique.

Hippo, Liwonde National Park, Malawi.

Tree roots, Lake Malawi, Malawi.

Mozambique

Much of Mozambique has — particularly during the war-ravaged years — seen considerable devastation, both by the forces of nature and at the hand of mankind. The universal value of this wilderness is undeniable, even to government officials, and international conservation and humanitarian organizations, safari operators and tour organizers are beating a hasty track to the country's wildlife terrain, which includes lucrative government-granted concession areas.

During the fight for liberation and the ensuing civil war of the 1980s and early 1990s, the land saw enormous devastation that threatened to all but obliterate every notable trace of Mozambique's wildlife. Overseas-based logging companies were tearing down trees at a disturbing rate, while Renamo soldiers in areas such as Gorongosa — once considered one of the continent's greatest legacies and, fortunately, today the country's most promising park — were utilizing game as a food source, effectively decimating stocks that had taken decades, if not centuries, to build up. As a result, the deterioration of visitors' facilities, fast-dwindling game populations, and the constant threat of attack meant that parks such as Gorongosa, Zinave and Banhine could no longer be visited by international tourists, and conservation areas slipped into decline. Fortunately, Mozambique was able to emerge from the internal conflict and, slowly but surely, foreign aid organizations and conservation efforts began to pool their resources to establish an assistance programme that helped stabilize endangered areas by, among other efforts, reintroducing the herds of buffalo and elephant that were once common here. Consequently, foreign travellers once again began to make their way back to Mozambique. Of the more than six tracts of land proclaimed as conservation areas in the revived Mozambique, Maputo Bay's elephant reserve was the first of the parks on the mainland to be rehabilitated, and Gorongosa and the marine wonderland of Bazaruto were the first to be reopened as national parks. Today, wildlife populations here and in similar areas are slowly growing, with more than 900 bird species crossing the southern skies, most notably in Mozambique's Mount Gorongosa region, Metangula, Cubùè, Gurué, Maputo Elephant Reserve and Milange. Herds of elephant traverse the Futi Channel in the south and along the banks of the Rovuma River in the far north, while small groups of buffalo, rhino and even lion and leopard may be spotted in the Zambezi Delta and the great Gorongosa National Park (the latter reopened in 1998). International conservation efforts may prove to be Mozambique's great saving grace, and its most spectacular success story has been the declaration of Africa's 'Superpark', the massive Gaza-Kruger-Gonarezhou Transfrontier Park, which spans the borders of three African countries: South Africa, Zimbabwe and Mozambique. The aim of the impressive new transfrontier conservation initiative is to share the economic benefits derived from conservation among the three nations by marrying environmental efforts with the all-important tourist market, thus realizing the commercial potential of protected areas in ecologically sound and economically viable ways for the benefit of all the players. The removal of the border fencing — including 150km (93 miles) of electrified fence between the Kruger National Park and Zimbabwe — that separates the individual regions of the three countries will allow the wild animals to roam freely across national boundaries, as well as allowing the visitors that flock to the southern subcontinent to see them. This is but the first phase in creating the world's largest conservation area, which will grow to a phenomenal 100,000km^2 (40,000 sq. miles). In the largest international effort to translocate wildlife, 'Operation Ark' saw some 1,000 elephants relocated — at a cost of about US$2-million — from the Kruger National Park to Mozambique and Zimbabwe, areas that in years gone by were home to these giants. The relocation of the elephants was the launching programme for the ambitious new reserve, and the first herd of about 30 individuals was placed in the Coutada 16 area, one of several designated regions in Mozambique to be incorporated into the phased development of the transfrontier park. At 40,000km^2 (15,500 sq. miles), the park — stretching some 500km (310 miles) from north to south — has already been described as the biggest game reserve in the world and is hailed as the 'world's biggest wild open space', an untamed wilderness of thick bushveld, untouched sandveld, and the mountainscape of the Lebombo range, the valleys of which are a well-watered landscape blessed with an abundant wildlife.

As a result of this initiative, other developments rapidly followed to help ensure the viability of the project. Projects are managed by the non-profit Peace Parks Foundation in association with the Mozambican government: the German government donated nearly US$5-million to train game rangers and build park headquarters; Japan has offered funds to eradicate the area of land mines remaining after the cessation of hostilities decades ago; and American investors have pledged some US$50-million for the development of Zimbabwe's Gonarezhou.

The development of, for example, Coutada means that there are more employment opportunities for local inhabitants as well as enormous potential for further tourist traffic, accessing Coutada 16 via new roads, camps and landing strips. The park is not only seen as a symbol of unification and a monument to peace, but it also brings with it the hope of a better future, which includes jobs and income for the rural poor of the area. Although this does not mean that the region's problems have disappeared entirely — there is still poaching, petty crime, and the occasional threat of foot-and-mouth disease — it does mean a shift of focus on the conservation of the area. The success of the venture depends, however, on a continued cooperation between the three participating nations.

Malawi

Malawi has traditionally placed much importance in protecting its wildlife heritage, and an impressive expanse of its land cover has been designated as protected land. The approximately 10 separate reserves and parks cover about 20 per cent of the country, and yet Malawi's national parks have never really featured among its top attractions. Given the history of inadequate governing bodies, it is little surprise that many of the country's wildlife areas are not particularly well developed, the game reserves even less so than the national parks, which have a slightly better infrastructure. A near disastrous combination of limited resources and a lack of commitment on the part of officials meant that much of the potential of these parks failed to come to fruition. Many conservation areas suffered enormously under a government that remained ineffectual, paying little attention to structures put in place to help preserve Malawi's natural heritage. Government funds that had apparently been set aside for the development of parks were channelled into other, more glamorous avenues — along with the revenue earned by these parks. Until recently, poaching was also an ongoing concern — and, to at least some degree, it still is. Many wild species were hunted, poached or raided from traditional lands. However, Malawi is slowly seeing a resurgence of foreign interest, and a number of areas are benefiting from a steady trickle of international funding. Germany has allocated funds for the development of Nyika, while Kasungu is receiving financial aid from the European Union and Liwonde from South Africa. Funds from these donor countries have helped reintroduce species to traditional roaming grounds, as well as establishing of anti-poaching campaigns, upgrading road access to the parks, and facilitating educational programmes. Park management has thus improved dramatically over the last decade or so, and this development has helped to improve domestic conditions of Malawians living in and around the parks and reserves.

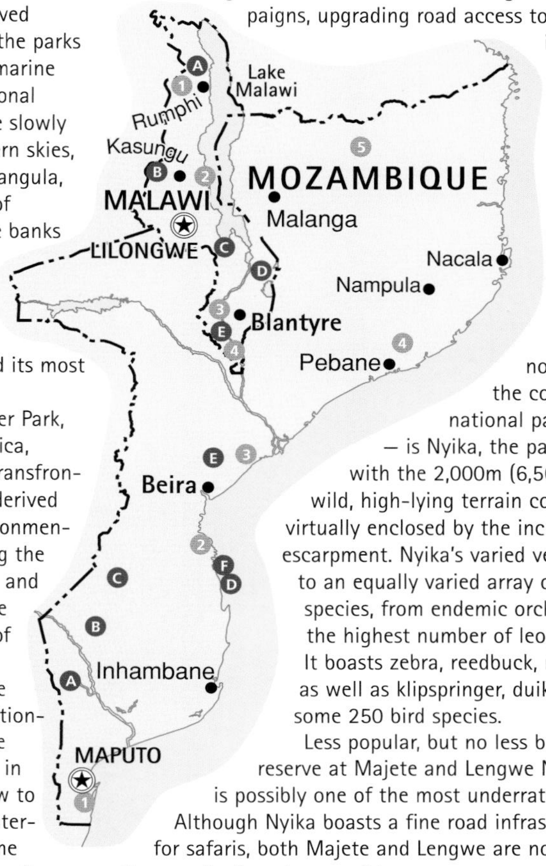

Almost hidden in the northwestern reaches of the country, Malawi's greatest national park — in extent, at least — is Nyika, the park that shares its name with the 2,000m (6,560ft) Nyika Plateau. The wild, high-lying terrain comprises hill and valley virtually enclosed by the inclines of the surrounding escarpment. Nyika's varied vegetation has given rise to an equally varied array of animal and plant species, from endemic orchids and chameleons to the highest number of leopards in southeast Africa. It boasts zebra, reedbuck, roan antelope and eland, as well as klipspringer, duiker, jackal and hyena, and some 250 bird species.

Less popular, but no less beautiful, are the game reserve at Majete and Lengwe National Park. The latter is possibly one of the most underrated parks in the country. Although Nyika boasts a fine road infrastructure that caters well for safaris, both Majete and Lengwe are not as well developed, but they are far from inaccessible.

Liwonde National Park, the smallest, most accessible and most rewarding of Malawi's parks, is also the best managed. Drastic improvements in the training of rangers and other staff have meant that the park is better patrolled than it has ever been. Liwonde was once plagued by poaching and suffered from rapidly declining wildlife populations. Thankfully, the ranging staff encounters fewer and fewer traps, and the threat of poaching has thus been curtailed — although, it must be said, some subsistence poaching continues to take place. There has been a discernible increase in mammal numbers, with elephant herds having more than quadrupled in less than 30 years. Today the 548km^2 (212-sq.-mile) stretch of land is home to more than 600 elephant, some 500 sable antelope and nearly 3,000 hippo. It also boasts healthy herds of bushbuck, impala and waterbuck, along with troops of vervet monkeys and yellow baboons. Although there are indeed leopards and there have been good sightings of the elusive spotted hyena, the numbers of predators do seem to be declining, and the lions that were once common prowlers on these plains have now been eradicated. However, following the success of reintroduction programmes focusing on zebra, eland, reedbuck, buffalo and even black rhino, attempts will be made to reintroduce lions once officials are satisfied that they can be contained within park borders.

Lake Malawi – which borders Malawi, Mozambique and Tanzania – is one of the subcontinent's most valuable assets, yet it remains one of its most threatened, and its precious resources are at constant risk from human intervention.

But conservation remains a precarious occupation, even when it is tackled with the best of intentions. Sadly, Lake Malawi seems to be one such failure. The great lake, with about 350 endemic cichlid species and some 650 others, is home to a precious freshwater fish population faced with almost certain extinction if the situation on its shores is allowed to persist. The destruction of the ecosystem is unparalleled, and the dire need for both education and environmental control is raising alarming concerns for the future of Lake Malawi.

ADV 310
NP 273

THE REGION

The history of conservation on the Indian Ocean Islands is a chequered one. While Madagascar, the world's fourth-largest island and a veritable wonderland of floral and faunal wealth, has set aside more than a million hectares as reserve land, the Comoros have registered no protected areas recognized by the United Nations, with the other island nations vacillating in between.

MADAGASCAR	Key
Andasibe-Mantadia National Park	D
Isalo National Park	A
Mananara Marine National Park	C
Mananara Terrestrial National Park	C
Montagne d'Ambre National Park	B
Ranomafana National Park	F
Andohahela Nature Reserve	22
Andringitra Nature Reserve	20
Ankarafantsika Nature Reserve	9
Marojejy Nature Reserve	15
Tsaratanana Nature Reserve	14
Tsimanampetsotsa Nature Reserve	1
Tsingy de Bemaraha Nature Reserve	4
Tsingy de Namoroka Nature Reserve	7
Zahamena Nature Reserve	17
Ambatovaky Special Reserve	E
Ambohijanahary Special Reserve	5
Analamazaotra (Périnet) Special Reserve	23
Analamerana Special Reserve	13
Anjanaharibe-Sud Special Reserve	15
Ankarana Special Reserve	12
Bemarivo Special Reserve	6
Kalambatritra Special Reserve	21
Katsijy Special Reserve	8
Mangerivola Special Reserve	18
Manongarivo Special Reserve	11
Marotandrano Special Reserve	D
Nosy Mangabe Special Reserve	24
Tampoketsa d'Analamaitso Special Reserve	10
Lake Kinkony Hunting Reserve	7
Périnet Rainforest	25
Ranomafana Rainforest Reserve	E
Midrongy-Sud Classified Forest	19
Zombitse Classified Forest	2
Kirindy-Kirindy Forest Reserve	3
Boucle du Baoule Reserve	16
Bemaraha Integral World Heritage Site	4

COMOROS

No UN-recognized protected area

MAURITIUS	
Black River Gorges National Park	A
Macchabée-Bel Ombre Nature Reserve	A

RÉUNION (FRANCE)	
Hauts de St Phillipe State Biological Reserve	A
Mazerin State Biological Reserve	A
Mare Longue-St-Philippe Nature Reserve	1

SEYCHELLES	
Morne Seychellois National Park	A
Praslin National Park	C
Baie Ternaie Marine National Park	A
Curieuse Marine National Park	C
Port Launay Marine National Park	A
St Anne Marine National Park	B
Vallée de Mai National Park	C
Aldabra Nature Reserve	1
Aldabra Atoll World Heritage Site	1
Vallée de Mai World Heritage Site	C

CLOCKWISE FROM TOP LEFT
Scuba diver, Seychelles.
Ankarana Special Reserve, Madagascar.
La Digue Island, Seychelles.
Leef-tailed ghecko, Madagascar.

Madagascar

The island's remote location has been a blessing in that it has resulted in a hothouse of evolution, where animal and plant species have evolved in splendid isolation, with many being indigenous to Madagascar alone. Of the less than 100 countries that boast populations of wild primates, for example, just four — Brazil, Indonesia, the DRC and Madagascar — harbour more than two-thirds of the world's primates. These nations also have the most endemics, with 100 per cent of Madagascar's 55 lemur species specific only to Madagascar. As a result, the island nation is one of just 17 countries that qualify for megadiversity status and, although slow in execution and not always successful, local and international conservation authorities are working together to save Madagascar's unique natural heritage. Government development programmes struggle to counter the general lack of resources and a less-than-adequate infrastructure, and environmental efforts are thus difficult to implement with efficiency. Over the centuries, all the megafauna have been exterminated, including lemurs the size of lions and the mammoth 3m-tall (10ft), 450kg (1,000lb) elephant bird, which had survived here after the break-up of Gondwana. In the period between the middle and late 1900s, for example, half of Madagascar's woods and forests were decimated to accommodate a population that had doubled in numbers and yet, despite the virtual collapse of the national economy, the Malagasy government remains committed to conservation. As a result, a number of established and highly regarded conservation organizations, — including the World Wide Fund for Nature (WWF) and the Jersey Wildlife Preservation Trust founded by the late Gerald Durrell — have offered their assistance by instituting integrated development programmes to preserve the wildlife remaining in the country's national parks and other wild areas.

One such project is the Maj National Reserve, established in 1998 and administered by the WWF. The aim here is not only to protect the biological diversity of the broader region, but also to accommodate the needs of locals who depend on the forest environment for their livelihood. Just 30 years ago, the ratio of forest to human inhabitant was 10ha (25 acres) per person, but this has now dwindled to more than 10 individuals for every hectare. Some 20 months before the park was gazetted, more than 70 villages were consulted on their requirements.

One of Madagascar's most remarkable success stories has been the majestic Isalo, the 81,540ha (200,000-acre) national park that was proclaimed as early as 1962. Today, the protected confines of Isalo, covering vast expanses of grassland punctuated with striking rock formations between the towns of Sakaraha and Ranohira, boasts an impressive record of sound ecological practices and, as the location of ancient sites held sacred by the Bara, it is a proud custodian of the country's anthropological heritage.

En route to Isalo, about 150km (93 miles) to the northeast of Tuléar, is the 21,500ha (53,000-acre) Zombitse forest, still enjoying considerable importance on WWF's priority list for Madagascar and one of the country's most favoured birding spots. Endemic to this stretch of forest land, for example, is the rare Appert's greenbul, along with a succession of other bird species — from the Madagascar partridge and sandgrouse to the *Thamnornis* warbler — plus a number of raptor species, including the goshawk, sparrowhawk and Madagascar gymnogene. This is the only place where the brown lemur, ring-tailed lemur and Verreaux's sifaka occur together naturally, and it is the exclusive retreat of the seriously endangered golden-crowned sifaka.

Although visitors' facilities in the national parks and reserves are generally basic, with rather poorly signposted routes and trails, they do offer the opportunity of experiencing first-hand the fascinating natural environments, including the rainforests of Nosy Mangabe and Périnet, the latter a winding two-hour drive from Tana, where you can see the indris and, especially on the night walks, the tenrec.

The pristine condition of these magical environments remains vital to the survival of Madagascar's unique species: spiny forests of endemic cactus-like plants dominate the southern deserts, while specially adapted plant species such as tree euphorbias, baobabs and pachypodia merge together to create impenetrable stands of vegetation which are home to sifaka lemurs and other endemic species.

Although the wild expanse of much of the island is the focus of Madagascar's conservation efforts, even bustling urban and semi-urban centres have tackled the prospect of sustainable tourism and are offering a viable alternative to Madagascar's untamed wilderness. The pretty Tsimbazaza Botanical and Zoological Park in Tana is one of the few places visitors can view most of the lemur species at close range — they tend to be elusive in the wild — and even the virgin forest of Lokobe near Nosy Bé, Madagascar's premier holiday destination, is being carefully watched given its proximity to the tourist mecca.

Comoros

Although remarkably picturesque in appearance, and hailed as the saving grace of the long-lost coelacanth, which was caught off its coast in the 1930s, the Comoros have a rather poor record of conservation and boasts no protected areas recognized by the United Nations.

Mauritius

Perhaps best known as the former home of the now extinct dodo, Mauritius has only one indigenous mammal species: the enigmatic Mauritius fruit, or golden, bat (the monkeys, deer and hare are here as a result of settlement by European colonists). As a result, conservation efforts on the island concentrate on its floral heritage. Although Mauritius has only two UN-recognized parks — Black River Gorges National Park and Macchabée-Bel Ombre — its protected land covers an impressive 9,000ha (22,000 acres), including (along with Rodrigues) at least 20 conservation areas smaller than 100ha (250 acres).

A number of urban oases, such as the botanical gardens of Curepipe, Balfour, and Le Réduit, as well as the Port Louis Company Gardens and Robert Edward Hart Gardens, make at least some attempt at preserving the local — and exotic — vegetation. Prime among these is the Sir Seewoosagur Ramgoolam Botanical Gardens, and one of the most significant efforts to protect the island's botanical heritage finds fruition in the 1,500ha (3,700-acre) Le Domaine du Chasseur, near Mahébourg.

Given the emphasis on the island's botany, the government nevertheless continues to sponsor a science-based avian conservation project at Rivière Noire. Known simply as the Government Aviary, it breeds rare bird species, including the only significant indigenous bird species found here today: the Mauritius kestrel, pink pigeon and echo parakeet. These programmes were slow to take off but, with the support of the Mauritius Wildlife Appeal Fund, have recorded considerable success in recent years. In 1980, the Mauritius Marine Conservation Society was formed to promote awareness and appreciation of the island's sealife and, apart from ongoing attempts to establish underwater parks, it continues to push for the enforcement of laws — already in existence — that control quotas, fishing methods, sea pollution and reef destruction.

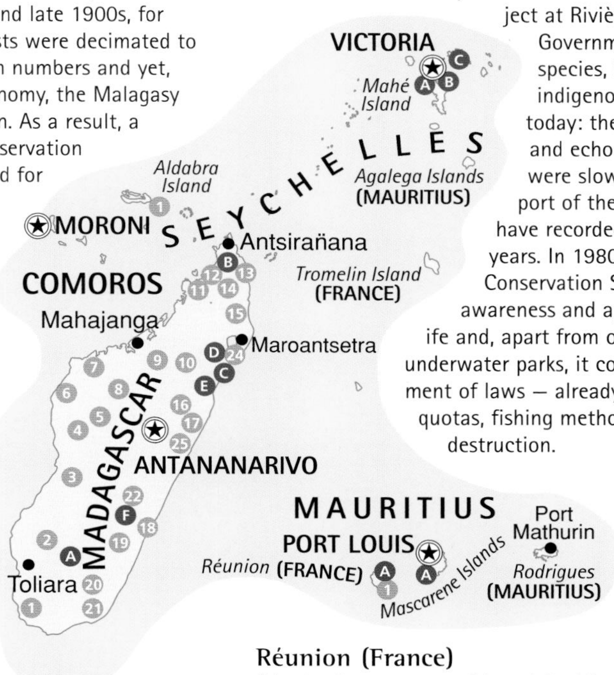

Listed as one of the world's 'hot spots' of biodiversity are Madagascar and the Indian Ocean Islands, which together have retained less than 10 per cent of their natural habitat in its original state.

Réunion (France)

Réunion boasts more of its original forest and wilderness areas than either of the others islands of the Mascarenes, and reserves and national parks (such as Hauts de St Phillipe and Mazerin), cover a total of 5,000ha (12,300 acres) of its land- and seascape. Indigenous flora and fauna, including a prolific bird life, are the focus of conservation efforts - most of the animal life was introduced during colonization - aimed at sustaining the island's tourist potential, but agriculture is the backbone of the economy and, as such, enjoys prominence over conservation. Amid the hills of St-Leu is the 7ha (17-acre) Mascarin National Botanical Conservatory, a lush and well-maintained sanctuary for Réunion's endangered plants and various exotic spices, while the Mare Longue Botanical Reserve — roughly the same size as the Conservatoire — is a tropical forest of giant trees.

Seychelles

Nearly half of Seychelles' land area has been set aside as national park or protected reserve, with some 40 per cent of its seascape declared marine conservation area. Morne Seychellois National Park, the nation's most impressive, is laced with hiking trails, while Praslin — home to Vallée de Mai, the 18ha (45-acre) World Heritage Site — boasts no fewer than six endemic palms, along with numerous other indigenous trees and plants. Even the smaller isles have their treasures, and a number of significant measures have been put into place to help regulate tourist traffic and preserve the balance of unique ecosystems.

Despite all these laudable efforts, the Seychelles have seen their fair share of ecological disasters. Tortoise populations have dwindled to alarmingly low numbers, as have fish and bird species, with several species now either endangered or extinct — often because of the competition they face from introduced species. All four of the indigenous turtle species — green, hawksbill, loggerhead and giant leatherback — also remain at risk. At the same time, concerted efforts to protect the Aldabra giant tortoise (both Arnold's and Marion's tortoises have long been extinct) have meant that further populations have been reintroduced on islands such as Cousin, Frégate and Curieuse. In its favour, the Aldabra Atoll has been declared a World Heritage Site and is thus administered by the Seychelles Islands Foundation, in turn sponsored by the Royal Society at the Smithsonian Institute. Tourism to the 34km-long (21-mile) atoll is extremely limited, and the relatively insignificant human population of islands such as these may account for the fact that the island-specific ecologies have been little influenced by human intervention. Where there is constant human activity on these paradise islands, a number of regulations have been established to help preserve the natural heritage of the region: on no fewer than nine of the islands the sea birds may not be disturbed, while spear fishing is forbidden throughout the island group, with fishing and the collection of seashells and corals prohibited in the marine parks. At the same time, meticulously planned reforestation schemes have been established on islands already disturbed by indiscriminate plantations.

ADV 312
NP 276

THE REGION

Although Namibia is about 250,000 square kilometres (96,000 square miles) larger than neighbouring Botswana, both countries have roughly the same amount of protected land, either in the form of national parks or nature and game reserves. Considering the extent of the harsh environment that comprises the two nations, these statistics are quite impressive.

NAMIBIA	Key
Etosha National Park	D
Fish River Canyon National Park	C
Mamili National Park	F
Mudumu National Park	E
Cape Cross Seal Nature Reserve	2
Hardap Game Reserve	3
Ai-Ais Hot Springs Game Park	C
Caprivi Game Park	7
Daan Viljoen Game Park	8
Khaudom Game Park	5
Mahango Game Park	6
Waterberg Plateau Game Park	4
Namib-Naukluft Park	B
Skeleton Coast Park	A
Damaraland Wilderness Reserve	1

BOTSWANA	
Chobe National Park	A
Nxai Pan National Park	B
Central Kalahari Game Reserve	5
Kgalagadi Transfrontier Park	8
Khutse Game Reserve	6
Mabuasehube Game Reserve	7
Makgadikgadi Pans Game Reserve	1
Moremi Game Reserve	2
Okavango Delta	4

CLOCKWISE FROM TOP LEFT

Dunes, Namib Desert, Namibia.
Gemsbok with giraffe drinking in the background, Etosha National Park, Namibia.
Okavango Delta, Botswana.
Elephant, Moremi Game Reserve, Botswana.

Namibia

In a land where water is scarce and vegetation sparse, it is impressive that some 15 per cent of Namibia's land cover has been set aside for conservation. Less than 50 years ago, conditions in Namibia were dire, but in the 1960s, authorities suggested turning over the ownership of the country's game to the landowners on whose lands the game roamed. This helped to initiate one of the most successful conservation drives in the subcontinent, providing an incentive for individuals to preserve the animals and plants on their land. Apart from laying the foundations for some of southern Africa's most lucrative game-farming operations, these tentative steps toward wildlife management sowed the seeds of sterling conservation efforts, many of which were established by the region's leading conservationists, such as the Southern African Nature Foundation, the Endangered Wildlife Trust, Save the Rhino and other organizations intent on preserving Namibia's wildlife.

Following the country's independence in 1990, conservation authorities in Namibia, in collaboration with the Ministry of Environment and Tourism, began to adopt a series of resource management programmes incorporating a number of community-based initiatives that included the enthusiastic cooperation of the private agricultural industry.

The relative calm and general sense of peace heralded by the emergence of self-determination has meant that the Namibian tourism industry has seen a considerable upturn and this has, in turn, been a further incentive to protect the natural heritage on which the hospitality industry relies so heavily. National treasures such as the dry and dusty plains of the Namib-Naukluft, the stark and unforgiving Etosha and the rugged landscape of game reserves – for example, those of Hardap and Khaudom – are today well established as important wildlife sanctuaries. These not only preserve the animals and plants that live there, but also contribute significantly to the national coffers.

Namibia's wildlife depends entirely on the generosity of the forces of nature. During the summer rains, water is relatively plentiful, but the dry winter brings with it a pitiful scarcity of water and it is then that the few remaining water holes and muddy pans offer the only relief in the parched landscape.

As the country's most prominent reserve, Etosha National Park in the northwest of Namibia comprises a vast depression of some 5,000 km² (2,000 sq. miles) that was once an enormous lake providing a vital source of nourishment for the wildlife of the area. Today, although the great pan is often no more than a semiarid depression in the sand, it remains virtually the only source of life for the animals that converge on its seasonal waters, migrating from one small water source to the next as scarce supplies evaporate during the dry spells. Desolate in both appearance and mood, the pans of Etosha fill only briefly with water during the rains – pools, shallows and even rivers revert to being little more than dust bowls in the dry season. Nevertheless, herds of springbok and other mammals find refuge here. Etosha is acclaimed not only for its small but thriving population of the tiny Damara dik-dik, but also the rare black-faced impala and even black rhino.

Despite the aridity of the region, the wild coast, the shifting dunes of the desert and even the arid expanse of the Kalahari are the home territory of an extraordinary array of wildlife. These range from mammals great and small to birds and insects, as well as an abundance of reptile species, all of which contribute to the unique ecology of the region. Some of the animals occur only in the wilderness of swamp, woodland and rivers in the northern regions, spreading across political boundaries. Certain inland areas are noted for their unique plants and diverse bird life, often gathering in huge flocks on the water's edges. Nonetheless, the relatively barren gravel and sand plains of the broader region boast a number of species that have adapted well to the demanding climate of the flat and apparently featureless landscape. Although no longer found in such great numbers, springbok remain the most abundant of southern Africa's antelope species. Herds still graze on the spring grasses that sprout on these plains and, most notably, on the river banks during the rain season, when the all-important water holes fill with life-giving water. The survival of the fittest is the instinct most prominent here in the harsh wilderness of Namibia.

From the vast countryside studded with mopane and thornbush to the gravel and quartz plains of the expansive Namib-Naukluft, and extending right up to the coastal dunes, the Namibian wilderness offers a varied panorama. Some far-flung areas have a very different mood and Damaraland, for example, is a region not blessed with an abundance of flora and fauna. Many of the creatures that have established themselves here rely on the delicate balance of the environment for survival, and are ever under the threat of poachers and hunters. In fact, few of the species that thrive in the country's wildlife sanctuaries are immune to the ravages of human intervention. Conservationists are forced to keep a wary eye on the existing populations of wildlife, among them the Hartmann's mountain zebra (a subspecies of the Cape mountain zebra), one of the most prolific game species in the Hardap Game Reserve and found only in this arid part of the subcontinent.

On the perimeter of the great Namib Desert stands the splendid Naukluft mountain range. The Naukluft mountains make up the escarpment that separates the wave-lashed shore from the dry interior which, in turn, forms the desert. Although the oppressive heat of both the Namib and the Kalahari are the most often cited reasons for discomfort, the icy cold nights are just as trying for both the animal life and visitors intent on exploring these lands, and further add to the many contrasts of Namibia's great landscape.

Botswana

With approximately 18 per cent of the country given over to conservation efforts, Botswana's conservation record is indeed one of the most impressive achievements in wildlife management on the continent. This has resulted in a resurgence in Botswana's tourism industry, and the country's reserves are now lauded as some of Africa's most significant.

The tourism industry is currently one of Botswana's most lucrative, accounting for some 42 per cent of its formal employment sector and bringing in no less than US$50 million a year. A vital element of this burgeoning business is ecotourism, an increasingly popular trend throughout Africa. Ecotourism has rapidly usurped Botswana's hunting industry as one of the country's top foreign-exchange earners. Hunting is now limited to relatively few reputable operations, practising – rather successfully – in allocated concession areas reserved specifically for this purpose. This has begged the eternal question of conservation versus sustainable resources and their revenue contribution to the national economy, a question much of Africa grapples with to this day. Botswana seems to have come to a widely accepted compromise regarding its land-usage policies, and is now one of Africa's leading ecotourism destinations. The sandy tracks first cut through this countryside by early explorers have given way, in parts, to a more developed infrastructure, but gravel and dust roads are still the paths most travelled in Botswana's wild areas. This adds to the rustic mood of untrammelled wilderness so sought after by travellers to Africa.

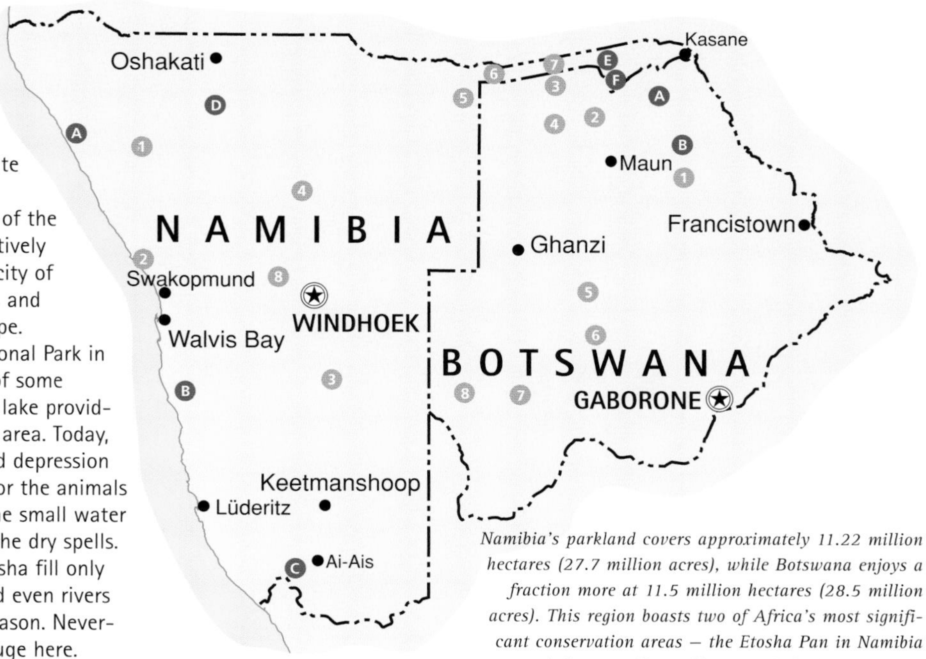

Namibia's parkland covers approximately 11.22 million hectares (27.7 million acres), while Botswana enjoys a fraction more at 11.5 million hectares (28.5 million acres). This region boasts two of Africa's most significant conservation areas – the Etosha Pan in Namibia and the magnificent Okavango Delta in Botswana.

Because so much of Botswana's land cover comprises arid and sparsely vegetated terrain, the ecological balance is a sensitive one, easily destabilized, yet it is these parched lands, unusually rich in game and bird species, that prove the great attraction. Game-viewing is at its finest in the dry winter from May to August, when wildlife congregates at the remaining water sources. The wet summers provide the animals with an abundance of water, making them far more reclusive from tourists, but this also introduces a greater risk of malaria. Nevertheless, this does little to detract from great wilderness areas such as the Okavango. The waters of the delta extend some 15,000 km² (5,800 sq. miles) when in flood, comprising a network of nutrient-rich channels and lagoons. These might not be home to large herds of wild game, but they certainly contain thriving populations of crocodiles, buffalo, hippo and antelope, such as lechwe and sitatunga, that have adapted well to this watery landscape. While herds of elephant plod through the unspoiled lands of northeastern Okavango, more than 500 bird species flit across the skies of the delta.

Whereas the Okavango region is predominantly wetland, the Moremi Game Reserve is a vast 2,000 km² (770-sq.-mile) expanse that includes flood plain and lagoon, dry bushveld and mopane woodland. The Moremi is roamed by typical big-game species, such as lion, leopard and cheetah, elephant, buffalo and wild dog, kudu, tsessebe and Botswana's ubiquitous lechwe. Like Moremi, Chobe National Park comprises a varied habitat, alternating between swamp and grassland, flood plain and bushveld. The northern border of its 10,000 km² (3,800-sq.-mile) wilderness is demarcated by the Linyanti-Chobe river system. The Chobe is Botswana's only perennial river and, although more than 30km (19 miles) of its banks have been given over to responsible tourism, it remains the life force for much wildlife. Most notable are the more than 35,000 elephants, but there are also over 450 bird species.

One of the most remarkable attempts to accommodate local communities has found fruition in the arid Kgalagadi Transfrontier Park between South Africa and Botswana. In an effort to preserve the natural habitat and its characteristic game species, government and conservation officials established this cross-border park, which is home to an amazing range of plant, mammal and even bird life. Covering an area of more than 2 million hectares (5 million acres), Kgalagadi effectively united South Africa's Kalahari Gemsbok National Park and Botswana's Gemsbok National Park. The Kgalagadi conservation area was Africa's first formally gazetted transboundary reserve, setting the precedent for many such parks on the continent.

NA 314
NP 278

THE REGION

Covering a total landmass of more than a million square kilometres (386,000 square miles), nearly 13 million hectares of South Africa, Lesotho and Swaziland comprise protected areas officially recognized by the United Nations, making the region one of the most conservation-conscious areas on the continent.

SOUTH AFRICA	Key
Addo Elephant National Park	L
Agulhas National Park	F
Augrabies Falls National Park	B
Bontebok National Park	G
Cape Peninsula National Park	E
Golden Gate Highlands National Park	P
Kgalagadi Transfrontier Park	O
Karoo National Park	H
Knysna National Lake Area	J
Kruger National Park	Q
Marakele National Park	R
Mountain Zebra National Park	M
Namaqua National Park	C
Pilanesberg National Park	U
Royal Natal National Park	S
Richtersveld National Park	A
Tankwa Karoo National Park	T
Tsitsikamma National Park	K
Vaalbos National Park	N
Vhembe-Dongola National Park	V
West Coast National Park	D
Wilderness National Park	I
Bonamanzi Game Ranch	33
Natal Drakensberg Park	30
Greater St Lucia Wetland Park	34
Botsalano Game Reserve	27
Borakalalo Game Reserve	54
Hluhluwe-Umfolozi Game Reserve	32
Itala Game Reserve	31
Makuya Game Reserve	48
Madikwe Game Reserve	55
Manyeleti Game Reserve	45
Mahushe Shongwe Game Reserve	40
Mkuzi Game Reserve	35
Mpofu Game Reserve	16
Ndumo Game Reserve	38
Qwaqwa Game Reserve	29
Songimvelo Game Reserve	41
Tembe Elephant Game Reserve	38
Tsolwana Game Reserve	13
Willem Pretorius Game Reserve	28
Bartolomeus Klip Private Reserve	5
Kapama Private Reserve	43
Klaserie Private Reserve	47
Lapalala Private Reserve	51
Mabula Private Reserve	53
Makalali Private Reserve	46
Phinda Resource Private Reserve	37
Sabi Sands Private Reserve	44
Timbavati Private Reserve	43
Thornybush Private Reserve	43
Touchstone Private Reserve	50
Tswalu Private Reserve	24
Welgevonden Private Reserve	52
Attakwaskloof Nature Reserve	9
Barberton Nature Reserve	26
Blouberg Nature Reserve	49
Blyde River Canyon Nature Reserve	42
Caledon Nature Reserve	21
Cwebe-Dwesa Nature Reserve	17
Doornkloof Nature Reserve	23
Double Drift Nature Reserve	14
De Hoop Nature Reserve	8
De Mond Nature Reserve	7
Gariep Dam Nature Reserve	22
Goegap Nature Reserve	1
Great Fish River Nature Reserve	15
Hluleka Nature Reserve	18
Hottentots Holland Nature Reserve	6
Kammanassie Nature Reserve	11
Karoo Nature Reserve	2
Kosi Bay Coastal Forest Nature Reserve	39
Malekgonyane Nature Reserve	20
Molopo Nature Reserve	25
Mkambati Nature Reserve	19
Pongola Nature Reserve	36
Witfontein Nature Reserve	10
Cedarberg Wilderness Area	3
Groot Winterhoek Wilderness Area	4
Groendal Wilderness Area	12

SWAZILAND	
Hlane Royal National Park	A
Mlilwane Wildlife Sanctuary	4
Malolotja Nature Reserve	1
Mkhaya Nature Reserve	2
Mlawula/Ndzindza Nature Reserve	3

LESOTHO	
Sehlabathebe National Park	A

CLOCKWISE FROM TOP LEFT
Meerkats, South Africa.
Protea and Sugarbird,
Table Mountain, South Africa.
Springbok and zebra at a water hole,
Kgalagadi Transfrontier Park.
Male lion, Kruger National Park,
South Africa.

South Africa

With no fewer than 17 national parks, and more than 1,000 private reserves and 500 privately owned game farms, some 12.5 million hectares (30 million acres) of South Africa is officially designated to the conservation of the region's extraordinary biodiversity. This extensive range of species diversity has been likened by many to the wild places of Indonesia and the rainforests of the Amazon Basin, and the vast extent of the subcontinent remains one of Africa's most significant wild areas, ensuring that the landscape here is home to one of the world's greatest panoramas of wildlife.

As a result, the northern stretches of the country are a natural paradise that includes within its boundaries the finest national parks and games reserves the continent has to offer.

With more than three million hectares (over seven million acres)of its total land area devoted almost exclusively to the preservation of indigenous flora and fauna, South Africa boasts a wide diversity of gazetted parkland. This ranges from the Eastern Cape's Addo Elephant National Park to the Free State's Golden Gate Highlands National Park, Mpumalanga's Blyde River Canyon to the Cape's Tsitsikamma and Cape Peninsula national parks, KwaZulu-Natal's Hluhluwe-Umfolozi Game Reserve and the private reserve of Sabi Sand in the Northern Province. These reserves hold some of the world's most impressive conservation records, and certainly some of the most comprehensive wildlife management systems on the continent. The intrinsically wild character of the land has also given rise to one of Africa's most impressive national parks, acclaimed worldwide for the sound principles adopted by its custodians in the management of its wildlife resources. Like many of the region's abundant private reserves and game farms, the Kruger National Park – comprising some 20,000km² (8,000 sq. miles) of the northern bushveld between the Crocodile and Limpopo rivers – boasts plenty of big game species, top among them lion, leopard, rhino, elephant and buffalo, which comprise the Big Five. It is also home to some 500 bird and 100 reptile species, 33 amphibians, 49 freshwater fish and, at about 147 species, nearly half of the national complement of mammals. In fact, South Africa's big cats, primates, rodents, carnivores, ungulates and other mammal species have proven to be the subcontinent's most enduring drawcards, attracting the attention of tourists and sightseers, conservationists and photographers to the country's bushveld, grasslands and savannas.

Despite the existence of great urban settlements that form the heart of Gauteng province, the landscape of South Africa's northern reaches is wild and relatively empty of people, absorbing much of its character from its undisputed rustic beauty. Dry and dusty plains give way to tracts of grassland interspersed with acacia and camelthorn, the eastern boundary delineated by the impressive expanse that is the Kruger National Park and the private reserves that skirt its boundaries. From here, the expansive Lowveld stretches south into the South African interior, a wild sweep of bushveld that spreads into the varying vegetation that makes up the South African landscape.

The remarkable diversity that is the face of South Africa presents a series of contrasting images, from the rugged mountainscape of the Western Cape, into the semidesert reaches of the Kalahari and the Northern Cape, and along the flower-bedecked shores of the east coast, spreading along the Eastern Cape and beyond the foothills of the Drakensberg in KwaZulu-Natal.

The nine provinces of South Africa cover no fewer than seven separate vegetation biomes, which include more than 15 protected wetland areas – prime among them the Kosi Bay and St Lucia systems in KwaZulu-Natal and the Wilderness Lakes on the Cape's Garden Route – and the biosphere reserves at Pongolapoort and the Waterberg. Dotted among these havens of relatively untainted wilderness is a succession of small but exclusive World Heritage Sites at the Cradle of Mankind, the Drakensberg mountain range, the St Lucia Wetlands, and Robben Island, some 11.5km (7 miles) off the coast of the Cape Peninsula. A handful of other sites, equally significant as conservation areas, are also under consideration for similar status.

The wealth of game parks and nature reserves in the southern subcontinent, justifiably renowned for some of the most spectacular scenery in Africa, is thus a haven for every type of conservationist and naturalist. The sensitive ecology of the area depends on a perfect balance within its fragile ecosystems, and thus was born a number of tireless conservation efforts that have required meticulous planning in order to marry the preservation of the wilderness with the needs of the all-important tourism market, which contributes quite considerably to the coffers of the broader region.

The highly successful Kgalagadi Transfrontier Park, between South Africa and Botswana, has lead to further efforts getting under way in the subcontinent. The Gaza-Kruger-Gonarezhou Transfrontier Park crosses South Africa's political boundaries with Mozambique and Zimbabwe, while the Maloti-Drakensberg Transfrontier Park links South Africa and Lesotho.

Swaziland

Considering its size, the 17,360km² (6,703 sq. miles) of Swaziland boasts no fewer than five conservation areas, which make a significant contribution to the national economy. However, due possibly to the general impoverishment of local communities, at least three of these reserves — Hlane, Malolotja and Mlilwane — have suffered at the hands of poachers and renegade hunters through the years.

The 14,000ha (35,000-acre) Hlane Game Reserve was established in the 1940s when the Swazi king secured a large tract of land on behalf of his people. However, this game-rich country attracted poachers and hunters, and once plentiful herds of zebra, impala, wildebeest, kudu and bushbuck were reduced to a couple of hundred of each. As a result, the king was compelled to declare the reserve a game sanctuary in 1967. With legal protection, however, numbers began to grow out of control, the land unable to sustain the populations, and small herds were relocated to Swaziland's other reserves.

The 4,500ha (11,000-acre) Mlilwane Wildlife Sanctuary is the nation's most significant, noted for its more than 200 bird species. But the largest and most impressive of Swaziland's reserves is the 18,000ha (44,000-acre) Malolotja Nature Reserve, founded in 1972 by the National Trust Commission in an attempt to consolidate the country's conservation effort. As a result, many species – most notably the white rhino – once prevalent in these regions were successfully reintroduced.

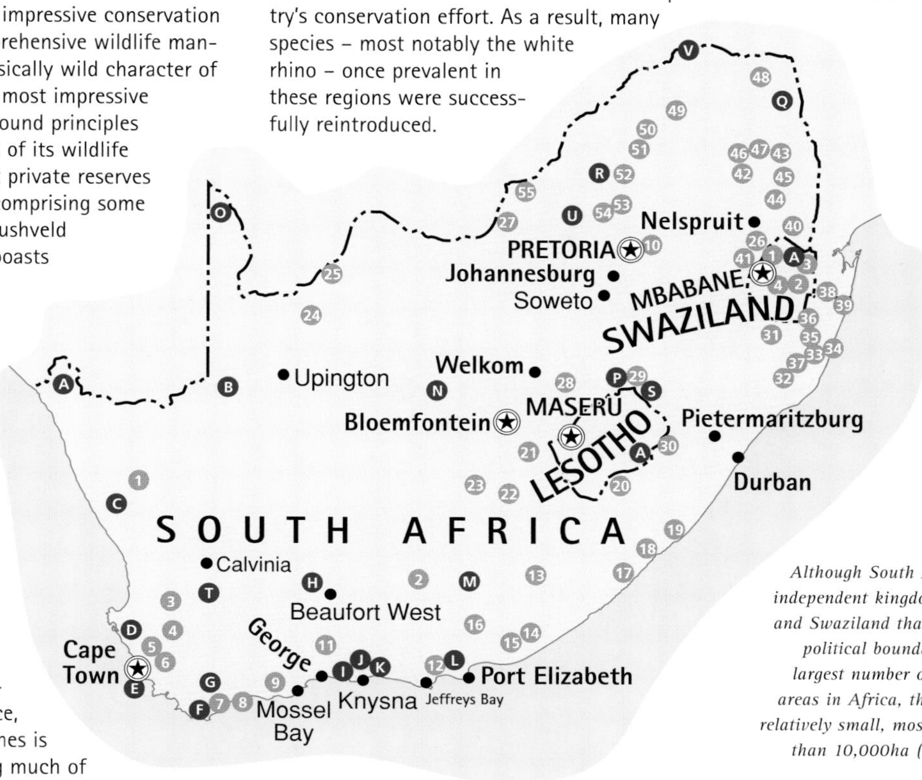

Although South Africa and the independent kingdoms of Lesotho and Swaziland that lie within its political boundaries boast the largest number of conservation areas in Africa, the majority are relatively small, most covering less than 10,000ha (24,700 acres).

Lesotho

More than 80 per cent of this small kingdom's 30,350km² (11,718 sq. miles) is made up of rugged mountain, boasting the highest point on the southern subcontinent — the peak of Thabana Ntlenyana is some 3,480m (11,400ft) above sea level. Scientific data and the rock paintings of ancient San artists provide evidence that the region was once the home of big game such as leopard, lion and a variety of antelope species. However, the relatively untrammelled landscape of rocky mountain slope and boulder-strewn grassland is today largely devoid of the once abundant wildlife. The country has only one national park, but considering the size and undeveloped infrastructure of the small kingdom, this is no small feat.

Sehlabathebe National Park comprises about 6,500ha (16,000 acres) of mountainous veld punctuated with sandstone outcrops dominated by the peaks of the Three Bushmen. It is home to small herds of wildebeest and reedbuck and is intersected by the winding Tsoelikana River and dotted with caves and the occasional dam stocked with exotic trout. There is also a small population of eland, oribi, jackal, baboon, wildcat and indigenous bird and fish species.

With the proposed establishment of southern Africa's third transfrontier park in the region, conservation appears to enjoy some priority for Lesotho, sometimes called the 'Roof of Africa'. There is enormous potential for the tourism market in a nation that draws much of its resources from income generated by a labour force that migrates between their homeland of Lesotho and South Africa. With an increased emphasis on the significance of local resources and an increasing awareness of the importance of conservation, the concept of the Maloti-Drakensberg Transfrontier Park was initiated in 1982 to preserve the area's biodiversity and help develop local communities through the promotion of the tourism potential. Financed in part by the World Bank, the Global Environment Facility and the Japanese government, a collaborative trans-border development and conservation programme has finally been established, and this cooperative attempt will lead to the foundation of a transfrontier park. This will incorporate South Africa's uKhahlamba-Drakensberg Park – itself declared a World Heritage Site in 2000 – and the Maloti Mountains of Lesotho. Apart from promoting the significant cultural heritage of the region's 600 sites of San rock art (boasting more than 40,000 individual works), the project will also extend the boundaries of the uKhahlamba-Drakensberg World Heritage Site and preserve the more than 2,000 plant, nearly 300 bird, 48 mammal and some 70 reptile and amphibian species that have established themselves in the mountainous kingdom.

National Park Maps

ALPHABETICAL LISTING FOR NATIONAL PARK AND KEY TOURIST MAPS

A herd of buffalo stampede across Ngorongoro Crater, Tanzania.

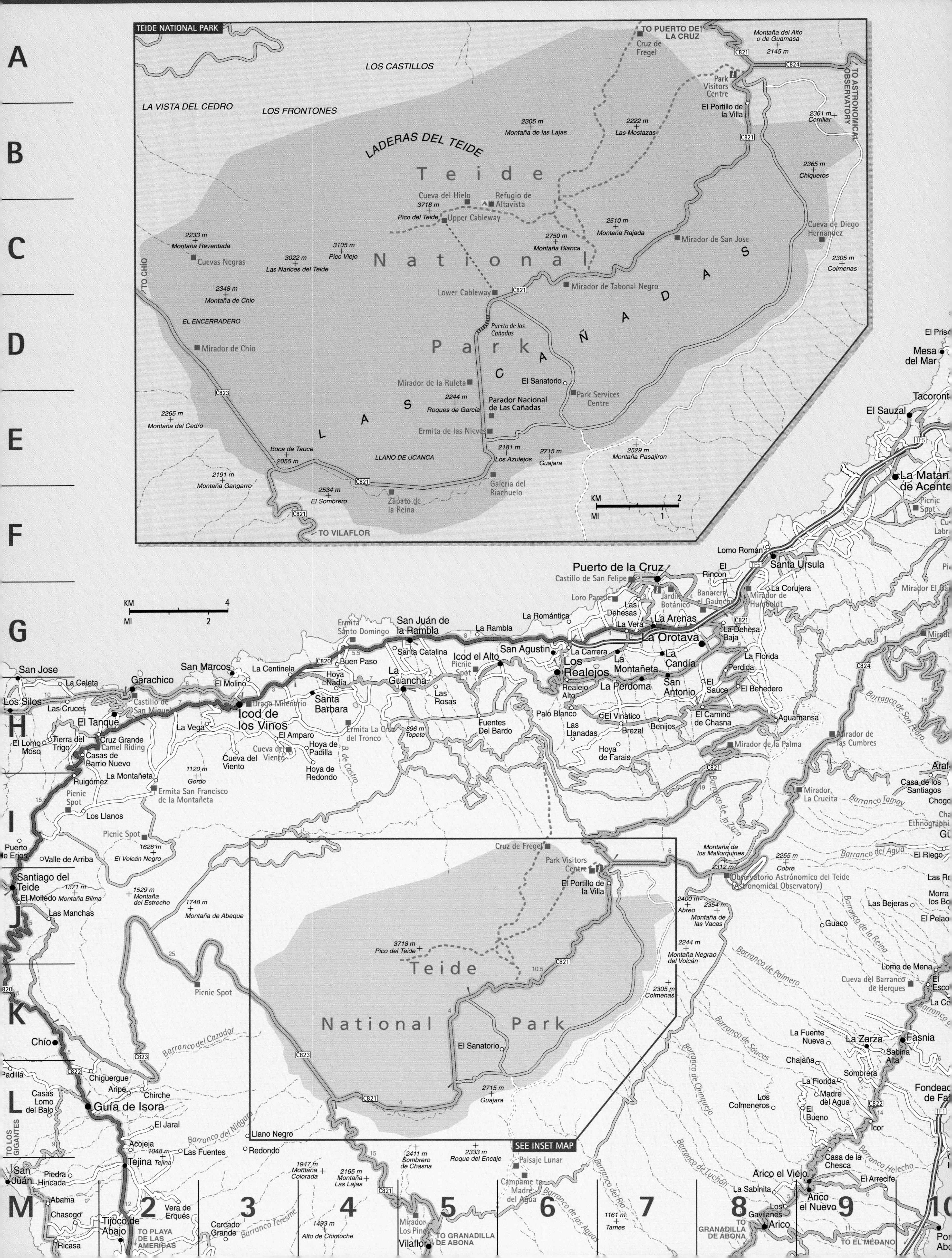
TEIDE NATIONAL PARK
TO PUERTO DE LA CRUZ
Cruz de Fregel
Montaña del Alto o de Guamasa 2145 m
LOS CASTILLOS
LA VISTA DEL CEDRO
LOS FRONTONES
Park Visitors Centre
El Portillo de la Villa
TO ASTRONOMICAL OBSERVATORY
2361 m Cerrillar
2305 m Montaña de las Lajas
2222 m Las Mostazas
LADERAS DEL TEIDE
Teide National Park
2365 m Chiqueros
Cueva del Hielo
Refugio de Altavista
3718 m Pico del Teide
Upper Cableway
2510 m Montaña Rajada
Mirador de San Jose
Cueva de Diego Hernandez
2233 m Montaña Reventada
Cuevas Negras
3022 m Las Narices del Teide
3105 m Pico Viejo
2750 m Montaña Blanca
2305 m Colmenas
TO CHIO
2348 m Montaña de Chio
Lower Cableway
Mirador de Tabonal Negro
EL ENCERRADERO
Puerto de las Cañadas
LAS CAÑADAS
Mirador de Chío
Mirador de la Ruleta
El Sanatorio
Park Services Centre
2244 m Roques de García
Parador Nacional de Las Cañadas
2265 m Montaña del Cedro
Ermita de las Nieves
Boca de Tauce 2055 m
LLANO DE UCANCA
2181 m Los Azulejos
2715 m Guajara
2529 m Montaña Pasajiron
2191 m Montaña Gangarro
2534 m El Sombrero
Zapato de la Reina
Galeria del Riachuelo
KM 2
MI 1
TO VILAFLOR
Puerto de la Cruz
Castillo de San Felipe
Loro Parque
Santa Ursula
La Orotava
Los Realejos
Icod de los Vinos
Garachico
San Juán de la Rambla
Santiago del Teide
Chío
Guía de Isora
Tejina
Arico el Viejo
Arico el Nuevo
Arico
Vilaflor
Fasnia
La Zarza
El Sauzal
La Matanza de Acentejo
Observatorio Astrónomico del Teide (Astronomical Observatory)
Picnic Spot
SEE INSET MAP
Paisaje Lunar
TO PLAYA DE LAS AMERICAS
TO GRANADILLA DE ABONA
TO EL MÉDANO
TO LOS GIGANTES

SPAIN
Gibraltar(UK)
MEDITERRANEAN SEA
Strait of Gibraltar
Tangier (Tanger)
Cap Spartel
Ceuta (SPAIN)
Ksar es Seghir
Restinga
Smir
Tetouan
Asilah
Arba des Beni Hassan
Oued Laou
Targa
Bou Hamed
Larache
Chechaouene
El Jebha
Torres de Alcala
Kalah Iris
Al Hoceima
Réserve de Merdja Zerga
Moulay Bousselham
Ksar el Kebir
Bab Taza
Cheferat
Bab Berred
Ketama
Targuist
Ouezzane
Souk el Arba du Rharb
Lalla Outka
Tidiquin
Boured
Taharsouk
RIF
Allal Tazi
Mechra Bel Ksiri
Barrage al Wahda
Rafsai
Aknoul
Mehdiya Plage
Sidi Slimane
Sidi Kacem
Mjara
Taounate
Kenitra
Oued Sebou
ROUTE DE L'UNITÉ
Abjelil
Taza
Sale
RABAT
Sidi Allal el Babraoui
Meknes (WHS)
Moulay Idriss
Fez
Skhirat
Tiflet
Khemisset
Bir Tam Tam
Sefrou
El Menzel
ATLANTIC OCEAN
Mohammedia
Ben Slimane
Bettache
Casablanca
Mediouna
Sidi Hajjaj
Rommani
Oued Bouregreg
El Hajeb
Imouzzer du Kandar
Ifrane
Azrou
Oulmes
Ez Zhiliga
Oued Sebou
Outat Oulad el Hajj
El Jadida
Azemmour
Bir Jhid
Berrechid
Boulemane
Timahdite
Enjil
Aguelmouss
Mrirt
Sidi Moussa
Benahmed
Oued Mellah
Oued Grou
Settat
Missour
Khenifra
Sidi Smail
Boulaouane
Khouribga
Oued Zem
Boujad
Itzer
Ksabi
Oualidia
Khemis des Zemamra
Sidi Bennour
Mechra Bnabbou
Guisser
Bouma
Midelt
Amersid
Cap Beddouza
El Boroudj
Fkih Ben Salah
Kasba Tadla
El Ksiba
MOYEN ATLAS
Ayachi 3737m
Skhour des Rehamna
Oued Oum er Rbia
Oued el Abid
Gourrama
Safi
Tlettai Sidi Bouguedra
Youssoufia
Benguerir
Beni Mellal
Oued Ziz
Rich
El Gorane Kadoussa
Sept des Gzoula
Chemaia
MOROCCO
El Kelaa Srarhna
Cascades d'Ouzoud
Azilal
Bin el Ouidane
Er Rachidia
Tamelelt
Oued Tensift
Demnate
Oued Dades
HAUT ATLAS
Aoufous
Taftecht
Sidi Mokhtar
Marrakech
Tabant
Goulmima
M'goun 4071m
Chichaoua
Kasbah Dar Caid Ouriki
Taddert
Tinerhin
Dar Caid Khoubbane
Tahanaoute
Arhbalou
Kasbah Telouet
Boumalne du Dades
Erfoud
Tizi n'Tiga Pass
Asni
Setti Fatma
Ait Moudzit
Rissani
Amizmiz
Oukaimeden
Agoulm
Imi n 'Tanoute
Jebel Toubkal 4167m
Toubkal NP
Skoura
2064m
JEBEL SARHRO
Alnif
Ijoukak
SEE INSET MAP
SEE PG 286
Dades Valley
Oued Rheris
Ouarzazate
Oued Drâa
Nkob
Argana
Tachakoucht
Askaoun
Ait Saadaut
Aoulouz
Sirwa 3305m
Agdz
Tazzarine
Taliouine
Tazenakht
Oued Daoura
Drâa Valley
Taroudant
Oulad Teima
Zagora
ANTI ATLAS
JEBEL BANI
2320m
Irherm
Foum Zguid
Ait Baha
1723m
Tagounit
Mhamid
Tata
Tafraoute
Hassi Bou Laadam eau bonne
ALGERIA
Akka
HAMADA DU DRÂA
Hassi el Khebi
TRANS-SAHARA "ROUTE DE LA MAURITANIE"
Foum el Hassane
Oued Drâa
TO NADOR
TO OUJDA
TO GUERCIF
TO BOUDENIB, FIGUIG
TO BECHAR, FIGUIG
KM 60
MI 30
A B C D E F G H I J K L M
1 2 3 4 5 6 7 8 9
TO MARRAKECH
TO ARHBALOU
Asni
Tassaft n Tizi
Agourii 2011m
Akerker
Tansghart
Iguenane
Ait el Qaq
Adrar n Tizrag
Setti Fatma
Taounirt n Ikis 3195m
2577m
Asloun
Imsker
Oukaimeden
Tadrart
Timichi
Tiourdiou
Arg
Jebel Oukaimeden 3273m
Jebel Angour 3616m
I'bbassene
Arjout 3741m
Ouaussaf
Ikis
Adrar n Ineghmar
3010m
Borj n Oufraou 3868m
Matat
Irkoubeline
Tacheddirt
Adrar Tazaina
Assif n Oufra
Ouaneskra
Tamatert
Bou Iguenouane 3615m
Imlil
Aroumd
Aksoual 3842m
Toubkal National Park
Azib Likemt
Adrar Taroukht
Adrar Mighiain
Tizi Oussem
Azib Tamsoult
Sidi Chamharouch
Azib Tifni
3674m
Aguelzim 3547m
Tichki 3753m
Adrar Tinilim 3670m
Tazaghart
Toubkal
Jebel Toubkal 4167m
Tissaldai
Tizi n Ourai
Adrar n Dern
3853m
Tizgui
3843m
4015m Tizi Melloul
Amrourough 3280m
Lac d'Ifni
Issoual
4088m Ouanoukrim
Azib Imi n Ouassif
Ifni
Az Izouggaghene
Imhilene
Amsouzart
KM 8
MI 4
TOUBKAL CIRCUIT HIKING TRAIL

A
B
C
D
E
F
G
H
I
J
K
L
M
2
3
4
5
6
7
8
9
ALGERIA
TUNISIA
MONTS DE TEBESSA
JEBEL TEBAGA
TO SOUK AHRAS
TO LE KEF
TO AIN BEIDA
TO BATNA
TO EL OUED
Daghbouche
Bayad
Mesloula
El Aouinet
Behir Chergui
Meskiana
Bou Khadra
Morsott
El Meridj
Kalat es Senan
Bou Jaber
Ain Senan
Table de Jugurtha
Sidi Amour Ben
Tajerouine
Jerissa
Mahjouba
Bir Salah
Oued Sarrath
Ain Mesria
Dahmani (Ebba Ksour)
Zannfour
El Ksour
Medeina
Elles
Kbor Klib
Souk Jemaa
Makthar
Mactaris
Kesra
Ain Mastour
Ousslatia
Ain Jlouia
Sidi Naji
El Jema
Sbikha
El Alam
Ain Ksibai
Kalaat Khasba
Haidra
Ammaedara
Thala
Remada (El Ayoun)
Rouhia
Jedelienne
Sufes
Sbiba
Barrage Sbiba
Ain Khamassia
Ain Sayada
Oued Jebbes
Haffouz
El Ala
Chebika
El Bathen
Aghlabite Pools
Hbabsa
Jebel Trozza
El Haouareb
Sidi Ali Ben Salem
Zaafrana
Menzel Mehiri
Bou Hajla
Nas Allah
Sidi Saad
Haleb el Ayoun
Ras el Aioun
El Kourf
Dhaiaa
Bir el Mkaddem
Hammamet
Youkous
Bir Mokadden
Tazbent
Tebessa
Bekkaria
Cheria
Elma Labiod
Tlidjen
Bou Chebka
Dernaia
Foussana
Chambi National Park
Bou Zegam
Qasserine
Cillium
Sbeitla
Sufetula
Jelma
Sebkhet el Bahira
Cherarda
Lessouda
Sidi Khelif
Ouled Halfouz
Sadaguia
Faid
Zaafria
Sidi Bou Zid
Fatnassa
Oum Ali
Bir Sbekia
Oglat Oulad Mahboub
Djeurf
Thelepte
Feriana
Ruins
Lac Lafiel
Bir el Hafey
Sidi Ai Ben Aoun
Mliket
Ouled Ahmed
Regueb
Rihana
Sebkhet Mecheguig
Bir el Ater
Djebel Onk
Oum el Ksab
Mejen Bel Abbes
Ksar Sidi Aich
Bir Ali Ben Khelifa
El Leben
Zabbeus
El Ghriss
Bordj Soukies
Sidi Boubaker
Bou Grad
Bou Alem
Dachret Majoura
Menzel Bou Zaine
Meknassy
Mezzouna
Negrine
Betita
Mides
Tamerza
Chebika
El Ouchika
Redeyef
Henchir Sovatir
Moulares
Garet ed Douza
Gafsa
El Ksar
Lalla
Sened Gare
Sened
Abdessadok
Zannouch
Viewpoints
Bou-Hedma NP
El Mech
Ghedir Rebaia
Borj Hachichina
Seldja Gorge
Metlaoui
Aioun Ameur
Sakket
El Guetar
Bou Saad
Castle
Bou Omrane
El Ayaycha
Sidi Haoual el Oued
Sebkhet en Noual
Souani
Mdhilla
El Amaiem
El Haffey
Mosque
Sidi Mansour
Akaziat
Sbih
Kentira
Sebkhet Dreiaa
Chott el Rahim
Chott Khalla
Chott el Gharsa
Chott Mejez Sfa
El Hamma Du Jerid
Chott Chtihatt Sghatt
Cedada
El Mahassen
Degache
Tozeur
El Haddar
Chabbia
Jujubier
Nefta
Corbeille de Nefta
Hazoua
Bordj Khanguet
Sebkhet Sidi Mansour
Zagrata
Oued Akarit
El Fejij
Ouali
Oudref
Metouia
Chott el Fedjaj
Bordj es Segui
El Hamma
Bou Chemma
Beni Ghilouf
Ksar Debbaba
Chenini
Spa
Eremathi
Chott el Jerid (Jerid Oasis)
SEE PG 287
Bir el Hamra
Debabcha
Bechri
Fatnassa
Oum es Somaa
Menchia
Stiftimia
Limaguess
Bordj Saidane
El Sboub
Ain Tamr
El Mansoura
Tombar
Telmine
Kebili
Chott Kebili
Bazma
Bchelli
Jemma
Blidet
Nouail
Oum Ech Chia
Ouled Khalifa
Nouvelle Matmata
Beni Aissa
Chemlali
Zeraoua
Tijma
Matmata
El Haddej
Tamezret
Troglodyte Houses
Techine
Toujane
Zmerten
Bir el Rtimi
Bir Faiza
Touiba
Douz
El Aouina
Zaafrane
Borj Zoumit
Chott el Ahzem
Chott el Franig
Chott Regoug
Bir Berbia
El Faouar
Es Sabria
Chott el Debaia
Chott el Toual
Bir oum Gounna
Bir el Touana
Chott Bou Charab
Bir Fegoussi
Bir el Grijima
Mouth Adora
Shott el Melah
Bir Soltane
Bir Zoui
Beni Kh
Ksar Tarcine
KM 25
MI 15

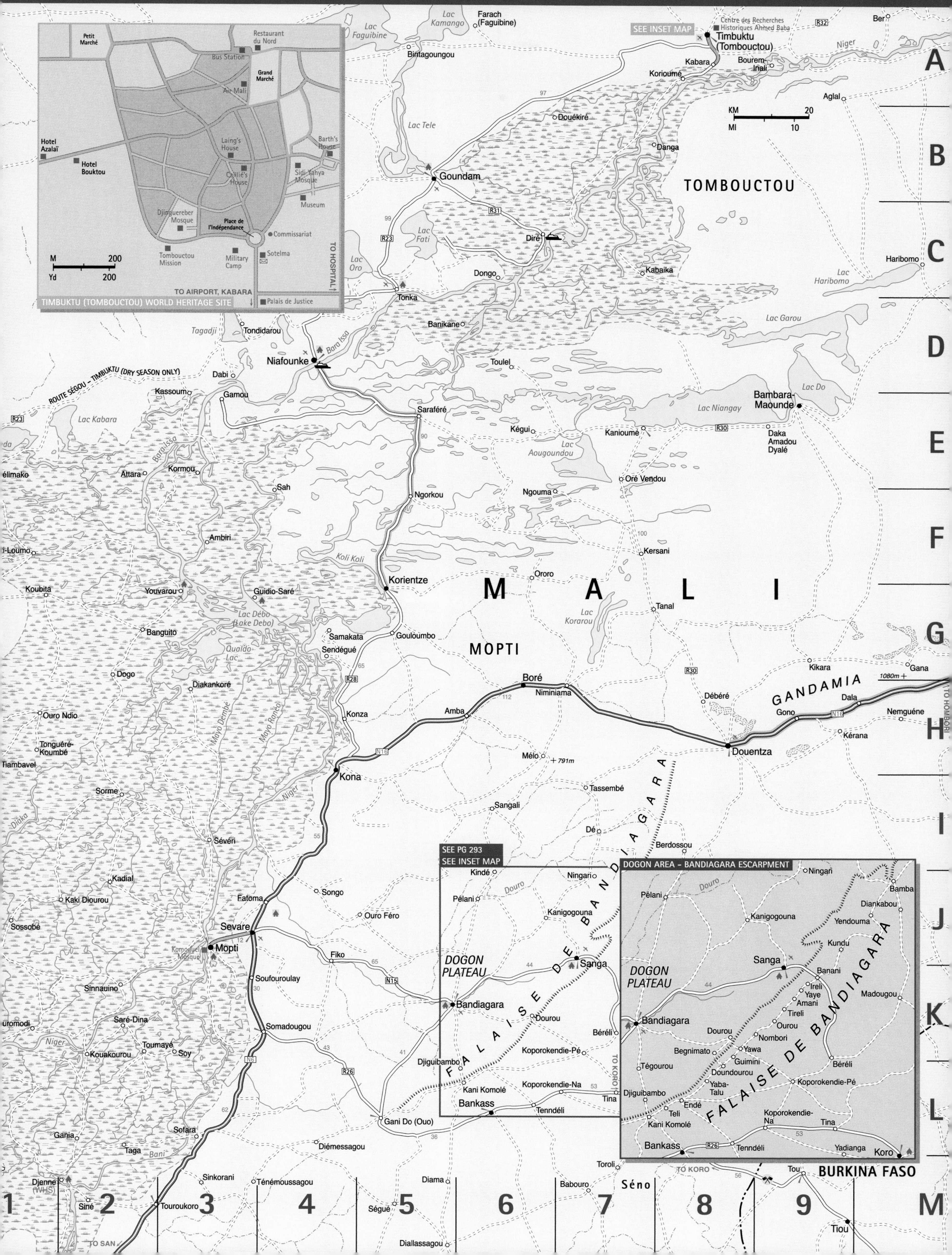
SEE INSET MAP
Timbuktu (Tombouctou)
Centre des Recherches Historiques Ahmed Baba
Kabara
Bourem-Inali
Korioumé
Niger
Ber
Aglal
Farach (Faguibine)
Lac Kamango
Lac Faguibine
Bintagoungou
Lac Tele
Douékiré
Danga
TOMBOUCTOU
Goundam
Lac Fati
Diré
Lac Oro
Dongo
Kabaika
Haribomo
Lac Haribomo
Lac Garou
Tonka
Banikane
Tagadji
Tondidarou
Niafounke
Bara Issa
Toulel
Dabi
ROUTE SÉGOU – TIMBUKTU (DRY SEASON ONLY)
Kassoum
Gamou
Saraféré
Lac Do
Lac Niangay
Bambara-Maounde
Kégui
Kanioumé
Daka Amadou Dyalé
Lac Kabara
Lac Aougoundou
Attara
Kormou
Sah
Ngorkou
Oré Vendou
Ngouma
Ambiri
Kersani
Koli Koli
Korientze
Ororo
M A L I
Koubita
Youvarou
Guidio-Saré
Lac Débo (Lake Débo)
Tanal
Lac Korarou
Banguito
Samakata
Sendégué
Goulouombo
MOPTI
Qualdo Lac
Dogo
Diakankoré
Boré
Niminiama
Kikara
Gana
1080m
GANDAMIA
Dala
Gono
Nemguéné
Kérana
Débéré
Ouro Ndio
Mayo Dembé
Mayo Ranéo
Konza
Amba
Douentza
Tonguéré-Koumbé
Tiambavel
Kona
Mélo
791m
Tassembé
Sorme
Sangali
Niger
Diaka
Dé
Séveri
Berdossou
SEE PG 293
SEE INSET MAP
Kindé
Ningari
Kadial
Songo
Pélani
Douro
Kaki Diourou
Fatoma
Ouro Féro
Kanigogouna
Sossobé
Sevare
Mopti
Komoguel Mosque
Fiko
Sanga
DOGON PLATEAU
Soufouroulay
Sinnauino
Bandiagara
FALAISE DE BANDIAGARA
Dourou
Béréli
Saré-Dina
Somadougou
Niger
Kouakourou
Toumayé
Soy
Djiguibambo
Koporokendie-Pé
TO KORO
Kani Komolé
Koporokendie-Na
Tina
Bankass
Tenndéli
Gani Do (Ouo)
Gania
Sofara
Taga
Bani
Diémessagou
Toroli
Djenne (WHS)
Sinkorani
Ténémoussagou
Diama
Babouro
Séno
TO KORO
Tou
BURKINA FASO
Siné
Touroukoro
Ségué
Tiou
TO SAN
Diallassagou
TO HOMBORI
KM 20
MI 10
TIMBUKTU (TOMBOUCTOU) WORLD HERITAGE SITE
Petit Marché
Restaurant du Nord
Bus Station
Grand Marché
Air Mali
Hotel Azalaï
Hotel Bouktou
Laing's House
Barth's House
Caillié's House
Sidi Yahya Mosque
Museum
Djinguereber Mosque
Place de l'Indépendance
Commissariat
Tombouctou Mission
Military Camp
Sotelma
TO HOSPITAL
TO AIRPORT, KABARA
Palais de Justice
M 200
Yd 200
DOGON AREA – BANDIAGARA ESCARPMENT
Bamba
Diankabou
Yendouma
Kundu
Banani
Ireli
Yaye
Amani
Tireli
Ourou
Nombori
Madougou
Begnimato
Yawa
Guimini
Doundourou
Yaba-Talu
Tégourou
Endé
Teli
Koporokendie-Na
Yadianga
Koro
A
B
C
D
E
F
G
H
I
J
K
L
M
1
2
3
4
5
6
7
8
9

LIBYA
SAHARA
NIGER
CHAD
SUDAN
CAMEROON
CENTRAL AFRICAN REPUBLIC
TO MARZUQ
TO AL JAWF
Korizo Pass
SEE INSET MAP
TIBESTI
Aozou
Bardaï
Palm Grove
Omchi
Kegufur Terbi 3082m
Toussidé 3447m
Palm Grove
Yebbi Bou
2295m
2908m
2954m Tarso Kobour
1286m
Zouar
3112m Tarso Ahon
3051m Arken-Ahon
3414m Koussi
DOHON
1291m
Séguédiné
Grand Bilma Dunes (Grand Erg de Bilma)
Gouro
Dirkou
Bilma
TIBESTI MOUNTAINS
Toudoulou
Cave Paintings
Orda
Madoa 1227m
Yebigue
Bardagué
ABO
Madiqué
1801m
Tombs
Zoumri
Tarso Ourari
Aderké
1548m
Tarso Emissi 3082m
Kegufur Terbi 3150m
1947m
Ehi Timi
1707m
3265m
Youbo
2746m
Tarso Toon 1829m
Soborom
2899m
Tarso Voon 2650m
Tarso Fieroko 3030m
Yega
Modra
Tarso Kobour 2954m
Gravures
Cave Paintings
Bini Madoa
1012m
Sherda
2121m
1341m
Falaise de l'Aguer-Tay
1652m
Miski
Arken-Ahon 3051m
Medouna
Ongur
Gouake
Doma
Yoo
Mao
KM 100
MI 50
TO FAYA-LARGEAU
ZAKOUMA NATIONAL PARK AND THE SALAMAT RIVER
Guedi 1600m
Mongo
Mangalmé
Alouf
Makokou
Abou Telfane Faunal Reserve
Telfane 1360m
TO BITKINE
TO GOZ BEÏDA
Fourdougou
Djiodat
Bali
Kataouare
Garat
Kitébil
Abgé
Salta
Goufo
Kilim
Dafra
792m
Saka
Zerab
Siref
748m
Azrak
Azoum
967m
Abou Deïa
Deresna
Mouray
Djebréne
Kamaday
Gagne
Ter
Korom
Djourt
Am Timan
Zakouma National Park
Zakouma
Am Djelato
Koubo Abou Azrak
Kourboutou
Koungouri
Bon
Marmak
Koubo Abou Gara
Zan
Kiéké
Djouna
Baïkoré
Salamat
Tiéau
Bola
Mindjik
Komo
Lake Iro
Salamat
Takalaou
Bonga
Doudéi
Kendegue
Malé
Dongo
TO SARH
Haraze-Mangueigne
Faya-Largeau
Mourdi Depression
ENNEDI
Fada
Fada Archeï Faunal Reserve
Mornou 1222m
Djourab Dunes
O. Archeï
Monou
O. Haouach
Oum Chalouba
O. Fama
Arada
Kapka 1270m
Iriba
Tiné
W. Aradeib
Haddad
Biltine
Guéréda
Enne
Haraz-Djombo
Djombo Kibbit
Abéché
Rime
Adré
Geneina
W. Barei
Djédaa
Oum Hadjer
Batha
Ati
Am Dam
Zalingei
Nguigmi
Diffa
Bol
Ngouri
Moussoro
Lake Chad
SEE PG 289
Karal
Massakory
Kalamaloué National Park
Ngoura
Lake Fitri
Ati Ardébé
Am Léiouna
Goz Beïda
Mongororo
Ngadda
Ngala
Massaguet
Moyto
Bokoro
N'DJAMENA
Maiduguri
Dikwa
Bama
Ngama
Bitkin
GUÉRA MASSIF
Kubbum
Hagar Banga
Rahad el Berdi
Waza National Park
Massenya
Boro
Kédédéssé
Gwoza
Mora
Maga
Logone
Gélengdeng
Boudamasa
Erguig
Melfi
Chari
Mokolo
Maga Dam
Yedseram
Roumsiki
Maroua
Yagoua
Ba Illi
Bousso
Sinianka-Minia Game Reserve
Mane Konjo
Mubi
Dourbeye
Kaélé
Bongor
Am Dafok
Tabur
Lake Mamoun
Birao
Léré
Fianga
Dik
Manda National Park
Kyabé
Dosseo
Kéita
Aouk
Mele
André Félix National Park
Garoua
Lagdo Reservoir
Pala
Binder-Léré Faunal Reserve
Kélo
Laï
Manovo-Gounda-St Floris National Park (WHS)
Tiroungoulou
Ouandjia-Vakaga Faunal Reserve
Ouanda Djallé
Radom National Park
Djoli Kere Forest Reserve
Sarh
Beka
Beinamar
Moundou
Doba
Koumra
Golongosso
Miaméré
Yata-Ngaya Faunal Reserve
Bénoué National Park
Bouba Ndjidah National Park
Faro Reserve
Moïssala
Maro
Bamingui-Bangoran National Park
Ndélé
Ouadda
Goré
Nana-Barya Faunal Reserve
Kabo
Gribingui-Bamingui Faunal Reserve
Bamingui
Mounguel
TO NGAOUNDÉRÉ
TO BOSSANGOA
TO KAGA BANDORO
TO BRIA
A
B
C
D
E
F
G
H
I
J
K
L
M
2
3
4
5
6
7
8
9
10

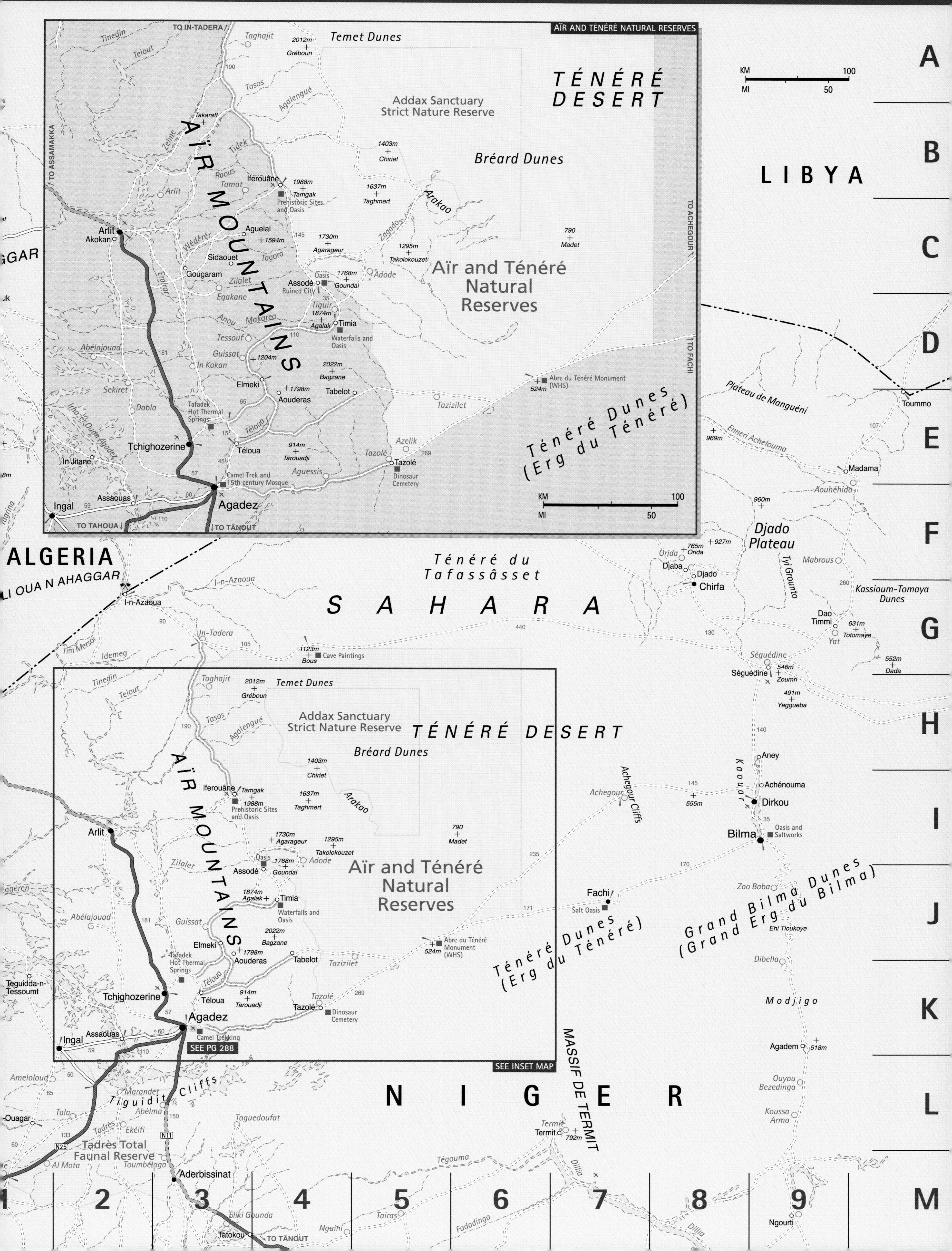
AÏR AND TÉNÉRÉ NATURAL RESERVES
TO IN-TADERA
Tinedin
Teiout
Taghajit
2012m
Gréboun
Temet Dunes
TÉNÉRÉ DESERT
Tasos
Agalengué
Addax Sanctuary
Strict Nature Reserve
Takaraft
AÏR MOUNTAINS
TO ASSAMAKKA
Zeline
Tidek
1403m
Chiriet
Bréard Dunes
Raous
Tamat
Iferouâne
1988m
Tamgak
Prehistoric Sites and Oasis
1637m
Taghmert
Arakao
Arlit
Akokan
Aguelal
1594m
Wédérér
1730m
Agarageur
Zagado
1295m
Takolokouzet
790
Madet
TO ACHEGOUR
Sidaouet
Tagora
Gougaram
Zilalet
Eralrar
Oasis
1768m
Goundai
Assodé
Ruined City
Adode
Aïr and Ténéré Natural Reserves
Egakane
Tiguir
1874m
Agalak
Timia
Anou Makarea
Tessouf
Waterfalls and Oasis
TO FACHI
Abélajouad
Guissat
1204m
In Kakan
2022m
Bagzane
Abre du Ténéré Monument (WHS)
524m
Elmeki
Sekiret
1798m
Aouderas
Tabelot
Tazizilet
Dabla
Tafadek Hot Thermal Springs
Ténéré Dunes (Erg du Ténéré)
Téloua
Inhazar Ouan Agadez
Tchighozerine
914m
Tarouadji
Azelik
Tazolé
In Uitane
Aguessis
Dinosaur Cemetery
Camel Trek and 15th century Mosque
Assaouas
Ingal
Agadez
TO TAHOUA
TO TÂNOUT
KM 100
MI 50
LIBYA
ALGERIA
Toummo
Plateau de Manguéni
969m
Enneri Achelouma
Madama
Aouhéhida
960m
Djado Plateau
Ténéré du Tafassâsset
765m
Orida
927m
Djaba
Djado
Chirfa
Tiyi Grounto
Mabrous
Kassioum-Tomaya Dunes
I-n-Azaoua
SAHARA
Dao Timmi
631m
Totomaye
Yat
In-Tadera
1123m
Bous
Cave Paintings
Tim Mersoï
Idemeg
Séguédine
546m
Zoumri
552m
Dada
491m
Yeggueba
Aney
Kaouar
Achegour
Achegour Cliffs
555m
Achénouma
Dirkou
Bilma
Oasis and Saltworks
Fachi
Salt Oasis
Zoo Baba
Grand Bilma Dunes (Grand Erg du Bilma)
Ehi Tioukoye
Dibella
Modjigo
Agadem
518m
SEE PG 288
SEE INSET MAP
Teguidda-n-Tessoumt
Ameloloud
Marandet
Tiguidit Cliffs
Abélma
Ekéifi
Tadrès Total Faunal Reserve
Tala
Ouagar
Al Mota
Toumbélaga
Taguedoufat
Aderbissinat
NIGER
MASSIF DE TERMIT
Termit
792m
Tégouma
Dillia
Ouyou Bezedinga
Koussa Arma
Eliki Gounda
Tatokou
Tairas
Nguihi
Fadadinga
Ngourti
N25
N11
A B C D E F G H I J K L M
1 2 3 4 5 6 7 8 9

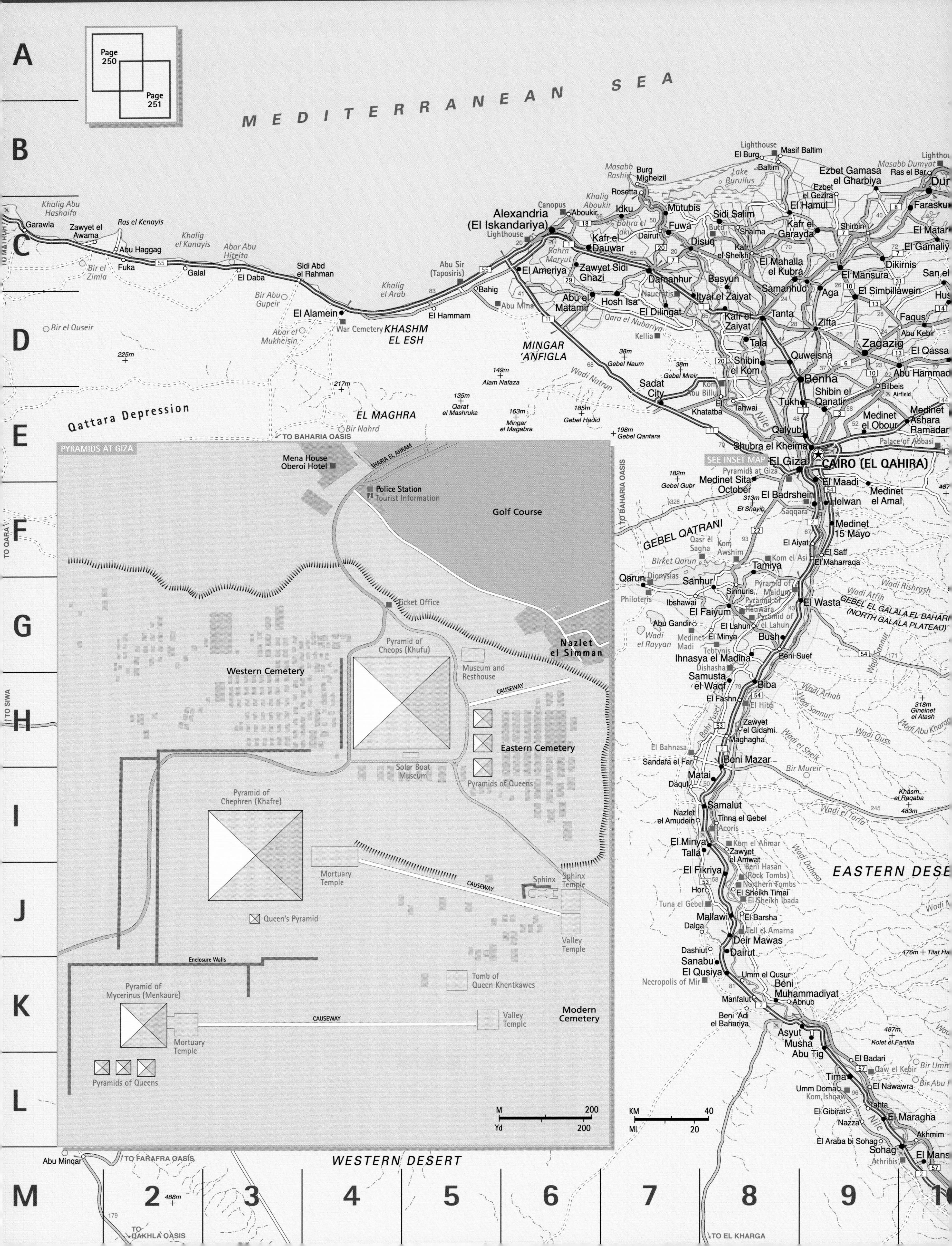

Page 250
Page 251
MEDITERRANEAN SEA
Alexandria (El Iskandariya)
Canopus
Aboukir
Rosetta
Burg Migheizil
Lighthouse
Masif Baltim
El Burg
Baltim
Lake Burullus
Ezbet Gamasa el Gharbiya
Ras el Bar
Damanhur
Kafr el Dauwar
Zawyet Sidi Ghazi
El Ameriya
Abu Sir (Taposiris)
Bahig
Abu Mina
El Hammam
El Alamein
War Cemetery
KHASHM EL ESH
Sidi Abd el Rahman
El Daba
Galal
Fuka
Abu Haggag
Zawyet el Awama
Ras el Kenayis
Garawla
Khalig Abu Hashaifa
Khalig el Kanayis
Abar Abu Hiteita
Bir el Zimla
Bir Abu Gupeir
Abar el Mukheisin
Bir el Quseir
Qattara Depression
EL MAGHRA
Bir Nahrd
MINGAR 'ANFIGLA
Wadi Natrun
Sadat City
Idku
Mutubis
Fuwa
Disuq
Sidi Salim
Kafr el Sheikh
El Mahalla el Kubra
Samanhud
Tanta
Basyun
Ityai el Zaiyat
Kafr el Zaiyat
El Dilingat
Hosh Isa
Abu el Matamir
Tala
Shibin el Kom
Quweisna
Benha
Zifta
Aga
El Mansura
El Simbillawein
Zagazig
Faqus
Abu Kebir
Abu Hammad
Bilbeis
Shibin el Qanatir
Tukh
Qalyub
Shubra el Kheima
Medinet el Obour
Medinet Ashara Ramadan
Palace of Abbasi
SEE INSET MAP
El Giza
CAIRO (EL QAHIRA)
Pyramids at Giza
El Maadi
Medinet el Amal
Helwan
Medinet 15 Mayo
El Badrshein
Saqqara
Medinet Sita October
GEBEL QATRANI
Qasr el Sagha
Kom Awshim
Birket Qarun
Qarun
Dionysias
Philoteris
Sanhur
Ibshawai
El Faiyum
Tamiya
Sinnuris
Pyramid of Maidum
Pyramid of Hauwara
Pyramid of el Lahun
El Lahun
El Wasta
Bush
Beni Suef
Medinet Madi
Tebtynis
Ihnasya el Madina
Samusta el Waqf
Biba
El Fashn
Beni Mazar
Matai
Samalut
El Minya
Tinna el Gebel
Kom el Ahmar
Zawyet el Amwat
Beni Hasan (Rock Tombs)
El Fikriya
Tuna el Gebel
Mallawi
Tell el Amarna
Deir Mawas
Dairut
Sanabu
El Qusiya
Umm el Qusur
Beni Muhammadiyat
Manfalut
Asyut
Musha
Abu Tig
El Badari
Tima
Tahta
El Maragha
Akhmim
Sohag
Athribis
El Mans
EASTERN DESERT
GEBEL EL GALALA EL BAHARI (NORTH GALALA PLATEAU)
Wadi Arabah
Wadi el Sheikh
Wadi el Tarfa
WESTERN DESERT
Abu Minqar
TO FARAFRA OASIS
TO DAKHLA OASIS
TO EL KHARGA
TO BAHARIA OASIS
TO QARA
TO SIWA
TO MATRUH
KM 40
MI 20
PYRAMIDS AT GIZA
Mena House Oberoi Hotel
SHARIA EL AHRAM
Police Station
Tourist Information
Golf Course
Ticket Office
Nazlet el Simman
Pyramid of Cheops (Khufu)
Museum and Resthouse
CAUSEWAY
Western Cemetery
Eastern Cemetery
Solar Boat Museum
Pyramids of Queens
Pyramid of Chephren (Khafre)
Mortuary Temple
Sphinx
Sphinx Temple
Valley Temple
Queen's Pyramid
Enclosure Walls
Tomb of Queen Khentkawes
Pyramid of Mycerinus (Menkaure)
Modern Cemetery
M 200
Yd 200
A
B
C
D
E
F
G
H
I
J
K
L
M
2
3
4
5
6
7
8
9
10

THEBES – VALLEY OF THE KINGS AND QUEENS
WESTERN VALLEY
VALLEY OF THE KINGS
EASTERN VALLEY
Tomb of Amenophis III
Tomb of Ay
Resthouse
Tomb of Tutankhamun
Tombs of the Kings
Deir el Bahari (Temple of Hatshepsut)
Temple of Mentuhotep
DRA ABU EL NAGA
Causeway
Resthouse
El Korn
EL ASASIF
Upper Enclosure
Lower Enclosure
Tombs of Sheikh Abd el Qurna
Temple of Ramses IV
Temple of Sethos I
QURNA
DEIR EL MEDINA
Temple of Ptolemaic
Temple of Tuthmosis III
Temple of Amenophis II
Tombs of the Queens
QURNET
Ramesseum (Temple of Ramses II)
VALLEY OF THE QUEENS
Temple of Tuthmosis IV
Temple of Merneptah
NECROPOLIS OF THEBES
Ticket Office
Temple of Amenophis III
Medinet Habu (Temple of Ramses III)
Pharaohs
Queen's
Habu
Colossi of Memnon (Amenophis III)
Palace of Amenophis III
Temple of Tuthmosis III
NEW QURNA
TO EL TARIF
TO ISNA
TO FERRY TO LUXOR
EASTERN DESERT
Limestone
Plateau
NILE
Asyut
Abu Tig
Tima
Sohag
El Manshah
Girga
El Balyana
Nag Hammadi
Qena
Qus
Luxor
SEE INSET MAP
SEE PG 291
Armant
Isna
Idfu
Kom Ombo
Daraw
Aswan
SEE PG 290
Lake Nasser
TO ABU SIMBEL
SINN EL KADDAB
LUXOR AND KARNAK
Temple of Montu
Grand Temple of Amun
Temple of Tuthmosis III
Sacred Lake
Temple of Amenophis II
Karnak
Temple of Mut
Temple of Ramses III
Chicago House Oriental Institute of Chicago University
Ticket Office for West Bank Sites
Luxor Museum
Temple of Luxor
Tourist Police
Luxor Railway Station
SHARIA EL KARNAK
SHARIA CORNICHE EL NIL
SHARIA EL MAHATTA
SHARIA EL SALAKHANA
TO SHERATON HOTEL

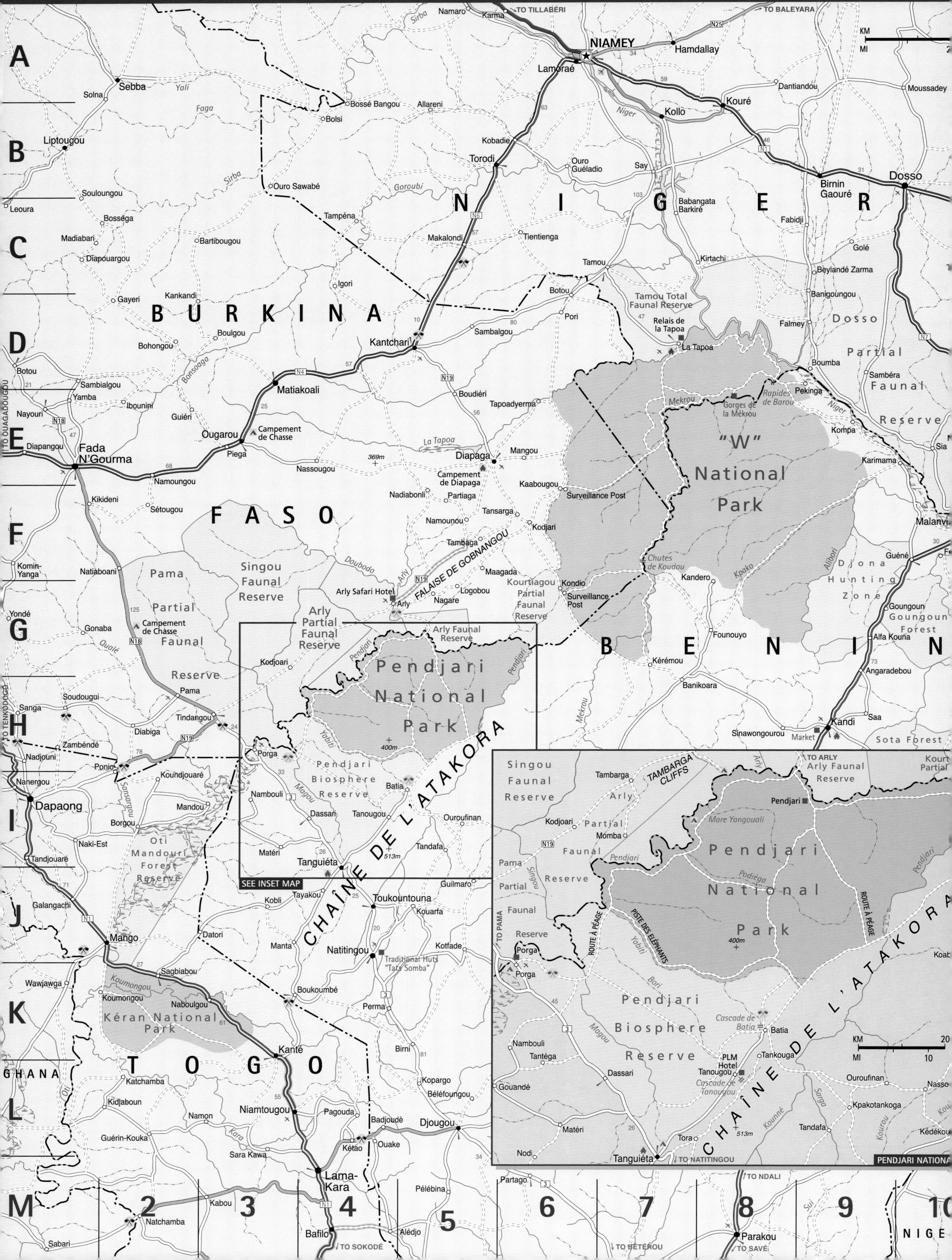
N
NIAMEY
TO TILLABÉRI
TO BALEYARA
Hamdallay
Lamordé
Kollo
Kouré
Dosso
Birnin Gaouré
Torodi
Say
Sebba
Liptougou
Kantchari
Matiakoali
Fada N'Gourma
Diapaga
N I G E R
B U R K I N A
F A S O
B E N I N
T O G O
GHANA
"W" National Park
Tamou Total Faunal Reserve
Dosso Partial Faunal Reserve
Singou Faunal Reserve
Pama Partial Faunal Reserve
Arly Partial Faunal Reserve
Arly Faunal Reserve
Pendjari National Park
Pendjari Biosphere Reserve
Djona Hunting Zone
Goungoun Forest
Oti Mandouri Forest Reserve
Kéran National Park
FALAISE DE GOBNANGOU
CHAÎNE DE L'ATAKORA
Arly Safari Hotel
Campement de Chasse
Campement de Diapaga
Surveillance Post
Relais de la Tapoa
La Tapoa
Gorges de la Mékrou
Rapides de Barou
Chutes de Koudou
Kandi
Banikoara
Natitingou
Tanguiéta
Porga
Batia
Dapaong
Mango
Kanté
Niamtougou
Lama-Kara
Djougou
Parakou
Bafilo
SEE INSET MAP
TAMBARGA CLIFFS
ROUTE À PÉAGE
PISTE DES ÉLÉPHANTS
Cascade de Batia
PLM Hotel Tanougou
Cascade de Tanougou
Mare Yangouali
TO ARLY
TO PAMA
TO NATITINGOU
PENDJARI NATIONAL
TO NDALI
TO SOKODÉ
TO BÉTÉROU
TO SAVÈ
TO OUAGADOUGOU
TO TENKODOGO
KM
MI
A
B
C
D
E
F
G
H
I
J
K
L
M
2
3
4
5
6
7
8
9
10

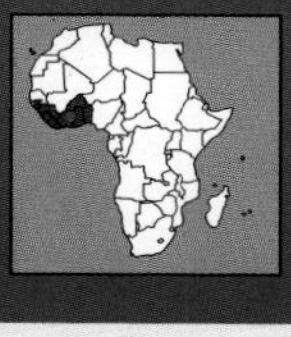

TO KAOUARA
TO GAOUA
KM 40
MI 20
Mangodara
Noumoukiedoumou
BURKINA FASO
Comoé
Batié
Doropo
Kalamon
Varalé
Namboukaha
Gbodonon
Ferkéssédougou
Korhogo
Tioroniaradougou
Kafolo
Comoé Safari Lodge
Bawé
Ouango-Fitini
Bombela
Téhini
Koebonou
Nassian
635m Mt Yévélé
PISTE DE OUANGO - FITINI
PISTE DE TÉHINI
Kolodio
Saye
Panzarani
Bouna Campsite
Bouna
Comoé National Park (WHS)
Carrefour de Bouin
PISTE DE SAYE
Gbadikaha
Viewpoint
Tobourougou
Kong
Kongolo
Blikaodi
Tafiré
Korohouita
Kolon
Koniéré
PISTE DE KONG
PISTE DE BANIA
Bania
Bineda
Kopingue
Iringou
Bandama Blanc
Toro Kinkane
589m Mt Boutourou
Niakaramandougou
625m Mt Potrou
Comoé Sogetel
Koutouba
Kinkane
Ganse
Kakpin
Banvayo
Dédi
Darhala
Nassian
Bonieredougou
Dabakala
Gbanhui
CÔTE D'IVOIRE
Tieningboue
Katiola
Timbe
Marabadiassa
Sanlo
TO WENCHI
Ganze
Sandegué
119
Satama Sokoura
Gouméré
Bodokro
Botro
Konandikro
Tanda
Béoumi
Bouaké
Asuefri
Brobo
Ouassadougou
Asriko
Prikro
Dior
Allangouassou
Sakassou
Tie-Ndiekro
Mbahiakro
Koun Fao
Ananda-Kouadiokro
Ouellé
TO SUNYANI
Lac de Kossou
Tiebissou
Didievi
Agnibilékrou
Bocanda
Daoukro
Apromprонou
Krégbe
Comoé
YAMOUSSOUKRO
Abengourou
Arrah
Dimbokro
Bongouanou
Bandama
Kokumbo
Toumodi
GHANA
Zaranou
Oumé
Lac de Taabo
Moronou
TO GAGNOA
TO ABIDJAN
TO AGOU
A
B
C
D
E
F
G
H
I
J
K
L
M
1
2
3
4
5
6
7
8
9

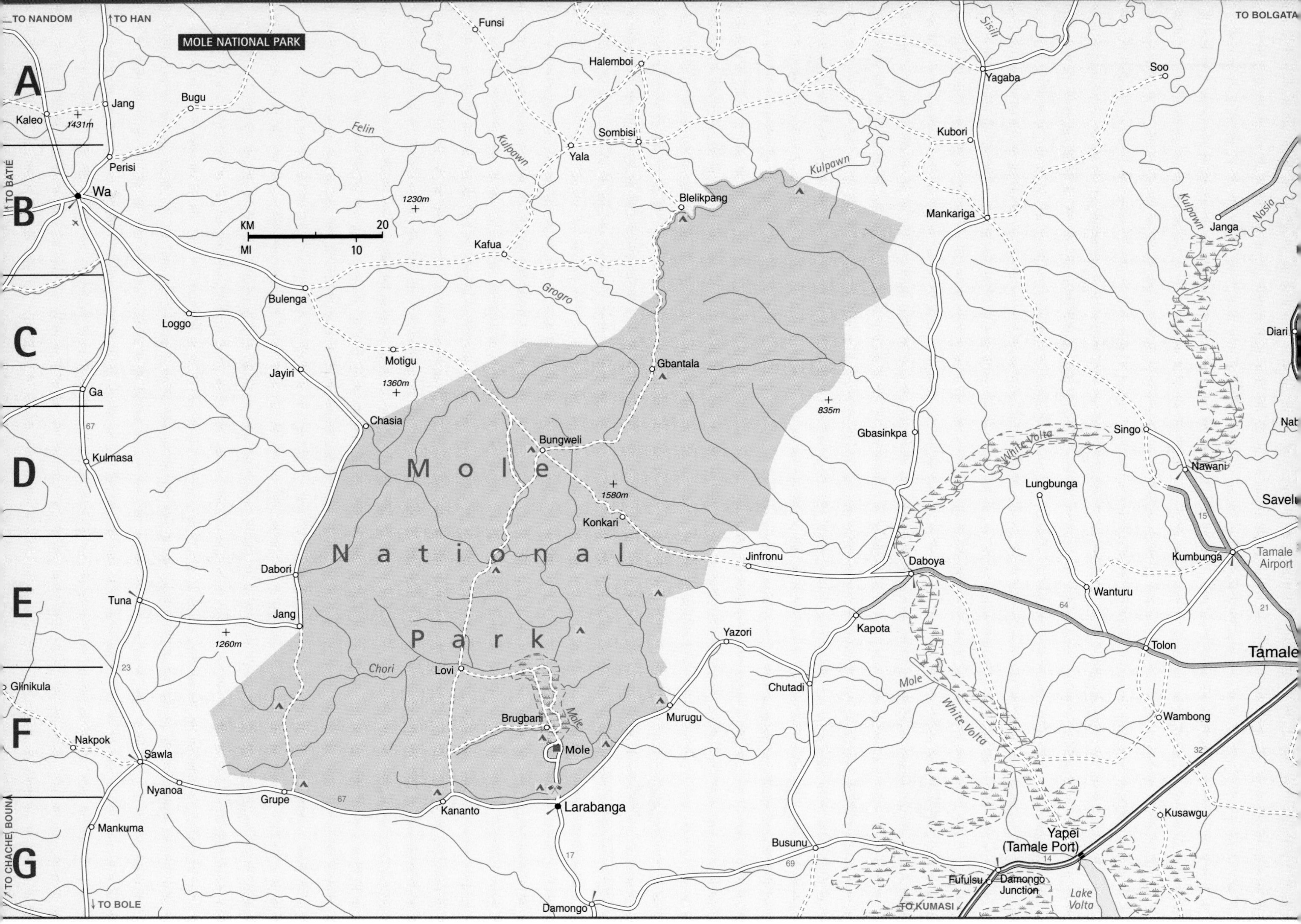
MOLE NATIONAL PARK
TO NANDOM
TO HAN
TO BOLGATA
TO BATIÉ
TO CHACHE, BOUNA
TO BOLE
TO KUMASI
KM 20
MI 10
Mole National Park
Kaleo
Jang
Bugu
1431m
Perisi
Wa
1230m
Felin
Kulpawn
Funsi
Halemboi
Sombisi
Yala
Sisili
Yagaba
Soo
Kubori
Mankariga
Blelikpang
Kafua
Bulenga
Grogro
Loggo
Motigu
Jayiri
1360m
Gbantala
835m
Gbasinkpa
Ga
Chasia
Bungweli
Kulmasa
1580m
Konkari
Dabori
Jinfronu
Daboya
Tuna
Jang
1260m
Chori
Lovi
Yazori
Kapota
Chutadi
Brugbani
Mole
Murugu
Nakpok
Sawla
Nyanoa
Grupe
Kananto
Larabanga
Mankuma
Damongo
Busunu
Fufulsu
Damongo Junction
Yapei (Tamale Port)
Lake Volta
Glinikula
White Volta
Nasia
Janga
Diari
Singo
Nawani
Lungbunga
Savelugu
Kumbunga
Tamale Airport
Wanturu
Tolon
Tamale
Wambong
Kusawgu
A
B
C
D
E
F
G

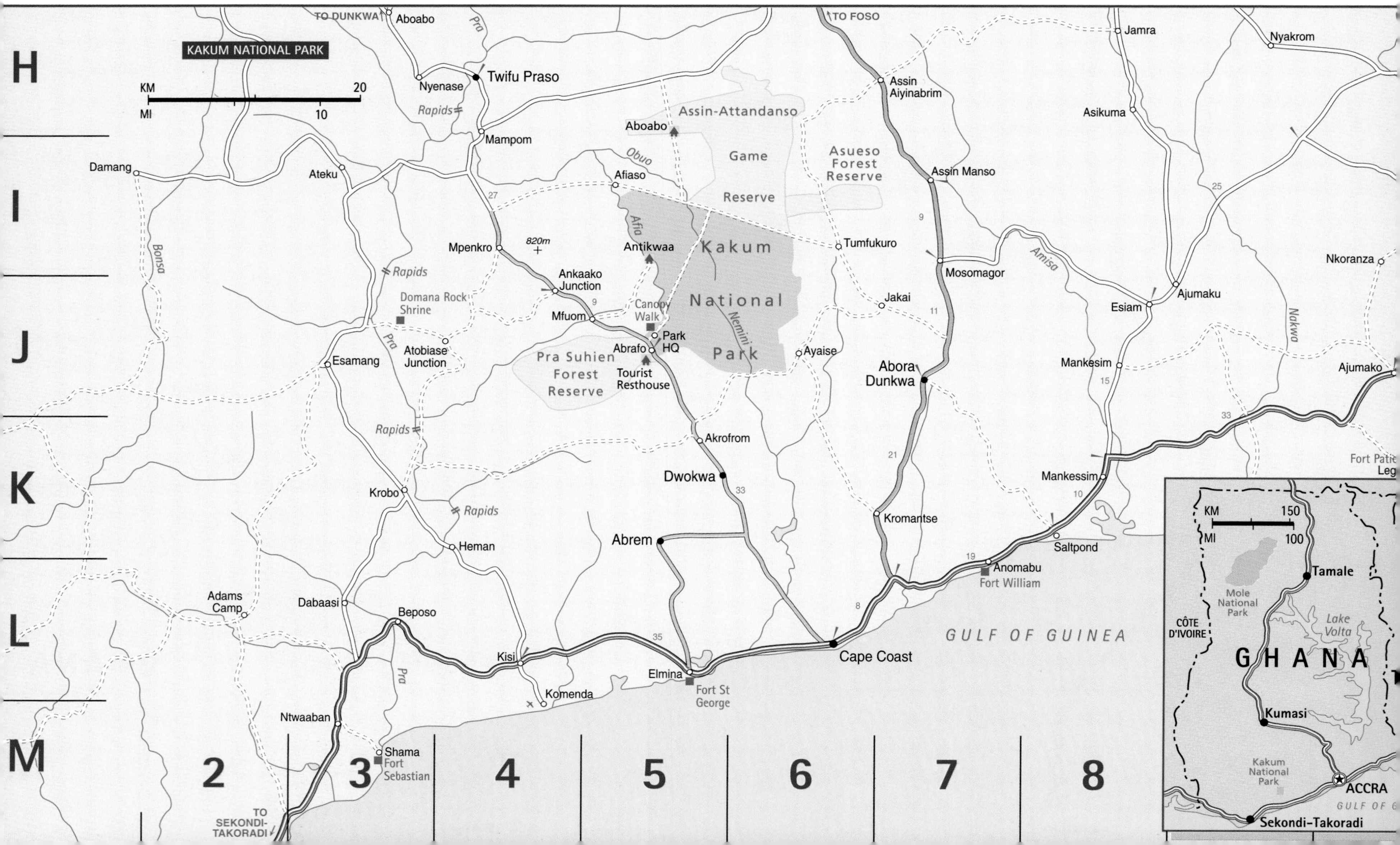
KAKUM NATIONAL PARK
TO DUNKWA
TO FOSO
TO SEKONDI-TAKORADI
KM 20
MI 10
Aboabo
Pra
Twifu Praso
Nyenase
Rapids
Mampom
Jamra
Nyakrom
Assin Aiyinabrim
Asikuma
Aboabo
Assin-Attandanso Game Reserve
Asueso Forest Reserve
Damang
Ateku
Obuo
Afiaso
Assin Manso
27
Bonsa
Mpenkro
820m
Antikwaa
Afia
Kakum National Park
Tumfukuro
Amisa
Nkoranza
Ankaako Junction
Domana Rock Shrine
Mfuom
Canopy Walk
Jakai
Mosomagor
Esiam
Ajumaku
Park HQ
Abrafo
Nemini
Ayaise
Nakwa
Esamang
Atobiase Junction
Pra Suhien Forest Reserve
Tourist Resthouse
Abora Dunkwa
Mankesim
Ajumako
Akrofrom
Dwokwa
Mankessim
Fort Patience
Legu
Krobo
Kromantse
Saltpond
Abrem
Heman
Anomabu
Fort William
Adams Camp
Dabaasi
Beposo
GULF OF GUINEA
Cape Coast
Kisi
Elmina
Fort St George
Komenda
Ntwaaban
Shama
Fort Sebastian
KM 150
MI 100
Tamale
Mole National Park
CÔTE D'IVOIRE
Lake Volta
GHANA
Kumasi
Kakum National Park
ACCRA
Sekondi-Takoradi
GULF OF GUINEA
H
I
J
K
L
M
2
3
4
5
6
7
8

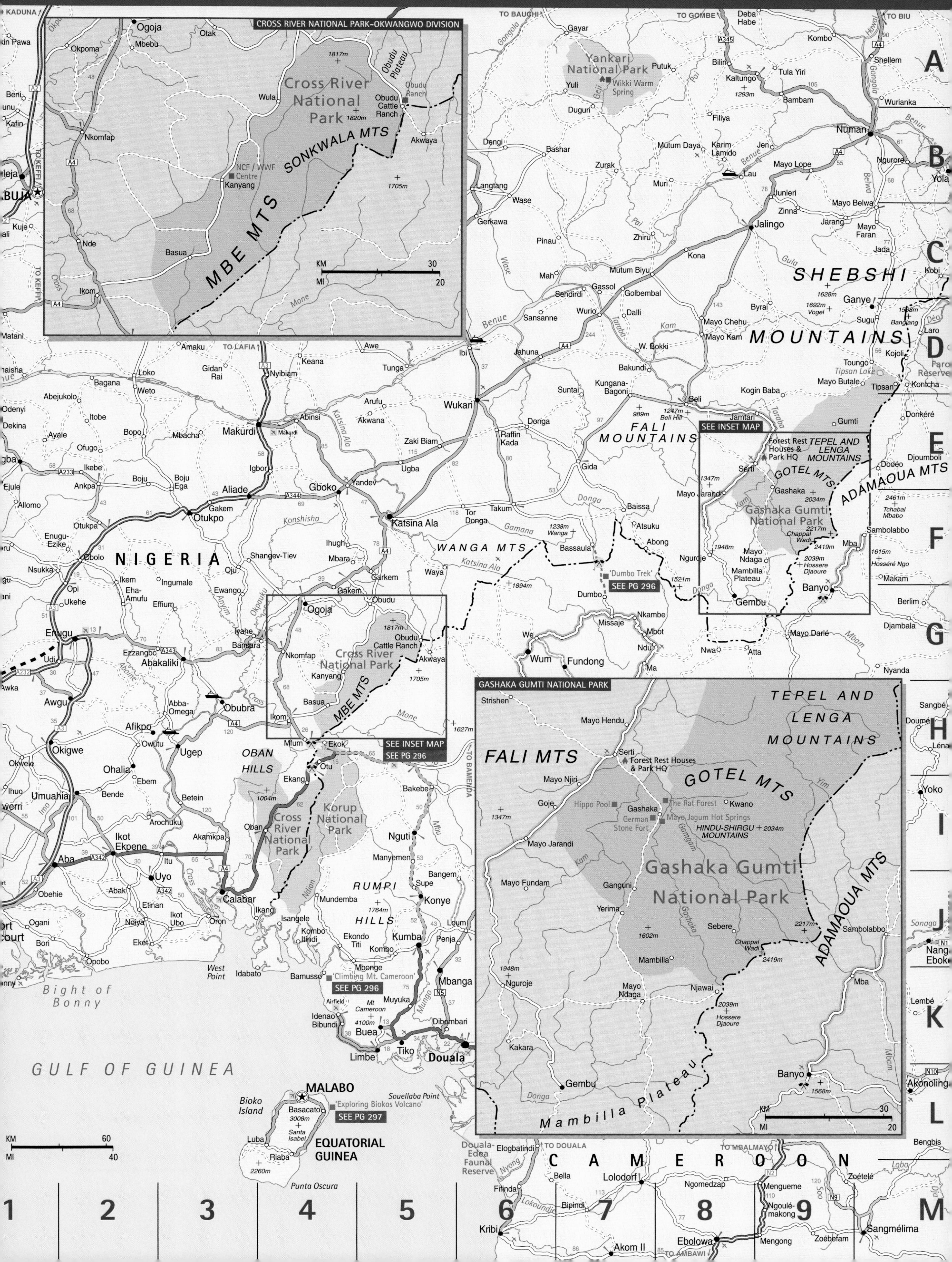
CROSS RIVER NATIONAL PARK–OKWANGWO DIVISION
Cross River National Park
Obudu Plateau
Obudu Ranch
Obudu Cattle Ranch
SONKWALA MTS
MBE MTS
NCF / WWF Centre
Ogoja
Okpoma
Mbebu
Otak
Wula
Nkomfap
Kanyang
Nde
Basua
Ikom
Akwaya
1817m
1820m
1705m
KM 30
MI 20
GASHAKA GUMTI NATIONAL PARK
TEPEL AND LENGA MOUNTAINS
FALI MTS
GOTEL MTS
ADAMAOUA MTS
Gashaka Gumti National Park
Forest Rest Houses & Park HQ
Hippo Pool
The Rat Forest
Mayo Jagum Hot Springs
German Stone Fort
HINDU-SHIRGU MOUNTAINS 2034m
Mambilla Plateau
Serti
Gashaka
Kwano
Mayo Njiri
Goje
Mayo Jarandi
Mayo Fundam
Ganguni
Yerima
Sebere
Chappal Wadi
Mambilla
Mayo Ndaga
Njawai
Hossere Djaoure
Nguroje
Kakara
Gembu
Banyo
Sambolabbo
Mba
Strishen
Mayo Hendu
NIGERIA
CAMEROON
EQUATORIAL GUINEA
GULF OF GUINEA
Bight of Bonny
Bioko Island
MALABO
Yankari National Park
Wikki Warm Spring
SHEBSHI MOUNTAINS
FALI MOUNTAINS
TEPEL AND LENGA MOUNTAINS
GOTEL MTS
ADAMAOUA MTS
WANGA MTS
OBAN HILLS
RUMPI HILLS
Korup National Park
Cross River National Park
Gashaka Gumti National Park
Tipsan Lake
Faro Reserve
Douala-Edea Faunal Reserve
Mt Cameroon 4100m
'Dumbo Trek' SEE PG 296
'Climbing Mt. Cameroon' SEE PG 296
'Exploring Bioko's Volcano' SEE PG 297
SEE INSET MAP
Benue
Cross
Katsina Ala
Gongola
Donga
Taraba
Makurdi
Enugu
Abakaliki
Calabar
Uyo
Aba
Umuahia
Jalingo
Wukari
Yola
Numan
Kumba
Buea
Limbe
Tiko
Douala
Katsina Ala
Gboko
Otukpo
Obudu
Ogoja
Ikom
Gembu
Banyo
Kribi
Ebolowa
Sangmélima
KM 60
MI 40
A B C D E F G H I J K L M
1 2 3 4 5 6 7 8 9

VILLAGES OF THE MANDARA MOUNTAINS
SEE INSET MAP
SEE PG 297
MANDARA MOUNTAINS
ALANTIKA MOUNTAINS
KAPSIKI
Mora Plain
Diamaré Plain
NIGERIA
CAMEROON
CHAD
Waza National Park
Bénoué National Park
Bouba Ndjidah National Park
Faro Reserve
Kalfou Reserve
Maga Dam
Lagdo Reservoir
Lac de Léré
Lac de Trene
Chutes Gauthiot
Sukur Cultural Landscape (WHS)
Podoko Village
Campement de Waza
TO MAIDUGURI
TO N'DJAMENA
TO GOMBE
TO NUMAN
TO NGAOUNDÉRÉ
TO GWOZA
TO MUBI
TO MAROUA
TO BOURRAH
Marguba
Wamuri
Bama
Gulumba Gana
Dipchari
Kumshe
Limani
Andaga
Kerawa
Kolotata
Ashigashiya
Gwoza
Madagali
Mora
Kourgui
Oudjilla
Tourou
Tokombere
Koza
Mokolo
Zamay
Meri
Mogode
Roumsiki
Gawar
Gazawa
Maroua
Salak
Mindif
Dogba
Mangafe Dobwol
Pete
Balaza
Bogo
Guirvidig
Maga
Pouss
Katoa
Waza
Ndiguina
Zina
Tchédé
Tchaskirou
Hinalé
Logone Gana
Mazera
Doreissou
Moulvouday
Gadjia
Yagoua
Kalfou
Bougay
Guidiguis
Doukoula
Dongrossé
Kaélé
Moutouroua
Binder
Fianga
Tikem
Gourmey
Mombaroua
Bongor Hanhan
Govin Lara
Torrock
Binder Nayri
Djodo Gassa
Lagon
Léré
Kebi
Figuil
Guider
Mayo Oula
Bossoum
Dourbeye
Douroum
Bourrah
Boukoula
Chidiri
Ouda
Hina
Mubi
Uba
Kuzum
Askira
Pupanyunyu
Shaffa
Garkida
Hong
Little Gombi
Gombi
Maiha
Holma
Zummo
Song
Sorau
Baché
Dembo
Baila
Boula-Ibib
Konkul
Belel
Demsa
Jiberu
Wuro Yolde
Gaschiga
Bilachi
Pitoa
Garoua
Bibémi
Adoumri
Mayo Lopé
Monbore
Joundi
Mayo Djoi
Béré
Dobinga
Ouarkla
Lagdo
Ngong
Tongo
Boki
Elephants
Tatou
Rey Bouba
le Grand Capitaine
Tcholliré
Gouna
Guidjiba
Bel Elan
Banda
Buffle Noir
Nigba
Bandjoukri
Mbé
le Faro
Pala
Sorga
Ngété
Moursale Banba
Lamé
Baida Baila
Tchangsou
Dari
Tchiming
Gagal
Goumadji
Vaimba
Diibao
Madingrin
Mayo Djarendi
Koum
Rhinoceros
Sorombeo
Ndok
Sora Mboum
Jimeta
Yola
Tépé
Gurin
Touroua
Tcheboa
Beka
Barasa
Kobi
Tchamba
Nyaourédou
Finyolé
Gode
Poli
Voko
Vokre
Bantadjé
Badir
Hawal
Benue
Bénoué
Mayo Tiel
Mayo Kebi
Mayo Binder
Mayo Sina
Mayo Godi
Mayo Vaimba
Mayo Senabou
Mayo Lidi
Rey
Goba
Faro
Déo
Luti
Yedseram
Logone
KM
MI
40
20

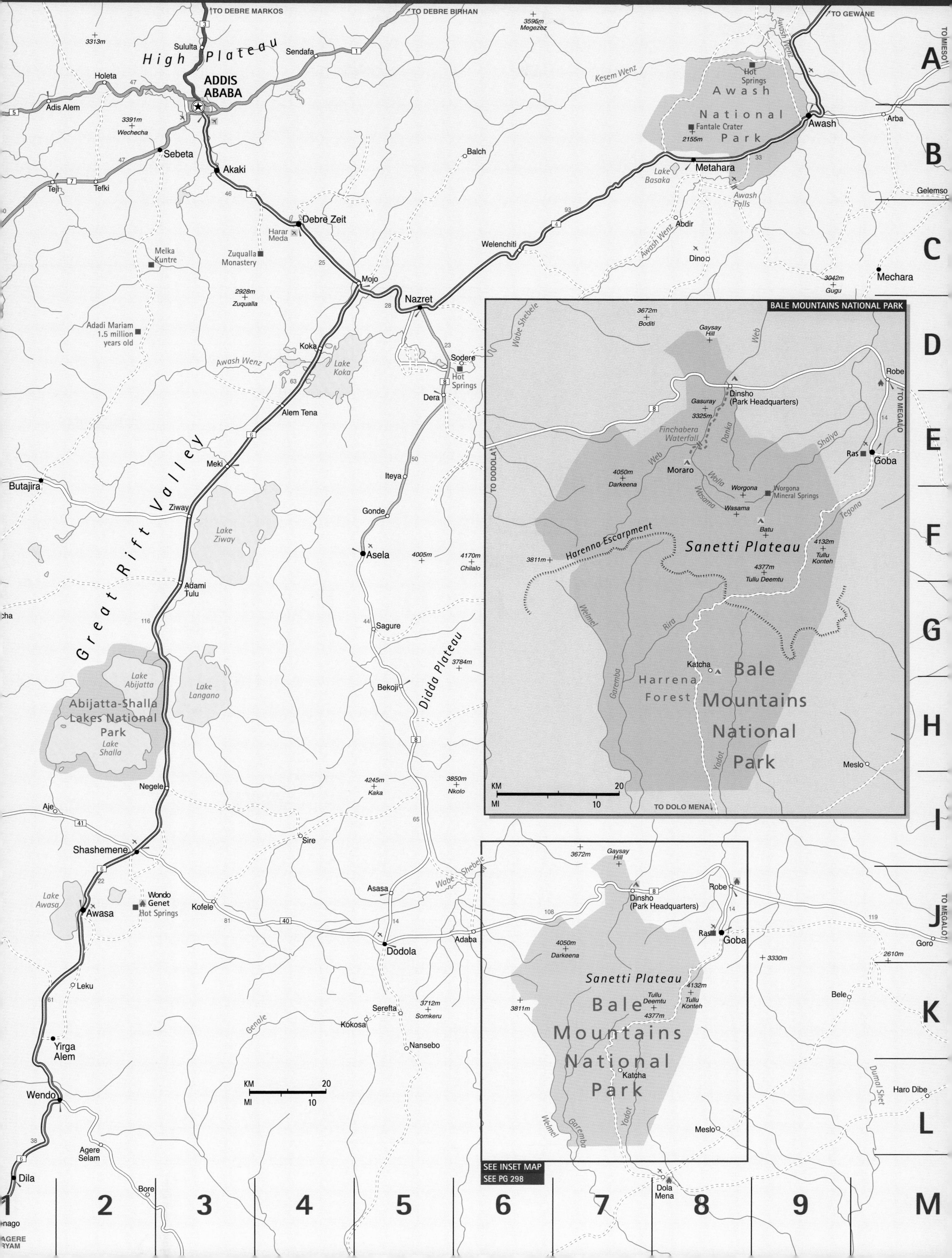
TO DEBRE MARKOS
TO DEBRE BIRHAN
TO GEWANE
TO MIESO
3313m
High Plateau
Sululta
Sendafa
3595m
Megezez
Holeta
ADDIS ABABA
Adis Alem
Kesem Wenz
Awash Wenz
Hot Springs
Awash National Park
Fantale Crater
2155m
Awash
Arba
3391m
Wechecha
Sebeta
Akaki
Balch
Lake Basaka
Metahara
Tefki
Teji
Gelemso
Awash Falls
Abdir
Harar Meda
Debre Zeit
Awash Wenz
Welenchiti
Melka Kuntre
Zuqualla Monastery
Dino
Mechara
3042m
Gugu
2928m
Zuqualla
Mojo
Nazret
Adadi Mariam
1.5 million years old
Koka
Lake Koka
Sodere
Hot Springs
Dera
Alem Tena
Great Rift Valley
Meki
Butajira
Iteya
Ziway
Lake Ziway
Gonde
Asela
4005m
4170m
Chilalo
Adami Tulu
Sagure
Didda Plateau
3784m
Lake Abijatta
Lake Langano
Abijatta-Shalla Lakes National Park
Lake Shalla
Bekoji
Negele
4245m
Kaka
3850m
Nkolo
Aje
Sire
Shashemene
Lake Awasa
Awasa
Wondo Genet
Hot Springs
Kofele
Asasa
Wabe Shebele
Dodola
Adaba
Leku
Serefta
3712m
Somkeru
Kokosa
Genale
Nansebo
Yirga Alem
Wendo
Agere Selam
Dila
Bore
KM 20
MI 10
BALE MOUNTAINS NATIONAL PARK
3672m
Boditi
Gaysay Hill
Wabe Shebele
Web
Robe
Dinsho
(Park Headquarters)
Gasuray
3325m
TO DODOLA
TO MEGALO
Finchabera Waterfall
Danka
Shaiya
Ras
Goba
4050m
Darkeena
Web
Moraro
Wolla
Wasama
Worgona
Worgona Mineral Springs
Wasama
Tegona
Batu
Harenna Escarpment
Sanetti Plateau
4132m
Tullu Konteh
3811m
4377m
Tullu Deemtu
Welmel
Rira
Katcha
Bale Mountains National Park
Harrena Forest
Garemba
Yadot
Meslo
KM 20
MI 10
TO DOLO MENA
3672m
Gaysay Hill
Dinsho
(Park Headquarters)
Robe
Ras
Goba
4050m
Darkeena
Sanetti Plateau
3811m
Tullu Deemtu
4377m
4132m
Tullu Konteh
Bale Mountains National Park
Katcha
Welmel
Garemba
Yadot
Meslo
SEE INSET MAP
SEE PG 298
Dola Mena
3330m
2610m
Goro
TO MEGALO
Bele
Dumal Shet
Haro Dibe
A
B
C
D
E
F
G
H
I
J
K
L
M
1
2
3
4
5
6
7
8
9

SIMIEN MOUNTAINS NATIONAL PARK
Simien Mountains National Park (WHS)
Imet Gogo
3926m
Viewpoint
Inatye
4070m
Chenek
Viewpoint
Bwahit
4200m
Argin
Geech
CLIFF EDGE
Jinbar
Geech Abyss
Michibi
Sankaber
Michotis Valley
Ambaras
Impassable road for vehicles
Chinkwanit
Lamalimu
3220m
Mule Trekking to the Simien Mountains
Debark
Lamma
Wazla
Beleghes
Serekawa
Meshaha
Chiro Leba
Ambikwa
Mizma
4543m
Ras Dashen
TO AKSUM
TO KEREN
TO ARKWASIYE
KM 10
MI 6
Keru
Massawa
RED SEA
Kassala
Sabderat
Gash
Tessenei
Gulch
Omhajer
Humera
Tekeze
May Barya
Adi Da'iro
1785m
Birkuta
Inda Silase
Dibaza
Aksum
Obelisks (WHS)
Adi Abun
Adwa
Enticcio
Adigrat
Mengela
2887m
Assale
Lake Assale
Idga Hamus
Sinkata
Hawzeni
Megab
Gelebeda
Tigray Rock-Hewn Churches
3068m
Debaina
Atsbi
Bere Ale
Sibuha
Wikro
SEE INSET MAP
Togo Ber
Akwi
2052m
Adi Remoz
2523m
Kaza
2745m
Amba Madre
Uri
Tembien Rock-Hewn Churches
Abiya Adi
Agulai
May Mekden
Mekele
Kwiha
Agbe
Gibai
3653m
Dukʼukʼo
Zaʼema
St Mikkae
3008m
Adi Arkay
Angereb
Simien Mountains NP (WHS)
4533m
Ras Dashen
Sankaber
Mule Trekking to the Simien Mountains
Debark
SEE INSET MAP
SEE PG 298
Arekwa
Samre
Adi Gudom
Debub
Enda Medhane Alem
2075m
Abergele
1333m
Dabat
3028m
Beleghes
Meshaha
2267m
3935m
Alage
Maychew
1815m
E T H I O P I A
DEN DES
TO METEMA
Amba Giyorgis
Wagna
1507m
Gendawa
Fasil Gebbi (WHS)
2811m
Gonder
3086m
Menna
2381m
Sekota
Lake Ashenge
Saloka
Rahad
Aykel
Azezo
Denk'ez
Walu
Dara
Tirare
Meskelo
Korem
2851m
Degoma
Nila
2804m
Mt Abune Yosef
3779m
Jirunzbo
Alamata
Ch'wahit
Waja
Hum
1302m
Sifani
1301m
Maryam Gimb
Gorgora
Lake Tana
Addis Zemen
Gwada
Bilbala
Hamusit
Kobo
Bahita
Sailing Lake Tana
SEE PG 299
Werota
Ibnat
3239m
Arema
Rock-Hewn Churches (WHS)
Lalibela
4284m
4008m
SEE INSET MAP
SEE PG 299
Awira
Dindar
Daga Istifanos Monastery
Daga
Aboja
Wemberya
Inkway Beret
Debre Tabor
Palace Ruins
Debre Zebrit
Dilbe
Weldiya
Kidhane Mohret Monastery
Zege
Mt Guna
4135m
Sali
3503m
Kunzila
Abay
Monastery Debre Maryam
Palace of Haile Selassie
Monastery of Kebran Gabriel
Bete Hor
Jita
Firida Mareja
Tenta
Beshlo
Wirgesa
Harbu
2705m
Bahir Dar
Blue Nile Falls
Beles
TO DESE
KM 20
MI
ROCK CHURCHES OF LALIBELA
KEDEMT HOTEL, SEKOTA
Lalibela Centre
Fikre Selam
Seven Olives
Asheton
Bus Station
Clinic
Bet Golgota
Bet Meskel & Bet Maryam
Bet Danaghel
Bet Medhane Alem
Bet Emanuel
Bet Merkorios
Bet Abba Libanos
Bet Gebriel-Rufael
Saturday Market
Beta Georgis (St George)
Cemetery
Jordan
Helen
Serke
TO LAL HOTEL, AIRPORT
TO ASHETON, MARYAM, NAKATALAPA
M 400
Yd 400
TO ADIGRAT
Sinkata
Adi Chewa
Arbuta Insesa
Takatisfi Cluster
Petrus & Paulos
Mikael Melehayzenhi
Adi Kesho Medhane Alem
3068m
Hawzeni
Takatisfi
Debaina
Mikael Debre
Abuna Yemata Guh
Megab
Maryam Korkor
Gheralta Cluster
Selasie Dugem
Dugem
Debre Tsion
Abuna Abraham
Mikael Mindae
Abreha Atsbeha
Yohannes Maikudi
Negash
Atsbi
Mikael Bote
Mikael Imba
Wikro Chirkos
Wikro
Sibuha
TO TEMBIEN CHURCHES
TO MEKELE
KM 20
MI 10
Dangla
Injibara
Chagne
2903m
Dura
Almusa
Borebo
Azena
Koli
Abay (Blue Nile)
Debre Markos
Dejen
Goha Tsiyon
TO ADDIS ABABA
Blue Nile
Jema
Wenchit
Awit
Mehal Meda
TO DESE
Jewaha
TO ADDIS ABABA
A B C D E F G H I J K L M
2 3 4 5 6 7 8 9 10

EQUATORIAL GUINEA
GABON
CONGO
TO BATA
TO NIEFANG
TO TEMELON
TO BITAM
TO MAYUMBA
TO YÉNEGANOU
Bolondo
Mbini
Senye
Evinayong
Mt de la Mitra 1200m
Midyobo
Acalayong
Cogo
Cocobeach
Isla de Corisco
Baie de Corisco
Mitémbié
Aboun
Akurenan
Médouneu
Mongomo
Sam
Nsoc
Oyem
Assok Ngomo
Konossoville
Bibas
Mvane
Nkolabona
Ndongolo
Assok Begue
Doumandzou
Égneng Melen
Mitzic
Saint-Germaine
Monts de Cristal
Assok
Song
Mvoum
Akok
Malibé
Engông Kouame
Andouk Foula
Alen Nkoma
Violainville
Kougouleu
Ntoum
Owendo
Pointe Denis
Mbél
Donguila
Estuaire de Gabon
Kango
Kafele
Eden Nzork
Mikongo
Zomoko
Lalara
Viafé
Yen
Mlanga
Bilo
Ébel Alémbé
Mevang
824m
Alémbé
Oyan
Ebouk-Village
Foulenzem
Mvam
Four-Place
Bifoum
Ebel Abanga
Ndjolé
Elarmekora (Junkville)
Ayem
Portes de l'Okanda
Kazamabika
Booué
Abelang
Ké
Koumameyong
Ovan
Ntenkélé
Minkouala
Makokou
Ipassa-Makokou Strict Nature Reserve
Chutes Kongou
Minkébé Forest Reserve
762m
937m
Mikongo Bushcamp
Primate Research Centre
Lopé Faunal Reserve
Offoué River Camp
Wonga Wongué
251m
Sangatanga
Wonga Wongué Presidential Reserve
Azingo
Lac Azingo
Benguie
Adané
Lambaréné
Boat trips to Ndjolé
Boat trips down the Ogooué River to Port Gentil
SEE PG 300
Lac Evaro
Lac Onangué
Lac Avanga
Lac Ezanga
Lac Aninguè
Issinga
Sindara
Ikobé
Fougamou
Yombi
Fanguindaka
Sika
Kili
Guidouma
Yeno
Mbari
Mandji
Saint-Martin
Mouila
Moulandoufala
Mbadi
Goumbi 820m
Lagune Nkomi
Lagune Iguéla
Iguela Hunting Reserve
Bongo
Akaka
Petit Loango Faunal Reserve
Ngové-Ndogo Hunting Reserve
Moukalaba-Dougoua Faunal Reserve
Guietsou
Doussala
Diela Vievi
Sounga
Setté Cama
Moukalaba Hunting Reserve
Moabi
Mourindi
Bokolo
Gamba
Setté-Cama Hunting Reserve
Bouda
Digoudou
Mouenda
Mayomani
Tchibanga
Difounda
Ouanga Plain Faunal Reserve
Lastoursville
Boundji
Mikouyi
Baniati
Mont Iboundji 972m
Iboundji
Mont Mimongo 875m
Koulamoutou
Ndanda
Mouli Pouli
Mougamou
Massif du Chaillu
Ovala
Massima
Étéké
Diyanga
Mimongo
Moukabou
Yéno
Popa
Pana
975m
Mbigou
Bilengui
Kotto
Matsanga
Grottes Bongolo
Lébamba
Mayoko
Ndendé
Malinga
Nyali
Doussala
Mbanda
Divénié
Moungoundou
Mont Fouari 651m
Mont Fouari Faunal Reserve
Nyanga Sud Hunting Reserve
Nyanga
Mossendjo
Mouyombi
KM 40
MI 20

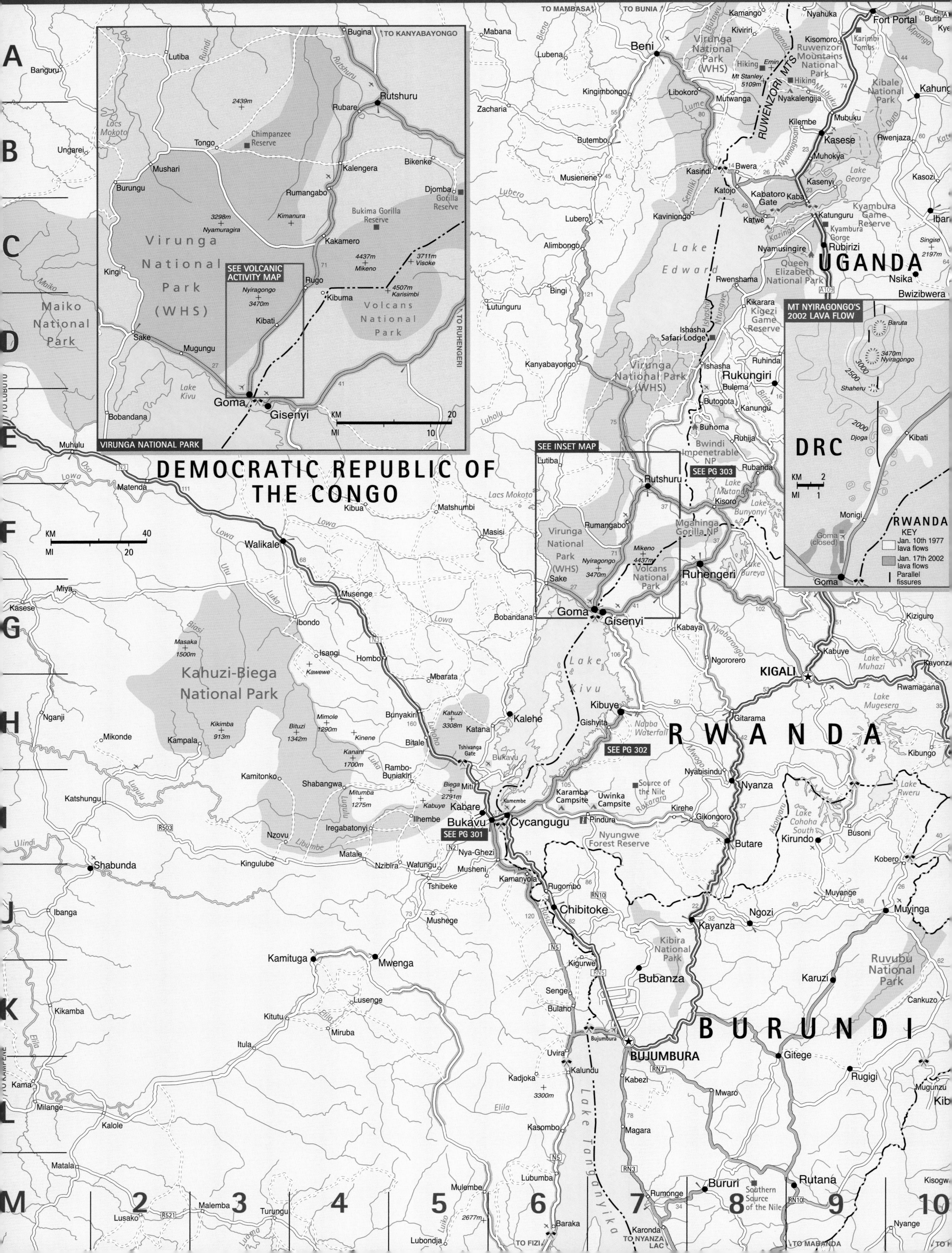

DEMOCRATIC REPUBLIC OF THE CONGO
UGANDA
RWANDA
BURUNDI
VIRUNGA NATIONAL PARK
Virunga National Park (WHS)
SEE VOLCANIC ACTIVITY MAP
Bugina
TO KANYABAYONGO
Lutiba
Rutshuru
Rubare
Tongo
Chimpanzee Reserve
Mushari
Burungu
Kalengera
Bikenke
Rumangabo
Djomba
Gorilla Reserve
Bukima Gorilla Reserve
Kimanura
3298m Nyamuragira
Kakamero
4437m Mikeno
3711m Visoke
4507m Karisimbi
Kingi
Rugo
Kibuma
Volcans National Park
Nyiragongo 3470m
Kibati
Sake
Mugungu
Lake Kivu
Goma
Gisenyi
Bobandana
TO RUHENGERI
KM 20
MI 10
Maiko National Park
Banguru
Ungarei
Muhulu
Matenda
Walikale
Miya
Kasese
Musenge
Ibondo
Isangi
Hombo
Mbarata
Masaka 1500m
Kahuzi-Biega National Park
Nganji
Mikonde
Kampala
Kikimba 913m
Bituzi 1342m
Mimole 1290m
Bunyakiri
Kahuzi 3308m
Katana
Kalehe
Bitale
Kinene
Kanani 1700m
Rambo-Buniakiri
Tshivanga Gate
Kamitonko
Shabangwa
Mitumba 1275m
Biega 2791m
Miti
Kabare
Katshungu
Kabuye
Ilhembe
Bukavu
Cycangugu
SEE PG 301
Nzovu
Iregabatonyi
Matale
Kingulube
Shabunda
Nzibira
Walungu
Nya-Ghezi
Musheni
Tshibeke
Kamanyola
Mushege
Ibanga
Kamituga
Mwenga
Lusenge
Kikamba
Kitutu
Miruba
Itula
Kama
Milange
Kalole
Matala
Lusako
Malemba
Turungu
Mulembe
Lubondja
2677m
Baraka
TO FIZI
Lubumba
Kasombo
Kadjoka
3300m
Uvira
Kalundu
Mabana
Lubena
Zacharia
TO MAMBASA
TO BUNIA
Beni
Kingimbongo
Butembo
Musienene
Lubero
Alimbongo
Bingi
Lutunguru
Kanyabayongo
Kaviniongo
Lake Edward
Kasindi
Katojo
Libokoro
Mutwanga
Virunga National Park (WHS)
Kamango
Kiviriri
Nyahuka
Fort Portal
Kisomoro
Rwenzori Mountains National Park
Karimbi Tombs
RUWENZORI MTS
Mt Stanley 5109m
Emin
Hiking
Nyakalengija
Kibale National Park
Kahunga
Kilembe
Mubuku
Kasese
Muhokya
Rwenjaza
Bwera
Kasenyi
Lake George
Kasozi
Kabatoro Gate
Katwe
Katunguru
Kyambura Game Reserve
Kyambura Gorge
Rubirizi
Nyamusingire
Queen Elizabeth National Park
Singiro 2197m
Ibanda
Nsika
Bwizibwera
Rwenshama
Kikarara
Kigezi Game Reserve
Ishasha
Safari Lodge
Ruhinda
Rukungiri
Bulema
Butogota
Kanungu
Buhoma
Bwindi Impenetrable NP
Ruhija
SEE PG 303
Rubanda
Lake Mutanda
Kisoro
Lake Bunyonyi
Mgahinga Gorilla NP
Ruhengeri
Lake Bureya
SEE INSET MAP
Lutiba
Rutshuru
Lacs Mokoto
Kibua
Matshumbi
Masisi
Rumangabo
Virunga National Park (WHS)
Nyiragongo 3470m
Mikeno 4437m
Volcans National Park
Sake
Bobandana
Goma
Gisenyi
MT NYIRAGONGO'S 2002 LAVA FLOW
Baruta
3470m Nyiragongo
Shaheru
Djoga
DRC
Kibati
KM 2
MI 1
Monigi
RWANDA
Goma (closed)
KEY
Jan. 10th 1977 lava flows
Jan. 17th 2002 lava flows
Parallel fissures
Goma
Kabaya
Ngororero
Kiziguro
Kabuye
Lake Muhazi
KIGALI
Kayonza
Rwamagana
Lake Mugesera
Lake Kivu
Kibuye
Gishyita
Ndaba Waterfall
SEE PG 302
Gitarama
Kibungo
Nyabisindu
Nyanza
Source of the Nile
Karamba Campsite
Uwinka Campsite
Kirehe
Lake Rweru
Pindura
Gikongoro
Lake Cohoha South
Kirundo
Busoni
Nyungwe Forest Reserve
Butare
Kobero
Rugombo
Chibitoke
Muyange
Muyinga
Ngozi
Kayanza
Kibira National Park
Kigurwe
Bubanza
Ruvubu National Park
Karuzi
Cankuzo
Senge
Bulaho
Bujumbura
BUJUMBURA
Gitega
Rugigi
Kabezi
Mwaro
Lake Tanganyika
Magara
Bururi
Southern Source of the Nile
Rutana
Rumonge
Karonda
TO NYANZA LAC
TO MABANDA
Nyange
Kisogwe
Mugunzu

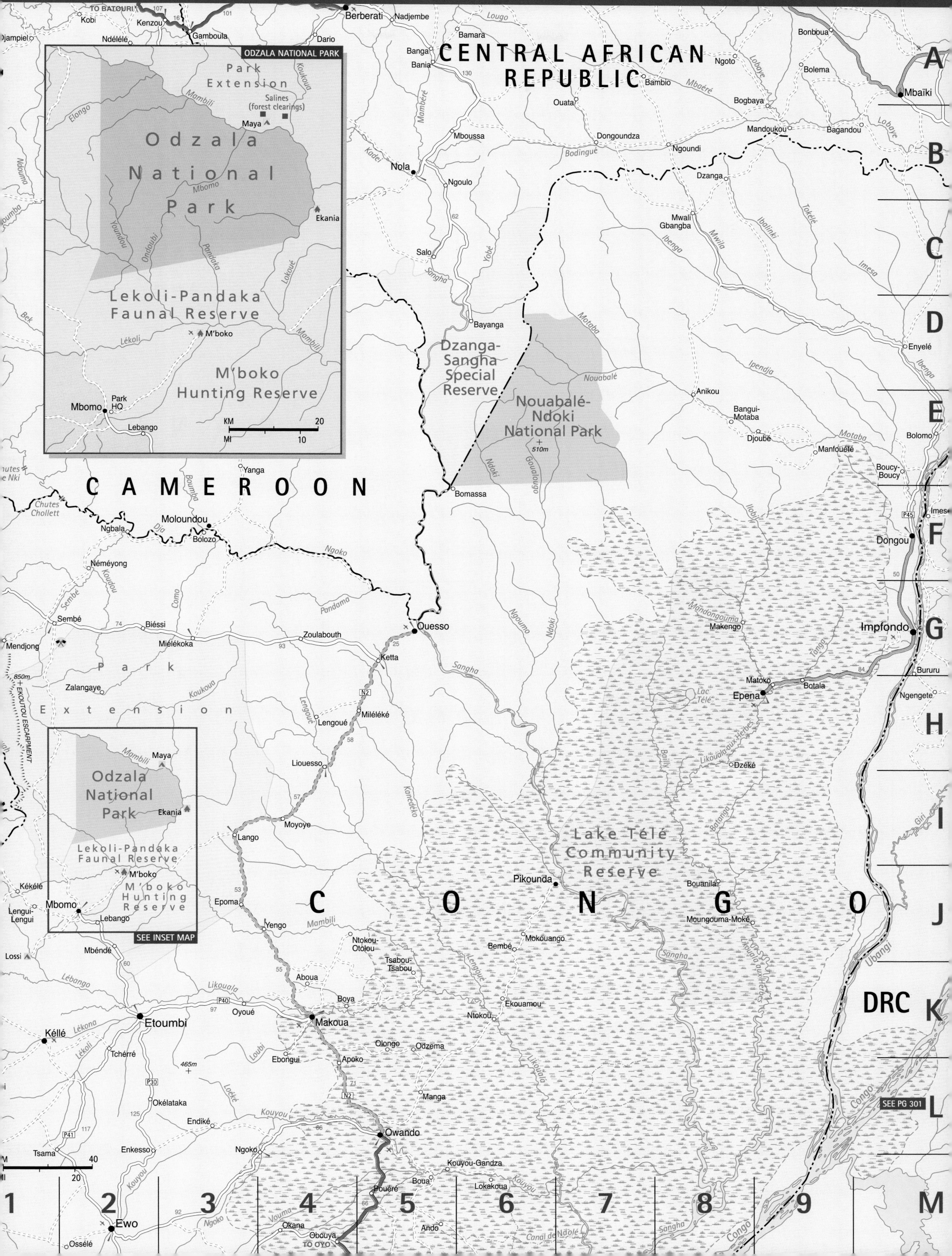
CENTRAL AFRICAN REPUBLIC
CAMEROON
CONGO
DRC
ODZALA NATIONAL PARK
Park Extension
Salines (forest clearings)
Maya
Odzala National Park
Ekania
Lekoli-Pandaka Faunal Reserve
M'boko
M'boko Hunting Reserve
Mbomo
Park HQ
Lebango
KM
MI
20
10
SEE INSET MAP
Dzanga-Sangha Special Reserve
Nouabalé-Ndoki National Park
510m
Lake Télé Community Reserve
Lac Télé
Berberati
Nadjembe
Bamara
Banga
Bania
Nola
Ngoulo
Salo
Bayanga
Bomassa
Mboussa
Ouata
Bambio
Ngoto
Bonbouia
Bolema
Mbaïki
Bogbaya
Mandoukou
Bagandou
Dongoundza
Ngoundi
Dzanga
Mwali Gbangba
Enyelé
Anikou
Bangui-Motaba
Djoubé
Manfouété
Bolomo
Boucy-Boucy
Dongou
Impfondo
Bururu
Ngengeté
Matoko
Epena
Botala
Makengo
Dzéké
Bouanila
Moungouma-Moké
Pikounda
Mokouango
Bembé
Ekouamou
Ntokou
Olongo
Odzema
Manga
Kouyou-Gandza
Lokakoua
Boua
Pouéré
Ando
Okana
Obouya
TO OYO
Owando
Ngoko
Apoko
Ebongui
Makoua
Boya
Aboua
Tsabou-Tsabou
Ntokou-Otolou
Yengo
Epoma
Lango
Moyoye
Liouesso
Lengoué
Miléléké
Ketta
Ouesso
Zoulabouth
Mélékoka
Biéssi
Sembé
Mendjong
Néméyong
Ngbala
Moloundou
Bolozo
Yanga
Chutes Chollett
Zalangaye
Park Extension
EKOUTOU ESCARPMENT
850m
Kékélé
Lengui-Lengui
Lossi
Mbéndé
Etoumbi
Oyoué
Kéllé
Tchérré
465m
Okélataka
Endiké
Enkesso
Tsama
Ewo
Ossélé
TO BATOURI
Kobi
Kenzou
Gamboula
Ndélélé
Djampiel
Dario
Sangha
Mambili
Likouala
Likouala aux Herbes
Ubangi
Congo
Motaba
Ibenga
Lobaye
Ngoko
Kouyou
Canal de Ndolé
SEE PG 301
N2
P40
P30
P41
P45
A
B
C
D
E
F
G
H
I
J
K
L
M
1
2
3
4
5
6
7
8
9

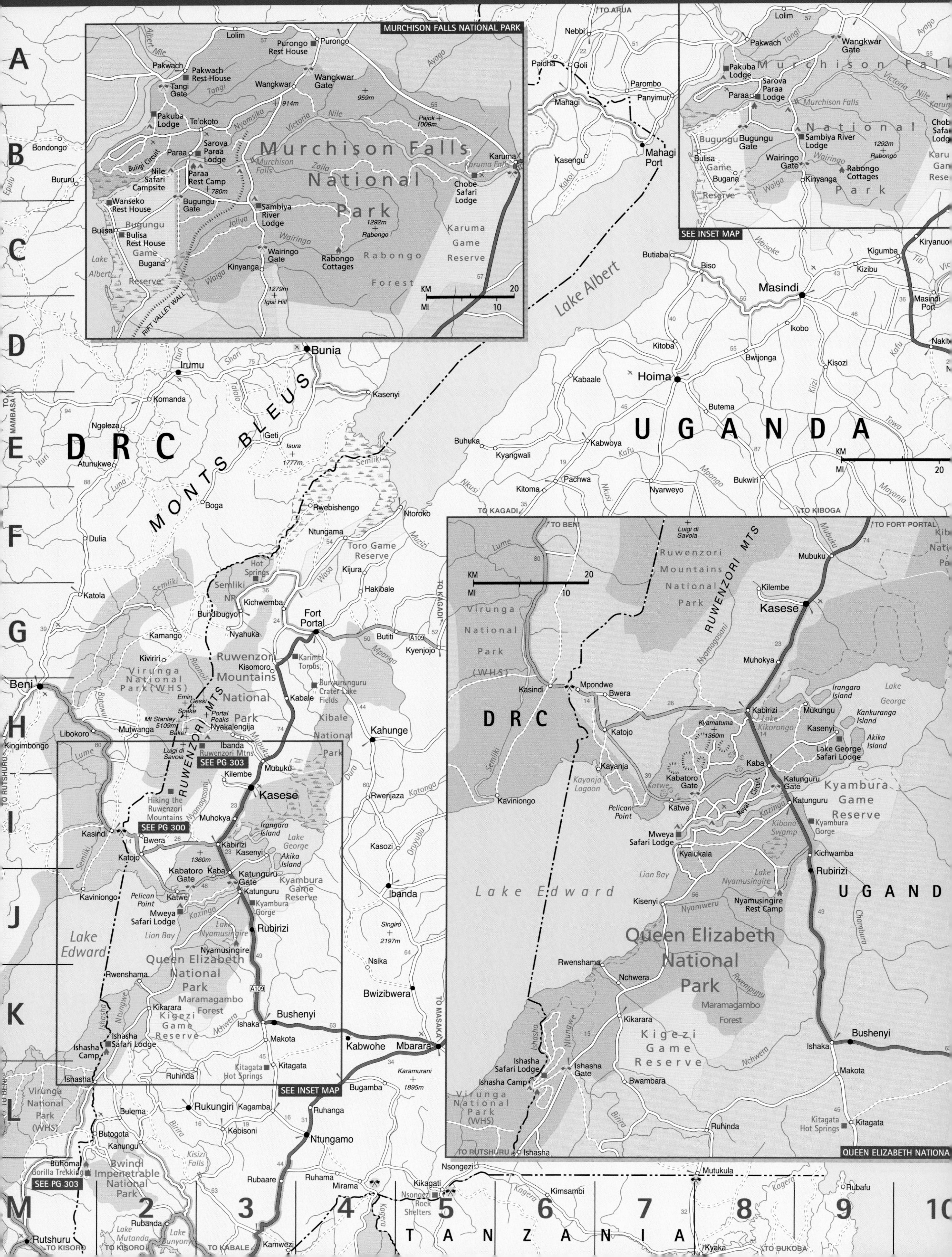
MURCHISON FALLS NATIONAL PARK
Murchison Falls National Park
Purongo Rest House
Purongo
Lolim
Pakwach
Pakwach Rest House
Tangi Gate
Wangkwar
Wangkwar Gate
Pakuba Lodge
Te'okoto
Sarova Paraa Lodge
Paraa
Paraa Rest Camp
Nile Safari Campsite
Buligi Circuit
Wanseko Rest House
Bugungu Gate
Sambiya River Lodge
Bugungu
Bulisa
Bulisa Rest House
Game Reserve
Bugana
Kinyanga
Wairingo Gate
Rabongo Cottages
Rabongo Forest
Karuma
Karuma Falls
Chobe Safari Lodge
Karuma Game Reserve
Igisi Hill
RIFT VALLEY WALL
Lake Albert
SEE INSET MAP
TO ARUA
Nebbi
Paidha
Goli
Mahagi
Parombo
Panyimur
Mahagi Port
Kasengu
Butiaba
Biso
Masindi
Masindi Port
Kigumba
Kiryanuo
Kizibu
Ikobo
Kitoba
Bwijonga
Hoima
Kabaale
Kisozi
Butema
Buhuka
Kyangwali
Kabwoya
Pachwa
Kitoma
Nyarweyo
Bukwiri
TO KAGADI
TO KIBOGA
UGANDA
DRC
MONTS BLEUS
Bunia
Irumu
Komanda
Kasenyi
Ngeleza
Geti
Atunukwe
Boga
Dulia
Katola
Bondongo
Bururu
Rwebishengo
Ntoroko
Ntungama
Toro Game Reserve
Kijura
Hakibale
Semliki NP
Hot Springs
Bundibugyo
Kichwemba
Fort Portal
Butiti
Kyenjojo
TO KAGADI
Nyahuka
Kamango
Kiviriri
Virunga National Park (WHS)
Ruwenzori Mountains National Park
RUWENZORI MTS
Kisomoro
Karimbi Tombs
Bunyaruguru Crater Lake Fields
Kabale
Kibale National Park
Kahunge
Beni
Libokoro
Mutwanga
Nyakalengija
Mt Stanley 5109m
Ibanda
Kilembe
Kasese
Mubuku
Hiking the Ruwenzori Mountains
SEE PG 303
SEE PG 300
Kasindi
Bwera
Katojo
Muhokya
Kabirizi
Kasenyi
Kaba
Katunguru
Kabatoro Gate
Kaviniongo
Katwe
Mweya Safari Lodge
Kyambura Game Reserve
Kyambura Gorge
Rubirizi
Lake Edward
Queen Elizabeth National Park
Maramagambo Forest
Kigezi Game Reserve
Rwenshama
Kikarara
Ishasha Safari Lodge
Ishasha Camp
Ishasha
Bushenyi
Ishaka
Makota
Kitagata Hot Springs
Kitagata
Ruhinda
Rwenjaza
Kasozi
Ibanda
Nsika
Bwizibwera
Kabwohe
Mbarara
TO MASAKA
Bugamba
Rukungiri
Kagamba
Ruhanga
Ntungamo
Bulema
Butogota
Kanungu
Kebisoni
Bwindi Impenetrable National Park
Buhoma
Rubaare
Ruhama
Mirama
Kikagati
Nsongezi
Rock Shelters
Kimsambi
Mutukula
Rubafu
TANZANIA
Rutshuru
Rubanda
Lake Mutanda
Lake Bunyonyi
TO KISORO
TO KABALE
Kamwezi
Kyaka
TO BUKOBA
TO RUTSHURU
TO BENI
TO MAMBASA
Kingimbongo
TO BENI
TO FORT PORTAL
Luigi di Savoia
Mpondwe
Kayanja
Kayanja Lagoon
Pelican Point
Kikorongo
Irangara Island
Kankuranga Island
Akika Island
Lake George
Lake George Safari Lodge
Kyamatuma
Kibona Swamp
Kyalukala
Kichwamba
Lion Bay
Lake Nyamusingire
Nyamusingire Rest Camp
Kisenyi
Nchwera
Ishasha Gate
Bwambara
QUEEN ELIZABETH NATIONA
TO RUTSHURU
A B C D E F G H I J K L M
1 2 3 4 5 6 7 8 9 10
KM 20
MI 10

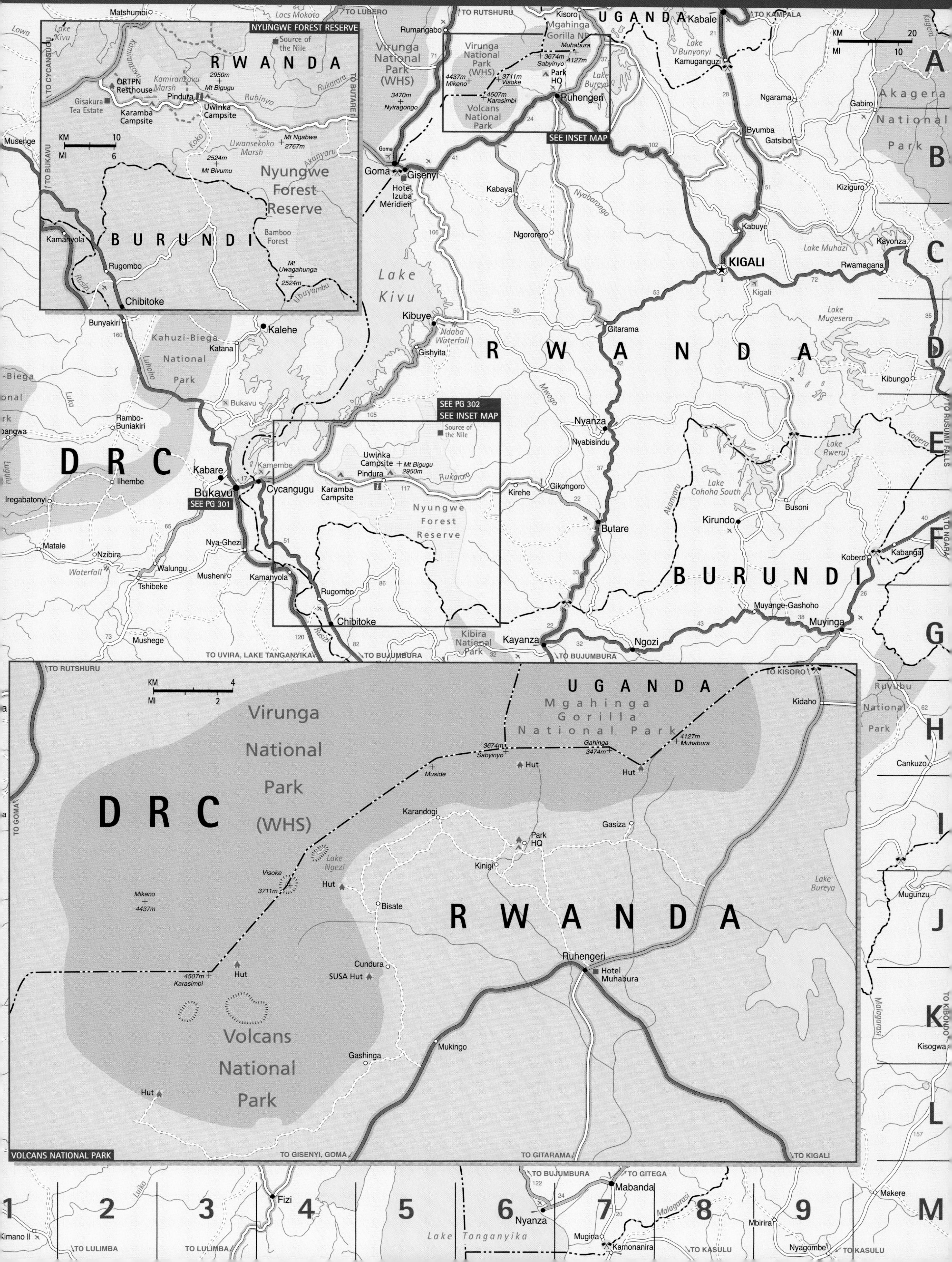
NYUNGWE FOREST RESERVE
RWANDA
BURUNDI
Source of the Nile
Kamiranzovu Marsh
ORTPN Resthouse
Gisakura Tea Estate
Karamba Campsite
Pindura
Uwinka Campsite
Mt Bigugu 2950m
Rubinyo
Rukarara
Uwansekoko Marsh
Mt Ngabwe 2767m
Mt Bivumu 2524m
Nyungwe Forest Reserve
Bamboo Forest
Mt Uwagahunga 2524m
Ubuyombu
Kamanyola
Rugombo
Chibitoke
TO CYANGUGU
TO BUKAVU
TO BUTARE
Matshumbi
Lacs Mokoto
TO LUBERO
TO RUTSHURU
Kisoro
UGANDA
Kabale
TO KAMPALA
Lake Bunyonyi
Kamunganguzi
Mgahinga Gorilla NP
Virunga National Park (WHS)
Volcans National Park
Rumangabo
Nyiragongo 3470m
Goma
Gisenyi
Hotel Izuba Méridien
Ruhengeri
SEE INSET MAP
Ngarama
Byumba
Gatsibo
Gabiro
Akagera National Park
Kiziguro
Kabaya
Nyabarongo
Ngororero
Kabuye
KIGALI
Kigali
Kayonza
Rwamagana
Lake Muhazi
Lake Kivu
Kibuye
Ndaba Waterfall
Gishyita
Gitarama
RWANDA
Lake Mugesera
Kibungo
Mwogo
Nyanza
Nyabisindu
Gikongoro
Kirehe
Butare
Lake Rweru
Lake Cohoha South
Akanyaru
Busoni
Kirundo
Kagera
TO RUSUMU FALLS
BURUNDI
Kobero
Kabanga
TO NGARA
Muyange-Gashoho
Muyinga
Ngozi
Kayanza
Kibira National Park
TO BUJUMBURA
SEE PG 302
Kamembe
Cycangugu
Bukavu
SEE PG 301
Kabare
Ilhembe
Iregabatonyi
DRC
Bunyakiri
Kalehe
Katana
Kahuzi-Biega National Park
Bukavu
Rambo-Buniakiri
Musenge
Matale
Nzibira
Waterfall
Walungu
Tshibeke
Nya-Ghezi
Musheni
Kamanyola
Rugombo
Chibitoke
Mushege
TO UVIRA, LAKE TANGANYIKA
VOLCANS NATIONAL PARK
TO RUTSHURU
TO KISORO
Kidaho
Mgahinga Gorilla National Park
Virunga National Park (WHS)
DRC
Sabyinyo 3674m
Gahinga 3474m
Muhabura 4127m
Muside
Hut
Karandogi
Gasiza
Park HQ
Kinigi
Lake Ngezi
Visoke 3711m
Bisate
Mikeno 4437m
RWANDA
Lake Bureya
Ruhengeri
Hotel Muhabura
Cundura
SUSA Hut
Karasimbi 4507m
Volcans National Park
Mukingo
Gashinga
TO GOMA
TO GISENYI, GOMA
TO GITARAMA
TO KIGALI
Ruvubu National Park
Cankuzo
Mugunzu
Malagarasi
Kisogwa
TO KIBONDO
Fizi
TO BUJUMBURA
TO GITEGA
Mabanda
Nyanza
Lake Tanganyika
Mugina
Kamonanira
Mbirira
Makere
Nyagombe
TO KASULU
TO LULIMBA
Kimano II
KM MI

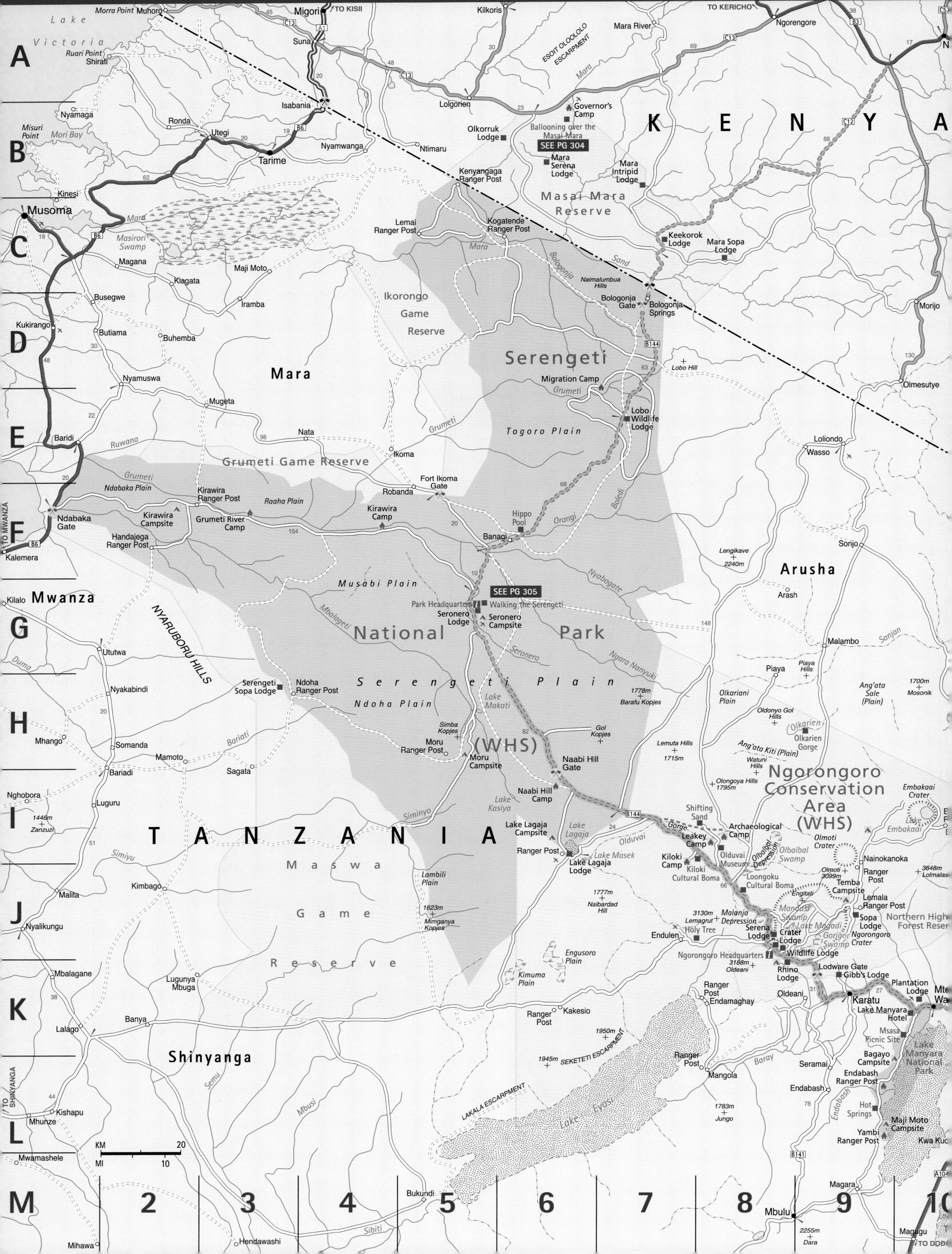
Lake Victoria
Morra Point
Muhoro
Migori
TO KISII
Kilkoris
TO KERICHO
Ngorengore
Mara River
Suna
Ruari Point
Shirati
ESOIT OLOOLOLO ESCARPMENT
Mara
Isabania
Lolgorien
Governor's Camp
Nyamaga
Ronda
Olkorruk Lodge
Ballooning over the Masai Mara
SEE PG 304
Misuri Point
Mori Bay
Utegi
Tarime
Nyamwanga
Ntimaru
Mara Serena Lodge
Mara Intripid Lodge
KENYA
Kinesi
Kenyangaga Ranger Post
Masai Mara Reserve
Musoma
Masirori Swamp
Lemai Ranger Post
Kogatende Ranger Post
Keekorok Lodge
Mara Sopa Lodge
Magana
Maji Moto
Kiagata
Sand
Bologonja
Naimalumbua Hills
Busegwe
Iramba
Ikorongo Game Reserve
Bologonja Gate
Bologonja Springs
Morijo
Kukirango
Butiama
Buhemba
Lobo Hill
Serengeti
Mara
Migration Camp
Grumeti
Olmesutye
Nyamuswa
Mugeta
Lobo Wildlife Lodge
Togoro Plain
Nata
Loliondo
Wasso
Baridi
Ruwana
Ikoma
Grumeti Game Reserve
Ndabaka Plain
Fort Ikoma Gate
Robanda
Kirawira Ranger Post
Raaha Plain
Boledi
TO MWANZA
Ndabaka Gate
Kirawira Campsite
Grumeti River Camp
Kirawira Camp
Hippo Pool
Orangi
Handajega Ranger Post
Banagi
Kalemera
Lengikave 2240m
Sonjo
Arusha
Musabi Plain
Nyabogate
Kilalo
Mwanza
SEE PG 305
Park Headquarters
Walking the Serengeti
Arash
Seronero Lodge
Seronero Campsite
NYARUBORU HILLS
Mbalageti
National
Park
Malambo
Sanjan
Utuwta
Duma
Seronero
Ngara Nanyuki
Piaya
Piaya Hills
Serengeti Sopa Lodge
Ndoha Ranger Post
Serengeti Plain
1778m Barafu Kopjes
Ang'ata Sale (Plain)
1700m Mosonik
Nyakabindi
Ndoha Plain
Lake Makati
Olkariani Plain
Oldonyo Gol Hills
Mhango
Somanda
Bariati
Simba Kopjes
Moru Ranger Post
(WHS)
Gol Kopjes
Olkarien Gorge
Lemuta Hills 1715m
Ang'ata Kiti (Plain)
Mamoto
Sagata
Moru Campsite
Naabi Hill Gate
Watuni Hills
Bariadi
Ngorongoro Conservation Area (WHS)
Olongoya Hills 1795m
Nghobora
Luguru
Naabi Hill Camp
Lake Kasiya
Embakaai Crater
1446m Zanzuzi
Siminyo
Lake Lagaja Campsite
Shifting Sand
Gorge
Archaeological Camp
TANZANIA
Lake Lagaja
Olduvai
Leakey Camp
Olbalbal Depression
Olbalbal Swamp
Olmoti Crater
Lake Embakaai
Simiyu
Maswa Game Reserve
Ranger Post
Lake Masek
Kiloleli Camp
Kiloki Cultural Boma
Olduvai Museum
Lake Lagaja Lodge
Nainokanoka
Lambili Plain
Loongoku Cultural Boma
Olmoti 3099m
Ranger Post
3648m Lolmalasin
Kimbago
Malita
Temba Campsite
1777m Naibardad Hill
Engitati
Lemala Ranger Post
1623m Mimganya Kopjes
3130m Lemagrut
Malanja Depression
Munge Swamp
Sopa Lodge
Northern Highlands Forest Reserve
Nyalikungu
Lake Magadi
Serena Lodge
Crater Lodge
Holy Tree
Endulen
Gorigor Swamp
Ngorongoro Crater
Engusoro Plain
Ngorongoro Headquarters
Wildlife Lodge
Mbalagane
3188m Oldeani
Lodware Gate
Rhino Lodge
Gibb's Lodge
Lugunya Mbuga
Kimumu Plain
Ranger Post
Plantation Lodge
Endamaghay
Oldeani
Karatu
Mto wa Mbu
Lake Manyara Hotel
Kakesio
Banya
Lalago
Ranger Post
Msasa Picnic Site
1950m
SEKETETI ESCARPMENT
1945m
Lake Manyara National Park
Shinyanga
Ranger Post
Baray
Seramai
Bagayo Campsite
Mangola
Endabash Ranger Post
Semu
Endabash
LAKALA ESCARPMENT
Lake Eyasi
Hot Springs
TO SHINYANGA
Kishapu
Mbusi
1783m Jungo
Maji Moto Campsite
Mhunze
Yambi Ranger Post
Kwa Kuchinja
Mwamashele
KM 20
MI 10
Magara
Bukundi
Mbulu
Sibiti
2255m Dara
Mihawa
Hendawashi
Magugu
TO DODOMA
A B C D E F G H I J K L M
2 3 4 5 6 7 8 9 10

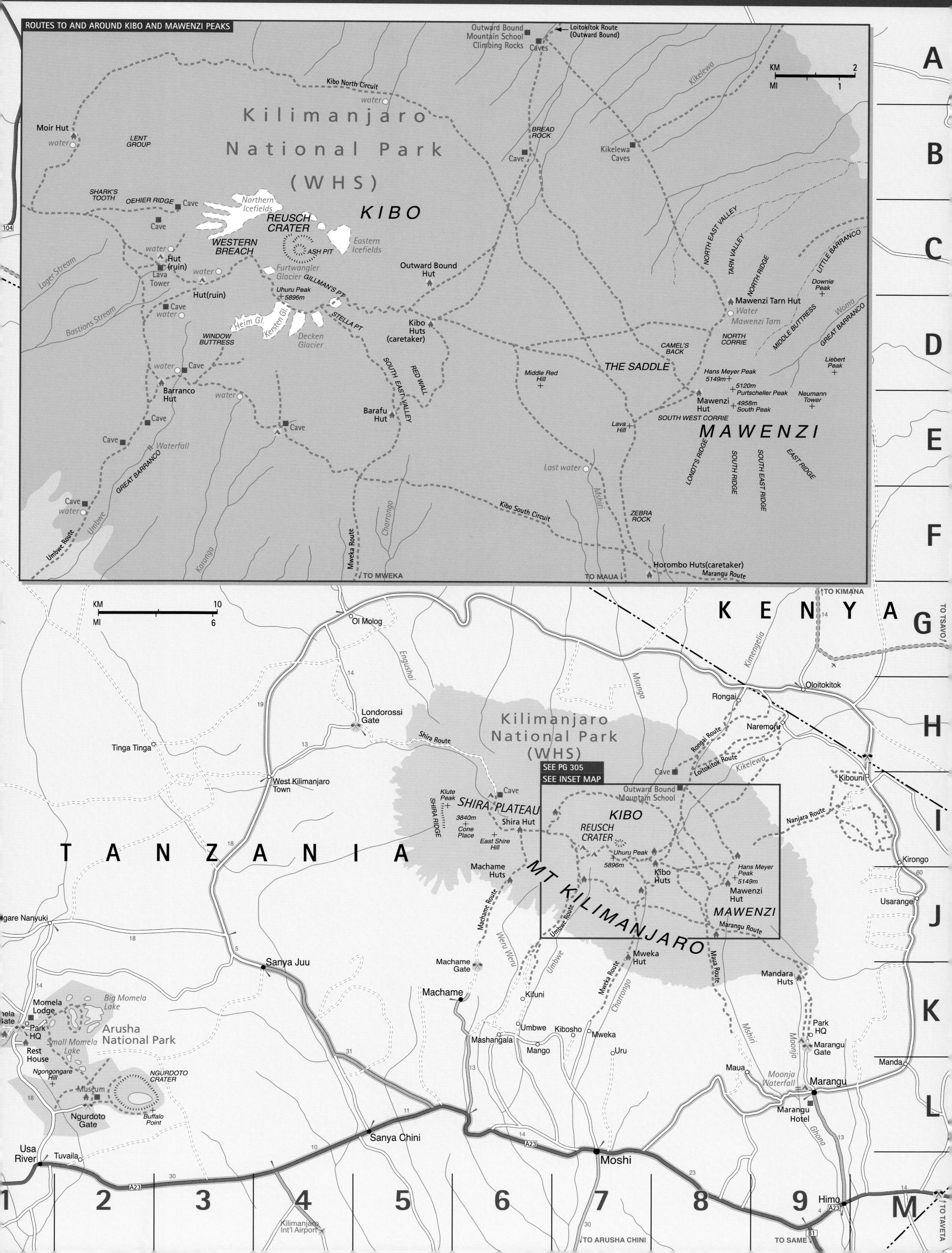
ROUTES TO AND AROUND KIBO AND MAWENZI PEAKS
Kilimanjaro National Park (WHS)
KIBO
REUSCH CRATER
ASH PIT
WESTERN BREACH
Northern Icefields
Eastern Icefields
Furtwangler Glacier
Uhuru Peak 5896m
GILLMAN'S PT
STELLA PT
Heim Gl.
Kersten Gl.
Decken Glacier
Kibo North Circuit
Kibo South Circuit
Outward Bound Mountain School Climbing Rocks
Caves
Loitokitok Route (Outward Bound)
Moir Hut
water
LENT GROUP
SHARK'S TOOTH
OEHIER RIDGE
Cave
Hut (ruin)
Lava Tower
Hut(ruin)
Lager Stream
Bastions Stream
WINDOW BUTTRESS
Barranco Hut
Waterfall
GREAT BARRANCO
Umbwe Route
Umbwe
Karanga
Mweka Route
TO MWEKA
Charrongo
Outward Bound Hut
Kibo Huts (caretaker)
SOUTH EAST VALLEY
RED WALL
Barafu Hut
BREAD ROCK
Kikelewa Caves
Kikelewa
Middle Red Hill
THE SADDLE
CAMEL'S BACK
Lava Hill
Last water
Mshiri
TO MAUA
ZEBRA ROCK
Horombo Huts(caretaker)
Marangu Route
NORTH EAST VALLEY
TARN VALLEY
NORTH RIDGE
LITTLE BARRANCO
Downie Peak
Mawenzi Tarn Hut
Water
Mawenzi Tarn
NORTH CORRIE
MIDDLE BUTTRESS
Woma
GREAT BARRANCO
Liebert Peak
Hans Meyer Peak 5149m
5120m Purtscheller Peak
4958m South Peak
Neumann Tower
Mawenzi Hut
SOUTH WEST CORRIE
MAWENZI
LONDT'S RIDGE
SOUTH RIDGE
SOUTH EAST RIDGE
EAST RIDGE
KM 2
MI 1
A B C D E F G H I J K L M
1 2 3 4 5 6 7 8 9
KM 10
MI 6
KENYA
TANZANIA
TO KIMANA
TO TSAVO
Ol Molog
Engushai
Londorossi Gate
Shira Route
Tinga Tinga
West Kilimanjaro Town
Kilimanjaro National Park (WHS)
SEE PG 305
SEE INSET MAP
Cave
Klute Peak
SHIRA PLATEAU
SHIRA RIDGE
3840m Cone Place
East Shire Hill
Shira Hut
Machame Huts
Machame Route
MT KILIMANJARO
Outward Bound Mountain School
KIBO
REUSCH CRATER
Uhuru Peak 5896m
Kibo Huts
Hans Meyer Peak 5149m
Mawenzi Hut
MAWENZI
Marangu Route
Umbwe Route
Msanga
Kimengelia
Rongai
Rongai Route
Loitokitok Route
Kikelewa
Oloitokitok
Naremoru
Kibouni
Nanjara Route
Kirongo
Usarange
Weru Weru
Umbwe
Mweka Hut
Mweka Route
Charrongo
Maua Route
Mandara Huts
Machame Gate
Machame
Kifuni
Umbwe
Kibosho
Mweka
Mashangala
Mango
Uru
Mshiri
Moonja
Park HQ
Marangu Gate
Maua
Moonja Waterfall
Marangu
Marangu Hotel
Manda
Ghona
Sanya Juu
Sanya Chini
Moshi
Himo
TO TAVETA
TO SAME
TO ARUSHA CHINI
Kilimanjaro Int'l Airport
Usa River
Tuvaila
Ngare Nanyuki
Momela Lodge
Big Momela Lake
Park HQ
Rest House
Small Momela Lake
Arusha National Park
Ngongongare Hill
Museum
NGURDOTO CRATER
Buffalo Point
Ngurdoto Gate
A23
B1

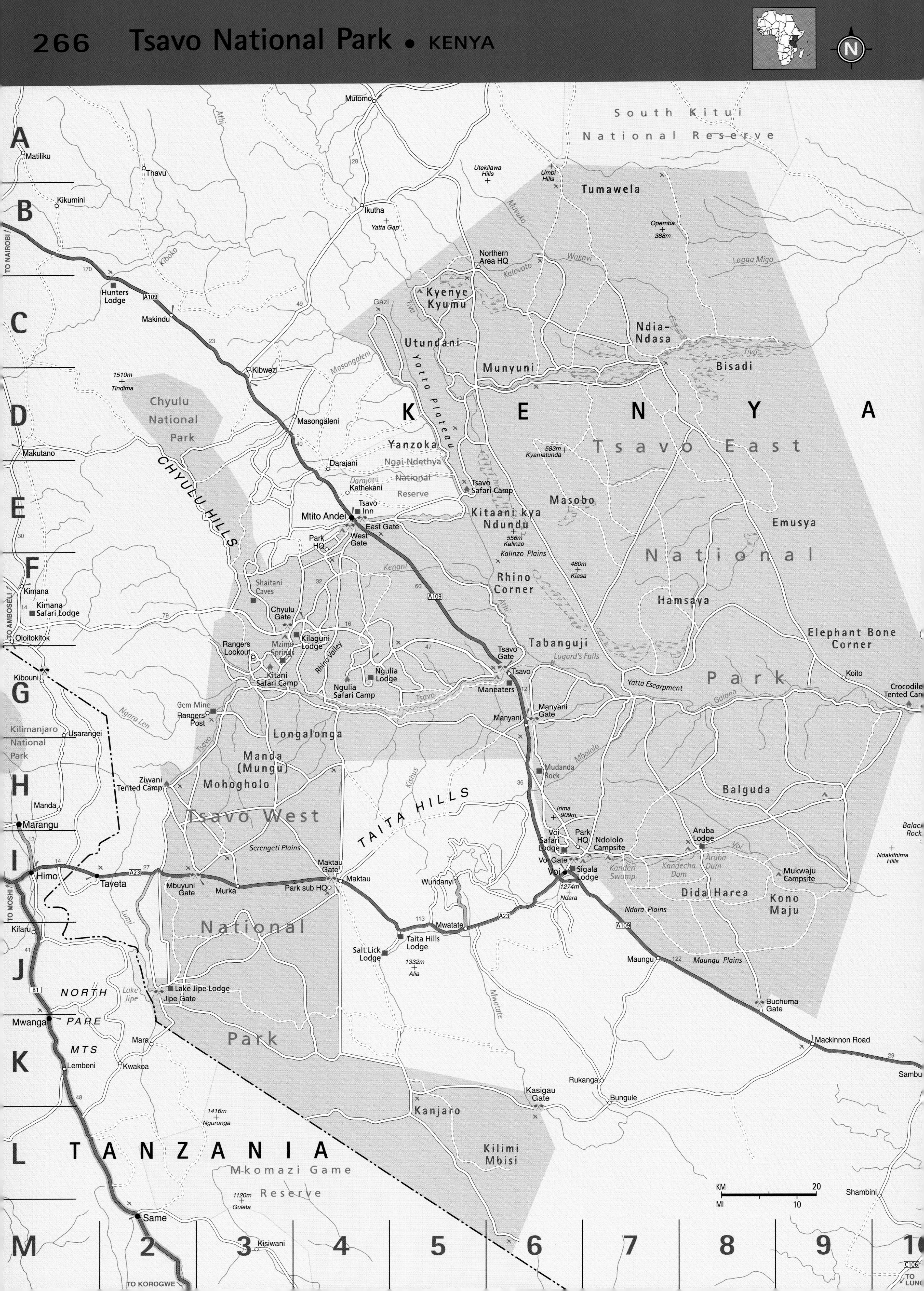

South Kitui
National Reserve
Mutomo
Matiliku
Thavu
Kikumini
Utekilawa Hills
Umbi Hills
Tumawela
Ikutha
Yatta Gap
Opemba
388m
Muvuko
TO NAIROBI
170
Hunters Lodge
A109
Makindu
Kiboko
Northern Area HQ
Kalovoto
Wakavi
Lagga Migo
Kyenye Kyumu
Gazi
Tiva
49
Ndia-Ndasa
Utundani
Yatta Plateau
Bisadi
Munyuni
23
Kibwezi
Masongaleni
1510m
Tindima
Chyulu National Park
K E N Y A
Masongaleni
Makutano
CHYULU HILLS
Yanzoka
Ngai-Ndethya National Reserve
583m
Kyamatunda
Tsavo East National Park
40
Darajani
Kathekani
Tsavo Safari Camp
Masobo
Tsavo Inn
Mtito Andei
East Gate
West Gate
Kitaani kya Ndundu
556m
Kalinzo
Kalinzo Plains
Emusya
30
Park HQ
Kenani
480m
Kiasa
Kimana
Kimana Safari Lodge
TO AMBOSELI
Oloitokitok
Shaitani Caves
32
60
A109
Rhino Corner
Hamsaya
Athi
79
Chyulu Gate
16
Mzima Springs
Kilaguni Lodge
Rangers Lookout
Rhino Valley
47
Tabanguji
Lugard's Falls
Elephant Bone Corner
Kibouni
Kitani Safari Camp
Ngulia Lodge
Ngulia Safari Camp
Tsavo Gate
Tsavo
Maneaters
Yatta Escarpment
Galana
Koito
Crocodile Tented Camp
Gem Mine Rangers Post
Ngara Len
Manyani Gate
Manyani
Kilimanjaro National Park
Usarangei
Longalonga
Manda (Mungu)
Mboiolo
Mudanda Rock
Ziwani Tented Camp
Mohogholo
36
Balguda
Manda
Marangu
Tsavo West National Park
TAITA HILLS
Irima
909m
Kishus
Serengeti Plains
Voi Safari Lodge
Park HQ
Ndololo Campsite
Aruba Lodge
Balach Rock
Ndakithima Hills
Voi Gate
Voi
Sigala Lodge
Kanderi Swamp
Kandecha Dam
Aruba Dam
Mukwaju Campsite
Himo
Taveta
A23
Maktau Gate
Maktau
Park sub HQ
Mbuyuni Gate
Murka
Wundanyi
1274m
Ndara
Dida Harea
Kono Maju
Ndara Plains
TO MOSHI
Lumi
113
Mwatate
A23
A109
Kifaru
Taita Hills Lodge
Salt Lick Lodge
Maungu
122
Maungu Plains
1332m
Alia
B1
NORTH PARE MTS
Lake Jipe
Lake Jipe Lodge
Jipe Gate
Mwanga
Mwatate
Buchuma Gate
Mara
Mackinnon Road
Lembeni
Kwakoa
29
Sambu
Rukanga
Kasigau Gate
Bungule
Kanjaro
48
1416m
Ngurunga
TANZANIA
Mkomazi Game Reserve
Kilimi Mbisi
1120m
Guleta
KM 20
MI 10
Shambini
Same
Kisiwani
TO KOROGWE
C106
TO LUNGA
A B C D E F G H I J K L M
2 3 4 5 6 7 8 9 10
N

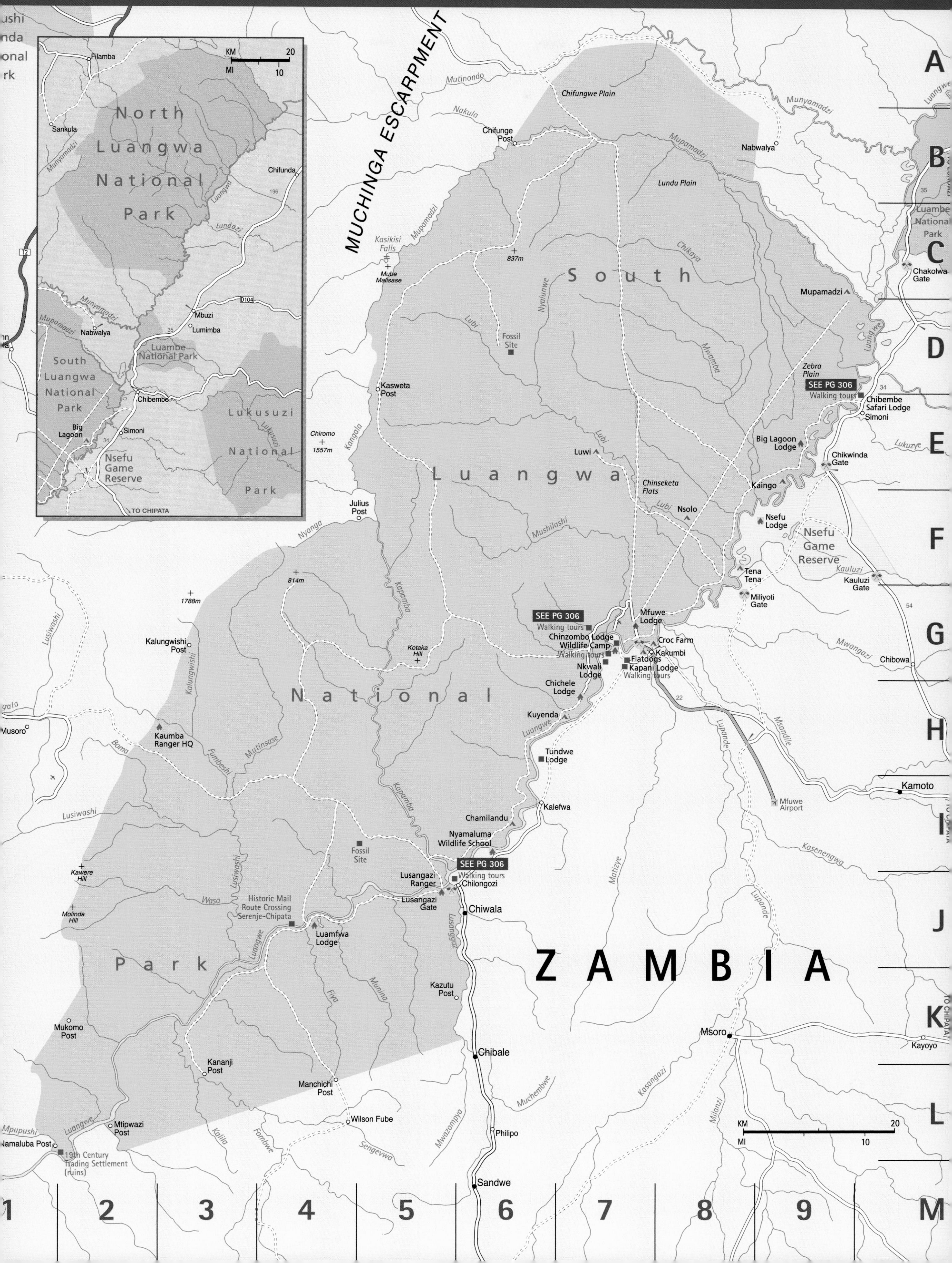
North Luangwa National Park
Filamba
Sankula
Munyamadzi
Chifunda
Lundazi
Luangwa
Mupamadzi
Nabwalya
Mbuzi
Lumimba
Luambe National Park
South Luangwa National Park
Chibembe
Big Lagoon
Simoni
Nsefu Game Reserve
Lukusuzi National Park
TO CHIPATA
KM 20
MI 10
MUCHINGA ESCARPMENT
Mutinondo
Nakula
Chifunge Post
Chifungwe Plain
Munyamadzi
Nabwalya
Lundu Plain
Kasikisi Falls
Mube Malisase
837m
South Luangwa National Park
Chikaya
Mupamadzi
Nyalunwe
Lubi
Fossil Site
Mwamba
Zebra Plain
SEE PG 306
Walking tours
Chibembe Safari Lodge
Simoni
Chakolwa Gate
Luambe National Park
Kasweta Post
Chiromo
1557m
Kangalo
Luwi
Big Lagoon Lodge
Chikwinda Gate
Lukuzye
Chinseketa Flats
Kaingo
Nsolo
Julius Post
Nyanga
Mushilashi
Nsefu Lodge
Nsefu Game Reserve
Tena Tena
Kauluzi
Kauluzi Gate
Miliyoti Gate
814m
1788m
Kapamba
Mfuwe Lodge
Chinzombo Lodge
Wildlife Camp
Croc Farm
Kakumbi
Flatdogs
Kapani Lodge
Nkwali Lodge
Kotaka Hill
Kalungwishi Post
Kalungwishi
Lusiwashi
Chichele Lodge
Kuyenda
Mwangazi
Chibowa
Musoro
Kaumba Ranger HQ
Boma
Fumbeshi
Mutinsase
Tundwe Lodge
Lupande
Msandile
Mfuwe Airport
Kamoto
Kalefwa
Chamilandu
Nyamaluma Wildlife School
Kasenengwa
Fossil Site
Lusangazi Ranger
Chilongozi
Lusangazi Gate
Chiwala
Kawere Hill
Molinda Hill
Wasa
Historic Mail Route Crossing Serenje-Chipata
Luamfwa Lodge
Lusangazi
Matizye
ZAMBIA
Fiya
Munima
Kazutu Post
Mukomo Post
Msoro
Kayoyo
Chibale
Kananji Post
Manchichi Post
Muchembwe
Kasangazi
Wilson Fube
Mwazampya
Philipo
Milanzi
Mtipwazi Post
Mpupushi
Namaluba Post
19th Century Trading Settlement (ruins)
Katila
Fombwe
Sengewwa
Sandwe
KM 20
MI 10
A B C D E F G H I J K L M
1 2 3 4 5 6 7 8 9

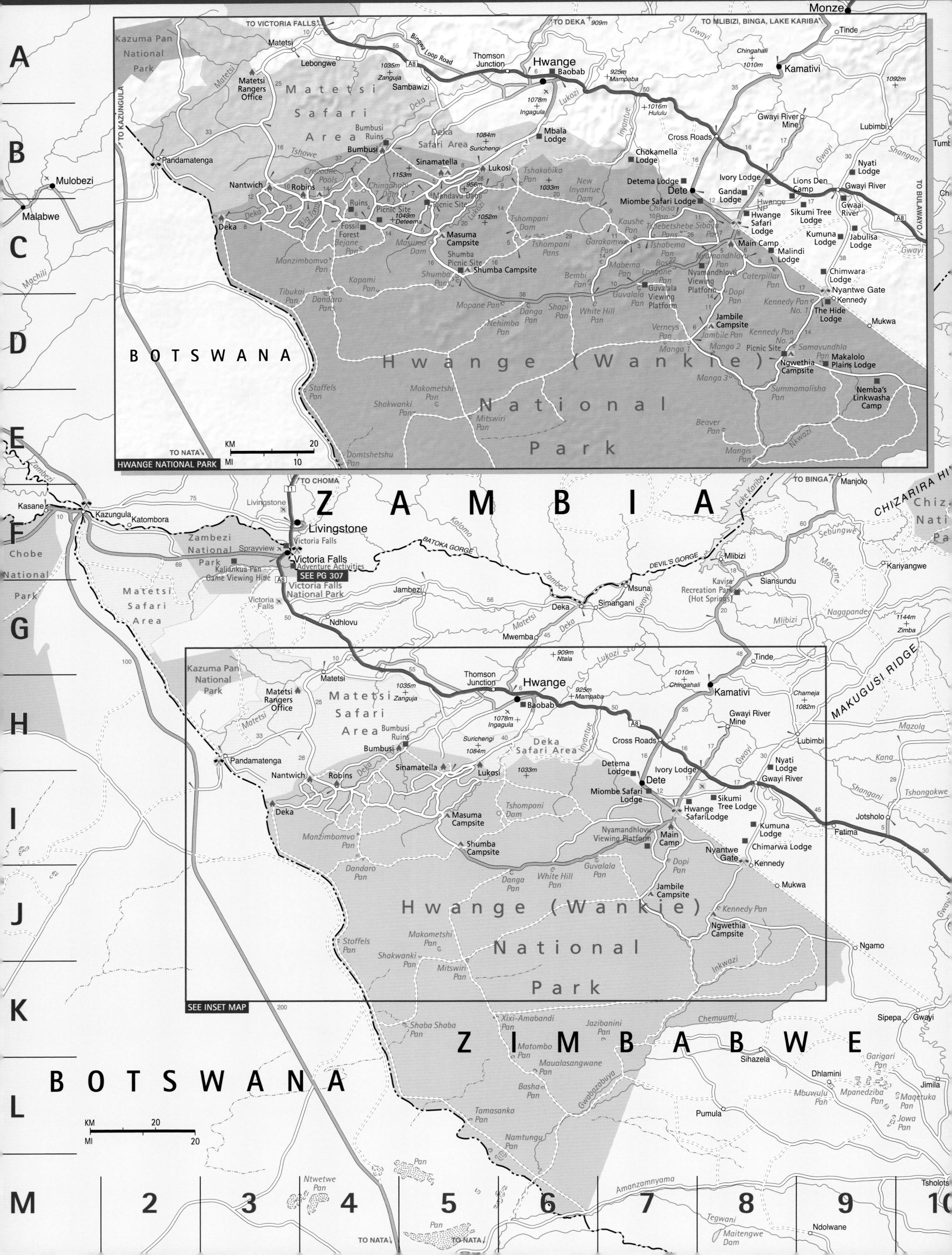

HWANGE NATIONAL PARK
TO VICTORIA FALLS
TO DEKA
TO MLIBIZI, BINGA, LAKE KARIBA
TO KAZUNGULA
TO BULAWAYO
TO NATA
TO CHOMA
TO BINGA
Kazuma Pan National Park
Matetsi
Lebongwe
Matetsi Rangers Office
Matetsi Safari Area
Sambawizi
Thomson Junction
Hwange
Baobab
Kamativi
Tinde
Monze
Pandamatenga
Mulobezi
Malabwe
Nantwich
Robins
Bumbusi Ruins
Bumbusi
Deka Safari Area
Mbala Lodge
Sinamatella
Lukosi
Mandavu Dam
Masuma Campsite
Shumba Campsite
Cross Roads
Chokamella Lodge
Detema Lodge
Dete
Miombe Safari Lodge
Ivory Lodge
Ganda Lodge
Lions Den Camp
Gwayi River
Gwaai River
Sikumi Tree Lodge
Hwange Safari Lodge
Main Camp
Kumuna Lodge
Jabulisa Lodge
Malindi Lodge
Chimwara Lodge
Nyantwe Gate
Kennedy
The Hide Lodge
Mukwa
Jambile Campsite
Ngwethia Campsite
Makalolo Plains Lodge
Nemba's Linkwasha Camp
Gwayi River Mine
Lubimbi
Nyati Lodge
Hwange (Wankie) National Park
BOTSWANA
ZAMBIA
ZIMBABWE
Livingstone
Victoria Falls
SEE PG 307
Victoria Falls National Park
Zambezi National Park
Chobe National Park
Kasane
Kazungula
Katombora
Jambezi
Ndhlovu
Deka
Simangani
Msuna
Mwemba
Mlibizi
Siansundu
Kavira Recreation Park (Hot Springs)
Kariyangwe
Manjolo
CHIZARIRA HILLS
MAKUGUSI RIDGE
Fatima
Jotsholo
Ngamo
Sipepa
Gwayi
Sihazela
Dhlamini
Jimila
Pumula
Ndolwane
Tsholotsho
SEE INSET MAP
KM 20
MI 10
KM 20
MI 20
A
B
C
D
E
F
G
H
I
J
K
L
M
2
3
4
5
6
7
8
9
10

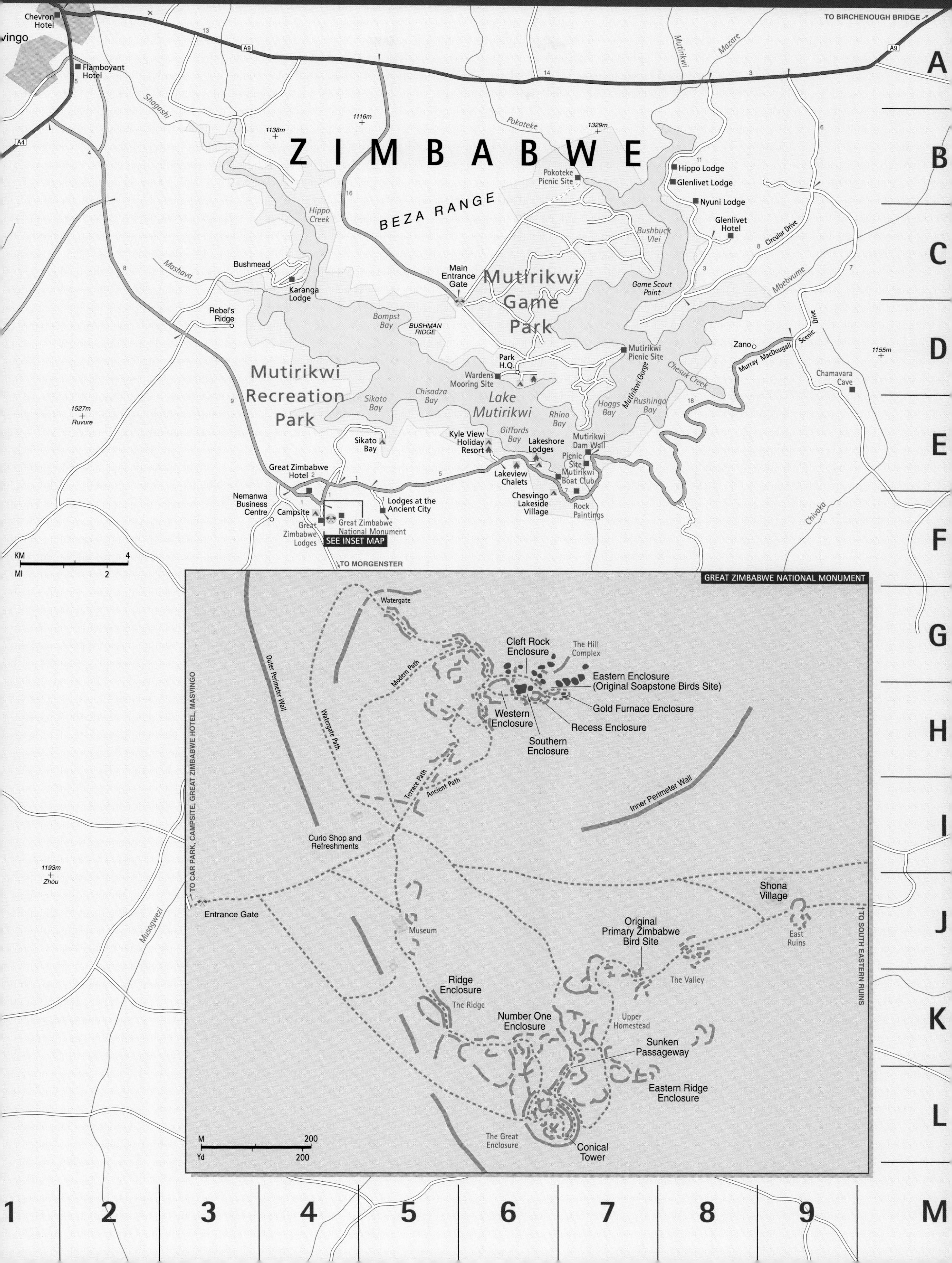

ZIMBABWE
TO BIRCHENOUGH BRIDGE
Chevron Hotel
Flamboyant Hotel
BEZA RANGE
Mutirikwi Game Park
Mutirikwi Recreation Park
Lake Mutirikwi
Hippo Lodge
Glenlivet Lodge
Nyuni Lodge
Glenlivet Hotel
Pokoteke Picnic Site
Bushmead
Karanga Lodge
Rebel's Ridge
Main Entrance Gate
Game Scout Point
Bushbuck Vlei
Hippo Creek
Bompst Bay
BUSHMAN RIDGE
Park H.Q.
Wardens Mooring Site
Mutirikwi Picnic Site
Zano
Murray MacDougall Scenic Drive
Circular Drive
Chamavara Cave
Chesuk Creek
Mutirikwi Gorge
Hoggs Bay
Rushinga Bay
Rhino Bay
Giffords Bay
Chisadza Bay
Sikato Bay
Kyle View Holiday Resort
Lakeshore Lodges
Mutirikwi Dam Wall
Picnic Site
Mutirikwi Boat Club
Lakeview Chalets
Chesvingo Lakeside Village
Rock Paintings
Great Zimbabwe Hotel
Nemanwa Business Centre
Campsite
Great Zimbabwe Lodges
Great Zimbabwe National Monument
SEE INSET MAP
Lodges at the Ancient City
TO MORGENSTER
1527m Ruvure
1193m Zhou
1155m
1138m
1116m
1329m
GREAT ZIMBABWE NATIONAL MONUMENT
Watergate
Cleft Rock Enclosure
The Hill Complex
Eastern Enclosure (Original Soapstone Birds Site)
Gold Furnace Enclosure
Recess Enclosure
Western Enclosure
Southern Enclosure
Outer Perimeter Wall
Watergate Path
Modern Path
Terrace Path
Ancient Path
Inner Perimeter Wall
Curio Shop and Refreshments
TO CAR PARK, CAMPSITE, GREAT ZIMBABWE HOTEL, MASVINGO
Entrance Gate
Museum
Shona Village
East Ruins
TO SOUTH EASTERN RUINS
Original Primary Zimbabwe Bird Site
The Valley
Ridge Enclosure
The Ridge
Number One Enclosure
Upper Homestead
Sunken Passageway
Eastern Ridge Enclosure
The Great Enclosure
Conical Tower

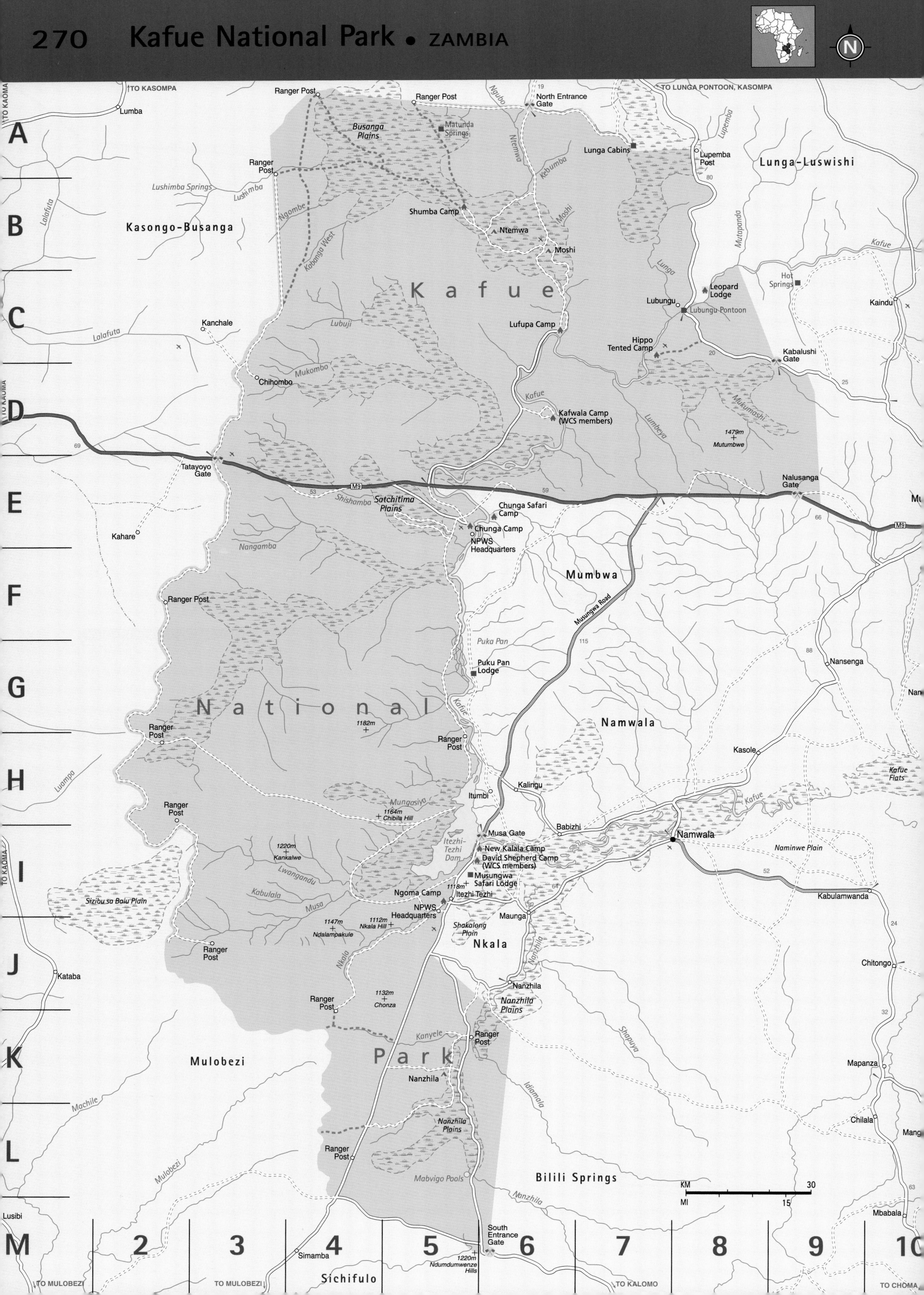

TO KASOMPA
TO KAOMA
Lumba
Ranger Post
Ranger Post
North Entrance Gate
TO LUNGA PONTOON, KASOMPA
Busanga Plains
Matunda Springs
Ngoba
Ntemwa
Lupemba
Lunga Cabins
Lupemba Post
Lunga-Luswishi
Ranger Post
Lushimba Springs
Lushimba
Kebumba
Lalafuta
Ngombe
Shumba Camp
Moshi
Kasongo-Busanga
Ntemwa
Moshi
Mutapanda
Kabanga West
Lunga
Kafue
Kafue
Hot Springs
Leopard Lodge
Lubungu
Lubungu Pontoon
Kaindu
Kanchale
Lubuji
Lufupa Camp
Lalafuta
Hippo Tented Camp
Kabalushi Gate
Mukombo
Chihombo
Kafue
Mukumashi
Kafwala Camp (WCS members)
Lumbeya
1479m Mutumbwe
Tatayoyo Gate
M9
Shishamba
Satchitima Plains
Nalusanga Gate
Chunga Safari Camp
Chunga Camp
NPWS Headquarters
Kahare
Nangamba
Mumbwa
Ranger Post
Musungwa Road
Puku Pan
Nansenga
Puku Pan Lodge
National
Kafue
1182m
Namwala
Ranger Post
Ranger Post
Kasole
Luampa
Kafue Flats
Kalingu
Itumbi
Mungasiya
Ranger Post
1164m Chibila Hill
Babizhi
Kafue
Musa Gate
Namwala
Itezhi-Tezhi Dam
New Kalala Camp
David Shepherd Camp (WCS members)
Naminwe Plain
1220m Kankalwe
Lwangandu
Musungwa Safari Lodge
TO KAOMA
Kabulala
Sizibu sa Balu Plain
Ngoma Camp
1118m Itezhi Tezhi
Kabulamwanda
Musa
NPWS Headquarters
1147m Ndalampakule
1112m Nkala Hill
Maunga
Shakalong Plain
Nkala
Ranger Post
Nkala
Nanzhila
Kataba
Chitongo
Nanzhila
Ranger Post
1132m Chonza
Nanzhila Plains
Kanyele
Ranger Post
Shapuya
Mulobezi
Park
Mapanza
Nanzhila
Idiamala
Machile
Chilala
Nanzhila Plains
Ranger Post
Mabvigo Pools
Bilili Springs
Mulobezi
KM 30
MI 15
Nanzhila
Lusibi
Mbabala
South Entrance Gate
Simamba
1220m Ndumdumwenze Hills
Sichifulo
TO MULOBEZI
TO MULOBEZI
TO KALOMO
TO CHOMA
A
B
C
D
E
F
G
H
I
J
K
L
M
2
3
4
5
6
7
8
9
10

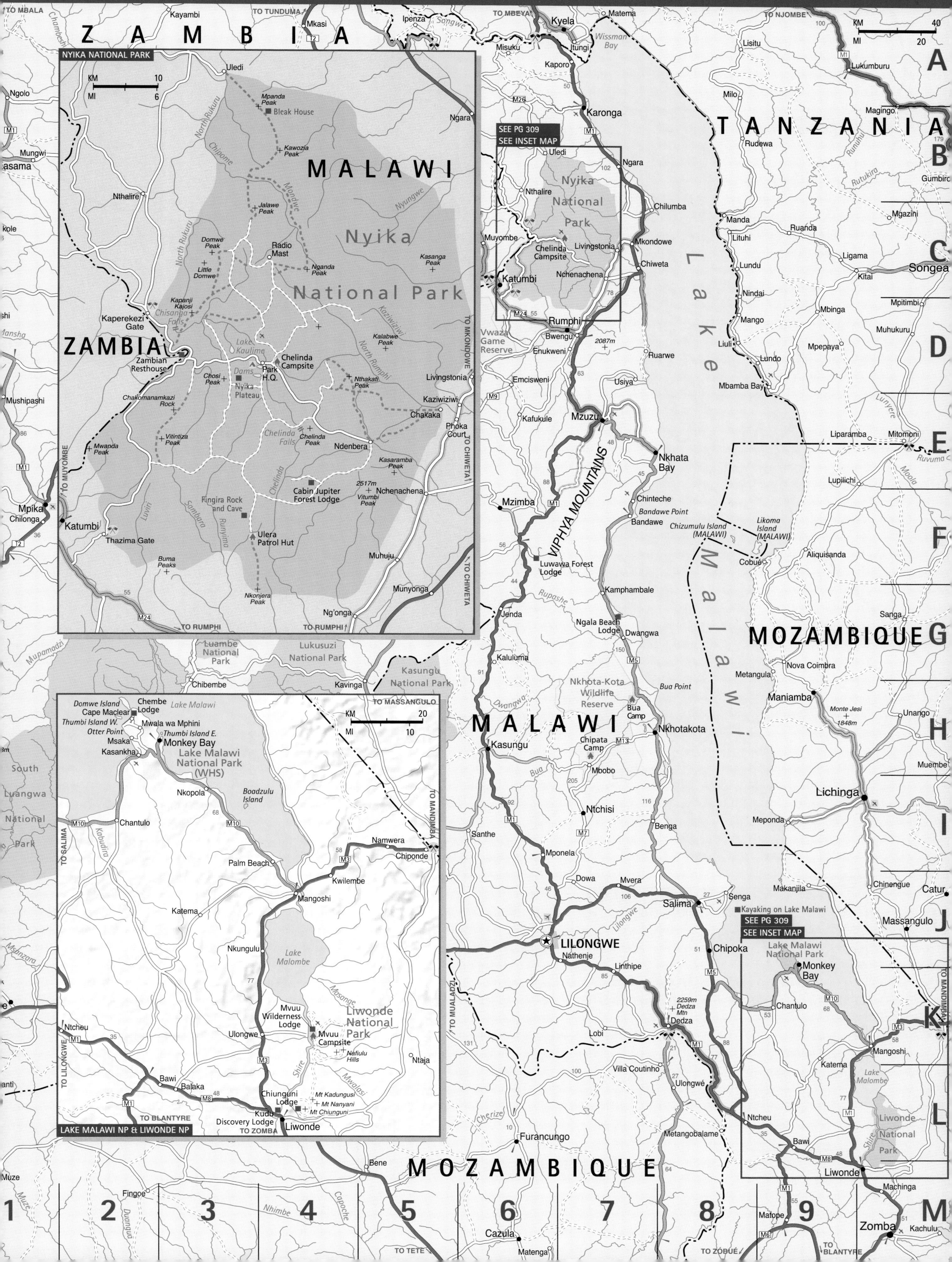
ZAMBIA
TANZANIA
MOZAMBIQUE
MALAWI
Lake Malawi
NYIKA NATIONAL PARK
Nyika National Park
Uledi
Mpanda Peak
Bleak House
Kawozia Peak
Ngara
Nthalire
Jalawe Peak
Domwe Peak
Little Domwe
Radio Mast
Nganda Peak
Kasanga Peak
Kapanji Kajosi
Chisanga Falls
Kaperekezi Gate
Zambian Resthouse
Lake Kaulime
Chelinda Campsite
Park H.Q.
Chosi Peak
Dams
Nyika Plateau
Kalabwe Peak
Nthakati Peak
Livingstonia
Kaziwiziwi
Chakaka
Phoka Court
Chakomanamkazi Rock
Vitintiza Peak
Mwanda Peak
Chelinda Falls
Chelinda Peak
Ndenbera
Kasaramba Peak
Cabin Jupiter Forest Lodge
2517m
Nchenachena
Vitumbi Peak
Fingira Rock and Cave
Ulera Patrol Hut
Katumbi
Thazima Gate
Buma Peaks
Nkonjera Peak
Muhuju
Munyonga
Ng'onga
TO RUMPHI
TO MUYOMBE
TO MKONDOWE
TO CHIWETA
SEE PG 309
SEE INSET MAP
LAKE MALAWI NP & LIWONDE NP
Domwe Island
Chembe Lodge
Cape Maclear
Thumbi Island W.
Mwala wa Mphini
Otter Point
Thumbi Island E.
Msaka
Monkey Bay
Kasankha
Lake Malawi National Park (WHS)
Nkopola
Boadzulu Island
Chantulo
Palm Beach
Namwera
Chiponde
Kwilembe
Mangoshi
Katema
Nkungulu
Lake Malombe
Mvuu Wilderness Lodge
Mvuu Campsite
Liwonde National Park
Nafulu Hills
Ntaja
Ncheu
Ulongwe
Bawi
Balaka
Chiunguni Lodge
Mt Kadungusi
Mt Nanyani
Mt Chiunguni
Kudu Discovery Lodge
Liwonde
TO MASSANGULO
TO MANDIMBA
TO SALIMA
TO LILONGWE
TO BLANTYRE
TO ZOMBA
Kayambi
Mkasi
Ipenza
Kyela
Matema
Wissman Bay
Misuku
Itungi
Kaporo
Karonga
Lisitu
Lukumburu
Milo
Magingo
Rudewa
Ngara
Chilumba
Manda
Ruanda
Mgazini
Lituhi
Ligama
Songea
Kitai
Lundu
Nindai
Mbinga
Mpitimbi
Mango
Muhukuru
Liuli
Mpepaya
Lundo
Mbamba Bay
Muyombe
Mkondowe
Chiweta
Rumphi
Bwengu
Enukweni
Vwaza Game Reserve
2087m
Ruarwe
Usiya
Emcisweni
Kafukule
Mzuzu
Nkhata Bay
VIPHYA MOUNTAINS
Chinteche
Bandawe Point
Bandawe
Chizumulu Island (MALAWI)
Likoma Island (MALAWI)
Cobué
Aliquisanda
Liparamba
Mitomoni
Lupilichi
Mzimba
Luwawa Forest Lodge
Kamphambale
Jenda
Ngala Beach Lodge
Dwangwa
Kaluluma
Nkhota-Kota Wildlife Reserve
Bua Camp
Bua Point
Nkhotakota
Kasungu
Chipata Camp
Mbobo
Ntchisi
Benga
Santhe
Mponela
Dowa
Mvera
Salima
Senga
LILONGWE
Nathenje
Linthipe
Chipoka
2259m Dedza Mtn
Dedza
Lobi
Villa Coutinho
Ulongwé
Ncheu
Metangobalame
Furancungo
Bene
Fingoe
Cazula
Matenga
Luambe National Park
Lukusuzi National Park
Kasungu National Park
Chibembe
Kavinga
South Luangwa National Park
Mpika
Chilonga
Katumbi
Mushipashi
Mungwi
Ngolo
Sanga
Nova Coimbra
Metangula
Maniamba
Monte Jesi 1848m
Unango
Muembe
Lichinga
Meponda
Makanjila
Chinengue
Catur
Massangulo
Kayaking on Lake Malawi
Lake Malawi National Park
Machinga
Zomba
Kachulu
Matope
TO TETE
TO ZÓBUÈ
TO BLANTYRE
TO MBALA
TO TUNDUMA
TO MBEYA
TO NJOMBE
TO MUALADZI
TO MANDIMBA
KM 40
MI 20

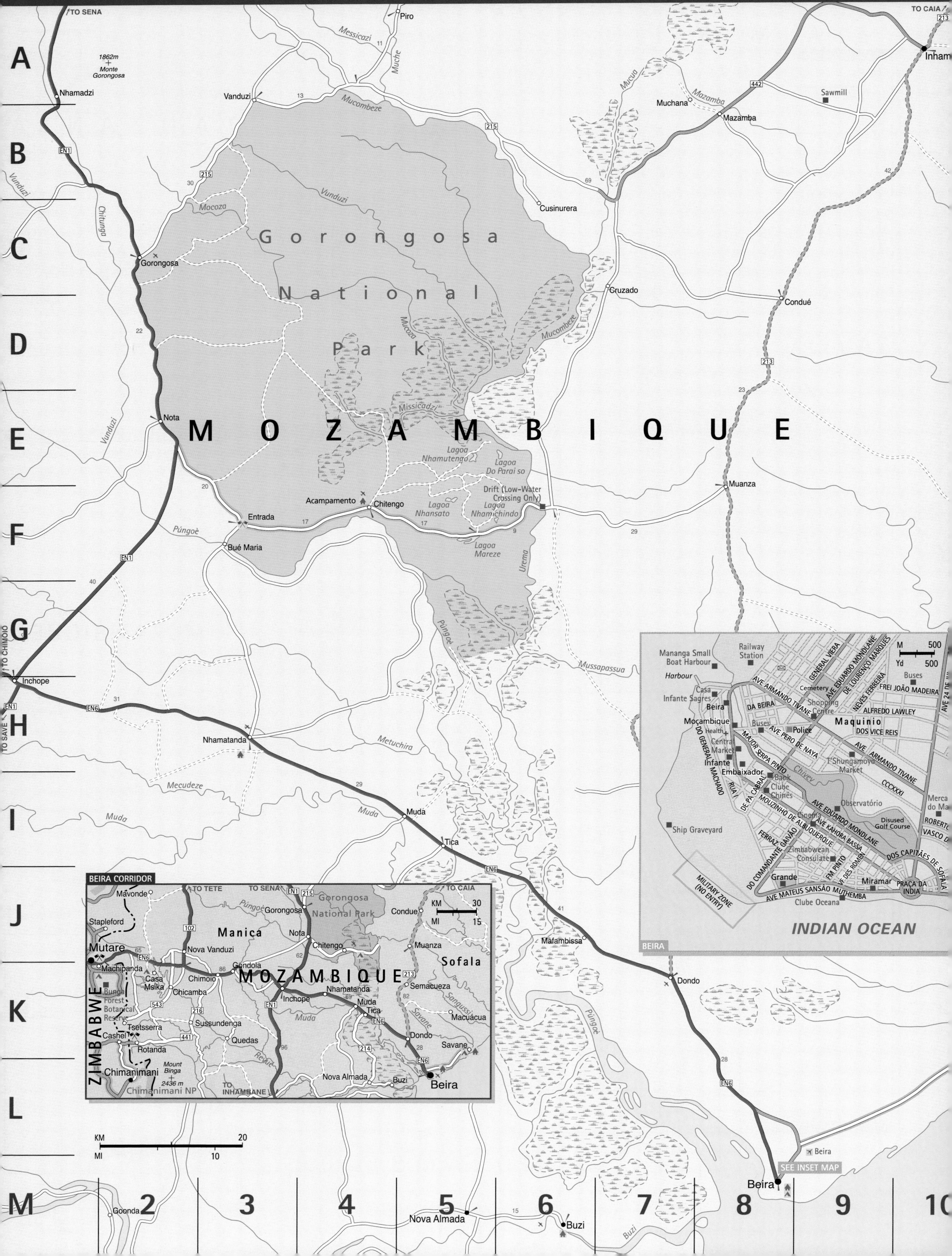
TO SENA
Piro
TO CAIA
Inhamb
1862m
Monte
Gorongosa
Nhamadzi
Messicazi
Muche
Vanduzi
Mucombeze
Mucua
Mazamba
Muchana
Mazamba
Sawmill
442
215
215
EN1
Vunduzi
Chitunga
Vunduzi
Mocoza
Cusinurera
Gorongosa
Gorongosa
National
Park
Cruzado
Condué
Mucombeze
Mucoza
213
Missicadzi
Nota
MOZAMBIQUE
Lagoa
Nhamutengo
Lagoa
Do Paraí so
Drift (Low-Water
Crossing Only)
Acampamento
Chitengo
Lagoa
Nhansato
Lagoa
Nhamichindo
Muanza
Entrada
Púngoè
Bué Maria
Lagoa
Mareze
Urema
Púngoè
Mussapassua
TO CHIMOIO
Inchope
TO SAVE
EN6
Nhamatanda
Metuchira
Mecudeze
Muda
Muda
Muda
Tica
EN6
Mafambissa
Dondo
Púngoè
EN6
Beira
SEE INSET MAP
Beira
Goonda
Nova Almada
Buzi
Buzi
KM 20
MI 10
A
B
C
D
E
F
G
H
I
J
K
L
M
2
3
4
5
6
7
8
9
10
BEIRA CORRIDOR
Mavonde
TO TETE
TO SENA
TO CAIA
Gorongosa
National Park
Púngoè
Gorongosa
Condue
KM 30
MI 15
Stapleford
Manica
Nota
Mutare
Nova Vanduzi
Chitengo
Muanza
Sofala
Machipanda
Gondola
Chimoio
MOZAMBIQUE
Casa
Msika
Chicamba
Nhamatanda
Semacueza
Sanguss
ZIMBABWE
Bunga
Forest
Botanical
Reserve
Inchope
Muda
Tica
Muda
Macuácua
Savane
Tsetsserra
Sussundenga
Dondo
Cashel
Quedas
Savane
Rotanda
Revué
Chimanimani
Mount
Binga
2436 m
Chimanimani NP
TO
INHAMBANE
Nova Almada
Buzi
Beira
Mananga Small
Boat Harbour
Railway
Station
M 500
Yd 500
Harbour
Casa
Infante Sagres
Beira
Moçambique
Health
Central
Market
Infante
Embaixador
Ship Graveyard
Buses
Police
Maquinio
Cemetery
Shopping
Centre
Buses
ALFREDO LAWLEY
DOS VICE REIS
FREI JOÃO MADEIRA
T'Shungamoyo
Market
Bank
Clube
Chinês
Observatório
Disused
Golf Course
Cinema
Zimbabwean
Consulate
Grande
Miramar
PRAÇA DA
INDIA
Clube Oceana
MILITARY ZONE
(NO ENTRY)
INDIAN OCEAN
BEIRA

INDIAN OCEAN
Beau Vallon Bay
VICTORIA
Pascal Village
Morne Seychellois National Park
Saint Anne Marine National Park
SAINT ANNE MARINE NP
Saint Anne
Cerf Island
Long Island
Round Island
Moyenne
Beacon Island
Saint Anne Channel
Cerf Passage
Vista do Mar
La Gogue
North Point
North East Point
Anse Nord-d'Est
Carana Beach
Machabée
Glacis
Le Niol
Bel Ombre
Danzil
Anse Jasmin Estate
Cap Ternay Estate
Cap Ternay
Baie Ternaie Marine National Park
Port Launay
Port Launay Marine National Park
La Passe Ternay
Conception
Thérèse Island
Port Glaud
La Plaine
Dugand
Mont d'Or
Mission
La Misere
Grande 'Anse
La Beolière
Barbarons
Anse Cimitière
Ile aux Vaches
Les Trios Dames
Quincy Village
Mare Anglaise
Union Vale
Pointe Conan
Sans Souci
Forbet Noire
Salazie
Brilliant
Les Mamelles
Fairview
Old Satellite Tracking System
Hermitage
New Port
Inner Harbour
SEE PG 310
SEE INSET MAP
Ferry to Praslin, La Digue
TO AIRPORT
MAHÉ (SEYCHELLES)
SEYCHELLES
SEE MAIN MAP
Curieuse Island
Praslin
La Digue
Mahé

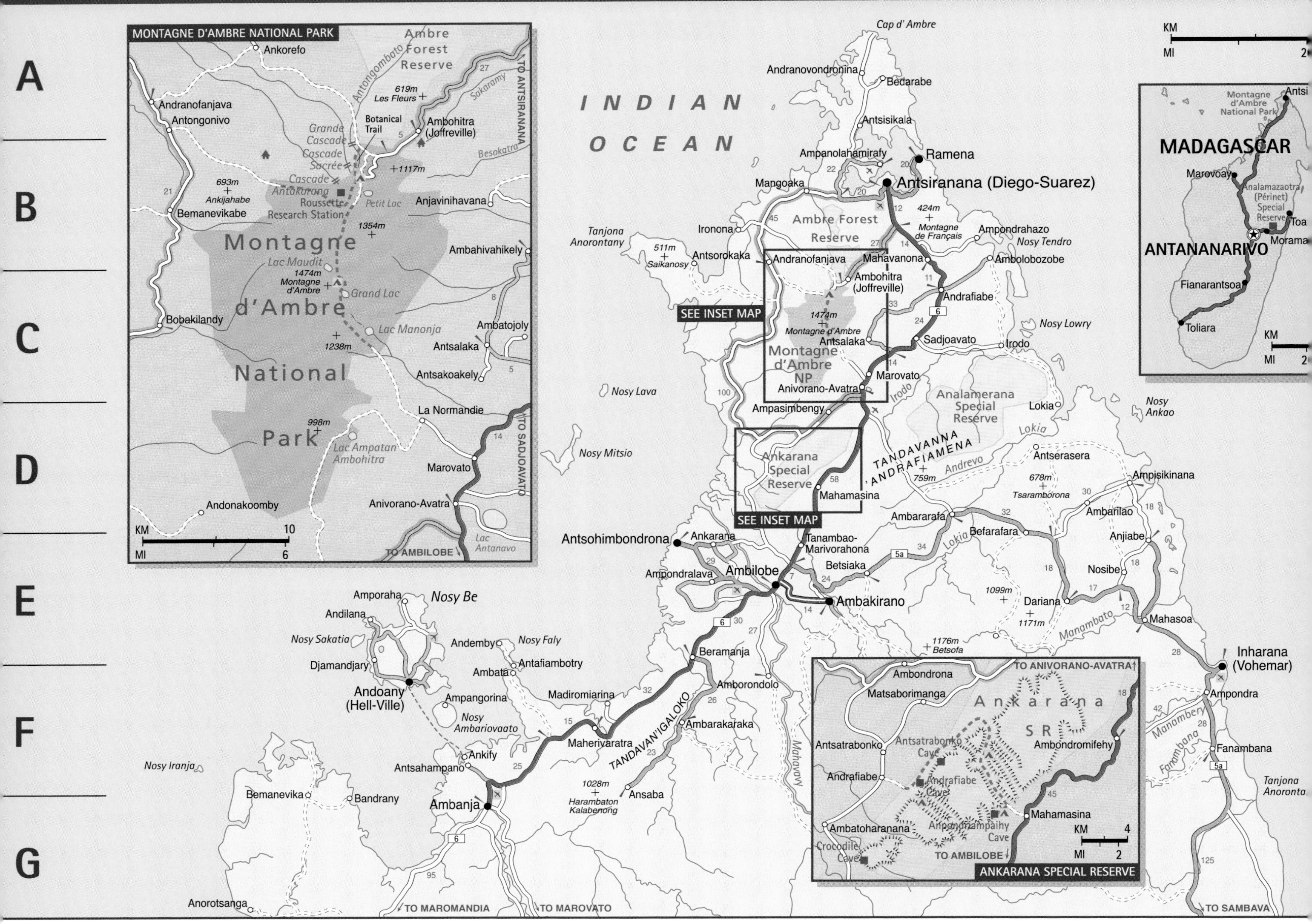

MONTAGNE D'AMBRE NATIONAL PARK
Ankorefo
Ambre Forest Reserve
Antongombato
619m Les Fleurs
Andranofanjava
Antongonivo
Botanical Trail
Ambohitra (Joffreville)
TO ANTSIRANANA
Sakaramy
Grande Cascade
Cascade Sacrée
Besokatra
Cascade Antakarana
1117m
693m Ankijahabe
Roussette Research Station
Petit Lac
Anjavinihavana
Bemanevikabe
1354m
Montagne d'Ambre National Park
Lac Maudit
1474m Montagne d'Ambre
Grand Lac
Ambahivahikely
Bobakilandy
Lac Manonja
1238m
Ambatojoly
Antsalaka
Antsakoakely
La Normandie
998m
Lac Ampatan Ambohitra
Marovato
TO SADJOAVATO
Andonakoomby
Anivorano-Avatra
Lac Antanavo
TO AMBILOBE
KM 10
MI 6
Cap d' Ambre
Andranovondronina
Bedarabe
INDIAN OCEAN
Antsisikala
Ampanolahamirafy
Ramena
Mangoaka
Antsiranana (Diego-Suarez)
424m Montagne de Français
Ampondrahazo
Nosy Tendro
Tanjona Anorontany
Ironona
Ambre Forest Reserve
511m Saikanosy
Antsorokaka
Andranofanjava
Mahavanona
Ambolobozobe
Ambohitra (Joffreville)
Andrafiabe
SEE INSET MAP
1474m Montagne d'Ambre
Montagne d'Ambre NP
Antsalaka
Sadjoavato
Irodo
Nosy Lowry
Nosy Lava
Marovato
Anivorano-Avatra
Ampasimbengy
Analamerana Special Reserve
Lokia
Nosy Ankao
Nosy Mitsio
Ankarana Special Reserve
TANDAVANNA ANDRAFIAMENA
759m
Andrevo
Antserasera
678m Tsaramborona
Ampisikinana
Mahamasina
SEE INSET MAP
Ambararafa
Ambarilao
Antsohimbondrona
Ankarana
Tanambao-Marivorahona
Befarafara
Anjiabe
Ampondralava
Ambilobe
Betsiaka
Nosibe
Ambakirano
1099m
Dariana
1171m
Manambato
Mahasoa
Amporaha
Nosy Be
Andilana
Nosy Sakatia
Andemby
Nosy Faly
Djamandjary
Ambatâ
Antafiambotry
1176m Betsofa
Beramanja
Inharana (Vohemar)
Andoany (Hell-Ville)
Ampangorina
Madiromiarina
Amborondolo
Ampondra
Nosy Ambariovaato
Maherivaratra
TANDAVAN'IGALOKO
Ambarakaraka
Mahavavy
Manambery
Fanambana
Nosy Iranja
Ankify
Antsahampano
1028m Harambaton Kalabenong
Ansaba
Bemanevika
Bandrany
Ambanja
Tanjona Anorontia
Anorotsanga
TO MAROMANDIA
TO MAROVATO
TO SAMBAVA
TO ANIVORANO-AVATRA
Ambondrona
Matsaborimanga
Ankarana SR
Antsatrabonko
Antsatrabonko Cave
Ambondromifehy
Andrafiabe
Andrafiabe Cave
Mahamasina
Ambatoharanana
Anjohimbalahy Cave
Crocodile Cave
TO AMBILOBE
KM 4
MI 2
ANKARANA SPECIAL RESERVE
KM
MI
Montagne d'Ambre National Park
MADAGASCAR
Marovoay
Analamazaotra (Périnet) Special Reserve
Toamasina
ANTANANARIVO
Moramanga
Fianarantsoa
Toliara
A
B
C
D
E
F
G

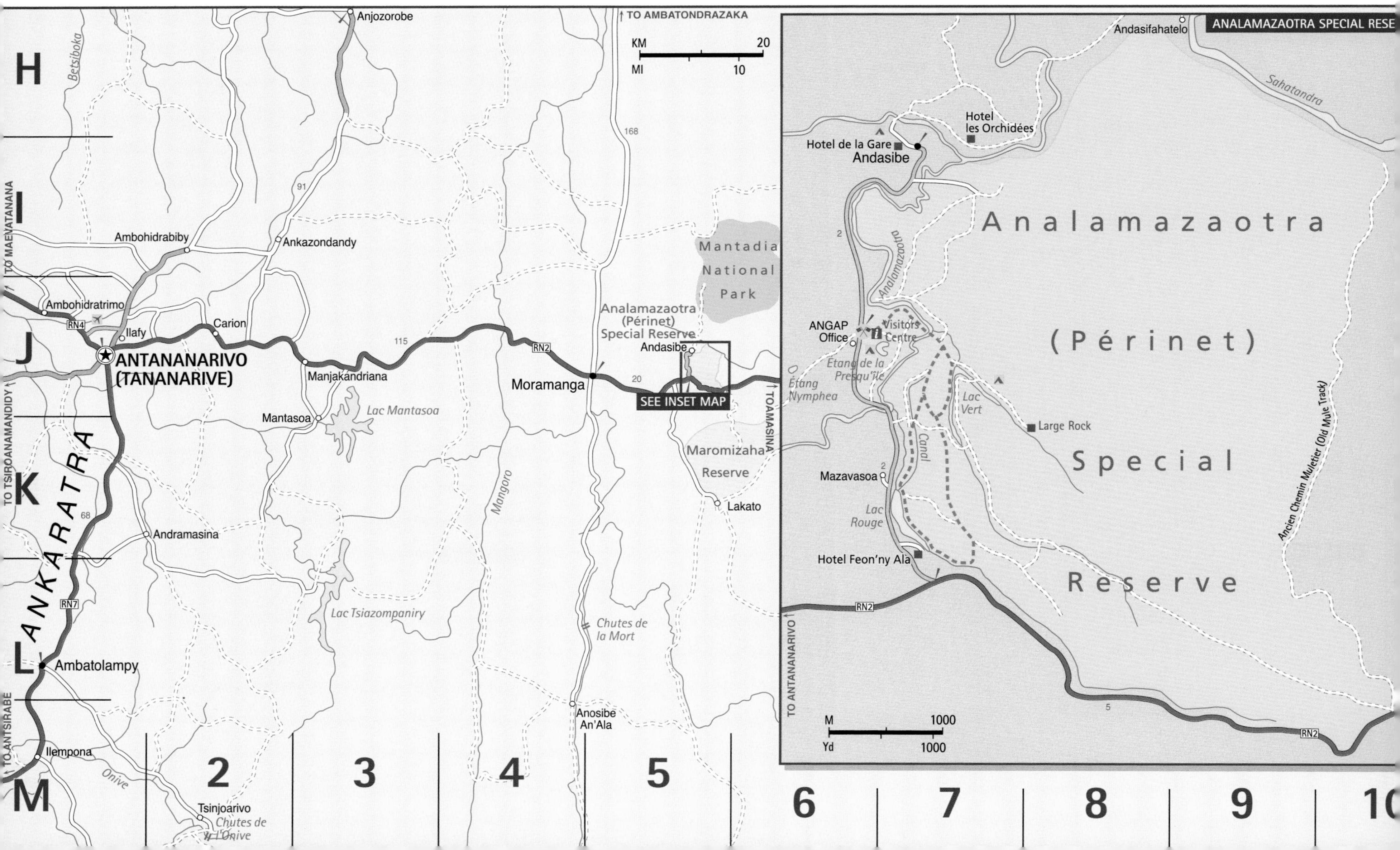

Anjozorobe
TO AMBATONDRAZAKA
Betsiboka
KM 20
MI 10
H
I
TO MAEVATANANA
Ambohidrabiby
Ankazondandy
Mantadia National Park
Ambohidratrimo
Ilafy
Carion
Analamazaotra (Périnet) Special Reserve
Andasibe
ANTANANARIVO (TANANARIVE)
Manjakandriana
Moramanga
SEE INSET MAP
TO TOAMASINA
Mantasoa
Lac Mantasoa
Maromizaha Reserve
TO TSIROANOMANDIDY
ANKARATRA
Mangoro
Lakato
Andramasina
Lac Tsiazompaniry
Chutes de la Mort
Ambatolampy
Anosibe An'Ala
TO ANTSIRABE
Ilempona
Onive
Tsinjoarivo
Chutes de l'Onive
J
K
L
M
2
3
4
5
Andasifahatelo
ANALAMAZAOTRA SPECIAL RESE
Sahatandra
Hotel les Orchidées
Hotel de la Gare
Andasibe
Analamazaotra (Périnet) Special Reserve
ANGAP Office
Visitors Centre
Etang de la Presqu'île
Étang Nymphea
Lac Vert
Large Rock
Canal
Ancien Chemin Muletier (Old Mule Track)
Mazavasoa
Lac Rouge
Hotel Feon'ny Ala
TO ANTANANARIVO
M 1000
Yd 1000
6
7
8
9
10

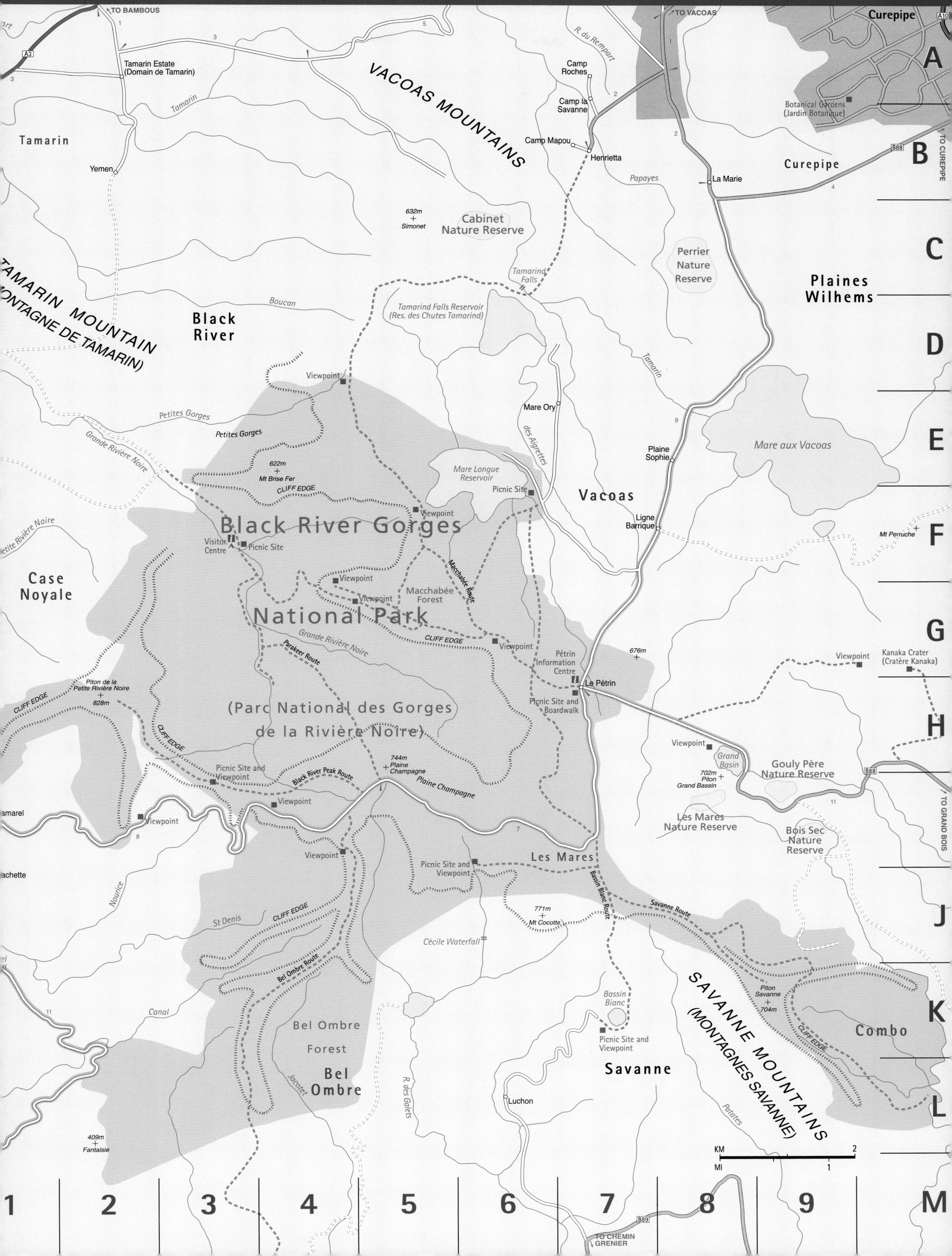
TO BAMBOUS
TO VACOAS
Curepipe
A3
A10
Tamarin Estate (Domain de Tamarin)
Tamarin
Yemen
VACOAS MOUNTAINS
R. du Rempart
Camp Roches
Camp la Savanne
Camp Mapou
Henrietta
Botanical Gardens (Jardin Botanique)
La Marie
Curepipe
B88
TO CUREPIPE
Papayes
632m Simonet
Cabinet Nature Reserve
Perrier Nature Reserve
Plaines Wilhems
TAMARIN MOUNTAIN (MONTAGNE DE TAMARIN)
Black River
Boucan
Tamarind Falls
Tamarind Falls Reservoir (Res. des Chutes Tamarind)
Viewpoint
Petites Gorges
Grande Rivière Noire
622m Mt Brise Fer
CLIFF EDGE
Mare Ory
des Aigrettes
Plaine Sophie
Mare aux Vacoas
Mare Longue Reservoir
Picnic Site
Vacoas
Ligne Barrique
Mt Perruche
Black River Gorges
Visitor Centre
Petite Rivière Noire
Case Noyale
Macchabée Forest
Macchabée Route
National Park
Parakeet Route
Pétrin Information Centre
676m
Le Pétrin
Kanaka Crater (Cratère Kanaka)
Piton de la Petite Rivière Noire 828m
(Parc National des Gorges de la Rivière Noire)
Picnic Site and Boardwalk
Grand Basin
702m Piton Grand Bassin
Gouly Père Nature Reserve
744m Plaine Champagne
Black River Peak Route
Plaine Champagne
Picnic Site and Viewpoint
Les Mares Nature Reserve
Bois Sec Nature Reserve
TO GRAND BOIS
Chamarel
Les Mares
Bassin Blanc Route
Savanne Route
Nourice
St Denis
771m Mt Cocotte
Cécile Waterfall
Bel Ombre Route
Canal
Piton Savanne 704m
Bassin Blanc
SAVANNE MOUNTAINS (MONTAGNES SAVANNE)
Combo
Bel Ombre Forest
Bel Ombre
Jacotet
R. des Galets
Savanne
Luchon
Patates
409m Fantaisie
KM 2
MI 1
B89
TO CHEMIN GRENIER
1 2 3 4 5 6 7 8 9
A B C D E F G H J K L M

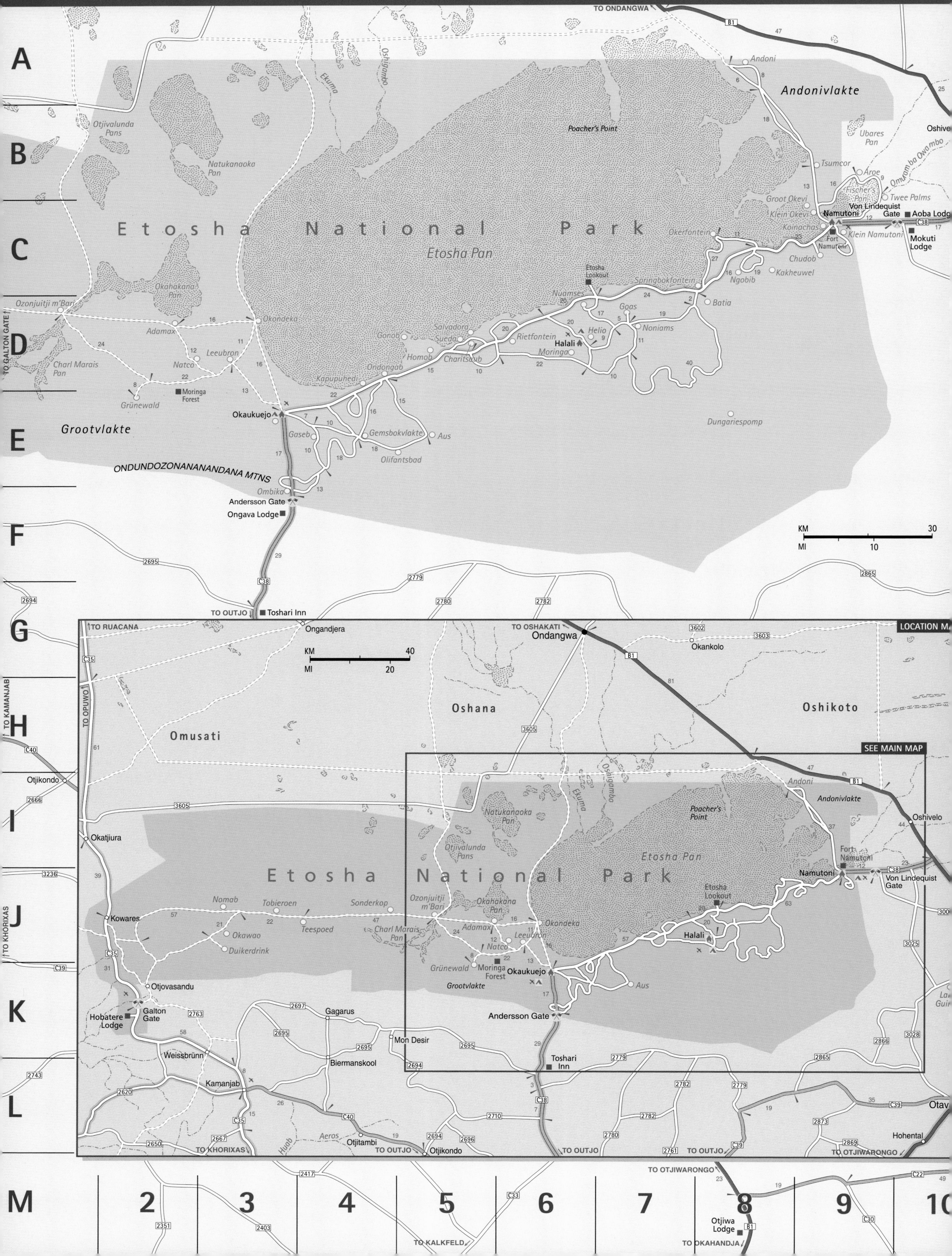
TO ONDANGWA
B1
Andoni
Andonivlakte
Oshivelo
Poacher's Point
Otjivalunda Pans
Natukanaoka Pan
Ubares Pan
Tsumcor
Aroe
Omuramba Owambo
Fischer's Pan
Twee Palms
Groot Okevi
Klein Okevi
Namutoni
Von Lindequist Gate
Aoba Lodge
Koinachas
Fort Namutoni
Klein Namutoni
Mokuti Lodge
C38
Etosha National Park
Etosha Pan
Okerfontein
Chudob
Kakheuwel
Ngobib
Etosha Lookout
Springbokfontein
Okahakana Pan
Ozonjuitji m'Bari
Nuamses
Batia
Goas
Noniams
Okondeka
Adamax
Salvadora
Sueda
Rietfontein
Helio
Halali
Moringa
Gonob
Homob
Charitsaub
Leeubron
Natco
Charl Marais Pan
Ondongab
Kapupuhedi
Moringa Forest
Grünewald
Okaukuejo
Grootvlakte
Dungariespomp
Gaseb
Gemsbokvlakte
Aus
Olifantsbad
ONDUNDOZONANANANDANA MTNS
Ombika
Andersson Gate
Ongava Lodge
TO GALTON GATE
Ekuma
Oshigambo
KM 30
MI 10
TO OUTJO
Toshari Inn
LOCATION MAP
TO RUACANA
Ongandjera
TO OSHAKATI
Ondangwa
Okankolo
KM 40
MI 20
Oshana
Oshikoto
Omusati
TO OPUWO
TO KAMANJAB
SEE MAIN MAP
Otjikondo
Okatjiura
Kowares
Nomab
Tobieroen
Sonderkop
Teespoed
Okawao
Duikerdrink
Otjovasandu
Galton Gate
Hobatere Lodge
Gagarus
Mon Desir
Weissbrünn
Biermanskool
Kamanjab
Aeros
Otjitambi
TO KHORIXAS
TO OUTJO
Otjikondo
Otav
Hohental
TO OTJIWARONGO
Otjiwa Lodge
TO KALKFELD
TO OKAHANDJA
TO KHORIXAS
A
B
C
D
E
F
G
H
I
J
K
L
M
2
3
4
5
6
7
8
9
10

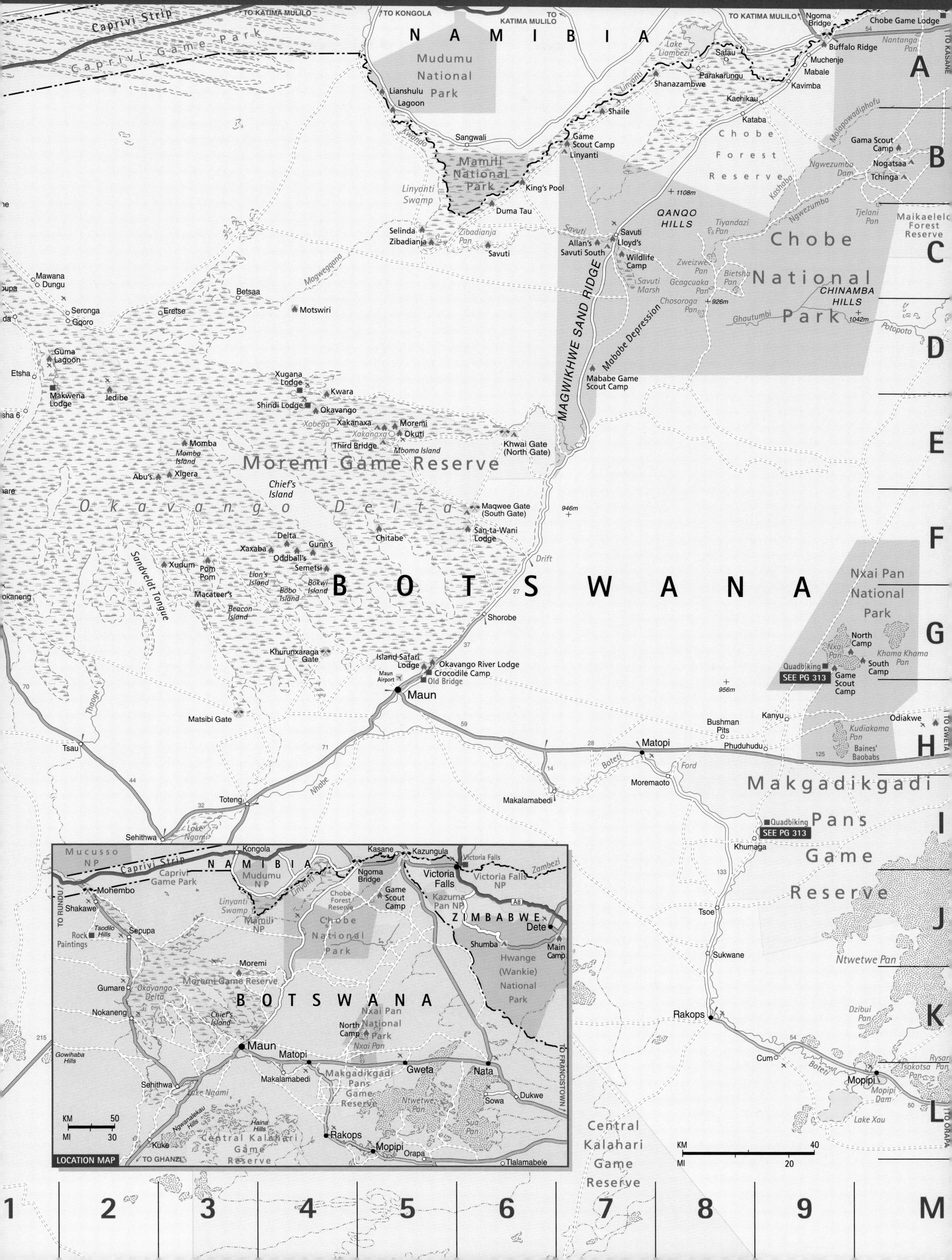
NAMIBIA
Caprivi Strip
Caprivi Game Park
TO KATIMA MULILO
TO KONGOLA
TO KATIMA MULILO
TO KATIMA MULILO
Mudumu National Park
Lianshulu Lodge
Lagoon
Sangwali
Kwando
Mamili National Park
Linyanti Swamp
King's Pool
Duma Tau
Selinda
Zibadianja
Zibadianja Pan
Savuti
Magweggana
Lake Liambezi
Linyanti
Satau
Parakarungu
Shanazambwe
Shaile
Game Scout Camp
Linyanti
Ngoma Bridge
Chobe Game Lodge
Buffalo Ridge
Muchenje
Mabale
Kavimba
Kachikau
Kataba
Nantanga Pan
TO KASANE
Chobe Forest Reserve
Malapowadiphofu
Gama Scout Camp
Nogatsaa
Tchinga
Ngwezumba Dam
Kashaba
Ngwezumba
Tjelani Pan
Maikaelelo Forest Reserve
1108m
QANQO HILLS
Savuti
Allan's Savuti South
Lloyd's
Wildlife Camp
Tiyandazi Pan
Chobe National Park
Zweizwe Pan
Bietsha Pan
Savuti Marsh
Gcagcuaka Pan
Chosoroga Pan
926m
CHINAMBA HILLS
1042m
Ghautumbi
Potopoto
MAGWIKHWE SAND RIDGE
Mababe Depression
Mababe Game Scout Camp
Mawana
Dungu
Seronga
Gqoro
Betsaa
Eretse
Motswiri
Guma Lagoon
Etsha
Makwena Lodge
Jedibe
Etsha 6
Xugana Lodge
Kwara
Shindi Lodge
Okavango
Xobega
Xakanaxa
Moremi
Okuti
Third Bridge
Mboma Island
Khwai Gate (North Gate)
Momba
Momba Island
Abu's
Xigera
Moremi Game Reserve
Chief's Island
Okavango Delta
Maqwee Gate (South Gate)
946m
San-ta-Wani Lodge
Chitabe
Delta
Gunn's
Xaxaba
Oddball's
Semetsi
Drift
Sandveldt Tongue
Xudum
Pom Pom
Lion's Island
Bobo Island
Bokwi Island
Macateer's
Beacon Island
BOTSWANA
Shorobe
Khurunxaraga Gate
Island Safari Lodge
Okavango River Lodge
Crocodile Camp
Maun Airport
Old Bridge
Maun
Thaoge
Matsibi Gate
Tsau
Nxai Pan National Park
North Camp
Nxai Pan
Khama Khama Pan
South Camp
Quadbiking
SEE PG 313
Game Scout Camp
956m
Kanyu
Odiakwe
TO GWETA
Bushman Pits
Phuduhudu
Kudiakama Pan
Baines' Baobabs
Matopi
Boteti
Ford
Moremaoto
Makalamabedi
Nhabe
Toteng
Sehithwa
Lake Ngami
Makgadikgadi Pans Game Reserve
Quadbiking
SEE PG 313
Khumaga
Tsoe
Sukwane
Ntwetwe Pan
Rakops
Dzibui Pan
Cum
Boteti
Mopipi
Mopipi Dam
Rysana Pan
Tsokotsa Pan
Lake Xau
TO ORAPA
Central Kalahari Game Reserve
KM 40
MI 20
Mucusso NP
Kongola
Caprivi Strip
NAMIBIA
Caprivi Game Park
Mudumu NP
Kasane
Kazungula
Victoria Falls
Ngoma Bridge
Victoria Falls
Victoria Falls NP
Zambezi
Mohembo
TO RUNDU
Shakawe
Linyanti Swamp
Chobe Forest Reserve
Game Scout Camp
Kazuma Pan NP
A8
ZIMBABWE
Dete
Tsodilo Hills
Rock Paintings
Sepupa
Mamili NP
Chobe National Park
Shumba
Main Camp
Hwange (Wankie) National Park
Moremi
Moremi Game Reserve
Gumare
Okavango Delta
BOTSWANA
Nokaneng
Chief's Island
Nxai Pan National Park
North Camp
Nxai Pan
Maun
Matopi
Gweta
Nata
Makalamabedi
Makgadikgadi Pans Game Reserve
Ntwetwe Pan
Sowa
Dukwe
Sua Pan
Sehithwa
Lake Ngami
Gowihaba Hills
Nqwanalekau Hills
Haina Hills
Central Kalahari Game Reserve
Rakops
Mopipi
Orapa
Tlalamabele
Kuke
TO GHANZI
TO FRANCISTOWN
KM 50
MI 30
LOCATION MAP
A B C D E F G H I J K L M
1 2 3 4 5 6 7 8 9

SKUKUZA CAMP
First Aid Doctor
Volkskas Guest House
Kitchen
Lion Guest House
Old Pontoon Crossing
Old Railway Bridge
Sabie
Shop
Restaurant
Parking
Moni Guest House
Nyathi Guest House
Waterkant 1 & 2
Huts 1-96
Amphitheatre
Kitchen
Huts 217-229
Car wash
Library
Selati Train Restaurant & Museum
Struben Guest House
Police Headquarters
Bathrooms
Student Accomodation Centre
Papenfus Clock Tower
Huts 97-209
Caravan & Camping Site
Parking
Bank
Kitchen
Reception
Huts 210-216
Bathrooms
Camping Site 300-320
Emergency Car repairs
Entrance Gate
Kitchen
SKUKUZA AREA
TO TOULON GATE
Sand
TO SATARA CAMP
Jakkalsbessie Bushveld Camp
Bird Hide
Mafunyana
Village
SEE INSET
Old Railway Bridge
LOWER SABIE ROAD
TO LOWER SABIE CAMP
TO PAUL KRUGER GATE
Viewpoint
Skukuza Camp
Nwaswitshaka
Camp Gate
TO PRETORIUSKOP CAMP, MALELANE GATE
Rest Camp
Concession Lodge
Bush Camp
Trails Camp
Messina
Limpopo
Mulaladrif
Pafuri Gate
Masisi
Makuya Game Reserve
Baboneni Drift
Viewpoint
Crooks Corner
Pafuri Picnic Site
Mutale
Nyalaland
Nkovakulu
Mazanje
Mashikiri
Punda Maria
Mandadzidzi
Muthati
Punda Maria Gate
Dzundwini
Magamba
Dokweni
Mphongolo
Babalala Picnic Site
Langtoon Dam
Sirheni
Sirheni Dam
Early Borehole
Biesiesvlei Dam
Phugwane
Wik-en-Weeg Dam
KaJilongo
Bububu
Shingwedzi
Bateleur
Rooibosrant Dam
Krapkuil Dam
Nkokodzi
Kruger
Olifantsbad Pan
Uitspan Pan
Nwambu Pan
Klein Letaba
Ntomeni Pan
Mopani
Grysbok
Pioneer Dam
Nshawu Dam
Boulders
Picnic Site
Letaba Ranch
Shimuwini
Letaba Ranch Game Reserve
Kaleka
Twisappel
Engelhard Dam
Letaba
Limpopo
Drift (Low-level crossings only)
MOZAMBIQ
Nationa
Park
Massi Dam
Waterpoort
Mara
Legkraal
Mphakane
Sebayeng
Politsi
Coach House
Tzaneen Dam
Tzaneen
GaMothiba
Leshwane
Veekraal
Ebenezer Dam
University of the North
Zion City Moria
GaMothapo
Boyne
Haenertsburg
Letaba
Letsitele
Mogoboya
Maake
Leydsdorp
Mulati
Kasteelkoppies
Murchison
MURCHISON RANGE
Gravelotte
Selati Game Reserve
Namakgale
Lulekani
Phalaborwa Gate
Phalaborwa
Masorini Museum and Picnic Site
Viewpoint
Olifants Wilderness Trail Base Camp
Balule
Nsumaneni
Tulani Safari Lodge
Selatirivier
Makalali Private Reserve
GaMashishimale
Wolkberg Wilderness Area
Pioneer Grave
Ofcolaco
Bewaarkloof Nature Reserve
GaMaja
The Downs
Trichardtsdal
Karongwi GR
Makhutswi
Safari Farm
Mica
Olifants
Gwalagwala
Klaserie Private Reserve
Pezulu
Motswari
Roodewal (Private)
Timbavati Picnic Site
Lekgalameetse Nature Reserve
Makutsi Conservancy
Lorraine
Balule Game Reserve
Makalali
M'bali
Tanda Tula
Blyde Olifants Conservancy
Tshukudu
Garonga
Matumi
Timbavati Private Reserve
Zeekoegat
Chuniespoort
Lebowakgomo
Penge
Olifants
Diphuti
Hoedspruit
Eastgate
Kambaku
Ngala Game Lodge
Satara
Mecklenburg
GaMankopane
Leolo
Tooseng
Tswaing
Battle of Sekhukhuneland (1879)
GaMasemola
J.G. Strijdom Tunnel
Kromellenboog
MPUMALANGA
Kapama GR
Kapama
Thornybush
Orpen
Orpen Gate
Phelwana
Museum
Picnic Site
Nwanetsi
Sweni
Abel Erasmus Pass
Aventura Swadini
Echo Caves
Blydepoort Dam
Klaserie
Timbavati
Khoka Moya
Talamati
Fairfield
Viewpoint
Nkaya Pan
Driekop
Mogaba
Aventura Blydepoort
Acornhoek
Cottondale
Andover GR
Manyeleti Game Reserve
Manyeleti
Imbali
Ngwenyeni Dam
Baobab Tree
Trichardt Memorial
Piet Gouws Dam
Tsatane
Old Voortrekker Road
Branddraai
Bourke's Luck Potholes
Blyde
DRAKENSBERG
LEOLO
Site of First Platinum Discovery
Burgersfort
Steelpoort
Jane Furse
Sekhukhune
Morone
Voortrekker Graves
Gethlane Lodge
Ohrigstad
River
Casteel
Rolle
Sabi Sands Private Reserve
Lugmag
Metsimetsi
Viewpoint
Tshokwane Picnic Site
Orpen Dam
Canyon
Vaalhoek
Ulusaba
Exeter
Londolozi
Mala Mala
Idube
Singita
Mulumuvi
Kirkmans Camp
Harrys Camp
Nkumbe
Memorial Tablets
Kennedy's Vale
Phokwane
Kokwaneng
Buffelsvlei
Mooiplaats
Krugerspos
Robbers Pass
Pilgrims Rest
Bushbuckridge
Gqweta
Bush
Huntington
Graskop
Marite
Mkhuhlu
Mount Sheba
Mount Sheba NR
Ohrigstad Dam
Ohrigstad Dam NR
Geological Exposure
Malaita
Maartenshoop
Waterval
Sabie River Sun
Hippo Pool
Paul Kruger Gate
Jakkalsbessie
Skukuza
SEE INSET MAP
Muntshe
Loskop
Mlondozi Dam
Rite
Hlogotlou
Gustav Klingbiel NR
Siesta Resort
Floreat Protea
Sabie
Kowyn Pass
Mac-Mac Falls
Hazyview
Albasini Ruins
Nwaswitshaka
Maleni
Numbi
Viewpoint Picnic Site
Park
Sehlakwane
Maleoskop
Lydenburg
Horseshoe Falls
Kiepersol
Nhlotini
Sunset Dam
Lower Sabie
Afgrond
Jaap-se-Hoogte
Sterkspruit NR
Long Tom Pass
eMahushu
Napi
Erts
Roossenekal
Die Berg
Die Berg Pass
Skdrwerant
Hendriksdal
Numbi
Pretoriuskop
Jock Safari Lodge
Skipberg
Viewpoint
Thomas Hart's Grave
Duke
Witklip Pass
Vermont
Pine Lake Sun
The Winkler
Renoster Pan
Picnic Site
Crocodile Bridge
Rooikraal
Laersdrif
Kwena Dam
Buffelskloof NR
Rosehaugh
White River
Biyamiti
Viewpoint
Hippo Pool
Asbes
Santa Pass
Sudwala Caves
Brondal
Plaston
Wolhuter
Lukimbi
Crocodile
Bothaberg
Stoffberg
Dullstroom
Schoemanskloof
Wonderkloof Pass
Sudwala Lodge
Hotel Bundu
Pienaar
Mthethomusha Game Reserve
Bushman
Berg-en-Dal
Malelane Sun Lodge
Hectorspruit
Tenbosch
Komati
Selons
Chameshoogte Pass
Patattanek
Old Joe
Madunusa
Montrose
Montrose Pass
Montrose Falls
Elandshoek
Nelspruit
KaNyamazane
Khandizwe
Malelane
Kaapmuiden
Thorn Hill
Karino
Selonsrivier
Palmer
Steelpoort
Ngodwana
Kaapsehoop
Kaapsehoop Pass
Klipspringer Lodge
Mpageni Pass
KROKODILPOORTSBERGE
Kaal Rug
Kwaggaskop
Crossroads Pass
N.Z.A.S.M. Tunnel
Spitskop
Wonderhoek
Machadodorp
Waterval-Boven
Krugerhof
Noordkaap
Louw's Creek
Buffelspruit
Mlumati
Mzinti
Squamans
Belfast
TO MIDDELBURG
TO PIETERSBURG

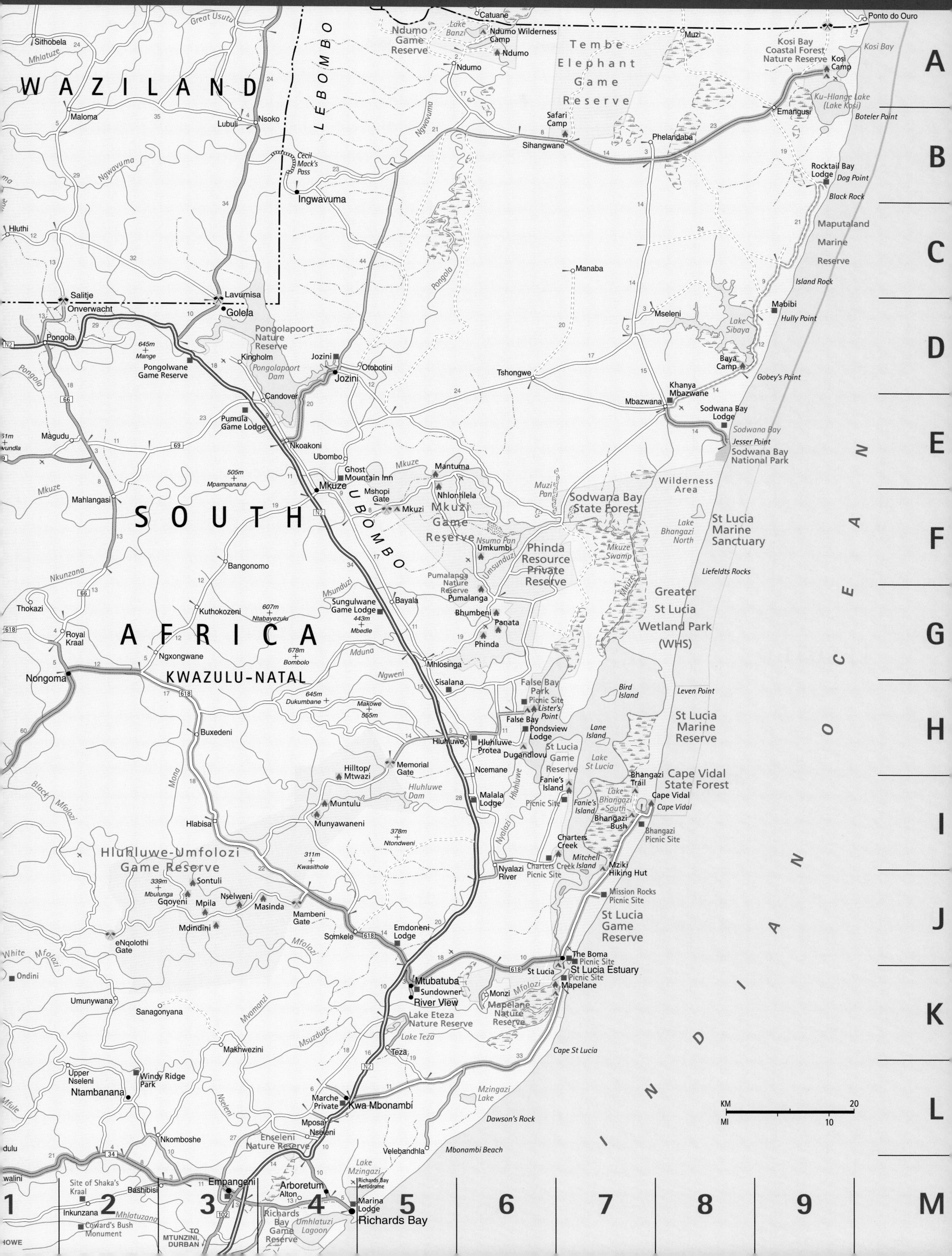

N
SWAZILAND
SOUTH AFRICA
KWAZULU-NATAL
INDIAN OCEAN
LEBOMBO
UBOMBO
Sithobela
Great Usutu
Mhlatuze
Maloma
Lubuli
Nsoko
Nawavuma
Cecil Mack's Pass
Ingwavuma
Hluthi
Salitje
Lavumisa
Onverwacht
Golela
Pongola
645m Mange
Pongolwane Game Reserve
Pongolapoort Nature Reserve
Kingholm
Pongolapoort Dam
Jozini
Otobotini
Candover
Pumula Game Lodge
Magudu
Nkoakoni
Ubombo
Ghost Mountain Inn
Mkuze
505m Mpampanana
Mahlangasi
Mshopi Gate
Mkuzi
Mantuma
Nhlonhlela
Mkuzi Game Reserve
Nsumo Pan
Umkumbi
Bangonomo
Kuthokozeni
607m Ntabayezulu
Thokazi
Royal Kraal
Sungulwane Game Lodge
443m Mbedle
Bayala
Pumalanga Nature Reserve
Pumalanga
Bhumbeni
Panata
Phinda
Phinda Resource Private Reserve
Ngxongwane
678m Bombolo
Mduna
Mhlosinga
Nongoma
Ngweni
Sisalana
645m Dukumbane
Makowe 555m
Buxedeni
Hluhluwe
Hluhluwe Protea
Memorial Gate
Hilltop/ Mtwazi
Hluhluwe Dam
Ncemane
Malala Lodge
Muntulu
Munyawaneni
Hlabisa
378m Ntondweni
311m Kwasithole
Hluhluwe-Umfolozi Game Reserve
Sontuli
339m Mbulunga
Gqoyeni
Mpila
Nselweni
Masinda
Mambeni Gate
Mdindini
eNqolothi Gate
White Mfolozi
Black Mfolozi
Ondini
Somkele
Emdoneni Lodge
Mtubatuba
Sundowner
River View
Lake Eteza Nature Reserve
Lake Teza
Teza
Umunywana
Sanagonyana
Makhwezini
Upper Nseleni
Windy Ridge Park
Ntambanana
Marche Private
Kwa Mbonambi
Mposa
Nseleni
Nkomboshe
Enseleni Nature Reserve
Velebandhla
Mbonambi Beach
Empangeni
Arboretum
Alton
Richards Bay Game Reserve
Umhlatuzi Lagoon
Lake Mzingazi
Richards Bay Aerodrome
Marina Lodge
Richards Bay
Site of Shaka's Kraal
Bashibisi
Inkunzana
Mhlatuzana
Coward's Bush Monument
TO MTUNZINI, DURBAN
Catuane
Ndumo Game Reserve
Lake Banzi
Ndumo Wilderness Camp
Ndumo
Tembe Elephant Game Reserve
Safari Camp
Sihangwane
Muzi
Phelandaba
Kosi Bay Coastal Forest Nature Reserve
Kosi Camp
Kosi Bay
Ponto do Ouro
Emangusi
Ku-Hlange Lake (Lake Kosi)
Boteler Point
Rocktail Bay Lodge
Dog Point
Black Rock
Maputaland Marine Reserve
Island Rock
Manaba
Mseleni
Mabibi
Hully Point
Lake Sibaya
Baya Camp
Gobey's Point
Tshongwe
Khanya Mbazwane
Mbazwana
Sodwana Bay Lodge
Sodwana Bay
Jesser Point
Sodwana Bay National Park
Wilderness Area
Muzi Pan
Sodwana Bay State Forest
Lake Bhangazi North
St Lucia Marine Sanctuary
Mkuze Swamp
Liefeldts Rocks
Greater St Lucia Wetland Park (WHS)
Bird Island
Leven Point
False Bay Park
Picnic Site
Lister's Point
False Bay
Pondsview Lodge
Dugandlovu
St Lucia Game Reserve
Lane Island
Lake St Lucia
St Lucia Marine Reserve
Fanie's Island
Fanie's Island
Lake Bhangazi South
Bhangazi Trail
Cape Vidal State Forest
Cape Vidal
Bhangazi Bush
Bhangazi Picnic Site
Charters Creek
Mitchell Island
Charters Creek Picnic Site
Nyalazi River
Mziki Hiking Hut
Mission Rocks Picnic Site
St Lucia Game Reserve
The Boma Picnic Site
St Lucia
St Lucia Estuary
Picnic Site
Mapelane
Monzi
Mfolozi
Mapelane Nature Reserve
Cape St Lucia
Mzingazi Lake
Dawson's Rock
Msunduzi
Mvamanzi
Msuzduze
Nseleni
Mona
Nyalazi
Hluhluwe
Mkuze
Pongola
Ngwavuma
Nkunzana
KM 20
MI 10
A B C D E F G H I J K L M
1 2 3 4 5 6 7 8 9

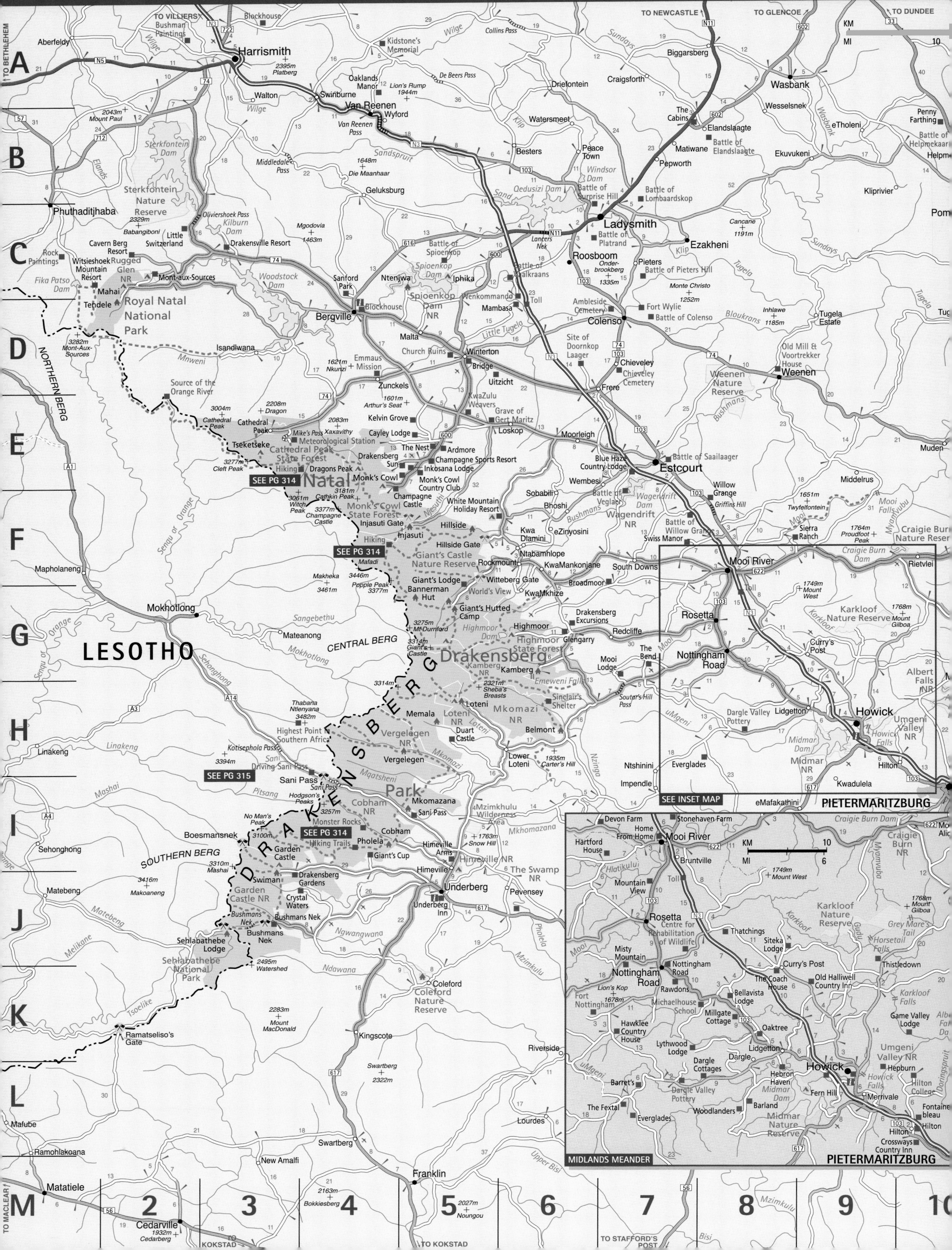
TO VILLIERS
TO NEWCASTLE
TO GLENCOE
TO DUNDEE
TO BETHLEHEM
KM
MI
Harrismith
2395m Platberg
Aberfeldy
Blockhouse
Bushman Paintings
Kidstone's Memorial
Collins Pass
Wilge
Sundays
Biggarsberg
Wasbank
Wesselsnek
Penny Farthing
Battle of Helpmekaar
eTholeni
Oaklands Manor
Lion's Rump 1944m
De Beers Pass
Driefontein
Craigsforth
Walton
Swinburne
Van Reenen
Wyford
Van Reenen Pass
2043m Mount Paul
Watersmeet
The Cabins
Elandslaagte
Battle of Elandslaagte
Matiwane
Ekuvukeni
Sterkfontein Dam
Elands
Besters
Peace Town
Pepworth
1648m Die Maanhaar
Middledale Pass
Sandspruit
Windsor Dam
Qedusizi Dam
Battle of Surprise Hill
Battle of Lombaardskop
Klip
Kliprivier
Geluksburg
Phuthaditjhaba
Sterkfontein Nature Reserve
Oliviershoek Pass
Kilburn Dam
2329m Babangiboni
Little Switzerland
Drakensville Resort
Mgodovia 1463m
Ladysmith
Battle of Platrand
Lancers Nek
Ezakheni
Cancane 1191m
Cavern Berg Resort
Rock Paintings
Witsieshoek Mountain Resort
Rugged Glen NR
Mont-aux-Sources
Battle of Spioenkop
Spioenkop Dam
Battle of Vaalkraans
Roosboom
Onderbrookberg 1335m
Pieters
Battle of Pieters Hill
Monte Christo 1252m
Tugela
Fika Patso Dam
Mahai
Tendele
Royal Natal National Park
Woodstock Dam
Sanford Park
Ntenjwa
Iphika
Spioenkop Dam NR
Wenkommando
Mambasa
Toll
Ambleside Cemetery
Fort Wylie
Battle of Colenso
Colenso
Bloukrans
Inhlawe 1185m
Tugela Estate
Bergville
Blockhouse
Malta
Little Tugela
3282m Mont-Aux-Sources
Isandlwana
Mnweni
Emmaus Mission
1621m Nkunzi
Church Ruins
Winterton
Bridge
Site of Doornkop Laager
Chieveley
Chieveley Cemetery
Weenen
Old Mill & Voortrekker House
Weenen Nature Reserve
NORTHERN BERG
Source of the Orange River
Zunckels
Uitzicht
Frere
Bushmans
1601m Arthur's Seat
KwaZulu Weavers
Grave of Gert Maritz
2208m Dragon
3004m Cathedral Peak
Cathedral Peak
Kelvin Grove
Loskop
Mike's Pass
2083m Xaxavithy
Meteorological Station
Cayley Lodge
Moorleigh
Tseketseke
Cathedral Peak State Forest
The Nest
Ardmore
Muden
3277m Cleft Peak
Hiking
Drakensberg Sun
Champagne Sports Resort
Dragons Peak
Inkosana Lodge
Blue Haze Country Lodge
Estcourt
Battle of Saailaager
SEE PG 314
Natal
Monk's Cowl
Monk's Cowl Country Club
Wembesi
Middelrus
Willow Grange
3181m Cathkin Peak
3061m Witch Peak
Champagne Castle
Sobabili
Battle of Vegleer
Wagendrift Dam
Griffins Hill
3377m Champagne Castle
Monk's Cowl State Forest
White Mountain Holiday Resort
Bhoshi
Wagendrift NR
1651m Twyfelfontein
Mooi Falls
Injasuti Gate
Hillside
Kwa Dlamini
eZinyoesini
Battle of Willow Grange
Swiss Manor
Sierra Ranch
1764m Proudfoot Peak
Craigie Burn Nature Reserve
Craigie Burn Dam
Sengu or Orange
Injasuti
Hillside Gate
Ntabamhlope
SEE PG 314
Mafadi
Giant's Castle Nature Reserve
Rockmount
KwaMankonjane
South Downs
Mooi River
Rietvlei
Mapholaneng
3446m Makheka
3461m
Popple Peak 3377m
Giant's Lodge
Bannerman Hut
Witteberg Gate
World's View
KwaMkhize
Broadmoor
1749m Mount West
Karkloof Nature Reserve
1768m Mount Gilboa
Mokhotlong
Sangebethu
Giant's Hutted Camp
Drakensberg Excursions
Rosetta
3275m Mt Durnford
Highmoor Dam
Highmoor
Highmoor State Forest
Glengarry
Redcliffe
Mateanong
CENTRAL BERG
3314m Giant's Castle
The Bend
Nottingham Road
Curry's Post
LESOTHO
Mokhotlong
Drakensberg
Kamberg NR
Kamberg
Mooi Lodge
Albert Falls NR
Schonghong
Emeweni Falls
2321m Sheba's Breasts
Sinclair's Shelter
Soutar's Hill Pass
3314m
Loteni
Mkomazi NR
Thabana Ntlenyana 3482m
Highest Point in Southern Africa
Memala
Loteni NR
Duart Castle
Belmont
Dargle Valley Pottery
Lidgetton
Howick
Umgeni Valley NR
Linakeng
Kotisephola Pass
3394m
Vergelegen NR
Vergelegen
Lower Loteni
1935m Carter's Hill
Ntshinini
Everglades
Midmar Dam
Midmar NR
Hilton
Sani
Driving Sani Pass
Mkomazi
SEE PG 315
Sani Pass
Sani Pass
Mqatsheni
Park
Impendle
Kwadulela
Mashai
Pitsang
Hodgson's Peaks
3257m
Cobham NR
Mkomazana
Sani Pass
Mzimkhulu Wilderness Area
SEE INSET MAP
eMafakathini
PIETERMARITZBURG
No Man's Peak
3100m
Monster Rocks
Cobham
SEE PG 314
Hiking Trails
Pholela
Mkhomazana
Boesmansnek
1763m Snow Hill
Himeville Arms
Sehonghong
SOUTHERN BERG
Garden Castle
Giant's Cup
Himeville NR
3310m Mashai
Swiman
Drakensberg Gardens
Himeville
The Swamp NR
3416m Makoaneng
Matebeng
Garden Castle NR
Crystal Waters
Underberg
Pevensey
Underberg Inn
Bushmans Nek
Bushmans Nek
Matebeng
Ngwangwana
Pholela
Melikane
Sehlabathebe Lodge
Bushmans Nek
Sehlabathebe National Park
2495m Watershed
Ndawana
Mzimkulu
Coleford
Coleford Nature Reserve
2283m Mount MacDonald
Tsoelike
Ramatseliso's Gate
Kingscote
Riverside
Swartberg 2322m
Lourdes
Mafube
Ramohlakoana
Swartberg
New Amalfi
Upper Bisi
Franklin
Matatiele
2163m Bokkiesberg
2027m Noungou
Mzimkulu
Cedarville
1932m Cedarberg
TO MACLEAR
TO KOKSTAD
TO KOKSTAD
TO STAFFORD'S POST
Bisi
Devon Farm
Stonehenge Farm
Craigie Burn Dam
Home From Home
Mooi River
Hartford House
Bruntville
Craigie Burn NR
Hlatikulu
Toll
1749m Mount West
Myamvuba
Mountain View
1768m Mount Gilboa
Karkloof Nature Reserve
Grey Mare's Tail
Rosetta
Centre for Rehabilitation of Wildlife
Thatchings
Siteka Lodge
Horsetail Falls
Misty Mountain
Nottingham Road
Nottingham Road
Rawdons
Curry's Post
Old Halliwell Country Inn
Thistledown
Lion's Kop 1678m
Fort Nottingham
Michaelhouse School
Bellavista Lodge
The Coach House
Karkloof Falls
Millgate Cottage
Game Valley Lodge
Hawklee Country House
Oaktree
Lythwood Lodge
Lidgetton
Umgeni Valley NR
Dargle
Dargle Cottages
Hebron Haven
Howick
Hepburn
Barret's
Dargle Valley Pottery
Midmar Dam
Howick Falls
Hilton College
Fern Hill
Merrivale
The Fextal
Barland
Fontainebleau
Everglades
Woodlanders
Midmar Nature Reserve
Hilton
Hilton
Crossways Country Inn
MIDLANDS MEANDER
PIETERMARITZBURG

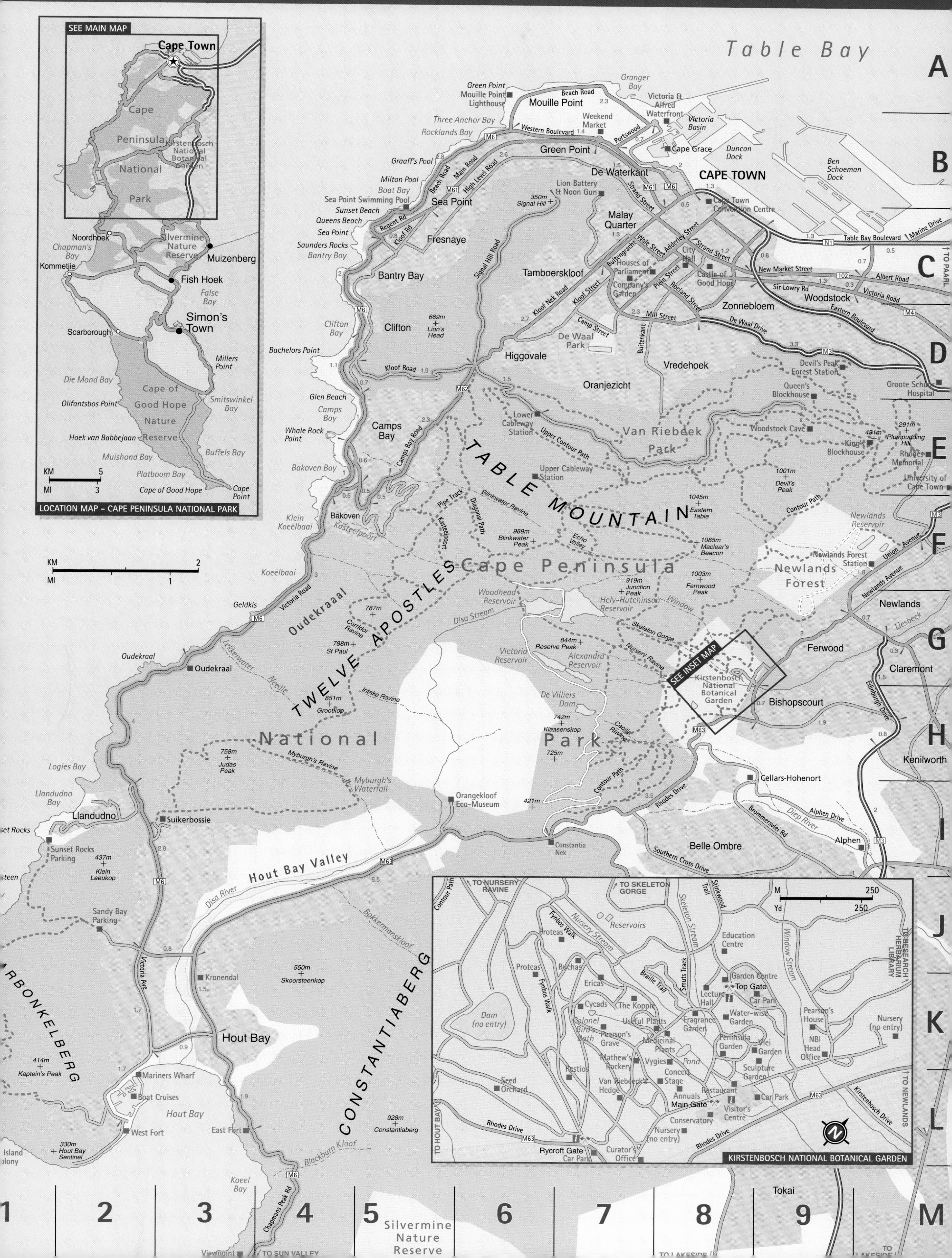

Table Bay
Granger Bay
Green Point
Mouille Point
Lighthouse
Beach Road
Mouille Point
Victoria & Alfred Waterfront
Victoria Basin
Weekend Market
Portswood
Western Boulevard
Three Anchor Bay
Rocklands Bay
Cape Grace
Duncan Dock
Ben Schoeman Dock
Green Point
Graaff's Pool
Main Road
High Level Road
Beach Road
De Waterkant
CAPE TOWN
Milton Pool
Boat Bay
Lion Battery & Noon Gun
Strand Street
Sea Point Swimming Pool
Sea Point
350m Signal Hill
Cape Town Convention Centre
Sunset Beach
Malay Quarter
Queens Beach
Regent Rd
Kloof Rd
Sea Point
Fresnaye
Wale Street
Adderley Street
Strand Street
Table Bay Boulevard
Marine Drive
Saunders Rocks
Bantry Bay
Signal Hill Road
Buitengracht
City Hall
Houses of Parliament
Plein Street
Castle of Good Hope
New Market Street
Albert Road
TO PAARL
Bantry Bay
Tamboerskloof
Company's Garden
Roeland Street
Sir Lowry Rd
Victoria Road
Woodstock
Kloof Street
Zonnebloem
Eastern Boulevard
Clifton Bay
Kloof Nek Road
Camp Street
Mill Street
De Waal Drive
Clifton
669m Lion's Head
De Waal Park
Buitenkant
Bachelors Point
Higgovale
Vredehoek
Devil's Peak Forest Station
Kloof Road
Oranjezicht
Groote Schuur Hospital
Queen's Blockhouse
Glen Beach
Camps Bay
Lower Cableway Station
Van Riebeek Park
Woodstock Cave
291m Plumpudding Hill
Whale Rock Point
Camps Bay
Camps Bay Road
Upper Contour Path
431m
King's Blockhouse
Rhodes Memorial
TABLE MOUNTAIN
Upper Cableway Station
1001m Devil's Peak
University of Cape Town
Bakoven Bay
Pipe Track
Blinkwater Ravine
1045m Eastern Table
Contour Path
Newlands Reservoir
Bakoven
Kasteelpoort
Diagonal Path
Klein Koeëlbaai
989m Blinkwater Peak
Echo Valley
1085m Maclear's Beacon
Newlands Forest Station
Union Avenue
Cape Peninsula
Newlands Forest
Koeëlbaai
919m Junction Peak
1003m Fernwood Peak
Newlands Avenue
Woodhead Reservoir
Hely-Hutchinson Reservoir
Window
Newlands
Liesbeek
Geldkis
Victoria Road
Oudekraal
787m
TWELVE APOSTLES
Disa Stream
Corridor Ravine
Skeleton Gorge
788m St Paul
844m Reserve Peak
Victoria Reservoir
Nursery Ravine
SEE INSET MAP
Ferwood
Alexandra Reservoir
Kirstenbosch National Botanical Garden
Claremont
Oudekraal
Oudekraal
Lekkerwater
Needle
Intake Ravine
De Villiers Dam
Bishopscourt
Edinburgh Drive
851m Grootkop
742m Klaasenskop
National
Park
Cecilia Ravine
758m Judas Peak
725m
Kenilworth
Myburgh's Ravine
Logies Bay
Myburgh's Waterfall
Contour Path
Cellars-Hohenort
Llandudno Bay
Orangekloof Eco-Museum
421m
Rhodes Drive
Alphen Drive
Llandudno
Suikerbossie
Diep River
Brommersvlei Rd
Sunset Rocks
Alphen
Sunset Rocks Parking
Constantia Nek
Belle Ombre
437m Klein Leeukop
Hout Bay Valley
Southern Cross Drive
Disa River
Sandy Bay Parking
Bokkemanskloof
Victoria Ave
550m Skoorsteenkop
Kronendal
KONKELBERG
414m Kaptein's Peak
CONSTANTIABERG
Hout Bay
Mariners Wharf
Boat Cruises
Hout Bay
West Fort
East Fort
928m Constantiaberg
330m Hout Bay Sentinel
Blackburn Kloof
Koeel Bay
Chapmans Peak Rd
Viewpoint
TO SUN VALLEY
Silvermine Nature Reserve
Tokai
TO LAKESIDE
KM 2
MI 1
SEE MAIN MAP
Cape Town
Cape Peninsula National Park
Kirstenbosch National Botanical Garden
Noordhoek
Chapman's Bay
Kommetjie
Silvermine Nature Reserve
Muizenberg
Fish Hoek
False Bay
Simon's Town
Scarborough
Millers Point
Die Mond Bay
Cape of Good Hope Nature Reserve
Olifantsbos Point
Smitswinkel Bay
Hoek van Babbejaan
Buffels Bay
Muishond Bay
Platboom Bay
Cape of Good Hope
Cape Point
KM 5
MI 3
LOCATION MAP - CAPE PENINSULA NATIONAL PARK
TO NURSERY RAVINE
TO SKELETON GORGE
Contour Path
Stinkwood Trail
Skeleton Stream
Reservoirs
Fynbos Walk
Nursery Stream
Proteas
Education Centre
Window Stream
TO RESEARCH HERBARIUM LIBRARY
Proteas
Buchus
Braille Trail
Smuts Track
Garden Centre
Top Gate
Ericas
Lecture Hall
Car Park
Dam (no entry)
Cycads
The Koppie
Water-wise Garden
Pearson's House
Nursery (no entry)
Colonel Bird's Bath
Useful Plants
Fragrance Garden
Pearson's Grave
Medicinal Plants
Peninsula Garden
Vlei Garden
NBI Head Office
Mathew's Rockery
Vygies
Pond
Restios
Concert Stage
Sculpture Garden
Seed Orchard
Van Riebeeck's Hedge
Annuals
Restaurant
Main Gate
Car Park
Visitor's Centre
TO NEWLANDS
Kirstenbosch Drive
TO HOUT BAY
Rhodes Drive
Conservatory
Nursery (no entry)
Rhodes Drive
Rycroft Gate Car Park
Curator's Office
KIRSTENBOSCH NATIONAL BOTANICAL GARDEN
M 250
Yd 250

Adventure Activities by Region

A kayaker braces himself for the stomach-churning drop over Thrombosis Falls, KwaZulu-Natal, South Africa.

FOR AN ALPHABETICAL LIST OF ADVENTURE MAPS IN THIS BOOK, PLEASE SEE OVERLEAF.

Nowhere in the world is the challenge of adventure more alive and inviting than in Africa. The vastness of its landscape, the towering peaks of its mountains, the depths of its great lakes and surrounding oceans, and the unpredictability of both its wilderness and its wildlife make for an apparently endless series of nail-biting excursions into parts unknown. While the continent continues to do battle with an ever-growing population and the encroaching development that is inevitably associated with expanding human settlement, the expansive land mass means that much of Africa remains uncharted and there is still much to be explored and discovered.

Although many parts of Africa are slowly beginning to realise the potential of its travel industry and have begun to capitalise on the lure of their adventure opportunities, most action sports and many other leisure activities inevitably lie beyond the immediate confines of Africa's cities, towns, villages and other human settlements. As a result, some of the finest surfing, hiking, snorkelling, rock climbing and river-rafting are to be found in remote wildernesses, far from the conveniences offered by golf greens, race tracks and diving schools typical of the established resort areas that attract caravans of tourists and holidaymakers to sparkling beach sands and idyllic isles. However, it is the solitude and tranquility of the parched hinterland, the inviting coral reefs of the warm Indian Ocean, the battered and windswept dunes, and the lonely dirt roads in the middle of nowhere that draw the intrepid adventurer.

Unlike Europe and even parts of North America, where space is at a premium and 'roughing it' means a three-man tent only minutes away from a bustling city or town, the vast majority of Africa's lazy lagoons, magnificent forests, horizon-less deserts and wild waters are seemingly lost to the rest of the world. This is the real playground of the windsurfers and waterskiers, divers and hikers, parasailors, paragliders and hang-gliders.

Despite the abject poverty of many of its people and the apparent neglect of many of its most historic settlements, the breathtaking sunsets, endless desert dunes and open savanna plains offer a contrasting view of the many faces of Africa, and its remarkable potential for adventure travel.

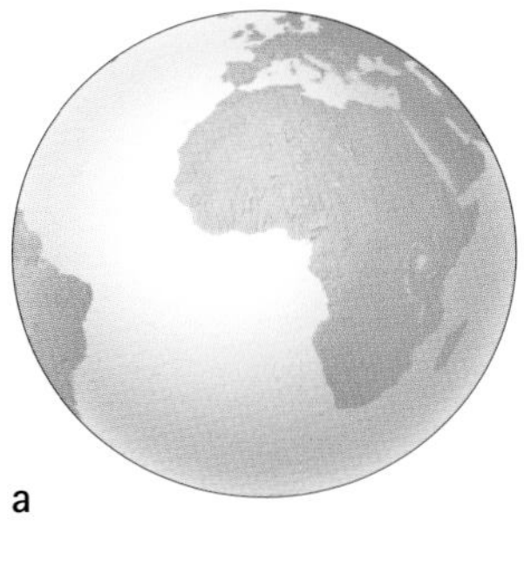

- Rwanda is Africa's most densely popu country (15th in the world), with 28 humans per square kilometre.
- Life expectancy for newborns in Zimb (at 1999) was 43 (males) and 42 (fe
- In 1995 Kenya had one post office fo 26,000 citizens. Chad had one for ev 200,000 citizens in 1994.

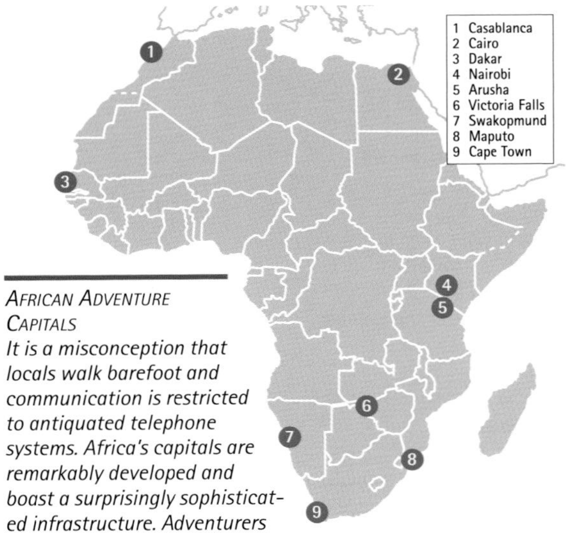

1 Casablanca
2 Cairo
3 Dakar
4 Nairobi
5 Arusha
6 Victoria Falls
7 Swakopmund
8 Maputo
9 Cape Town

AFRICAN ADVENTURE CAPITALS
It is a misconception that locals walk barefoot and communication is restricted to antiquated telephone systems. Africa's capitals are remarkably developed and boast a surprisingly sophisticated infrastructure. Adventurers should enjoy success with most of their information needs, particularly in the more popular travel destinations, as indicated on the map. These destinations are the main adventure activity hotspots or serve as the best point of entry to specific adventure regions.

CANNED HUNTING

An alarming number of unscrupulous 'safari operators' offer the 'thrill of the hunt' to equally conscience-deficient travellers determined to leave Africa with a trophy of a lion skin or zebra pelt. While there are a number of officially sanctioned and approved hunting operations scattered throughout Africa – the merits of which are best determined by individuals – there are increasing reports of 'canned hunting'. Here lions are enclosed in restricted areas with little chance of escape, and are easily trapped in the sites of a firearm. Even pro-hunting organisations such as Safari Hunters International have condemned canned hunts as barbaric.

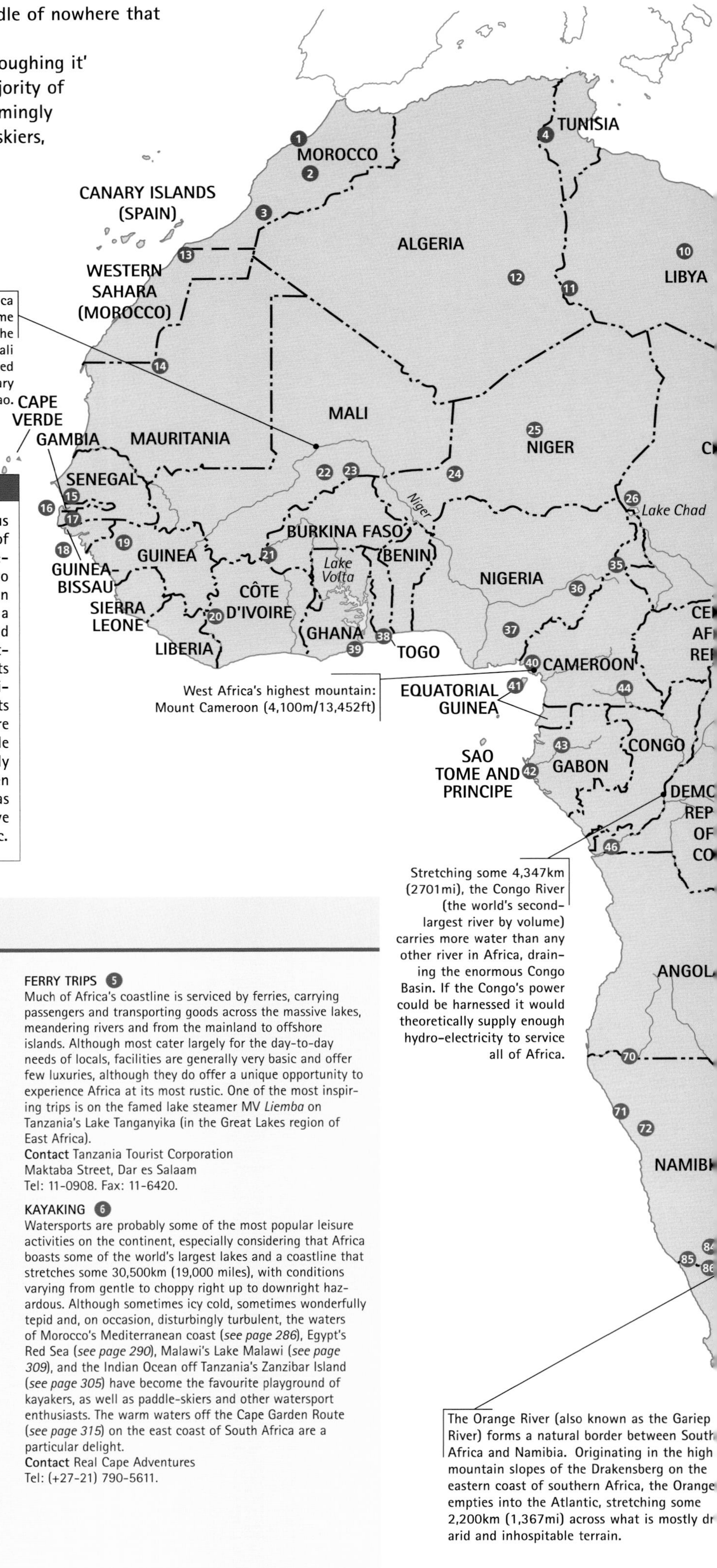

The Niger River is the third largest in Africa and, from its source in Guinea, extends some 4,200km (2,600mi) to its outlet in the Atlantic in Nigeria. The capitals of Mali (Bamako) and Niger (Niamey) are located along its length, as are the legendary settlements of Timbuktu and Gao.
MOROCCO
TUNISIA
CANARY ISLANDS (SPAIN)
ALGERIA
LIBYA
WESTERN SAHARA (MOROCCO)
MALI
CAPE VERDE
GAMBIA
MAURITANIA
NIGER
SENEGAL
Lake Chad
Niger
BURKINA FASO
BENIN
GUINEA
GUINEA-BISSAU
Lake Volta
NIGERIA
CÔTE D'IVOIRE
SIERRA LEONE
GHANA
LIBERIA
TOGO
CAMEROON
West Africa's highest mountain: Mount Cameroon (4,100m/13,452ft)
EQUATORIAL GUINEA
SAO TOME AND PRINCIPE
GABON
CONGO
Stretching some 4,347km (2701mi), the Congo River (the world's second-largest river by volume) carries more water than any other river in Africa, draining the enormous Congo Basin. If the Congo's power could be harnessed it would theoretically supply enough hydro-electricity to service all of Africa.
ANGOL
NAMIBI
The Orange River (also known as the Gariep River) forms a natural border between South Africa and Namibia. Originating in the high mountain slopes of the Drakensberg on the eastern coast of southern Africa, the Orange empties into the Atlantic, stretching some 2,200km (1,367mi) across what is mostly dr arid and inhospitable terrain.

SOME AFRICAN ADVENTURE HOT-SPOTS

TRAIN JOURNEYS 1
Travelling Africa's rugged terrain is most memorable when enjoyed from the rhythmic motion of a train steaming across the seemingly endless countryside. The continent boasts a number of these journeys, varying from the rudimentary comforts of the journey from Wadi Halfa to Khartoum in Sudan (*see page 291*) and the Red Lizard Train Journey in Tunisia to the ultimate luxury of South Africa's Blue Train or the Pride of Africa rail trip between Kenya and South Africa. To experience 'Real Africa', take the Tazara Express between Zambia and Tanzania.
Contact Passenger Services, Lusaka
Tel: (+260-5) 27-1019 ext. 209.

ELEPHANT-BACK SAFARIS 2
Elephants are as much a part of the African landscape as the baobab and the desert dune. Apart from the famed Dumbo Trek (*see page 296*) in Nigeria to its border with Cameroon, a number of African nations - particularly in southern Africa — offer wildlife safaris from the backs of these great beasts. The most popular excursions are those that carry visitors around the Victoria Falls in Zimbabwe, and through the floodplains of Botswana's Okavango Delta.
Contact Elephant Back Safaris
Private Bag 332, Maun, Botswana,
Tel: (+267) 66-1260. Fax: (+267) 66-1005
e-mail: ebs@info.bw.

WHALE WATCHING 3
Whales are popular visitors to the African coast, with many of the southern species such as the Southern Right making their way from the cold waters of the Antarctic to the warmer climes further north during the southern winters. Here they mate and calve before returning to their home territories. South Africa and virtually all the Indian Ocean Islands are much-favoured stopovers for these giant mammals, and there are a number of land-based viewing points along the coast.
Contact South Africa-based MTN Whale Hotline
Tel: 0800-22-8222.

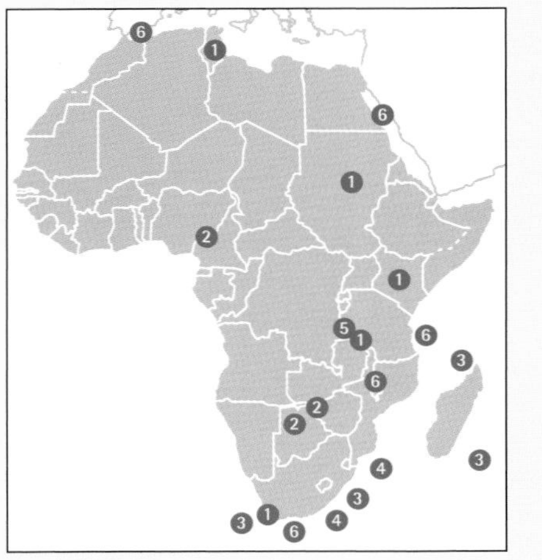

SHARK DIVING 4
A number of prominent stretches of the African coastline are bathed by warm waters — particularly those of the Indian Ocean — which makes for ideal shark conditions. Many of these form natural breeding grounds for seals and an abundance of seabirds, and — because of the plentiful prey – are the hunting ground of the Great White and other sharks. Although it is always advisable to be on the lookout for these much-feared and often-seen predators, relatively few attacks have been reported in recent years and a number of private operators — most notably in South Africa, a much-favoured haunt of these hunters — offer excursions to view sharks and even dive (in reinforced metal cages) to see them up close.
Contact White Shark Ecoventures
Cape Town, South Africa
Tel: 082 658 0185.

FERRY TRIPS 5
Much of Africa's coastline is serviced by ferries, carrying passengers and transporting goods across the massive lakes, meandering rivers and from the mainland to offshore islands. Although most cater largely for the day-to-day needs of locals, facilities are generally very basic and offer few luxuries, although they do offer a unique opportunity to experience Africa at its most rustic. One of the most inspiring trips is on the famed lake steamer MV *Liemba* on Tanzania's Lake Tanganyika (in the Great Lakes region of East Africa).
Contact Tanzania Tourist Corporation
Maktaba Street, Dar es Salaam
Tel: 11-0908. Fax: 11-6420.

KAYAKING 6
Watersports are probably some of the most popular leisure activities on the continent, especially considering that Africa boasts some of the world's largest lakes and a coastline that stretches some 30,500km (19,000 miles), with conditions varying from gentle to choppy right up to downright hazardous. Although sometimes icy cold, sometimes wonderfully tepid and, on occasion, distinctly turbulent, the waters of Morocco's Mediterranean coast (*see page 286*), Egypt's Red Sea (*see page 290*), Malawi's Lake Malawi (*see page 309*), and the Indian Ocean off Tanzania's Zanzibar Island (*see page 305*) have become the favourite playground of kayakers, as well as paddle-skiers and other watersport enthusiasts. The warm waters off the Cape Garden Route (*see page 315*) on the east coast of South Africa are a particular delight.
Contact Real Cape Adventures
Tel: (+27-21) 790-5611.

The Nile River (the longest in the world at 6,671km/4,145mi) covers a vast area that, combined, would be greater in size than most countries in Europe. The river is formed as a result of the unification of the Blue Nile (which has its source in Ethiopia's Lake Tana), and the White Nile, which arises in Sudan and helps support more than 100 million Africans who live along its cultivated banks.

BE RESPONSIBLE

Africa continues to be plagued with all sorts of environmental issues and the almost unstoppable degradation of its vast resources. Travellers to the continent are urged to follow the principles of ecotourism by treating both the land and its people with sensitivity and respect, whether it is in the inner-city or in the heart of No Man's Land. Damage to the environment here is, more often than not, irreversible – Africa simply does not have the means or the infrastructure to 'clean up' after its visitors.

Much the same is true when it comes to issues of security. While much of the continent is now much more readily accessible (and traversable), economic and political stability are still faraway dreams for many African nations, and many continue to suffer under the enormous strain of violent crime and factional fighting. As a result, the infrastructure in certain areas may fall well short of Western standards, and it is here that travellers should be entirely self-sufficient, especially when it comes to matters of personal safety. Emergency services may be few and far between, equipment archaic and dangerously inefficient, and visitors' facilities extremely basic.

A large number of even popular tourist destinations are also susceptible not only to the elements of nature, but to pestilence and disease such as malaria (see below) and yellow fever, and adventurers should take all the necessary precautions to avoid themselves becoming another statistic.

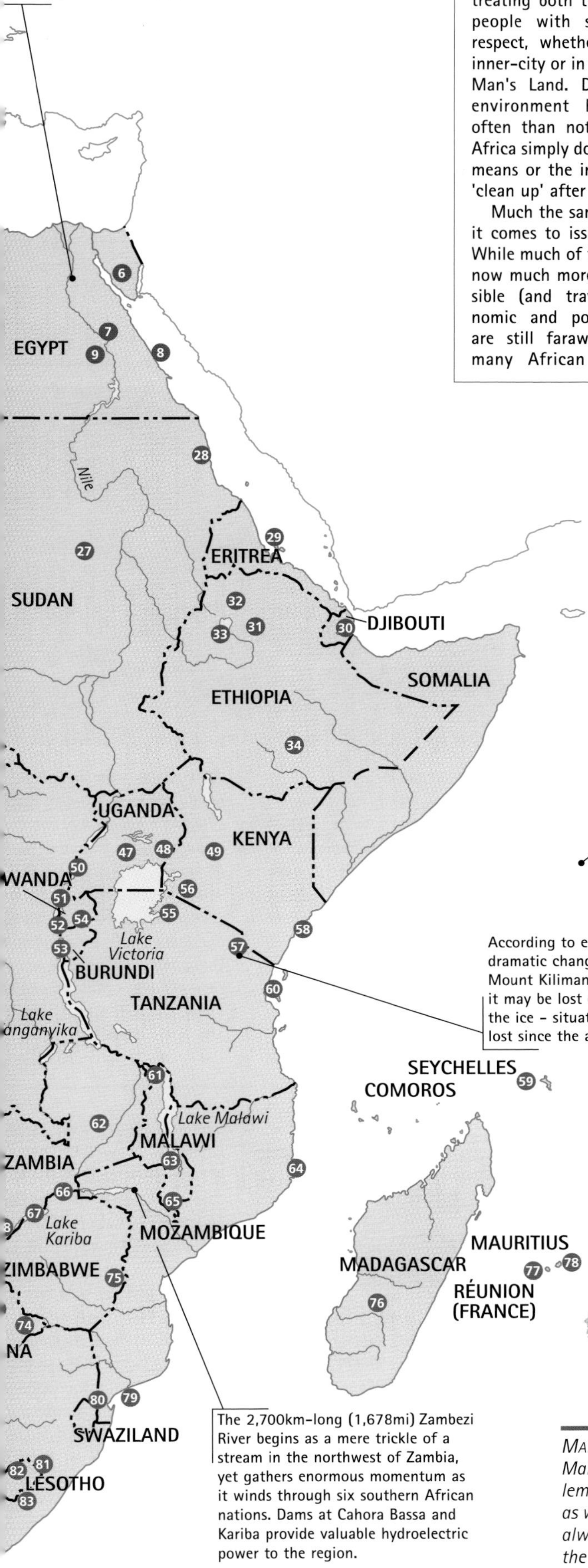

The oceans cover nearly three quarters of the Earth's surface and, despite countless research and conservation efforts, constitute some of the least explored areas of the planet's natural life. The world's highest mountain is, in fact, Mount Kea (10,203m/33,476ft) but, as it stands on the seabed, it is mostly unreachable by travellers.

According to environmental activists affiliated to Greenpeace, dramatic changes in latter-day climate may mean that towering Mount Kilimanjaro's ice field could retreat to such a degree that it may be lost entirely by the year 2015. Some 80 per cent of the ice – situated virtually on the equator – has already been lost since the area was first mapped almost 100 years ago.

The 2,700km-long (1,678mi) Zambezi River begins as a mere trickle of a stream in the northwest of Zambia, yet gathers enormous momentum as it winds through six southern African nations. Dams at Cahora Bassa and Kariba provide valuable hydroelectric power to the region.

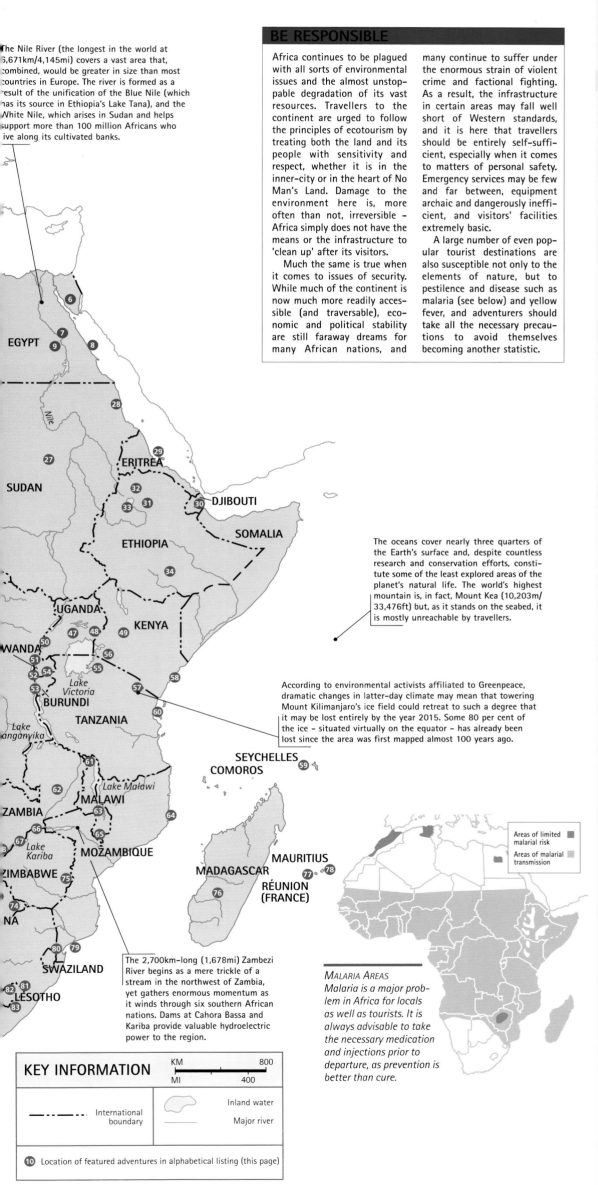

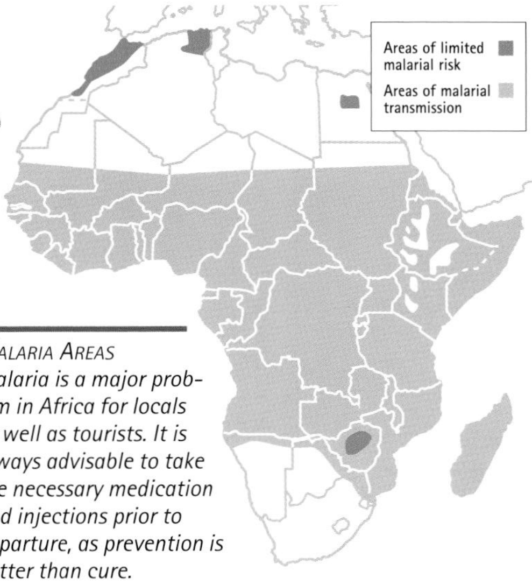

MALARIA AREAS
Malaria is a major problem in Africa for locals as well as tourists. It is always advisable to take the necessary medication and injections prior to departure, as prevention is better than cure.

KEY INFORMATION

KM 800
MI 400

International boundary
Inland water
Major river

⑩ Location of featured adventures in alphabetical listing (this page)

ALPHABETICAL ADVENTURE LISTING

KEY
Animal transport
Big-game fishing
Bungee jumping
By air
By sail
Gorilla trek
Mild waters
Mountain climbing
On foot
On four wheels
On two wheels
Surfing and windsurfing
Train journeys
Underwater exploring
Wild waters

LOCATION	COUNTRY	PAGE NO.	MAP
Acacus Mountains	Libya	289	11
Accra	Ghana	295	39
Adrar Plateau	Mauritania	293	14
Atlas Mountains	Morocco	286	2
Bale Mountains	Ethiopia	298	34
Banfora Region	Burkina Faso	295	21
Basse-Casamance	Senegal	292	17
Bazaruto	Mozambique	308	79
Big-game fishing	Mauritius	310	78
Bioko's Volcano	Equatorial Guinea	297	41
Burundi	Burundi	302	53
Chimanimani	Zimbabwe	307	75
Chott el Jerid	Tunisia	287	4
Congo River	DRC	301	46
Cunene River	Namibia	313	70
Dahlek Archipelago	Eritrea	298	29
Dja Reserve	Cameroon	297	44
Dogon Plateau	Mali	293	22
Drâa Valley	Morocco	286	3
Drakensberg Mountains	South Africa	314	81
Fish River Canyon	Namibia	312	84
Fouta Djalon Plateau	Guinea	294	19
Gambia River	Gambia	292	15
Garden Route	South Africa	315	87
Guinea Coast	Guinea-Bissau	294	18
Hombori Mountains	Mali	293	23
Ilha de Mozambique	Mozambique	308	64
Kaokoland	Namibia	312	72
Kenya (camel safaris)	Kenya	304	49
Kenyan Coast	Kenya	304	58
Khartoum to Wadi Halfa	Sudan	291	27
Laayoune	Western Sahara	287	13
Lac Togo	Togo	295	38
Lake Chad	Chad	289	26
Lake Kariba	Zimbabwe	306	67
Lake Malawi	Malawi	309	63
Lake Tana	Ethiopia	299	33
Lalibela	Ethiopia	299	31
Libya's coast	Libya	288	5
Libya's desert towns	Libya	289	10
Lowland Forests	DRC	301	52
Madagascar	Madagascar	311	76
Makgadikgadi Pans	Botswana	313	73
Maluti Mountains	Lesotho	315	82
Man Region	Côte d'Ivoire	294	20
Mandara Mountains	Cameroon	297	35
Maputo Province	Mozambique	308	80
Masai Mara	Kenya	304	56
Mauritius	Mauritius	311	78
Mount Cameroon	Cameroon	296	40
Mount Elgon	Uganda	303	48
Mount Kilimanjaro	Tanzania	305	57
Mount Mulanje	Malawi	309	65
Niger camel trekking	Niger	288	25
Niger River	Niger	288	24
Nigeria's 'Dumbo Trek'	Nigeria	296	36
Nigeria's rainforests	Nigeria	296	37
Nile River	Egypt	290	9
Nyika Plateau	Malawi	309	61
Nyungwe Forest	Rwanda	302	54
Orange River	South Africa	314	86
Poubara Falls	Gabon	300	43
Ogooué river	Gabon	300	42
Red Sea	Egypt	290	8
Réunion	Réunion	311	77
Richtersveld	South Africa	314	85
Riverboat on the Congo	DRC	301	45
Rwenzori Mountains	DRC	300	50
Rwenzori Mountains	Uganda	303	50
Rwanda's waterways	Rwanda	302	51
Sani Pass	Lesotho	315	83
Senegal's waterways	Senegal	292	16
Serengeti	Tanzania	305	55
Seychelles (surfing)	Seychelles	310	59
Seychelles (scuba)	Seychelles	310	59
Simien Mountains	Ethiopia	298	32
Sinai Plateau	Egypt	290	6
Skeleton Coast	Namibia	312	71
South Luangwa	Zambia	306	62
Sudanese coast	Sudan	291	28
Tadjoura	Djibouti	299	30
Tassili	Algeria	287	12
Tuli Block (horseback)	Botswana	313	74
Uganda (gorilla)	Uganda	303	47
Victoria Falls	Zambia/Zimbabwe	307	69
West Bank	Egypt	291	7
West Coast	Morocco	286	1
Driving the Zambezi	Zambia/Zimbabwe	306	68
Zambezi River	Zambia	307	66
Zanzibar	Tanzania	305	60

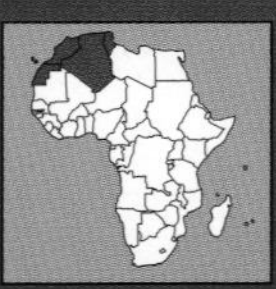

2 DAYS+ MOROCCO

TREKKING THE ATLAS

Travel Info

Destination: High Atlas Mountains
Requirements: Valid passports (6 months); citizens of EU countries, USA, Australia, Canada and New Zealand do not need visas for stays of less than 90 days. Consult your local embassy. No hiking permits are required.
Currency: Moroccan dirham (100 centimes)
Climate: Best time to trek is summer (May-October), when nights are cool and days warm to hot, with seasonal storms.
Risk factor: Although the Atlas does not offer easy walking, it is neither too technical nor too inaccessible for the determined hiker.
Health: No immunizations are required, unless visitors are travelling through or from countries with a recent history of yellow fever. There is a moderate Aids risk in the area.
Pack: Sturdy but comfortable walking boots, a sleeping bag and tent are essential, as are sunscreen and bottled water. Shorts are not recommended.
Facilities: Apart from a tent and sleeping bag, most other requirements for the trek are usually provided by the operators' guides. Overnight accommodation, although simple, is comfortable.
Contact: Club Alpin Francais, B.P. 6178, Casablanca. Tel: 09212-02-270090

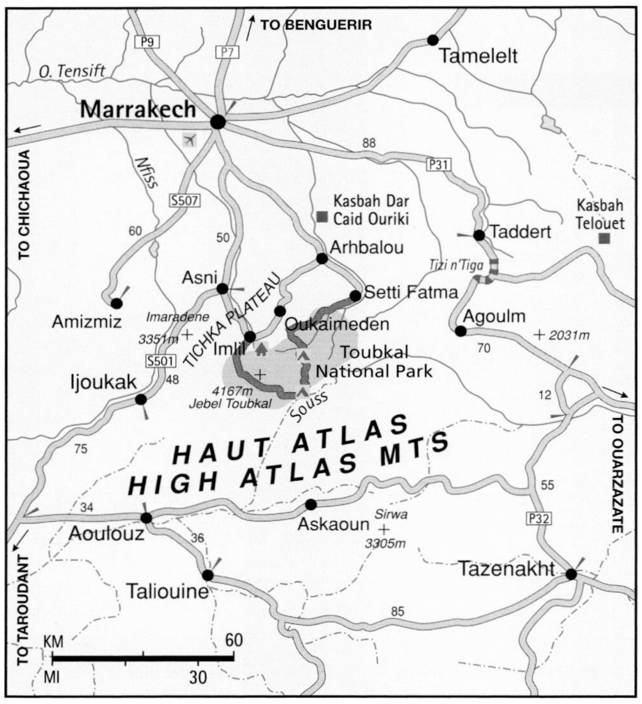

Most hikers and trekkers will head directly from the airport at Marrakech for the start of The Wonder Walk, the challenging but not impossible trek from Tichka to Jebel Toubkal, the 4,167m (13,670ft) pinnacle first climbed by a French party in 1923. The 140km (80-mile) Tichka-to-Toubkal route, arduous in parts but generally uncomplicated, takes at least a fortnight to complete. It takes you through scenic areas, from the isolated Tichka to the impressive Jebel Toubkal. This breathtaking peak dominates the Atlas range for hundreds of miles and provides limitless trekking opportunities, with hikes to the summit taking two to three days from Imlil village alone. Ascents to areas such as Tizi n' Tiga (3,000m/9,843ft) and Imaradene (3,351m/10,995ft) are inevitably steep and take hours to complete.

Accompanying mule "wranglers" are a godsend, and overnight stays at bustling centres such as Ijoukak are a welcome respite. Although this hike is more draining than it is demanding, it should not take too much out of you if you are fit. There are, however, a number of alternative routes, and the Rif also offers some outstanding walks. However, the accessibility of these may also depend on seasonal snowfall (local weather is generally pleasant, but Toubkal experiences snows in June) and the availability of pack mules and Berber guides, who offer invaluable assistance with cooking and setting up camp.

Many of Morocco's more than 75 official camp sites are along the trekking routes and, although rather unsophisticated, are generally very well priced for the budget traveller. The Moroccan National Tourist Office (MNTO) holds comprehensive lists of camping facilities.

3 HOURS+ MOROCCO

SURFING MOROCCO'S COAST

Travel Info

Destination: West Coast
Requirements: Valid passports (6 months); citizens of EU countries, USA, Australia, Canada and New Zealand do not need visas for stays of less than 90 days. Consult your local embassy.
Currency: Moroccan dirham (100 centimes)
Climate: Balmy and sunny with good surfing conditions virtually year-round.
Risk factor: Fun far surpasses risk.
Health: No immunizations are required, unless visitors are travelling through or from countries with yellow fever. There is a moderate Aids risk in the area.
Pack: Sunscreen and surfboards and/or windsurfers, but local surfing schools may offer equipment to hire. Women should cover legs and arms as beachwear may be frowned upon in public places.
Facilities: Main holiday towns have plenty of accommodation, ranging from the basic to the plush, while more out-of-the-way destinations have simple overnight hostels for backpackers. Ablution facilities are virtually non-existent along undeveloped coastal areas.
Contact: Royal Moroccan Surfing Federation. Tel: 09212-02-259530 Fax: 09212-02-236385

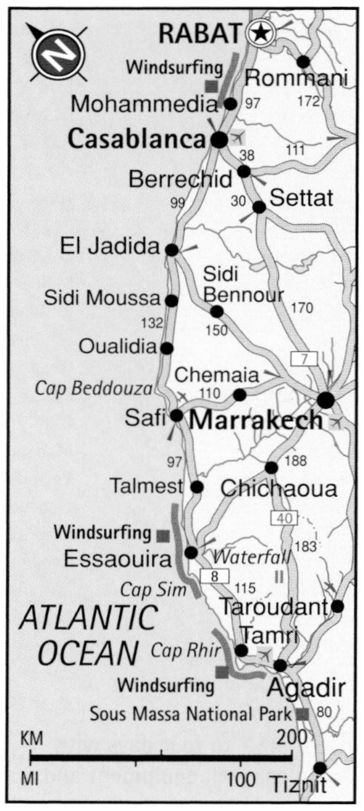

Although much of Morocco's 3,500km (2,200-mile) coastline comprises what is in effect one extended beach, mercifully little of it has become commercialized in a European sense, although popular resort developments dot the horizons of Casablanca, Tangier and Plage des Nations at Rabat. Travellers with a thirst for adrenaline sports – particularly those water-based – find a virtually untouched haven here, with sublime weather and the convenience of hotel complexes should the need arise. The purpose-built resort city of Agadir, set against a magnificent backdrop of sand dunes and lapped by the waves of the Atlantic, is the nation's beach sport mecca, with good facilities for anything from waterskiing and sailing to windsurfing and wavesurfing. Some 350km (215 miles) south is Essaouira – not for nothing known as The Windy City – a vital centre for water sports and a world-class windsurfing hot spot where the beach sands stretch for more than 10km (6 miles) south to Cap Sim. The most ardent windsurfers flock to favoured spots such as Sidi Kaouki, blessed with weather conditions ideally suited to windsurfing, Force 4-7 winds pummelling the 20°C (68°F) seas and waves reaching to about 2.5m (8ft) and higher. Conditions are a little tamer at Taghazout – like Essaouira, also first discovered by French windsurfers – so many beginners start out in the waves here, with more experienced enthusiasts heading for the more taxing waves at points known as Killer and Mystery about 1km (½ mile) to the south. Other coastal spots known for their thrilling wave action include Mehdia Plage at Kenitra, Plage de Safi, Plage de Bouznika between Rabat and Casablanca, Plage de Mirlet near Tiznit, and

Sidi Bouzid at El Jadida.

The long, sandy, unspoiled beaches of Morocco generally boast good to very impressive windsurfing and surfing conditions for most of the year, with peak season corresponding more or less with the high holiday season. Surfing first arrived on these shores with holiday-makers in the early 1970s and has become one of the most important attractions along the country's west coast — the rocky reef sandy banks and beach brea offering considerably more e ing conditions than on the Mediterranean coast to the north. A number of clubs, su schools and organizations ha become so well established there seems to be a never-e series of competitions and t naments catering for both lo and visiting surfers.

1-14 DAYS MOROCCO

CAMEL TREKKING THE DRÂA VALLEY

Travel Info

Destination: Drâa Valley
Requirements: Valid passports (6 months); citizens of EU countries, USA, Australia, Canada and New Zealand do not need visas for stays of less than 90 days. Consult your local embassy.
Currency: Moroccan dirham (100 centimes)
Climate: Valleys are cooler and more hospitable to visitors than the often oppressive heat beyond the Oued Drâa. Best times are September-February.
Risk factor: Minimal, but riding and negotiating skills are an advantage; 4x4 vehicles are recommended for travel beyond camel routes.
Health: No immunizations are required, unless visitors are travelling through or from countries with yellow fever. There is a moderate Aids risk in the area.
Pack: Cool, comfortable and light clothes for the day, and warm gear for nights. If hiring camels from private individuals, take water, bedding and sunscreen.
Facilities: Even small towns and villages have simple but adequate overnight facilities, but few beyond the larger centres have anything remotely luxurious.
Contact: Best of Morocco (UK-based). Tel: 0944-1380-828533, Fax: 0944-1380-828630. www.realmorocco.com

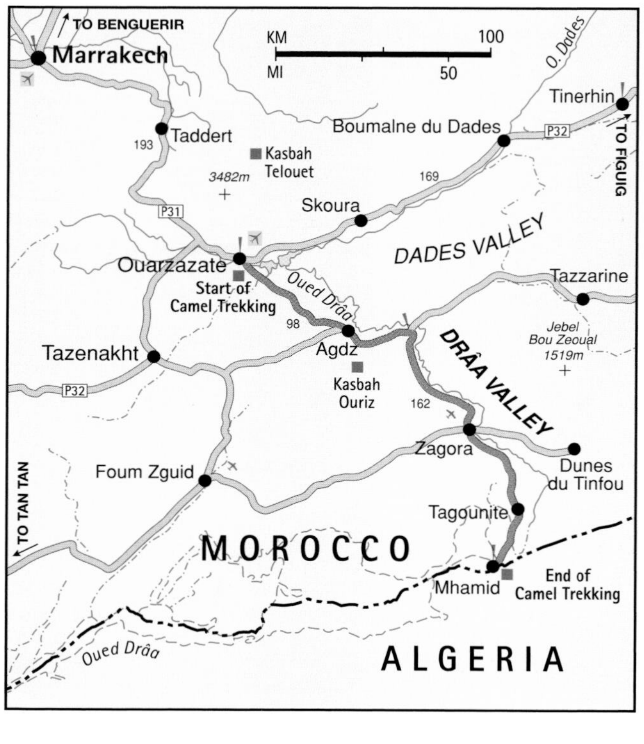

The 1,100km (680-mile) Oued Drâa is Morocco's longest river – a linear oasis of the Drâa Valley that meanders through parched land towards the Sahara, back out of the desert and finally merges into the Atlantic at Cape Drâa, just north of Tan Tan.

Just over 200km (125 miles) from Marrakech on the P31 highway, the most prominent settlement is Ouarzazate, the principal starting point for the camel trekking industry here. The routes followed by camel caravans cross a variety of landscapes – through hilly mountainscapes, up dramatic passes and along rocky plains, finally descending to the tiny hamlet of Agdz, gateway to the Drâa Valley.

These courses trace the line created by the river and drift through about 200km (125 miles) of palm groves, croplands and orchards, while looming overhead are the valley slop The vistas enjoyed by travell are unparalleled, and the jou is interspersed with little ka and other remnants of ancie civilizations. However, the ex rience of the camel trek – ta between one day and two w – makes them even more remarkable. Few other exper ences, particularly those offe at Zagora and Tinfou, can m sitting astride these intrigui beasts, bobbing about in the saddle as the sun sets behin valley walls.

The nearly 100km (60 mil along the Drâa Valley betwe Zagora and Agdz is said to b the most memorable of the camel treks. These exception animals can walk between 5 (30 miles) and 90km (60 mil in a single day, carrying a lo up to 200kg (440 lb) and sta without water for up to a m however, it is unlikely that a trek you undertake will put t endurance statistics to the te

1-4 DAYS
TUNISIA

SAILING TUNISIA'S CHOTT EL JERID

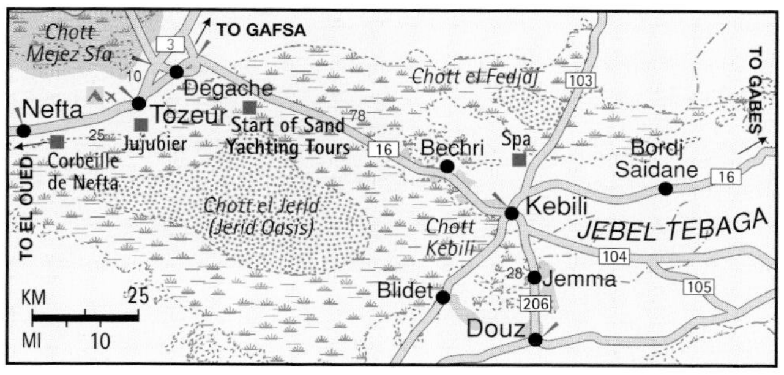

Travel Info
)estination: Chott el Jerid, Tunisia
ements: Valid passports should be
ient for short stays, but visas may
equired for travellers from certain
ies for visits of longer than a few
‹s. Consult your local embassy. No
and yachting permits are required.
ıcy: Tunisian dinar (100 centimes)
e: Generally hot and windy on the
‹posed *chott* and dunes. Best from
ember, but March–May are idyllic.
factor: No risks, other than a few
mps and bruises, but be sensible –
ergency help can be problematic –
ware of sunburn and dehydration.
h: No immunizations are required,
jiene levels are generally poor and
erborne disease is not uncommon.
s a moderate Aids risk in the area.
Sunscreen, hardwearing clothing,
protective gear, and bottled water.
acilities: Adequate introduction by
tors connected to upmarket hotels
arby towns, such as Tozeur, Gabès,
Douz, Degache and Kebili.
Contact: Hotel El Jerid*, B.P. 201,
Tozeur, Tunisia, 2200.
Tel: 09216-76-450488,
Fax: 09216-76-454356
: Most hotels around the principal
s offer sand yachting expeditions.

Whereas Tunisia's coastline has proved to be its most alluring attraction, with yachts and sailing boats dotting its picturesque horizon, an entirely different kind of sailing and yachting is fast gaining popularity as its most innovative pastime. Although history has shown that venturing across the massive *chott*, or salt-crusted lake, was once a tortuous task, the 85km (53-mile) route between Degache and Kebili is today a well-maintained tar road. The dangers are now considerably less than they were for early travellers. In a region where 4x4 excursions seem to be the dominant feature of the local tourism industry, it is indeed a find to discover the sand yachting facilities of Chott el Jerid. This is located between Gabès and the Algerian border, about 20km (12 miles) from Tozeur, from which expeditions can be arranged as most hotels have access to operators.

Although the western extremes of El Jerid are grotty and littered with the debris of irreverent travellers, the colours of the *chott* and its dunes stand in stark contrast to the endless flatness of boulder-strewn, sandy hills and rocky plains. The idyllic desert provides an inspiring setting for this adventure sport.

Harnessing the power of the wind and sand – and there is plenty of both here – is not as easy as it seems, and novices would be well advised to be patient during the learning process. Bumps and falls are frequent – and the resulting aches and bruises decidedly uncomfortable – but the exhilaration of conquering the elements is reward in itself.

'Yachting' tours operate from November to May, with the best sailing conditions prevailing between March and May, whereafter days become too hot to enjoy the experience properly. Be sure to dress appropriately and, if you feel the need (although the locals seldom do, of course), take your own protective gear to shield you from the desert sands, which can be surprisingly hard when you take a fall. Some long runs can be tough and gruelling, but casual trips are far from taxing and pose very little risk of danger. Clothes should be light but hard wearing, and it may be a good idea to tie up long hair and abandon any thoughts of wearing jewellery.

Sailing in the early evenings (few operators take enthusiasts out at night) will require that you use a reliable insect repellent. Be aware of the effects of the sun during the day: the combination of wind and constant exposure to the sun can result in very severe sunburn (use a high-factor sunscreen), heat exhaustion and dehydration can be deadly. Don a hat (with a strap to keep it on when travelling at high speed) and drink plenty of bottled water.

1-4 DAYS
ALGERIA

EXPLORING TASSILI

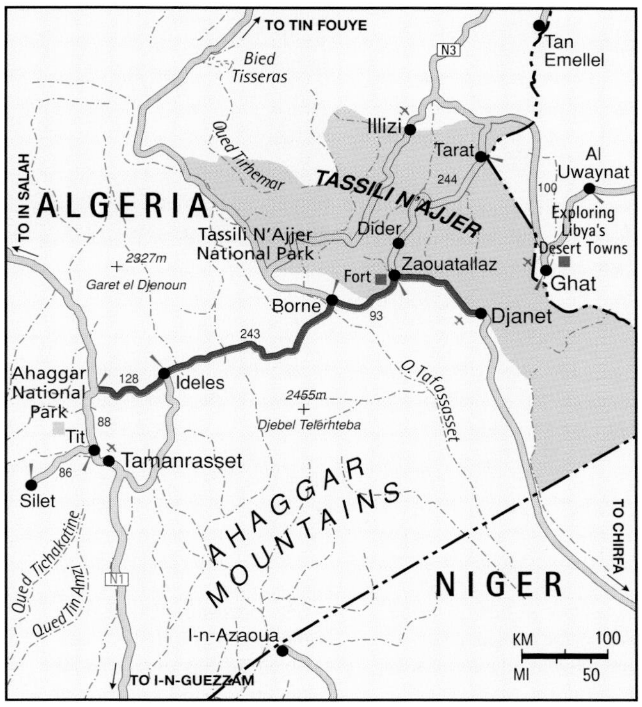

Travel Info
Destination: Tassili, Algeria
ements: Given the political insta-
ity, travel may be perilous or even
icted. Consult your local embassy.
ıcy: Algerian dinar (100 centimes)
ate: Day temperatures are searing,
e nights can be icy. Rain is scarce.
factor: Risks are very high indeed,
vate travel to and through Algeria
is tenuous at best and extremely
angerous at worst, exacerbated by
cessibility and harsh desert condi-
virtually throughout the country.
h: No immunizations are required,
less visitors are travelling through
or from countries with a recent
y of yellow fever. The risk of Aids
is uncertain.
Take with you virtually every day-
necessity, from drinking water to
vehicle parts and spares.
es: Overnight and visitor facilities
improving, but continued internal
means that existing amenities may
ing. Camping and hiking in small,
ected private parties is ill-advised.
Contact: US Embassy, B.P. 408,
Algiers, 16000.
: 09213-21-691-425 / 255 / 186
Fax: 09213-21-693-979

The monuments at Tassili and Ahaggar are the most popular attractions in the entire country, and the area around Tamanrasset is the closest the country gets to an organized hospitality industry – the northern reaches around Algiers are extremely dangerous for foreign travellers. Travel options are limited and the easiest way to get around would probably be with your own vehicle. Getting your vehicle there and travelling safely are, however, an entirely different matter, although things do seem to be picking up a little and it is possible to drive yourself. Travelling from Europe, the roughly 2,500km (1553-mile) route between the coast at Algiers and Djanet (near Tassili N'Ajjer) has been upgraded and allows for some pleasant days of driving. Certain areas remain out of bounds to private vehicles (such as the plateau at Tassili N'Ajjer) but the region is fast gaining popularity for its walks and hiking trails. Your guide will inevitably be a Tuareg (communication is a real difficulty), who knows the land well – his knowledge and expertise as a guide having been passed down from his father and, in all probability, from his father before him.

Trails vary from a single day – one will take you to the famed rock art at Jabberen, others to the historic sites at Tinterhert and Terarart – to four days with mules to carry all equipment and supplies. Given the dry, sweltering conditions and steep inclines, some of the longer treks (such as the 600m/2,000ft to the plateau) are strenuous: attempt them under cooler conditions and rest when the sun is at its fiercest.

The area around Tassili is best known for its ancient art, and it is largely to see these sites that hikers set off to the small town. Most routes to far-off sites may take three to five days, the return journey the most laborious. Temperatures soar and then plummet as night falls.

1-6 DAYS
TERN SAHARA (MOROCCO)

DRIVING THE DUNES OF LAAYOUNE

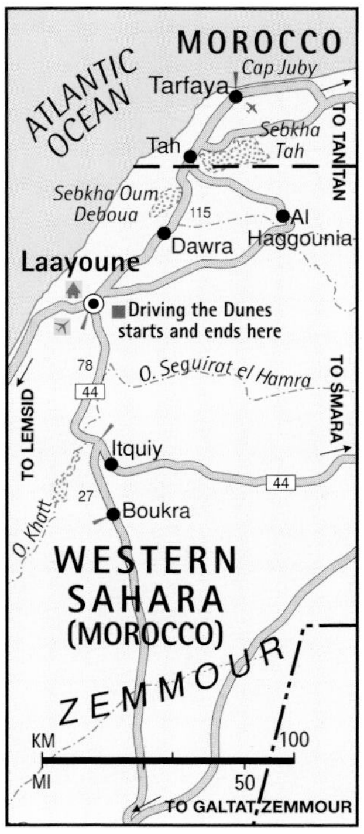

Travel Info
Destination: Laayoune
Requirements: Valid passports (6
hs); citizens of EU countries, USA,
ralia, Canada and New Zealand do
eed visas for stays of less than 90
ys. Consult your local embassy. No
driving permits are required.
Currency: Moroccan dirham
(100 centimes)
te: Best time to visit is April/May,
but days can become very hot.
factor: There should be few risks
ound Laayoune, but deal only with
reputable operators affiliated with
upmarket hotels.
h: No immunizations are required,
s visitors are travelling through or
countries with a recent history of
yellow fever. Moderate Aids risk.
Pack: Cool, lightweight clothing is
tial. The harsh desert demands the
a hat and sunscreen, while bottled
is a good idea. Don't wear shorts.
es: Private excursions are not rec-
ended. Operators provide vehicles.
out comfortable accommodation is
available in and around Laayoune.
Contact: Delegation Regionale du
sme, B.P. 471, Morocco, Laayoune.
Tel: 09212-4-889-1694
Fax: 09212-4-889-1695

Although the people of the Western Sahara have long claimed independence from Morocco, it remains a protectorate of its northern neighbour. Moroccan officials do, however, encourage interaction between its citizens and those of the Western Sahara and, in fact, actively promote tourism to what it essentially considers its southernmost province. There is a surprising amount of tourist traffic in this western extreme of the great desert.

The most impressive attraction in a region of undulating sands parched by the African sun is the sea of rolling dunes that presents one of the most memorable images of North Africa. A very small number of the settlements along this stretch have any real facilities for travellers beyond simple food stalls, cafés, camp sites and other budget accommodation – though this may be the charm of a region that counts its natural heritage as its prime attraction. The main centre at Laayoune – with its apparent military and UN presence – is considered the 'economic hub' of the Western Sahara and is heavily subsidized by Moroccans intent on developing the region for the tourism trade. However, it remains rather insignificant by world standards and, perhaps fortunately, it is hardly a bustling holiday destination. Surrounded by desert, the endless sea of dunes is virtually its only saving grace – but what a gem it is. A number of private individuals and even a few small tour operators work from Laayoune, taking every opportunity to show off the splendour of its desert sands. Although there are a few hikes, desert treks and walking trails that start and end here, it is the dune riding experience that is the principal attraction. Bumping down miles and miles of trackless sand across the vast expanse is indeed a thrill, and many of the small hotels (and all the more upmarket ones, although they are few and far between) offer 4x4 excursions north to Tarfaya. The experience will certainly be fun and memorable – few sunsets can compare. Remember that carefully managed ecotourism has the potential to be one of Africa's most significant income producers.

Ecosystems such as the fragile desert environment are vital to the tourism trade, and the success of official conservation programmes lies almost entirely in the hands of visiting travellers to sensitive areas such as the Western Sahara. It is important to be responsible when navigating these dunes – avoid fly-by-night operators who have no regard for the fragility of the desert landscape.

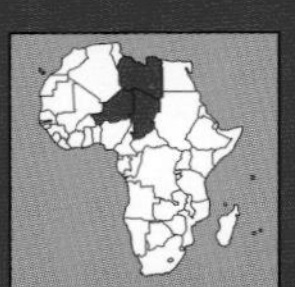

DISCOVERING THE NIGER

1–14 DAYS
NIGER

Travel Info
Destination: Niamey
Requirements: Passports, visas and yellow-fever certificates are essential – officials may want to see a return ticket. Although the capital is relatively safe, take no chances with bureaucracy.
Currency: Franc CFA (100 centimes)
Climate: Days can be warm, but being on the water means that temperatures are moderate, particularly during the rains. Best time to canoe is October–May, when the water levels have risen.
Risk factor: Although large tracts wind through open savanna, certain sections cut through forested banks and there may be several rapids. Most are simple to navigate, but a few may be challenging, especially after good rains.
Health: The Niger is relatively clean with no real health hazards for swimmers. Hippos should be avoided, although they tend to stay well clear of boats.
Pack: You will need your own tent, camping equipment and food rations, with a set of waterproof clothing for canoeing and a set of warm clothing.
Facilities: Facilities are generally basic but adequate, with no five-star treatment. Aim to be entirely self-sufficient.
Contact: Niger Car Voyages, Avenue de l'Afrique. Tel: 09227-732-331, Fax: 09227-733-539

Coursing through a diverse range of habitats and extending for 4,184km (2,600 miles), much of the Niger is navigable by canoe and the 36,260km² (14,000 sq. mile) delta has plenty of exploration opportunities.

Most river-based excursions start in and around Niamey, which has sound tourist facilities and reliable transport.

Despite the disappointing trickle that is the source of the Niger, by the time the river has made its way into Niger, it is quite impressive and a number of river-riders start their trip here. It is essential that travellers utilize local guides. In Niger, the reliable guides may be found in Niamey, and most small towns en route should be able to offer accommodation and food.

Visitors heading for the Niger will not need to take long and bumpy road trips to get there. Transport opportunities are quite varied – from taxis to market trucks – and the glorified dirt paths are relatively easy to negotiate, even on a bicycle. A hike to the river, although not challenging, may prove difficult only because – despite short distances – it takes longer than imagined (some hikers can take only a few hours to get to there).

Some adventurers opt for a simple plank as a 'vessel' which, although cheap and easy to handle, can accommodate only one, so most choose a dugout canoe. The waters are easy to navigate and the trip will make no demands on physical strength. Villages are few on certain sections, so travellers have to b self-reliant. All along the ri there are hindrances and, although relatively easily ov come, this is not for the ser traveller: if the canoe does capsize, you will certainly g wet enough to be uncomfo

Depending on individual eraries, some parts of the ri can be completed in a day o few hours between stops. O require a lot more time and effort – some stretches can up to two weeks to comple and are sure to sap at least of your energy.

CAMEL TREKKING IN NIGER

3–7 DAYS
NIGER

Travel Info
Destination: The Ténéré
Requirements: Passports, visas and yellow-fever certificates are essential – officials may want to see a return ticket. To cross the Ténéré you need a local guide, and police insist you travel in convoy. Take no chances.
Currency: Franc CFA (100 centimes)
Climate: Conditions are unbelievably hot and dry. Best times to visit are the coolest months: November–January.
Risk factor: At certain points you will have to report to the Gard Nomadique, the Niger desert police, but this is simply a formality and there should be no complications, especially if travelling with a local guide. Extreme caution is advised in the desert, with careful planning.
Health: Drink lots of fluids. Respect the environment and the military.
Pack: Pack clothes to cater for extreme temperatures, plus sunscreen, protective headgear, water and a first-aid kit.
Facilities: A number of international agencies offer carefully planned and well-executed tours into desert regions. Niamey and other large settlements offer alternatives, but are not always reliable.
Contact: Nigercar-Voyages, Avenue de l'Afrique. Tel: 09227-73-2331, Fax: 09227-73-3539

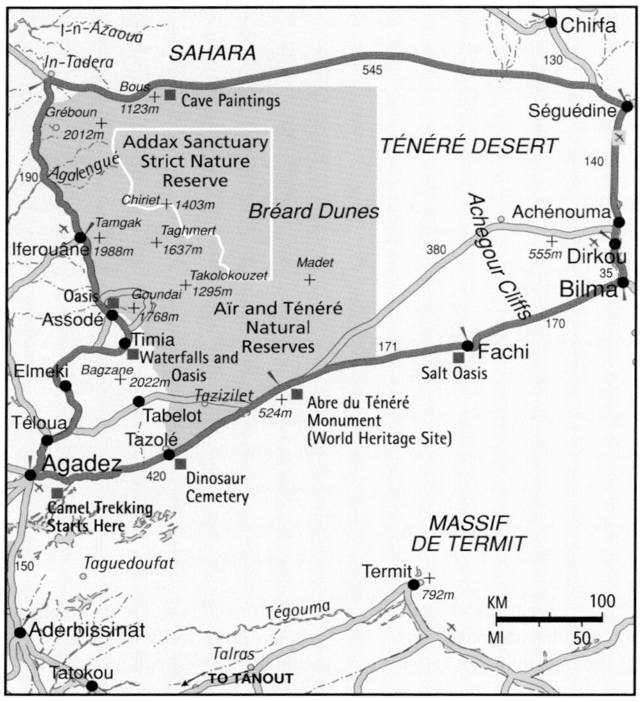

Even the best-planned operation along the easiest of the Ténéré's routes will present challenges. Camels are the most convenient and rewarding way of travelling from one isolated oasis to another. The sun is harsh, the heat often unbearable and the air dry, and the going both demanding and slow. The journey will be long and uncomfortable unless you are accustomed to riding, yet camels are a better option than 4x4 vehicles on the desert sands.

The most frequently used routes across Niger's Ténéré wind their way between high sand dunes that tower some 300m (1,000ft) – buffeted by the same harmattan winds that bring a chill to the desert night – into giant crests that are difficult to ascend and unnerving to descend. When the air isn't stiflingly hot and still, winds sweep across the sand and rocks. Most camel treks start at Agadez or Bilma or other 'urban' settlements. Dry desert grasses and small and insignificant acacia are swallowed up by the emptiness beyond the towns. As you trek deeper into the Sahara there is very little else for miles around, other than the scattering of black boulders – just sand and sky. One endless ridge of sand looks much like the next, so orientation is a constant battle that becomes increasingly difficult as the winds pick up or night begins to settle. It is at these times that one abandoned oil rig looks eerily similar to an outcrop of rocks left behind hour or two previously. You not rely on instinct here, be it will not be reliable – as e denced by a plane wreck or gravestone in the sand.

The trek will almost certa be a long one of at least 50 (310 miles) and, given the t of the desert people, you ar unlikely to encounter any m than the most basic amenit right up until you find yours at the foot of the giant cliff that pinpoint the outer limi the Ténéré.

DRIVING LIBYA'S COAST

3–5 DAYS
LIBYA

Travel Info
Destination: Mediterranean coast, Libya
Requirements: Visitors will need a letter of invitation from a Libyan citizen and a visa – neither are easy to obtain. Extreme caution should be taken when travelling and all necessary documentation must be verified and approved prior to departure. You need a permit to drive on Libya's roads, plus a desert permit and a local guide to ride off-road.
Currency: Libyan dinar (1,000 dirhams)
Climate: Best time to drive the coast is November–January.
Risk factor: Libya is difficult to travel in, so visitors are urged to use an operator with reliable links to a Libyan agency. Off-road driving is controlled and fuel stops congregate on main routes only.
Health: There are few health risks, but confirm with your operator in advance.
Pack: The coast is well developed, so items should be available in big towns.
Facilities: English is rarely spoken, so independent travel is near impossible. Without a knowledgeable guide, even basic requirements are hard to obtain.
Contact: Libyan Tourism Treasures, 25 Shari'a, Istanbul, Tripoli. P.O. Box 5144, Tripoli. Tel: 09218-21-444-9199 Fax: 09218-21-333-9486

The Tripolitanian coast, commonly referred to as the Jezirat al Maghreb by locals, makes for an ideal scenic drive and is wonderfully devoid of tourists, although driving in Libya can be hair-raising: Libyans are very bad drivers, with scant regard for safety. Visitors should drive very cautiously even on empty roads in isolated areas. You do not want to be forced into an encounter with the local police or traffic officials. Apart from the fact that it is the nation's capital, Tripoli is the obvious starting point for a trip along Libya's coast. It is also busy and noisy, but delightfully cosmopolitan.

The Tripolitanian coast is a fertile stretch scattered with ancient Greek and Roman ruins and highlighted by the grand Italian-style architecture of the capital, but it also covers a vast distance that can seem to go on forever. Long trips along the Mediterranean – extending east from the capital to Tobruk and onward to Egypt – should be carefully planned, especially if they do not entail returning to a large settlement overnight. The route is, however, a pleasant one and is lined with citrus orchards and stands of olive trees. Much of this area is also covered by a well-maintained road network that offers unparalleled views across the Mediterranean, and smaller coastal towns offer more-than-adequate amenities. One of the finest is Sabratah, best known for the beauty of its landscape and the magnificence of its surviving ruins, a legacy of the Roman occupation of Libya. Better known is, of course, Leptis Magna, a series of Roman baths, ruined amphitheatres and other archaeological sites of enormous historical significance. Further east lie the Greek cities of Cyrene and Appollonia, as well as the splendour of Jbel Akhdar, a beautiful 'peninsula' jutting out into the Mediterranean, which provides some rewarding driving.

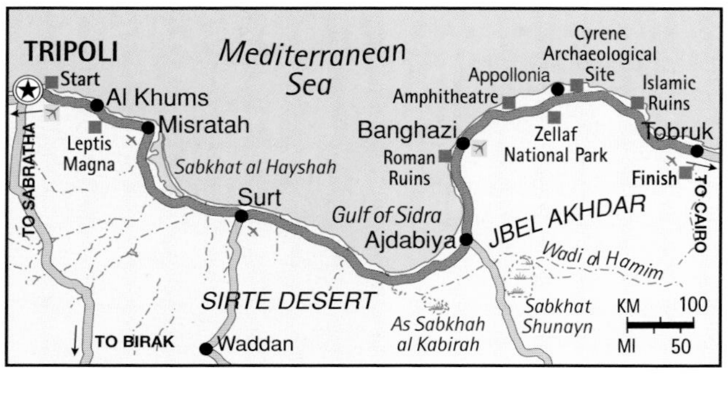

Given the popularity of the coastal region, it is remarkably uninhabited – particularly the stony plateau inland – and the drives are blissfully uninterrupted. In most areas you will travel for kilometres on lonely, isolated roads and rough tracks that seem endless, with hardly another person in sight. This may make for some excellent driving, but realize that should anything happen – particularly when ing off-road – the chances help are limited to your gui and his network of contacts which, although generally re able, may prove quite exper Off-road driving means taki your own spares, winches a sand ladders and, because y will have to cross either the dunes slightly inland or the Mediterranean beach sands, should have at least some s when negotiating soft sands other obstacles.

1 DAY+ LIBYA

Travel Info
Destination: Birak
rements: Visitors will need a letter tation from a Libyan citizen and a visa – neither are easy to obtain. n should be taken when travelling necessary documentation must be d and approved prior to departure. u need a desert permit and a local guide to ride off-road.
ency: Libyan dinar (1,000 dirhams)
ate: Best time to enter the Libyan t is in winter, when conditions are oler. Nights and early mornings are enerally cold throughout the year.
ctor: Libya is difficult to travel in, sitors are urged to use an operator h reliable links to a Libyan agency. road driving is controlled and fuel s congregate on main routes only.
: Other than standard precautions, e should be few health risks when sing the desert. Confirm the status he area as conflicts tend to erupt. Be as self-reliant as possible, even when travelling with an operator.
ilities: English is rarely spoken, so ependent travel is near impossible.
Contact: Coast and Desert Travel, P.O. Box 3139, Tripoli. Tel: 09218-21-444-0029, Fax: 09218-21-444-8979

EXPLORING LIBYA'S DESERT TOWNS

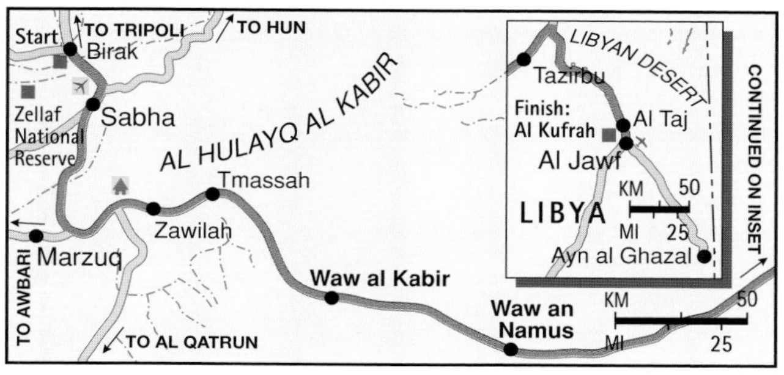

Although travel from Tripoli to Gharyan and onward to Birak is via a long, narrow road lined with terraced farming land, the route will take you further and further into what is clearly desert and some of the most remarkable landscape Libya has to offer. The people are generally ardent followers of Islam and, although the towns are extraordinarily quaint and steeped in a fascinating history, some Westerners may feel out of place amid the harsh lifestyle of these people. Alcohol is strictly forbidden (especially in smaller, conservative communities) and women are clearly the underlings in the village, with most required to cover up completely. Disregard of these social rules is frowned upon and actively discouraged.

Some local norms are less rigid in coastal towns such as Sirt, which is also one of the entry points into the desert. The Sirt route will lead from the coast to Houn and again down to Birak, Libya's centre and the heart of desert life. From here, all the settlements east to the Acacus mountains of the Fezzan, south to the desert towns of Sabha and Zuela and west to Waw al Kabir, War an Namus, Tazirbu and finally Al Kufrah, in the southeast of the country, rich in cultural history and staunchly Muslim. All routes south from the Libyan capital or Sirt on the Tripolitanian coast are long and tiring, and much of the terrain is difficult to cover and not at all 'user-friendly' for Westerners. Leading increasingly further from civilization, the isolated roads to Sabha and Wadi al Hayat are dotted with a sprinkling of oasis towns and villages from which travellers may venture out onto the endless desert sands of the Sahara, and the extraordinary rock art that lies scattered there. Most notable of these settlements are Teshwinet and Wadi

Matkhandoush, most famed for their stylized scripts and other depictions of life in the region more than 3,000 years ago. While some of the rocks show signs carved by elements such as the wind and even the sea – much of the region was covered by the erosive waves of the ocean millennia ago – some of the depictions carved by human hands show evidence of elephant and other plains mammals that lived here some 6,000 years ago.

Etched into the rock faces are rural scenes that show farming with domestic cattle, hunting expeditions, village life and even the camel caravans that passed through as they plied the trade routes. Although fewer than in the past, still scattered among the pebbles, stones and decaying ruins are arrow heads, shards of pottery and other ancient artefacts, making the sands and the desert settlements a wonderland for exploration.

3 DAYS+ LIBYA

Travel Info
Destination: Acacus Mountains
ements: Visitors will need a letter tation from a Libyan citizen and a visa – neither are easy to obtain. n should be taken when travelling necessary documentation must be d and approved prior to departure. u need a desert permit and a local guide to ride off-road.
ncy: Libyan dinar (1,000 dirhams)
te: The Acacus Mountains and the ezzan are hot, dry and windswept.
ctor: Desert winds can play havoc th vehicles and movement may be severely restricted. Civilization is ic, and any supplies or spare parts some time to reach these outposts all. Off-road driving is controlled, uel stops tend to congregate only around principal towns.
Other than standard precautions, e should be few health risks when ing the desert. Confirm the status e area as conflicts tend to erupt. Be as self-reliant as possible, even n travelling with an operator – an ption that is highly recommended.
ilities: English is rarely spoken, so ependent travel is near impossible.
ntact: Akakus Tours, Tripoli, Libya. Tel: 09218-274-2813 / 04

CROSSING THE ACACUS MOUNTAINS

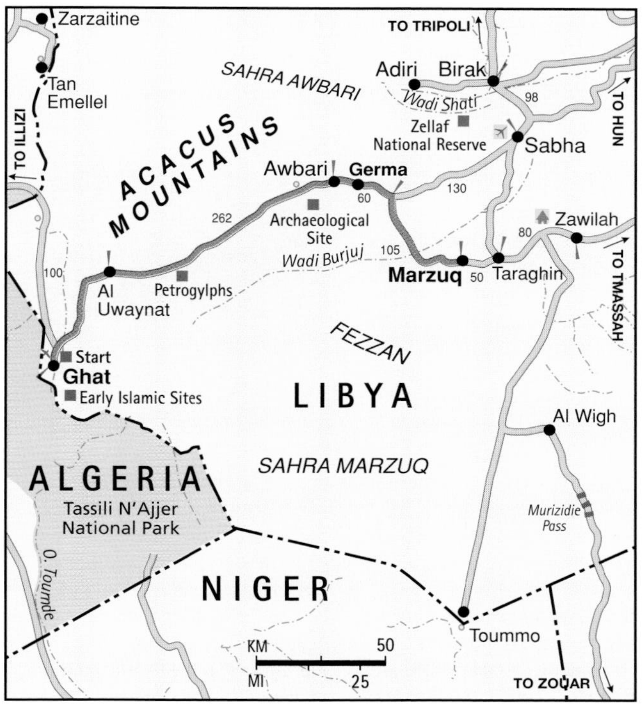

The Acacus Mountains extend from the Awbari Sand Sea north to the country's southern border with Algeria, and reach a height of 1,000-1,500m (3,300-5,000ft) in the southwestern corner of Libya. At their foot lie the gravel plains and desert dunes of the region known as the Fezzan, a dry and empty expanse of rocks, sand and salt lakes. On the face of it, the Fezzan may appear uninspiring and, apart from the historical significance of its rock art, much of it is little more than arid plain. It does, however, include the Acacus Mountains. The faces of the mountains are riddled with long-forgotten caves and alcoves, the boulder-strewn terrain ideal for off-road adventure. This prime 4x4 terrain, with its fantastical rock formations and – like so many of the surrounding desert towns – ancient rock art, is excellent for camping. The region has changed much over the millennia, the relatively dense vegetation replaced by open savanna plains, and the herds of elephant, giraffe, ostrich, rhino and antelopes have long gone.

Today, many of the towns – Ghat, Marzuq and Germa – exist largely as a result of the trade routes that crisscrossed the Sahara. A number of these well-worn paths are still utilized in modern Libya and have become much used routes, with an equal number left to be covered by the sands, or rediscovered by off-road enthusiasts. Crossing the mountains means making your way across fine sand – let your tyres down to help traverse the sand here – and along winding passes that skirt nail-biting freefalls. Many 4x4 enthusiasts tend to take a team of camels along as emergency back-up, but if this is not possible it is wise to travel with at least two vehicles. Excursions last a few days at

least, taking you far from reliable spare-part suppliers and other conveniences. The journey will be demanding, with plenty of soft sand and rocky outcrops to cover. You need experience, a guide and good equipment – so it may not be a cheap experience.

4 HOURS+ CHAD

Travel Info
Destination: Lake Chad
ements: A yellow-fever certificate ential and you may be required to ce proof of a cholera inoculation.
itors – except French and German s – need a visa. Travellers need to ster immediately with N'Djamena's immigration office.
rrency: Franc CFA (100 centimes)
: Days can be uncomfortably hot, me on the water allows for cooler onditions. October–April are best.
factor: Although much of Chad is , N'Djamena and its surrounds are tively trouble-free. Confirm status ur agent and relevant authorities.
ealth: Malaria remains a problem. a is a hazard, but it is unlikely to leeting visitors aware of the dan- s. Take water purification tablets. Take anything you think you may s the region is virtually devoid of ructure. Sunscreen and protective clothing are advisable.
ilities: Western-style facilities are non-existent, and what is avail- basic and best avoided. Try to be as self-sufficient as possible.
ntact: Department of Tourism and Parks, B.P. 86, N'Djamena, Chad. 235-512303, Fax: 09235-572261

DISCOVERING LAKE CHAD

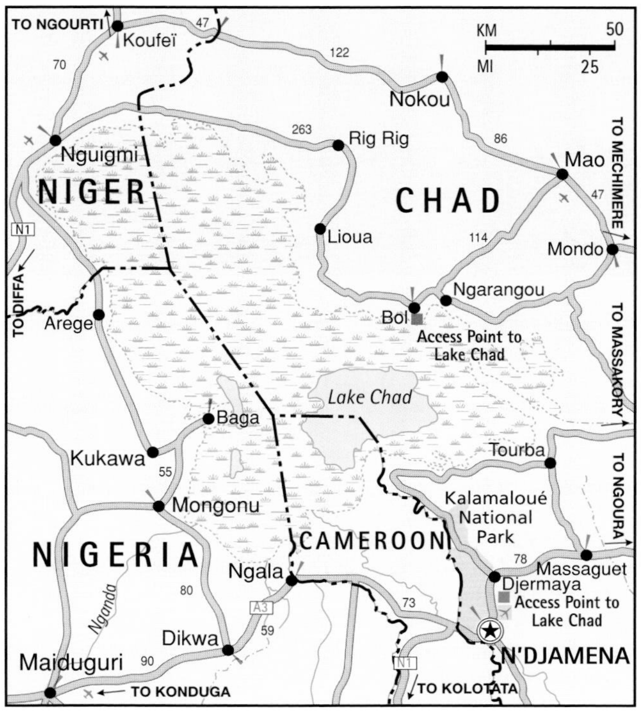

Lake Chad is undoubtedly the top attraction in this difficult-to-travel country. The rewards are, however, unique and the isolation and inaccessibility make the destination that much more alluring. The lake remains a favourite escape even for locals and its shores can get quite congested. The endlessly frustrating bureaucracy of Chad's officialdom inevitably hampers visits to the lake, and it is for this reason that Lake Chad remains unravaged by modern commercialism. The shores are remarkably untouched by development and are easily explored, especially with the assistance of locals who spend so much of their time on the waters. The surrounding area is one of the few in Chad that are relatively safe from the crime and violence that seem to pervade much of the north. The sheer size of the lake is perhaps its most notable attribute, extending some 10,000 to 26,000km² (4,000 to 10,000 sq. miles), depending on the amount of rain that has fallen, but it has on occasion all but dried up during dry seasons.

The terrain consists mostly of scrub and sand, but this does little to deter the determined adventurers. Because of the volatile political situation, few surveys have been conducted on the viability of the lake, but this has not stopped travellers who continue to row, sail and even swim these waters. This may prove a little reckless, but any number of boats big and small, used mostly to fish the lake, can be hired on the shore, and the vastness of the lake surface means that it is not difficult to spend a full day soaking up the sun. There are, however, plenty of opportunities to explore the lake's shores, hike the immediate surrounds and discover the cultural element of village life.

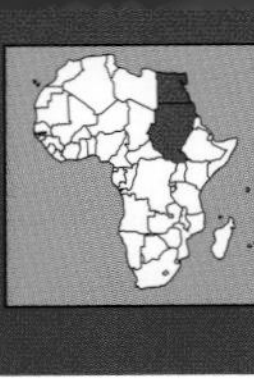

1 DAY+ EGYPT

Travel Info

Destination: Red Sea
Requirements: Most visitors will need a passport and an easy-to-obtain visa.
Currency: Egyptian pound (100 piastres)
Climate: The climate is dry and hot all year, with temperatures reaching 40°C (75°F) in summer and seldom falling below 15°C (30°F) in winter.
Risk factor: The inadequacies of divers pose the most danger. Know your own limits and level of expertise and never dive alone in unknown waters.
Health: Wash all raw fruit and vegetables and drink only bottled water. Pollution is present but should pose little danger to divers using common sense.
Pack: Dive operators are generally well equipped and knowledgeable about what is required on diving expeditions. Be sure to use only reputable operators who are well established. Equipment may be hired, often at an additional charge.
Facilities: Diving facilities range from adequate to impressive. Most dive schools or centres offer courses of various durations and degrees of skill. Accommodation and other amenities are more limited but are also generally more comfortable the further south you dive.
Contact: Red Sea Diving Club. Tel: 0920-3-601342

DIVING THE RED SEA

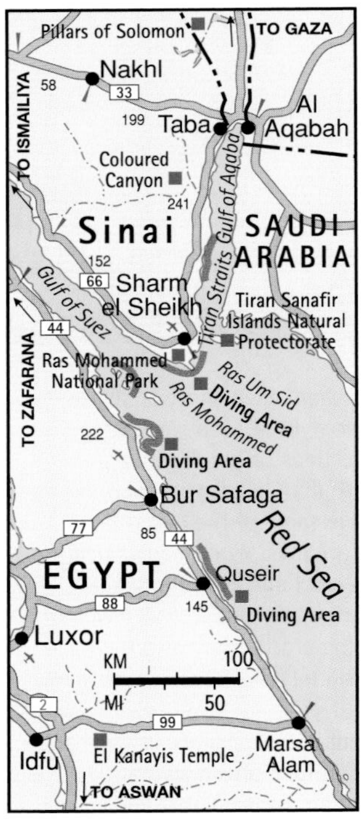

With water temperatures reaching no lower than 20°C (38°F) in winter and averaging 30°C (56°F) in summer, the Red Sea is all it is made out to be. Because the sea is relatively undisturbed by rain and current, the water is crystal clear, with excellent visibility on descents as far as 40m (130ft) in summer and 25-30m (82-98ft) in winter. Currents are quite gentle and the reefs and underwater inclines are, for the most part, in good condition. Despite a relatively sparse population and the responsible practices adopted by many dive operations, the burgeoning popularity of diving has exerted considerable pressures on the marine ecosystem.

The remarkable Near and Middle gardens and, in particular, the Far Garden are easily accessed by divers with a modicum of skill and experience, while the underwater world around the Tiran Straits and Ras Mohammed may require more than the basics. The latter is notorious for powerful currents and abrupt inclines that make snorkelling hazardous. Snorkelling, on the other hand, is more accessible further south, with virtually all tourist-oriented sites – such as Ras um Sid at Sharm el Sheikh – catering for all levels. Although there are many well-known coral-festooned wrecks to explore, the magic lies in the natural wonders: a paradise of lionfish, parrotfish, stingrays, fans, Spanish dancers and other nudibranchs. Because of the appeal of these waters, there is no shortage of dive clubs, dive schools and diving centres – many of which offer night dives – and most are well versed in the demands of diving the Red Sea. As a result, popular dive sites around Sinai are now soundly based in commercialism, so it is the less explored southern region around Hurghada that

may offer a better experience. The sea is generally as calm as glass, while activities are carefully monitored by the Hurghada Environmental Protection and Conservation Association. One of the most spectacular stretches is the 300km (185-mile) section extending from Quseir to the Egyptian border with Sudan. Although not very well serviced, it is wonderfully empty of other visitors and boasts a number of (pricey) 'hotel' boats that cater well for visitors. These unspc areas are supreme in their appeal: vertical walls that d some 100m (330ft) and are cled by colourful clownfish, racuda, masked butterflyfish moray eels and turtles. The walls and not easily accesse the novice – diving here is n leisurely pastime and you w need some sort of advanced ing qualification if you inter tackle this marine wonderla

2-3 DAYS EGYPT

Travel Info

Destination: Nile Valley
Requirements: Almost all foreign visitors will require a valid passport and a relatively easy-to-obtain visa.
Currency: Egyptian pound (100 piastres)
Climate: The air is hot and humid, so the cooler climes of the Nile Valley have attracted the most attention from visiting adventurers. It can get a little windy, but not enough to cause discomfort.
Risk factor: Risks are few, but bilharzia is a scourge of the Nile. Both the river and its delta are infested with the disease-carrying mollusc, so swimming is not advised; any protracted contact with the water may be risky.
Health: Wash all the raw fruit and vegetables you eat and drink only bottled water. Do not swim in the Nile.
Pack: Take lightweight travelling clothes, and your own bottled water.
Facilities: Other than the boat ride, few amenities are offered by felucca operators, and you will generally be expected to be self-sufficient. Areas such as Aswan are fairly well geared towards the foreign traveller.
Contact: Egyptian Tourist Authority, 5 Sharia Adly St, Cairo. Tel: 0920-2-3913454 Fax: 0920-2-6854363 / 6854788

SAILING DOWN THE NILE

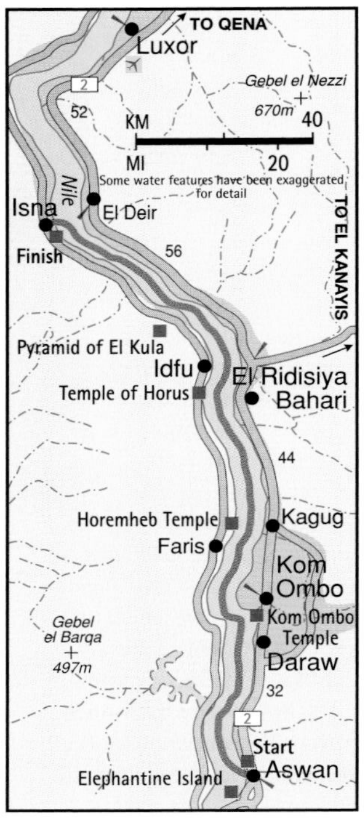

The most famous river in all of Africa, the Nile has been the focal point of Egypt since the most ancient of days, yet the fertile valley through which the river snakes remains in stark contrast to the dry surrounds of the arid lands beyond.

The river is plied by every conceivable vessel able to negotiate its waters, but it is the ancient felucca (the traditional wooden sailing boat with two sails) that remains the most common on the waters of the Nile. Still used by the locals for transport, fishing and even recreation, the felucca has adapted to changing times to become the means by which visitors sail the Nile. To hire a felucca is as easy as clicking your fingers as they are present every few metres along the banks of the river, and their skippers-cum-owners are eager to please and equally eager to get back out on the water. Tickets are easily obtained from the self-styled operators working the Corniche and, although prices vary, are generally inexpensive. The starting point is usually the southern town of Aswan, where hundreds of budget travellers gather to hire the 600-plus feluccas that ply these waters. The most popular excursions entail a two- to three-day trip on the Nile from the southern town of Aswan to Idfu, Kom Ombo and Esna. Although others may be shorter – some lasting only a few hours, such as exploratory trips to the Nile islands of Kitchener's and Elephantine – the three-day trips offer a unique opportunity to unwind and escape the chaos of Cairo and other bustling cities. Because the vessels are rather small, these trips are best taken in small groups of no more than six individuals, although the operator – who has the potential

to earn 20 times the average wage in Cairo – may try to persuade you to take more for the ride. There will be an additional fee for police registration, and you will in all likelihood have to pay for your own food en route, especially if you are utilizing the services of private felucca owners or other fly-by-nigh

The trip itself is likely to b gentle, lazy cruise down a ri lined with date palms, bana trees and mango stands – th view only occasionally interrupted by the sight of a gra cruise liner blotting the hori

1-2 DAYS EGYPT

Travel Info

Destination: Sinai Peninsula
Requirements: Almost all visitors need a passport and an easy-to-obtain visa.
Currency: Egyptian pound (100 piastres)
Climate: The climate is dry and hot all year, with temperatures reaching 40°C (75°F) in summer and seldom falling below 15°C (30°F) in winter. Nights on the peninsula can be extremely cold.
Risk factor: Land mines and bandits are present, so travel in groups or hire an overland operator who knows the area.
Health: Wash fruit and vegetables and drink bottled water. To avoid heat exhaustion, cover up and drink plenty of fluids.
Pack: Lightweight (days) and warm (nights) clothing – temperatures drop rapidly. Take sturdy hiking boots and essentials to walk Mount Sinai; a torch and warm clothing for the 'sunrise hike'.
Facilities: Accommodation is not varied but is adequate – book through a reputable operator. Entry to certain areas, such as Ras Mohammed, will not automatically form part of your Sinai trip – separate arrangements must be made. Special permits are required for camping.
Contact: Egyptian Tourist Authority, 5 Sharia Adly St, Cairo. Tel: 0920-2-3913454 Fax: 0920-2-6854363 / 6854788

CROSSING THE SINAI DESERT

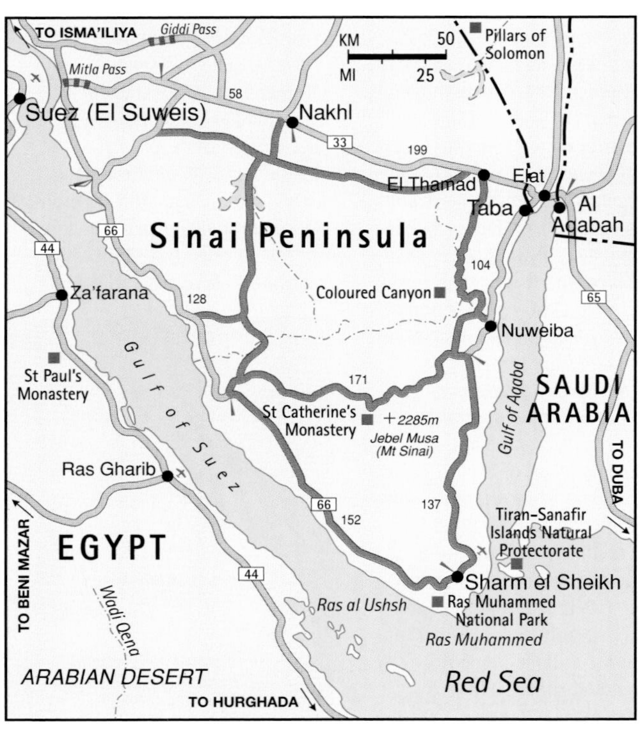

Although the Sinai Peninsula is virtually surrounded by the Red Sea, it is most noted for the beauty of its sandy plains and rocky mountain slopes.

The inland tourist trade centres around the arid mountains. Bordered in the north by the Mediterranean and the southern peninsula by the Red Sea, the hinterland is characterized by dry plains punctuated by oases, the five largest of which are increasingly popular among travellers. They remain relatively unscathed by development and are valuable as stopovers for at least some of the tourist traffic travelling across the Sinai. Overlanding Sinai is neither arduous nor hazardous: the trick is to stick to secure, well-established routes. Reliable and up-to-date road maps are essential as routes are not well signposted and are easily confused with other less safe and detours and alternatives.

The most visited spot is the 2,285m (7,500ft) Mount Sinai where, according to the Bible, God gave Moses the Ten Commandments. Known loc as Jebel Musa, the mountai neither difficult to climb no ticularly demanding. Access the easily traversed trail, bu it also be reached via the St of Repentance. According to local legend, the Steps were forged by a monk who painstakingly cut the 3,000 step hand, and hiking this route rather, walking it!) should ta no more than three hours. M travellers across the Sinai m an excursion of it, stopping night on the slopes.

The going, be it by 4x4, b camel, is slow – the sands c play havoc with inexperienc drivers – but not too uncom able. It is the oppressive hea rather than substandard tra that get the better of travel not accustomed to battered vehicles or temperamental camels. Poverty is everywhe and many locals traders dep on the passing tourists.

1 DAY

SUDAN

WRECK DIVING OFF THE SUDANESE COAST

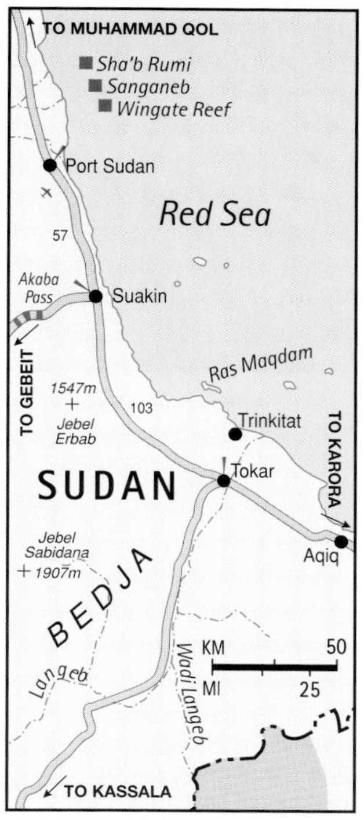

Travel Info

Destination: Port Sudan
...rements: All travellers need a visa, ...btaining one can be a lengthy and ...ting process. Travel permits (avail... ...n Khartoum) are required for trips ...nd the capital. Never rely on flight ...edules, and be aware that customs ...ry strict with even everyday items.
...cy: Sudanese pound (100 piastres)
...te: Temperatures are warm to hot, ...the best months to dive June–July. ...er temperatures, partly because of ...erground volcanic activity, are very ...arm, peaking at about 30°C (86°F).
...actor: Sharks, lionfish and stinging ...are present, so never take chances.
...th: Take standard precautions such ...drinking only bottled water. Divers ...e susceptible to ear infections and ...ual risks of diving and snorkelling.
...k: Facilities are limited, and divers ...vised to take their own equipment ...d accessories to be self-sufficient.
...es: There are few diving operators, ...l equipment is non-existent. Bring ...own! The best way to dive is from live-aboard boats in Port Sudan.
Contact: Olympia Travel Agents P.O. Box 2068, Khartoum, Sudan ...249-11-778580, Fax: 09249-11-...241, olympiatravel@hotmail.com

The waters off Sudan are not nearly as well serviced as those off Egypt, and the environment enjoys far less protection. Nonetheless, this part of the Red Sea remains one of the region's most rewarding diving areas. The temperate waters sustain over 400 species of coral and a plethora of fish and invertebrates. The relative isolation and the awkward geography have resulted in fewer visitors, which has protected the ecosystem.

Getting into and travelling around Sudan may not be easy, but the rewards are great: the water is crystal clear, as there is little run-off from the land. The sea remains largely undisturbed by humans as there is almost no fishing, although this in turn means that there are a greater number of sharks. The water off Port Sudan is some of the deepest in the world, reaching over 3,000m (9,970ft), resulting in the marine life in the area being one of the world's most diverse, with fish such as rainbow runners, tuna, jacks, unicornfish, sailfin surgeonfish, parrotfish and barracuda swimming the coral-encrusted reefs. Although most diving activity takes place in the winter months – summer sees strong currents and whirlpools – water temperatures average 28°C (82°F) virtually throughout the year. The more experienced divers can dive as deep as 40m (130ft), yet much of the marine splendour is also on offer at 25m (80ft). The reef wall at Sha'b Rumi – about 40km (25 miles) from Port Sudan – is said to provide one of the finest dive sites in the world and is particularly remarkable between 20m (65ft) and 36m (120ft). Lionfish, lagoon rays and sharks roam among the remnants of pioneering equipment from Jacques Cousteau's underwater expedition in the 1970s and, open to exploration, the site still provides some unique 'wreck'-diving opportunities. There is plenty of fish, but it is better to stick to the wall of the reef than to open spaces if you don't want sharks to mistake you for prey. Further afield are old diving cages and fish pens also open to investigation, but it may be worth your while to move on to the 8km (5-mile) atoll of Sanganeb, where the waters are more than 25m (80ft) deep. As a result, both North Point and Southwest Point are hailed as two of the top dives: both are carpeted with coral life and an abundance of marine animals, but are surpassed by the experience of exploring the wreck of the *Umbria*, visible from the surface of the water at Wingate Reef off Port Sudan.

The sea here is still and warm, with plenty of colour and life. The length of the wreck extends from 15–35m (50–120ft), but is quite easily accessed via a number of entry points – although some areas of the ship are more difficult to access and are thus less explored.

7 DAYS+

SUDAN

TRAIN JOURNEY FROM KHARTOUM TO WADI HALFA

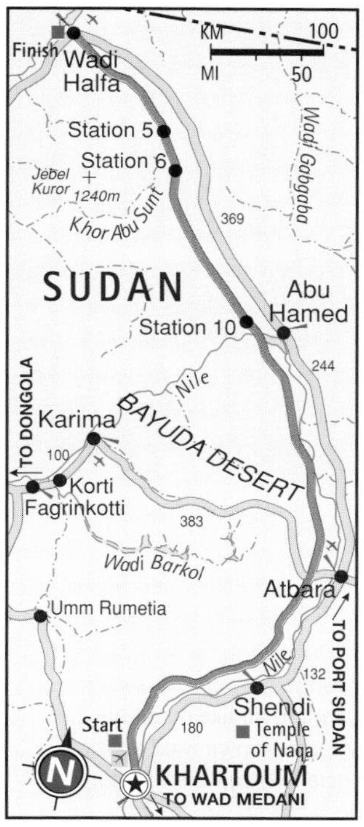

Travel Info

Destination: Khartoum
...ements: All travellers need a visa, ...btaining one can be a lengthy and ...frustrating process. Travel permits ...able in the Khartoum) are required for trips beyond the capital.
...cy: Sudanese pound (100 piastres)
...e: Dry and inhospitable, with little ...rain or relief from the harsh sun.
...factor: With some common sense ...sensible itinerary, travellers should ...ew risks and the train trip is rela...ly hassle-free. There may be other ...s in Sudan (check with authorities ... travel agents prior to departure).
...h: Health risks are few, apart from ...andard precautions such as drink...g only the bottled drinking water.
...k: Days can be sweltering even on the train, but nights are icy. Take ...own bedding and food if travelling ...nomy class', although the latter is ...y available at the stopover towns.
...es: Amenities are adequate, albeit ...with a few more comforts enjoyed ...n the 'luxury class' compartments.
Contact: Olympia Travel Agents P.O. Box 2068, Khartoum, Sudan
Tel: 09249-11-778580
Fax: 09249-11-781241
olympiatravel@hotmail.com

The train trip from the bustling capital of Khartoum is one of the best opportunities to see Sudan.

Little remains of the once impressive network of trains that crisscrossed Sudan, and the existing state-owned and -run rail infrastructure is little more than a practical means of getting produce and merchandise from one point to another. One of the few existing lines is the route from Khartoum, which stretches north to Wadi Halfa (also, incidentally, serviced by a fairly regular bus route that is considerably less enticing!), with branch lines to Port Sudan and Karima, and another that extends from Er-Rahad to Nyala.

The train from Khartoum to Wadi Halfa is scheduled to depart every Monday, but do not allow the rest of your trip to depend on the punctual departure or arrival of the train – or, indeed, any other form of transport. The trip itself is not very expensive and there are a number of options from which to choose: the 'sleeper' class which, although still cheap, is double the cost of first- and second-class compartments. In the former, you are likely to get some peace, quiet and, with a little luck, some rest, whereas the first-class and second-class compartments are usually filled to capacity (which is theoretically limited to six in first class!). The trip is already cheap for foreigners and much in demand among locals (discounts are seldom granted), but there are many diversions to justify the already negligible outlay.

The train stops at Atbara – where Lord Kitchener first encountered the Mahdists – from where it will divert either to Port Sudan or Wadi Halfa. Once-thriving Atbara is now little more than a final resting place for run down locomotives but, by all accounts, is still charming. Accommodation is quite seedy, so be choosy rather than cheap – alternatively, stay aboard the Wadi Halfa-bound train rather than wait the week out for the next locomotive. The final destination of Wadi Halfa may not be as diverse in interest as Khartoum, but it is considerably more laid-back. The town is the convergence point of the Khartoum train, bus and road transport service, and serves as the final stop for the Lake Nasser steamer. The infrastructure here is, nonetheless, generally substandard, and accommodation options are limited.

1-3 HOURS

EGYPT

BALLOONING OVER THE NILE'S WEST BANK

Travel Info

Destination: Luxor/Qena
...rements: Most visitors will need a ...ssport and an easy-to-obtain visa.
...cy: Egyptian pound (100 piastres)
...limate: Dry and hot all year, with ...peratures reaching 40°C (75°F) in ...ner and seldom falling below 15°C (30°F) in winter.
...actor: Risks are few, especially as ... balloon trips are short. Pilots are ...rts who have flown for years, and ...ws do this every day of their lives.
...h: Ballooning over Egypt provides ...lth hazards, as long as passengers ...a head for heights. Early-morning air is crisp and generally clean.
...k: Dress warmly on departure, but ...ents should be easily removable as temperature rises. Binoculars and cameras are invaluable.
...ties: These excursions are popular ...th established package-tour com... and over the peak tourist seasons ...seems eternally popular with visi... balloon enthusiasts should make ...tions well in advance. Most oper...are well organized and hospitable.
Contact: Balloons Over Egypt, ...x 52, Sharia Khaled Ibn el-Walid.
Tel: 0920-95-376515
Fax: 0920-95-370638 / 376515

Under the darkness of pre-dawn Africa, just before the sun peeps over the horizon of an endless desert, teams of balloonists gather on the open sands around Luxor, heartland of Egypt's great legacy of tombs and temples. It is from here that the most popular early-morning balloon flights lift off, launching from the West Bank about 3km (2 miles) from where the ferry docks, and float high above the valleys.

Most of the flights take off in the tranquil coolness of early morning but, prior to departure, passengers are run through the motions, with emphasis on landing and emergency procedures. The balloon crew help secure the giant wicker basket while their passengers board, after which the basket is released into the weightlessness of the Egyptian morning. Light gusts gently disturb the air as flame bursts from overhead to ensure that the basket ascends gracefully, often some 300m (1,000ft) in the air. This rather isolated wilderness of spectacular beauty stretches over about 10km² (3.6 sq. miles) of dry mountain slopes through cane

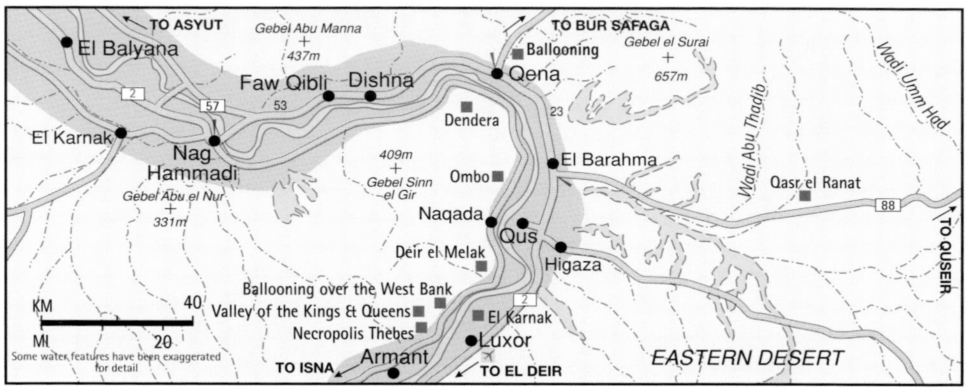

fields and groves of palm trees and – between these extremes – the columns, pillars and age-old ruins that characterize ancient Egypt. Fortunately, ballooning has virtually no effect on the environment: the people, the wildlife or the ancient structures. The baskets, seldom carrying more than three of four passengers, skirt the world of the ancients, drift over the already steamy land and head for the hills of Qena. From these heady heights the vivid colours of the remaining mud-brick houses of Qena – only a fragment of the ancestral homes that were once spread across this area – become apparent as touchdown approaches. The landings can be either remarkably gentle or hair-raising, depending on the prevailing winds, but the touchdown, even in unexpected winds, seldom means more than a bump and a bruise, usually forgotten over the champagne breakfast that awaits.

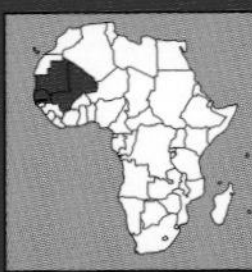

4 HOURS+
SENEGAL

Travel Info

Destination: Basse-Casamance
Requirements: A valid passport, visa and yellow fever vaccination are all essential. Keep your travel documents with you at all times, especially when travelling in areas considered unsafe.
Currency: CFA francs (100 centimes)
Climate: The heat and humidity can be rather uncomfortable. The best times to travel are between October and May.
Risk factor: Malaria is a constant problem throughout the region, and tap water is not safe to drink. Independent travel beyond Dakar is generally considered risky, so make the necessary enquiries before departure.
Health: Malaria-carrying mosquitoes are a constant irritation. Drink only bottled water, and eat no raw foodstuffs. Carry a personal first-aid kit for emergencies.
Pack: Lightweight clothing should be sufficient for the first six months of the year, but be sure to pack sunscreen, a sun hat and a first-aid kit.
Facilities: Food and accommodation are both inexpensive and good, but expect few additional facilities beyond the larger, established towns.
Contact: Ministry of Tourism, B.P. 4049, Ave Peytavin, Dakar. Tel 09221-821-1126, info@senegal-online.com, www.senegal-tourism.com

CYCLING IN BASSE-CASAMANCE

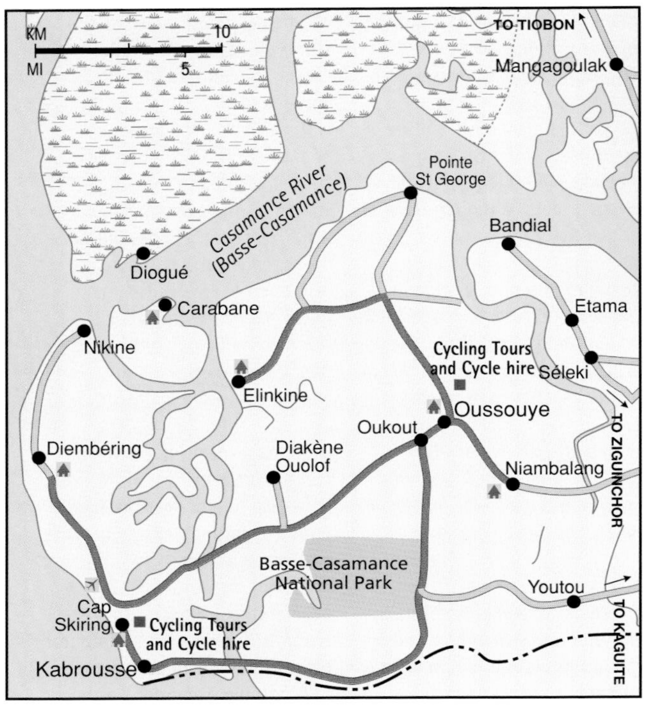

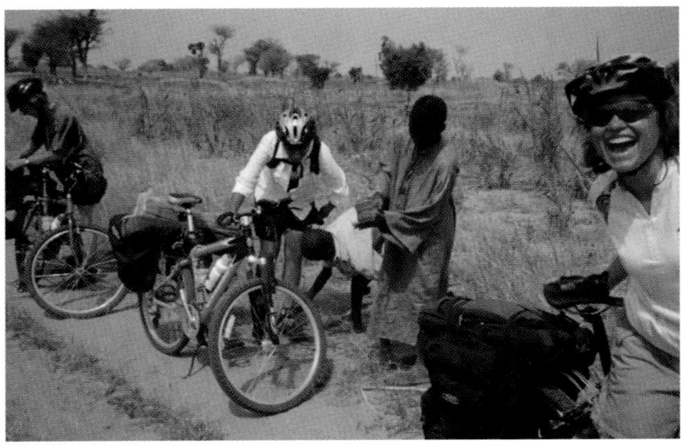

Although much of Senegal is not entirely safe for travel, it is remarkably beautiful, and nowhere is that more evident than at the lower Casamance River, known locally as the Basse-Casamance. This is a world of wooded slopes, thick tropical vegetation and sparkling waters.

The best way to explore the region is by bicycle. Most visitors hire bicycles in Oussouye or the resort capital at Cap Skiring, although this may also be done inland at Ziguinchor. The latter is, however, a little out of the way and just getting to your destination will eat at your time. Much of the land among the network of streams and mud flats has been reclaimed in order to grow rice, and many areas are protected by dikes that aid in the flooding of the paddies. As a result, the wet ground is not always easy to cross. Large tracts of the coast are broken by ti[dal] inlets, making the area arou[nd] the river mouth challenging [and] difficult to cover by bike. It i[s] nevertheless a popular way o[f] getting around, and a numbe[r of] sandy tracks offer a unique opportunity to explore.

Although the southern str[etch] around Cap Skiring is busier [and] more geared towards the tra[vel]ler, it is also the best place t[o] explore, with plenty of place[s to] hire bikes, and – although th[ere] are some good roads that le[ad to] settlements inland – you sho[uld] count on cycling on long, sa[ndy] tracks. The area is relatively [small] and can be covered in a day, [but] keep in mind that Cap Skirin[g is] a holiday resort and, despite [the] fact that there are plenty of opportunities for cycling and sailing, it can get quite busy.

6 HOURS+
SENEGAL

Travel Info

Destination: Basse Casamance
Requirements: A valid passport, visa and yellow fever vaccination are essential. Keep travel documents with you at all times, especially when in 'unsafe' areas.
Currency: CFA franc (100 centimes)
Climate: Heat and humidity can be oppressive, and is only slightly less uncomfortable on the Casamance and its tributaries. Best times are October–May.
Risk factor: Malaria is a constant threat; tap water is undrinkable. Parts of the river are polluted, but don't take your cue from the locals. Independent travel beyond Dakar is considered risky; make relevant enquiries before departure.
Health: Malaria-carrying mosquitoes are a constant irritation. Drink only bottled water, and eat no raw foodstuffs. Carry a personal first-aid kit for emergencies.
Pack: Lightweight clothing should do for the first six months of the year, but pack sunscreen, a sun hat and a first-aid kit.
Facilities: Food and accommodation are both inexpensive and good, but one can expect few additional facilities beyond the confines of Cap Skiring.
Contact: Ministry of Tourism, B.P. 4049, Ave Peytavin, Dakar. Tel 09221-821-1126, info@senegal-online.com, www.senegal-tourism.com

NAVIGATING SENEGAL'S WATERWAYS

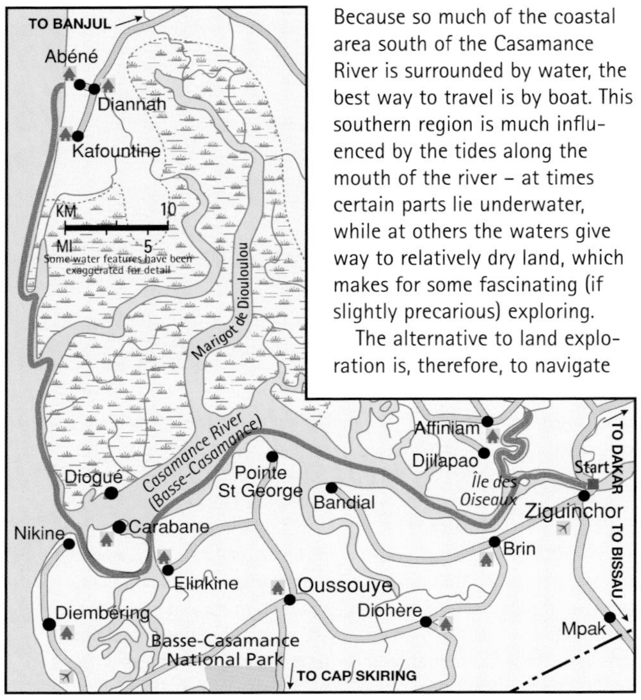

Because so much of the coastal area south of the Casamance River is surrounded by water, the best way to travel is by boat. This southern region is much influenced by the tides along the mouth of the river – at times certain parts lie underwater, while at others the waters give way to relatively dry land, which makes for some fascinating (if slightly precarious) exploring.

The alternative to land exploration is, therefore, to navigate the waterways – and there are plenty of these. Aside from the Casamance River leading inland from the Atlantic, there are also various creeks and streams that make for rewarding sailing. One of the most popular options is a day excursion on the MV *Joola*, which sails regularly up to Ziguinchor, itself a thriving little town with abundant accommodation which is cheap yet comfortable. Using Ziguinchor as your base will afford you ample opportunities for river travel. One option is the pirogue trip up to Affiniam. The vessel departs from the jetty mid-morning three times a week (Monday, Wednesday and Friday) and follows the meandering river up to the small town. It is a relatively short trip and you should be back by lunchtime, with perhaps enough time to jump on the next outgoing pirogue to Ile aux Oiseaux, crossing the Casamance to Djilapao. Both excursions are

inexpensive and offer fine opportunities to see the sites along the river bank, as well as to stop off at the tourist spots along the way.

Situated between the river and the border with Guinea-Bissau, Basse Casamance National Park is one of Senegal's most favoured stopovers, yet it is the Atlantic coastline that offers the mos[t to] adventurers. There are plenty [of] budget options for food and accommodation in the north[ern] area between Abéné and Ka[foun]tine, which provide small bu[t] interesting little stops that c[reate] the perfect foil for the more sophisticated activities avail[able] at Cap Skiring in the south.

1 DAY+
GAMBIA

Travel Info

Destination: Gambia River
Requirements: A passport and visa and/or visitor's pass are required, but no vaccinations are necessary.
Currency: Dalasi (100 butut)
Climate: Tropical, with oppressive heat and high humidity levels.
Risk factor: Travelling on the Gambia River offers few risks, other than those usually associated with water adventures. Take precautions against malaria and drink bottled water.
Health: Malaria is present and parts of the river may be polluted, but the most serious concern is the heat and humidity, especially when travelling on the water.
Pack: A high-factor sunscreen and personal water supply is essential and, although it can be uncomfortably hot on the water, night temperatures have been known to drop sharply.
Facilities: In the more tourist-oriented centres – such as Cap Skiring – there are many good operators from which choose, although some may be rather pricey. Locals also offer a more informal service, but are not as well organized.
Contact: Ministry of Tourism, New Administrative Bldg, State House, Banjul, Gambia, Tel: 09220-227881, Fax: 09220-27753, www.gambiatourism.info

SAILING THE GAMBIA RIVER

With so much of the nation centred around the river that shares its name, the Gambia River is the primary tourist attraction in the country, providing a number of varying options for the traveller.

Day trips on the river – in anything from the simple pirogues to larger commercial vessels – are, for the most part, a time of leisure rather than a means of getting from A to B. Stretching some 500km (310 miles) from its source in Guinea's Fouta Djalon highlands, the entire length of the river is a frenzy of activity, mostly locals making a living from these waters – fishing, growing rice, and offering river trips to adventurous visitors. Most of these

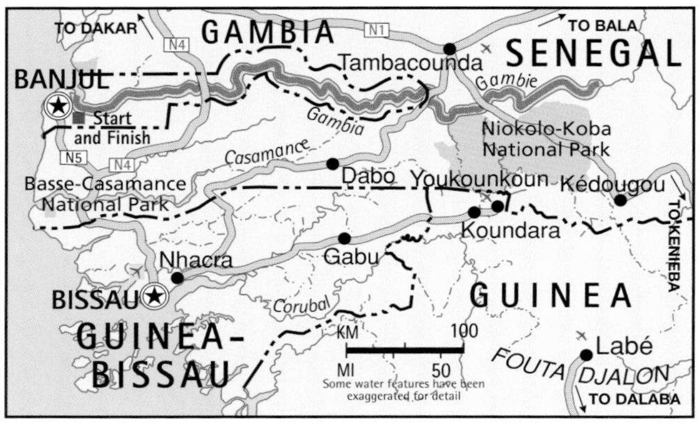

trips are cheap - the extreme poverty in parts keeps the prices low – and are by far the best means of exploring the country. Although the skippers of these vessels are both enthusiastic and knowledgeable, language may prove to be a serious obstacle, especially in the less developed areas. The locals are extremely helpful and know the best areas of the river and its tributaries to explore – although these are usually the popular tourist traps. Unlike on the coastal stretch, which depends to a large extent on the often frenetic tourist season, conventional 'tour agents' are rare along the less developed tributaries, which are largely the terrain of enterprising locals keen to show off their river and its habitat. Be warned, however, that in some parts the locals can be quite demanding when it comes to rewards or hand-o[uts].

The people in some areas [along] the river bank have indeed t[aken] advantage of the fact that f[or]eigners do venture here, and small riverside lodges and in[for]mal overnight facilities have sprung up sporadically along [the] banks of the river and its tri[bu]taries – notably the Lamin – [to] cater for tourists. It is, howe[ver,] the unspoiled nature of the terrain and the unpredictabi[lity] of the isolated wilderness sp[ots] that are the river's principal attractions, and there is still plenty of wildlife – from rive[r] crabs to monkeys – in the ar[ea]. River excursions to even out[-of-]the-way places feature prom[i]nently on the packaged itine[r]aries of local operators, so v[iew]ing the aquatic animals and plants of the swamps and m[ud] flats, woodlands and savann[a is] quite possible.

2 DAYS+

MAURITANIA

Travel Info

Destination: Atar, Adrar Plateau
Requirements: Most visitors need a ort and visa, which is not difficult to come by. No vaccinations are ired, but check prior to departure.
Currency: Ouguiya (5 khoums)
Climate: Oppressively hot April–ember, with days peaking at about C (122°F). Best November–January.
Risk factor: Risks are few, but the erty means that some vehicles may entirely safe. Unscrupulous operators may offer unreliable vehicles.
: Heat and humidity are more of a mfort than a risk, but drink plenty ids. Local water may not be palat- for Westerners. Malaria is present light. Emergency medical facilities e limited – so don't take chances.
Light clothing for steamy days and arm cover-up for evenings. If you do serious walking, take boots, a at, sunscreen and your own water.
cilities: Atar will probably cater to eeds – from car and camel hire to rnight stays – but beyond there is y little. Fuel stations are very rare.
tact: Adrar Voyages, P.O. Box 926, Nouakchott. Tel: 09222-5251717 Fax: 09222-5291818, adrarvoyages@toptechnology.mr

DRIVING THE ADRAR REGION

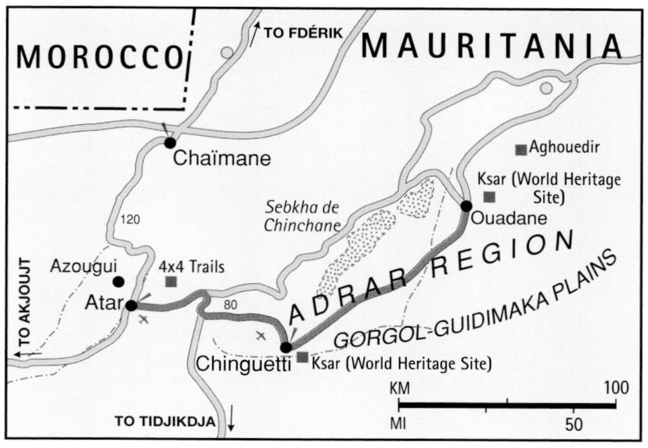

Four-wheel-drive excursions are fairly common on the Adrar plateau, far-off horizons skirting an endless panorama of dune and escarpment broken only occasionally by a green oasis.

The villages here are miraculously free of commercialism, which makes for some fine exploring. Lonely and isolated, the Adrar is a far cry from Nouakchott, but it is in tiny remote spots in this region that the Mauritanian legacy lives on.

The Adrar is rich in a cultural heritage that includes prehistoric rock art, historical forts, ancient stone circles and other archaeological sites well worth the bumpy ride to reach them. The landscape is punctuated with ancient sites – such as the Berber ruins at Azougui – and is best traversed by 4x4 vehicles, donkey or camel. The roads and tracks are difficult to negotiate, arduous and demanding even with a 4x4. They stretch across hard rock and flat grey sands, through winding bends and narrow passes to golden dunes and steep gorges. Private car hire is a good alternative to the package tours and works out cheaper, with up to half a dozen passengers sharing the costs. Local guides are relatively easy to come by and may know a camel trek operator – the best way to explore the surrounds – who is both reliable and inexpensive.

The desert oases offer a welcome respite from the harshness of the sun and the often uncomfortable undulation of the dune landscape; they stand in sharp

contrast to the green belt that forms the southern region and which comprises little more than the great Chemama flood plain and the plains of the Gorgol-Guidimaka. The flora and fauna – notably the endangered addax antelope – are fast making way for the creeping desert sands, but even the least scenic routes offer sightings of gazelles and antelope such as the oryx, wild sheep, ostriches and, of course, plenty of domesticated camels.

A notable exception to the dusty little rural outposts of the Adrar is the lively settlement of Atar, which acts as a base for many travellers to the area. Atar is the closest you will get to Western civilization on the plateau. Many tour operators in the town hire out Land Rovers, other 4x4 vehicles and even camels, but the more established ones tend to be rather more expensive than those offered by the small hotels and bed-and-breakfast-type operations.

1 DAY+

MALI

Travel Info

Destination: Dogon Plateau
irements: All visitors, except citins of France, need standard travel ents, including a visa and a yellow vaccination. Overland drivers need a special tourist visa for vehicles.
urrency: CFA franc (100 centimes)
ate: Dogon Country is usually very and uncomfortably so, with little of shade beyond local settlements.
actor: Trekking the Dogon is rela- safe for level-headed and discreet rs. Some sort of formal tour pack- advised as the police and military best handled by those in the know.
: The water at the villages is rela- safe, but it is best to use purifica- tablets or to boil drinking water.
ck: Water, light clothing and good ng shoes, not special hiking boots.
ties: Apart from the overland tour ors, who are generally well organ- ed, there are few options through to visit the Dogon, and the alter- s seldom meet Western standards.
act: Wilderness Travel (California-based). Tel: 1-510-558-2488 or 1-800-368-2794 info@wildernesstravel.com, www.wildernesstravel.com

TREKKING THE DOGON PLATEAU

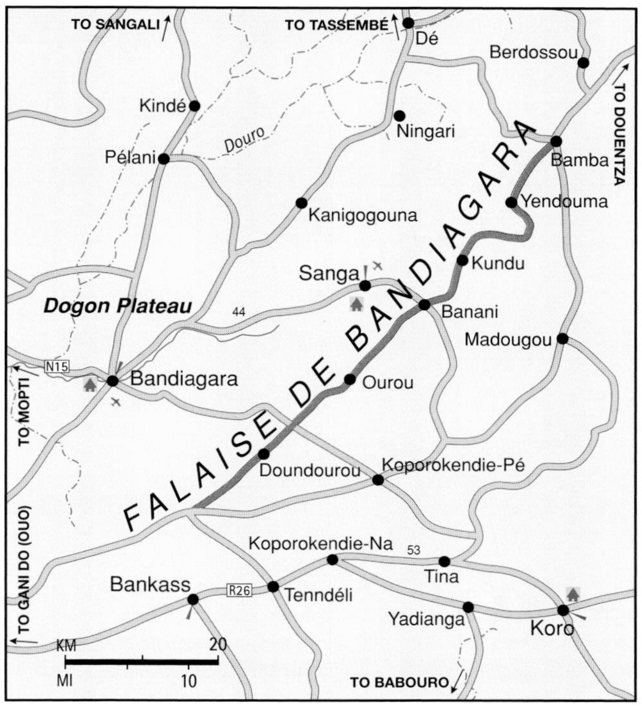

The Dogon people build their villages from mud and it is these fascinating structures that are most characteristic of a trek across the plateau stretching northwest of the Bandiagara. The family huts and outbuildings that comprise each village and the cave shelters that have been etched into the rock faces feature high on most package tours, although most are easily accessible on private treks.

The going here is tough and most travellers opt for an organised party rather than making their own way. Thick sand, unpredictable winds and the heat from the Sahara may prove too much for the inexperienced traveller. Operators and the locals who act as guides and trackers know the area well and can read the signs sent by nature to forewarn of potential disaster. The guides are well versed in cultural aspects such as the many taboos, and they will probably be some of the few comprehensible English speakers. Some operators may offer a motorcycle, moped or even a 4x4, but as long as you don't try to carry too much – porters come at a small price, but are not essential unless they act as guides too – the trek is hardly an impossible exercise.

Because it is so sandy and the routes neither well marked nor well maintained, cycling and even off-road driving are not worth the effort. The rocky face of the escarpment can be the most daunting aspect on foot, but once that has been conquered there are also rocky outcrops and stretches of sand. These challenges are, however, minor and, although they call for some stamina and perseverance, are surmountable. One element that poses few dangers is the wildlife, simply as it is limited to

birds and a few mammal species. Apart from the other services offered by guides, this is also one of the reasons why they are so essential to appreciating this region: there is not a bird call or animal track the guide will not recognize immediately.

1 DAY+

MALI

Travel Info

Destination: Hombori
irements: All visitors, except citi- France, will need standard travel ments, including a visa and a yel- ever vaccination. Overland drivers a special tourist visa for vehicles.
urrency: CFA franc (100 centimes)
te: Northeastern Mali is extremely nhospitable, with conditions often oppressively hot and dry.
k factor: The climb up Le Main de is for skilled climbers. Beyond the Mopti to Gao route, travel (rela- ly secure) can be confusing and is ackled with a local guide. There is rong police and military presence.
th: Apart from physical dangers of mb, dehydration is a threat. Water villages is relatively safe, but it is best to stick to bottled water.
Take all your equipment and gear make sure they are in good order.
ies: Apart from a handful of gen- lly well-organized local operators, re are few options. Do not rely on cal shops to stock any equipment.
act: Wilderness Travel (California-based). Tel: 1-510-558-2488 or 1-800-368-2794 info@wildernesstravel.com, www.wildernesstravel.com

ROCK CLIMBING AT HOMBORI

The northeastern corner of Mali is austere and far off the beaten track, which makes for difficult travelling. It is a harsh and sparsely populated region and sandwiched on these arid lands is the tiny hamlet of Hombori which, had it not been for its adventure opportunity, would otherwise be overlooked by even the most ardent of travellers. Although it is situated on the N16 highway between Mopti and Gao (less than 250km/155 miles from the latter), Hombori offers little for the visitor, except the rugged terrain of the 1,150m (3,775ft) mountain of Hombori Tondo on which it has been established, in addition to its position as a gateway to the enormous monolith that is Le Main de Fatma.

Just over 10km (6 miles) from the little town, the great rock is the area's one claim to fame and is hailed as the finest of Africa's rock-climbing challenges. Those adventurers not following the principal route would be advised to take a guide as the tracks are confusing and difficult to navigate without a 4x4.

Climbing Le Main de Fatma is strictly for the most skilled rock climber. In parts near-vertical and in others riddled with nooks, crannies and awkward angles and overhangs, the giant rock presents a huge challenge. Novices are advised to admire the 'professionals' and move right along. These surfaces demand a finely honed skill, years of experience and patience with yourself and the challenges of the rock face. It should be tackled with only the most sophisticated equipment and gear, following a meticulously planned route. Because of the difficulties, the costs can be astronomical, with the least amount of outlay spent on overnighting. Once adventurers reach the summit, few can deny the thrill of conquering the demanding rock face.

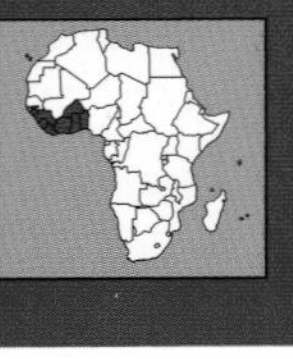

1 DAY+
GUINEA-BISSAU

WINDSURFING GUINEA-BISSAU'S COAST

Travel Info
Destination: Bijagós Archipelago
Requirements: Apart from standard travel documents, most visitors need a one-month visa (easily extended). A yellow fever certificate is also required.
Currency: CFA franc (100 centimes)
Climate: Although generally hot, very high rainfall which makes December–January the best time to visit the coast.
Risk factor: There are few risks to windsurfing off Guinea Bissau – as long as you know what you are doing or have a local expert with you! These are unfamiliar waters with a temperament of their own – take no foolhardy chances.
Health: Malaria is a real risk in Guinea Bissau – even on the offshore islands – and certain of the muddy waters have been known to carry bilharzia. Take all the necessary precautions.
Pack: Water purification tablets, and a first-aid kit for emergencies. Take your own equipment and gear if you prefer.
Facilities: Accommodation in and around the capital is rather good, but generally costly, with the less expensive options centred around the offshore islands, where the standard is quite high.
Contact: Guiné Tours, Avenue Amílcar, Bissau. Information Centre, Bissau, Tel: 09245-21-3282

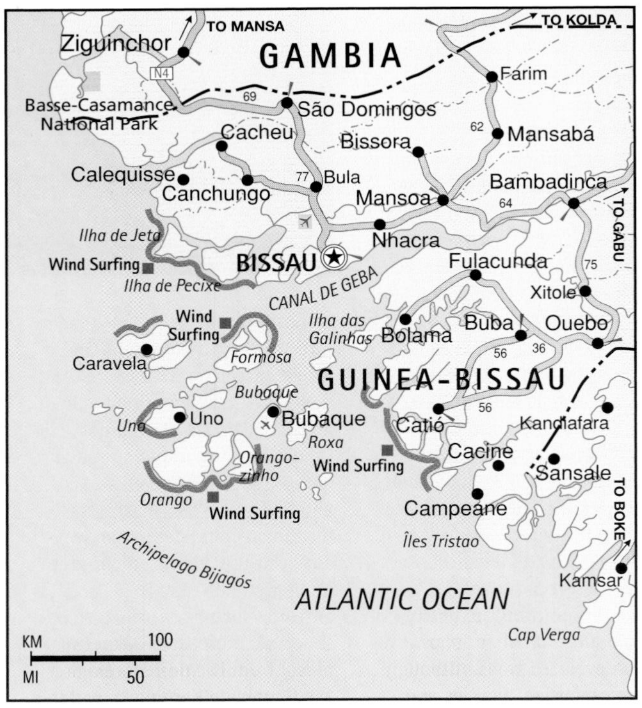

Guinea-Bissau is noted for its picture-perfect beaches and islands. Activity here revolves around the mud flats, lakes and lagoons of the coastal stretch, and much of the fledgling tourist industry is water-based. Although average rainfall is high, conditions are hot, which makes for outstanding leisure activity on the beaches and coastal waters as well as off Cape Verde.

Regular ferries and boats carry visitors to and from outlying islands, which offer some excellent beaches with fine waves. Most notable are the islands of the Bijagós Archipelago, rapidly becoming a highlight on the windsurfer's itinerary.

Some of the islands are largely uninhabited, while others – Bolama, Bubaque and Galinhas – are pleasantly undeveloped. While Cape Verde and Praia are relatively sophisticated, some islands offer only small hotel although many locals will ha ly offer a meal and overnight accommodation.

The best time to hit the b is early morning when the s are deserted and the winds i Tides change rapidly, and lo tide will mean that an expan of mud separates the beach the ocean, which makes for ing windsurfing. The trick is throw convention to the win literally – and to control the rather than the wind. This is very difficult as, armed only the board, there is little to restrain you. Windsurfing he a fusion of two disciplines: learning to control the boar the waves while enjoying th scenery. Flat water and light winds are seldom a problem. Top-class windsurfers make look so effortless, but this c a very dangerous sport. Novi should take lessons first.

2 DAYS+
GUINEA

HIKING THE FOUTA DJALON PLATEAU

Travel Info
Destination: Fouta Djalon Plateau
Requirements: A valid passport and visa are required, although you may also need an invitation from a citizen. Keep travel documents with you always, especially when travelling in 'unsafe' areas.
Currency: Guinean franc (100 centimes)
Climate: Days can be very warm, but the valleys are moderate, particularly during the rains. Best hiking is early in the year.
Risk factor: As long as travellers are prepared and do not take chances when hiking in this rugged and often precarious terrain, there should be few hazards.
Health: Much of the abundant water may not be suitable for Western stomachs, so avoid drinking the water unless it has been boiled or purified.
Pack: Hikers will probably need to take their own tent, camping equipment and food rations, as well as a change of warm clothing for chilly nights.
Facilities: Facilities are rather basic and hikers should be self-reliant, and prepared for any eventuality. Some command of French will be useful.
Contact: National Tourism Office, B.P. 1275, Six Avenue de la Republique, Immeuble Al-aman, Conakry, Guinea Tel: 09224-455-161/3, Fax: 09224-455-164

Guinea's highlying Fouta Djalon plateau is its top drawcard. Comprising a series of flat outcrops that form sandstone plateaux, this expanse dips into valleys of dense thickets, is sliced by cliffs, and evens out in places to cover open plains peppered with bare rocks and scrubby vegetation. This is typical of the topography of much of Guinea and makes the Fouta Djalon ideal adventure terrain.

Although December to May receive a lower rainfall, June to December see heavy rains, with the heaviest falls around August. Guinea is one of the region's wettest countries – the capital receives an annual rainfall of 4m (13ft) – and the high-lying plateau inland is laced with small rivers, streams and creeks, in addition to being the source of a number of significant water sources, including the Gambia and Senegal rivers.

The undulating landscape of the plateau ensures that hiking is not easy, with long distances that require regular ascents and descents. The terrain is rugged and tough, but may be ideal for some vigorous cycling, although off-road driving is not a viable option, with far too many practi-

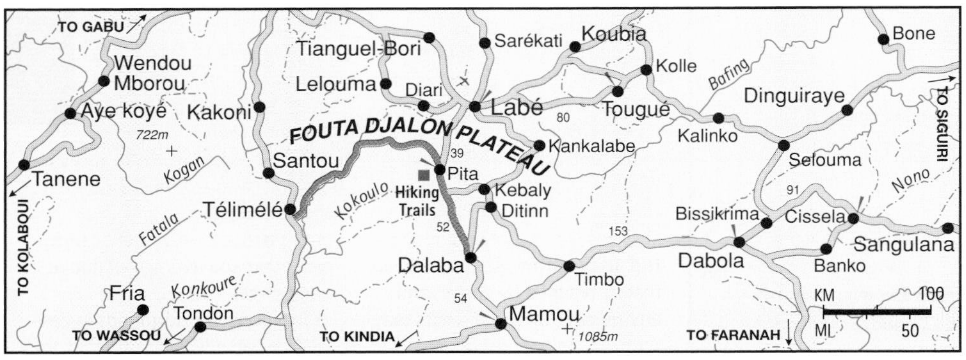

cal hazards to overcome. Most visitors to the region opt to travel on foot, and trails and paths wind relentlessly down into the gullies and up again to stretch along the open plains. Popular hiking and mountain-biking areas include the waterfalls at La Voile de la Mariée and Les Chutes de Kinkon, and the welcoming hamlets of Pita and Dalaba. Mountain-bikers particularly enjoy the trail between Pita and Télimélé. Hiking demands little practical skill but will require stamina and perseverance, with few oppo nities to turn back or pull o favour of a comfortable hot room. Although local inhabi are known to be hospitable, trailists have to rely on their initiative as well as their ow day-to-day essentials. The b method of overnighting in t Fouta Djalon is camping. Although hiking and campin relatively safe adventures, k in mind that many of the lo live from hand to mouth an may be tempted by the pros of petty crime.

5 HOURS+
CÔTE D'IVOIRE

HIKING THE MAN REGION

Travel Info
Destination: Man Region
Requirements: Most visitors need a visa, but all require yellow fever vaccination. Visitors from the US who stay less than three months may not need a visa, but verify prior to departure.
Currency: CFA franc (100 centimes)
Climate: Harmattan winds plague the dry season, while rains fall April–July and again October–November; many of the national parks close during this time.
Risk factor: Beyond the standard precautions for hiking in an unfamiliar terrain with a limited infrastructure, risks are few in the mountains around Man.
Health: Although water is usually safe, take bottled water. There are few health risks, although AIDS is a growing concern, particularly in outlying areas.
Pack: Lightweight clothing should be fine for days, but pack extra clothes for nights on the mountain, where temperatures drop steeply and quickly. Hiking boots and other essentials are needed.
Facilities: Much of Côte d'Ivoire is well geared towards tourists, and many operators are well established. Do not to rely on facilities in Man, Danané and Biankouma.
Contact: Bourse de Tourisme. Tel: 09225-202-51600

Hiking in what is arguably the most picturesque region of the Côte d'Ivoire – aside from its splendid coastline – is an invigorating experience, even for the hiker who claims to have seen it all. The thickly wooded mountains that make up the far western reaches around Man are the only real climbing spots in a country that is otherwise characterized by small hills and plains. Lushly forested mountains make the Man region one of the most romantic in the Côte d'Ivoire, with an impressive variation of hikes and trails that make walking here enormously rewarding. While some of the hikes require little more than a few hours of gentle walking – even Mont Sangbé National Park is ideal for walking safaris – the generally high temperatures and undulating landscape also mean that there are many other opportunities for a vigorous climb that will take the serious hiker up the 1,752m (5,750ft) of Mount Nimba, 1,223m (4,000ft) of Mount Tonkoui and the 1,278m (4,200ft) of Mount Toura, the most prominent of the many peaks that virtually enclose the town of Man.

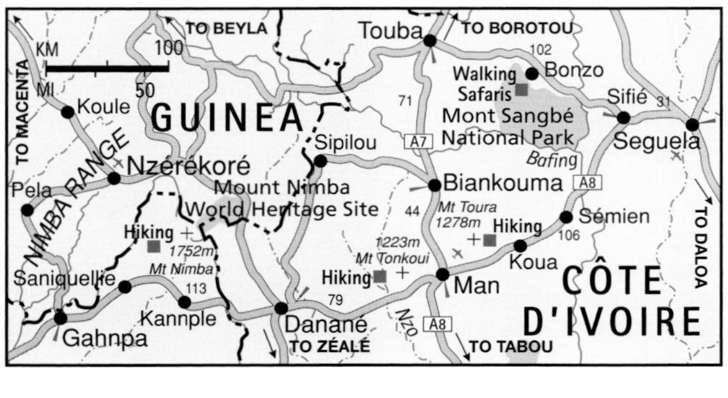

While the settlements of Danané – best known for its old vine bridges – and Biankouma provide good starting points for hikes into the surrounding mountains, Man is the commercial heart of the region and most of the favoured sites are within comfortable walking distance of the town. The more out-of-the-way starting points are most easily accessed by vehicle, but the vast majority are little more than a brisk, not too challenging walk away. Hitchhiking is easy and safe along the main routes, although not always reliable.

The region is laced with a number of scenic waterfalls, streams and rivers – most

notably the River Nzo to the southwest – and just beyond the limits of Man, en route to Tonkoui, travellers will inevitably pass the popular cascade waterfalls. Although part of the slopes leading to the summit of Mount Tonkoui are out of bounds and guarded, the 32km (20 miles) between the town of Man and the peak are laced with a string of hikes and trails varying considerably in degrees of difficulty. Most are conquered without too much exertion, but heavy ra can make hiking more diffic particularly if you are ill-pre pared. Much the same can b said for the ever-popular La Dent, the rather peculiarly shaped rock formation little than 10km (6 miles) from to that is said to watch over th people of Man. The amble u slope is not easy and most h will need a guide (easily hire the little village of Glogouin the views are spectacular.

1 DAY+
BURKINA FASO

Travel Info
Destination: Banfora Region
irements: Apart from the standard travel documents, all visitors will re a visa and proof of yellow fever vaccination.
urrency: CFA franc (100 centimes)
ate: Best time to tour the Banfora region is in January or February, when the rains have largely passed and high temperatures and winds have not yet settled.
factor: Dehydration – the physical ertion combined with soaring temperatures can take their toll.
: Much of the natural waters that ow in the region are contaminated bilharzia. Malaria is ever-present.
: The standard hiking and camping ipment should suffice. Ensure that you have sunscreen and bottled drinking water.
ities: Many of the principal towns ffer adequate enough facilities for idget travellers, but take your own ing equipment and stock up on all essary supplies before heading off into the hills.
act: Office du Tourisme Burkinabe, P.O. Box 2765, Bobo, Bukina Faso
Tel: 09226-97-1986
Fax: 09226-97-1987

TOURING THE BANFORA REGION

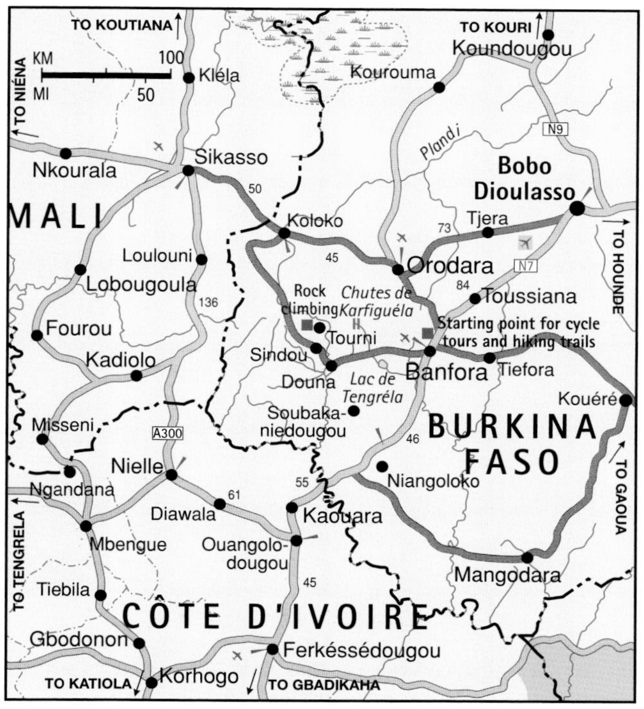

Hilly and well vegetated, the Banfora region is very different from the rest of Burkina Faso, which comprises mostly flat grassland. It has become a prime rambling destination, with a variety of outdoor pursuits, including cycle tours, canoe trips and a series of routes and paths best explored on a moped.

Although the regional 'capital' is at Bobo-Dioulasso, it is the town of Banfora that is the best starting point for the area's cycle routes and hiking trails. Emanating from Banfora is a number of popular excursions taking visitors on foot or two wheels to waterfalls, lakes and mountain slopes. Undeveloped and rugged, the going is tough but rewarding. Road travel is not easy, for purely practical reasons, such as military checkpoints. Enlist one of the local guides, who are useful when following the convoluted trails. Although quite expensive, bicycles and

mopeds, known as *mobylettes*, may be hired from any prominent little town in the area.

No more than 7km (4 miles) from Banfora is Lac de Tengréla, skirted by a 2km (1 mile) track ideal for cycling. You can also take a boat across the lake to see resident hippos – fisherfolk are be more than willing to take you out onto the waters in traditional dug-out pirogues and may also offer you accommodation.

A little more than 10km (6 miles) from Lac de Tengréla are the Chutes de Karfiguéla, waterfalls that are particularly impressive after heavy rains. They are easily reached via a narrow path that is easy to walk but awkward to cycle. Also nearby are the Domes de Febedougou, stony peaks that are undemanding when it comes to the ascent, but time-consuming and surprisingly draining – not unlike the 3km (2 mile) of rugged crests of Sindou, famed for its rock-climbing. This terrain may be explored on foot, by bicycle or on a moped, but is quite exhausting as the roads are in poor condition.

1 DAY+
TOGO

Travel Info
Destination: Lac Togo
quirements: Standard travel documents. Most visitors need a visa and proof of yellow fever vaccination.
urrency: CFA franc (100 centimes)
te: Rain falls largely mid-year, yet ons around the lake area are generally moderate, with the average temre 27°C (80°F) December–January.
factor: Considered relatively safe, is recovering from the turmoil it nced towards the end of the 20th tury. Blockades are still regular on prominent cross-country routes.
lth: Lake Togo is considered to be bilharzia, but don't take chances.
Pack only essentials, such as sun- and changes of clothing – travel What you don't have you will be to buy in Lomé – what you don't nd there, you probably don't need.
es: Few of the water-sport operaaround Lac Togo will have up-toear and equipment, but what they tock and hire out should be suffihe area's market towns have adeaccommodation and food outlets.
Contact: Lomé Tourism Office, P.O. Box 1289, Lomé, Togo
Tel: 09228-221-4313
Fax: 09228-221-8927

ON THE WATERS OF LAC TOGO

Lac Togo (about 30km (19 miles) to the east of the capital) is relatively shallow, which does not make ideal conditions for diving, but there are plenty of other diversions. A number of small but relatively efficient – and certainly helpful – operators have established something of a reputation on the shores of the lake, hiring out windsurfer, bicycles and other sports equipment.

True to its reputation, Lac Togo is a holiday retreat with an abundance of water sports, including the mostly Western staple – water-skiing. A number of the operators have contacts who may act as guides on the lake or exploring beyond its shores, and it may be useful to enlist one of them if you venture into the towns. Market towns are scattered along the lake shore and even Lomé is not too long a trip. Many of the settlements are readily reached by canoe, and any number of casual touts may, for a fee, take one or two individuals at a time.

The excursion is laid-back, with a romantically scenic backdrop.

A prominent town is Togoville, long hailed as the voodo capital. Many locals are fierce believers but visitors have little to fear as the authentic beliefs of voodooism are not nearly as sinister as Hollywood would have us believe.

Aside from those across the waters of Lac Togo, many smaller settlements are not easy to reach by road, unless you happen to be visiting on markets days. As so much of the surrounding land is rural, markets are the only significant feature on local calendars and are an attraction all of their own, with plenty of indigenous crafts and other souvenirs available at good prices.

Exploring the surrounds is easily done on a bicycle, which

inevitably ensures that you will not be overly harassed at the police control points. This mode of transport might prove more of a problem during and after heavy seasonal rains, when many of the subsidiary routes and even main thoroughfares suffer greatly.

1 DAY+
GHANA

Travel Info
Destination: Accra
uirements: Standard travel documents. Most visitors need a visa and proof of yellow fever vaccination.
Currency: Cedi (100 pesewas)
imate: Temperatures can climb to uncomfortable levels, but Accra is generally moderate.
factor: Although there have been of pickpocketing and other petty ne, safety is not really an issue in Police presence can be irritating, ten when hinting at a bribe for a minor transgression of the law.
There should be few health hazut although tap water in the city nkable it is safer to drink bottled Many of the beaches are plagued tile currents – never swim alone!
ack no more – and no less – than any other African city. Standards sunscreen, bottled water and the like are readily available.
ities: Despite the deterioration of city towards the end of the 20th ury, Accra has seen a turnaround, facilities – along with their price vary from adequate to luxurious.
Contact: Scantravel, P.O. Box 4969, Accra, Ghana
Tel: 09233-21-663134

DRIVING SCENIC ACCRA

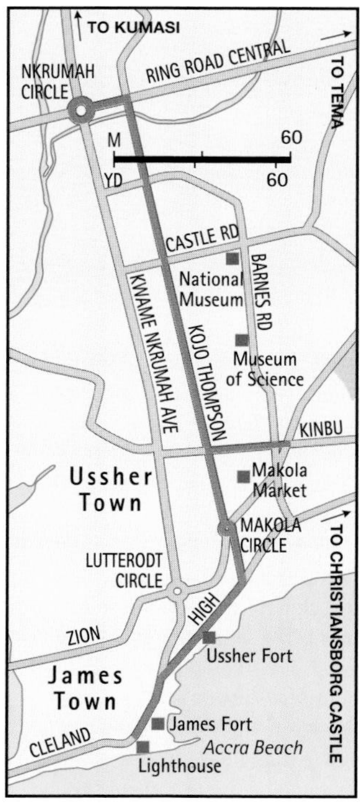

There are not many capital cities in Africa that have quite the same sense of adventure, but Accra has it all – and more. Not only is it set against one of the most spectacular backdrops on the south coast of West Africa – and, as such, was once one of the premier holiday destinations in the region – it also boasts an extraordinarily rich legacy of historical and cultural significance, and it is this comprehensive package that makes it so alluring. Surprisingly green for such a big city, Accra's main attractions are the natural splendour of the surrounds and the historical importance of the ancient structures that are so characteristic of the capital. As a result, the combination of these two fine assets means that tourism here centres on the scenic routes through the principal historic sites. The most significant of the latter are Chistiansborg Castle and the James and Ussher forts, the three fortresses that stand guard over the city. These are not open to the public (James Fort serves as a prison and the castle as the president's office) and are heavily guarded by the military.

From a starting point within James Town in the heart of the city, make your way from High Street to Kojo Thompson Road, where the music and excited voices will inevitably lead you to the market stalls of Makola. The immediate area is generally known for its inexpensive lodgings and, although some may be rather substandard, others are delightfully comfortable and good value for money. Just beyond lies Nkrumah Circle and within easy walking distance lies a variety of restaurants and other traditional eateries, but scattered along these quaint streets is a string of museums and art galleries interspersed with theatres that offer a unique look at the cultural activity of the inner city. Much of the city is easily covered on foot, but a more comprehensive view of authentic Accra may require road travel. Buses and taxis are fairly regular and reliable, although a taxi may have a better chance of getting through the road blocks on the outskirts of the city. These are usually little more than a formality and well worth conquering your fear of surly police officials in the heart of an African city. Beyond the outer limits of the city lies a world that is uniquely beautiful, best known perhaps for the fine beaches at Labadi and Kokrobite and especially Coco Beach. Also within easy reach are the serene Aburi Botanical Gardens, which are over a century old. Car rental can be outrageously expensive, so it is perhaps best to utilize the public transport that departs from the junction of Barnes and Kinbu roads.

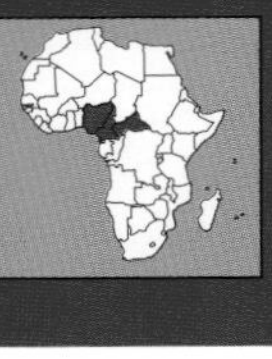

1 DAY+ NIGERIA

EXPLORING NIGERIA'S RAINFORESTS

Travel Info

Destination: Obudu Cattle Ranch
Requirements: Most visitors will require a pre-arranged visa and proof of a yellow fever and (occasionally) cholera vaccination. If travelling by vehicle, special clearance by way of a Carnet de Passage en Douane is required.
Currency: Naira (100 kobo)
Climate: The southern regions are hot and wet, with rains falling March–November and the dry period December–March, when harmattan winds blow.
Risk factor: Hitchhiking is potentially dangerous, but there are few other risks. You will inevitably need a local guide to help navigate the routes and to help you out of any trouble.
Health: Malaria is particularly rampant in the hot, wet rainforest conditions.
Pack: Take malaria medication, provisions and supplies, and all the necessary camping gear to be self-sufficient.
Facilities: Visitors' amenities in Nigeria are appalling, and few of the 'luxuries' are operational. You need to be self-reliant, especially in 'undeveloped' areas such as the parks. English widely spoken.
Contact: Nigeria Tourist Board P.O. Box 167, Abuja, Nigeria. Tel: 09234-9-523-0420, Fax: 09234-9 523 0419, www.nigeria.com

Although certain sections of the rainforests in the southwest have been cleared for plantations of palm trees, the wooded valleys and hills around Ikom, Mfum and Enugu provide an extraordinary opportunity to explore: climb the peaks, take a horse back ride, or hike through dense vegetation to view mountain elephants, gorillas and other forest primates.

Many visitors depart from 500-year-old Calabar or from Ikom, which are linked by share-taxis. Ikom is merely a stopover and does not have many attractions, but on its outskirts lie 300-odd 1,800-year-old stone monoliths adorned with abstract human shapes. The grand prize, however, is Obudu Cattle Ranch on the Oshie Ridge of the Sonkwala range. The 'ranch' is a combination of cattle station and resort and the surrounds, encircled by forested hills, offer wilderness excursions. Included among the facilities are guided trips into the forests to see the gorillas – more evidence of their presence than actual sightings – and treks that range from simple day walks to extended hikes over vast distances. One 13km (8-mile) trek takes you to the Gorilla Camp, and other local attractions, through thick bush and up steep inclines as well as descents into misty valleys. Although some routes are arduous, they make for great hiking. This is also true of Cross River National Park's Okwangwo Division, where gorillas have only recently been rediscovered in the Mbe Mountains. By all accounts, guided treks here can take a few days as many trails wind through the forests, and make for some exhausting hiking. Thick foliage, abundant water and steep inclines mean you will get dirty and tired, cold and damp, and scratched and bruised. The park does, however, have two forest camps where tents may alsc hired. There are 1,500 wildli species, including primates.

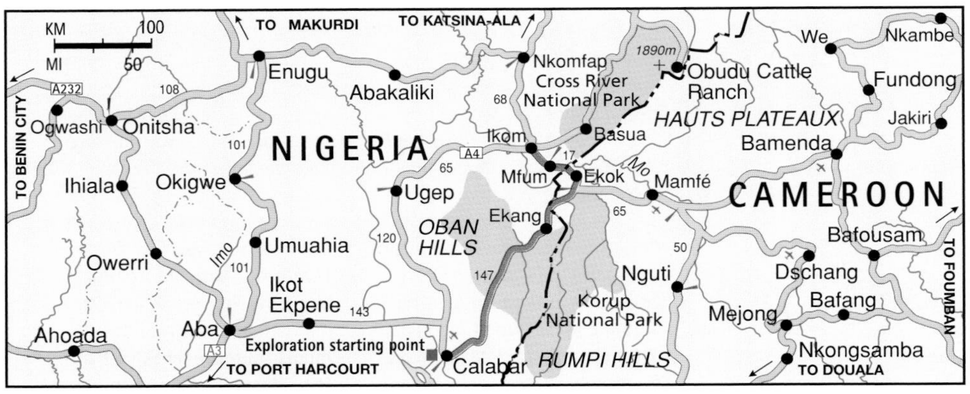

2 DAYS NIGERIA

NIGERIA'S DUMBO TREK

Travel Info

Destination: Bassaula
Requirements: Most visitors need a pre-arranged visa and proof of yellow fever and (occasionally) cholera vaccination. If travelling by vehicle, a Carnet de Passage en Douane is required.
Currency: Naira (100 kobo)
Climate: The southern regions are hot and wet, with rains falling March–November and the dry period December–March, when harmattan winds blow.
Risk factor: Other than the overgrown route of the Dumbo Trek, there are few risks. Porters and guides know the route and may be of help when you enter Cameroon, where immigration authorities are not accustomed to tourists.
Health: Malaria is particularly rampant in the hot, wet rainforest conditions.
Pack: Take malaria medication, provisions and supplies, and all the necessary camping gear to be self-sufficient.
Facilities: English is not widely spoken in the border region with Cameroon. Bassaula has basic accommodation, but most trekkers camp in villages en route. This is basic, but quite safe.
Contact: Nigeria Tourist Board P.O. Box 167, Abuja, Nigeria. Tel: 09234-9-523-0420, Fax: 09234-9 523 0419, www.nigeria.com

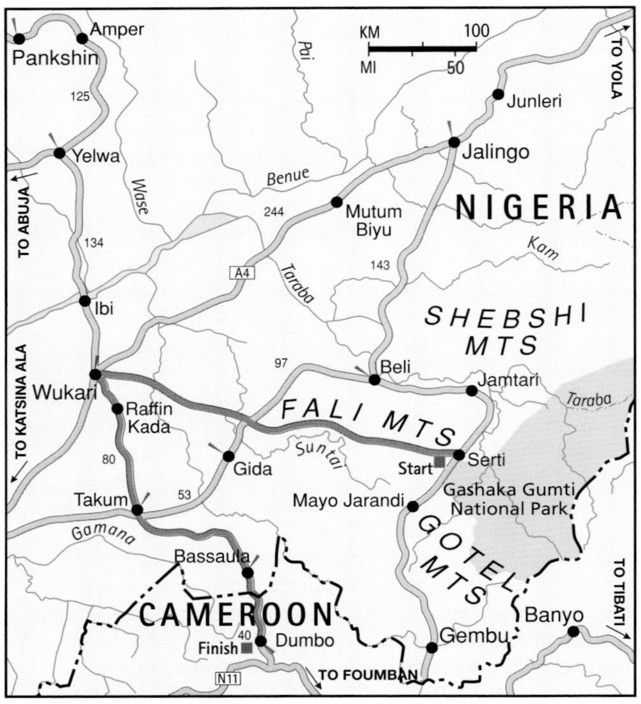

So much of the southern reaches are so isolated that it would be safest to report your itinerary to officials at Wukari, Jalingo, Yola or even Bassaula. Travelling from Bassaula, take the expensive option of a rented vehicle, as public transport from the towns in the region is unreliable. Avoid hitchhiking where possible in favour of the cheap buses and share-taxis. Travel at night is only for the foolhardy as the dangers are considerable: bad roads, reckless driving, and road-blocks. Although navigable in 4x4 vehicles, many roads are just dry tracks, and the local communities are rural, with no expertise when it comes to off-road driving. As a result, the only alternative is to explore the surrounds on 'established' routes rarely utilized by Westerners. The most popular option is the Dumbo Trek, a two-day adventure from southeastern Nigeria, just west of the Gashaka-Gumti park, to Dumbo in Cameroon.

The 'official' route of the Dumbo Trek crosses some of Nigeria's least explored areas and passes through fascinating rural settlements. First stop is Wukari, the last point of 'civilization' before hitting trekking country. Beyond lies the jungle around Takum and an open expanse crossed only by streams and dirt tracks. The next stop is the hamlet of Bassaula, departure point for the Dumbo Trek. The 40km (25-mile) hike to Cameroon is a trying one, and travellers should go prepared for a challenging adventure. Although the init section is a recognized route is no more than a rough pat leading through harsh terrai The ground is scattered with rocks, intertwined with root heavily wooded, and even th hardiest of vehicles will find near-impossible to cross. Th only access is on foot, and t dense vegetation and incons tent path make it easy to lo your way. The climbs are ne steep nor demanding, and th only physical exertion is the tance and the route itself.

2 DAYS+ CAMEROON

CLIMBING MOUNT CAMEROON

Travel Info

Destination: Mount Cameroon
Requirements: Virtually all Westerners need a passport and visa, although no particular immunizations are required.
Currency: CFA franc (100 centimes)
Climate: Although warm and humid, the best time to climb Mount Cameroon is December–April, when everything is dry.
Risk factor: Guides will help to avoid any dangers you may encounter on the slopes of the mountain, and practical common sense should keep you out of danger.
Health: Malaria is rife and the water is seldom drinkable, but prophylactic medication and bottled water are available in most of the larger towns.
Pack: Your own rations, along with sturdy hiking shoes or boots and good quality camping gear – sleeping bag, tent, warm clothing, cooking equipment.
Facilities: This is hiking and trekking country aimed largely at the budget traveller, and although some equipment and gear may be hired in Buea and similar settlements in the area, they offer only rudimentary accommodation at basic camp sites and the like.
Contact: Common Board of Eco Tourism, Mount Cameroon Project, Buea, Cameroon. Tel: 09237-95-407339

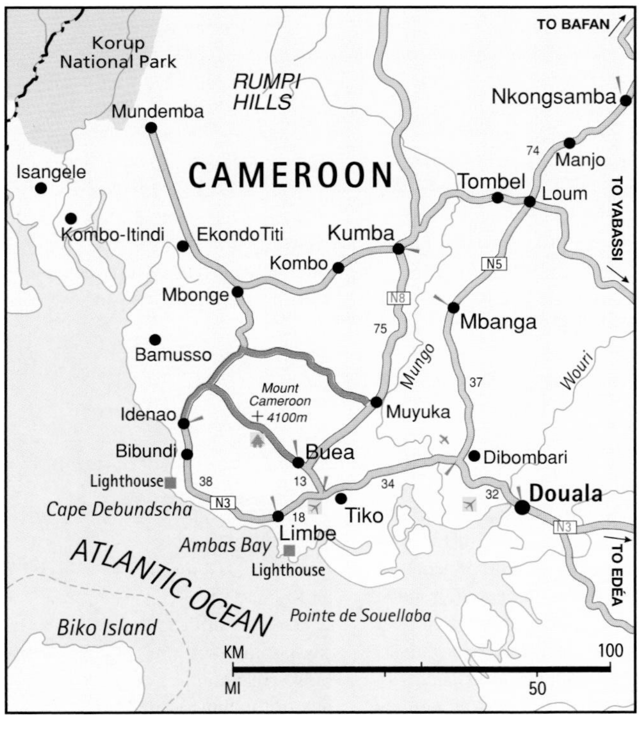

Mount Cameroon in southwestern Cameroon is, at 4,100m (13,452ft), the highest in West and Central Africa. Situated at the foot of a vast plateau virtually covered with forests, the landscape here is spectacular, and it is for this reason that the great hulk has become a not-so-secret climbing destination.

The departure point for adventures is Douala, Cameroon's most important urban centre (not the capital) and a vital link to exploring Mount Cameroon. Skirted by beaches covered in black sand, Douala has facilities that will make expeditions easier, but your final stop before venturing onto the mountain is Buea, 79km (49 miles) west of Douala. It is here that climbers finalize the logistics of their climb, book their guide at the tourist office, buy provisions – and get their rest. The best option is to make your booking through the Common Board of Eco Tourism, which provides porters, guides and useful information. There are various routes up and down, with many options for overnighting and attractions en route – including the elusive forest elephants.

The region between the summit and the coast enjoys a moderate climate tempered by high rainfall. The landscape is a scenic wonder and the volcano is seldom active, but do not be fooled – the climb up Mount Cameroon is not entirely easy. You will certainly need a guide to lead the way across stony gradient, t demanding at least some lev fitness and resilience on the ascent. The extreme weathe patterns on the other slopes mean that the eastern side the mountain provides the e est access point. A number relatively new trails have be forged into the rocky face, p viding alternatives to the tri and-tested Guinness Trail. Th high slopes can become bitt cold, with plenty of rain, hig speed wind and even snow.

2 DAYS+
CAMEROON

Travel Info
Destination: Mandara Mountains
uirements: Virtually all Westerners
d a passport and visa, although no
icular immunizations are required.
urrency: CFA franc (100 centimes)
te: Although warm and humid, the best time to climb the Mandara
untains is December to April, when everything is still reasonably dry.
actor: Guides should help to avoid dangers you may encounter on the
tain slopes, and practical common
se should keep you out of danger.
alth: Malaria is rife throughout the
ntry and the water is seldom drink-
e, but prophylactic medication and water are available in large towns.
k: Your own rations, sturdy hiking
or boots, and good quality camp-
g gear – sleeping bag, tent, warm clothing, cooking equipment.
cilities: This is hiking and trekking
ountry aimed largely at the budget
ler. Some equipment and gear can be hired in Maroua and similar
ements in the area, but they offer
ly rudimentary accommodation at basic camp sites and the like.
act: Star Voyages, Boulevard de la Renouveau, Maroua, Nigeria
Tel: 09237-229-25-22

WALKING THE MANDARA MOUNTAINS

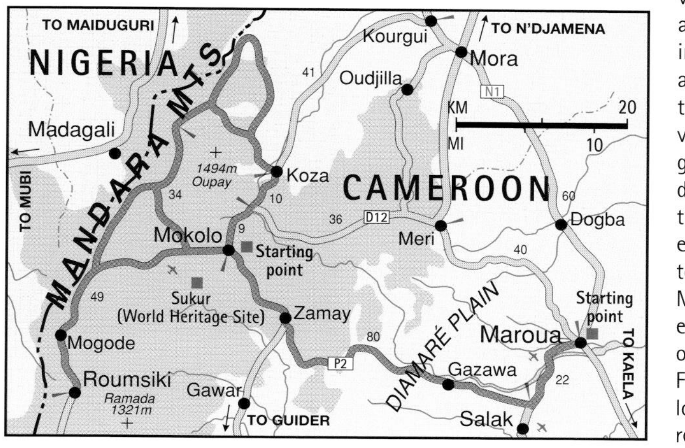

Situated to the west of Maroua and south of Mokolo – the most logical starting points for an exploratory venture – the mountains and volcanic plugs of Mandara are far removed from the standard tourist circuit. The threat of cultural clashes in the area seems to scare away many prospective adventurers. However, there is a promising emergence of adventure travel with the rough formalization of ecotourism that may be the light at the end of the tunnel, and the area is one of the most scenic in the region.

A few forward-thinking individuals have recognized the value of this pristine wilderness, and the fledgling adventure industry has settled well into the area, with a number of walking tours emanating from mountain villages – 'towns' may be too grand a description for these dusty little outposts. Although there are formal accommodation establishments in and around the towns of Mokolo, Mora and Maroua, the most memorable experience is overnighting with one of the mountain families. Fuel is expensive here, so for the locals donkeys and even horses remain the only alternative to walking, although the latter is indeed rewarding. Tracks and paths through the mountains are apparently endless, but apart from the occasional steep climb and equally steep descent, traversing these routes is not too difficult given some time and determination. The roads to and from mountain hamlets are dot-

ted with the stalls of produce vendors and the small thatched huts of rural families, but there is seldom any further activity for miles around. As you progress deeper into the valleys, the scenery becomes increasingly spectacular, taking on an almost Gothic appearance as the rustic rural shelters blend with the stony face of the mountain slopes. Walking is somewhat more arduous than on the range's outer reaches, but the rewards are huge, and the feeling of isolation quite overwhelming. It is little wonder that even the prerequisite tourist stops at Roumsiki, Koza and Oudjilla can come as somewhat of a culture shock, with the prying eyes of the villagers and the excited chatter of children following your every move. Although these are seldom the intended destination of true adventurers, the cultural experience – festivals, handicrafts and traditional lifestyles – is unmatched.

1 DAY+
CAMEROON

Travel Info
Destination: Dja Faunal Reserve
irements: Virtually all Westerners
a passport and visa, although no
cular immunisations are required.
rrency: CFA franc (100 centimes)
te: The southern areas can be wet
, and the tree canopy offers little
spite even during the end-of-year
ins. Humidity is high year-round.
actor: There are virtually no dan-
s in the Dja Reserve. The Baka are
ble and well able to placate fears.
: Malaria is rife and water is sel-
inkable, but prophylactic medica-
and bottled water are available in towns. Stock up well beforehand.
c: Although visitors to the reserve
y want to pack camping gear and
overnighting with the Baka means
ay have little need for provisions.
cilities: Dja is somewhat isolated,
ng in the accommodation offered
udimentary. Other options include
g at the existing camp or seeking
basic hospitality of the pygmies.
act: Ecosystem Forestier d'Afrique
entrale, P.O. Box 13844, Yaoundé,
Cameroon. Tel: 09237-220-9472
Fax: 09237-220-9472
fac@tamnet.cm, www.ecofac.org

EXPLORING THE DJA RESERVE

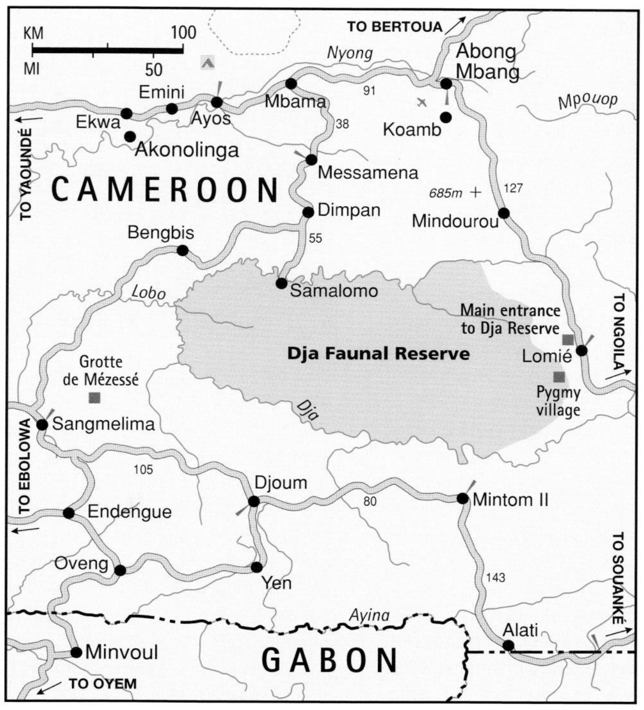

Hailed as the most significant of Cameroon's remaining natural forests, the thick woods of Dja Faunal Reserve are some of the best preserved in West and Central Africa, their heavy undergrowth, towering canopy and life-giving waters playing an all-important role in the fragile ecosystem. The reserve is neatly enclosed by the meandering Dja River, and the wooded landscape – protected by law – boasts populations of forest elephant, buffalo, and gorillas and other primates, although those that have survived the sporadic hunting are all elusive and unlikely to be spotted amid dense vegetation. Despite its beauty, the reserve is pleasantly devoid of tourists, who seldom venture as far as south as Lomié and towns such as Sangmélima and Mintom in the south, Abong Mbang a little further to the north, and the village of Somalomo on the border of the reserve. These isolated spots were once virtually inaccessible, but today see at least some traffic and, as a result, Lomié has become the base for venturing into the reserve's rainforests and the journeys to visit the pygmy villages on its eastern fringes.

Baka pygmies still live in mostly traditional homesteads influenced little by the modern-day trappings that have infiltrated other traditional groups throughout the continent. Organized trips to these unusual settlements are led by guides from the Baka community – they know what they are talking about and offer first-hand experience of the customs and ancestral lifestyle of the pygmies (noted for their hunting skills) and the still largely unexplored realm of their forest culture. The Baka are extremely hospitable and it is possible to overnight in their simple but comfortable homes. Show some respect for the customs and traditions that have been passed down the generations – and cherish the memory of time spent with one of the world's oldest intact civilizations.

1 DAY+
EQUATORIAL GUINEA

Travel Info
Destination: Bioko Island
ements: Virtually all visitors need
port and visa, and those climbing
peaks of Bioko require a special
it from government authorities – expect delays!
rency: CFA franc (100 centimes)
: Humidity levels are high during
ns, with the heaviest rains falling
st three/four months of the year.
tor: Visitors should encounter no
on Bioko, as long as they remain
e, keep an eye on prevailing con-
and plan their routes in advance.
alth: The island habitat poses no
health risks, apart from heat and
ustion on the uphill trail. Visitors
vised to drink only bottled water.
k: Sturdy hiking boots, sunscreen,
rations and warm clothes to pro-
if a chill settles over the slopes.
lities: Accommodation in Malabo
rom the basic to the comfortable
unless you looking for the ultra-
ous, you will find what you need
her essentials – such as food and
er supplies – are generally readily available in the capital.
act: Ministry of Culture, Tourism
ancophony, Malabo, Bioko Norte,
torial Guinea, Tel: 09240-92903

EXPLORING BIOKO'S VOLCANOES

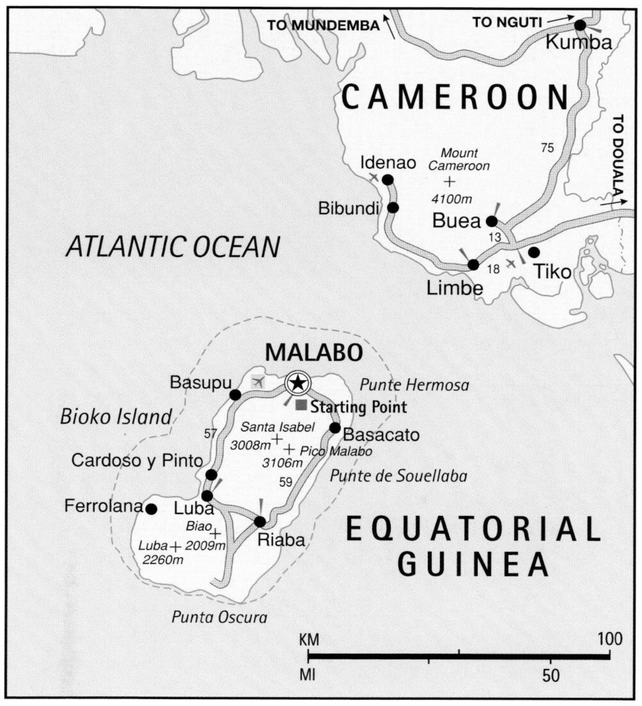

The capital of Equatorial Guinea is Malabo, on picturesque Bioko, an island that evolved on what was a trio of volcanic peaks, today skirted by a succession of attractive beaches – the most significant is at Luba, some 57km (35 miles) from Malabo – and a string of quaint fishing villages.

Bioko is much closer to the Cameroon mainland than it is to the country it serves. Visitors from Rio Muni, the collective name of the country's mainland, will inevitably be forced to the island on the *Acacio Mañe*, which leaves for the capital every day to return to Bata on the mainland at night. Getting around Malabo is just as easy: although taxis do operate in Malabo, the capital is so small that it is easily covered on foot. Towering high above – beyond the outer limits of the capital – are the fertile slopes, their dark soil and lush vegetation characteristic of volcanic terrain. It is these dipping valleys and lofty crests that are the destination of hikers and mountaineers. The mountain is laced with walking paths and hiking trails, but because Bioko's 3,106m (10,200ft) Pico Malabo volcano serves as a military installation it remains out of bounds for anyone lacking the prerequisite clearance permit.

Although many route markers are in need of attention – some are barely legible – they can hardly be considered misleading or confusing, and the trails are all rather straightforward (if not perfectly straight!). The ascent is not difficult, but the winding course of existing routes means that it may take longer than anticipated. Despite the fact that the Bioko volcano remains one of the most visited areas of Equatorial Guinea, you will probably not encounter too many other tourists.

1-3 DAYS
ERITREA

DIVING THE DAHLAK ARCHIPELAGO

Travel Info

Destination: Dahlak Archipelago
Requirements: Eritrean authorities are notoriously relaxed about documentation; nonetheless, all visitors require a valid passport and visa.
Currency: Eritrean nakfa (100 cents)
Climate: Coastal conditions hot and, June–August extremely humid, with day temperatures averaging 40°C (104°F). Best times are December to February, when temperatures average 30°C (86°F).
Risk factor: Apart from the usual risks of diving in unfamiliar waters, there are few other dangers, and much of Eritrea is relatively risk-free – apart from land mines that remain following the war.
Health: Malaria and dengue fever are both prevalent in the coastal regions, and the sun can be fierce in summer.
Pack: Unlike other areas along the Red Sea, not many dive operators work the Eritrean coast. Those who do are usually well equipped and knowledgeable. Equipment may be hired, but it may be best to take your own basics.
Facilities: Diving amenities are modest but usually adequate, with a few dive centres offering courses and diving expeditions that are well serviced.
Contact: Petros, Dahlak Sea Touring. Tel: 0929-11-552-489

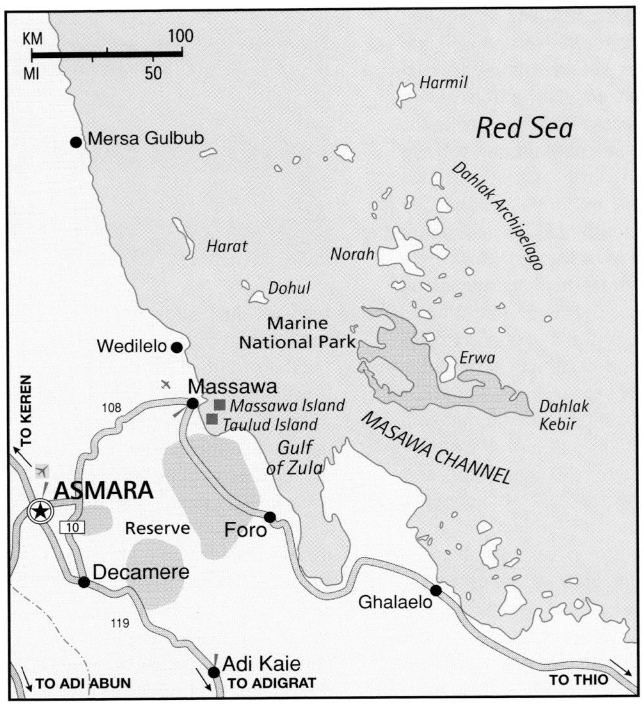

The Dahlak Archipelago off Eritrea's west coast is part of the diver's playground that is the Red Sea. The shoreline provides some of the most unspoiled beaches on this coast, and is dotted with tiny beaches popular with divers who swim out to the coral reefs to explore the marine life for which the Red Sea is renowned. The majority of Eritrea's beaches are isolated and unpopulated, although divers and snorkellers in the know tend to congregate here to extract the sea life or explore the ecosystem. Despite the fact that large tracts of these waters form part of a marine reserve, they are indeed open to divers. Permits are, however, required, so confirm this with one of the local diving centres.

Much of the coast forms a peaceful strip of sparkling sand that has a distinctly European feel. This is particularly true of Massawa, which in its heyday was famed for the richness of its pearl cache. The small urban centre suffered enormously in the war, but it is now reclaiming some of its stature and remains popular, especially over weekends and holidays when the islands of Taulud and Massawa (or Batsi) off the mainland become getaway retreats. As a result, the islands are punctuated with cheap hotels that are adequate if not luxurious, although Taulud does have much more comfortable – and more expensive – hotels. The most easily acce is Gurgusum, less than 10km miles) north of Massawa, bu is also one of the busiest. Di fishing and even camping ex sions to Dahlak and beyond launch from here, taking loa four to six passengers to the islets of Dahlak. Boats carry only four are cheaper to hir Diving conditions are excell but permits are valid for on three days and are costly.

1-7 DAYS
ETHIOPIA

HIKING THE BALE MOUNTAINS

Travel Info

Destination: Bale Mountains
Requirements: All travellers – except Kenyans – will need a valid passport and visa, in addition to permits to hike the mountain ranges. Cholera and yellow fever vaccinations may also be required.
Currency: Ethiopian birr (100 cents)
Climate: Temperatures are surprisingly moderate even in the interior, and the climate is generally comfortable year-round, apart from the heavy rains between July and September.
Risk factor: Apart from the usual health risks (see below), there have been some reports of banditry in outlying areas, although not particularly in daylight.
Health: Bilharzia (and other waterborne diseases) is prevalent throughout the country; extreme caution should be exercised with drinking water and fresh foods. AIDS is ever-present.
Pack: Water purification tablets are essential, as are a sunscreen and comfortable but sturdy hiking gear. Do not depend on your guide for anything.
Facilities: Access is limited and in need of some upgrading. Amenities are poor to adequate, with only a few basics.
Contact: Bale Mountains National Park. Tel: 09251-1-516938

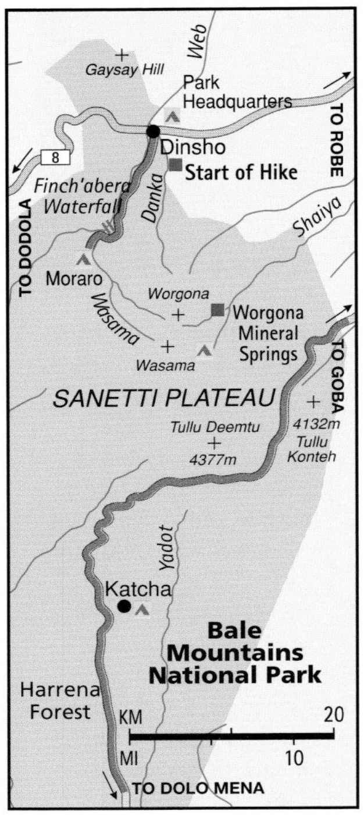

Because the Bale Mountains National Park was only gazetted in 1970, it remains largely unexplored. In parts rugged and austere, Bale's tranquil beauty provides a haven of some 2,400km² (925 sq. miles) to unique indigenous wildlife on the rather flat expanse. With hardly a blade of grass or tree in sight, but punctuated with heather and pale-hued shrubs, the Sanetti Plateau is – at 4,000m (13,125ft) – Africa's highest moor, while the 4,377m (14,360ft) Tullu Deemtu is the second-highest mountain in the country. Some 400km (250 miles) to the south of the capital at Addis Ababa, the Afro-alpine moorlands form the centre of the mountain range, and the wild animals here show little fear for hikers and trailists who traipse their lands. Blue-winged geese and other unique avifauna make their home on the numerous tarns, and the Bale Mountains National Park is also host to klipspringers, grey duikers, jackals and leopard and, very occasionally, the Abyssinian lion. Also in abundance are rodents, which comprise the chief diet of the near extinct Simien wolf (a third of which still reside on the Bale mountainside). These endangered carnivores are relatively safe here from the environmental degradation and human encroachment that have affected other home territories. Many hikers make it a point to see these creatures.

Bale is extensive and the ground covered by the hiking trails – some little more than vague tracks – includes the misty 'valley' to the south of the Sanetti Plateau and the Harena forest that lies at the foot of the Bale range, with its heavy undergrowth, high canopy and excitable primate populations.

The woodlands of Harena are protected, which explains why outsiders have explored relatively little of what they have to offer. The forest is home to unique faunal species, including the Menelik's bushbuck, the mountain nyala, and Rouget's rail. Virtually all are spotted with relative ease, and during the course of the hike – which may last from less than a day to nearly a week – hikers may expect to see any number of these, often in abundance. The treks are usually on foot, an may also be on the back of mule, but need to be sancti by park officials based at Di Some routes are demanding most are easily accessible fo moderately fit and, for the l adventurous, there is also th option of shorter trails (som more than a mile or two). In case, accommodation at the lodge, camp or self-catering will be necessary.

1-10 DAYS
ETHIOPIA

MULE TREKKING IN THE SIMIEN MOUNTAINS

Travel Info

Destination: Simien Mountains
Requirements: All travelers – except Kenyans – need a passport and visa, in addition to permits to hike the mountain. Cholera and yellow fever vaccinations may also be required.
Currency: Ethiopian birr (100 cents)
Climate: Temperatures are moderate even in the interior and, apart from the heavy rains July–September, the climate is generally comfortable year-round.
Risk factor: Apart from usual health risks (see below), there have been reports of banditry in outlying areas; this is not common, particularly not in daylight.
Health: Bilharzia (and other waterborne diseases) is prevalent, and caution should be exercised with drinking water and fresh foods. AIDS is ever-present.
Pack: Water purification tablets are essential, as are a sunscreen and comfortable but sturdy hiking gear. Do not depend on your guide for anything.
Facilities: Amenities are rudimentary to adequate, but the experience is worth any discomfort travellers may experience as a result of spending too many hours on the back of a mule trudging across a rocky landscape.
Contact: National Tour Operations (NTO). Tel: 09251-1-514838 / 512923. Fax: 09251-1-1517688

Ethiopia's magnificent Simien Mountains form the heart of the national park and World Heritage Site that shares its name. It is indeed a spectacular region, with a limited but fascinating array of indigenous wildlife that has become its principal attraction. The mammal and bird life here is restricted to relatively few species, but those that have set up home here are in abundance, and include endemic creatures such as baboon, ibex, raptors such as the lammergeier, and the increasingly threatened Simien wolf. In fact, the area boasts one of the most viable populations of these carnivores. As a result, it is popular among not only hikers, but also other naturalists such as trekkers who make their way across the mountain on mules.

Mule trekking has now become one of the most popular ways to explore the Simien Mountains, and a number of locals have gravitated towards catering for the needs of an increasing numbers of visitors. Fortunately, much of the 'tourist' infrastructure remains truly basic and the surrounds are wonderfully unspoiled. Unlike Bale Mountains National Park, which is not only a wildlife reserve but also a Controlled Hunting Area, the Simien Mountains National Park is best known as a trekking destination, and the rough and stony terrain of the slopes is laced with a series of trails.

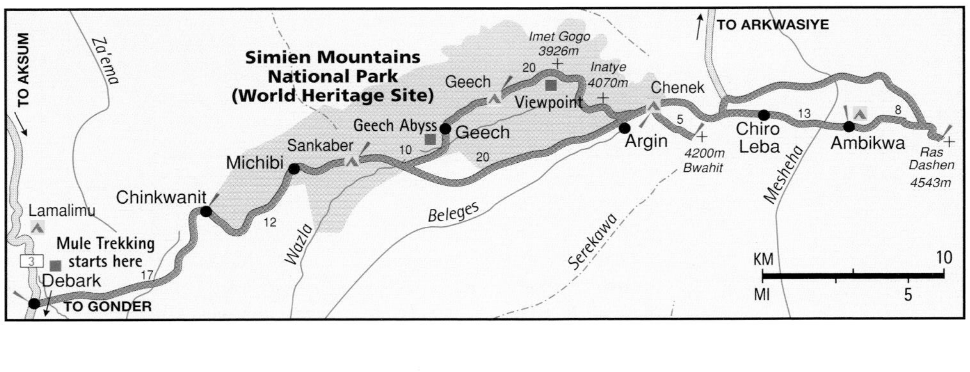

Most of the treks start at Debark, some 100km (62 miles) from Gondar. The length of time spent on the mountains and the degree of fitness and/or stamina required vary. Some excursions may require only one or two nights in the Simien Mountains, while other treks – such as that to Ras Dashen, at 4,620m (15,160ft) the third highest peak in Africa – can take up to 10 days. Travellers unsure abou week on the back of a mule should avoid the gruelling t and opt for day outings.

Naturally, the costs vary may change from time to ti and, although mule treks ac the range can hardly be con sidered expensive, they usu do entail a number of separ costs that mount up: park 48-hour entry fee, camping guard fee, guide fee, mule f and tent costs, plus gratuiti and daily incidentals.

1-5 HOURS
ETHIOPIA

Travel Info
Destination: Lake Tana
quirements: All travellers – except
enyans – need a passport and visa.
olera and yellow fever vaccinations
may also be required.
urrency: Ethiopian birr (100 cents)
mate: Temperatures are moderate,
d the climate is comfortable year-
und (heavy rains July–September).
sk factor: Apart from usual health
(see below) associated with water-
pastimes, Tana holds few dangers.
h: Bilharzia (and other waterborne
eases) is prevalent throughout the
try, and extreme caution should be
ised with drinking water and fresh
foods. AIDS is ever-present.
ack: Water purification tablets are
al, as are a sunscreen and a set of
m, dry clothing. Do not depend on
your guide for anything.
cilities: Facilities at Lake Tana are
lly good, with a variety of options
able to travellers. Accommodation
ies from basic to comfortable, but
s are equally extreme, so it is best
n through a reliable tour operator.
ontact: Experience Ethiopia Travel.
09251-1-152336 / 519291, Fax:
1-1-519982, eet@telecom.net.et,
www.telecom.net.et/eet

SAILING LAKE TANA

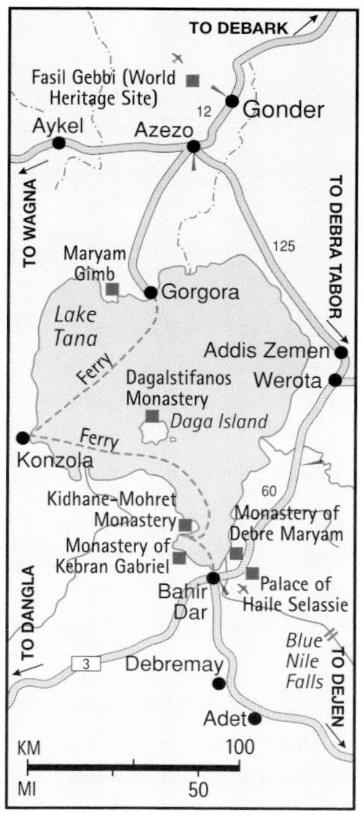

The waters of Lake Tana are gentle, the air still and the mood distinctly African, with a sense of timelessness that only Ethiopia can offer. Tana lies in the heart of the Ethiopian Highlands in the north of the country, and its 3,600km^2 (1,400 sq. miles) are dotted with nearly 40 islets best seen from one of Haile Selassie's palaces on the hilltop above Bahar Dar, the small settlement on the southern banks. Although the area may seem remote and laid-back, it is one of Ethiopia's most fascinating, with a number of added attractions beyond the lake. En route to the lake, stop off at one of Africa's most impressive waterfalls, the Blue Nile Falls, about 30km (19 miles) from its source at Bahar Dar. The falls are 400m (1,300ft) wide and are known here as Tis Isat – 'the Smoke of the Nile' – and plummet nearly 50m (165ft) in a spectacle of colour that 'bursts' through the water as it is broken by the light. The falls are remarkable at virtually any time of the year, but are arguably at their finest following the heavy rains between October and December (the Tourist Information Centre at Tis Abbay may be able to offer more practical information).

However, the waters and 37 islands of Lake Tana remain the most magical attraction in central Ethiopia. Apart from the natural beauty of the surrounds, the lake also boasts some of the nation's most remarkable cultural sites, for it is on the numerous islands that some of Africa's oldest monasteries lie scattered – some dating from 500 to nearly 1,000 years back. Sailing along these waters is thus a truly enriching experience, although it can also be an impoverishing one: trips to the islands can be alarmingly expensive for the budget traveller. Trips usually last

between one and five hours (or longer), and there are a number of options. The best – at half the price of 'official' tours – are the private entrepreneurs. Although the atmosphere is more relaxed, the guides may not be as knowledgeable as those crewing the boats of the Marine Transport Authority. The latter are more expensive but, because their boats can take up to two dozen passengers, may work out just as cheap in the long run, if you are prepared to wait for the boat to be filled before sailing. Skippers will inevitably stop off at a number of the island monasteries, most popularly Kebran Gabriel and Debre Maryam, and most tourists will expect to be taken out to Kidhane Mohret on the Zege Peninsula, which is best known for its unusually erotic paintings atypical of the Muslim communities here.

4 HOURS
ETHIOPIA

Travel Info
Destination: Lalibela
quirements: All travellers – except
nyans – need a passport and visa.
lera and yellow fever vaccinations
lso be required; church custodians
may want to see a touring permit.
rrency: Ethiopian birr (100 cents)
e: Temperatures are moderate, and
from heavy rains July–September,
climate is comfortable year-round.
ctor: Apart from the usual health
e below), there have been reports
of banditry in outlying areas.
n: Bilharzia (and other waterborne
s) is prevalent and caution should
exercised with drinking water and
fresh foods. AIDS is ever-present.
ack: Water purification tablets are
essential, as are a sunscreen and
omfortable but sturdy hiking gear.
ies: Because Lalibela is one of the
urist attractions in Ethiopia, facil-
re fair to good, with a number of
ate tour agents – and locals mas-
ing as such. Established operators
offer a far better service than the
siderably cheaper fly-by-nighters.
ntact: Experience Ethiopia Travel.
09251-1-152336 / 519291, Fax:
1-1-519982, eet@telecom.net.et,
www.telecom.net.et/eet

HISTORIC LALIBELA

The rock churches of Lalibela are probably the most famous of Ethiopia's cultural and historical sites – and justifiably so. They form part of what is commonly known as the country's Historic Route, which takes in some of the most significant places of worship and Christian-based sites on the continent.

In the heart of Ethiopia's dustlands lies small groups of unusual, stone-walled churches that were meticulously chopped from the surrounding countryside by human hands in an extraordinary manifestation of devotion and the unshakable religious beliefs of the Ethiopian Orthodox Church. Some of the most remarkable of these unique structures are the 11 churches scattered on the outskirts of Lalibela, once the capital of the medieval Zagwe dynasty. While Ethiopia boasts identical cave-like churches elsewhere - notably at Tigray - Lalibela's structures

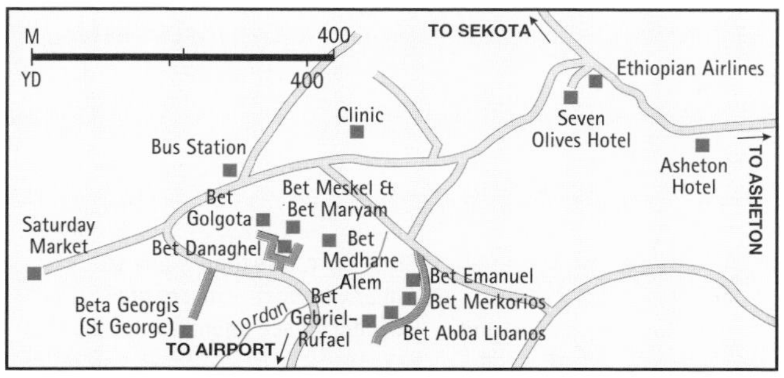

are widely regarded as some of the finest examples of indigenous religious architecture in Africa. These cavernous churches excavated from the bedrock of a craggy mountain face provide an amazing spectacle. Protected by a series of deep furrows and linked by underground passages and tunnels, they are treasured sites of ancient Ethiopian culture and worship, the finding places of a host of illustrated Bibles, ceremonial parchments, sacred works of art and ornate crucifixes particular to this region. The series of winding passages are said to have taken a decade to complete, with some 50,000 faithful followers working full-time on the labyrinth.

These cave-like structures remain the place of worship for a number of orthodox Christians who not only continue to celebrate mass as they have done for centuries, but also stand watch over the ancient relics, preserving them for posterity.

Originally known as Roha – it was changed to Lalibela after a king of that name who was instructed in a dream to construct his 12th-century capital here – the town is rather modest in size, yet the churches are grand and imposing, the largest of which – Bet Medhane Alem – looms some 11.5m (38ft) and covers an area of no less than 800m^2 (8,606 sq. ft). Other impressive sites include the massive Bet Abba Libanos and Bet Giorgis, a monolith in the shape of a 15m (50ft) cross and encircled by a trough nearly as deep as the towering structure is high.

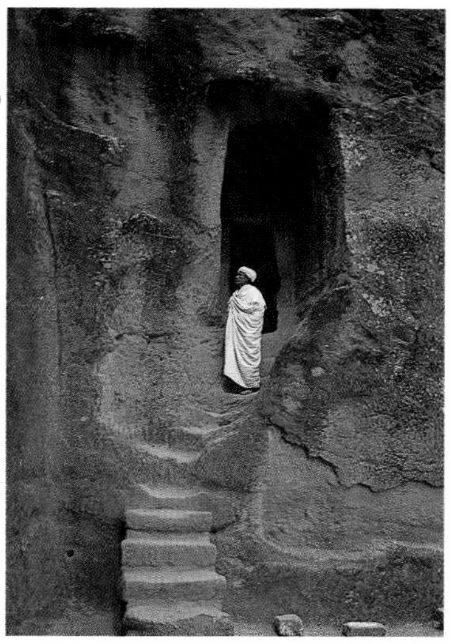

A tour of the precinct is hardly demanding and inordinately breathtaking, and some walking is involved to get from church to church – most visitors end up a little tired rather than thoroughly exhausted. To save you from doubling back to the more prominent features, it is best to utilize the services of a guide to walk you through the churches. The entry fee allows access to all 11 churches, which should take no more than four hours to complete – much the same time it would take to do the round trek to Asheton Maryam monastery, an equally enthralling diversion.

1 DAY+
DJIBOUTI

Travel Info
Destination: Gulf of Tadjoura
ments: All visitors (except French
s) require a passport and the necessary one-month visas on entry.
y: Djiboutian franc (100 centimes)
e: Humid and very hot, with day-
emperatures in even the moderate
er months peaking at 25°C (77°F).
factor: There are almost no risks
nd the main centre, but venturing
afield – particularly the northern
reas – may present some dangers.
There are few health risks, but it
st to drink only bottled water and
exual contact with the prostitutes
ating in and around Djibouti City.
k: Take light holiday clothing and
of sunscreen, particularly if much
the holiday is to be spent on the
r. To avoid high hiring costs, take
n equipment, such as scuba gear.
ties: Visitors' facilities in Djibouti
quate, but are certainly no match
en for countries such as Ethiopia.
e locals speak virtually no English
l, travel can be frustrating, and is
ery expensive – especially for the
budget traveller.
Contact: La Caravane du Sel (The
of Salt), P.O. Box 2098, Djibouti
53-35-3752, Fax: 09253-35-6618

EXPLORING TADJOURA

Situated as it is at the mouth of the Red Sea, Djibouti's Gulf of Tadjoura is indeed a unique find for the determined adventurer. Ruled by Arabs and, latterly, the French (as French Somaliland), Djibouti has seen its fair share of turmoil, even in recent times.

Although hardly a bastion of political stability, it has emerged to become an increasingly popular adventure destination. Much of the activity, naturally, centres on the capital and the waters of the Gulf of Tadjoura, the small inlet off the Gulf of Aden.

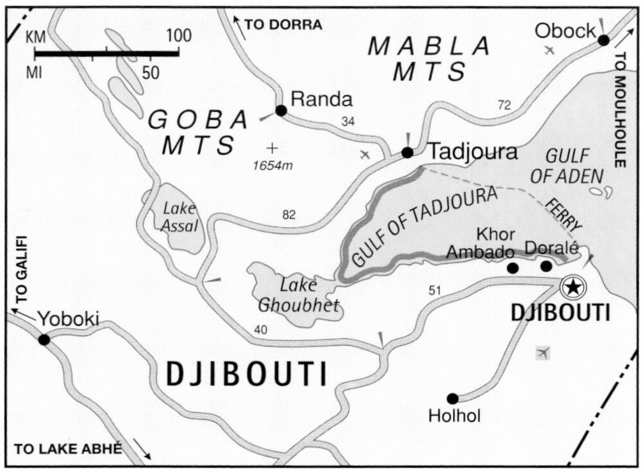

The port at Djibouti is largely commercial and there are few opportunities to take advantage of industry-based cargo ships that frequent the harbour (crew seldom if ever take paying travellers). Dhow operators may be persuaded to take budget travellers to other ports along the Red Sea but, for safety reasons, all travel documents should be in perfect order.

The north is still unsafe and the south uninspiring, so travellers inevitably congregate at Tadjoura, the comparatively small settlement on the opposite side of the bay that once formed the barrier between the Issas and the Afars. The ferry from L'Escale will take you to Tadjoura, which offers the best holiday opportunities and is a district capital, despite its size. A popular beach is the out-of-the-way Khor-Ambado, although it is the sands at Doralé that have proven to be the most enticing. The waters of the gulf are open to a variety of

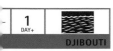

water-based activities, including its most highly regarded attraction: diving and snorkelling some of the most outstanding coral reefs of northern Africa and yet within metres of the picturesque shoreline. Also within easy reach are Lake Assal and Lake Ghoubhet, equally famed for their underwater wilderness.

The town itself is rather quiet and not particularly exciting, but is set against Djibouti's finest landscape, which includes a hiking haven of no fewer than four mountain peaks of over 1,000m (3,300ft) high that are accessed by hiking trails and nature walks.

The small capital has a charm of its own and is easily accessible from Tadjoura, most notably across the bay on a series of small vessels. For adventures further afield, such as windsurfing on the sands of Petit and Grand Bara or a 4x4 expedition to Lac Abbé, it is best to utilize the services of package-tour operators.

GABON

EXPLORING THE POUBARA FALLS

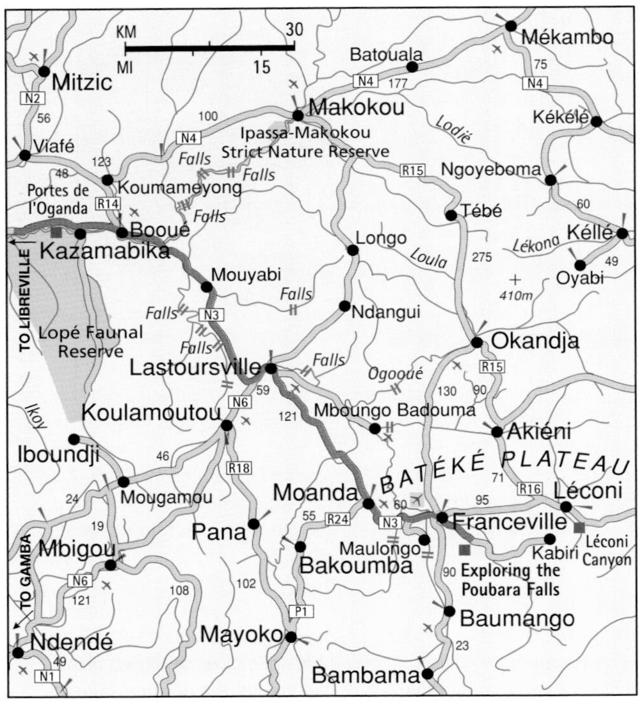

Travel Info

Destination: Franceville
Requirements: All visitors require a visa – which can take weeks – and, theoretically, a written invitation from a resident to visit. Although not always essential, it is best to follow rules. Yellow fever and cholera immunizations are required.
Currency: CFA franc (100 centimes)
Climate: Hot and very humid virtually year-round throughout the country, especially in the forested zones.
Risk factor: The wilds of Gabon are relatively safe – although a reliable guide will help facilitate matters – so it is the volatility of animal life that poses the most risks. Do not take chances.
Health: The nature of the environment brings with it health risks, such as waterborne diseases; consult a doctor familiar with tropical conditions.
Pack: Lightweight, protective clothing. Sturdy, protective shoes – preferably boots – if you intend doing a lot of walking (inevitable in Gabon's forests).
Facilities: Facilities are usually extremely rudimentary, and few operators are able to offer anything other than the basics.
Contact: Mistral Voyages, B.P. 2106, Libreville, Gabon.
Tel: 09241-760421, Fax: 09241-747780, mistral.lbv@internetgabon.com

Many adventurers flock to the forests of Gabon – and few are disappointed. While the coastal region, where dense tropical forests reach down to the beaches, is the most obvious stopover - parts of Libreville are well geared towards tourism – it is the forests around Franceville that provide some of the most fascinating diversions.

With the heavily canopied forests of Gabon receiving an average of 3,000mm (120in) of rain in a year, it is not surprising that the woods of Franceville are lined with lichens, moss, fungi and ferns, and laced with rivers and streams punctuated by rapids and waterfalls. Walking here is precarious, not the least because the undergrowth is thick, wet and, in parts, steaming. Hikers will need some sort of machete or cutting tool to clear overgrown areas, but routes are well trod, even though distances are vast. Carry as light a load as possible: there are few donkeys

or other beasts of burden as the sleeping sickness carried by the tstetse fly would quickly mean the end of them. Be prepared to haul your own backpack, water and equipment. You are likely to encounter an array of forest inhabitants, from chimpanzees and mangabey monkeys to hornbills and dwarf crocodiles, plus spiders and snakes. The gorillas are less easy to spot unless you are on a 'gorilla tour', but you

will stumble across – literall
elephant and leopard droppi

Beyond the forest lie the Poubara Falls with their thu
ing 3m (10ft) rapids, but it n
take some courage to ventu
across the nearly 100-year-c
vine bridge to the falls. The
bridge is sturdy but unnervi
if you want to see waterfall
may need to settle for those
Djuma, far more accessible v
boat chartered in Franceville

GABON

DOWN THE OGOOUÉ RIVER

Travel Info

Destination: Port-Gentil/Lamberene
Requirements: All visitors require a visa – which can take weeks – and, theoretically, an invitation to visit, so it is best to follow rules to the letter. Yellow fever and cholera immunizations are required.
Currency: CFA franc (100 centimes)
Climate: Hot and very humid year-round, especially in the forests. Temperatures on the river are more moderate.
Risk factor: Although generally safe, the Ogooué River is best experienced with a local at your side. The forests receive a very high rainfall (3,000mm / 118 inches), making the waters are powerful.
Health: The Ogooué does pose risks, including diseases carried by water used frequently for industry.
Pack: Clothing must be waterproof and comfortable, as you will be spending a lot of time on the water.
Facilities: Facilities are adequate, with Lamberene and Port Gentil well serviced by river-trip operators – be they 'official' or private. There is seldom any real difference between first- and second-class fares on the more formal excursions.
Contact: Mistral Voyages, B.P. 2106, Libreville, Gabon.
Tel: 09241-760421, Fax: 09241-747780, mistral.lbv@internetgabon.com

The 970km (683-mile) Ogooué River rises in the east and stretches across the width of Gabon, spilling into the Atlantic south of Port-Gentil, and it is here that much of the river-based activity is centred. Although it is a small settlement, with little excitement, it is a fascinating place, where all sorts of river excursions can be arranged with enterprising locals. One of the most popular excursions – largely because it is so cheap – is a 'cruise' up the Ogooué (although vessels travel in both directions). Locals have used the pirogue – traditional dugout – as transport for centuries, and trips on these simple vessels offer an insider's view of the river.

There are plenty of commercial vessels taking the trip up and down for practical and leisure purposes. The obvious choice – especially for visitors arriving from Libreville – is the trip from Lamberene to Port Gentil. Any number of craft (used for fishing and day-to-day transport) depart daily, but specialized 'cruise' vessels leave twice a week – usually on Monday and Friday – and take about 10 hours. These are inexpensive and, although hardly luxurious, are comfortable. More expensive but the preferred option is a trip on the large *Azingo*, which leaves Port Gentil for Lamberene on Mondays, returning to port on a Thursday. This trip is the most popular, especially because there is so much to see and do en route. The vessels is said to be like a village in its own right, with plenty of on-board distractions, but the leisurely trip is broken by a number of stop-offs at local villages. The trip up the river to Lamberene can take nearly two days, although the return trip to Port Gentil – following the direction of the seaward river – takes only a day (albeit a full 24 hours). Trips beyond Lamberene to Ndjolé are not very well organized or especially pleasant, and will mean hitching a ride on a rather grimy oil barge, where you will pay for the ride only – no services, no food and no English-speaking crew. Although this trip can be economical, more comfortable options can be quite expensive if travelling in a small

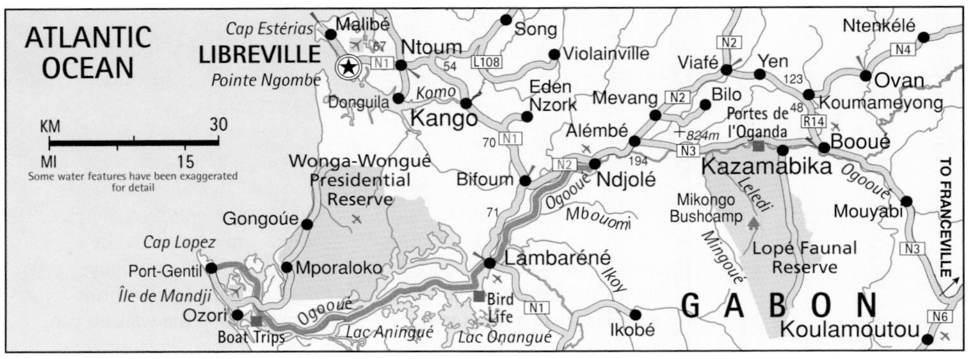

party. Virtually the entire riv
however, populated by hipp
other wildlife. This is particu
true in the dry season – or a
as it gets in Gabon – betwe
May and September.

DEMOCRATIC REPUBLIC OF THE CONGO

HIKING THE RUWENZORIS

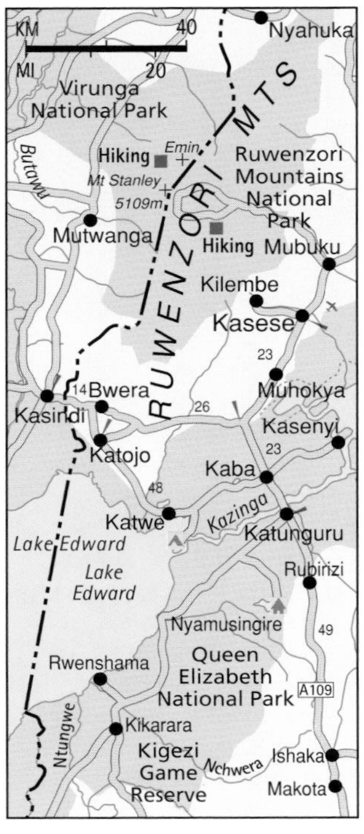

Travel Info

Destination: Ruwenzori Mountains
Requirements: Although standard entry conditions apply, be prepared for complications. The DRC is not an easy place in which to travel – and not particularly safe – so keep your visa-stamped passport and yellow fever vaccination certification with you at all times.
Currency: Congo franc (100 centimes)
Climate: Hot, humid and wet throughout the year, often uncomfortably so.
Risk factor: Security remains risky and travellers should enquire beforehand.
Health: Malaria is a real danger, and most Westerners may be susceptible to other diseases. Take precautions.
Pack: Antimalarial medication, plus light, warm clothing that is waterproof as well as easily removable as the humidity increases and the temperature rises.
Facilities: Facilities are simple, with no luxuries, although Virunga headquarters are well geared towards visitors. Specialized tours to see the gorillas can be expensive, but Virunga permits are usually valid for at least seven days.
Contact: Uganda Tourist Board, P.O. Box 722, Kampala, Uganda.
Tel: 09243-41-342196 / 7
Fax: 09243-41-342196

Of all the great parks in the Democratic Republic of the Congo, the most acclaimed is the 8,000km² (3,000 sq. mile) Virunga National Park and World Heritage Site, the nation's first park established some 80 years ago. This magnificent natural heritage site – as well as many other parks, conservation areas and wildlife sanctuaries – fell victim to the ravages of the civil war, resulting in only a small proportion of its abundant fauna surviving, yet it remains one of the few viable options for adventure travellers. Even so, caution should be observed. Some areas have been reopened to the public, one of which is the great Ruwenzori Mountains, perhaps the DRC's most notable attraction.

Situated in the far north of Virunga National Park (known locally as Parc National des Virunga), the Ruwenzoris were once high on the list of the world's hiking destinations, but today even the most ardent adventurers tend to tackle them from Uganda rather than the DRC. Some stability has returned to the region, yet few travel agents and tour operators are comfortable recommending these mountains for hiking. The safety and security problems that ravaged the DRC also affected 'gorilla tourism' – more sensible alternative's are Uganda's Mgahinga National Park or Bwindi Impenetrable Forest.

More is the pity, as the undulating slopes of the Ruwenzoris are probably some of the most spectacular in Central Africa. Despite the fact that the mountains are linked to neighbouring Uganda as they straddle the border between the two countries, together the Ruwenzoris – inevitably lush and densely wooded – form one of the four principal administrative centres of the DRC. Swathed in mists for

much of the year, the slippery slopes are almost always wet and difficult to navigate without some experience, making hiking extremely arduous, with local conditions posing the most challenges. Although the hiking routes – few are marked out and even fewer negotiated by the uninitiated – are not for the faint-hearted, the extra effort and careful planning required will pay handsome dividends. The central regions of the range comprise a number of individual

peaks, many of which are pe
nently covered in snow and
ted with glaciers – even in t
heart of Africa. Conquering
slopes of these mountains, v
extend some 100km (62 mil
into Uganda, is some feat a
should not be approached li
but the rewards are enormo
not the least of which is the
relief and sense of achiever
if you are able to ascend the
towering peaks of Mount St
which, although officially in
Uganda, is right on the bord

2 DAYS+

CRATIC REPUBLIC OF THE CONGO

Travel Info

Destination: Kinshasa/Congo River
rements: Although standard entry
ons apply, be prepared for compli-
s. The DRC is not an easy place in
ch to travel – and not particularly
– so keep your visa-stamped passport and yellow fever vaccination
certification with you at all times.
ency: Congo franc (100 centimes)
te: Hot and humid, and exploring
ongo River can add to discomfort.
Risk factor: Apart from the usual
ity risks, rapids are graded one to
one being tame with few risks, six
virtually impassable) and much of
ngo falls dangerously close to the
more challenging classification.
alth: Malaria is a real danger, and
Westerners are susceptible to other
seases. Whitewater rafters should
carry a well-stocked first-aid kit.
Antimalarial medication and com-
e, waterproof clothing, with a dry
set for after a day on the water.
ities: Facilities vary from good to
ood, but are expensive. Sadly, this
he only option worth considering.
ntact: ONATRA, B.P. 98, Kinshasa.
Tel: 09243-12-23424

WHITEWATER RAFTING ON THE CONGO

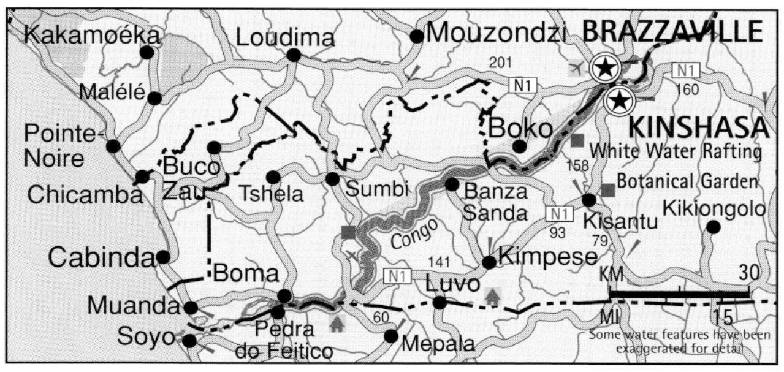

The wild waters of the Congo – even those near to the capital of Kinshasa – are said to be some of the most thrilling and fearsome in Africa, and Central Africa is fast becoming one of the world's top whitewater rafting destinations. The torrential waters and the unforgiving rapids that cascade down the length of the river offer a remarkable challenge set among some of the least explored stretches of water in the world – access to much of the Congo is restricted by the political situation, in addition to the thick vegetation that crowds much of its banks. Nonetheless, the experience remains unparalleled.

Virtually encircled by an overgrown jungle, the principal departure points around Kinshasa are relatively easily reached by adventurers, with many opting for the riverboat excursion from Kisangani to the capital. From here, many of the most popular whitewater destinations on the river are, at the most, just hours away. Many of Africa's whitewater rapids remain largely unexplored, and this is particularly true of the Congo River's many tributaries, which offer some unrivalled river experiences. The tributaries of the Congo total some 14,500km (9,000 miles), many of them winding their way around an apparently endless series of nearly 4,000 tiny islands, each as densely vegetated as the next. Some of the most breathtaking of the Congo's impressive offshoots are the Kafubu and Luapula rivers, where some rapids – one of which is appropriately called Big Eyes – extend about 500m (550yd), while the Lofoi River plummets more than 350m (1,150ft) from the surrounding tablelands at Lakoba Falls.

Although the upper parts are indeed interrupted by daunting stretches of challenging rapids,

the Congo starts out as a fairly tame and relatively peaceful stretch of water. However, it soon races through some of the continent's most fearsome gorges, each pummelled by its own relentless whitewater rapids, highlighted by the seven cataracts of Boyoma (Stanley Falls). It eventually culminates in the massive drop at Livingstone Falls, just outside Kinshasa.

While the Congo is only 2km (1 mile) wide in parts, its width can be an intimidating 16km (10 miles) in others and the 320km (200-mile) stretch between the capital and the ocean is punctuated with no fewer than 30 cataracts. While pioneering trips took months to conquer the river's waterways, the strength of the Congo depends on seasonal rainfall, although nowhere along its lengths can its waters be considered gentle. The enormous force of the hurtling waters and the strength of the river's pull has seen many a daredevil's efforts end in tragedy. The services of an experienced guide are vital, irrespective of what waters you decide to ride, but especially when tackling unfamiliar territory – of which the Congo will provide an abundance!

1 DAY

CRATIC REPUBLIC OF THE CONGO

Travel Info

ation: Kahuzi-Biega National Park
rements: Although standard entry
ons apply, be prepared for compli-
s. The DRC is not an easy place in
ch to travel – and not particularly
– so keep your visa-stamped passport and yellow fever vaccination
certification with you at all times.
ency: Congo franc (100 centimes)
e: Hot, humid and wet throughout
the year, often uncomfortably so.
factor: Security remains risky and
vellers should enquire beforehand.
alth: Malaria is a real danger, and
Westerners are susceptible to other
diseases. Take precautions.
ack: Antimalarial medication, plus
eight but waterproof clothing and
mfortable but sturdy hiking boots.
ties: Facilities are extremely basic
d, even though the special gorilla
e expensive, travellers should not
pect any frills. Accommodation is
ted and lacks even the most basic
ties. Take your own camping gear,
food and water rations.
Contact: National Tourism Office,
B.P. 9502, Kinshasa.
Tel: 09243-12-30070

TREKKING THE LOWLAND FORESTS

Although many gorilla enthusiasts opt for alternatives offered by neighbouring countries, there are still some options available to visitors to the DRC, even though travel here is rather precarious. The best bet is Kahuzi-Biega National Park, between Goma and Bukavu. It is at the latter that permits and other essential preparations can be arranged, but be warned that the entire exercise can be trying.

The park was established more than 30 years ago in order to preserve the natural habitat of the endangered primates that now serve as its principal attraction. It started out as a rather small conservation area of about 600km² (375 sq. miles), but within five years it had grown to some 6,000km² (3,750 sq. miles) and still serves as one of the last remaining refuges for the lowland gorilla. Although there are some 20 breeding troops in the park, less than a quarter are accustomed to human contact

and accessible to visitors. As a result, although there are no seasonal limits to the visits, preteens are specifically excluded from the walking safaris that set out in search of the elusive primates. Hikes, led by experienced trackers and hosted by knowledgeable guides (both of which are compulsory), can often take the better half of a day, although most of the guides do this so often that they can usually locate a gorilla family within two to three hours. The walking can, nevertheless, be tough and demanding and requires considerable effort and patience. The vegetation is undeniably dense and difficult to negotiate, especially with a full backpack, so be prepared. Bookings have to be finalized in advance through the Institut Zairose our la Conservation de la Nature at Bukavu, and the trip, although extremely rewarding, is not cheap. Not only are there park fees, camera permits and additional incidentals, but your local entourage will also expect to be tipped at the end of the day.

3 DAYS+

CRATIC REPUBLIC OF THE CONGO

Travel Info

Destination: Kinshasa
rements: Although standard entry
ons apply, be prepared for compli-
s. The DRC is not an easy place in
ch to travel – and not particularly
– so keep your visa-stamped passport and yellow fever vaccination
certification with you at all times.
ency: Congo franc (100 centimes)
e: Hot, humid and wet throughout
the year, often uncomfortably so.
factor: A trip on the river means
will mix with people such as con
Watch your baggage, and keep a
file. Cameras could cause trouble.
h: Malaria and other tropical dis-
ases may be rife. Take precautions.
k: Antimalarial medication, light-
t but waterproof clothing, as well
as bedding if travelling third class.
ities: Facilities in first and second
are adequate, but third class may
whelming for Westerners. Trading
selling supplies visit the riverboat
larly, but treat the food and water
ht from these locals with caution.
ntact: ONATRA, B.P. 98, Kinshasa.
Tel: 09243-12-23424

A RIVERBOAT ON THE CONGO

Considerably less adventurous – but no less enjoyable – is a lazy and relatively hassle-free trip down the Congo River on board one of the many riverboats that ply the waters of the mighty river. This is a unique, eye-opening experience and is usually extremely laid-back and not at all demanding, providing a rare chance to catch your breath amid the flurry of on-board activity. Widely acclaimed as one of the Classic African Journeys, a trip on the imposing *Le Grand Poseur* provides nonstop entertainment, with hundreds of fellow passengers relaxing in the time-honoured African way: dancing and drinking. The entourage has been described as a floating village, with a tug leading the way with barges trailing in its wake.

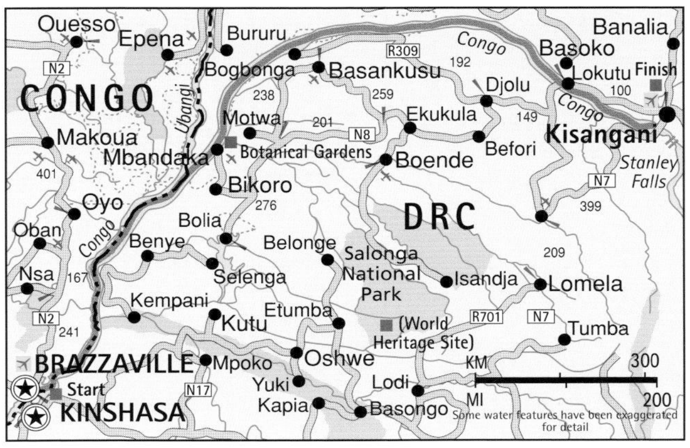

Life on board the riverboat is a microcosm of what life is like on the banks of the Congo River, and an assortment of characters litter the decks, ranging from vendors to curio tradesmen, prostitutes to loan sharks.

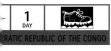

So popular are these remarkable trips that booking is essential, and you will need to make prior arrangements long before your departure dates. Be sure to confirm your reservation before you arrive in Kinshasa, from where the riverboat departs – albeit less frequently nowadays. Everything and everyone here operates on African time, so don't plan your itinerary to the minute, particularly if you are relying on public transport to get to and from the capital. Although time spent on board is leisurely, the Congo's riverboat makes numerous stops, and exploring the river banks can entail lots of walking – be sure to get back to the vessel in time for its departure (it is not unknown for the vessel to next pass only after a month a two!).

For first-class passengers, time spent on the riverboat is quite comfortable, with twin bunks and private ablution facilities, but second-class berths sleep four and have communal showers. Third class is basically the deck, and travelling companions can be rather dicey, so are best avoided – especially if you are travelling all the way to Kisangani, which can take nearly two weeks.

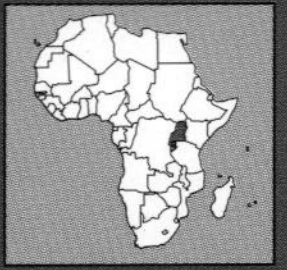

1 DAY+ RWANDA

RWANDA'S WATERWAYS

Travel Info

Destination: Lake Kivu
Requirements: Apart from standard documents (including yellow fever certification), visitors need a one-month visa.
Currency: Rwandan franc (100 centimes)
Climate: Hot and humid year-round. The best times are in the rains, March–May (but most uncomfortable time to travel).
Risk factor: Dangers posed by whitewater rafting are enormous, and sections of Rwanda's rivers are not even navigable for experts. Parts are still a security risk – enquire when planning your trip.
Health: AIDS and malaria are rampant. Tap water is not safe, with bilharzia a problem in certain slow-moving waters.
Pack: Take everything you need (apart from food) for a minimum stay of a week or two, as consumables are generally scarce and outlets for adventure gear are virtually non-existent.
Facilities: Like most things in Rwanda, accommodation is expensive and few tour operators cater for budget travellers. Most operators rent out the most basic equipment, provide a guide and offer few other services.
Contact: Rwandan National Tourism and Parks Office, P.O. Box 905, Kigali. Tel: 09250-576514, Fax: 09250-576515 ortpn@rwanda1.com, www.visitrwanda.gov.rw

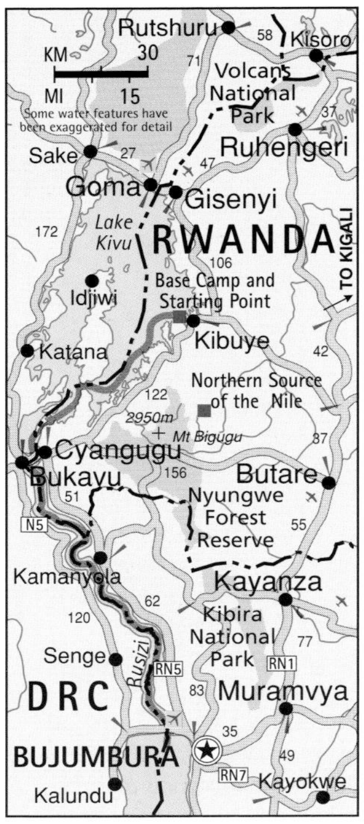

Although the attractions of Volcans National Park in the far north and the Nyungwe Forest in the south remain the most popular, it is the rivers and stream that lead to and from Lake Kivu in the far west, Lake Bulera in the north and Lake Muhazi in the east that provide some of the finest adventure thrills.

Only a small section of the mighty Nile falls within the boundaries of Rwanda, and the most eagerly anticipated water rides might be found beyond the country's borders in Uganda on the portion of the Nile known as Victoria Nile around Lake Victoria and Lake Mobutu (previously Lake Albert). The Rwandan section has its fair share of thrills and spills – certain sections are relatively gentle in comparison to those in Uganda, while others are hair-raising, with a number of obstacles to be negotiated with

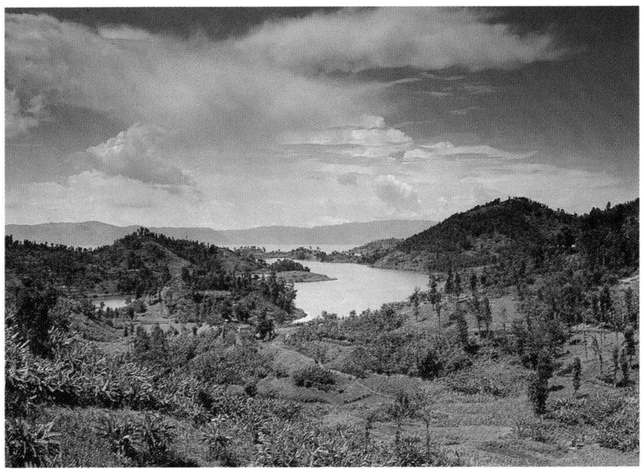

considerable skill and perfect timing. Some parts are downright dangerous, and if whitewater rafters successfully conquer the steep rapids and avoid the literally thousands of crocodiles lurking on the river bed or on its banks, a number of sections will demand that you simply get out and walk – portaging some rapids and man-made interruptions along the river course such as dams is inevitable.

Much of the Rwandan landscape comprises undulating mountains and hills, so the land is generally terraced – both naturally and to accommodate the necessary farm lands – and there is thus a succession of rapids and waterfalls along the courses of the country's rivers.

For whitewater rafters these vary considerably according the international grading sy tems, ranging from a mere s in the river's course to towe – and unrideable – falls. It i best to consult a touring op tion that specializes in excu sions down Rwanda's water courses. The risks are usuall minimal and allow for some tively gentle waters, but in places the dangers are life-threatening and should not taken lightly.

Rwanda's water-based ac ities tend to extend way bey the confines of its short stri the Nile, and focus largely o lakes. However, there are so breathtaking falls on the Ru River, and many adventurers establish some sort of base the lake shore town of Kibu thriving little settlement no known for the quality and d sity of its water-sport pursu on the banks of Lake Kivu.

1 DAY RWANDA

HIKING THE NYUNGWE RAINFOREST

Travel Info

Destination: Nyungwe National Park
Requirements: Standard documents (including yellow fever certification), and visitors require a one-month visa.
Currency: Rwandan franc (100 centimes)
Climate: Hot and humid year-round. The best times are in the rains, March–May (but most uncomfortable time to travel).
Risk factor: Parts of the country are still a considered a security risk (check status before arriving) and, according to reports, land mines may still be found.
Health: AIDS and malaria are rampant. Tap water is not safe, with bilharzia a problem in certain slow-moving waters.
Pack: Take all the equipment and gear you will require for walks and hikes, which tend to vary greatly in difficulty and distance. Especially important are waterproof clothing and hiking shoes.
Facilities: Good accommodation is expensive, and few tour operators cater for budget travellers. While operators in nearby towns and authorities at the forest station will provide a guide, forest camps offer nothing beyond the basic site and some toilet facilities.
Contact: Rwandan National Tourism and Parks Office, P.O. Box 905, Kigali. Tel: 09250-576514, Fax: 09250-576515 www.visitrwanda.gov.rw

Nyungwe is a haven for a huge diversity of flora and fauna, from brilliant insects – notably butterflies – to nearly 300 bird species, 50 mammal species and a number of tree varieties.

Although the nearly 1,000km² (390 sq. mile) area has not been declared a national park, it remains one of the largest protected rainforests of its kind in Africa. The Nyungwe Forest Conservation Project is already nearly two decades old and, although parts of the forest are still threatened, steady progress is being made. Butare and Cyangugu are fast becoming departure points for hikes, trails, and gorilla treks, but offer little beyond basic requirements. Some tours into the forests, starting from Butare and Cyangugu or the forest station at Uwinka, take only an hour or two, departing three times a day and covering only the periphery, while others – such as that to the marshes of Kamiranzovu to see the forest elephants – are longer, taking you into the deepest sections. Other guided tours may cover anything from 10km (6 miles) to 25km (15 miles). There are also half a dozen self-guided trails that range in difficulty from a hassle-free stroll to 10km (6 miles) of forest negotiation. The most prominent hiking trails

require two or three hours o atively tiring walking, but th are no steep climbs and few obstacles. Most established routes wind their way throu hardwoods and skirt occasic waterfalls, but some may le through damp swampland. C you reach the end there ma some cleaning up to do, but rest will be well deserved.

1 DAY+ BURUNDI

RAFTING BURUNDI'S WHITE RIVERS

Travel Info

Destination: Luvironza River
Requirements: Apart from standard documents, most visitors need a one-month visa and yellow-fever certification.
Currency: Burundi franc (100 centimes)
Climate: Inevitably hot and humid throughout the year, temperatures can average some 30°C (86°F), with the heaviest rains mid-October to April.
Risk factor: Burundi's river waters are potentially hazardous to even experienced whitewater rafters, and every precaution should be taken. Political instability means independent travel beyond the capital also poses dangers.
Health: Malaria is a serious problem, especially along rivers and lakes. Drink only bottled water. Parts of Lake Tanganyika may be bilharzia infected.
Pack: Take all the gear and equipment you will need, rather than rely on the inevitably limited tourist infrastructure.
Facilities: Facilities are generally poor, and are usually limited to catering for backpackers and budget travellers, all of whom would be well advised to be self-sufficient wherever possible.
Contact: Burundi Tourist Office, P.O. Box 902, Bujumbura, Burundi. Tel: 09257-222023, Fax: 09257-229390, ontbur@cbinf.com

River rafting in Central Africa – with its abundance of water sources and undulating terrain – is one of the great whitewater experiences. Despite the enormous power of the river in the latter reaches of its winding course, the section of the Nile that makes its way across the Burundi landscape is far from impressive and, although it does offer at least some opportunity for leisurely exploration, it is not the waters of the Nile that provide thrilling whitewater rafting.

Although this is a claim fiercely opposed by Ugandans, the people of Burundi consider the southernmost source of the river to emerge at what they have aptly called Source de Nile, less than 10km (6 miles) from the small settlement of Rutana in the southeastern corner of the country. The waters here are very tame indeed, however, and will

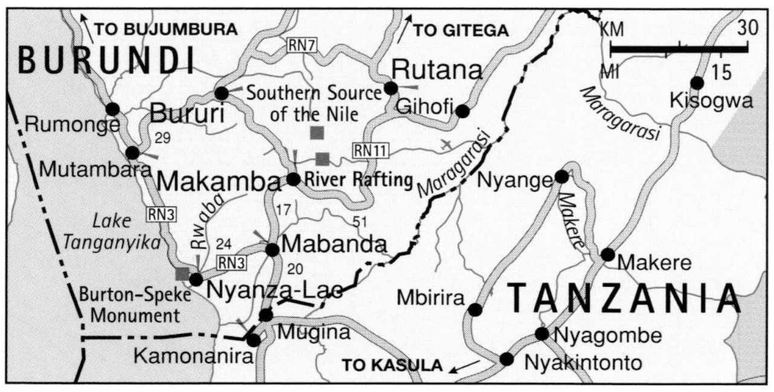

disappoint even the most determined young river rafter. Most of the rafting expeditions on the section of the Nile that crosses this terrain operate, in fact, from the waters of what is essentially the Kagera River before it stretches some 500km (300 miles) into Rwanda and beyond. Burundi's claim to fame is the Luvironza River in the far south of the country. Although the lay of the land here is rugged and bumpy, it is delightfully green in places and surprisingly hospitable to the traveller, especially given the isolated location. Few operators have established themselves in the region and many of the waterways are largely uncharted, making for some invigorating – but potentially hazardous – rafting that demands careful planning and nerves of steel. While some tions may be misleadingly g in appearance, others are cl the playgrounds of only the skilled, with one potentially astrous series of rapids after another, accompanied by ma of frothing water. Not even able gear and equipment co trolled by experienced hands any guarantee of safety, mac the more precarious by the f that emergency services are tually non-existent this far f 'civilization'. Adventurers ply these waters are entirely on own, and all sorts of precaut should be taken to ensure sc level of safety. Be sensible, r your itinerary and whereabo to local officials, and – abov – take no chances. While so sections are indeed relatively tame and pose few risks, the unfamiliar waters and the la any sort of reliable support i structure mean that even th gentlest of stretches may sp a few surprises.

1 DAY+ UGANDA

Travel Info
nation: Mount Elgon National Park
rements: Although all visitors will
ed a passport, some require a visa.
ee (starting at US$15) required to
enter Mount Elgon National Park.
ency: Ugandan shilling (100 cents)
e: Rains fall almost all year, and it
to climb and hike from December
to early March, and in mid-year.
actor: Apart from a few precarious
s, risks are few. It can be cold and
windy on the mountain at night.
: High incidence of AIDS, bilharzia
alaria, but risks are low if you take
ations. Water should be purified or
l, and expect mild altitude-related
adaches and the like near summits
Pack only personal items and com-
dities such as sunscreen. Food can
e purchased in Mbale and camping
gear may be hired in Kolongi.
ies: The nearby settlements should
e the needs of climbers and hikers
enturing onto the slopes of Mount
on, but aim to be self-sufficient –
especially once in the mountain.
ontact: Uganda Wildlife Authority,
P.O. Box 3530, Kampala, Uganda.
Tel: 09256-41-346287 / 0,
Fax: 09256-41-346291,
wa@uwa.org.ug, www.uwa.org.ug

CLIMBING MOUNT ELGON

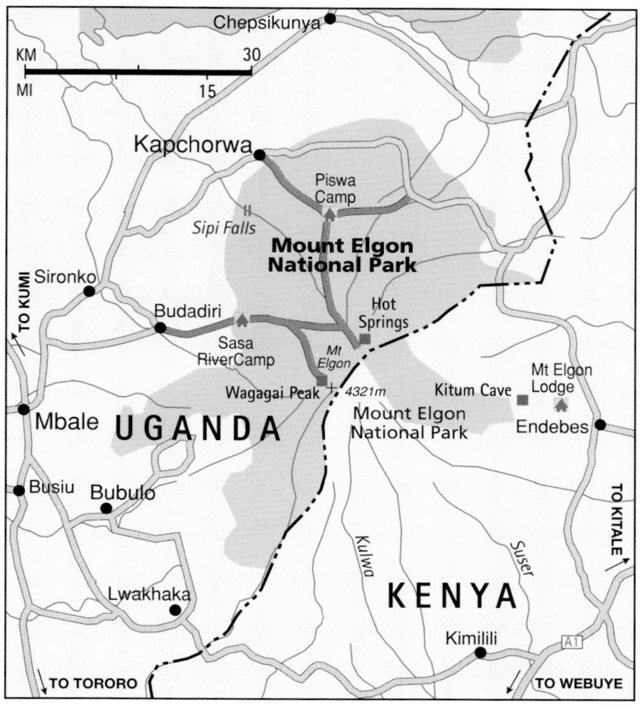

The 1,145km² (440-sq. mile) park at the foot of Mount Elgon – thought to have once been higher than Kilimanjaro – is one of the main bases from which travellers depart en route up the mountain. As an extinct volcano last active millennia ago, Elgon's summit now comprises a lake-filled crater enclosed by craggy peaks, the tallest of which is the 4,321m (14,200ft) crest of Wagagai, the destination for many climbers.

Trips generally start at the park headquarters at Budadiri (guides and porters are available) or, 20km (12 miles) away, from Mbale. The staff know where to go, what to do and how to do it, and costs are minimal, with little outlay beyond the park fees and a fee for guides and porters.

There are a number of different ways to reach the summit — most are variations of only two direct routes — and the majority are quite tame, although the

escarpment climb is not for nothing known as the Wall of Death and should entice only experienced climbers with some expertise at high altitudes. Generally, however, most of the peaks are accessible to novice climbers with moderate strength.

All routes commence with a 6-hour walk from Budadiri, passing through Bumasifwa village and heading for the camp on the Suser River, where you overnight, to depart the following morning on a half-day trek to one of two camps below Jackson's Summit. The trek from here to Wagagai's top takes three to four hours, whereafter you return to the Suser camp. The two main routes take no fewer than four days, one going to the springs and one to the summit of Wagagai, with another taking an additional day to include both sites en route. A further option requires an additional two days and follows the same initial route but ends at Kaporchwe, returning via the overnight hut at Piswa.

1-6 DAYS UGANDA

Travel Info
Destination: Ruwenzori Mountains
ements: Although all visitors need
a passport, some require a visa for
Uganda. Enquire well in advance.
ency: Ugandan shilling (100 cents)
ate: Despite their equatorial loca-
n, the Ruwenzoris can be cold and
with heavy rains mid-September to
November and March to late April.
ctor: Dangers are numerous and a
al part of hiking the Ruwenzoris –
y should not be taken lightly. Only
for the most skilled mountaineer.
: Altitude sickness is a concern on
e peaks; malaria, yellow fever and
mosquito-carried diseases (such as
oing sickness) have been recorded.
k: Protective clothing is essential,
items should be waterproof. Take
hiking boots, protective headgear
and rain gear.
ities: Facilities are generally good
en it comes to the actual hike, but
nodation and other amenities may
ely lacking if you are not prepared
gh it, especially in the mountains.
tact: Ruwenzori Mountain Service
(RMS), P.O. Box 33, Kasese.
Tel: 09256-0483-44015,
Fax: 09256-0483-44077,
info@traveluganda.co.ug

TREKKING THE RUWENZORIS

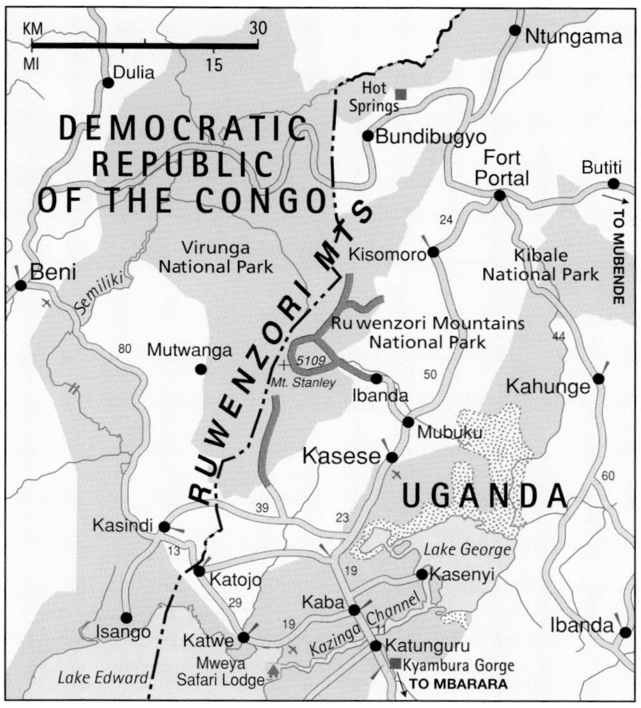

Although the groups of gorillas are restricted to the immediate surrounds of Kisoro and Kabale in the deep south, the extremes of the Ruwenzoris are home to the primates that have made 'gorilla trekking' popular. The infrastructure is still quite basic for the traveller, but there is an abundance of beautiful scenery. Because of the relative accessibility of the gorillas just to the south and the hiking opportunities around the Ruwenzoris, the mountains in the country's western reaches are attracting increasing numbers of travellers.

The entire region is extremely mountainous, with the highest peaks of the Ruwenzori Mountains – which extend more than 100km (62 miles) – towering 5,109m (16,762ft) and often covered with snowfall for much of the year. Conditions are regularly icy – the glacial peaks are Uganda's coldest – and extremely wet, even in what is almost called the 'dry season'.

Underfoot, the ground is very wet, almost waterlogged in parts, and the climb is challenging, often exacerbated by thick mists over the mountains. Some short walks take only a day or two, while some extend for as long as three or four days. Anything longer will, however, mean that the degree of difficulty climbs as steep as the mountainface, and you are in for serious mountaineering. The loop trail will take no fewer than six days and, with the difficulties experienced in orientation and a threat of altitude sickness, is regarded as demanding. Aimed at the serious hiker, this route can work out to be expensive, especially as you will need a guide and a porter to carry necessary equipment, in addition to the park fees – even transport to the foothills can be costly. It is a tough hike, many parts bogged down in thick mud or thick vegetation, and only those well up to the challenge – and able to handle the distance and the degree of difficulty – need even attempt the longer, more demanding trails.

1 DAY UGANDA

Travel Info
stination: Bwindi Impenetrable NP
ements: Although all visitors need
a passport, some require a visa. A
orilla-tracking permit (US$150 or
must be obtained at the National
ks Office in Kampala. Entry fee of
US$15 is required for Bwindi.
ncy: Ugandan shilling (100 cents)
ate: Rains fall almost all year, and
ng is best from December to early
and mid-year. Nights can be cold.
factor: Hazards are negligible, as
re led by experienced guides. This
of Uganda's most rugged terrain,
so do not take chances.
th: To protect the gorillas anyone
ng symptoms of illness will not be
itted within range of the animals.
k: Clothing that will protect legs,
s and torso from the heavy — and
nvasive — vegetation. Take sturdy
protective headgear and rain gear.
ities: Facilities are generally good
the hike, but accommodation and
r amenities may be sorely lacking,
pecially in the depths of the park.
ntact: Uganda Wildlife Authority,
P.O. Box 3530, Kampala, Uganda.
Tel: 09256-41-346287 / 0,
Fax: 09256-41-346291,
wa@uwa.org.ug, www.uwa.org.ug

GORILLA TREKKING IN UGANDA

A number of adventure destinations in central and eastern Africa claim to be the home of family groups of gorillas, and while many do play host to these great beasts, tracking them down and actually laying eyes on them – watching their movements and deciphering their habits – is seldom a reality, especially given their unobtrusive travel patterns and the inaccessibility of their natural habitats. This is not true, however, of the Ruwenzori range in Uganda, where hiking through the dense vegetation with an experienced 'gorilla guide' could well lead to one of your most memorable experiences in Africa.

The town of Kabale, in the deep south of Uganda, acts as what is essentially the 'gateway' to the region's mountain gorilla reserves, offering many guided walks on well-marked trails to see chimpanzees and other primates. The gorillas in these regions form essentially two distinct groups – one in Uganda's Bwindi Impenetrable National Park and the other in the mountainous landscape of the Virunga range in the Mgahinga National Park that crosses the borders between Uganda, the DRC and Rwanda, all of which have taken advantage of the draw card that is their gorilla population.

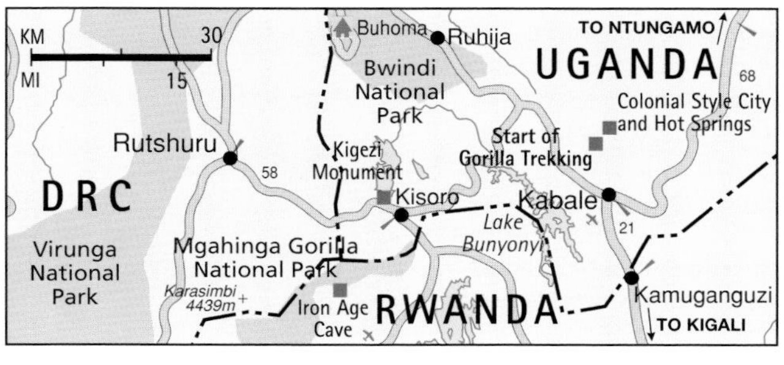

It is, however, magnificent Bwindi that does this with the greatest effect. Quite apart from the fact that it is home to an extraordinary number of other mammal species, plus more than 300 species of bird and butterfly, it is also set in remarkably beautiful surrounds that are well serviced by a comprehensive network of trails and hikes, making gorilla trekking all the more easier and attainable in densely vegetated terrain that is not easily traversed by the unwary Westerner.

Bwindi offers numerous hikes, but the most popular remain the Ivo River Walk (eight hours), the Waterfall Trail (three hours), the Mazubijiro Trail (three hours), the Rushara Trail (also three hours), and the considerably shorter route of the Muyanga River Trail (30 minutes).

To get to see the gorillas of Bwindi, you have to book well in advance in order to obtain one of only 10 permits issued on a particular day (a further two are available on a first-come-first-served basis at the park, but this may be taking an expensive chance). Groups may not exceed half a dozen individuals, but the potential rewards are indeed worth the wait and frustration. You will almost certainly get to see these unusual mammals at first hand, but for no longer than the stipulated 60 minutes (in order to preserve the status quo). Without doubt, the hour that you spend observing these magnificent creatures in their natural habitat will be your most memorable in Africa.

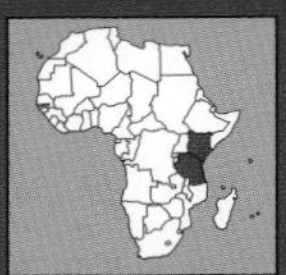

1 HOUR+ KENYA

BALLOONING OVER THE MASAI MARA

Travel Info

Destination: Masai Mara Reserve
Requirements: Passports and, for citizens of some countries, visas are required. Only immunization required is for visitors travelling through or from countries with a recent history of yellow fever.
Currency: Shilling (100 cents)
Climate: Hot and dry, with heavy rains from December–April.
Risk factor: No more risk than would usually be associated with adventure sports. Nerve-wracking, but safe.
Health: Malaria is rife, except at Nairobi and on the highlands, where risk is lower. Seafood such as shellfish may be a little risky. Drink only bottled water.
Pack: For safaris, light cotton clothes, a sun hat and solid walking boots should be sufficient, but early-morning balloon trips can be affected by wind-chill.
Facilities: Luxury lodges and comfortable tented camps cater for an extremely upmarket tourist trade. Budget camp sites run by local Masai (such as Musiara, Talek, Olooloo, Sekenani and Ololaimutiek) are inexpensive but basic.
Contact: Gametrackers, P.O. Box 62042, Nairobi. Tel: 09254-2-338927 / 222703 Fax: 09254-2-330903 game@southafricaonline.co.ke www.gametrackers.com

The Masai Mara's 1,680km^2 (650 sq. miles) is little more than an extension of Tanzania's Serengeti. It is also the traditional homeland of the Masai nation, but much of the land has now been given over to the wildlife that has made the Masai Mara Reserve one of the most highly regarded in the world.

Thousands of visitors make their way here every year to witness first-hand the magnificence of Kenya's wildlife in what is acclaimed as the finest game-viewing experience in Africa. They cross the great savanna plains on foot, on horseback, via four-wheel drive and, most memorably, in a hot-air balloon.

At the crack of dawn, travellers converge around the deflated balloon and the roaring apparatus that will fill it up. As the sun emerges, the burners are ignited and passengers board for a brief lecture on the etiquette of ballooning, which is essentially a dangerous pastime if rules aren't followed. Looking down from the morning sky, the view is breathtaking. Below stretch the wilds of the bushveld, dotted with astonishing numbers of wild animals. Scattered across the veld are the Big Five — elephant, lion, leopard, buffalo and black rhino — as well as big-game species such as cheetah, giraffe and zebra. There are also wildebeest, ranging the veld by the thousands, as well as impala, hartebeest, bushbuck, waterbuck and reedbuck. Braving the wind-chill factor — even in Africa you'll feel this up in a hot-air balloon — will allow you an unparalleled view of nearly 100 mammal species, at the same time bringing you into close contact with no fewer than 500 bird species, among them hawks and falcons, bustards, vultures and sunbirds. Game-viewing is outstanding almost all year, but especially good in January and February. The highlight of the year is the migration of wildlife – notably wildebeest – which cross from Tanzania between December and May in search of pastures.

The aerial flit of about an hour across the bushveld will inevitably end with a sumptuous champagne breakfast, after which you will be driven back to the lodge on an early-morning game-drive. Memorable as the balloon safari is, you should expect to pay a lot for the experience. There is no budget accommodation in the park and, if you do decide t sacrifice the luxury of an up market lodge or tented cam order to rough it at the cam sites, be sure to budget for expenses such as entry fees, guide fees, porter fees, cam fees, guard fees and firewo The cheapest way is to tag an organized safari led by o the many competitive priva operators working the regio

4 DAYS+ KENYA

CAMEL SAFARIS

Travel Info

Destination: Safari routes
Requirements: Passports and, for citizens of some countries, visas are required. Only immunization required is for visitors travelling through or from countries with a recent history of yellow fever.
Currency: Shilling (100 cents)
Climate: Usually hot and dry throughout the country, and relatively humid along the coastal stretches.
Risk factor: Generally risk-free and, besides stubborn camels and the usual dangers of nights in the bush, safari operators take good care of clients.
Health: Malaria is rife throughout most of Kenya, except at Nairobi and on the highlands where the risk is considerably lower. Dehydration can be an issue, but be sure to drink only bottled water.
Pack: Lightweight clothes, sun hat and sturdy walking boots are essential for trekking safaris.
Facilities: Luxury lodges and very comfortable tented camps cater largely for the upmarket tourist visiting national parks and reserves. More basic and substantially cheaper options may be found throughout the country.
Contact: Let's Go Travel Nairobi, Nairobi, Kenya. Tel: 09254-24-441030 / 447151

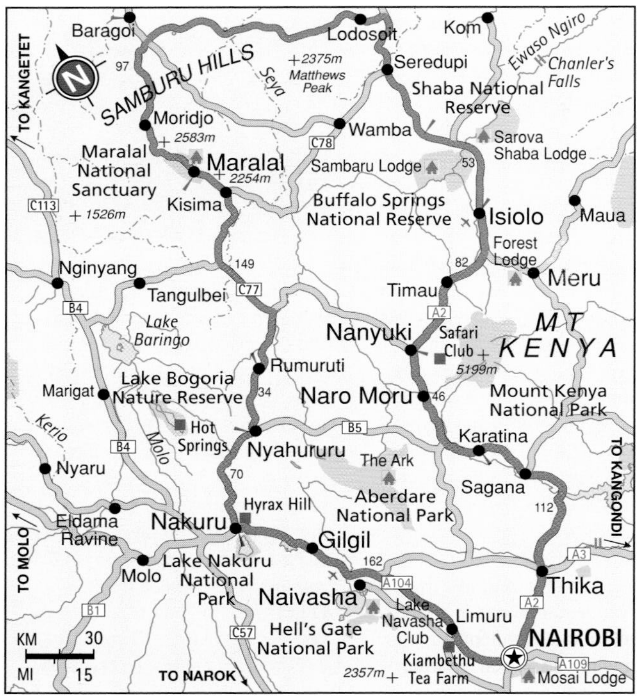

Camel safaris provide a unique alternative to 4x4. Escorted by an armed guide, you ride and walk alongside the camels throughout the day. This way, you get to see plenty of wild animals. Although you get to travel through otherwise inaccessible areas, many 'camel safaris' may mean little more than a hike alongside the great beasts as they lumber across the veld. This does not, however, detract from the experience.

Most operators allow trekkers to hitch rides on the backs of the camels, which are constantly tended by expert handlers who are keen to help and eager to please. Many local safari guides may don traditional dress for the benefit of the tourists, but they are well versed in the lore and the lie of the land, and you would do well to trust their instincts. The pace of the walk is usually brisk, but the guides are able to point out all the wildlife,

including countless bird species. At night, the caravan sets up camp on the river banks or alongside a water hole where wildlife congregates in the evening hours. Nights are spent under a big, white mosquito net, or in one of the tents carried by the camels. Most camel treks will last five to six days or longer and, although shorter safaris may be available, don't be tempted to take the one- or two-day option. Although it may be hard on your body, go for a safari that will take a few days. Apart from fact that it will give you a f better feel for the land and people – a glimpse is never enough – the longer the saf the cheaper the per-day rat There is plenty of competiti among the individual opera but fees and costs are gene similar and, although there always chancers, most of th larger, more established saf companies based in Kenya h sound track records and off variety of exciting options.

3 HOURS+ KENYA

DHOW SAILING ON THE KENYAN COAST

Travel Info

Destination: Mombasa
Requirements: Passports and, for citizens of some countries, visas are required. Only immunization required is for visitors travelling through or from countries with a recent history of yellow fever.
Currency: Shilling (100 cents)
Climate: Conditions are usually hot and humid along the tropical coast.
Risk factor: Risks are minimal, but stick to basic hygiene with food and water.
Health: Malaria is rife throughout most of Kenya, except at Nairobi and on the highlands, where the risk is considerably lower. Dehydration can be an issue when you are under the harsh sun all day, but be sure to drink only bottled water.
Pack: You will need little more than standard touring clothes, which should include light cotton clothing, sunscreen and sun hat, as well as some form of cover if you will be cruising at night.
Facilities: Lodges, resorts and upmarket hotels — the base for many tour operators — take very good care of clients, but dhow taxis and small, one-man businesses offer little in "creature comforts".
Contact: Tamarind Dhow Safaris, P.O. Box 95805, Mombasa. Tel: 09254-11-474600 / 1, Fax: 09254-11-471948

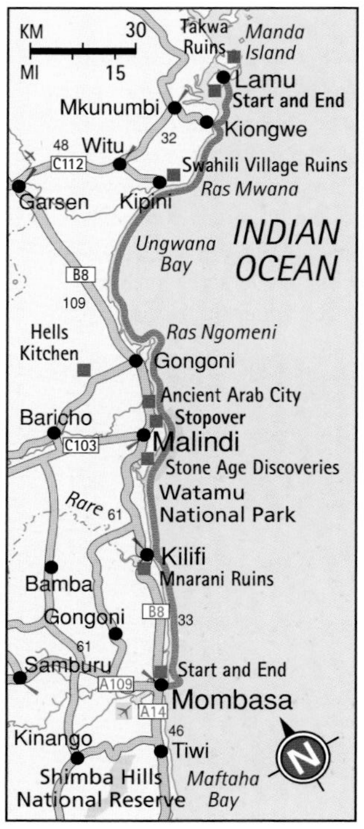

Most of the Kenya's offshore islands, notably Mombasa, Lamu and Malindi, offer day trips on dhows. These can either be arranged by mainland lodge managers or hired privately on the beaches of East Africa. These wind-powered craft offer a tempting alternative to the dusty roads of coastal villages.

Whether you are taking an extended overnight journey along the Kenyan coast, an afternoon excursion into the bay, a pleasure cruise, or simply using the dhow as a means of getting from Point A to Point B, there will inevitably be plenty of opportunities to weigh anchor virtually anywhere along the shore. Dhow taxis are simple affairs with no frills and tend to line up for trade along the docks of the main harbour towns, where others from as far afield as Arabia and India may lie at anchor. Impromptu excursions with a party of about half a dozen passengers sharing the cost may result in a delay, as skippers will often wait until the dhow is full before he sails. There are, however, comfortable vessels for more leisurely trips, although even these are still quite basic, with few facilities on board. If you need to sleep, you will be expected to bunk down on the floor of the boat with only the sail and the sky overhead. The only food served may be the fish caught from the dhow en route, and passengers are expected to bring their own water as well as any luxuries they require. Formal tours offer a very different experience, however, with a number of good operators based in Mombasa and Lamu, among other places. Organized cruises, such as those offered by Tamarind Dhow Safaris and other operators, usually depart twice a day – once at about midday and again in the early evening – with lunch and/or dinner included in the fare. Lit either by the midday sun or the silver moon, these trips are usually lively affairs, with hearty seafood dishes on offer and on-board entertainment in the form of a local band. En route to the islands or on mainland stops, the dhow will, in all probability, be approached by the many floating markets in dugout canoes that make their way from vessel to vessel, touting and bartering their wares, which range from brightly coloured kikois and basketware to *objets d'art* and exotic sp Operators will also offer – usually as part of their pack sumptuous meals, live musi entertainment and guided t of the historic sites at stopo such as Mombasa's Old Tow Malindi, and the villages of Shela and Matondoni on La where builders and sailors practise the timeless skills o building and maintaining th ancient vessels using age-ol equipment which dates bac hundreds of years.

5 DAYS TANZANIA

CLIMBING KILIMANJARO

Travel Info

ation: Mount Kilimanjaro, Marangu
irements: Most visitors need pass-
and visas from their local embassy.
lers from South America and most
of Africa are required to present a
ow fever immunization certificate.
ncy: Tanzanian shilling (100 cents)
nate: Avoid the rains in April, May
and November.
actor: Cheap package deals may be
s reliable and less safe than estab-
ed operators. Irresponsible tourists
degrading the trail in Kilimanjaro
ational Park through constant use.
n: Exhaustion, fatigue and altitude
s are the most serious complaints.
accinated against cholera, tetanus,
atitis and polio. AIDS is prevalent.
Warm, waterproof and windproof
es, sturdy hiking boots, a sleeping
sunscreen and water. Sweets help
ntain energy. A head torch for the
-morning stretch. A kikoi (sarong)
that can act as a scarf and pillow.
lities: Reliable operators offer the
est service and provide equipment.
ntact: Wild Frontiers (RSA-based),
O. Box 844, Halfway House, 1685.
0927-11-468165, Fax: 0927-11-
702-2035, wildfront@icon.co.za,
www.wildfrontiers.com

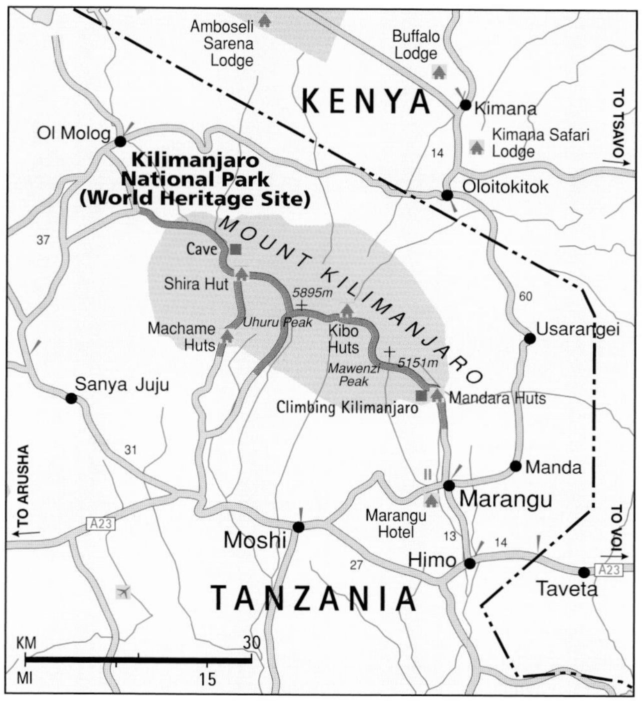

Although there are difficult areas on Kili's slopes, it is unlikely you will need ropes, ice axes and picks, and the more followed routes are relatively trouble-free. In fact, the greatest challenge is overcoming the heat of the sun and the icy chill of the summit – the most reported danger is the altitude sickness that sets in at about 3,500m (10,500ft). The only way to combat it is to climb slowly and stop often to allow your body to acclimatize.

Climbing Kilimanjaro is an expensive exercise: although tour operators should see to transfers, accommodation, and equipment, you need to hire registered guides and porters as well as pay the US$20 rescue fee. There are also park and camping fees, yet the standard five-day climb is so popular that it may be overbooked (the park sees 20,000 visitors pass through a year). The first day of the ascent departs from the park and comprises an undemanding three- or four-hour hike through rainforest to the A-frame huts at the first rest stop. You then plough on to the night stop at Mandara Hut, from where you will progress to Horombo on day two where, at 3,720m (12,200ft), the first signs of altitude sickness strike. The day's five-hour trek will take you to the rim of Maundi Crater and up an incline to the highlands. The trek becomes tougher by the third day as you pass the Last Water and Zebra Rocks and move onto The Saddle, the bridge connecting the peaks of Kibo and Mawenzi. The last stretch of the six-hour walk up to Kibo Hut at 4,700m (15,4400ft) can be arduous. Kibo is dreary and cold, and the last two days are mentally and physically demanding. In the icy morning, you head for Gillman's Point on the crater. Oxygen is very thin, making the walk tougher, but a mere 210m (700ft) further is the great reward: Kilimanjaro's true summit, Uhuru Peak.

1-2 DAYS TANZANIA

WALKING THE SERENGETI

Travel Info

stination: Serengeti National Park
uirements: Most visitors will need
ports and visas, so enquire at your
local embassy before departure.
ers from South America and most
of Africa are required to present a
ow fever immunization certificate.
cy: Tanzanian shilling (100 cents)
te: Coolest June–October, but this
so the busiest and most expensive
January–February may be better –
ough hot, it's the best time to see
migration in the southern park.
actor: The day-to-day life is filled
with the dangers of wildest Africa.
th: Be vaccinated against cholera,
nus, hepatitis and polio. Malaria is
n the lowlands. AIDS is prevalent.
Most operators supply basics, but
e light hiking gear, warm clothes,
walking boots, and sun protection.
ities: Expensive tented camps and
es; 18 simple camp sites ('special'
p sites and wilderness camp sites,
asonable amenities), and 12 pub-
camps (including Seronera, Lobo,
ka and Bologonja) where facilities
are virtually non-existent.
act: Tropical Tours, P.O. Box 727,
a, Tanzania. Tel: 09255-57-8353
Fax: 09255-57-8907

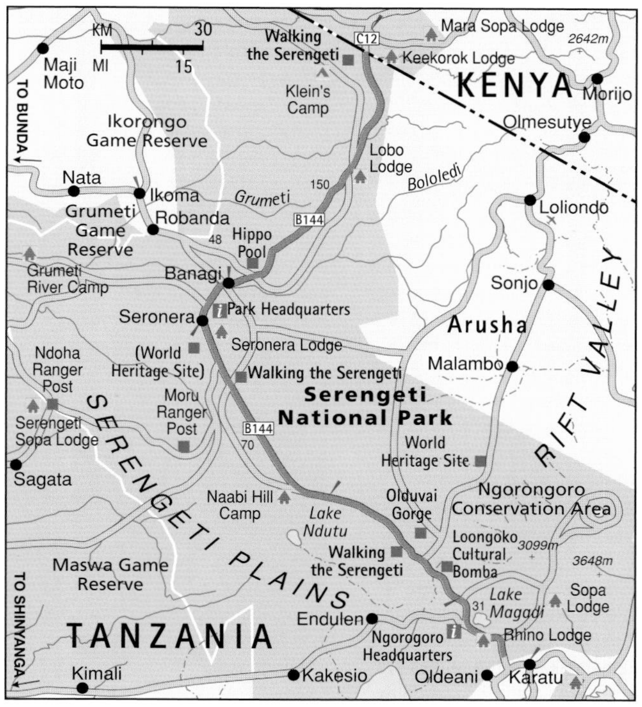

The 14,763km² (5,700 sq. mile) Serengeti is surrounded by Ngorongoro, Kenya's Masai Mara and other parks of the same ilk, but is far more than the endless savanna. Although this is indeed home to some of the most impressive herds of wildlife on the continent, the Serengeti also has valleys, rolling hills and patches of scrubby woodland. The plains are the most memorable and the easiest to cross. The prospect of walking this wild countryside is at once intimidating and enthralling. One way of avoiding the tourist trap is to explore the land on foot – almost within touching distance of more than a million wildebeest, hundreds of thousands of Thomson's gazelle, and tens of thousands of zebra, impala and topi. These herds are all stealthily stalked by the great predators of Africa, including not only lion, cheetah and even leopard, but also wild dog, jackal, spotted hyena and bat-eared fox.

Even the best roads are, however, poor and the distances vast. Hitchhiking will prove futile – there are no private vehicles and high-priced safari operations ignore stragglers. It is best to opt for a tour company. Arusha has plenty of options, but only some hiking tours are based on responsible ecotourism. What you do not want to do is end up in the middle of the Serengeti without shelter and without a guide. Reliable operators charge more, but the package includes park fees, camping fees, food and fuel costs, plus they provide drivers, cooks, porters, and guides.

Choose the operator and itinerary well: as you will spend up to two days getting to and from your destination, remember that the shorter the excursion, the less you will get to see. By choosing to walk, you will be faced with limited facilities such as long-drop toilets and basic camp sites, and will not have at your disposal the luxuries offered by the exclusive lodges and tented camps favoured by most well-heeled travellers to Tanzania.

1 DAY+ TANZANIA

EXPLORING THE WATERS OFF ZANZIBAR

Travel Info

estination: Zanzibar Town, Unguja
rements: Most visitors need pass-
and visas – enquire at your local
sy. Travellers from South America
ost of Africa are required to pres-
yellow fever immunization certifi-
Travel documentation is checked
on entry to Zanzibar. Some diving
rsions may require qualifications.
cy: Tanzanian shilling (100 cents)
e: Tropical and hot, so best times
December–January (peak holiday
and June–October. Ocean condi-
ary according to location, and the
me to dive is October–November.
sk factor: Theft and mugging are
ning more frequent – keep an eye
ipment and accessories. Exposure
sun exacerbated by wind and sea.
aria remains a threat. Currents on
the east coast may be dangerous.
Malaria is a risk. AIDS is prevalent.
anzibar is Muslim, so exposed flesh
rowned upon beyond tourist spots.
es: Many hotels have local guides
and a number of operators offer-
ter-based excursions keep offices
e Town. Many offer PADI courses.
Contact: Indian Ocean Divers,
ni Road, P.O. Box 2370, Zanzibar.
Tel/fax: 09255-24-33860

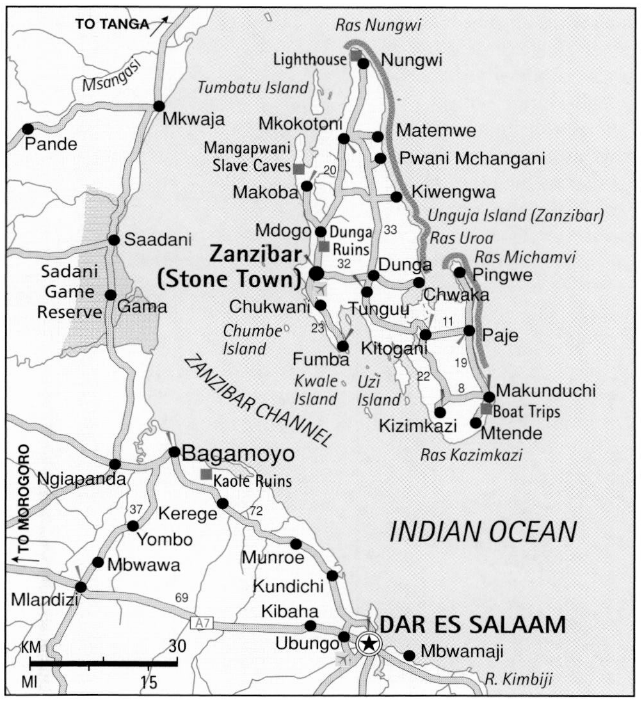

Some 85km (53 miles) long and 25km (16 miles) wide, Zanzibar's coast of rocky coves, mangroves, lagoons, pristine beaches and astonishing coral reefs is home to many leisure activities, from kayaking to deep-sea game fishing and, more recently, diving and snorkelling. Visibility from a kayak is virtually unobstructed and you will see right down to the corals and reefs.

Not for nothing is this area known as The Sunrise Coast, and this is most true of Bwejuu and Makunduchi. There are numerous boat trips to offshore islets and even Pemba. Exploring these by boat provides a unique glimpse of coastal Tanzania, and offers some of the best scuba diving and snorkelling in East Africa. The corals are virtually unscathed and the reefs teem with sea creatures. Although diving is extraordinary, few operators are based on the eastern shore – locals will rent out their own vessels, and equipment may be hired from the dive schools on the west coast. Conditions at the latter are better and, because it is so sheltered, visibility makes for excellent diving.

The beach at Chuumbe Island Coral Park is punctuated with 'eco-bungalows', and a network of walking and diving trails laces the coast. There are also wrecks, and the Stone Town' harbour is dotted with 200 of them. However, conditions in the harbour are poor and it is best to explore wrecks elsewhere on the coast.

Modern Unguja is geared toward the needs of divers, with schools offering all levels of NAUI- and PADI-accredited courses along with boat-based expeditions. The east coast of the island, however, remains undeveloped, and most lodgings are rustic, but tour operators also offer other rewards, including increasingly popular big-game fishing and deep-sea diving, as well as the magical opportunity to dive with dolphins and turtles – and even the occasional shark.

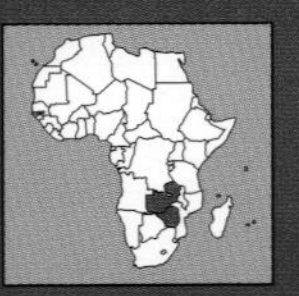

2 DAYS+ ZAMBIA

WALKING SOUTH LUANGWA

Travel Info
Destination: South Luangwa National Park
Requirements: Most visitors require visas, unless with an organized tour.
Currency: Kwacha (100 ngwee)
Climate: September to November can be unbearably hot in the valley, but June to November are dry and thus provide the best game-viewing opportunities.
Risk factor: Distances are vast and may be challenging in parts, with the usual risks posed by wilderness safaris, so it is best to take a pre-arranged tour with guides.
Health: Malaria is rife throughout the country year-round, as are waterborne diseases.
Pack: Antimalarial medication, water purification tablets, protective clothing and good hiking shoes. Tour operators should provide a list of essentials.
Facilities: Facilities are generally very good – even impressive – in the lodges, but some hiking stopovers can be quite basic. Lodge service and amenities are beyond reproach.
Contact: Lilongwe-based (Malawi) Ulendo Safaris.
Tel: 09265-74-3507,
Fax: 09265-74-3492,
rob@ulendo.malawi.net

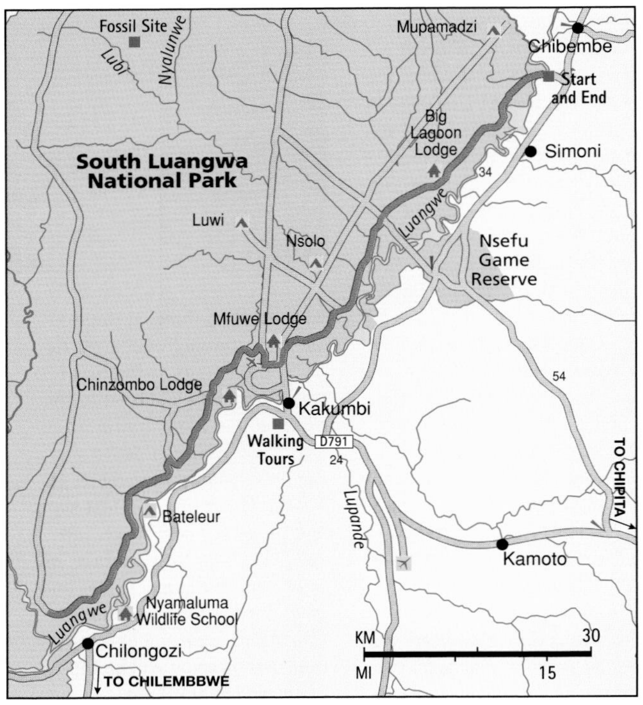

More easily reached than its northern neighbour, South Luangwa National Park is most popular among fly-in visitors, but may also be accessed via road, from Malawi via Chipata or from Lusaka along the Great East Road. The latter is worthy of its name, but certain areas remain tricky to navigate and, despite the repair work, are riddled with potholes. For hikers on walking safaris, this poses few problems, but the undulating roads offer some suggestion as to what the wilderness may offer. The ground varies from soft sand to hard-baked stretches that can take their toll on the legs on five-day guided walks or even shorter excursions. Hikers – and, of course, self-drivers – will have to cross stretches of scrubby veld and dry river beds and, because there are no accessible bridges, this may take some stamina (and, for drivers, considerable skill behind the wheel).

Generally, guides stick to open areas, where it is easier to spot predators and where escape routes are open. Both the vegetation and the wildlife vary enormously, and South Luangwa is rightfully renowned for its lion, leopard, elephant, buffalo, zebra, puku, crocodiles and hippos.

The park has seen some development and is no longer as laid-back as before, with a number of visitors intent on experiencing the bird life, including hero[...] storks, goliath heron, egrets[...] marabou, jacana, and ibis.

There are a number of si[...] lodges and camp sites, but [...] safari-goers head for the lo[...] on the Luangwa River's eas[...] banks on the outskirts of th[...] park. Most have isolated fly[...] camps within the park, whi[...] have been set up to accom[...] date guests on walking safa[...]

1 DAY+ ZIMBABWE

SAILING LAKE KARIBA

Travel Info
Destination: Lake Kariba
Requirements: Few visitors will require a visa, but a valid passport is essential.
Currency: Zimbabwe dollar (100 cents)
Climate: Temperatures are the highest in the country and can be especially high on the water. Nights can, however, be cold, especially mid-year.
Risk factor: Because the waters and shores of Kariba are well serviced by the local travel industry, risks are few – beware of the usual pickpockets and adhere to the standard safety precautions when on the water.
Health: Malaria, bilharzia and, of course, AIDS are prevalent throughout much of the country, but drinking water is relatively safe.
Pack: Malarial prophylactics, sunscreen and personal supplies if unsupervised.
Facilities: Amenities are generally very good to excellent (especially at Kariba's upmarket lodges), but even the most rustic of camp sites and overnight accommodation will offer the basic facilities.
Contact: Chete Island Safaris.
Tel: 09263-4-499783
Fax: 09263-4-499060
westisl@id.co.zw

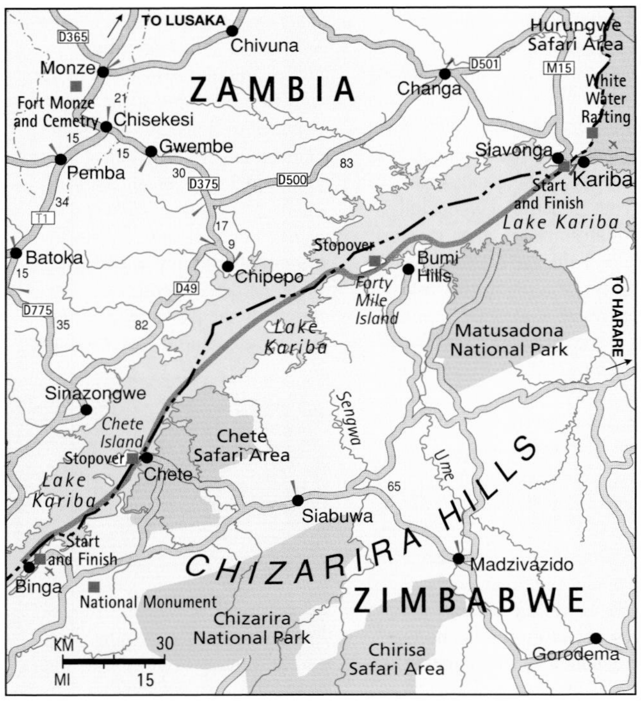

Lake Kariba – 282km (175 miles) long and straddling the Zambezi River – covers about 5,000km^2 (1,950 sq. miles) and remains Zimbabwe's principal source of hydroelectricity. The heart of the lake's leisure industry is Matusadona National Park, which has attractive resorts that offer fine game-viewing, walking trails, boat cruises and sailing safaris.

Although the harvesting of fish such as *kapenta* is the mainstay of locals, it is activities such as sport fishing that attract visitors. There are plenty of marinas, boat yards and anchorages, and the game lodges on the water's edge boast excellent facilities, including yachting and fishing.

Game-viewing and birdwatching from the water is very rewarding, with buffalo, crocodile, fish eagles, cormorants, kingfishers, darters and herons, and even elephant and buffalo. The water, punctuated with drowned trees, and the shores are, in fact, a wildlife sanctuary, and the neighbouring parks of Matusadona and Chizarira are extremely rich in game. Given the lake's location and popularity, certain parts of the shore are very expensive. Prices vary from the outrageous to budget picnic cruise, many of which depart regularly from the lake's marinas. There are many 'backpacker cruises' and a number of tour operators offer excursions to the islands, including Fothergill and Spurwing and even Matusadona. The *Chaminuka* ferry leaves Kariba town once a week (Thursday), and takes to three days to reach Bing[...] Costs are low and the game viewing very good, but ame[...] are usually basic and you sh[...] bring your own supplies. Tri[...] the 30-foot *Searunner* trim[...] skirt Chete Island and it is [...] unusual to spot wildlife fro[...] deck. Other operators offer special day packages for sm[...] groups, usually including a [...] on the water. Accommodati[...] including tents, is not hard [...] come by, but you may want [...] book these in advance.

1 DAY+ ZAMBIA / ZIMBABWE

DRIVING THE ZAMBEZI

Travel Info
Destination: Zambezi Valley
Requirements: Zambia – Most visitors require visas, unless they are part of an organized tour; Zimbabwe – Few visitors require a visa; a valid passport is essential.
Currency: Zambia – Kwacha (100 ngwee) Zimbabwe – Zimbabwe dollar (100 cents)
Climate: The valley can be hot and humid, and is particularly wet in December.
Risk factor: Summer rains in and around December can make driving hazardous.
Health: Malaria is rife throughout the region year-round, as are waterborne diseases, such as bilharzia. AIDS is prevalent throughout.
Pack: Lightweight clothing for driving, and warm clothes for cold nights. Drivers not part of an organized tour are well advised to take extra precautions and plan with great care, especially for the maintenance and repair of vehicles.
Facilities: Beyond established and well-patronized tourist destinations such as Mana Pools in Zimbabwe, facilities may not be up to standard and refuelling and restocking may be problematic.
Contact: Backpackers Africa, P.O. Box 44, Victoria Falls. Tel/Fax: 09263-13-42208, Mobile: 09263-11-404968
backpack@africaonline.co.zw
lvhwalkingsafaris@esmartbiz.com

The land through which the 2,700km (1,700 miles) Zambezi River cuts is some of Africa's finest wilderness area, but can also be among the most treacherous, especially when navigating the shores of the river. For the most part, the tracks and roads are lined with trees and the escarpment on both the Zimbabwean and Zambian sides can be steep and dangerous. Some roads and paths have been forged along the river, but certain sections have fallen prey to erosion and, occasionally, flooding. All 4x4 drivers should take precautions and ensure they have vehicle sparess. During the arid season, flood plains are dry, grass cover minimal, and a fine dust covers much of the land. Although lush after the rains, the rushing waters can be hazardous, and the wildlife present their own risks, while armed poachers may follow in their tracks.

Although the route of the Zambezi is not an easy drive, areas such as the Mana plains may be less challenging. Mana is renowned for its hiking and foot safaris under the protection of

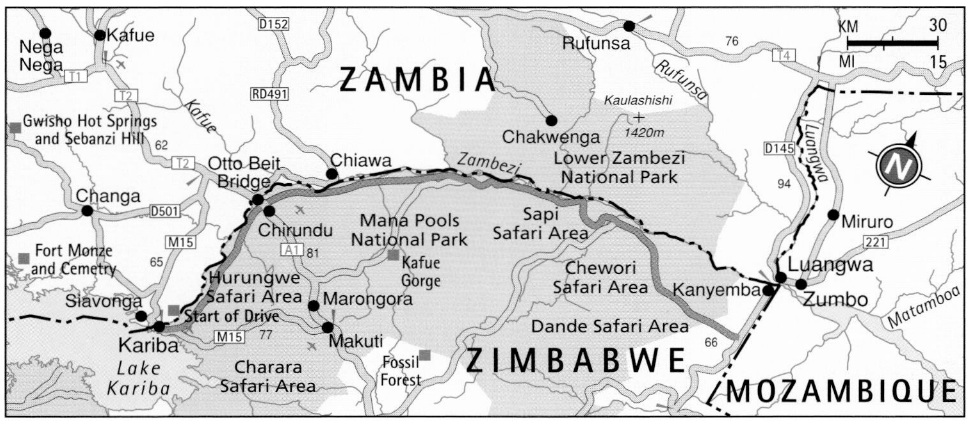

armed guards. Because the region is well developed, facilities are good, with regular opportunities to refuel, restock and repair vehicles. Also en route are fishing camps and other tourism-based activities.

While the section below Kariba is one of the least tamed, much of the hospitality industry centres around Mana Pools National Park. The terrain varies from the rocky Zambezi escarpment to plains, and althoug[...] may be explored on foot, it [...] closed to the public from M[...] October. An alternative rou[...] the wilderness between Mo[...] and Mwinilunga in Zambia. Known as the Source of the Zambezi, the veld varies fro[...] relatively comfortable drive [...] level ground to some extre[...] demanding stretches that r[...] considerable driving skill.

1-10 DAYS
ZAMBIA / ZIMBABWE

Travel Info
Destination: Zambezi Valley
uirements: Zambia – Most visitors
re visas, unless they are part of an
zed tour; Zimbabwe – Few visitors
a visa, but a passport is essential.
cy: Zambia – Kwacha (100 ngwee)
we – Zimbabwe dollar (100 cents)
te: The Zambezi Valley is both hot
umid, and the summer rains mean
ater levels rise, while certain areas
can experience torrential flows.
actor: Risks are generally few, but
some swimming ability is advised.
th: Malaria is rife throughout the
ion year-round, as are waterborne
diseases, such as bilharzia. AIDS is
prevalent throughout the region.
Day trips require little planning as
ntials are usually covered by oper-
Overnight excursions and trips of
lays will require warm, waterproof
ng. Check with your tour operator.
ties: Trips of two or three days or
more are usually well established.
ors take good care of their guests,
gh some overnight stops may be a
more basic than some may expect,
so be prepared to rough it.
Contact: Shearwater Adventures.
Tel: 09263-14-735712
Fax: 09263-14-735716

ON THE WATERS OF THE ZAMBEZI

The majesty of the Zambezi River is surpassed perhaps only by the thrill of its waters, and it is far and away the favourite playground of water-sport adventurers in southern Africa. While the river can be gentle and tranquil in parts, it can also be breathtakingly fearsome and others and, as a result, offers something for everyone, from laid-back canoe trips on the open water to exhilarating whitewater rafting down nail-biting rapids. As it is the focal point of river adventure in both Zambia and Zimbabwe, tour operators abound.

The gentler option – although not always entirely 'gentle' – is canoeing or kayaking, the way local inhabitants have done for centuries. While some tour agents opt for the traditional dugout canoes, most rely on two-man Canadian canoes made of fibreglass, and accomplished river guides take parties out in groups of two or three. The level of skill required is basic and, as long as you don't have a fear of water, it can be enjoyed by all.

Canoeing and kayaking the gentler waters above the famed Victoria Falls is the most popular choice, and several adventure companies have based themselves here. Excursions last from a few hours on the water – usually twice-daily excursions, in the morning and evening when the heat is less oppressive – to four days or even more than a week, covering about 20km (12 miles) a day. As only a single party is permitted on each section of the river in a day, you will be unlikely to encounter anyone else.

A number of Zimbabwe-based trips launch from the Kariba vicinity, and may take you as far as Chirundu (which also offers river excursions), with a further three days taking you to Mana Pools, and yet another three days to Kenyamba. A more daring option would be to tackle the whirlpools at Mupata Gorge, but these demand considerably more skill to negotiate and can be very hazardous for the inexperienced.

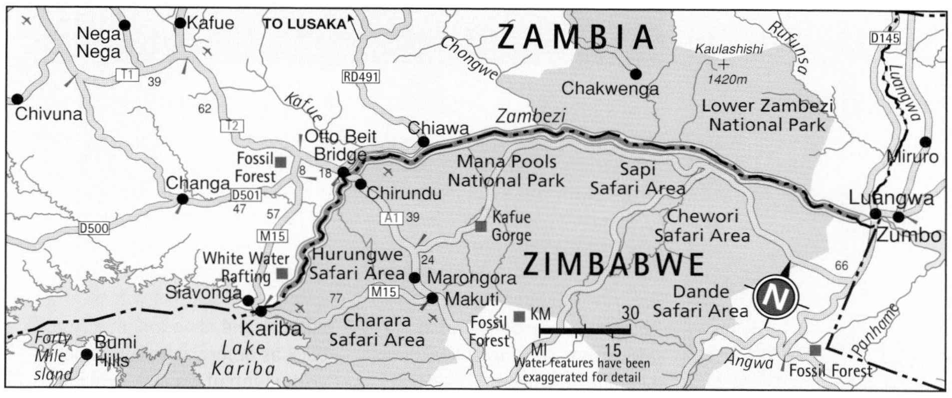

1 DAY+
ZAMBIA / ZIMBABWE

Travel Info
Destination: Victoria Falls
iirements: Zambia – Most visitors
e visas, unless they are part of an
zed tour; Zimbabwe – Few visitors
a visa, but a passport is essential.
y: Zambia – Kwacha (100 ngwee)
we – Zimbabwe dollar (100 cents)
: Hot and humid all year, but the
falls are best February–August.
sk factor: Risks are plentiful, like
lging hippos and battling some of
rica's most fearsome rapids. Some
xcursions require little more than
ination; others can be deadly and
re considerable skill on the water.
h: Malaria is rife; AIDS remains a
n; waterborne diseases (bilharzia)
sk; bumps, grazes and bruises are
par for the course on the river.
ntimalarial medication and water
urification tablets and protective,
proof clothing. Most reliable tour
operators provide the necessities.
ities: River operators tend to plan
to make the trip comfortable, and
es are few, but basics are covered.
Contact: Safari Par Excellence.
P.O. Box 5920, Harare
9263-4-700911 / 2, Fax: 09263-
4-706318, Cell: 263-91-24-233
es@mweb.co.zw, www.safpar.com

VICTORIA FALLS ADVENTURE

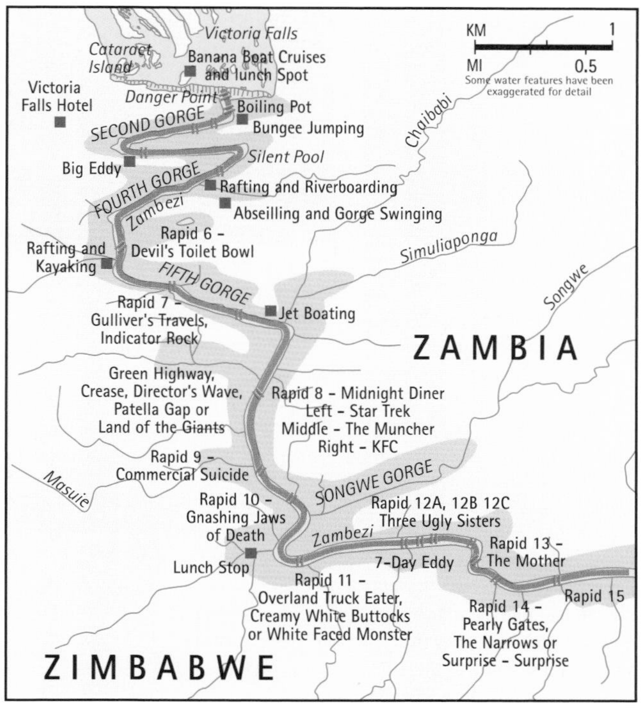

Everything is bigger and better, deeper and steeper at the much-publicized junction of Zimbabwe and Zambia. Whitewater rafting can be terrifying, bungee-jumping breathtaking, elephant-back safaris out of this world and the overhead flights in a plane or helicopter are the stuff of lifetime memories. There are also walking routes, hiking trails, 4x4 excursions, sundowner cruises and game-viewing safaris. While the Falls are undeniably a tourist trap, the facilities here are unparalleled.

The Zimbabwean side is particularly well serviced by the hospitality industry and is, therefore, not cheap. The Zambian side is less 'developed' and not as spectacular, but it does offer a different, less glitzy view, with a better opportunity to get close to the waters of the falls.

Highlights are undoubtedly the awesome 110m (360ft) bungee jump, hailed as the highest commercial bridge leap in Africa. Although queues may be long, the wait frustrating and the cost expensive, the experience is unbeatable. Another memorable experience is a flight in a sea-plane, helicopter, microlight or, in the case of the much vaunted Flight of Angels, in a twin-engined aircraft over the falls. Prices depend on the agent and/or aircraft and how long you stay in the air (the Flight of Angels departs every 15 minutes), but the experience is exhilarating – although flips are frowned upon by conservationists.

The main attraction is, however, the whitewater rafting, and the Zambezi Gorge is known to be one of the wildest whitewater spots in the world. High-water trips are available from the Zimbabwean or Zambian sides, but are, depending on the rains, restricted to July and early August, while low-water runs are tackled between mid-August and end December. While the waters above the falls are shallow, more than 20 rapids punctuate the waters below. When the waters are low, the dangers are greater, and August to December are graded 5 – extremely demanding (Grade 6 is given to rapids that are unridable). The three-day, 65km (40-mile) whitewater trail from Kazungula ends at Big Tree at the Falls.

1 DAY+
ZIMBABWE

Travel Info
ation: Chimanimani National Park
Requirements: Few visitors
a visa, but a passport is essential.
ncy: Zimbabwe dollar (100 cents)
Climate: Best time to hike is
eptember, when it is sunny but not
t. Can be windy and cold at night.
actor: It is generally safe to walk
nanimani, but never hike alone or
en in pairs and plan well. Keep to
vn routes as you may wander into
bique. Watch for sudden changes
eather. Give your itinerary to park
thorities in case you don't return.
n: Malaria, bilharzia and AIDS are
valent. Although drinking water is
tively safe even on the mountain,
rification tablets as a precaution.
k: Take your own supplies such as
nd equipment (collecting of fire-
d is prohibited, so you will need a
s cooker), plus warm clothes, sun
protection and a sleeping bag.
ies: Do not expect luxury accom-
ation, but amenities are generally
and overnight stays comfortable.
t: National Parks Central Booking
ffice, P.O. Box CY 140, Causeway,
Tel: 09263-4-706077 / 707624,
Fax: 09263-4-726089
natparks@africaonline.co.zw

EXPLORING CHIMANIMANI

Relatively small, Zimbabwe's Chimanimani National Park — and the mountains and village that share its name — is the focal point for excellent walking and is especially popular among backpackers. Today, it is probably the most popular hiking destination in Zimbabwe. The region is blessed with an extraordinary splendour, and a rich floral and faunal life, including baboons and antelope species such as klipspringer and blue duiker. Within easy reach are two of the area's top tourist attractions: the wildlife of Chimanimani Eland Sanctuary, and the natural beauty of the forest-enclosed Bridal Veil Falls. It is, however, the mountain range that holds the allure for hikers: a huge granite massif that towers some 2,200m (7,200ft) crowned by the impressive 2,436m (7,995ft) peak of Mount Binga (also known as Kweza), which lies on the other side of the Mozambique border. Virtually all the paths and trails are faultless, taking hikers through a delightfully unspoiled mountain wilderness dotted with caves, gorges, streams, and slopes blanketed with grassy plains punctuated by msasa trees. To reach the lofty heights of Mount Binga can take three to four hours of rather arduous climbing, but access to the plateau via Bailey's Folly may require only two to three hours.

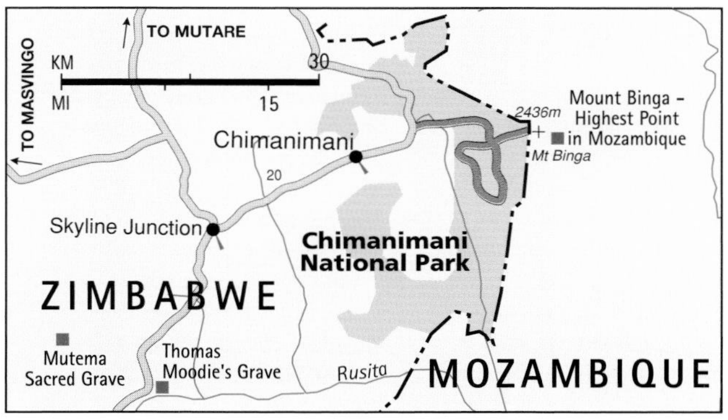

There are, however, various hiking options, including a one-day walk to the Southern Lakes by way of the Banana Grove Trail and the relatively gentle walk up Skeleton Pass, which should take less than an hour. While many trails take one up – and/or down – some demanding inclines and may be considered challenging by most, some walks require only moderate fitness, although few should ever be tackled alone.

Chimanimani has more than adequate visitor facilities, especially since the surrounds are generally free of humans. About 20km (12 miles) from Chimanimani village is Mutekeswane Base Camp, the starting point of no fewer than three separate mountain routes winding some 500m (1,640ft) up the slopes. Camps sites here have warm showers and basic overnighting requirements, but perhaps the most popular accommodation options are offered at caves such as Digby's Falls, North Cave and Peterhouse Cave. All provide easy access to some of the most spectacular hikes in the area.

The good news is that Chimanimani National Park is well serviced by a sound tourist infrastructure such as shuttle services and well-informed operators, and even offers the services of search parties in case of emergencies.

1 DAY+ MOZAMBIQUE

DIVING BAZARUTO

Travel Info

Destination: Bazaruto Archipelago
Requirements: Passports, visas and, if travelling by car, a driver's licence, which may have to be presented on request. Visitors travelling through or from countries with a recent history of yellow fever need a vaccination certificate.
Currency: Metical (100 centavos)
Climate: Humid and tropical, with high summer temperature and moderate rains.
Risk factor: No real danger beyond the usual risks posed by ocean sports. Be prepared, take precautions, and be sensible, as rescue services are limited.
Health: Malaria is rife and AIDS is a very real threat. Waterborne diseases include hepatitis, typhoid, cholera and dysentery. The local water is not drinkable.
Pack: Winter evenings can be chilly, but carrying plenty of clothing should not be a priority. Take malarial prophylactics and sunscreen, as well as diving gear if you're on a budget (renting is costly).
Facilities: Bazaruto is an upmarket destination and, although facilities are adequate, most lodges and resorts range from good to excellent, albeit pricey.
Contact: Mozambique National Tourism Company, C.P. 2446, Maputo. Tel: 09258-1-650001, Fax: 09258-1-431346 entur@virconn.com, mitur@virconn.com

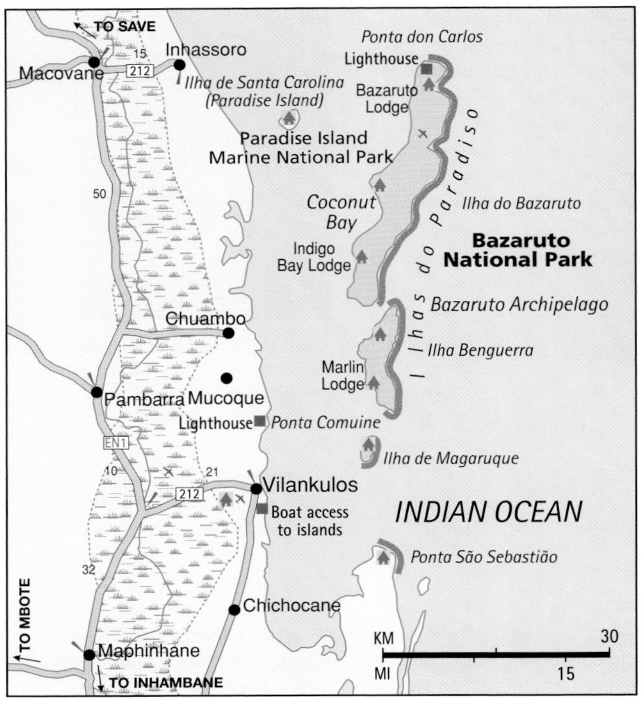

About 20km (12 miles) off the coast of Mozambique lies the chain of tiny islands that make up the Bazaruto Archipelago. Rehabilitated after the Mozambican conflict, the archipelago comprises four principal islands – Bazaruto Island, Magaruque, Benguerra, and St Carolina, perhaps better known as Paradise Island — and several smaller reef-lined islands, which make up the national park. Bazaruto, Magaruque and Benguerra are the largest of the group.

Buffeted by fluctuating sea levels, powerful currents and strong winds, the unique ecosystem is relatively isolated and, as such, remains unscathed by development. The waters, heated by the warm Benguella current that emanates from near th equator, are crystal clear an splashed with colour in the of tropical sea life, such as brightly coloured corals, anemones, fish and turtles. makes for an unparalleled u water experience, providing extraordinary opportunities explore. The diving, outstan beaches, upmarket accomm tion and fishing and birding opportunities have earned t archipelago a reputation as favourite tourist spot. Idyllic Bazaruto is most popular a fly-in travellers, and only vi with reservations at one of lodges are permitted to ove on the islands themselves. to these protected waters is boat from Vilankulos, some 500km (300 miles) south of Beira. Camping is permitted is not recommended, as the so many choices for more comfortable lodgings on the magical islands.

3 HOURS+ MOZAMBIQUE

WALKING ILHA DE MOZAMBIQUE

Travel Info

Destination: Ilha de Mozambique
Requirements: Passports and visas required. Visitors travelling through or from countries with a recent history of yellow fever need a vaccination certificate.
Currency: Metical (100 centavos)
Climate: Generally hot and humid, with cooler weather June–August.
Risk factor: Petty crime may be a problem in the south of the island. Vandalizing historic sites is punishable.
Health: Malaria is rife on the mainland and AIDS is a real threat. Waterborne diseases include hepatitis, typhoid, cholera and dysentery. The water is not drinkable.
Pack: Lightweight clothing should be sufficient, but be sure to pack good walking shoes. The Muslim community will frown on female travellers who expose any flesh. Sunscreen is recommended and bottled water is essential.
Facilities: Very, very basic to adequate. Harassment and theft means that the rudimentary lodgings are a better bet than camping. Reservations are advised.
Contact: Mozambique National Tourist Company, P.O. Box 31991, Braamfontein, 2017. Tel: 0927-11-339-7275, Fax: 0927-11-339-7295 moz-tour@netactive.co.za

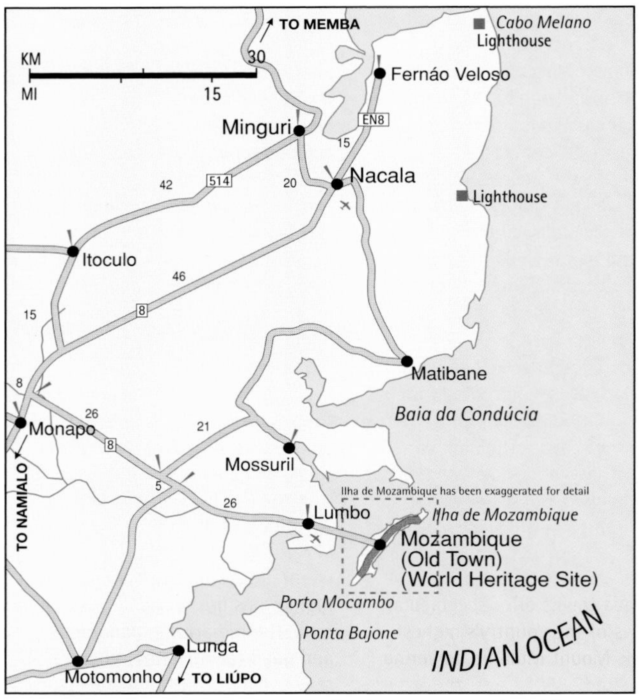

No more than 2.5km (1.5 miles) long, picture-postcard Ilha de Mozambique is linked via a bridge to the mainland 3km (2 miles) away, its coastline offering unsurpassed views across the Indian Ocean. Unfortunately, the waters here are severely polluted – a contrast to the diving spots further along the shore.

Like much of Mozambique, the island that shares its name is impoverished, and conditions on parts of Ilha de Mozambique are no better than some of the worst on the mainland. Although most islanders in the southern reaches of the island live in small, tightly packed shelters in shack towns, the rest of the island – particularly the northern parts – comprises splendid colonial buildings, mosques, forts, palaces and churches. In fact, so vast in number are these buildings that Mozambique Island, once the nation's capital, is a World Heritage Site. In keeping with its

historic past, the streets and alleyways of the Old Town are edged by quaintly dilapidated structures that appear to have been standing here for millennia. Although the urban heart is slowly losing its colonial atmosphere to the ambience of the traditional Muslim community that is reclaiming its stronghold on the island, there are still many remnants of yesteryear.

The best preserved is the 16th-century Fort of São Sebastião, erected around a spring that remains the island's only reliable source of drinking w Within its confines is the im sive Church of Nossa Senho Baluarte, erected in 1522 a thus the southern hemisphe oldest European building st standing. Also notable in th exquisite detail and historic significance are the Palace Chapel of São Paulo (which ed as the governor's residen the 18th century) and the J College of São Paulo, with i almost Gothic pulpit dating to the days when Portugues Catholics held the island.

4 HOURS+ MOZAMBIQUE

EXPLORING MAPUTO PROVINCE

Travel Info

Destination: Maputo
Requirements: Passports and visas are required. Visitors travelling through or from countries with a recent history of yellow fever need a vaccination certificate. Beach driving requires a permit.
Currency: Metical (100 centavos)
Climate: Hot and humid, with cool weather and coastal breezes June–August.
Risk factor: Experienced mechanics specializing in 4x4 maintenance are hard to come by, and language is an obstacle.
Health: Malaria is rife and AIDS is a real threat. Waterborne diseases include hepatitis, typhoid, cholera and dysentery. Water is not drinkable.
Pack: Lightweight summer clothing and sunscreen. Bottled water is essential. Ensure you are familiar with your vehicle's requirements (bring your own spares). Vehicle hire is not recommended.
Facilities: Facilities vary from basic to very comfortable; out-of-the-way stops offer budget accommodation. Roads are navigable but are generally in poor condition and best suited for 4x4 vehicles.
Contact: Mozambique Tours (RSA-based), P.O. Box 38359, Point, 4069. Tel: 0927-31-303-2190, Fax: 0927-31-303-2396, mit@iafrica.com, www.mozambiquetravel.co.za

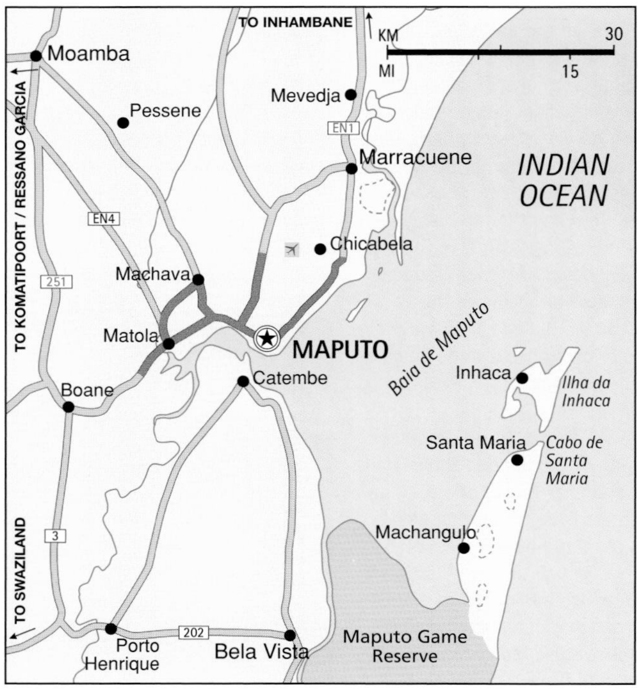

Readily accessible by road from South Africa, Maputo province has everything: well-stocked reserves, historic old towns, magical beaches, outstanding diving, and miles of endless road that create an unparalleled adventure playground.

For most 4x4 enthusiasts — this is the only real way to explore the south — the departure point is Komatipoort in South Africa's Mpumalanga province, and entry is via Ressano Garcia in the far south. Life here centres around the capital, a bustling, contemporary urban settlement that, although dilapidated, is well thought out yet charming in character and mood. The war-ravaged streets remain much as they were during the civil war, but are now peopled by laughing children, earnest street vendors and sarong-clad women. Despite the tourist traffic, language remains an obstacle even in the capital, and Portuguese, the official language, is spoken only by a few.

Lined by groves of cashew trees and a series of villages of bamboo-and-palm huts, the scarred roads in the south a generally in poor condition, ing four-wheel-drive vehicle preferable to sedans. Be on lookout for potholes — a re warning sign is sandy patch gouged into the grass on th sides of the tarred roads, an cation that vehicles have be compelled to scramble off t road. Off-road, the sand is a fine as castor sugar and tra lers reluctant to break a sw are advised to pack up and home. Even in the best-maintained areas, driving ca demanding and the slightes falter can end in spinning w and flying sand. This is espe true on the shoreline, where beach sand is very fine.

The coast is extremely fra and a permit is required to along the beach. Edge forwa very slowly, with diff-locks engaged and tyres deflated, drive on the compact sand the high-water mark.

3 HOURS+

MALAWI

KAYAKING ON LAKE MALAWI

Travel Info

Destination: Lake Malawi

ements: Passports and, for citizens e countries, visas are required. No health certificates are required.

Currency: Kwacha (100 tambala)

ate: Warm and pleasant: tempera- verage 24°C (75°F) November–April and 30°C (86°F) May–October.

ctor: Health risks are considerable ime is a problem: tents have been ned during robberies and there has an increase in muggings. Be alert.

: Malaria is a very real threat, and areas are entirely free of pollution diseases such as bilharzia. Water- activities are rewarding, but many advisors are reluctant to encourage swimming and snorkelling. Take malarial prophylactics and a uito net. Drink bottled water, and ry a supply of purification tablets.

ities: Amenities are generally very , and the area is serviced by well- ished hotels and resorts as well as reliable tour operators, although ng facilities can be too basic to be considered comfortable.

ntact: Lake Malawi National Park. 927-21-7831955, Fax: 0927-21- 31954, let'sgo@kayakafrica.co.za, www.kayakafrica.co.za

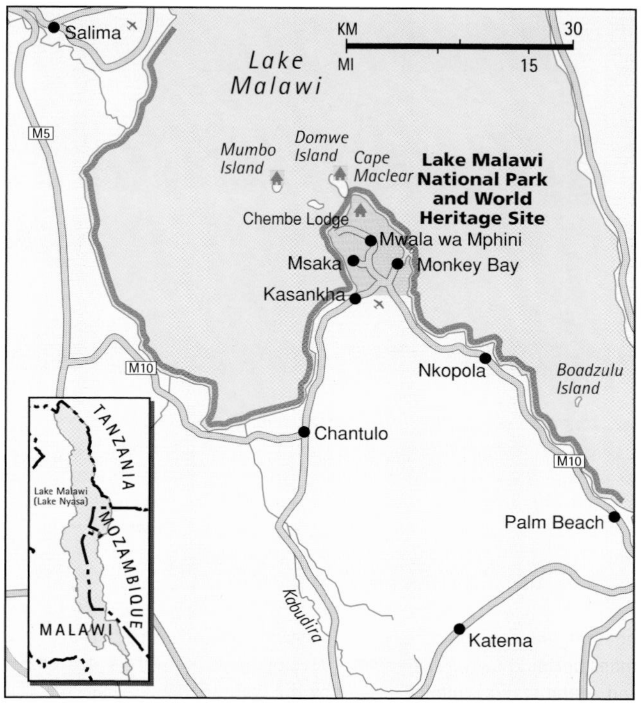

The shores of Lake Malawi have one of the worst records of malaria infection in the African interior, and bilharzia is a constant threat, yet the lake's waters remain the region's favoured leisure destination. The hospitality industry has found a well-established home here: an ever growing number of hotels, lodges and camp sites offer anything from windsurfing and kayaking to sailing, snorkelling and diving.

The best way to experience the lake's varied habitat is by kayak, exploring the fish-filled waters and shoreline caves and stopping to snorkel among the luminous creatures. Most of the lake's islands offer guided kayaking expeditions, and the sport is fast gaining popularity among adventurers. Private operators have, in recent years, been permitted to lead kayaking trips between the islands in the concession areas, and basic camps have been established on two or three of the stopovers. Facilities here are, if hardly luxurious, then comfortable. There is little to beat the gentle sway of a hammock and the warm showers provided by water buckets well placed among the lower branches of trees. The camp sites at Domwe and Mumbo, for example, offer a welcome base for energetic kayakers returning from the water after what is essentially a rather demanding pastime. Hopping from island to island, rock to rock, and flitting from one pool or cove to the next is a lot more draining than you may think, especially when the sun is high and the water bottle is low. Stopovers on the islands may be occupied by rock climbing, beachcombing, bird-watching, and even swimming, but be warned that, although the risk is minimal, there is the possibility of a chance encounter with a crocodile.

Sadly, despite local assurances, the waters of Lake Malawi are not disease-free, and extreme caution should be exercised when using the lake.

1 DAY+

MALAWI

CLIMBING MOUNT MULANJE

Travel Info

Destination: Mount Mulanje

ements: Passports and, for citizens e countries, visas are required. No health certificates are required.

Currency: Kwacha (100 tambala)

imate: Climbing is best in the dry s April–November, although tem- res, especially September/October, high. Summer rains render many s impassable without 4x4 vehicle.

ctor: The climb can be demanding es, but trekking Mount Mulanje is erally risk-free, and the only real ers are those brought upon themselves by foolhardy hikers.

: Malaria is a real threat and, like Malawi, many water sources may contain diseases such as bilharzia. Vater purification tablets, malarial ylactics and a mosquito net, espe- lly if you are overnighting on the ountain. Drink only bottled water.

ties: Overnight accommodation in untain huts is basic but comfort- kers and trekkers are well advised self-sufficient – even if you are using the services of a guide.

Contact: Central African Safaris, P.O. Box 489, Lilongwe, Malawi Tel: 09265-1-771393 Fax: 09265-1-771397

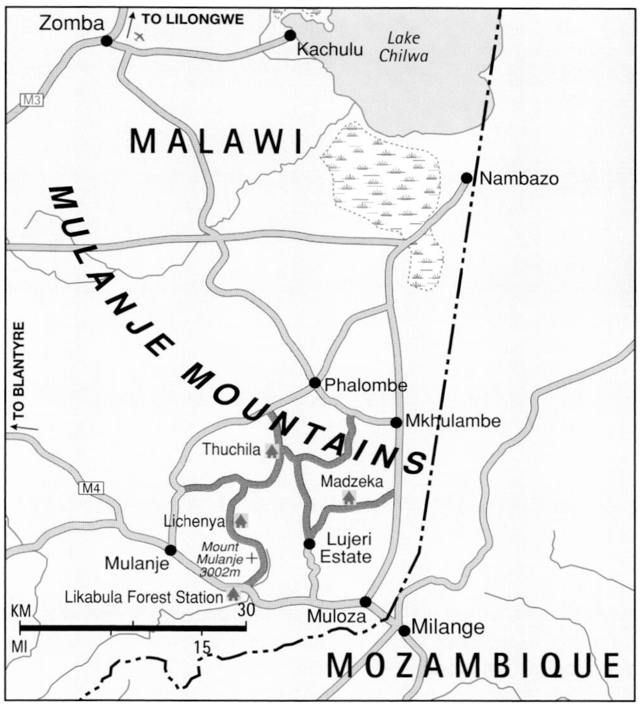

The Mulanje region in the south of the country lies at the heart of Malawi's tea industry. The slopes of the Mulanje Massif are covered with a patchwork of verdant plantations, yet the majestic highlands that stretch up from the Zomba Plateau are ideal hiking territory. Mulanje and Zomba towns offer spectacular views of the country's highest peak, Mount Mulanje, towering 3,002m (9,850ft) over the region.

The network of walks and trails – with many undiscovered routes – provides endless opportunities to wonder at Malawi's natural heritage. All are accessed via well-marked and reliable paths dotted intermittently with a good number of well-maintained and serviced overnight stops in the shape of small huts. The remarkable panorama and good facilities that characterize Mount Mulanje have made it the country's top hiking destination, as well as a reserve (hikers must obtain permission at Likabula Forest Station). The going is seldom too tough for even the moderately fit (certain sections require determination, rock-climbing skill and perseverance), and a number of short, relaxed meanders in the lower reaches of the montane forest will satisfy casual walkers. To reach the top of the mountain will take at least one full day, but it is not too arduous and the rewards at the top are worth the effort. Local weather is extremely impetuous and it is easy to lose your way on the mountain. The peak is often wrapped in billows of cloud (notably May to July, when thick mist, heavy cloud cover and relentless precipitation cause drastic drops in night temperatures) and can be virtually impenetrable on foot. Consult the officers at Likabula or knowledgeable climbers affiliated to local mountain clubs.

4 HOURS+

MALAWI

RIDING NYIKA

Travel Info

Destination: Nyika National Park

ements: Passports and, for citizens e countries, visas are required. No health certificates required.

Currency: Kwacha (100 tambala)

te: Moderately warm to hot, with eratures ranging from 20°C (68°F) 27°C (80°F) throughout the year.

sk factor: Risks are few, but most rseback safari operators will insist ents have some skill on horseback.

ealth: Malaria is a real threat and ter sources may contain bilharzia.

ck: Professional operators provide st of your needs and all necessary equipment, but for extended trips ck your own comfortable gear and wear, malarial prophylactics and a uito net. Drink only bottled water, p a supply of purification tablets.

Facilities: Private safari operators rvedly pride themselves on service nce. Remember that the nature of rseback safari means that you will hing it! Overnight stays are com- ble at worst and luxurious at best.

Contact: Nyika Safari Company, P.O. Box 2338, Lilongwe, Malawi Tel: 09265-1-752379 Fax: 09265-1-757316 tions@nyika.com, www.nyika.com

At an altitude of about 2,000m (6,560ft) above sea level, the face of Nyika Plateau – part of Malawi's biggest national park, Nyika National Park, that nestles in the far north of Nyika province – is unlike anything you may see elsewhere in Malawi. Its flat, horizonless plains, waving with high savanna grasses interrupted only in the distance with the occasional forest grove and a lone hill, dip down into rugged gorges. A series of jagged mountain peaks neatly encircles the grass-covered plateau and lends the wilderness a quiet, even melancholy feel. Road access to Nyika is somewhat lacking, providing a rather uncomfortable journey to the national park along the more established route that, although short in distance, can take longer than five hours.

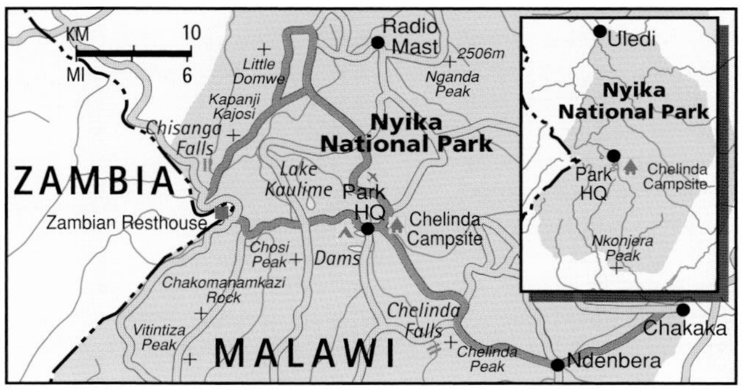

Many roads – particularly those in, around and to the park – are impassable during the wet season, yet road travel is your only choice, and no visitors (no matter how brave the attempt) may enter on foot.

Although wildlife populations are well represented at Nyika, hikers following the numerous walks and trails that cross the plateau tend to lose out on sightings of zebra, roan antelope, reedbuck, waterbuck, eland, and kudu. The high, golden grasses provide ample camouflage for these animals and, in addition, provide shelter to about 450 bird species, among them wattled cranes and francolins. As a result, horseback safaris have proven to be the best way to spot the various game species scattered across Nyika National Park. Quite at home here are herds of elephant, buffalo, kudu and plenty of roan antelope, plus the occasional lion and leopard. Exploring on horseback is thus the most rewarding vantage point to experience the wide, open veld of Nyika and view the carpets of wild flowers that blanket its spring landscape. Atop a steed and high above the tall grasses, the wilderness and the creatures it harbours are far more accessible and even tangible. Private operators such as that at Chelinda keep their own stables and offer various routes and trails that include excursions to Lake Kaulime, the plateau's only natural lake, among other sites. The horseback trails can take a few hours, a few days, or even a few weeks – provided your pocket and levels of endurance are up to it. Most operators will insist that you take a mounted guide, and these scouts are more often than not an enormous help, as well as being friendly, knowledgeable and willing to assist with any request.

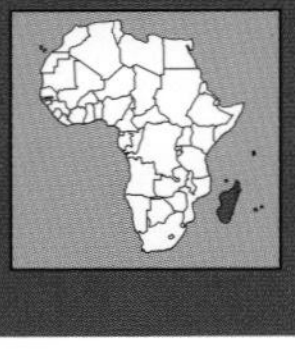

2 HOURS+
SEYCHELLES

SURFING THE SEYCHELLES

Travel Info

Destination: Grand 'Anse, Mahé
Requirements: Valid passport only – and your surfboard, although local schools based on Mahé may provide them at a nominal cost.
Currency: Seychelles rupee (100 cents)
Climate: Generally warm to hot, with some tropical humidity. Trade winds offer the best surfing conditions from April to October.
Risk factor: Virtually no risks, other than the occasional hungry shark and the breakneck speed of the waves.
Health: No vaccinations are necessary and malaria poses no threat. The combination of wind and sea can cause severe dehydration and sunburn.
Pack: Boardshorts and sunscreen are the most important, but be safe by taking a light beach shirt and/or sarong, as well as your own bottled water to the beach.
Facilities: Waves are excellent, as are all the visitors' amenities on a group of islands that depends on its tourism income. Even the remotest of beaches has comfortable facilities for tourists.
Contact: Travel Services Seychelles, P.O. Box 356, Victoria. Tel: 09248-32-2414, Fax: 09248-32-1366 tss@tss.sc, www.tss.sc

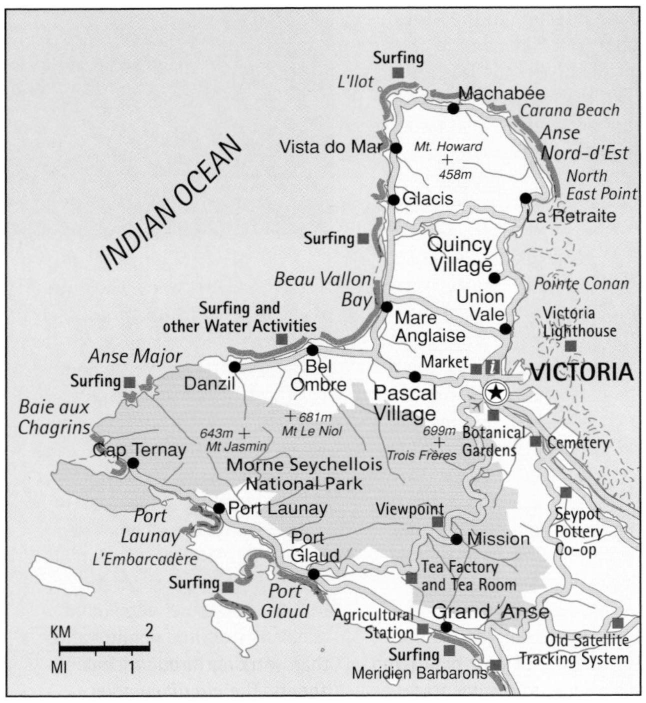

The waters off the Seychelles are supreme for surfing, and prove most popular during the south-east trade winds. At stretches of unspoiled coastline such as those at Beau Vallon and particularly Grand 'Anse, the wind and waves should be enough to get any surfer pumped. You won't need technical support crews critical in other adrenaline sports; all you need is the wind and the waves. Despite the increasing number of visitors, there are no desperate attempts to find a lift on a wave. Boards most typically seen plying these waters rely on function more than they do on fashion, and many locals have resigned themselves to the fact that any board is better than none at all. You still see the big, rather ungainly boards that helped pioneer the sport, bu smaller boards, which rely le volume and more on control skill, are more and more com

Although waters vary fron gentle to nerve-wracking (th may be precarious undercurr off Grand 'Anse), dangers are few. Sharks are virtually imp ble to avoid, however, and it your best interest to steer cl of the murky waters during ing times around early morn and evening if you do not wa to end up as shark bait. Give the often neck-breaking spe reached on these waves, it is best not to take chances in the least intimidating waves Generally, if you are surfing the right places and with the right people who know what they're doing, then these wa are perfectly safe, and you should be able to prevent th injuries that tend to end car – and lives.

2 HOURS+
SEYCHELLES

SCUBA OFF THE SEYCHELLES

Travel Info

Destination: Mahé
Requirements: Valid passport only. Scuba-diving schools and operators do provide diving equipment.
Currency: Seychelles rupee (100 cents)
Climate: Weather is pleasantly hot all year, with sea temperatures seldom less than 18°C (64°F); November–February is humid, with heavy monsoon rains occasionally affecting water clarity. Diving is good all year, but best in October.
Risk factor: The only risk is the inexperience of novice divers. Dangers from marine life are minimal – brush up on those presented by stone fish and the like.
Health: No vaccinations required and malaria poses no threat.
Pack: Swimwear and beach clothing should be enough, but pack your own scuba gear to avoid high costs of hiring.
Facilities: Scuba facilities are good to excellent, and available through the main hotels and specialist operators. There are dive schools for novices as well as advanced dives for certified divers (take proof). Accommodation standards are high, and no camping is permitted.
Contact: Indian Ocean Explorer Cruises, P.O. Box 384, Victoria. Tel: 09248-34-4223, Fax: 09248-32-2414, divesy@seychelles.net

The reefs off Seychelles teem with fish of every colour and size, and the islands – from the corals and coves that circle Praslin to tiny Denis, for example – offer a breathtaking opportunity to dive and snorkel among an extraordinary diversity of marine life and geological structures.

Every one of the islands seems to be entirely different to the next, making for some spectacular diving. The creatures that make the Seychelles such a memorable scuba destination are but a sample of the wealth of sea life around the islands. The fish are entirely familiar with onlookers and pay little attention to divers, allowing not only easy contact between man and fish, but also a diversion from the profusion of colour – although bleaching has discoloured corals in some areas – and texture of the coral life. In places, powerful sea currents have been known to stir up murky waters, and this creates the ideal home for reclusive nurse sharks and feathertail stingrays sheltering in niches, crevices and caves.

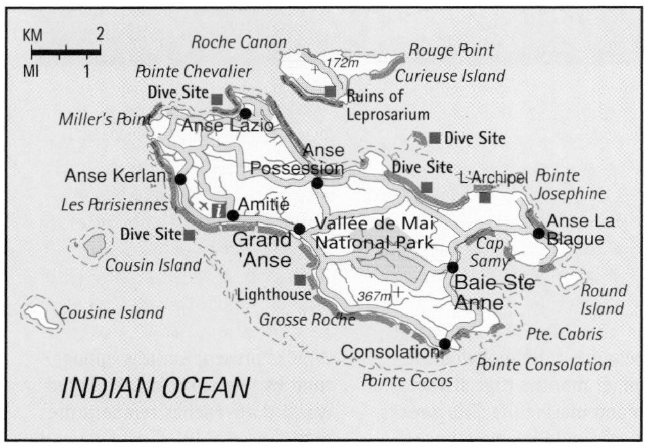

On Aldabra, the world's largest raised coral atoll, schools of black-tipped reef sharks hunt the shallows of the lagoon for small fish, while anemones litter the sea bed, and little angelfish dash in and out of the crevices as the tides recede. In the deeper waters, schools of triggerfish and parrotfish feed placidly as scuba divers skirt the reefs, drifting over some of the most colourful expanses ever to be experienced in the Indian Ocean. The trick here is to take your time as you make your way across the undulating seascape, watching for skittish marine creatures and dodging currents so strong that they can suck you in toward the mouths of small caves that punctuate the rock face.

Off Astove, one of the four islands in the Aldabra group, the steep inclines of the Astove Wall stretch some 5km (3 miles), dropping abruptly to awesome depths that cover a dark and forbidding realm of rough terrain.

The wall itself is pleasantl unblemished by human inter ence, but, in a world such as it is not the human inhabita that pose the problem: this i home, too, of silver-tipped a hammerhead sharks.

Most of the more promin hotels that dot the islands a able to provide scuba instru and are well connected to private operators based here Even the smaller islands, suc Denis, boast good diving sch with highly qualified dive masters and reliable equipm

2 HOURS+
MAURITIUS

BIG-GAME FISHING IN MAURITIUS

Travel Info

Destination: West Coast
Requirements: A valid passport, as well as a return or onward air ticket. Visas, where required, are very easily obtained.
Currency: Seychelles rupee (100 cents)
Climate: Weather is generally good all year, but the west coast fishing grounds are dry and hot, especially from Jan–March, with Feb–March the wettest.
Risk factor: Few to no risks, but big-game fishing is a specialized activity that demands both expertise and strength – novices should be accompanied by a skilled angler.
Health: No vaccinations are necessary and malaria poses no threat, but sunburn can cause considerable discomfort.
Pack: If travelling on a deep-sea fishing trip in a private capacity, make sure that you are fully prepared and well equipped. The services of a professional operator are highly recommended, and these will provide all the necessary gear.
Facilities: Accommodation, be it budget or high-end, is seldom a problem, and hotels and private tour operators are generally extremely well equipped.
Contact: Organisation de Pêche du Nord (Corsaire Club), Trou aux Biches, Mauritius. Tel: 09230-261-6267, Fax: 09230-265-5209

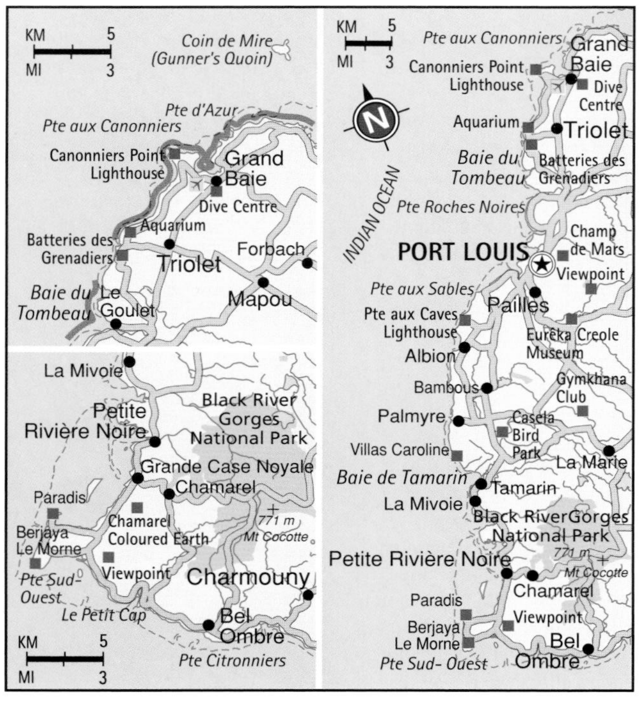

The waters off Mauritius are home to an endless stream of sailfish, tuna, kingfish, barracuda and marlin, most of which are caught in huge numbers. The deep-sea fishing here is some of the best in the world, and the season extends throughout the year, peaking between October and December. La Pirogue hosts the annual 555 Big-Game Fishing World Cup, and many world records have been set in waters less than a kilometre (half a mile) off the west coast. There are a number of options, and each offers opportunities to hook fish such as wahoo, shark, sailfish, tuna and marlin in waters known to reach some 600m (2,000ft) deep. At the height of the season, usually October to April, currents around Le Morne establish ideal conditions for bait species that attract game fish like marlin and tuna.

Many reputable operation based in Mauritius and, depe ing on the season and the si the party, they all offer boat well maintained and fully ki – for private excursions, be i half-day trip or longer. Some trips to the deep waters off either the west or north of t island depart from Grand Ba Most can accommodate up five anglers, and will take novices (because of the skill strength required, few opera encourage or even permit younger sailors to tag along) further option is to approac local fishermen; for a nomin cost, they will rent out their vessels. They are also a hand source of information: when start out, what bait to use, where to go for the best cat and what you can expect to catch in which waters. Most game fishing is, however, do through established operato who have years of experienc the Indian Ocean.

1 HOUR
RÉUNION

Travel Info
Destination: St Gilles les Bains
uirements: Valid passport only, but
: nationals may also require a visa.
Consult your local embassy.
rency: French franc (100 centimes)
imate: Balmy to hot with seasonal
s and warm sea temperatures. Best
time to visit May–October.
factor: Buckle up – and avoid the
cyclone season January–March.
th: No immunizations are required,
s visitors are travelling through or
countries with a recent history of
cholera or yellow fever.
Light, summer clothing, and some
gear if travelling in the warm wet
riod between November and April.
lities: Generally good to very good
' amenities, and most of the independent helicopter companies are
remely knowledgeable and helpful.
Contact: Helilagon, 97867 St Paul,
CIDEX, Altiport de l'Eperon,
St Gilles les Hauts.
Tel: 09262-555-555,
Fax: 09262-228-678

RÉUNION BY AIR

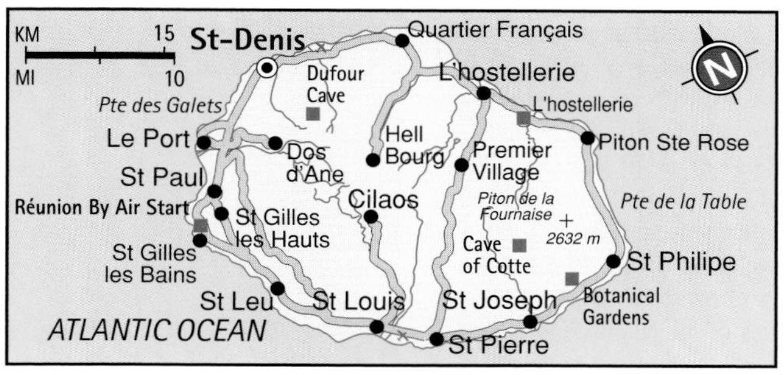

This tiny island is surprisingly sophisticated in its infrastructure, perhaps because it remains a *department* of France. The knowledge and skill of the few adventure specialists based on Réunion have resulted in a plethora of top-flight outdoor pursuits and yet one of the most memorable is what you see from the air: gloriously rugged mountainfaces cracking through the highlands, dormant or extinct volcanoes brooding alongside massive amphitheatres, and cirques carved into the magnificent landscape. This volcanic island is, geologically speaking, the youngest in the Mascarenes, which includes Mauritius and Rodrigues. Little more than 2,500km² (940 sq. miles) in land area, 72km (45 miles) long and 65km (40 miles) wide, the entire expanse is a breathtaking panorama of natural beauty, best experienced from the lofty comfort of a helicopter or light aircraft.

From amid the clouds – or so it seems, the island is so small – the land is pinpointed by the 3,069m (10,069ft) peak of Piton des Neige, highest in the Indian Ocean, and the 2,632m (8,635ft) Piton de la Fournaise, which remains one of the world's most active volcanoes. The rugged interior of plains and gorges is crowned by cirques and mountains, and Réunion's natural heritage is made that much more fascinating by an adrenaline-pumping helicopter flip, taking in the magical beauty from a bird's-eye view. Virtually all the natural arenas and other out-of-the-way spots sprinkled across the topography are inaccessible by vehicle, and may only be reached on foot, an often arduous and time-consuming means.

Helicopters and other aircraft excursions take off at St Gilles les Bains. The skill (and, quite often, daring) of your pilot (who gives a running commentary

during the trip) flitting you across this remote part of the Indian Ocean is breathtaking: skimming the waters, flipping across vast amphitheatres, diving from dizzying heights, or gently drifting on the sea breeze. Light aircrafts in particular can cruise at low speeds.

Your best bet may be to reserve your seat with a helicopter company that takes direct bookings from the public, rather than working through local agents. The *circuit complet* across the entire island will take less than an hour, but will fly you over everything you could possibly want to see: waterfalls and rivers, cirques and mountains, beaches and sea, the gorges of Maïdo and the craters of the Plaine des Sables, and you may even choose to lunch in the heart of the great Mafate Cirque. Although the complete tour can be pricey, shorter flights take in one or two of the cirques and are cheaper, depending on the amount of time spent in the air.

2 HOURS+
MAURITIUS

Travel Info
Destination: Grand Baie
irements: A valid passport, as well
return or onward air ticket. Visas,
required, are very easily obtained.
ency: Mauritian rupee (100 cents)
ate: Weather is generally good all
, but the west can be dry and hot,
especially from Jan–March, with
Feb–March the wettest.
k factor: Deep-sea diving can be a
dangerous pastime; obey the rules
f safety and etiquette, even in the
c waters of Mauritius, and employ
vices of professional dive masters.
lth: No vaccinations are necessary
malaria poses no threat. Sunburn
can cause considerable discomfort.
All equipment and accessories will
ovided by established dive schools
dive operators; private diving trips
e not recommended, especially for
hose who are not seasoned divers.
ities: Accommodation is generally
o outstanding, and hotels and pri-
tour operators are more than able
accommodate diving expeditions.
Contact: Paradise Diving,
PLM. Mont Choisy, Coastal Rd,
Grand Baie, Mauritius.
Tel: 09230-265-6070,
Fax: 09230-265-6749

DIVING OFF MAURITIUS

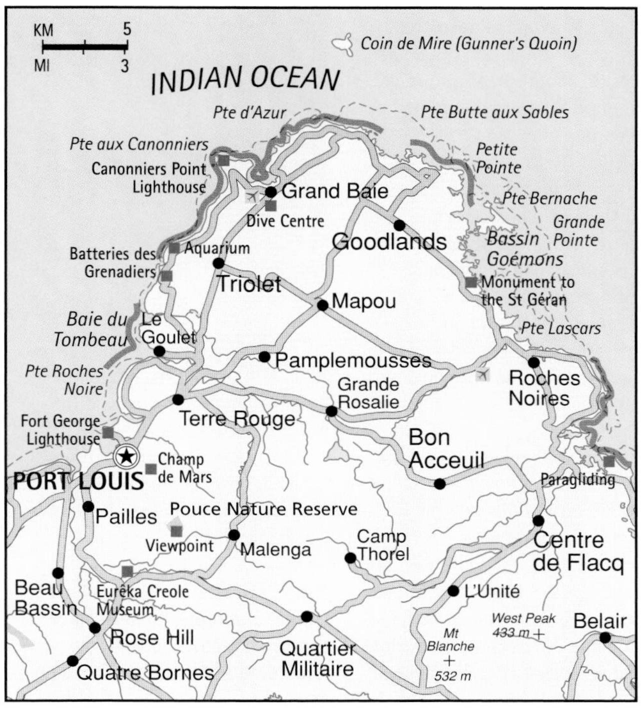

Mauritius provides some of the best diving off the African coast: wreck dives, shelf dives, night dives as well as diving excursions to nearby island dive sites. The sea bed and even wrecks are covered with sponges and corals, and are home to fan worms, sea urchins and anemones. Visibility is best in winter, but it is the summer months that attract the fish and marine life. The wrecks, some floundering here in the 1700s and 1800s and others actually dropped here to create artificial reefs, are popular attractions. Most sites present few dangers, other than injuries from sea urchins, the lethal stonefish and poisonous-finned lionfish, so if you're diving independently, bring protective gear. Wrecks present endless opportunities to explore a submerged world that reaches temperatures of about 27°C (81°F) and beyond.

To dive warm surface waters and even colder waters 20m (66ft) below, it is seldom necessary to wear a wetsuit, and most diving schools will not require rigorous protection. These operators offer the best and safest dives, providing reliable equipment, expert advice and high safety standards.

Nowhere in Mauritius are spear guns permitted, and the removal of shells and corals from reefs and lagoons is forbidden.

For visitors with no previous experience, a standard introductory course in a swimming pool is a prerequisite; experienced divers are allowed to bypass the learners' course if they can provide proof of their certification. Unlike other water sports offered by leisure operations, the costs for deep-sea diving are seldom incorporated into package holidays, and holiday budgets should include provision for boat fees, hiring equipment and any number of optional extras.

1 DAY+
MADAGASCAR

Travel Info
Destination: Isalo National Park
uirements: A valid passport and a
visa are both required.
rency: Malagasy franc (0.2 ariary)
te: Although the climate may vary
onsiderably, tropical Madagascar is
lly hot and humid throughout the
articularly in the forested regions.
ember–December provides the best
ons for hikers, but avoid the rains
between January–March.
actor: Malaria is rife, and rabies is
non among wild dogs. The water is
rinkable, and bilharzia and giardia
present. AIDS is an increasing risk.
h: No immunizations are required,
s visitors are travelling through or
countries with a recent history of
cholera or yellow fever.
ck: Comfortable but solid walking
lightweight clothing (days), warm
hing and a flashlight (nights), and
terproof gear for the rainy season.
acilities: The infrastructure is very
modest, affording few luxuries.
Contact: Unusual Destinations,
P.O. Box 97508, Petervale.
Tel: 09261-706-1991,
Fax: 09261-463-1469,
info@unusualdestinations.com
www.unusualdestinations.com

HIKING MADAGASCAR

The continent-in-miniature boasts a unique community of plant and animal life that evolved slowly in a protected environment that has been effectively isolated from the world. Perhaps most famed for its chameleons and more than 30 species of lemur, Madagascar is covered with singular habitats spread across its numerous parks and conservation areas, from Nosy Komba, Montagne d'Ambre and Ankarana to the private reserves of Amboasary-Sud and Berenty.

The opportunities for hikes and walks are innumerable, and one of the top destinations is Isalo, accessed via nearby Ranohira, a small but poorly serviced settlement on the park's outskirts. The walks here are breathtaking and vary from simple one-day excursions to extended trips.

The guides – based at the hotels in Ranohira – are skilled and informed, yet other facilities are simple at best, and Isalo is one of the few areas on the island that may be affected by petty crime such as theft. Compared to most other parks, animals are generally scarce at Isalo, but its Monkey Canyon trail remains popular with hikers, taking in lemur sightings and the gentle pools of l'Oasis and Piscine Naturelle, both of which have pleasant camp sites.

Although equally untamed, Zombitse, on the other hand, has no demarcated trails, camp sites or guides, yet offers a relatively hassle-free stroll through thick woods. A number of small operations offer excursions into the heart of Madagascar. The variety of mammals, birds, reptiles and amphibians is unparalleled and, with trained locals acting as guides, the experience is unmatched. Some of the best opportunities are at dusk and nightfall (many tour companies offer this alternative), when nocturnal creatures emerge to hunt and forage. You will encounter lemurs and perhaps even the aye-aye, but flitting in the canopy overhead will be a series of endemic night birds such as nightjars and owls, and crossing your path are the giant jumping rat and the secretive fossa. These excursions are most rewarding from October to March, when the hibernating inhabitants venture out after the cooler winter months. Some – in the more visited regions – have become quite accustomed to human presence, but direct contact with these essentially wild creatures is discouraged. Unfortunately, humankind's interference has meant that large animals have now been obliterated, and Madagascar's natural heritage is at great risk.

Although a regulated tourism industry contributes enormously to conservation, it also tends to put it at risk – visitors are urged to take extreme care when walking its landscape.

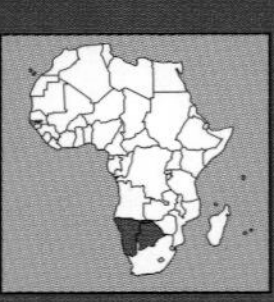

2 DAYS+ NAMIBIA

DRIVING NAMIBIA'S SKELETON COAST

Travel Info

Destination: Skeleton Coast Park
Best times: May–August.
Requirements: Valid passport; visa for non-RSA, -US and -EU visitors (confirm with your travel agent).
Currency: Namibian dollar (100 cents)
Climate: Generally moderate, often misty. Heavy summer rains (Jan–March) with flash floods and high temperatures.
Risk factor: Private trips should be well planned, taking into account the volatility of desert and ocean.
Health: Only visitors travelling from or through areas where yellow fever is endemic need to provide proof of vaccination; no other vaccinations are required. Malaria is endemic in the northern areas, so prophylactic treatment is essential. There is a risk of AIDS and bilharzia in this area.
Pack: Warm clothing for the fog-laden coast; sunscreen is essential; comfortable lightweight clothing for hot days.
Facilities: Some plush private operations, but generally simple to very rustic camping and overnight facilities.
Contact: Wilderness Safaris Namibia. P.O. Box 6850, Windhoek, Namibia. Tel: 09264-61-225178, Fax: 09264-61-239455, info@nts.com.na, www.wilderness/safaris.com

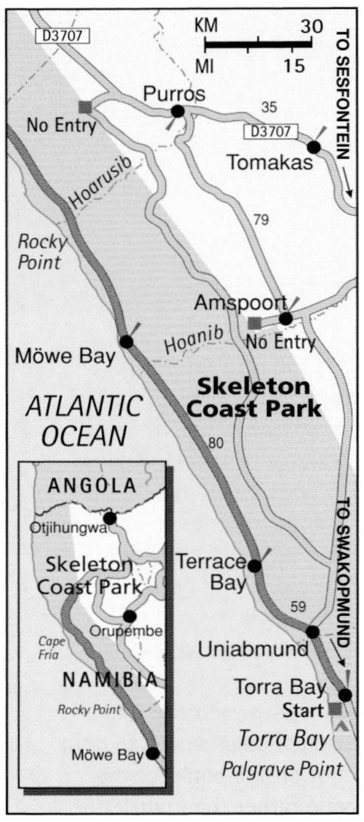

Of all Namibia's spectacular vistas, the most extraordinary must be the vast stretch of desert shore that is the Skeleton Coast. Although sparsely vegetated and apparently inhospitable to both flora and fauna, it boasts a unique array of life forms – albeit somewhat scanty – that have made unusual adaptations to life on this sandy, dry and wind-blown shore. The rolling desert sands attract adventurers to this eerie expanse of beach that stretches from the country's northernmost border with Angola down to the south, where it joins the dry and dusty plains of the Namib Desert in the Namib-Naukluft Park. Flanked on the west by the cold waters of the Atlantic and on the east by the parched hinterland, this place of solitude covers some 1.6 million hectares (4 million acres) that, together, form the Skeleton Coast Park. It is an extensive wilderness and a traveller's paradise.

The rocky coast is battered by the winds and pummelled by the ocean waters, and much of it is traversed with roads, some little more than bumpy dirt roads, others tarred but in a sad state of disrepair. All of this makes for a sound yet challenging four-wheel drive. The southern reaches are covered by the sandy dunes of the Namib, and the gravel plains of the north are liberally sprinkled with boulders and rocks, laced, on occasion, with rivers – the volatile nature of which bring little relief to this apparently barren coast.

The hardy surfaces here pose potential problems for wild drivers: visitors travelling in a 4x4 through the region are advised to drive carefully, particularly in areas that have seen no rain for some time or that have had too much rain. It is also essential to pack all the spares and parts you may need to help

yourself out of situations that may seem run-of-the-mill at home. The scenic beauty of colours and contrasts that dot the seascape up and down the beach seem idyllic, yet they are considerably less hospitable when you are stranded and helpless under the blazing sun.

Despite the aridity of the broader region, the Namibia coast and certain inland are are a haven for adventurers but the golden rules are to your homework first so that may be prepared for any eventuality.

---

3 DAYS NAMIBIA

DRIVING THROUGH KAOKOLAND

Travel Info

Destination: Kaokoland
Climate: Moderate to hot throughout the year, but best May–August
Requirements: Valid passport; visa for visitors other than those from RSA, US and EU.
Currency: Namibian dollar (100 cents)
Climate: Winters are moderate but cool, with heavy summer rains January–March.
Risk factor: Isolated and inhospitable to the ill-prepared traveller. Party of at least two 4x4s essential on roads that are essentially dust tracks. Professional assistance in planning is advised.
Health: Only visitors travelling from or through areas where yellow fever is endemic need provide proof of vaccination. Malaria endemic to northern areal. There is a risk of AIDS and bilharzia in this region.
Pack: Sunscreen and comfortable lightweight clothing essential, as are first-aid supplies, water rations and vehicle parts.
Facilities: Although locals are generally accommodating, guesthouses are few and far between – visitors need to be entirely self-sufficient. Some reliable tour operators service this area.
Contact: Kaokohimba Safaris. P.O. Box 11580, Windhoek, Namibia Tel/Fax: 09264-61-222 378

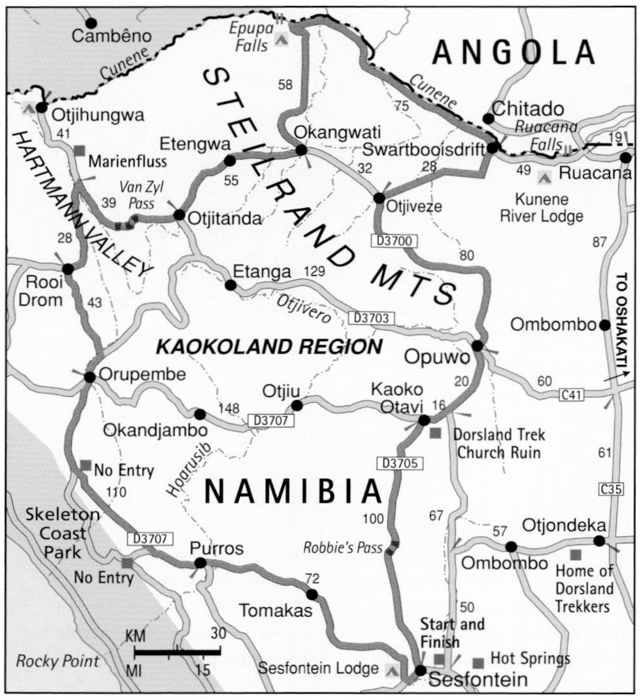

The immediate interior from the northern strip of the Skeleton Coast is known as Kaokoland. The nearly 50,000km^2 (19,500 sq. miles) of rough roads and rocky, mountainous terrain are not immediately inviting to the traveller. The tracks are unpredictable and difficult to navigate, and the landscape is wild and, to a large degree, empty of inhabitants other than the local Himba.

Still isolated from Western influence, the Himba are simple subsistence farmers who remain true to custom, so problems with your vehicle here are not going to be solved by the locals. The locals are friendly, approachable and hospitable, but it is best not to rely on them for anything more than a welcome drink and a cheery smile. At the same time, however, they know their home best and if you find yourself lost – and can decipher the elaborate hand gestures of the locals (few speak English) – you may decide

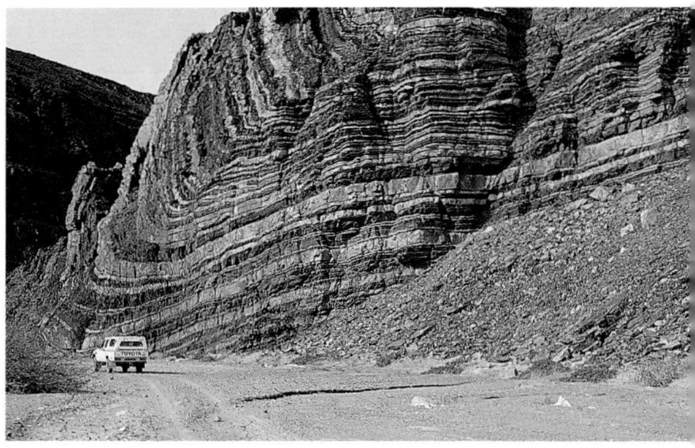

to ask for directions. Remember, however, that locals have different names to those on maps.

Apart from the perils of the desert landscape, the natural splendour remains the attraction. Although mistakenly considered an entirely separate species from the African elephant, Namibia's desert-dwelling elephants have simply adapted to the harsh Kaokoland. Of the most notable deviations from other elephants

is, of course, their diet. Here browse on indigenous Ana t The elephants may spend da search of water while they trudge in excess of 60km (3 miles) for a drink. Many wil mals will make their way fr one water supply to anothe the supplies dry up in the dr season. Travellers should be aware that this instinct has honed over millennia – take own reliable water rations.

---

2 DAYS+ NAMIBIA

HIKING THE FISH RIVER CANYON

Travel Info

Destination: Fish River Canyon
Best time: May–September
Requirements: Valid passport; visa for visitors not from RSA, US and EU. Hiking permits required from Nature Conservation.
Currency: Namibian dollar (100 cents)
Climate: Summers are blistering, but winter night temperatures can plummet.
Risk factor: Terrain is hard-going and tough, with plenty of dangers for the uninitiated. Professional assistance in planning is advised.
Health: Only visitors travelling from or through areas where yellow fever is endemic need to provide proof of vaccination; no other vaccinations are required. AIDS and bilharzia in this area.
Pack: Sunscreen and comfortable lightweight clothing are essential, as are comprehensive first-aid supplies and plenty of water rations.
Facilities: Varying from comfortable to very simple, but there are plenty of agents operating from Lüderitz and Keetmanshoop. Hiking is seasonal and is permitted only from May–August.
Contact: Namibia Tourism Board, Private Bag 13306, Windhoek, Namibia. Tel: 09264-61-2842111 Fax: 09264-61-282364 infos@namibiatouism.com.na

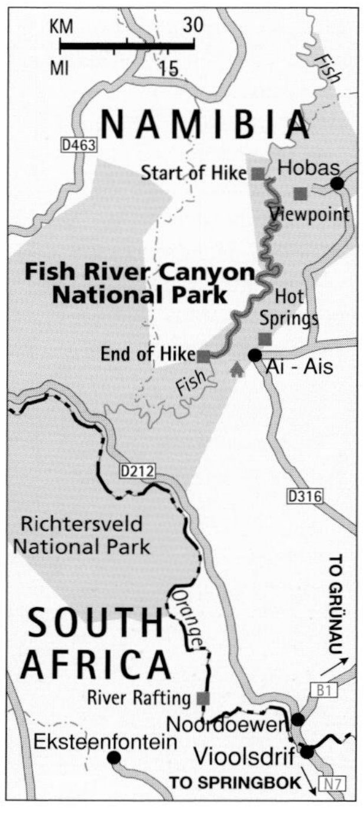

The steep inclines and roughly hewn rock faces of the Fish River Canyon, eroded over time by the forces of nature and its ravaging elements, are second in size only to the Grand Canyon of North America. It is a wild and spectacularly unspoiled wilderness of geological formations carved from layers of sandstone, shale and lava over a period of some 1,800 million years. The canyon is just over 160km (100 miles) long, and in parts it is 600m (2,000ft) deep and 27km (17 miles) wide. Its grandeur lies more in the spectacle than in the geological records and data that make up this natural phenomenon.

Eroded by the flow of the Fish River – which rises in the Khomas Hochland Mountains southwest of Windhoek and flows some 800km (500 miles) before it meets the Gariep (Orange) far to the south – these

remarkable rock surfaces boast a network of paths and trails carved into the rock and sand by countless footprints. The last 160km (100 miles) of the river's fierce and often breathtaking course winds through the deep canyon that forms the backdrop to Namibia's most challenging hiking trail. Although these trails are popular with ardent walkers and climbers, they are not standard tourist fare and remain entirely unspoiled – unlike the mass-orientated tourism drawcards of the big cities.

For the first 65km (40 miles) of its course, the gorge of the Fish River Canyon is, in effect, a canyon within a canyon, making for some remarkable walkin Almost in retaliation agains forces that shifted the rocks sediment millennia ago, the River began to cut a deep c nel in the bed of the origina trough – only much deeper, rower and far more spectac In places, the canyon floor i more than 500m (1,640ft) b the level of the plateau. Fortunately, it is a relatively gentle world of placid pools mighty boulders strewn acro beds of sand, with little evi of life. Naturally, this sort o lation – in a spot that is rel tively inhospitable – presen dangers of its own. As long wary travellers use their co sense and take no chances i landscape that has carved s threatening gorge from the surface, there should be litt worry about – just the endl stretch of undulating path, always particularly well sign posted, that lies ahead.

2 DAYS+
NAMIBIA

Travel Info
Destination: Cunene River
Best times: May–August
uirements: Valid passport; visa for visitors not from RSA, US and EU.
ency: Namibian dollar (100 cents)
te: Winters are moderate but cool, with heavy summer rains January–rch, which may bring flash floods.
sk factor: Relatively dangerous to remely dangerous in places, with a ber of risks that may prove serious f not fatal) if handled incorrectly. sional operators are recommended.
th: Only visitors travelling from or hrough areas where yellow fever is ic need to provide proof of vacci-. Malaria is endemic to the north, ere is a risk of AIDS and bilharzia.
: Sunscreen and comfortable, light thing essential; waterproofing and equipment a must. First-aid sup-nd water rations required in parts.
es: Rough and physically demand-but most operations (many RSA-ed) provide some simple comforts.
Contact: Felix Unite, P.O. Box 2807, Clareinch 7700. Tel: 09264-63-297161, reservations@felixunite.co.za, www.felixunite.com

RIVER-RAFTING ON THE CUNENE

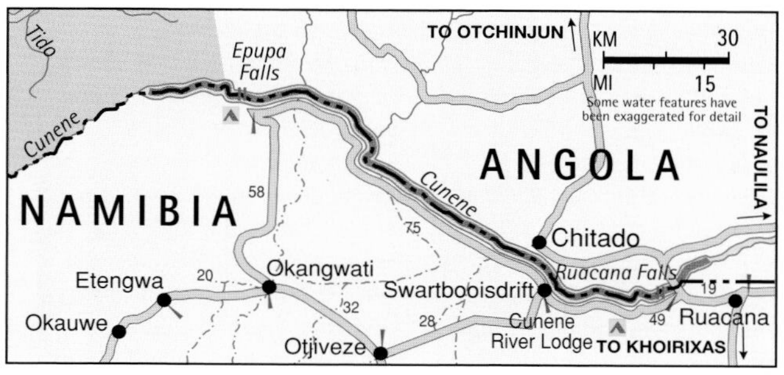

The mighty Cunene in the north of Namibia forms part of its border with Angola for about 325km (200 miles). Winding and twisting through a rough primeval landscape, the great river is characterized by fearsome crocodiles, thundering waterfalls, tranquil streams and, of course, the raging white-water rapids that have made this river one of the continent's premier rafting destinations.

The savanna that surrounds the small town of Khoirixas in the Cunene district in the west of the country forms the setting for the rugged Ugab Valley – a vast and wild country studded with mopane and thornbush and dominated by the 35m (115ft) tower of Finger Rock. However, the river remains the lifeblood of the region. Its untamed waters, in parts almost entirely white from the turbulence that roars beneath the surface, cascade over all-time favourite adventure thrills – the renowned Epupa and Ruacana falls and the nail-biting rapids at Enyandi and Ondorusu. Although the rapids that form the initial stretch are relatively placid and tame, the best are yet to come. Further on downstream, the Cunene gouges a torturous course through the weathered landscape, and several exciting rapids have to be negotiated, calling on all your strength and skill. All, of course, have fearful names – The Crusher, Dead Man's Grave, and Smash – but they are not impassable, and some have even been ridden by rafters with only a few days' training and limited experience. There are, however, some treacherous cascades, but most tour operators will insist on testing the skills of rafters before they allow them onto these stretches.

The section of river further downstream takes you through some magnificent scenery and through waters that are home to the Nile or water monitor, acclaimed as the continent's biggest lizard. They can grow to as long as 2m (6ft) and are extremely strong swimmers. This expanse of turbulent river, with its exhilarating white waters and tremulous course, is, however, not for the faint-hearted. Some claim that the more sensible traveller should choose to do it on foot on the banks of the Cunene rather than tackle the fearsome waters, but the stalwarts will inevitably brave the raging torrent. Be warned, though, that you should take every care not to take the river lightly – it can be cruel to the unprepared. The route is clearly marked and most published maps and route planners pinpoint the real dangers, but this is not child's play – your life may be at risk should you underestimate the strength of the river and the pull of its undercurrent.

2 DAYS+
BOTSWANA

Travel Info
ation: Makgadikgadi and Nxai Pan National Park
Best times: Winter (May–August)
uirements: Valid passport; visa for visitors not from RSA, US and EU. A 4x4 vehicle is essential.
Currency: Pula (100 thebe)
e: Generally sunny and hot. Heavy r rains December–February; freezing ight-time temperatures in winter.
factor: Private excursions are ill-l; thin-crusted pans are very dan-us; inexperienced bikers can cause severe environmental damage.
h: Malaria is endemic, so prophy-tic treatment is essential. Tickbite common after the first rains, and have been reports of hepatitis A. AIDS and bilharzia are widespread. Sunscreen and lightweight protective clothing are essential.
Facilities: Simple but comfortable lodges and designated camp sites self-drive visitors; luxury San and 's camps are in a concession area.
Contact: Uncharted Africa Safari mpany, P.O. Box 173, Francistown, Botswana. Tel: 09267-241-2277, Fax: 09267-241-3458, office@unchartedafrica.co.bw, www.unchartedafrica.com

QUADBIKING ACROSS MAKGADIKGADI

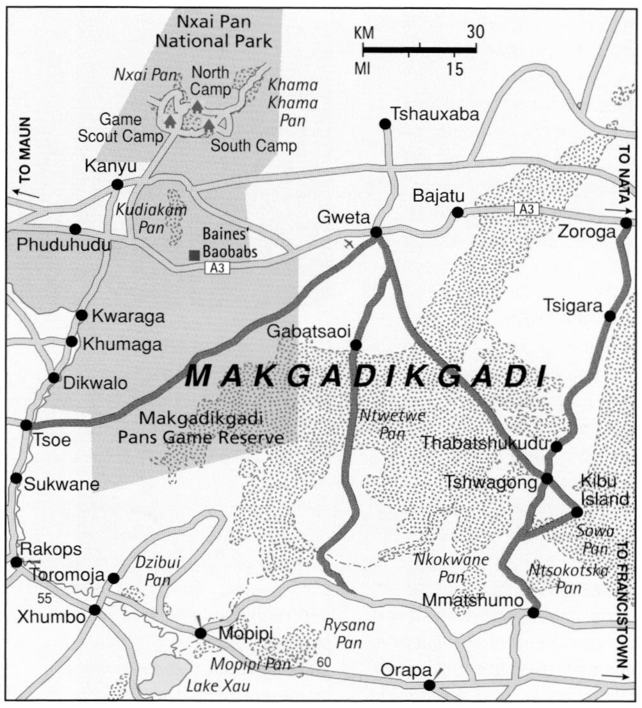

The plains of the Makgadikgadi and Nxai Pan National Park cover 7,500km² (2,850 sq. miles) of dry, lifeless land that, ironically, once formed one of the supercontinent's great lakes. Following changes in climate and immense seismic shifts, the waters that covered this landscape have receded, leaving seasonal salt pans that extend 12,000km² (4,600 sq miles). Winters see a spare and desolate land that is arduous in its crossing. Established operators here know the region and are quick to warn of the dangers of the dry pans and the havoc they may wreak. The general mode of transport in Makgadikgadi is the quadbike, a small, sturdy but reliable four-wheel vehicle with limited impact on the sands – almost all other vehicles cause irreparable damage to the ecosystems. Because of the unforgiving terrain, travellers (usually in pairs) are given impromptu lessons on how to handle quadbikes – be warned that it is not as simple as pushing the pedal and steering.

Beyond Kibu Island, mirages appear and disappear under the harsh sun as the 'caravans' negotiate shallow but bone-rattling gullies and crests on the hard salty clay, a deceiving lid on the water that lies below the surface. This is clearly no ride in the park, and there are pitifully few, if any, landmarks to navigate by, so every inch further into the pans means another inch further away from help. Travellers making their way across the pans need to be self-sufficient in every respect – even if you did have the foresight to bring a winch, there is simply nothing to which to attach the rope! It is for this reason that it is highly inadvisable to travel alone in a private capacity. Tour operators (recommended by reliable travel agents) have, inevitably, learnt the hard way, and know all the tricks – and probably every furrow and ridge of the land – so paying for their services and expert advice is undoubtedly your best option.

3–10 DAYS
BOTSWANA

Travel Info
Destination: Tuli Block
Best times: Winter (May–August)
uirements: Valid passport; visa for visitors not from RSA, US and EU.
Currency: Pula (100 thebe)
e: Generally sunny and hot. Heavy r rains December–February; freezing ight-time temperatures in winter.
Risk factor: Private excursions are dvised, and visitors are required to competent riders – outfitters will to take novices throughout what is essentially treacherous territory.
h: Malaria is endemic, so prophy-tic treatment is essential. Tickbite common after the first rains, and have been reports of hepatitis A. AIDS and bilharzia are widespread in the area. Sunscreen and lightweight protective clothing is essential.
acilities: Mostly luxurious private and safari-style tented camps, but atered and self-catered operations for the budget-conscious.
Contact: Mawana Horse Safaris, P.O. Box 200, Skeerpoort 0232. Tel: 09267-207-1440, Fax: 09267-207-1439, lvhs@infotech.co.za, www.lvhsafaris.co.za

ON HORSEBACK THROUGH TULI

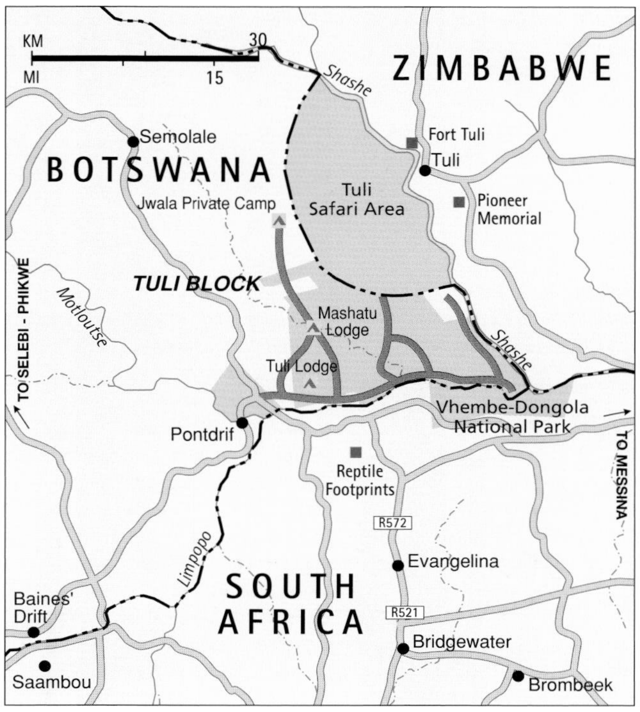

The Tuli Block comprises reserves, concession areas and agricultural land covering 12,000ha (300,000 acres). This is indeed big-game country, and the primitive landscape has contributed much to making Botswana one of Africa's top wildlife safari destinations.

Riding horseback through Tuli is one of those experiences that can overshadow even the plushest private safaris. The open veld, wide blue skies and plethora of wildlife in an untamed wilderness are all at hand: lion, leopard, cheetah, Burchell's zebra, wildebeest, hippo and the Tuli elephant all have a home here. The horizon is punctuated with clusters of boulders and baobabs, while impala, klipspringer, honey badgers and bat-eared foxes dart in and out of sight. Much of the land here is private, so venturing off gravel roads is not encouraged, but there are also adventure operators offering diversions into the wilds. While some established concerns pride themselves in providing every luxury, the smaller ones offer the most tactile – and most memorable – experiences that may take anything between three and 10 days. Night drives are not permitted in Botswana, and the Tuli trail is reserved for days only.

Most family cars are able to negotiate the well-signposted roads, but game-viewing is then rather limited. Horseback safaris also increases the chance of encountering wild animals. No inexperienced horse riders are permitted on the trails, and even those who are fairly well versed in horsemanship need to heed the warning of guides. In most cases, even the horses are carefully screened for their controlled temperament and ability to withstand the perils of the veld. Groups are advised to stick to the tracks already etched into the dry river beds.

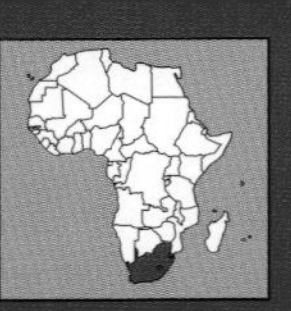

2–5 DAYS
SOUTH AFRICA

CROSSING THE RICHTERSVELD

Travel Info

Destination: Richtersveld National Park
Requirements: Valid passport only. Permits for hiking, angling and 4x4 trails in the Richtersveld National Park can be obtained from the park warden.
Currency: Rand (100 cents)
Climate: Winter (May–August) is best, as summer heat can be oppressive, with sandstorms and strong winds.
Risk factor: Moderate to high-risk driving, and easy to physically demanding hiking routes.
Health: Visitors travelling through areas where yellow fever is endemic need to provide proof of vaccination; no other vaccinations are required. There is no malaria risk in the dry Richtersveld.
Pack: Sunscreen is essential, along with a high fluid intake. Strong winds and very basic facilities necessitate a tent that can be sealed.
Facilities: Amenities within the park vary from basic camp sites with no facilities at all to comfortable self-catering, fully equipped accommodation. Official routes and trails are clearly signposted.
Contact: Park Warden, Richtersveld National Park, P.O. Box 406, Alexander Bay 8290. Tel: 0927-27-831-1056, Fax: 0927-27-831-1575.

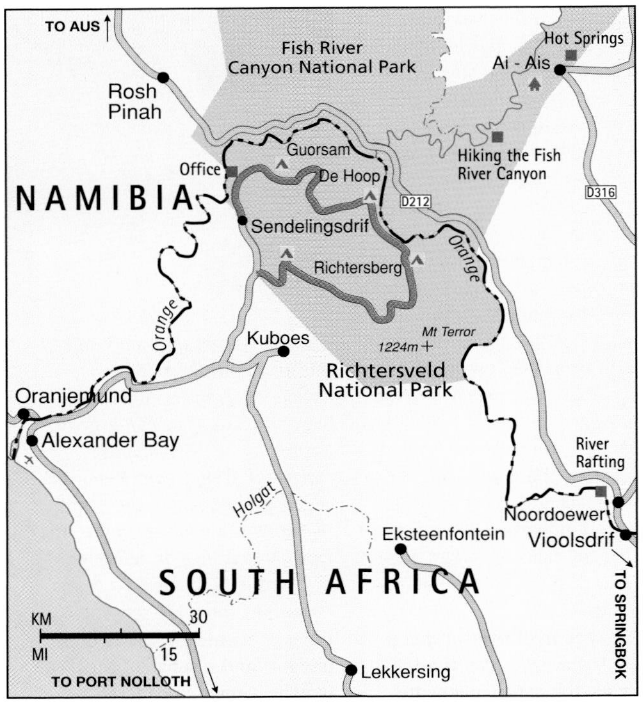

Although accessible from a number of points in South Africa and along the Namibian border, many roads leading to the 160,000ha (395,400-acre) Richtersveld National Park may not be numbered, while routes within the park can only accommodate high-clearance and 4x4 vehicles. Situated more than 200km (125 miles) from Springbok, the region is remote, its plains dotted with granite boulders and desert landscape lined with mountains. As such, crossing the Richtersveld — on foot or by road — demands planning and careful navigation, making good use of the few existing facilities at the camp sites and overnight stopovers. The 4x4 routes and hiking trails that crisscross the veld, compact sands and rocky passes vary in intensity and it is not for nothing that natural features such as Mount Terror have earned a fearful reputation. The fact that the tracks are rough and unsophisticated and that the heat can be unbearable has served only to add to its popularity as one of the region's most formidable wilderness areas.

The national park that shares the name of the broader region was proclaimed in 1991 and, with its geological extremes and variety of succulent vegetation, remains the traditional home of the pastoralist Nama. They still own the land and continue to farm with livestock, retaining some remnants of their customs.

Many of the existing 4x4 trails are the legacy of early pioneers who left their tracks here during the prospecting days of the early 20th century. In order to preserve the delicate ecosystem, off-road driving is limited to these numbered tracks. Because the park's official routes are relatively new, the opportunity to explore some spectacularly unspoiled wilderness is unique and, to keep it that way, the number of vehicles is restricted to three, carrying no more than a dozen travellers at a

time. The hiking routes are limited to specially demarca zones, and from April to Oc special guided hikes take pa of between five and 12 indi uals on two- to five-day ex sions. Appropriate levels of ness are required for these

2 DAYS+
SOUTH AFRICA

HIKING THE DRAKENSBERG

Travel Info

Destination: Drakensberg
Requirements: Valid passport only. Permits, where required, are available at the various park entrances. Booking is essential virtually throughout the area.
Currency: Rand (100 cents)
Climate: Snowfalls in the icy winters and heavy downpours in the hot summer, so spring (August–November) is best.
Risk factor: Simple walking trails to very demanding hikes across varied terrain.
Health: Visitors travelling through areas where yellow fever is endemic need to provide proof of vaccination; no other vaccinations are required.
Pack: Camping equipment, comfortable and solid hiking boots, warm, protective clothing and sleeping bags for the freezing winters or lightweight clothing and rain gear for blistering summer days.
Facilities: Relatively sophisticated, varying from basic camp sites with ablutions to very comfortable overnight huts and private lodges. Many routes and trails are well signposted.
Contact: KwaZulu-Natal Wildlife, P.O. Box 1750, Winterton 3200. Tel: 0927-33-845-1000, Fax: 0927-33-845-1001, mchunub@kzn.wildlife.com, www.kznwildlife.com

The ridge of high peaks that forms the escarpment between South Africa's east coast and the mountainous hinterland is one of Africa's most remarkable, boasting grand formations and extraordinary rock sculptures. The air here is soft, gentle and silent, while the earth beneath your hiking boots is studded with rocks, stones and plant life that dates back thousands of years. The steep ravines and rugged inclines of the Drakensberg remain one of Africa's most remarkable geological features, and the environmental awareness of its custodians makes it a pristine wilderness.

This wild country is a hiker's dream, offering relatively undemanding walking trails, rolling hills and rugged cliffs that require some resilience, while the most arduous climbs require supreme fitness and commitment. High peaks and rocky routes take their toll, and even casual hikers are advised to

familiarize themselves with some of the dangers of areas such as Mzimkhulu, Bushman's Nek, Giant's Castle and the state forests. Scenic beauty abounds, but then so do precarious drops, steep slopes and sheer isolation of many routes and trails. The foothills of the southern region, part of which borders Lesotho and its remarkable Sani Pass (see page 315), provide a fractionally gentler alternative to the hikes of the northern Drakensberg.

Nevertheless, they require d gence and an ability to nav the rigorous inclines. There few short hikes and overnig walks, such as the Giant's C Hiking Trail, which takes ab five days, but even 'simple' routes have dangers. The 3, (11,000ft) peak of Giant's C for example, requires a hig of fitness, endurance and ex ence. The rewards are unpa leled and the views that str forever are a welcome pana

1–5 DAYS+
SOUTH AFRICA

RAFTING THE ORANGE RIVER

Travel Info

Destination: Orange River
Requirements: Valid passport. All necessary documentation and permits to raft are obtained via commercial operators. Booking is essential.
Currency: Rand (100 cents)
Climate: Best during the summer rains (November–January) when waters are high. Intense heat can cause discomfort.
Risk factor: Moderate to challenging, but professional river guides provide valuable instruction and guidance.
Health: Visitors travelling through areas where yellow fever is endemic need to provide proof of vaccination; no other vaccinations are required. Basic swimming ability recommended.
Pack: Protective, waterproof clothing adds to your comfort levels; tour operators will provide most of your requirements. Sunscreen is essential.
Facilities: Facilities offered by operators are generally good to very good, although the nature of the adventure means that participants should be willing to rough it in the wilderness.
Contact: Felix Unite, P.O. Box 2807, Clareinch 7700. Tel: 0927-21-670-1300, Fax: 0927-21-683-6488, reservations@felixunite.co.za, www.felixunite.com

Slicing through an apparently lifeless landscape is the winding course of the mighty Orange, South Africa's greatest river and 'homeland' of its river-rafting adventures. It is the most revered by water-sport enthusiasts and, with its succession of tortuous bends, breathtaking rapids and raging waters, is justifiably one of South Africa's premier adventure destinations. As such, its waters are plied by a number of reputable commercial operators who offer competitive rates — especially during the holiday season, November to January. Time spent on the Orange is unmatched in excitement and wonder, not the least of which is the scenic beauty of its banks. Although not beautiful in the conventional sense, the often parched landscape is simply spectacular — taking it all in from a canoe on the river makes it all the more memorable.

Although known more for its spectacular white waters and adrenaline-pumping rapids, canoe trails and circular routes that include the impressive Augrabies Falls National Park, the Orange does have less demanding routes, where little experience is required. Bear in mind that this is one of the subcontinent's most powerful watercourses in many parts of its snaking route, so be sure to keep your wits about you. It is little wonder that certain sections

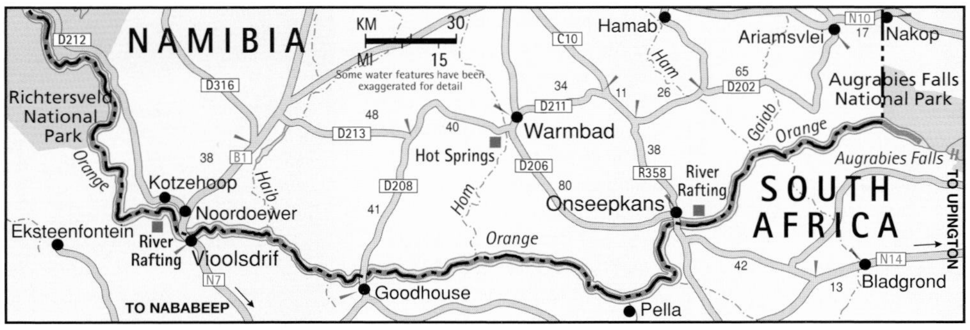

have been named as fair warning of their perils. Rollercoaster, Crunch and Crusher, and others, will call on all your strength, knowledge of the river and application of the important pointers dispensed by the experienced water guides and instructors during the comprehensive introductory lecture offered by operators. Although you are not expected to have extensive rafting experience to tackle the Orange, organized excursions can be anything from one to five

days (sometimes longer), ar novice canoeists should rat stick to routes and trips in ing with their ability. What essentially a fun and exhila adventure can end in disast you take the river too light Water levels fluctuate acco to the season — the river fl in summer and the rocky riv bed below the cascading w presents dangers of its own Sensible handling and the r equipment should ensure a and invigorating trip.

1–5 DAYS
SOUTH AFRICA

KAYAKING THE GARDEN ROUTE

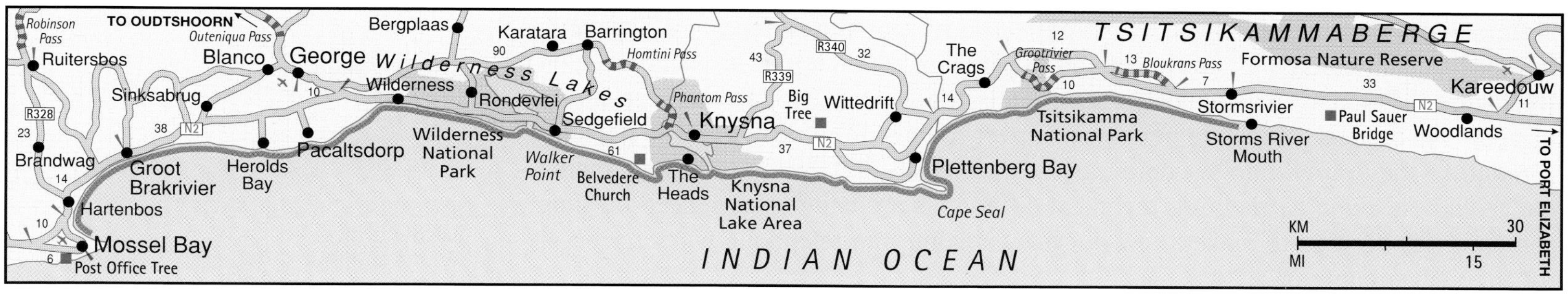

The more than 200km (125-mile) stretch of scenic coastline between Mossel Bay and the Storms River Mouth is remarkably undeveloped: craggy cliffs, soft beaches, gentle inland waters and endless ocean.

Barricaded from the arid interior by the Outeniqua and Tsitsikamma mountains, the Garden Route is a world of cliffs and coves, lakes and lagoons fed by the Indian Ocean, and a playground for the canoeist and kayaker. The wild ocean, placid inlets and lazy lagoons offer many water sports: surfing to sailing, waterskiing to angling and, most notably, kayaking and canoeing.

The beaches and ocean, blessed with sunny summers and mostly temperate winters, are set against a verdant backdrop. True to its name, the region is known for its natural bounty. Thousands of hectares of reserves and conservation areas, such as the Wilderness Lakes Area, lie along these beaches, but it is the salty sea air and gentle winds that lure kayakers. Operators are relatively few, but those who do work these shores are knowledgeable and helpful – perhaps because so much of this coast depends on the seasonal patronage of visitors in a hospitality industry that has seen enormous growth. The best times to take to the waters are at sunset, when dolphins cavort in the waves, seals ply the ocean and gentle 'white horses' ripple across the sea. However, remember that the ocean is untamed, and beach-based lifesavers and rescue units are not on duty in the off-season. It is not unheard of for kayaks to be surrounded by relatively harmless hammerhead sharks and even the occasional great white. The weather, although generally faultless, can be temperamental, waves unpredictable and sun harsh, but these may be a small price to pay.

Travel Info
Destination: Garden Route
Requirements: Valid passport only.
…nits obtained via commercial operators. Booking is essential.
Currency: Rand (100 cents)
…ate: Conditions are generally good …ear-round, but winter rains can be …some. Summer is the peak holiday …eriod and can be terribly crowded.
…isk factor: Usually gentle, but the warm ocean can pose a shark risk.
…h: Visitors travelling through areas …re yellow fever is endemic need to …vide proof of vaccination; no other …cinations are required. Basic swimming ability and some kayaking experi… are recommended (not essential). Some waterproof clothing may be …od idea, but operators should pro…e necessary equipment. Sunscreen …commended, especially in summer.
…ties: Facilities offered by operators are generally good to very good, …ough the nature of the adventure …s that participants should be pre…ed to get at least a little wet, with discomfort in cold winter months.
Contact: Real Cape Adventures, …ox 51508, Waterfront, Cape Town … 556 2520, Fax: 0927-21-790-5611, …@mweb.co.za, www.seakayak.co.za

2–5 DAYS
LESOTHO

PONY TREKKING IN THE MALUTIS

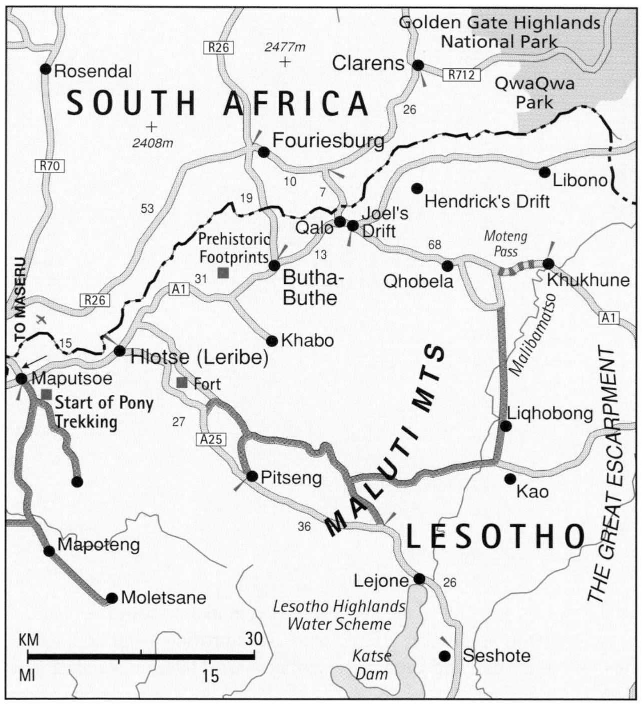

The western extreme of South Africa's KwaZulu-Natal province is demarcated by a series of crests that makes up the KwaZulu-Natal Drakensberg, which forms the Great Escarpment that separates South Africa from Lesotho. The landscape here, traditional home of the Basotho people, is wild and rugged. Its open veld and golden grassland are skirted by rocky ridges, and much of the land is untamed and inaccessible, even on foot or by four-wheel-drive. The largely rural Basotho use horses and the sure-footed Basotho pony to navigate this terrain. These tough and hardy mounts are the most dependable way to traverse Lesotho, and an entire industry – albeit rather basic – has grown around the Basotho pony and its strengths.

In the summer, the mountain is carpeted in indigenous plants, while winter brings snow to the mountain peaks that still shelter pastoral herdsmen wearing little more than ornately decorated blankets for which the Basotho are renowned. Although the people of Lesotho are at home on horseback on these hilly plains, this does not mean that crossing the countryside is easy. The going is extremely tough in places – you do not have to be a practised horseman to take advantage of the unspoiled wilderness, but familiarize yourself with some of the basics of horse riding. The logistics of most pony-trekking tours are carefully planned by operators based in Lesotho and South Africa. It is best to make use of their services rather than rely on your own abilities to interpret local conditions in a landscape that is both volatile and deceiving. Every care needs to be taken to avoid complications on a trip into such an isolated world, making trained guides your most vital 'accessory'. Amenities on the South African side are far more sophisticated, and the foothills of the Drakensberg are dotted with some fine lodges, private reserves and overnight facilities.

Travel Info
Destination: Maluti Mountains / Drakensberg
…Requirements: Valid passport only. …order crossings can be problematic …out the correct documentation, so thorough planning is essential.
Currency: Loti (100 lisente)
…e: Winter temperatures can be icy, formidable wind-chill factor con…ing enormously to freezing condi…ns. Summers are moderate to hot.
…actor: At least some riding ability …ecommended, but pony-trekking is generally risk-free.
…h: Visitors travelling through areas …re yellow fever is endemic need to …ide proof of vaccination; no other vaccinations are required.
…ck: Warm clothing for winter, and weight clothing for summer. Solid …ing and/or riding boots are advis…le. Bottled water is recommended.
…ilities: Facilities are virtually non…tent; those available are extremely simple, yet charming. Be prepared.
Contact: Basotho Pony Trekking, P.O. Box 12118, Brandhof, 9324. Tel: 09266-31-4156, …l: 082 552 4215, 082 77 555 60, malealea@mweb.co.za, www.malealea.co.ls

1–4 DAYS
SA / LESOTHO

DRIVING SANI PASS

Undoubtedly one of the most revered and panoramic passes in southern Africa, Sani Pass is the highest in the country and provides unsurpassed views over vast tracts of South Africa. The world here is a lost one, whipped by winds that emit a ghostly wail as they batter the rugged slopes and pummel every nook and crevice. Extremes of weather and vegetation make the countryside all the more picturesque, and the long, winding Sani Pass forms the lifeline of this remote expanse of the steep escarpment.

Cut by breathtaking hairpin bends carved into the rocky slopes, even at its least trying the pass is an arduous and difficult climb, twisting and slicing its way along the steep inclines of the valley formed by the meandering Mkhomozana River. This is the simplest way to ascend the 2,875m (9,500ft) mountain face and the vistas, from even relatively low down on the pass will knock your breath away. This is not a place for sufferers of even mild vertigo. The drops are long and hard and the 6km (4-mile) route from the South African border post carries the traveller no less than 1,000m (3,280ft), so it is not surprising that no standard sedan vehicle is permitted beyond that point. This is 4x4 terrain in the very truest sense, and every conceivable ability of an off-road vehicle is put to the test here.

A few private individuals operate from the nearby hamlets of Underberg and Himeville. They offer the next best thing to negotiating yourself up the perilous pass to the mountainous heights of Lesotho.

The pass itself is a small but significant chink in the great mountain. Once little more than a rough bridle path crafted by man and beast, and mostly by blanketed Basotho horsemen and the occasional adventurer, Sani Pass is today the only road link between KwaZulu-Natal and the remote Lesotho highlands. It is so precipitous that even the Basotho ponies struggle a little – especially when the rocky ground is covered by a soft mantle of snow. Although local townsfolk know the lie of the land well and are ready for most emergencies, winter snow can play havoc with even the most meticulously planned excursion.

Travel Info
…stination: Sani Pass, South Africa/ Lesotho border
…Requirements: Valid passport only. …er crossings require all the proper …entation, so planning is essential. …s, where required, can be arranged …rators in Himeville and Underberg.
…rrency: South Africa – Rand (100 …ents); Lesotho – Loti (100 lisente)
…: Snowfalls in the icy winters and …vy downpours in the hot summers …ke spring (Aug–Nov) the best bet.
…sk factor: Not for the uninitiated, … with less than impressive driving …r with no head for heights. Route may close in adverse conditions.
…: Visitors travelling through areas …e yellow fever is endemic need to provide proof of vaccination.
…ck: Warm clothing is essential for …vernight stays during the freezing …er months. You should carry every …vable necessary spare vehicle part.
Facilities: Comfortable overnight …ties in foothill towns, but accom…odation in Lesotho is rudimentary.
Contact: Sani Pass Tours, P.O. Box 12, Himeville 3256. Tel/Fax: 0927-33-701-1064. sanipass@futurenet.co.za www.sanipasstours.com

The following listings cover all the African countries and islands featured in this Atlas. Dialling codes for each country appear in brackets (dial 09 followed by the +000 number listed), and are followed by listings for local tourist information offices and relevant foreign embassies, consulates and so on in each country. Numbers are subject to change throughout Africa more often than in the western world, mostly as a result of upgrades of local telephone networks. Expect to encounter difficulties in getting through to the desired number on occasion, as lines are frequently conjested, maintenance work is being carried out, technical difficulties are being experienced or, simply, someone has decided to make a few bucks by stealing the telephone wires to recycle for their silver content!

ALGERIA +213
NATIONAL OFFICE of TOURISM
25-27 Khelifa Boukhalfa, Algiers, Algeria. Tel: 21 792 301
www.i-cias.com/m.s/algeria

ANGOLA +244
NATIONAL TOURIST AGENCY
C.P. 1240, Palácio de Vidro, Luanda, Angola. Tel: 2 310 065
www.angola.org, angola@angola.org

BENIN +229
MINISTRY of TOURISM
B.P. 2037, Cotonou, Benin
Tel: 307 010

BOTSWANA +267
DEPT. of TOURISM
Private Bag 0047,
Gaborone, Botswana
Tel: 395 3024, Fax: 390 8675
botswanatourism@gov.bw
www.gov.bw/tourism
www.botswanatourism.org

ANGOLA EMBASSY
Tel: 397 5089, 390 0204
Fax: 397 5089

BRITISH HIGH COMMISSION UK
Tel: 395 2841/2/3, Fax: 395 6105
british@bc.bw

FRANCE EMBASSY
Tel: 397 1518, 395 7119
Fax: 397 7133, ambbots@info.bw

GERMANY EMBASSY
Tel: 395 3143, Fax: 395 3038

ITALY & SPAIN HON. CONSULATE
Tel: 391 2641, Fax: 397 3441
icc@iccdc.info.bw

LIBYA EMBASSY
Tel: 395 2481, Fax: 395 6928

NAMIBIA EMBASSY
Tel: 390 2181, Fax: 390 2248

NIGERIA HIGH COMMISSION
Tel: 391 3561

SOUTH AFRICA HIGH COMMISSION
Tel: 390 4800/1/2/3, Fax: 390 5502

UNITED STATES OF AMERICA EMBASSY
Tel: 395 3982, Fax: 395 6947
usembgab@mega.bw

ZAMBIA EMBASSY
Tel: 395 1953, 397 1718
Fax: 391 5929

ZIMBABWE EMBASSY
Tel: 391 4495, 391 2500
Fax: 395 9229

BURKINA FASO +226
TOURISM & HOTELS BOARD
B.P. 624, Ougadougou 01,
Burkina Faso
Tel: 324 788, Fax: 324 786

BURUNDI +257
NATIONAL TOURISM OFFICE
B.P. 902, Bujumbura, Burundi
Tel: 2 22023, Fax: 2 29390

CAMEROON +237
MINISTRY of TOURISM
B.P. 266, Yaoundé, Cameroon
Tel: 2 224 411, 2 222 137
Fax: 2 221 295
mintour@camnet.cm
www.camnet.cm/mintour/tourism

CANARY ISLANDS (SPAIN)+34
CANARY ISLAND PROMOTION of TOURISM, NATURE & LEISURE
Tel: 34 928 306 510

SPANISH NATIONAL TOURIST OFFICE
United Kingdom 57-58 St James's st, London, SW1A 1LD
Tel: 171 499 0901 / 1169
Fax: 171 629 4257

CAPE VERDE +238
TOURISM CENTRE (PROMEX)
Avenue Oua, C.P. 89c, Praia, Santiago, Cape Verde
Tel: 622 621, *622 736*,
Fax: 622 657
promex@cvtelecom.cv

ANGOLA EMBASSY
Tel: 623 235 / 6, Fax: 62323

BRITISH CONSULATE
Tel: 322 584, Fax: 326 629
elisabete.e.soares@scv.simis.com

FRANCE EMBASSY
Tel: 616 001, Fax: 612 114

SOUTH AFRICA EMBASSY
Tel: 445 963

UNITED STATES OF AMERICA EMBASSY
Tel: 615 616, Fax: 611 355

CENTRAL AFRICAN REPUBLIC (CAR) +236
MINISTRY of TOURISM
B.P. 1988, Bangui, CAR
Tel: 611 055, Fax: 617 653

CHAD +235
DEPT. of TOURISM & PARKS
B.P. 86, N'Djaména, Chad
Tel: 512 303, Fax 572 261

COMOROS +269
DEPT. of TOURISM & HOTELS
B.P. 97, Moroni, Comoros
Tel: 732 927
dg.tourisme@snpt.km

BRITAIN CONSULATE
Tel: 733 182

BRITAIN EMBASSY
Tel: 49378/9, 49380, Fax: 49381
ukembant@simicro.mg (no more a british embassy in the comores)

FRANCE EMBASSY
Tel: 730 753, Fax: 730 922

SOUTH AFRICA EMBASSY
Tel: 732 812

UNITED STATES OF AMERICA EMBASSY
Tel: 202 4400, Fax: 208 9534
usembass@intnet.mu

Herd of zebra, Ngorongoro Crater, Tanzania

CONGO +242
MINISTRY of TOURISM
B.P. 456, Brazzaville, Congo
Tel: 830 802

CÔTE D'IVOIRE +225
MINISTRY of TOURISM
Plateau in Immeuble de la Corniche, Blvd de Gaulle, Abidjan
Tel: 202 0651

DEMOCRATIC REPUBLIC OF THE CONGO (DRC) +243
NATIONAL TOURISM OFFICE
B.P. 9502, 2a / 2b Avenue des Orangers, Kinshasa-Gombe
Tel: 12 300 70

DJIBOUTI +253
MINISTRY of TOURISM
B.P. 79, Djibouti
Tel: 352 540, Fax: 353 290

EGYPT +20
MINISTRY of TOURISM
Misr Travel Tower, Abassia Square, Abassia, Cairo, Egypt
Tel: 2 682 8467, 2 282 8457
Fax: 2 285 9551
www.interoz.com/egypt

ALGERIA EMBASSY
Tel: 2 755 3907, Fax: 2 735 7359

ANGOLA EMBASSY
Tel: 2 337 7602, Fax: 2 337 8663

BRITAIN EMBASSY
Tel: 2 794 0850/4, Fax: 2 795 1235
www.britishembassy.org.eg

BURKINA FASO EMBASSY
Tel: 2 380 6974

BURUNDI EMBASSY
Tel: 2 337 8523, Fax: 2 302 4302

CAMEROON EMBASSY
Tel: 2 344 1114. Fax: 2 344 1101

CENTRAL AFRICAN REPUBLIC EMBASSY
Tel: 2 346 1702

CHAD EMBASSY
Tel: 2 337 3232

DJIBOUTI EMBASSY
Tel: 2 336 6435, Fax: 2 749 6225

DRC EMBASSY
Tel: 2 336 8339

ERITREA EMBASSY
Tel: 2 344 1955

ETHIOPIAN EMBASSY
Tel: 2 335 5937

FRANCE EMBASSY
Tel: 2 570 3917, Fax: 2 573 8170

GERMAN EMBASSY
Tel: 2 736 5813, Fax: 2 736 4594

ITALY EMBASSY
Tel: 2 773 0119

KENYA EMBASSY
Tel: 2 305 6507

LIBYA EMBASSY
Tel: 2 735 5439

MAURITIUS EMBASSY
Tel: 2 748 8275

MOROCCO EMBASSY
Tel: 2 735 9677

MOZAMBIQUE DIPLOMATIC MISSIONS & CONSULAR OFFICES
Tel: 2 748 6389, Fax: 2 748 6378
emozcai@intouch.com

NIGERIA EMBASSY
Tel: 2 735 6042

SOMALIA EMBASSY
Tel: 2 337 4038

SOUTH AFRICA EMBASSY
Tel: 2 571 7234 / 5, Fax: 2 571 7238

SUDAN EMBASSY
Tel: 2 794 5043, Fax: 2 794 5012

TANZANIA EMBASSY
Tel: 2 337 4155
INFO: tanrepcairo@infinity.com.eg

TUNISIA EMBASSY
Tel: 2 735 4940, Fax: 2 736 1412

UGANDA EMBASSY
Tel: 2 380 2504

UNITED STATES OF AMERICA EMBASSY
Tel: 2 794 8211, cacairo@state.gov
www.usembassy.easynet.net

EQUATORIAL GUINEA +240
MINISTRY of CULTURE, TOURISM, FRANCOPHONY
Malabo, Bioko Norte,
Equatorial Guinea
Tel: 92903

ERITREA +291
MINISTRY of TOURISM
P.O. Box 1010, Asmara, Eritrea
Tel: 1 126 997, Fax: 1 126 366
ona12@eol.com.er

ETHIOPIA +251
ETHIOPIAN COMMISSION FOR HOTELS AND TOURISM
P.O. Box 2183, Addis Ababa, Ethiopia.
Tel: 1 513 144/5, Fax: 1 513 899

GABON +241
NATIONAL TOURISM OFFICE
P.O. Box 161, Libreville
Tel: 724 229

GAMBIA +220
MINISTRY of TOURISM
New Administrative Bldg,
State House, Banjul, Gambia
Tel: 227881, Fax: 27753
www.gambiatourism.info

GHANA +233
TOURIST BOARD
National Culture Centre, Kumasi
Tel: 51 262 43, 51 244 794
gtb@africaonline.com.gh

GUINEA +224
NATIONAL TOURISM OFFICE
B.P. 1275, Six Avenue
De La Republique, Immeuble Al-aman, Conakry, Guinea
Tel: 455 161/3, Fax: 455 164

GUINEA-BISSAU +245
INFORMATION CENTRE
Avenida Domingos Ramos, Bissau
Tel: 21 3282

KENYA +254
KENYA TOURIST BOARD
P.O. Box 30630, Nairobi
Tel: 2 271 262, Fax: 2 719 925
info@kenyatourism.org
www.magicalkenya.com

ALGERIA EMBASSY
Tel: 2 565 173
algerianembassy@form-net.com

BURUNDI EMBASSY
Tel: 2 729 275, 2 575 113 / 249

COMOROS EMBASSY
Tel: 2 24 73 65, Fax: 2 33 17 92
austria@africaonline.co.ke

CÔTE D' IVOIRE HONORARY CONSULATE
Tel: 220 179, Fax: 211 677

DJIBOUTI EMBASSY
Tel: 2 339 640

DRC EMBASSY
Tel: 2 229 771 Fax: 2 334 539

ERITREA EMBASSY
Tel: 2 443 163 / 4, Fax: 2 443 165

ETHIOPIA EMBASSY
Tel: 2 723 401, Fax: 2 722 091

EGYPT EMBASSY
Tel: 2 570 360, Fax: 2 570 383

FRANCE EMBASSY
Tel: 2 339 410, Fax: 2 339 977
iekenya@form-net.com

GABON EMBASSY
Tel: 2 261 004

GERMANY EMBASSY
Tel: 2 712 527 / 9
bavaria@form-net.com

HUNGARY EMBASSY
Tel: 2 444 2499 / 2 444 2612

ITALY EMBASSY
Tel: 2 337 777, Fax: 2 337 056
afra@form-net.com

LESOTHO EMBASSY
Tel: 224 876, Fax: 337 493

LIBERIA EMBASSY
Tel: 2 249 354, Fax: 2 803 898

LIBYA EMBASSY
Tel: 2 250 380

MADAGASCAR EMBASSY
Tel: 2 445 0432

MALAWI EMBASSY
Tel: 2 444 0569, Fax: 2 444 0568

MAURITIUS EMBASSY
Tel: 2 330 215

MOROCCO EMBASSY
Tel: 2 765 574
embassymorocco@form-net.com

MOZAMBIQUE EMBASSY
Tel: 2 512 610

NIGERIA EMBASSY
Tel: 2 564 116, Fax: 2 564 117

RWANDA DIPLOMATIC MISSIONS
Tel: 2 575 975, Fax: 2 575 976

RWANDA EMBASSY
Tel: 2 331 412, Fax: 2 336 365

SEYCHELLES EMBASSY
Tel: 2 441 150

SEYCHELLES CONSULATE
Tel: 2 560 165, 575 814

SOMALIA EMBASSY
Tel: 2 580 165, 2 581 683

SOUTH AFRICA EMBASSY
Tel: 2 320 63100,
Fax: 2 320 63219

SUDAN EMBASSY
Tel: 2 720 054, 2 720 854

SWAZILAND EMBASSY
Tel: 2 339 231

TANZANIA EMBASSY
Tel: 2 331 056, Fax: 2 218 269

UGANDA EMBASSY
Tel: 2 330 801, Fax: 2 330 970

UNITED KINGDOM EMBASSY
Tel: 2 335 944
bhcinfo@iconnect.co.ke
www.britain.or.ke

UNITED STATES OF AMERICA EMBASSY
Tel: 2 537 800, Fax: 2 537 810

ZAMBIA EMBASSY
Tel: 2 724 850, Fax: 2 724 796

ZIMBABWE EMBASSY
Tel: 2 272 6503, Fax: 2 272 3035

LESOTHO +226
LESOTHO TOURIST BOARD
P.O. Box 1378, Maseru 100, Lesotho
Tel: 22 316 307, 22 321 426

LIBERIA +231
NATIONAL BUREAU of TOURISM
P.O. Box 3223, 14th St. & Cheeseman Ave, Monrovia, Liberia
Tel: 222 081

LIBYA +218
THE GENERAL BOARD of TOURISM
P.O. Box 71981, Tripoli, Libya
Tel: 503 041

MADAGASCAR +261
MINISTRY of TOURISM
15 Ruepatrice Lumumba,
Tsaralalana, Antananarivo, 101
Tel: 2022 27292
mtm@simicro.mg

MALAWI +265
DEPARTMENT of TOURISM
P.O. Box 402, Blantyre, Malawi
Tel: 1 620 902, Fax: 1 621 923
INFO: tourism@malawi.net

EGYPT EMBASSY
Tel: 1 794 657

GERMANY EMBASSY
Tel: 1 772 555, Fax: 1 770 250

MOZAMBIQUE EMBASSY
Tel: 1 774 100, Fax: 1 771 342
INFO: mozambique@malawi.net

SOUTH AFRICA EMBASSY
Tel: 1 772 571, Fax: 1 773 722

UNITED KINGDOM EMBASSY
Tel: 1 772 400, Fax: 1 772 657
bhc@wissmw.com

UNITED STATES OF AMERICA EMBASSY
Tel: 1 773 166, Fax: 1 774 976
consularlilong@state.gov
http://usembassy.state.gov/malawi

ZAMBIA EMBASSY
Tel: 1 772 100, 1 782 100
Fax: 1 774 349

ZIMBABWE EMBASSY
Tel: 1 774 988, Fax: 1 772 382

MALI +223
MINISTRY of TOURISM
B.P. 4075, Bamako, Mali
Tel: 221 5725, Fax: 221 5727
info@culture.gov.ml

TOURIST OFFICE of MALI
B.P. 191, Bamako, Mali
Tel: 225 673, Fax: 225 541
tombouctou2000@tourisme.gov.ml
www.tourisme.gov.ml

MAURITANIA +222
SOCIETY of MAURITANIA TOURISM AND HOTELS (SMTH)
B.P. 552, Nouakchott, Mauritania
Tel: 222 53351

MAURITIUS +230
MAURITIUS TOURISM (MTPA)
11th Floor, Air Mauritius Building,
President John Kennedy Street,
Port Louis, Mauritius
Tel: 210 1545, 210 1015
mtpa@intnet.mu, www.mauritius.net

BRITISH HIGH COMMISSION
Tel: 202 9400, Fax: 202 9408
bhc@intnet.mu

EGYPT EMBASSY
Tel: 686 5775

FRANCE EMBASSY
Tel: 202 0100, Fax: 202 0120

ITALY EMBASSY
Tel: 207 7844

MADAGASCAR EMBASSY
Tel: 686 5015

SEYCHELLES CONSULATE
Tel: 211 1688
gfok@intnet.mu

Tuareg man, Western Sahara dunes

SOUTH AFRICA HIGH COMMISSION
Tel: 212 6925 / 28, Fax: 212 9346
saecon@intnet.mu

UNITED STATES of AMERICA EMBASSY
Tel: 208 2347, Fax: 208 9534
usembass@intnet.mu

MOROCCO +212
MOROCCAN NATIONAL TOURIST OFFICE (INCL. WESTERN SAHARA)
B.P. 19, Angle 31 Rue Ouid Fès et avenue, al Abtal, Agdal, Rabat, Morocco
Tel: 37 681 531, Fax: 37 681 527
visitmorocco@onmt.org.ma
www.tourism-in-morocco.com

ALGERIA EMBASSY
Tel: 37 765 591, Fax: 37 762 237

EGYPT EMBASSY
Tel: 37 731 833

FRANCE EMBASSY
Tel: 37 689 700, Fax: 37 689 701

GERMANY EMBASSY
Tel: 37 637 000
amballma@mtds.com

ITALY EMBASSY
Tel: 37 706 597

MALI EMBASSY
Tel: 37 759 121

MAURITANIA EMBASSY
Tel: 37 656 678

SENEGAL EMBASSY
Tel: 37 754 149

SOUTH AFRICA EMBASSY
Tel: 37 706 760, Fax: 37 730 758

TUNISIA EMBASSY
Tel: 37 660 251

UNITED KINGDOM EMBASSY
Tel: 37 729 696, 720 905
britemb@mtds.com

UNITED STATES OF AMERICA EMBASSY
Tel: 37 762 265
www.usembassy-morocco.org.ma

MOZAMBIQUE +258
MOZAMBIQUE NATIONAL TOURISM COMPANY (ENT)
C.P. 2446, Avda 25 de Setembro 1203,
Maputo, Mozambique
Tel: 1 650 001, 1 427 204
Fax: 1 431 346
entur@virconn.com
mitur@virconn.com

NAMIBIA +264
NAMIBIA TOURISM
c/o Ministry of Environment & Tourism, P/Bag 13244, Windhoek
Tel: 61 284 2111, 61 209 6000
Fax: 61 229 936, 61 254 848
info@namibiatourism.com.na
www.namibiatourism.com

NAMIBIA TOURISM OFFICE
P/Bag 13346, Windhoek, Namibia
Tel: 61 220 241, 61 284 2330,
Fax: 61 221 930
www.ahj.addr.com

ALGERIA EMBASSY
Tel: 61 236 376

ANGOLA EMBASSY
Tel: 61 220 302, 61 227 535
Fax: 61 221 498

BOTSWANA EMBASSY
Tel: 61 221 941, Fax: 61 236 034

EGYPT EMBASSY
Tel: 61 222 408, 61 221 501
Fax: 61 228 856

FRANCE EMBASSY
Tel: 61 276 700

GERMANY EMBASSY
Tel: 61 273 100 / 2, 61 273 133
Fax: 61 222 981
info@german-embassy-windhoek.org
www.german-embassy-windhoek.org

GHANA EMBASSY
Tel: 61 221 341

ITALY EMBASSY
Tel: 61 228 602, Fax: 61 229 860

KENYA EMBASSY
Tel: 61 226 836

MALAWI EMBASSY
Tel: 61 221 391 / 3
Fax: 61 221 392

NIGERIA EMBASSY
Tel: 61 232 103

SOUTH AFRICA EMBASSY
Tel: 61 205 7111

UNITED KINGDOM EMBASSY
Tel: 61 223 022, Fax: 61 228 895

UNITED STATES OF AMERICA EMBASSY
Tel: 61 221 601, Fax: 61 229 792
kopfgb@state.gov

ZAMBIA EMBASSY
Tel: 61 237 610, Fax: 228 162

ZIMBABWE EMBASSY
Tel: 61 227 738, Fax: 61 226 859

NIGER +227
NATIONAL TOURISM OFFICE
Ave Luebke, B.P. 612, Niamey
Tel: 732 447, Fax: 733 940

NIGERIA +234
NIGERIA TOURIST BOARD
Blocks 378 & 381, Zone 4
P.O. Box 167, Abuja, Nigeria
Tel: 9 523 0420, Fax: 9 523 0419
www.nigeria.com

RÉUNION +262
RÉUNION TOURISM COMMITTEE
Place du 20 Decembre 1848,
B.P. 615, 97472 Saint-Denis, Réunion
Tel: 210 041, Fax: 210 021
ctr@la-reunion-tourisme.com
www.la-reunion-tourism.com

RWANDA +250
TOURISM & NATIONAL PARKS
B.P. 905, Kigali, Rwanda
Tel: 576 514, 573 396, Fax: 576 515
ortpn@rwanda1.com
www.visitrwanda.gov.rw

SAO TOME & PRINCIPE +239
TOURISM OFFICE
CP40, Avenue Marginal 12de, Julho, São Tomé
Tel: 2 24245, 2 21542
tourism@saotome.st, www.saotome.st

ANGOLA EMBASSY
Tel: 222 376

BRITAIN CONSULATE
Tel: 2 21026, Fax: 2 21372
hblyth@cstome.net

CAPE VERDE
Tel: 12 227 28

DRC EMBASSY
Tel: 317 0533, Fax: 317 0580
stp@un.int, www.saotome.org

GABON EMBASSY
Tel: 224 434, 224 164

UNITED STATES of AMERICA EMBASSY
(in Gabon, + 241)
Tel: 762 003 / 4, Fax: 745 507
www.usembassy.state.gov/libreville

SENEGAL +221
MINISTRY of TOURISM
B.P. 4049, Ave Peytavin
Tel: 821 1126
info@senegal-online.com
www.senegal-tourism.com

SEYCHELLES +248
SEYCHELLES TOURISM (STMA)
P.O. Box 1262, Bel Ombre, Mahé, Seychelles
Tel: 620 000, Fax: 620 214
seychelles@aspureasitgets.com
dgtmtca@seychelles.net
www.seychelles.com

BRITAIN HIGH COMMISSION
Tel: 283 666, Fax: 225 127
bhcsey@seychelles.net
www.bhcvictoria.sc

FRANCE EMBASSY
Tel: 38250

GERMANY EMBASSY
Tel: 224 666, Fax: 224 065

MADAGASCAR CONSULATE
Tel: 34403

MAURITANIA CONSULATE
Tel: 76441

Table Mountain and Constantia winelands, Cape Town, South Africa

UNITED STATES of AMERICA CONSULAR AGENCY
Tel: 225 256, Fax: 225 189
usoffice@seychelles.net

UNITED STATES OF AMERICA EMBASSY
Tel: 255 256, Fax: 255 189

SIERRA LEONE +232
NATIONAL TOURIST BOARD
P.O. Box 1435, International Conference Centre, Aberdeen Hill, Freetown, Sierra Leone
Tel: 272 709 / 250 , Fax: 272 197
ntbinfo@sieratel.sl
www.sierra-leone.org

SOMALIA +252
MINISTRY of TOURISM
P.O. Box 533, United Nations Avenue, Mogadishu, Somalia
Tel: 1 26016, 1 39004
www.somaliwebsite.com

SOUTH AFRICA +27
SOUTH AFRICAN TOURISM
Bojanala House, 12 Rivonia Road, Illovo, Johannesburg, 2196
Private Bag X10012, Sandton, 2146, South Africa
Tel: 11 778 8000, Fax: 11 778 8001
info@southafrica.net
www.southafrica.net

SOUTH AFRICAN TOURISM BOARD
Cape Tourism Authority (CAPTOUR)
Tourist Info Centre, Adderley St, Cape Town, 8000
Tel: 21 483 4165, 487 2718

ALGERIA EMBASSY
Tel: 12 342 5074 / 75
Fax: 12 342 6479, 342 5078
embalgpta@intekom.co.za

ANGOLA EMBASSY
Tel: 12 342 0049 / 51
Fax: 12 342 7039

FRANCE EMBASSY
Tel: 12 429 7000 / 7029

GABON EMBASSY
Tel: 12 342 4376 / 7
Fax: 12 342 4375

GERMANY EMBASSY
Tel: 12 427 8900, Fax: 12 343 9401
Tel: 21 424 2410, Fax: 424 9403

GHANA HIGH COMMISSION
Tel: 12 342 5847 / 9
Fax: 12 342 5863

HUNGARY EMBASSY
Tel: 12 430 3020 / 30
Fax: 12 430 3029
hunem@cis.co.za

ITALIAN EMBASSY
Tel: 21 424 1256, 423 5157
Fax: 21 424 0146

UNITED KINGDOM EMBASSY
Tel: 12 483 1200
Fax: 12 483 1302

UNITED STATES of AMERICA EMBASSY
Tel: 12 342 1048, 21 421 4280
Fax: 12 342 2299, 21 425 4151

SUDAN +249
TRAVEL & TOURIST AGENCY
P.O. Box 769, Khartoum, Sudan
Tel / Fax: 11 70949
US: www.sudanembassy.org
www.sudan.net

SWAZILAND +268
GOVERNMENT TOURIST OFFICE
P.O. Box 451, Mbabane, Swaziland
Tel: 404 4556
www.swazi.com/tourism

TANZANIA +255
TANZANIA TOURIST BOARD
P.O. Box 2485, Dar es Salaam, Tanzania.
Tel: 22 211 1244 / 5, 22 212 0373
ttb2@ud.co.tz, md@ttb.ud.or.tz
www.tanzania-web.com

ALGERIA EMBASSY
Tel: 22 211 7620

ANGOLA EMBASSY
Tel: 22 211 7674, 22 213 9235

BURUNDI EMBASSY
Tel: 22 211 7615

DRC EMBASSY
Tel: 66010

EGYPT EMBASSY
Tel: 22 211 3591

FRANCE EMBASSY
Tel: 22 266 6021, Fax: 22 266 8435
ambfrance@africaonline.co.tz

GERMANY EMBASSY
Tel: 22 211 7411
german.emb.dar@raha.com

ITALY EMBASSY
Tel: 22 211 5935, Fax: 22 211 5938
italdipl@raha.com

KENYA EMBASSY
Tel: 22 270 1748

MALAWI EMBASSY
Tel: 22 266 7664

MOZAMBIQUE EMBASSY
Tel:22 213 3063

NIGERIA EMBASSY
Tel: 22 260 2843

RWANDA DIPLOMATIC MISSIONS
Tel: 511 158 89, Fax: 511 158 88

RWANDA EMBASSY
Tel: 22 277 5444, 22 213 0119

SEYCHELLES CONSULATE
Tel: 22 266 8113

SOUTH AFRICA HIGH COMMISSION
Tel: 22 260 1800
essaemb@idsc.gov.eg

SUDAN EMBASSY
Tel: 22 215 2154

UGANDA EMBASSY
Tel: 22 266 7391

UNITED KINGDOM EMBASSY
Tel: 22 211 0101, Fax: 22 211 0102
bhc.dar@dar.mail.fco.gov.uk

UNITED STATES OF AMERICA EMBASSY
Tel: 22 266 7836 / 6010
Fax: 22 266 6701
usembassy-dar1@raha.com
www.usembasst.state.gov

ZAMBIA EMBASSY
Tel: 22 211 2977, 22 211 8481

ZIMBABWE EMBASSY
Tel: 22 211 2913, 22 213 0933

TOGO +228
NATIONAL TOURISM OFFICE
B.P. 1289, Lomé, Togo, West Africa
Tel: 221 4313
www.republicotogo.com

TUNISIA +216
TUNISIAN NATIONAL TOURISM OFFICE (ONTT) 1, Ave Mohamed V, 1001, Tunis, Tunisia
Tel: 71 341 077, Fax: 71 350 997
www.tourismtunisia.com
www.tunisietourisme.com.tn
info@tourismtunisia.com

ALGERIA EMBASSY
Tel: 71 783 166, Fax: 71 788 804

EGYPT EMBASSY
Tel: 71 792 283, Fax: 71 794 389
FRANCE EMBASSY
Tel: 71 333 027, Fax: 71 351 967

GERMANY EMBASSY
Tel: 71 788 242, Fax: 71 786 455

ITALY EMBASSY
Tel: 71 321 811

LIBYA EMBASSY
Tel: 71 781 913, Fax: 71 780 866

MOROCCO EMBASSY
Tel: 71 782 775, Fax: 71 787 103

SEYCHELLES CONSULATE
Tel: 71 383 266, Fax: 71 382 257

SOUTH AFRICA EMBASSY
Tel: 71 798 449

UNITED KINGDOM EMBASSY
Tel: 71 341 444
www.british-emb.intl.tn

UNITED STATES OF AMERICA EMBASSY
Tel: 71 107 000, Fax: 71 962 115
www.usembassy.state.gov/posts/ts1/wwhmain.html
consulartunis@state.gov

UGANDA +256
UGANDA TOURIST BOARD
IPS Building, Parliament Avenue, P.O. Box 7211, Kampala
Tel: 41 342 196 / 7, Fax: 41 342 188
utb@starcom.co.urg
www.visituganda.com

ZAMBIA +260
ZAMBIAN NATIONAL TOURISM BOARD
P.O. Box 30017, Lusaka
Century House, Cairo Rd, Lusaka
Tel: 1 22 9087 / 90
Fax: 1 22 9090
zntb@zamnet.zm

ZIMBABWE +263
ZIMBABWE TOURISM DEVELOPMENT CORPORATION
P.O. Box 8052, Harare
Tel: 4 758 730

ZIMBABWE TOURISM (ZTA)
P.O. Box, CY286, Causeway, Harare
Tel: 4 751 720 / 2, 4 752 570
Fax: 4 758 828, 4 758 826
info@ztazim.co.zw
www.zimbabwetourism.co.zw

ZIMBABWE COUNCIL FOR TOURISM
P.O. Box 7240
Tel: 4 708 836, 4 708 822

ALGERIA EMBASSY
Tel: 4 702 532

ANGOLA EMBASSY
Tel: 4 770 070 / 7

BOTSWANA EMBASSY
Tel: 4 729 551, 4 705 814

BRITAIN HIGH COMMISSION
Tel: 4 774 700, 772 990
Fax: 4 774 617
bhcinfo@africaonline.co.zw *or* british.info@fco.gov.uk
www.britainzw.org

CONGO EMBASSY (Brazzaville)
Tel: 4 730 705

DRC EMBASSY (Zaire)
Tel: 4 724 494

EGYPT EMBASSY
Tel: 4 303 444 / 5

ETHIOPIA EMBASSY
Tel: 4 725 822 or 4 701 514 / 4

FRANCE EMBASSY
Tel: 4 703 216

GERMANY EMBASSY
Tel: 4 308 655 / 6

GHANA EMBASSY
Tel: 4 738 652

HUNGARY EMBASSY
Tel: 4 733 210

ITALY EMBASSY
Tel: 4 498 327

KENYA EMBASSY
Tel: 4 741 414 or 4 704 820 / 33

LIBYA EMBASSY
Tel: 4 728 381 / 3, 4 774 885 / 6

MALAWI EMBASSY
Tel: 4 798 589 / 7, Fax: 4 752 137

MOZAMBIQUE DIPLOMATIC MISSIONS AND CONSULAR OFFICES
Tel: 4 79837 / 9, Fax: 4 73898
embamoc@utande.co.zw

MOZAMBIQUE EMBASSY
Tel: 4 253 871 / 4

NAMIBIA EMBASSY
Tel: 4 885 841, 4 304 856

NAMIBIA EMBASSY
(High Commission)
Tel 4 722 113, Fax 4 722 114

NIGERIA EMBASSY
Tel: 4 253 976, 4 253 877 / 8

SOUTH AFRICA EMBASSY
Tel: 4 251 040

SOUTH AFRICA HIGH COMMISSION
Tel: 4 753 147, Fax: 4 753 185
sahcecon@ecoweb.co.zw

SENEGAL EMBASSY
Tel: 4 304 980

SUDAN EMBASSY
Tel: 4 725 240, 4 702 002

TANZANIA EMBASSY
Tel: 4 792 726, Fax: 4 724 172

UNITED KINGDOM EMBASSY
Tel: 4 799 760 / 2

UNITED STATES OF AMERICA EMBASSY
Tel: 4 250 593 / 5, Fax: 4 796 488
consularharare@state.gov
www.usembassy.state.gov/posts/zi1/wwhemb.html

ZAMBIA EMBASSY
Tel: 4 773 777, 4 740 936

Sleeping under the stars, Dogon Plateau, Mali.

AFRICA – PEOPLE AND PLACES

Page numbers in italics refer to pictures

Antique beer bottle hanging on rusty nail, Kolmanskop ghost town, Namibia.

African (Jackass) penguins, Boulders beach, Cape Town, South Africa

AFRICA – ADVENTURES

1st Cataract, *Nile* 55 L17
3rd Cataract, *Nile* 61 E17
4th Cataract, *Nile* 61 F19
5th Cataract, *Nile* 62 G2
6th Cataract, *Nile* 62 I1

A

Aalwynsfontein, 150 H8
Aandster, 146 H3
Aansluit, 145 F13
Aasvoëlbad, 113 L12
Aasvoëlnes, 115 L15
Aba, *DRC* 69 K15
Aba, *Nigeria* 66 I8
Abadla, 52 D1
Aba-Huab, 125 F16
Abaiat, 69 C18
Abaji, 66 E8
Abak, 66 I8
Abakaliki, 66 H9
Abala, *Congo* 72 D10
Abala, *Nigeria* 58 J7
Abalak, 58 J10
Abalessa, 58 A9
Abali, 248 F1
Abama, 244 M1
Abanga, 259 D5
Abar Abu Hiteita, 250 C3
Abar el Kanayis, 55 E11
Abar el Mukheisin, 250 D3
Abattekh, 51 H11
Abay, 70 B3
Abba, 67 I17
Abba Kella, 70 G3
Abba-Omega, 66 H9
Abbotsdale, 156 H9
Abdelcader, 70 C10
Abdessadok, 246 G6
Abdi, 60 M8
Abdir, 257 C8
Abdoulaye Faunal Reserve, 66 E1
Abdourta, 68 A4
Abebo, 69 F20
Abéché, 60 L7
Abejukolo, 66 F8
Abélajouad, 249 D2
Abelang, 259 E7
Abel Erasmus Pass, 139 I19
Abélma, *river* 249 L2
Abélma, 249 G3
Abelti, 70 F4
Abenab, 114 L6
Abengourou, 65 G14
Abeokuta, 66 G4
Aberdare National Park, 83 K16
Aberdeen, 158 D8
Aberfeldy, 147 L16
Abergele, 62 M8
Abgé, 248 E3
Abgue, 68 A3
Abidjan, 65 I14
Abiekwasputs, 144 H5
Abijatta-Shalla Lakes National Park, 70 G5
Abinsi, 66 F10
Abiya Adi, 62 L8
Abjelil, 49 F14
Abnub, 55 I16
Abo, 248 A7
Aboabo, 254 I5
Aboine, 255 G2
Aboisso, 65 I15
Aboja, 258 I4
Aboke, 69 D17
Abomey, 66 G2
Abong, 67 G12
Abong Mbang, 67 K15
Abora Dunkwa, 254 J6
Aboua, 72 B10
Abou Deïa, 68 B2
Aboukir, 250 C6
Aboun, 72 B3
Aboundji, 72 C8
Abou Telfane Faunal Reserve, 68 A2
Abrafo, 254 J5
Abre du Ténéré Monument (WHS), 59 G15
Abrem, 65 I17
Abreo, 244 J7
Abri, 61 D18
Ab Touyour, 68 A1
Abu Ballas, 55 L12
Abu Dis, 62 F2
Abu Dom, 61 G19
Abu Durba, 55 G18
Abu el Matamir, 250 D6
Abu Gabra, 69 B11
Abu Gandir, 250 G7
Abu Gubeiha, 69 B16
Abu Haggag, 250 C2
Abu Hamed, 62 E2
Abu Hammad, 250 E9
Abu Hashim, 69 B16
Abuja, 66 E8
Abu Kabisa, 61 L14
Abu Kebir, 55 E16
Abu Matariq, 69 B11
Abu-Mendi, 70 B2
Abu Mina, 250 D6
Abu Minqar, 250 M1
Abumombazi, 68 K6
Abunakombo, 73 B14
Abu Sari, 61 D18
Abu Simbel, 61 B19
Abu Simbel Temple, 63 J12
Abu Sir, 250 D5
Abu Sunt, 60 K10
Abu Tabari Oasis, 61 G15
Abu Tig, 55 I16
Abu Zabad, 69 A14
Abu Zayyan, 53 C17
Abwong, 69 E17
Abyad, 61 L14
Abydos, 251 G3
Abyei, 69 D13
Acalayong, 259 C2
Acampamento da Cameia, 76 H7
Accra, 65 I19
Achaacha, 49 C19
Achegour, 59 E17
Achelouma, 248 B1
Achénouma, 249 I9
Acholibur, 78 I1
Acojeja, 244 L2
Acoris, 250 I8
Acornhoek, 140 J1
Aculo, 76 F4
Adaba, 70 G6
Adachai, 82 A6
Adad, 71 D14
Adadi Mariam, 257 D2
Adadle, 71 D12
Adaigba, 66 H7
Adamax, 113 K16
Adams Mission, 155 F12
Adané, 72 C3
Adani, 66 G8
Adar, 68 B4
Adarama, 62 H4
Ad Darsia, 54 C4
Addax Sanctuary Strict Nature Reserve, 59 F14
Addi, 67 G16
Addis Ababa, 70 E5
Addis Zemen, 70 A4
Addo, 159 H13
Addo Elephant National Park, 159 G12
Ad Dubasi, 61 K20
Adefa, 65 G20
Adelaide, 159 D16
Adel Bagrou, 57 J15
Adele, 70 F7
Aden, 63 M15
Adendorp, 158 C10
Aderbissinat, 59 J12
Aderké, 248 B8
Adet, 70 B4
Adi Abun, 62 K8
Adi Arkay, 62 L7
Adiaso, 65 H18
Adi Daro, 62 K7
Adidome, 65 H19
Adigala, 70 C9
Adigrat, 62 K9
Adi Gudom, 62 L9
Adi Kaie, 62 K9
Adikas, 70 H2
Adilang, 78 K4
Adi Remoz, 258 E3
Adiri, 53 H17
Adis Abeba, *see Addis Ababa*
Adis Alem, 257 B1
Adi Ugri, 62 J8
Ado Awaiye, 66 F3
Adode, 249 D5
Ado-Ekiti, 66 F6
Adok, 69 F15
Adoru, 66 G8
Adoumandjali, 67 K18
Adoumri, 67 D15
Adranga, 69 L15
Adrar, 52 H2
Adrar des Iforhas, 58 E6
Adrar Plateau, 57 D11
Adrar Tinilim, 245 C3
Adra Sout Touf, 56 C6
Adré, 60 L9
Adriandampy, 48 K5
Aduka, 82 B1
Adunu, 66 D8
Adura, 66 D9
Adusa, 74 A5
Adwa, 62 K8
Adwari, 78 L3
Adzopé, 65 H15
Af'abet, 62 I8
Afferi, 65 H14
Afgooye, 71 M13
Afgrond, 278 K3
Afgundud, 80 J6
Afguns, 138 G8
Afia, 254 I5
Afiaso, 254 I5
Afikpo, 66 H9
Aflou, 52 A6
Afmadu, 85 H19
Afole, 66 F1
African Banks, 46 B10
Afwein, 84 H9
Aga, 250 D9
Agadem, 249 K9
Agadez, 59 H12
Agadir, 51 E13
Agaete, 45 I17
Agago, 78 J2
Agaie, 66 E7
Agalak, 249 D4
Agalengué, 249 B4
Aganga, 262 C10
Agarageur, 249 C4
Agaru, 69 B20
Agbar Bajiboji, 66 H7
Agbe, 258 F7
Agbelouve, 66 G1
Agboville, 65 H14
Agdz, 51 E16
Agere Maryam, 70 I5
Agere Selam, 257 L2
Aggeneys, 150 C9
Aghlabite Pools, 246 B10
Aghouedir, 57 C11
Agiert, 57 I12
Agiri, 59 L18
Aglal, 247 B9
Agnibilékrou, 65 G15
Ago-Are, 66 E4
Agogo, 65 G18
Agona, 65 H17
Agona Junction, 65 I16
Agona-Swedru, 65 I18
Agoro, *Ethiopia* 70 F3
Agoro, *Uganda* 78 G2
Agou, 65 H14
Agouénit, 57 H14
Agoulm, 245 I4
Agoumar, 68 I7
Agourii, 245 A3
Agter Sneeuberg, 159 B12
Agtertang, 153 I13
Aguamansa, 244 H8
Aguelal, 249 C4
Aguelhok, 58 E5
Aguelmouss, 245 F7
Aguelzim, 245 C2
Aguessis, 249 F4
Aguié, 59 L12
Agüimes, 45 K19
Agula, 62 L9
Agulai, 258 E8
Agule, 82 D5
Agulhas National Park, 157 M13
Agulo, 44 B8
Agwampt, 62 E4
Agwara, 66 C5
Agwata, 82 B2
Agwei, 69 F18
Agweri, 66 H7
Agwok, 69 F13
Ahaggar, 58 A10
Ahaggar (Hoggar) National Park, 58 A9
Aha Hills, 128 C3
Ahenkro, 65 G19
Ahero, 82 J9
Ahimahamasina, 48 J6
Ahmar Mountains, 70 D8
Ahoada, 66 I7
Ahrens, 155 C13
Ahsaad, 54 D9
Ai-Ais, 143 K15
Ai-Ais Hot-Springs Game Park, 143 J15
Aim Touta, 49 J14
Ain Beida, 49 J16
Ain Benian, 49 I12
Aïn Benimathar, 49 F16
Aïn Ben Tili, 51 J12
Ain Bousef, 49 J12
Ain Defla, 49 J11
Ain Deheb, 49 E20
Ain el Auoda, 49 F12
Ain el Hadjar, 49 E19
Ain el Hadjel, 49 J12
Ain el Hamara, 49 L11
Ain el Hammoth, 49 I13
Ain el Orak, 49 F19
Ain Fekan, 49 D19
Ain Jloula, 246 B9
Ain Khamassia, 246 C6
Ain Ksibai, 246 B5
Ain Madhi, 49 L11
Ain Mastour, 246 A8
Ain Mesria, 246 A5
Ain M'lila, 49 J15
Ain Oulmene, 49 J14
Aïn Oussera, 49 J12
Ain Sayada, 246 C7
Ain Sefra, 52 B3
Ain Senan, 246 B4
Ain Sukhna, 55 F16
Ain Tamr, 246 J7
Ain Temouchent, 49 D17
Ain Tounine, 246 K10
Aioun Ameur , 246 H3
Aïr Mountains, 59 G12
Aïr & Ténéré Natural Reserves, 59 G14
Ait Baha, 245 K1
Ait el Qaq, 245 B3
Ait Mellou, 51 E13
Ait Moudzit, 245 I6
Ait Saadaut, 51 E18
Aiyetoro, 66 F7
Ajai Game Reserve, 69 L16
Ajaokuta, 66 F7
Ajasse, 66 F5
Ajdabiya, 54 E4
Aje, 257 I1
Ajir, 67 B14
Ajumako, 254 J10
Ajumaku, 65 I18
Akaba, 66 F1
Akabli, 52 J4
Akagera National Park, 86 D2
Akaka, 72 E3
Akaki, 70 E6
Akamkpa, 66 I9
Akanous, 135 J18
Akanyaru, 263 F8
Akasha, 61 D18
Akatsi, 65 H20
Akaziat, 246 H8
Akbou, 49 I13
Akchar, 56 E6
Akelo, 69 G19
Akerker, 245 A4
Aketi, *river* 68 L8
Aketi, 68 L8
Akhmim, 55 J16
Akiéni, 72 D8
Akika Island, 262 H9
Akjoujt, 56 E7
Akka, 245 L3
Akkedisberg Pass, 157 K12
Aklampa, 66 F2
Aknoul, 49 E15
Akobo, *river* 70 G2
Akobo, 69 F18
Akok, 67 L11
Akokan, 249 C2
Akokora, 69 M13
Akom II, 67 L12
Akono, 67 K12
Akonolinga, 67 K14
Akonyaru, 260 I8
Akop, 69 F14
Akor, 57 K15
Akosombo, 65 H19
Akot, 69 G15
Akoupe, 65 H15
Akplabanya, 65 H19
Akra, 254 K9
Akrofrom, 254 K5
Aksoual, 245 C3
Aksum, 62 K8
Aksum (WHS), 62 K8
Akubu, 69 F19
Akula, 68 L3
Akum, 82 C6
Akurdet, 62 J7
Akure, 66 G6
Akurenan, 72 A4
Akwana, 255 E5
Akwanga, 66 E9
Akwaya, 255 B5
Akwi, 258 E2
Ala, 66 F10
Al Adam, 54 C8
Ala Draham, 49 I17
Alafiarou, 66 E2
Alage, 258 G8
Alaill Dadda, 70 A10
Alajeró, 44 D7
Alak Itenina, 48 J6
Alakuko, 66 G4
Alamata, 62 M9
Alam Nafaza, 250 E5
Alantika Mountains, 67 E14
Alaotra, 48 F9
Alapa, 66 E5
Al Aqabah, 55 F19
Alaska, 119 F17
Alati, 67 L15
Al Atshan, 62 L3
Alawa, 66 C8
Alawa Game Reserve, 66 D7
Al Aziziyah, 53 C17
Al Barun, 69 B19
Albasini Ruins, 278 K7
Albatross Island, 142 G6
Al Bayda, 54 C5
Albayzin Granada, 49 B16
Albert Falls, 155 D12
Albert Falls Dam, 280 H10
Albert Falls Nature Reserve, 155 D11
Albertinia, 157 K18
Albert Nile, 69 K17
Alberton, 147 D14
Albertshoek, 146 G4
Al Bidia, 68 C3
Albion, 46 J2
Alboran, 49 D16
Albrechts, 126 L3
Aldabra Atoll, 46 D7
Aldabra Atoll (WHS), 46 D6
Aldeia Chioco, 120 B8
Alderley, 160 B5
Aldinville, 155 D14
Alédjo, 252 M5
Aleg, 56 H7
Alegranza, 50 F9
Aleheride, 66 E1
Alel, 69 H16
Alemaya, 70 D9
Alemb, 72 D9
Alémbé, 72 C4
Alem Tena, 257 E4
Alen Nkoma, 259 E3
Alere, 66 F6
Alerek, 78 K5
Alettasrus, 146 E1
Alexander Bay, 143 M11
Alexandra, 147 C14
Alexandra Reservoir, 281 G7
Alexandria, *Egypt* 55 D13
Alexandria, *South Africa* 159 H15
Alexeck, 127 I18
Alfa Kouna, 252 G9
Alfândega, 72 K10
Al Gamamiya, 62 E1
Al Garef, 69 A20
Al-Gargara, 56 C5
Algarve, 49 B11
Algeciras, 49 C13
Alger, *see Algiers*
Algeria, 49 K12
Al Ghaba, 61 G18
Algiers, 49 I12
Al Haggounia, 50 H9
Alhambra Generalife, 49 B16
Al Harabah, 53 D15
Al Hasa Bay, 63 J17
Alheit, 132 C4
Al-Hilla, 61 L14
Al Hoceima, 49 D14
Al-Hudaida, 63 K12
Al Hulayq al Kabir, 54 I1
Ali, 68 H9
Alia, 266 J5
Alia Bay, *bay* 70 K2
Alia Bay, 70 K2
Aliade, 66 G10
Alibo, 70 D3
Alibori, 252 F9
Alicante, 49 A19
Alice, 159 E17
Alicedale, 159 G15
Alikalia, 64 E6
Alima, 73 D11
Alimbongo, 74 C6
Alindao, 68 I5
Aliquisanda, 101 I16
Ali Sabien, 70 B10
Aliwal North, 153 I17
Al Jabal al Akhdar, 54 D5
Al Jadidah, 55 G13
Al Jaghbub, 54 F9
Aljanare, 66 B4
Al Jawf, *Libya* 54 L7
Al Jawf, *Saudi Arabia* 63 B20
Al Jaws al Kabir, 53 C15
Al Kab, 62 E1
Alkamari, 59 L15
Al Kararim, 53 C19
Al Kawa, 62 L1
Al Khums, 53 C18
Allada, 66 G2
Allal Tazi, 49 E12
Allamanda, 46 F5
Allandale, 153 B19
Allangouassou, 65 F14
Allanridge, 146 J8
Allareni, 58 L5
Allbori, 66 B3
Alldays, 139 B14
Allemanskraal Dam, 147 L11
Allep, 153 E12
Allia Bay, *bay* 79 G15
Allia Bay, 79 G15
Allomo, 255 F1
All Saints Nek, 154 M2
Alma, *Mauritius* 46 J4
Alma, *South Africa* 138 I10
Alma, *South Africa* 146 J9
Almagro, 45 I17
Al Mahbas, 51 H13
Almahel, 70 B1
Al Maqrun, 54 D4
Al Marj, 54 C5
Almeria, 49 B17
Al Mota, 249 M2
Almusa, 258 L1
Alnif, 51 D18
Aloi, 78 M3
Alojera, 44 B5
Alouf, 248 D3
Alpha, 148 J5
Alphonse, 46 D10
Alphonse Islands, 46 D9
Al Qala's, 53 D18
Al Qaryah ash Shargiyah, 53 E17
Al Qatrun, 53 L18
Al-Qulayd Bahri, 61 F18
Al Quwaisi, 62 L3
Al Rahibat, 53 D16
Al Taj, 54 L8
Al Tamini, 54 C7
Alta Vista, 244 J10
Altenstein, 127 M12
Alto Cuilo, *Angola* 76 F5
Alto Cuito, *Angola* 76 J4
Alto de Chimoche, 244 M4
Alto Hama, 75 H20
Alto Ligonha, 110 K9
Alto Molócu, 110 K6
Alton, 279 M4
Alua, 111 D16
Aluakluak, 69 H15
Aluk, 69 E12
Al Uwaynat, 53 K14
Alwero, 69 F19
Al Wigh, 53 L18
Al Wittyah, 53 C15
Amabele, 159 D20
Amach Kalo, 58 J8
Amada Gaza, 67 J17
Amada Temple, 63 J13
Amadi, *DRC* 69 K11
Amadi, *Sudan* 69 I15
Amake, 57 J11
Amaku, 255 D3
Amala, 83 M12
Amaler, 83 C13
Amalia, 146 H3
Amamula, 74 C5
Amandas, 119 F20
Amani, 247 K9
Amanzamnyama, 268 M7
Amanzimtoti, 155 F13
Amatikulu, 155 B15
Amaya, 83 E16
Amba, 247 H5
Amba Giyorgis, 258 G3
Ambahivahikely, 274 C4
Ambakirano, 274 E7
Ambalabe, 48 E7
Ambalavao, 48 J6
Ambam, 67 L12
Amba Madre, 258 E4
Ambanja, 48 C8
Ambarakaraka, 274 F5
Ambararafa, 274 E7
Ambaras, 258 C5
Ambarilao, 274 E8
Ambata, 274 F4
Ambatafinandrahana, 48 I6
Ambato Boeny, 48 E7
Ambatoharanana, 274 G6
Ambatojoly, 274 C4
Ambatolahy, 48 H5
Ambatolampy, 48 H7
Ambatomainty, 48 F5
Ambatondrazaka, 48 F8
Ambe, 74 E2
Ambidédi, 56 K9
Ambikwa, 258 B9
Ambilobe, 48 B9
Ambinaninony, 48 G8
Ambinanitelo, 48 D9
Ambiri, 247 F3
Ambleside Cemetery, 280 D6
Amboahangy, 48 L5
Amboasary, 48 G7
Ambodiatafana, 48 F9
Ambodifotatra, 48 F9
Ambodiriana, 48 G8
Ambohidrabiby, 274 I1
Ambohidratrimo, 48 G7
Ambohimanga Atsimo, 48 I7
Ambohinihaonana, 48 J7
Amboiva, 75 G18
Ambolobozobe, 274 C8
Ambondromamy, 48 E7
Ambondromifehy, 274 F8
Ambondrona, 274 F7
Amboni, 95 E17
Amboni Caves, 95 E16
Amborondolo, 274 F6
Amboseli Biosphere Reserve, 88 H9
Amboseli National Park, 88 H10
Ambositra, 48 I6
Ambovombe, 48 M4
Ambre Forest Reserve, 274 A3
Ambriz, 75 C17
Ambriz Protected Reserve, 75 D17
Ambrose Bay, 125 G12
Am Dafok, 68 C7
Am Dam, 60 M6
Am Deressa, 60 M7
Am Djelato, 248 G4
Am Djéména, 60 L3
Am Doutile, 68 B4
Amelia Bay, 101 C14
Am el Melh, 49 K13
Ameloloud, 249 L1
Amentego Megauda, 61 G18
Amersfoort, 148 G1
Amersid, 245 G9
Ameya, 70 G3
Amhara, 70 C3
Amino, 81 D18
Aminuis, 135 F16
Amirantes Islands, 46 C9
Amisa, 254 I7
Amitié, 47 B15
Amizmiz, 51 D15
Am Khoumi, 60 M6
Am Léiouna, 60 M8
Ammaedara, 246 C4
Amman, 55 C19
Amolitar, 82 C1
Amos, 158 E4
Amou Oblo, 65 G20
Amourj, 57 I15
Amoya, 65 H16
Ampangorina, 274 F4
Ampanihy, 48 L3
Ampanolahamirafy, 48 A9
Ampara, 133 E16
Ampasimanolotra, 48 G8
Ampasimbengy, 274 D6
Ampasinambo, 48 I7
Amper, 67 D11
Ampisikinana, 48 B10
Ampitatafika, 48 H6
Ampondra, 274 F9
Ampondrahazo, 274 B8
Ampondralava, 274 E5
Amporaha, 48 B8
Ampotaka, 48 M3
Amrourough, 245 D3
Amsouzart, 245 D3
Amspoort, 112 L7
Amsterdam, 148 E4
Am Timan, 68 C3
Amudat, 82 B9
Amuria, 82 B4
Am Zoer, 60 K8
Anaba, 66 C6
Anakao, 48 L3
Analafolaka, 48 J6
Analalava, 48 D7
Analamazaotra (Périnet) Special Reserve, 48 G8
Analamerana Special Reserve, 48 B9
Analavory, 48 G6
Ananda-Kouadiokro, 65 G14
Anantsono, 48 K3
Anataka, 48 D7
Ancuabe, 103 M15
Ancuaze, 121 D15
Andaga, 67 B15
Andaingo Gara, 48 G8
Andalatanosy, 48 L5
Andapa, 48 D9
Andara, 115 G19
Andasibe, 274 I6
Andasifahatelo, 274 H8
Andavaka Caves, 48 L3
Andemby, 274 F4
Anden Verde, 45 J16
Andéramboukane, 58 J6
Andilamena, 48 F8
Andilana, 48 B8
Andilanatoby, 48 G7
Andjou, 68 H5
Ando, 261 M5
Andoany, 48 C7
Andohalela, 48 L5
Andohalela Nature Reserve, 48 M5
Andohara, 48 G7
Andonakoomby, 274 D2
Andoni, *oasis* 114 I2
Andoni, 114 I1
Andonivlakte, 276 B8
Andouk Foula, 259 D3
Andover Game Reserve, 140 J1
Andrafiabe, 274 F6
Andrafiabe Cave, 274 G7
Andramasina, 274 K2
Andranofanjava, 274 B2
Andranolava, 48 K4
Andranomafana, 48 J3
Andranomavo, 48 E5
Andranomena, 48 G8
Andranopasy, 48 I3
Andranosamonta, 48 C7
Andranovondronina, 274 A6
Andranovory, 48 K4
Andrea, 48 F5
André Félix National Park, 68 D7
Andrevo, 274 D7
Andriba, 48 F6
Andrieskraal, 158 I9
Andriesvale, 144 G6
Andringitra Nature Reserve, 48 J6
Androka, 48 M3
Androranga, 48 C9
Andudu, 69 L13
Andújar, 49 A15
Andulo, 76 G1
Anefis I-n-Darane, 58 G4
Anécho, 66 H1
Aneker, 58 J9
Aney, 59 E18
Angaradebou, 66 B3
Angíata Kiti, 264 H8
Anger, 70 D3
Angereb, *river* 62 L6
Angereb, 62 L6
Ango, *river* 68 J10
Ango, 68 J10
Angoche, 123 A16
Angola, 75 F18
Angu, 68 K8
Angwa, 119 A18
Anhanca, 113 B17
Anie, 66 F1
Anikou, 261 E8
Aninous Pass, 150 C5
Anivorano-Avatra, 274 D3
Anja-Belitsaka, 48 L3
Anjahambé, 48 F8
Anjavinihavana, 274 B4
Anjiabe, 274 E9
Anjiamangirana, 48 D8
Anjo, 80 H10
Anjohibe Caves, 48 D6
Anjomá Ramartina, 48 H5
Anjozorobe, 48 G7
Anka, 66 A7
Ankaako Junction, 254 J4
Ankarana, 274 E5
Ankarana Special Reserve, 48 B9
Ankaratra, 274 L1
Ankarena, 48 F9
Ankavandra, 48 G5
Ankazoabo, 48 J4
Ankazobe, 48 G6
Ankazomborona, 48 E7
Ankazomiriotra, 48 H6
Ankazondandy, 274 I2
Ankify, 274 F4
Ankijahabe, 274 B2
Ankililioka, 48 K3
Ankilizato, 48 H4
Ankorefo, 274 A2
Ankoro, 77 B13
Ankpa, 66 G9
Annaba, 49 I16
Ann's Villa, 159 G13
An Nuba, 61 G17
Anomabu, 254 L7
Anorotsanga, 274 G2
Anosibe An'Ala, 274 M4
Anou, 249 D3
Anpondriampaihy Cave, 274 G7
Ansaba, 48 C9
Anse aux Anglais, 47 G18
Anse aux Pins, 46 D5
Anse Boileau, 46 E4
Anse Boileau Church, 46 E4
Anse Boudin, 47 B15
Ansebu, 62 I7
Anse de Grand Sable, 46 K6
Anse Etoile, 273 E8
Anse Grand Var, 47 I18
Anse Jasmin Estate, 273 G3
Anse Kerlan, 47 B14
Anse La Blague, 47 B17
Anse Lazio, 47 B15
Anse Major, 46 B2
Anse Nord-d'Est, 46 A4
Anse Polite, 46 E3
Anse Possession, 47 B15
Anse Quitor, 47 J17
Anse Royale, 46 E5
Anse Royale Bay, 46 F5
Anse Soleil Beach, 46 E3
Anse Volbert Village, 47 B15
Ansongo, 58 J4
Antaeopolis, 55 I16
Antafiambotry, 274 F4
Antalaha, 48 D10
Antananarivo, 48 H7
Antanifotsy, 48 J6
Antanimenabaka, 48 F8
Antat, 273 J5
Antejévez, 45 K16
Anti Atlas, 51 F14
Antikwaa, 254 I5
Antiwirifa, 65 G16
Antoetra, 48 I7
Antoncojo, 44 D7
Antongila Bay, *Madagascar* 48 E9
Antongila Bay, *Malawi* 97 L15
Antongombato, 274 A3
Antongonivo, 274 B2
Antonibe, 48 D7
Antranoambo, 48 E8
Antsahabe, 48 D8
Antsahampano, 274 B6
Antsakabary, 48 D8
Antsakoakely, 274 D4
Antsalaka, 274 C4
Antsalova, 48 G5
Antsambalahy, 48 D9
Antsatrabonko, 274 F6
Antsatrabonko Cave, 274 F7
Antserasera, 274 D8
Antsiafabositra, 48 F7
Antsirabato, 48 D10
Antsirabe, 48 H7
Antsiranana, 48 B9
Antsisikala, 274 B7
Antsoha, 48 H5
Antsohihy, 48 D7
Antsohimbondrona, 48 B8
Antsondrovava, 48 G4
Antsorokaka, 274 C6
Anum, *river* 65 H18
Anum, 65 H19
Anyama, 65 I14
Anyau, 69 K16
Anyeke, 69 L18
Anyinam, 65 H18
Anyirawase, 65 H19
Anysberg, 157 H16
Anysspruit, 148 G4
Anzi, 73 D19
Aouderas, 249 E4
Aoufous, 51 D19
Aouhéhida, 249 F9
Aouinat er Rajjat, 57 I15
Aoukale, 68 D4
Aoukar, 57 G11
Aoukâr, 57 B17
Aoulouz, 51 E15
Aourou, 56 J9
Aozou, 60 C3
Apac, 69 M18
Apam, 254 K10
Apawanta, 74 A6
Aphroditopolis, 55 K17
Api, 68 K10
Aplahoue, 66 G1
Apoka, 78 G5
Apoko, 72 C10
Apolu, 66 E4
Aprompronou, 65 G15
Aqiq, 62 G7
Araa, 94 E4
Ara Arba, 70 H8
Arab, 62 G4
Arabia, 81 H17
Arada, 60 J7
Arafali, 62 J9
Arafo, 244 I10
Arage, 66 E9
Arago, 78 J1
Araka, 69 J15
Arakao, 249 C5
Arandis, 124 A9
Aranos, 135 H15
Araouane, 57 F19
Arash, 264 G8
Ara Terra, 70 H8
Arawale National Reserve, 90 C2
Arba, 257 B10
Arba'at, 62 E5
Arba des Beni Hassan, 49 D13
Arba Minch, 70 H4
Arbole, 57 M20
Arboretum, 279 M4
Arboutchatak, 67 A19
Archer's Post, 84 G2
Arcturus, 120 H2
Arebi, 69 L14
Arege, 59 L18
Arekwa, 62 L8
Arema, 258 I6
Arendsness, 113 K15
Arero, 80 C6
Arg, 245 B2
Argana, 245 J2
Argent, 147 C17
Argin, 258 B7
Argo, 61 E18
Arguas de Firgas, 45 I18
Arguayoda, 44 D6
Argungu, 58 M8
Arhbalou, 245 I4
Ariamsvlei, 144 K4
Aribinda, 58 K2
Arico, 244 M8
Arico el Nuevo, 244 M8
Arico el Viejo, 244 M8
Arinaga, 45 L20
Aripe, 244 L2
Aris, 134 B8
Arjo, 70 E3
Arjout, 245 B5
Arken-Ahon, 248 D9
Arli, 66 B1
Arlington, 147 K13
Arlit, 59 F12
Arly, *river* 252 G5
Arly, 252 G4
Arly Faunal Reserve, 66 B2
Arly Partial Faunal Reserve, 66 B1
Armant, 55 K17
Armony, 47 K15
Arniston, 157 L14
Aroab, 144 F3
Arochuku, 66 I8
Aroe, 114 J2
Aroma, 62 J5
Aroumd, 245 C2
Arquipélago dos Bijagós, 64 C1
Arrah, 65 G14
Arrecife, 45 E14
Arrieta, 45 C14
Ar-Ruat, 69 A17
Artemou, 56 J9
Artenara, 45 J17
Arthur's Seat, 280 E4
Aru, 69 L16
Arua, 69 L16
Aruba Dam, 266 I8
Arucas, 45 I19
Arufu, 66 F10
Arumbi, 69 L15
Arure, 44 B6
Arusha, *admin.* 94 B6
Arusha, 88 K7
Arusha National Park, 88 J8
Aruwimi, 73 A20
Arzew, 49 D18
Asa, *DRC* 68 J10
Asa, *Kenya* 89 F19
Asab, 135 M11
Asahaha, 81 H15
Asankranguaa, 65 H16
Asasa, 257 J5
Asawinso, 65 H16
Asbes, 278 L3
Asbesberge, 145 M15
Asbe Teferi, 70 E8
Asbospan, 143 E12
Asedjrad, 52 K4
Asela, 70 F6
Asembe, 82 J7
Asendobo, 70 F3
Asfun el Matana, 251 H3
Asha, 66 G4
Ashburton, 155 E11
Ashigashiya, 256 C5
Ashira, 71 C19
Ash Pit, 265 C4
Ash-Shuheit, 62 L4
Ash Shuwayrif, 53 F18
Ashton, 157 I14
Asikuma, 254 H8
Asilah, 49 D13
Askaoun, 245 J3
Askeaton, 153 M20
Askham, 144 G7
Askira, 67 C14
Askraal, 157 J16
Asla, 52 B4
Asmara, 62 J8
Asnet, 60 L5
Asni, 51 D15
Asosa, 69 C20
Asriko, 65 F13
Assa, 51 G13
Assab, 63 M13
As Sabkhah al Kabirah, 54 F3
Assa Gaila, 70 A10
Assaikio, 66 E10
Assale, 258 D10
Assamakka, 58 E10
Assaouas, 249 F2
Assaq, 50 L6
Assdadah, 53 D18
Assegaaibos, 158 I9
Assen, 138 L7
As Sidr, 54 E2
Assif n'Ait Mizane, 245 B2
Assif Tizgui, 245 D3
Assin Aiyinabrim, 254 H7
Assin-Attandanso Game Reserve, 254 H5
Assinie, 65 I15
Assin Manso, 254 I7
Assodé, 249 D4
Assok, 72 B4
Assok Begue, 259 C7
Assok Ngomo, 259 A7
As Sultan, 54 D2
As-Sumay, 69 D12
Assumption, 46 E7
Aston Bay, 158 J10
Astove, 46 E8
Astroea, 46 L4
Asuefri, 65 F15
Asueso Forest Reserve, 254 I6
Aswan, 55 L18
Aswan High Dam, 55 M18
Asyut, 55 I15
Atakpamé, 66 F1
Atar, 56 D9
Atasi Nkwanta, 65 H17
Atbara, *river* 62 H3
Atbara, 62 G2
Atchewa, 62 H8
Atebubu, 65 F18
Ateku, 254 I3
Ateppi, 69 K17
Atesa, 65 H16
Athanese, 273 G5
Athi, 89 D12
Athi River, 88 C9
Athribis, 251 F2
Ati, 60 L4
Atiak, 69 K17
Ati Ardébé, 60 M3
Atiedo, 69 F12
Atim, 60 L7
Atira, 82 C4
Atlanta, 138 L7
Atlante del Sol, 45 E11
Atlantic Ocean, 64 G2
Atlantis, 156 H8
Atobiase Junction, 254 J3
Atome, 75 H18
Atongo Bakari, 68 H5
Atsbi, 258 E8
Atsuku, 255 F7
Atta, 67 H13
Attara, 247 E2
Atteridgeville, 147 B14
Atunukwe, 262 E1
Atura, 69 M18
Atwiy, 50 L7
Aúbe, 123 B16
Auchi, 66 G7
Augrabies, 151 A15
Augrabies Falls, 144 M5
Augrabies Falls National Park, 144 L4
Auheib, 127 M16
Aujara, 67 A11
Aulia, 62 J1
Auma, 68 L7
Auna, 66 C5
Auno, 67 A14
Auob, 135 I13
Aus, *oasis* 113 L19
Aus, 142 E10
Ausnek, 143 F11
Austin's Post, 153 D15
Avabuki, 74 A4
Avindi, 68 I4
Avoca, 148 B6
Avond, 126 G4
Avondrust, 157 H14
Avontuur, *South Africa* 145 F15
Avontuur, *South Africa* 158 I5
Awae, 67 K13
Awakaba, 68 E3
Awara Plain, 70 K8
Aware, 71 F12
Awasa, 70 G5
Awash, 70 E7
Awash Falls, 257 C8
Awash National Park, 70 E6
Awash Wenz, 70 C7
Aw Dheegle, 71 J19
Awe, 66 F10
Aweil, 69 E12
Awfist, 50 K6
Awgaro, 62 K6
Awgu, 66 H8
Awjilah, 54 G5
Awka, 66 H8
Awsard, 56 B8
Axim, 65 J16
Ayachi, 245 G8
Ayagaures, 45 L17
Ayaise, 254 J6
Ayale, 255 E2
Ayame, 65 I15
Ayamikem, 67 M11
Ayanfure, 65 H16
Ayangba, 66 F8
Aye Koyé, 64 B4
Ayem, 259 F6
Ayina, 67 L14
Ayinwafi, 65 G18
Aykel, 62 M6
Ayn al Ghazal, 61 C11
Ayn al Ghazalah, 54 C7
Ayod, 69 F16
Ayorou, 58 K4
Ayos, 67 J14
Ayoun el Atrous, 57 H12
Aysha, 70 C9
Azaough, 58 H8
Azare, 67 B11
Azarori, 58 K10
Azazga, 49 I13
Azefal, 56 D7
Azelik, 249 E5
Azemmour, 51 B15
Azena, 258 L2
Azer n Fad, 249 E1
Azezo, 62 M7
Azib Imi n Ouassif, 245 D2
Azib Likemt, 245 C4
Azib Tamsoult, 245 C2
Azib Tifni, 245 C3
Azilal, 245 H6
Azingo, 259 G2
Az Izouggaghene, 245 D2
Azoum, 248 E5
Azrak, 248 E4
Azrou, 51 B18
Az Zawiyah, 53 C16
Az Zintan, 53 D16

B

Baadjie, 112 L10
Baanta, 71 K16
Baantama, 65 F18
Baardheere, 70 L10
Baardskeerdersbos, 157 L12
Baba, 67 H19
Bababe, 56 I7
Babaera, 75 I19
Bab al Maknusah, 53 J16
Babana, 66 C4
Babanango, 148 L5
Babangata Barkiré, 252 C7
Babangiboni, 280 C2
Babanusa, 69 B12
Babar, 49 K15
Babati, 94 B4
Bab Berred, 245 C9
Babelegi, 138 M10
Babia, 69 J12
Babi-Babi, 135 A17
Babile, 70 E9
Babile Elephant Sanctuary, 70 E9
Babizhi, 270 I6
Babomeni Drift, 140 A2
Babonde, 69 L12
Babongena, 74 B2
Babongo, 67 G16
Baboua, 67 H17
Babouro, 247 M7
Bab Taza, 49 E14
Babuatse, 132 L7
Babura, 59 M13
Bacaadweyn, 71 G16
Bachalo, 64 F4
Baché, 256 G4
Bachelors Point, 281 D4
Bachuo Akakbe, 67 I11
Bactili, 85 C16
Bada, 70 F6
Badagri, 66 H3
Badanga, 67 B19
Badda Rogghie, 70 E4
Badeggi, 66 E7
Bader, 59 K11
Badera, 85 K19
Badeyuicheri, 58 K9
Badi, 64 D4
Badinko Faunal Reserve, 57 L12
Badir, 67 C14
Badjer, 67 H16
Badjoud, 252 L4
Badogo, 64 B10
Badou, 65 F20
Badplaas, 148 C4
Badzere, 67 H16
Baediam, 56 J9
Bafang, 67 I11
Bafatá, 64 A3
Bafia, 67 J12
Bafilo, 66 D1
Bafing, 64 A8
Bafing-Makana, 64 A8
Bafoulabe, 56 L10
Bafousam, 67 I12
Bafu Bay, 64 I8
Bafut, 67 H11
Bafwabalinge, 74 B4
Bafwaboli, 74 B3
Bafwagadi, 74 A2
Bafwasende, 74 A3
Baga, 59 L19
Bagaji, 58 L7
Bagamayo, 93 K16
Bagamoyo, 95 K16
Bagana, 66 F8
Bagandou, 261 B9
Bagani, 116 I4
Bagaroua, 58 K8
Bagata, 73 G13
Bagaya, 68 H4
Bagbara, 68 I2
Bagega, 66 B7
Bageya, 58 M10
Bagodo, 67 H15
Bagoe, 65 E12
Bagoé, 65 B12
Baguineda, 57 M14
Bagzane, 249 E4
Bahdur Island, 62 G7
Bahi, 94 I2
Bahia de Avila, 45 E12
Bahia de las Calcosas, 44 J3
Bahia de los Roques, 44 F4
Bahia de Naos, 44 M2
Bahia de Tijimiraque, 44 K4
Bahig, 250 D5
Bahinga, 74 I4
Bahir Dar, 70 B3
Bahi Swamp, 94 J1
Bahita, 258 I2
Bahn, 64 G9
Bahra el Manzala, 250 C10
Bahra Maryut, 250 C6
Bahr Azoum, 68 B5
Bahr Azrak, 68 B4
Bahr Bola, 68 C3
Bahr Dosseo, 68 D4
Bahr-el-Arab, 68 C10
Bahr el Arab, 69 D13
Bahr el Ghazal, *Chad* 60 K3
Bahr el Ghazal, *Sudan* 69 F11
Bahr el Jebel, 69 J17
Bahr ez Zaraf, 69 F16
Bahr Kéita, 68 D3
Bahr Salamat, 68 D2
Baía da Condúcia, 111 H19
Baía de Cabinda, 72 I5
Baía de Fernão Veloso, 111 F19
Baia de Inhambane, 141 F17
Baía de Maputo, 149 C12
Baía de Memba, 111 E19
Baía de Pemba, 103 L19
Baía de Pomene, 141 C18
Baía de Setúbal, 49 A11
Baía de Sofala, 133 E16
Baía do Bengo, 75 D17
Baía dos Tigres, 112 A1
Baía Farta, 75 I17
Baía Massane, 133 E16
Baía Metizane, 133 F16
Baibokoum, 67 F18
Baida Baila, 256 I9
Baidou, *CAR* 68 G5
Baidou, *CAR* 68 H4
Baie aux Chagrins, 46 C1
Baie aux Hutres, 47 H17
Baie de Corisco, 72 B2
Baie de l'Est, 47 H20
Baie de Sangareya, 64 D3
Baie de Tamarin, 46 K1
Baie du Cap, 46 L2
Baie du Nord, 47 H17
Baie du Tombeau, 46 I2
Baie Lazare Village, 46 F4
Baie Ternaie Marine National Park, 273 I2
Baie Topaze, 47 I17
Baikoré, 248 G4
Baila, 56 M4
Bailey, 159 A17
Bailly, 261 H7
Bailundo, 75 H20
Baines' Baobabs, 129 E17
Baines' Drift, 139 A12
Baissa, 67 G12
Baixo Longa, 76 L3
Bajoga, 67 C13
Bajone, 122 E9
Baka, 68 J3
Bakala, 68 H4
Bakaore, 60 J8
Bakebe, 67 H11
Bakel, 56 K8
Baker, 262 H2
Bakerville, 146 C7
Bakin Birji, 59 K13
Bako, *Côte d'Ivoire* 65 E11
Bako, *Ethiopia* 70 E4
Bakordi, 69 J13
Bakori, 66 B8
Bakouma, 68 H7
Bakoumba, 72 E7
Bakoven, 281 F4
Bakoy, 64 A9
Bakundi, 255 D7
Bakwa-Kenge, 73 H17
Bala, *Senegal* 56 L8
Bala, *Uganda* 82 A1
Balabaiba, 75 H18
Balachu Rocks, 266 I10
Balaka, 109 I15
Balaki, 64 A6
Balama, 111 B11
Balangala, 73 B15
Balat, 55 K14
Balaza, 256 D7
Balch, 257 B6
Bale, *river* 64 A8
Bale, 76 K1
Balelesberg, 148 I2
Bale Mountains National Park, 70 H7
Baleni, 99 D19
Balesa, 79 G19
Balesa Kulai, 79 L18
Baleyara, 58 L7
Balfour, *South Africa* 147 E16
Balfour, *South Africa* 159 D17
Balgowan, 154 D10
Balguda, 266 H8
Bali, 67 H11
Balifondo, 68 I7

(Bal-Bri) Touring Index 321

Balili, 67 C18
Balise 250 Poste Weygan, 52 L3
Balisson, 46 K4
Balle, 57 J13
Ballengeich, 148 J1
Ballito, 155 D14
Ba Illi, 248 K4
Balloul, 49 E19
Balmoral, 147 B17
Balo, 64 A8
Balombe, 76 K2
Balombo, *river* 75 H19
Balombo, 75 H18
Baltim, 55 D15
Baltimore, 139 D11
Balule Game Reserve, 139 H20
Balunda, 73 F14
Balunga, 74 I2
Bam, 67 F18
Bama, 67 B15
Bamake, 64 J10
Bamako, 57 M13
Bamara, 261 A5
Bamba, *Congo* 73 I13
Bamba, *DRC* 69 J11
Bamba, *Kenya* 89 K19
Bamba, *Mali* 58 H2
Bambadinca, 64 A3
Bambam, 67 D13
Bambama, 72 E7
Bambara, 68 E2
Bambara-Maounde, 57 J20
Bambaran, 57 L12
Bambari, 68 H4
Bambesi, 69 D20
Bambey, 56 K4
Bambili, 68 K10
Bambio, 261 B7
Bamboi, 65 F16
Bambos de Sonhe, 72 L10
Bambous, 46 J2
Bambous Mountains, 46 K5
Bambouti, 69 I12
Bambui, 67 H11
Bamenda, 67 H11
Bame Town, 64 I8
Bamingui, *river* 68 E2
Bamingui, 68 F4
Bamingui-Bangoran National Park, 68 F2
Bamusso, 66 J10
Bana Danied, 56 K7
Banagi, 87 G19
Banalia, 68 M9
Banamba, 57 L14
Banandje, 65 E11
Banangui, 68 I9
Banani, 247 K9
Banankoro, *Guinea* 64 E8
Banankoro, *Mali* 57 L16
Banarera el Gaunche, 244 G7
Banc d'Arguin National Park (WHS), 56 E5
Banc du Geyser, 48 B7
Banda, *Burundi* 91 C15
Banda, *Congo* 67 F15
Banda, *DRC* 72 G6
Bandabe, 48 D9
Bandae, 65 I16
Bandaka, 73 C15
Bandakami, 72 H8
Bandal, 67 G16
Bandama, *river* 65 E13
Bandama, 45 J19
Bandama Blanc, 253 E2
Bandama Rouge, 65 E11
Bandana, 65 H14
Bandar, *Ghana* 65 F16
Bandar, *Mozambique* 121 C13
Bandarbeyla, 71 D19
Bandawe, 101 H12
Bandawe Point, 101 H13
Bande, 68 H10
Bandelierkop, 139 E16
Bandia, 67 I11
Bandiagara, 57 K19
Bandjoukri, 67 F16
Bandjoun, 67 I12
Ban Donige, 69 C18
Bandrany, 274 G3
Bandrélé, 48 B6
Bandua, 133 D15
Bandula, 120 M8
Bandundu, *admin.* 73 F14
Bandundu, 73 F11
Bandur, 139 B15
Banfele, 64 C7
Banfora, 65 C13
Bang, 67 G18
Banga, *Angola* 72 L9
Banga, *DRC* 73 H15
Banga, *DRC* 73 I15
Banga, *river* 68 H6
Bangadi, 69 J12
Bangala Dam Recreational Park, 132 G2
Banga Melo, 68 K3
Bangana, 68 F7
Bangangte, 67 I12
Bangare, 58 L4
Bangari Pinza Range, 132 G6
Bangassou, 68 J6
Bangbali, 68 E4
Bangem, 255 J5
Banghazi, 54 C4
Banglang, 255 D10
Bangolo, 64 G10
Bangonomo, 279 F3
Bangoran, *river* 68 E3
Bangoran, 68 F4
Bangouren, 67 H11
Bangu, 76 E9
Bangue, 67 L17
Bangui, 68 J2
Bangui-Motaba, 261 E8
Banguito, 247 G3
Bangula, 121 C17
Banguru, 74 B4
Bangweulu Swamps, 77 G17
Banh, 57 K20
Banhine National Park, 140 C7
Bani, *Burkina Faso* 58 L3
Bani, *CAR* 68 G6
Bani, *river* 65 A11
Bania, 67 J18
Baniati, 259 H9
Bani Bangou, 58 J6
Banie, 64 B8
Banifing, 65 C11
Banigoungou, 252 D9
Banikane, 247 D5
Banikoara, 66 B2
Banima, 68 I8
Banissa, 70 K7
Bani Walid, 53 D17
Banjul, 56 L3
Bank, 147 D12
Bankass, 57 K19
Bankberg, 159 B11
Banket, 119 F18
Bankilare, 58 K4
Bankim, 67 H13
Bankkop, 148 E3
Banko, *Guinea* 64 C7
Banko, *Mali* 65 A12
Bankon, 64 B9
Banmaanka Saraar, 71 D14
Banner Rest, 154 K10
Bansara, 66 H9
Bantadjé, 67 F15
Bantakoto, 57 M11
Bante, 66 E2
Bantry Bay, 281 C5
Banvayo, 65 E15
Banvo, 76 E5
Banya, 87 K16
Banya Fort, 79 D15
Banyo, 67 G13
Banza, 68 L2
Banza Sanda, 72 H8
Banza Sosso, 72 I9
Bao, 67 E18
Baoro, 67 H18
Baoule, 57 L12
Baoulé, 65 A11
Bape, 137 B14
Bapsfontein, 147 C16
Bara, *Nigeria* 67 C12
Bara, *Sudan* 61 L18
Baraawe, 71 K18
Baraboulé, 58 K1
Barafu Kopjes, 264 H7
Baragli, 89 H20
Baragoi, 83 B17
Bara Issa, 57 I18
Baraka, *river* 62 I6
Baraka, 91 A12
Barakke, 159 C11
Baranga, 69 K11
Barani, 57 L18
Baraoueli, 57 L15
Barasa, 256 J1
Baray, 264 L8
Barbarons, *area* 273 L9
Barbarons, *peak* 46 D4
Barbarons, *river* 273 M9
Barbarons Beach, 273 L8
Barberspan, 146 E5
Barberspan Nature Reserve, 146 E5
Barberton, 148 B5
Bardagué, 248 A7
Bardaï, 60 C3
Bare, 70 J10
Barentu, 62 J7
Bargoni, 90 F5
Bari, *river* 68 K2
Bari, 66 C6
Bariadi, 87 H16
Bariati, 264 H3
Baricho, 89 J20
Baridi, 87 F16
Barika, 49 K14
Baringa, 73 B16
Baris, 55 L15
Barkedji, 56 J6
Barkewo el Ablod, 56 H9
Barkly East, 154 J1
Barkly Pass, *pass* 154 K2
Barkly West, 146 M1
Barland, 280 L8
Barmou, 58 J9
Baro, *river* 70 F1
Baro, 66 E7
Baroda, 159 B13
Baroe, 158 G10
Barotse Flood Plain, 104 K6
Barotseland, 104 K8
Baroua, 68 I8
Barqah al Bayda, 54 E4
Barqat al-Bahriya, 54 D9
Barra do Dande, 75 D17
Barraga Sbiba, 246 C6
Barrage al-Massire, 51 C16
Barrage al Wahda, 245 D8
Barrage de Poubara, 72 E8
Barrage Djorf-Torba, 52 D1
Barrage Mohamed V, 49 E16
Barranco de Castro, 244 H4
Barranco de Chinquejo, 244 K7
Barranco de Herques, 244 K10
Barranco del Agua, 244 I9
Barranco de la Reina, 244 J9
Barranco de las Aguas, 244 M6
Barranco de la Zaza, 244 I8
Barranco del Cazador, 244 K2
Barranco del Niágara, 244 L2
Barranco del Rio, 244 L6
Barranco de Luchón, 244 L7
Barranco de Palmero, 244 J8
Barranco de San Pedro, 244 H9
Barranco de Santiago, 44 D8
Barranco de Sáuces, 244 K8
Barranco Helecho, 244 L9
Barranco Tamay, 244 I9
Barranco Teresme, 244 M3
Barra Peninsula, 141 G18
Barret's, 280 L7
Barrington, 158 I4
Barry Church, 157 K16
Barrydale, 157 I16
Barsalago, 58 L2
Barsaloi, 83 D17
Bartibougou, 252 C3
Basacato, 66 K10
Basali, 73 A19
Basanga, 74 I1
Basankusu, 73 A14
Basase, 73 I20
Basha Pan, 268 L6
Bashar, 67 D11
Bashee, 160 B4
Bashee Bridge, 160 A3
Bashibisi, 279 M2
Bashimuke, 73 I20
Basoko, 73 A19
Basongo, 73 G15
Basopdesh, 94 B1
Basotu, 93 C20
Bassar, 65 E20
Bassaula, 67 G11
Basse-Casamance National Park, 56 M3
Basséga, 72 C7
Bassigbiri, 69 I11
Bassikounou, 57 I15
Bassila, 66 E2
Bassin Bianc, 275 K7
Bassin Goémons, 46 H5
Basso, 66 C4
Bastions Stream, 265 D2
Basua, 66 H10
Basubuke, 73 H20
Basyun, 250 D8
Bas-Zaire, 72 I7
Bata, *Eq. Guinea* 67 M11
Bata, *Uganda* 82 A3
Batabi, 66 D6
Bataillor, 73 K16
Batama, 74 B3
Batamba, 67 J12
Batanga, 261 I8
Batangafo, 68 G1
Batcham, 67 I11
Batchenga, 67 J13
Bate, 128 C3
Batéké Plateau, 72 D8
Batemba, 73 H19
Bate-Nafadi, 64 C8
Batha, 60 M5
Bathurst, 159 H17
Bati, 70 B7
Batia, *oasis* 114 K1
Batia, 66 C2
Batibo, 67 H11
Batié, 65 D16
Batna, 49 J15
Batoka, 118 D6
Batoka Gorge, 118 H2
Batoua, 67 I14
Batouala, 72 B7
Batouri, 67 J16
Batsari, 59 M11
Batshamba, 73 I14
Batteries des Grenadiers, 46 H2
Battlefields, 119 K15
Battle of Blood River 1838, 148 K3
Battle of Colenso, 154 A10
Battle of Driefontein 1900, 153 B14
Battle of Elandslaagte, 148 M1
Battle of Gingindlovu, 155 B15
Battle of Helpmekaar, 280 B6
Battle of Lombaardskop, 280 C7
Battle of Magersfontein 1900, 153 B11
Battle of Paardeberg 1900, 153 B12
Battle of Pieters Hill, 280 C7
Battle of Platrand, 280 C6
Battle of Poplar Grove 1900, 153 B13
Battle of Saailaager, 154 B10
Battle of Sekhukhuneland (1879), 139 I16
Battle of Spioenkop, 280 C5
Battle of Surprise Hill, 280 C6
Battle of Talana, 148 K2
Battle of Tugela 1838, 155 C15
Battle of Vaalkraans, 280 C6
Battle of Vechtkop, 147 I14
Battle of Veglaer, 280 F6
Battle of Willow Grange, 280 F7
Batu, 257 F8
Bauchi, 67 C11
Baumango, 72 E7
Bauta, 73 B16
Bauyrat al Hasun, 53 D19
Baviaanskloofberge, 158 G6
Bawa, 66 B7
Bawdie, 65 I17
Bawé, *river* 253 C6
Bawé, 253 B6
Bawi, 109 I15
Bawiti, 55 H13
Bawku, 65 B19
Bawo, 64 H9
Bay, 57 L19
Baya Bwanga, 73 H17
Bayad, 246 A3
Bayadi, 72 F5
Bayala, 148 J9
Bayanga, 67 L18
Baydhabo, 71 K11
Bay of Anfile, 62 K10
Bayota, 65 H12
Bay Reserve, 57 L18
Bayuda Desert, 62 F1
Bayun Islands, 71 M17
Bayzo, 58 L8
Bazaruto Archipelago, 133 K18
Bazaruto Island, 133 J19
Bazaruto National Park, 133 J18
Baze, 68 J10
Bazian-Bea, 67 H19
Bazma, 246 K6
Bchelti, 246 K6
Be, 48 B8
Beacon Bay, 160 F2
Beacon Island, 46 B5
Bealanana, 48 D9
Beatrice, 119 I20
Beau Bassin-Rose Hill, 46 J2
Beau Bois, 46 L3
Beau Champ, 46 J6
Beaufort West, 158 C3
Beau Soleil, 47 H18
Beauty, 138 D9
Beau Vallon, 273 F6
Beau Vallon Bay, 46 B2
Beaver Pan, 268 E7
Bébédjia, 67 E18
Bebeka, 70 G2
Bebowa III, 67 G19
Bechar, 52 D2
Bechri, 246 J5
Bedarabe, 274 A7
Bedele, 70 E2
Bederwanak, 71 D12
Bedford, 159 D15
Bediako, 65 G16
Bedja, 62 G5
Beer Sheva, 55 D18
Beervlei Dam, 158 F5
Beeshoek, 145 L15
Beestekraal, 138 M8
Befale, 73 B16
Befandriana, 48 D8
Befarafara, 274 E7
Befori, 73 B17
Befotaka, 48 C8
Befoza, 274 G7
Begi, 69 D20
Begnimato, 247 K8
Begon, 67 H17
Begoro, 65 H19
Beheloka, 48 L3
Behir Chergui, 246 B2
Behulpsaam, 158 C10
Beila, 56 G6
Beilul, 63 L12
Beinamar, 67 E17
Beira, 133 C16
Beirut, 55 A19
Beitbridge, 131 M17
Beja, 49 K18
Bejaia, 49 I14
Bejane Pan, 268 C4
Beji, 66 D7
Bek, 67 L16
Beka, 67 G15
Bekapaika, 48 F7
Beke, 77 F12
Bekily, 48 L4
Bekipay, 48 E6
Bekitro, 48 L4
Bekkaria, 246 C3
Bekker, 145 J18
Bekoji, 70 F6
Bekondja, 68 F1
Bekondji, 73 C14
Bekopaka, 48 H4
Bekoropoka-Antongo, 48 J3
Bekuy, 65 B15
Bekwai, 65 H17
Bekyem, 65 G17
Bela-Bela, 138 K10
Bélabo, 67 I15
Belair, 46 J5
Bélaka Mbéré, 67 G17
Belasko, 57 M15
Belamoty, 48 K4
Belas, 72 M7
Bela Vista, 149 D11
Belbedji, 59 K12
Bele, 70 G7
Beledweyne, 71 J13
Beléfoungou, 252 L5
Beleges, 62 M7
Belehede, 58 K2
Belel, 67 D15
Beles, 70 B3
Beleya, 64 C7
Belfast, 148 B2
Belfodiyo, 70 C1
Belgo, 69 D17
Belhirane, 52 D10
Beli, *Guinea-Bissau* 64 B4
Beli, *Nigeria* 67 F12
Belifang, 67 H11
Beli Hill, 255 E8
Belize, 72 H6
Bell, 159 G19
Bella, 255 M7
Belle Mare Plage, 46 I6
Belle Ombre, 281 I8
Bellevue, 159 G14
Bellville, 156 I9
Belmont, 152 D10
Belo, 48 I4
Belobaka, 48 H5
Beloha, 48 M4
Beloko, 67 H17
Bel Ombre, *Mauritius* 46 M2
Bel Ombre, *Seychelles* 46 C3
Bel Ombre Forest, 275 K4
Belonge, 73 E15
Belo-Tsiribihina, 48 H4
Belvedere Church, 158 J4
Belwa, 255 B10
Bemal, 67 F19
Bemanevika, 274 G2
Bemanevikabe, 274 B2
Bembe, *river* 68 J2
Bembe, 72 K8
Bembé, 261 J6
Bembéréké, 66 C3
Bembesi, 131 A11
Bembezi, 118 M8
Bembi Pan, 268 D6
Bembou, 56 M9
Beme, 57 J12
Ben, 57 M17
Bena, 66 B7
Benahmed, 51 B16
Ben Alberts Nature Reserve, 138 J6
Benane, 84 H6
Bena-Tshadi, 73 H18
Ben Badie, 49 E18
Bende, 255 I2
Bendela, 73 F12
Bendugu, 64 D6
Bene, *Mozambique* 77 K20
Bene, *Mozambique* 108 I7
Bene-Dibele, 73 G18
Bénéna, 57 M17
Benenitra, 48 K4
Benga, *Malawi* 109 B13
Benga, *Mozambique* 121 A12
Bengamisa, 74 B2
Bengbis, 67 K14
Bengi Spring, 132 J5
Bengo, *admin.* 72 K7
Bengo, *river* 72 M8
Bengo, 75 D18
Benguela, 75 I17
Ben Guerdane, 53 B14
Benguerir, 51 C15
Benguie, 259 F4
Benha, 55 E15
Beni, 74 B6
Beni 'Adi el Bahariya, 250 K8
Beni Aissa, 246 K9
Beni Ghilouf, 246 J8
Beni Hasan, 55 H15
Benijos, 244 H7
Beni Kheddache, 246 L10
Beni Mazar, 55 G15
Beni Mellal, 51 C17
Beni Muhammadiyat, 250 K8
Benin, 66 E2
Beni Ounif, 52 C3
Beni Saf, 49 D17
Benisheikh, 67 B14
Beni Slimane, 49 J12
Beni Suef, 55 G15
Ben Zellten, 246 K10
Ben Lavin Nature Reserve, 139 D17
Ben Mehidi, 49 I17
Benoni, 147 C16
Bénoué, 67 E15
Bénoué National Park, 67 E16
Benoy, 67 E18
Ben Schoeman Dock, 281 B9
Bensekou, 66 B4
Ben Slimane, 51 A17
Ben S'Rour, 49 K13
Bentiaba, 75 K16
Bentiu, 69 E15
Benty, 64 E4
Benue, 67 D14
Benye, 73 E11
Benza, 72 J7
Béoliere, 273 J7
Beolire, 273 K7
Béoumi, 65 F13
Beposo, 65 I17
Ber, 247 A10
Beraketa, 48 L5
Beramanja, 48 C9
Beravina, 48 G5
Berber, 62 G2
Berbera, 71 C12
Berberati, 261 A4
Berberati, 67 J17
Berbice, 148 H5
Berdale, 71 G16
Berdossou, 247 I8
Bere, 67 D18
Béré, 256 J7
Bere Ale, 258 E9
Bereaville, 157 J11
Bérébi, 65 J11
Berebuda, 69 J12
Bereeda, 71 B19
Bereko, 94 C3
Berekum, 65 F16
Béréli, 247 K9
Berenice, 63 I16
Berg Aukas Mine, 114 M7
Bergland, 134 C8
Bergplaas, 158 I3
Bergrivier, 156 E7
Bergsig, 125 E15
Bergville, 154 A8
Berjaya Le Morne, 46 L1
Berjaya Mahé Beach, 46 D2
Berkane, 49 E16
Berlim, 255 G10
Berlin, 159 E20
Bermolli, 145 M14
Bernique, 47 C18
Bero, 75 L16
Beroroha, 48 J5
Berrahal, 49 I16
Berrechid, 51 B16
Berriane, 52 B7
Berrouaghia, 49 J11
Berseba, 143 C16
Bertoua, 67 J15
Besakay, 48 G6
Besalampy, 48 E4
Beshlo, 70 B5
Bessao, 67 F18
Besse, 68 D3
Bessi, 56 L4
Besters, 147 M19
Betafo, 48 H6
Betanatanana, 48 G4
Betanty, 48 M4
Bétaré Oya, 67 I16
Bete Hor, 258 J6
Betein, 66 I9
Bétérou, 66 E2
Bethal, 147 E19
Bethanie, *Namibia* 143 E14
Bethanie, *South Africa* 147 A13
Bethel, 159 D20
Bethelsdorp, 159 I12
Bethesdaweg, 158 A10
Bethlehem, 147 L14
Bethulie, 153 H15
Betioky, 48 L4
Betita, 246 G2
Betongwe, 69 L13
Beto Shet, 70 C5
Bétou, 68 L1
Betrandraka, 48 F7
Betroka, 48 K5
Betsaa, 277 D3
Betsiaka, 48 B9
Betsiboka, 48 G7
Betsofa, 274 F7
Bettache, 49 F12
Bettiesdam, 147 F19
Betty's Bay, 156 K10
Beu, 72 J10
Beungas, 72 J10
Bevato, 48 G6
Bevedere, 273 H9
Bevoalavo, 48 M3
Bewaarkloof Nature Reserve, 139 H16
Bewley, 146 A6
Beyla, 64 E9
Beylandé Zarma, 252 C9
Beyra, 71 G15
Bezaha, 48 K4
Bhalekane, 148 C8
Bhoshi, 280 F6
Bhunya, 148 E5
Bia, 65 H15
Bianga, 68 J4
Biankouma, 64 F10
Biaro, 74 B1
Biasi, 74 D4
Biba, 55 G15
Bibas, 72 A5
Bibe, 67 J14
Bibémi, 67 D16
Bibiani, 65 H16
Bibundi, 66 J10
Bichi, 66 A9
Bida, 66 E7
Bidon V, 58 B5
Bié, 76 I2
Bied Tisseras, 52 I9
Bienge, 73 I15
Bier, 138 K6
Biermanskool, 113 M15
Biesiesfontein, 150 J7
Biesiespoort, 152 M5
Biesiesvlei, 146 D6
Biesiesvlei Dam, 278 C8
Biéssi, 261 G2
Bietsha Pan, 277 D8
Bifoum, 72 C4
Big Bend, 148 F8
Bigene, 56 M5
Biggarsberg, 148 L1
Bighel, 66 E10
Bight of Benin, 66 I4
Bight of Bonny, 66 J7
Big Momela Lake, 265 K2
Bignona, 56 M4
Bigori, 69 B20
Big Toms, 268 C4
Biharamulo, 86 H4
Biharamulo Game Reserve, 86 G6
Bihawana, 94 J3
Bijoutier, 46 D10
Bikenke, 260 B5
Bikita, 132 D4
Bikoro, 73 C13
Bikuar National Park, 75 L19
Bilachi, 256 H2
Bilanga, 58 M3
Bilassana, 64 E9
Bilate, 70 G5
Bilau, 74 D5
Bilbala, 258 H6
Bilbeis, 55 E16
Bilénqui, 72 E5
Bilesha Plain, 85 G13
Bili, *river* 68 J7
Bili, 68 J3
Bilili Springs, 270 L6
Bilini, 67 D12
Bilis Quogaani, 85 H18
Billaouar, 57 H11
Bilma, 59 F18
Bilo, *Ethiopia* 70 E3
Bilo, *Gabon* 72 B5
Biloo, 71 L17
Biltine, 60 K7
Bima, 69 I11
Bimasa, 58 M9
Bimba, 67 J16
Bimbe, 75 H20
Bimbila, 65 E19
Bimbo, 68 J1
Bin, 49 I12
Binde, 65 B18
Binder, 67 D16
Binder-Léré Faunal Reserve, 67 D17
Binder Nayri, 256 H8
Bindu, 73 K14
Bindura, 120 F3
Bineda, 65 E16
Bin el Ouidane, 245 H6
Binga, *Tanzania* 99 B17
Binga, *Zimbabwe* 118 G6
Bingi, 260 D6
Bin-Houye, 64 G10
Bini Madoa, 248 C6
Binkolo, 64 E6
Bintagoungou, 57 H18
Bioko Island, 66 K9
Biougra, 51 E14
Bipindi, 67 L11
Bipok, 67 J12
Bir Abbad, 251 I5
Bir Abu Gupeir, 250 D3
Bir Abu Haleifa, 251 E2
Birak, 53 H17
Bir al Ghanam, 53 C16
Bir Ali Ben Khelifa, 246 F9
Bir Allaq, 53 D16
Birao, 68 C6
Bir Berbia, 246 L3
Birbir, 70 E1
Bir Buerak, 251 A3
Birchenough Bridge, 132 D7
Bircot, 71 F11
Bir Dhufan, 53 C18
Bir Di, 69 F14
Bird Island, 148 K10
Bire Kpatua Game Reserve, 69 J12
Bir el Ater, 49 K16
Bir el Grijima, 246 L6
Bir el Hafey, 49 K18
Bir el Hammamat, 251 G6
Bir el Hamri, 246 J1
Bir el Mkaddem, 246 C2
Bir el Qreiya, 251 F5
Bir el Quseir, 250 D1
Bir el Rtimi, 246 K1
Bir el Touana, 246 L3
Bir el Zimla, 250 D1
Bir Faiza, 246 K1
Bir Fegoussi, 246 L5
Bir Gandouz, 56 C5
Bir Gidami, 251 F6
Bir Hasana, 55 E18
Biri, 68 F10
Birini, 68 F6
Birira, 260 E8
Biriwiri, 109 H13
Bir Jhid, 245 F3
Birkat Saira, 60 L10
Birket Qarun, 55 F15
Birkuta, 258 D3
Bir Mogreïn, 50 K10
Bir Mokadden, 246 C2
Bir Mureir, 250 I8
Bir Nahrd, 250 E4
Birni, 66 D2
Birnim, 59 K14
Birnim Lalle, 59 K11
Birnin Gaouré, 58 M6
Birnin Gwari, 66 C7
Birnin Kebbi, 58 M8
Birnin Kudu, 67 B11
Birnin Nkonni, 58 L9
Birnin-Yauri, 66 C5
Bir oum Gounna, 246 L2
Bir Quleib, 55 M19
Bir Salah, 246 B4
Bir Sbekia, 246 E3
Bir Seiyala, 55 J18
Bir Shalatein, 63 I17
Bir Soltane, 246 L8
Bir Tam Tam, 51 A19
Bir Umm Dud, 251 E2
Bir Umm Hibai, 251 K5
Bir Zar, 53 D13
Bir Zoui, 246 L10
Bisadi, 266 D8
Bisanadi National Reserve, 84 I4
Bisate, 263 J5
Bise, 88 F8
Bisellia, 69 F12
Bisho, 159 E20
Bishopscourt, 281 H9
Bisi, 154 H9
Biskra, 49 K14
Biso, 69 M17
Bissandougou, 64 D9
Bissau, 64 A2
Bissikrima, 64 C6
Bissora, 64 A2
Bita, 68 G9
Bitale, 91 D15
Bitam, 67 M13
Bitata, 70 I6
Bitilifondi, 68 I10
Bitkin, 68 A1
Bitou, 65 B19
Bitoutouk, 67 K11
Bitterfontein, 150 J7
Bitterwater, 113 K14
Bityi, 160 A4
Biu, 67 C14
Bivane, *river* 148 I5
Bivane, 148 I4
Biyamiti, 278 L8
Bizana, 154 J9
Bizerte, 49 H19
Bla, 57 M16
Blackburn Kloof, 281 L4
Black Mfolozi, 148 K7
Black Mountain, 54 H3
Black Nossob, 135 C14
Black River Gorges National Park, 46 L2
Black Rock, *point* 142 H7
Black Rock, 145 G14
Black Volta, 65 E17
Bladgrond, 151 B13
Blairbeth, 138 L2
Blaka, 248 C1
Blama, 64 F6
Blanca, 45 F17
Blanche Mountains, 46 J5
Blanco, 158 I2
Blanfla, 65 G12
Blantyre, 109 L15
Bleak House, 271 B4
Blebo, 64 J10
Bleha, 65 B17
Blelikpang, 254 B5
Blendio, 65 B12
Blesmanspos, 145 J19
Bletterman, 152 I8
Blida, 49 I12
Blidet, 246 K5
Blikaodi, 65 E16
Blinkfontein, 145 J18
Blinkklip, 145 L16
Blinkwater, *South Africa* 139 D14
Blinkwater, *South Africa* 159 D16
Blinkwater Bay, 150 K6
Blinkwater Peak, 281 F6
Blitta, 65 F20
Bloemfontein, 153 C15
Bloemhoek, 151 D11
Bloemhof, 146 I5
Bloemhof Dam, 146 J5
Bloemhof Dam Nature Reserve, 146 I5
Blolekin, 64 G10
Blood River, 148 J3
Blouberg, 139 D13
Blouberg Nature Reserve, 139 C13
Bloubergstrand, 156 I8
Bloudrif, 146 K9
Blouhaak, 139 D15
Bloukrans, 151 M12
Bloukrans Monument, 154 B10
Bloukrans Pass, 151 M12
Blue Bay, 46 L5
Bluecliff, 159 H12
Bluegums, 153 H19
Blue Lagoon National Park, 106 K4
Blue Lagoon Ranch, 106 J4
Blue Mountain Pass, 154 D3
Blue Nile, 62 J1
Bluewater Bay, 159 I13
Blukwa, 69 M16
Blumenfelde, 135 F12
Blyde Olifants Conservancy, 139 I19
Blydepoort Dam, 278 I5
Blyde River Canyon Nature Reserve, 139 J20
Bnagola, 73 E16
Bo, 64 F6
Boadzulu Island, 109 F16
Boali, 68 J1
Boali Falls, 68 I1
Boanda, 67 I13
Boane, 148 C10
Boangi, 73 E16
Boa Vista, 56 B4
Bobakada, 68 I2
Bobakilandy, 274 C2
Bobala, 68 I1
Boban, 68 I1
Bobandana, 260 E2
Bobi, 69 L18
Bobo Dioulasso, 65 B14
Bobo Island, 277 G4
Bobonong, 131 L11
Bobuk, 69 B19
Boca de Tauce, 244 E3
Bocanda, 65 G14
Bocaranga, 67 G17
Bochum, 139 D13
Bocolo, 75 H18
Bocota, 76 L5
Boda, 67 J20
Bodélé Depression, 60 I1
Bodenhausen, 134 A10
Bodenstein, 146 D8
Bodhei, 90 E5
Bodi, 65 H16
Bodibeng, 128 F9
Bodiki, 67 J20
Boditi, 257 D7
Bodo, 65 H14
Bodokro, 65 F13
Bodoukpa, 67 I19
Boe, 64 B3
Boegoeberg, 152 B2
Boegoeberg Dam, 152 B2
Boeke, 73 B16
Boekenhoutfontein, 147 A11
Boende, 73 C16
Boendu, 73 B15
Boenze, 72 I8
Boerboonfontein, 157 I15
Boesmanshoek, 153 L16
Boesmanskop, 153 F18
Boesmansnek, 154 E6
Boesmansriviermond, 159 I17
Boetsap, 146 K1
Boffa, 64 C3
Bofossou, 64 E8
Boga, 74 A7
Bogandé, 58 M3
Bogangolo, 68 I1
Bogbaya, 261 B8
Bogbode, 68 M10
Bogbonga, 68 M3
Bogo, 67 C16
Bogol Manyo, 81 D17
Bogoro, 97 M18
Bogose, 68 K3
Bogoso, 65 I16
Bogué, 56 H7
Boguera, 67 J19
Bohicon, 66 G2
Bohlokong, 147 L15
Bohodou, 64 D9
Bohong, 67 H18
Bohongou, 252 D2
Boi, 67 D11
Boila, 111 M15
Boileau Bay, 46 E4
Boin National Park, 65 H15
Bois Sec Nature Reserve, 46 L3
Bojatau, 129 D19
Boju, 66 G9
Boju Ega, 66 G9
Bokada, 68 J2
Bokandi, 68 F1
Bokatola, 73 C14
Boke, 70 D8
Boké, 64 C3
Bokele, 73 D15
Boken, 58 M1
Bokhara, 144 J6
Bokhol Plain, 80 K8
Boki, 67 E15
Bokito, 67 J12
Bokkeveldberge, 150 H8
Bokkiesberg, 280 M4
Boknesstrand, 159 I16
Boko, 72 H9
Bokoko, 69 I11
Bokolako, 56 L8
Bokol Mayo, 70 J8
Bokolo, 259 L3
Bokolongo, 73 B15
Bokondji, 68 L2
Bokondo, 73 B18
Bokong, 154 D4
Bokora Game Reserve, 78 M6
Bokoro, 60 M3
Bokote, 73 C15
Bokoute, 68 H2
Bokpunt, 156 H8
Boksburg, 147 D15
Bokspits, 144 F7
Bokspuits, 151 B19
Bokuma, 73 C13
Bokungu, 73 C17
Bokwi Island, 277 G4
Bol, 59 L20
Bola, 248 H2
Bolama, 64 B1
Bolay 1, 67 J19
Bolbol, 58 M7
Bole, *Ethiopia* 70 H4
Bole, *Ghana* 65 E16
Boleka, 73 D14
Bolema, 261 A9
Bolero, 101 E11
Bolgatanga, 65 C18
Boli, *DRC* 74 C5
Boli, *Zimbabwe* 132 J4
Bolia, 73 D13
Bolo, *river* 68 E3
Bolo, 160 C1
Bolobo, 73 E11
Bologonja, 264 C6
Bologonja Springs, 264 D7
Boloi, 79 F19
Bololedi, 88 E2
Bolomba, 73 B14
Bolombo, 73 A17
Bolomo, 261 E10
Bolona, 65 C12
Bolondo, 67 M11
Bolonguera, 75 J17
Bolotwa, 159 B19
Bolozo, 261 F3
Bolsi, 58 L5
Bolton, 120 K2
Boma, *river* 107 A20
Boma, 72 I7
Bomadi, 66 I6
Bomassa, 261 F5
Boma ya Lindi, 98 J3
Bombakabo, 68 L3
Bombe, 68 I2
Bombela, 65 D14
Bombi, 68 L6
Bombo, 72 H10
Bombolo, 279 G4
Bombo-Makuka, 73 I11
Bomboyo, 67 A18
Bomet, 83 M11
Bomili, 69 M11
Bomokandi, 69 K12
Bomongo, 68 M1
Bompst Bay, 269 D5
Bomu, 68 J8
Bon, 248 G3
Bon Acceuil, 46 I4
Bon Accord, 147 A15
Bonam, 58 M2
Bonapabli, 64 H7
Bonboua, 261 A9
Bondo, 68 K8
Bondongo, 262 B1
Bondoukou, 65 F16
Bondoukui, 65 B15
Bone, 64 B7
Bonga, 70 G3
Bongandanga, 68 M4
Bongimba, 73 F15
Bongo, 76 I6
Bongor, 67 C17
Bongor Hanhan, 256 G10
Bongouanou, 65 H14
Bongoui, 68 E5
Boni, 57 J20
Bonieredougou, 65 E13
Boni National Reserve, 90 D7
Bonkoukou, 58 K6
Bonny, 66 J8
Bonny Ridge, 154 H7
Bonou, 66 G3
Bonoua, 65 I15
Bonsa, 254 I2
Bonsaaga, 58 M4
Bontebok National Park, 157 J15
Bonthe, 64 G4
Bontioli Faunal Reserve, 65 C15
Bontrand, 154 H9
Bonyere, 65 I16
Bonza Bay, 160 F2
Bonzan, 65 B16
Bonzo, *Côte d'Ivoire* 65 F11
Bonzo, *Zimbabwe* 120 K7
Boola, 64 E9
Boons, 147 C11
Boorama, 70 D10
Boosaaso, 71 B17
Booué, 72 C6
Bopo, 66 F9
Bor, *river* 80 K9
Bor, 69 H17
Bora, *mountains* 62 M9
Bora, 68 E10
Borakalalo Game Reserve, 138 L8
Borchers, 139 D18
Bordj Bou Arreridj, 49 J13
Bordj Bounaama, 49 D20
Bordj es Segui, 246 I6
Bordj Khanguet, 246 I6
Bordj le Prieur, 58 C5
Bordj Messouda, 53 E12
Bordj Omar Idriss, 52 H10
Bordj Saidane, 246 J7
Bordj Soukies, 246 G1
Bore, *Botswana* 136 B6
Bore, *Ethiopia* 70 H5
Boré, 57 J19
Borebo, 258 L1
Borgou, 252 I2
Borgu Game Reserve, 66 D4
Bori, 66 D3
Boriziny, 48 D6
Borj, 53 E14
Bo Rjeimât, 56 F6
Borj Hachichina, 246 G10
Borj Machened Salth, 53 C14
Borj n Oufraou, 245 B5
Borj Zoumit, 246 K8
Borkou, 60 F4
Borne, 53 L11
Boro, *river* 68 E9
Boro, *river* 129 C11
Boro, 68 J3
Borol, 68 B1
Boromata, 68 D6
Boromo, 65 B16
Boron, 65 E12
Borotou, 65 E11
Bort Bourgulba, 53 C13
Boshoek, 138 M5
Boshof, 146 M4
Boskuil, 146 H6
Bosobolo, 68 J3
Bososama, 68 J3
Boso-Semodja, 73 B14
Bosoport, 146 E7
Bospoort Dam, 147 A12
Bossangoa, 67 H20
Bossé Bangou, 252 B4
Bosséga, 252 C2
Bossembélé, 67 I19
Bossentele, 67 I19
Bosseoui, 67 J19
Bossiekom, 151 D13
Bossiesvlei, 134 K7
Boss Longone Pan, 268 D7
Bossoum, 256 F5
Bosua Pass, 134 B3
Bosumba, 73 A14
Botala, 261 H9
Botata, 64 G8
Boteke, 73 C14
Botelenza, 68 K4
Boteler Point, 149 G12
Boteti, 129 E13
Bothaberg, 278 L1
Bothashoop, 148 G5
Bothasnek, 148 B5
Bothas Pass, 147 I20
Bothatogo, 128 G9
Bothaville, 146 H8
Bothithong, 145 G18
Botlhapatlou, 137 G19
Botlokwa, 139 E15
Bot Makak, 67 K12
Botou, 58 M3
Botrivier, 157 K11
Botrivier Vlei, 157 K11
Botro, 65 F13
Botsalano Game Park, 146 A6
Botshabelo, 153 C17
Botswana, 138 D2
Botterkloof, 151 M11
Bou, 65 E12
Boua, 261 M5
Bouafle, 65 G12
Bouaké, 65 F13
Bou Alem, 49 K17
Boualem, 52 B6
Bouam, 67 J15
Bou Anane, 51 C20
Bouanga, 72 E10
Bouanila, 261 J8
Bouar, 67 H17
Bou Arfa, 52 C2
Bouba Ndjidah National Park, 67 E16
Boubélé, 65 J11
Bouboury, 65 I13
Bouca, 68 H1
Boucan, 275 D4
Bou Chebka, 246 D4
Bou Chemma, 246 I9
Bouchia, 68 K1
Bouchouayinly, 56 B5
Boucy-Boucy, 261 F10
Bouda, 259 L4
Boudamasa, 248 K4
Boudamassa, 67 C18
Boudenib, 51 D20
Boudeuse, 46 C9
Boudi, 81 E12
Boudiéri, 252 E5
Boudoua, 67 J18
Bouénguidi, 259 I9
Bouenza, 72 G8
Bougaa, 49 I14
Bou Gadoum, 57 I14
Bougay, 256 F9
Boughessa, 58 E6
Bougoui, 67 G17
Bougouni, 65 B11
Bougouriba, 65 B16
Bougouribi, 65 C15
Bou Grad, 246 G6
Bougtob, 52 A4
Bougzoul, 49 J11
Bou Hajla, 49 J18
Bou Hamed, 49 D14
Bou-Hedma National Park, 49 L18
Bou Iguenouane, 245 C3
Bouili, 66 C3
Bouinandjé, 72 B7
Bouira, 49 I13
Bou Izakarn, 51 G13
Bou Jaber, 246 B4
Boujad, 51 B17
Boujdour, 50 J7
Bou Kadir, 49 C19
Boukanda, 58 L6
Boukas, 52 C1
Bou Khadra, 246 B3
Boukoula, 67 C15
Boukoumbé, 252 K3
Boula-Ibib, 67 D16
Boulal, 56 J5
Boulankio, 72 G9
Bou Lanouar, 56 C6
Boulaouane, 51 B15
Boulbi, 57 J16
Boulemane, 51 B19
Boulgou, 66 A1
Boulou, 68 F8
Boulsa, 58 M2
Bouma, 51 B18
Boumaine du Dades, 51 D17
Boumba, 67 K16
Boumbe I, 67 J17
Boumboum, 58 J1
Boumdeït, 56 H10
Boume, 72 E6
Boumeoul, 64 A5
Bouna, 65 D15
Boundi, 68 H9
Boundiali, 65 D12
Boundji, 72 D10
Boune, 59 L15
Bounga, 68 I5
Boungou, 68 F5
Bounkiling, 56 M4
Bounou, 57 L19
Bou Ormane, 246 H6
Boupom Wildlife Sanctuary, 65 G17
Boura, 65 B16
Boured, 245 D10
Boureimi, 58 I7
Bourem, 58 H3
Bourem-Inali, 247 A8
Bourg El-Arab, 55 D13
Bourke's Luck Potholes, 278 J5
Bouroum, 58 L2
Bourrah, 67 C15
Bourzanga, 58 L2
Bous, 249 G4
Bou Saad, 246 H7
Bou Saada, 49 K13
Bou Sfer, 49 D18
Bousso, 67 C19
Boussouma, 58 M2
Boutilimit, 56 G7
Boutougou Fara, 56 L8
Boutouli, 68 J1
Bouye, 68 H10
Bouza, 58 K10
Bou Zegam, 246 D5
Bouzghaia, 49 C20
Bo-Wadrif, 157 C14
Bowwood, 118 E2
Boya, 261 K4
Boyabo, 68 K2
Boyne, 139 G16
Boyo, 68 I5
Boza, *CAR* 68 I2
Boza, *Tanzania* 95 G17
Bozene, 68 L2
Bozoum, 67 H19
Brack, 134 B9
Braemar, 155 H11
Brak, *river* 139 B16
Brak, *river* 150 B7
Brak, *river* 151 I16
Brakbos, 152 D1
Brakpan, *Namibia* 135 M16
Brakpan, *South Africa* 147 D15
Brakpoort, 152 L6
Brakspruit, 146 E9
Brakwater, 134 A8
Brandberg Nature Reserve, 125 I17
Brandberg West Mine, 125 H15
Branddraai, 139 J18
Brandfort, 153 A17
Brandkop, 151 K11
Brandvlei, 157 I17
Brandvlei, 151 H15
Brandwag, 158 J1
Bransan, 56 I8
Bras Panon, 47 K15
Brass, 66 J7
Braunschweig, *South Africa* 148 H3
Braunschweig, *South Africa* 159 E19
Braunville, 153 M19
Brava, 56 C2
Bray, 137 M12
Brazzaville, 72 G9
Bread Rock, 265 B6
Breakfast Vlei, 159 F18
Bréard Dunes, 249 B6
Bredasdorp, 157 L14
Breede, 157 J15
Breidbach, 159 E19
Breipaal, 153 E15
Bresoanu, 65 F18
Brewaniase, 65 F19
Brewerville, 64 H6
Breyten, 148 D2
Brezal, 244 H7
Brezina, 52 B5
Bria, 68 H6
Bridgewater, 139 A14
Brieville, 48 F7
Brikama, 56 L3
Brilla, 273 I10

C

D

Dakawa, 95 K11
Dakhla, 50 M4
Dakingari, 66 B4
Daki Tagwas, 66 A6
Dakoro, 59 K11
Dala, 76 G5
Dalaba, 56 M7
Daleside, 147 E14
Dalga, 250 J7
Dali, 57 J14
Dali Sharafat, 62 M2
Dalli, 67 F12
Dallol Fago, 58 L7
Dallol Mouri, 58 L7
Dalmanutha, 148 B3
Daloa, 65 G11
Dalocha, 257 G1
Dalton, 155 D12
Damagaram-Takaya, 59 K13
Damakar, 59 M18
Damakuli, 67 A15
Damang, 254 I1
Damanhur, 55 E14
Damara, 68 I1
Damasak, 59 L17
Damascus, 55 B20
Damaturu, 67 B13
Damba, 72 J9
Dambai, 65 F19
Dambam, 67 B12
Dambarta, 66 A9
Damboa, 67 B14
Dam Gamad, 61 L15
Damietta, *see Dumyat*
Damongo, 65 E17
Damongo Junction, 254 G8
Dams, 271 D3
Dana Bay, 158 K1
Danakil, 62 K10
Danakil Desert, 62 M10
Danané, 64 G10
Dandaro Pans, 268 D4
Dandau, 76 H2
Dande, 79 C15
Dando, 76 G2
Danga, 57 I19
Danga Pan, 118 L3
Dangavo, 68 F4
Dange, *river* 72 L8
Dange, 58 M9
Dangla, 70 B3
Dan Gona, 58 K9
Dan-Gulbi, 66 B7
Dangur, 70 B2
Daniëlskuil, 145 L17
Danielsrus, 147 K15
Danie Theron Monument, 147 E11
Danisa Hills, 70 K8
Danka, 257 E8
Dankalou, 68 D1
Dankhayo Bay, 101 F13
Dan Mairo, 59 L11
Dannhauser, 148 K1
Danot, 71 F13
Dan Sadau, 66 B7
Dans Galets Beach, 273 M8
Dans Gravier, 46 E4
Dan Tchiao, 59 M13
Dante, *see Xaafuun*
Dantiandou, 252 B8
Danzil, 46 C2
Dao Timmi, 249 G9
Daoud, 49 E18
Daouenle, 70 C10
Daoukro, 65 G15
Dapaong, 65 C19
Dapchi, 59 M16
Daquf, 250 I7
Dara, *mountains* 88 M3
Dara, *peak* 264 M9
Dara, 258 H7
Daradou, 68 H9
Daraina, 48 C9
Darajani, *river* 266 E4
Darajani, 266 E4
Darambue, 92 K10
Daramombe, 120 M2
Daraw, 251 J5
Darazo, 67 B11
Dar Bel Ouar, 246 A10
Darburruk, 71 D11
Dar Caid Khoubbane, 245 I1
Dar Chebika, 51 H11
Dar Chioukh, 49 K12
Dar el Leqceiba Barka, 56 H6
Darer, 79 D18
Dar es Salaam, 95 L18
Darfur, 68 C8
Dargle, 280 K8
Dargle Cottages, 280 L7
Dargo, 58 M3
Dargol, *river* 58 L4
Dargol, 58 K5
Darhala, 65 E14
Dari, 256 I8
Dariana, 274 E8
Dario, 261 A4
Darkeena, 70 G6
Darling, 156 G8
Darlington Dam, 159 G12
Darnah, 54 C7
Darnall, 155 C15
Darouma, 57 L11
Darou-Mousti, 56 J5
Darro, 71 C18
D'Arros, 46 C10
Darul, 64 F7
Darwendale, 119 G18
Dase, 62 J7
Dashiut, 250 J7
Daskop, 158 I3
Dass, 67 C11
Dassa, 66 F2
Dassari, 252 L7
Dassen Island, 156 G6
Dasville, 147 F15
Datori, 65 C20
Dauban, 273 L9
Daura, 59 M12
Davel, 147 E20
Davo, 65 I12
Dawa, 80 C9
Dawadawa, 65 F17
Dawn, 160 F1
Dawqah, 62 E10
Dawson's Rock, 279 L6
Daza, 60 J6
d'Azagny National Park, 65 I13
Dé, 247 I7
De Aar, 152 I8
Dead Sea, 55 D19
Dealesville, 153 A15
Deali, 56 J5
Debabcha, 246 J5
Deba Habe, 255 A8
Debaina, 258 E9
Debarei, 68 A7
Debark, 62 L7
Deba-Sima, 63 M12
Debdou, 52 A1
De Beers, 146 H2
De Beers Pass, 147 L18
Debel, 80 I8
Débéré, 247 H8
De Berg Pass, 139 L17
Debra, 127 C20
Debre Birhan, 70 D6
Debre Markos, 70 C4
Debremay, 70 B4
Debre Tabor, 70 A4
Debre Zebit, 70 B5
Debre Zebrit, 258 I5
Debre Zeit, 70 E6
Debre Zeyit, 70 C2
De Brug, 153 C15
Debub, 258 F8
Decamere, 62 J8
Deception Pan, 129 J14
Decken Glacier, 265 D4
Dedda, 62 J7
Deder, 70 D9
Dédi, 253 E7
De Doorns, 157 H12
Dédougou, 65 A16
Dedza, 109 F13
Dedza Mountain, 109 F13
Deelfontein, 152 J7
Deelpan, 146 D5
Degache, 246 I3
Dega Medo, 70 F10
de Gaulle, 67 G17
Degeh Bur, 71 F11
Degema, 66 J7
Degoma, 258 H4
De Gracht, 139 B13
Dehibat, 53 C14
De Hoek, 156 F9
De Hoop Nature Reserve, 157 K15
Deim Bukhit, 69 G11
Deim Zubeir, 68 F10
Deir el Melak, 251 G4
Deir Mawas, 250 J8
Dejen, 70 D4
Deka, *river* 118 J2
Deka, 118 I4
Deka Safari Area, 118 K2
Dekese, 73 G17
Dekina, 66 F8
Dekoa, 68 H2
Delaa, 52 B8
Delami, 69 B15
Delareyville, 146 F5
Delep, 60 M5
Delgo, 61 D18
Deli, 67 E18
Dellya, 49 I13
Delmas, 147 C17
Delportshoop, 145 L19
Delta du Saloum, 56 L3
Delta du Saloum National Park, 56 L3
Del Verine Falls, 70 I7
Demba, 73 I17
Demba Koli, 56 L8
Dembecha, 70 C4
Dembeldoro, 80 E10
Dembéni, 48 A4
Dembi, 70 F3
Dembia, 68 I8
Dembi Dolo, 70 E1
Dembo, 67 D15
Dembos, 72 L9
Demi, 70 D2
Demistkraal, 158 H10
Demnate, 245 H5
Demsa, 67 D15
Denakil Depression, 62 K10
Denakil Desert, 258 G10
Denan, 71 H11
Dendera, 251 G4
Dendoudi, 56 J7
Dendron, 139 E14
Deneysville, 147 F14
Denge, 69 K13
Dengebe, 66 A7
Dengi, 67 D11
Dengu, 68 J8
Denguiro, 68 I6
Denk'ez, 258 H4
Dennilton, 139 L13
Deo, 68 F4
Déo, 255 D10
Deou, 58 K2
Déposé, 46 E9
Dera, 70 E6
Derbissaka, 68 H9
Derby, 147 B11
Derdepoort, 138 J3
Deresna, 248 F3
Dérésa, 60 L7
Derkali, 81 F12
Derm, 135 F12
Dernaia, 49 K17
Derre, 122 D2
Derri, 71 J14
Derudeb, 62 H5
De Rust, 158 H3
des Aigrettes, 275 E6
Dese, 70 B6
Deseada Nambroque, 44 F3
Désert, 273 J6
Desnoefs, 46 D10
Despatch, 159 I13
Desroches, 46 C10
Destinée Island, 47 J17
Dete, 118 K4
Deteema, 268 C4
Deux Balé National Park, 65 B16
Devedso Hills, 120 K4
De Villiers Dam, 281 H6
Devil's Peak Forest Station, 281 D9
Devon, 147 D17
Devon Farm, 280 I7
Devonlea, 146 E2
Devure, 132 C5
De Waal Park, 281 D6
De Waterkant, 281 B7
Dewetsdorp, 153 D17
De Wildt, 147 A14
Dhaiaa, 246 C1
Dhaya, 49 E18
Dhaym-al-Khayl, 50 K8
Dhlamini, 130 B8
Dhooble, 85 H16
Dhoomadheere, 70 M8
Dhuudo, 71 D19
Dhuusamarreeb, 71 I14
Dia, 57 L13
Diabiga, 252 H2
Diabo, 65 A19
Diaca, 103 G17
Diadioumbera, 56 K10
Diaka, 57 K17
Diakankoré, 247 H3
Diakon, 57 K11
Dialafara, 56 L10
Dialakoto, 56 L8
Diallassagou, 247 M5
Diama, 247 M5
Diambo, 68 L2
Diamou, 56 K10
Diamounguel, 56 J8
Diana, 56 L8
Diana Malari, 56 M5
Dianfa, 65 E12
Dianpounte-Kamara, 57 K11
Diankabou, 247 J10
Dianra, 65 E12
Diapaga, 66 A2
Diapangou, 252 E1
Diapouargou, 252 C1
Diarabala, 65 F12
Diari, 64 B5
Dias, 101 M17
Dias Cross, 159 H16
Diawala, 65 D13
Diaz Point, 142 E6
Dibaya, 76 B8
Dibaya Lubue, 73 G15
Dibaza, 258 D5
Dibebe, 277 C1
Dibella, 249 J9
Dibeng, 145 I14
Dibete, 138 F4
Dibi, 67 G15
Dibombari, 67 J11
Dida Galgalu Desert, 80 J3
Dida Harea, 266 I7
Didda Plateau, 70 G6
Dider, 53 K11
Didesa, 70 D2
Didieni, 57 L13
Didievi, 65 G13
Didigsala, 62 M10
Didimtu, 70 L7
Dido, 90 A2
Didoko, 65 H13
Didy, 48 G8
Didyr, 65 A16
Die Berg, 278 K3
Die Berg Pass, 278 L3
Die Bos, 157 B12
Diébougou, 65 C15
Die Dam, 157 M12
Diego Garcia Island, 47 D19
Diego-Suarez, *see Antsiranana*
Die Kalk, 135 K11
Diela Vievi, 259 K3
Diélimako, 247 F1
Diema, 57 K12
Die Maanhaar, 280 B4
Diemansputs, 151 F19
Diémessagou, 247 L4
Diepsloot Nature Reserve, 147 C14
Dieput, 152 I8
Diere, 56 I6
Die Venster, 157 G13
Die Vlug, 158 I5
Dif, 85 F15
Diffa, 59 L17
Difoundia, 72 F4
Difuma, 74 G2
Digalu, 80 C4
Digba, 68 J10
Digoudou, 259 L5
Digui, 68 I4
Digya National Park, 65 G18
Dihimba, 103 B17
Diibao, 67 E17
Diinsoor, 71 L11
Dik, 67 D20
Dikabeya, 138 A7
Dikhil, 70 B9
Dikirnis, 250 C9
Dikodougou, 65 E12
Dikokwana Pan, 137 I15
Dikulwe, 77 F13
Dikwa, 67 A16
Dikwalo, 129 F15
Dila, 70 H5
Dilbe, 70 B6
Dili, 69 K11
Dilli, 57 J14
Dillia, 59 J17
Dilling, 69 A14
Dilolo, 76 G8
Dima, 70 C5
Dimako, 67 J15
Dimbelenge, 73 I19
Dimbi, 68 J5
Dimbokro, 65 G13
Dimlik, 67 C19
Dimonika-Mayombe Biosphere Reserve, 72 G5
Dimpam, 67 K14
Dinangourou, 57 K20
Dinas, 84 H8
Dinchiya, 70 G2
Dinder, 62 M3
Dinder National Park, 70 A1
Dindima, 67 C12
Dindiza, 140 E10
Dineiqil, 251 L2
Dinga, 68 G6
Dingba, 69 K13
Ding Ding, 69 E18
Dingila, 68 K10
Dingueteri, 64 B4
Dinguiraye, 64 B7
Dinka, 69 E13
Dino, 257 C8
Dinokwe, 138 E5
Dinsho, 70 G7
Diobahika, 86 J6
Dioila, 65 A11
Dion, 65 A11
Diongoï, 57 K12
Dioniqu, 72 J7
Dionysias, 250 G7
Dior, 253 I9
Diore, 65 F15
Dioro, 57 L16
Diosso, 72 H5
Dioulatiedougou, 65 E11
Diouloulou, 56 M4
Dioura, 57 K16
Diourbel, 56 K4
Dipchari, 256 B6
Diphuti, 139 I19
Diré, 57 H19
Dire Dawa, 70 D9
Dirico, 115 G17
Dirinbaji, 66 B6
Dirj, 53 E14
Dirkiesdorp, 148 G3
Dirkou, 59 F18
Dirra, 61 L13
Disa, 94 C4
Dis Al, 127 I14
Disa River, 281 J3
Dishasha, 250 H8
Dishna, 63 F13
Disuq, 250 C7
Ditche, 64 A3
Ditinn, 64 C5
Ditshipeng, 145 F18
Ditsinane Pan, 130 J2
Divénié, 72 F5
Divinhe, 133 G16
Divo, 65 H13
Divuma, 76 F8
Dixcove, 65 J17
Diyanga, 259 I8
Dizangue, 67 K11
Diziva, 76 L2
Dja, 67 L14
Djaba, 249 F8
Djado, 59 C17
Djado Plateau, 59 C17
Djafarabe, 57 K16
Dja Faunal Reserve (WHS), 67 K14
Djalasiga, 69 L15
Djale, 73 E18
Djamaa, 49 M14
Djamandjary, 274 F3
Djamba, 73 L19
Djambala, 72 F9
Djampiel, 67 J16
Djanet, 53 L12
Djebel Onk, 246 F3
Djebok, 58 I4
Djebréne, 248 F2
Djédaa, 60 L4
Djelfa, 49 K12
Djema, 68 H9
Djemila, 49 I14
Djenen Krater, 52 B2
Djeniene Bou Rezg, 52 C3
Djenné (WHS), 57 L17
Djerem, 67 G15
Djermaya, 59 M20
Djeurf, 246 E1
Djeve, 256 E5
Dji, 68 G7
Djibasso, 57 M18
Djibo, 58 K1
Djiborosso, 65 E11
Djibouti, *country* 70 A9
Djibouti, 70 B10
Djidja, 66 G2
Djigueni, 57 J13
Djiguibambo, 247 L7
Djilbe, 67 A17
Djim, 67 J13
Djinko, 64 A8
Djiodat, 248 E3
Djion, 64 D9
Djiroutou, 65 I11
Djohong, 67 G17
Djoku-Punda, 73 I15
Djoli Kere Forest Reserve, 67 E20
Djolu, 73 B18
Djomba, 260 C5
Djombo Kibbit, 60 L6
Djonaba, 56 H9
Djona Hunting Zone, 66 B3
Djoua, 72 A7
Djouah, 261 H1
Djoubé, 261 E8
Djoubissi, 68 H4
Djoudj National Bird Sanctuary (WHS), 56 I4
Djougou, 66 D2
Djouk, 56 H10
Djoukou, 68 I3
Djoum, 67 L14
Djoumboli, 67 F14
Djouna, 248 G4
Djourab Dunes, 60 I5
Djourt, 248 F3
D'Kar, 128 J6
Dlolwana, 155 A13
Doa, 121 C15
Doba, 67 E19
Dobe, 115 M18
Dobinga, 67 E16
Doda, 95 E17
Dodéo, 255 E10
Dodo, 65 I11
Dodola, 70 G6
Dodoma, *admin.* 94 D4
Dodoma, 94 J4
Dodori National Reserve, 90 E6
Dodowa, 65 H19
Dogba, 256 D7
Dogbo, 65 I11
Dogbo-Toto, 66 G2
Dogo, 65 B11
Dogoba, 69 H15
Dogondoutchi, 58 L7
Dogonkirya, 58 K8
Dogon Plateau, 57 K18
Dogon Tapki, 58 L8
Dog Point, 279 B9
Dohne, 159 D20
Dohon, 248 B10
Dohul, 62 I9
Doinyo Lengai, 264 I10
Doka, 62 L5
Doko, 64 B9
Dokolo, 82 B3
Dokpam, 65 E19
Dokweni, 278 C7
Dola Mena, 257 M7
Dolo Bay, 81 E20
Dolo Mena, 257 I9
Dolomietpoort, 113 K12
Doma, 119 C17
Domaine du Chasseur, 46 K5
Domaine du Chasseur Nature Reserve, 46 K5
Domana Rock Shrine, 254 J3
Doma Safari Area, 119 B17
Dombe, 133 D11
Dombe Grande, 75 I16
Dombia, 56 M10
Dombiadji, 64 A4
Domboshawa, *mountains* 120 G1
Domboshawa, 120 G2
Dominase, 65 H19
Domiongo, 73 H16
Domo, 71 F15
Domoni, 48 B5
Dompem, 65 I16
Domtshetshu Pan, 268 E4
Domwe Island, 109 D15
Domwe Peak, 271 C3
Dona Ana Bridge, 121 F16
Dondée, 273 M9
Dondo, 133 B16
Dondon, 90 B5
Dondotsha, 148 M7
Donga, *Benin* 66 D2
Donga, *Nigeria* 67 F11
Dongo, 75 K20
Dongodesh, 94 B2
Dongola, 61 F17
Dongou, 68 M1
Dongoundza, 261 B7
Dongrossé, 256 F8
Dongue, 75 L18
Donguila, 72 B3
Dongur, 70 B2
Dongwe, *DRC* 76 J10
Dongwe, *Namibia* 105 D11
Dongwe Range, 131 B18
Donkéré, 255 E10
Donkerpoort, 153 H13
Donko, 66 B6
Donnybrook, 154 F9
Donzi, 68 H2
Doolow, 81 E20
Doornadraai Dam, 139 I12
Doorndraai Dam Nature Reserve, 139 H11
Doornrivier, 157 I11
Dordabis, 134 C9
Dordrecht, 153 L18
Doreenville, 135 C12
Doreissou, 256 E9
Dorey, 58 I3
Dori, 58 K3
Doring Bay, 156 A7
Doringbos, 157 B11
Doringbult, 146 E7
Doringspruit, 280 L10
Doro, 58 I3
Doropo, 65 D15
Doros Crater, 125 G16
Dorowa, 120 M4
Dorra, 70 A9
Dorsale Camerounaise, 67 H12
Dorsland Trek Church Ruin, 112 H8
Doruma, 69 J12
Dos d'Ane, 47 K14
Dos Hermanas, 49 B13
Dosseo, 248 L7
Dosso, 58 M7
Dosso Partial Faunal Reserve, 58 M6
Douako, 64 D7
Douala, 67 J11
Douala-Edéa Faunal Reserve, 67 K11
Doualayal, 67 G14
Douaouir, 57 D20
Doubanga, 72 D4
Doubelma, 58 K5
Doubodo, 66 A1
Doudéi, 248 H5
Douékiré, 247 B7
Douentza, 57 J19
Dougga (WHS), 49 I17
Douglas, 152 C8
Dougol, 67 G18
Dougountoun, 64 B5
Doui, 68 F8
Doukoula, 67 C17
Doulouyaba, 56 L8
Doum, 68 E4
Doumandzou, 259 C5
Doum Doum, 60 L1
Doumé, *river* 261 A1
Doumé, 67 H14
Douna, 65 C13
Dounde Bague, 56 K8
Doundourou, 247 L8
Doura, 57 K15
Dourbali, 67 B18
Dourbeye, 67 D15
Dourdoura, 68 B5
Dourou, 247 K8
Douroum, 256 F5
Doussala, 72 E4
Dousséous, 259 M6
Doutoufouk, 59 K14
Douz, 49 M17
Dover, 147 G13
Dovesdale, 146 E10
Dowa, 109 C11
Downie Peak, 265 D9
Drâa Valley, 245 J6
Draghoender, 152 D2
Drago Milenario, 244 H3
Dragon, 280 E3
Drakensberg, 154 H3
Drbatte, 79 B20
Drennan, 159 D13
Driefontein, 147 L19
Driekop, 278 I3
Drimiopsis, 127 L14
Driver's Drift, 159 A18
Droërivier, 158 C3
Droëspruit, 145 J15
Drolvtakte, 157 K18
Drummondlea, 139 I12
Dry, 146 H2
Dschang, 67 I11
Dua, 68 K5
Duale, 73 B18
Duamangaga, 94 E1
Duangua, 108 J3
Duba, 63 E17
Dubela, 69 L14
Dubie, 74 L5
Dubreka, 64 D3
Dubreuil, 46 K4
Duchess Hill, 119 J17
Dududu, 155 G11
Dudup, 85 F15
Due, 73 G13
Duékoué, 65 G11
Dufour Cave, 47 K14
Dugand, 273 J6
Dugdug, 69 F13
Duge, 64 H9
Duguri, 67 D12
Duhun Tarsu, 60 C5
Duikerdrink, 113 L14
Duiker Island Seal Colony, 281 L1
Duineveld, *oasis* 113 K13
Duineveld, 134 G9
Duiwelskloof, 139 F17
Duiwelsvuur, 113 K15
Dûjuuma, 71 K17
Dukambio, 62 K7
Dukana, 79 F19
Duke, 278 L10
Duk Faiwil, 69 F17
Dukku, 66 B5
Duk'uk'o, 258 F4
Dukul, 67 C13
Dukumbane, 279 H4
Dukwe, 130 F4
Dulala, 77 F11
Dulia, *DRC* 68 L8
Dulia, *DRC* 74 B6
Dullstroom, 139 M16
Duma, *Botswana* 116 K8
Duma, 55 E13
Duma, *Sudan* 69 J11
Duma, *Tanzania* 87 H14
Dumbo, 67 G11
Dumela, 130 I7
Dumyat, 55 D16
Duna, 76 J6
Duncan Dock, 281 B8
Dundee, 148 K2
Dundo, 73 K16
Dunga, 95 J18
Dungariespomp, 276 E8
Dunga Ruins, 95 I17
Dungas, 59 L14
Dungu, *Botswana* 116 K6
Dungu, *DRC* 69 K13
Dungu, *river* 69 K13
Dungunab Bay, 62 D6
Dunkassa, 66 C3
Dunkwa, 65 H17
Dunqul, 251 L2
Du Plessis Pass, 157 J20
Dupleston, 153 G15
Dupuy, 273 M10
Dur al Fawakhir, 54 F5
Durban, 155 F13
Durbanville, 156 I9
Durissa Bay, 125 I13
Du Riz, 273 H2
Durra, 70 G3
Duru, *river* 69 K13
Duru, 69 J13
Durukhsi, 71 E13
Durumo, 93 C18
Dusa Marreeb, *see Dhuusamarreeb*
Dush, 55 L15
Duta, 77 G18
Dutlwe, 137 G14
Du Toitskloof, 157 H11
Dutse, 67 B11
Dutsin Ma, 59 M12
Dwaal, 153 J11
Dwaalboom, 138 J4
Dwangwa, *river* 101 L11
Dwangwa, 101 K13
Dwarsberg, 138 K4
Dwarskersbos, 156 E8
Dwarskloof, 157 J12
Dwesa Nature Reserve, 160 C5
D West, 67 B15
Dwokwa, 65 I17
Dwyka, *river* 157 F19
Dwyka, 157 F19
Dysseldorp, 158 H2
Dzanga, 261 B8
Dzaoudzi, 48 B6
Dzata Ruins, 139 C18
Dzéké, 261 I8
Dzibui Pan, 129 H17
Dzioua, 52 B9
Dzita, 65 I20
Dzodze, 65 H20
Dzumeri, 139 F19
Dzundwini, 278 B6

E

Eask, 51 G13
Easter Cliffs, 124 M9
Eastern, *Kenya* 83 K19
Eastern, *Zambia* 108 D2
Eastern Bomu Wildlife Reserve, 68 J8
Eastern Cape, 159 B14
Eastern Desert, 55 I17
Eastern Icefields, 265 C4
Eastern Table, 281 F8
East Fort, 281 L3
East London, 160 F2
East London Coast Nature Reserve, 160 F1
Eastnor, 131 B12
Eastpoort, 159 D14
East Ridge, 265 E9
East Shire Hill, 265 I6
Eban, 66 D5
Ebanga, 75 I19
Ebangalakata, 73 C16
Ebba Ksour, *see Dahmani*
Ebebiyin, 67 L12
Ebel Abanga, 259 F4
Ebel Alémbé, 259 E5
Ebelle, 66 H7
Ebem, 66 I9
Ebende, 160 B3
Ebeneerde, 135 K11
Ebenezer Dam, 139 G17
Ebola, 68 K5
Ebolowa, 67 L12
Ebonda, 68 L6
Ebongui, 72 C9
Ebony, 125 L20
Ebouk-Village, 259 F4
Eboundja, 67 L11
Echambot, 67 K16
Echedo, 44 J4
Echo Caves, 139 I18
Écija, 49 B15
Ed Daein, 68 B10
Ed Damazin, 69 B19
Ed Damer, 62 H2
Ed Dueim, 61 L20
Edéa, 67 K11
Edenburg, 153 E15
Edendale, 155 E11
Eden Nzork, 72 C4
Edenvale, 147 C15
Edenville, 147 I13
Edingeni, 100 I10
Edjérir, 58 G5
Eedsamub, 143 A14
Eendekuil, 156 D9
Eenhana, 113 E19
Eensgevonden, 146 M8
Effium, 255 G3
Egakane, 249 D3
Egbe, 66 F6
Egbunda, 69 L11
Egito Praia, 75 H17
Egmont Dam, 153 G18
Egneng Melen, 259 C6
Egypt, 55 H11
Eha-Amufu, 66 G9
Ehi Timi, 248 B7
Ehomba, 112 E9
Eidukal, 62 E3
Eiffel Flats, 119 J16
Eindpaal, 135 M15
Eintracht, 127 M12
Eirup, 135 H12
Eiseb, 128 F2
Ejeda, 48 L4
Ejidogari, 66 E5
Ejisu, 65 G17
Ejule, 66 G8
Ejura, 65 G17
Ekang, 66 I10
Ekangala, 147 B17
Ekata, 72 B8
Ekéifi, 249 L2
Eket, 66 J9
Ekismane, 249 M1
Ekok, 66 H10
Ekoko, 114 F4
Ekoli, 73 C20
Ekondo Titi, 66 J10
Ekouamou, 73 B11
Ekouata, 72 C2
Eksteenfontein, 150 A4
Eku, 66 D5
Ekukola, 73 C14
Ekuku, 73 C17
Ekukula, 73 B16
Ekuma, 276 A4
Ekumakoko, 73 E19
Ekuvukeni, 148 M2
Ekwa, 67 K14
Ekyiumenfuro, 65 G18
El Abiodh Sidi Cheikh, 52 B5
El Agaba, 56 H10
El Adayma, 251 H4
El Aioun, 49 E16
El Aiyat, 250 F8
El Ala, 246 C8
El Alam, 246 A10
El Alamein, 55 E13
El Alia, 52 C9
El Amaiem, 246 H6
El Ameriya, 250 D6
El Amparo, 244 H3
Elands, 139 K13
Elands Bay, 156 C7
Elandsdrif, 159 C15
Elandsdrift, 146 L2
Elands Height, 154 I3
Elandshoek, 278 M5
Elandskraal, 148 M3
Elandskuil, 278 B7
Elandslaagte, 148 L1
Elandspulte, 146 C7
Elands River Valley, 139 M18
El Aouina, 246 K6
El Aouinet, 49 J16
El Araba bi Sohag, 251 F1
El Araba el Madfuna, 63 F12
El Arco, 45 C14
El Aricha, 52 A3
El-Arish, 55 D18
Elarmekora, 259 F6
El Arrecife, 244 M9
El Arrouch, 49 I15
El Ashmunein, 55 H15
Elat, 55 F19
El Atrun Oasis, 61 G14
El Ayaycha, 246 H7
El Ayoun, *see Remada*
El Badari, 55 I16
El Badrshein, 250 F8
El Bahnasa, 250 H7
El Balyana, 251 F3
El Ban, 70 D9
El Barsha, 250 J8
El Basaliya Qibli, 55 K17
El Bathen, 246 B9
El Bayadh, 52 B5
El Bayadiya, 55 K17
El Behedero, 244 H8
El Beher, 57 I13
El Beru Hagia, 70 L8
El Bes, 79 H18
El Boibou, 57 I14
Elboitong, 70 M3
El Borouj, 245 G4
El Bueno, 244 L9
El Bulma, 49 J14
El Burg, 250 B8
El Cabrito, 44 C8
El Camino de Chasna, 244 H7
Elche, 49 A18
El Daba, 55 E12
El Dabba, 61 G18
Eldama Ravine, 83 I12
El Deir, 55 K17
El Der, 80 F10
El Dilingat, 250 D7
El Dimugrat, 251 H3
El Djouf, 57 D13
El Doctoral, 45 L19
Eldoret, 83 H11
Elefanteberg, 126 C7
Elele, 66 I8
El Encerradero, 244 D2
Elephant Bone Corner, 266 G9
Elephantes, 140 G6
Elephantine Island, 55 L18
Elephants of Kaniama, 74 K1
El Escobonal, 244 K10
El Faiyum, 55 G15
El Fans, 49 I18
El Faouar, 53 B13
El Fasher, 61 L12
El Fashn, 55 G15
El Fejj, 246 I8
El Fifi, 68 C9
El Fikriya, 250 J7
El Fud, 70 G10
El Gaga, 55 K15
Elgal, 85 D11
El Gamaliya, 250 C10
El Geili, 62 I1
El Ghriss, 246 F9
El Giara, 85 L17
El Gibirat, 251 E1
Elgin, 156 J10
El Giza, 55 F15
El Gleita, 56 J10
El God God, *Kenya* 70 L9
El God God, *Somalia* 81 J17
El Gof, 80 F7
El Golea, 52 E7
El Gorane Kadoussa, 245 H10
El Guetar, 246 H6
El Gulut, 62 M5
El Haddar, 246 J3
El Haddej, 246 K10
El Hadjar, 49 I16
El Haffey, 53 A13
El Hajeb, 51 A18
El Hamel, 49 K13
El Hamma, 53 A13
El Hamma Du Jerid, 246 I3
El Hammam, 55 E14
El Hamul, 250 C8
El Hamurre, 71 G17
El Haouareb, 246 C9
El Haouaria, 49 I19
El Haouita, 52 B7
El Harar, 71 L18
El Hawata, 62 L3
El Hiba, 250 H8
El Hidjer, 68 B3
Elias Garcia, 73 M15
El Idar, 70 A9
El Idisat, 55 K17
El Iein, 85 K14
Eliki, 59 J11
Eliki Gounda, 249 M3
Elila, 74 F2
Elim, 139 D17
Elipa, 73 D20
El Iskandariya, *see Alexandria*
Eliye Springs, 79 I13
Elizabeth Bay, 142 G6
Elizabeth Bay Ghost Town, 142 F6
El Jadida, 51 B15
El Jaral, 244 L2
El Jebelein, 62 M1
El Jebha, 245 C9
El Jema, 246 A9
El Jemm, 49 K19
El Julán, 44 L2
El Kab, 251 I5
El Kadada, 62 H2
El Kala, 49 I17
El Kanayis, 55 K18
El Kanayis Temple, 55 L18
El Karnak, 55 J17
El Katulo, 70 L7
El Kelaa Srarhna, 51 C16
El Kere, 70 H9
El Khandaq, 61 F17
El Kharga, 55 K15
El Khatatba, 55 E14
El Khattara, 251 J5
El Khroub, 49 J15
Elki, 68 B2
El Kilh Sharq, 251 I5
El Koin, 61 E18
El Kourf, 246 C3
El Ksar, 246 G5
El Kseur, 49 I14
El Ksiba, 51 C18
El Ksour, *place of interest* 246 A7
El Ksour, 246 A6
El Kubra, 55 E15
El Kure, 70 I10
El Lageita, 251 G5
El Lagowa, 69 B13
El Lahun, 250 G8
El Leben, 246 F8
El Leh, 80 G8
Elles, 246 A6
Elliot, 154 K2
Elliotdale, 160 B4
Ellisras, *see Lephalale*
El Lomo Moso, 244 H1
El Maadi, 250 F9
El Maghra, 250 E4
El Mahalla el Kubra, 250 D8
El Mahamid, 55 K18
El Maharraqa, 250 G9
El Mahassen, 246 I3
Elma Labiod, 49 K16
El Malan, 49 D18
El Manaqil, 62 K2
El Manshah, 251 F3
El Mansour, 52 H2
El Mansoura, 246 J6
El Mansura, 55 D16
El Maragha, 251 E2
El Matariya, 55 D16
El Maya, 52 B6
El Mdou, 246 J10
El Mech, 246 G8
El Medo, 70 I9
El Meghaier, 52 A9
Elmeki, 59 G13
El Melemm, 69 D13
El Menzel, 245 E9
El Meridj, 246 B3
Elmeston, 138 G8
El Mhaijrat, 56 F5
El Milia, 49 I15
Elmina, 65 I17
El Minya, 55 H15
El Molino, 244 H3
El Molledo, 244 J1
El Molnto, 44 C9
El Mreyye, 57 G15
El Nasser, 55 L18
El Nawawra, 251 E2
El Obeid, 61 L17
El Odaiya, 69 A13
Eloff, 147 D16
Elogbatindi, 67 K11
El Ogla Gasses, 49 K16
Elogo, 67 M16
El Ouata, 52 F2
El Ouchika, 246 G3
El Oued, 53 B11
El Pelao, 244 J10
El Pinar, *see Taibique*
El Portillo de la Villa, 244 B8
El Pris, 244 D10
El Qahira, *see Cairo*
El Qasr, 55 K13
El Qassasin, 250 D10
El Qusiya, 250 K7
El Ridisiya Bahari, 251 I5
El Riego, 244 I10
El Rincon, 244 G7
El Rio, 44 L3
El Rizeiqat, 55 K17
El Saff, 55 F16
El Salhiya, 55 E16
El Sanatorio, 244 E6
El Sauce, 244 H8
El Sauzal, 244 E9
El Sboub, 246 J7
El Shayib, 250 F8
El Sheikh Ibada, 250 J8
El Sheikh Timai, 250 J8
El Sibu Temple, 61 A19
El Simbillawein, 250 D9
El Sombrero, 244 F4
El Suweis, *see Suez*
El Tanque, 244 H1
El Tarf, 49 I17
El Thamad, 55 F18
El-Tina Bay, 55 D17
Elubo, 65 I16
El Vinatico, 244 H7
El Volcán, 45 D12
El Volcán Negro, 244 I2
El Wak, 70 L8
El Wasta, 250 G9
El Wuz, 61 J17
eMafakathini, 280 I8
Emahlatini, 148 F5
eMahusha, 278 K6
Emali, 89 F11
Emangusi, 149 G11
Embakaai Crater, 264 I9
Embu, 83 L20
Embundo, 76 M2
Emcisweni, 101 F11
Emeweni Falls, 280 H6
Emin, 260 A8
Emini, 67 K14
Emmaus Mission, 280 D4
Empakaai Crater, 88 I4
Empangeni, 155 A16
Empress Mine, 119 J14
Emusya, 266 E8
Enangiperi, 83 L14
Enaniliha, 48 L6
Enchereda, 44 B8
Encoje, 72 K9
Endabash, *river* 264 L9
Endabash, 264 L8
Endamaghay, 264 K8
Enda Medhane Alem, 62 M9
Endau, 89 C15
Endé, 247 L8
Endebes, 82 E10
Endengue, 67 L14
Endesh, 93 D20
Endibar, 70 F4
Endiké, 261 L3
Endom, 67 K13
Endulen, 88 J1
Enfida, 49 J19
Engaruka, 88 I4
Engaruka Basin, 88 J6
Engaruka Ruins, 88 I5
Engcobo, 154 M2
Engelhard Dam, 278 F8
Engitati, 264 J8
Engong Kouame, 259 D3
Engushai, 265 G5
Engusoro Plain, 264 K6
Enjil, 51 B19
Enkesso, 261 L2
En Nahud, 61 M16
Enne, 248 H6
Ennedi, 248 E8
Ennerdale, 147 D13
Enneri Achelouma, 59 B18
Enneri Blaka, 59 C18
Enseleni Nature Reserve, 155 A17
Entebbe, 74 C10
Enticcio, 258 D7
Entrada, 272 F3
Entre Deux, 47 L14
Entre Lagos, 109 I19
Entumeni, 155 B14
Enugu, 66 H8
Enugu-Ezike, 255 F2
Enukweni, 101 E12
Enyamba, 74 G1
Enyelé, 68 L1
Epako, 126 I3
Epe, 66 H4
Epemba, 113 F19
Epembe, 112 E8
Epena, 261 H8
Epéna, 73 A12
Epina, 44 B6
Epini, 74 A5
Epokiro, 127 K16
Epoma, 72 B10
Epukiro, 127 J17
Epulu, 69 L14
Epupa, 126 F1
Epupa Falls, 112 C7
Equateur, 73 B14
Equatorial Guinea, 67 M11
Eralrar, 249 C3
Ere, 67 D18
Eref, 68 A2
Ereke, 67 G18
Eremathi, 246 J9
Eremutua, 126 H3
Erer, 70 F9
Erese, 44 K4
Eretse, 277 D3
Erfenis Dam, 146 M9
Erfoud, 51 D19
Erg Check, 51 M18
Erg du Djourab, 60 I5
Erg du Ténéré, 59 H14
Erg er Raoui, 51 F19
Erg Iguidi, 51 K14
Erg-n-Ataram, 52 M4
Erguig, 248 J4
Erima, 82 D1
Eritrea, 62 I6
Ermelo, 148 E1
Ermil Post, 61 L14
Ermita de la Caridad, 44 K3
Ermita de la Magdalena, 45 E12
Ermita de las Nieves, 45 D13
Ermita de Nuestra Señora de la Peña, 45 G16
Ermita de San Francisco, 45 G17
Ermita de San Juan, 44 B8
Ermita de San Lorenzo, 44 D7
Ermita de San Marcos, 44 A7
Ermita de San Pedro, 45 I17
Ermita de San Sebastián, 45 D13
Ermita de Santiago, 45 K17
Ermita La Cruz del Tronco, 244 H4
Ermita NS de Guadalupe, 44 C7
Ermita NS del Buen Paso, 44 C7
Ermita NS de Lourdes, 44 C7
Ermita San Francisco de la Montañeta, 244 I2
Ermita San Pedro, 44 J3
Ermita Santo Domingo, 244 G4
Erongo, 126 J1
Er Rachidia, 51 D19
Er Rahad, 61 M18
Errego, 110 M4
Errocef, 246 E5
Erts, 139 L16
Erufa, 66 E6
Erundu, *river* 126 F4
Erundu, 126 G5
Eruwa, 66 F3
Esamang, 254 J3
Escade Vacances, 47 H18
Escravos, 66 I5
Eséke, 67 K12
Eshowe, 155 B15
Esiam, 254 J8
Esiama, 65 I16
Esigodini, 131 E13
Esira, 48 L6
Espagsdrif, 146 K1
Esparagos, 56 B4
Esperana, 140 M7
Espinheira, 112 B4
Esprit, 46 E7
Espungabera, 132 F9
Es Sabria, 246 L5
Essaouira, 51 D13
Essau, 56 L4
Essé, 67 J13
Estcourt, 154 B10
Estima, 108 L6
Estivane, 140 H6
Estuaire, 72 C3
Etaga, 123 B12
Etaka, 113 E13
Etaka, 261 I1
Etanga, 112 F7
Étang de la Presqu'Île, 274 J6
Étang Nymphea, 274 J6
Etéké, 72 D5
Etéké, 259 I7
Etemba, 126 J2
Etendeka, 112 H5
Etengwa, 112 E7
Ethiopia, 70 E2
Ethiopian Highlands, 70 C3
eTholeni, 280 B9
Etilyasa, 113 G14
Etinan, 255 J2
Etjo, 126 I5
Etoile, 46 C10
Etosha, 126 A2
Etosha National Park, 113 J13
Etosha Pan, 113 J19
Etoumbi, 72 C9
Etrobeke, 48 L3
Etsa Pan, 137 E11
Etsha, 277 E1
Etsha 13, 116 L6
Etsha 6, 116 M6
Etumba, 73 F15
Eurîka Creole Museum, 46 J3
Euthini, 100 G10
Euwo, 68 I5
Evale, 113 A17
Evander, 147 E18
Evangelina, 139 A14
Evaton, 147 E13
Everglades, 280 L7
Evero, 126 I7
Evinayong, 72 A4
Ewango, 66 G9
Ewaso Ngiro, *river* 83 G19
Ewaso Ngiro, 88 B3
Ewbank, 145 D17
Ewo, 72 D9
Excelsior, 153 B19
Eye of Kuruman, 145 I16
Eyl, *river* 71 E18
Eyl, 71 F18
Ezakheni, 280 C7
Ezbet el Gezira, 250 C9
Ezbet Gamasa el Gharbiya, 250 C9
Ezgueret, 58 H6
eZinyosini, 280 F6
Ezo, 69 I12
Ezzangbo, 66 H9
Ez Zhiliga, 51 B17

F

Faans Grove, 145 H13
Fabidji, 252 C8
Facauma, 76 C7
Fachi, 59 G16
Fada, 60 H8
Fada Archeï Faunal Reserve, 60 H8
Fadadinga, 249 M6
Fada N'Gourma, 65 A20
Fafa, *river* 68 G1
Fafa, 58 J4
Fafakourou, 56 L6
Fafaya, 64 B6
Fafen, 71 E11
Faga, 58 L4
Faggo, 67 B11
Fagrinkotti, 61 G19
Faguibine, *see Farach*
Faid, 49 K18
Fairfield, 157 K12
Fairview, 273 J9

L

M

N

Naboulgou, 252 K2
Nabuganyi, 82 F2
Nabusanke, 74 C9
Nabwalya, 100 K4
Nacala, 111 G19
Nacaroa, 111 F15
Nachikufu Cave, 100 H1
Nachingwea, 103 B12
Nachorugwai Desert, 79 J15
Nacumua, 110 F5
Nadawali, 65 C16
Nadiabonli, 252 F4
Nadjembe, 261 A5
Nadjouni, 252 H1
Nador, 49 D16
Nafada, 67 B13
Nafadji, 56 M9
Nafiulu Hills, 271 K4
Nafka Wildlife Reserve, 62 I8
Naga, 51 G15
Nagapande, 268 G9
Nagara, 56 J10
Nagare, 252 G5
Nag el Sarabgi, 251 J5
Nag Hammadi, 251 G3
Nagichot, 78 E4
Nagojje, 82 H2
Nagpotpot, 78 C5
Nahoro, 102 C1
Nahr Baru, 69 E19
Naiams Fort, 143 F15
Naibardad Hill, 264 J6
Naidor, 94 E9
Naimalumbua Hills, 264 D6
Nainokanoka, 264 I9
Naiopue, 110 L5
Nairi, *admin.* 72 F6
Nairi, *river* 72 G7
Nairobi, 88 C8
Nairobi National Park, 88 C8
Nairoto, 103 J13
Naivasha, 83 L15
Naiwangaa, 99 I17
Nakalatlou Pan, 136 H8
Nakalatlou/Urwi Pan, 135 D19
Nakanya, 104 K9
Nakapanya, 102 E8
Nakapiripirito, 82 B8
Nakasongola, 74 A9
Nakayembe, 105 J12
Nakfa, 62 H8
Nakhl, 55 F18
Naki-Est, 65 C20
Nakiloro, 78 K9
Nakitoma, 69 M17
Nakiwa, 120 F4
Nakonde, 96 J10
Nakop, 144 K4
Nakosa, 107 B16
Nakpanduri, 65 C19
Nakpok, 254 F1
Nakuijit, 82 C10
Nakuru, 83 K14
Nakwa, 254 J9
Nalatale Ruins, 131 C16
Nalazi, 140 G9
Naledi, 137 H15
Nalume, 110 H4
Nalut, 53 D14
Nam, 67 D19
Namaacha, 148 C9
Namacala, 110 G9
Namacunde, 113 D17
Namacurra, 122 F5
Namajani, 103 D12
Namakgale, 140 G1
Namaluba Post, 267 L1
Namalulu, 94 C9
Namanga, 88 H8
Namanyere, 96 C3
Namapa, 111 C16
Namaponda, 111 L15
Namaqualand, 150 C6
Namaqua National Park, 150 F5
Namaro, 252 A5
Namarrói, 110 L3
Namasagali, 82 F2
Namatakwarra, 128 C2
Nambazo, 109 K18
Nambinda, 99 L11
Nambiranji, 99 L17
Namboukaha, 65 D13
Nambouli, 252 K6
Nambuangongo, 75 C18
Nambunga, 103 D14
Nambunju, 99 K15
Nambwa, 102 B8
Nametil, 111 K13
Namgorab, 134 L4
Namialo, 111 H16
Namib, 124 B8
Namib Desert, 124 F8
Namibe, 75 L16
Namibe Reserve, 75 L16
Namibia, 125 G15
Namib-Naukluft Park, 134 K1
Namib Rand Nature Reserve, 134 L3
Namichiga, 99 M16
Namidobe, 122 H5
Namies, 151 C11
Namina, 111 H11
Naminwe Plain, 106 L2
Namiroe, 110 L8
Namitete, 108 E9
Namon, 66 D1
Namoungou, 252 F2
Namounou, 252 F5
Nampala, 57 J17
Nampevo, 122 B6
Nampula, *admin.* 111 H12
Nampula, 111 I12
Namtungu Pan, 268 L6
Namuhi, 103 B16
Namuiranga, 103 C19
Namukumbo, 106 J3
Namunda, 103 B16
Namuno, 111 C12
Namuxinda, 76 B5
Namwala, *area* 270 H7
Namwala, 106 L1
Namwera, 109 F17
Namwiwa, 82 E4
Nana, *river* 67 H17
Nana, 67 G17
Nana Bakassa, 67 G19
Nana Barya, 67 F20
Nana-Barya Faunal Reserve, 67 F20
Nana Candundo, 76 H8
Nanania Plateau, 134 K8
Nandi, 132 H5
Nandom, 65 C16
Nanergou, 252 I1
Nangade, 103 E15
Nanga Eboko, 67 J14
Nangamba, 270 F3
Nanganga, 103 B14
Nangano, 103 A11
Nangaru, 99 L17
Nangbeto, 66 G1
Nangolet, 78 B4
Nangomba, 103 D11
Nangua, 102 D10
Nangulangwa, 99 F15
Nangurukuru, 99 H17
Nanguruwe, 103 C18
Nanjirinji, 99 L16
Nankoma, 82 H4
Nankova, 76 M4
Nansebo, 257 K5
Nansenga, 270 G9
Nansimo, 87 F13
Nansio, 87 F12
Nantanga Pan, 277 A10
Nantulo, 103 K12
Nantwich, 268 C3
Nanyamba, 103 D16
Nanyuki, 83 J18
Nanzhila, 105 M18
Nanzhila Plains, 270 K6
Naos, 134 D7
Napaha, 111 B12
Napeitom, 83 C14
Napier, 157 L13
Naqada, 251 G4
Nara, 57 J14
Naremoru, 265 H8
Narena, 64 A10
Narengmor, 79 F11
Narib, 134 H10
Nariep, 150 I5
Narira, 120 M1
Narok, 134 H7
Narok, 88 B4
Naro Moru, 83 J18
Narosura, 88 C4
Narubis, 143 G19
Nas Allah, 246 D9
Nasarawa, 66 E8
Nasia, *river* 65 C19
Nasia, 65 D18
Nasir, 69 E18
Nasmah, 53 D17
Nasolot Nature Reserve, 83 B11
Nasondoye, 77 F11
Nassian, 65 D14
Nassougou, 252 E3
Nassoukou, 252 L10
Nassoulé, 261 A3
Nata, *Botswana* 130 E3
Nata, *river* 130 D3
Nata, *Tanzania* 87 E17
Natal Drakensberg Park, 154 E5
Natchamba, 65 D19
Natco, 276 D2
Nathenje, 109 E11
Natiaboani, 65 B20
National Park, 46 C3
National West Coast Tourist Recreational Area, 124 A7
Natis, 113 K17
Natitingou, 66 C2
Natukanaoka Pan, 113 I17
Natukoma, 116 B7
Nauchas, 134 F5
Naucratis, 250 D7
Naudesnek, 154 I3
Nauela, 110 K5
Naukluft, 134 I3
Naulila, 113 D13
Naute Dam, 143 G17
Naute Recreation Area, 143 G16
Nauzerus, 134 G5
Nava, 69 L11
Navrongo, 65 C18
Nawani, 254 D9
Nawinda Kuta, 117 C15
Nayazwidzi, 132 A3
Nayouri, 252 E1
Nayuchi, 109 I18
Nazlet el Amudein, 250 I7
Nazombe, 103 F12
Nazret, 70 E6
Nazza, 251 F2
Nbâk, 254 F1
Nbeika, 56 G9
Ncamasere, 116 J3
Ncanaha, 159 H14
Ncaute, 115 H13
Ncemane, 279 I6
Nchenachena, 101 D12
Nchwera, 262 K7
Ncojane, 135 D19
Ncojane Ranches, 135 D20
Ncora Dam, 154 M1
Ndabaka Plain, 264 F2
Ndaba Waterfall, 260 H7
Ndagaa, 95 I18
Ndakithima Hills, 266 I9
Ndala, 93 D13
Ndalambo, 96 I9
Ndalampakule, 270 J4
N'dalantando, 75 E19
Ndali, 66 D3
Ndambissoa, 68 H6
Ndanda, *CAR* 68 I6
Ndanda, *Tanzania* 103 C13
Ndande, 56 J4
Ndanga, 67 J20
Ndangane, 56 K3
Ndangui, 72 C7
Ndara, 266 I6
Ndara Plains, 266 I7
Ndareda, 94 B3
Nde, 255 C2
Ndedo, 94 E8
Ndedu, 69 K13
Ndeji, 66 E6
Ndekesha, 73 J17
Ndéko, 73 D11
Ndélé, 68 E4
Ndelele, 67 J16
Ndélélé, 261 A2
Ndembe, 67 J15
Ndembera, 97 F18
Ndembo, 99 L11
Ndembera, 101 D12
Ndendé, 72 E5
Ndhlovu, 268 G4
Ndia, 56 K8
Ndiago, 56 I4
Ndia-Ndasa, 266 C7
Ndiguina, 67 B17
Ndikinimeki, 67 J12
Ndikoko, 67 J12
Ndim, 67 G18
Ndindi, *Gabon* 72 G4
Ndindi, *Senegal* 56 J4
Ndioum Guent, 56 K6
Ndiri, 68 F4
Nditam, 67 I13
Ndiwe, 67 K17
Ndiya, 66 J9
N'Djamena, 67 A17
Ndjole, 67 J13
Ndjolé, 72 C4
Ndlozane, 148 F6
Ndoha Plain, 87 H18
Ndok, 67 F16
Ndokama, 67 J11
Ndokayo, 67 H16
Ndoki, 67 M19
Ndola, 77 I15
Ndolwane, 268 M9
Ndom, 67 J12
Ndombi Bay, 101 D14
Ndonga, 115 G15
Ndongolo, 72 A5
Ndon Kota, 67 H19
Ndop, 67 H11
Ndoto Mountains, 83 C19
Ndoumbou, 68 G1
Ndoussi, 65 H13
Ndu, 67 H12
Nduguti, 93 B18
Nduluku, 89 D11
Ndumbwe, 103 B17
Ndumo, 148 G9
Ndumo Game Reserve, 148 F9
Ndunda, 100 D9
Ndundu, 99 E16
Ndundulu, 155 A16
Nduye, 69 L14
Ndwedwe, 155 D13
Nebbi, 262 A6
Nebbou, 65 B17
Nebo, 139 K15
Nebulu, 69 M11
Nechisar National Park, 70 H4
Necropolis of Mir, 250 K7
Necropolis of Thebes (WHS), 55 K16
Necungas, 121 A14
Necuto, 72 H6
Nedatra, 70 C5
Needle, 281 G4
Nefta, 53 A12
Negage, 75 C19
Negala, 57 M13
Nega Nega, 106 L7
Neganisi, 66 C4
Negele, 70 I6
Negezi, 87 L14
Negomane, 103 F11
Negrine, 49 K16
Negro Bay, 71 F18
Nehimba Pan, 268 D5
Nehone, 113 A18
Neilersdrif, 151 A17
Neineis, 125 J19
Nejo, 70 D2
Nekemte, 70 E3
Nekheb, *see El Kab*
Nelshoogte, 148 B4
Nelspoort, 158 B4
Nelspruit, 139 M20
Néma, 57 H15
Neméyong, 261 F2
Nemguéne, 247 H10
Nemini, 254 J5
Nemtungu Pan, 130 C4
Nengo, 104 F1
Nepara, 114 F8
Nepoko, 69 L13
Neriquinha, 76 L7
Nerston Sandlane, 148 E5
Nessona, 121 L18
Netia, 111 H16
Neuhof, 134 K4
Neumann Tower, 265 E9
Neuras, 134 I5
Newala, 103 E14
New Amalfi, 154 G6
Newcastle, 148 J1
New England, 154 J1
New Featherstone, 119 K19
New Grove, 46 L4
New Halfa, 62 J4
New Hanover, 155 D12
Newington, 140 K2
New Inyantue Dam, 268 C6
Newlands, 281 G10
Newlands Forest, 281 G9
Newlands Forest Station, 281 F9
Newlands Reservoir, 281 F9
New Machavie, 146 F10
New Port, 273 H9
New Savy, 273 K10
Nezet, 273 E7
Ngabé, 72 F10
Ngabeni, 154 J8
Ngabwe, 106 E4
Ngadda, 67 A15
Ngagau, 98 F3
Ngaide II, 68 D4
Ngala, 68 I5
Ngalambula, 97 E16
Ngalia, 68 I5
Ngalwa, 59 L17
Ngam, 67 C18
Ngama, *CAR* 68 J5
Ngama, *Chad* 67 B20
Ngambé, 67 J12
Ngambe Tikar, 67 H13
Ngamdu, 67 B14
Ngamiland, 128 C8
Ngamo, 118 M6
Nganda, *Senegal* 56 L5
Nganda, *Tanzania* 97 J17
Ngandana, 65 C12
Nganda Peak, 271 C4
Ngangala, 69 J17
Ngangora, 99 L11
Nganji, 74 E4
Nganzi, 72 I6
Ngaoundal, 67 F15
Ngaoundéré, 67 G15
Ngara, *Malawi* 101 B13
Ngara, *Tanzania* 86 G2
Ngara Len, 266 G2
Ngarama, 263 B8
Ngarangou, 59 L20
Ngare Nanyuki, 265 J1
Ngaso Plain, 80 H4
Ngasumet, 94 C10
Ngatataik, 88 F8
Ngato, 67 K17
Ngayu, 69 M13
Ngbala, 67 M17
Ngelani, 88 C10
Ngeleza, 262 E1
Ngengete, 261 H10
Ngerengere, 95 L12
Ngesi, 131 B19
Ngété, 256 H10
Ngezi, 131 C16
Ngezi Dam, 131 E17
Ngezi Recreational Park, 119 K18
Nghobora, 87 I15
Ngiapanda, 95 K15
Ngidinga, 72 I9
Ngina, 69 K13
Ngo, 72 E10
Ngoa, 69 L14
Ngobib, 114 J1
Ngodwana, 278 M5
Ngog Mapubi, 67 K12
Ngogwe, 82 I2
Ngohowe Pan, 137 F14
Ngoila, 67 L15
Ngoilanga, 98 I4
Ngoko, *river* 72 D9
Ngoko, 72 C10
Ngola, 67 K17
Ngolo, 96 L4
Ngolo Waterfall, 68 I6
Ngoma, 117 H15
Ngoma Bridge, 117 H15
Ngomba, 97 F11
Ngombe, 270 B3
Ngome, 148 J6
Ngomedzap, 67 K12
Ngong, *Cameroon* 67 E15
Ngong, *Kenya* 88 C8
Ngonga, 67 J11
Ng'onga, 271 G4
Ngongo, 96 H9
Ngongongare Hill, 265 L1
Ngongoro, 93 C15
Ngonini, 148 B7
Ngonye Falls, 117 C11
Ngora, 82 D5
Ngorengore, 88 B3
Ngorkou, 247 F5
Ngoro, 67 I13
Ngorongoro Conservation Area (WHS), 87 K20
Ngororero, 260 G8
Ngoso, 73 H14
Ngoto, 67 J20
Ngotwane, 138 G5
Ngoubi, 68 H5
Ngoui, 56 I7
Ngoulémakong, 67 L12
Ngoulo, 261 C5
Ngouma, 57 J19
Ngoumo, 261 G6
Ngoundi, 261 B8
Ngouni, 72 D8
Ngounié, *admin.* 72 D5
Ngounié, *river* 72 D4
Ngoura, *Cameroon* 67 I16
Ngoura, *Cameroon* 67 J16
Ngouri, 60 L1
Ngourti, 59 J18
Ngouyo, 68 I10
Ngové-Ndogo Hunting Reserve, 72 E3
Ngoyeboma, 72 B8
Ngozi, 74 F7
Ngqeleni, 154 M6
Ngqungqu, 160 A5
Ngubalo, 87 K11
Ngubo, 270 A6
Ngudu, 87 I13
Ngulemendouka, 67 J14
Nguema, 76 B8
Ngui, 68 H6
Nguia Bouar, 67 I17
Nguigmi, 59 K18
Nguila, 67 J13
Nguini, 249 M4
Ngundu, 132 G1
Nguni, 84 M4
Ngurdoto Crater, 88 K9
Ngurojé, 67 G13
Ngurore, 67 D13
Nguru, *peak* 93 L20
Nguru, 59 M15
Nguruliro, 97 C13
Ngurumahiga, 102 B8
Nguru Mountains, 94 J10
Ngusa, 266 L3
Nguti, 67 I11
Ngwale, 102 A9
Ngwanalekau Hills, 128 H9
Ngwanche Pan, 138 H1
Ngwane Pan, 138 H1
Ngwavuma, 279 C2
Ngwempisi, 148 E4
Ngwenyeni Dam, 278 I8
Ngwesi, 130 H9
Ngweze, 117 F20
Ngwezumba, *river* 117 J15
Ngwezumba, 117 J16
Ngwezumba Dam, 277 B9
Ngxongwane, 279 G3
Nhabe, 129 E11
Nhachengue, 141 C16
Nhacolo, 121 C14
Nhacra, 64 A2
Nhamadzi, 272 B1
Nhamalabue, 121 F17
Nhamatanda, 133 A14
Nhamitenguere, 133 A17
Nhandugue, 121 H12
Nharia, 76 G2
Nhia, 75 F18
Nhimbe, 108 J5
Nhlabane Lake, 148 M9
Nhlangano, 148 G6
Nhlazatshe, 148 K5
Nhlotini, 278 K8
Nhoma, *river* 115 L14
Nhoma, 115 J17
Niababri, 65 I12
Niable, 65 G15
Niada, 68 I5
Niafounke, 247 D4
Niafounké, 57 I18
Niagassola, 64 A9
Niakaramandougou, 65 E13
Niambezaria, 65 I12
Niamey, 58 L5
Niamina, 57 L14
Niamtougou, 66 D1
Niamvoudou, 67 J14
Niandan Koro, 64 B8
Niandat, 64 D8
Niangandu, 99 E11
Niangara, 69 K12
Niangoloko, 65 C14
Nia-Nia, 74 A4
Niansour, 68 B5
Niantan, 64 C7
Niantanina, 64 C9
Niapu, 69 L11
Niari, 72 G8
Niassa, 102 M2
Niassa Game Reserve, 102 J3
Niau, 56 L5
Nicondocho, 102 K10
Nicuadala, 122 G4
Nicupa, 111 F17
Niega, 58 M2
Niekerkshoop, 152 D3
Nielle, 65 C13
Niem, 67 H17
Niemba, *river* 77 B14
Niemba, 77 A15
Niembe, 91 J11
Niéna, 65 B12
Nietverdiend, 138 K2
Nieu Bethesda, 158 A9
Nieuwoudtville, 150 L10
Nieza, 49 I18
Nigba, 256 L4
Nigel, 147 D15
Niger, *river* 58 H2
Niger, 59 I12
Nigeria, 66 F5
Nigramoep, 150 D5
Nikki, 66 D4
Nikoemvon, 67 L12
Nikonga, 92 A6
Nila, 258 H5
Nile, 63 G14
Niminiama, 247 H6
Nimjat, 56 H6
Nimule, 69 K17
Nimule National Park, 69 K16
Nina, 135 C12
Ninda, 76 K7
Nindai, 271 D8
Ninette, 135 A14
Ningari, 247 J9
Ningi, 67 B11
Nioasamoridu, 64 E9
Nioka, *DRC* 69 M16
Nioka, *DRC* 73 K19
Niokhi, 73 F12
Niokolo-Koba, 56 L8
Niokolo-Koba Biosphere Reserve (WHS), 56 M7
Niono, 57 K16
Niorenge, 110 D8
Nioro du Rip, 56 L5
Nioro du Sahel, 57 J11
Nioumachoua, 48 B4
Nipepe, 110 E8
Nipiodie, 122 E8
Nipiodi, 122 A7
Nisseko, 65 C15
Nizi, 69 M15
Njagi, 98 F5
Njawai, 255 K8
Njazidja, 48 A3
Njesuthi, 280 F5
Njiapanda, 97 I13
Njinjo, 99 H15
Njoge, 94 I7
Njogonjwa, 98 J4
Njoko, 117 A16
Njombe, *river* 97 A18
Njombe, *Tanzania* 97 J18
Njoro, *Kenya* 83 K14
Njoro, *Tanzania* 94 F6
Njunga, 101 D19
Nkala, *area* 270 J5
Nkala, *river* 270 J4
Nkala Hill, 270 J4
Nkam, 72 B5
Nkamba Bay, *bay* 96 G2
Nkamba Bay, 96 H1
Nkambe, 67 G12
Nkandla, 148 M5
Nkawkaw, 65 H18
Nkaya Pan, 278 I9
Nkayi, 119 L12
Nkeni, 72 E9
Nkhata Bay, *bay* 101 G13
Nkhata Bay, 101 G13
Nkhotakota, 101 M12
Nkhota-Kota Wildlife Reserve, 109 A12
Nkoakoni, 279 E4
Nkoam-bang, 67 J14
Nkob, 51 E17
Nkokanjiru Tombs, 74 C7
Nkokodzi, 278 D7
Nkokwane Pan, 129 H19
Nkolabona, 72 A5
Nkole, 100 C1
Nkolmengboua, 67 L13
Nkolo, 257 I5
Nkomboshe, 279 L3
Nkomfap, 66 H10
Nkomo, 139 E20
Nkondwe, 92 I3
Nkongjok, 67 I11
Nkongsamba, 67 J11
Nkonjera Peak, 101 D11
Nkonko, 93 J19
Nkonkoni, 148 I8
Nkon Ngok, 67 J12
Nkopola, 109 E15
Nkoranza, 65 F17
Nkoshya, 77 E16
Nkoteng, 67 J14
Nkoué, 72 G9
Nkourala, 65 B12
Nkovakulu, 278 B6
Nkulumane Junction, 131 D13
Nkulumbeni, 140 B3
Nkumbi, 96 D5
Nkungulu, 109 G16
Nkungwe, 77 A17
Nkunzana, 279 G1
Nkunzi, 280 D4
Nkurenkuru, 114 E8
Nkusi, 74 A8
Nkwalini, 155 A16
Nkwanta, 65 F19
Nlaklan, 64 I9
Nnewi, 66 H8
Nobantu, 154 L5
Nobere, 65 B18
Nobokwe, 160 A1
Nodi, 252 L6
Nodwengu, 148 L6
Noel Hunt Bridge, 119 L12
Noenieput, 144 I4
Nohana, 154 F2
Nokaneng, 128 C7
Nokong, 154 C3
Nokou, 59 K20
Nola, 67 K18
Noli, 103 B11
Noll, 158 I4
Nomab, 113 K13
No Man's Peak, 280 I3
Nombori, 247 K9
Nomtsas, 134 I7
Nondo, 96 K4
Nondwa, 94 K2
Nondweni, 148 K4
Nongoma, 148 J7
Noniams, 114 K1
Nono, 64 C7
Nooitgedacht Dam Nature Reserve, 148 C2
Noordhoek, 156 J8
Noordkaap, 148 A6
Noordkuil, 156 D8
Noordoewer, 150 A5
Norah, 62 I9
Norassoba, 64 C8
Nordeste, 76 C7
Norman, 126 J3
Normandien, 147 K19
Northam, 138 K6
North Corrie, 265 D8
North East, *Botswana* 130 H7
North East, *Kenya* 85 B12
North East Point, 46 B4
North East Valley, 265 C8
Northern, *Malawi* 101 E12
Northern, *Zambia* 100 C4
Northern Cape, 151 H13
Northern Icefields, 265 C3
Northern Tombs, 55 H15
Northern Tuli Conservation Area, 131 L13
North Horr, 79 H18
North Island, 79 E14
North Kitui National Reserve, 84 K5
North Luangwa National Park, 100 I4
North Pare Mountains, 89 K11
North Point, 66 I5
North Rumphi, 271 D4
North West, 146 F2
Norton, 119 H19
Norvalspont, 153 I13
Nosibe, 274 E8
Nosivolo, 48 I7
Nossob, 126 M10
Nossombougou, 57 M13
Nosy Ambariovaato, 274 F4
Nosy Ankao, 48 B10
Nosy Barren, 48 G4
Nosy Be, 274 E4
Nosy Be Archipelago, 48 C8
Nosy Faly, 274 E4
Nosy Iranja, 274 F2
Nosy Lava, 274 D5
Nosy Mitsio, 48 B8
Nosy Sainte Marie, 48 F9
Nosy Sakatia, 274 E3
Nosy Tendro, 274 C8
Nosy-Varika, 48 I8
Nota, 121 L13
Notintsila, 154 M6
Notocoto, 123 D11
Notsé, 66 G1
Nottingham Road, 154 D9
Nouabalé, 261 E7
Nouadhibou, 56 D5
Nouail, 246 K6
Nouakchott, 56 G5
Nouamrhar, 56 E5
Nouhao, 65 B19
Noumoukiedoumou, 65 D14
Noun, 67 I12
Nouna, *river* 67 M14
Nouna, 57 M18
Noungou, 280 M5
Noupoort, 153 K11
Noupoortsnek, 147 L14
Nourice, 275 J2
Nouvelle Matmata, 246 J9
Nova Almada, 133 C15
Nova Caipemba, 72 K8
Nova Coimbra, 101 K15
Nova Golegã, 133 E13
Nova Guarda, 109 C18
Nova Mambone, 133 H17
Nova Nabúri, 123 C13
Nova Sentarém, 109 C19
Nova Vandúzi, 120 L9
Noya, 72 B4
Noyace, 46 L2
Nqabara, 160 C4
Nqabeni, 154 I9
Nqamakwe, 160 B1
Nqoga, 116 M8
Nqutu, 148 L4
Nsa, 72 E10
Nsakaluba, 77 F15
Nsalu Caves, 77 I17
Nsama, 77 D17
Nsambi, 73 D12
Nsami Dam, 139 D20
Nsanje, 121 D17
Nsasane, 278 I9
Nsawam, 65 H18
Nsawkaw, 65 F16
Nsefu Game Reserve, 100 M4
Nsele, 72 H10
Nseleni, 279 L4
Nshawu Dam, 278 E8
Nshongezi, 86 A3
Nshongweni Dam, 155 F12
Nsika, 74 C7
Nsiza, 131 C14
Nsoc, 72 A5
Nsoko, 148 G8
Nsokolo, 96 J6
Nsombo, 77 G17
Nsongezi, 262 M5
Nsontin, 73 F13
Nsukka, 66 G8
Nsumbu, 96 G1
Nsumbu National Park, 96 G1
Nsumo Pan, 279 F6
Ntabamhlope, 154 C9
Ntabayezulu, 279 G3
Ntabazinduna, 131 D13
Ntabebomvu, 148 K4
Ntaja, 109 H18
Ntambanana, 279 L2
Ntambu, 77 H11
Ntambenethe, 73 E11
Ntcheu, 109 H14
Ntchisi, 109 B12
Nteko, 96 J9
Ntem, 67 L12
Ntemwa, 270 A6
Ntenkélé, 72 B6
Nthalire, 101 B11
Nthunga, 101 K12
Ntibane, 154 M4
Ntimaru, 87 C19
Ntobo, 86 L9
Ntokou, 261 K6
Ntokou-Otolou, 72 B10
Ntomeni Pan, 278 E7
Ntondweni, 279 I5
Ntoroko, 262 F5
Ntoum, 72 B3
Ntshilini, 154 M7
Ntshingwayo Dam, 147 K20
Ntshinini, 280 H7
Ntsokotsa Pan, 130 H1
Ntsou, 72 E10
Ntsumaneni, 278 G9
Ntui, 67 J13
Ntumba, 96 F8
Ntungama, 74 B7
Ntungamo, 86 A1
Ntungwe, 260 D8
Ntunjambili, 155 B14
Ntusi, 74 C8
Ntwaaban, 254 M2
Ntwemwa, 105 E19
Ntwetwe Pan, 129 G19
Ntywenka, 154 K4
Nuamses, 276 D6
Nuba, 69 B15
Nubian Desert, 62 D1
Nugubaes, 126 D3
Nulli, 131 L19
Numan, 67 D14
Numatinna, 69 G12
Numbi, 74 E6
Nun, 66 J7
Nungo, 110 B7
Nungwe, 86 I7
Nungwi, 95 H18
Nuon, 64 G9
Nurei, 60 L9
Nursery Ravine, 281 G7
Nutfield, 139 K12
Nuu, 89 B15
Nuwefontein, 144 K1
Nuweiba, 55 G19
Nuwerus, 150 K7
Nuwe Smitsdorp, 139 H14
Nuweveldberge, 157 D18
Nuy, 157 H12
Nwa, 67 H12
Nwambu Pan, 278 E8
Nwanedi Dam, 139 B19
Nwanedi Game Reserve, 139 B18
Nwaswitshaka, 278 K8
Nwayfadh, 50 K6
Nwera, 99 E19
Nxabe, 129 C13
Nxai Nxai, 128 C3
Nxai Pan National Park, 129 D17
Nxaunxau, 116 L2
Nya, 67 E18
Nyabessan, 67 L11
Nyabira, 119 G20
Nyabisindu, 74 E7
Nyadiri, 120 D6
Nya-Ghezi, 260 I5
Nyagombe, 91 C17
Nyagui, 120 F3
Nyahanga, 87 G14
Nyahua, *river* 93 H12
Nyahua, 93 G13
Nyahuka, 260 A9
Nyahururu, 83 I15
Nyakabindi, 87 H16
Nyakagomba, 86 I7
Nyakahura, 86 I3
Nyakalengija, 260 B8
Nyakaliro, 86 G9
Nyakanazi, 86 J4
Nyakintonto, 91 C17
Nyakisogo, 92 B2
Nyakitasi, 99 F16
Nyakrom, 254 H9
Nyala, *Sudan* 68 A9
Nyala, *Zimbabwe* 132 L4
Nyalazi, 148 L9
Nyalazi River, 279 J6
Nyali, 72 E5
Nyalikungu, 87 H13
Nyamaga, 87 B15
Nyamagasani, 262 G7
Nyamandhlovu, 131 C11
Nyamandhlovu Pan, 268 C7
Nyamapanda, 120 D8
Nyamassila, 66 F1
Nyamazugu, 86 H9
Nyamba, 103 B13
Nyambi, 105 J13
Nyambiti, 87 I13
Nyamgalika, 92 C4
Nyamhanga, 98 G6
Nyamirembe, 86 G7
Nyamlell, 69 E11
Nyamoko, 67 I12
Nyamsika, 262 B3
Nyamtumbo, 102 C2
Nyamuragira, 260 C3
Nyamuswa, 87 E15
Nyamwage, 99 F16
Nyamwanga, 87 D18
Nyamweru, 262 J7
Nyanatakara, 86 J5
Nyanda, 255 G10
Nyandekwa, 86 M10
Nyanga, *admin.* 72 G4
Nyanga, *Congo* 72 F5
Nyanga, *river* 72 F6
Nyanga, *Zimbabwe* 120 I7
Nyangamara, 103 B15
Nyanga National Park, 120 J8
Nyanga Sud Hunting Reserve, 72 F5
Nyange, 91 B18
Nyangolo, 98 C3
Nyanguge, 87 H12
Nyanhonge, 87 J12
Nyanoa, 254 G2
Nyanza, *admin.* 82 I7
Nyanza, 260 I8
Nyanza Lac, 74 H6
Nyanza-Lac, 91 C14
Nyaoruédou, 256 K3
Nyaru, 83 H12
Nyarweyo, 262 F7
Nyasa, 74 I3
Nyassar, 67 F16
Nyatande, 108 G2
Nyawa, 120 G2
Nyazura, 120 K5
Nyé, 67 M13
Nyenase, 65 I17
Nyeri, *Kenya* 83 K18
Nyeri, *Uganda* 69 K17
Nyero Rock Shelters & Paintings, 82 D5
Nyibiam, 66 F9
Nyiel, 69 H16
Nyika, 132 D4
Nyika National Park, 101 D12
Nyika Plateau, 101 D11
Nyimba, 107 G18
Nyiragongo, 260 D3
Nyiri Desert, 88 G10
Nyiru Range, 79 L17
Nylstroom, *see Modimolle*
Nyokana, 160 C4
Nyong, 67 J14
Nyoni, 155 C15
Nyouanga, 68 G10
Nyungwe, 271 C5
Nyungwe Forest Reserve, 74 F6
Nyunzu, 74 I4
Nyuruandanga, 99 C17
Nzako, 68 H6
Nzambi, 72 G5
Nzara, 69 J13
NZASM Tunnel, 148 A3
Nzebela, 64 F9
Nzega, 93 B12
Nzeka, 96 F6
Nzérékoré, 64 F8
N'zeto, 72 K6
Nzhelele, 139 A18
Nzhelele Dam, 139 B17
Nzibira, 260 J4
Nzili, 68 B6
Nzima, 87 K11
Nzo, *river* 64 G10
Nzo, 64 F10
Nzoia, 82 H7
Nzopi, 69 K14
Nzoro, *river* 69 K15
Nzoro, 67 G18
Nzovu, 260 I3
Nzwani, 48 B5

O

Oaktree, 280 K8
Oangwa, 115 M18
Oatlands, 158 E8
Oba, 66 G6
Obaba, 73 E11
Obala, 67 J13
Oban, 66 I10
Oban Hills, 66 I9
Obehie, 66 I8
Obi, 66 F10
Obo, *river* 69 L14
Obo, 69 I11
Obobogorap, 144 H5
Obock, 70 A10
Obokote, 74 D3
Oboli, 72 E9
Obolo, 255 F2
Obouya, 72 D10
Observatorio Astrónomico del Teide, 244 J8
Obubra, 66 H9
Obudu, 66 G10
Obudu Cattle Ranch, 255 B5
Obudu Ranch, 255 B5
Obuo, 254 I5
Oburi, 82 C3
Occidental, 76 B6
Ochero, 82 C2
Ocua, 111 C15
Oda, 65 H18
Odendaalsrus, 146 J9
Odenyi, 255 E1
Odienné, 65 D11
Odjala, 72 C8
Odonkawkron, 65 G18
Odrus, 62 E5
Odzala National Park, 72 B9
Odzema, 261 K5
Odzi, 120 L6
Odziba, 72 G10
Oehier Ridge, 265 C2
Ofcolaco, 139 H18
Ofe, 66 E6
Ofere, 66 F7
Offoué, 259 F7
Offumpo, 65 H14
Ofin, 65 H17
Ofinso, 65 G17
Ofoase, 65 H18
Ofugo, 66 F9
Ogaden, 71 G11
Ogani, 66 J8
Ogbomosho, 66 F4
Ogembo, 82 M9
Ogies, 147 C18
Ogoja, 66 G10
Ogooué, 72 C5
Ogooué-Ivindo, 72 B6
Ogooué-Lolo, 72 C6
Ogooué-Maritime, 72 D3
Ogoué, 259 F4
Ogoulou, 259 I7
Ogun, *river* 66 F4
Ogun, 66 E4
Ogur, 78 L2
Ogurugu, 66 G7
Ogwashi, 66 H7
Ohalia, 66 I9
Ohanet, 53 G12
Ohe Pan, 136 E5
Ohiya, 85 D12
Ohrigstad, 139 J19
Ohrigstad Dam, 139 K18
Ohrigstad Dam Nature Reserve, 139 K18
Oju, 66 G9
Oka, 66 G6
Okadja, 68 A6
Okahakana Pan, 113 K17
Okahandja, 126 L6
Okahao, 113 G14
Okakarara, 126 F8
Okakombo, 126 I3
Okalongo, 113 E15
Okamatapati, 127 E11
Okana, 261 M4
Okandja, 72 C8
Okandjambo, 112 H6
Okangoho, 126 E10
Okangwati, 112 D7
Okankolo, 113 G19
Okano, 259 C8
Okanono, 126 J3
Okapi National Park, 69 M12
Okaputa, 126 D7
Okarukurume, 127 I13
Okasewa, 135 A12
Okata, 66 F4
Okatjiura, 113 J11
Okatjoruu, 114 M9
Okatumba, 112 I9
Okatuwa, 127 J18
Okauwe, 112 E6
Okavango, *admin.* 115 H12
Okavango, *river* 114 E7
Okavango Delta, 128 A8
Okave, 126 E6
Okavewa, 113 K13
Okazize, 126 K5
Oke-Iho, 66 F3
Okélataka, 261 L2
Okene, 66 F7
Okere, 78 L6
Okerfontein, 114 J1
Okiep, 150 E6
Okigwe, 66 H8
Okok, 78 L6
Okoloria, 82 C6
Okola, 67 K13
Okollo, 69 L16
Okombahe, 126 I1
Okondeka, 113 K18
Okondethe, 113 K11
Okondjatu, 127 H12
Okongo, 114 E3
Okovarumendu, 127 J14
Okoyo, 72 D9
Okozondara, 127 J13
Okozongoro, 126 I4
Okpoma, 255 A2
Okrouyo, 65 H12
Oku, 74 E4
Okuta, 66 E4
Okwa, *Botswana* 129 M14
Okwa, *Nigeria* 66 F9
Okwangalete, 82 D2
Okwa Pan, 136 I10
Okweke, 255 H1
Olbalbal Depression, 264 J8
Olbalbal Swamp, 264 J8
Old Bunting, 154 M6
Old Dongola, 61 G18
Oldeani, 88 K3
Old Hartley, 119 I18
Old Joe, 278 L4
Old Matare, 120 L6
Old Mkushi, 107 F12
Old Morley, 160 B6
Old Nariam, 82 B6
Ol Doinyo Drok, 88 G7
Ol Doinyo Lengai, 88 H4
Ol Doinyo Lenkiyio, 83 D19
Ol Doinyo Ngiro, 83 G18
Ol Doinyo Sabuk National Park, 88 B10
Oldonyo Gol Hills, 264 H8
Old Ovo Game Reserve, 66 E5
Old Petauke, 107 E19
Old Rhenish Mission Church, 124 C6
Old Shinyanga, 87 L13
Olduvai, 264 I7
Olduvai Gorge, 88 I2
Olduvai Museum, 264 J8
Olenguruone, 83 L12
Oli, 66 C4
Olifants, *Namibia* 134 B9
Olifants, *Namibia* 135 G13
Olifants, *South Africa* 140 H2
Olifants, *South Africa* 150 M7
Olifants, *South Africa* 158 H4
Olifantsbad, 113 L18
Olifantsbad Pan, 278 E7
Olifantshek Dam, 147 B11
Olifantshoek, 145 K14
Olifants River Irrigation Scheme, 156 A9
Olifantsrus, 113 K13
Olinga, 122 E7
Olive Schreiner House, 152 I8
Olive Schreiner's Grave, 159 C13
Olivia, 46 K5
Oliviershoek Pass, 147 M17
Ol Joro Orok, 83 J15
Olkarien, 264 H8
Olkarien Gorge, 264 H8
Olmesutye, 88 E4
Ol Molog, 88 I9
Olmoti, 88 J3
Olmoti Crater, 264 I9
Olodio, 64 J10
Oloitokitok, 89 I11
Olomandou, 64 E9
Olongo, 261 K5
Olongoya Hills, 264 I8
Olorgasailie National Monument, 88 D7
Oloserri, 88 F7
Oltepesi, 88 D7
Ol Tukai, 88 H10
Olukondo, 113 G18
Olumbe, 103 E19
Olyfberg, 139 F16
Omaheke, 127 K13
Omahoro, 126 G2
Omaruru, *river* 126 I4
Omaruru, 126 J3
Omarurumond, 125 L15
Omatako, *Namibia* 126 H7
Omatako, *river* 115 G15
Omatako, *river* 126 H6
Omatjene, 126 E5
Omatjete, 126 H1
Omawewozonyanda, 127 J16
Ombala-io-Mungo, 113 C14
Ombalantu, 113 E14
Ombatjipuro, 126 G6
Ombika, 113 L17
Ombo, 251 G4
Ombombo, *Namibia* 112 J10
Ombombo, *Namibia* 113 G11
Ombonde, 113 M11
Ombo Show Ostrich Farm, 126 K7
Ombotozu, 126 J5
Omboué, 72 E2
Omchi, 60 C4
Omdraaisvlei, 152 G5
Omdurman, 62 I1
Omhajer, 62 K6
Omitara, 127 M11
Omo, 79 B14
Omoku, 66 I7
Omo National Park, 70 I2
Omoro, *river* 78 G4
Omoro, 78 M3
Ompupa, 75 M17
Omu-Aran, 66 F5
Omumborombongapan, 113 K12
Omuo, 66 F6
Omuramba, 114 I5
Omuramba Onaiso, 113 J15
Omurumendu, 127 M12
Omusati, 113 G15
Onaanda, 113 G16
Oncócua, 112 A7
Ondangwa, 113 G18
Ondekaremba, 134 A9
Onderombapa, 135 C16
Onderstedorings, 151 G16
Onderstepoort Nature Reserve, 147 A15
Ondini, 148 L7
Ondjiva, 113 C17
Ondo, 66 G5
Ondombo, 126 H4
Ondongab, 113 K18
Ondoto, 112 D9
Ondoubi, 261 C2
Ondundozonananandana Mountains, 276 E2
Onema, 73 H20
Onema-Okolo, 73 G19
Onema Ututu, 73 G18
Onesi, 113 E12
Ongandjera, 276 G4
Ongeluksnek, 154 H4
Ongenga, 113 D16
Ongers, *river* 152 J5
Ongers, 152 G5
Ongoka, 74 D2
Ongongoro, 127 D11
Ongoro Gotjari, 126 M9
Onguia, 72 D9
Ongwediva, 113 F17
Oniipa, 113 F18
Onilahy, 48 K3
Onitsha, 66 H8
Onive, 274 M1
Onoko, 67 C18
Onour, 248 D9
Onoy, 72 D5
Onquenha, 75 L19
Onrus, 157 K11
Onseepkans, 151 A11
Ons Hoop, 138 F8
Ontmoeting, 144 G9
Onverwacht, 148 H7
Oodweyne, 71 D13
Oorkruis, 151 B19
Oorlogskloof, 151 L12
Oorwinning, 139 C16
Oosgam, 157 H19
Oostermoed, 138 J5
Opala, 73 C20
Opepe Fort, 82 D5
Opemba, 266 B7
Operet, 114 I3
Opi, 66 G8
Opienge, 74 B4
Opobo, 66 J8
Opono Lake, 113 G17
Oppermans, 153 D11
Opuwo, 112 G9
Oraba, 69 K16
Orah, 66 H6
Oran, 49 D18
Orange, *Lesotho* 154 G2
Orange, *Namibia* 150 B9
Orange, *South Africa* 143 L14
Orange, *South Africa* 144 M5
Orange, *South Africa* 152 C6
Orangekloof Eco-Museum, 281 I5
Orango, 64 C1
Orangozinho, 64 C1
Orania, 152 E9
Oranjefontein, 138 E8
Oranjemund, 143 M11
Oranjerivier, 152 E9
Oranjeville, 147 G14
Oranjezicht, 281 E7
Orapa, 129 I19
Orda, 248 A9
Oré Vendou, 247 F7
Oribi Gorge Nature Reserve, 154 I10
Orida, *oasis* 249 F8
Orida, 249 F8
Orihuela, 49 A19
Orkadiere, 56 J8
Orkney, 146 G9
Orle River Game Reserve, 66 G7
Orodara, 65 C13
Orom, 78 I4
Oron, 66 J9
Ororo, 247 F6
Orpen Dam, 140 K4
Orpen Plaque, 278 J9
Ortum, 83 D11
Orumo, 78 L3
Orupembe, 112 G5
Oruwanje, 112 H8
Oruyubu, 260 C10
Orzola, 45 C14
Osamba, 127 M11
Osborn, 148 M5
Oséle, 72 D10
Oshakati, 113 F17

Oshana, 113 G17
Oshigambo, 113 F18
Oshikango, 113 D17
Oshikoto, 114 G2
Oshikuku, 113 F16
Oshititu, 114 F2
Oshivelo, 114 I3
Oshoek, 148 D5
Oshogbo, 66 F5
Oshwe, 73 G14
Osire, 126 H8
Osizweni, 148 J2
Oso, 74 D5
Ososo, 66 G7
Osse, *Angola* 75 K20
Osse, *Nigeria* 66 G6
Ossélé, 261 M2
Otak, 255 A3
Otavi, 126 C8
Otchinjau, 112 A9
Otechifengo, 112 A5
Oti, 65 D19
Oti Mandouri Forest Reserve, 65 C20
Otimati, 155 C14
Otjasondu, 126 I10
Otjihaenena, 114 M6
Otjihajavara, 126 M7
Otjihorongo, 126 G1
Otjikango, 126 E7
Otjikondavirongo, 112 J8
Otjikondo, 126 C1
Otjimbingwe, 134 A4
Otjimbingwe Historical Monument, 126 M4
Otjinene, 127 H14
Otjinhungwa, 112 D4
Otjinoko, 127 H16
Otjisemba, 126 K5
Otjitaimo, 112 J9
Otjitambi, 125 C19
Otjitanda, 112 E6
Otjitasu, 126 F4
Otjitoko, 113 I11
Otjitunduwa, 113 I11
Otjiu, 112 H7
Otjivalunda Pans, 276 B1
Otjivalunda Saltpan 1, 113 I15
Otjivero, *river* 112 F6
Otjivero, 127 M11
Otjiveze, 112 E8
Otjiwarongo, 126 F6
Otjiyarwa, 127 I16
Otjomatemba, 112 J9
Otjondeka, 113 I11
Otjongundu, 125 H20
Otjovasandu, 113 L12
Otjozondjou, 127 F13
Otjozondjupa, 126 E9
Otobotini, 279 D5
Otse, 137 K20
Otta, 66 G3
Otter Point, 271 H2
Otto Beit Bridge, 106 M10
Ottosdal, 146 F6
Ottoshoop, 146 B6
Otu, 66 H10
Otukpa, 66 G8
Otukpo, 66 G9
Otumba, 112 B3
Otuwe, 126 H4
Oua, 259 B10
Ouacha, 59 L14
Ouadane, 57 D11
Ouadda, 68 F6
Ouadi Archei, 60 H8
Ouadi Haouach, 60 I8
Ouadi Howar, 60 I10
Ouadimi, 68 H4
Ouad Naga, 56 G6
Ouagadougou, 65 A18
Ouahigouya, 57 L19
Ouahire, 65 C11
Ouaka, 68 G4
Ouake, 66 D1
Oualâta Rini, 57 H15
Ouali, 246 I9
Oualia, 57 L11
Oualidia, 51 B14
Ouallam, 58 K5
Ouana, 259 G9
Ouanda Djallé, 68 E7
Ouandago, 68 G2
Ouandjiia-Vakaga Faunal Reserve, 68 E6
Ouandja, 68 E7
Ouandjia, 68 D6
Ouando, 68 H10
Ouaneskra, 245 C3
Ouanga Plain Faunal Reserve, 72 F3
Ouango, 68 J6
Ouango-Fitini, 253 B6
Ouangolodougou, 65 D13
Ouanoukrim, 245 D2
Ouarak, 56 J5
Ouarâne, 57 D12
Ouargaye, 65 B19
Ouargla, 52 C9
Ouaritoufoulout, 58 I7
Ouarkla, 67 E16
Ouarkoye, 65 A15
Ouarzazate, 51 E16
Ouassa Bamvele, 67 I14
Ouassadougou, 65 F14
Ouata, 261 B6
Ouatagouna, 58 J4
Ouatere Galafondo, 68 I2
Ouaussaf, 245 B2
Oubangui, 68 L1
Ouda, 68 H1
Oudekraal, 281 G4
Oudekraal, 281 G2
Oudref, 246 I9
Oudtshoorn, 158 H2
Ouebo, 64 B3
Oued Akarit, 246 I9
Oued Amded, 58 B8
Oued Bou Ali, 52 D7
Oued Bou-Rouhat, 52 B2
Oued Dades, 51 D17
Oued Daoura, 245 I9
Oued Drâa, 51 E17
Oued El-Betoun, 52 A2
Oued el Fahl, 52 D8
Oued el Fekka, 246 E6
Oued el Ferch, 246 J10
Oued el Hallail, 49 K16
Oued el Hamma, 246 J8
Oued el Hattab, 246 C7
Oued el Hogueff, 246 E5
Oued el Kebir, 246 F5
Oued el Kerd, 246 G7
Oued el Khatt, 50 J8
Oued el Leguene, 246 K9
Oued el Melch, 246 H4
Oued el Rharbi, 52 C4
Oued en Namous, 52 D3
Oued Enne, 60 K5
Oued en Nsa, 52 C8
Oued es Seggeur, 52 C6
Oued Fama, 60 J6
Oued Grou, 51 B18
Oued Guellouar, 56 H8
Oued Haouach, 248 F8
Oued in Sokki, 52 H7
Oued Jebbes, 246 B8
Oued Jenein, 53 D13
Oued Kadja, 248 I8
Oued Khalifa, 246 J9
Oued Laou, 245 B8
Oued Mahaiguene, 52 B6
Oued Mial, 52 G6
Oued Moulouya, 49 E15
Oued Mya, 52 F7
Oued Retem, 52 A9
Oued Safsaf, 52 F7
Oued Saoura, 52 F2
Oued Sarrath, 246 B5
Oued Simbi, 68 B6
Oued Sous, 51 E15
Oued Takisset, 53 L13
Oued Tigseri, 51 H12
Oued Tilmeldjame, 52 G6
Oued Tin Amzi, 58 C9
Oued Touil, 49 K11
Oued Zbayra, 50 K8
Oued Zem, 51 B17
Oued Zizi, 51 E19
Ouelessebougou, 65 A11
Ouella, 58 K7
Ouellé, 65 G14
Ouenkoro, 57 L18
Oue-Oue, 66 D2
Ouessa, 65 B16
Ouesse, 66 E2
Ouesso, 72 A10
Ouezzane, 49 E13
Ougarou, 66 A1
Ougarta, 52 F1
Ouham, 67 H19
Ouihi, 68 F4
Ouin, 68 G1
Oujda, 49 E16
Oukaimeden, 245 B2
Oukraal, 157 K12
Oulad Teïma, 51 E14
Ould Yenje, 56 J9
Ouled Achour, 246 D10
Ouled Ahmed, 246 E8
Ouled Ameur, 246 A10
Ouled Djellal, 49 L14
Ouled Halfouz, 246 D9
Ouli, 67 I16
Oulmes, 49 F13
Oumache, 49 K14
Oum Ali, 246 E4
Oumba, 72 D5
Oum Chalouba, 60 J7
Oumé, 65 H12
Oum Ech Chia, 246 K8
Oum el Bouaghi, 49 J16
Oum el Ksab, 246 F4
Oum es Somaa, 246 J5
Oum Hadjer, 60 L6
Oumm el Khez, 57 H11
Ounara, 245 I1
Oundja, 68 D6
Ouo, *see Gani Do*
Ouogo, 67 F20
Ourafane, 59 K12
Ourar, 66 E7
Oure-Kaba, 64 D6
Ouro Amat, 56 K8
Ouro Féro, 247 J5
Ouro Guéladio, 252 B6
Ouromodi, 247 K1
Ouro Ndio, 247 H2
Ouro Sawabé, 252 C3
Ourou, 247 K9
Ouroufinan, 252 L9
Oursi, 58 K3
Ousslatia, 246 B8
Oussoumbidiaga, 57 K11
Outamba-Kilimi National Park, 64 D5
Outeniekwaberge, 157 H19
Outjo, 126 D4
Outo Sogui, 56 J7
Ouyou Bezedinga, 249 L9
Ovala, 72 D5
Ovambo, 114 I5
Ovan, 72 B6
Oveng, 67 L14
Overyssel, 138 F10
Oviston, 153 I14
Oviston Nature Reserve, 153 I14
Owando, 72 C10
Owena, *river* 66 G6
Owena, 66 G5
Owendale, 145 L17
Owendo, 72 B2
Owerri, 66 I8
Owo, 66 G6
Owutu, 66 H8
Oyabi, 72 C8
Oyan, 259 E4
Oyem, 67 M13
Oyo, *Egypt* 63 K17
Oyo, *Nigeria* 66 F4
Oyoué, 72 B9
Oyster Bay, 158 J9
Ozondati, 125 M20
Ozongombo, 126 G3
Ozonjuitji m'Bari, 276 D1
Ozori, 72 D2
Ozoro, 66 I7

P

Pa, 65 B16
Paarl, 156 H10
Pacaltsdorp, 158 J2
Pachwa, 262 F6
Pacuária da Barra do Longa, 75 F16
Paddock, 154 I10
Padibe, 78 H1
Padilla, 244 L1
Padjou, 67 D19
Pafuri Gate, 140 A2
Pager, 78 H3
Pagode, 46 E8
Pagouda, 252 L4
Pagui, 68 I4
Pahaguibi, 60 K8
Pahn Wroal, 64 I9
Pai, 67 E12
Paidha, 262 A6
Paiko, 66 D7
Pailles, 46 J3
Paimol, 78 I4
Paisaje Lunar, 244 L6
Paiva, 122 F7
Pájara, 244 J10
Paje, *Botswana* 130 M5
Paje, *Zanzibar* 95 J19
Pajok, 262 B5
Pajule, 78 J2
Pakelle, 69 K17
Pakhuis Pass, 156 B10
Paki, 66 B9
Pakwach, 69 L16
Pala, 67 D17
Palace of Abbasi, 250 E9
Palace of Haile Selassie, 258 J3
Palala, *Liberia* 64 G8
Palala, *South Africa* 139 H11
Palamakoloi, 136 E8
Palapye, 138 B6
Paleisheuwel, 156 D9
Palgrave Point, 125 F12
Palingpan, 145 K15
Pallisa, *admin.* 82 E5
Pallisa, 82 E4
Palma, *Mauritius* 46 J2
Palma, *Mozambique* 103 D19
Palma del Rio, 49 A14
Palm Beach, *Malawi* 109 F16
Palm Beach, *South Africa* 154 J10
Palmeira, 140 M7
Palmeirinhas, 75 E16
Palmer, 278 M3
Palmeria, 56 B3
Palmerton, 154 K7
Palmietfontein, 154 H1
Palmwag, 125 D14
Palmwag Lodge, 125 D14
Palmyre, 46 K2
Palo Blanco, 244 H6
Paloich, 69 C17
Pama, *Burkina Faso* 65 B20
Pama, *CAR* 68 I4
Pama, *river* 67 J20
Pama Partial Faunal Reserve, 66 B1
Pambani, 87 I12
Pambarra, 133 K16
Pambeguwa, 66 C9
Pambuke, 131 F16
Pampierstad, 146 J1
Pamplemousses, 46 I4
Pampoenpoort, 152 J3
Pampoenpoort Dam, 131 C12
Pamula, 130 C7
Pana, 72 E6
Panbult, 148 F3
Panda, 141 H15
Pandamatenga, 117 K18
Pandambili, 94 J7
Pandane, 141 H17
Pande, 95 H15
Pandogari, 66 C7
Pandu, 68 I2
Panga, 69 M11
Panga Falls, 69 K11
Pangala, 72 F9
Pangale, 92 F10
Pangani, 95 G16
Pangar, 67 H15
Pangar Djerem Reserve, 67 H15
Pangi, 74 F3
Pango Aluquem, 75 D18
Pangonda, 68 G5
Pania Mutombo, 73 H19
Pania-Mwanga, 77 C14
Pankshin, 67 D11
Pan Point, 113 J16
Pansdrif, 147 A13
Pantelleria, 49 I20
Panther Huk, 142 K8
Panu, 73 G14
Panyam, 66 D10
Panyangara, 78 J7
Panyimur, 262 B7
Panza Island, 95 G19
Panzarani, 65 D16
Panzi, 73 K12
Paoua, 67 G19
Paouignan, 66 F2
Papane, 129 C13
Papendorp, 150 M7
Papiesvlei, 157 L12
Papkuil, 145 M17
Paraa, 262 B2
Paradis, 46 L1
Paradise, 146 F2
Paradise Beach, 159 J11
Paradise Island, 133 J18
Paradise Island Marine National Park, 133 J18
Paradise Pools, 120 F2
Paradise Sun, 47 B15
Parador Nacional de Las Cañadas, 244 E5
Paradyspan, 113 J16
Parakarungu, 277 A8
Parakou, 66 D3
Paresis, 126 F5
Park Rynie, 155 H12
Parombo, 262 B7
Parow, 156 I9
Parque Natural de Los Isolotes del Norte de Lanzarote y Riscos de Famara, *Alegranza, Canary Islands* 45 A12
Parque Natural de Los Isolotes del Norte de Lanzarote y Riscos de Famara, *La Graciosa, Canary Islands* 45 C12
Partago, 252 M6
Partiaga, 252 F5
Parys, 147 F12
Pascal Village, 46 C3
Pata, *CAR* 68 F5
Pata, *CAR* 68 J2
Pata, *Senegal* 56 L5
Patambalu, 73 E13
Patani, 66 I7
Patattanek, 139 M18
Paté, 90 F6
Pategi, 66 E6
Pate Island, 90 F6
Patensie, 158 I10
Pâté Reynieux, 47 I19
Paternoster, 156 E6
Paterson, 159 G14
Patick, 56 K4
Patlong, 154 F4
Patongo, 78 K3
Pauila, 101 H19
Paula's Cave, 126 J3
Paul Kruger Gate, 140 K2
Paulpietersburg, 148 I4
Paul Roux, 147 L13
Pawa, 69 L12
Payar, 56 K5
Pearly Beach, 157 L11
Pearston, 159 D12
Pebane, 122 F10
Peddie, 159 F18
Pediva, 75 M16
Pedra do Feitico, 72 I7
Pedras Negras, 75 E20
Pedro Barba, 45 B14
Pehonko, 66 C2
Peili, 69 G12
Peka, 154 B2
Pekabrug, 154 B2
Pekinga, 252 E8
Pela, 64 F8
Pélébina, 252 M5
Pelekech, 79 G11
Pelenge, 73 F18
Pelezi, 65 G11
Pelican Point, 124 C7
Pella, 151 B11
Pellissier House & Museum, 153 H15
Peloyakukama/Ocwa Pan, 129 L15
Pemba, *Mozambique* 111 A18
Pemba, *Zambia* 118 B6
Pemba Channel, 95 G18
Pemba Island, 95 F19
Pembe, 141 F15
Pende, *river* 67 G18
Pende, 67 G18
Pendé, 67 F19
Pendembu, 64 E5
Pendjari, 252 I8
Pendjari Biosphere Reserve, 66 C1
Pendjari National Park, 66 B2
Pene Mende, 74 G5
Penge, *DRC* 69 L13
Penge, *DRC* 73 I20
Penge, *South Africa* 139 I18
Penhalonga, 120 L7
Penhoek Pass, 153 L17
Penja, 255 J5
Penjua, 73 D14
Pennington, 155 H12
Pensa, 58 L2
Penzele, 73 C13
Pepa, 77 C17
Pepworth, 147 M20
Peramiho, 101 C18
Perard, 273 I7
Percy Fyfe Nature Reserve, 139 H12
Perdekop, 147 G19
Perdida, 244 H8
Perere, 66 D3
Perisi, 254 B1
Perma, 66 C2
Perrier Nature Reserve, 275 D8
Persnip, 135 L14
Pescara Cassiano, 109 F18
Pessene, 149 A11
Petauke, 107 F20
Pete, 67 C16
Peter Pan, 129 I11
Petersburg, 159 C11
Petit Butte, 47 I17
Petite Île, 273 K5
Petite Pointe, 46 H5
Petite Polyte, 46 E8
Petite Revire, 46 J2
Petite Rivière Noire, 46 L1
Petites Gorges, *gorge* 275 E3
Petites Gorges, *river* 275 E2
Petite Soeur, 47 A18
Petit Gabriel, 47 I18
Petit Gravier, 47 I20
Petit Lac, 274 B3
Petit Loango Faunal Reserve, 72 E2
Petrusburg, 153 C13
Petrus Steyn, 147 I14
Petrusville, 152 G10
Peu-Peu, 113 A14
Pevensey, 280 J6
Phalaborwa, 140 G1
Phalombe, 109 L18
Phamong, 154 G1
Phelandaba, 279 B7
Philadelphia, 156 H9
Philae Island (WHS), 53 C18
Philae Temple, 251 K4
Philipo, 267 L6
Philippolis, 153 G12
Philippolis Road, 153 G13
Philips Cave, 126 K1
Philipstown, 152 H10
Philoteris, 250 G7
Phinda Resource Reserve, 148 J10
Phitsane Molopo, 146 B4
Phoenix, 155 E13
Phoka Court, 271 E5
Phokwane, 139 K15
Phonda, 278 D7
Phuduhudu, 129 E16
Phuduhudu Borehde, 136 F10
Phugwane, 140 C2
Phuthaditjhaba, 147 M16
Piankana, 73 F13
Pian Upe Game Reserve, 78 M8
Piaya, 264 H8
Piaya Hills, 264 H8
Pibor, 69 G18
Pibor Post, 69 G18
Picard, 46 E7
Pico de las Nieves, 45 K18
Pico del Teide, 44 G7
Pico Viejo, 244 C4
Pied du Morne, 273 G7
Piedra Hincada, 244 M1
Piega, 252 E3
Piekenaarskloof, 156 D10
Pienaar, 278 L7
Pienaar Nature Reserve, 138 M2
Pienaarsrivier, 138 L10
Pierrot Island, 47 J19
Pietermaritzburg, 155 E11
Piet Meintjies, 157 G15
Pieters, 280 C7
Pietersburg, *see Polokwane*
Pietersburg Game Reserve, 139 G15
Piet Gouws Dam, 278 I1
Pietia, 64 I10
Piet Plessis, 146 D1
Piet Retief, 148 G4
Piggs Peak, 148 C6
Pigu, 65 D18
Piketberg, 156 E9
Pikounda, 73 B11
Pilane, 138 I2
Pilanesberg National Park, 138 L5
Pilemane, 64 C10
Pilgrims Rest, 139 K19
Pilikwe, 138 B6
Pilipili, 69 J13
Pillars of Solomon, 55 E19
Pinanga, 73 F13
Pinau, 255 C6
Pinda, 121 F18
Pindura, 260 I6
Pinetown, 155 E13
Pingwe, 95 J19
Pintades Island, 47 I18
Piodi, 77 C11
Pioka, 72 H8
Pioneerdam, 125 A17
Pioneer Gate, 146 A5
Pionierdam, 113 L13
Pipi, 68 E6
Piro, 121 J14
Pissila, 58 M2
Piste des Eléphants, 252 J7
Pita, 64 B5
Pitoa, 67 D15
Piton de la Fournaise, 47 L15
Piton de la Petite Rivire Noire, 275 H2
Piton des Neiges, 47 L14
Piton du Milieu, 46 K4
Piton Grand Bassin, 275 I8
Piton Maïdo, 47 L14
Piton Savanne, 275 K8
Piton Ste Rose, 47 L16
Pitsane, 137 M20
Pitseng, 154 B4
Pitu, *river* 98 L2
Pitu, 98 J4
Pizhi, 66 D6
PK Rouge, 72 G10
Plage de la Blondine, 259 D1
Plage du Remorquer, 259 D1
Plainalto de Chimoio, 120 L9
Plaine Champagne, *peak* 275 I5
Plaine Champagne, 275 I5
Plaine Corail, 47 J17
Plaine Magnien, 46 L4
Plaine Sophie, 275 E7
Plaisance, *river* 273 I9
Plaisance, 273 H9
Planalto de Lichinga, 101 L16
Planalto de Morvia, 108 G4
Planalto Moçambicano, 110 L2
Plandi, 65 B14
Plaston, 139 M20
Platbakkies, 150 G8
Platberg, 280 A3
Plateau de Jef-Jef, 60 D8
Plateau de Manguéni, 59 A17
Plateau du Tademat, 52 H4
Plateau of Yorubaland, 66 E3
Plateau Sud-Camerounis, 67 J14
Plateaux, 72 E9
Plathuis, 157 H17
Platjan, 139 A13
Platrand, 147 G19
Platte, 47 B18
Platte Island, 47 C12
Platveld, 126 D7
Playa Amanay, 45 G15
Playa Bajas de Zamora, 44 F2
Playa Blanca, 45 F12
Playa de Alojera, 44 B5
Playa de Avalo, 44 C9
Playa de Cofete, 45 H15
Playa de Guasimeta, 45 E13
Playa de la Arena, 44 G6
Playa de la Arenas, 44 D5
Playa del Abrigo, 44 G8
Playa de la Caleta, 44 B8
Playa de la Cocina, 45 C13
Playa de la Garita, 45 D14
Playa de la Madera, 45 D11
Playa de la Rajita, 44 D6
Playa de la Salvajita, 44 E7
Playa de las Coloradas, 44 L2
Playa de la Tia Vicenta, 45 D14
Playa del Cantadal, 44 K3
Playa del Castillo, 45 G17
Playa del Inglés, 45 M18
Playa del Moro, 45 F18
Playa del Paso, 45 E11
Playa del Pozo, 44 L3
Playa del Rincón Grande, 44 A7
Playa de Miguel, 44 L3
Playa de Montaña Roja, 45 F11
Playa de Negrin, 44 A5
Playa de San Sebastián, 44 D9
Playa de Santa Catalina, 44 B8
Playa de Santiago, *beach* 44 D8
Playa de Santiago, 44 D8
Playa de Suárez, 44 D8
Playa de Tacorón, 44 L2
Playa de Vallehermoso, 44 A7
Playa Honda, 44 G8
Playa Lambra, 45 B14
Playa Quemada, 45 E12
Playa Zamora, 44 C9
Plettenberg Bay, 158 J5
Plooysburg, 152 B9
Plumpudding Hill, 281 E10
Plumpudding Island, 142 I7
Plumtree, 130 F9
PL Uys Memorial, 148 J3
Pniel, 156 I10
Pô, 65 B18
Poacher's Point, 276 B6
Pobe, 66 G3
Pobe Mengao, 58 L1
Pochala, 69 G19
Podor, 56 H6
Pofadder, 151 C11
Pogge Falls, 73 J16
Poie, 73 F18
Pointa da Cruz, 56 B2
Pointe Almina, 49 D14
Pointe au Sel, 46 E5
Pointe aux Canonniers, 46 H3
Pointe aux Caves Lighthouse, 46 J1
Pointe aux Cornes, 47 G19
Pointe aux Roches, 46 M2
Pointe aux Sables, 46 I2
Pointe Bambou, 46 K5
Pointe Belize, 47 C18
Pointe Bernache, 46 H5
Pointe Brocus, 46 L5
Pointe Butte aux Sables, 46 H4
Pointe Cabris, 47 C16
Pointe Cap Barbi, 47 B17
Pointe Capucins, 46 G5
Pointe Cèdre, 273 E8
Pointe Chevalier, 47 A14
Pointe Citronniers, 46 M2
Pointe Cocos, *Mahé* 46 G6
Pointe Cocos, *Praslin Island* 47 C16
Pointe Conan, 46 B4
Pointe Consolation, 47 C16
Pointe Corail, 47 J17
Pointe Corps de Garde, 46 L5
Pointe Coton, *point* 47 H20
Pointe Coton, 47 H20
Pointe d'Azur, 46 H3
Pointe de la Batterie, 46 K6
Pointe de la Rivèire St Etienne, 47 M13
Pointe de la Table, 47 M15
Pointe de l'Embarcadre, 46 I5
Pointe Denis, 259 E1
Pointe des Châteaux, 47 L13
Pointe des Galets, 47 K13
Pointe de Tamarin, 46 K1
Pointe du Diable, 47 H17
Pointe Golette, 46 G4
Pointe Jacques, 47 D18
Pointe Josephine, 47 B17
Pointe La Farine, 47 B17
Pointe Lafayette, 46 I5
Pointe La Rue, 46 D5
Pointe Lascars, 46 I5
Pointe Lazare, 46 F3
Pointe L'Escalier, 273 J3
Pointe Ma Flore, 47 C18
Pointe Manioc, 47 H16
Pointe Maravi, 46 F4
Pointe Matoopa, 273 I1
Pointe Moyenne, 46 J2
Pointe-Noire, 72 H5
Pointe Palmiste, 47 I16
Pointe Pongara, 72 B2
Pointe Poursuite, 47 I18
Pointe Raffin, 47 I18
Pointe Roche Noire, 47 I20
Pointe Roches Noires, 46 I2
Pointe Source d'Argent, 47 C17
Pointe Sud-Ouest, 46 L1
Pointe Vacoas, 46 L5
Pointe Zanguilles, 47 B15
Poivre Atoll, 46 C10
Poko, *river* 69 L12
Poko, 69 K11
Pokoteke, 132 C2
Pokuma, 118 G3
Polentswe Pan, 135 L19
Poli, 67 E15
Politsi, 139 F17
Polokwane, 139 G13
Polymnie, 46 D7
Poma, 74 D2
Pomene, 141 C18
Pomeroy, 148 M2
Pomfret, 145 B17
Pomona Island, 142 H6
Po National Park, 65 B17
Pônfi, 108 I10
Pongo, 69 E12
Pongola, *river* 148 H5
Pongola, 148 H7
Pongola Nature Reserve, 148 H3
Pongolapoort Dam, 148 H9
Pongolapoort Nature Reserve, 148 I8
Pongo Memorial, 131 C16
Pongore, 118 K3
Pongwe, 95 K14
Poni, 65 C16
Ponio, 65 C20
Ponondougou, 65 D12
Ponta Albina, 75 L15
Ponta Bajone, 111 I18
Ponta da Barra, 141 F18
Ponta da Marca, 112 A1
Ponta das Palmeirinhas, 75 D16
Ponta das Salinas, 75 I16
Ponta de Barra Falsa, 141 C18
Ponta Dobela, 149 E12
Ponta do Diablo, 103 L19
Ponta don Carlos, 133 J18
Ponta do Ouro, *point* 149 F12
Ponta do Ouro, 149 F12
Ponta do Padrão, 72 J6
Ponta Dundo, 133 K18
Ponta Freitas Morna, 72 K6
Ponta Lipobane, 123 D14
Ponta Macalonga, 123 E13
Ponta Maunhane, 103 M19
Ponta Metacáua, 111 C19
Ponta Monaepa, 122 F9
Ponta Mualadi, 123 C15
Ponta Namalungo, 111 K18
Ponta Nangata, 111 E19
Ponta Nantagala, 123 B17
Ponta Pandera, 123 D14
Ponta São Sebastião, 133 L18
Ponta Selala, 111 L16
Ponta Timbue, 122 K2
Ponta Závora, 141 I16
Ponte Colville, 46 L3
Pontdrif, *Botswana* 131 M13
Pontdrif, *South Africa* 131 M14
Pont Naturel, 46 L5
Ponto do Ouro, 279 A10
Ponto Mocambo, 111 I18
Pool, 72 G9
Pools, 156 E10
Popa, *Gabon* 72 D6
Popa, *Namibia* 116 I3
Popa Falls, 116 I3
Popenguine, 56 K3
Popple Peak, 280 G4
Porga, 66 C1
Pori, 252 D6
Poris de Abona, 244 M10
Poror, 83 E17
Port Alfred, 159 H17
Portal Peaks, 262 H3
Port Beaufort, 157 L16
Port-Berge Sofia, *see Boriziny*
Port Edward, 154 K10
Port Elizabeth, 159 I13
Porterville, 156 F10
Portes de l'Oganda, 72 C5
Portes de l'Enfer, 74 I4
Port-Gentil, 72 D2
Port Glaud, *bay* 46 D2
Port Glaud, 46 C3
Port Grosvenor, 154 L9
Port Harcourt, 66 J8
Port Launay, *bay* 46 C2
Port Launay, 46 C2
Port Launay Marine National Park, 273 I3
Port Loko, 64 E4
Port Louis, 46 J3
Port Mathurin, 47 H17
Port Nolloth, 150 C2
Porto Amboim, 75 F17
Porto Condo, 76 F1
Porto Henrique, 148 D10
Porto Ingles, 56 C3
Porto-Novo, 66 H3
Porto Rinao, 56 C3
Porto Santo, 50 B8
Port Said, 55 D16
Port Shepstone, 155 I11
Port St Johns, 154 M8
Port Sudan, 62 E6
Port Sud-Est, 47 I19
Portugal, 49 A12
Port Victoria, 82 I6
Possel, 68 I2
Possession Island, 142 G6
Post Chalmers, 159 B13
Postmasburg, 145 L15
Posto Antigo do Luxico, 76 C5
Potchefstroom, 146 F10
Potfontein, 152 G9
Potgietersrus, *see Mokopane*
Potiskum, 67 B13
Potoru, 64 G6
Potsdam, 160 F1
Poubara Falls, 72 E7
Pouce Nature Reserve, 46 J3
Poudjo, 68 I5
Pouéré, 72 C10
Pouma, 67 K11
Poumale, 68 I3
Poupan, 152 F9
Pouss, 67 C17
Pouytenga, 65 A19
Povoaão Velha, 56 B3
Pozo de la Salud, 44 K2
Pozo de las Calcosas, 44 J3
Pra, 254 J3
Praia, 56 C3
Praia de Jangamo, 141 H17
Praia de Zalala, 122 H5
Praia do Bilene, 140 L8
Praia do Chongoene, 141 L11
Praia do Tofo, 141 G18
Praia do Xai-Xai, 140 L10
Praslin Island, 47 B15
Prasuhien Forest Reserve, 65 I16
Preguia, 56 B3
Premier Mine Dam, 147 B17
Premier Village, 47 L15
Prend Town, 64 I9
Pretoria, 147 B15
Pretoriuskloof Bird Sanctuary, 147 L15
Prickly Pear Plantations, 45 D14
Prieska, 152 E3
Prieskapoort, 152 E3
Prikro, 65 F15
Prince Albert, 158 G1
Prince Albert Road, 157 F19
Prince Alfred Hamlet, 157 G11
Prince Imperial 1879 Monument, 148 K4
Principe, 66 M8
Pringle Bay, 156 K9
Priors, 153 H13
Protected Public Reserve of Longo-Mavinga, 116 C1
Protected Public Reserve of Luengué, 115 C12
Protected Public Reserve of Mucusso, 115 F15
Protem, 157 K14
Proudfoot Peak, 280 F9
Providential Pass, 132 D1
Pru, 65 G18
Ptoyo, 83 C11
Puchapucha, 102 E8
Pudimoe, 146 H2
Puercos, 45 L18
Puerto de Erjos, 244 I1
Puerto de la Cruz, 44 F7
Puerto de la Estaca, 44 K4
Puerto de las Cañadas, 244 D5
Puerto del Carmen, 45 E13
Puerto del Rosario, 45 F17
Puerto de Mogán, 45 L16
Puerto Rico, 45 L17
Puig, 69 E15
Pujehun, 64 G5
Pukota, 106 B10
Puma, 93 E19
Pumalanga Nature Reserve, 279 G5
Pumula, 268 L7
Punda Maria, 140 B1
Pundanhar, 103 D17
Púngo, 121 M14
Púngoe, 120 K10
Pungwe Falls, 120 J8
Punia, 74 D3
Punta Arenas Blancas, 44 K2
Punta Casa Blanca, 45 J20
Punta de Amacas, 44 J4
Punta de Camello, 44 H8
Punta de Fuencaliente, 44 F3
Punta de Góngora, 45 J16
Punta de Jandía, 45 I15
Punta de la Aldea, 45 J16
Punta del Agua, 45 B13
Punta de la Restinga, 44 M3
Punta de la Sal, 44 K1
Punta de la Salinas, 45 I19
Punta de la Tiñosa, 45 E17
Punta del Becerro, 44 D6
Punta del Cangrejo, 44 G6
Punta del Cardonal, 45 I16
Punta del Cerrillo, 45 D14
Punta del Corcho, 44 D4
Punta del Hidalgo, 44 E8
Punta del Jurado, 44 F7
Punta del Parchel, 45 M17
Punta del Sordo, 44 H8
Punta del Tarajalito, 45 G16
Punta del Tumas, 45 I16
Punta del Volcán, 45 E11
Punta de Maspalomas, 45 M18
Punta de Puerto Rico, 45 L16
Punta de Teno, 44 F5
Punta de Tierra Negra, 45 D14
Punta Falcones, 44 D6
Punta Gaviota, 45 D12
Punta Ginés, 45 F11
Punta Gorda, *Gomera* 44 D8
Punta Gorda, *La Palma* 44 E2
Punta Grieta, 45 A13
Punta Guerra, 45 C13
Punta Majona, 44 B9
Punta Norte, 44 J4
Punta Oscura, 66 K9
Punta Paloma, 45 H15
Punta Paso Chico, 45 F16
Punta Pesebre, 45 H15
Punta Prieta, 45 C13
Punta Salema, 44 H7
Punta Salinas, 44 E4
Punta Sardina, 45 I17
Punta Tamadite, 44 E9
Punta Usaje, 45 C14
Puntjie, 157 I17
Puntland, 71 E17
Punto Campo, 66 L10
Pupanyunyu, 256 D2
Purongo, 262 A4
Purros, 112 I6
Purtscheller Peak, 265 E8
Putsonderwater, 151 C20
Putuk, 255 A7
Pwaga, 94 L7
Pwalugu, 65 C18
Pwani, 95 M17
Pwani Mchangani, 95 I18
Pwela, 96 E6
Pweto, 77 D15
Pyramid of El Kula, 251 I4
Pyramid of el Lahun, 250 G8
Pyramid of Hawara, 250 G8
Pyramids at Giza, 55 F15
Pyramids of Meroe, 62 H2

Q

Qacentina, 49 I15
Qacha's Nek, 154 G5
Qairouan, 49 J18
Qala en Nahl, 62 L4
Qallabat, 62 M5
Qalo, 154 A4
Qalyub, 250 E8
Qamata, 159 B19
Qaminis, 54 D4
Qandala, 71 B18
Qanqo Hills, 277 C7
Qara el Nubariya, 250 D7
Qarat el Mashruka, 55 E13
Qardho, 71 D17
Qarun, 250 G7
Qaryat Abu Nujaym, 53 E19
Qaryat Abu Qurays, 53 D18
Qaryat Shumaykh, 53 D17
Qasr al Qarn, 54 F8
Qasr ash Shaqqah, 54 E9
Qasr Bu Hadi, 53 E20
Qasr el Banat, 251 G5
Qasr el Sagha, 250 F7
Qasr Farafra, 55 I12
Qasr Ibrim, 61 B19
Qassabat, 53 C17
Qasserine, 49 K17
Qattara Depression, 55 F12
Qedusizi Dam, 280 C6
Qena, 55 J17
Qhobela, 154 A5
Qiba, 154 L2
Qift, 55 J18
Qobong, 154 G2
Qolora Mouth, 160 D3
Qombolo, 160 B1
Qoqodala, 153 M18
Qora Mouth, 160 D4
Qoton, 71 D19
Qsour Essaf, 49 J19
Qu, 75 J19
Quaggasfontein Poort, 151 M17
Qualdo Lac, 247 G3
Qualé, 252 G2
Quara, 68 H10
Quarenta, 76 F1
Quarra, 68 I9
Quartier Franais, 47 K15
Quartier Militaire, 46 J4
Quatre Bornes, *Mauritius* 46 J3
Quatre Bornes, *Seychelles* 46 F5
Qubi, 115 M18
Qudeni, 148 M4
Quedas de Agua da Binga, 75 G17
Quedas do Calandula, 72 M10
Quedas do Lúrio, 111 C17
Queen Elizabeth National Park, 74 C6
Queen Elizabeth Park, 155 D11
Queens Beach, 281 C4
Queen's Blockhouse, 281 E9
Queensburgh, 155 F12
Queen's Mine, 131 C12
Queenstown, 159 A18
Quela, 76 E2
Quelimane, 122 H4
Quelo, 72 J6
Quembo, 76 J5
Queve, 75 G19
Quiama National Park, 75 F17
Quiangala, 72 K9
Quibala, 75 F19
Quibengue, 72 J10
Quibocolo, 72 J9
Quicabo, 72 L8
Quiculungo, 72 L9
Quicungurr, 72 K9
Quifuma, 75 J16
Quihita, 75 L18
Quilemba, 75 K17
Quilenda, 75 F18
Quilengues, 75 J18
Quilona, 72 K7
Quilua, 123 B16
Quimbele, 73 J11
Quimbi, 72 J8
Quimbriz, 72 J6
Quimbumbe, 72 K7
Quincy Village, 46 B3
Quinga, 111 F14
Quinhamel, 64 B1
Quionga, 103 C19
Quipaza, 72 J10
Quipedro, 72 L9
Quipungo, 75 K16
Quirima, 76 G3
Quirimba Archipelago, 103 E19
Quissanga, 103 K18
Quissico, 141 J14
Quissonga, 75 F19
Quitapa, 76 F3
Quitende, 72 L9
Quiterajo, 103 H18
Quiteve, 75 L19
Quitubia, 75 F20
Quixaxe, 111 J16
Quko, 160 D2
Qumbu, 154 K5
Quoin Point, 157 M12
Quoxo, 137 B15
Qurayd, 69 C17
Qurdud, 69 C14
Qureida, 68 B9
Qus, 55 J17
Quseir, 55 J19
Quthing, *see Moyeni*
Quweisna, 250 D8
Qwaqwa Game Reserve, 147 M15

R

Raaha Plain, 264 F3
Raas Binne, 71 B19
Raas Cabaad, 71 H17
Raas Gabbac, 71 F18
Raas Ilig, 71 F18
Raas Khansiir, 71 C13
Raas Xaafuun, 71 C20
Rabaable, 71 F16
Rabah, 58 M9
Rabak, 62 L1
Rabat, 49 F11
Rabongo, 69 M17
Rabongo Forest, 262 D4
Rachid, 56 F10
Radisele, 138 C5
Radium, 138 L10
Radom National Park, 68 E8
Rafai, 68 I8
Raffingora, 119 D18
Raffin Kada, 67 F11
Rafin-Cabas, 66 E9
Rafsai, 49 E14
Raga, *river* 68 F9
Raga, 68 E10
Rahad, 62 K2
Rahad el Berdi, 68 B7
Rahama, 66 C10
Raheita, 63 M13
Rahole National Reserve, 84 I6
Rahouia, 49 D19
Rakay, 65 B17
Rako, 71 D18
Rakops, 129 H16
Ralebona, 154 H2
Ramatlabama, *river* 146 B4
Ramatlabama, 146 A5
Ramatseliso's Gate, 154 G6
Rambo-Buniakiri, 260 I4
Ramena, 48 B9
Ramis, 70 E9
Ramohlakoana, 280 L1
Ramokgonami, 138 C7
Ramokgwebane, *river* 130 G9
Ramokgwebane, 130 F8
Ramotswa, 138 K1
Ramsgate, 155 J11
Ramu, 81 F16
Ran, 67 A16
Ranaka, 137 K19
Randa, 70 B9
Randalhurst, 148 M5
Randberge, 134 F2
Randburg, 147 C13
Randfontein, 147 D12
Rand Rifles, 124 C8
Randvaal, 147 E14
Ranérou, 56 J7
Rangnom, 69 D15
Rankin's Pass, 138 I8
Rano, 66 B10
Ranohira, 48 K5
Ranomafana National Park, 48 I7
Ranotsara Ava, 48 K5
Rantabe, 48 E9
Rao, 56 I4
Rapale, 111 I12
Rapides de Barou, 252 E8
Rapides de Elephant, 68 J2
Raqdalin, 53 B15
Raraga, 122 E7
Rare, 89 K20
Ras, 257 E9
Ras Abu Gallum National Park, 55 G19
Ras Abu Shagara, 62 C6
Ras al Hamamah, 54 B5
Ras al Hilal, 54 B6
Ras al Ushsh, 55 H18
Ras Asis, 62 F7
Ras Attabil, 53 D17
Ras Banas, 63 H17
Ras Dashen, 258 B10
Ras Dejen, 62 M7
Ras Dumera, 63 M13
Ras el Aioun, 246 C4
Ras el Bar, 250 C9
Ras el Kenayis, 250 C2
Ras el Ma, 49 E18
Ras Gharib, 55 H17
Ras Gurmal, 62 J10
Rashad, 69 A16
Ras Hadarba, 63 K18
Rashid, *see Rosetta*
Ras Kasar, 62 G7
Ras Kazimkazi, 95 K19
Ras Kigomasha, 95 E19
Ras Kimbiji, 99 A19
Ras Kiuyu, 95 E20
Ras Kosar, 63 K11
Ras Maqdam, 62 F6
Ras Mbanura, 99 M19
Ras Michamvi, 95 J18
Ras Mkumbuu, 95 F17
Ras Mohammed, 55 H19
Ras Mohammed National Park, 55 H18
Ras Mombi, 99 J19
Ras Mwana, 90 H4
Ras Ngomeni, 90 I3
Ras Nungwi, 95 H18
Rass Ajdir, 53 B15
Ras Shakhs, 63 K11
Ras Simeta, 63 L12
Ras Upembe, 95 G20
Ras Uroa, 95 I18
Rateldraf, 113 K12
Ratelfontein, 156 B8
Ratombo, 139 D18
Ravine, 281 H7
Rawana, 80 G4
Rawdons, 280 K7
Rawsonville, 157 I11
Rayton, 147 B16
Realejo Alto, 244 H6
Rebel's Ridge, 269 D3
Redcliff, 119 L15
Redcliffe, 154 D9
Reddersburg, 153 E16
Redelinghuys, 156 D8
Redeyef, 49 L16
Redlands, 152 F5
Redondo, 244 L3
Redoubt, 154 J9
Red Sea, 63 E15
Red Wall, 265 D5
Reebokrand, 153 F11
Reef, 46 D5
Regaia, 49 D13
Reggane, 52 I3
Regina Mundi Mission, 130 A9
Regone, 123 C12
Regua, 140 C5
Regueb, 246 F8
Rehoboth, 134 E7
Reitz, 147 J15
Reitzburg, 147 G11
Reivilo, 145 I19
Relizane, 49 D19
Remada, 53 C14
Rembo Ngové, 259 K3
Rembo Nkomi, 259 J2
Remboué, 259 E3
Remhoogte Pass, 134 G5
Rémire, 46 C10
Renco, 132 F2
Renk, 69 B18
Renoster, *South Africa* 147 G11
Renoster, *South Africa* 157 B16
Renosterkop, 158 C4
Renoster Pan, 278 L8
Renostersspruit, 146 F7
Renostervlei, 113 L12
Reo, 65 A16
Repembe, 133 I12
Reqqada, 246 C10
Réserve de Merdja Zerga, 49 E12
Reserve Peak, 281 G6
Ressano Garcia, 140 M4
Restinga, 49 D14
Restvale, 158 B4
Reteta, 110 C10
Réunion, 47 K13
Reusch Crater, 265 C4
Révia, 110 B3
Revubu, 108 L10
Revué, 133 A11
Rey, 67 F16
Rey Bouba, 67 E16
Rhenosterspruit Nature Reserve, 147 B13
Rhino Bay, 269 E6
Rhino Camp, 69 L17
Rhino Corner, 266 F6
Rhodes, 154 I2
Rhodes' House, 155 G11
Rhodes' Memorial, 281 E10
Rhodes' Summer House, 131 E12
Rhoufi, 49 K15
Rhourd el Baguel, 53 D11
Riaba, 66 K10
Riabela, 76 L4
Ria Tawny Game Production Reserve, 65 H15
Riba, 85 B14
Ribah, 66 B6
Ribáuè, 110 H9
Ribeira da Cruz, 56 A2
Ricasa, 244 M1
Rich, 51 C19
Richards Bay, 155 A18
Richards Bay Game Reserve, 155 B17
Richard Toll, 56 I5
Richelieu, 46 J2
Richmond, *see Boknesstrand*
Richmond, *South Africa* 152 L7
Richmond, *South Africa* 155 F11
Richtersveld National Park, 143 L13
Riebeeckstad, 146 J9
Riebeek East, 159 F15
Riebeek-Kasteel, 156 G10
Riebeek-Wes, 156 G9
Riekertsdam, 138 M2
Riet, *South Africa* 153 C11
Riet, *South Africa* 157 B18
Rietbron, 158 E5
Rietfontein, *Namibia* 128 K2
Rietfontein, *oasis* 113 K19
Rietfontein, *South Africa* 144 F5
Riethuiskraal, 157 K18
Rietkolk, 139 G15
Rietkuil, 147 I17
Rietoog, 134 G6
Rietpoel, 157 K12
Rietpoort, 150 J7
Riet se Vloer, 151 I16
Rietvlei, 155 C11
Rietvlei Dam, 147 B15
Rietvlei Nature Reserve, 147 C15
Rif, 49 E14
Rift Valley, *admin.* 83 D13
Rift Valley, 70 L2
Rig Rig, 59 K19
Rihana, 246 F8
Rijau, 66 B6

Sokoto, 58 M9
Sokoumba, 68 E4
Sokoy Yakoma, 68 H10
Sole, 58 K1
Solenzo, 65 A15
Solesia, 96 H7
Soli, 59 K12
Solio, 83 K17
Solitaire, 134 G3
Solna, 58 L3
Solola, 85 I18
Sololo, 80 H6
Solomondale, 139 F16
Solowu, 94 H4
Solusi, 131 E11
Solwezi, 77 H12
Somabhula, 131 C16
Somadougou, 57 K18
Somalia, 71 H14
Somali Basin, 46 B9
Somaliland, 71 C12
Somali Peninsula, 71 E15
Somali Plateau, 70 F9
Somanda, 87 H16
Somanga, 99 F17
Sombisi, 254 B5
Sombrera, 244 L9
Sombrero de Chasna, 244 M5
Somerset West, 156 J10
Somil, 104 K1
Somkele, 279 J4
Somkeru, 257 K5
Somokoro, 65 E12
Somra, 246 C10
Sonaco, 56 M6
Sonanga, 57 L15
Sondang, 83 D12
Sonderkop, 113 K15
Sonderpan, 151 C20
Sondu, 82 K10
Song, 67 D14
Songa, 77 D11
Songaw Lagoon, 65 H20
Songe, 94 G10
Songea, 101 D19
Songimvelo Game Reserve, 148 C5
Songo, 108 K7
Songo Mnara Island (WHS), 99 I18
Songo Songo Island, 99 G18
Songwe, 97 H12
Sonji, 96 F6
Sonjo, 88 G3
Sonop, 147 A13
Sonstraal, 145 G13
Sonta, 77 F15
Soo, *river* 255 M9
Soo, 254 A9
Sóo, 45 D13
Sooya, 71 L17
Sopo, 68 F10
Sora Mboum, 67 F17
Sorau, 256 G3
Sorefta, 70 G6
Sorga, 256 H9
Sori, 66 C3
Soria, 45 K17
Sorme, 247 I2
Sorombeo, 67 F16
Soroti, *admin.* 82 B6
Soroti, 82 C4
Sorris Sorris, 125 H18
Sosso, 67 K18
Sosso (31 de Janeiro), 72 K9
Sossobé, 247 J1
Sossusvlei, 134 J1
Sota, 66 C4
Sota Forest, 252 H9
Sotik, 82 L10
Sotouboua, 66 E1
Souani, 246 H9
Souanké, 67 M16
Soubakaniedougou, 65 C13
Soubré, 65 I11
Soudougui, 252 H1
Souellaba Point, 67 K11
Souffleur, 46 L4
Soufouroulay, 247 K4
Souguéur, 49 D20
Souillac, 46 M3
Souk Ahras, 49 J16
Souk el Arba du Rharb, 49 E12
Soukies, 246 G2
Souk Jemaa, 246 B6
Soukoukoutane, 58 K7
Soulabali, 56 L6
Soulemaka, 68 E6
Souloungou, 252 C1
Sounga, 72 E3
Soungrougrou, 56 L5
Sountat, 60 L5
Source of the Nile, 74 E6
Sour el Ghozlane, 49 J13
Sousse, 49 J19
Souss-Massa National Park, 51 F13
Sout, *South Africa* 150 K9
Sout, *South Africa* 151 C15
Soutar's Hill Pass, 280 H7
South Africa, 146 G6
Southbroom, 155 J11
South Downs, 154 C10
South East, 137 L20
South East Island, 46 D5
South East Ridge, 265 E8
South East Valley, 265 D5
Southern, *Botswana* 137 L15
Southern, *Zambia* 118 B3
Southern, 109 I14
Southern Kashiji, 104 C6
Southern National Park, 69 H13
Southern Source of the Nile, 74 G6
Southern Tombs, 55 H15
Southeyville, 159 A19
South Horr, 83 A18
South Island, 79 K16
South Island National Park, 79 K16
South Kitui National Reserve, 89 E16
South Luangwa National Park, 100 L2
South Pare Mountains, 95 B12
South Peak, 265 E8
Southport, 155 I11
South Ridge, 265 E8
South Sand Bluff, 154 L9
South Turkana National Reserve, 83 B13
Southwell, 159 H16
South West Corrie, 265 E7
Soutpan, 153 A16
Soutpansberg, 139 C15
Sowa, 130 F3
Soweto, 147 D13
Soy, 83 G11
Soyo, 72 J6
Spain, 49 B15
Spanwerk, 138 G5
Speelmanskraal, 158 I4
Speke, 262 H2
Speke Gulf, 87 G13
Spencer Bay, 142 A4
Spes Bona, 147 G11
Sphinx (WHS), 55 F15
Spioenkop Dam, 154 A8
Spioenkop Dam Nature Reserve, 154 A8
Spitskop, 278 M5
Spitskop Nature Reserve, 144 L8
Spitskopvlei, 159 A11
Spitzkoppe, 125 K20
Spoegrivier, 150 H5
Spreetshoogte Pass, 134 F4
Sprigg, 144 M9
Springbok, 150 E6
Springbokfontein, 113 K19
Springbokwasser, 125 E14
Springbokwater Gate, 125 E13
Springfontein, 153 G14
Springs, 147 D16
Spring Valley, 159 C16
Spruitdrif, 150 M8
Spytfontein, 153 B11
Squamans, 278 M9
Staansaam, 144 G7
Stafford's Post, 154 H9
Stampriet, 135 I13
Standerton, 147 G18
Stanford, 157 K11
Stanger, 155 D15
Stanmore, 131 G14
Stapleford, 120 K8
Station 5, 61 C19
Station 6, 61 D19
Station 10, 62 E1
Steekdorings, 145 H19
Steelpoort, 139 J17
Steenbokpan, 138 F7
Steilloopbrug, 139 E11
Steilrand, 148 J6
Steilrand Mountains, 112 F7
Steilwater, 139 E12
Steinhausen, 127 K11
Steinkopf, 150 C5
Stella, 146 E3
Stella Point, 265 D4
Stellenbosch, 156 J9
Sterk, 139 H12
Sterkfontein Dam, 147 M17
Sterkfontein Dam Nature Reserve, 147 M17
Sterkspruit, 153 H19
Sterkspruit Nature Reserve, 139 L18
Sterkstroom, 153 L16
Sterkwater, 139 H12
Sterling, 151 K18
Steynsburg, 153 K14
Steynsrus, 147 J11
Steytlerville, 158 G9
Stiftimia, 246 J6
Stile, 49 L14
Stilfontein, 146 F9
Still Bay East, 157 K18
Still Bay West, 157 K18
Stinkwater, 114 I1
Stockpoort, 138 F7
Stoffberg, 139 M16
Stoffels Pan, 268 E4
Stompneus Bay, 156 E6
Stompneuspunt, 156 D6
Stonehaven Farm, 280 I7
Stone Town, *see Zanzibar*
Stoneyridge, 154 L5
Stormberg, *mountains* 153 L17
Stormberg, *river* 153 K16
Stormberg, 153 K16
Stormsrivier, 158 J7
Stormsvlei, 157 J14
Straatsdrif, 138 M3
Strait of Gibraltar, 49 D13
Strand, 156 J9
Strandfontein, 150 M7
Strandfonteinpunt, 150 H4
Strip Memorial National Monument, 131 H19
Strishen, 255 H6
Struis Bay, *bay* 157 M14
Struis Bay, 157 M14
Strydenburg, 152 F7
Strydpoort, 146 G6
Strydpoortberge, 139 H15
Studtis, 158 H8
Stutterheim, 159 D19
Suakin, 62 F6
Suam, 82 E9
Suana, 73 J15
Subida Grande, 75 L15
Subugo, 88 D4
Sudan, 62 H2
Sudd, 69 F16
Sud-Quest, 46 E7
Sudr, 55 F17
Sudwala Caves, 139 M19
Sue, 69 G13
Sueda, 113 K19
Suez, 55 F17
Suez Canal, 55 E17
Sufes, 246 C6
Sufetula, 246 D6
Sugu, 255 D10
Suguta, *river* 83 C16
Suguta, 94 J7
Suguta Valley, 83 C16
Suguti, 87 E14
Suguti Bay, 87 D14
Sui, 252 M9
Suikersbosrand Nature Reserve, 147 E15
Sukses, 126 H6
Sukuku, 73 J12
Sukuma Museum, 87 G12
Sukur Cultural Landscape (WHS), 67 C16
Sukwane, 129 G16
Suleja, 66 E8
Sulima, 64 G6
Sullivan, 273 G6
Sulu, 73 H19
Sululta, 70 E5
Suluq, 54 D4
Sumba, 68 L4
Sumbawanga, 96 E6
Sumbe, 75 G17
Sumbi, 72 H7
Sumbu, 96 G1
Sumbu Bay, 96 G1
Sumbuya, 64 F5
Summamalisha Pan, 268 E8
Summerdown, 127 I13
Summerstrand, 159 J13
Summit, 62 F5
Suna, 87 B17
Sunate, 103 M16
Sun City, 138 M5
Sundays, 148 M2
Sundra, 147 D16
Sunga, 95 C13
Sungawula, 92 L9
Sunginge, 76 D2
Sungo, 121 C13
Sungue, 132 I7
Sunland, 159 H13
Sunset Beach, 46 B2
Sunset Dam, 278 K9
Sunset Rocks, 281 I1
Suntai, 67 F12
Suntal, 67 F12
Suntu, 70 F3
Sunyani, 65 G16
Supe, 255 J5
Suqa el Gamal, 61 M14
Sura, 70 G8
Sure, 81 F11
Surichengi, 268 B5
Surman, 53 B16
Surt, 53 D20
Suser, 82 F9
Susijinda, 93 D15
Sussendenga, 133 B11
Susua, 88 B6
Suswe, 120 E7
Sutherland, 157 C15
Suther Peak, 281 K1
Sutti, 58 L9
Sutton, 145 H14
Sutukoba, 56 L7
Suurberg, 159 G13
Suurbraak, 157 J16
Swaershoek, 159 D13
Swahili Village Ruins, 90 G4
Swakop, 126 K8
Swakopmund, 124 B7
Swana-Mume, 77 G13
Swartberg, 154 G7
Swartberg Nature Reserve, 157 G19
Swartbooisdrift, 112 D9
Swartdoring, 150 J6
Swartkolkvloer, 151 J14
Swartkops, 159 I12
Swartmodder, 144 K6
Swartplaas, 146 C10
Swartputs, 145 K18
Swartruggens, 146 A9
Swart Umfolozi, 148 K6
Swartwater, 138 C10
Swaziland, 148 F5
Swedru, 254 I10
Swellendam, 157 J14
Swempoort, 153 K19
Swimming Pool, 44 J4
Swinburne, 147 L18
Sybrandskraal, 139 M12
Sydney-on-Vaal, 145 M19
Syfergat, 153 L16
Syria, 55 B20

T

Taabo, 65 H13
Taal Monument, 153 J16
Taba, 55 F19
Tabanguji, 266 G6
Tabankulu, 154 J7
Tabant, 245 I6
Tabatka, 49 I17
Tabelbala, 51 G19
Tabelot, 59 G13
Taberdga, 49 K15
Table Bay, 156 I8
Table de Jugurtha, 246 B4
Table Mountain, 156 I8
Tabligbo, 66 G1
Tabora, *admin.* 93 E11
Tabora, 93 E11
Tabou, 65 J11
Tabourougou, 253 D5
Tabuk, 63 C17
Tabur, 68 C7
Tachakoucht, 245 J4
Tacheddirt, 245 B3
Tacoronte, 244 E10
Tacuane, 122 B4
Taddert, 51 D15
Tadist, 58 I9
Tadjemout, 49 L11
Tadjmout, 52 K7
Tadjoura, 70 B10
Tadjroua, 49 F20
Tadrart, 245 B4
Tadrés Total Faunal Reserve, 59 J11
Tafadek Hot Thermal Springs, 59 H12
Tafelberg, 153 M12
Tafiré, 253 D3
Tafnidilt, 51 G11
Tafraoute, 51 F13
Taftecht, 245 I1
Taga, 247 L2
Tagab, 61 E17
Tagadji, 247 D3
Tagal I, 256 H10
Tagau, 59 M16
Taghajit, 249 A4
Taghaoumit, 57 H14
Taghit, 52 E2
Taghmert, 249 C5
Tagounit, 245 K7
Tagounite, 51 F17
Taguedoufat, 249 L3
Taguelmit, 53 B15
Tagulluche, 44 B5
Tahanaoute, 245 I3
Tiharsouk, 49 E14
Tahiche, 45 D13
Tahomi, 64 H9
Tahoua, 58 J9
Tahta, 55 I16
Tahwai, 250 E8
Tai, 64 H10
Tai National Park (WHS), 64 I10
Taibique, 44 L2
Taidalt, 51 G12
Taïmana, 57 L15
Taï National Park (WHS), 64 I10
Tainton, 160 E2
Tairas, 249 M5
Taita Hills, 89 K14
Taiyara, 61 L18
Taizz, 63 L14
Tajarhi, 53 L17
Tajerouine, 246 A5
Takaba, 81 H12
Takai, 67 B11
Takalama, 68 C6
Takalaou, 248 H3
Takaloi, 94 I8
Takamaka, *Réunion* 47 L15
Takamaka, *Seychelles* 46 F4
Takara, 68 F4
Takaraft, 249 B3
Takatokwane, 137 G14
Takatshwaane, 136 B6
Takiéta, 59 L13
Takoanda, 68 G4
Takochi, 58 K10
Takolokouzet, 249 C5
Takoon 1823, 145 G19
Takorka, 58 L10
Takpamba, 65 D20
Takpolma, 64 G7
Takum, 67 G11
Takundi, 73 H11
Takwa Ruins, 90 F6
Tala, *oasis* 249 L2
Tala, 88 C10
Tala Mellet, 249 C1
Talata Mafara, 58 M10
Talcho, 58 K7
Taleni, 160 B4
Talguharai, 62 F4
Taliouine, 51 E15
Tali Post, 69 H15
Talismanis, 128 K2
Talla, 250 I7
Talmest, 51 D14
Talodi, 69 C15
Talras, 59 J14
Tama, 59 M12
Tamaduste, 44 J4
Tamale, 65 D18
Tamale Port, *see Yapei*
Tamanar, 51 E13
Tamanhint, 53 I18
Tamani, 57 L15
Tamanrasset, 58 A9
Tamarin, 46 K2
Tamarind Falls, 275 D6
Tamarind Falls Reservoir, 275 D5
Tamarin Estate, 275 A2
Tamarou, 66 D3
Tamasanka Pan, 130 B4
Tamat, 249 C3
Tamatert, 245 C3
Tama Wildlife Reserve, 70 H2
Tamayye, 50 L5
Tamba, 131 I16
Tambach, 83 G12
Tambacounda, 56 L6
Tambaga, 252 F5
Tambakara, 56 I10
Tambankulu, 148 C8
Tambarga, 66 B1
Tamboerskloof, 281 C6
Tambohorano, 48 F4
Tambor, 75 M16
Tamboura, 68 I9
Tambura, 69 I12
Tamchaket, 57 H11
Tamelelt, 51 D16
Tamerna, 52 B10
Tamerza, 246 H2
Tames, 244 M7
Tamesna, 58 F9
Tamezret, 246 K9
Tamgak, 249 C4
Tamiya, 250 G8
Tamota, 95 H11
Tamou, 252 C6
Tamou Total Faunal Reserve, 252 D7
Tampéna, 252 C4
Tamri, 51 E13
Tamsu, 115 I16
Tanal, 57 J19
Tanambao-Marivorahona, 274 E6
Tanambe, 48 F8
Tanandava, 48 J4
Tanantou, 64 E10
Tana River Primate National Reserve, 90 E2
Tanda, 65 F15
Tandafa, 252 L9
Tandala, 97 J16
Tanderiouel, 58 J3
Tandjile, 67 D18
Tandjouaré, 65 C19
Tan Émellel, 53 H13
Tanene, 64 B3
Tanezrouft, 58 B3
Tanga, *admin.* 95 D15
Tanga, 95 F17
Tanganasoga, 44 K2
Tanger, *see Tangier*
Tangier, 49 D13
Tangoutranat, *see Ti-n-Aguelhaj*
Tanguiéta, 66 C1
Tangulbei, 83 F15
Taninga, 140 L7
Tanis, 250 D10
Tanjona, 48 E9
Tanjona Anorontany, 274 C5
Tankouga, 252 K8
Tankuw, 65 F17
Tankwa, 157 D14
Tanougou, 252 L8
Tânout, 59 J13
Tansarga, 252 F5
Tansghart, 245 A2
Tanta, 55 E15
Tan Tan, 51 H11
Tan Tan Plage, 51 G11
Tantéga, 252 K6
Tanzania, 94 F3
Tao, 45 D13
Taoudenni, 57 B19
Taounate, 49 E14
Taourirt, 52 I3
Taourirt n Ikis, 245 A4
Tapeta, 64 H9
Tapili, 69 K12
Tapoadyerma, 252 E5
Tapol, 67 E17
Taposiris, *see Abu Sir*
Taqatu Hayya, 62 G5
Tara, 118 D4
Taraba, 67 F13
Tarabulus, *see Tripoli*
Taraghin, 53 J18
Tarangire National Park, 94 C5
Tarat, 53 J12
Taratara, 115 G15
Tarbaj, 81 M12
Tarfa, 63 D12
Tarfaya, 50 H9
Targa, 44 D7
Targuist, 49 E14
Tarhacha, 60 L7
Tarhunah, 53 C17
Tarime, 87 C17
Tarka, 159 B15
Tarkastad, 159 B15
Tarkwa, 65 I17
Tarn Valley, 265 D8
Tarouadji, 249 E4
Taroudant, 51 E14
Tarrafal, 56 B2
Tarso Ahon, 248 C9
Tarso Emissi, 248 B9
Tarso Kobour, 248 C8
Tarso Ourari, 248 B8
Tarso Tieroko, 248 C9
Tarso Voon, 248 C8
Tarteri, 67 B14
Taru, 93 F20
Tarube, 116 M6
Tasawah, 53 J16
Tasker, 59 J15
Tassa, 252 C10
Tassatt nTizi, 245 A2
Tassara, 58 H10
Tassembé, 247 I7
Tassili N'Ajjer, 52 J10
Tassili N'Ajjer National Park, 52 L9
Tassili Oua N Ahaggar, 58 F8
Tata, 51 F15
Tataguine, 56 K4
Tatakpani, 68 H2
Tataouine, 53 B14
Tati, 130 I9
Tatokou, 59 J13
Tatou, 256 K6
Taufikia, 69 D16
Taula, 131 J17
Taung, 146 I2
Tauro, 45 L17
Taveta, *Tanzania* 89 K11
Taveta, *Tanzania* 98 I3
Taweisha, 61 M14
Tawilah, 61 L12
Tawurgha, 53 C19
Tayakou, 252 J3
Tayeeglow, 71 J12
Tayma, 63 D19
Taza, 49 F15
Tazaghart, 245 C1
Tazbent, 246 C2
Tazenakht, 51 E16
Tazirbu, 54 K5
Taziziiet, 249 E5
Tazo, 44 B6
Tazolé, 249 E5
Tazra, 50 H10
Tazrouk, 52 M9
Tazzarine, 51 E17
T Bakare, 66 C4
Tchabal Mbabo, 255 F10
Tchafchou, 66 E3
Tchamba, 67 E14
Tchangsou, 67 E17
Tchaourou, 66 E2
Tchaskirou, 256 C8
Tchatchako, 65 E20
Tcheboa, 256 I3
Tchédé, 256 C9
Tcheriba, 65 A16
Tchérré, 72 C9
Tchetti, 66 F2
Tchibanga, 72 F4
Tchighozerine, 59 H12
Tchilounga, 72 G5
Tchiming, 256 I8
Tchin-Tabaradene, 58 I10
Tchollíré, 67 E16
Tcht, 57 F13
Tebarat, 58 K8
Tébé, 72 C8
Tebessa, 49 J16
Teboulbou, 246 J10
Teborba, 49 I18
Tebourba, 49 I18
Tebursouk, 49 I18
Tebtynis, 250 G8
Techaza, 75 L19
Techiman, 65 F17
Techine, 53 B14
Techinoca, 76 K2
Techirimba, 75 H19
Techissanha, 76 K2
Techla, 56 C7
Techongolola, 76 F1
Ted, 71 J12
Tedzani Falls, 109 K15
Teekloof Pass, 157 B19
Teespoed, 113 K14
Tefki, 257 C2
Tegina, 66 D7
Tégouma, 59 I14
Tégourou, 247 L7
Teguidda-n-Tessoumt, 59 H11
Teguise, 45 D14
Tehezgorou, 58 J5
Téhini, 65 D15
Teide National Park, 44 G7
Teiskot, 58 H4
Teiti, 61 F18
Tejeda, 45 J17
Teji, 257 C1
Tejiade, 44 D8
Tejina, *peak* 244 M2
Tejina, 244 M2
Tejira, 59 K14
Tekeze, 62 K6
Tela, 77 H15
Telagh, 49 E18
Tel Aviv, 55 C18
Telde, 45 J19
Tele, 68 L8
Telebrug, 154 H1
Telfane, 248 E2
Teli, 247 L8
Télimélé, 64 C4
Tell el Amarna, 250 J8
Tell el Maskhuta, 250 E10
Telmine, 246 J5
Telomita, 48 F7
Téloua, 249 E3
Teltele, 79 B20
Tely, 69 K12
Tema, 65 I19
Temba, 138 M10
Tembe, 148 D10
Tembe Elephant Game Reserve, 149 G11
Tembien Rock-Hewn Churches, 258 E6
Tembisa, 147 C15
Tembo, 73 K12
Tembo Aluma, 73 K11
Tembwe, 100 F8
Temcha, 70 C4
Temelon, 67 M12
Temera, 58 H2
Temki, 68 B1
Temple Amara, 61 D17
Temple of Hathor, 55 J17
Temple of Horus, 63 H13
Temple of Kawa, 61 F18
Temple of Khnum, 251 H3
Temple of Naqa, 62 I2
Temple of Seddenga, 61 D17
Temple of Sesibi, 61 D17
Temple of Sulb, 61 D17
Temples of Sethos I & Ramses II, 63 F12
Tenado, 65 A16
Tenbosch, 278 L9
Tendaho, 70 B7
Tendelti, 61 M19
Tendrara, 49 G16
Ténémoussagou, 247 M4
Ténéré Desert, 59 C15
Ténéré Dunes, 59 H14
Tenerife, 44 F6
Tenes, 49 C20
Tengue, 76 L2
Te-n-Guembou, 57 I12
Tenika Caves, 48 J5
Tenkodogo, 65 B18
Tenndeli, 247 L8
Tenoya, 45 I19
Tenta, 70 B6
Te'okoto, 262 B2
Tepa, 65 G16
Tépé, 256 H2
Tepere, 111 E12
Tepi, 70 G2
Ter, 248 F3
Téra, 58 L4
Terakeka, 69 I16
Terhazza, 51 M16
Termesse, 64 A5
Termit, 59 I16
Teror, 45 I18
Terrace Bay, 125 D11
Terra Firma, 145 A16
Terre Rouge, 46 I3
Ter Shet, 70 F8
Teselima, 65 F16
Teselinde, 44 B6
Tesenane, 141 B12
Teshi, 66 D5
Tessalit, 58 E5
Tessaoua, 59 L12
Tessenei, 62 J5
Tessit, 58 J3
Tessolo, 133 K13
Tessouf, 249 D3
Testour, 49 I18
Tete, *admin.* 108 J4
Tete, 108 M9
Tetouan, 49 D14
Teturi, 74 A6
Teufelsbach, 126 M7
Teviot, 153 M14
Tewane, 138 C6
Teyateyaneng, 154 C2
Teza, 148 M9
Thaba Bosiu, 154 D2
Thaba Chitja, 154 H4
Thabana Ntlenyana, 154 D7
Thaba Nchu, 153 C18
Thaba Phatshwa, 153 C19
Thaba Putsoa, 154 F2
Thabatshukudu, 130 G1
Thabazimbi, 138 J7
Thabong, 146 K9
Thakadu, 130 H5
Thala, 49 J17
Thale, 128 B7
Thamaga, 137 J19
Thaoge, 116 L6
Tharaka, 84 K3
Thatganyana Rock, 130 M4
Thatchings, 280 J8
Thavu, 89 F12
Thebes (WHS), 251 G3
The Bluff, 155 F14
The Crags, 158 I6
The Downs, 139 H17
Theewaterskloof Dam, 157 J11
The Fextal, 280 L6
The Garden Route, 158 K2
The Haven, 160 C5
The Heads, 158 J4
Thelepte, 49 K17
Thenia, 49 I13
Theniet el Had, 49 J11
The Ranch, 155 B13
The Range, 120 L1
The Rat Forest, 255 I8
Theron, 146 L9
Thérse, 273 K4
Thérse Island, 273 K3
The Saddle, 265 D7
The Swamp Nature Reserve, 280 J6
Theunissen, 146 L8
The Winkler, 139 L20
Thika, *river* 88 A10
Thika, 88 B9
Thilogne, 56 I7
Thio, 62 K10
Thiou, 57 L19
This, 56 K3
Thistledown, 280 K9
Thitani, 89 A12
Thohoyandou, 139 C18
Thokazi, 148 J7
Thomas Hart's Grave, 278 L7
Thomas Moodie's Grave, 132 D9
Thomson Junction, 268 A5
Thorndale, 139 F16
Thornhill, 159 I11
Thorn Hill, 278 M8
Thornville, 155 E11
Thornybush Private Reserve, 140 I1
Three Sisters, 158 A5
Thua, 89 C18
Thuli, 131 J13
Thumbi Island East, 271 H3
Thumbi Island West, 109 E14
Thyolo, 109 M16
Thyou, 65 A17
Tiagua, 45 D13
Tiama, 72 J10
Tiambavel, 247 H1
Tianguel-Bori, 64 B5
Tiankoura, 65 C15
Tiaret, 49 D20
Tias, 45 E13
Tiassale, 65 H13
Tibati, 67 H14
Tiberghamine, 52 G4
Tibesti, 60 D3
Tibo, 69 K13
Tibukai Pan, 268 D3
Tica, 133 A15
Tichki, 245 C3
Tidiguin, 245 C9
Tidjikdja, 57 F11
Tido, 112 B5
Tiéau, 248 H3
Tiebila, 65 D13
Tiebissou, 65 G13
Tiebli, 65 B18
Télimélé, 64 C4
Tiefora, 65 C14
Tiegba, 65 I14
Tiel, 56 J6
Tieme, 65 D11
Tie-Ndiekro, 65 G14
Tieningboue, 65 F12
Tienko, 65 C11
Tientienga, 252 C6
Tierfontein, 146 K7
Tierkloof, 146 G2
Tierpoort, 153 D15
Tierra del Trigo, 244 H1
Tiettai Sidi Bouguedra, 51 C13
Tiflet, 51 A17
Tigaday, 44 K3
Tiga Reserve, 66 B10
Tignre, 67 G14
Tigray, 62 L8
Tigray Rock-Hewn Churches, 62 L9
Tiguent, 56 G5
Tiguezefene, 58 J7
Tiguidit Cliffs, 249 L2
Tiguir, 249 D4
Tiji, 53 C15
Tijma, 246 K10
Tikem, 67 D17
Tiko, 66 J10
Tilat Hassan, 250 J10
Tilemses, 58 I9
Tillabéri, 58 K5
Tillia, 58 I9
Tilrhemt, 52 B7
Tima, 251 E2
Timahdite, 49 G13
Timanfaya National Park, 45 D11
Timau, 83 I19
Timbavati, 140 I2
Timbavati Game Reserve, 140 H2
Timbe, 65 F14
Timbédra, 57 I13
Timbo, 64 C6
Timbuktu, 57 H19
Timgad, 49 J15
Timia, 59 G13
Timichi, 245 B4
Timimoun, 52 G3
Tim Mersoï, 249 A2
Timmoudi, 52 F2
Tina, 154 J6
Tina Bridge, 154 K6
Ti-n-Aguelhaj, 57 H19
Tinajo, 45 D12
Ti-n-Akof, 58 J3
Ti-n-Azabo, 58 I4
Tindangou, 65 B20
Tinde, 118 J5
Tindima, 266 D2
Tindila, 64 C10
Tindouf, 51 H14
Tiné, 60 J9
Tinedin, 249 A2
Tinerhin, 245 I7
Tinerhir, 51 D18
Tinfouchy, 51 G17
Tin Fouye, 53 H11
Tinga Tinga, 88 I8
Tingréla, 65 C12
Tingya, 69 C17
Tinkisso, 64 B8
Tinna el Gebel, 250 I8
Tiñor, 44 K4
Tintane, 57 I12
Tintioulen, 64 C9
Ti-n-Toumma, 59 I17
Tioribougou, 57 L14
Tioroniaradougou, 65 D13
Tiou, 247 M9
Tiouilit, 56 F5
Tiourdiou, 245 B4
Tipaza, 49 I11
Tipsan, 255 E10
Tipsan Lake, 255 D9
Tiran & Sanafir Islands Protectorate, 55 H19
Tirant, 273 D7
Tireli, 247 K9
Tiri, 68 E3
Tiriri, 82 B4
Tirriro, 64 C9
Tirmini, 59 L13
Tiro, 64 D7
Tiroungoulou, 68 D6
Tissa, 51 A19
Tissaldai, 245 C3
Tissemsilt, 49 D20
Tit, 58 A10
Titao, 57 L20
Titepesaare, 83 C18
Titi, 262 C10
Titule, 68 K10
Tiva, 89 B12
Tivaouane, 56 J3
Tiwal, 68 C7
Tiwi, 95 B19
Tiyandazi Pan, 277 C8
Tizgui, 245 D5
Tizgui Remt, 51 H13
Tizi, 68 H5
Tizi Melloul, 245 D2
Tizi n Ourai, 245 D3
Tizi n'Tiga Pass, 245 I4
Tizi Oussem, 245 C1
Tizi Ouzou, 49 I13
Tiznit, 51 F13
Tjelani Pan, 277 C9
Tjera, 65 B14
Tlalamabele, 130 I3
Tlapeng Pan, 136 E6
Tlatsa, 278 E3
Tlemcen, 49 E17
Tlhabane Sun, 147 A11
Tlhakgameng, 145 E20
Tlidjen, 246 D2
Tlokweng, 138 J1
Tmassah, 53 J19
To, 65 B17
Toamasina, 48 G9
Tobago Hills, 61 K13
Tobieroen, 113 K14
Tobli, 64 H9
Tobre, 66 C2
Tobruk, 54 C8
Tod, 251 H4
Todenyang, *peak* 79 D13
Todenyang, 79 D13
Todin, 57 M19
Toeguin, 58 M1
Toep, 66 E10
Toeslaan, 144 L6
Toesse, 65 B18
Togbo, 68 H6
Togga Miriye, 71 C13
Tognuf, 62 I6
Togo, *CAR* 68 H4
Togo, *DRC* 69 K13
Togo, 66 G1
Togobala, 64 D10
Togo Ber, 258 E5
Togoro Plain, 264 E6
Togou, 57 L16
Tog Wajaale, 71 D11
Tokai, 281 M9
Tokar, 62 F6
Tokeh, 67 K20
Tokong Pan, 136 J10
Tokounou, 64 D8
Tokwe, 131 B19
Tölanaro, 48 M6
Tole, 67 H18
Toliara, 48 K3
Tolo, 73 F13
Tolode, 64 H9
Tolon, 254 E9
Tolwe, 139 C12
Toma, 57 M19
Tomakas, 112 J7
Tombar, 246 J5
Tombat, 62 K4
Tombe, 76 I3
Tombel, 67 J11
Tombo, 154 M7
Tomboco, 72 J7
Tombouctou, *see Timbuktu*
Tombs of the Nobles, 63 H13
Tombua, 75 L15
Tom Burke, 138 D9
Tome, 141 A14
Tominian, 57 L17
Tomori, 67 K17
Tompi Seleka, 139 K14
Tonash, 139 B12
Tonde, 107 D11
Tondidarou, 247 D3
Tondidji, 57 L11
Tondi Kwindi, 58 K5
Tondon, 64 C4
Tondoro, 114 F9
Tonga, 67 I12
Tongaat, 155 D14
Tonganda, 132 D7
Tongo, *Cameroon* 256 J4
Tongo, *DRC* 260 B3
Tongomayel, 58 L2
Tongora, 98 F5
Tonguéré-Koumbé, 247 H1
Tongwe, 95 G15
Tonj, 69 G13
Tonka, 57 I18
Tonota, 130 J8
Tontelbos, 151 J14
Tooseng, 278 I1
Topete, 244 H5
Tora, 252 L7
Tor Donga, 255 F6
Torit, 69 J18
Tornoy, 60 L4
Torodi, 58 M5
Toro Game Reserve, 74 A8
Toro Kinkane, 65 E14
Toroli, 247 M7
Toromoja, 129 H16
Tororo, *admin.* 82 F6
Tororo, 82 G6
Torra Bay, 125 E12
Torres de Alcala, 245 C9
Torrock, 67 D17
Tosamaganga, 98 D2
Tosca, 145 B18
Toscanini, 125 G13
Tosi, 69 C16
Tosing, 154 H2
Tot, 83 E13
Toteng, 128 E10
Toto, 66 F8
Totoe, 97 G11
Totomaye, 249 G9
Totota, 64 G8
Tou, 57 L19
Touajil, 56 B10
Touba, *Côte d'Ivoire* 64 F10
Touba, *Senegal* 56 J5
Toubacouta, 56 L4
Toubere Bafal, 56 K7
Toubkal, 245 D2
Toubkal National Park, 51 D15
Touboro, 67 F17
Toudoulou, 248 B7
Tougan, 57 M19
Touggourt, 52 B9
Tougouri, 58 L2
Tougué, 64 B6
Touiba, 246 K5
Touil, 57 J11
Toujane, 246 K10
Toukoto, 57 L11
Toukountouna, 66 C1
Toulel, 247 D6
Touléples, 64 H9
Toumayé, 247 K3
Toumbélaga, 249 M2
Toummo, 59 B19
Toumodi, 65 H13
Toumoundjila, 64 C10
Toungo, 67 F13
Tourassine, 50 L9
Tourba, 60 M1
Tour de Merkala, 51 G14
Tourist, 125 J15
Tourni, 65 C13
Touroua, 67 E15
Tourougoumbe, 57 J12
Touroukoro, 247 M3
Toussiana, 65 C14
Toussidé, 248 B7
Touws River, 157 G14
Toworth, 69 H20
Tozeur, 49 L16
Tradouws Pass, 157 I15
Tranomaro, 48 L5
Trarza, 56 H5
Trawal, 156 A9
Trekkopje, 124 A9
Trena, 70 C8
Triangle, 132 H3
Trichardt, 147 E18
Trichardt Memorial, 140 J4
Trichardtsdal, 139 H18
Trinkitat, 62 F7
Triolet, 46 H4
Tripoli, 53 B17
Trois Frres, 46 C3
Trole, 76 L6
Trompsburg, 153 F14
Trooilapspan, 151 A18
Trou d'Eau Douce, 46 J5
Troutbeck, 120 I8
Tsama, 72 C9
Tsandi, 113 F13
Tsangano, 109 I13
Tsaobis Leopard Nature Park, 134 A2
Tsaramandroso, 48 E7
Tsaramborona, 274 D8
Tsarantanana, 48 E8
Tsaraxaibis, 144 H2
Tsarisberge, 134 J4
Tsarishoogte Pass, 134 K5
Tsatane, 278 I2
Tsatsu, 137 L18
Tsau, 128 E8
Tsauchab, 134 I4
Tsau Hills, 128 I8
Tsaukaib, 142 E8
Tsavo, 89 I15
Tsavo East National Park, 89 I15
Tsavo West National Park, 89 J13
Tsawe Pan, 136 G7
Tsawisis, 143 D17
Tsazo, 154 M2
Tseikuru, 84 K4
Tsembou, 72 G6
Tses, 143 B17
Tsesame, 137 G17
Tsetsebjwe, 139 A11
Tsetseng, 136 E10
Tsetserra, 132 A9
Tsévié, 66 H1
Tshabema Pan, 268 C7
Tshabong, 145 C13
Tshakabika Pan, 268 C6
Tshakhuma, 139 C18
Tshaka, 76 E9
Tshala, 76 D8
Tshane, 136 H6
Tshaneni, 148 C8
Tshani, 160 A6
Tshauxaba, 129 D19
Tshebetshebe Pans, 268 C7
Tshela, 72 H7
Tshenge-Oshwe, 73 G18
Tshesebe, 130 G8
Tshibala, 76 B8
Tshibamba, 76 E8
Tshibambula, 73 I17
Tshibeke, 74 F5
Tshibiritsheke Pan, 136 E6
Tshibuka, 73 I15
Tshibwika, 76 E8
Tshidilamolomo, 146 B1
Tshidiwe, 76 B4
Tshie, 76 D10
Tshikando Pan, 117 L17
Tshikapa, 73 J16
Tshikula, 73 J18
Tshilenge, 73 J19
Tshimbalanga, 76 E9
Tshimbi, 68 L7
Tshimboko, 73 K20
Tshimbulu, 73 J18
Tshimbungu, 76 E9
Tshinka Pan, 137 I15
Tshintshanku, 73 J18
Tshipise, 139 B18
Tshisenge, 73 K16
Tshisonge, 76 C8
Tshitadi, 73 J17
Tshitanzu, 76 D9
Tshiturapadsi, 131 M19
Tshofa, 74 H2
Tsholotsho, 130 C9
Tshompani Dam, 268 C6
Tshompani Pan, 118 K2
Tshompani Pans, 268 C6
Tshongwe, *DRC* 77 C11
Tshongwe, *South Africa* 148 H10
Tshootsha, 128 L2
Tshopo, 74 B2
Tshotswa Pan, 136 H3
Tshuapa, 73 D18
Tshunga Falls, 74 B2
Tshwagong, 130 G1
Tsia, 137 F16
Tsiaki, 72 G8
Tsigara, 130 E1
Tsineng, 145 G15
Tsingy de Bemaraha Nature Reserve (WHS), 48 G5
Tsinjoarivo, 48 G6
Tsintsabis, 114 J6
Tsiombe, 48 M4
Tsiroanomandidy, 48 G5
Tsitondroina, 48 I6
Tsitsa Bridge, 154 K5
Tsitsikammaberge, 158 I5
Tsitsikamma National Park, 158 J6
Tsitsikamma Point, 158 J9
Tsivory, 48 L5
Tsodilo Hills, 116 L3
Tsoe, 129 G15
Tsoelike, 154 F5
Tsokotsa Pan, 129 I18
Tsolo, 154 K5
Tsomo, *river* 160 C2
Tsomo, 160 B2
Tsoulou Faunal Reserve, 72 G6
Tsuli, 130 D4
Tsumbiri, 73 F11
Tsumcor, 276 B9
Tsumeb, 114 L5
Tsumis Park, 134 F9
Tsumkwe, 115 M16
Tsunuye Pan, 137 F15
Tswaane, 136 A6
Tswaane Pan, 137 G13
Tswaing, *South Africa* 138 M9
Tswaing, *South Africa* 139 I15
Tswaing Pan, 137 K17
Tubeya, 76 C9
Tubmanburg, 64 G7
Tubo, 66 C8
Tubruq, *see Tobruk*
Tudun Wada, 66 B10
Tugela, *river* 155 B14
Tugela, 155 C15
Tugela Estate, 280 D9
Tugela Ferry, 155 A12
Tugela Gorge, 155 A13
Tugela Mouth, 155 C15
Tuinplaas, 139 K11
Tukh, 250 E8
Tukuyu, 97 J13
Tula, 84 M10
Tula Yiri, 67 D13
Tulbagh, 157 G11
Tuli, 131 K14
Tulia, 93 B17
Tuli Block, 131 M12
Tuli Safari Area, 131 L14
Tullu Deemtu, 257 G8
Tullu Konteh, 257 F9
Tullus, 68 B9
Tulu Bolo, 70 E5
Tululusia, 265 K1
Tulume, 76 C8
Tum, 79 M17
Tumawela, 266 B6
Tumba, 73 F19
Tumbatu Island, 95 H17
Tumbe, 73 E12
Tumbili, 93 G11
Tumbi Point, 101 E14
Tumbo, 268 B10
Tumbu Ancient Site, 95 C19
Tumbwe, 77 G13
Tumfukuro, 254 I6
Tumu, 65 C17
Tumungu, 74 G5
Tuna, 65 D16
Tuna el Gebel, 250 J7
Tunaydah, 55 K14
Tundulu, 77 E16
Tunduma, 96 J10
Tunduru, 102 E7
Tunga, *Angola* 114 B5
Tunga, *Nigeria* 66 F10
Tungaru, 69 C15
Tunguru, 87 M12
Tunguu, 95 J18
Tunis, 49 I18
Tunisia, 49 K17
Turda, 69 C13
Turiani, 95 J11
Turkana, 78 F9
Turkwel, 79 I13
Turkwell Gorge Reservoir, 83 C11
Turmi, 70 I3
Turners Peninsula, 64 G4
Turtle Pond, 47 A15
Turton, 155 H12
Turungu, 260 M3
Turutoko, 78 L6
Tussen-die-Riviere Game Farm, 153 H16
Tutu, 74 D1
Tutukpene, 65 F19
Tutume, 130 F6
Tuvaila, 265 M2
Tuzule, 76 B9
Tweefontein, 157 C12
Tweelina Rambuka, 135 K20
Tweeling, 147 I15
Twee Palms, 276 C9
Tweeputte, 127 C19
Twee Rivier, 135 M16
Tweespruit, 153 C18
Twelve Apostles, 281 H4
Twifu Praso, 254 H4
Twilight, 134 I10
Twingi, 77 H16
Twisappel, 278 F8
Twyfelfontein, 280 F8
Twyfelfontein Rock Engravings, 125 G16
Txenga Pan, 128 G9
Tyi Grounto, 249 F9
Tylden, 159 B18
Tzaneen, 139 G17
Tzaneen Dam, 139 F17

U

Uaco Cungo, 75 G19
Uagoscia, 71 J16
Uamba, 73 L13
Uangando, 113 C19
Uape, 110 M8
Uba, 67 C15
Ubangi, 73 B12
Ubares Pan, 114 I2

ALL PHOTOGRAPHS ARE LISTED IN ORDER OF THEIR APPEARANCE ON EACH PAGE, STARTING FROM THE TOP LEFT AND RUNNING FROM TOP TO BOTTOM

Cover *See inside cover flap*
2 A Chanan Weiss
4 A galloimages/gettyimages.com
B galloimages/gettyimages.com
5 A galloimages/gettyimages.com
B galloimages/gettyimages.com
C galloimages/gettyimages.com
8 A David Rogers David Rogers Photo.
10 A Jason Laure Gallo Images
B Mary Duncan
C Photo Access/Pictor
D Rudolf Pigneter Tony Stone/Gallo
11 A Photo Access/Pictor
B Chris North Sylvia Cordaiy PL
C Jason Laure
D David Wall DavidWallPhoto.com
E Chris van Lennep Gallo Images
F Robert van der Hilst Tony Stone/Gallo
12 A Gallo Images
B Justin Fox
C Photo Access/Pictor
13 A R Daly Photo Access
B Gable Sylvia Cordaiy PL
C National Geographic Image Collection
D Gable Sylvia Cordaiy PL
E Ariadne van Zandbergen
F National Geographic Image Collection
14 A David Rogers David Rogers Photo.
B David Rogers David Rogers Photo.
C David Rogers David Rogers Photo.
D Wayne Griffiths Gallo Images
15 A F Jack Jackson
B F Jack Jackson
C F Jack Jackson
D Justin Fox Photo Access
E Wayne Griffiths Gallo Images
16 A Ariadne van Zandbergen
B Ariadne van Zandbergen
C Ariadne van Zandbergen
D Ariadne van Zandbergen
17 A Gable Sylvia Cordaiy PL
B Chanan Weiss
C Ariadne van Zandbergen
18 A Gable Sylvia Cordaiy PL
B Pierre Hinch Gallo Images
19 A Chanan Weiss
B Gable Sylvia Cordaiy PL
C Chanan Weiss
D Chanan Weiss
E Chanan Weiss
20 A Will Curtis Tony Stone/Gallo
B Kerstein Geier Gallo Images
C Gable Sylvia Cordaiy PL
D Gable Sylvia Cordaiy PL
21 A David Wall DavidWallPhoto.com
B Gable Sylvia Cordaiy PL
C Marco Turco Gallo Images
D Jason Laure
E galloimages/gettyimages.com
22 A Gill Shapley
B Ariadne van Zandbergen
C Ariadne van Zandbergen
23 A Jason Laure
B Andrea Booher Tony Stone/Gallo
C Jason Laure
D Gill Shapley
E P Wagner Photo Access
F Ariadne van Zandbergen
24 A Duncan Butchart
B Duncan Butchart
C National Geographic Image Collection
25 A Martin Harvey Gallo Images
B Jason Laure
C Martin Harvey
D Gill Shapley
E National Geographic Image Collection
F Gerald Cubitt
26 A Ariadne van Zandbergen
B Ariadne van Zandbergen
C David Steele Photo Access
D Chanan Weiss
27 A Alan Binks Gallo Images
B Ariadne van Zandbergen
C Ariadne van Zandbergen
D Alan Binks Gallo Images
E Ariadne van Zandbergen
F Jacques Marais
28 A Andrew Bannister Struik Image Lib
B Chanan Weiss
C Andrew Bannister Struik Image Lib
D Gerald Cubitt
29 A Anthony Bannister Gallo Images
B Peter Ribton Struik Image Library
C Ariadne van Zandbergen
D Andrew Bannister Struik Image Lib
E David Rogers David Rogers Photo.
F Richard Surman Tony Stone/Gallo
30 A P Wagner Photo Access
B Martin Harvey
C David Rogers David Rogers Photo.
D Jason Laure
31 A Gerald Cubitt
B Loretta Steyn Gallo Images
C Roger de la Harpe Gallo Images
D Ariadne van Zandbergen
E Ariadne van Zandbergen
F Ariadne van Zandbergen
32 A Daryl Balfour Gallo Images
B Tom Peschak
C Jacques Marais
D Ariadne van Zandbergen
33 A P Wagner Photo Access
B Ariadne van Zandbergen
C Jacques Marais
D Ariadne van Zandbergen
E David Rogers David Rogers Photo.
F Jacques Marais
34 A Gerald Cubitt
B Gerald Cubitt
C Gerald Cubitt
D Claudio Velásquez
35 A Jéan du Plessis
B Justin Fox
C Roger de la Harpe Africa Imagery
D David Steele Photo Access
E Gerald Cubitt
F Claudio Velásquez
36 A Jéan du Plessis
B Jéan du Plessis
C Jéan du Plessis
D Willie and Sandra Olivier
E Jéan du Plessis
37 A Claudio Velásquez
B P Wagner Photo Access
C Roger de la Harpe Africa Imagery
D David Rogers David Rogers Photo.
E Claudio Velásquez
38 A Lanz van Horsten
B Roger de la Harpe Africa Imagery
C Roger de la Harpe Africa Imagery
D Erhardt Thiel Struik Image Library
E D Bristow Photo Access
39 A Tom Peschak
B Walter Knirr Struik Image Library
C Willie and Sandra Olivier
D P Wagner Photo Access
40 A Johan Kloppers
161 A Studio shots Struik Image Library
B Weiss Inpra
162 A Jeanetta Baker Photo Bank
208 A Martin Harvey
212 A F Jack Jackson
B Peter Timmermans Tony Stone/Gallo
C galloimages/gettyimages.com
D Photo Access/Pictor
214 A David Wall DavidWallPhoto.com
B Martin Harvey
C F Jack Jackson
D Martin Harvey
216 A Geoff Spiby
B David Rogers David Rogers Photo.
C Photo Access/Pictor
D Chanan Weiss
218 A Chanan Weiss
B Ariadne van Zandbergen
C Justin Fox Photo Access
D Ariadne van Zandbergen
220 A Marco Turco Gallo Images
B Ariadne van Zandbergen
C Colin Paterson-Jones
D Gable Sylvia Cordaiy
222 A Gable Sylvia Cordaiy
B David Wall DavidWallPhoto.com
D Jason Laure
C galloimages/gettyimages.com
224 A Ariadne van Zandbergen
B Ariadne van Zandbergen
C Ariadne van Zandbergen
D Gavin Thomson Gallo Images
226 A Geoff Spiby
B National Geographic Image Collection
C National Geographic Image Collection
D galloimages/gettyimages.com
228 A P Blackwell Photo Access
B P Wagner Photo Access
C Claudio Velásquez
D Ariadne van Zandbergen
230 A Anthony Bannister Gallo Images
B Ariadne van Zandbergen
C Ariadne van Zandbergen
D Ariadne van Zandbergen
232 A David Wall DavidWallPhoto.com
B P Blackwell Photo Access
C Ariadne van Zandbergen
D Martin Harvey Gallo Images
234 A Ariadne van Zandbergen
B Geoff Spiby
C Claudio Velásquez
D Ariadne van Zandbergen
236 A Geoff Spiby
B Nigel Dennis Gallo Images
C Claudio Velásquez
D Claudio Velásquez
238 A Lanz van Horsten
B Martin Harvey
C Claudio Velásquez
D David Rogers David Rogers Photo.
240 A Nigel Dennis Africa Imagery
B Claudio Velásquez
C Nigel Dennis
D Martin Harvey
242 A Martin Harvey
282 A Michael Neuman
286 A Mary Duncan
B Sue Strange Pictures Colour Library
C Peter Baker Photobank
287 A Chris North Sylvia Cordaiy PL
B F Jack Jackson
C Sue Strange Pictures Colour Library
288 A Justin Fox
B Justin Fox
C D Pinnock Photo Access
289 A Gable Sylvia Cordaiy PL
B R Daly Photo Access
C National Geographic Image Collection
290 A F Jack Jackson
B Wayne Griffiths Gallo Images
C David Rogers David Rogers Photo.
291 A Linda Pitkin
B F Jack Jackson
C Johnathan Smith Sylvia Cordaiy PL
292 A David Mozer iBike.org
B Chanan Weiss
C Ariadne van Zandbergen
293 A Gable Sylvia Cordaiy PL
B Chanan Weiss
C Chanan Weiss
294 A Jérôme Boggio-Pasqua
B Jacques Marais
C Jacques Marais
295 A Chanan Weiss
B Andrew Bannister Struik Image Lib.
C Chanan Weiss
296 A Gable Sylvia Cordaiy PL
B Ian Michler Struik Image Library
C Topham INPRA
297 A John Blair Camtour UK
B Gable Sylvia Cordaiy PL
C Jacques Marais Struik Image Lib.
298 A Geoff Spiby
B Ariadne van Zandbergen
C Guy Marks Sylvia Cordaiy PL
299 A F Jack Jackson
B Ariadne van Zandbergen
C Jason Laure
300 A Duncan Butchart
B Duncan Butchart
C Dave van Smeerdijk Photo Access
301 A David Pluth FotoGrafx
B Chanan Weiss
C David Wall DavidWallPhoto.com
302 A David Pluth FotoGrafx
B Ariadne van Zandbergen
C David Pluth FotoGrafx
303 A David Pluth FotoGrafx
B John Cleare Mountain Camera PL
C David Pluth FotoGrafx
304 A D Steele Photo Access
B P Wagner Photo Access
C Photo Access
305 A Chanan Weiss
B Lanz van Horsten
C C Lanz Photo Access
306 A David Rogers Photo Access
B Lanz van Horsten
C galloimages/gettyimages.com
307 A Roger de la Harpe Africa Imagery
B P Wagner Photo Access
C B&L Worsley Photo Access
308 A David Steele Photo Access
B Ariadne van Zandbergen
C Ariadne van Zandbergen
309 A David Rogers David Rogers Photo.
B Ariadne van Zandbergen
C Ariadne van Zandbergen
310 A Jacques Marais
B P Wagner Photo Access
C galloimages/gettyimages.com
311 A Ariadne van Zandbergen
B Geoff Spiby
C Jacques Marais
312 A Jéan du Plessis
B Willie and Sandra Olivier
C Hein van Horsten Gallo Images
313 A P Wagner Photo Access
B J Nel Photo Access
C R Daly Photo Access
314 A Mark Gush Photo Access
B Walter Knirr Struik Image Library
C Geoff Spiby
315 A Roger de la Harpe Africa Imagery
B P Wagner Photo Access
C David Rogers David Rogers Photo.
316 A Lanz van Horsten
317 A Heather Green
318 A Simon Lewis
B Chanan Weiss
319 A Simon Lewis
B Jéan du Plessis

Published by Maps International

In association with National Geographic Maps

National Geographic Maps United States of America

Frances Marshall President
Allen Carroll Senior Vice President, Chief Cartographer
Daniel Ortiz Vice President, General Manager
Kevin Allen Director of Map Services
Michael Horner Senior Editor
Alan Warner Graphic Designer

Map Studio South Africa

Lois O'Brien Managing Director Map Studio
John Loubser Project Manager
Simon Lewis Managing Editor
Sean Fraser Author
Elaine Fick Senior Cartographer
Elmari Kuyler DTP Operator
Ryan Africa DTP Operator
Denielle Lategan Researcher
Myrna Collins Production Manager
Liesel Brown Researcher
John Hall National Parks Cartographer
Peter Bosman Design Concept
Steven Felmore Regional Map Art, Adventure Icons
Thea Grobbelaar Proofreading Mary Duncan Text Index
Carl Germishuys Database
Daniella Levin, Maria Wedgewood,
Tanya Lessing, Maryna Beukes Database DTP

Lovell Johns United Kingdom

Ben Hill Managing Director LovellJohns
David Stevens Operations Director LovellJohns
Richard Hewish New Business Director LovellJohns
Neil Hanson Production Manager
Christine Bond Database Manager
Liz Donnelly Project Editor
Chris Bates Senior Cartographer
Leanne Wright Senior Cartographer
Wil Adnams Senior Digital Cartographer
David Murray Software Development

Special Thanks

Anderson Geographics Ltd. for the creation of shaded relief on Touring Maps (pages 49-160)
New Holland Publishers SA for the use of Globetrotter base mapping, www.newhollandpublishing.com
Carmen Swanepoel, Struik Image Library
Globe Views on Pages 42, 164, 210, 284
Copyright Digital Wisdom

Copyright Information

Reproduction by Hirt & Carter (Pty) Ltd
Printed in Singapore by Tien Wah Press (Pte) Ltd
ISBN 1-56695-173-9
10 9 8 7 6 5 4 3 2 1

Forward any comments on this product to
ngatlascomments@mapstudio.co.za

African Travels with National Geographic

On this page you'll find an array of other quality travel products from National Geographic. Venture to far-flung corners of the globe with NATIONAL GEOGRAPHIC magazine and spectacular National Geographic videos. Plan great vacations with the award-winning NATIONAL GEOGRAPHIC TRAVELER magazine and the Society's fact-filled, illustrated travel guides. In all the outstanding products below, you'll enjoy dazzling images, incomparable maps, and detailed travel information just like you find in the African Adventure Atlas.

Available Now

TOLL-FREE: 1-800-962-1643 INTERNATIONAL: 1-303-670-3457

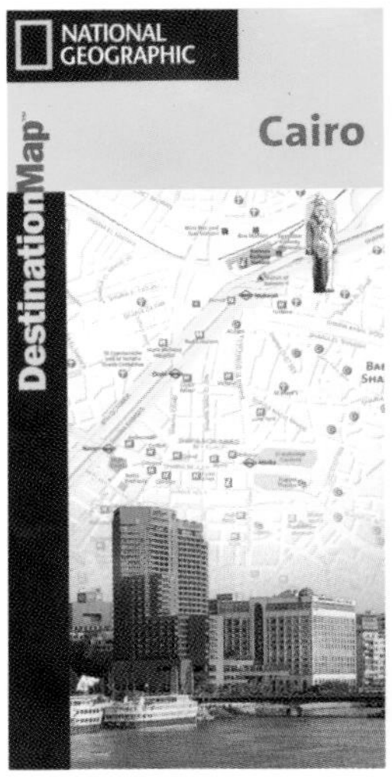

ISBN 1-56695-171-2

Once the seat of the great empires of the pharaohs, Cairo has much to offer. 'The Pyramids at Giza', 'Egyptian Antiquities Museum' and 'Museum of Islamic Art' are covered in this Destination map. Also featured are a number of old mosques, including 'Mosque of Muhammed Ali', and town plans of Aswan, Thebes and Luxor.

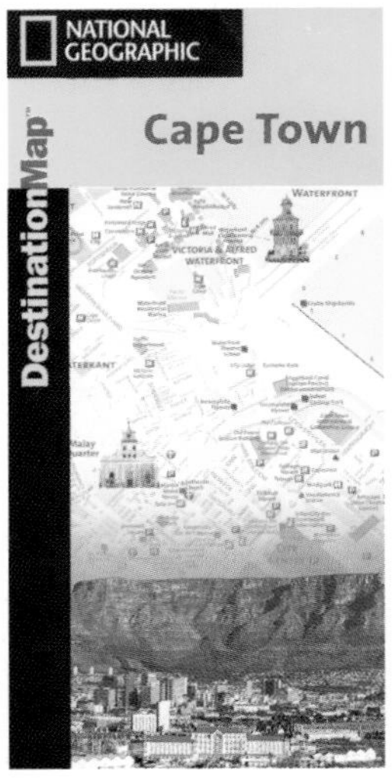

ISBN 1-56695-168-2

Cape Town is known for its Winelands, which are the pride of South Africa. Other places of interest featured are Table Mountain (a beacon to the Cape), the Victoria & Alfred Waterfront and the spectacular Kirstenbosch National Botanical Garden. Included in this destination map is a map of Cape Town international Airport.

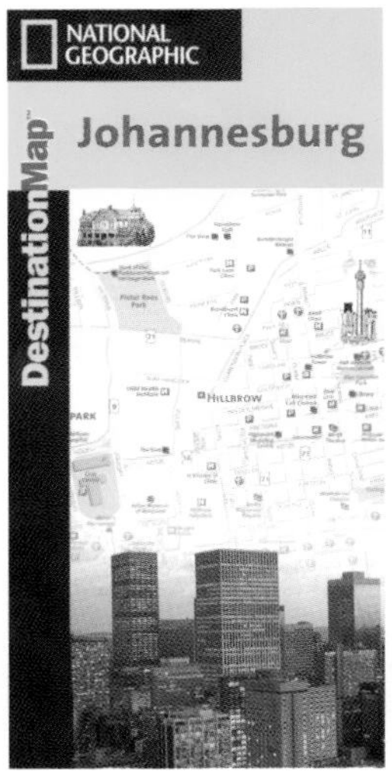

ISBN 1-56695-169-0

Known as South Africa's 'City of Gold', Johannesburg is the focal point of the Gauteng Province. With exciting places to visit such as 'Gold Reef City' (a casino and entertainment complex) and the famed 'Palace of the Lost City' (the grandest hotel in the country) you will have no excuse not to visit this cosmopolitan environment.

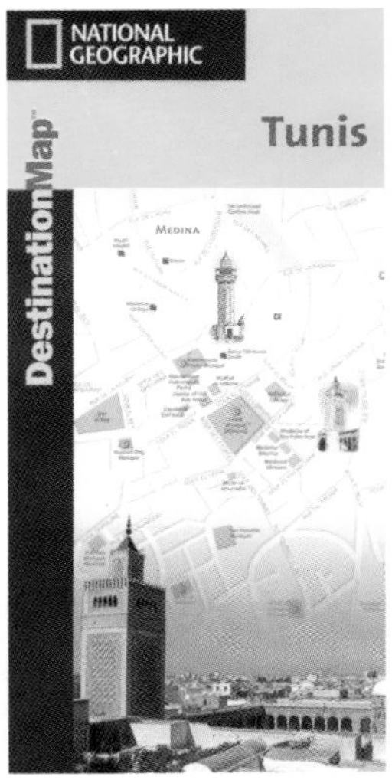

ISBN 1-56695-172-0

Tunis, one of the most important sea ports in Africa, is also the spiritual centre of the Tunisian nation. Besides all the mosques that dot the inner city (such as 'Kasbah Mosque' and 'Zitouna Mosque') there are also numerous Museums to visit, including the Bardo Museum (a floorplan of which is shown in this Destination map).

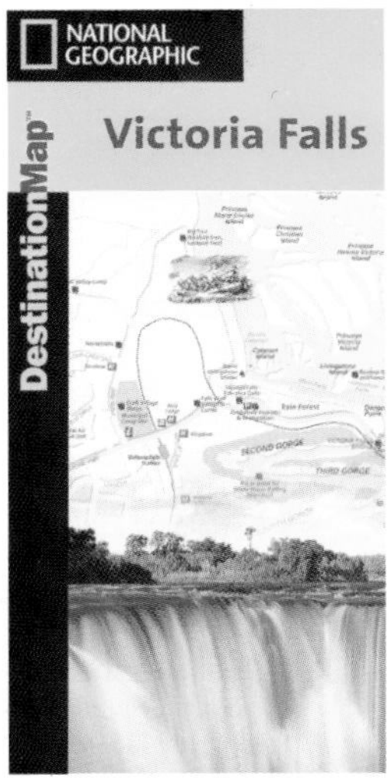

ISBN 1-56695-170-4

The mighty Victoria Falls is one of Africa's greatest natural wonders, and the area provides endless adventures opportunities, ranging from white-water rafting on the Zambezi to bungee jumping and flights over the falls. There's hiking and 4x4 trails, gameviewing and safaris in the National Park and even leisure cruises on the mighty river.

MAPSTUDIO SOUTH AFRICA TOLL-FREE: 0860 10 50 50

Next Up

DESTINATION MAPS

Durban
ISBN 0-7922-3322-0

Dar es Salaam & Surrounds
ISBN 0-7922-3321-2

Rabat, Marrakech & Fez
ISBN 0-7922-3323-9

Maputo & Surrounds
ISBN 0-7922-3328-X

Nairobi & Surrounds
ISBN 0-7922-3327-1

ADVENTURE MAPS

Cape Town
ISBN 1-56695-168-8

Kilimanjaro
ISBN 1-56695-167-4

Fish River Canyon
ISBN 1-56695-166-6

TO BECOME A MEMBER OF THE NATIONAL GEOGRAPHIC SOCIETY CALL: 1.800.NGS.LINE USA/CANADA
813.979.6845 INTERNATIONAL

Other National Geographic Products

PURCHASE ONLINE: www.nationalgeographic.com

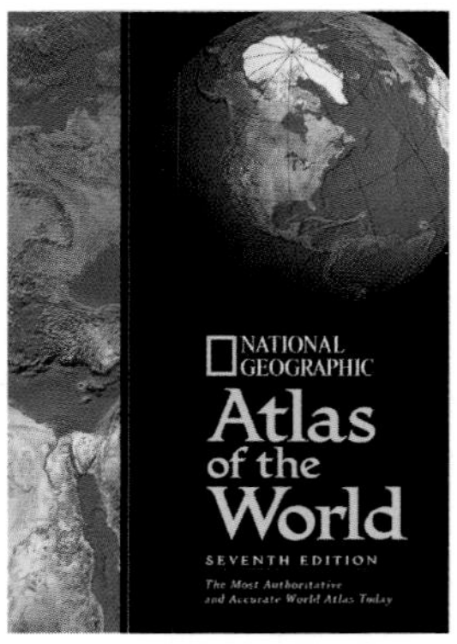

7th EDITION WORLD ATLAS

National Geographic's World atlas that has set the standard for cartographic excellence for more than a generation. The 7th Edition carries this tradition forward, with highly accurate political, urban, regional, thematic, and ocean-floor maps, as well as stunning satellite images. Also included are maps and illustrated articles on Earth's processes and resources, flags and facts for every country, new maps of the moon, the solar system, the Milky Way, and the universe. The index has more than 155,000 place-names, enabling the reader to easily locate any place on Earth.

To order: www.nationalgeographic.com/maps

MAPS

National Geographic's diverse range of maps and software take you from your neighborhood to the worlds most exotic locations. National Geographic maps are world renowned for their beauty, accuracy, and attention to detail. Whether you are an adventurer or an armchair traveler, our maps enable you to see the world, explore the seven continents, discover fascinating facts about countries, learn more about history and nature, and plan your next backcountry excursion. From the trail to the universe, we have the maps you need.

To receive a catalog or to order:
www.nationalgeographic.com/maps
Toll-free 1-800-962-1643
International 1-303-670-3457

MAGAZINE

Dream it. Plan it. Do it. *National Geographic Adventure* magazine takes you all over the globe with articles, in-depth stories, first-person accounts from some of the world's most well known adventurers, and regular features to help you get the most out of any excursion. *Adventure* helps you find that out-of-the-way spot and then provides you with expert facts and advice about activities and gear. Whether you are a novice or a pro, *Adventure* magazine gives you accessibility, awesome photography, and first-person features that capture the spirit of modern adventure. Everyone wants their life to be an adventure ... we show them how.

To subscribe or learn more:
www.nationalgeographic.com/adventure